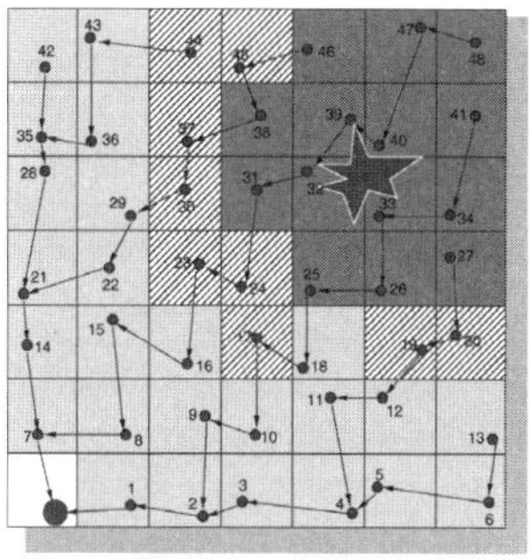

HANDBOOK ON SENSOR NETWORKS

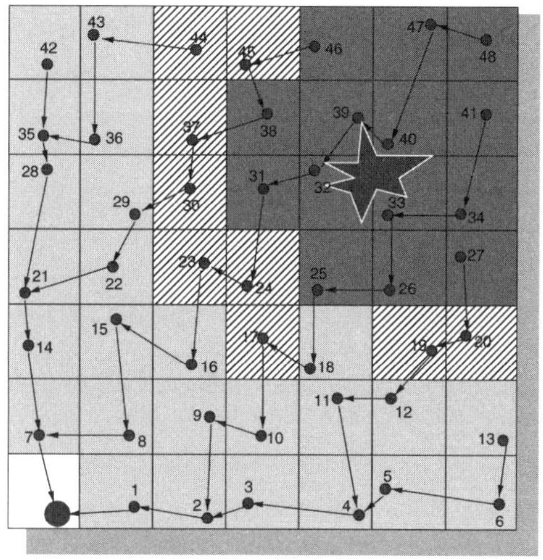

HANDBOOK ON SENSOR NETWORKS

editors

Yang Xiao
University of Alabama, USA

Hui Chen
Virginia State University, USA

Frank Haizhon Li
University of South Carolina Upstate, USA

World Scientific

NEW JERSEY • LONDON • SINGAPORE • BEIJING • SHANGHAI • HONG KONG • TAIPEI • CHENNAI

Published by

World Scientific Publishing Co. Pte. Ltd.

5 Toh Tuck Link, Singapore 596224

USA office: 27 Warren Street, Suite 401-402, Hackensack, NJ 07601

UK office: 57 Shelton Street, Covent Garden, London WC2H 9HE

British Library Cataloguing-in-Publication Data
A catalogue record for this book is available from the British Library.

HANDBOOK ON SENSOR NETWORKS

ISBN-13 978-981-283-730-1
ISBN-10 981-283-730-2

Desk Editor: Tjan Kwang Wei

Typeset by Stallion Press
Email: enquiries@stallionpress.com

Printed by FuIsland Offset Printing (S) Pte Ltd. Singapore

Preface

As computing and networking technologies are gradually integrated with every aspect of human lives and activities, networked sensing technology is becoming pervasive. Evidently, we are witnessing the emergence of the integration of networked sensing technology with various physical systems. Continuous development of networked sensing technologies leads to exciting applications, which continuously improve human lives and productivity, and help pursue our understanding on the physical world. Nevertheless, we are motivated to provide the community with a reference book of recent advances in this exiting field.

This edited book presents a collection of recent advances in sensor networks areas. It is a contribution of many prominent researchers working on the sensor networks field around the world. The book contains 35 chapters which are divided into 10 parts, and it covers almost wide spectrum of sensor networks, including but not limited to, physical layer issues, media access control, routing, architecture, design and implementation, testbed, security, localization and location discovery, energy efficiency, data gathering and processing, monitoring and detection, multimedia sensor networks, social-economic issues, and medical sensors. Nevertheless, we believe this book will be a good reference for researchers, practitioners, and students who are interested in the research, development, design, and implementation of sensor networks.

This book is made possible by the great efforts of our contributors and publishers. We are indebted to our contributors, who have sacrificed days and nights to put together these chapters for our readers. We would like to thank our publishers. Without their encouragement and quality work, we could not have this book. Finally, we are grateful that our families have continuously supported us.

Yang Xiao
Department of Computer Science
The University of Alabama
101 Houser Hall
Box 870290
Tuscaloosa, AL 35487-0290 USA
E-mail: yangxiao@ieee.org

Hui Chen
Department of Mathematics and Computer Science
Virginia State University
P.O.Box 9068
Petersburg, VA 23806 USA
E-mail: huichen@ieee.org

Haizhon Frank Li
Division of Mathematics and Computer Science
University of South Carolina Upstate
Spartanburg, SC 29303, USA
E-mail: fli@uscupdate.edu

About Editors

Yang Xiao worked in industry as a MAC (Medium Access Control) architect involving the IEEE 802.11 standard enhancement work before Dr. Xiao joined Department of Computer Science at The University of Memphis in 2002. He is currently with Department of Computer Science at The University of Alabama. He was a voting member of IEEE 802.11 Working Group from 2001 to 2004. He is an IEEE Senior Member. He is a member of American Telemedicine Association. He currently serves as Editor-in-Chief for *International Journal of Security and Networks* (IJSN), *International Journal of Sensor Networks* (IJSNet), and *International Journal of Telemedicine and Applications* (IJTA). He serves as a referee/reviewer for many funding agencies, as well as a panelist for NSF and a member of Canada Foundation for Innovation (CFI)'s Telecommunications expert committee. He serves on TPC for more than 100 conferences such as INFOCOM, ICDCS, MOBIHOC, ICC, GLOBECOM, WCNC, etc. He serves as an associate editor for several journals, e.g., *IEEE Transactions on Vehicular Technology.* His research areas are security, telemedicine, sensor networks, and wireless networks. He has published more than 300 papers in major journals, refereed conference proceedings, book chapters related to these research areas. Dr. Xiao's research has been supported by the US National Science Foundation (NSF), U.S. Army Research, Fleet & Industrial Supply Center San Diego (FISCSD), and The University of Alabama's Research Grants Committee.

Hui Chen is a geophysicist turned computer programmer and computer science researcher. From 1996 to 2001, he spent most of his time in research on computational aspects of geophysics. He late worked as a software developer in industry. Out of his interest in research and teaching, and his desire to learn, he joined the faculty of the Department of Mathematics and Computer Science at Virginia State University in 2007. While retaining interest in computational problems in Earth sciences, he primarily works on computer systems, networking, and security areas such as design and analysis wireless networks, sensor networks, caching for wireless systems, operating system and network security as well as applied computing. He served and is serving as technical program committee member for many conferences such as IEEE Globecom and IEEE ICC. He was and is a guest editor of a few journals, such as special issues of "Wireless Telemedicine and Applications" and "Wireless Network Security" of the EURASIP Journal on Wireless Communications and Networking. He is member of IEEE and ACM. Email: huichen@ieee.org

Frank Haizhou Li is an assistant professor of Computer Science at the University of South Carolina Upstate. He received his Ph.D. degree from the University of Memphis. Prior to pursuing his career in Computer Science, he has worked as a chemical engineer for four years. His research interests include modeling and analysis of mobile, wireless, ad hoc and sensor networks, Quality of Service and MAC enhancement for IEEE 802.11 wireless LANs, adaptive network services, multimedia services and protocols over wireless networks, and Computer Security. Frank has served as technical program committee member for many conferences such as IEEE ICC and IEEE WCNC. Email: fli@uscupstate.edu

Contributors

Ozgur B. Akan
Next generation Wireless Communications Laboratory (NWCL),
Department of Electrical and Electronics Engineering,
Middle East Technical University, 06531 Ankara
Turkey

Prathima Agrawal
Department of Electrical and Computer Engineering
Auburn University, Auburn, AL 36849
USA

Stefano Basagni
Department of Electrical and Computer Engineering
Northeastern University
Boston, MA
USA

Alper Bereketli
Next generation Wireless Communications Laboratory (NWCL),
Department of Electrical and Electronics Engineering,
Middle East Technical University
06531 Ankara
Turkey

Hatem Bettahar
Compiegne University of Technology
Computer Science Department
Heudiasyc lab.
France

Abdelmadjid Bouabdallah
Compiegne University of Technology
Computer Science Department
Heudiasyc lab.
France

R. R. Brooks
Holcombe Department of Electrical and Computer Engineering
Clemson University
P.O. Box 340915, Clemson, SC 29634-0915
USA

S. Buchegger
Deutsche Telekom Laboratories
Ernst-Reuter-Platz 7
D-10587 Berlin
Germany

ChihYung Chang
Department of Computer Science and Information Engineering,
Tamkang University
Taiwan

Hsiao-Hwa Chen
Department of Engineering Science
National Cheng Kung University
Hsin-Chu, Taiwan
ROC

Jiming Chen
College of Information Science and Engineering, Zhejiang University
Hangzhou
China

Ling-Jyh Chen
Institute of Information Science, Academia Sinica
Taiwan

Min Chen
Department of Electrical and Computer Engineering, Univ. of British Columbia
V6T 1Z4
Canada

Dingzhu Du
Department of Computer Science, University of Texas at Dallas
800 W. Campbell Road
Richardson, TX 75080
USA

Miguel A. Erazo
School of Computer and Information Sciences
Florida International University, Miami, FL 33199
USA

S. Esswein
Forestry Department, Clemson University
P.O. Box 340915, Clemson, SC 29634-0915
USA

Nelson L. S. da Fonseca
Institute of Computing, State University of Campinas
Av. Albert Einstein, 1251, Campinas SP
Brazil

Xiaofeng Gao
Department of Computer Science, University of Texas at Dallas,
800 W. Campbell Road
Richardson, TX 75080
USA

Mikhail I. Gofman
Department of Computer Science
State University of New York at Binghamton
Binghamton, NY
USA

Fabrizio Granelli
DISI – University of Trento
Via Sommarive 14, I-38050 Trento
Italy

N. Guo
Wireless Networking Systems Laboratory
Department of Electrical and Computer Engineering
Center for Manufacturing Research
Tennessee Technological University
Cookeville, TN 38505
USA

Shuo Guo
Department of Computer Science and Engineering
The University of Minnesota
200 Union Street SE, Minneapolis, MN 55455
USA

Tian He
Department of Computer Science and Engineering
The University of Minnesota
200 Union Street SE, Minneapolis, MN 55455
USA

Z. Hu
Wireless Networking Systems Laboratory
Department of Electrical and Computer Engineering
Center for Manufacturing Research
Tennessee Technological University
Cookeville, TN 38505
USA

M. Talha Isik
Next generation Wireless Communications Laboratory (NWCL)
Department of Electrical and Electronics Engineering
Middle East Technical University
06531 Ankara
Turkey

Jaehoon Jeong
Department of Computer Science and Engineering
The University of Minnesota
200 Union Street SE, Minneapolis, MN 55455
USA

Xiaohua Jia
Computer Science, City University of Hong Kong
Hong Kong

Kyoung-Don Kang
Department of Computer Science
State University of New York at Binghamton
Binghamton, NY
USA

Sampada Karandikar
Holcombe Department of Electrical and Computer Engineering,
Clemson University
P.O. Box 340915, Clemson, SC 29634-0915
USA

Muhi Ahmed Ibne Khair
University of Manitoba
Winnipeg, Manitoba
Canada

Rahul Khanna,
Intel Corporation, 2111 NE 25th Ave.
Hillsboro, OR 97124
USA

Donghyun Kim
Department of Computer Science, University of Texas at Dallas
800 W. Campbell Road
Richardson, TX 75080
USA

Jang Young Kim
Department of Computer Science
State University of New York at Binghamton
Binghamton, NY
USA

Dzmitry Kliazovich
DISI – University of Trento
Via Sommarive 14, I-38050 Trento
Italy

S. Krishnamurthy
Deutsche Telekom Laboratories
Ernst-Reuter-Platz 7
D-10587 Berlin
Germany

Yu-Kwong Kwok
Colorado State University
Fort Collins, CO 80526
USA

Chun-Fai Law
MTR Corporation
Hong Kong

Chonho Lee
Department of Computer Science
University of Massachusetts
Boston, MA
USA

Yuehhua Lee
Computer Science Department, University of Victoria
Canada

Victor C.M. Leung
Dept. of Electrical and Computer Engineering, Univ. of British Columbia
V6T 1Z4
Canada

Yihan Li
Department of Electrical and Computer Engineering
Auburn University, Auburn, AL 36849
USA

Nia-Chiang Liang
Google Inc.
USA

Dandan Liu
Computer School, Wuhan University
Wuhan, Hubei
China

Huaping Liu
School of EECS, Oregon State University
Corvallis, OR 97331
USA

Kejie Lu
3Department of Electrical and Computer Engineering
University of Puerto Rico at Mayag¨uea
Mayag¨uez, PR 00681

Boushra Maala
Compiegne University of Technology
Computer Science Department
Heudiasyc lab.
France

Shiwen Mao
Department of Electrical and Computer Engineering
Auburn University
Auburn, AL 36849
USA

Scott F. Midkiff
Bradley Department of Electrical and Computer Engineering
Virginia Tech
Blacksburg, VA 24061
USA

Jelena Mišić
University of Manitoba
Winnipeg, Manitoba
Canada

Vojislav B. Mišić
University of Manitoba
Winnipeg, Manitoba
Canada

S. A. V. Satya Murty
Indira Gandhi Center for Atomic Research
Kalpakkam
India

P. Gireesan Namboothiri
Indian Institute of Technology Madras
Chennai
India

Maurizio A. Nanni
Department of Electrical and Computer Engineering
Northeastern University
Boston, MA
USA

Jisu Oh
Department of Computer Science
State University of New York at Binghamton
Binghamton, NY
USA

Meng-Shiuan Pan
Department of Computer Science
National Chiao Tung University
Hsin-Chu, 30010
Taiwan

Dongming Peng
Department of Computer and Electronics Engineering,
University of Nebraska – Lincoln, NE
USA

C. Post
Forestry Department, Clemson University
P.O. Box 340915, Clemson, SC 29634-0915
USA

Yi Qian
National Institute of Standards and Technology
Gaithersburg, MD 20899-8920
USA

R. C. Qiu
Wireless Networking Systems Laboratory
Department of Electrical and Computer Engineering
Center for Manufacturing Research
Tennessee Technological University
Cookeville, TN 38505
USA

Byrav Ramamurthy
Department of Computer Science and Engineering
University of Nebraska-Lincoln
Lincoln, NE 68588-0115
USA

Domingo Rodriguez
Department of Electrical and Computer Engineering
University of Puerto Rico at Mayag¨uea
Mayag¨uez, PR 00681

B. M. Sadler
Wireless Networking Systems Laboratory
Department of Electrical and Computer Engineering
Center for Manufacturing Research
Tennessee Technological University
Cookeville, TN 38505
USA

Divya Sakamuri
Ford Motor Company
USA

Taka Sakurai
Stichting IMEC Nederland, PO Box 8550,
5605 KN Eindhoven
Netherlands

Prasan Kumar Sahoo
Department of Information Management
Vanung University
Chungli
Taiwan

S. Selvakennedy
School of Information Technologies J12
University of Sydney, NSW 2006
Australia

Hamid Sharif
Department of Computer and Electronics Engineering,
University of Nebraska – Lincoln, NE
USA

Jang-Ping Sheu
Department Computer Science, National Tsing Hua University Hsin-Chu
Taiwan

Zhijie Jerry Shi
Department of Computer Science and Engineering,
University of Connecticut
Storrs, CT 06269
USA

Feng Shu
Stichting IMEC Nederland, PO Box 8550,
5605 KN Eindhoven
Netherlands

Krishna M. Sivalingam
University of Maryland, Baltimore County
Baltimore, MD
USA

Min Song
Electrical and Computer Engineering Department
Old Dominion University
Norfolk, VA 23529
USA

Y. Song
Wireless Networking Systems Laboratory
Department of Electrical and Computer Engineering
Center for Manufacturing Research
Tennessee Technological University
Cookeville, TN 38505
USA

Ivan Stojmenovic
SITE, University of Ottawa
Canada

Tony Sun
PacketMotion Inc.
USA

Junichi Suzuki
Department of Computer Science
University of Massachusetts
Boston, MA
USA

Yu-Chee Tseng
Department of Computer Science
National Chiao Tung University
Hsin-Chu, 30010
Taiwan

Li-Ping Tung
Institute of Information Science, Academia Sinica
Taiwan

Hai L. Vu
Stichting IMEC Nederland, PO Box 8550,
5605 KN Eindhoven
Netherlands

Bing Wang
Department of Computer Science and Engineering,
University of Connecticut, Storrs, CT 06269
USA

Honggang Wang
Department of Computer and Electronics Engineering,
University of Nebraska – Lincoln, NE
USA

Wei Wang
Department of Computer and Electronics Engineering,
University of Nebraska – Lincoln, NE
USA

Yong Wang
Department of Computer Science and Engineering
University of Nebraska-Lincoln
Lincoln, NE 68588-0115
USA

Kui Wu
Computer Science Department, University of Victoria
Yuyan Xue
Department of Computer Science and Engineering
University of Nebraska-Lincoln

Lincoln, NE 68588-0115
USA

Lun-Wu Yeh
Department of Computer Science
National Chiao Tung University
Hsin-Chu, 30010
Taiwan

Fan Zhang
Department of Computer Science and Engineering,
University of Connecticut, Storrs, CT 06269
USA

Hongwei Zhang
Department of Computer Science, Wayne State University
USA

P. Zhang
Wireless Networking Systems Laboratory
Department of Electrical and Computer Engineering
Center for Manufacturing Research
Tennessee Technological University
Cookeville, TN 38505
USA

Q. Zhang
Wireless Networking Systems Laboratory
Department of Electrical and Computer Engineering
Center for Manufacturing Research
Tennessee Technological University
Cookeville, TN 38505
USA

Ziguo Zhong
Department of Computer Science and Engineering
The University of Minnesota
200 Union Street SE, Minneapolis, MN 55455
USA

C. Zhou
Wireless Networking Systems Laboratory
Department of Electrical and Computer Engineering
Center for Manufacturing Research
Tennessee Technological University
Cookeville, TN 38505
USA

Ting Zhu
Department of Computer Science and Engineering
The University of Minnesota
200 Union Street SE, Minneapolis, MN 55455
USA

Feng Zou
Department of Computer Science, University of Texas at Dallas,
800 W. Campbell Road
Richardson, TX 75080
USA

Moshe Zukerman
Stichting IMEC Nederland, PO Box 8550,
5605 KN Eindhoven
Netherlands

Yang Xiao
Department of Computer Science
The University of Alabama
101 Houser Hall
Box 870290
Tuscaloosa, AL 35487-0290
USA

Fei Hu
Department of Computer Engineering,
RIT, Rochester, New York,
USA

Alexandru Samachisa
Department of Computer Engineering,
RIT, Rochester, New York,
USA

Marcin Lukowiak
Department of Computer Engineering,
RIT, Rochester, New York,
USA

Daniel Philips
Electrical Engineering,
RIT, Rochester, New York,
USA

Acknowledgement

Prof. Yang Xiao's work is supported in part by the US National Science Foundation (NSF) under the grant numbers CCF-0829827, CNS-0716211, and CNS-0737325.

Contents

Part I

Chapter 1

Architectures and Cross-Layer Design for Cognitive Networks

Dzmitry Kliazovich* and Fabrizio Granelli†

DISI, University of Trento
Via Sommarive 14, I-38050 Trento, Italy
**granelli@disi.unitn.it*
†kliazovich@disi.unitn.it

Nelson L. S. da Fonseca

Institute of Computing, State University of Campinas
Av. Albert Einstein, 1251, Campinas SP, Brazil
nfonseca@ic.unicamp.br

Network evolution towards self-aware autonomous adaptive networking attempts to overcome the inefficiency of configuring and managing networks, which leads to performance degradation. In order to optimize network operations, the introduction of self-awareness, self-management, and self-healing into the network was proposed. This created a new paradigm in networking, known as cognitive networking.

This chapter describes state-of-the-art, as well as future directions in cognitive networking. Fundamental techniques for enabling cognitive properties, such as, adaptation, learning, and goal optimization processes are detailed in this text. A comparison of available research proposals leads to the design of a promising cognitive network architecture capable of incorporating cognitive network techniques. Finally, a discussion on the required properties of the cross-layer design for cognitive networks and deployment issues are specified.

1.1. Introduction

Requirements and expectations on network services have constantly evolved. The evolution of communication technologies, especially in the wireless domain, introduced a paradigm shift from static to mobile access, from centralized to distributed infrastructure, and from passive to active networking.

Technological advances have brought networking a step forward towards the goal of service provision on an "anytime, anywhere" basis, while ensuring instantaneous and secure communications. However, such innovation is bound by the constraints included in the original Internet (and TCP/IP) design, which does not include, for example, mobility support, security, and active networking. For this reason, technological advancements were achieved at the cost of increased network complexity and limited performance.[1] The fundamental reason for performance inefficiency is the difficulty in configuring and managing networks — a task traditionally performed by network operators and technicians.[2]

Self-awareness, self-management, and self-healing characteristics have been proposed in order to optimize network operation, reconfiguration, and management, as well as to improve data transfer performance by bringing "intelligence" into the network, thereby creating a new paradigm known as *cognitive networking*, which is expected to become a key part of 4th generation wireless networks (4G).[3]

The term *cognitive* is related to the ability of a network to be aware of its operational status and adjust its operational parameters to fulfill specific tasks, such as detecting changes in the environment and user requirements. Cognition requires support from network elements (routers, switches, base stations, etc.), which should host active tasks to perform measurements to reconfigure the network. These characteristics are related to the paradigm of *active networks*,[4] which differ from cognitive networks service in that they do not include a *cognitive process* that considers adaptation and learning techniques.

The main challenges in cognitive networks range from the limitations of wireless technologies to network complexity, heterogeneity, and Quality of Service.

Network complexity is a function of the number of nodes and alternate routes, as well as the number of communication mediums and protocols running in the network. The introduction of wireless links in the network increased its complexity, since it changed the notion of connectivity.

Wireless nodes communicate over radio channels, which are subject to frequent fading and signal interference. In wireless networks, nodes can join and leave the network in ad hoc manner. Furthermore, mesh type connections can be established.

In addition, mobility allows wireless terminals to dynamically change their location, as well as their point of attachment to the network core. Mobility affects path availability, making it difficult to reach stability in a reasonable timeframe. Consequently, network management and optimization must add functionalities for self-healing.

Heterogeneity: The Internet is composed of combinations of different transmission technologies and a large variety of applications and transmission protocols (see Fig. 1.1). However, there is no layer in the TCP/IP that accounts for heterogeneity.

One of the most widely used approaches for performance improvement is the division of a connection into segments, each optimized for a particular domain. Despite several attempts to address heterogeneous paths in the Internet,[5] application performance will remain poor until the deployment of such capability on the majority of existing domains.

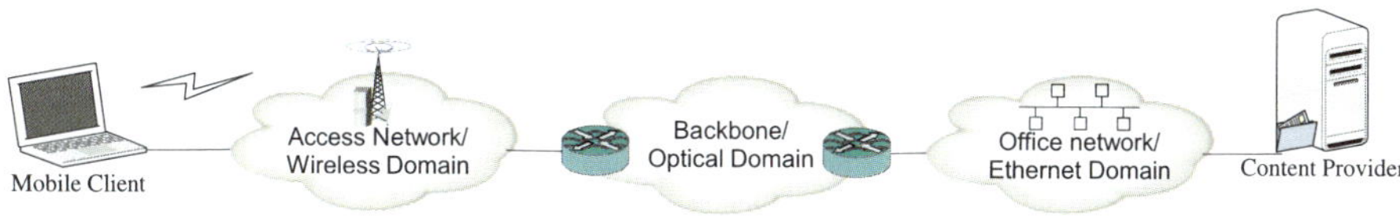

Fig. 1.1. Heterogeneous network path.

Enhancing performance requires awareness of underlining transmission technologies over the entire path between sender and receiver nodes. The optimization process should be distributed across multiple domains and optimization should achieve the goals defined at the connecting ends.

Quality of Service (*QoS*): Limited provisioning of delay bounds and bandwidth unavailability require the implementation of different reservation control mechanisms to support QoS requirements of different applications and users. Firoiu *et al.*[6] provides a comprehensive survey of available QoS mechanisms from the technical and the business perspective. No complete QoS solution can be performed within a single protocol layer.[6,7]

The two main driving forces for cognitive networks are technological and business oriented.

From the technological perspective, cognitive networking is envisioned as a logical evolution towards the definition of a unified QoS-aware environment, encompassing multiple technologies already available in the wireless network domain. The diversity of network configurations, involved technologies, and objectives dictated by the requirements of user applications is the main motivation behind cognitive networking.

From the business perspective, cognitive networks are envisioned as the way to increase profits for wireless service providers through cost reduction and development of new revenue streams obtained by the offer of heterogeneous wireless access solutions. The benefits enabled by cognitive networking include: the possibility to rely on common hardware and software platforms while supporting the evolution of radio technologies, development of new services, minimization of infrastructure upgrades, accelerated innovation, and maximization of return-on-investment through the reuse of already available network equipment.[2]

The business case offered by cognitive technologies provides network operators with the possibility to continuously analyze the configuration and the performance of a network segment, aiming at efficient service provision. Moreover, reconfiguration can be triggered by application requirements, policies, or billing plans. Cognitive networking offers extended sets of operation choices, creating new ways for interactions between network operators and end-users.[8]

The rest of this chapter provides fundamental concepts on cognitive networks. Novel cognitive network architecture is proposed after a discussion on current research trends. Finally, cross-layer techniques for improving current proposals on cognitive networks are introduced.

1.2. Fundamental Concepts on Cognitive Networks

Interest in cognitive networks gained momentum in the research community just some years ago. One of the first works that underlined the relevance of the concept of cognitive networks dates back to August 2003.[2] Clark *et al.*[2] proposed a network knowledge plane with cognitive techniques, such as "representation, learning, and reasoning that allow the knowledge plane to be "aware" of the network and its actions."

The following subsections define the cognitive network concept and related fundamental concepts.

1.2.1. *Definition*

The term *cognition* (from Latin, *cognoscere*, "to know") is used in many disciplines to describe the phenomenon closely related to the concepts of knowledge, intelligence, and learning. In networking, cognition is primarily motivated by system complexity and difficulty to use simple decision-making elements, such as those based on the closed form system models.

The principle of cognitive networking was conceived in association with cognitive radio. Mitola *et al.*[9] discussed the possibility of the adaptation of a network of cognitive radio devices where decisions are based on the knowledge obtained through the use of the unsupervised learning process.[9] They defined the cognitive cycle as consisting of six processes: observation, orientation, planning, learning, decision making, and action. According to the authors, a cognitive system is considered to...

> *"employ model-based reasoning to achieve a specified level of competence in radio-related domains."*

As illustrated in Ref. 10, such processes can envisage a reconfigurable network node with observation and action functionalities, while the remaining functionalities (such as orientation, planning, decision making, and learning) could constitute a "cognitive engine." As a result, a reconfigurable node constitutes a platform for the implementation of cognitive networks. Observations and actions should be flexible and bring the required degree of freedom for the design of cognitive elements. However, the precise concept of cognitive networking was first introduced by Clark *et al.*[2] who defined:

> *"the knowledge plane: representation, learning, and reasoning that allow the knowledge plane to be "aware" of the network and its actions in the network."* (*by Clark et al.*)

The knowledge plane should be designed to function properly in the presence of incomplete or misleading information, account for different high-level goals, and operate with future network technologies. These requirements cannot be satisfied using simple closed form expressions demanding complex or "cognitive" techniques. This definition is considered as one of the first for cognitive networking, due to its explicit reference of such notions as "knowledge" and "awareness" within a network-wide scope.

The scope of operation is what distinguishes a cognitive network from other systems, such as a network of cognitive radios. Cognitive radios focus on the optimization of wireless channel(s) access, thus limiting the scope to the node's vicinity, while cognitive networking aims at network-wide optimization and end-to-end network-wide goals. The PhD dissertation of Thomas[11] introduces new goals to the definition given by Clark[2]:

> "*... a network with a cognitive process that can perceive current network conditions, and then plan, decide and act on those conditions. The network can learn from these adaptations and use them to make future decisions, all while taking into account end-to-end goals.*"

The end-to-end user or application-defined goals are achieved through adaptation and cognition that involve all network elements (routers and switches) and communication techniques from the physical to the application layer across the data path.

1.2.2. *Cognitive network fundamentals*

The fundamental techniques enabling cognitive properties of networking algorithms can be summarized as the following functions: observation, analysis, decision making, and action.

In Fig. 1.2, these functionalities are presented as elements of a pyramid. The functional elements located closer to the pyramid foundation are typically more distributed across the network. For example, observation elements could simply keep track of node physical characteristics (such as signal level) and variables (such as the size of TCP windows). Alternatively, action elements could perform simple operations, such as tuning Network Interface Card (NIC) transmission parameters. These functional elements are typically passive, while most of the intelligence is located closer to the top of the pyramid. In this way, analysis and decision-making functions receive feedback obtained from the observation and issue action commands to the action elements.

Consequently, functional elements located closer to the bottom of the pyramid can be widely spread in the network, while those located closer to the top of the pyramid are commonly less spread.

Another important aspect of functional elements of cognitive networks is the property of scaling. For example, their behavior and implementation trend

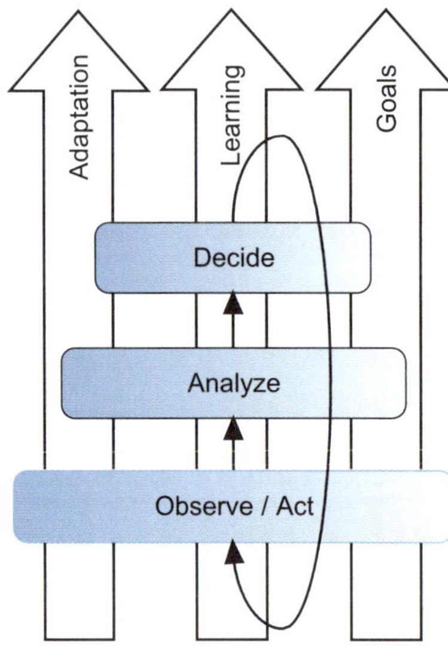

Fig. 1.2. Cognitive process essentials.

(centralized or distributed) is repeated on different scales, either at node or at network level. For example, at node level, observation and action elements correspond to intra-protocol layer agents able to control internal layer parameters, while the analysis or decision making process run as more generic processes, typically in parallel to the protocol stack.

At network layer, network nodes as a whole could be considered as observation and action elements, in which case measurements gathered at different protocol layers are aggregated at the node and sent as a single report to analysis. They can also be considered a decision-making engine, which, in the case of hierarchical implementation, provide aggregation and localization at network layer before passing information to more global entities.

Additionally, the pyramid of cognitive network functional elements is driven by three planes: adaptation, learning, and goals.

Adaptation is an essential part of all functional elements, enabling themselves to respond to changes in their environment. For example, the observation element could be requested to perform measurements of certain parameters within the protocol stack of the node and report it to the analysis module in a given interval of time. Then, the adaptive observation element could adjust this interval based on the operation scenario and network setup.

Commonly, small reporting intervals are used for parameters with frequently changed values, while large reports are considered for more static parameters. The observation element controls the reporting interval, which is the first instance of measurement.

However, high frequency of reporting increases signaling between observation and analysis elements. In this case, both observation and analysis are performed at the same network node and messages are transferred internally, causing overhead which could be neglected, while analysis is performed at another network node, signaling consuming relevant network resources.

The Learning plane is the core of the cognitive system. Learning enables functional elements of the pyramid to perform different actions based on past experience. An essential part of the learning process is the feedback adaptation loop, enabling the cognitive system to study reactions to the performed actions through observation, analysis, and decision making, yielding conclusions that are stored in the system and that can influence future decisions.

Two classes of learning can be performed by the cognitive system: informal and formal. Informal learning is implicit and can be performed by the same cognitive cycle on a regular basis during its normal operation. An example of such learning is the cognitive cycle implemented in a wireless node that increases the transmission rate when it perceives performance degradation. This is considered knowledge obtained by an informal learning procedure.

Formal learning is the process of knowledge transfer directly from the entity which obtained the knowledge. An example of formal learning in cognitive networks is that obtained by network nodes by gathering, aggregating, and broadcasting to other nodes of the network. Alternatively, it could be a simple exchange of knowledge between neighboring nodes.

The *Goal* plane provides a set of objectives that should be reached or approached by the cognitive optimization process. As suggested by Thomas *et al.*[12] the goals should be end-to-end and have network-wide scope. Optimization goals can be defined in a network-centric way by the network operator based on a chosen business model. They may correspond to personal preferences of an end user or can come from user application requirements (QoS). It is important that the goal plane resolves the conflicts between goals by taking into account their diversity and priority level and by providing a set of objectives using high-level languages.[13] The specification of goals for cognitive network is a difficult task and it is currently poorly addressed in literature. The questions that should be answered are: How are the rules described? Who (regulatory authority, network operator, users, applications, etc.) specifies them? How goals are made conflict-free? How fast are these goals disseminated in the network?

In summary, the adaptation and the goals planes take observation, analysis, and the decision making process into account, in order to choose a proper set of actions to adjust the basis of cognitive process for achieving specified network goals. Furthermore, the learning process is responsible for the reconfiguration of cognitive process elements based on experience and future prediction.

Another important point is the existence of a quality control feedback channel, which for every optimization step should perform an analysis of resulting network performance, compare it against the set of targeted objectives, and confirm that the optimization process is progressing in the right direction. Conversely, the cognitive process should backtrack; in the case of actions, it should verify that the system is one step behind its objectives. This process can be repeated at different scales in the network.

Cognitive network management should include well-defined operational metrics, allowing control of the optimization process and its possible backtracking procedures.

1.2.3. *Similarities to cognitive radio*

There has been some source of misunderstanding about the scope of cognitive networks and the scope of cognitive radios. Cognitive radio provides efficient and dynamic spectrum access by adaptively changing transmission and reception parameters to avoid interference with other communication systems. According to Ref. 14, the main functions of a cognitive radio are: *spectrum sensing*, aimed at detection of primary users and available spectrum "holes"; *spectrum management*, in order to select the best-suited frequency channel among spectrum holes; *spectrum sharing*, for fair coordination of spectrum usage with other cognitive nodes; and *spectrum mobility*, for leaving spectrum usage, in case primary licensed users are detected.

The main motivation behind cognitive radios is the need to enable dynamic spectrum sharing (as opposed to the traditional fixed allocation policy), while facing growing demands for high data rates and as a result, more flexibility and automation in the management of the available spectrum. Additional restrictions on the operational spectrum band are related to the nature of electromagnetic waves propagation and limitations on the size of antenna and mobile terminals.[15] Practically speaking, cognitive radio technologies are designed to overcome this limitation by enabling operations in the portions of spectrum sensed to be free from other transmissions.

Cognitive radios focus on the optimization of spectrum usage for increasing spectrum utilization, both at the physical layer (spectrum sensing) and at the link layer (scheduling and coordination). Even when management involves a joint effort of several cognitive radio devices, optimization is pursued in the vicinity of a node.

Moreover, the scenarios targeted by cognitive networks are far more complex and network-intensive, including several communication technologies (wire line, optical, and wireless), as well as different network elements (nodes and routers), which may or may not be designed to cooperate. In this scenario, optimization procedures are distributed across different layers of the protocol stack and across different networks.

Therefore, the main difference between cognitive radios and cognitive networks lies in scope of the optimization performed; while cognitive radios operate locally at the radio link level, cognitive networks aim at end-to-end optimization.[12] This consideration underlines the network-wide scope of a cognitive network, separating it from other local adaptation and optimization approaches.

However, the main common denominator between cognitive radios and cognitive networks is the definition of a cognitive process based on observations and measurements for optimizing reconfiguration of operating parameter.

1.3. Current Research Initiatives on Cognitive Network

Research on cognitive networks was embraced by several efforts, both in the United States[16] and in Europe, being relevant within the European Sixth and Seventh Research Framework Programmes (FP6[17] and FP7[18]).

Initially, research projects in cognitive networks considered Beyond-3G (B3G) network architectures, given the full control of the network core and the ease of including additional functionalities. The research projects in this category are E^2R[19] and m@ANGEL platform.[20]

The E^2R (End-to-end Reconfigurability) project[19] capitalizes on the benefits of Next Generation Network (NGN) and exploits a wide range of network technologies, such as cellular, fixed or WLAN. The ultimate goal of E2R is an all-IP network fully integrated with reconfigurable equipment.[21] However, the assumption of simultaneous reconfigurability support at all the layers for all the involved actors/devices represents a drawback and limits its incremental deployment.

The m@ANGEL platform[20] introduces a special approach for solving mobility problems in heterogeneous network environments with the support of cognition. The cognitive process is considered to be implemented in the access part of the network, between base stations and mobile users. The structure of the access network consists of two planes: the infrastructure plane, which includes reconfigurable elements (such as hardware transceivers, base stations, and the network core) and the management plane, composed of m@ANGEL entities. Each m@ANGEL entity is responsible for monitoring, resource brokerage, goals management, and reconfigurable element control functionalities.

A certain degree of cooperation is considered between m@ANGEL elements. However, this cooperation is usually performed within the scope of network elements located in neighboring cells and it is not propagated to the network core, somehow limiting the scope of a unified solution.

Differently than the B3G-focused approaches, researchers from Trinity College of Dublin presented a general framework for implementing the cognitive functionality.[10] This work focuses on node architecture enabling reconfigurable properties, implying logical separation between network nodes and the cognitive engine running in the network. While the cognitive engine performs learning, orientation, planning, and decision-making functions, observation and action are left to the reconfigurable node.

Node reconfiguration can be requested by the cognitive engine and performed by the Stack Manager component, which is the core of the reconfigurable node architecture. The stack manager builds a customized protocol from the layer components provided by the Component Inventory. Layer components are the software modules implementing functionalities of an entire protocol layer or a part of the layer (like a digital modulator, for example). They aim at interconnection with other layer components and communication with the stack manager.

This approach relies on the techniques to make the cognitive node capable of modifying or adjusting its protocol stack as a function of the dynamics of network environment. Moreover, the logical separation of the cognitive network primitives, such as learning or decision making outside reconfigurable nodes (into cognitive engine), can potentially limit the benefits from local optimization and can increase the amount of signaling traffic.

CogNet (Cognitive Complete Knowledge Network) is an ongoing research project funded by NSF.[22] It proposes new cognitive network architecture designed to maintain layered abstraction of TCP/IP protocol stack. In CogNet, each protocol layer is extended with so-called Intra-layer Cognition Modules, which are software agents performing intra-layer monitoring, control, and coordination functions. Modules are interconnected through the Cognitive Bus, part of the Cognitive Plane, to coordinate the cognition modules and are implemented in parallel to the protocol stack.

A unique property of the proposed architecture is the fact that the cognitive functions implemented in intra-layer cognitive elements are distributed between different protocol layers. Such design simplifies the cognitive processes running in the network and reduces signaling overhead.

However, the performance of the proposed architecture seems to be highly dependent on Cognitive Plane operation, which is responsible for translation of end-to-end goals into objectives and configuration parameters at each layer. Consequently, the lack of proper coordination or intra-layer cognitive agents monitoring could lead to unpredictable performance results.

The CogNet project develops the IEEE 802.11[23] and CDMA[24] testbeds for gaining understanding and identifying relationships among different parameters at different layers in a real operation environment.

The cognitive network model proposed by Thomas *et al.*[12] is composed of three horizontal layers. The top level is responsible for specification and translation of user/application requirements into goals understandable by cognitive process.

Several cognitive processes can run in the immediate plane, with implementation potentially distributed between several network nodes. The cognitive process involves learning, knowledge, and decision-making and operates when information about the network is limited.

The bottom layer of the model corresponds to the Software Adaptable Network (SAN), consisting of modifiable network elements and sensors. The communication between modifiable elements and the cognitive plane is performed using the software adaptable network API. Such an architectural solution brings modularity and flexibility into the design of modifiable elements.

Gelenbe *et al.*[25] proposed the idea of cognitive packet networks, which basically moves routing and flow control capabilities from network nodes into packets. Such packets, called cognitive packets, "route themselves" and learn to avoid congestion and avoid being destroyed. Each cognitive packet contains a cognitive map and a piece of code that is executed every time the packet arrives at the network node (router). Routing decisions are taken relying on the cognitive map, as well as mailbox messages left by other packets or by the network node.

The idea of cognitive packets bears similarities to the concept of active networking,[26] related to custom code execution. However, a unique feature of cognitive packets is their ability to change their behavior based on the state of the network.

Another approach to overcoming limitations of traditional IP networks was presented by Lake *et al.*[27] The Software Programmable Intelligent Network (SPIN) merges concepts from IP, PSTN, cellular, and ad hoc networks for overcoming the fundamental limitations of IP networks (such as in-band signaling and impact of long and nested feedback loops on network performance).

SPIN architecture consists of three planes interconnected by layer-2 transport infrastructure:

- *Forwarding plane*: This plane is responsible for switching and monitoring and it can provide connectionless packet forwarding, connection oriented packet forwarding, tag switching, and label switching. Additionally, it performs active and passive measurements, such as packet loss, jitter, bandwidth, and one-way latency.
- *Control/management plane*: It manages forwarding plane devices targeting data, forwarding optimization based on the received measurements. This plane also has the advantage of physical separation from the forwarding plane, including high availability, reliability, and fault tolerance.
- *Cognitive plane*: This plane resides on top of control/management and forwarding planes, providing intelligence for and administration of the entire system. It operates multiple functions dedicated to performing single tasks, including schemas for optimal routing and load balancing, as well as managing responses to legacy control protocols.

A brief comparison of the cognitive network proposals overviewed previously is provided in Table 1.1. The following parameters were used in the comparison: consistency with TCP/IP, stack reconfigurability, cognitive process, network support, and goals.

Consistency with TCP/IP gives the degree of modifications required to work on a standard layered TCP/IP protocol reference model; for example, how easy it is to deploy the proposed approach. Most of the approaches are not "TCP-friendly," mainly due to the reliance on reconfigurable elements of the protocol

Table 1.1. Cognitive network research proposals comparison.

Approach	Consistency with TCP/IP	Reconfigurable elements	Cognitive process	Required level of support from the network	Goal
E^2R	No	Entire protocol stack	Centralized or partially distributed	High	All-IP B3G network with seamless mobility
m@ANGEL	No	Lower protocol stack layers	In access network	High in access network	Resource allocation and mobility management in heterogeneous networks
Sutton *et al.*[10]	No	Entire protocol stack	No a part of reconfigurable node	Moderate	Reconfigurable node architecture with dynamic protocol stack
CogNet	Yes	Intra-layer modules	Distributed (at the node level)	Moderate	
Thomas *et al.*[12]	No	Reconfigurable elements and network sensors	Distributed (at the network level)	Moderate	Design of generic cognitive network framework
SPIN	No	Separate cognitive/ management plane	Distributed in the network	High	Combines properties of IP and PSTN network architectures using cognition

stack. The only TCP-friendly approach is CogNet, which was specifically designed to maintain TCP/IP layer abstraction. This is achieved by introducing a cognitive network interface at each protocol layer, which ensures smooth interaction between internal elements to the layer functionalities with the cognitive engine.

Reconfigurability specifies the required degree of reconfiguration needed by the proposed cognitive network framework. Solutions such as m@ANGEL, furnish reconfigurability at the lower protocol stack layers close to hardware. As a consequence, incremental deployment in existing networks is possible, while other proposals like E^2R, Sutton *et al.*,[10] and SPIN, require entire protocol stack reconfigurability.

Cognitive process implementation ranges from centralized to distributed implementations. Centralized implementations are able to provide better control and optimization properties, while distributed ones lead to reduced operational complexity and more failures. Most of the proposals combine centralized and distributed implementation for the cognitive process, attempting to achieve an optimal trade off.

Required level of support from the network means that the cooperation from different network elements (switches and routers) is required by the approach in order to work properly. Approaches like E^2R, m@ANGEL, and SPIN rely on a high level of cooperation from network elements, while other solutions like Sutton *et al.*,[10] CogNet, and Thomas *et al.*[12] reduce the level of requested cooperation to a moderate level. In any case, it is clear that cognitive network frameworks tend to break end-to-end Internet principle by adding intelligence to the network core rather than keeping it at the end nodes.

Goals involve configuration, optimization of data flow, and its performance metric.

1.4. A Reference Cognitive Network Architecture

Presented in this section is a proposal for cognitive network architecture, shown in Fig. 1.3, derived as a combination of the key concepts from other research initiatives previously presented. The objectives are to maintain consistency with the TCP/IP protocol stack, to be simple in managing reconfigurable elements, to have a distributed cognitive process, to need a minimum level of network support, and to optimize end-to-end performance.

All these imply that cognitive network elements should be implemented in a transparent and incremental way to the existing protocol stack.

To operate with a standard protocol stack, each protocol layer is enhanced with a small software module able either to obtain internals to the layer information (observation) or to tune internal parameters (action). The information sensed at the protocol layers is delivered to the cognitive plane implemented at the cognitive node. This cognitive plane runs data analysis and decision making processes.

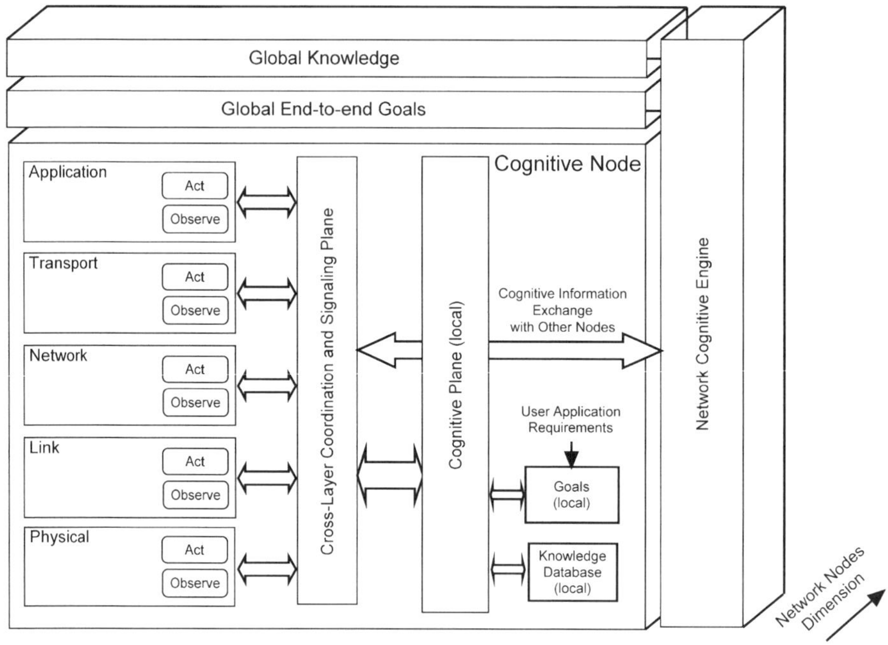

Fig. 1.3. Cognitive network framework.

Results of data analysis could lead to information classified as knowledge, storable in the local knowledge database.

The decisions made by the cognitive plane at the node aim to optimize the protocol stack and are driven by the Goals specified in the local database. The scope of these goals is local (at node level). Most of them are generated by the demands and QoS requirements of user applications running at a given cognitive node.

While goals and knowledge databases are directly connected to the cognitive plane of the node and allow instant information exchange, the cognitive plane communication with the protocol stack is performed by the Cross-layer Coordination and Signaling Plane (CCSP). CCSP is responsible for providing a proper way for signaling information delivery. An example of such functionality is the immediate delivery of parameter values. Another example is the use of a predefined threshold. Completely different signaling methods are required for parameters at different layers associated with a particular packet traveling. In summary, CCSP should provide optimal signaling information delivery and interconnecting elements of the cognitive node architecture.

The proposed architectural concepts are related to cognitive process running in a single network node. However, as defined in previous sections, the main property of cognitive networking is its network-wide scope. Therefore, the network of cognitive nodes is driven by a Network Cognitive Engine (NCE), which is capable of communicating with cognitive planes of different network nodes coordinating and managing them. NCE is responsible for harvesting cognitive information available at cognitive nodes. This information includes local goals of the node and applications demands, the knowledge obtained by the node, or direct values of specific protocol stack parameters. NCE information harvesting, which corresponds to the observation function, could be performed on a scheduled basis or by using instant requests. Moreover, information could be node related or parameters associated with a particular flow transmission.

The analysis of information gathered from cognitive nodes helps the NCE to construct global knowledge and goals after definition and upon every adjustment, which are reported back to cognitive nodes so that they can adjust their appropriate local databases and, as a result, their behavior.

A main characteristic of the cognitive network architecture is scalability, assured by the use of a combination of centric (at node level) and distributed (at network level) techniques. In particular, at node level the core cognitive techniques, such as data analysis, decision making, and learning, are concentrated in the cognitive planes of the nodes and implemented in a centralized manner. Furthermore, observation and action software add-ons to the protocol layers serve only as instruments and cognitive planes are typically "non-intelligent" ones. This constitutes one of the main differences of cognitive network architecture presented in Ref. 28, which is that it adopts cognitive processes inside a single protocol layer. Distributing cognitive process among the protocol layers (especially the learning and decision making functions) would require complex algorithms for synchronization and coordination between intra-layer cognitive processes. Alternatively, it seems that a single centralized cognitive process at node level brings a simpler solution, while implementation of cognitive process at network layer (CNE) must be distributed or clustered implemented.

A similar approach is considered for aggregation of all kinds of signaling data. Data such as that observed at the local protocol stack, user application requirements, and knowledge obtained by cognitive plane are aggregated at node level before being delivered to the CNE.

1.5. Cross-Layer Design for Cognitive Networks

An essential element of cognitive network architecture presented in the previous section is the cross-layer coordination and signaling plane, which is recognized for providing information exchange between the cognitive primitives, observation, and action performed, either at the node or across the network. For example, in Ref. 28, the availability of the Cognitive Bus, which is responsible for signaling information exchange between different layers of the protocol stack, is considered. However, communication techniques implemented by the Cognitive Bus are left out of the scope of this text.

In the following sections, an overview of the available approaches for cross-layer signaling and techniques most appropriate for cognitive networking is given.

1.5.1. *Cross-layer design proposals*

Information exchange between two or more layers of the protocol stack raises important issues concerning the implementation of different cross-layer solutions inside the TCP/IP protocol reference model, their coexistence, and interoperability.[29]

The principles behind implementation of common cross-layer signaling models are directed towards rapid prototyping, portability, and efficient implementation of cross-layer entities, while maintaining TCP/IP modularity.[30]

In this framework, several cross-layer signaling architectures have been proposed:

Interlayer signaling pipe is one of the first approaches used for implementation of cross-layer signaling,[31] allowing the propagation of signaling messages layer-to-layer along with packet data flow. Signaling information, included in an optional portion of packet headers, follows the packet processing path to another in the protocol stack, either in a top-bottom or a bottom-top manner.

An important property of this signaling method is that signaling information inserted into a packet header can be associated with this particular packet either at the ingress or at the egress path of the protocol stack.

The main disadvantage of the Interlayer Signaling Pipe method is the limitation of the propagation of the signaling information to the direction of the packet flow, making it unsuitable to cross-layer schemes which require instant signaling.

Direct Interlayer Communication is another signaling method which was proposed in Ref. 31 to improve the interlayer signaling pipe method by the introduction of signaling shortcuts performed out of band. In this way, the proposed Cross-Layer Signaling Shortcuts (CLASS) approach allows non-neighboring layers of the protocol stack to exchange messages, skipping processing at every adjacent layer.

Along with reduced processing overhead, CLASS avoids insertion of signaling information into packet headers, which makes it suitable for bidirectional communication. Signaling messages use the Internet Control Message Protocol (ICMP).[32,33]

Despite the advantages of direct communication between protocol layers and a standardized way of signaling, the ICMP-based approach involves operation with heavy protocol headers (IP and ICMP), as well as significant protocol processing overhead. Moreover, it appears to be limited to request-response actions, while more complicated signaling should be adapted to handle asynchronous events. To this aim, a mechanism which uses callback functions can be employed. This mechanism allows a given protocol layer to register a specific procedure (callback function) with another protocol layer, whose execution is triggered by a specific event at that layer.

Central Cross-Layer Plane, implemented in parallel to the protocol stack, is probably the most widely proposed cross-layer signaling architecture. Implementation

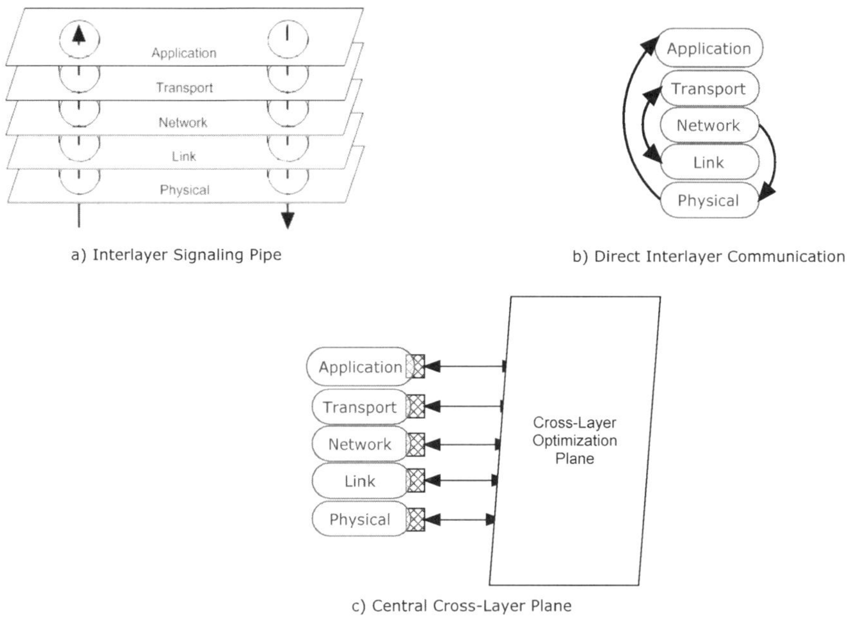

of this signaling method could be as simple as a shared database accessed by all the layers.[34] More advanced implementations introduce signaling interfaces as each protocol level internally provides access to the internal protocol layer parameters and functions. Communication with the central cross-layer plane is maintained by using a predefined set of API functions.[30,35]

1.5.2. *Cross-layer design for cognitive networks*

Most of the existing cross-layer signaling proposals employ cross-layer signaling between different layers within the protocol stack of a single node. However, as emphasized in Ref. 12, true cognitive networking should maintain a network-wide scope with cognitive process operating based on end-to-end goals. Consequentially, most of the cross-layer signaling approaches currently available in literature are not appropriate to support cognitive networks which require network-wide propagation of cross-layer signaling information. In addition, there is the question of how cross-layer signaling can be performed.

A set of proper techniques required for network-wide cross-layer signaling is discussed next.

Among the overviewed methods, an encapsulation of signaling information into packet headers or ICMP messages can be considered appropriate. Their advantages, underlined in the single-node protocol stack scenario, become more significant for network-wide communication. For example, the way of encapsulating cross-layer signaling data into optional fields of the protocol headers does not produce any additional overhead and keeps the association of signaling information with a specific packet. However, this method limits propagation of signaling information to packet paths in the network. For that reason, it is desirable to combine packet headers signaling with ICMP messages, which are well suited for explicit communication between network nodes.

One of the early examples of cross-network cross-layering is the Explicit Congestion Notification (ECN) presented in Ref. 36. It realizes in-band signaling approach by marking in-transit TCP data packet with congestion notification bit. However, due to the limitation of signaling propagation to the packet paths, this notification needs to propagate to the receiver first, which echoes it back in the TCP ACK packet outgoing to the sender node. This unnecessary signaling loop can be avoided with explicit ICMP packets signaling. However, it requires traffic generation capability from network routers and it consumes bandwidth.

An example of the adaptation of Central Cross-Layer Plane-like architecture to the cross-network cross-layer signaling is presented in Ref. 37. This reference suggests the use of a network service which collects parameter values related to the wireless channel located at the link, as well as at the physical layer and the provisioning of this information to adaptive mobile applications.

A unique combination of local and network-wide cross-layer signaling approaches called Cross-Talk is presented in Ref. 38. CrossTalk architecture consists of two cross-layer optimization planes, where one is responsible for the organization of cross-layer information exchange between protocol layers of the local protocol stack and their coordination. The other plane is responsible for network-wide coordination, considered the aggregation of cross-layer information provided by the local plane. It serves as an interface for cross-layer signaling over the network. Most of the signaling is performed in-band, using the packet headers method, making it accessible not only at the end host but at the network routers as well. Cross-layer information received from the network is aggregated and then can be considered for the optimization of local protocol stack operation based on global network conditions.

Main problems associated with deployment of cross-layer signaling over the network, also pointed in Ref. 39, include security issues, problems with non-conformant routers, and processing efficiency. Security considerations require the design of proper protective mechanisms, avoiding protocol attacks attempted by non-friendly network nodes, which furnish incorrect cross-layer information in order to trigger specific behavior. The second problem addresses misbehavior of network routers. It is pointed out that in 70% of the cases IP packets with unknown options are dropped in the network or by the receiver protocol stack. Finally, the problem with processing efficiency is related to the additional costs of the routers hardware for cross-layer information processing. While it is not an issue for the low-speed links, it becomes relevant for high speed ones where most of the routers decrement only the TTL field to maintain a high packet processing speed.

1.5.3. *Co-existence and integration*

An important challenge of the design of cognitive network solutions corresponds to the implementation of cognitive network primitives in current networking environments, given the limitations of the widely spread TCP/IP stack and of proper solutions of the implementation in "non-friendly" network environments.

Indeed, cognitive networking relies on active network nodes which cooperate for observation, analysis, decision making, and action elements. However, an assumption that all the network nodes are friendly to cognitive networking can be verified. Moreover, some of the nodes capable of cognitive networking may not be willing to cooperate.

The possibility of deployment of cognitive networks in widely IP networks depends on the fundamental characteristics of the cognitive network solutions overviewed in Sec. 2.2.3.

One of the main issues is the consistency with TCP/IP node between the network node implementing cognitive network functionalities and an ordinary network node running unmodified TCP/IP stack. A potential solution to obtain compatibility is the introduction of a cognitive network interface at each protocol stack layer to provide access to the internal layer parameters and functions to the cognitive engine.

The limitation of reconfigurable elements to lower protocol layers only will help avoiding modification of the core of the protocol stack implemented in the operating system, which obviously will facilitate the deployment. However, this approach may lead to limitations in the design of cognitive network algorithms leading to the reduced performance.

Another important factor affecting co-existence with TCP/IP and incremental deployment of cognitive networks is related to the level of support required from the network elements. In the case of high reliance required implementation, it is possible only in networks (or parts of networks) with cognitive-friendly switches and routers, requiring the deployment of additional equipment. This is not always possible, especially in the widely deployed IP networks. However, it is feasible in isolated networks such as the cellular network environment.

1.6. Conclusions and Future Directions

Network evolution towards self-aware autonomous adaptive networking resolves inefficiency of network configuration and management. In order to optimize network operation, reconfiguration, management, and improving performance, it has been proposed to introduce self-awareness, self-management, and self-healing properties by bringing "intelligence" into the network, creating a new paradigm in networking, referred to as cognitive networking.

This chapter provides a detailed survey of state-of-the-art and future directions in cognitive networking by defining fundamental techniques, enabling cognitive properties and unveiling details of adaptation, learning, and goal optimization processes.

Comparison of available research proposals motivated the design of a promising cognitive network architecture capable of fully implementing cognitive network techniques.

Finally, discussion on the required properties of the cross-layer design for cognitive networks and corresponding deployment issues are discussed.

References

1. C. Barakat, E. Altman and W. Dabbous, On TCP performance in a heterogeneous network: A survey, *IEEE Communications Magazine*, **38**(1), 40–46 (January 2000).
2. D. D. Clark, C. Partridge, J. C. Ramming and J. T. Wroclawski, A knowledge plane for the Internet, *ACM SIGCOMM*, Karlsruhe, Germany (August 2003).
3. *Clash of the Titans — WiMAX and 4G: The Battle for Convergence is Joined*, Maravedis Market research and analysis (July 2006).
4. D. L. Tennenhouse, J. M. Smith, W. D. Sincoskie, D. J. Wetherall and G. J. Minden, A survey of active network research, *IEEE Communications Magazine*, **35**(1), 80–86 (January 1997).
5. D. Kliazovich, F. Granelli, G. Pau and M. Gerla, APOHN: Subnetwork layering to improve TCP performance over heterogeneous paths, *IEEE Next Generation Internet Design and Engineering (NGI)*, Valencia, Spain (April 2006).
6. V. Firoiu, J.-Y. Le Boudec, D. Towsley and Z.-L. Zhang, Theories and models for Internet quality of service, *IEEE Proceedings*, **90**(9), 1565–1591 (2002).
7. H. Zhu, M. Li, I. Chlamtac and B. Prabhakaran, A survey of quality of service in IEEE 802.11 networks, *IEEE Wireless Communications*, **11**(4), 6–14 (2004).
8. P. Demestichas, G. Dimitrakopoulos and J. Strassner, Introducing reconfigurability and cognitive networks concepts in the wireless world, *IEEE Vehicular Technology Magazine*, **1**(2), 32–39 (2006).
9. J. Mitola, *Cognitive Radio: An Integrated Agent Architecture for Software Defined Radio*, PhD thesis, Royal Institute of Technology (2000).
10. P. Sutton, L. E. Doyle and K. E. Nolan, A reconfigurable platform for cognitive networks, *1st International Conference on Cognitive Radio Oriented Wireless Networks and Communications*, 1–5 (June 2006).
11. R. Thomas, *Cognitive Networks*, PhD dissertation, Virginia Tech (June 2007).
12. R. W. Thomas, D. H. Friend, L. A. DaSilva and A. B. MacKenzie, Cognitive networks: Adaptation and learning to achieve end-to-end performance objectives, *IEEE Communications Magazine*, **44**(12), 51–57 (December 2006).
13. P. Surana, *Meta-Compilation of Language Abstractions*, PhD Thesis Dissertation, Northwestern University, Illinois (2006).
14. I. F. Akyildiz, W.-Y. Lee, M. C. Vuran and S. Mohanty, Next generation/dynamic spectrum access/cognitive radio wireless networks: A survey, *Computer Networks*, **50**, 2127–2159 (May 2006).
15. W. Krenik and A. Batra, Cognitive radio techniques for wide area networks, *Design Automation Conference*, 409–412 (June 2005).
16. *National Science Foundation — Funding opportunities*, available at http://www.nsf.gov/funding/aboutfunding.jsp.

17. *Sixth Framework Programme Research* — FP6 home page, http://ec.europa.eu/research/fp6/ (2002).
18. *Seventh Framework Programme Research* — FP7 home page, http://cordis.europa.eu/fp7 (2007).
19. D. Bourse, S. Buljore, A. Delautre, T. Wiebke, M. Dillinger, J. Brakensiek, K. Moessner, K. El-Khazen and N. Alonistioti, *The End-to-End Reconfigurability* (E^2R) *Research*, SDR Forum Technical Conference, Orlando, USA (2003).
20. P. Demestichas, V. Stavroulaki, D. Boscovic, A. Lee and J. Strassner, m@ANGEL: autonomic management platform for seamless cognitive connectivity to the mobile internet, *IEEE Communications Magazine*, **4**(6), 118–127 (June 2006).
21. D. Bourse and K. El-Khazen, End-to-end reconfigurability (E^2R) research perspectives, *IEICE Transactions on Communications, Special Section on Software Defined Radio Technology and Its Applications*, 4148–4157 (2005).
22. Cognet Project, http://adaptive5.ucsd.edu/cognet/.
23. P. Baumgart, *Building an IEEE 802.11 Testbed for the CogNet: Cognitive Complete Knowledge Network,* available at http://adaptive5.ucsd.edu/cognet/Documents.
24. R. Rao and B. S. Manoj, Cognitive cellular network testbed development, Internal report, 2007, available at http://ece-classweb.ucsd.edu:16080/fall07/ece291/Descriptions/cog.%20wifi_Fall07.doc.
25. E. Gelenbe, Z. Xu and E. Seref, Cognitive packet networks, *11th IEEE International Conference on Tools with Artificial Intelligence*, 47–54 (November 1999).
26. S. F. Bush and A. Kulkarni, *Active Networks and Active Network Management: A Proactive Management Framework,* Kluwer Academic/Plenum Publishers, New York, Boston, Dordrecht, London, Moscow (2001).
27. S. M. Lake Sr., Cognitive networking with software programmable intelligent networks for wireless and wireline critical communications, *IEEE Military Communications Conference* (*MILCOM*), 1693–1699 (October 2005).
28. B. S. Manoj, R. R. Rao and M. Zorzi, *Architectures and Protocols for Next Generation Cognitive Networking*, Frank H. P. Fitzek and Marcos D. Katz (eds.), *Cognitive Wireless Networks Concepts, Methodologies and Visions Inspiring the Age of Enlightenment of Wireless Communications*, Springer (November 2007).
29. V. Srivastava and M. Motani, Cross-layer design: A survey and the road ahead, *IEEE Communications Magazine*, **43**(12), 112–119 (2005).
30. V. T. Raisinghani and S. Iyer, Cross layer feedback architecture for mobile device protocol stacks, *IEEE Communications Magazine*, **44**(1), 85–92 (2006).
31. Q. Wang and M. A. Abu-Rgheff, Cross-layer signaling for next-generation wireless systems, *IEEE Wire-less Communications and Networking* (*WCNC*), 1084–1089 (2003).
32. A. Conta and S. Deering, *Internet Control Message Protocol* (*ICMPv6*) *for the Internet Protocol Version 6* (*IPv6*) *Specification*, RFC 2463 (1998).
33. J. Postel, *Internet Control Message Protocol*, RFC 792 (1981).
34. K. Chen, S. H. Shah and K. Nahrstedt, Cross-layer design for data accessibility in mobile ad hoc networks. Wireless personal communications, Special Issue on *Multimedia Network Protocols and Enabling Radio Technologies*, **21**, 49–75 (2002).
35. K. M. El Defrawy, M. S. El Zarki and M. M. Khairy, Proposal for a cross-layer coordination framework for next generation wireless systems, *ACM International Conference on Communications and Mobile Computing*, 141–146 (2006).
36. K. Ramakrishnan, S. Floyd and D. Black, *The Addition of Explicit Congestion Notification* (*ECN*) to IP, RFC 3168 (2001).

37. B.-J. Kim, A network service providing wireless channel information for adaptive mobile applications: I: Proposal, *IEEE International Conference on Communications (ICC)*, 1345–1351 (2001).
38. R. Winter, J. H. Schiller, N. Nikaein and C. Bonnet, CrossTalk: cross-layer decision support based on global knowledge, *IEEE Communications Magazine*, **44**(1), 93–99 (2006).
39. P. Sarolahti and S. Floyd, *Cross-layer Indications for Transport Protocols*, Internet draft draft-sarolahti-tsvwg-crosslayer-00.txt (2007).

Chapter 2

A Cross-Layer Approach to Reducing Delay and Energy Consumption Based on Data Importance in Sensor Networks

Jisu Oh*, Kyoung-Don Kang†, Jang Young Kim‡ and Mikhail I. Gofman§

Department of Computer Science
State University of New York at Binghamton
**joh@cs.binghamton.edu*
†kang@cs.binghamton.edu
‡jkim31@binghamton.edu
§mgofman1@binghamton.edu

It is essential to reduce the end-to-end delay and energy consumption in wireless sensor networks, so in this chapter, we design and evaluate a cross-layer approach for integrated packet scheduling, data aggregation, and medium access control. Our protocol considers data semantics to deliver more important data with shorter delays and higher resolution. The results of our performance evaluation in TOSSIM show that our approach can reduce the average delay for delivering important data packets by up to several orders of magnitude compared to the tested baseline approaches, while improving energy efficiency.

2.1. Introduction

In a number of WSN applications, such as assisted living, fire detection, structural monitoring, and surveillance, it is critical to reduce the end-to-end (E2E) delay and energy consumption. However, E2E delay reduction and energy conservation may pose conflicting requirements. Immediate packet transmission without in-network processing may reduce the E2E delay. However, it increases the energy consumption due to redundant data transmissions causing collisions and network congestion. In-network processing improves energy efficiency by aggregating similar data packets. However, a sensor node may have to delay the delivery of a data packet to aggregate it with incoming packets. As a result, the E2E delay may increase.

To resolve potential conflicts between the delay and aggregation, we present a novel concept of the *most important data first* to deliver important data with shorter delays and higher resolution. In contrast, a node delays the delivery of a redundant

†Contact Author

packet to aggregate it with other incoming packets that may contain similar sensor data values. To support the most important data first concept, we present a new cross-layer protocol called highest importance first (HIF). Our protocol takes advantage of data importance levels, which can be obtained at the application layer, for efficient packet scheduling, data aggregation, and medium access control. Despite the importance, relatively little prior work has been done to significantly improve WSN performance and energy efficiency based on data criticality.

There are several ways to determine the importance of sensor data. First, the importance of a sensor data can be determined by its value. For example, a high temperature reading can be more important than a normal temperature value for fire detection. Also, in disaster recovery, a sensor data indicating vital signs of survivors in a disaster area are critical. Second, multiple sensor data can be fused to detect an event of interest such as fire. The confidence of a detected event can be expressed as a number in [0, 1] where confidence 1 confirms the detected event with the highest possible confidence.[1] The higher the confidence, the greater the importance. Alternatively, data packets can be associated with E2E deadlines, for example, to support battlefield monitoring. In this case, a packet with a shorter deadline is more important. The key contribution of this paper is not to develop a new method to determine the importance of sensor data. Instead, we aim to develop and evaluate a cross-layer protocol, which seamlessly integrates packet scheduling, data aggregation, and medium access control to support the most important data first concept. Therefore, in the rest of this chapter, we assume that data importance is given and focus on the design, implementation, and evaluation of the HIF protocol.

For packet scheduling, HIF employs multilevel fixed priority queues to deliver important data with high resolution and short delays. The importance of data is quantized into several levels equal to the number of the fixed priority queues. According to the importance level, a data packet is added to the corresponding queue. Due to fixed priority scheduling, a data packet in a low priority queue can be transmitted only when there is no data packet in the higher priority queue(s). Data aggregation is applied to the data in each queue, if their sensor values are similar and sensing ranges overlap. Thus, redundant data in a low priority queue will be delayed longer for further data aggregation. As a result, important data will experience relatively short delays. Further, the resolution of important data is more probable to be high due to less in-network aggregation. One may argue that low priority packets may starve due to fixed priority scheduling; however, suppressing redundant data transmissions can enhance the timeliness of delivering important packets, while saving energy. Also, via data aggregation, we alleviate potential starvation at a low priority queue. If there are a large number of high importance data, our protocol will aggregate them together rather than transmitting them one by one. Generally, less network congestion can enhance the reliability of data delivery too.

In addition to packet scheduling and in-network processing at each node, HIF supports prioritized-MAC layer service to ensure that the node with the most important data in the neighborhood has the highest probability to access the wireless channel first. In distributed MAC protocols, e.g., the Distributed Coordination Function (DCF) in 802.11, carrier sensing and collision avoidance are required to coordinate concurrent channel access by multiple nodes. In this chapter, we differentiate MAC based on data importance. Especially, we adapt the 802.11e[2] protocol — an extension of 802.11 for QoS enhancement — to allocate a small DCF Interframe Space (DIFS) and back-off window size for a high priority queue. As a result, the node with the most important data will have the shortest DIFS before channel access. Further, it will have probabilistically the smallest random back-off upon a collision.

Our protocol is implemented in TinyOS[3] and evaluated in TOSSIM.[4] In our performance evaluation, HIF incorporating scheduling, in-network aggregation, and differentiated MAC services based on data semantics reduces the average E2E delay of the high and medium priority packets by orders of magnitude compared to the tested baseline approaches. Also, HIF considerably enhances energy efficiency.

The rest of the chapter is organized as follows. Section 2.2 describes the HIF protocol design and implementation. Section 2.3 presents our performance evaluation results. Related work is presented in Sec. 2.4. Finally, Sec. 2.5 concludes the chapter and discusses future work.

2.2. Design and Implementation of the Highest Importance First Protocol

This section presents the design of our cross-layer protocol to support the most important data first concept via efficient packet scheduling, in-network processing, and medium access control. It also describes the implementation of the HIF protocol in TinyOS.

2.2.1. *Data importance-aware scheduling*

The importance level of a data packet can be determined based on the sensor data value as previously discussed. Alternatively, the confidence level of an event, e.g., fire, can be computed using multi-modal sensor readings such as the temperature, light, and noise values.[1] Given the confidence c ($\in [0, 1]$) of a data packet, the packet is added to queue i if $\frac{n-i}{n} < c \leq \frac{n-i+1}{n}$ where $1 \leq i \leq n-1$. Note that $0 \leq c \leq 1/n$ for $i = n$.

For packet scheduling, we apply the fixed priority scheduling algorithm. Let us assume that there are n fixed priority queues where queue 1 is the highest priority queue. A data packet is added to a queue according to its importance level. Packets in queue i ($2 \leq i \leq n$) can be transmitted only after all the packets in the higher priority queue(s) are transmitted. Hence, important data packets are transmitted before less critical ones.

By delaying lower priority packets, important packets can be transmitted with shorter delays. Further, low importance data can be aggregated further while waiting in the queue. When the network is congested, it is acceptable to degrade the resolution of low importance data, because relatively noncritical information is conveyed by them.

2.2.2. *Data semantic-aware in-network processing*

Energy efficiency is a major design requirement in WSNs consisting of battery-powered sensor nodes such as MICA motes. Since the packet transmission cost dominates energy consumption in WSNs, in-network aggregation has been applied to reduce energy consumption by reducing the number of packet transmissions.[5,6] Aggregation, however, requires a data packet to be delayed until a new sensor reading becomes available or packets arrive from different nodes. As a result, the E2E delay may increase as previously discussed. To handle these conflicts, our in-network processing cooperates with packet scheduling to improve both E2E delay and energy efficiency.

We perform in-network aggregation based on the value similarity and spatial proximity between two sensor readings, similar to ESCAN.[7] Each data packet contains a sensor reading value and its coverage, $\langle value, coverage\rangle$. *value* is a pair of the minimum and maximum sensor readings, $(vmin, vmax)$, in an area covered by *coverage*. *coverage* is a region represented by a circle whose center is (x, y) and radius is r. In Fig. 2.1, for example, packet p_1 has value $\langle(vmin_1, vmax_1)$ and coverage $(x_1, y_1, r_1)\rangle$, while packet p_2 consists of $\langle(vmin_2, vmax_2)$ and $(x_2, y_2, r_2)\rangle$. To aggregate two arbitrary packets p_1 and p_2 into one packet, we define the value

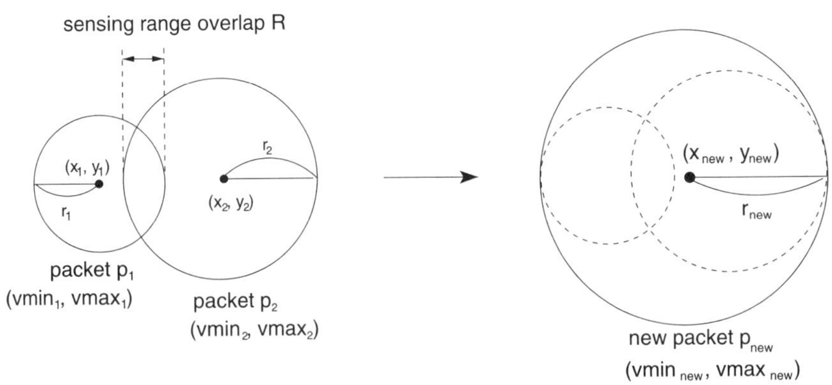

Fig. 2.1. Aggregation two packets into one packet.

difference between p_1 and p_2:

$$T = \frac{max(vmax_1, vmax_2) - min(vmin_1, vmin_2)}{average(vmin_1, vmax_1, vmin_2, vmax_2)}. \tag{2.1}$$

Further, we define the sensing range overlap:

$$R = r_1 + r_2 - distance((x_1, y_1), (x_2, y_2)) \tag{2.2}$$

where *distance* is the Euclidean distance. To aggregate p_1 and p_2 into p_{new} in Fig. 2.1, two aggregation conditions should be satisfied: (1) $T \leq T_{threshold}$ and (2) sensing range overlap $R \geq R_{threshold}$ where $R_{threshold} > 0$.

If the two aggregation conditions are met, p_1 and p_2 are aggregated and a new packet p_{new} is generated with a new value and coverage as follows:

$$value_{new} : vmin_{new} = min(vmin_1, vmin_2) \tag{2.3}$$
$$vmax_{new} = max(vmax_1, vmax_2),$$

$$coverage_{new} : r_{new} = \frac{r_1 + r_2 + distance((x_1, y_1), (x_2, y_2))}{2} \tag{2.4}$$
$$x_{new} = (x_1 + x_2)/2$$
$$y_{new} = (y_1 + y_2)/2.$$

2.2.3. *Prioritized MAC (P-MAC)*

Wireless channel access by multiple network nodes is controlled by the MAC layer. In HIF, channel access is also differentiated according to the importance of data to transmit.

To differentiate MAC layer service, we determine the random wait before channel probing and contention window size, similar to 802.11e.[2,8–10] A node with a high priority packet to forward waits for a shorter amount of time before probing the channel. Upon a collision, it randomly picks the back-off delay within the contention window $CW = [CW_{min}, CW_{max}]$. The size of CW is determined by the priority of the packet to be forwarded. In Table 2.1, for example, the contention window size is differentiated among three priority levels: high, medium and low.

2.2.4. *Implementation of the highest importance first protocol*

Figure 2.2 shows key components of the HIF protocol implemented in TinyOS. At every sampling period, each node gets a sensor reading such as temperature via

Table 2.1. Contention window size.

Priority	High	Medium	Low
CW_{min}	7	16	32
CW_{max}	15	31	524

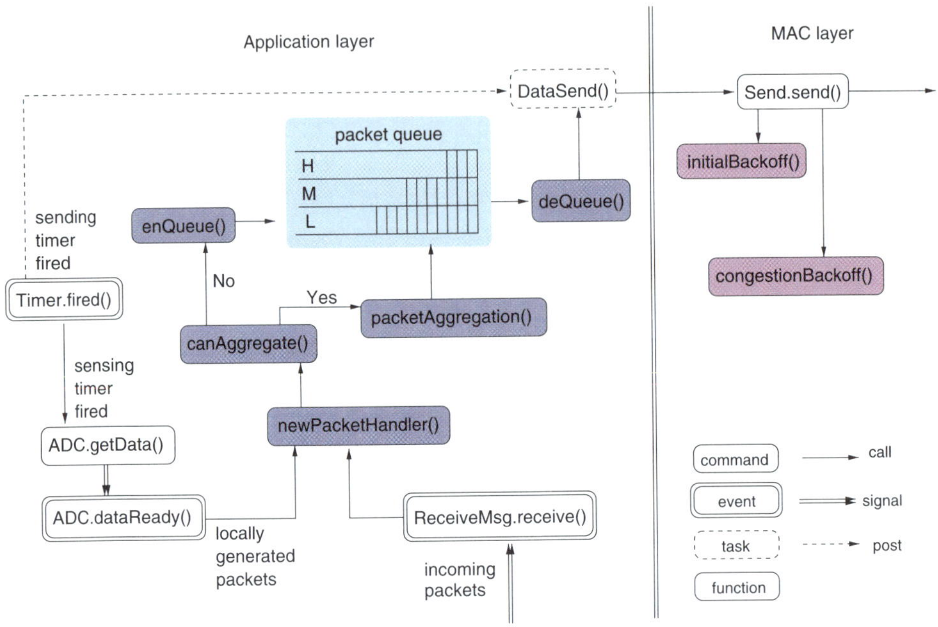

Fig. 2.2. HIF protocol components.

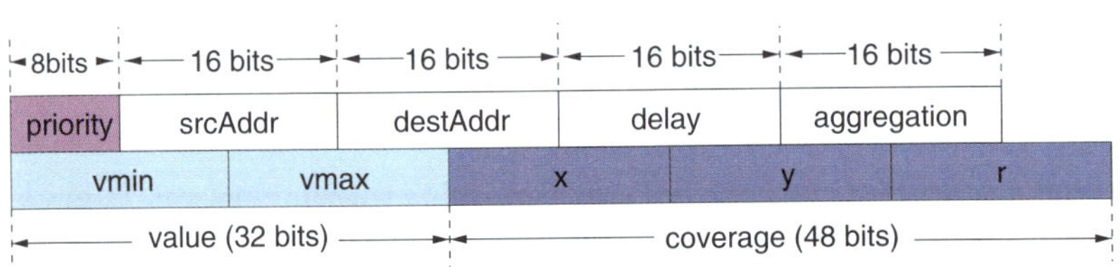

Fig. 2.3. HIF packet format.

ADC.getData( ) and *ADC.dataReady*( ) and generates a new HIF data packet. Figure 2.3 shows the format of a HIF packet, in which *delay* measures how much time the packet has spent in the network since it was generated. When two packets are aggregated into one, we set the longer delay of the two to the new packet's delay. The aggregation field in Fig. 2.3 shows the total number of packets aggregated into the current packet.

A new packet is generated using the sensor reading taken at each sampling period and it is passed to *newPacketHandler*( ) in Fig. 2.2, which determines the new packet's importance. After that, *canAggregation*( ) is called to check whether or not the new packet can be aggregated with any packet already in the corresponding queue based on the aggregation rules described in Sec. 2.2.2. If the new packet can be aggregated with a packet in the queue, *packetAggregation*( ) aggregates the two packets into one. Otherwise, *enQueue*( ) adds the new packet at the end of the corresponding queue. *ReceiveMsg.receive*( ) receives a packet arriving from a different sensor node and handles the packet according to its importance in a way similar to managing a locally generated packet. As discussed in Sec. 2.2.1, each node schedules packet transmissions in the highest importance first manner via *deQueue*( ).

2.3. Performance Evaluation

Experimental settings and performance evaluation results are discussed in this section. The performance of HIF is evaluated in TOSSIM. Especially, we use PowerTOSSIM[11] to measure the energy consumption in addition to measuring the delay.

For performance evaluation, we assume that there are three fixed priority queues, i.e., high, medium, and low priority queues. Due to resource constraints, we limit the maximum queue length to be 60 packets per priority level. Thus, maximum 180 data packets can be queued at each node. Also, packets in each queue are transmitted in a FIFO manner. In this way, we reduce the memory consumption and computation time overhead for maintaining the queues.

Also, we use the contention window sizes specified in Table 2.1. For performance evaluation purposes, we set $T_{threshold} = 0.35$ (Eq. (2.1)) and $R_{threshold} = 10\,\text{ft}$ (Eq. (2.2)). Further, we use the TOSSIM radio model that simulates realistic radio characteristics. A description of the other experimental settings follows:

- Every sensor node is stationary and each node knows its own physical location.
- The simulated area is divided into equal-size cells and one sensor node is randomly located in each cell.
- We use the tree network topology. We assume that there is a single base station and all sensor nodes report to the base station. The base station is located in the left bottom cell. Figures 2.4 and 2.8 show our network topologies with 25 and 49 nodes used for our experiments.
- Each sensor node creates high, medium, and low priority packets with the probability 0.1, 0.3 and 0.6, respectively. We claim this setting is reasonable, as critical events, e.g., fire or earthquakes, could be relatively infrequent.
- We compare the performance of HIF to two baselines: BASE and ESCAN[7] — a well known approach for data aggregation in WSNs. In BASE, a single queue is used to hold up to 180 packets. Thus, the notion of data importance is not supported. Further, packets are scheduled in a FIFO manner. Neither data aggregation nor differentiated MAC is supported. In ESCAN, a single queue is used and packets are scheduled in a FIFO fashion. Data packets are aggregated, if their values are not different by more than the specified threshold and their sensing ranges overlap, similar to HIF.

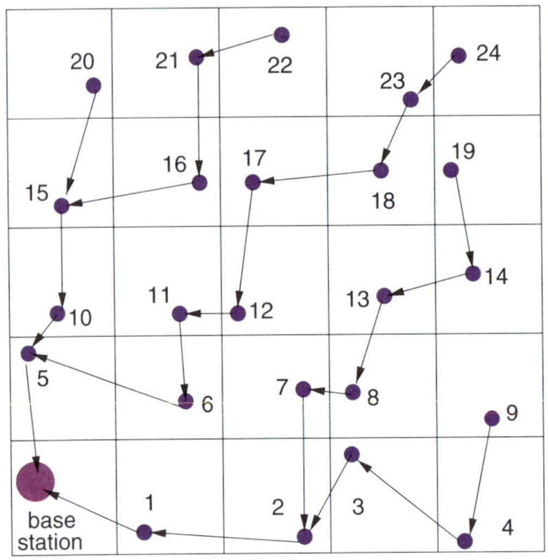

Fig. 2.4. Network topology with 25 nodes (Exp. Set 1).

Each simulation run is executed for 300 s. At every 0.5 s, each node samples the environment to generate a sensor reading. Each performance data presented in this section is the average of 5 simulation runs. 90% confidence intervals are also derived and presented by vertical lines in the figures. Our experiments consist of two sets with 25 and 49 simulated sensor nodes. The results are described next.

2.3.1. *Experiment set 1*

In this subsection, the E2E delay, number of the packets received by the base station, and energy consumption are measured for the network setting shown in Fig. 2.4.

2.3.1.1. *End-to-end delay*

Figure 2.5 shows the average E2E delay of the tested approaches. In the figure, hif_h, hif_m, and hif_l indicate the average E2E delay of the high, medium, and low priority packets in HIF, respectively. As shown in the figure, our cross-layer protocol reduces the average E2E delay of the high and medium priority packets by orders of magnitude compared to BASE and ESCAN. In HIF, the average E2E delay is 115.87 ± 9.62 ms and 458.16 ± 50.6 ms for high and medium priority packets, respectively. As shown in Fig. 2.5, the average E2E delay of low priority packets in HIF is similar to the E2E delay of ESCAN. This demonstrates that HIF significantly reduces the E2E delay for important packets without excessively increasing the delay of low priority packets.

The E2E delay of BASE in Fig. 2.5 is remarkably long. Specifically, its average E2E delay is 13,986.96 ± 664.31 ms. This is because BASE transmits all raw

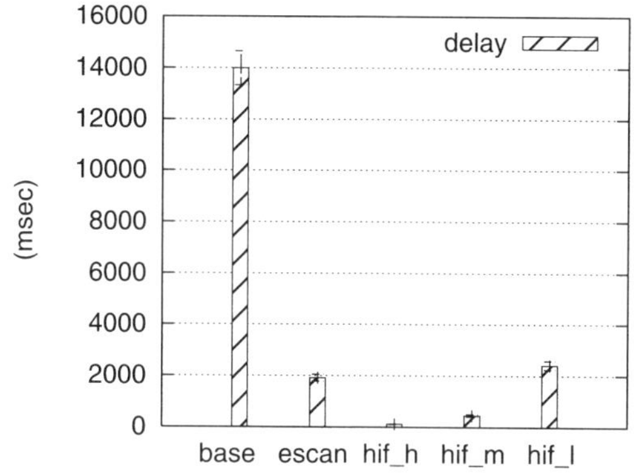

Fig. 2.5. Average E2E delay (Exp. Set 1).

packets in a FIFO manner with no in-network aggregation. By aggregating data, HIF and ESCAN decrease the E2E delay. HIF further reduces the delay of the high and medium packets via efficient packet scheduling and MAC based on data importance. Unlike HIF, BASE and ESCAN do not differentiate packets based on data semantics. Consequently, important packets are delayed and lost or dropped with the same probability as less critical packets.

2.3.1.2. *Energy consumption*

Figure 2.6 shows the per node average energy consumption for all the tested approaches. Both ESCAN and HIF significantly reduce the energy consumption, via data aggregation, compared to BASE. Specifically, each node in HIF and ESCAN consume 1,473.23 mJ and 1,700.17 mJ in average. As expected, BASE with no mechanism to reduce radio communication depletes battery quickly. The per node energy consumption of BASE is approximately 10,273.48 mJ, which is higher than ESCAN

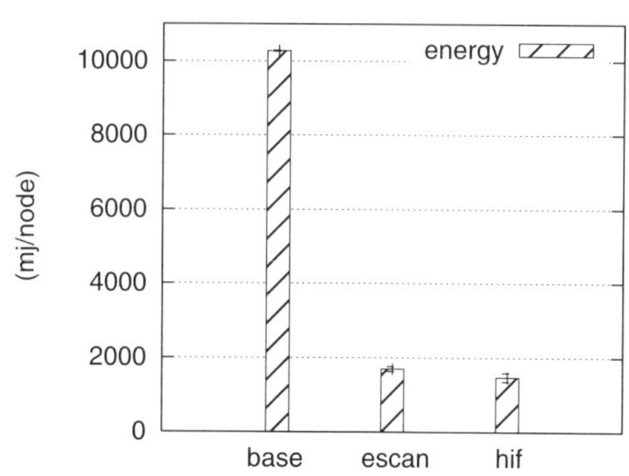

Fig. 2.6. Average per-node energy consumption (Exp. Set 1).

and HIF by an order of magnitude. Unlike ESCAN, HIF reduces energy consumption by aggregating less critical data packets more aggressively by the cross-layer approach based on data semantics.

Since we use Mica2 mote as our energy model, we can calculate approximate mote lifetime for each approach. Typically one AA battery capacity is 4.3 watt-hour (1 watt-hour = 1,000 mJ/s ×3,600 s).[12] As each mote runs using two AA batteries, the total energy capacity of one mote is 8.6 watt-hour. Given the total capacity and the measured average energy consumption per node in Fig. 2.6, we have got 10.46 days lifetime for BASE, 63.30 days for ESCAN, and 72.98 days for HIF. Therefore, HIF can prolong the network lifetime by more than seven times compared to BASE.

2.3.1.3. *Number of received packets*

ESCAN and HIF aggregate data packets based on their value and spatial proximity. In this way, ESCAN and HIF can reduce energy consumption and packet losses due to channel contention and network congestion. In Fig. 2.7, the dashed bars indicate the total number of packets received at the base station. For ESCAN and HIF, we also show the number of generated packets by gray bars. As shown in the figure, ESCAN and HIF significantly reduce the total number of transmitted packets. In BASE, more than 1,000 packets are delivered to the base station. In contrast, less than 200 packets are transmitted to the base station in ESCAN and HIF.

Figure 2.7 shows that, in HIF, the medium and low priority packets are more aggressively aggregated than the high priority packets due to the fixed priority scheduling and differentiated MAC based on data importance. We have observed that the queue in BASE and ESCAN overflows more often near the base station due to the increased traffic. In HIF, we have not observed any overflow in the high priority queue. In contrast, we have observed that ESCAN and BASE lose packets with equal probability regardless of their importance.

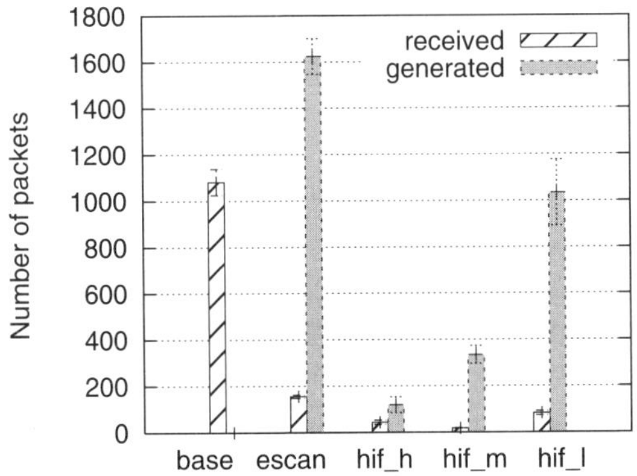

Fig. 2.7. Number of received packets (Exp. Set 1).

2.3.2. *Experiment set 2*

Figure 2.8 shows the second experimental scenario considered in this chapter. Especially, in this scenario, a fire event is placed at upper-right corner the sensor node 40. The radius of the simulated fire is 10 ft and sensor nodes near the fire generate high priority data as shown in Fig. 2.8. Also, nodes around the fire boundary generate medium priority data. The remaining nodes in the network transmit low priority data to the base station.

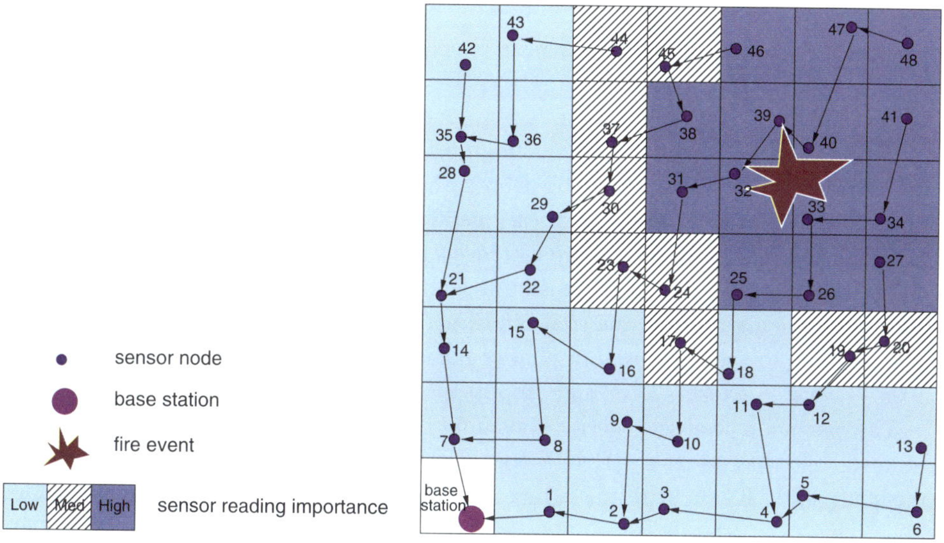

Fig. 2.8. Network topology with 49 nodes (Exp. Set 2).

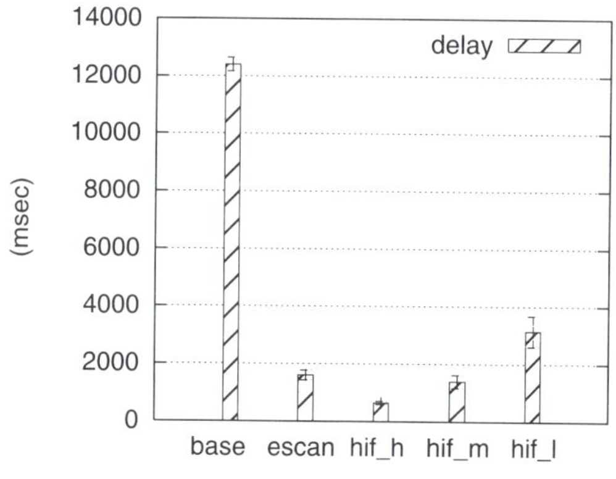

Fig. 2.9. Average E2E delay (Exp. Set 2).

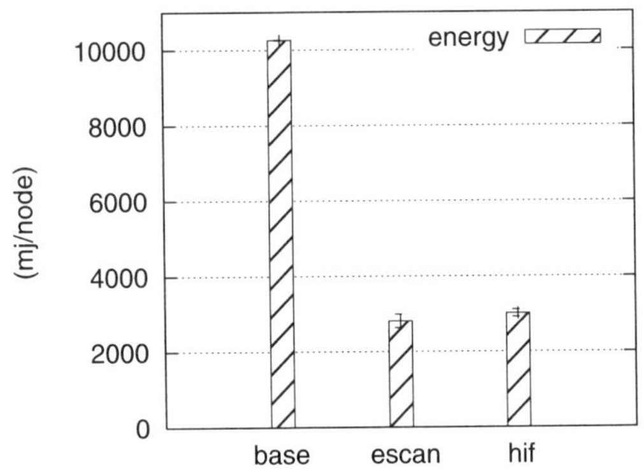

Fig. 2.10. Average per-node energy consumption (Exp. Set 2).

As shown in Fig. 2.9, HIF delivers high priority packets considerably faster than the other packets. In HIF, the E2E delay of high, medium and low priority packets is 648.01 ± 56.10 ms, $1,390.14 \pm 227.67$ ms, and $3,144.50 \pm 538.38$ ms, respectively. Overall, HIF's delays for all the priority levels in Fig. 2.9 have increased compared to the delays shown in Fig. 2.5. This is because more than 29% (=14/48) of the sensor nodes generate high importance data in Experiment Set 2. Further, the hop count is increased due to the increased number of nodes. In the Experiment Set 1, only 10% of the generated packets have high importance and the network only has 25 nodes.

The per-node average energy consumption is shown in Fig. 2.10. Similar to the result of experiment set 1, HIF considerably reduces power consumption. HIF consumes $3,017.63 \pm 97.66$ mJ which results in 35.62 days of the network lifetime. This is a significant energy saving compared to BASE that consumes $10,262.28 \pm 9.99$ mJ. Using BASE, the network life time reduces to only 10.47 days. HIF consumes slightly more energy than ESCAN does as shown in Fig. 2.10. However, HIF ensures that important packets experience shorter E2E delays and higher data resolution unlike ESCAN (or BASE).

In Fig. 2.11, ESCAN and HIF remarkably reduce the number of packets received by the base station, similar to Fig. 2.7. Compared to Fig. 2.7, Fig. 2.11 shows that HIF aggregates high priority packets more often because more nodes generate high priority packets and they are geographically close as shown in Fig. 2.8. Thus, high priority packets in HIF leaves room for the delivery and in-network processing of medium and low priority packets.

2.4. Related Work

A number of protocols are developed to support timely delivery of data in WSNs.[13–16] Because these protocols do not take data semantics into account, redundant packets can be queued up in front of important packets. Head of line

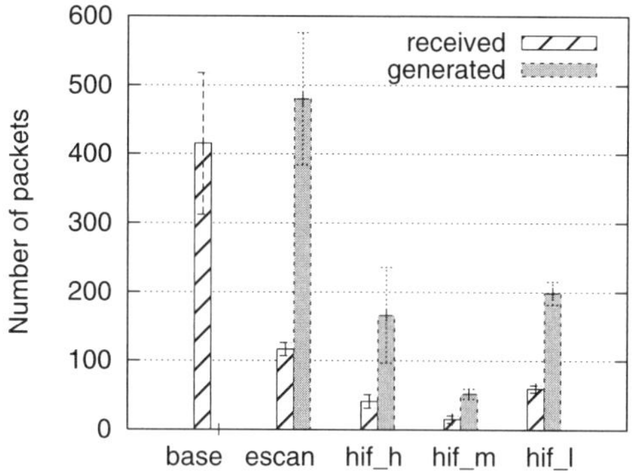

Fig. 2.11. Number of received packets (Exp. Set 2).

blocking by redundant packets may cause priority inversions that delay important data transmissions. Several protocols are developed to differentiate communication channel access in ad-hoc wireless networks.[17–21] However, they do not consider data semantics for service differentiation. By applying fixed priority scheduling, HIF avoids priority inversions. Also, HIF ensures that the node with the most important packet to transmit gets the highest probability to access the channel first.

Johnsson *et al.*[22] developed a new packet scheduling algorithm to minimize the total delay cost. In their approach, there are several priority levels. Each priority level is associated with a specific delay bound. For each packet, the estimated transmission delay is computed based on the packet size and link quality. Using the estimated delay, the delay cost, i.e., the estimated delay divided by the delay bound specified for the packet's priority level, is computed. To minimize the total cost, a node transmits the packet with the smallest delay cost first. In this approach, however, urgent packets with tight delay bounds can be transmitted after less urgent ones that have lower delay costs. Our approach can avoid priority inversions via efficient scheduling and medium access control when E2E deadlines are used to determine data importance levels.

In-network data aggregation can reduce energy consumption in wireless sensor networks.[5–7,23,24] Unlike HIF, in these approaches, packets are transmitted in a FIFO manner. They do not support differentiated aggregation or medium access control too. To reduce network traffic and energy consumption, sensory values are estimated using prediction models.[25–27] In these approaches, each sensor node and the base station share a probabilistic model. A new sensor reading is transmitted to the base station only if the base station cannot predict it using the shared model with the specified accuracy. These approaches, however, require a high accuracy prediction model. Also, the overhead for building and maintaining a statistical model in each resource-constrained sensor node is not negligible. Compared to these approach, we take a lightweight in-network approach to reduce the delay and energy consumption based on data importance.

Event detection schemes are developed in sensor networks.[1,28,29] Multi-modal sensor data fusion is applied to derive the confidence of a detected fire.[1] A database table for event detection is partitioned and shared by neighboring sensor nodes to collaboratively detect events of interest.[28] An efficient data fusion protocol is presented in Ref. 29. HIF is complementary to these approaches in that data importance levels can be derived by using one of (or a combination of) them. Given the importance of data, our protocol can reduce the delay and energy consumption. Overall, relatively little work has been done to develop a cross-layer approach that can significantly enhance the timeliness and energy efficiency considering data semantics.

2.5. Conclusions and Future Work

In wireless sensor networks, decreasing the end-to-end delay and energy consumption is essential. In this chapter, we present a new notion of the most important data first. To support shorter delays and higher resolution for important data, we develop a cross-layer approach that seamlessly integrates packet scheduling, data aggregation, and medium access control based on data semantics. The design and implementation of our protocol are discussed in detail. The performance of our approach is thoroughly evaluated in TOSSIM. The performance analysis results show that our approach can significantly reduce the end-to-end delay for delivering important data packets, while considerably improving energy efficiency. In the future, we will further investigate data-centric approaches to enhancing performance and energy efficiency. We will also explore how to provide robust real-time routing, while supporting in-network data aggregation.

References

1. S. Li, Y. Lin, S. H. Son, J. A. Stankovic and Y. Wei, Event detection services using data service middleware in distributed sensor networks, *Telecommunication Systems*, **26**(2–4), 351–368 (June 2004).
2. *International Standard for Information Technology. Telecommunications and Information Exchange Between Systems — Local and Metropolitan Area Networks. Specific Requirements Part 11: Wireless LAN Medium Access Control (MAC) and Physical Layer (PHY) Specifications.* IEEE 802.11 WG and IEEE std 802.11 (1999).
3. J. Hill, R. Szewczyk, A. Woo, D. Culler, S. Hollar and K. Pister, System architecture directions for networked sensors, *Architectural Support for Programming Languages and Operating Systems*, 93–104 (2000).
4. P. Levis and N. Lee, *TOSSIM: A Simulator for TinyOS Networks*, Technical report, University of California at Berkeley (2003).
5. S. Madden, M. J. Franklin, J. M. Hellerstein and W. Hong, TAG: A tiny AGgregation service for ad-hoc sensor networks, *ACM SIGOPS Operating Systems Review*, **36**, 131–146 (Winter, 2002).

6. H. Jiang and S. Jin, Scalable and robust aggregation techniques for extracting statistical information in sensor networks, *Proceedings of the 26th IEEE International Conference on Distributed Computing Systems* (2006).
7. Y. J. Zhao, R. Govindan and D. Estrin, Residual energy scan for monitoring sensor networks, *IEEE Wireless Communications and Networking Conference* (2002).
8. S. Choi, Overview of emerging IEEE 802.11 protocols for MAC and above, *Sp. Issue on Wireless Communications and Broadcasting*, **11**, 105–126, *SK Telecom Telecommunications Review* (2003).
9. S. Choi, J. del Prado and S. Mangold, IEEE 802.11e contention-based channel access (EDCF) performance evaluation, *IEEE International Conference on Communications*, **2**, 1151–1156 (May 2003).
10. G. Bianchi, T. V. I. Tinnirello and L. Scalia, Understanding 802.11e contention-based prioritization mechanisms and their coexistence with legacy 802.11 stations, *IEEE Network*, **29**(4), 28–34 (July/August 2005).
11. V. Shnayder, M. Hempstead, B. R. Chen, G. W. Allen and M. Welsh, Simulating the power consumption of large-scale sensor network applications, *The 2nd ACM Conference on Embedded Networked Sensor Systems* (November 2004).
12. Battery. http://www.prc68.com/I/batt.shtml.
13. C. Lu, B. Blum, T. Abdelzaher, J. Stankovic and T. He, RAP: A real-time communication architecture for large-scale wireless sensor networks, *Proceedings of 8th Real-Time and Embedded Technology and Application Symposium*, 55–66 (2002).
14. T. He, J. A. Stankovic, C. Lu and T. Abdelzaher, SPEED: A stateless protocol for real-time communication in sensor networks, *Proceedings of the 23rd International Conference on Distributed Computing Systems*, 46–55 (May 2003).
15. E. Felemban, C.-G. Lee and E. Ekici, MMSPEED: Multipath Multi-SPEED Protocol for QoS guarantee of reliability and timeliness in wireless sensor networks, *IEEE Transactions on Mobile Computing*, **5**(6), 738–754 (June 2006).
16. H. Li, P. Shenoy and K. Ramamritham, Scheduling messages with deadlines in multi-hop real-time sensor network, *Proceedings of the 11th IEEE Real Time and Embedded Technology and Applications Symposium*, 415–425 (March 2005).
17. A. Veres, A. T. Campbell, M. Barry and L.-H. Sun, Supporting service differentiation in wireless packet networks using distributed control, *IEEE Journal on Selected Areas in Communications*, **19**(10), 2081–2093 (October 2001).
18. A. Pal, A. Dogan and F. Ozguner, MAC layer protocols for real-time traffic in ad-hoc wireless networks, *Proceedings of the International Conference on Parallel Processing*, 539–546 (2002).
19. R. O. Baldwin, N. J. Davis and S. F. Midkiff, A real-time medium access control protocol for ad hoc wireless local area networks, *ACM SIGMOBILE Mobile Computing and Communications Review*, **3**(2), 20–27 (April 1999).
20. D.-J. Deng and R.-S. Chang, A priority scheme for IEEE 802.11 DCF access method, *IEICE Transactions on Communication*, **E82-B**(1), 96–102 (January 1999).
21. M. C. Vuran and I. F. Akyildiz, Spatial correlation-based collaborative medium access control in wireless sensor networks, *IEEE/ACM Transactions on Networking*, **14**(2), 316–329 (April 2006).
22. K. B. Johnsson and D. C. Cox, An adaptive cross-layer scheduler for improved QoS support of multiclass data services on wireless systems, *IEEE Journal on Selected Areas in Communications*, **23**(2), 334–343 (February 2005).

23. N. Shrivastava, C. Buragohain, D. Agrawal and S. Suri, Medians and beyond: New aggregation techniques for sensor networks, *Proceedings of the 2nd International Conference on Embedded Networked Sensor Systems*, 239–249 (2004).
24. R. D. Nowak, Distributed EM algorithms for density estimation in sensor networks, *IEEE International Conference on Acoustics, Speech, and Signal Processing* (April 2003).
25. D. Chu, A. Deshpande, J. M. Hellerstein and W. Hong, Approximate data collection in sensor networks using probabilistic models, *Proceedings of the 22nd International Conference on Data Engineering*, 48 (2006).
26. S. Santini and K. Romer, An adaptive strategy for quality-based data reduction in wireless sensor networks, *Proceedings of the 3rd International Conference on Networked Sensing Systems* (2006).
27. A. Deshpande, C. Guestrin, S. R. Madden, J. M. Hellerstein and W. Hong, Model-driven data acquisition in sensor networks, *Proceedings of the 30th International Conference on Very Large Data Bases*, **30**, 588–599, Toronto, Canada (2004).
28. D. J. Abadi, S. Madden and W. Lindner, REED: Robust, efficient filtering and event detection in sensor networks, *Proceedings of the 31st International Conference on Very Large Data Bases*, 769–780 (2005).
29. Q. Wu, N. S. Rao, J. Barhen, S. S. Iyengar, V. K. Vaishnavi, H. Qi and K. Chakrabarty, On computing mobile agent routes for data fusion in distributed sensor networks, *IEEE Transactions on Knowledge and Data Engineering*, **16**(6), 740–752 (June 2004).

Part II

Medium Access Control

Chapter 3

Performance Evaluation of MAC Mechanisms in Wireless Sensor Networks

Prasan Kumar Sahoo

Department of Information Management
Vanung University, Chungli, Taiwan
pksahoo@msa.vnu.edu.tw

Jang-Ping Sheu

Department of Computer Science
National Tsing Hua University, Hinchu, Taiwan
sheujp@cs.nthu.edu.tw

Performance analysis of wireless sensor networks in terms of data transmission capacity and lifetime of the networks are critical research issues towards the design of optimal deployment strategies of the sensor networks. In contrast to other types of wireless networks, nodes in wireless sensor networks are densely deployed and organize themselves in an ad hoc fashion. Due to limited transmission ranges, any two nodes cannot reach each other directly and rely on other sensor nodes to relay data between them. Hence, the data packets between the source and destination are routed through multi-hops. Besides, sensor nodes are normally small in size and have constrained energy sources. Hence energy consumption analysis is an important performance measure in wireless sensor networks. In this chapter, the contention free and contention based channel access mechanism in wireless sensor networks is discussed. Considering different MAC mechanisms in wireless sensor networks, mathematical models for the energy consumption issues are analyzed.

3.1. Introduction

In wireless sensor networks (WSNs), normally nodes are randomly deployed over certain regions such as harsh terrains and dense forests. After deployment of the nodes, they organize among themselves in a distributed fashion to form the network. However, all nodes of the network are battery powered and run with limited energy resources. Because of the harsh working environments and geographical condition of the monitoring region, recharging or replacing the sensors battery may be inconvenient, or even impossible. Thus, when a node exhausts its energy, it cannot help but ceases sensing and routing data, possibly reducing the coverage and connectivity level of the network and thereby degrading the performance of the whole network. This implies that making good use of energy resources is a must in wireless sensor networks. Besides, sensor nodes have limited transmission ranges and organize themselves in an *ad hoc* fashion. Although sensors may be mobile, they can be considered to be stationary after deployment and normally far away from the sink. Hence, they deliver their data through multihop communications, i.e., using intermediate nodes as relays and act as a data source and a data router. In general, data packets from the source to the destination node traverse through multiple hops before they reach at the destination and therefore consume more energy. Moreover, any protocol to be deployed in sensor networks need to be aware of energy usage. Hence, energy consumption and multi-hop routing are two characteristics of the wireless sensor networks, as they have important implications to the performance of the network.

In the research field of performance evaluation, primarily, network performance is measured by monitoring certain parameters such as throughput, energy consumption and latency. Subsequently, the performance data are evaluated and consequences for the network configuration are derived. The performance metrics are measured for the contention free or contention based channel access, duration of a node in the backoff and collision state. A Medium Access Control (MAC) protocol specifies how nodes share the channel, and hence plays a central role in the performance of a sensor network. Recently developed wireless personal area networks (WPANs) specify the communication mechanism among the short range wireless nodes built from small, energy-efficient devices operating on battery power, which require little infrastructure to operate, or none at all. The IEEE 802.15.4[1] standard proposes the wireless medium access control (MAC) and physical layer specifications for the low-rate wireless personal area networks, which can be used in some applications such as home automation, industrial sensing and control, environment monitoring and sensing. These applications have more relaxed throughput requirements under tens of Kbps and lower power consumption requirements. The main concern of these applications is that of extremely low power consumption, since it is impossible or undesirable to replace or recharge batteries for the devices. For these applications, IEEE 802.15.4 specifies the channel access mechanism among the densely deployed sensor nodes, which could be designed for the single hop star topology or for a multi hop peer-to-peer network.

3.2. Related Work

With regard to performance evaluation of large scale stationary ad hoc networks (note that sensor networks can be viewed as large ad hoc networks), analytical studies are presented in Ref. 2. In their work, two network scenarios such as one for the arbitrarily located nodes and traffic patterns, the other one with randomly located nodes and traffic patterns are analyzed. A discrete time Markov chain model for the sensor sleep/active dynamics is developed in Ref. 3, in which the model predicts the sensor energy consumption; by acquiring the sleep/active modes of each sensor. In their model, a central controller constructs the network energy map representing the energy reserves available in the various parts of the system. In the past research, various solutions have been proposed to reduce the sensors energy expenditure. For instance, energy-efficient MAC layer schemes can be found in Refs. 4 and 5. Traffic routing and connectivity issues in sensor networks are addressed in Refs. 6–8, while energy-aware strategies for data dissemination and data collection appear in Refs. 9–11. From the energy consumption viewpoint, an effective technique is to place sensors in sleep mode during idle periods. The benefits of using sleep modes at the MAC layer are presented in Ref. 4, where the authors describe the so-called PAMAS scheme that allows a node to turn off its RF apparatus when it overhears a packet that is not destined for it. The work in Refs. 5, 12 and 13 propose wake-up scheduling schemes at the MAC layer which wake up sleeping nodes when they need to transmit/receive, thus avoiding a degradation in network connectivity or quality of service provisioning.

Performance analysis for IEEE 802.15.4 with focus on beacon-enabled mode and star-topology is studied in Ref. 14. They have analyzed energy consumption, throughput and latency with different parameterizations. Analysis of the organization mechanisms[15] revealed that association of networks (star or peer-to-peer) and recovery from orphaning has a good efficiency in IEEE 802.15.4 networks. Earlier investigations in Ref. 16 consider a multi-hop network with a low duty cycle protocol. They found that with higher numbers of devices and higher arrival rates instabilities can occur. In Ref. 14, the performance of the IEEE 802.15.4 standard in terms of throughput and energy efficiency is assessed based on simulation. However, this work focuses on a scenario with few nodes and low load, which diverges significantly from the conditions encountered in wireless microsensor networks. In Ref. 21, the authors construct network topologies for the IEEE 802.15.4 enabled WSNs, with small number of coordinators while still maintaining network connectivity. By reducing the number of coordinators, the average duty cycle is reduced and the battery life is prolonged. In Ref. 18, authors evaluate the potential of an IEEE 802.15.4 radio for use in an ultra low power sensor node operating in a dense network. The first simulation-based performance evaluations of the new medium access control protocol in IEEE 802.15.4, focusing on its beacon-enabled mode for small and low loaded star-topology network is evaluated in Ref. 14 and for the dense networks is evaluated in Ref. 18. Their performance evaluation study reveals some of the key throughput-energy-delay tradeoffs inherent in the MAC protocol.

In Ref. 19, under moderate data rate and non-beacon enabled mode, IEEE 802.15.4 shows clear advantage over 802.11 regarding control overhead and transaction latency. In that work, the performance evaluation is made with evenly distributed nodes, instead of randomly distributed. We are of the point that these assumptions are not quite reasonable for many applications of wireless sensor networks. In Ref. 20, the results show that the IEEE 802.15.4 can be used for medical sensor networking, which is configured in non-beacon mode with low data rate asymmetric traffic. Beacon mode may also be used, but with more severe restrictions on data rate and crystal tolerance. In Ref. 21, three topology control algorithms are proposed to construct network topologies with small number of coordinators, while still maintaining network connectivity. In their work, the average duty cycle is reduced and the battery life is prolonged. In Ref. 22, authors have developed a simplified analytical procedure to calculate packet service time in a beacon-enabled IEEE 802.15.4 sensor cluster, which can be used to implement a simple admission control algorithm to be run at the cluster coordinator. Performance analysis in a beacon enabled IEEE 802.15.4 network is made in Ref. 23 under two duty cycle management distributed algorithms. The authors model and evaluate both policies using the theory of discrete time Markov chains and M/G/1/K queues with vacations. In Ref. 24, the same authors, model the WPAN with uplink transmissions, considering the devices with buffers of finite size, where packets may be rejected if the buffer is full.

Performance of an IEEE 802.15.4 compliant network operating in the beacon enabled mode with both downlink and uplink traffic is analyzed in Ref. 25 through discrete time Markov chains and the theory of M/G/1 queues. In Ref. 26, the authors numerically simulate the performance of relative location for both single-hop and multihop networks. However, they have not considered the energy consumption issues of the network during such estimations of relative locations and thereby node locations. In Ref. 27, authors have examined the reliability of the point to point communication with a real IEEE 802.15.4 hardware and run lengths distribution both in indoor and outdoor environments. In Ref. 28, the paper provides a simple, but nevertheless extremely accurate, analytical model to compute the IEEE 802.11 DCF throughput in the assumption of finite number of terminals and ideal channel conditions. The proposed analysis applies to both packet transmission schemes employed by DCF, namely the basic access and the RTS/CTS access mechanisms. The form of the analysis given in Ref. 29, is similar to that of Ref. 28 for IEEE 802.11 DCF, but the key difference in the main approximation assumption is that each device's carrier sensing probability, rather than its packet sending probability is assumed independent. In Ref. 30, authors analyze the performance limits of the slotted CSMA-CA mechanism of IEEE 802.15.4 in the beacon-enabled mode for broadcast transmissions in WSNs.

In Refs. 31 and 32, authors have established the realistic environment for the preliminary performance evaluation of the IEEE 802.15.4 wireless networks, taking several sets of practical experiments to study the effects of direct and indirect data transmissions, CSMA-CA mechanism, data payload size, and beacon-enabled mode. A new Markov chain model of the IEEE 802.15.4 is proposed in Ref. 33, and the throughput and energy consumption in saturation conditions are analyzed.

The proposed model utilizes the probability of a device in the channel sensing states instead of the channel accessing states. A saturation throughput analysis of an IEEE 802.15.4 sensor network with a star topology is carried out in Ref. 34, under the assumption that each sensor has an infinite backlog of packets. A discrete time Markov chain model of a sensor network is developed Ref. 35 without considering IEEE 802.15.4 or IEEE 802.11 MAC methods. In their work, authors have used the model to investigate the system performance in terms of energy consumption, network capacity, and data delivery delay taking sleep and active mode of the nodes. Though, several analytical methods are proposed to model the performance of the wireless sensor networks, to find a suitable model for achieving better energy consumption and throughput is difficult. In Ref. 36, the authors have investigated experimentally the coexistence problems of IEEE 802.11b and IEEE 802.15.4 wireless networks. The main goal of their work is to deduce the correlations between interfering effects and systems configuration to be used in the design of coexisting networks. However, they have not made any performance study about such coexistence issues.

The authors in Ref. 37 have proposed an adaptive message passing MAC protocol for wireless sensor network. The proposed MAC protocol modifies the message passing mechanism of SMAC to make the size of the small fragment adjusted according to different traffic load by using the information of the control packet and achieves a significant decrease in energy consumption. The packet error rate of the IEEE 802.15.4 under the interference of the IEEE 802.11b is analyzed Ref. 38 using the bit error rate and the collision time. The bit error rate is obtained from signal to interference and noise ratio. In this work, the power spectral density of the IEEE 802.11b is considered in order to determine the in-band interference power of the IEEE 802.11b to the IEEE 802.15.4. They have not considered any performance analysis using both IEEE 802.11 and IEEE 802.15.4 MAC mechanisms. In Refs. 31 and 32, the authors have established the realistic environment for the preliminary performance evaluation of IEEE 802.15.4 wireless networks, taking several sets of practical experiments to study the effects of direct and indirect data transmissions, CSMA-CA mechanism in the beacon-enabled mode. It is to be noted that the effect of backoff mechanism with binary exponential contention windows on the performance of the sensors has not been studied yet. Concept of binary contention windows introduced in IEEE 802.11 is normally used by the nodes during backoff procedure. The binary exponential contention window concept of IEEE 802.11 could be used in wireless sensor network in the post collision scenarios with initial channel access mechanisms of IEEE 802.15.4.

Though several works propose analytical models for the WSNs using IEEE 802.15.4 channel access mechanisms, it is interesting to analyze the energy model and thereby to evaluate the performance of the network based on the number of backlogged nodes with exponential backoff windows and halting procedures during the channel access mechanism of IEEE 802.15.4. Hence, a contention based hybrid

CSMA-CA mechanism Ref. 40 for the WSNs that combines the initial channel assessment procedure of IEEE 802.15.4 and binary exponential contention windows of IEEE 802.11 in the post collision situation is described in this chapter. Besides, the energy consumption issues due to a cluster based WSN and hybrid MAC are analyzed.

3.3. Medium Access Control (MAC) Protocols

The medium access control (MAC) protocol specifies how nodes in a sensor network can access a shared communication channel. Normally, MAC is a logical entity that can control or coordinate the access of the stations into the medium, i.e., the radio channels and can utilize mainly structures and protocols to enhance communications over the medium. It provides the core framing operation and handles the data moving between physical and network layers. The MAC protocols for WSN usually trade off performance in terms of latency, throughput and fairness and for cost in terms of energy efficiency and reduced algorithmic complexity, while providing a good scalability and some limited adaptability for topology changes. But, for accessing channel to transmit data from one node to another, a node has to use either a contention based MAC and competes with other nodes to get the channel access or uses a contention free MAC to avoid collision. We are discussing the mechanisms of contention free and contention-based MAC mechanisms as follows.

3.3.1. *Contention free MAC*

A MAC protocol is said to be contention-free if it does not allow any collisions. Most of the existing contention-free MAC protocols assume that the sensor nodes are time-synchronized in some way, which is usually not possible on account of the large scale of sensor networks. Wireless sensor nodes are typically operated in energy constrained environments and should be able to operate with much lower average power consumption than the existing wireless network components. Because of the limited battery life associated with each device, as well as the difficulty involved in performing frequent battery replacement for a very large number of devices scattered over a large area, energy efficient MAC is highly essential. In contention-free MAC protocols, the nodes follow some particular schedule, which guarantees the collision-free transmission times. Typical examples of such protocols are: Frequency Division Multiple Access (FDMA); Time Division Multiple Access (TDMA)[41]; Code Division Multiple Access (CDMA).[42] In addition to TDMA, FDMA and CDMA, various reservation based[43] or token based schemes[44,45] are also proposed for distributed channel access control. Among these schemes, allocation of TDMA slots is well studied and there are many centralized[46,47], and distributed[48–50] schemes for TDMA slot assignments. All these existing protocols are either centralized or rely on a global time reference.

In TDMA, the channel is divided into fixed number of slots that comprises a frame, which repeats cyclically. In each slot, only one node is allowed to transmit. The slotted TDMA is frequently used in cellular wireless communication systems, such as GSM. Within each cell, a base station allocates time slots and provides timing and synchronization information to all mobile nodes. The major advantage of TDMA is its energy efficiency, because it directly supports low-duty-cycle operations on nodes. However, there are some limitations to use TDMA in wireless sensor networks, since it requires nodes to form clusters, analogous to the cells in the cellular communication systems. One of the nodes within the cluster is selected as the cluster head, and acts as the base station. Nodes are normally restricted to communicate with the cluster head within a cluster; peer-to-peer communication is not directly supported. However, TDMA has a natural advantage of collision free medium access. If wireless sensor network is operated in conjunction with a TDMA based scheme, the QoS requirements in each allocated time duration must be also satisfied in the physical transmissions through coarse wireless channels. These requirements are mapped to the corresponding parameters in the MAC layer and can be satisfied by selecting the optimum combination of transmission power, modulation level, and fragment size, between the physical and MAC layers.

TDMA is very attractive for applications in sensor networks because of their energy efficiency. Since slots are pre-allocated to individual nodes, they are collision-free. There is no energy wasted on collisions due to channel contention. TDMA naturally supports low-duty-cycle operation and a node only needs to turn on its radio during the slot that it is assigned to transmit or receive. Finally, overhearing can be easily avoided by turning off the radio during the slots of other nodes. In general, TDMA can provide good energy efficiency, but they are not flexible to changes in node density or movement, and lack of peer-to-peer communication. The difficulties with TDMA systems are synchronization of the nodes and adaptation to topology changes when these changes are caused by insertion of new nodes, exhaustion of battery capacities, broken links due to interference, the sleep schedules of relay nodes, and scheduling caused by clustering algorithms. The slot assignments, therefore, should be done with regard to such possibilities. However, it is not easy to change the slot assignment within a decentralized environment for traditional TDMA, since all nodes must agree on the slot assignments. Hence, the TDMA schemes though provide excellent energy-efficiency due to minimization of idle listening, elimination of overhearing and collision free operation, they are not considered as practical solutions for sensor networks because of the complications of providing WSN time synchronization and difficulties to address scalability challenges.

Inter-cluster communications and interference need to be handled by other approaches, such as FDMA or CDMA. FDMA offers a collision-free medium access, but it requires additional circuitry to dynamically communicate with different radio channels. This increases the cost of the sensor nodes, which is contrary to the objective of sensor network systems. CDMA also offers a collision-free medium, but its high computational requirement is a major obstacle for the less energy-consumption objective of sensor networks. In pursuit of low computational cost for wireless CDMA sensor networks, there has been limited effort to investigate source and modulation schemes, particularly signature waveforms, designing simple receiver models, and other signal synchronization problems. If it is shown that the high computational complexity of CDMA could be traded-off against its collision-avoidance feature, CDMA protocols could also be considered as candidate solutions for sensor networks.

3.3.2. *Contention based MAC*

In wireless sensor network, nodes are deployed densely and are typically dispersed at high, possibly non-uniform, densities. The nodes may turn on and off in order to conserve energy and the communication traffic is space and time correlated. Contention occurs when two nearby sensor nodes both try to access the communication channel. It causes message collisions, which are very likely to occur when traffic is frequent and correlated, and they decrease the lifetime of a sensor network. Contention-based MAC protocols are also known as random access protocols, requiring no coordination among the nodes accessing the channel. Colliding nodes back off for a random duration and try to access the channel again. Such protocols first appeared as Pure ALOHA[51] and Slotted ALOHA. The throughput of Aloha-like protocols was significantly improved by the Carrier Sense Multiple Access (CSMA) protocol.[52] The CSMA methods have a lower delay and promising throughput potential at lower traffic loads, which generally happens to be the case in wireless sensor networks. However, additional collision avoidance or collision detection methods should be employed.

CSMA is an important contention based protocol. In CSMA, the central idea is listening before transmitting. The purpose of listening is to detect if the medium is busy, also known as carrier sense. In CSMA, if a node detects a busy channel, it delays access and retries later. The CSMA protocol has been widely studied and extended and today it is the basis of several widely-used standards including IEEE 802.11[53] and IEEE 802.15.4. There are several variants of CSMA, including non-persistent, 1-persistent, and p-persistent CSMA. In non-persistent CSMA, if a node detects an idle medium, it transmits immediately. If the medium is busy, it waits a random amount of time and starts carrier sense again. In 1-persistent CSMA, a node transmit if the medium is idle. Otherwise it continues to listen until the medium becomes idle, and then transmits immediately. In p-persistent CSMA, a node transmits with probability p if the medium is idle, and with probability $(1 - p)$ to back-off and restart carrier sense. A sensor in a contention-based MAC requests and competes for the access to the medium. Although a contention-based protocol inherits good scalability necessary for node changes in wireless sensor networks, its major drawback is energy inefficiency due to idle listening, collision, overhearing, and control-packet overhead. Unlike a TDMA-based MAC protocol, a contention-based MAC protocol suffers collision and control overhead. However, it is more flexible in reducing idle listening and thus increasing throughput. Some of the recently-proposed energy-efficient contention-based MAC protocols are S-MAC (Sensor-MAC),[54] T-MAC (Timeout-MAC),[55] and PMAC (Pattern-MAC).[56]

Contention based MAC has several advantages compared to contention free MAC mechanism. First, because contention MAC allocates resources on-demand, they can scale more easily across changes in node density or traffic load. Second, contention based MAC can be more flexible as topologies change. There is no requirement to form communication clusters, and peer-to-peer communication is directly supported. Finally, contention based MAC does not require fine-grained time synchronization as in TDMA protocols. The major disadvantage of a contention protocol is its inefficient usage of energy. It normally has all the sources of energy waste as nodes listen at all times and collisions and contention for the media can waste energy. Overcoming this disadvantage is required if contention-based protocols are to be applied to long-lived sensor networks. The performance of contention based MAC protocols is weak when traffic is frequent or correlated and these protocols suffer from stability problems.

3.4. IEEE 802.15.4 and IEEE 802.11 MAC Mechanisms

IEEE 802.15.4 standard is meant to offer the specification for the lower network layers of a type of wireless personal area network (WPAN), which focuses on low-cost, low-speed ubiquitous communication between devices. The basic framework conceives a 10-meter communications area with a transfer rate of 250 kbit/s, and even lower rates can be considered with the resulting effect on power consumption. Hence, several features of this standard can be used for the extremely low manufacturing and operation costs with technological simplicity and are quite suitable for the wireless sensor networks. In contrast, IEEE 802.11 is the de facto standard for wireless local area networks (WLAN) that provides specification for the nodes with data rates of 1 and 2 Mbit/s and can operate in Industrial Scientific and Medical (ISM) frequency band at 2.4 GHz. Though, contention based carrier sense multiple access with collision avoidance (CSMA/CA) protocol has proposed as the MAC mechanisms for both standards, several features of medium access are different due to the density, scalability and energy constraints of the network. Hence, following subsections illustrate the medium access methods of both standard to compare and contract their MAC mechanisms.

3.4.1. *IEEE 802.11 MAC mechanism*

The 802.11 standard specifies a common medium access control (MAC) layer, which provides a variety of functions that support the operation of 802.11-based wireless

LANs. In general, the MAC layer manages and maintains communications between 802.11 stations by coordinating access to a shared radio channel and utilizing protocols that enhance communications over a wireless medium. 802.11 MAC layer uses an 802.11 Physical (PHY) layer, such as 802.11b or 802.11a, to perform the tasks of carrier sensing, transmission, and receiving of 802.11 frames. IEEE 802.11 standard defines two modes. They are the mandatory distributed coordination function (DCF) based on the carrier sense multiple access with collision avoidance (CSMA/CA) protocol and the optional point coordination function (PCF). Although the PCF is designed for real-time traffic, it is not widely deployed due to its inefficient polling schemes, limited QoS provisioning, and implementation complexity. In practice, most of the WLANs deploy DCF as the MAC protocol. An important aspect of the DCF is a random back off timer that a station uses if it detects a busy medium. If the channel is in use, the station must wait a random period of time before attempting to access the medium again. This ensures that multiple stations wanting to send data do not transmit at the same time. The random delay causes stations to wait different periods of time and avoids all of them sensing the medium at exactly the same time, finding the channel idle, transmitting, and colliding with each other. The back off timer significantly reduces the number of collisions and corresponding retransmissions, especially when the number of active users increases.

When a station has a frame at the MAC sublayer buffer, it first senses the channel. If the channel is busy, it will backoff with a randomly chosen number of time slots, where a slot is uniformly distributed over $[0, CW_r)$, and CW_r is the contention window for retransmission stage r. After the channel becomes idle for a duration of DCF-interframe-space (DIFS), the backoff counter counts down for each time slot when the channel is idle. In DCF the backoff counter (BC) freezes when the channel is busy due to a successful transmission or collisions from other stations, and it resumes after the channel turns idle again. When the BC reaches zero, the station transmits immediately. A station resets its CW to the minimum value $CW_{min} = 32$ after each successful transmission. If two or more stations transmit at the same time slot, a collision occurs and all involved stations double their CWs, which is upper-bounded by $CW_{max} = 1{,}024$ in the standard, and backoff again. The frame is discarded if retransmission fails after a pre-defined retry limit, which depends on the frame length. Usually a sender transmits data frames directly when its backoff counter reaches zero, and the receiver will reply with an explicit acknowledgment (ACK) after a duration of short interframe space (SIFS) if the data frame is successfully decoded. This is called the basic access mode.

To improve the efficiency of transmitting long frames, the standard also defines an optional request-to-send/clear-to-send (RTS/CTS) access mode. When the frame length is larger than a threshold, the source station sends out an RTS frame to its intended destination station, which replies with a CTS frame if the RTS is correctly decoded. After that, the source transmits the data frame and waits for the corresponding ACK frame from the destination. There are periods of short-interframe-space (SIFS) in between the RTS, CTS, data and ACK frames. As DIFS is longer than SIFS, an ongoing transmission sequence is not interrupted by a new transmission. In case of a collision, the source stations in the basic mode waits for duration of (ACK timeout + DIFS) before resuming their backoff procedure. In the RTS/CTS mode, the source stations wait a duration with the same length because the CTS frame has the same length as the ACK frame. In both basic and RTS/CTS access modes, neighboring stations that detect a collision defer a duration of extended-interframe-space (EIFS) before resuming their backoff procedure. The EIFS equals the summation of SIFS, DIFS and the transmission time of the CTS or ACK frame with the lowest mandatory transmission rate so that all the stations will resume their backoff procedure at the same time. The CTS/ACK timeout and EIFS mechanism serves as an implicit N_ACK in DCF.

In addition to the above physical carrier sense (PCS) mechanism, a virtual carrier sense (VCS) mechanism is also introduced in the DCF. It is implemented by means of the so-called network allocation vector (NAV), which is maintained by every station that is not currently involved in any transmission or reception of frames. Each such station may set the NAV according to the information in the Duration/ID field of the RTS or Data frame. In the RTS/CTS mode, stations may reset its NAV to zero if a transmission does not start during a period with a duration of (2 SIFS + CTS + 2 Slot) after the NAV is set according to the duration value of the RTS frame. Before the NAV expires, the station may stop the physical carrier sensing activity to save energy. As a condition to accessing the medium, the MAC layer checks the value of its network allocation vector (NAV), which is a counter resident at each station that represents the amount of time that the previous frame needs to send its frame. The NAV must be zero before a station can attempt to send a frame. Prior to transmitting a frame, a station calculates the amount of time necessary to send the frame based on the frame's length and data rate. The station places a value representing this time in the duration field in the header of the frame. When stations receive the frame, they examine this duration field value and use it as the basis for setting their corresponding NAVs. This process reserves the medium for the sending station.

With radio-based LANs, a transmitting station cannot listen for collisions while sending data, mainly because the station cannot have it's receiver on while transmitting the frame. As a result, the receiving station needs to send an acknowledgement (ACK) if it detects no errors in the received frame. If the sending station does not receive an ACK after a specified period of time, the sending station assumes that there is a collision (or RF interference) and retransmits the frame. For supporting time-bounded delivery of data frames, the 802.11 standard defines the optional point coordination function (PCF) where the access point grants access to an individual station to the medium by polling the station during the contention free period. Stations cannot transmit frames unless the access point polls them first. The period of time for PCF-based data traffic (if enabled) occurs alternately between contention (DCF) periods. The access point polls stations according to a polling list, then switches to a contention period when stations use DCF. This process enables support for both synchronous (i.e., video applications) and asynchronous (i.e., e-mail and Web browsing applications) modes of operation. No known wireless NICs or access points on the market today, however, implement PCF.

3.4.2. *IEEE 802.15.4 MAC mechanism*

The MAC layer in the IEEE 802.15.4 standard specifies two types of data transfer modes, which may occur between the device and a coordinator. Those transfer modes are: non-beacon-enabled mode and a beacon-enabled mode. The mechanisms for each transfer type depend on whether the network supports the transmission of beacons. A beacon-enabled network is used for supporting low-latency devices. If the network does not need to support such devices, it can elect not to use the beacon for normal transfers. However, the beacon is still required for network association. In the non-beacon-enabled mode, nodes in the network use a non-slotted CSMA with collision avoidance (CSMA/CA) mechanism to contend for channel access. If the channel is sensed to be idle, the transmission of a frame will begin immediately; otherwise the node will backoff and try to access the channel in a future slot. This mechanism has been extensively studied in the literature and its performance is well understood.[57] In the beacon-enabled mode, if a device wishes to transfer data to a coordinator, it first listens for the network beacon. When the beacon is found, the device synchronizes to the device. At the appropriate point, the device transmits its data frame, using slotted CSMA-CA to the coordinator. The coordinator transmits a beacon periodically to form the so-called "superframe" time structure. A superframe consists of a beacon that enables the beacon-enabled mode, contention access period (CAP), contention free period (CFP), and an optional inactive portion in which all the nodes may enter a sleep mode to reduce power consumption. The CAP and CFP together form the active portion of the superframe, during which all communication among the nodes should take place. In the CFP, the network coordinator alone controls entirely the contention-free channel access by assigning guaranteed time slots (GTS) to those nodes with their GTS requests granted. The assignment of the GTS to those nodes is determined by the scheduling scheme adopted by the network coordinator, which is open in the standard. The coordinator acknowledges the successful reception of the data by transmitting an optional acknowledgment frame and the transaction is completed. In the slotted CSMA-CA of IEEE 802.15.4, the MAC sublayer first initializes three variables i.e., the number of backoffs (NB), contention window (CW) and backoff exponent (BE). These three variables need to be maintained for each frame before it is successfully transmitted. According to this MAC mechanism, a node with a frame waiting for transmission at the MAC buffer is required to backoff a random number of slots first, with CW set at a value

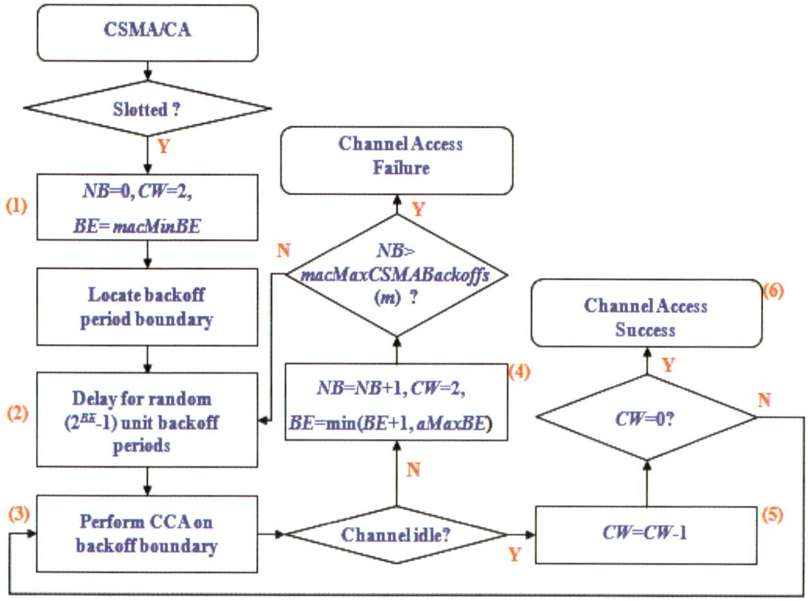

Fig. 3.1. Flow chart of IEEE 802.15.4 channel access mechanism.

of two, as shown in step 1 of Fig. 3.1. At the end of this backoff stage, the node will do the first channel clear assessment (CCA). If the channel is sensed idle, CW is decremented by one and the node will do the second CCA in the next slot. Only when both CCAs indicate an idle channel (thus CW reaches zero), will the node start the transmission in the next slot; otherwise, it will enter the next backoff stage and reset CW to two. The value of backoff exponent (BE) shall be either initialized to the value of *macMinBE* or initialized to the lesser of 2 and the value of *macMinBE*. The variable *macMinBE* means the minimum value of the backoff exponent (BE) in the CSMA-CA algorithm and as per the standard, its value can be 0 through 3. However, the value of *BE* shall not be more than *aMaxBE*, which means the maximum value of *BE* in the CSMA-CA algorithm and its value can be taken up to 5 as per the standard. It is to be noted that if this value is set to 0, collision avoidance is disabled during the first iteration of the algorithm. The MAC sublayer in a slotted CSMA-CA system shall also reset *CW* to 2. Then the MAC sublayer shall delay for a random number of complete backoff periods in the range 0 to $(2^{BE} - 1)$ units, as shown in step 2 of Fig. 3.1 and then perform the first clear channel assessment (CCA), as shown in step 3 of Fig. 3.1. In a slotted CSMA-CA system, the CCA shall start on a backoff period boundary.

If the channel is assessed to be idle during the first CCA, the MAC sublayer in a slotted CSMA-CA system shall ensure that the contention window has expired before commencing transmission. To do this, the MAC sublayer shall first decrement

CW by one, as shown in step 5 of Fig. 3.1 and then determine whether it is equal to 0. If it is not equal to 0, the CSMA-CA algorithm shall return to perform the second CCA, as shown in step 3 of Fig. 3.1. However, if it is equal to 0, the MAC sublayer assumes the channel access is a success and shall begin transmission of the frame on the boundary of the next backoff period. As per the standard, herewith the packet transmission is considered as a success and the procedure is terminated. However, upon performing the first CCA, if the channel is assessed to be busy, the MAC sublayer shall increment the value of both *NB* and *BE* by one, ensuring that *BE* shall be no more than *aMaxBE*, as shown in step 4 of Fig. 3.1. If the value of *NB* is less than or equal to the variable *macMaxCSMABackoffs*, the CSMA-CA algorithm shall return to step 2, as shown in Fig. 3.1. Here, the variable *macMaxCSMABackoffs* represents the maximum number of times the CSMA-CA algorithm is required to backoff while attempting the current transmission and its value can be taken up to 3 as per the standard. If the value of *NB* is greater than *macMaxCSMABackoffs*, the CSMA-CA algorithm shall terminate with a *Channel Access Failure* status. As per the standard, herewith the packet transmission is considered as a failure and the procedure is terminated.

3.5. Energy Consumption Issues

Total energy consumption is one of the critical performance parameters of a wireless sensor networks as it directly affects the lifetime of the network. Since most of sensors are micro-electronic devices, the constrained energy source at each node is taken as <0.5 Ah, 1.2 V. Though scalability, node density, routing and clustering methods, data aggregation, modes of power saving and so on are various parameters that affect the network lifetime, suitable channel access mechanisms also play important role on the performance of the network. Addressing several issues of MAC mechanisms, our original contributions in this chapter are to discuss the energy consumption budgeting for a hybrid MAC and clustering mechanism of a wireless sensor networks.

3.5.1. *Energy budget for a cluster based WSN*

The impact of contention based MAC on the performance of wireless sensor network is studied in Ref. 58 that addresses the medium access control and energy efficiency analysis of randomly distributed sensors over a space with density ρ. In their proposal, prior to any transmission, each node randomly chooses one of the available time slots. All nodes of the network organize themselves into clusters with one node acts as a cluster head (CH) in each cluster, which rotate randomly in each round. Considering the packet overhead to be negligible with respect to the payload, let duration of sending each packet by nodes during a round be T units, which is same for all nodes. The sink transmits triggering packet to the surrounding sensors, with power $P_t = \frac{E_H}{T}$, where E_H be the energy spent to transmit a bit with high power level. A random number of nodes n_t, with mean N_t may receive the power from the sink and those nodes n_t are termed as the triggered sensors. The triggered nodes initiate the self-election phase and elects itself as a CH with probability x. If n_{ch} represents the number of CHs, the mean of n_{ch} can be $N_{ch} = x \cdot N_t$. Hence, the mean round energy consumption is given as $E_{round} = (1 - x)E_{non-CH} + x\ E_{CH}$, where E_{CH} and E_{non-CH} are the amount of energy consumed by the CH and Non-CH, respectively.

To notify the election, each CH transmits a broadcast packet and upon receiving the packet sent by the CHs, each sensor decides which cluster it has to subscribe to. It is to be noted that the number of CHs receive response from the nodes and the number of nodes that are associated with a given cluster are random variables and are denoted as n_{ach} and n_p, respectively; with their means as N_{ach} and N_p, respectively. As proposed in Ref. 59, the channel access in a contention based MAC has to follow several phases. They are: (1) *Triggering*, where sink sends the triggering packet to the nodes, and no collision is possible. (2) *Broadcasting*, where each CH sends the broadcast packet to the nodes to form the cluster. Here, the broadcast packet is divided into W slots, and each CH chooses one of the W available slots randomly. (3) *Transmission*, where the nodes in each cluster transmits data packets. Here, Z is available slots, which is divided among the nodes for intra-cluster transmissions and the slot duration (T_d), is taken as the time required to transmit a packet θ_d.

Since, $W \geq N_{ch}$, the inter-cluster collision is neglected. If E_L is the energy spent to transmit a bit with low power level, E_{rx} is the energy spent to receive a bit, θ_c and θ_d are the size of control and data packets, respectively and Z is the size of the broadcast packet sent by the CHs, we can have

$$E_{non-CH} = E_{rx}\theta_c + [E_{rx}\theta_c N_{CH} + E_L \theta_d N_{tx_{non-CH}} + E_{rx}Z](1-p), \qquad (3.1)$$

where $N_{tx_{non-CH}} = (1-p_Z)+2p_Z = 1+p_Z$ is the number of transmission that each non-CH has to perform to transmit the packet correctly to the CH. The collision probability (p_Z) is given by

$$p_Z = \sum_{n_p=2}^{\infty}\left[1-\left(1-\frac{1}{Z}\right)^{n_p-1}\right] Prob(n_p) = \frac{e^{-N_p} - 1 + Z - Ze^{-\frac{N_p}{Z}}}{Z-1}, \qquad (3.2)$$

where, n_p is Poisson distributed and is the statistical distribution of the number of nodes which transmit to the same CH. *Prob*(n_p) is the Poisson distribution with N_p and is given by

$$Prob(n_p) = e^{-N_p} \cdot \frac{N_p^{n_p}}{n_p!}. \qquad (3.3)$$

It is to be noted that each CH consumes energy when it receives requests from the sink data packets from the non-CHs, the sink's retransmission requests and when it transmits two broadcast packets. The first broadcast packet is to inform nodes of its role and the second is to inform nodes of the correct reception of the packets. The amount of consumed energy is given by

$$\begin{aligned} E_{CH} &= E_{rx}\theta_c + E_L\theta_c + E_{rx}\theta_d \cdot N_p \\ &\quad + E_L Z + (N_p + 1) \cdot E_H\theta_d \cdot N_{tx_{CH}} \\ &\quad + E_{rx}W \cdot (N_{tx_{CH}} - 1), \end{aligned} \tag{3.4}$$

where $N_{tx_{CH}}$, is the number of transmissions made by every CH to the sink.

3.5.2. *Energy budget for a hybrid MAC*

It is to be noted that as discussed in Sec. 1.4, IEEE 802.11 channel access mechanism is quite different from CSMA-CA procedure of IEEE 802.15.4. In IEEE 802.15.4 CSMA-CA, the standard specifies the conditions for the successful and failure status of the channel access mechanism based on its two *CCAs*. However, the standard does not consider the condition of collision after channel access is a success. Besides, it suggests that the packet is rejected if both *CCAs* are failed. However, in WSN, nodes are densely deployed over certain region and it is obvious that several nodes can compete with each other for the same channel to transmit data. Hence, few nodes may get chance to transmit their data and may collide with each others. Moreover, the nodes who fail to get the channel or to transmit data due to collision may go to the backlogged states and wait for re-accessing the channel. Hence, the backoff procedure of IEEE 802.11 for the collide nodes can be considered to evaluate total energy consumption of the network.

3.5.2.1. *The hybrid CSMA-CA mechanism*

Consider a homogeneous and fully connected wireless sensor network with N number of nodes. As shown in Fig. 3.2, when a device is turned on and is ready to transmit, it first delays for a random number of backoff periods in the range of 0 to $(2^{BE} - 1)$ units. After the initial random backoff period is over, the device has to perform the clear channel assessment (CCA) for two consecutive slots to access the channel similar to the CSMA-CA mechanism of IEEE 802.15.4. If the channel is sensed idle upon two successful *CCAs*, transmission begins immediately. Otherwise, a node defers channel access, remains in the backlogged state and waits for the random maximum $(2^{BE} - 1)$ units backoff periods. During the backoff procedure, the backoff timer is halted, if channel busy is detected and resumes immediately, if the channel becomes idle. For reliable communications, the acknowledgment message is considered, which is sent out by the destination node upon successfully receiving the packet.

3.5.2.2. *A discrete-time Markov chain model*

Based on the hybrid CSMA-CA mechanism, let us consider an extended linear feedback model, as shown in Fig. 3.3. The nodes may be in *thinking* or in *backlogged*

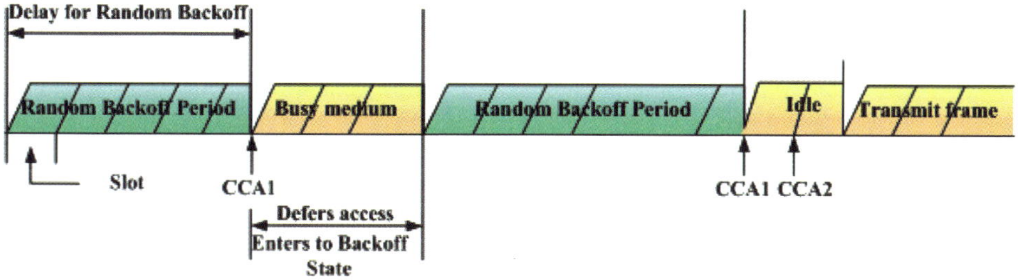

Fig. 3.2. Basic channel access procedure in the hybrid CSMA-CA mechanism.

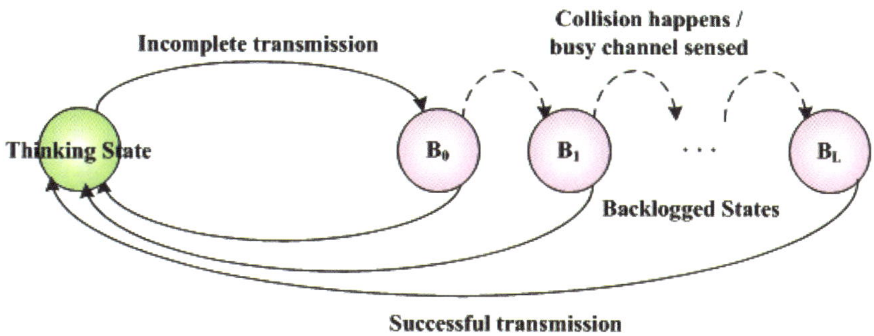

Fig. 3.3. The extended linear feedback model.

states, alternatively. Let $L+1$ number of backlogged states be considered, where L is the retry limit. If W_0 is the initial contention window size, which is doubled for each retransmissions, the maximum contention window size (W_m) for the mth retransmission can be $W_m = W_0 \times 2^m$. Each backlogged user can sense the channel in the current slot of mth retransmission with a probability of $v_m = 2/W_m$. Note that a node generates a new packet with probability g to transmit in the thinking state, whereas it remains in the backlogged state, if it senses the channel busy. As per the extended linear feedback model, $L+1$ number of backlogged states are present in the system represented by $B_0, B_1, \ldots, B_L$, respectively. Let us assume that i_0, $i_1, \ldots, i_L$ be the number of backlogged nodes present within the backlogged states $B_0, B_1, \ldots, B_L$, respectively and X_t denotes the total number of backlogged nodes present in those backlogged states B_m, $\forall\, m \in \{0, 1 \ldots, L\}$. Hence, $X_t = \sum_{m=0}^{L}(i_m)$, for all $t \in [t, t+I]$, where I is the duration of each idle period. If N represents total number of nodes in the network, the total number of backlogged nodes X_t may range from 0 to N and those $L+1$ number of backlogged states can be represented in a discrete-time Markov chain, as shown in Fig. 3.4. The transition from state i to j ($i \leq j$) implies that some thinking nodes are entering to the backlogged state. Similarly, transition from state $i+1$ to i represents that there is a successful packet transmission. Considering the communication channel consists of a sequence

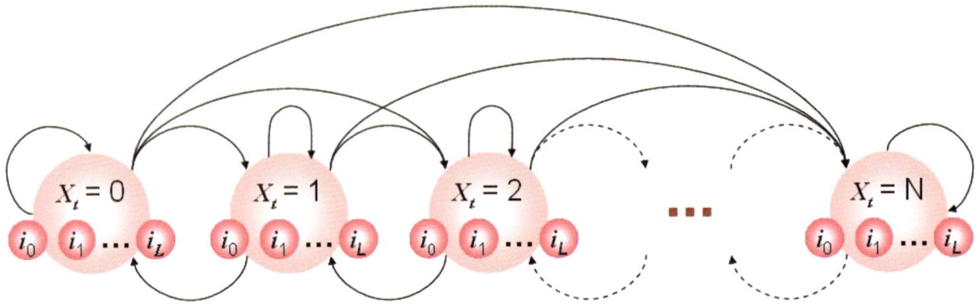

Fig. 3.4. A discrete time Markov chain model for the system status.

of regeneration cycles that is composed of idle and busy periods, the state transition probability of the discrete-time Markov chain model can be found out. Let, duration of the busy period for the successful and unsuccessful transmission be T and C slots, respectively. The transmission matrix[60,61] P can be expressed as

$$P = SQ^T J + FQ^C, \tag{3.5}$$

where $S = (s_{ik})$, $F = (f_{ik})$, and $Q = (q_{ik})$ are the transition matrices. Let, $\Pi = (\pi_0, \pi_1, \ldots, \pi_N)$ be the stationary probability distribution of X_t at the embedded points, where π_i represents the probability that there are i nodes in the backlogged state at the current slot. Then, we can have $\Pi = \Pi P$, which can be obtained from the recursive solution of $\Pi = \Pi P$.

3.5.2.3. *Energy consumption model*

The energy consumption model of each transmission attempts of a node can be designed using the hybrid CSMA-CA mechanism as the underlying medium access control. Let us consider an example as shown in Fig. 3.5, where maximum retry limit of the packet retransmission is equal to two. Under such condition, four possible cases may arise for the failure or successful transmission. Without loss of generality, as shown in Fig. 3.5, Case 1 is a successful transmission attempt without any further retransmission. In Case 2, the packet is successfully transmitted after only one retransmission. Similarly in Case 3, successful transmission occurs only after two retransmissions. But, in Case 4, the transmission attempt is failed, even after two retransmissions. Based on the above example, a generalized energy consumption model for L number of trials can be found out. Let, $\bar{P}_s(m)$: be the expected successful probability of the m-th retransmission of transmission attempts, for $m \in \{1, \ldots, L\}$.

$\bar{P}_s(0)$: be the expected successful probability of the first transmission.

$\epsilon_s(m)$: be the total energy consumption of the successful transmission attempt with m number of retransmissions.

$\epsilon_f(m)$: be the total energy consumption of the failed transmission attempts with m number of retransmissions.

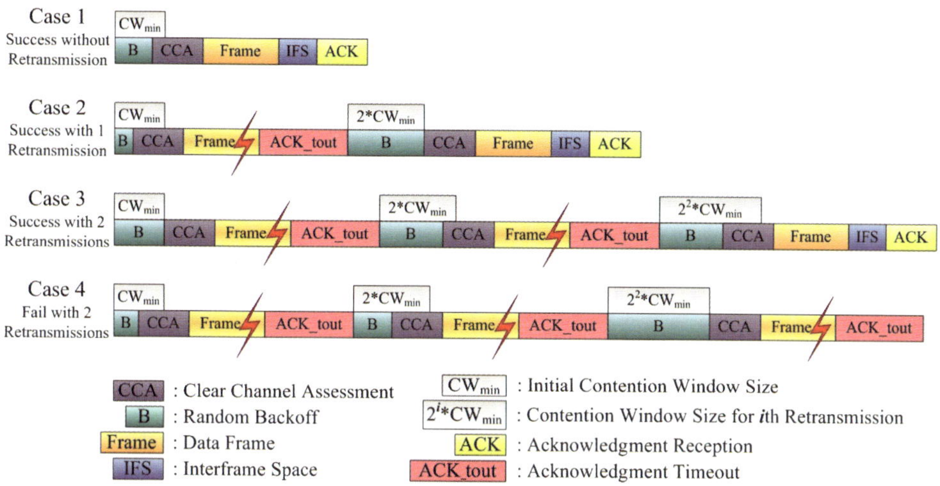

Fig. 3.5. Example of an energy consumption model with retry limit $L = 2$.

Then, the expected energy consumption for any transmission attempts, i.e., either for the successful or failure transmission due to 2-retransmission attempts can be calculated as follows:

$$\begin{aligned}\bar{\epsilon} &= \bar{P}_s(0)\epsilon_s(0) + \left[1 - \bar{P}_s(0)\right]\bar{P}_s(1)\epsilon_s(1) + \left[1 - \bar{P}_s(0)\right]\left[1 - \bar{P}_s(1)\right]\bar{P}_s(2)\epsilon_s(2) \\ &\quad + \left[1 - \bar{P}_s(0)\right]\left[1 - \bar{P}_s(1)\right]\left[1 - \bar{P}_s(2)\right]\epsilon_f(2). \end{aligned} \tag{3.6}$$

However, by generalizing the retry limit from 2 to L, the expected total energy consumption can be expressed as

$$\begin{aligned}\bar{\epsilon} = \bar{P}_s(0)\epsilon_s(0) &+ \sum_{m=1}^{L}\left(\prod_{j=0}^{m-1}\left[1 - \bar{P}_s(j)\right]\right)\bar{P}_s(m)\epsilon_s(m) \\ &+ \left(\prod_{m=0}^{L}\left[1 - \bar{P}_s(m)\right]\right)\epsilon_f(L). \end{aligned} \tag{3.7}$$

It is to be noted that a transmission is completed successfully, if no other transmission is being performed simultaneously. Hence, consequently the successful probability of a transmission is equal to the probability, when only one node transmits at the same time. Since, the system status varies with time, we have the expected successful probability of the mth retransmission of the transmission attempts as follows:

$$\bar{P}_s(m) = \sum_{i=0}^{N}\pi_i P_s(m, i), \tag{3.8}$$

where, π_i is the probability that the system status X_t equals to i. $P_s(m, i)$ is the successful probability of the mth retransmission of the transmission attempt while there are i number of nodes in the backlogged state.

Now the energy consumption due to each failure and successful transmission of each retransmission attempts can be found out. Taking Fig. 3.5 as a case study, it is to be estimated that the total energy consumption in Case 1 is $\epsilon_s(0)$, which can be calculated as $\bar{\epsilon}_{backoff}(0) + \epsilon_{cca} + \epsilon_{data} + \epsilon_{ifs} + \epsilon_{ack}$. The total energy consumption $\epsilon_s(1)$ in Case 2, equals to $\bar{\epsilon}_{backoff}(0) + \epsilon_{cca} + \epsilon_{data} + \epsilon_{ack\_tout} + \bar{\epsilon}_{backoff}(1) + \epsilon_{cca} + \epsilon_{data} + \epsilon_{ifs} + \epsilon_{ack}$. The total energy consumption $\epsilon_s(2)$ in Case 3, is $2 \times (\epsilon_{cca} + \epsilon_{data} + \epsilon_{ack_tout}) + \epsilon_{cca} + \epsilon_{data} + \epsilon_{ifs} + \epsilon_{ack} + \sum_{m=0}^{2} \bar{\epsilon}_{backoff}(m)$. The total energy consumption $\epsilon_f(2)$ in Case 4, is $3 \times (\epsilon_{cca} + \epsilon_{data} + \epsilon_{ack\_tout}) + \sum_{m=0}^{2} \bar{\epsilon}_{backoff}(m)$. Generalizing the above example for any number of retry limit m, the total energy consumption is given by

$$\epsilon_s(m) = m \cdot \epsilon_f + \epsilon_s + \sum_{k=0}^{m} \bar{\epsilon}_{backoff}(k), \tag{3.9}$$

$$\epsilon_f(m) = (m+1) \cdot \epsilon_f + \sum_{k=0}^{m} \bar{\epsilon}_{backoff}(k), \tag{3.10}$$

where $\epsilon_s = \epsilon_{cca} + \epsilon_{data} + \epsilon_{ack}$ and $\epsilon_f = \epsilon_{cca} + \epsilon_{data} + \epsilon_{ack\_tout}$. ϵ_s is the energy consumption of a successful transmission excluding the energy consumption during the backoff periods. The value of ϵ_s comprises the energy spent for performing CCA (ϵ_{cca}), transmitting data frame (ϵ_{data}), the interframe space time (ϵ_{ifs}), and for receiving the acknowledgment message (ϵ_{ack}). On the contrary, ϵ_f is the energy consumption of a failed transmission excluding the energy consumption during backoff periods. The value of ϵ_f considers the energy spent for performing CCA (ϵ_{cca}), transmitting data frame (ϵ_{data}), and waiting for the acknowledgment timeout (ϵ_{ack_tout}). Let, P_{tx_mode} and P_{rx_mode} denote the power consumption in the transmitting and receiving modes, respectively. Then, the energy consumption due to individual operation could be estimated as follows:

$$\begin{aligned} \epsilon_{cca} &= P_{rx\_mode} \times T_{cca}, \\ \epsilon_{ifs} &= P_{rx\_mode} \times T_{ifs}, \\ \epsilon_{ack} &= P_{rx\_mode} \times T_{ack}, \\ \epsilon_{ack\_tout} &= P_{rx\_mode} \times T_{ack\_tout} \\ \epsilon_{data} &= P_{tx\_mode} \times T_{data} \end{aligned} \tag{3.11}$$

where T_{cca} is the time for performing the clear channel assessment (CCA). T_{ifs} is the interframe space time. T_{ack} is the duration within which an acknowledgment message is received. T_{ack_tout} is the duration of acknowledgment timeout. T_{data} is the duration of transmitting data. To be more accurate, the analysis of the expected energy spent during the backoff period ($\bar{\epsilon}_{backoff}(m)$) in the mth retransmission of all transmission attempts is divided into two parts: the energy consumption, while the backoff counter is decreasing ($\bar{\epsilon}_{decrease}(m)$) and the energy consumption, while the backoff counter is halted ($\bar{\epsilon}_{halt}(m)$) due to the busy medium. The energy consumption in both of the cases could be estimated as follows:

$$\bar{\epsilon}_{backoff}(m) = \bar{\epsilon}_{decrease}(m) + \bar{\epsilon}_{halt}(m), \tag{3.12}$$

where energy consumption $\bar{\epsilon}_{decrease}$ for the fixed contention window is estimated as

$$\bar{\epsilon}_{decrease}(m) = P_{rx\_mode} \times T_{slot} \times \frac{1 + W_0}{2}, \tag{3.13}$$

and $\bar{\epsilon}_{decrease}$ for the exponentially increased contention window is estimated as

$$\bar{\epsilon}_{decrease}(m) = P_{rx\_mode} \times T_{slot} \times \frac{1 + 2^m W_0}{2}, \tag{3.14}$$

where $0 \leq \mathrm{m} \leq \mathrm{L}$ and T_{slot} is the duration of each slot. Similarly, the energy consumption due to halting the backoff counter can be estimated as follows

$$\bar{\epsilon}_{halt}(m) = P_{rx\_mode} \times \bar{T}_{halt}(W) \times T_{data}. \tag{3.15}$$

3.6. Conclusion

In this chapter, we have studied the contention free and contention based MAC mechanisms for the wireless sensor networks. Besides, the popularly used MAC mechanisms of IEEE 802.11 and IEEE 802.15.4 are compared to find their contrasting features. Since, energy is the important constraint of WSN, the standard energy consumption parameters are explained for the cluster based and non-clustered based network with a hybrid channel access mechanism. In the hybrid MAC, it is explained how to combine the idea of CSMA-CA mechanism of IEEE 802.15.4 and backoff procedure of IEEE 802.11 during collision. Analytical models based on the extended linear feedback and Markov chain models are developed for the fixed and binary exponential contention windows to analyze and improve the energy efficiency of wireless sensor network.

References

1. IEEE. Wireless Medium Access Control (MAC) and Physical Layer (PHY) specifications for low-rate wireless personal area networks (LR-WPANs) (IEEE 802.15.4) (2003).
2. P. Gupta and P. R. Kumar, The capacity of wireless networks, *IEEE Trans. on Information Theory*, **46** (2000).
3. A. F. Mini, B. Nath and A. A. F. Loureiro, A probabilistic approach to predict the energy consumption in wireless sensor networks, *Proc: 4th Workshop de Comunicao sem Fio e Computao Mvel*, Brazil (October 2002).
4. S. Singh and C. S. Raghavendra, PAMAS: Power aware multi-access protocol with signaling for ad hoc networks, *ACM Computer Communication Review*, 5–26 (1998).

5. W. Ye, J. Heidemann and D. Estrin, An energy efficient MAC protocol for wireless sensor networks, *Proc. IEEE INFOCOM*, New York, June (2002).
6. C. Intanagonwiwat, R. Govindan and D. Estrin, Direct diffusion: A scalable and robust communication paradigm for sensor networks, *Proc. IEEE/ACM MobiCom*, Boston (2000).
7. R. Jain, A. Puri and R. Sengupta, Geographical routing for wireless ad hoc networks using partial information, *IEEE Personal Comm.* (2001).
8. B. Chen, K. Jamieson, H. Balakrishnan and R. Morris, Span: An energy-efficient coordination algorithm for topology maintenance in ad hoc wireless networks, *Proc. IEEE/ACM MobiCom*, Italy (July 2001).
9. J. Kulik, W. Rabiner Heinzelman and H. Balakrishnan, Negotiation based protocols for disseminating information in wireless sensor networks, *Proc. ACM/IEEE MobiCom*, Seattle (1999).
10. F. Ye, H. Luo, J. Cheng, S. Lu and L. Zhang, A two-tier data dissemination model for large-scale wireless sensor networks, *Proc. ACM/IEEE MobiCom*, Atlanta (2002).
11. C. Florens and R. McEliece, Packet distribution algorithms for sensor networks, *Proc. IEEE INFOCOM*, San Francisco (2003).
12. C. Schurgers, V. Tsiatsis, S. Ganeriwal and M. Srivastava, Topology management for sensor networks: Exploiting latency and density, *Proc. 3rd ACM International Symposium on Mobile Ad Hoc Networking and Computing* (2002).
13. R. Zheng, J. Hou and L. Sha, Asynchronous wakeup for power management in ad hoc networks, *Proc. IEEE MobiHoc*, Annapolis, MD (June 2003).
14. G. Lu, B. Krishnamachari and C. S. Raghavendra, Performance evaluation of the IEEE 802.15.4 MAC for low-rate low-power wireless networks, *Proc. IEEE Workshop on Energy-Efficient Wireless Communications and Networks* (2004).
15. J. Zheng and M. J. Lee, Will IEEE 802.15.4 make ubiquitous networking a reality?: A discussion on a potential low power, low bit rate standard, *IEEE Communications Magazine*, **42**(6), 140–146 (2004).
16. J. Huang, Y. Huang, E. Callaway, Q. Shi and B. O'Dea, Simulation of a low duty cycle protocol, *Proc. OPNETWORK*, USA (2001).
17. J. Ma, M. Gao, Q. Zhang, L. M. Ni and W. Zhu, Localized low-power topology control algorithms in IEEE 802.15.4-based sensor networks, *Proc. 25th IEEE International Conference on ICDCS* (June 2005).
18. B. Bougard, F. Catthoor, D. C. Daly, A. Chandrakasan and W. Dehaene, Energy efficiency of the IEEE 802.15.4 standard in dense wireless micro sensor networks: Modeling and improvement perspectives, *Proc. Design Automation and Test in Europe Conference and Exhibition*, 196–201 (2005).
19. J. Zheng and M. J. Lee, A comprehensive performance study of IEEE 802.15.4, *IEEE Press Book* (2004).
20. N. F. Timmons and W. G. Scanlon, Analysis of the performance of IEEE 802.15.4 for medical sensor body area networks, *Proc. 1st IEEE International Conference on Sensor and Ad Hoc Communications and Networks* (2004).
21. J. Ma, M. Gao, Q. Zhang, L. M. Ni and W. Zhu, Localized low-power topology control algorithms in IEEE 802.15.4-based sensor networks, *Proc. 25th IEEE International Conference on Distributed Computing Systems*, 27–36 (2005).
22. J. Misic, S. Shafi and V. B. Misic, Admission control in 802.15.4 beacon enabled clusters, *Proc. International Conference on Communications and Mobile Computing*, July (2006).

23. J. Misic and V. B. Misic, Duty cycle management in sensor networks based on 802.15.4 beacon enabled MAC, *Journal of Ad Hoc and Sensor Wireless Networks*, **1**, 207–233 (2005).
24. J. Misic, V. B. Misic and S. Shafi, Performance of IEEE 802.15.4 beacon enabled PAN with uplink transmission in non-saturation mode — Access delay for finite buffers, *Proc. 1st IEEE International Conference on Broadband Networks*, 416–425 (2004).
25. S. Shafi, Performance of a beacon enabled IEEE 802.15.4 cluster with downlink and uplink traffic, *IEEE Transactions on Parallel and Distributed Systems*, **17**(4), 361–376 (2006).
26. Q. Shi, S. Kyperountas, N. S. Correal and N. Feng, Performance analysis of relative location estimation for multihop wireless sensor networks, *IEEE Journal on Selected Areas in Communications*, **23**(4), 830–838 (2005).
27. M. Petrova, J. Riihijarvi, P. Mahonen and S. Labella, Performance study of IEEE 802.15.4 using measurements and simulations, *Proc. IEEE Wireless Communications and Networking Conference*, **1**, 487–492 (2006).
28. G. Bianchi, Performance analysis of the IEEE 802.11 distributed coordination function, *IEEE Journal on Selected Areas in Communications*, **18** (2000).
29. S. Pollin, M. Ergen, S. C. Ergen, B. Bougard, L. V. der Perre, F. Catthoor, I. Moerman, A. Bahai and P. Varaiya, Performance analysis of slotted IEEE 802.15.4 medium access layer, http://www.soe.ucsc.edu/research/ccrg/DAWN/papers/ZigBee MACvPV.pdf.
30. A. Kouba, M. Alves and E. Tovar, A comprehensive simulation study of slotted CSMA/CA for IEEE 802.15.4 wireless sensor networks, *Proc. 6th IEEE International Workshop on Factory Communication Systems* (2006).
31. J. S. Lee, An experiment on performance study of IEEE 802.15.4 wireless networks, *Proc. IEEE 10th International Conference on Emerging Technologies and Factory Automation* (2005).
32. I. Howitt, R. Neto, J. Wang and J. M. Conrad, Extended energy model for the low rate WPAN, *Proc. 2nd IEEE International Conference on Mobile Ad Hoc and Sensor Systems* (2005).
33. T. R. Park, T. H. Kim, J. Y. Choi, S. Choi and W. H. Kwon, Throughput and energy consumption analysis of IEEE 802.15.4 slotted CSMA-CA, *IEE Electronics Letters*, **41**(18) (2005).
34. C.K. Singh and A. Kumar, Performance evaluation of an IEEE 802.15.4 sensor network with a star topology, ece.iisc.ernet.in/anurag/papers/anurag/singh-kumar05submitted-detailed.pdf.gz.
35. C.-F. Chiasserini and M. Garetto, Modeling the performance of wireless sensor networks, *Proc. Conference of the IEEE Computer and Communications Societies*, **1**, 231 (2004).
36. L. Angrisanil, M. Bertocco, D. Fortin and A. Sona, Assessing coexistence problems of IEEE 802.11b and IEEE 802.15.4 wireless networks through cross-layer measurements, *Proc. IEEE Instrumentation and Measurement Technology Conference* (May 2007).
37. J. Xiao and G. Zeng, An adaptive message passing MAC for wireless sensor networks, Proc. *IEEE Wireless Communications, Networking and Mobile Computing Conference*, 2448–2451 (2007).
38. S. Y. Shin, H. S. Parky, S. Choi and W. H. Kwon, Packet error rate analysis of IEEE 802.15.4 under IEEE 802.11b interference, *Lecture Notes in Computer Science* (May 2005).

39. J.-S. Lee, An experiment on performance study of IEEE 802.15.4 wireless networks, *Proc. IEEE International Conference on Emerging Technologies and Factory Automation* (2005).
40. J.-P. Sheu, P. K. Sahoo and Y.-C. Chang, *Performance Evaluation of Wireless Sensor Network with Hybrid Channel Access Mechanism*, Technical Report, submitted to Dept. of Computer Science and Information Engineering, National Central University, Taiwan (2006).
41. J. Martin, *Communication Satellite systems*, Prentice Hall, New Jersey (1978).
42. A. J. Viterbi, *CDMA, Principles of Spread Spectrum Communication*, Addison-Wesley, Reading, MA (1995).
43. L. Kleinrock and M. O. Scholl, Packet switching in radio channels: New conflict-free multiple access schemes, *IEEE Transactions on Communications*, **28**(7), 1015–1029 (1980).
44. I. Chlamtac, W. R. Franta and K. Levin, BRAM: The broadcast recognizing access method, *IEEE Transactions on Communications*, **27**(8) (1979).
45. D. Farber, J. Feldman, R. Heinrich, D. Hopwood, K. Larson, D. Loomis and L. Rowe, The distributed computing system, *Proc. IEEE COMPCON*, San Francisco, CA, 31–34 (1973).
46. R. Nelson and L. Kleinrock, Spatial TDMA: A collision free multihop channel access protocol, *IEEE Transactions on Communications*, **33**(9), 934–944 (1985).
47. T. V. Truong, *TDMA in Mobile Radio Networks*, 504–507 (1984).
48. M. H. Ammar and D. S. Stevens, A distributed TDMA rescheduling procedure for mobile packet radio networks, *Proc. IEEE ICC*, Denver, 1609–1613 (June 1991).
49. I. Cidon and M. Sidi, Distributed assignment algorithms for multihop packet radio networks, *IEEE Transactions on Computers*, **38**(10), 1353–1361 (1989).
50. V. Rajendran, K. Obraczka, J. J. Garcia and L. Aceves, Energy-efficient, collision-free medium access control for wireless sensor networks, *Proc. SENSYS* (2003).
51. N. Abramson, Development of the ALOHANET, *IEEE Transactions on Information Theory*, **31**(2), 119–123 (1985).
52. L. Kleinrock and F. Tobagi, Packet switching in radio channels: Part I — carrier sense multiple access modes and their throughput delay characteristics, *IEEE Transactions on Communications*, **23**(12), 1400–1416 (1975).
53. LAN MAN Standards Committee of the IEEE Computer Society, Wireless LAN medium access control (MAC) and physical layer (PHY) specification, IEEE, New York, USA, *IEEE Std 802.11-1999 Edition* (1999).
54. W. Ye, J. Heidemann and D. Estrin, Medium access control with coordinated adaptive sleeping for wireless sensor networks, *IEEE/ACM Transactions on Networking* (2004).
55. T. V. Dam and K. Langendoen, An adaptive energy-efficient MAC protocol for wireless sensor networks, *Proc. ACM SenSys*, November (2003).
56. T. Zheng, S. Radhakrishnan and V. Sarangan, PMAC: An adaptive energy-efficient MAC protocol for wireless sensor networks, *Proc. IEEE International Parallel and Distributed Processing Symposium* (2005).
57. D. Bertsekas and R. Gallager, Data Networks, Prentice Hall, 2nd edition (1992).
58. A. Conti, D. Dardari, C. Buratti, D. Sangiorgi and R. Verdone, Impact of contention based MAC on the performance of a wireless sensor network for environmental monitoring, *Proc. Second European Workshop on Wireless Sensor Networks*, 400–404 (2005).

59. R. Vedrdone, A. Conti, D. Sangiorgi and D. Dardari, Process estimation through self-organizing collaborative wireless sensor network, *IEEE Globecom*, Dallas (2004).
60. L. Kleinrock, *Queuing Systems: Vol. I. — Theory*, John Wiley and Sons, New York (1976).
61. X. Li and Q. A. Zeng, Performance analysis of IEEE 802.11 MAC protocols over WLANs with capture effect, *Proc. 2nd International Conference on Mobile Computing and Ubiquitous Networking* (2005).

Chapter 4

Toward Efficient Wireless Medium Access Control

Shiwen Mao*, Yihan Li*, Prathima Agrawal* and Scott F. Midkiff†

*Department of Electrical and Computer Engineering
Auburn University, Auburn, AL 36849, USA

†Bradley Department of Electrical and Computer Engineering
Virginia Tech, Blacksburg, VA 24061, USA

Medium access control (MAC) protocols play an important role in coordinating channel access among the terminals. There have been a large number of MAC schemes proposed in the literature for wired and wireless networks. This research regained considerable interests recently, largely due to the dominant adoption of the IEEE 802.11 protocols and Bluetooth for wireless LANs as well as multi-hop wireless networks. One problem of these MAC schemes in a wireless network is their inefficiency, which sometimes makes them the performance bottleneck of the protocol stack. In this chapter, we first discuss the inefficiency problem of existing wireless MAC schemes. We then review several general approaches to improving the MAC efficiency in the literature. As case studies, we next introduce a location assisted enhancement to the IEEE 802.11 MAC, which can schedule feasible concurrent transmissions within a small neighborhood, thus leveraging spatial reuse, and a polling service-based MAC scheme (termed PSMAC), which amortizes the high control overhead of channel access over multiple data frames. We present performance studies that clearly demonstrate the efficacy of these schemes.

4.1. Introduction

In wireless networks, medium access control (MAC) protocols are the "workhorse" of the protocol stack. As they play an important role in coordinating channel access among wireless terminals, their efficiency is very important for higher layer protocols (e.g., TCP or video streaming) to savor the benefits of emerging physical layer technologies. In order to accommodate current and emerging bandwidth-intensive applications, it is thus crucial to improve the efficiency of wireless MAC protocols (as indicated by Amdahl's Law[a]), while new physical layer technologies are being adopted for higher channel data rates.

[a]A form of Amdahl's Law states that to improve the performance of a system, its components with respect to the most frequently encountered states must be improved. Conversely, performance gain is delimited by such components.

During the everlasting quest for more efficient medium access, many MAC protocols have been proposed. Currently, the CSMA/CA-based IEEE 802.11 MAC has become the most popular MAC protocol for single- or multi-hop wireless networks. However, as a drastic contrast to its dominant role, there is strong evidence showing that the 802.11 MAC is becoming the performance bottleneck, largely due to the spatial reuse-related inefficiency and high control overhead associated with its medium access mechanism.[1–4] For example, Woo and Culler[4] find that the RTS-CTS-DATA-ACK handshake series in transmitting a frame can constitute up to 40% overhead in a sensor platform. In addition, the interesting study in Ref. 1 shows that such problems are inherent in the IEEE 802.11 MAC. By simply increasing the data rate without reducing overhead, the enhanced performance is still bounded even when the nominal data rate goes to infinity. It is therefore crucial to make such wireless MAC protocols more efficient.

In this chapter, we consider the problem of improving the efficiency of wireless MAC protocols. We first discuss the causes of inefficiency in wireless MAC schemes and protocols in Sec. 4.2. We then review several general and effective approaches in the literature to improve the MAC performance in Sec. 4.3. As case studies, we introduce a location assisted enhancement to the IEEE 802.11 MAC in Sec. 4.4, which can schedule feasible concurrent transmissions within a small neighborhood, thus leveraging spactial reuse, and a polling service-based MAC scheme (termed PSMAC) in Sec. 4.5, which amortizes the high control overhead of channel access over multiple data frames. We present performance studies that clearly demonstrate the efficacy of these schemes.

4.2. The Low Efficiency Problem of Existing Wireless MACs

In this section, we discuss the inefficiency problem of the reservation-based p-Persistent CSMA (due to its similarity to the IEEE 802.11 MAC[5,6]) and IEEE 802.11 MAC. We will see that the MAC inefficiency is mainly due to its scheduling overhead.

4.2.1. *Throughput limit of reservation-based p-Persistent CSMA*

We consider a slotted-time system, where each time slot is the combined transmission time of an RTS frame and a CTS frame. In p-Persistent CSMA, a node with backlogged data frames, say Node A, first senses the medium at the beginning of the next time slot. If the medium is idle, Node A will transmit an RTS with probability p in the first half of the time slot. In the RTS, node A specifies the destination of its head of line frame, say Node B. If this is the only RTS sent in that time slot, Node B will reply with a CTS in the second half of the time slot; otherwise, there is collision of multiple RTS frames and no CTS will be returned.

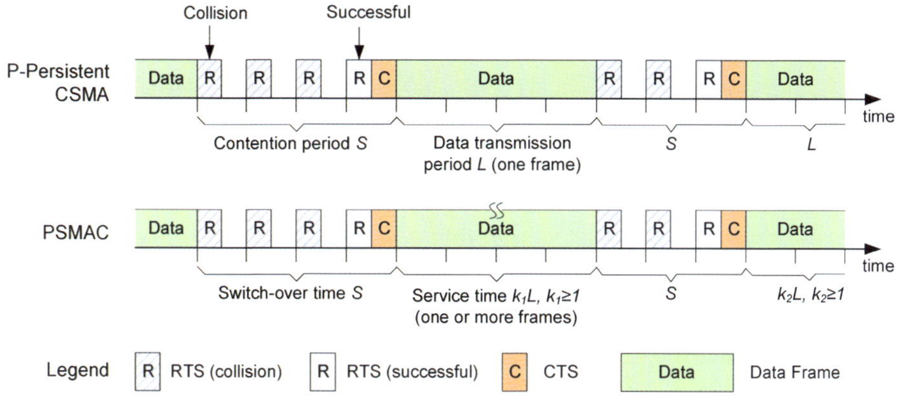

Fig. 4.1. Time-line illustration of p-Persistent CSMA and the proposed PSMAC schemes.

Frame transmissions are aligned to the beginning of the time slots. We assume fixed frame length of L time slots. If the RTS/CTS dialog is successful, a data frame will be transmitted in the following L time slots, right after the time slot of the successful RTS/CTS dialog. The operation of this mechanism is illustrated in Fig. 4.1. For simplicity, we ignore the protocol components such as Inter-Frame-Spaces (IFS) and ACK frames that are used as in the IEEE 802.11 MAC. However, these components can be modeled as a fixed amount of overhead and can be easily incorporated into the model.

For such random access networks, performance limits can be derived by studying the system under heavy load. Therefore, we make the *heavy traffic assumption* in the following analysis, assuming each node has at least one data frame to transmit at any time. Let S be the time measured from the time when the previous service finishes to the time when one pair of RTS/CTS succeeds (see Fig. 4.1). The operation of p-Persistent CSMA can be modeled as a *alternating renewal process*:[7] every contention period of S will be followed by a service period of L, and S is the overhead for transmitting L time slots of data. Therefore, the average throughput of the system is

$$T = \frac{L}{L + E(S)}. \tag{4.1}$$

For a given network of N nodes, T is a function of the transmission probability p. The optimal transmission probability and the maximum throughput are derived as[8]

$$p^* = \frac{1}{N} \quad \text{and} \quad T^*(N) = \frac{L(1-\frac{1}{N})^{N-1}}{L(1-\frac{1}{N})^{N-1}+1}, \quad N \geq 2. \tag{4.2}$$

It can be easily shown that the optimal value p^* ensures that, on average, there is only one RTS transmitted in each competition slot, which leads to the highest throughput.

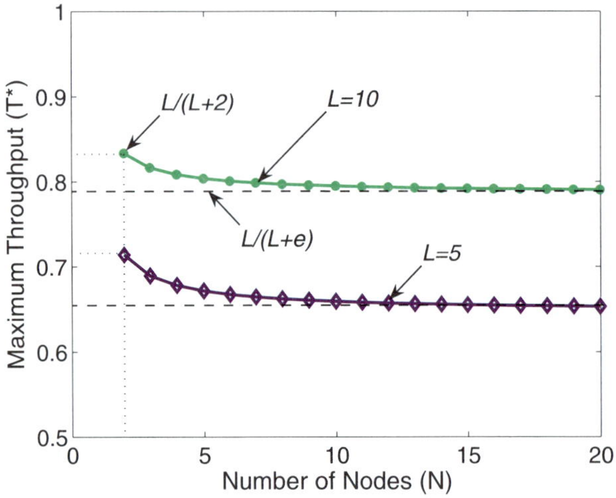

Fig. 4.2. The maximum throughput of p-Persistent CSMA ($L = 10$ and $L = 5$).

In Fig. 4.2, $T^*(N)$ versus N are shown for the case $L = 10$ and $L = 5$. It can be seen that, in the simplest case of $N = 2$, the throughput achieves its maximum of $T^*(2) = L/(L+2)$. Here the slight reduction in throughput is caused by the collision when both nodes send RTS to compete for the channel. As the number of nodes increases, the maximum throughput decreases due to the higher chance of collision. When $N \to \infty$, the maximum throughput approaches from above to a limit of $T^*(\infty) = L/(L+e)$, where e is Euler's number. For example, if $L = 10$ and $N = 20$, the maximum throughput is 79%; when $N \to \infty$, the throughput reaches its limit 78.6%. The p-Persistent CSMA scheme clearly does not achieve 100% throughput. When $L = 5$, the throughput limit is 64.8%, as shown in Fig. 4.2.

Clearly the maximum throughput (4.2) is also a function of frame length L. It is possible to achieve a reasonably high throughput with p-Persistent CSMA by increasing the frame length. Can we reduce the protocol overhead by disabling the RTS/CTS mechanism? If data frames are directly used in contention resolution, the system reduces to Slotted ALOHA. It can be verified that the optimal throughput is $T^* = 1/e = 36.8\%$ as $N \to \infty$, the well-known upper bound for Slotted ALOHA, which may be even lower than (4.2).

4.2.2. *Throughput limit of IEEE 802.11a*

The CSMA/CA-like IEEE 802.11 MAC has become the most popular protocol for single- or multi-hop wireless networks. However, the IEEE 802.11 MAC has a limited throughput because of a considerable control overhead. Xiao and Rosdahl show in Ref. 1 that, for a given payload size and a given set of overhead parameters, the throughput upper limit (TUL) and the delay lower limit (DLL) exist and are given as below independently of the data rate:

$$TUL = \frac{8L_{DATA}}{2T_P + 2T_{PHY} + 2\tau + T_{DIFS} + T_{SIFS} + \frac{1}{2}CW_{min}T_{slot}}, \tag{4.3}$$

$$DLL = T_P + T_{PHY} + \tau + T_{DIFS} + \frac{1}{2}CW_{min}T_{slot}, \tag{4.4}$$

The symbols used in the above equations are defined as follows:

Symbol	Definition
T_{DATA}	Transmission time for payload
T_{H_DATA}	Transmission time of MAC overhead
T_P	Transmission time of the physical preamble
T_{PHY}	Transmission time of the PHY header
T_{slot}	A slot time
T_{DIFS}	DIFS time
T_{SIFS}	SIFS time
L_{DATA}	Payload size in bytes
τ	Propagation delay
CW_{min}	Minimum backoff window size

According to the above results, for example when the payload size is 1000 bytes, the maximum achievable throughput for IEEE 802.11a is only 24.7 Mb/s, which is about 45.7% of the nominal link capacity of 54 Mb/s.

4.2.3. *Overhead in a wireless sensor network*

Similar observation has been made when adopting the IEEE 802.11-like MAC in wireless sensor networks. For example, Woo and Culler[4] find that the RTS-CTS-DATA-ACK handshake required in transmitting a packet can constitute up to 40% overhead in a sensor network. When used in a multi-hop environment, the problem gets even worse due to carrier sensing and spatial reuse, making it hard to provide sufficient end-to-end throughput for paths with a large number of hops.[2]

Finally, the interesting study in Ref. 1 shows that by simply increasing the data rate without reducing overhead, the enhanced performance is bounded even when the data rate goes to infinity. It is therefore crucial to reduce the control overhead of such wireless MAC protocols.

4.3. General Approaches to More Efficient MAC

In this section, we briefly review several existing approaches for improving wireless MAC efficiency, including using directional antennas, using multiple channels and reducing scheduling overhead.

4.3.1. *Wireless MAC using directional antennas*

Usually omni-directional antennas are assumed for mobile nodes in a wireless network. With an omni-directional antenna, radio signal is transmitted to all directions. To avoid collision, all other nodes are required to remain silence when two nodes are communicating, which leads to a lower network capacity with more nodes in the network.[9] A directional antenna works differently, where its main lobe has much higher gain than its side and back lobes. With directional antennas, it is possible for two pair of nodes to communicate simultaneously even when they are close to each other. The network capacity can be therefore increased.

Since current MAC protocols, including IEEE 802.11, do not support directional antenna, new protocols need to be designed and resolve three new problems: a different kind of hidden node problem, a deafness problem and a higher directional interference. When directional antennas are used, the hidden node problem may occur when two nodes are nearby but invisible to each other while their antennas pointing in different directions. This does not happen when omni-directional antennas are used, since nearby nodes can detect each other if they are within each other's transmission ranges. When a sender try to communicate to a receiver while the receiver's antenna is pointing in another direction, the receiver cannot hear and the deafness problem occurs. Higher directional interference is due to the higher antenna gains. Most MAC protocols using directional antennas comprise the RTS/CTS/DATA/ACK handshake and overcome the problems by combining directional and omni-directional messages.

Ko *et al.*[10] proposed one of the first MAC protocols, Directional MAC (D-MAC), with which each node has several directional antennas but only one is allowed to transmit at a time. RTS, DATA and ACK are sent directionally, while CTS is sent omni-directionally to deal with the hidden node problem. The other choice is to send RTS omni-directionally and other messages directionally. It is assumed that each node knows its own location and its immediate neighbors' locations. D-MAC achieves higher throughput compared to IEEE 802.11 since more nodes are allowed to transmit at a time.

In the scheme proposed by Nasipuri *et al.*[11] if a node has data waiting, it first sends out an RTS in all directions by every antenna. The receiver also sends out the CTS in all directions by every antenna if it is available. Only one transceiver in a node can transmit at a time. The sender learns the relative direction of the receiver by discerning which antenna picks up the strongest CTS signal. The DATA message is then sent directionally from the sender by the corresponding antenna to the receiver. There is no need for a node to know location information in advance.

In Multi-hop RTS MAC(M-MAC),[12] RTS packets can be sent to the destination in multi-hops, while CTS, DATA and ACK messages are sent in a single hop. The reason for doing this is that directional antennas have a higher gain than omni-directional antennas. In Directional Virtual Carrier Sensing (DVCS),[13] three primary capabilities are added to the original IEEE 802.11 MAC protocol for directional communication with DVCS: caching the Angle of Arrival (AOA), beam locking and unlocking, and use of directional NAV (DNAV). The network capacity increases 3 to 4 times with DVCS compared with omnidirectional communication as shown in experimental results.

With the tone-based directional MAC (Tone DMAC) protocol, all RTS, CTS, DATA and ACK messages are transmitted directionally, while omni-directional out-of-band tones are used to indicate deafness to blocked nodes.[14] In the Circular Directional RTS, the RTS is transmitted directional in a circular way until it covers all the directions.[15] The RTS contains the duration of the intended four way handshake (as in 802.11). The neighbors are therefore informed about the intended transmission as the information is spread around by the circular RTS. The neighbors then decide if they will defer their transmission in the direction of transmitter or receiver. Thus, the number of hidden terminals can be significantly reduced since the neighbors are aware of the intended handshake.

4.3.2. *Wireless MAC with multiple channels*

Multi-channel multi-interface wireless networks receive considerable interests recently, largely due to the availability of multiple wireless cards at a mobile host, as well as the compelling need of larger throughput.[16–26] Although the use of multiple channels offers great potential for higher throughput, it also brings about challenging scheduling problems, since now connectivity also depends on channel assignment, in addition to mobility/distance and channel dynamics.[19,26]

In the multi-channel CSMA protocol by Nasipuri *et al.*,[27] the total available bandwidth is divided by multiple channels. When a node has a data packet to transmit, it first consider the channel it used in its previous transmission. If the channel is not free, it randomly selects a free channel to transmit. It has been shown that this protocol is more efficient than single channel CSMA schemes. However, it is interesting to see that, when the traffic load is low or the number of nodes is small, its performance is not as good as the latter. The reason is that, when the traffic load is low or the number of nodes is small, some channels are not in use, which leads to bandwidth waste.

In many multi-channel MACs, handshake is used between sender and receiver to select a channel for transmission. One approach is the dynamic channel assignment (DCA),[25] where the total bandwidth is divided into a common control channel and multiple data channels. The control channel is used for control packets. Each node is equipped with two half-duplex transceivers, one for the control channel and the other for data channels. An RTS/CTS/RES five way handshake is used to indicate the data channel to use and reserve the channel. For channel selection, each node maintains a channel usage list (CUL) and a free channel list (FCL) by listening to all its neighbors in the control channel. In the RTS message from the sender, a list of free channels are included. The receiver then checks the list and select one channel for data transmission, and indicates it in the CTS message. Before sending the data packet, the sender first sends out a reservation (RES) message to inform all its neighbors of the data channel reservation.

4.3.3. *Reducing MAC overhead*

As leveraging concurrent transmissions improves the wireless MAC performance, another effective way is to reduce their control overhead. In Ref. 28, Xiao proposed two mechanisms, concatenation mechanism (CM) and piggyback mechanism (PM), to improve the throughput and delay performance by reducing overhead of the IEEE 802.11 protocols. This interesting scheme is extended in Ref. 29 for multimedia data transmissions.

In CM, data frames with the same source and destination addresses are concatenated into a large virtual frame for a single transmission. The destination node will receive all concatenated frames and acknowledge the last concatenated frame only. The maximum number of concatenated frame in a virtual frame is bounded by a threshold, called *concatenated threshold*. In this way, a scheduling overhead is incurred for a virtual frame instead of each individual frame, at the additional cost of a relative smaller CH frame.

In PM, a receiver is allowed to piggyback a data frame to the sender if it has a frame available for the sender. The piggybacked frame should be the one arrived the earliest among all frames to the sender. The sender needs to acknowledge the piggyback frame after an SIFS time. The overhead is reduced since the piggyback frame does not need to compete for the medium.

4.3.4. *Remarks*

We can see that the above schemes reviewed so far can be roughly categorized as either (i) reducing collisions domain and leveraging concurrent transmissions or (ii) reducing the control overhead. Some of the techniques requires specific hardware (e.g., directional antennas) or additional resource (e.g., multiple orthogonal channels), and thus may not be suitable for wireless sensor nodes that have stringent space, energy, processing, and hardware constraints. On the contrary, the CM and PM schemes[28] are better suited for the wireless sensor network environment since they only require change of the scheduling, which can be implemented by modifying the device driver of the wireless interface.

In the remainder of this chapter, we present two schemes as case studies. The first scheme schedules concurrent transmissions by exploiting location information,[30] while the second scheme employs efficient polling service to amortize control overhead.[8] For both schemes, there is no need for extra hardware or resource. In addition, both schemes are complementary to the existing techniques. That is, they can be adopted to further improve the MAC performance when extra hardware or resource are available.[31]

4.4. Leveraging Concurrent Transmissions

In most of wireless MAC schemes, the virtual carrier sensing mechanism to resolve the hidden-terminal problem. However, the so-called "exposed-terminal" problem still remains. An exposed terminal, i.e., a node located within the RTS range but not in the CTS range, is refrained from transmission, even if its transmission will not interfere the other receiver. The exposed terminal problem hinders spatial reuse in scheduling and is a key problem for network throughput in a multi-hop wireless network.

Considerable effort has been made to mitigate the exposed node problem. For example, it has been found that carrier sensing range is an important parameter for spatial reuse, while using the optimal carrier sensing range will certainly help to reduce the number of exposed nodes.[32–36] In addition, researchers also exploited efficient power control for leveraging spatial reuse.[37–41] In the so-called MACA-P protocol,[42] a control gap is introduced between the RTS-CTS exchange and the subsequent DATA-ACK exchange, such that exposed nodes can transmit RTS-CTS in this control interval to schedule their concurrent DATA frame transmissions. Additional control messages called Request-To-Send-Simultaneously (RTSS) and Clear-To-Send-Simultaneously (CTSS) are also used for scheduling concurrent transmissions in a recent work.[43]

4.4.1. *Location-assisted MAC*

In the following, we present an approach to improve spatial reuse in multi-hop wireless networks. This approach exploits location information to schedule concurrent transmissions. The objective is to allow exposed node to schedule concurrent transmissions in order to improve network throughput and delay performance. Here each node is assumed to have its location information, either through GPS or many available localization algorithms,[44–46] and each node is able to exchange its location information with its neighbors. We first discuss the key steps in the proposed scheme, then present the complete distributed protocol.

4.4.1.1. *Identifying exposed terminal*

When a node first overhears an RTS and then a DATA frame from the same transmitter, it can be identified as an exposed terminal with regard to the overheard transmission. In practice, however, information such as frame type will be only available at the MAC layer after the entire frame is received and verified by checking the FCS (frame check sequence) trailer. When a node recognizes itself as an exposed terminal in this manner, it will be too late to schedule any concurrent transmission. In

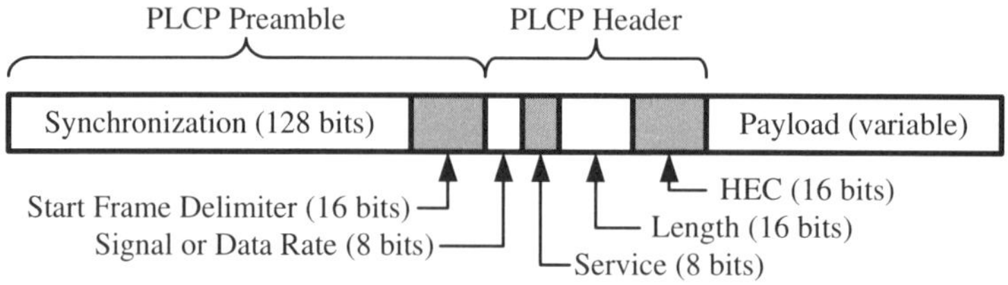

Fig. 4.3. The IEEE 802.11 PHY frame structure when DSSS is used.

order to schedule concurrent transmissions, exposed terminals should be identified *before* the current DATA frame transmission begins.

A cross-layer approach is adopted to identifying exposed terminals, which exploits PHY frame header information for early DATA frame identification. The IEEE 802.11 PHY frame structure is shown in Fig. 4.3 for direct spread spectrum sequencing (DSSS). As soon as the PLCP (physical layer convergence protocol) header, which precedes the current MAC DATA frame, is completely received and verified (by checking HEC, a 16-bit CRC code), the exposed node will know the MPDU (MAC protocol data unit) length. The exposed node can determine if the MAC frame is DATA from the length information since DATA frames are always longer than control frames (i.e., RTS, CTS, and ACK). By comparing the *Length* value with that in the preceding RTS, the exposed node can infer if the RTS and the DATA frame are from the same sender. It can further validate its inference if the interval between the DATA frame and the RTS is (SIFS + CTS + SIFS) plus some propagation delay.

4.4.1.2. *Validating scheduled transmission*

When a node is identified as an exposed terminal, its transmission should be validated first. Such validation is necessary since a scheduled transmission may not always be feasible. By exploiting location information, we can correctly identify scheduled transmissions that will not be interfered by the current transmission (see Fig. 4.4(a)). Furthermore, for both DATA frames to be delivered successfully, the corresponding ACK transmissions should not interfere with each other either. In the case of ACK transmission, the roles of transmitter and receiver are switched, as shown in Fig. 4.4. Therefore, in order to prevent collision between the two ACK frames, the current receiver should be out of the interference range of the scheduled transmitter, and the scheduled receiver should be out of the interference range of the current transmitter (see Fig. 4.4(b)).

Figure 4.5 presents procedure `validate_schdTx()`. It evaluates the feasibility of a scheduled transmission by considering both DATA and ACK frames. Recall that the location information of a node's neighbors is available, which is used in the validation procedure. In Fig. 4.5, d_1 is the distance between the scheduled

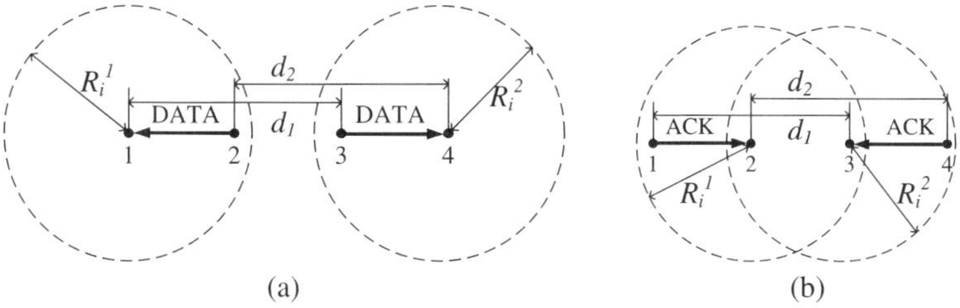

Fig. 4.4. DATA and ACK transmissions for the current transmission from Node 2 to Node 1 and the scheduled transmission from Node 3 to Node 4. (a) DATA frame transmission. (b) ACK frame transmission. Reprint from[30] ©2008 IEEE.

Procedure validate_schdTx()

calculate d_1 and d_2 ;
estimate R_i^1 and R_i^2 ;
if ($d_1 > R_i^1$ **AND** $d_2 > R_i^2$ **AND** $d_1 > R_i^2$ **AND** $d_2 > R_i^1$)
  return 1 ; *// the scheduled transmission is allowed*
else
  return 0 ; *// the scheduled transmission is cancelled*
endif

Fig. 4.5. Procedure validating a scheduled transmission. The variables d_1, d_2, R_i^1 and R_i^2 are shown in Fig. 4.4. Reprint from[30] ©2008 IEEE.

transmitter and the current receiver, while d_2 is the distance between the current transmitter and the scheduled receiver. These can be easily computed from the coordinates of these nodes. Furthermore, R_i^1 and R_i^2 are the interference ranges of the current receiver and the scheduled receiver, respectively; R_i^1 and R_i^2 are also the interference ranges of the current transmitter and the scheduled receiver, respectively. These interference ranges can be estimated using a proper propagation model.[30] The first two conditions in Line 3 test the feasibility of the concurrent DATA transmission, while the last two conditions in Line 3 check the feasibility of the concurrent ACK transmission. An exposed node will not proceed to schedule a concurrent transmission if either of the above conditions is violated.

4.4.1.3. *Scheduling concurrent transmission*

If the validation is passed, the exposed terminal will try to schedule its concurrent transmission. Figure 4.6 provides an example. The starting time of a scheduled transmission is determined as follows. First, the value *schdTx_margin* is computed as:

$$\begin{aligned} schdTx\_margin = {} & \text{current\_duration} - \text{SIFS} - \text{CTS} - \text{SIFS} \\ & - (\text{PLCP reading time}) - (\text{scheduled data duration}) \\ & - \text{SIFS} - \text{ACK} - (\text{round-trip propagation delay}), \end{aligned} \tag{4.5}$$

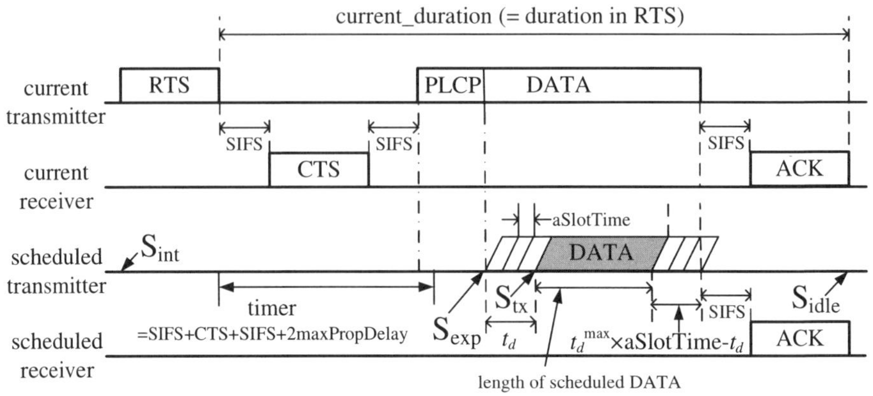

Fig. 4.6. A time-line illustration for the operation of the proposed protocol. Reprint from[30] ©2008 IEEE.

where current_duration represents the duration carried in the preceding RTS of the current transmission.

Suppose that there are multiple nodes near the current transmitter. Then more than one node can be identified as exposed terminals. Since we are developing a fully distributed protocol, each exposed node may start to transmit and there may be collision among themselves. To play on the safe side, we take a conservative approach to introduce a random delay in order to differentiate the starting times of potential concurrent transmissions. A random value t_d is generated similar to the backoff mechanism:

$$t_d = (random\_integer \ \% \ t_d^{max}) \times aSlotTime, \tag{4.6}$$

where t_d^{max} is an upper bound for t_d computed as

$$t_d^{max} = \lceil schdTx\_margin/aSlotTime \rceil .$$

Note that the random delay is a multiple of $aSlotTime$ (20 μs in IEEE 802.11b[47]). If $schdTx\_margin$ is negative, the scheduled transmission cannot fit into the current data transmission period, and it will not be scheduled. Otherwise, the scheduled data frame may be transmitted following the received PLCP preamble and header, after an additional delay t_d. If t_d^{max} is sufficiently large, the probability that multiple scheduled transmissions start concurrently will be negligible.

Once an exposed terminal gets a positive $schdTx\_margin$ value, it will start a timer with value t_d after detecting the beginning of the current DATA frame transmission. During the interval, it will keep on detecting if there is scheduled transmission from another exposed terminal (in addition to the current transmission).[b] If it detects a scheduled transmission, it will cancel its timer as well as its

[b]We assume the radio device of an exposed node can detect such events. For example, a concurrent transmission from another exposed node (with a smaller timer value) can be detected by a sudden

DATA frame. Otherwise, when the timer times out, it will start to schedule its concurrent transmission.

Due to the introduction of random delay t_d, two ACKs for the current and scheduled transmission may not be aligned. In order to let the scheduled receiver know when to transmit ACK, we introduce a new frame type for the scheduled DATA. The new frame type has one extra field, termed T_{info}, for carrying the random delay value $(t_d^{max} - t_d/aSlotTime)$. We can use the reserved value of Type and Subtype, e.g., value "11" for this type of frames.[47] When a normal DATA frame is received, ACK frame is sent after SIFS. When a DATA frame of type "11" is received, ACK is sent after SIFS plus $(T_{info} \times aSlotTime)$.

4.4.1.4. *A distributed protocol*

Now we are ready to put all the pieces together. The basic operation of this MAC protocol resembles that of IEEE 802.11 MAC. By incorporating the identification, validation, and scheduling procedures described above, it can schedule concurrent transmissions from exposed nodes, thus leveraging spatial reuse and improving network throughput.

The state-transition diagram of the proposed protocol is given in Fig. 4.7, where the solid arrows indicate the state transition path of a successfully scheduled transmission. First, based on the frames overheard from the medium, a node

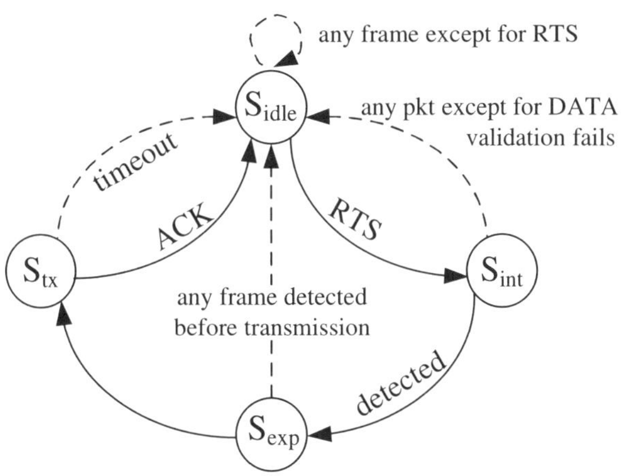

Fig. 4.7. State-transition diagram of the location-assisted MAC protocol, which has four states: (i) the initial state S_{idle}, (ii) the intermediate state S_{int}, (iii) the exposed terminal state S_{exp}, and (iv) the scheduled transmission sate S_{tx}. Reprint from[30] ©2008 IEEE.

increase in the instant Received Signal Strength Indicator (RSSI).[47] The exposed node can also decode the received current DATA frame (rather than discarding it). It can infer the presence of a concurrent transmission when the PHY bit error rate suddenly increases.

may identify itself as an exposed terminal. Specifically, after receiving an RTS destined to some other node, the node enters the intermediate state S_{int}. If a DATA frame from the same sender is detected as discussed, the node enters state S_{exp}. However, only nodes passing the validation process of the scheduled transmission will remain in S_{exp}. The validation process determines: (i) whether or not the scheduled transmission will collide with the current transmission by running procedure `validate_schdTx()` as shown in Fig. 4.5; (ii) whether or not the scheduled data frame can fit into the transmission period of the current data frame. That is, if $schdTx\_margin$ is non-negative.

A timer with value t_d will start if and only if both conditions are satisfied. However, the timer could be canceled if multiple concurrent transmissions (i.e., the current transmission and other scheduled transmissions) are detected before it expires, as indicated by the vertical dash arrow in Fig. 4.7. Otherwise, the scheduled DATA frame will be transmitted when the timer expires. The loop is closed when the scheduled receiver returns an ACK to the scheduled transmitter successfully. Otherwise, the scheduled sender will time out and try to retransmit the DATA frame. It is worth noting that although the scheduled transmission does not use an RTS to reserve the scheduled receiver, the scheduled receiver should not be involved in an ongoing transmission. This is because otherwise the scheduled transmitter should have overheard a CTS from the scheduled receiver (since it is a one-hop neighbor) in response for an earlier RTS from some other transmitter.

4.4.2. *Simulation studies*

To demonstrate the performance of the proposed protocol, we implement it with `ns-2.30` and perform extensive simulation studies. In addition to the proposed protocol, a companion mechanism is also implemented to distribute location information. In this implementation, each node maintains a table storing its location information and that of its one-hop neighbors. We modify RTS to piggyback the coordinates of the sender itself and its target receiver. An alternative approach is to adopt a special control message for distributing location information, which is discussed in Ref. 30.

Throughout this section, the antenna parameters are set to the default values in `ns-2.30`, i.e., $R_{tx} = 250$ m and $R_{cs} = 550$ m. The channel rate is set to 1 Mb/s. In all the simulations, data flows start at $t = 10$ s, and last for about 15 minutes. For throughput, we focus on the number of bytes successfully transmitted at the "agent" level (i.e., excluding protocol overhead, and end-to-end throughput rather than one-hop throughput). Each simulation is repeated five times with different random seeds. Each result reported in this section is the average of the corresponding five trials, with 90% confidence intervals plotted. Other simulation parameters will be given when the results are discussed.

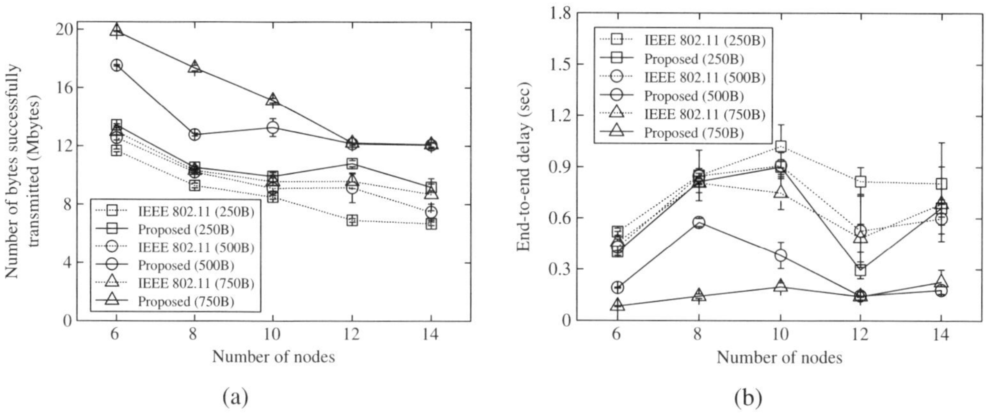

Fig. 4.8. Simulation results for chain networks. (a) Number of bytes successfully transmitted over an 890-second interval. (b) Average end-to-end delay. Reprint from[30] ©2008 IEEE.

4.4.2.1. *Chain networks*

The first simulation study is performed with the chain network topology, where the distance between any two adjacent nodes is set to 200 m. In the simulation, the forward flow (from Node 1 to Node N) is a CBR session with a stream of 1000-byte frames, while the backward flow (from Node N to Node 1) is a CBR session with smaller packet size.

The simulation results for chain networks with various packet sizes for the backward flow are plotted in Fig. 4.8(a). Here the data rates of the flows for the 6-, 8-, 10-, 12-, and 14-node chain networks are set to 90 Kb/s, 80 Kb/s, 70 Kb/s, 55Kb/s, and 55 Kb/s, respectively. These data rates are chosen according to the simulations presented in Ref. 2. A performance measure, *normalized throughput improvement*, is defined as

$$\alpha = \frac{throughput\_proposed - throughput\_802.11}{throughput\_802.11}.$$

We have $\alpha = 67.89\%$ for the 8-node chain when the frame size of the backward flow is 750 bytes. For the 6-, 10-, 12-node and 14-node chain networks, the normalized improvements achieved by the proposed scheme are found to be 52.93%, 58.26%, 27.25%, and 39.27%, respectively. When the packet size of the backward flow is reduced, the improvement ratio tends to be smaller. For example, when the packet size of the backward flow is 500 bytes, the throughput improvement ratio ranges from 24.94% to 61.22%, for chain networks with increasing number of nodes. When the packet size of the backward flow is 250 bytes, the throughput improvement ratio ranges from 13.47% to 56.18% for the chain networks.

The average end-to-end delay is shown in Fig. 4.8(b). We observe significantly reduced average end-to-end delays when the proposed MAC is used. Let β

denote the ratio of the end-to-end delay of the proposed MAC over that of IEEE 802.11 MAC, i.e.,

$$\beta = \frac{delay\_proposed}{delay\_802.11}.$$

In the 6-node chain with 750-byte backward flow, we have $\beta = 18.36\%$. Significant delay improvement is also achieved for other chain networks we examined. When the packet size of the backward flow is equal to 750 bytes, the β values are 17.68%, 26.48%, 29.13%, and 33.06%, for the 8-, 10-, 12-, and 14-node network, respectively.

4.4.2.2. *Random networks*

We perform the scheme with random network topologies. In this setting, 64, 81, 100, and 121 nodes are randomly located in a 1,000 m × 1,000 m area, respectively. 16, 18, 20, and 22 nodes are selected as the source nodes for the 64-, 81-, 100-, and 121-node random networks, respectively. The data rates are set to 300 Kb/s for all the cases. AODV protocol is used for routing.[48]

We use variable packet sizes in the simulation, where packet size is uniformly distributed within range [100, 1,100] bytes, and the data rate is uniformly distributed within range [100, 200] Kb/s. Figure 4.9 shows the simulation results for the four random networks with variable packet sizes. The packet size is uniformly distributed within range [100, 1,100] bytes, and the data rate is uniformly distributed within range [100, 200] Kb/s. The throughput improvements α are 14.50%, 14.77%, 25.01%, and 30.44%, respectively, while the delay ratios β are 82.95%, 86.57%, 88.52%, and 76.48%, respectively. These are consistent with those observed for the random networks with fixed packet size and data rates.[30]

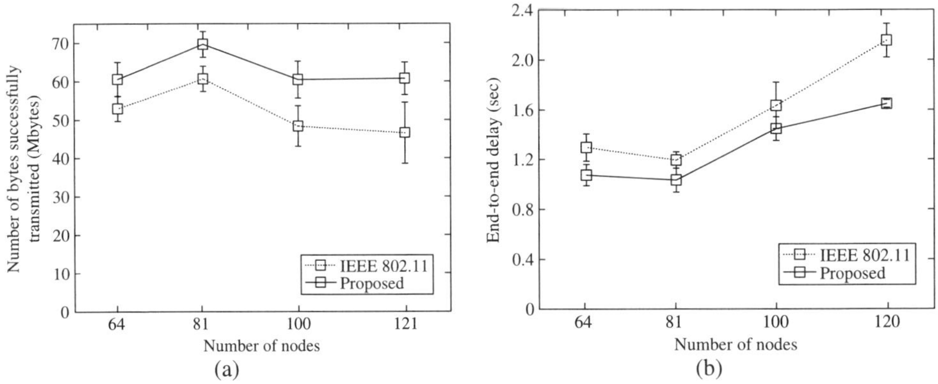

Fig. 4.9. Simulation results for random networks with randomly chosen packet sizes and data rates. (a) Number of bytes successfully transmitted over an 890-second interval. (b) Average end-to-end delay. Reprint from[30] ©2008 IEEE.

4.5. Distributed Polling Service-Based MAC

The second case study is the distributed polling service-based MAC (termed PSMAC) that uses efficient polling service in a wireless network.[8] Polling is a general way of multiplexing service requests for a single server from multiple stations.[49] A polling system can be centralized, where a server polls the stations and controls channel access (as in Bluetooth[50]), or distributed, where stations follow a distributed protocol to contend for channel access. Once a station accesses the channel, there are three types of service policies to serve its packets: (i) *exhaustive policy*, where the server serves a station until its buffer is emptied; (ii) *gated policy*, where the server serves for a station only those requests which are already buffered in the station when this service period begins; and (iii) *limited-k policy*, within which a station is served until either the buffer is emptied or the first k buffered requests are served, whichever occurs first. One special case of the limited-k service is the limited-1 service, where at most one request is served during each service period. It has been shown that both exhaustive service and gated service are more efficient than the limited-k service, and they can guarantee bounded delay as long as the offered load is strictly less than 100%.[49,51]

Limited-k service is actually used in the CM MAC,[28] where k equals to the design parameter *concatenated threshold.* Limited-1 service, which has the lowest efficiency among polling service disciplines, is used in most of the existing wireless MAC protocols. Motivated by insights from polling system theory, PSMAC is proposed in Ref. 8 to improve the MAC efficiency by using the gated polling service. In the following, we first introduce three variations of the PSMACs, and then present a performance study that demonstrates the achievable gains in throughput, delay, energy savings, and fairness.

4.5.1. *Polling service-based MACs*

4.5.1.1. *PSMAC 1*

The first polling service-based scheme, termed PSMAC 1, incorporates a *gated service* for frame scheduling.[49] More specifically, all arriving frames (transit or locally generated) are queued in a common transmission buffer (or, the *global queue*). Nodes send out RTS/CTS as in p-Persistent CSMA. In the RTS, the source node specifies the destination MAC address of its *head-of-line* frame, say Node B. If this is the only RTS in the time slot, Node B will return a CTS. In the RTS, Node A will also specify how many packets will be transmitted, so that all other nodes will get this information. However, instead of sending one data frame after a successful RTS/CTS pair, all frames that have arrived at the source node before the RTS transmission, will be served back-to-back in the following slots. Other nodes will start a new round of competition (using the p-Persistent method) when the current sequence of frame transmissions is over. The operation of PSMAC 1 is illustrated in Fig. 4.1.

As will be shown in simulation results, PSMAC 1 achieves 100% throughput when the arrival rate is not larger than the medium capacity.

4.5.1.2. *PSMAC 2*

For wireless terminals (e.g., disposable sensor nodes), it is generally crucial to conserve energy. It has been shown that a node in the sleep state consumes far less energy than in the idle, transmit, or receive state. It is therefore desirable to schedule nodes to sleep whenever possible, be it a Wireless LAN,[47] a wireless sensor network[4,52] or an ad hoc network.[53] It is also appealing to schedule nodes to sleep without sacrificing delay and throughput performance, which, however, is generally hard to achieve.[4,52,53]

In PSMAC 2, each node maintains $N-1$ *virtual queues*, one for each of its neighbors. If there are one or more non-empty virtual queues, the node first selects one of them. The selection strategy can be round robin, uniform, or by following a priority order (e.g., longest-queue-first). The node then attempts to transmit RTS as in p-Persistent CSMA to contend for service. In the RTS, it specifies K, the number of frames backlogged in the selected virtual queue at this time, and the ID of Node B, the destination node corresponding to the selected virtual queue. If the RTS succeeds, Node B will return a CTS and *gated service will be used for this virtual queue* (i.e., K frames will be transmitted back-to-back to Node B). All other nodes which are not involved in this transmission, can be scheduled to sleep during this period and wake up when the K frame transmissions are over.[c]

The PSMAC 2 throughput is very close to 100% but not as high as PSMAC 1, since it uses gated service only for one virtual queue instead of the global queue. However, it has the advantage if energy conservation is a major consideration. Since a node only sleeps when it is not involved in a transmission, there is no additional delay or throughput degradation incurred. It is also interesting to see that its delay performance is very close to that of PSMAC 1 under bursty traffic.

4.5.1.3. *PSMAC 3*

For the two PSMAC schemes, PSMAC 1 is more bandwidth efficient, while PSMAC 2 is amenable for energy conservation. To obtain both advantages, PSMAC 3 combine the two schemes. In PSMAC 3, each node maintains $N-1$ virtual queues, and nodes compete for the channel by sending RTS as in PSMAC 2. When a sender successfully wins the channel, it first broadcasts an *announcement frame*.

[c]Note that we can set a threshold $\bar{K}$ and schedule a node to sleep only if the expect sleep period is longer than $\bar{K}$ time slots, in order to avoid frequently switching between sleep and awake modes with very short periods.

The announcement frame notifies its neighbors the lengths of all the non-empty virtual queues at the source node, as well as the order in which the virtual queues will be served. Therefore, each destination node will be notified how many frames it will receive, as well as the starting and ending times for reception. The sender then starts data transmission, clearing the virtual queues one at a time in the order as specified in the announcement frame. All other nodes, except the corresponding destination of the virtual queue currently being served, can be scheduled to sleep and to wake up when its corresponding virtual queue is to be served. If a node is not one of the announced destinations, it can go to sleep and wake up when all the virtual queues at the source node are cleared.

This way, PSMAC 3 has a similar service as in PSMAC 1, as well as the energy conservation capability as in PSMAC 2. There is only one additional frame (the announcement frame) as extra overhead for each burst of data transmission, compared to PSMAC 1. Thus PSMAC 3 achieves approximately the same delay and throughput performance as PSMAC 1, and approximately the same energy savings as PSMAC 2.

4.5.1.4. *Multi-hop networks*

Among the three schemes, it is straightforward to adopt PSMAC 2 for a multi-hop wireless network. Its operation is similar to that of IEEE 802.11: each time one receiver is reserved by a successful RTS/CTS dialog, but a gated service is used for the virtual queue corresponding to the target receiver. A question to ask is "how about its performance?" Simulation results show that PSMAC 2's performance on throughput, delay, and fairness approaches to those of PSMAC 1 and 3 as traffic gets bursty. This makes PSMAC 2 highly suitable for the multi-hop wireless environment, where traffic usually gets burstier as traversing more hops due to large variations on wireless channel capacity.[54]

4.5.2. *Performance evaluation*

The average delay, energy saving and fairness performance of PSMAC were studied by simulation in Ref. 8 under uniform i.i.d. Bernoulli traffic, uniform on–off bursty traffic, uniform LRD traffic and nonuniform traffic. We present selected results here and refer interested reader to Ref. 8 for a comprehensive study.

4.5.2.1. *Delay performance*

The average delay of the three PSMAC schemes are plotted in Fig. 4.10 for different traffic models. In the simulation, it was assumed that there were 20 nodes in the system and the transmission time for each data frame is 10 time slots. It can be seen that PSMAC 1 and PSMAC 3 have the same delay performance under the entire range of load examined and for all the three traffic models. These are expected

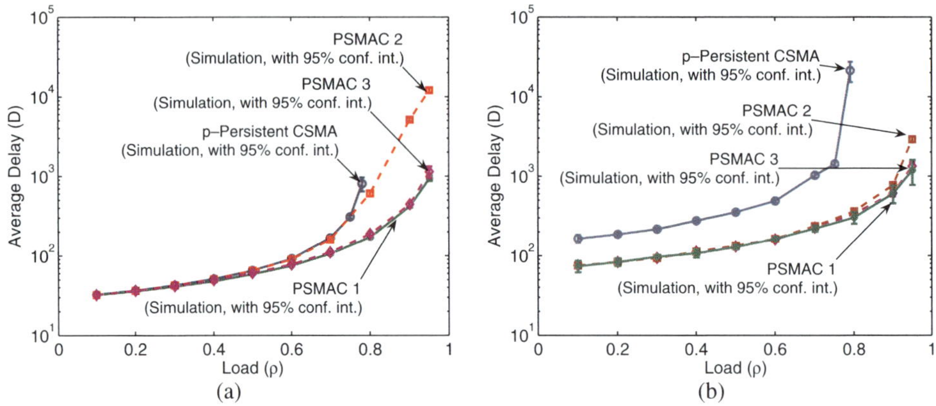

Fig. 4.10. Average delays under various traffic models. (a) i.i.d. Bernoulli traffic. (b) On–off bursty traffic. Reprint from[8] ©2008 IEEE.

results, since from the descriptions in Sec. 4.5.1, both PSMACs use gated service for the global queue at a winning node, while the only difference is the order at which frames are served (the additional control frame in PSMAC 3 is negligible). That is, first-come-first-serve or one virtual queue at a time.

The delay achieved by p-Persistent CSMA is plotted in Fig. 4.10 as benchmarks. In all the three figures, the PSMAC schemes outperform p-Persistent CSMA in delay performance, and the improvements are bigger when traffic gets burstier. Specifically, the p-Persistent CSMA curve diverges when ρ is close to 79%, while the PSMAC delays are all bounded for all the traffic models and all the loads examined.

From Fig. 4.10(a), we also find that all the four schemes have similar average delay in the low load region. This is because under a light load, the queues or virtual queues are less likely to build up. Although gated service is used in the three proposed schemes, it usually serves queues with a single frame and thus reduces to limited-1 service as in p-Persistent CSMA. However, for the more interesting heavy load region, the PSMAC 1 and 3 delays are significantly smaller than that of p-Persistent CSMA. This is because under a heavy load, the queues are more likely to build up and gated service will be more efficient than the limited-1 service. For PSMAC 2, although load is higher, the average rate to each virtual queue, $\mu = \rho / [N(N-1)]$, is still not big enough to build up large backlogs. Thus a gated service for a virtual queue is still more like a limited-1 service, and its delay curve remains close to that of p-Persistent CSMA. Nevertheless, it still achieves a higher throughput than p-Persistent CSMA.

When traffic gets bursty, as shown in Fig. 4.10(b), all the PSMACs achieve significantly smaller delay over p-Persistent CSMA. Under a bursty traffic, the backlogs of the global queues or virtual queues are more unevenly distributed. There is a high chance for the PSMACs to find a queue (or a virtual queue in the case of PSMAC 2) with a large number of backlogged frames, and gated service will achieve a much better delay performance in these scenarios. A somewhat *counter-intuitive* observation is that, as traffic gets burstier, the PSMAC 2 delay curve almost completely overlaps with the PSMAC 1 curve, although it only uses gated service for a chosen virtual queue (see Fig. 4.10(b)). This implies that under highly bursty traffic, the frames backlogged at a node are more concentrated in a small number of virtual queues (destined to a small subset of neighbors). In these cases, gated service for the global queue rather than a heavily loaded virtual queue does not make much difference.

4.5.2.2. *Energy savings*

The energy savings of the PSMACs is examined by using the power consumption model from[55] in the simulations. The transmit, receive, idle, and sleep powers are 1,400 mw, 1,000 mw, 830 mw, and 130 mw, respectively. Note that we use a time slot as unit of time, and the normalized powers (in units per time slot) are used in our simulations, which are 1.4, 1.0, 0.83, and 0.13 for the transmit, receive, idle, and sleep state, respectively.

In Fig. 4.11, the simulated average energy consumption, i.e., the average normalized energy consumed per node per time slot, is shown for all the four schemes under the i.i.d. Bernoulli traffic and the on–off bursty traffic. Similar results are obtained for the LRD traffic model. The traffic load is $\rho = 0.7$ for both figures and the number of nodes N is from 2 to 20.

It can be seen that p-Persistent CSMA and PSMAC 1 consume almost the same amount of energy per node per time slot, while PSMACs 2 and 3 are much more energy efficient due to their capability of scheduling nodes to sleep. For example,

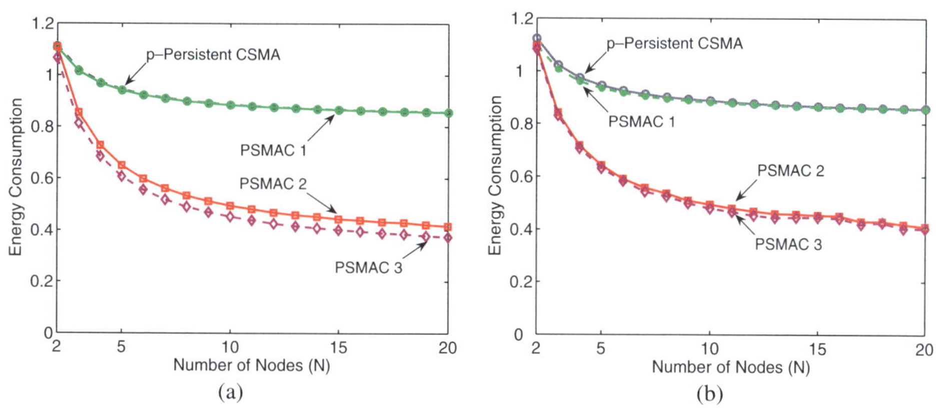

Fig. 4.11. Energy consumption under various traffic models. (a) i.i.d. Bernoulli traffic ($\rho = 0.7$). (b) On–off bursty traffic ($\rho = 0.7$). Reprint from[8] ©2008 IEEE.

in Fig. 4.11(a), when $N = 20$, the average energy consumption of p-Persistent CSMA is 0.8590, while the average energy consumption of PSMAC 2 is 0.4166. The normalized reduction is $(0.8590 - 0.4166)/0.8590 = 51.5\%$. Note that when $N = 2$, all the schemes have similar energy consumptions. This is because there is no way to schedule nodes to sleep when $N = 2$; when one node is transmitting, the other node must be receiving. Finally, it is worth noting that the PSMAC 2 curve approaches the PSMAC 3 curve when traffic gets burstier, as observed in the delay and throughput performance studies.

4.5.2.3. *Fairness performance*

A general concern of using gated service is fairness. Compared to limited-1 service, one may expect that gated service favors heavily loaded users. Various fairness definitions have been used in the literature. We consider the ultimate user experienced performance metric, node delay, in fairness definition. The first fairness index is defined as,[56]

$$f(D_1, D_2, \ldots, D_N) = \frac{(\sum_{i=1}^{N} D_i)^2}{N \sum_{i=1}^{N} D_i^2}, \tag{4.7}$$

where D_i is the average delay of Node i, $i \in [1, 2, \ldots, N]$. This fairness index generally varies from 0 to 1. When all nodes have the same average delay, we have that $f = 1$ and the system is 100% fair. As disparity increases, fairness decreases for schemes which favor only a few selected nodes. For example, when the delay of one node is dominant (i.e., $D_1 \gg D_i, \forall i \neq 1$), the fairness index is $f \approx 1/N$ (and $\lim_{N\to\infty} f = 0$ in this case). We also use the so-called worst-case fairness index, which is defined as

$$f(D_1, D_2, \ldots, D_N) = \frac{\min_{i=1,\ldots,N}\{D_i\}}{\max_{i=1,\ldots,N}\{D_i\}}. \tag{4.8}$$

This fairness index also varies between one and zero. When all the node delays are equalized, we have $f = 1$; when one node's delay is dominant, we have $f \approx 0$.

Under the uniform traffic pattern, simulations show that all the schemes have a similar fairness index. Now let's consider the more interesting *nonuniform* traffic pattern as follows. Recall that ρ is the arrival rate to the system and μ_i the arrival rate to Node i. The arrival rates to the nodes are determined as

$$\mu_i = \begin{cases} \dfrac{\rho}{2}, & i = 1 \\ \dfrac{\rho}{2(N-1)}, & 2 \le i \le N \end{cases} \quad \text{and} \quad \sum_{i=1}^{N} \mu_i = \rho. \tag{4.9}$$

With this non-uniform traffic pattern, Node 1 is heavily loaded, while all the other nodes are lightly and equally loaded.

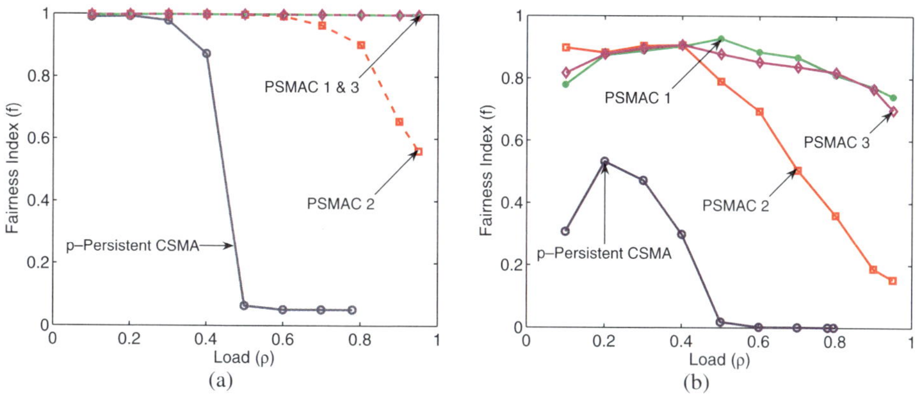

Fig. 4.12. Fairness indices under the on–off bursty traffic model. (a) Fairness definition (4.7). (b) Fairness definition (4.8). Reprint from[8] ©2008 IEEE.

Figure 4.12 shows the fairness indices achieved by the four schemes under the on–off bursty traffic. Similar results for the Bernoulli and LRD traffic are obtained but omitted for brevity. It can be seen from Fig. 4.12(a) that when load ρ is low, the fairness indices of all the schemes are almost the same. For increased ρ, the p-Persistent CSMA curve drops quickly, while the fairness curves of PSMACs 1 and 3 remain at high values close to 1. Specifically, the p-Persistent CSMA fairness index drops to $f = 1/N = 5\%$, when ρ is beyond 50%. This indicates that one of the nodes, i.e., Node 1, has a large delay that dominates the delays of all other nodes. Similar observations can be made from Fig. 4.12(b) when the worst-case fairness index is used. Although in this case the PSMAC indices are lower than one, they are still quite higher than the p-Persistent CSMA curve, which falls to zero when the load exceeds 50%.

The node delays are presented in Fig. 4.13 for the case of $\rho = 0.7$ under the on–off bursty traffic. When p-Persistent CSMA is used, the Node 1 delay is 18147.5, which is much larger than the delays of other nodes (ranging from 320 to 350). We also find that the average node delays achieved by the three PSMACs are all lower than the corresponding p-Persistent CSMA node delay. Furthermore, the Node 1 delay is slightly lower than those of all the other nodes when PSMACs 1 and 3 are used, and slightly higher than those of all the other nodes when PSMAC 2 is used. The PSMAC fairness indices are much larger than that of p-Persistent CSMA for all the cases we studied.

These are quite *counter-intuitive results*, since, contrary to the common belief, the use of gated service does not result in poor fairness performance. Rather, the three PSMAC schemes achieve better fairness performance than p-Persistent CSMA. This is largely due to the high efficiency of the PSMAC schemes and the reduced overhead. *All* the queues are efficiently served and the delays of those lightly loaded

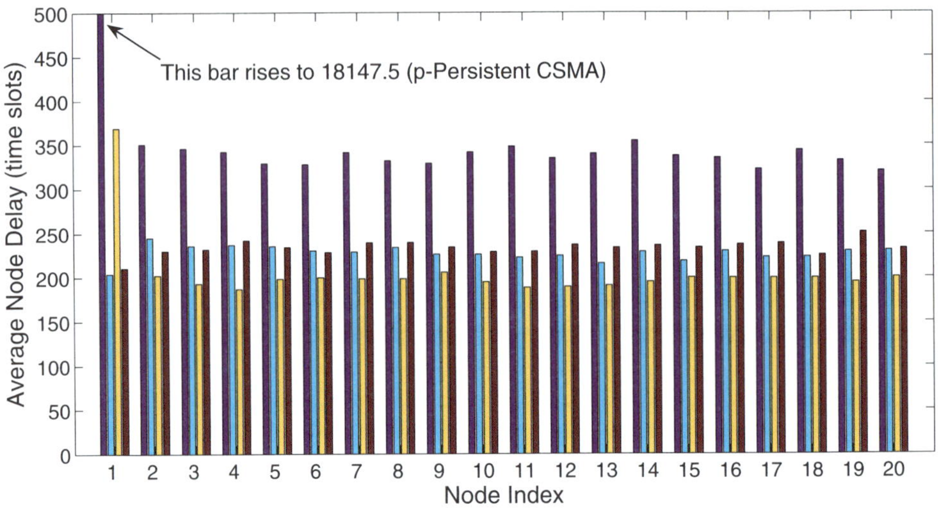

Fig. 4.13. Average node delays achieved by the four schemes under non-uniform on–off bursty traffic ($\rho = 0.7$). The bars in each group, from left to right, are for p-Persistent CSMA, PSMAC 1, PSMAC 2, and PSMAC 3, respectively. Reprint from[8] ©2008 IEEE.

nodes are only slightly increased (due to the heavily loaded node). Thus the benefit introduced by gated service to a heavily loaded node does not seriously increase the delays of other nodes. Fairness is not sacrificed for improved delay and throughput performance.

4.5.2.4. *PSMAC in multi-hop wireless networks*

As discussed, PSMAC 2 can be easily adopted for multi-hop wireless networks. In this section we examine its performance using a grid network topology. The 25-node network consists of a grid of 5 by 5 nodes. The transmission range is chosen such that each node has at most 8 neighbors. Note that now winning the channel also depends on possible transmissions two hops away, and RTS/CTS can effectively solve the hidden terminal problem.

Figure 4.14 shows the average delay of PSMAC 2 and p-Persistent CSMA under the on–off bursty traffic model and the uniform traffic pattern. The offered load ρ can be larger than 1 due to spatial reuse. The RTS transmission probability for Node i is set to $p_i^* = 1/N_i$ where N_i is the number of its neighbors. As expected, PSMAC 2 outperforms p-Persistent CSMA in throughput and delay. The p-Persistent CSMA delay becomes unbounded when ρ is close to 2, while the PSMAC 2 delay is still bound when ρ is 2.6 in our simulations. There is over 30% improvement in throughput without any additional hardware requirements. When $\rho = 2.0$, the PSMAC 2 delay is only about 5.9% of the corresponding p-Persistent CSMA delay. Similar

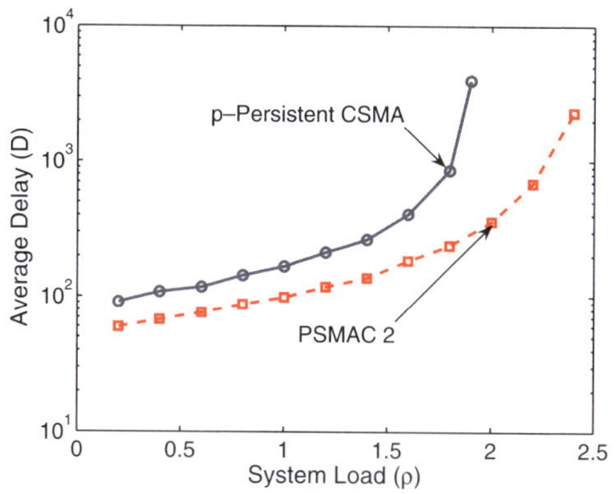

Fig. 4.14. Average delays of PSMAC 2 in a 25-node multi-hop grid network under the on–off bursty traffic. Reprint from[8] ©2008 IEEE.

observation are made for the other two traffic models and for energy and fairness performance, but are omitted due to lack of space.

4.6. Conclusion

In this chapter, we examine the important problem of improving the efficiency of wireless MAC protocols. After revealing the inefficiency problem of two representative MAC protocols, we review existing techniques that address this problem. As case studies, we present a location assisted MAC scheme for leveraging spatial reuse, and a polling service-based MAC for amortizing the high control overhead. For both schemes, there is no need for extra hardware or resource. In addition, both schemes are complementary to the existing techniques; they can be incorporated to further improve the MAC performance when extra hardware or resource are available.

Acknowledgments

This work has been supported in part by the National Science Foundation (NSF) under Grant ECCS-0802113, and through the Wireless Internet Center for Advanced Technology (WICAT) at Auburn University.

References

1. Y. Xiao and J. Rosdahl, Throughput and delay limits of IEEE 802.11, *IEEE Commun. Letters*, **6**(8), 355–357 (August 2002).
2. J. Li, C. Blake, D. Coute, H. Lee and R. Morris, Capacity of ad hoc wireless networks, *Proc. ACM MobiCom'01*, 61–69, Rome, Italy (July 2001).
3. Z. Fu, H. Luo, P. Zerfos, S. Lu, L. Zhang and M. Gerla, The impact of multihop wireless channel on TCP performance, *IEEE Transactions on Mobile Computing*, **4**(2), 209–221 (March/April 2005).

4. A. Woo and D. Culler. A transmission control scheme for media access in sensor networks, *Proc. ACM MobiCom'01*, 221–235, Rome, Italy (July 2001).
5. R. Bruno, M. Conti and E. Gregori, Optimization of efficiency and energy consumption in p-persistent CSMA-based wireless LANs, *IEEE Trans. Mobile Computing*, **1**(1), 10–31 (January/March 2002).
6. F. Cali, M. Conti and E. Gregori, Dynamic tuning of the IEEE 802.11 protocol to achieve a theoretical throughput limit, *IEEE/ACM Trans. Networking*, **8**(6), 785–799 (December 2000).
7. S. Ross, *Applied Probability Models with Optimization Applications*, Dover Publications, New York, NY (1970).
8. Y. Li, S. Mao, S. Panwar and S. Midkiff, On the performance of distributed polling service-based wireless mac protocols, *IEEE Transactions on Wireless Communications*. to appear.
9. P. Gupta and R. R. Kumar, The capacity of wireless networks, *IEEE Trans. Inform. Theory*, **46**(2), 388–404 (March 2000).
10. Y.-B. Ko, V. Shankarkumar and N. Vaidya, Medium access control protocols using directional antennas in ad hoc networks, *Proc. IEEE INFOCOM'00*, **1**, 13–21, Tel-Aviv, Israel (March 2000).
11. A. Nasipuri, S. Ye, J. You and R. Hiromoto, A MAC protocol for mobile ad hoc networks using directional antennas, *IEEE WCNC*, Chicago, IL (September 2000).
12. R. R. Choudhury, X. Yang, R. Ramanathan and N. H. Vaidya, Using directional antennas for medium access control in ad hoc networks, *Proc. ACM MOBICOM* (September 2002).
13. M. Takai, J. Martin, A. Ren and R. Bagrodia, Directional virtual carrier sensing for directional antennas in mobile ad hoc networks, *Proc. ACM MobiHoc 2002*, pp. 183–193, Lausanne, Switzerland (June 2002).
14. R. R. Choudhury and N. H. Vaidya, Deafness: A mac problem in ad hoc networks when using directional antennas, *Proc. 10th IEEE International Conference on Network Protocols (ICNP)*, (2004).
15. T. Korakis, G. Jakllari and L. Tassiulas, A mac protocol for full exploitation of directional antennas in ad-hoc wireless networks, *Proc. ACM MobiHoc 2003*, 98–107, Annapolis, MD (June 2003).
16. V. Bhandari and N. Vaidya, *Connectivity and Capacity of Multi-Channel Wireless Networks with Channel Switching Constraints*, Technical report, University of Illinois at Urbana-Champaign (January 2007).
17. V. Bhandari and N. Vaidya, *Capacity of Multi-Channel Wireless Networks with Random Channel Assignment: A Tight Bound*, Technical report, University of Illinois at Urbana-Champaign (October 2006).
18. P. Kyasanur and N. Vaidya, *Capacity of Multichannel Wireless Networks: Impact of Channels, Interfaces and Interface Switching Delay*, Technical report, University of Illinois at Urbana-Champaign (October 2006).
19. P. Kyasanur, J. So, C. Chereddi and N. Vaidya, Multi-channel mesh networks: Challenges and protocols, *IEEE Wireless Communications*, **13**(2), 30–36 (April 2006).
20. P. Kyasanur and N. Vaidya, Routing and interface assignment in multi-channel multi-interface wireless networks, *Proc. IEEE WCNC'05*, 2051–2056, New Orleans, LA (March 2005).
21. X. Gong, S. Midkiff and S. Mao, A cross-layer approach to channel assignment in wireless ad hoc networks, *ACM/Kluwer Mobile Networks and Applications Journal (MONET)*, **12**(1), 43–56 (February 2007).

22. X. Gong, S. Midkiff and S. Mao, On-demand routing and channel assignment in multi-channel wireless ad hoc networks, *Elsevier Ad Hoc Networks Journal*, to appear.
23. J. Deng, Y. Han and Z. Haas, Analyzing split channel medium access control schemes, *IEEE Trans. Wireless Commun.*, **5**(5), 967–971 (May 2006).
24. Y. Han, J. Deng and Z. Haas, Analyzing multi-channel medium access control schemes with ALOHA reservation, *IEEE Trans. Wireless Commun.*, **5**(8), 2143–2152 (August 2006).
25. S.-L. Wu, C.-Y. Lin, Y.-C. Tseng and J.-P. Sheu, A new multichannel mac protocol with on-demand channel assignment for multihop mobile ad hoc networks, *Proc. International Symposium on Parallel Architectures, Algorithms and Networks (ISPAN) 2000*, 232–237, Dallas/Richardson, TX (December 2000).
26. J. So and N. Vaidya, Multi-channel mac for ad hoc networks: Handling multi-channel hidden terminals using a single transceiver, *Proc. ACM MOBIHOC'04*, 222–233, Roppongi, Japan (May 2004).
27. A. Nasipuri, J. Zhuang and S. R. Das, A multichannel CSMA mac protocol for multihop wireless networks, *Proc. IEEE WCNC*, 183–193 (September 1999).
28. Y. Xiao, IEEE 802.11 performance enhancement via concatenation and piggyback mechanisms, *IEEE Trans. Wireless Commun.*, **4**(5), 2182–2192 (September 2005).
29. M. Li, H. Zhu, Y. Xiao, I. Chlamtac and B. Prabhakaran, Adaptive frame concatenation mechanism for qos in multi-rate wireless ad hoc networks, *Proc. IEEE INFOCOM'08*, Phoenix, AZ (April 2008).
30. S. M. Hur, S. Mao, Y. T. Hou, K. Nam and J. H. Reed, On exploiting location information for concurrent transmission in multi-hop wireless networks, *IEEE Transactions on Vehicular Technology*, to appear.
31. Y. Li, S. Mao, P. Agrawal and S. F. Midkiff. Low-complexity channel-aware scheduling for multi-channel wireless networks, *Proc. 2008 IEEE Conference on Automation Science and Engineering (IEEE-CASE)*, Washington D.C. (August 2008).
32. F. Ye, S. Yi and B. Sikdar, Improving spatial reuse of IEEE 802.11 based ad hoc networks, *Proc. IEEE GLOBECOM'03*, 1013–1017, San Francisco, CA (December 2003).
33. J. Deng, B. Liang and P. K. Varshney. Tuning the carrier sensing range of IEEE 802.11 MAC, *Proc. IEEE GLOBECOM'04*, 2987–2991, Dallas, TX (2004).
34. J. Zhu, X. Guo, L. L. Yang and W. S. Conner, Leveraging spatial reuse in 802.11 mesh networks with enhanced physical carrier sensing, *Proc. IEEE ICC'04*, 4004–4011 (June 2004).
35. X. Yang and N. Vaidya, On physical carrier sensing in wireless ad hoc networks, *Proc. IEEE INFOCOM'05*, 2525–2535, Miami, FL (March 2005).
36. H. Zhai and Y. Fang, Physical carrier sensing and spatial reuse in multirate and multihop wireless ad hoc networks, *Proc. IEEE INFOCOM'06*, Barcelona, Spain (April 2006).
37. J. P. Monks, V. Bharghavan and W.-M. W. Hwu, A power controlled multiple access protocol for wireless packet networks, *Proc. IEEE INFOCOM'01*, 219–228, Anchorage, AK (April 2001).
38. M. Cesana, D. Maniezzo, P. Bergamo and M. Gerla, Interference aware (IA) MAC: An enhancement to IEEE 802.11b DCF, *Proc. Fall 2003 IEEE Vehicular Technology Conference*, 2799–2803, Orlando, FL (October 2003).
39. C.-H. Yeh, The heterogeneous hidden/exposed terminal problem for power-controlled ad hoc MAC protocols and its solutions, *Proc. Fall 2004 IEEE Vehicular Technology Conference*, 2548–2554, Los Angeles, CA (September 2004).

40. S. V. D. Heuvel-Romaszko and C. Blondia, Enhancements of the IEEE 802.11, a MAC protocol for ad hoc network with history of power adjustment, *Proc. 2005 IEEE International Conference on Wireless Networks, Communications, and Mobile Computing*, 48–54, Maui, HI (June 2005).
41. Y. Zhou and S. M. Nettles, Balancing the hidden and exposed node problems with power control in CSMA/CA-based wireless networks, *Proc. 2005 IEEE Wireless Communications and Networking Conference*, 683–688, New Orleans, LA (March 2005).
42. A. Acharya, A. Misra and S. Bansal, MACA-P: A MAC for concurrent transmissions in multi-hop wireless networks, *Proc. 2003 IEEE International Conference on Pervasive Computing and Communications*, 505–508, Dallas-Fort Worth, TX (March 2003).
43. K. Mittal and E. Belding, RTSS/CTSS: Mitigation of exposed terminals in static 802.11-based mesh networks, *Proc. 2nd Workshop on Wireless Mesh Networks*, 3–12, Reston, VA (September 2006).
44. H. Akcan, V. Kriakov, H. Brnnimann and A. Delis, GPS-free node localization in mobile wireless sensor networks, *Proc. the 5th International ACM Workshop on Data Engineering for Wireless and Mobile Access*, 35–42, Chicago, IL (June 2006).
45. A. Haeberlen, E. Flannery, A. Ladd, A. Rudys, D. Wallach and L. Kavraki, Practical robust localization over large-scale 802.11 wireless networks, *Proc. ACM MobiCom'04*, 70–84, Philadelphia, PA (September 2004).
46. D. Niculescu and B. Nath, VOR base stations for indoor 802.11 positioning, *Proc. ACM MobiCom'04*, 58–69, Philadelphia, PA (September 2004).
47. IEEE, Wireless LAN media access control (MAC) and physical layer (PHY) specifications, (1999).
48. C. Perkins, E. Belding-Royer and S. Das, Ad hoc on-demand distance vecor (AODV) routing (July 2003), IETF RFC 3561.
49. H. Takagi and L. Kleinrock, *A Tutorial on the Analysis of Polling Systems*, Technical report, Computer Science Department, UCLA Report No. 850005 (February 1985).
50. Specification of the Bluetooth system version 1.2 (November 2003). Bluetooth Special Interest Group, [online] Available: http://www.bluetooth.com.
51. L. Kleinrock and H. Levy, The analysis of random polling systems, *Operations Research*, **36**(5), 716–732 (September/October 1988).
52. W. Ye, J. Heidemann and D. Estrin, Medium access control with coordinated, adaptive sleeping for wireless sensor networks, *ACM/IEEE Trans. Networking*, **12**(3), 493–506 (June 2004).
53. R. Zheng and R. Kravet, On-demand power management for ad hoc networks, *Elsevier Ad Hoc Networks J.*, **3**(3), 51–68 (January 2005).
54. I. Lee and A. Fapojuwo, Estimating heavy-tails in long-range dependent wireless traffic, *Proc. IEEE VTC 2005-Spring*, 2132–2136, Stockholm, Sweden (June 2005).
55. B. Chen, K. Jamieson, H. Balakrishnan and R. Morris, Span: An energy-efficient coordination algorithm for topology maintenance in ad hoc wireless networks, *Proc. ACM MOBICOM'01*, 85–96, Rome, Italy (July 2001).
56. R. Jain, A. Durresi and G. Babic, *Throughput Fairness Index: An Explanation* (February 1999), ATM Forum Document Number: ATM_Forum/99-0045.

Part III

Network Formation, Topology Discovery, and Routing

Chapter 5

QoS Aware Routing in Wireless Sensor Networks

Feng Zou, Donghyun Kim, Xiaofeng Gao and Dingzhu Du

Department of Computer Science
University of Texas at Dallas
Richardson, TX, 75080

Wireless Sensor Network (WSN), named as one of the top technologies that will change the world, has more and more significant impacts on our life nowadays. Initially driven by military applications, its applications have reached fields like environment, health, etc. Although having applications in many fields, WSN is restricted by its own. The specialty of the sensors put strict restrictions on energy consumption in WSNs. Therefore, the design of it is affected by quite a lot factors. WSN design in network layer, i.e., routing protocol design, has got a lot of attentions recently because of its specialty. In literature, a lot of research has been done on several important aspects of WSNs, while supporting Quality of Sercive(QoS) in WSNs is still a largely unexplored research field. We discuss the challenges of QoS support in WSNs and give a detailed survey of QoS routing protocols in this chapter. Open research issues about QoS routing are also presented at last of this chapter.

5.1. Wireless Sensor Networks (WSNs)

Named by MIT's Technology Review as one of the 10 technologies that will change the world,[1] wireless sensor network (WSN) is starting to have a significant impact on our everyday life right now.

5.1.1. *WSNs applications*

Initially, the research of it is driven by military applications such as battle-field surveillance and enemy tracking. These systems aggregate data from multiple sensors to monitor events in an area of interest. For example, as illustrated in Fig. 5.1, in a battle-field surveillance, sensors can be deployed by helicopters initially. Networking of these sensors assists operations by locating active objects on the battle field. Such application of sensor network could not only increase the efficiency of monitoring, also assure the safety of people operating it.

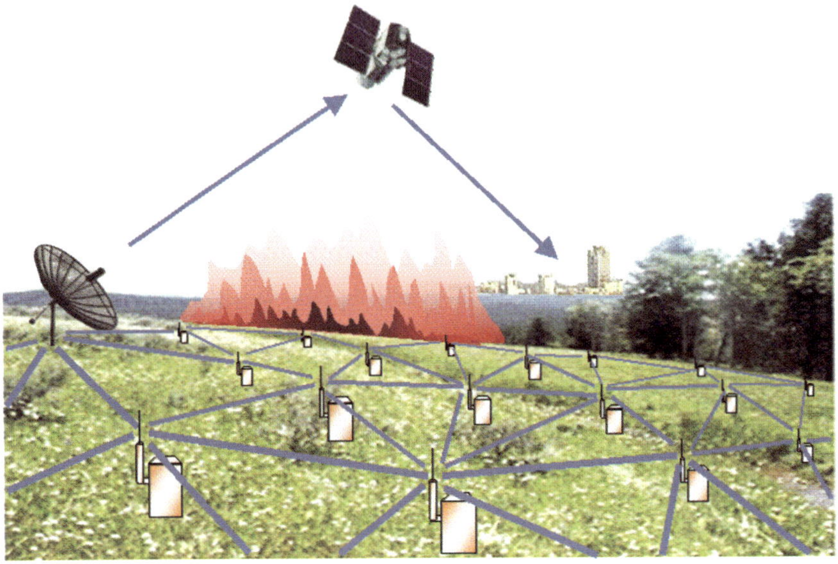

Fig. 5.1. An example of battle-field surveillance system.

Potential applications for WSNs are numerous, which could be classified into several categories like military applications, environment applications, health applications, home applications and other commercial applications.[2] In the military aspect, WSNs could help to monitor forces, detect biological and chemical attack, assess battle damage, or target. In the environmental research field, WSNs could help to detect forest fire and flood, model the agriculture process. For health applications, tele-monitoring of physiological data tracking, monitoring doctors and patients inside a hospital, or drug administration could be candidates for WSN applications. At home, WSN helps to make home automation, smart environment into reality. Some commercial applications are environmental control in office buildings, interactive museums detecting, monitoring car thefts, inventory control, vehicle tracking and detection.

5.1.2. *Factors influencing WSN design*

Briefly speaking, sensor is a device which measures a physical quantity and converts it into a signal which can be read by an observer or by an instrument. For accuracy, all sensors need to be calibrated against known standards. A sensor's sensitivity indicates how much the sensor's output changes when the measured quantity changes. For instance, if the mercury in a thermometer moves 1cm when the temperature changes by 1, the sensitivity is 1 cm/1. So obviously, sensors that measure very small changes must have very high sensitivities. Recent advantages in micro-electro-mechanical systems (MEMS) and low power and highly integrated

Fig. 5.2. Sensor could have a size of as little as a penny.

digital electronics have led to the development of micro sensors.[2–6] In most cases, a micro sensor reaches a significantly higher speed and sensitivity compared with macroscopic approaches.

Though having all these advantages, sensors are restricted by their own. They could have a very small size as little as a penny (see Fig. 5.2), and be of low cost and low power as well. Therefore, each sensor node is constrained in energy supply and bandwidth, which poses many challenges to the design and management of WSNs.

Callawan *et al.* claimed that a successful WSN design must have several unique features: (1) low power consumption; (2) low cost; (3) worldwide availability; (4) network topology type; (5) good fault-tolerance; (6) flexible scalability; (7) high security; (8) enough data throughput; (9) low message latency; and (10) mobility.[7] We will explain several of them in detail in the following.

5.1.2.1. *Low power consumption*

The wireless sensor node, being a micro-electronic device, can only be equipped with a limited power source (< 0.5 Ah, 1.2 V). In some application scenarios, replenishment of power resources might be impossible. Sensor node lifetime, therefore, shows a strong dependence on battery lifetime. In a multihop WSN, disfunction of several nodes in it could cause serious topology changes, which might require recalculations and reorganizations. Hence, the power conservation and the power management is seriously important. Many existing work,[8–11] has studied about this factor in the literature.

The main task of a sensor node in a sensor field is to detect events, perform quick local data processing, and transmit the data. Therefore, the power consumption of a WSN can be divided into three domains: sensing, communication, and data processing. Sensing power varies with the nature of applications. Sporadic sensing might consume lesser power than constant event monitoring. A sensor node spends maximum energy in data communication domain, which involves both data transmission and reception. In this domain, a sensor node must have built-in computational abilities and be capable of interacting with its surroundings. The energy expenditure in data processing is much less compared to the data communication.

5.1.2.2. *Low cost*

As the WSNs contain a large number of sensor nodes, a cost of a single sensor will have great impact on the cost of the whole system. So the price of the sensor has to be kept low. The state-of-the-art technology allows a Bluetooth radio system to be less than $10.[12] Also, the price of a PicoNode is targeted to be less than $1.[13] It is claimed that the price of a sensor should be less than $1 in order for the WSNs to be feasible.[13] Please note that a sensor might be equipped with other devices like sensing and processing units, or with a location find system, which depends on the requirements of the applications. Therefore, lowering the cost is a very challenging issue that could be solved with the help of engineers in the field of electronics.

To lower the cost from another perspective is to reduce the total number of sensors used in the design. The fewer sensors used in the network, the fewer energy consumption we will have. Therefore, we need to optimize the total number of sensors in the network design as well.

5.1.2.3. *Fault tolerance*

One thing that needs to be noted is that fault tolerance is the ability to sustain sensor network functionalities without any interruption due to sensor node failures.[5,16,17] As sensor nodes may fail or be blocked due to lack of power, or some environmental change, the failure should definitely not affect performing overall task of the system. This is the fault tolerant issue concerned by researchers nowadays. Fault tolerance levels in WSNs could be different from each other according to specific applications. For example, sensor nodes being deployed in a battlefield for surveillance and detection, have to have high fault tolerance because the sensed data are critical and sensor nodes can be destroyed by hostile actions. While for the WSNs designed depolyed for home automation, fault tolerance requirements are much lower.

5.1.2.4. *Scalability*

As the number of sensor nodes in the WSNs could vary from several hundreds to millions and the densities of nodes vary from each other as well, the designed. The designed schemes for the WSNs should be able to grow so that they could be applied to these different WSNs.

5.2. Routing in WSNs

The WSNs design is related to different layers in network infrastructure. In physical and link layers, research has been focused on system-level power awareness such as dynamic voltage scaling, radio communication hardware, low duty cycle issues, energy aware MAC protocols.[19–24] In network layer, research has been focused on finding ways for route setup and reliable relaying of data from the sensor nodes to the sink. It usually involves multi-hop communications and has been studied as part of the network layer problems.[14,25,26]

Due to the its own characteristics distinguishing it from contemporary communication and wireless ad-hoc networks, routing in WSNs is still a very challenging task. First, it is impossible to build a global addressing scheme for the deployment of a large number of sensor nodes. Thus, classical IP-based protocols cannot be applied to WSNs. Second, almost all the applications of sensor networks require the flow of data from multiple sensors to a sink, which is quite different from typical communication networks. Third, data generated by sensors has a high level of redundancy in it since multiple sensors might take care of same vicinity of a phenomenon and generate same data about it. Such redundancy needs to be exploited by the routing protocols to improve energy and bandwidth utilization. Fourth, sensors are constrained by their power and storage restrictions, which require special and careful resource management.

As a consequence, many new algorithms have been proposed for the problem of routing in WSNs. They consider the characteristics of WSNs as well as the application and architecture requirements. People classify existing research on routing in WSNs into the different categories according to different classification method.

One way is to classify them into two categories as (1) cluster-based routing and (2) cat routing protocols. In cluster-based protocols, some elected cluster-heads discover and maintain the routing information; in cat routing protocols, all the nodes in the network participate in route discovery and maintenance. Most of the cluster-based routing protocols[4,18] propose to transmit data from the cluster head to the base station directly. It is well known[9] that the energy spent in transmission over a wireless medium is directly proportional to d^c, where d is the transmission range and c is a constant between 2 to 4. Moreover, simulation results show that increasing the transmission range beyond certain value decreases the lifetime of the sensor network. Thus, cluster-based protocols are typically not scalable to large-scale sensor networks.

Another way for classification, classifies them into data-centric protocols, hierarchical protocols, location-based protocols and network flow or QoS awareness protocols. We will talk about this in detail in the follows.

5.2.1. *Data-centric protocols*

Data-centric protocols are query-based and depend on the naming of desired data, which helps in eliminating many redundant transmissions. Since in many applications of sensor networks, it is not feasible to assign global identifiers to each node due to the large number of nodes deployed. It becomes hard to select a specific set of sensor nodes to be queried. Therefore, data is transmitted from every sensor node in the region with significant redundancy. As this is very inefficient in terms of energy consumption, routing protocols that are able to select a set of nodes and aggregate the data during the relaying have been considered, which led the idea of data-centric protocols.

Data-centric protocols are quite different from traditional address-based routing where routes are created between addressable nodes. In detail, in data-centric protocols, the sink sends queries to certain regions and waits for data from the sensors located in the selected regions. SPIN[25] is the first data-centric protocol that ever considers data negotiation between nodes in order to eliminate redundant data and save energy. SPIN solves these shortcomings of conventional approaches like flooding and gossiping using data negotiation and resource-adaptive algorithms. Nodes running SPIN assign a high-level name to their data, called meta-data, and perform meta-data negotiations before any data is transmitted so that no redundant data is sent throughout the network. In addition, SPIN has access to the current energy level of the node and adapts the protocol it is running based on how much energy is remaining. Simulation results show that SPIN is more energy-efficient than flooding or gossiping while distributing data at the same rate or faster than either of these protocols. Directed diffusion[14] was developed later and became a breakthrough in data-centric routing. Afterwards, many other protocols are proposed either based on it[27,28] or follow a similar concept.[16,26,29,30]

5.2.2. *Hierarchical protocols*

Different from data-centric protocols, hierarchical routing aims at efficiently maintaining the energy consumption of sensor nodes by involving them in multi-hop communication within a particular cluster and also by performing data aggregation and fusion in order to decrease the number of transmitted messages to the sink.

LEACH[31] is one of the first hierarchical routing protocols for sensors networks and also one of the most popular hierarchical routing algorithms. The idea is to form clusters of the sensor nodes based on the received signal strength and use local cluster heads as routers to the sink. This strategy is designed for sensor networks where an end-user wants to remotely monitor the environment. It saves energy because the transmissions are only done by cluster heads in this case, which is a much smaller number than total number of nodes. Distributed cluster formation, local processing and randomized rotation of the cluster-heads are included to reduce global communication. Simulations show that LEACH is an energy-efficient protocol that extends system lifetime. The idea proposed in LEACH inspired many other hierarchical routing protocols[29,32,33] later. Also there are some other protocols developed independently[34,35] in this category.

5.2.3. *Location-based protocols*

Most of the routing protocols for WSNs require location information in order to calculate the distance between two particular nodes so that energy consumption could be estimated. As we explained before that there is no addressing scheme for WSNs like IP-addresses and they are spatially deployed in a region. So using the location of sensors, the query can be diffused only to the particular region. This will eliminate the number of transmission messages significantly.

Some of the existing routing protocols for ad hoc network is applicable for WSNs here, especially those energy-aware routing protocols like GAF, MECN and SMECN.[36–38] Take GAF for an example. In GAF, the whole network is partitioned into virtual grids and each sensor node associates itself with a point in the grid according to its position. Those nodes associated with same grid point are considered equivalent. All the nodes have three different status, sleeping, discovery and active. Sleeping state is for energy saving. In discovery state, each node broadcast messages to its equivalent nodes. The transition between these states are decided by time. The sleeping time could be adjusted according to the active time. When routing, each point in the vitual grid acted as the router to communicate with the base station for each nodes. GAF protocol is not scalable since the distance to the base station will increase with the increasing of the network size. Besides, since only the active nodes sense and report data, the data accuracy is not guaranteed.

5.2.4. *Network flow protocols*

In fact, not all of the approaches fit into the several categories we just discussed. There are some of them that is solved as a network flow problem.

Maximum lifetime energy routing proposed by Chang *et al.*[39] is an solution to the problem of routing in WSNs based on network flow approach. The target is to maximize the network lifetime by carefully defining link cost as a function of node remaining energy and required transmission energy using that link. Different from this protocol, Kalpakis *et al.*[40] modeled the routing problem as the maximum lifetime data-gathering problem and presented a polynomial time algorithm for it. Another example is the minimum cost forwarding protocol,[41] which aims at finding the minimum cost path in a large sensor network. Strictly speaking, this is not a network flow protocol, while since data flows over the minimum cost path and the resources on the nodes are updated after each flow, it is included here.

5.2.5. *QoS aware protocols*

While a lot of research has been done on some important aspects of WSNs, supporting Quality of Sercive(QoS) in WSNs is still a largely unexplored research field.

Few protocols have been proposed to support QoS in routing, since most of them focus on the energy-awareness aspect. Most of the protocols we talked about in the above sections focus on the energy-aware routing as well. We will talk about some existing protocols here for a simple example. Further discussion about QoS aware routings will be addressed in the next section in detail.

Protocols like SAR[42] and SPEED[43] are examples of QoS aware protocols. They not only consider the energy constraint and also take the factor of good QoS performance into consideration. They consider the end-to-end delay in their schema so that the system could meet certain such kind of requirements during the connection. This is especially useful for large WSN systems that need to transfer multimedia data.

5.3. QoS Aware Routing in WSNs

As we mentioned in the previous section, even though a lot of research work has been done on some important aspects of WSNs such as architecture and protocol design, or energy conservation and locating, supporting Quality of Service (QoS) in WSNs is still a largely unexplored research field. In routing, few protocols has been proposed to meet the QoS requirements. Most of them take energy constraint as the most important requirement for their protocols design because of the special characteristics of the WSNs.

5.3.1. *QoS support in networks*

In fact, QoS is an overused term with various means and perspectives. Different technical communities may interpret it in different ways. In application communities, QoS generally means the quality perceived by the user or the application. While in the networking community, researchers take it as a measure of the service quality that the network offers to the applications or the users, which is easy to understand if you put yourself into the positions. Since usually, what applications or users care about is not how the network manages resources to provide QoS support. They only concern about the services that networks provide which will have direct impact on the quality of the application. On the opposite, from the networks perspective, their goal is to provide the QoS services while maximizing network resource utilization.

One thing we need to notice about is that the constraints for QoS support in different kind of networks vary from each other.

In wired network, with the rising popularity of the end-to-end bandwidth-hungry multimedia applications, QoS support becomes more and more important, and necessary. Therefore the network is required to provide best effort service, such as guaranteed services (hard QoS) and differentiated services (soft QoS), for end-to-end users/applications. QoS support in wired network usually could be achieved by over-provisioning of resources and/or traffic engineering.[17,44] Over-provisioning usually is implemented by adding abundant resources in the network. It is easy to realize that all the users are served at the same service class. Therefore, the service could be unpredictable during peak traffic. For the traffic engineering methodology, there are two approaches to support QoS, reservation-based approach and reservation-less approach and they use different strategies to obtain QoS.

In the infrastructure-based wireless networks, as an extension for wired networks, we could integrate with wireless MAC protocols to provide QoS support, since wireless MAC protocols may provide data traffic of differentiated classes with corresponding access priorities over the shared wireless medium.

While in wireless ad hoc networks, mechanisms in wired data networks could not be applied to support QoS directly because of the bandwidth constraint and dynamic network topology. This is the same for supporting QoS requirements in WSNs. QoS support in WSNs has its own challenges. We will talk about it in the following section.

5.3.2. *Challenges for QoS support in WSNs*

Except those challenges inherited from general wireless networks, QoS support in WSNs have its own unique challenges:[45,46]

(1) *Resource constraints*: The constraints on resources involve energy, bandwidth, memory, buffer size, processing capability, and limited transmission power. Energy is the most critical concern among all of these constraints. Considering the specialty of the sensor node, it might be infeasible to replace or recharge the battery for sensor nodes in real applications (e.g., remote environment or inhospitable environment). As a result, requirement on QoS support in WSNs should be simple.

(2) *Removal of redundancy*: As we discussed before, WSNs are characterized with high redundancy in the data generated. Though this redundancy does help to loose the reliability/robustness requirement of the system, it costs much more energy unnecessarily. In unconstrained traffic, it is easy to eliminate the redundant data messages since simple aggregation functions would suffice. While it is not easy to aggregate data for QoS traffic. Though data fusion or aggregation is a solution to solve the problem while maintaining the robustness, comparison of images and video streams is still computationally trivial and will consume significant energy resources. So a combination of system and sensor level rules would be necessary to make aggregation of QoS data feasible. For example, data aggregation of image data can be selectively performed for traffic generated by sensors pointing to same direction since the images maybe very similar.

(3) *Energy balance*: In order to reach a life-long network, it is smart to let energy evenly distributed in the network so that energy at a single node won't be drained out very soon.

(4) *Multiple traffic types*: As WSNs could include heterogeneous sets of sensors, it raises multiple technical issues related to routing. For example, in some applications, a diverse mixture of monitoring sensors is required for capturing different target data, like temperature, pressure, tracking of movement, or image capture. Therefore, different reading rates at these sensors might be needed, subject to diverse quality of service constraints and multiple data delivery models. Thus, such an environment makes QoS much more challenging in WSNs.

(5) *Buffer size limitation*: As we know, sensor nodes are usually restricted by processing and storage capabilities because of their specialty. Though the use of multi-hop routing in WSNs dramatically reduces the energy consumed for data collection, it heavily relies on intermediate nodes storing incoming packets for forwarding. Obviously, buffering of multiple packets has several advantages in WSNs. The transition of the radio circuitry between transmission and reception modes consumes considerable energy. Thus it is better to receive many packets prior to forwarding them. In addition, data aggregation and fusion should involve multiple packets. Multi-hop routing of QoS data would typically require long sessions and buffering of even larger data. So the buffer size limitation will increase the delay variation that packets incur while traveling on different routes and even on the same route. Such an issue will make it difficult to meet QoS requirements.

(6) *Network dynamics*: In WSNs, nodes could die because of power restriction. Meanwhile, each node in the network could move around as long as it remains in the network. Such kind of scenarios greatly affect the network topology, and also increase the complexity of QoS support.

(7) *Scalability*: As each WSN could consist of hundreds or thousands of sensor nodes densely distributed in a terrain. Therefore, QoS support should be designed to scale up to a large number of sensor nodes. QoS support should maintain stable performance with the increasing of the node numbers.

(8) *Different QoS levels*: As sensors in the WSNs vary from each other in functions and requirements, especially for sinks. Multiple sinks in the network could ask for different requirements. One sink may ask sensors located in the north to give temperature report every minute, while another sink might only interested in information from sensors at south about the highest temperature among a period. WSNs should be able to support different QoS levels for this kind of situation.

(9) *Energy and delay trade-off*: As we know, because of the characteristics of transmission power of the radio in noisy environments of the non-flat terrain, multi-hop routing is necessary in WSNs and it has claimed its domination in WSNs. Although multi-hop routing reduces the energy consumed for data collection, it causes serious accumulative packet delay. And compared with propagation delay, packet queuing delay is much stronger. In real application, the increase of the number of hops in the route can not only slow down packet delivery, not also

complicate the analysis and handling of the delay-constrained traffic. Thus, it is expected that QoS routing could meet delivery requirements by sacrificing energy efficiency to some extent. To low the high error rate in wireless communication, sometimes redundant data routing is needed. This further complicates the trade-off between energy consumption and delay of packet delivery.

5.3.3. *QoS aware routing protocols*

To meet these challenges, researchers have proposed different kinds of QoS aware routing protocols, which could be classified according to various criteria.

One way of classification categorizes all protocols into two categories.[46] One category focuses on the energy and delay trade-off without much consideration to the other issues. The second category focuses on spreading the traffic so that effective boosting the bandwidths and lowering the delay.

Another way categories into three kinds: traditional end-to-end QoS, reliability assurance, and application-specific QoS, according to the different targets.[45] We will talk about this in detailing sections in the following entries.

5.3.3.1. *Traditional end-to-end QoS*

The Sequential Assignment Routing(SAR)[6] is universally acknowledged as the first protocol in WSNs that mentioned a notion of QoS. In this protocol, each sensor needs to make selection using SAR algorithm from multiple paths directing to the sink nodes. For each path, the protocol takes into account of its energy, QoS factors, and priority level of a packet. It computes a weighted QoS metric by multiplying the additive QoS metric and a weighted coefficient came from the priority level of the packet. The SAR algorithm will object to minimize the average weighted QoS metric throughout the lifetime of the network.

SPEED,[43] a QoS routing protocol that could provide soft real-time end-to-end guarantee, is proposed by He *et al.* in 2003. Each node in the protocol is required to maintain the information of its neighbors and should figure out geographic forwarding to find the paths itself. Meanwhile, the protocol thrives at ensuring a certain speed for each packet delivery so that each application could estimate the end-to-end delay for the packets by considering the distance to the sink and the speed of the packet delivery before making the admission decision.

Another example is the QoS-aware protocol proposed by Akayya *et al*[47] also in 2003. The end-to-end requirements come from multimedia applications such as image or video data. This protocol targets at finding the path that costs the least and is energy efficient so that it could meet the end-to-end delay requirement.

The problem of protocols in this category is that the end-to-end requirement might not be necessary in WSNs. Besides, mechanisms in all these protocols are quite complex and the costs that each sensor need to consume in the network is too much.

5.3.3.2. *Reliability assurance*

Some protocols concern about the reliability issues in WSNs.[48,49] Different from other work, they consider the need for information-awareness and adaptability to channel errors along with differentiated allocation of network resources based on the criticality of data. Different priority levels are assigned based on the criticality of data inside a packet and the priority level maps to a reliability for data delivery. This reliability still is based on end-to-end service. And in fact, QoS concerns should include latency, energy, and bandwidth as well, not only including reliability.

ESRT is a novel transport scheme proposed by Y. Sankarasubramaniam *et al.*.[50] Compared with the protocols mentioned above, it not only considers the reliability, also energy factor. This is mainly achieved by a congestion control component which not only guarantee to achieve reliability, not also energy conservation. More importantly, this solution is not based on end-to-end concept, which brings up the non-end-to-end service concept for future work. While it has the same short-coming, not concerning about other factors like latency or bandwidth.

5.3.3.3. *Application-specific QoS*

QoS could have other explanations in different applications as well. It was once defined as the optimum number of sensors that should send information at any given time by Iyer *et al.*[51] They communicate the information of QoS to sensors around utilizing the base stations by a broadcast channel and also try to dynamically adjust the optimum number of sensors by exploiting the mathematical paradigm.

QoS also has been studied from the perspective of the joint optimization of sensor scheduling and data routing in the paper wrote by Perillo *et al.*[52] In their paper, they target to balance the application reliability with efficient energy consumption. They define QoS as the application reliability only in their paper.

In some other papers such as Refs. 53 and 54, QoS is defined as coverage or exposure, which is explained as covering the desired area of interest or leaving no sensing holes so that sensors can detect unexpected events as quickly as possible and as reliably as possible. The QoS support in their methods does not relate to the QoS support from the underlying network, which is quite differently.

5.4. Open Research Issues

With its special characteristics, for example, limited energy supply and dynamic network infrastructure, QoS routings in WSN have to be treated quite differently from other networks. As we have discussed in the sections above, they have quite a few challenges themselves. General QoS routings in traditional networks attempt to do the followings:

(1) QoS requirements from applications or users will be ensured without breaking the policy of ensuring an efficient resource usage, i.e., bandwidth utilization.
(2) The QoS requirements of the most important traffic will be definitely satisfied even during network overload.

Efficient resource usage in WSNs, in fact, not only means efficient bandwidth utilization, also include a minimal usage of energy. Considering from this aspect, QoS support in WSNs should not only cover the assurance mechanisms also employ control mechanisms at mean time. By doing so, we can eliminate unnecessary energy consumptions while delivering the data. Same as the second attempt illustrated above, while a little more than that, routing in WSNs should satisfy the requirements of applications/users even in the presence of different types of network dynamics, since the mobility of the WSNs makes some of the following situations happen, i.e., node failure, wireless link failure. So accordingly, we have several open research issues for QoS routings in WSNs.[45,46]

(1) Simpler models: Lots of existing protocols for traditional networks are not applicable for WSNs due to their complexity. Novel and simple routing protocols are required to be designed for WSNs to support QoS. Instead of traditional layered design, cross layer design might be much more helpful for model design here.
(2) Integration: Future research for routing protocols might includes integration of WSNs with IP-based networks (e.g., Internet). It is quite possible that the WSNs need to take the requests from users made to the sensor sinks through internet. Also data collected from sensors usually need to be transmitted to the servers on internet to do further analysis. In both cases, we need to deal with integration of different kinds of networks.
(3) QoS control mechanisms: As we mentioned before, besides QoS assurance mechanisms, QoS control mechanisms are absolutely necessary in WSNs. Sometimes, sensors will send out excessive data which waste a lot unnecessary energy. Also energy will be wasted when sensors send out inadequate data which will reduce the quality of the application.
(4) Trade-offs: As known, data collected by sensors in WSNs has a high redundancy. To reduce the redundancy of the data and improve the information reliability. we could make use of data fusion to save energy. While the disadvantage is that it will cause much delay in the network. So what is the optimum trade-off? Does it exist or not?
(5) Service differentiations: The criteria of differentiation could vary from each other a lot. Possible choices are traffic types, data delivery models, sensor types, application types, or the content of packets. While it is not affordable to maintain

so many different classes. It is desired to control the resource allocation so that a desired maximum resource utilization could be achieved.

(6) Node mobility: Due to node mobility, routings in WSNs become a lot more difficult than in traditional networks. Most of these existing protocols assume that the sensor nodes and all the sinks are stationary, which simplifies the scenarios for routing. While in some situations, like in battle field, sensors and sinks are mobile, which could excessively drain the energy of nodes by propagating the information through the network. Smart QoS routing protocols are required in these cases in order to handle the overhead of mobility and dynamic topology.

(6) Adaptive QoS assurance: Instead of having a gradual decaying performance quality as time progresses, it is much desirable to maintain QoS throughout the network life time. This will prevent gaps in data received by sinks, which are caused by network dynamics.

5.5. Conclusion

As a lot of research has been done on some important aspects of WSNs (e.g., energy aware), supporting Quality of Sercive(QoS) in WSNs is still a largely unexplored research field. Few protocols have been proposed to support QoS in routing. Inherited from general wireless networks, QoS support in WSNs have its own unique challenges like resources constraints, redundancy removal, multiple traffic types and etc. Existing QoS aware routing protocols are categorized into three kinds, which are traditional end-to-end QoS, reliability assurance QoS and application-specific QoS, according to the different QoS targets. Future work for QoS aware routing protocols design will focus on solving some open research issues like giving simpler models, dealing with network integration, service differentiations and trade-offs between data redundancy and network delay, etc.

References

1. G. Huang, Casting the wireless sensor net, *2003 MIT Technology Review.*
2. I. F. Akyildiz *et al.*, Wireless sensor networks: A survey, *Computer Networks*, **38**, 393–422 (March 2002).
3. R. H. Katz, J. M. Kahn and K. S. J. Pister, Mobile networking for smart dust, *Proceedings of the 5th Annual ACM/IEEE International Conference on Mobile Computing and Networking* (*MobiCom99*), Seattle, WA (August 1999).
4. R. Min *et al.*, Low power wireless sensor networks, *Proceedings of International Conference on VLSI Design*, Bangalore, India (January 2001).
5. J. M. Rabaey *et al.*, PicoRadio supports ad hoc ultra low power wireless networking, *IEEE Computer*, **33**, 42–48 (July 2000).
6. K. Sohrabi *et al.*, Protocols for self-organization of a wireless sensor network, *IEEE Personal Communications*, **7**(5), 16–27 (October 2000).

7. E. H. Callawan and Jr., Wireless sensor networks: Architectures and protocols, Auerbach Publications, 1–40 (2004).
8. T. Pering, T. Burd and R. Brodersen, The simulation and evaluation of dynamic voltage scaling algorithms, *Proceedings of International Symposium on Low Power Electronics and Design ISLPED98*, 76C81 (August 1998).
9. G. J. Pottie and W. J. Kaiser, Wireless integrated network sensors, *Communications of the ACM* **43**(5), 551C558 (2000).
10. E. Shih, S. Cho, N. Ickes, R. Min, A. Sinha, A. Wang and A. Chandrakasan, Physical layer driven protocol and algorithm design for energy-efficient wireless sensor networks, *Proceedings of ACM MobiCom01*, Rome, Italy, 272C286 (July 2001).
11. A. Sinha and A. Chandrakasan, Dynamic power management in wireless sensor networks, *IEEE Design and Test of Computers* (March/April 2001).
12. J. M. Rabaey, M. J. Ammer, J. L. da Silva Jr., D. Patel and S. Roundy, PicoRadio supports ad hoc ultra-low power, wireless networking, *IEEE Computer Magazine*, 42C48 (2000).
13. J. Rabaey, J. Ammer, J. L. da Silva Jr. and D. Patel, Pico- Radio: Ad-hoc wireless networking of ubiquitous lowenergy sensor/monitor nodes, *Proceedings of the IEEE Computer Society Annual Workshop on VLSI* (*WVLSI00*), Orlanda, Florida, 9C12 (April 2000).
14. C. Intanagonwiwat, R. Govindan and D. Estrin, Directed diffusion: A scalable and robust communication paradigm for sensor networks, *Proceedings of the ACM MobiCom00*, Boston, MA, 56C67 (2000).
15. E. Shih, S. Cho, N. Ickes, R. Min, A. Sinha, A. Wang and A. Chandrakasan, Physical layer driven protocol and algorithm design for energy-efficient wireless sensor networks, *Proceedings of ACM MobiCom01*, Rome, Italy, 272C286 (July 2001).
16. Y. Yao and J. Gehrke, The cougar approach to in-network query processing in sensor networks, *SIGMOD Record* (September 2002).
17. D. Zeinalipour, S. Aristeidou and S. Kazeli, *IP Quality of Services* (in Greek), http://www.cs.ucr.edu/csyiazti/downloads/papers/ipqos/papers/ip-qos.pdf (1999).
18. G. Hoblos, M. Staroswiecki and A. Aitouche, Optimal design of fault tolerant sensor networks, *IEEE International Conference on Control Applications*, Anchorage, AK, 467C472 (September 2000).
19. E. Crowley, R. Nair, B. Rajagopalan and H. Sandick, *A Framework for QoS Based Routing in the Internet*, Internet-draft, draft-ietf-qosr-framework-06.txt (August 1998).
20. Q. Ma and P. Steenkiste, Quality-of-Service routing with performance guarantees, *Proceedings of the 4th International IFIP Workshop on Quality of Service* (May 1997).
21. R. Querin and A. Orda, QoS-based routing in networks with inaccurate information: Theory and algorithms, *Proc. IEEE INFOCOM97*, Japan, 75–83 (1997).
22. Z. Wang and J. Crowcraft, QoS-based routing for supporting resource reservation, *IEEE Journal on Selected Area of Communications* (September 1996).
23. W. Ye, J. Heidemann and D. Estrin, An energy-efficient MAC protocol for wireless sensor networks, *Proceedings of the 21st International Annual Joint Conference of the IEEE Computer and Communications Societies* (*INFOCOM'02*), New York, 1567–1576 (June 2002).
24. L. Zhang *et al.*, RSVP: A new resource reservation protocol, *IEEE Network* (September 1993).
25. W. Heinzelman, J. Kulik and H. Balakrishnan, Adaptive protocols for information dissemination in wireless sensor networks, *Proc. 5th Annual ACM/IEEE International Conference on Mobile Computing and Networking* (*MobiCom*), (1999).

26. R. Shah and J. Rabaey, Energy aware routing for low energy ad hoc sensor networks, *Proceedings of the IEEE Wireless Communications and Networking Conference* (*WCNC02*), Orlando, FL (March 2002).
27. D. Braginsky and D. Estrin, Rumor routing algorithm for sensor networks, *Proceedings of the 1st Workshop on Sensor Networks and Applications* (*WSNA*), Atlanta, GA (October 2002).
28. C. Schurgers and M.B. Srivastava, Energy efficient routing in wireless sensor networks, *MILCOM Proceedings on Communications for Network-Centric Operations: Creating the Information Force*, McLean, VA (2001).
29. A. Manjeshwar and D. P. Agrawal, TEEN: A protocol for enhanced efficiency in wireless sensor networks, *Proceedings of the 1st International Workshop on Parallel and Distributed Computing Issues in Wireless Networks and Mobile Computing*, San Francisco, CA (April 2001).
30. N. Sadagopan *et al.*, The ACQUIRE mechanism for efficient querying in sensor networks, *Proceedings of the 1st International Workshop on Sensor Network Protocol and Applications*, Anchorage, Alaska (May 2003).
31. W. Heinzelman, A. Chandrakasan and H. Balakrishnan, Energy-efficient communication protocol for wireless sensor networks, *Proceeding of the Hawaii International Conference System Sciences*, Hawaii (January 2000).
32. S. Lindsey and C. S. Raghavendra, PEGASIS: Power efficient gathering in sensor information systems, *Proceedings of the IEEE Aerospace Conference*, Big Sky, Montana (March 2002).
33. A. Manjeshwar and D. P. Agrawal, APTEEN: A hybrid protocol for efficient routing and comprehensive information retrieval in wireless sensor networks, *Proceedings of the 2nd International Workshop on Parallel and Distributed Computing Issues in Wireless Networks and Mobile Computing*, Ft. Lauderdale, FL (April 2002).
34. L. Subramanian and R. H. Katz, An architecture for building self configurable systems, *Proceedings of IEEE/ACM Workshop on Mobile Ad Hoc Networking and Computing*, Boston, MA (August 2000).
35. M. Younis, M. Youssef and K. Arisha, Energy-aware routing in cluster-based sensor networks, *Proceedings of the 10th IEEE/ACM International Symposium on Modeling, Analysis and Simulation of Computer and Telecommunication Systems* (*MASCOTS2002*), Fort Worth, TX (October 2002).
36. L. Li and J. Y Halpern, Minimum energy mobile wireless networks revisited, *Proceedings of IEEE International Conference on Communications* (*ICC01*), Helsinki, Finland (June 2001).
37. V. Rodoplu and T. H. Ming, Minimum energy mobile wireless networks, *IEEE Journal of Selected Areas in Communications*, **17**(8), 1333–1344 (1999).
38. Y. Xu, J. Heidemann and D. Estrin, Geography-informed energy conservation for ad hoc routing, *Proceedings of the 7th Annual ACM/IEEE International Conference on Mobile Computing and Networking* (*MobiCom01*), Rome, Italy (July 2001).
39. J.-H. Chang and L. Tassiulas, Maximum lifetime routing in wireless sensor networks, *Proceedings of the Advanced Telecommunications and Information Distribution Research Program* (*ATIRP'2000*), College Park, MD (March 2000).
40. K. Kalpakis, K. Dasgupta and P. Namjoshi, Maximum lifetime data gathering and aggregation in wireless sensor networks, *Proceedings of IEEE International Conference on Networking* (*NETWORKS '02*), Atlanta, GA (August 2002).
41. M. Chu, H. Haussecker and F. Zhao, Scalable information-driven sensor querying and routing for ad hoc heterogeneous sensor networks, *The International Journal of High Performance Computing Applications*, **16**(3) (August 2002).

42. K. Sohrabi, J. Gao and V. Ilawadhi, Protocols for self-organization of a wireless sensor network, *IEEE Personal Communications*, **7**(5), 16–27 (2000).
43. T. He, C. Lu and F. A. Tarek, SPEED: A stateless protocol for real-time communication in sensor networks, *Proceedings of International Conference on Distributed Computing Systems* (*ICDCS 2003*), Providence, Rhode Island, USA, 46–55 (May 2003).
44. Z. Demetrios, *A Glance at Quality of Services in Mobile Ad-Hoc Networks*, http://www.cs.ucr.edu/csyiazti/cs260.html (November 2001).
45. D. Chen and P. K. Varshney, QoS support in wireless sensor networks: A Survey, *Proc. of the 2004 International Conference on Wireless Networks* (*ICWN 2004*), Las Vegas, Nevada, USA, June 21–24 (2004).
46. M. Younis, K. Akayya, M. Eltowiessy and A. Wadaa, On handling QoS traffic in wireless sensor networks, *Proc. HICSS*, 90292C90302, *Big Island, USA* (January 2004).
47. K. Akayya and M. Younis, An energy-aware QoS routing protocol for wireless sensor networks, *Proceedings of IEEE Workshop on Mobile and Wireless Networks* (*MWN2003*), Providence, RI (May 2003).
48. S. Bhatnagar, B. Deb and B. Nath, Service differentiation in sensor networks, *Proceedings of 4th International Symposium on Wireless Personal Multimedia Communications* (September 2001).
49. B. Deb, S. Bhatnagar and B. Nath, ReInForM: Reliable information forwarding using multiple paths in sensor networks, 28th *Annual IEEE conference on Local Computer Networks* (*LCN 2003*), Bonn, Germany (October 2003).
50. Y. Sankarasubramaniam, B. Akan and I. F. Akyildiz, ESRT: Event to sink reliable transport in wireless sensor networks, *MobiHoc 2003*, Annapolis, Maryland (June 2003).
51. R. Iyer and L. Kleinrock, QoS control for sensor networks, *ICC 2003* (May 2003).
52. M. Perillo and W. Heinzelman, Providing application QoS through intelligent sensor management, *Proceedings of the 1st IEEE International Workshop on Sensor Network Protocols and Applications* (*SNPA 03*), (May 2003).
53. S. Meguerdichian, F. Koushanfar, G. Qu and M. Potkonjak, Exposure in wireless ad-hoc sensor networks, *Mobile Computing and Networking*, 139–150 (2001).
54. S. Meguerdichian, F. Koushanfar, M. Potkonjak and M. B. Srivastava, Coverage problems in wireless ad-hoc sensor networks, *Proceedings of IEEE Infocom*, 1380–1387 (2001).

The following references are not cited in the text

55. R. Min, T. Furrer and A. Chandrakasan, Dynamic voltage scaling techniques for distributed microsensor networks, *Proceedings of ACM MobiCom95* (August 1995).
56. T. Nandagopal, T. Kim, X. Gao and V. Bhargavan, Achieving MAC layer fairness in wireless packet networks, *Proceedings of the ACM MobiCom00*, Boston, MA (2000).
57. Srisathapornphat and C. Jaikaeo, Sensor information networking architecture and applications, *IEEE Personal Communications*, 52C59 (August 2001).

Chapter 6

Obstacle-Resist Routing Protocols for Wireless Sensor Networks

Chih-Yung Chang

Department of Computer Science and Information Engineering
Tamkang University

Jang-Ping Sheu

Department of Computer Science, National Tsing Hua University

The well known location-aware routing protocols utilize the local location information for constructing an efficient route with low control overheads in wireless sensor networks (WSNs). However, their performance drops significantly when obstacles exist. To reduce the impact of obstacles on routing performance, developing obstacle-resist routing protocols is one of the most important issues in WSNs and has recently received much attention. The major goal of an obstacle-resist routing protocol is to guide the packets along a route without visiting the concave areas of obstacle. Existing passive routing protocols can only lead the packets away from the obstacles, but cannot guide the packet to the best route. Alternatively, a number of active obstacle-resist routing protocols automatically detect and maintain the obstacle information when the obstacle is formed and then establishes a forbidden region for each concave area to improve the performance of location-aware routings. This chapter reviews obstacle-resist location-aware routing protocols from both concept and technique points of view. The location-aware routing protocols, obstacle boundary detection algorithms as well as passive and active routing protocols are reviewed. Finally, we point out some possible future directions and open issues related to the obstacle-resist routing problem.

6.1. Introduction

Wireless sensor networks (WSNs) have a wide range of potential applications, including environmental monitoring, object tracking, military, smart home, and remote medical system. A WSN comprises a sink node and an extremely large of sensor nodes that communicate with each other in order to perform a broader sensing task. Sensor node is a tiny device with capabilities of sensing, data processing and storing, and communication but is constrained in energy. The sink node is an interface between the observer and WSNs through which observer can dispatch queries to the sensor nodes. Upon receiving the query request, sensor nodes report their readings to the sink node in a multi-hop manner.

In a WSN, each node is typically assumed to be aware of its own location information. The greedy forwarding routing has been widely applied for forwarding the sensors' readings to the sink node hop-by-hop using location information. In the greedy forwarding routing protocol,[1,2] a node delivers the message to the neighbor closest to the destination until the message is arrived at the destination node. With the good use of location information, the greedy forwarding routing creates a small amount of control packets and usually constructs an efficient route. However, the performance of greedy forwarding routing highly depends on the obstacles. Obstacles can be dynamically formed in a WSN due to several reasons. First, the random deployment causes a non-uniform distribution of WSN where some region might not contain any sensor node. Second, some sensor nodes exhaust their energy after working for a relatively long period of time, resulting in some region without functionality of sensing and communication. Third, physical obstacle such as mountains or buildings also can be treated as an obstacle which potentially blocks the communications. Fourth, all sensor nodes in some region could not work normally owing to the animus signal interference. Finally, groups of animals-passing or strong breeze blowing also cause some sensor nodes failure or sweeping away, and hence dynamically form an obstacle. Since the greedy forwarding routing protocol did not take obstacles into consideration, packets that encounter a concave region of an obstacle will be propagated or blocked in the region where greedy forwarding is impossible.

In the past few years, a number of routing protocols that take obstacles into consideration have been addressed. Depending on the timing of coping with the obstacle problem, these researches can be classified into *passive* and *active* categories. In the passive approaches,[3,4] obstacle-resisting mechanism is involved in the design of routing protocols and will be applied to overcome the obstacle when the packets encounter an obstacle. However, there is no preprocessing for the obstacle as it forms and the obstacle information is usually not maintained by the WSN. Packets will be routed around the perimeter of the obstacle according to the predefined obstacle handling rules which aim to prevent the transmission of packet from blocking. Since the passive approaches lack for global obstacle information, packets can be routed to the destination successfully by an inefficient path rather than the shortest path.

Alternatively, the active approaches[1,2,5–12] automatically detect and maintain the obstacle information. To minimize the impact of obstacles on existing routing protocols, obstacle-detection[13,14] is an essential task. Sensors nearby the obstacle cooperatively maintain the obstacle information when the obstacle is formed. With the knowledge of obstacle shape and size, the active approaches are able to guide packets toward the shorter route and prevent the packets from entering a concave region where greedy forwarding is impossible.

The first task for maintaining the obstacle information is to detect the obstacle by identifying border nodes that are located around the obstacle. Two obstacle detection algorithms[13,14] are reviewed in Sec. 6.2. Existing routing protocols that take obstacles into consideration are classified into passive and active categories and are reviewed in Secs. 6.3 and 6.4, respectively. In addition to reviewing the basic concepts and designing principles of the existing obstacle-resist routing mechanisms, some possible future directions and open issues related to the obstacle-aware routing problem are presented.

6.2. Obstacle Boundary-Detection Algorithms

Boundary recognition is an important issue which might improve the route efficiency since the boundary nodes of an obstacle can guide the packets moving along an efficient route whenever the packets encounter an obstacle. In addition, the boundary nodes can virtually change the shape from a concave region to a convex region and therefore the packets will not be forwarded to the dead end nodes where no neighbor is closer to the destination than itself. Y. Wang, J. Gao, and S. B. Mitchell proposed a boundary recognition algorithm[13] to identify the boundary nodes of an obstacle or hole and connect them into meaningful boundary cycles by using only connectivity information. The proposed boundary recognition is mainly composed of the following four steps.

(1) Flood the network from an arbitrary node, say r. Each node records the minimum hop count to r. This step implicitly builds a shortest path tree rooted at r. The r is generally preferred to be selected on the boundary of the monitoring region. Figure 6.1(a) shows an example of the constructed shortest path tree.
(2) In the shortest path tree constructed in step 1, determine the nodes that form the *cut*, where the shortest paths of distinct homotopy type meet after passing around holes. Informally, the nodes of a branch of the cut have their least

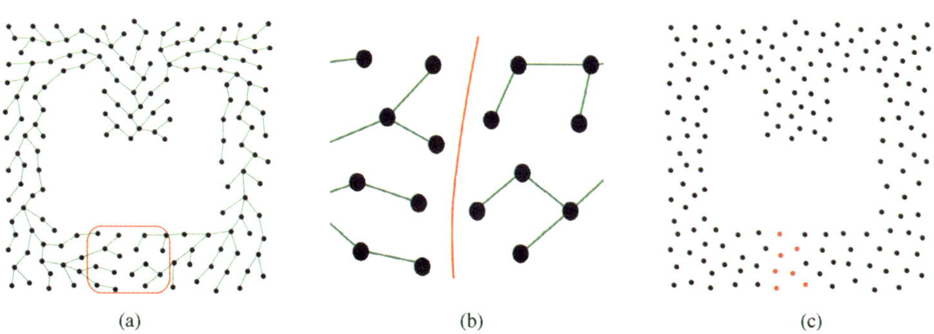

Fig. 6.1. The *cut* in the monitoring region. (a) The nodes within the red rectangular region are cuts, (b) the cut and (c) the cuts are marked with red color.

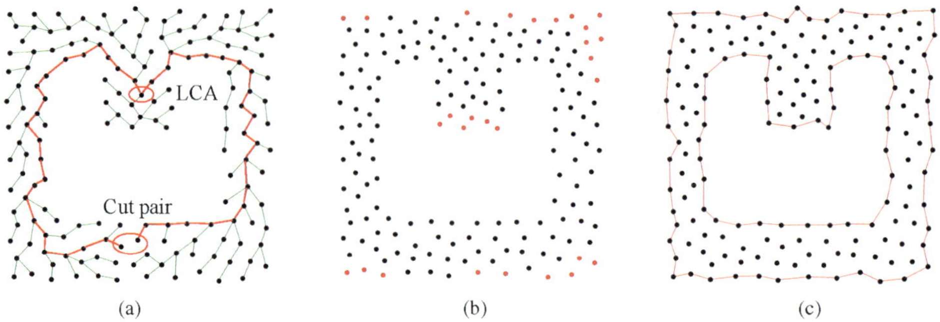

Fig. 6.2. The process of refining the obstacles. (a) The shortest cycle R, (b) the extreme nodes and (c) the tight inner and outer boundaries.

common ancestor (LCA) relatively far away and their paths to the LCA well separated as shown in Figs. 6.1(a)–(c). If there are multiple branches of the cut, corresponding to multiple holes, delete nodes on branches of the cut in order to merge holes, until there is only one composite hole left in the sensor field.

(3) Determine a shortest cycle, R, enclosing the composite hole; R serves as a coarse inner boundary and is constructed from the *cut* pair to their LCA as shown in Fig. 6.2(a). After constructing the coarse inner boundary, it floods the network from the cycle R to each node. Every node in the network records in its minimum hop counts to R by receiving the flooding information.
(4) Detect the "extreme nodes" whose hop counts to R are locally maximal as shown in Fig. 6.2(b), and then refines the coarse inner boundary R to provide tight inner and outer boundaries. These boundaries are in fact cycles of shortest paths connecting adjacent extreme nodes as shown in Fig. 6.2(c).

Overall, Y. Wang, J. Gao, and S. B. Mitchell proposed a boundary recognition algorithm to identify the boundaries of obstacles or holes existed in the monitoring region by using only the connectivity information. However, the communication overhead of the proposed algorithm is significant since network flooding operations are required.

P. K. Sahoo, K. Y. Hsieh, and J. P. Sheu[14] proposed two algorithms to identify the boundary of a given WSN where sensors are random deployed. The identified boundary nodes are therefore responsible for executing the target detection task which aims to capture the entry and exit of single target through the monitoring region. Two boundary selection algorithms, named sequential boundary node selection algorithm (SBNS) and distributed boundary node selection algorithm (DBNS), are proposed in Ref. 14.

In the proposed SBNS, the sink node initially plays the role of boundary node and then broadcasts the *Request_Info* packet to its one-hop neighbors. The broadcasted packet contains the location information, sensing range and unique

ID of the sink. Upon receiving the packet, each of its one-hop neighbors replies to the sink node with a *Reply_Info* packet which includes the same information as *Request_Info* packet. Thereafter, the sink node compares its location with the locations of its one-hop neighbors and determines the next boundary node. Herein, we assume that each node has a straight line to find a BN among its neighbors. The line is assumed to be vertical on the right or left side of the sink, if the sink has maximum ($x_0 = X_{max}$) or minimum ($x_0 = X_{min}$) value in its x-coordinate, respectively or horizontal on the top or bottom side of the sink, if the sink has maximum ($y_0 = Y_{max}$) or minimum ($y_0 = Y_{min}$) value in its y-coordinate, respectively. Then the sink applies the right-hand rule to rotate the line along clockwise direction. The first node whose sensing range intersects with the rotating line will be selected as the next boundary node. The sink node then broadcasts the selected boundary node. Each selected boundary node will subsequently select a new boundary node by further constructing a straight line connecting to the previous boundary node and itself. This procedure for boundary node selection is repeatedly done by the selected boundary node until the starting node is visited again.

In the aforementioned SBNS, the node that plays role of the boundary node is determined by the previous boundary node. Different from SBNS, the boundary nodes in the DBNS are determined by themselves. To accomplish this, the sink node in DBNS broadcasts a *BN_Start* packet to its one hop neighbors with the same information as *Request_Info*. Upon receiving the *BN_Start* packet, sensors add their ID and locations to the packet and then broadcast the modified packets to their one-hop neighbors. After that, each node determines whether it is an *extreme node* or not based on its maximum or minimum value in its x or y or both coordinates. The extreme node will be a candidate of boundary nodes. Each candidate boundary node then collects its neighboring information and check if there are two candidate boundary nodes located in its left and right sides, respectively. If it is the case, each candidate boundary node broadcasts a *BN_Msg* to its one-hop neighbors to declare that it plays a role of boundary node.

6.3. Passive Obstacle-Resist Routing Protocols — LBM, OFSGP and OFMGP

Location-aware greedy routing protocol makes good use of the location information for reducing the control overheads raised from network flooding. However, the efficiency of a location-aware routing will be significantly impacted by the communication hole or obstacles which can make the greedy forwarding impossible and therefore block the packet forwarding. In Ref. 3, Ko and Vaidya proposed a LBM method to cope with the geocasting problem with the consideration of obstacle-resistance. Different from unicast or multicast service, geocasting service is defined by sending messages from the source to all hosts located in a specific geographical region. In a geocasting service, the source host is capable of defining a specific geocasting region and all hosts located in this region are considered to be receivers. Message flooding from source to the geocasting region is the simplest method to overcome the obstacles. However, message spread from the source host to the geocasting region is very costly, and creates serious redundancy, contention, and collision. The most efficient way to provide a geocasting service with low control overhead and high success rate is using location-aware routing in the first phase for delivering the packet from source to any node in the geocasting region. Then the second phase is to execute a packet flooding operation over the predefined geocasting region. However, an outdoor environment might contain unpredictable obstacles, such as mountains, lakes, buildings, or subregions without any host. These obstacles will impede or block messages.

The developed LBM in Ref. 3 aims to deliver a message from source to a geocasting region with low control overhead and high success rate. According to the source host location and destination region, a sender defines a forwarding zone and attempts to flood the message in that zone. If no obstacles exist, the message can be successfully flooded to all hosts in the destination region. However, if the estimated forwarding zone cannot cover the obstacle, the message will be blocked. In this situation, Ko used a threshold δ to enlarge the forwarding zone so that it can cover the obstacle. A large value of δ results in a large forwarding zone, and thus achieves a high success rate, but it also causes contention and collision problems. As shown in Fig. 6.3, when the variable δ is zero, the forwarding zone does not cover the obstacle. The LBM will enlarge the value of variable δ until the forwarding zone can cover all obstacles and the message can be transmitted to all hosts in the geocasting region. The performance of geocasting service depends on the value of δ, which is unknown and is defined through trial-and-error. To overcome unpredictable obstacles, setting δ as a large value achieves a high success rate but creates many flooding packets in MANET.

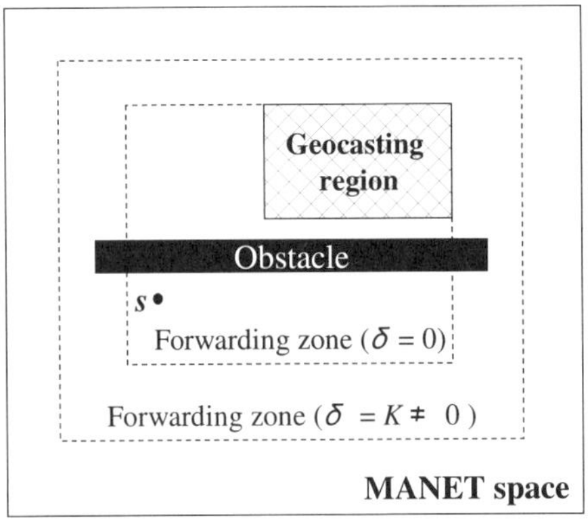

Fig. 6.3. The execution of LBM protocol.

A geocasting protocol, named OFSGP (Obstacle-Free Single-Destination Geocasting Protocol),[4] is proposed aiming to keep messages away from obstacles by creating a very small flooding region. Even in cases involving unpredictable obstacles, OFSGP relays the message from the source host to all hosts in a single destination region with a high success rate and low flooding cost. Additionally, the multi-destination geocasting problem with more than two disconnected destination regions is also investigated in Ref. 4. Initially, the network region is equally partitioned into several disjoint cells. Each cell is assigned with a unique Cell-ID. The OFSGP assumes that each host is aware of its own location information which can be used to identify the cell it is located. In each cell, the host located closest to the center of that cell will be selected as a manager for executing information exchange. An appreciate cell size is determined to guarantee that the manager of each region is able to communicate directly with the managers of neighboring cells. Each manager will periodically broadcast an "*existence*" message so that the neighboring managers know its existence. If a manager does not receive the "existence" message from a neighboring manager for a long time, it will mark the corresponding neighboring cell as an obstacle region and record the information in its table.

The OFSGP mainly consists of two phases, the *reaching phase* and *broadcasting phase*. In the reaching phase, the source host attempts to send the message to one host in the destination region. To accomplish this, the source host first identifies the destination regions and then evaluates the center location of the destination region. Let C_s denote the cell-ID of the cell where the source host is located, and let C_d denote the cell-ID of the center of the destination region. In the reaching phase, the cell region C_d is considered to be the virtual destination. Managers that receive the short message attempt to relay the message to the cell region C_d. The *promising cells* of a cell are the three neighboring cells that are closest to the destination cell C_d. Managers of the promising cell are called *promising managers*. The direction that links the current cell and the promising cells is called *promising direction*. A manager, say M that is not located in the destination region and receives the short message packet should apply the following three rules in reaching phase to determine the next packet forwarders.

Rule 1. *Manager M should relay the message to the promising managers.*

Rule 2. *If the three promising cells are obstacles, manager M should relay the message to the other three neighboring managers. If manager M receives an already received packet, it will not relay or broadcast the message again.*

Rule 3. *If Rules 1 and 2 fail, the message will be returned to the neighboring manager who sent the short message to manager M.*

Upon receiving a message returned from a neighboring manager due to the execution of *Rule 3*, the manager marked the corresponding neighboring cell as an obstacle.

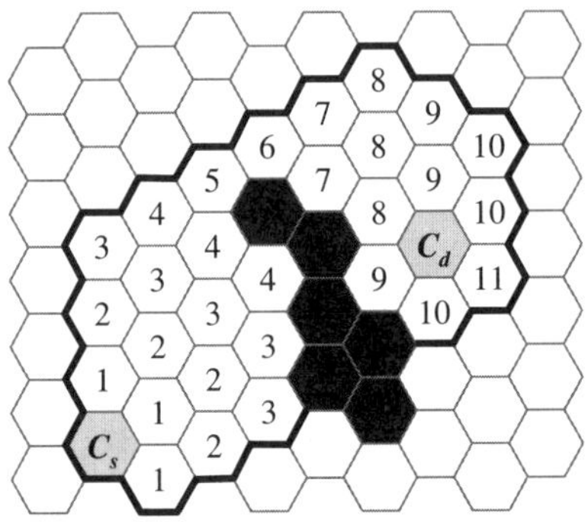

Fig. 6.4. An example of OFSGP.

Figure 6.4 shows an example of OFSGP. The number labeled on each cell denotes the order of packet forwarding from source cell to the virtual destination cell.

The reaching phase of the OFSGP guarantees that the packet can be successfully delivered to at least one cell belonging to the geocasting region. The second phase of OFSGP is the *Broadcasting phase* which aims to deliver the packet to all hosts in the geocasting region, even if the obstacles create difficulties. Let the managers of the cells surrounding the geocasting regions be the *around manager*. Let M_a denote the around manager, while M_d represents the manager located in the geocasting regions. Once M_a or M_d receives the "*forwarding*" packet, they initiate the following *broadcasting protocol*.

When receives packet, manager M_a treats the geocasting region as a large virtual obstacle and makes two copies of the packet, one labeled "*forwarding*" and the other labeled "*around*". Similar to *Rule 1* of *reaching phase* protocol, the manager M_a selects three promising managers. Manager M_a sends the "*forwarding*" packet to promising managers located in the geocasting region. The manager M_a then sends the "*around*" packet to other promising managers that are not located in the geocasting region, intending to route the packet along the boundary of the geocasting region. Similar to the *Rule 2* of reaching phase, if the three promising managers are located in the destination regions, M_a sends the "*around*" packet to the other three neighboring managers to ensure that the "*around*" packet could be transmitted along the boundary of the geocasting region. In this way, manager M_a treats the destination region as a virtual obstacle and applies the *Rule 2* and *Rule 3* of the Reaching Phase Protocol. In case that a manager M_a receives the "*around*" packet three times, or a manager is neither M_d nor M_a, it will do nothing. When manager M_d receives the "*forwarding*" packet, it simply broadcasts the packet to neighbors by flooding.

Compared to LBM, the OFSGP creates a smaller flooding area and achieves a higher success rate for relaying a packet to the geocasting region. In addition to OFSGP, a protocol, named OFMGP, is developed to cope with the multi-destination geocasting problem. The OFMGP creates a shared path for multiple geocasting destinations so that the number of flooding packets can be reduced.

6.4. Active Obstacle-Resist Routing Protocols

Though the aforementioned location-aware routing protocols take obstacles into consideration, however, they cannot prevent the packets from entering the concave region of an obstacle. A more efficient policy to reduce the impact of obstacles on routing is to maintain the obstacle information before routing. Several routing protocols that fall in the category of *active obstacle-resist routing protocols* have been proposed to maintain of the obstacle information or to virtually change the shape of obstacle before the execution of routing operation. This subsection reviews these important routing protocols.

6.4.1. *Face-based routing protocols-GFG and GPSR*

A big hole might block the communication and significantly impact the routing performance in a WSN. To our knowledge, Greedy-Face-Greedy (GFG)[1] is the first algorithm that guarantees packet delivery in a connected WSN that contains hole. The GFG is a face-based routing algorithm that initially constructs a phase for each hole and guides packet toward the destination against the existing holes. Figure 6.5 depicts the constructed faces F_1, F_2 and F_3 for the existing holes. Since face edges might be the boundary of a hole, packet can be guaranteed to be delivered to the destination if it routes along the face edges while encountering a big hole.

Initially, the source s establishes a line connecting itself and destination t. In case the established line intersects with some faces, these faces will be visited by the packet routing from node s to t. As shown in Fig. 6.5, the GFG initially constructs faces F_1, F_2 and F_3 after the WSN has been deployed. When a source s intends to

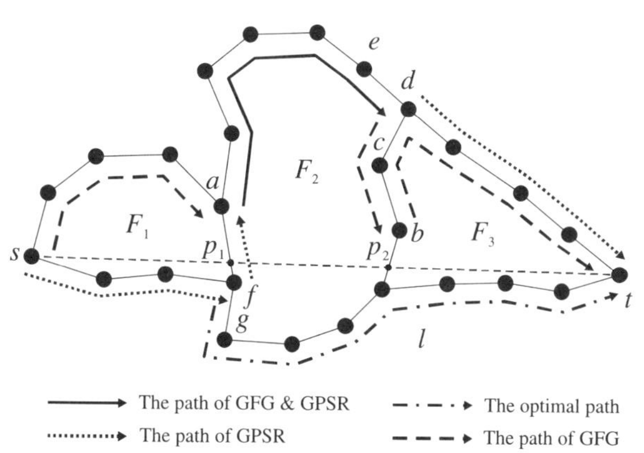

Fig. 6.5. The routing paths created by the GFG and GPSR.

send a packet to a destination t, it established a line $\overline{st}$ which intersects with faces F_1, F_2 and F_3 at intersection points p_1, p_2 and t, respectively. The first phase of packet routing is to forward the packet to point p_1 in a node-by-node manner using left-hand rule. By this way, the packet will be subsequently forwarded to node a. Upon encountering the intersection point p_1, the packet switches to another phase at node a and will be forwarded to the second intersection point p_2 along the edges of face F_2. Similarly, the packet will be forwarded to node b by applying the left-hand rule and then switches to another phase which aims to deliver the packet to the destination t. Finally, the GFG is able to overcome the existing holes and successfully delivers the packet to the destination node t.

The face routing guarantees the packet delivery from a source to a destination. However, it increases the end-to-end delay due to the redundant routing path it traversed. As shown in Fig. 6.5, path *d-c-b* is a redundant path by applying the GFG for sending packet from node s to node t.

B. Karp proposed another face routing protocol, named Greedy Perimeter Stateless Routing (GPSR)[2] which considers the existence of holes in a WSN. The GPSR combines Greedy Forwarding and Face Routing to reduce the path length. Similar to GFG, the GPSR initially construct faces for a given WSN. When a source node s intends to send a packet to node t, it firstly assigns the packet with a Greedy Forwarding mode. Upon receiving a packet with Greedy Forwarding mode, each forwarding node chooses the neighbor closest to the destination as the next hop forwarder. In this way, the packet can be forwarded node by node until it encounters a hole where no neighbor closer to node t than itself. In this case, the forwarding node, say n, will switch the packet from Greedy Forwarding to Perimeter mode and append its location to the packet. Upon receiving a packet with the Perimeter mode, the forwarding node applies the Right-Hand Rule to select the first counter-clockwise neighbor as the forwarding node. The routing mode of the packet will be switched back to the Greedy Forwarding mode if the forwarding node is closer to destination than node n. Consider the example shown in Fig. 6.5. The packet is sent from source s to node f hop-by-hop in the Greedy Forwarding mode. Since node f cannot find a closer neighbor to t than itself, the routing mode of that packet will be changed to Perimeter mode. Similar to GFG, packet in Perimeter mode will travel edges of face F_2. When the packet reaches node e which is closer to node t than node f, the routing mode is switched back to Greedy Forwarding mode to prevent the packet from traversing the redundant path *d-c-b*.

The face routing protocol such as GFG and GPSR can overcome the dead-end problem and successfully forward the packet to the destination. However, the routing path constructed by face routing might be inefficient due to the lack of global holes information. As shown in Fig. 6.5, node f forwards the packet to node a, resulting in an inefficient route. A better route marked by l can be constructed if node f forwards the packet to node g. Moreover, both GFG and GPSR did not take physical obstacle into consideration.

6.4.2. *Routing protocol for locating and bypassing routing holes*

The Greedy Forwarding Routing might be failure because that the dead-end node nearby a hole fails to find a closer relay node to destination than itself. Q. Fang *et al.*[5] proposed a hole-detection and bypassing algorithm to cope with the dead-end problem.

A node p is called *stuck node* if a point q is outside the transmission range of p so that there exists no 1-hop neighbor of p that is closer to q than p. The stuck node is a node that may cause the failure of Greedy Forwarding Routing. In Ref. 5, the *Voronoi diagram* is utilized to identify such stuck node in a distributed manner. The Voronoi diagram constructed by all sensor nodes partitions the network plane into a set of convex regions, called Voronoi cells, such that all points inside a cell are closest to the node that constructs the Voronoi cell. To identify the stuck node, each node constructs the Voronoi diagram with its neighbors to check whether or not at least one Voronoi vertex outside its transmission range. If it is the case, the node plays the role of stuck node. Figure 6.6(a) depicts the identification of stuck node s_1 since Voronoi vertex v of node s_1 is outside the transmission range of node s_1.

After identifying all stuck nodes, each stuck node starts the *BoundHole* algorithm for constructing the boundary of a hole. At first step, each stuck node, say s_1, which contains one Voronoi vertex v outside its transmission range, takes itself as the center and rotates line s_1v around s_1 counterclockwise, as shown in Fig. 6.6(a). Assume the neighbor of node s_1, say s_2, is the first node touched by line s_1v. Node s_2 continues the boundary identification process using line s_1s_2. When the touched node returns to node s_1, the *BoundHole* algorithm is terminated and the boundary identification of a hole is completed.

The two cases shown in Figs. 6.6(a) and 6.6(b) depict the robustness of the proposed *BoundHole* algorithm. In the first case, node s_5 is outside the transmission range of nodes s_2 and s_3. An invalid hole-boundary will be constructed by traversing $s_1 \to s_2 \to s_3 \to s_4 \to s_5 \to s_6 \to s_3 \to s_2 \to s_6 \to s_5 \to s_4 \to s_3 \to s_6 \to s_2 \to s_1$. Therefore, the edge from s_2 to s_3 is eliminated to avoid the invalid boundary. In the second case, as shown in Fig. 6.6(b), node s_1 is outside the transmission range of

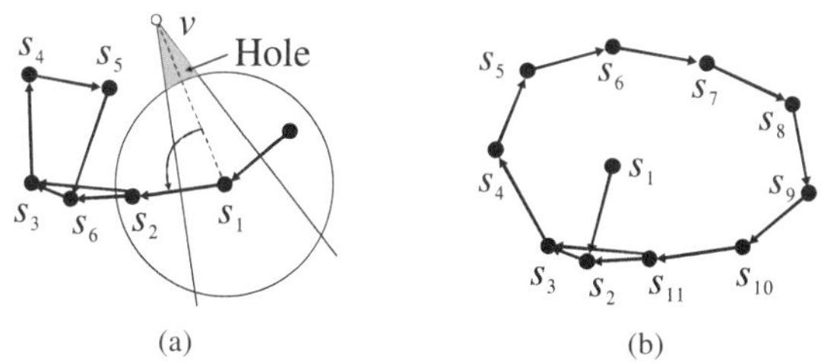

Fig. 6.6. Two special cases of *BoundHole* algorithm. (a) The stuck node s_1 and (b) a special case that *BoundHole* algorithm might not be terminated.

nodes s_{11} and s_3. The *BoundHole* algorithm won't be terminated since the packet for identifying hole-boundary cannot returns to node s_1. Therefore, the edge from s_{11} to s_3 is eliminated to avoid the loop.

The paper proposed an algorithm to find the stuck node with low control overheads since each node only requires one-hop information. However, it did not take the physical obstacle into consideration and cannot guarantee the correctness for identifying the stuck nodes that are nearby the physical obstacle.

6.4.3. *Weight-based routing protocols — PAGER and DUA*

In literature, some other researchers developed weight-based routing algorithms aiming to cope with the dead-end problem. L. Zou *et al.*[6] proposed a weight-based routing algorithm, called PAGER, which overcomes the dead-end problem when the Greedy Forwarding Routing is applied. The PAGER works well in both MANET and WSN environments. Initially, each sensor holds a cost which is determined by the distance from itself to the closest sink node. The sender chooses the neighbor with the smallest cost as the forwarding node to relay the packet. A node is a dead-end node if no neighbor is closer to sink than itself. Hence, all neighbors of a dead-end node have larger costs than its cost. Therefore, the cost reassignment process, called *Cost Spread Phase*, is initiated by the dead end node to reassign the costs of nodes within the concave region of a hole or an obstacle until every node at least has a neighbor with lower cost than itself.

In the Cost Spread Phase, each dead end node, say s, increases its cost to be higher than the maximum cost of its neighbors by Δ, where Δ is a user-defined incremental step size. After cost reassignment, node s broadcasts its new cost to its neighbors. Upon receiving the new cost message from node s, each node updates the cost record of node s, then checks whether or not itself is a new dead-end node. If yes, the new dead-end node executes Cost Spread Phase. Take Fig. 6.7 as an example. Node a is a dead-end node since its neighbors b and c have larger costs than itself. Assume that Δ is set at 3 in this example. Node a increases its cost to 16 since the maximum cost of its neighbor is 13, as shown in Fig. 6.7(b). After

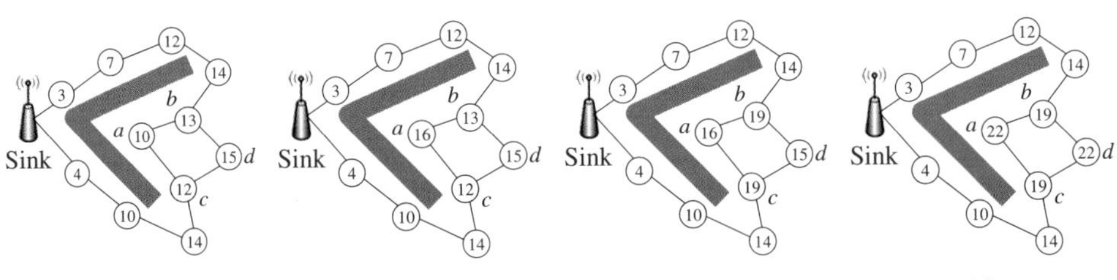

Fig. 6.7. The execution of PAGER. (a) Original cost on each node, (b) the dead-end node a changes its cost, (c) nodes b and c change their costs and (d) node a again changes its cost.

reassigning the cost, node a broadcasts its new cost to neighbors b and c. Upon receiving the new cost message from node a, nodes b and c become new dead-end nodes. Therefore, they subsequently execute the Cost Spread task and reassign their costs with 19, as shown in Fig. 6.7(c). Figure 6.7(d) depicts the final cost of each node. It can be observed that each node has at least one neighbor with smaller cost and hence all dead-end nodes are eliminated. Since the obstacle is dynamically formed in the network, the PAGER maintains the cost of each node periodically. Each node periodically checks whether or not it is a dead-end node according to its neighboring information and executes the operations defined in the Cost Spread Phase if it is a dead-end node.

The PAGER algorithm guarantees that there is no dead-end node, provided that the network is connected. The path length constructed by weight-based routing protocol is near optimal. However, the Cost Spread task may raise the ping-pong effect where the cost of a node is reassigned once more. For example, as shown in Fig. 6.7, node a has a ping-pong effect since it updates cost twice and hence it raises significant control overheads. In addition, the packet routing based on the cost value might be inefficient and hence increase the overheads including the energy consumption and end-to-end delay.

S. Chen *et al.*[7] proposes another weight-based routing algorithm, called DUA, which actively detects the dead-end node and further improves the routing performance of PAGER in terms of path length. Similar to PAGER, each sensor node in DUA maintains a cost that is determined by the distance from the node to the closest sink node. Then a cost reassignment task is performed on those nodes that are located in the concave region of an obstacle or a hole. As a result, each node has a neighbor with lower cost than itself. When a sensor or a forwarder intends to send its reading to the sink node, it chooses the neighbor with smallest cost to act as a relay node. The packet therefore can be successfully transmitted to the sink node in a hop-by-hop manner.

The details of cost reassignment task are described below.

Case 1: If sensor s is a dead-end after node deployment, it updates its cost to be higher than the maximum cost of its neighbors by Δ, where Δ is a constant that is greater than the largest Euclid distance from any sensor to its closest sink node.

Case 2: If sensor s becomes a dead-end after some neighbors have upgraded their costs, it updates its cost just below the smallest value of the upgraded neighbor costs.

Case 3: If sensor s becomes a dead-end after all neighbors have upgraded their costs, it increases its cost by double Δ.

Case 4: If the cost of sensor s is larger than a neighbor x by the difference of their original costs, it sets its cost to the cost of node x addition the difference of their original costs.

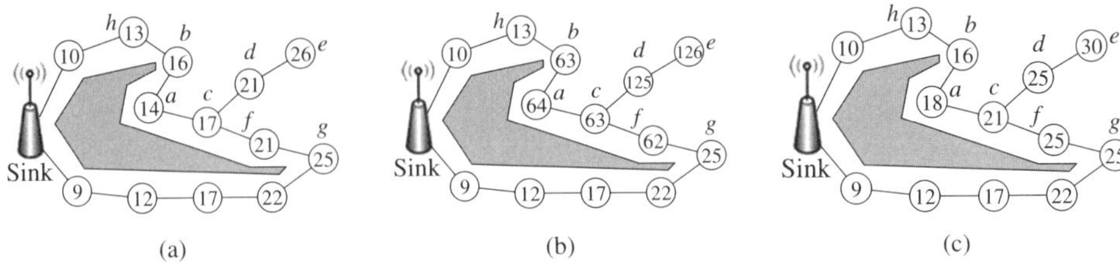

Fig. 6.8. (a) The initial cost of each node, (b) the cost reassignment of cases 1 to 3 and (c) the cost reassignment of case 4.

Figure 6.8 depicts examples of cases 1–4 by applying the cost reassignment with $\Delta = 50$. Initially, each node maintains a cost according to the distance from itself to the sink node. Since node a is a dead-end, it applies case 1 and updates its cost to 64. Upon receiving the new cost message from node a, nodes b and c match case 2 and thus update their costs to a common value of 63. After node d updating its cost to 62 because it satisfies case 2, node e becomes a dead-end in case 3. Therefore, it updates its cost to 126. Since node d becomes a dead-end again, it applies case 2 to change its cost to 125 as shown in Fig. 6.8(b). Although all dead-end are eliminated as shown in Fig. 6.8(b), node a might create an inefficient routing path a-c-f-$\cdots$-sink. Case 4 is proposed to cope with this problem. As shown in Fig. 6.8(b), nodes b, f, d satisfy case 4 and thus they change their costs to 16, 29, 67, respectively. After that, nodes a, c and e change their costs to 18, 33, 72 since they match case 4. The operations defined in case 4 are repeatedly executed by nodes c, d, e and f until all cases are failed. Figure 6.8(c) shows the final costs of all nodes.

Though DUA obtains a better routing performance than PAGER, however, it cannot always guarantee an efficient path. For example, the path f-c-a-b-$\cdots$-sink constructed by DUA is not efficient since a better path f-g-$\cdots$-sink exists. Moreover, the ping-pong effect of DUA raises significant control overheads.

6.4.4. *Angle-based routing protocols — NEAR and LARGER*

As discussed previously, the advantage of greedy forwarding routing is that an efficient route can be constructed to deliver a packet from source to destination based on local position information without keeping network-wild information. However, an obstacle that contains a concave region might block the packet forwarding. A major issue in greedy routing algorithm is how to proceed when a concave node is reached. A NEAR (Node Elevation Ad-hoc Routing) algorithm[8] is proposed based on angle information. The NEAR identifies the concave nodes and reposition their coordinates such that packets applying the greedy forwarding routing will not be forwarded to the concave nodes.

The NEAR consists of identifying and repositioning processes. In identifying process, if the angle between two adjacent node's neighbors exceeds 180 degrees,

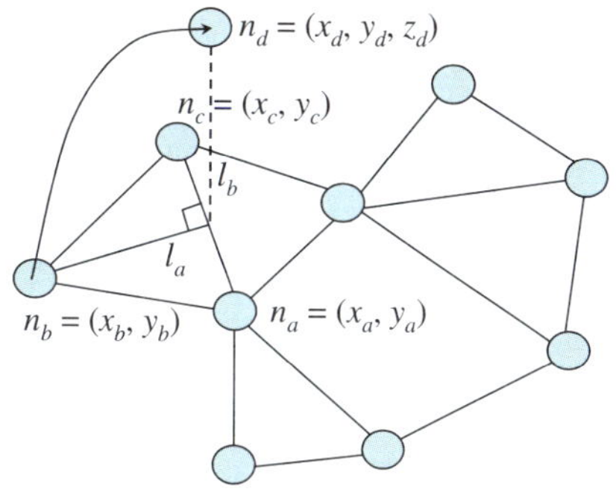

Fig. 6.9. An example of node repositioning process.

the node is necessarily concave for routing in this direction. Assume the location of each node is represented by an N-dimension coordinate system. In repositioning process, an $N + 1$ dimension is added such that the node is virtually repositioned if its coordinate is non-zero. Figure 6.9 demonstrates a simple repositioning of a node n_b. Each node has X and Y coordinates. Since the angle of node n_b with its neighbors is larger than threshold value, node n_b treats the length of l_b, which is the value of Z coordinate for node n_d, as the length of l_a. The X and Y coordinates of node n_d are the cross point's X and Y coordinates of n_b's perpendicular bisector on the line of n_a and n_c. As a result, node n_b is replaced by node n_d. By this way, all concave nodes become floating nodes. Greedy routing algorithm can therefore avoid getting stuck in the concave area.

Similar with the GPSR, a routing packet in NEAR might stay in either greedy or recovery modes. When receiving a packet in greedy mode, the forwarding node can only select non-floating node as its next forwarding node. This way, the routing can avoid the concave areas until it reaches the destination or its vicinity. If the source or destination nodes are floating nodes, the routing switches to a recovery mode. In case that the source node is a floating node, it sets up a threshold value, say Z_{max}, which will always be set lower than the source node height, in order to force descent towards ground level. The threshold value of Z_{max} will be updated with every hop until a non-floating node is reached. During the packet routing, each forwarding node can only select the next forwarding node from the neighbor whose value of Z coordinate is smaller than threshold Z_{max}. When a message has to reach a floating destination, Z_{max} is set to the destination height. The packet can then climb along z axis until it reaches the destination.

The previously discussed DUA and WRGP algorithms mainly use a weight to represent whether or not a node is suitable to play the forwarding node role. However, they assume the destination node is the sink node which is fixed and known by all sensor nodes. In case the destination nodes are not fixed, a node might be a dead-end node for a pair of source and destination but might not be a dead-end node for another pair. Therefore, the destination location determines whether a node should play the role of dead-end node. A destination-region-based local minimum aware geometric routing (LARGER) algorithm[9] has been proposed to improve the accuracy of the local minima prediction. The LARGER partitions the network into k destination regions. Each node maintains a status vector of length k to indicate whether or not the node is local minimum for these k destination regions. If a node is a local minimum for the ith destination region, the ith status in the status vector is set to 1. Otherwise, it is 0. For a given destination region, a node is labeled as a destination-region-based predicted local minimum if the percentage of the destination region that is covered by the node's local minimum angle is greater that a constant threshold p (the local minimum threshold). The LARGER uses a destination-region-based local minimum prediction scheme to increase the accuracy of the local minimum prediction and prevents routing failures caused by the inaccurate prediction of some local minima.

The routing algorithm of LARGER is almost the same as the existing geographic routing and stays in either greedy forwarding mode or face forwarding mode. In the greedy forwarding, a node that receives the message will select the neighbor closest to the destination as its next forwarding node, with a constraint that the local minimum cannot be selected as a receiver. In case that there is no neighboring node closer to the destination than itself, the routing switches to the face forwarding mode, which forwards the message along face until the greedy forwarding is possible.

6.4.5. *Route guiding protocols — RGP and MRGP*

Actively identifying and maintaining the obstacle shape can help guide the packet to an efficient route. C. Y. Chang *et al.*[10] proposes route guiding protocols, named RGP and MRGP, which identify the shape of obstacles and guide the packet to overcome single and multiple obstacles, respectively. The packets are guided routing along the shortest path from the encountered border node to the sink node where the border node is defined as a node that is nearby the obstacle. The RGP mainly consists of four phases: Obstacle Detection, Normalization, Forbidden Region Construction and Packet Guiding phases.

Phase I: Obstacle detection phase

In the obstacle detection phase, the RGP proposes Check Rules 1 and 2 to determine the border nodes nearby the concave and convex regions of an obstacle, respectively.

Check Rule 1: Node s should serve as a border node if it has any Voronoi edge with infinite length.

Check Rule 2: While sensor s doesn't belong to the condition in Check Rule $R1$, for each Voronoi vertex $v^s_{n_i,n_{i+1}}$ of s, if n_i cannot construct $v^{n_i}_{s,n_{i+1}}$ or n_{i+1} cannot construct $v^{n_{i+1}}_{s,n_i}$, then node s should serve as a border node.

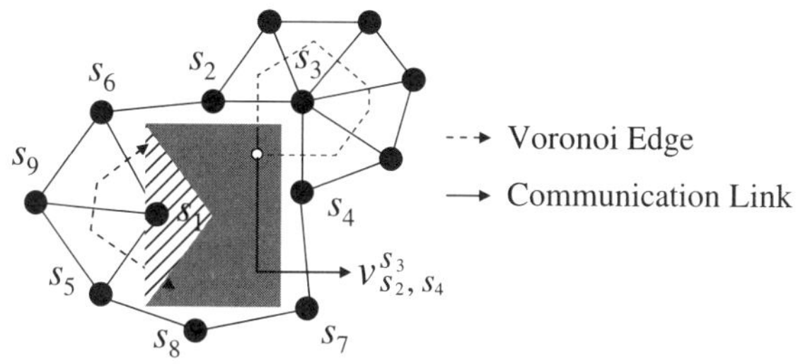

Fig. 6.10. An example for illustrating the Check Rules 1 and 2.

Figure 6.10 shows an example for illustrating the Check Rules 1 and 2. Node s_1 satisfies Check Rule 1 since it has two Voronoi edges with infinite length while node s_3 satisfies Check Rule 2 since nodes s_2 and s_4 cannot construct $v^{s_2}_{s_3,s_4}$ and $v^{s_4}_{s_2,s_3}$. As a result, nodes s_1 and s_3 are border nodes. By applying the proposed Check Rules, all border nodes can be identified in a distributed manner. The RGP further proposed a Self Pruning Rule to minimize the number of border nodes. A border node will abandon its border role if its left and right border nodes can communicate with each other. As shown in Fig. 6.1, nodes s_6 is a neighbor of s_5, making node s_1 abandoning its border node role according to the Self Pruning Rule.

Phase II: Normalization phase

In this phase, some border nodes are selected to serve as the corner nodes for regularizing the obstacle shape. For example, nodes s_1, s_6, s_3, s_7, s_5 in Fig. 6.10 will play the role of corner nodes. Let *turning angle* denotes the angle sweeping from two neighboring border nodes of a border node counterclockwise. The *accumulated angle* is defined as the sum of turning angles of a set of successive border nodes. The border node whose turning or accumulated angles larger than a predefined threshold will play the role of corner node. The shape of obstacle can be represented by the connection of all corner nodes. The identified corner nodes will be further used in later phase for constructing forbidden regions.

Phase III: Forbidden region construction phase

A forbidden region is a concave region of an obstacle. An example of concave region is the shadow region as shown in Fig. 6.10. Since the concave region might raise the dead end problem, this phase aims to construct a forbidden region for each concave region to prevent the packet from being delivered into concave region. For example, the corner node s_1 asks its two neighboring corner nodes s_6 and s_5 to construct a boundary of forbidden region by applying Greedy Forwarding routing. Each corner node executes the same process until the routing passing through the asked border node. As shown in Fig. 6.10, corner nodes s_1, s_6, s_5, s_9 finally construct a forbidden region that packet won't delivered to node s_1 since node s_1 locates in the forbidden region. The forbidden region is regarded as an obstacle. Therefore, node s_1 abandons its border node role while node s_9 becomes a new border node.

Phase IV: Packet guiding phase

Since the obstacle might lead the packet to an inefficient route, Packet Guiding Phase is proposed to guide the packet to the best route. Let *extreme corner nodes be the nodes* located at the extreme east, west, south and north locations of all corner nodes and be denoted as C_E, C_W, C_S, and C_N, respectively. Each border will evaluate the best path according to the information of extreme corner nodes. When a packet arrives at a border node, that border node therefore is able to guide the packet to the sink along a better path. In this phase, the extreme corner nodes will be firstly identified. Afterward, the node C_N sends a *guide probe packet* that traverses all border nodes and forbidden boundary nodes to collect the information of other extreme corner nodes. The collected information is again sent by C_N to all border nodes so that all border nodes have the information of four extreme corner nodes. According to this information, each border node can select a better route that passes through the extreme corner nodes to the destination.

An extension of RGP, named MRGP, is proposed in Ref. 10 to cope with the multiple obstacles problem. To guide the packet to an efficient route and bypassing these obstacles, all obstacles encountered by a packet are virtually treated as a large obstacle. Each border node can guide the visited packet to a better route according to the information of four extreme corner nodes of the virtual obstacle. The proposed RGP and MRGP guide packets along an efficient route and avoid the dead end problem. However, RGP and MRGP did not consider the cases that the source or destination fall in the forbidden region.

6.4.6. *Weight-aware route guiding protocol: WRGP and M-WRGP*

Another weight-based study, named WRGP that considers the shape of obstacle and guides the packet to a better route is proposed in Ref. 11. The weight value denotes the priority for selecting a relay node from neighbors. A neighbor with the smallest weight value will be selected to help relay packet to the sink node. The WRGP proposed the weight reassignment procedure to construct a forbidden region for each concave region of an obstacle. Then a set of border nodes that are nearby the obstacle is identified to further guide the packet along the best route. Moreover, WRGP also considers multiple obstacles.

The WRGP is mainly composed of two phases: Weight Modification Phase and Packet Guiding Phase. Initially, each node maintains a weight value that denotes the distance from itself to the sink node. A node should forward a visited packet to the neighbor with smallest weight value. In order to avoid the packet encountering the dead end, initially, the WRGP identifies a set of border nodes by executing the Weight Modification Phase. The Weight Modification Phase is mainly designed to construct a forbidden region. The following presents the details of this phase. Since the dead-end node has no neighbor with smaller weight than itself, it changes its weight value from w to $2\Delta - w$, where Δ denotes the distance from the farthest point in the monitoring region to the sink node. As a result, all dead-end nodes will be eliminated so that packet can be delivered to the sink node without visiting the forbidden region. Although the Weight Modification Phase construct a forbidden region for each concave area of obstacles, however, the packet might be delivered along an inefficient route since it might be forwarded along the longer path around the obstacle. For this reason, the Packet Guiding Phase is further proposed to guide the packet to an efficient route. Let the effective border node denote the node that might deliver a packet to an inefficient route with pure weight-based routing. Each effective border node maintains a *path_cost* value that is determined by the path length from itself to the sink. Therefore, the packet can be guide to the best route according to the *path_cost* of each effective border node.

In addition to single obstacle, the WRGP also considers the environment containing multiple obstacles. The M-WRGP is proposed to guide the packet to the best route even if the environment contains multiple obstacles. The critical border node is defined as a border node that is successful to deliver the packet to the sink node using Greedy Forwarding routing. To find the best route to the sink node, the critical border nodes of an obstacle O sends the probe packets toward the sink to detect the other obstacles that block the probe path. When a previous obstacle is encountered by the probe packet, each effective border node of obstacle O updates its *path_cost* according to the effect of the previous obstacle. Therefore, the packet can be guided by the effective border nodes along the best route after the M-WRGP has been applied by all nodes around the obstacles.

6.4.7. *Prolonging lifetime of obstacle boundary nodes — HVC*

Most applications of wireless sensor networks discussed in literature are working in an outdoor environment which might contains unknown obstacles. Routing across the obstacles using GPSR will raise a considerable overload on the boundary nodes. These boundary nodes will easily exhaust their energy and hence the increasing failure nodes enlarge the obstacle size. Distributing the workload of network routing to the nodes nearby the boundary nodes will prolong the lifetime of boundary nodes and prevent the obstacle size from change rapidly. J. P. Sheu and M. L. Ding[12] proposed a distributed protocol, named Hexagonal Virtual Coordinate (HVC), for distributing the workload of boundary node to the other neighboring nodes. The developed HVC initially constructs a virtual coordinate system and finds some landmarks surrounding an obstacle. When the virtual coordinates is constructed, the nodes in the network will be aware of the relative coordinates among the landmarks. A source node can therefore find multiple paths which bypass the obstacle and are with the same length to the destination. The source node then selects one path from the multiple paths aiming to achieve a load-balance routing.

In the virtual coordinate construction, the HVC finds out some specific nodes to play the role of landmarks. The landmark selection process is presented below

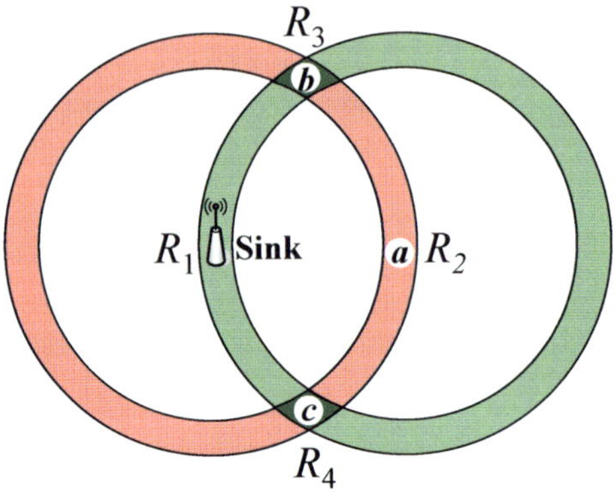

Fig. 6.11. The landmarks are elected form the intersecting regions of the ring areas with radius = r hops.

using an example shown in Fig. 6.11. Initially, the sink node is assigned as the first landmark and then floods a control packet to the entire network. Upon receiving the control packet, each node records the landmark ID and the hop count to the landmark. After the control packet floods over the r hops, a ring-shaped area will exist in which the nodes in this area will have r hops distance to the sink node. Assume the maximum ID in the ring-shaped area R_1 is node a. Node a will become the second landmark of the network. The second landmark then locally floods a control packet for r hops. As a result, the two rings centered at the first and second landmarks will have two intersection regions. As shown in Fig. 6.11, the intersection regions of the two rings with centers sink node and a are R_3 and R_4, respectively. Two nodes b and c which have maximum ID within regions $R3$ and $R4$ will be elected as the third and fourth landmarks, respectively. The aforementioned operations for finding the landmarks will be executed subsequently until no new landmark is formed in the network. In case that the ring is broken by hole into several disconnected segments, the node with maximum ID in each segment will become the landmark too.

After that, each landmark sends the sink node a packet containing stored landmark IDs and hop count to landmarks. Upon receiving the packets from each landmark, the sink constructs the HVC chart. The HVC chart is composed of the landmarks of the network and the hop distances between each pair of closer landmarks. Figure 6.12 shows an example of the constructed landmarks. Note that the hole will be surrounded by the constructed landmarks. Finally, the sink node broadcasts the constructed HVC chart to all nodes in the network to let them know the relative locations between the landmarks.

Upon receiving the HVC chart, each node finds a shortest path, called the Auxiliary Routing Path (ARP), from itself to the landmark nearest to destination node. The landmarks in the ARP will guide the packet to be greedy forwarded to its destination hop by hop. As shown in Fig. 6.12, the source s will construct an ARP

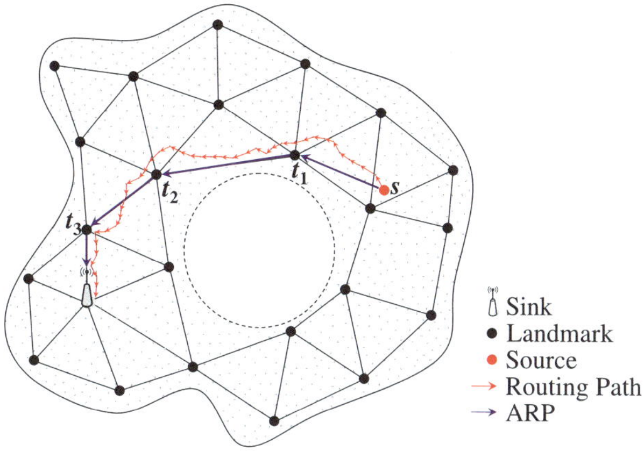

Fig. 6.12. The ARP from the source node s to sink node is $s \to t_1 \to t_2 \to t_3 \to$ sink.

$s \to t_1 \to t_2 \to t_3 \to$ sink which guides the direction of routing from s to sink node, where t_1, t_2, and t_3 are landmarks. Each node then further applies greedy forwarding to relay the packet to the neighbor nearest to the landmark which is nearest to sink node in the ARP. As shown in Fig. 6.12, the routing path from s to *sink* is shown as a sequence of red arrows. Since the distance between any pair of adjacent landmarks is likely equal, a source can randomly choose one of the paths with the same path length to be ARP to achieve better load balancing.

Overall, the landmarks found by proposed protocol are uniformly located in the network and can surround holes even if some holes exist. In addition, a load balanced routing path can be constructed to the destination even if this path comes across holes in the network.

6.5. Conclusion and Future Work

Routing protocols that take obstacle-resist into consideration can significantly improve the performance in terms of routing length, end-to-end delay and success rate. This chapter reviews the obstacle boundary detection algorithms and a number of passive and active obstacle-resist routing protocols. The passive routing protocols, including LBM, OFSGP and OFMGP, are developed for improving the success rate with a reasonable control overhead. However, there is no preprocessing for the obstacle before routing hence the packets might be routed around the perimeter of the obstacle.

A number of active obstacle-resist routing protocols has been developed to reduce the impact of obstacles on routing. The face-based routing protocols, including GFG and GPSR, establish faces and route the packets along face when packets reach a dead end node. Some other weight-based routing algorithms, such as PAGER and DUA, are proposed aiming to overcome the dead-end problem when the Greedy

Forwarding Routing is applied. The NEAR and LARGER routing protocols consider that any sensor node could be the destination node and resolve the dead-end problem by establishing angle-based obstacle information. Some other route guiding protocols, including RGP, MRGP, WRGP and M-WRGP, are developed for the purposes not only making the obstacle information to be transparent but also guiding the packet along the best route when the packets encounter the boundary nodes of an obstacle. The common cost for these routing protocols is the overhead required for establishing the forbidden region for each concave areas of an obstacle. However, packet routing can be more efficient when the active obstacle-resist routing protocols are applied.

Although the aforementioned articles devote themselves to develop obstacle-resist routing protocols, however, most of them consider each obstacle individually. The routing path guided by the boundary node of an obstacle might be inefficient because the boundary node did not maintain the global information of multiple obstacles. In addition, when two obstacles geographically close to each other, they can be virtually treated as a big obstacle and hence the control overheads required for established the individual obstacle can be further saved. Another open issue is developing obstacle-resist routing protocols for location-aware multicast routing protocols. A multicast tree with a high degree of path sharing can save the energy consumption and reduce redundant data transmission. However, the capability for resisting obstacle might be decreased along with the shared degree. How to create a multicast tree that resist multiple obstacles as well as reduce the redundant transmissions will be another interesting and important open issue in the future.

References

1. I. Stojmenovic and X. Lin, GEDIR: Loop-free location based routing in wireless networks, *International Conference on Parallel and Distributed Computing and Systems*, 1025–1028 (November 1999).
2. B. Karp and H. T. Kung, GPSR: Greedy perimeter stateless routing for wireless networks, *Proceedings of the 6th Annual International Conference on Mobile Computing (MOBICOM)*, 243–254 (August 2000).
3. Y. B. Ko and N. H. Vaidya, Geocasting in mobile ad hoc networks: Location-based multicast algorithm, *IEEE Workshop on Mobile Computer Systems and Applications* (Februray 1999).
4. C. Y. Chang, C. T. Chang and S. C. Tu, Obstacle-free geocasting protocols for single/multi-destination short message services in ad hoc networks, *Springer Netherlands Wireless Networks*, **9**(2) (March 2003).
5. Q. Fang, J. Gao and L. J. Guibas, Locating and bypassing routing holes in sensor networks, *23rd Annual Joint Conference of the IEEE Computer and Communications Societies (INFOCOM)*, **4**, 2458–2468 (March 2004).
6. L. Zou, M. Lu and Z. Xiong, A distributed algorithm for the dead end problem of location based routing in sensor networks, *IEEE Transactions on Vehicular Technology*, **54**(4), 1509–1522 (July 2005).

7. S. G. Chen, G. B. Fan and J. H. Cui, Avoid 'Void' in geographic routing for data aggregation in sensor networks, *International Journal of Ad Hoc and Ubiquitous Computing (IJAHUC), Special Issue on Wireless Sensor Networks*, **2**(1), 169–178 (2006).
8. N. Arad and Y. Shavitt, Minimizing recovery state in geographic ad-hoc routing, *Proceedings of the 7th ACM International Symposium on Mobile Ad Hoc Networking and Computing (MobiHoc)*, (May 2006).
9. C. Liu and J. Wu, Destination-region-based local minimum aware geometric routing, *Proceedings of the 4th IEEE International Conference on Mobile Ad-hoc and Sensor Systems (MASS)*, (October 2007).
10. C. Y. Chang, K. P. Shih, S. C. Lee and S. W. Chang, RGP: Active route guiding protocol for wireless sensor networks with obstacle, *Proceedings of the 3rd IEEE International Conference on Mobile Ad-hoc and Sensor Systems (MASS)*, (October 2006).
11. C. Y. Chang, W. C. Ju and Y. C. Chen, WRGP: Weight aware route guiding protocol for wireless sensor networks with obstacles, *Proceedings of the IEEE International Conference on Communication (ICC)*, (May 2008).
12. J. P. Sheu and M. L. Ding, Routing with hexagonal virtual coordinates in wireless sensor networks, *Proceedings of the IEEE wireless communications and networking conference (WCNC)*, (March 2007).
13. Y. Wang, J. Gao and J. S. B. Mitchell, Boundary recognition in sensor networks by topological methods, *Proceedings of the 12th Annual International Conference on Mobile Computing and Networking (MOBICOM)*, (September 2006).
14. P. K. Sahoo, K. Y. Hsieh and J. P. Sheu, Boundary node selection and target detection in wireless sensor networks, *Proceedings of the 4th IEEE and IFIP International Conference on Wireless and Optical Communications Networks (WOCN)*, (July 2007).

Chapter 7

Cooperative Geographical Routing in Wireless Sensor Networks

Min Chen[*,‡], Victor C.M. Leung[*,§] and Shiwen Mao[†,¶]

[*]*Department of Electrical and Computer Engineering*
University of British Columbia, V6T 1Z4, Canada

[†]*Deptartment of Electrical and Computer Engineering*
Auburn University, Auburn, AL 36849, USA

[‡]*minchen@ece.ubc.ca*

[§]*vleung@ece.ubc.ca*

[¶]*smao@ieee.org*

Reliable delivery of sensory data to a sink node in large scale sensor networks is a challenging problem. This chapter tackles this problem by assuming dense deployment of sensors, which allows us to exploit diversity in choosing intermediate nodes for reliability and energy-efficiency. The proposed reliable and energy-efficient routing (REER) protocol is based on the geographic routing approach. The central idea of REER is the notion of reference nodes (RNs), which means the nodes closest to the ideal locations between the source and the sink. The multiple Cooperative Nodes (CNs) around RNs will contend to relay data packets; thus, there is no overhead of route discovery and REER is resilient to node failures and transmission errors. By adjusting the distances between RNs, we can control the trade-off between reliability and energy-efficiency, which is validated by both analysis and simulation.

7.1. Introduction

Sensor networks are usually subject to high failure rate: connectivity between nodes can be lost due to environmental noise and obstacles; nodes may die due to battery depletion, environmental changes or malicious destruction. In such environments, reliable and energy-efficient data delivery is crucial because sensor nodes operate with limited battery power and error-prone wireless channels. However, the goal of reliability and energy-efficiency often conflict each other. We consider two extremes of routing protocols in terms of these two design objectives: unicast routing and flooding. Unicast routing is energy-efficient for reliable networks, but is not robust for dynamic networks. Flooding is very robust for dynamic and error-prone networks, but incurs a high overhead for sensor networks. Some routing protocols try to achieve a trade-off between the two extremes to make this adaptive to different types of networks (with different link/node failure rate, node density, etc.). For example, in directed diffusion (DD),[1] exploratory data is periodically flooded for reliability. When a path is reinforced, it is used for a while with unicast routing in order to save overhead.

In this chapter, a reliable energy-efficient routing (REER) protocol is proposed to construct a "unicast-like" path, while exploiting broadcast to attain high reliability during data dissemination. The goal of REER is to achieve both reliable and energy-efficient data delivery for dense wireless sensor networks (WSNs). When sending a packet from source to the sink over multiple hops, REER controls the distance r between two adjacent hops. At each hop, an appropriate number of nodes for cooperatively forwarding the data is selected. The smaller is r, the more common nodes are shared by two adjacent hops, thus, the more cooperative nodes (CNs) can be selected for cooperative data forwarding. Since r decides how many nodes will be selected, it efficiently provides a tradeoff between reliability and energy cost. When r is equal to the transmission range of data packet, REER behaves almost like a unicast fashion. By comparison, if r is very small, REER can be deemed as scope-controlled flooding around the path from the source to the sink. Unlike directional/controlled flooding, REER only selects the nodes which need to participate data broadcasting to achieve required reliability in a hop-by-hop fashion. Thus, the number of nodes involved in data delivery can be minimized while achieving required reliability. Furthermore, the unselected nodes will enter sleeping mode to save energy. We present extensive simulations to show that REER normally yields higher reliability than traditional geographical routing scheme while achieving less energy consumption. In REER, the overall performance gain in terms of reliability, lifetime, and data delivery latency increases as the link/node failure rate increases.

The remainder of this chapter is organized as follows. Section 7.2 presents the background of reliable data transmission using geographical routing over WSNs. Section 7.3 describe the proposed REER design issues and algorithm. Sections 7.4 and 7.5 present simulation model and experiment results, respectively. Section 7.6 summarizes the chapter.

7.2. Related Work

Our work is closely related to the reliable data transfer scheme in WSNs, and geographic routing in WSNs. We will give a brief review of the exsiting work in these two aspects.

7.2.1. *Reliable data transmission over WSNs*

There are increasing research efforts on studying the issue of reliable data transfer in WSN.[2–8] In these work, hop-by-hop recovery,[2,3] end-to-end recovery,[7,8] and multi-path forwarding[4–6] are the major approaches to achieve the desired reliability by previous work.

PSFQ[2] works by distributing data from source nodes in a relatively slow pace and allowing nodes experienced data loss to recover any missing segments from immediate neighbors aggressively. PSFQ employs hop by hop recovery instead of end to end recovery. RMST[3] is a selective NACK-based protocol that can be configured for in-network caching and repair. Several acknowledgement based end-to-end reliable event transfer schemes are proposed to achieve various levels of reliability in Ref. 8. A virtual MIMO based cross layer design is proposed in Ref. 9. In the design, the nodes can form adaptively the cooperative nodes set to transmit data among clusters. Then, the hop-by-hop recovery scheme and multi-hop routing scheme are integrated into the virtual MIMO scheme to jointly provide energy efficiency, reliability and end-to-end QoS guarantee.

In,[4] multiple disjoint paths are set up first, then multiple data copies are delivered using these paths. In,[5] a protocol called ReInForM is proposed to deliver packets at desired reliability by sending multiple copies of each packet along multiple paths from sources to sink. The number of data copies (or, the number of paths used) is dynamically determined depending on the probability of channel error.

Instead of using disjoint paths, GRAB[6] uses a path interleaving technique to achieve high reliability. It assigns the amount of credit α to the packet at the source. α determines the "width" of the forwarding mesh and should be large enough to ensure robustness but not to cause excessive energy consumption. However, finding a suitable value of α for various reliability requirements of sensor networks is not trivial. Furthermore, when the quality of channel changes frequently, out-of-date α makes GRAB either waste energy to unnecessarily use more paths or fail to achieve the required reliability. It is worth noting that although GRAB[6] also exploits data broadcasting to attain high reliability, it may not be energy-efficient because it may involve many next-hop nodes in order to achieve good reliability and an unnecessarily large number of packets may be broadcast. By comparison, in REER a data packet is only broadcast once at each hop, and it is quite robust to link/node failures.

Some researchers explore the special features of sensor applications in reliable protocol design. For example, considering asymmetric many-to-one communication pattern from sources to sink in some sensor applications, data packets collected for a single event exhibit high redundancy. Thus, some reliable techniques[2,3] proposed for WSN would either be unnecessary or spend too much resources on guaranteeing 100% reliable delivery of data packets. Exploiting the fact that the redundancy in sensed data collected by closely deployed sensor nodes can mitigate channel error and node failure, ESRT[7] intends to minimize the total energy consumption while guaranteeing the end-to-sink reliability. In ESRT, the sink adaptively achieves the expected event reliability by controlling the reporting frequency of the source nodes. However, in the case that many sources are involved in reporting data simultaneously to ensure some reliability (e.g., in a high unreliable environment), the large amount of communications are likely to cause congestion.

7.2.2. *Geographical routing in WSNs*

Geographical (position-based) routing[10] is a routing scheme in which each sensor node is assumed to be aware of its geographical location using GPS or distributed location services, and packet forwarding is performed based on the locations of the nodes. Each node broadcasts a hello message periodically to notify its neighbors of its current position; based on this information, each node sets up a neighbor information table that records the positions of its one-hop neighbors.

In general, each packet is routed to a neighbor closer to the sink than the forwarding node itself until the packet reaches the sink. If a node does not have any neighbors closer to the sink, a fallback mechanism is triggered to overcome this local minimum. Bose *et al.* proposed Greedy-Face-Greedy (GFG) routing,[11] in which upon arriving at a void, the protocol switches from greedy mode to face mode to circumnavigate the void. When the current node is closer to destination than the node initially starting the face mode,[12] the protocol returns to greedy mode (the void is considered circumnavigated), and chooses the next hop using the left/right hand rule. The right hand rule consists in "rolling" to the right along the edges. GFG has been reinvented in Refs. 12 and 13, respectively. As the reinvention, a new name GPSR was given in Ref. 12.

7.3. System Architecture and Protocol Design

This section presents the architecture and design of the REER protocol. We first give an overview of the network organization, and then describe the key REER components in detail. Lastly, we present an analysis that derive the key performance metrics for the proposed protocol.

7.3.1. *Overview*

Consider a large scale, dense wireless sensor network, within which a source node, say, node s, generates reports on detected events in Fig. 7.1. These reports will be delivered to the sink node t via multi-hop routing. Usually sensor networks are deployed in the harsh environments, and thus the wireless links/nodes are failure prone. In addition, the sensor nodes are severely energy constrained due to the low-cost and disposable nature. Therefore, we choose reliability and energy efficiency as the two most important design objectives for REER.

The operation of REER is illustrated in Figs. 7.1(a)–(c). A set of nodes, termed reference nodes (RNs) between the source and the sink (source and the sink themselves are also RNs) are first selected, such that the distance between two adjacent RNs is sought to be an application-specific value (denoted by r). Note that, more closely are the RNs located to the straight line from the source node to the sink, less hop count should be obtained. In performing RN-selection, upstream RN will broadcast a probe message (PROB) with the transmission range of R. Its neighbors,

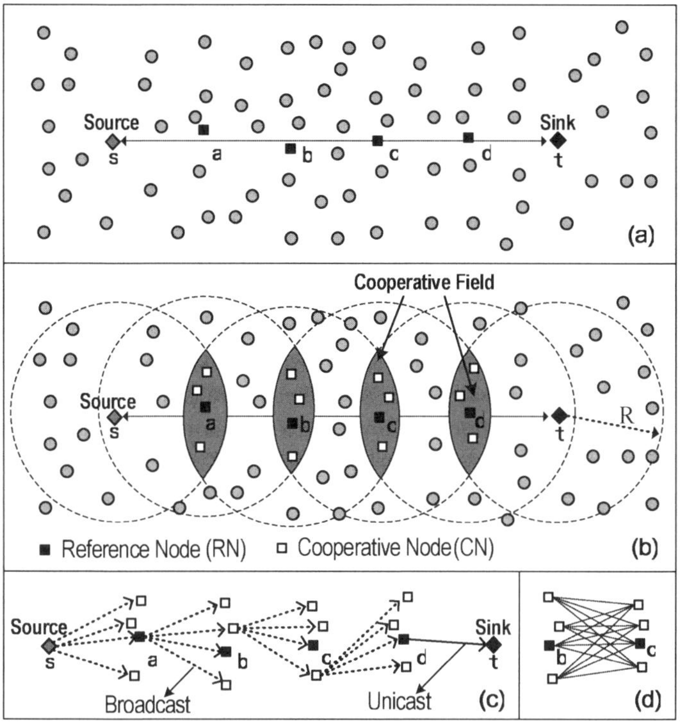

Fig. 7.1. Illustration of the REER routing protocol: (a) *RN*s along the shortest path; (b) *CN*s in the cooperative fields; (c) cooperative data forwarding; (d) the forwarding mesh between two cooperative fields.

which receive this PROB and within the *RN*-selection area in Fig. 7.3, are called "reference node candidates" (*RNC*s). The *RN*s are determined sequentially, starting from the source node. When a node is selected as the *RN* by its upstream *RN*, it will perform the *RN*-selection mechanism again to find its downstream *RN*, and so forth. In Fig. 7.1, since the source node s itself is an *RN*, it initiates *RN*-selection first to find its downstream *RN*, i.e., node a. The *RN* selection mechanism will be detailed in Sec. 7.3.2.

After a certain timer expires, the *RN*s determine a set of cooperative nodes (*CN*s) around each of them based on the coverage of the PROB messages they sent during *RN*-selection period. Note that the *CN*-selection does not need any control overhead.

As shown in Fig. 7.1(b), for *RN* b, the area covered by the transmissions of its upstream *RN* a will be a disk centered at a and have a radius of R, while the area covered by the transmissions of its downstream *RN* c will be a disk centered at c with the radius of R. As r is set to be smaller than R, these two disks will overlap, and node b will be located within the overlapping area. This overlapping area is deemed as the *cooperative field* of *RN* b (denoted by CF_b). That is, the sensor nodes in CF_b are the *CN*s for *RN* b. The *CN*-selection mechanism will be detailed in Sec. 7.3.3.

After the *RN*s and *CN*s are determined, each data packet will be forwarded toward the sink node by relaying between groups of *CN*s (i.e., group-by-group, rather than hop-by-hop), as illustrated in Fig. 7.1(c). REER exploits data broadcasting to attain high reliability. More specifically, each data packet is broadcast at each hop, such that the *RN* and all the *CN*s with a good signal-noise-ratio (SNR) in the next *CF* will receive this data packet. *RN*s and *CN*s play the same role in data relaying. This strategy provides an effective tradeoff between traditional multipath routing and single path routing schemes. That is, it has the advantage of error resilience as in multipath (or mesh) routing schemes, but without the associated overhead of sending multiple copies of the same packet.

Figure 7.1(d) shows all the possible wireless links between two consecutive cooperative groups, while the quality of each of the links is varying. With the proposed scheme, the link with the best quality is used. Such a strategy makes our scheme robust to link dynamics.

Upon reception, a node (*RN* or *CN*) will be selected randomly to broadcast the data packet towards the next cooperative field, and so forth. The data dissemination mechanism will be detailed in Sec. 7.3.4. The nodes, which are neither selected as *RN* nor *CN*, will enter the sleeping mode to save energy during data dissemination.

7.3.2. *Reference node selection strategy*

In the global coordinate system (o is the origin) of Fig. 7.2, node h is an *RN*. Its position (x_h^o, y_h^o) is piggybacked in the PROB message sent by h. Thus, a neighbor node i knows its position (x_i^o, y_i^o), the position of its upstream *RN* h, and the sink's location (x_t^o, y_t^o).

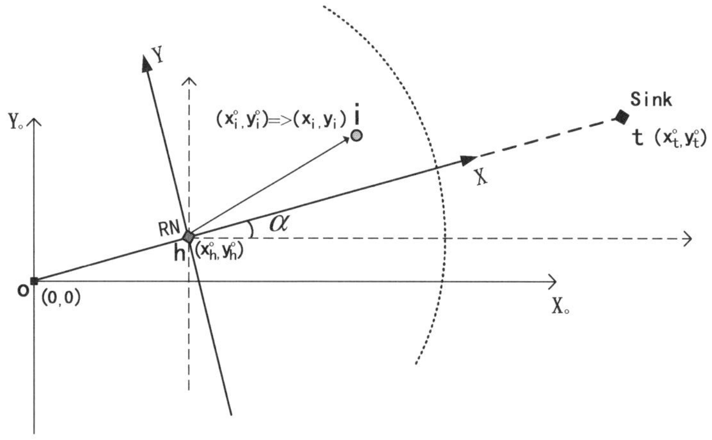

Fig. 7.2. Obtaining virtual coordinates by means of GPS.

In this chapter, we employ the *virtual coordinates* proposed in Ref. 14. The *virtual coordinates* of a node (e.g., i in Fig. 7.2) are defined as the coordinates in the virtual two-dimensional coordinate system where the node's upstream node (e.g., h in Fig. 7.2) is the origin, and the X-axis is the line between the upstream node (e.g., h in Fig. 7.2) and the sink. In the example shown in Fig. 7.2, the *virtual coordinates* of i is denoted by (x_i, y_i), which can be calculated by Eq. (7.1).

$$\begin{cases} x_i = \cos(\alpha)\cdot(x_i^o - x_h^o) + \sin(\alpha)\cdot(y_i^o - y_h^o) \\ y_i = \cos(\alpha)\cdot(y_i^o - y_h^o) - \sin(\alpha)\cdot(x_i^o - x_h^o) \\ \alpha = \arctan(\frac{y_t^o - y_h^o}{x_t^o - x_h^o}). \end{cases} \tag{7.1}$$

The RN-selection is performed according to (x_i, y_i) and r. Let $A(d, r_1, r_2)$ denote the size of an area intersected by two circles with radius being r_1 and r_2, respectively, and the distance between their centers being d. Let D_i be the distance between the RN_i and the sink. Then, the area covers the CNs of RN_i is equal to $A(D_{i-1} - D_{i+1}, R, R)$. Assume nodes are densely and nearly uniformly distributed; then, the density of sensor nodes can be deemed as a constant ρ approximately. The number of CNs in the CF_i with center being RN_i is equal to:

$$N_i = A(D_{i-1} - D_{i+1}, R, R)\cdot\rho. \tag{7.2}$$

Let f be the failure probability of each link/node. Then, the hop reliability that data packet successfully passes CF_i can be given by:

$$p = 1 - f^{N_i}. \tag{7.3}$$

Based on Eqs. (7.2) and (7.3), p is a decreasing function of $(D_{i-1} - D_{i+1})$. If required hop reliability is an application-specific constant, $(D_{i-1} - D_{i+1})$ is fixed, i.e. the specified hop distance $r = r_i = D_i - D_{i+1}$ is a constant. In the following section, we describe the algorithm in such condition.

The point $(r, 0)$ is called strategic position in Fig. 7.3, which is r away from the upstream RN and located in the line between source and the sink to maximize hop length. Denote the distance between node i and the strategic position $(r, 0)$ by $\Delta D_i = \sqrt{(x_i - r)^2 - (y_i)^2}$. The smaller is ΔD_i, the higher possibility that i should be selected as the RN. Nodes within the shadow area (RN-selection-area) of Fig. 7.3 are deemed as RN-candidates (RNCs). A threshold TH is set to limit the RN-selection-area, and the x coordinate of a RNC should be smaller than r to obtain the required hop reliability approximately. Thus, RN-selection-area is a half circle with radius TH in Fig. 7.3.

Upon the reception of a PROB message from h, node i will discard the packet under any of the following conditions:

C1 the node has already received this packet;
C2 $x_i > r$;
C3 $\Delta D_i > TH$.

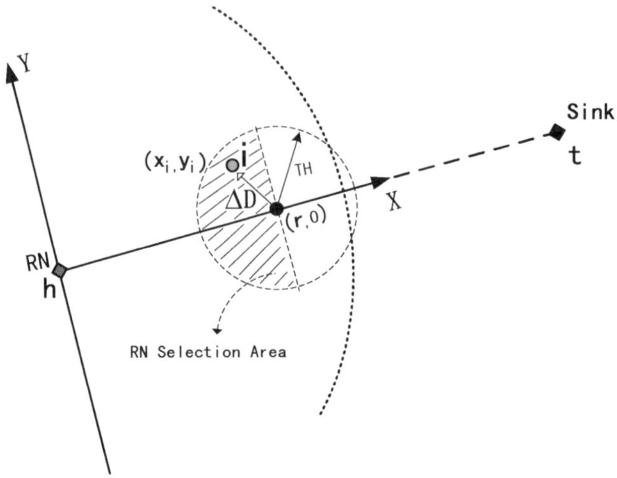

Fig. 7.3. Illustration of *RN*-selection.

If the packet is not discarded, i will start a backoff timer. In order to guarantee that the one closest to strategic position has highest possibility to be selected as the next *RN*, the timeout value for the backoff timer (t_{rnc}) is proportional to ΔD. t_{rnc} is calculated in Eq. (7.4).

$$t_{rnc} = \tau \times \Delta D + \text{rand}(0, \mu), \tag{7.4}$$

where τ is the time value of a fixed unit slot. rand$(0, \mu)$ returns a random value uniformly distributed in $[0, \mu)$, and μ is a small constant.

Assume i has the smallest t_{rnc} value among all the *RN*Cs and its backoff timer expires first, it will unicast a "reply" message (REP) to its upstream reference node h. When node h receives the REP, it broadcasts a "selection" message (SEL) with the identifier of node i (already piggybacked in the REP). To guarantee that only one *RNC* is selected as the downstream *RN*, node h only accepts the first REP while ignoring the later ones. If node i receives the SEL, it is selected as the downstream *RN* for h. When other *RNC*s receive the SEL or REP, they will cancel their backoff timers. When the sink receives PROB, it will broadcast a notification packet immediately to terminate *RN*-selection.

To reduce the possibility of collision of REP messages, we can set τ a sufficiently large value, while low value of τ decreases the time needed to setup *RN*s. The setting of τ is shown in Table 7.2. Since the *RN* selection is a relatively infrequent task as compared to the period of data transmission, even the use of large τ will not increase the data latency.

7.3.2.1. *The structure of route discovery packet*

The information contained in a PROB is shown in Fig. 7.4. The set of *SourceID*, *SinkID* and *SeqNum* is used to identify the PROB message. *SinkPOS* indicates

Fixed Attributes

SourceID	SinkID	SeqNum	SinkPOS	HopDistance

Variable Attributes

RN_ID	RN_POS	HopCount

Fig. 7.4. The packet structure of PROB message.

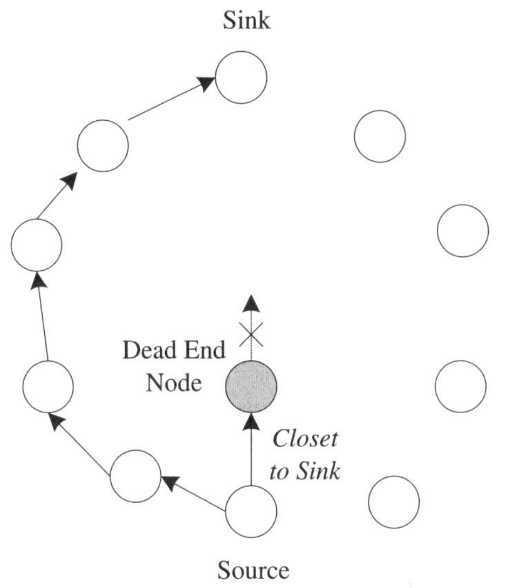

Fig. 7.5. Illustration of dead end problem.

the absolute coordinates of the sink. *HopDistance* indicates the expected per hop distance. The fixed attributes are set by the source and not changed while propagated across the network. On the other hand, when an *RN* broadcasts a PROB message, it will change variable attributes. *RN_ID* is the identifer of current reference node. *RN_POS* is the absolute coordinates of the *RN*. *HopCount* is the hop count from current node to the source. *RN_ID* and *HopCount* are used in Sec. 7.3.3.

7.3.2.2. *The dead end problem during* RN-*selection*

The so-called dead end problem[15,16] arises when a packet is forwarded to a local optimum, i.e., a node with no neighbor of closer hop distance to the destination as illustrated in Fig. 7.5. In REER, if there are no *RNC*s located in the *RNC*-area, it will enter greedy mode to select the node among all its neighbors that is geographically closest to the sink as the downstream *RN*. If an *RN* does not have any neighbor closer to the sink in the greedy mode, REER meets the dead end problem and *RN*-selection will be performed in recovery mode, i.e., the downstream *RN* is selected according to the right-hand rule to recover from the local minimum.[12] The right-hand rule is a well-known concept for traversing mazes. To avoid loops, the downstream *RN* is selected in recovery mode on the faces of a locally extracted planar subgraph, namely the Gabriel graph. The *RN*-selection returns to greedy mode when an *RN* is closer to the sink than the *RN* where RN-selection entered the recovery mode. Furthermore, if the *RN* has *RNC*(s) in its *RNC*-area, the *RN*-selection switches to normal selection mode described in Sec. 7.3.2 rather than greedy mode.

If an *RN* is selected by greedy mode or recovery mode, the corresponding cooperative field will be distorted seriously. In this case, the cooperative field is not constructed and data packet will be forwarded by unicasting, and the responsibility of reliability is shifted to MAC layer.

7.3.3. *Cooperative node selection strategy*

As shown in Fig. 7.1(a), PROBs are broadcast by the *RN*s along the path from the source to the sink, starting from the source node. Note that PROB is sent only during the cooperative field establishment phase and each *RN* will broadcast PROB only once.

Upon the reception of the first PROB, an intermediate node will become a *CN* candidate (*CNC*), and start a "CN-decision" timer (*CN-Decision-Timer*). Assume node i is one of such *CNC*s. As *RN* selection proceeds toward the sink, i will receive more PROBs. When its *CN-Decision-Timer* expires, i is expected to receives all the PROBs and performs a CN-decision procedure. In this procedure, i checks how many PROBs it has received. If the number of PROBs is three or more, node i induces that it becomes a *CN*. Then, it will figure out which *RN* it belongs to.

The detailed *CN*-Decision-Mechanism is shown in the flowchart in Fig. 7.6 where the *RN-table* is used for a *CNC* to store information of received PROBs from different *RN*s. The *EntryIdx* is the index of the *RN*-entry (RE) in the *RN-table*. Each RE includes the following information: (1) the hop count to the source node (hc_s); (2) the identifier of the *RN* (id_{rn}) sending the PROB; (3) the distance from the *RN* to the sink (D_t), which is calculated based on *SinkPOS* and *RN_POS* in the PROB message.

The stored information is used for the *CN*-decision procedure and the following data dissemination (in Sec. 7.3.4). In the example of Fig. 7.7(a), *CNC* i is closest to node b among all the *RN*s. It receives the first PROB from a and set the id_{rn} of the first RE ($RE[1].id_{rn}$) to a; then it receives the second PROB from b and set $RE[2].id_{rn}$ to b; lastly, it receives the third PROB from c and set $RE[3].id_{rn}$ to c. In this example, node i knows it is a *CN* since its *EntryIdx* is equal to 3, and selects the *RN* indicated in the second RE (i.e. node b) as its *RN*. There also exists "four-PROBs" case in which a *CN* receives four PROBs. Fig. 7.7(b) shows such an

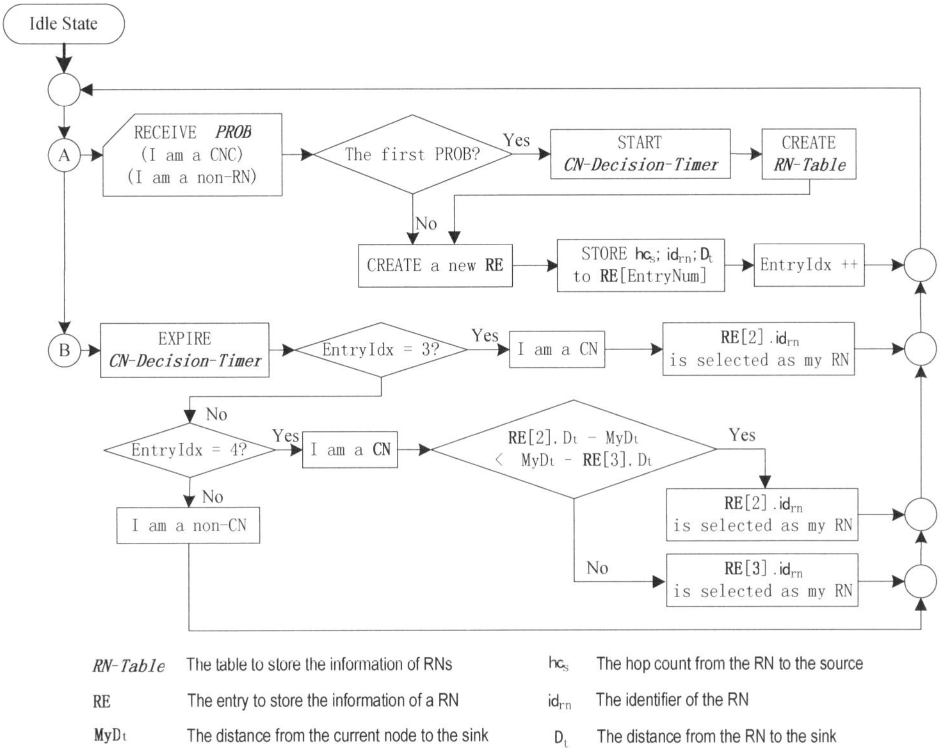

Fig. 7.6. Flowchart of the *CN* decision mechanism.

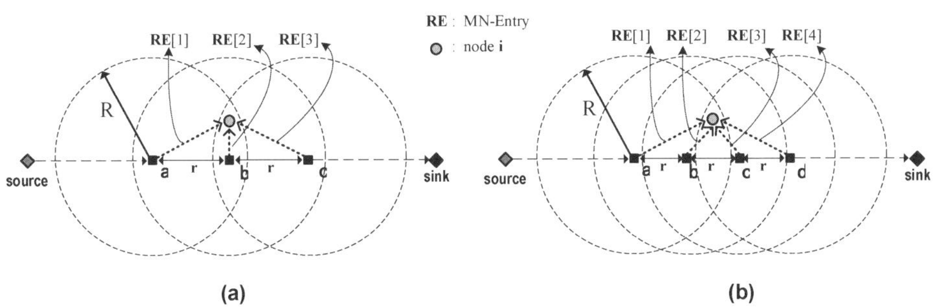

Fig. 7.7. The cases of three-PROBs and four-PROBs.

example. However, there should be no five(or more)-PROBs cases, which means r is set to too small a value inefficiently.

In Four-PROBs case, only nodes $RE[2].id_{rn}$ and $RE[3].id_{rn}$ are eligible as the *RN* for the *CN*. The *CN* makes the decision by comparing which one is closer to itself as shown in Fig. 7.6 where MyD_t denotes the distance from the current *CN* to the sink.

Note that this section only considers the case of a single flow. If multiple flows coexist, REER creates an *RN-table* for each flow with a unique identifer (flow-id).

7.3.4. *Data dissemination in REER*

When the *RN*s and *CN*s are determined, data reports are forwarded by the cooperation of the group of *CN*s at each hop. The data packet format contains the following information: the identifier of the source s; the identifier of the sink t; the identifier of the node broadcasting the packet h; the hop count from source to current node $Data.hc_s$; the sequence number *Data.SeqNum*.

Assuming a node i receives a broadcast data packet. Let Seq^i_{data} be the largest sequence number of the data packets that node i has so far received. It first compares Seq^i_{data} with *Data.SeqNum*. If *Data.SeqNum* is not larger than Seq^i_{data}, the data packet is either a stale one or broadcast by i's downstream node. In this case, node i will drop the data.

Then, node i will randomly choose a backoff time (t_b) in Eq. (7.5), and set its *Backoff-Timer* to t_b to perform a two phase contention procedure.[17]

$$t_b = \text{rand}(0, T_{max}). \tag{7.5}$$

In Eq. (7.5), T_{max} denotes the maximum backoff timer value. Assume N_{cf} denotes the number of *CN*s in the cooperative field. In order to be differentiated with other nodes in the same cooperative field, at least the length of time slot ΔT should be reserved for each node to content the channel in the same cooperative field. Thus,

$$T_{max} = N_{cf} \cdot \Delta T. \tag{7.6}$$

Large ΔT helps to reduce the possibility of simultaneous data broadcasting, while a small value of ΔT decreases the data latency. Once i's *Backoff-Timer* expires, it transmits a jamming signal for a short time t_j which is calculated in Eq. (7.7), where β is a small constant.

$$t_j = \text{rand}(0, \beta T_{max}), \quad 0 < \beta \ll 1. \tag{7.7}$$

As an adverse example shown in Fig. 7.8, *CN2* and *CN3* happen to choose the same t_b to start jamming the medium simultaneously while the *Backoff-Timer* of *CN*1 does not expire yet. *CN*1 listens a jamming signal either from *CN2* or *CN3*; Then, it cancels its *Backoff-Timer* to quit the contention. After *CN3* finishes jamming the medium, it detects the jamming signal from *CN2* and gives up the contention of forwarding the data. Finally, *CN2* wins the contention.

When node i hears the forwarding of a packet, it also compares hc^i_s (i's hop count to the source) with $Data.hc_s$ (the hop count of the received packet). If ($hc^i_s = Data.hc_s$)&& ($Seq^i_{data} = Data.SeqNum$), it deduces that the transmission is successful since an immediate downstream node broadcasts the data packet.

```
A. Handle DATA
procedure process_data(DATA(h,t,hc_s^h,SeqNum))
  i is the identifier of the current node;
  hc_s^h is the hop count from s to h;
  SeqNum is the sequence number of the data packet;
begin
if ((f_cn^i=TRUE)||(f_rn^i=TRUE)) then
  if (DATA.SeqNum > Seq_data^i)
   && (DATA.hc_s^h+1=hc_s^i) then
     Store DATA;
     t_b ← rand(0, T_max);        //refer to Eq. (7.5)
     Set Backoff-Timer to t_b;
  else if (DATA.SeqNum = Seq_data^i)
   && (DATA.hc_s^h = hc_s^i) then
    Cancel Backoff-Timer (if it's valid);
    Cancel ReTx-Timer (if it's valid);
  else
    Discard DATA;
  endif
else
 Discard DATA;
endif
end

B. Backoff-Timer Expires
procedure send_jamming(void))
begin
h ← i;
SeqNum ← Seq_data^i;
t_j ← rand(0, βT_max);        //refer to Eq. (7.7)
Broadcast JAM(h,SeqNum) signal for t_j;
Set Jamming-Timer to (t_j);
end

C. Handle JAM
procedure process_jam(JAM(h,SeqNum))
begin
Cancel Jamming-Timer (if it's valid);
Discard the stored DATA;
end

D. Jamming-Timer Expires
procedure broadcast_data(void))
begin
h ← i;
hc_s^h ← hc_s^i;
if (I can reach sink in one hop) then
  Unicast DATA(h,t) to t;
else
  Broadcast DATA(h,t,hc_s^h,SeqNum);
  Set ReTx-Timer to (T_max);
  RetryIdx ← 1;
endif
end

E. ReTx-Timer Expires
procedure rebroadcast_data(void))
begin
RetryIdx + +;
Broadcast DATA again;
if (RetryIdx ≤ RetryLimit_data) then
  Start ReTx-Timer;
endif
end
```

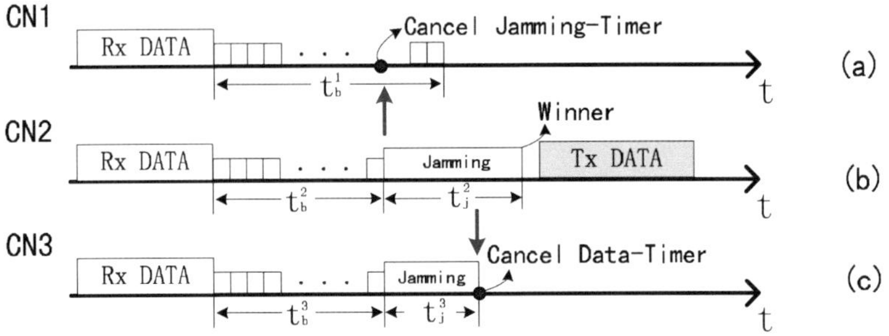

Fig. 7.8. The time flow of broadcasting data packet.

Otherwise, node i will rebroadcast the data packet when a retransmission-timer (*ReTx-Timer*) expires, and starts the timer again until the retry limit reaches.

The pseudo-code of the data dissemination of REER protocol is shown in Table 7.1 where "←" denotes an assignment operation. f^i_{cn} is a flag that indicates whether a sensor node i is a cooperative node or not, while f^i_{rn} is a flag that indicates whether i is a reference node or not.

7.3.5. *Performance analysis*

In this section, we present the analysis that derives the key performance metrics of REER, including the probability of successfully delivering data packet to the sink, P, the cumulative energy consumption involved in forwarding a data packet to the sink, E, and the cumulative delay for a data packet, T_{ete}. And show the impact of hop distance on these performance metrics.

To simplify analysis, we consider an ideal scenario where the hop distance r is identical between each adjacent RNs, and all the cooperative fields have the same shape, as shown in Fig. 7.9. We set up a two-dimensional coordinate system where the X-axis is the line between reference node b and the sink, and node b is at the origin of the coordinate system. The alphabet index of each node is equal to the one in Fig. 7.1.

Let R be the maximum transmission range of a PROB message. Let h_{cf} and v_{cf} be the horizontal and vertical radius of the cooperative field in Fig. 7.9, respectively. They are equal to:

$$h_{cf} = R - r \tag{7.8}$$

$$v_{cf} = \sqrt{R^2 - r^2}. \tag{7.9}$$

Let r_{max} be the possible maximum distance among all the CN pairs between two adjacent cooperative fields (e.g., CF_c and CF_d). Then,

$$r_{max} = \sqrt{r^2 + (2 \cdot v_{cf})^2} = \sqrt{4R^2 - 3r^2}. \tag{7.10}$$

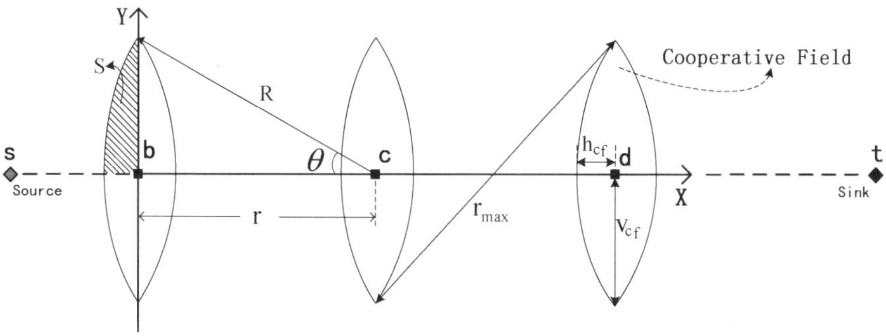

Fig. 7.9. An ideal scenario in REER.

To guarantee any pairs of *CN*s in adjacent cooperative fields can communication with each other, the maximum transmission range of a data packet R_{data} is set to r_{max}. In this case, R_{data} is also larger than $2v_{cf}$ which is the maximum distance between any two nodes in the same cooperative field. Thus, all *CN*s within the the same cooperative field can hear each other, so that they can cancel their timers when one of them is forwarding the packet. This fact is used in Sec. 7.3.4, where jamming signal broadcast by any node in a cooperative field (*CF*) will make any other nodes in the same *CF* cancel broadcasting the same data.

Let S_{cf} be the size of the area of a cooperative field, and let S be the size of the shaded area in Fig. 7.9. Then S_{cf} is equal to:

$$S_{cf} = 4 \cdot S = 4 \cdot \left(\theta \cdot R^2 - \frac{1}{2} \cdot \sqrt{R^2 - r^2}\right). \tag{7.11}$$

In Eq. (7.11), $\theta = cos^{-1}(r/R)$. Assume the node density is δ. Then, the number of *CN*s in cooperative field (N_{cf}) is equal to:

$$N_{cf} = S_{cf} \cdot \delta. \tag{7.12}$$

Let d be the distance between the source and the sink. Then, the hop counts between the source and the sink (H) is equal to:

$$H = \left\lceil \frac{d}{r} \right\rceil. \tag{7.13}$$

The number of cooperative fields between the source and sink is equal to $H - 1$. Let f be the failure probability of each link/node. Let p denote the successful delivery probability of data packet at each hop. Then,

$$P = p^H = (1 - f^{N_{cf}})^H. \tag{7.14}$$

Let e_{tx} and e_{rx} be the energy consumption of transmitting and receiving a data packet, respectively. Then, the cumulative energy consumption E involved in successfully forwarding a data packet to the sink is

$$E = e_{tx} \cdot H + e_{rx} \cdot [3(H-2) \cdot N_{cf} \cdot (1-f) + 2N_{cf} \cdot (1-f) + 1]. \tag{7.15}$$

Note that $H-2$ numbers of *CF*s will listen to the data broadcasting three times and only the last *CF* listens to the data two times. One of *CN*s in the last *CF* will unicast the data to the sink.

Let t_{data} be the time to transmit a data packet; Let $\overline{t_b}$ be the average of backoff time before data forwarding. Then, the end-to-end latency for a data packet is equal to:

$$T_{ete} = t_{data} \cdot H + \overline{t_b} \cdot (H-1). \tag{7.16}$$

Given all other parameters fixed, P, E, and T_{ete} are decreasing functions of r. The smaller is r, the larger will be N and H, the higher reliability p is achieved. However, for small r values, more energy E is consumed for each data packet, and T_{ete} also becomes larger. Thus, r provides a control knob to trade-off robustness and energy efficiency (and latency). r should be adaptively selected to achieve required reliability while meeting the application-specific QoS requirements (e.g. reliability, and end-to-end latency bound).

7.3.6. *Control overhead compared with shortest path based geographical routing*

Let n_s be the number of sensor nodes in the network. The number of neighbors k of a node is equal to:

$$k = \pi R^2 \rho. \tag{7.17}$$

Let e_{ctrl} be the energy consumption of transmitting a control message. Let o_g be the control overhead for setting up neighbor information table in a shortest path based geographical routing (e.g., GPSR). Let o_r be the control overhead for establishing *RN*s and *CN*s in REER. Then,

$$o_g = n_s \cdot e_{ctrl}. \tag{7.18}$$

$$o_r = H \cdot 3e_{ctrl}. \tag{7.19}$$

In GPSR, each node beacons a hello message for setting up or updating the neighbor information table; In REER, three messages (i.e. PROB, REP, and SEL) are needed to construct *RN* and *CN*s per hop. In general, n_s is much larger than $3H$. In GPSR, each node needs to store k number of neighbor entries in its local memory, while in REER, each node does not require neighbor information except for the identifier of the *RN*. Once cooperative fields are established, *RN*/*CN* does not need to store any routing-relevant information, while other nodes can enter sleeping mode to save energy. Thus, REER scales well in dense sensor network, where the sensors have low storage capacity.

7.4. Simulation Model

7.4.1. *Simulation settings*

We implemented our scheme using OPNET[18,19] to evaluate the performance of REER and GPSR. The hop distance is specified. During the data dissemination, the nodes outside the cooperative fields will enter sleeping mode to save energy. In GPSR, a greedy forwarder will be selected out of the list of neighbors. If the selected neighbor fails to receive a packet, its previous hop node tries to retransmit the packet until the retry limit reaches. Then, a backup node is selected from the neighbor table, and the MAC layer tries to deliver the packet to the this node. We use IEEE 802.11 DCF as the underlying MAC. Six hundreds of sensor nodes are randomly placed over a 500 m × 200 m area. The rectangular shape of the simulation area is chosen to obtain longer paths, i.e. a higher average hop count. The transmission range of sensor node is 60 m. As we take a conservative approach in evaluation, we do not assume sensor node can adjust transmission range in REER, i.e. $R_{data} = R$. The sensor nodes are battery-operated. The sink is assumed to have infinite energy supply. We assume both the sink and sensor nodes are stationary. The sink located close to one corner of the area, while the target sensor nodes are specified at the other corner. Each source generates sensed data packets using a constant bit rate with a 5 second interval.

We use the energy model in Ref. 20. In,[22] Gilbert-Elliot model is used to model the link failure. We adopt an ON-OFF two state Gilbert-Elliot model. State ON represents that the link is in "good" status, while state OFF represents a "link failure" state. Let f be the link failure rate. With the time duration of state ON (T_{on}) fixed to 100 s, that of state OFF (T_{off}) is calculated as a function of f ($T_{off} = T_{on} \times f/(1-f)$). The parameter values used in the simulations are presented in Table 7.2. The basic settings are common to all the experiments. To decrease the influence of one special topology on the results, each experiment was repeated 10 times with different topologies; For each result, we simulate for 20 times with different random seeds. For the evaluation, the mean values of these 10 × 20 runs were taken.

7.4.2. *Performance metrics*

In this section, five performance metrics are evaluated:

- *Reliability (Packet delivery ratio)* — It is denoted by P. It is the ratio of the number of data packets delivered to the sink to the number of packets generated by the source nodes.
- *Energy Consumption per Successful Data Delivery* — It is denoted by e. It is the ratio of network energy consumption to the number of data packets successfully delivered to the sink. The network energy consumption includes all the energy consumption by transmitting and receiving during simulation. As in Ref. 21, we

Basic Specification	
Network Size	500 m × 200 m
Topology Configuration Mode	Randomized
Total Sensor Node Number	600
Data Rate at MAC layer	1 Mbps
Transmission Range of Sensor Node	60 m
Time Duration of State ON	Default: 10 s
Node failure rate	Default: 0%
Packet loss rate	Default: 0%
Sensed Traffic Specification	
Size of Sensed Data	Default: 1 Kbytes
Size of Control Message	Default: 128 bytes
Sensed Data Packet Interval	5 s
REER Specification	
r	Default: 40 m
τ in Eq. (7.4)	Default: 2.5 ms
μ in Eq. (7.4)	Default: 5 ms
ΔT in Eq. (7.6)	Default: 10 ms

do not account energy consumption for idle state, since this part is approximately the same for all the schemes simulated. Let E be the all the energy consumption by transmitting, receiving, and overhearing during simulation. Let n_{data} be the number of data packets delivered to the sink. Then, e is equal to:

$$e = \frac{E}{n_{data}}. \tag{7.20}$$

- *Average End-to-end Packet Delay* — It is denoted by T_{ete}. It includes all possible delays during data dissemination, caused by queuing, retransmission due to collision at the MAC, and transmission time.
- *Number of the Control Messages per Successful Data Delivery* — It is denoted by n_{ctrl}. It is the ratio of the number of control messages transmitted to the number of data packets delivered to the sink before lifetime.
- *Energy*delay/Reliability* — In sensor networks, it is important to consider both energy and delay. In,[21] a combined metric can reflect the impact of several performances. Considering the reliability is also an important metric in unreliable environment, this chapter adopts the following metric to evaluate the integrated performance of reliability, energy and delay:

$$\eta = \frac{e \cdot T_{ete}}{P}. \tag{7.21}$$

7.5. Performance Evaluation

In Sec. 7.5.1, we examine the impact of node density on the REER performance. In Sec. 7.5.2, GPSR and REER with varying r are evaluated in terms of link failure rate.

7.5.1. *Effect of normalized node density on the REER performance in unreliable environments*

In the following experiments, link failure rate is set to 0.3; r is set to $0.8R$; Let δ_q be the normalized node density, i.e. the ratio of the current node density to the default one ($\frac{600\ nodes}{500\times200\ m^2}$). δ_q is changed from 0.25 to 2 by controlling the number of sensor nodes in the fixed size of network.

In Fig. 7.10(a), the higher is δ_q, the larger is N_{cf}, the higher is the hop reliability and P. When δ_q is beyond 1.5, REER has a delivery ratio near 100%.

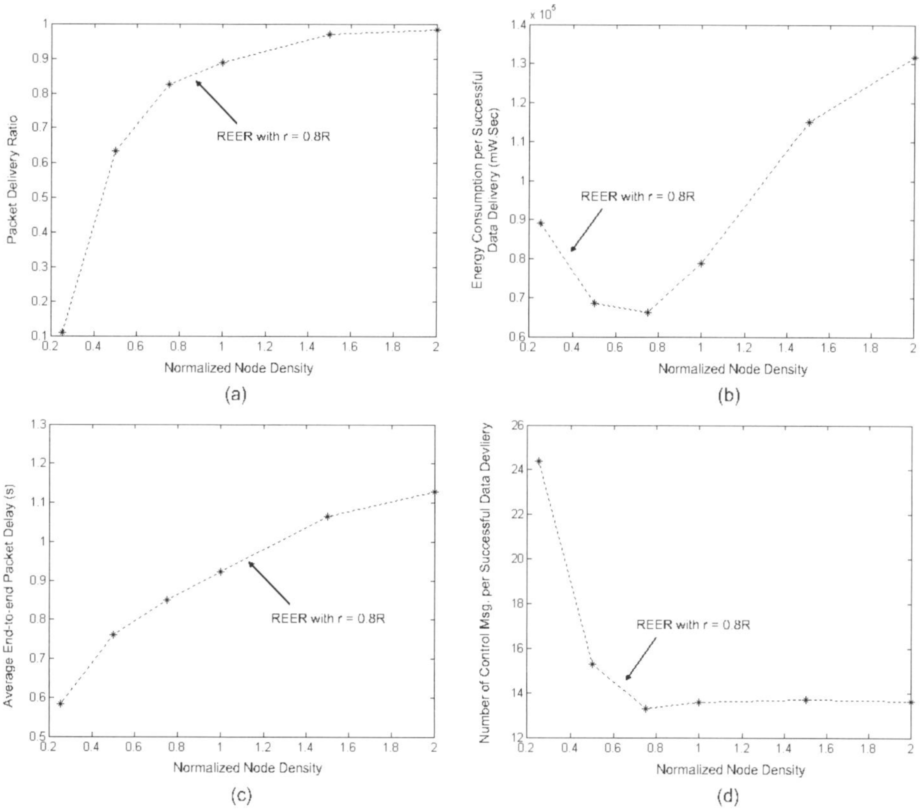

Fig. 7.10. The impact of normalized node density (δ_q) on performances: (a) Packet delivery ratio (P); (b) Energy consumption per successful data delivery (e); (c) Average end-to-end packet delay (T_{reer}); (d) Number of control messages per successful data delivery (η).

According to Eqs. (7.14) and (7.15), P is increasing function of N_{cf}, while E is linearly increasing function of N_{cf}. When N_{cf} is too small to overcome the 30% link failure rate, P increases exponentially with N_{cf} increased. Thus, $n_{data} = P \cdot TotalDataSendNum$ dominates Eq. (7.20) to make e_{reer} decrease. When δ_q is equal to 0.75, e_{reer} reaches its minimum. If δ_q goes beyond 0.75, P does not increase much (see Fig. 7.10(a)). However, E always linearly increases in proportion to δ_q, and dominates Eq. (7.20). Thus, e increases again, as shown in Fig. 7.10(b).

Recall that T_{max} denotes the maximum backoff timer value during data dissemination. T_{max} has a large impact on the data latency. It is set according to N_{cf} in Eq. (7.6). With δ_q increased, N_{cf} increases. The larger is N_{cf}, the larger T_{max} will be set to avoid collisions. Thus, in Fig. 7.10(c), T_{ete} of REER increases with δ_q increased. Currently, we adopt a simple backoff time function as shown in Eq. (7.6), we believe a better function can lower the data latency extensively.

In Fig. 7.10(d), η reaches its minimum value when δ_q is equal to 0.75. The smaller is η, the better is the integrated performance of REER. It is unnecessary to increase δ_q more if the value is large enough to achieve required reliability.

7.5.2. *Comparison of REER and GPSR with variable link failure rates*

In this section, six groups (i.e. GPSR and REER with r set to $0.67R$, $0.75R$, $0.85R$, $0.93R$, and R respectively) of simulation are evaluated. In each group of experiments, we change f from 0 to 0.9 by the step size of 0.1 with all the other parameters in Table 7.2 fixed.

The smaller is r, the larger number of *CN*s in each cooperative field are exploited. Thus, in Fig. 7.11, REER yields higher reliability as r decreased. When r is equal to $0.67R$, REER keeps achieving more than 90% packet delivery ratio until f is larger than 0.6. Since GPSR depends on periodically beaconing to perform local repair, it is not robust to high link failure rate. Thus, the reliability is low if the link failure rate goes beyond 0.3.

GPSR selects a next hop in its neighbor table and the MAC-layer tries to deliver the packet to this node. However, this node is not reachable in case of link failure, and the MAC-layer sends a failure notification back to the network layer to make the routing protocol selects another next hop. In case of high link failure rate, GPSR had to select several times a next hop until finally the MAC-layer was able to deliver the packets. By comparison, REER broadcast a data packet only once at each hop. Furthermore, the nodes which are not selected as *RN*s/*CN*s can enter sleeping mode to save energy. Thus, in Fig. 7.12, e_{reer} is almost always lower than e_{gpsr} with varying f.

According to Eq. (7.15), E decreases with f increases, i.e. the link failure helps to save energy for receiving data packet. If the number of *CN*s is large enough to

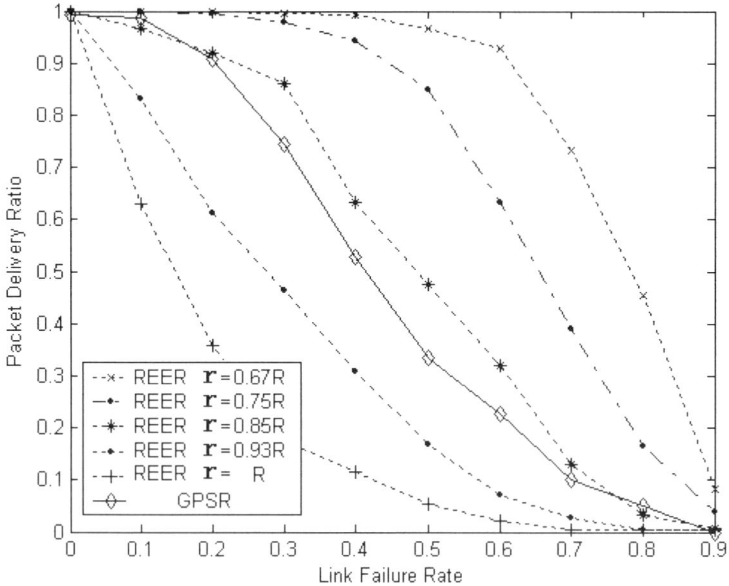

Fig. 7.11. The comparison of P.

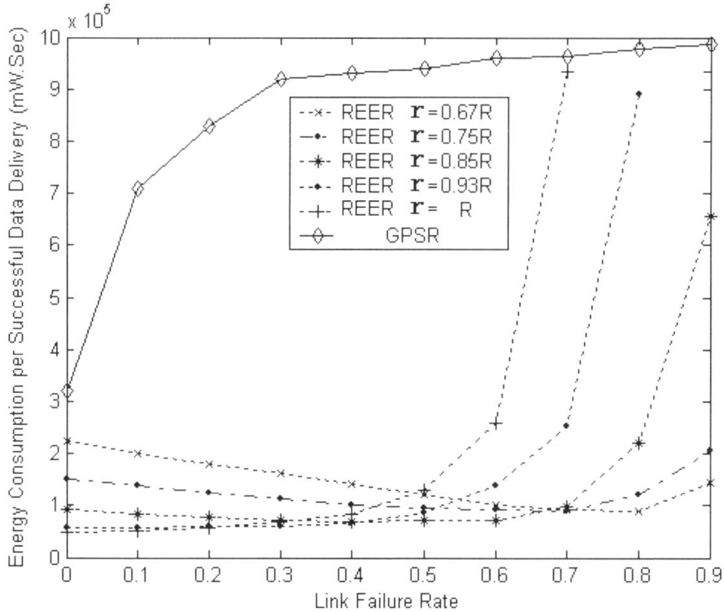

Fig. 7.12. The comparison of e.

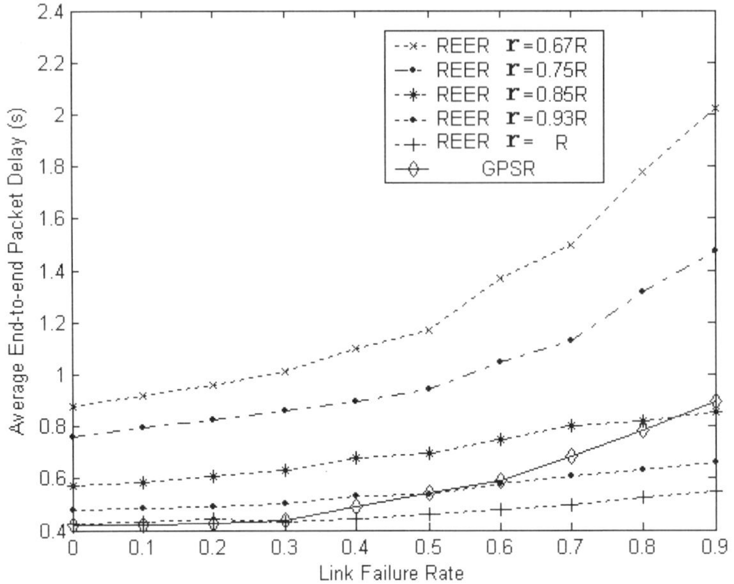

Fig. 7.13. The comparison of T_{ete}.

overcome the link failure, a large f helps to lower e_{reer}. The reason is n_{data} does not change much, while E decreases. Thus, in Fig. 7.12, given r fixed, there is a certain value of f to make e reach its minimum. If f goes beyond that point, the number of *CN*s is insufficient to antagonize the high link failure rate, which causes n_{data} decrease exponentially. Thus, e_{reer} increases fast again.

In Fig. 7.13, the delay of GPSR increases with higher f. The responsibility for this effect lies again in the increasing number of link layer retransmissions. Given r fixed, the delay of REER also increases with higher f. It is because REER performs a backoff process at each hop during data dissemination. In Fig. 7.16, the number of *CN*s is six. When f is low, the *CN* with low t_b is more likely to forward the data packet, which makes hop latency low. As an example in Fig. 7.16(a), *CN1* is selected to forward the data packet. In contrast, *CN4* is selected in Fig. 7.16(b), where the hop latency is equal to $t_{data} + t_b^4 > t_{data} + t_b^1$.

On the other hand, given f fixed, the delay of REER is inversely proportional to r, as shown in Fig. 7.13. It is because that the smaller is r, the higher is the number of *CN*s in a *CF*, the higher T_{max} are needed to differentiate the *CN*s according to Eq. (7.6), the longer backoff time is yielded, and the higher is the delay of REER. Another reason is that the hop count between source and sink increases as r decreases.

In Fig. 7.14, n_{ctrl} of REER is lower than that of GPSR, since REER never uses control message beaconing to repair a route.

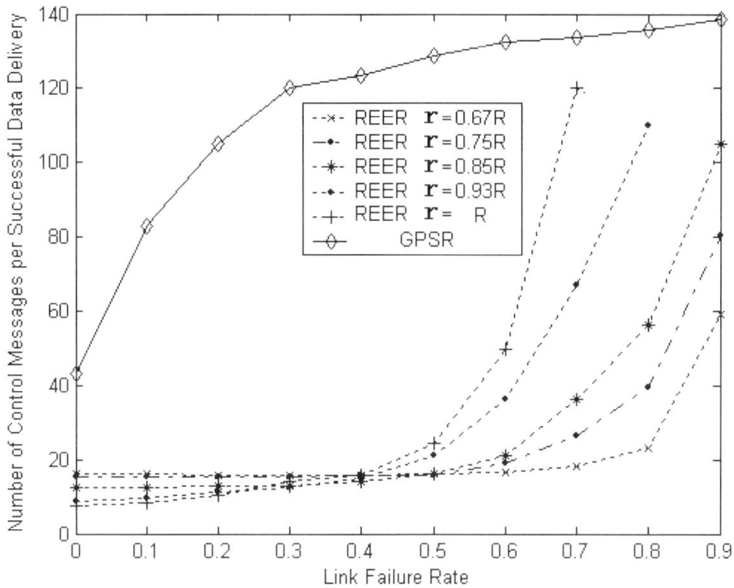

Fig. 7.14. The comparison of n_{ctrl}.

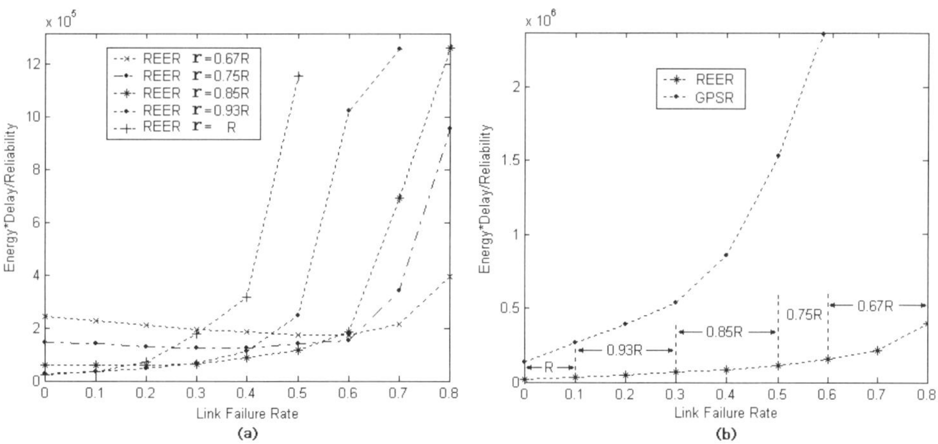

Fig. 7.15. The comparison of η.

Observed in Figs. 7.12–7.14, REER exhibits more consistent and relatively higher reliability, lower energy-consumption than GPSR by compromising end-to-end delay bound. These figures also give hints that REER should choose r adaptively for different f. To find optimal r in terms of η, Fig. 7.15(a) is plotted. Then, in Fig. 7.15(b), the optimal r for variable f are selected. The overall performance gain of REER further improves with the strategy of adaptive r selection.

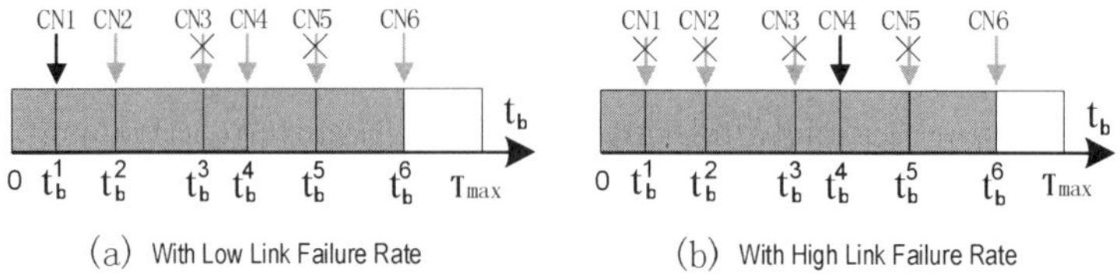

Fig. 7.16. The comparison of backoff time: (a) with low link failure rate; (b) with high link failure rate.

7.6. Conclusion

This chapter proposes REER to achieve both reliability and energy-efficiency simultaneously. In REER, we first select reference nodes (*RN*s) between source and sink. Then, multiple cooperative nodes (*CN*s) are selected for each reference node. The smaller is the distance (r) between two adjacent *RN*s , the larger number of *CN*s will be selected for each flow. r provides a control knob to trade off robustness, energy-efficiency and data delay. In unreliable communication environments, traditional routing protocols may fail to deliver data timely since link/node failures can be found out only after trying multiple transmissions. In REER, each data is relayed by broadcasting at each hop, such that among all the *CN*s at next hop that received the data successfully, only one *CN* will rebroadcast the data.

We have evaluated the REER protocol through both analysis and extensive simulation. According to the simulation results, we observe the following: (1) With the link failure rate increased, r should be set small enough to achieve required reliability but not so small as to incur unnecessary large energy consumption and end-to-end packet delay; (2) REER is unsuitable to perform in low node density environments; (3) in a reliable environment, both GPSR and REER with large r exhibit higher reliability; (4) REER exhibits more consistent and relatively higher reliability, less energy consumption than GPSR in unreliable environments. The extensive simulations also show reliability is achieved by sacrificing the energy-efficiency and delay performance. Thus, the relevant parameters should be selected carefully to achieve reliability with energy-efficiency while minimizing the delay.

A better backoff time function used in data dissemination should help to lower the data latency while not increasing the possibility of simultaneous data broadcasting. To find such a function will be one part of our future work.

References

1. C. Intanagonwiwat, R. Govindan and D. Estrin, Directed diffusion: A scalable and robust communication paradigm for sensor networks, the *Proceedings of the 6th Annual ACM/IEEE MobiCom* (2000).
2. C. Y. Wan and A. T. Campbell and L. Krishnamurthy, Pump-slowly, fetch-quickly (PSFQ): A reliable transport protocol for sensor networks, *IEEE Journal of Selected Areas in Communications*, Vol. 23, pp. 862–872 (2005).

3. F. Stann and J. Heidemann, RMST: Reliable data transport in sensor networks, *Proceedings of the IEEE International Workshop on Sensor Network Protocols and Applications*, pp. 102–112 (2003).
4. D. Ganesan, R. Govindan, S. Shenker and D. Estrin, Highly resilient, energy efficient multipath routing in wireless sensor networks, In *Mobile Computing and Communications Review (MC2R)*, **1**(2), pp. 10–24 (2002).
5. B. Deb, S. Bhatnagar and B. Nath, ReInForM: Reliable information forwarding using multiple paths in sensor networks, *IEEE LCN*, pp. 406–415 (2003).
6. F. Ye, G. Zhong, S. Lu and L. Zhang, GRAdient broadcast: A robust data delivery protocol for large scale sensor networks, accepted by *ACM Wireless Networks (WINET)*, **11**(2), 285–298 (2007).
7. Y. Sankarasubramaniam, O. B. Akan and I. F. Akyildiz, ESRT: Event-to- Sink Reliable Transport in Wireless Sensor Networks, in *ACM MobiHoc*, pp. 177–188 (June 2003).
8. N. Tezcan, E. Cayirci and M. U. Caglayan, End-to-end reliable event transfer in wireless sensor networks, In *IEEE PIMRC'04*, Vol. 2, pp. 989–994 (2004).
9. Y. Yuan, Z. He and M. Chen, Virtual MIMO based cross-layer design for wireless sensor networks, *IEEE Transactions on Vehicular Technology*, **55**(3), 856–864 (2006).
10. I. Stojmenovic, Position-Based Routing in Ad Hoc Networks, *IEEE Comm. Magazine*, **40**(7), 128–134 (2002).
11. P. Bose, P. Morin, I. Stojmenovic and J. Urrutia, Routing with guaranteed delivery in ad hoc wireless networks, *Proc. ACM DIAL 1999*, pp. 48–55, Seattle, USA (1999).
12. B. Karp and H. T. Kung, GPSR: Greedy perimeter stateless routing for wireless networks, *Proc. of ACM MobiCom 2000*, pp. 243–254 (2000).
13. H. Frey and I. Stojmenovic, On delivery guarantees of face and combined greedy-face routing algorithms in ad hoc and sensor networks, *ACM MOBICOM*, pp. 390–401 2006.
14. M. Chen, X. Wang, V. Leung and Y. Yuan, Virtual coordinates based routing in wireless sensor networks, *Sensor Letters*, Vol. 4, pp. 325–330 (2006).
15. L. Zou, M. Lu and Z. Xiong, A distributed algorithm for the dead end problem of location-based routing in sensor networks, *IEEE Trans. Vehicular Technology*, **54**, pp. 1509–1522 (2005).
16. Q. Fang, J. Gao and L. J. Guibas, Locating and bypassing routing holes in sensor networks, *IEEE Infocom*, **23**(1), 2458–2468 (2004).
17. Zakhia G. Abichar and J. M. Chang, CONTI: Constant-Time contention resolution for WLAN access, *LNCS*, Vol. 3462, pp. 358–369 (2005).
18. M. Chen, OPNET network simulation, *Press of Tsinghua University*, China, April 2004, ISBN 7-302-08232-4, 352 pages.
19. http://www.opnet.com.
20. M. Chen, T. Kwon and Y. Choi, Energy-efficient differentiated directed diffusion (EDDD) for real-time traffic in wireless sensor networks, *Elsevier Computer Communications*, Special Issue On Dependable Sensor Network, **29**(2), 231–245 (2006).
21. M. Chen, V. Leung, S. Mao and Y. Yuan, DGR: Directional geographical routing for real-time video communications in wireless sensor networks, *Computer Communications*, **30**(17), 3368–3383 (2007).
22. H. S. Wang and N. Moayeri, Finite-state markov channel — a useful model for radio communication channels, *IEEE Transaction on Vehicular Technology*, **43**(1), 163–171 (1995).

Chapter 8

The Impact of Node Heterogeneity on ZigBee Network Routing

Ling-Jyh Chen and Li-Ping Tung

Institute of Information Science, Academia Sinica, Taiwan

Tony Sun

PacketMotion Inc.

Nia-Chiang Liang

Google Inc.

Based on the IEEE 802.15.4 LR-WPAN standard, the ZigBee standard has been proposed to interconnect simple, low rate, and battery powered wireless devices. The deployment of ZigBee networks is expected to facilitate numerous applications, such as home-appliance networks, home healthcare, medical monitoring, consumer electronics, and environmental sensors. An effective routing scheme in a ZigBee network is particularly important in that it is the key to achieve resource (e.g., bandwidth and energy) efficiency in ZigBee networks. Routing in a ZigBee network is not exactly the same as in a MANET. In particular, while Full Function Devices (FFD) can serve as network coordinators or network routers, Reduced Function Devices (RFD) can only associate and communicate with FFDs in a ZigBee network. Therefore, different from traditional MANET routing algorithms, which only take into account node mobility to figure out a best route to a given destination, node heterogeneity plays an important role in ZigBee network routing. In this chapter, we firstly perform extensive evaluation, using NS-2 simulator, to study the impact of node heterogeneity on ZigBee mesh network routing. The results show that the ZigBee mesh routing algorithm exhibits significant performance difference when the network is highly heterogenous. Then, we study the mesh routing and its support of device mobility with different mobility cases. Under a rich set of preliminary tests, our results indicate that ZigBee device type plays a significant role in determining the routing performance in most mobile scenarios.

8.1. Introduction

With wireless networking technologies permeating into the very fabrics of our working and living environment, simple appliances and numerous traditional wired services can now be wirelessly and efficiently connected. This provides simple yet effective control/monitoring conveniences, while allowing very interesting applications to be developed on top of these wireless gadgets. The ZigBee standard,[1] designed to interconnect simple devices that previously have not been networked, is the latest attempt to address this wireless network vision. In the context of a business environment, this wireless movement can facilitate better automated control/management of facilities and assets. Moreover, there are also many applications for home-appliance networks, as well as in the area of home healthcare, medical monitoring, consumer electronics, and environmental sensors.

ZigBee is a network and application layer specification developed by a multi-vendor consortium called the ZigBee Alliance.[2] Backed by 150+ member companies, the ZigBee standard was ratified in late 2004, and was publicly released for non-commercial use in June of 2005. Various ZigBee compliant product prototypes and application scenarios have already been developed by the industry, yet the performance and the supporting facilities of ZigBee networks have not been thoroughly evaluated. In particular, knowledge of how nodal mobility and nodal diversity (i.e., nodes of different networking capabilities) affects the workings of the ZigBee routing protocols is of significance.

Routing in a ZigBee enabled network is very similar to the one in a Mobile Ad hoc NETwork (MANET). In both cases, maintaining an end-to-end route is challenging since the network topology may change very frequently due to node failures, mobility, and many other factors. Various MANET routing protocols have been proposed in the last few years.[3–9] Among them, Ad hoc On-demand Distance Vector Routing (AODV)[3] and Dynamic Source Routing (DSR)[4] are two of the most popularly deployed schemes. These routing algorithms of MANET aim to figure out the best route, even if the network is highly dynamic, toward a given destination at any time by consuming minimal messages/time overhead. Moreover, every participating node in MANET routing is implicitly assumed to be MANET router capable, and assumed to operate with the same set of functionalities.

However, such general yet implicit assumption in MANET routing does not hold in ZigBee networks. In a ZigBee network, each participating node plays the role as either a Full Function Device (FFD) or a Reduced Function Device (RFD), depending on its function capabilities (e.g., amount of memory, computation capability, energy level, and etc). While FFDs can serve as network coordinators or network routers (thus capable of routing), RFDs can only associate and communicate with FFDs (and are not allowed to participate in network routing). As a result, traditional MANET routing schemes can't be applied to ZigBee networks. It turns out that node heterogeneities must be taken into account in designing an effective routing scheme for ZigBee networks.

In this chapter, we firstly study the impact of network heterogeneity on ZigBee mesh routing. Particularly, we are interested to find out how different mixture of mobile ZigBee routers and mobile ZigBee end devices influences the performance of ZigBee mesh routing. We present a rich set of simulation results illustrating the effect caused by the diversity in node capabilities. Our results reveal that routing performance does degrade when the network is comprised of an increasing number of ZigBee end devices. Moreover, compared to AODV routing results, we do see significant differences in routing performance when network nodes are not assumed to be equally capable. Additionally, we found that the routing performance is closely tied to the ZigBee node type used.

Moreover, we study the mesh routing and its support of device mobility with different mobility cases. Without a doubt, mobility support is important to the proper function of many envisioned ZigBee applications. Since mobility is anticipated and unavoidable, adequate mobility support is important in ensuring ubiquitous connection to/from the mobile devices. Our simulation results reveal that existing ZigBee provisions for mobility is inadequate, and mobility problem was not thoroughly considered by the standard. Furthermore, we found that the current recovery mechanisms are not reliable, or responsive enough in all mobility cases. The situation worsens when there are multiple instances of mobility in the ZigBee network, yet routing performance in ZigBee network is closely tied to the ZigBee node types used.

The rest of this chapter is organized as follows. In Sec. 8.2, we give a brief overview of IEEE 802.15.4 and the ZigBee mesh routing specifications. Section 8.3 presents simulation results, illustrating the behavior of ZigBee mesh routing under different level of nodal diversity both in the moderately and highly mobile ZigBee network. Then, in Sec. 8.4, we show simulation results which study the mobility support of ZigBee mesh routing in several mobility scenarios as well as under different mobility speed. Finally, Sec. 8.5 summarizes the impact of nodal diversity in ZigBee mesh network, the mobility support of mesh routing, and concludes the chapter.

8.2. Overview

8.2.1. *IEEE 802.15.4*

Based on the PHY and MAC layers specified by IEEE 802.15.4 WPAN standard,[10] the ZigBee specification establishes the framework for the Network and Application layers. The protocol stack of ZigBee networks is detailed in Fig. 8.1. Specifically, at the MAC layer, IEEE 802.15.4 controls access to the radio channel using Carrier Sense Multiple Access with Collision Avoidance (CSMA/CA) or the optional slotted CSMA/CA mechanism, as respectively utilize by the beaconless and beaconed modes. At the PHY layer, IEEE 802.15.4 defines a total of 27 channels: 16 channels at a maximum rate of 250 kbps in the ISM 2.4–2.4835 GHz band, 10 channels at 40 kbps in the ISM 902–928 MHz band, and one channel at 20 kbps in the 868.0–868.6 MHz band. Table 8.1 summarizes the high level characteristics of the IEEE 802.15.4 standard.

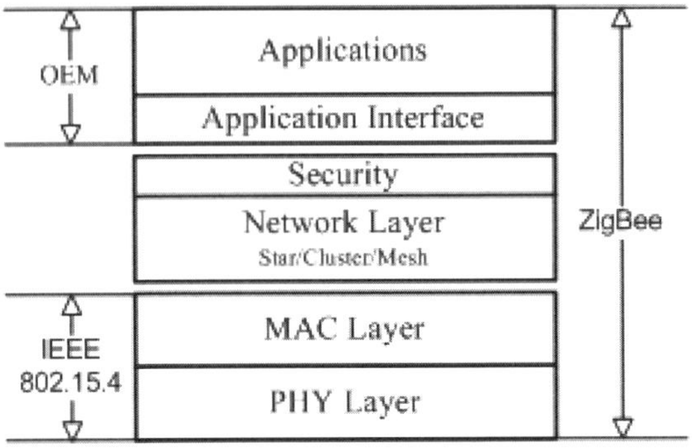

Fig. 8.1. ZigBee protocol stack in relation to IEEE 802.15.4 standard.

Table 8.1. Characteristics of IEEE 802.15.4 standard.

Frequency Band	868–868.6 MHz	1 channel; 20 kbps
	902–928 MHz	10 channels; 40 kbps
	2.4–2.4835 GHz	16 channels; 250 kbps
Channel Access	Slotted/Unslotted CSMA-CA	
Range	10 to 30 meters	
Addressing	Short 16-bit or IEEE 64-bit	

Two device types are specified within the IEEE 802.15.4 framework: full function device (FFD) and reduced function device (RFD). An FFD generally has more responsibilities in that they must maintain routing tables, participate in route discovery and repair, maintain beaconing framework, and handle node joins. Moreover, an FFD has the capability of communicating with any other devices within its transmission range. On the other hand, an RFD simply maintains the minimum amount of knowledge to stay on the network, and it does not participate in routing. RFDs can only associate and communicate with FFDs. FFDs and RFDs can be interconnected to form star or peer-to-peer networks.

8.2.2. *ZigBee mesh routing*

Based on IEEE 802.15.4, the ZigBee Alliance specifies the standards for the network layer and the application layer. More specifically, the ZigBee network layer defines how the network formation is performed and how the network address is assigned to each participating ZigBee node. Note that the assigned network address is the *only* address that is used for routing and data transmission in ZigBee networks. Three device types are defined in ZigBee: ZigBee coordinator, ZigBee routers, and ZigBee end devices. An RFD can only be a ZigBee end device; whereas an FFD can be either a ZigBee coordinator or ZigBee router. The ZigBee coordinator is responsible for starting a new network. ZigBee coordinator and routers are "routing capable", while the ZigBee end devices can't participate in routing and have to rely on their corresponding ZigBee parent routers for that functionality.

Every node in a ZigBee network has two addresses, namely a 16-bit short network address and a 64-bit IEEE extended address. The 16-bit network address is assigned to each node dynamically by its parent coordinator/router upon joining the network. This address is the only address that is used for routing and data transmission. It is analogous to the IP addresses that we use on the Internet; whereas the extended address is similar to the MAC address, which is a unique identification of each device and is mostly fixed at the time the device is manufactured.

There are two addressing schemes (of the 16-bit short network address) allowed in ZigBee mesh networks, namely the static address allocation scheme and the tree address allocation scheme. Both schemes work in similar fashion. In both schemes, the parent nodes assign an address "block" to their child router, which is in turn allocated to their respective decedents. The ZigBee coordinator/router is responsible to maintain the amount of free address spaces left, the address block size, and the address to be assigned next.

Two routing schemes are available in ZigBee networks, namely mesh routing and tree routing. The mesh routing scheme is similar to the Ad hoc On Demand Vector (AODV) routing algorithm,[3] while the tree routing scheme resembles the cluster tree routing algorithm as described in Ref. 11. In this chapter, we will only focus on mesh routing in ZigBee mesh networks. In ZigBee mesh routing, route requests ($RREQ$) are broadcasted on-demand when data is to be transmitted to a destination of an unknown path. Routes are constructed based on the route replies ($RRPL$ from intermediate nodes and destination node), and a route error ($RERR$) message is transmitted to the user when a path can't be found. The route repair mechanism repairs invalid routes when a previous route can not be found. Since only coordinators/routers (FFDs) can actively participate in mesh routing, the end devices (RFDs) have to rely exclusively on their parent nodes to perform mesh routing on their behalves.

The performance of AODV algorithm has been extensively studied (e.g., Refs. 12–14 and etc). Yet, previous evaluation studies are mostly IEEE 802.11 centric and would consider all participating nodes routing capable nodes. However, under the innate properties of IEEE 802.15.4 and ZigBee networks (i.e., the addressing structure and service assumptions), the performance bound of ZigBee mesh routing (which is AODV-like) is thus expected to be different than the ones from previous AODV studies. More specifically, when a node "associates" with a new parent node (when the node attaches to a new parent node in range), a new 16-bit network address will be inherited by the child node, and the routing protocol has to react accordingly in order to keep the routing table updated. Moreover, the fact that the ZigBee mesh routing accommodates different device types (device with unequal routing capacities) distinguishes itself from traditional AODV networks. We will examine the impact of node mobility and heterogeneity in ZigBee mesh networks in the next section, and to the best of our knowledge, this issue has not yet been considered in the literature.

8.3. Evaluation I: Impact of Nodal Diversity on ZigBee Routing

This section presents extensive simulation results that illustrate the impact of nodal diversity on the properties of ZigBee mesh routing and the original AODV routing. In particular, we will compare how the nodal composition of a network affects the workings of ZigBee mesh routing. AODV routing performance is used for baseline comparison on how a typical homogenous network would perform as oppose to a heterogenous network environment. We use the NS-2 simulator with Samsung's IEEE 802.15.4 extension,[15] and wrote our own ZigBee mesh routing schemes according to the ZigBee standard. We will compare the delivery ratio of various ZigBee network configurations, focusing on the impact caused by various node types.

The simulation is set to closely mimic the settings of a household/factory deployment. Nodes are initially aligned in an equally spaced grid before a selected percentage of nodes become mobile. Nodes move within the set topology according to the random waypoint model developed and described in Ref. 16 and all results are averaged across 50 independent trials of the same configuration. We make use of the static addressing scheme described in Sec. 8.2 for mesh routing. The percentage of ZigBee end devices to ZigBee router varies, while the mobile nodes are randomly chosen. Other standard ZigBee network settings apply, and general parameters used is summarized in Table 8.2.

The parameters *nwkMaxDepth*, *nwkMaxChildren* and *nwkMaxRouter* are network values defined by the ZigBee standard, and are set at install time. *nwkMacDepth* denotes the maximum depth of the network from the coordinator, *nwkMaxChildren* is the maximum number of children allowed at each router, and *nwkMaxRouter* specified the maximum number of routers a parent may have as children. Since ZigBee networks were intended to operate at low data rates, our simulation uses CBR flows of 10 Kbps. We use packet delivery ratio as our performance

Table 8.2. General simulation parameters.

Network Size	45 m × 45 m
Number of Nodes	36 nodes
Transmission Range	10 meters
Network Setup Time	30 seconds
Simulation Duration	300 seconds
Number of Concurrent Data Flows	2
Transmission Rate	10 packets/sec
Mobility Model	Random Waypoint
Traffic Type, Packet Size	CBR, 127 bytes
$nwkMaxDepth(L_m)$	5
$nwkMaxChildren(C_m)$	10
$nwkMaxRouter(R_m)$	10

evaluation matrices. Packet delivery ratio is averaged over the number of flows in the network to reflect the mean per-flow delivery ratio.

8.3.1. *Varying heterogeneity in moderately mobile ZigBee network*

This subsection studies the routing performance of ZigBee mesh routing scheme when there are varying amount of ZigBee end devices in the network, focusing on the scenario when only 20% of the network are mobile nodes. AODV routing results are also graphed as a basis for performance comparison although AODV is run on an all router topology (since AODV requires routing capability from all nodes), and does not change to the percentage of ZigBee end devices in the network. 20% of the network nodes are randomly chosen as mobile nodes, all moving at a speed of 1m/s using the random waypoint model. Two general mobility cases were simulated, focusing on the responses of different node types. In the first scenario, we keep the receiver stationary while setting senders to be mobile. In the second scenario, the sender remains stationary while the receiver is mobile. We repeat the same simulations with two node types, ZigBee router and ZigBee end devices. Source and destination are randomly chosen, but all networking settings remain the same for all simulations. We vary the percentage of ZigBee end devices from 0% to 50% in order to observe the response of ZigBee mesh routing to increasing percentages of ZigBee end devices.

Because end devices do not participate in ZigBee mesh routing, when the total number of devices is fixed, increasing the percentage of end devices effectively decreases the number, and hence density, of ZigBee mesh routing capable devices in the network. This forces all devices to have fewer choices in potential end-to-end paths, and thus may end up using paths at lower qualities and/or more susceptible to path breakages. Reflected in Figs. 8.2 and 8.3, all curves of the delivery ratio in

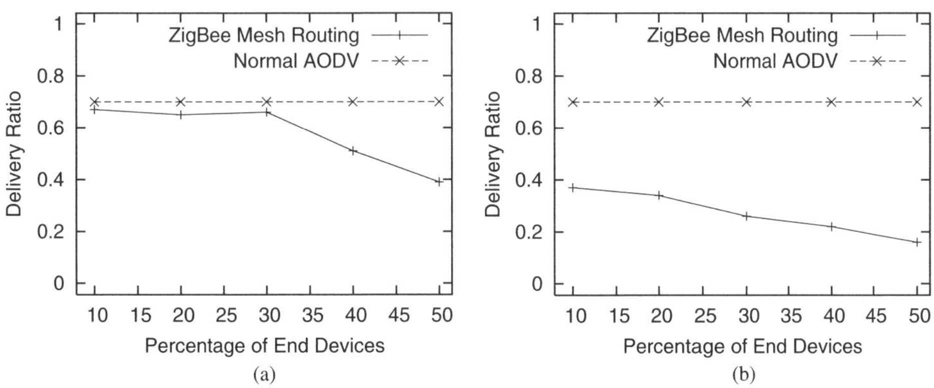

(a) (b)

Fig. 8.2. Packet delivery ratio for network with 20% mobile nodes, ZigBee router and end device acting as mobile sender, sending to a stationary destination. (a) ZigBee router acting as sender and (b) ZigBee end device acting as sender.

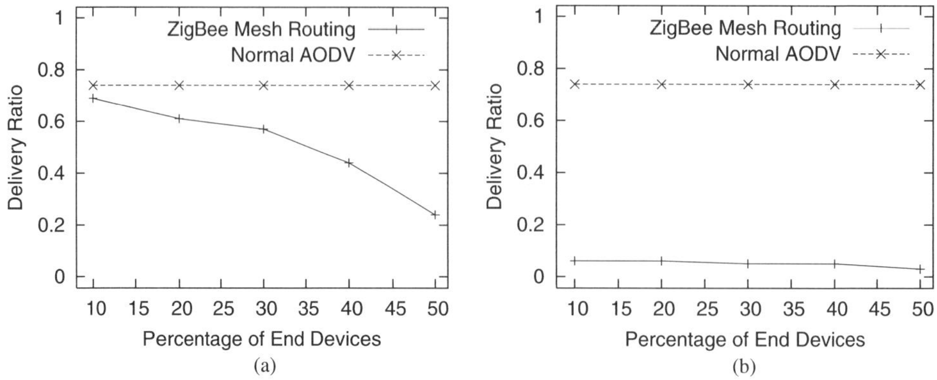

Fig. 8.3. Packet delivery ratio for network with 20% mobile nodes, ZigBee router and end device acting as mobile receiver, receiving from a stationary sender. (a) ZigBee router as receiver and (b) ZigBee end device as receiver.

ZigBee mesh routing share the same trend of going lower as the percentage of end devices grows. However, the AODV performs relatively well under assumption that all nodes are router capable.

Compared with the cases where a ZigBee end device acts as an end host of the path (either sender or receiver), having a router as the end host tends to show a better performance. This is obvious since the router directly participates in the ZigBee mesh routing, while an end device must always associate itself with a router and changes its own address every time it switches to a new router. When a path is broken, the router can usually re-establish the path faster. Note that the delivery ratio in the case where an end device acts as the receiver is particularly low. This is due to the fact that when the end-to-end path becomes broken, the receiver suffers the aforementioned overhead of router reassociation and address acquiring, as in other cases. In the meantime, the sender has to rediscover the receiver, now with a new address, using application layer recovery mechanisms, further degrading the performance. As expected, AODV assumes all devices as routing capable, therefore changing the percentage of end devices has no impact on the data delivery ratio in both sender and receiver cases.

8.3.2. *Varying heterogeneity in highly mobile ZigBee network*

Following the same methodology, we now study the performance of ZigBee mesh routing when more devices are mobile. Specifically, we increase the percentage of mobile nodes from 20% to 50%, all moving at 1m/s under the random waypoint model. All other settings remain the same.

Similar to Figs. 8.2 and 8.3, Figs. 8.4 and 8.5 show that as the percentage of end devices increases, the number of routing capable devices in ZigBee mesh routing decreases, so does the delivery ratio. Moreover, a larger percentage of mobile devices

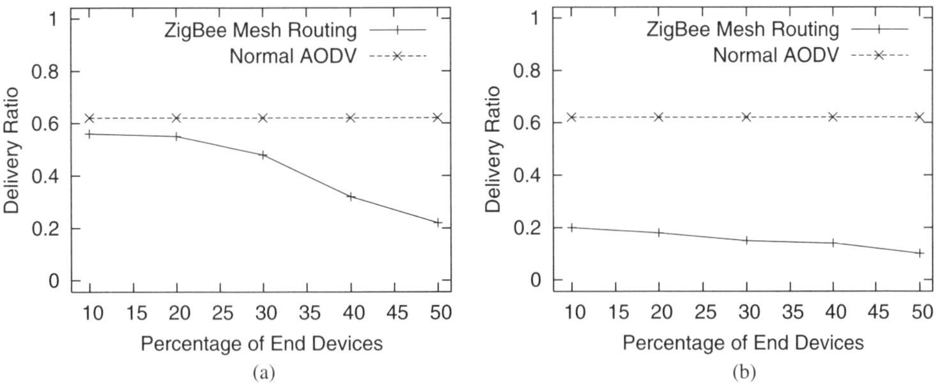

Fig. 8.4. Packet delivery ratio for network with 50% mobile nodes, ZigBee router and end device acting as mobile sender, sending to a stationary destination. (a) ZigBee router acting as sender and (b) ZigBee end device acting as sender.

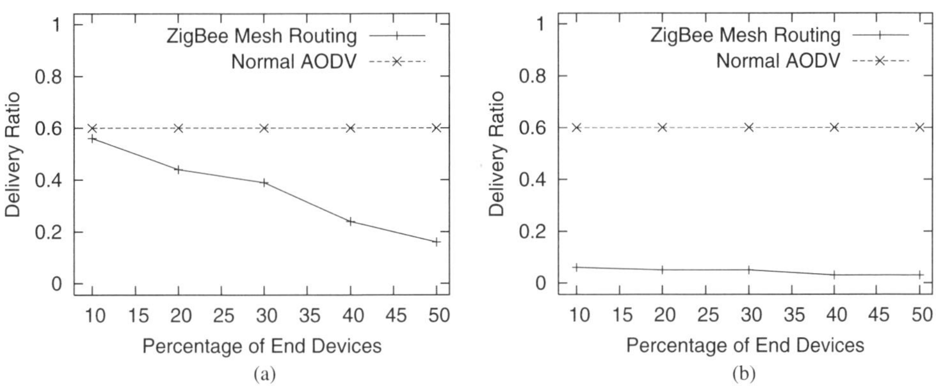

Fig. 8.5. Packet delivery ratio for network with 50% mobile nodes, ZigBee router and end device acting as mobile receiver, receiving from a stationary sender. (a) ZigBee router as receiver and (b) ZigBee end device as receiver.

tends to increase the chance of path breakages, so the absolute delivery ratios are lower, seen in both AODV and ZigBee mesh routing mechanisms.

8.4. Evaluation II: Mobility Support in ZigBee Mesh Routing

In this section, we discussed the ZigBee mesh routing scheme and its support for device mobility. For all of our simulations, the network used in our simulation consists of 70% routers and 30% end devices, which are all randomly chosen. All networking settings and general simulation parameters are the same as described in Sec. 8.3 and Table 8.2. Here, we also use packet delivery ratio and relative routing overhead as our performance evaluation matrices. Packet delivery ratio is averaged over the number of flows in the network to reflect the mean per-flow delivery ratio. On the other hand, routing overhead is denoted by a normalized value of the total overhead of the network with respect to the traffic in the network.

8.4.1. *Scenarios with varying percentage of mobile nodes*

This section studies the performance when there are varying amount of mobile nodes in the network. Mobile nodes move at a speed of 1 m/s randomly. Like the previous simulations, two general mobility cases were simulated. In the first scenario, we keep the receiver stationary while setting senders to be mobile. In the second scenario, the sender remains stationary while the receiver is mobile. We repeat the same simulations with two node types, i.e., ZigBee routers and end devices. Source and destination are randomly chosen, but all networking settings remain the same for all simulations. We vary the percentage of mobile nodes from 0 to 50% to observe the response of mobile nodes in the network.

From the results depicted in Fig. 8.6(a), it is clear that the device type plays a critical role in determining the delivery ratio for mobile senders. ZigBee routers can typically transmit out more data, while ZigBee devices can only send out half of the amount compare to the routers. Furthermore, the ZigBee end devices are more heavily influenced by the percentage of mobile nodes in the network compare to the ZigBee router. This is due to the fact the ZigBee end devices need to associate with a new parent when it moves, the extra association time actually degrades the packet delivery ratio. On the other hand, from Fig. 8.6(b), we see that ZigBee routers actually incurs more routing overhead compare to the end devices. The additional routing overhead is from route repair messages that routers send/receive to repair the route.

As the destination of data streams, all ZigBee receivers encounters some performance degradation (in terms of data delivery ratio) when it is mobile as illustrated in Fig. 8.7(a). Mobile receiver would clearly benefit if it is a ZigBee router. The

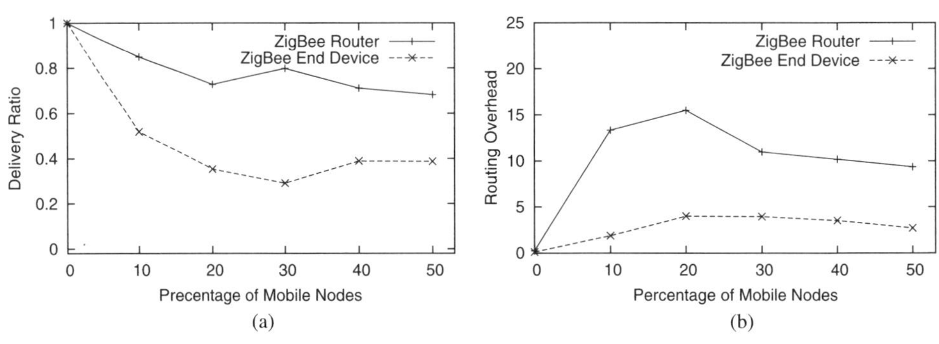

Fig. 8.6. ZigBee router or ZigBee end device as mobile sender, data to stationary destination. (a) Packet delivery ratio and (b) relative routing overhead compared to the actual data throughput.

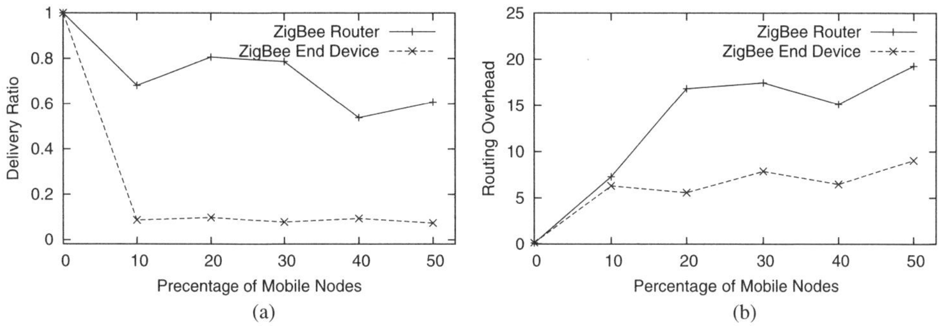

Fig. 8.7. ZigBee router or ZigBee end device as mobile receiver, data from stationary source. (a) Packet delivery ratio and (b) relative routing overhead compared to the actual data throughput.

reason is that ZigBee routers are route capable and the route repair mechanism in mesh routing can repair some of the mobility induced damages in a timely manner. Results also confirm the intuition that mesh routing consumes more overhead when there are more mobile nodes in the network as shown in Fig. 8.7(b).

8.4.2. *Scenarios with mobile nodes of varying speed*

Following the same methodology in the previous subsection, this subsection studies the routing performance when the mobile nodes in the network are moving at varying speeds. The ZigBee network in question consist of 70% routers and 30% end devices, and 20% of the nodes in the network are selected randomly as mobile nodes. Specifically, we evaluate for packet delivery ratio when the nodes are moving from 1 m/s to 5 m/s in 1 m/s increments.

Figure 8.8(a) clearly show that the device type plays a critical role in determining the delivery ratio in mesh routing. ZigBee routers can typically transmit out more data, while ZigBee devices can only send out half of the amount compare to the

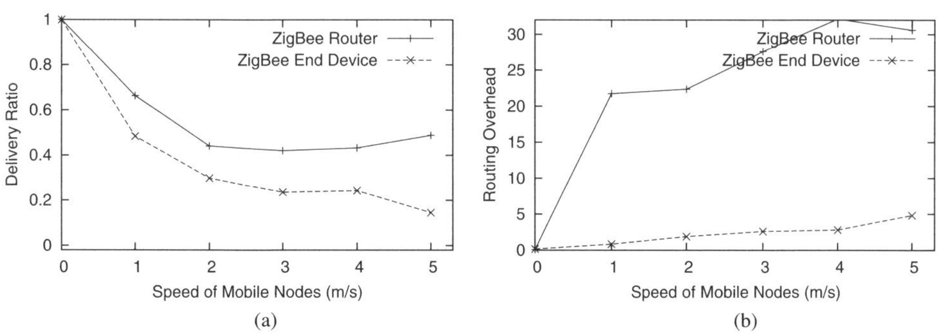

Fig. 8.8. ZigBee router or ZigBee end device as mobile sender, data to stationary destination. (a) Packet delivery ratio and (b) relative routing overhead compared to the actual data throughput.

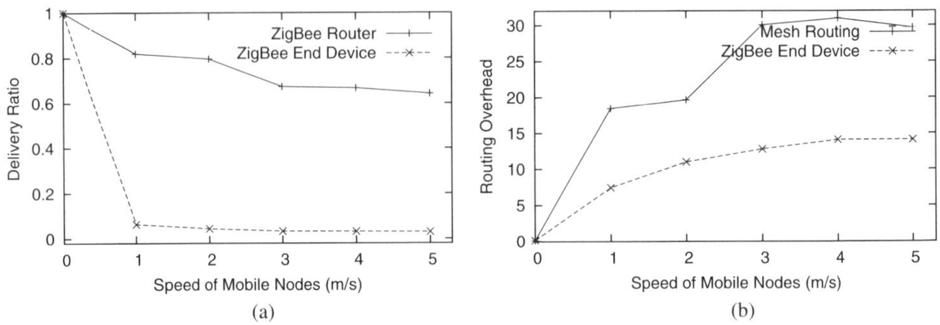

Fig. 8.9. ZigBee router or ZigBee end device as mobile receiver, data from stationary source. (a) Packet delivery ratio and (b) relative routing overhead compared to the actual data throughput.

routers. On the other hand, from Fig. 8.8(b), we see that ZigBee routers actually incurs more routing overhead compare to the end devices. The additional routing overhead is from the various route repair messages that routers send/receive to repair the route. We also see that as node speed increases, the delivery ratio decreases.

As the previous results, Fig. 8.9(a) also shows that the device type plays a critical role in determining the delivery ratio in mesh routing. In addition, ZigBee receivers tend to encounter more severe performance degradation when it is traveling at higher speeds. As depicted in Fig. 8.9(a), ZigBee router as the mobile receiver exhibited more resiliency against high node speeds, even though it consumes more overhead than ZigBee end device as the mobile receiver as illustrated in Fig. 8.9(b). ZigBee router typically suffers less packet losses under mobile scenarios. This behavior is closely related to the fact that ZigBee routers are routing capable, while the ZigBee end devices are not.

8.5. Conclusions

Routing in a ZigBee network is not exactly the same as in a MANET. In particular, while Full Function Devices (FFD) can serve as network coordinators or network routers, Reduced Function Devices (RFD) can only associate and communicate with FFDs in a ZigBee network. Therefore, different from traditional MANET routing algorithms, which only take into account node mobility to figure out a best route to a given destination, node heterogeneity plays an important role in ZigBee network routing.

In this chapter, we firstly study the impact of network heterogeneity on ZigBee mesh routing. Particularly, we are interested to find out how different mixtures of mobile ZigBee routers and mobile ZigBee end devices influence the performance of ZigBee mesh routing. We performed extensive evaluation using NS-2 simulator, with our own ZigBee implementation. The results indicate that the ZigBee mesh routing algorithm exhibits significant performance difference when the network is highly heterogenous. Routing performance in ZigBee network does degrade when the network comprises of an increasing number of ZigBee end devices. Moreover, the delivery ratio worsens when there are more instances of mobility in the network (in highly mobile scenarios). Furthermore, comparing to AODV routing results, we do see significant difference in routing performance when network nodes are not assumed to be equally capable. We also reveal that the ZigBee end devices tend to perform worse than ZigBee routers in both sending and receiving packets, since the end devices incur much overhead in associating with new parents when there is network mobility. On the other hand, ZigBee routers typically suffer less packet loss when there are intensive amounts of mobility in the ZigBee network, yet the additional service overhead of ZigBee (such as association with children devices) still degrades the performance of ZigBee routers in almost all scenarios.

In addition, we study the mesh routing and its support of device mobility with different mobility cases. Our evaluation results indicate that ZigBee end devices experiences detrimental packet losses in almost all mobility scenarios. This situation worsens under multiple instances of mobility, and when mobile nodes travel at higher speeds. Yet, ZigBee router typically suffers less packet losses under mobile scenarios. This behavior is closely related to the fact that ZigBee router are routing capable, while the ZigBee end devices are not. We also realized that the current recovery mechanism is inadequate in accommodating multiple instance or rapid mobility. Additional design work should be proposed to resolve the various problems pointed out in this chapter.

References

1. Z. Alliance, Zigbee specification v1.0 (June 2005).
2. Z. Alliance, Zigbee alliance. http://www.zigbee.org/.
3. C. Perkins and E. Royer, Ad hoc on-demand distance vector routing, *2nd IEEE Workshop on Mobile Computing Systems and Applications*, 90–100 (1999).
4. D. B. Johnson and D. A. Maltz, *Dynamic Source Routing in Ad Hoc Wireless Networks*, eds. Homasz Imielinski and H. Korth, *Mobile Computing*, **353**(5), 153–181. Kluwer Academic Publishers (1996).
5. P. Jacquet, P. Muhlethaler, A. Qayyum, A. Laouiti, L. Viennot and T. Clausen, Optimized link state routing protocol (olsr). RFC 3626 (October 2003).
6. I. Chakeres, E. Belding-Royer and C. Perkins, Dynamic manet on-demand routing protocol (dymo), Internet Draft, draft-ietf-manet-dymo-03.txt (October 2005).
7. V. Park and S. Corson, Temporally-ordered routing algorithm (tora) version 1, Internet Draft, draft-ietf-manet-tora-spec-03.txt (June 2001).
8. Z. J. Haas, M. R. Pearlman and P. Samar, The zone routing protocol (zrp) for ad hoc networks, Internet Draft, draft-ietf-manet-zone-zrp-04.txt (July 2002).
9. B. N. Karp and H. T. Kung, Gpsr: Greedy perimeter stateless routing for wireless networks, *ACM Mobicom*, 243–254 (August 2000).
10. I. 802.15.4. IEEE 802.15.4: Mac and phy specifications for lr-wpans. http://www.ieee802.org/15/pub/TG4.html (2003).

11. A. A. O. A. L. Hester and Y. Huang, Neurfon netform: A self-organizing wireless sensor network, *11th IEEE ICCCN Conference* (October 2002).
12. X. Hong, K. Xu and M. Gerla, Scalable routing protocols for mobile ad hoc networks, *IEEE Network Magazine*, 11–21 (July–August 2002).
13. C. E. P. Samir R. Das and E. M. Royer, Performance comparison of two on-demand routing protocols for ad hoc networks, *IEEE Conference on Computer Communications (INFOCOM)* (March 2000).
14. E. M. Royer and C. E. Perkins. An implementation study of the aodv routing protocol, *IEEE Wireless Communications and Networking Conference*, (2000).
15. J. Zheng and M. J. Lee, *A Comprehensive Preformance Study of IEEE 802.15.4*, *IEEE Press Book* (2004).
16. J.-Y. L. B. Santashil PalChaudhuri and M. Vojnovic, Perfect simulations for random trip mobility models. *38th Annual Simulation Symposium* (April 2005).

Chapter 9

ZigBee Wireless Sensor Network and Its Network Formation Problem

Lun-Wu Yeh*, Meng-Shiuan Pan† and Yu-Chee Tseng‡

Department of Computer Science
National Chiao Tung University, Hsin-Chu, 30010, Taiwan
**lwyeh@cs.nctu.edu.tw*
†mspan@cs.nctu.edu.tw
‡yctseng@cs.nctu.edu.tw

ZigBee is a communication standard which is considered to be suitable for low-rate and low-power wireless sensor networks. When forming a ZigBee network, a device is said to join a network successfully if it can obtain a network address from a parent device. The parent device can locally decide addresses for its child devices by the ZigBee address assignment scheme. The assignment scheme is easy to implement, but the network address utilization may be low. In another words, some devices can not join the network. This chapter describes the ZigBee network formation problem and introduces a solution.

9.1. Introduction

The recent progress of wireless communication and embedded micro-sensing MEMS technologies has made wireless sensor networks (WSNs) more attractive. A WSN normally consists of many inexpensive wireless nodes, each capable of collecting, processing, and storing environmental information, and communicating with neighboring nodes. Many applications of WSNs have been developed, such as emergency guiding,[1,2] smart living space,[3,4] and environmental monitoring.[5,6]

Recently, many WSN platforms have been developed, such as MICAz, MICA2,[7] Tmote,[8] and Dust Network.[9] In order to allow different systems to communicate with each other, standards are needed. The ZigBee/IEEE 802.15.4 protocols have been proposed for the purpose. The ZigBee/IEEE 802.15.4 standards are developed for low-cost, low-power, low-rate, and scalable wireless networking. The IEEE 802.15.4 is defined by IEEE 802.15 LR-WPAN (Low Rate Wireless Personal Area Network) Task Group 4. It defines the data and physical layers. The upper layers including network, security, and application framework are defined by the ZigBee Alliance.[10] These standards resolve the interoperability issues from the physical

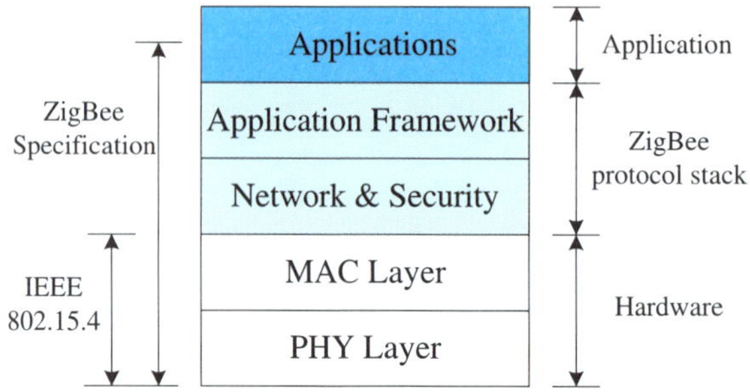

Fig. 9.1. The protocol stack of ZigBee/IEEE 802.15.4.

layer to the application layer. Figure 9.1 shows the relationship of ZigBee/IEEE 802.15.4.

The ZigBee standard has evolved since the first released version in 2004. The ZigBee Alliance releases the ZigBee 1.0[11] in December 2004. After several comments and modifications from some manufacturers, ZigBee alliance releases ZigBee 1.1[12] in December 2006. According to several product deployments and trial experiments, the newest version, announced in early 2007, is called ZigBee Pro.[13] The evolvement of ZigBee standard is toward the goal of providing the consumers with ultimate flexibility, mobility, and ease of use by building wireless intelligence and capabilities into everyday devices. Several companies, such as Chipcon,[14] Ember,[15] and Jennic,[16] have developed their ZigBee protocol stacks. These companies provide a complete system-on-chip solutions for ZigBee/IEEE 802.15.4 for sensor networking applications.

As shown in Fig. 9.2, ZigBee supports three kinds of networks, namely star, tree, and mesh networks. A *ZigBee coordinator* is responsible for initializing, maintaining,

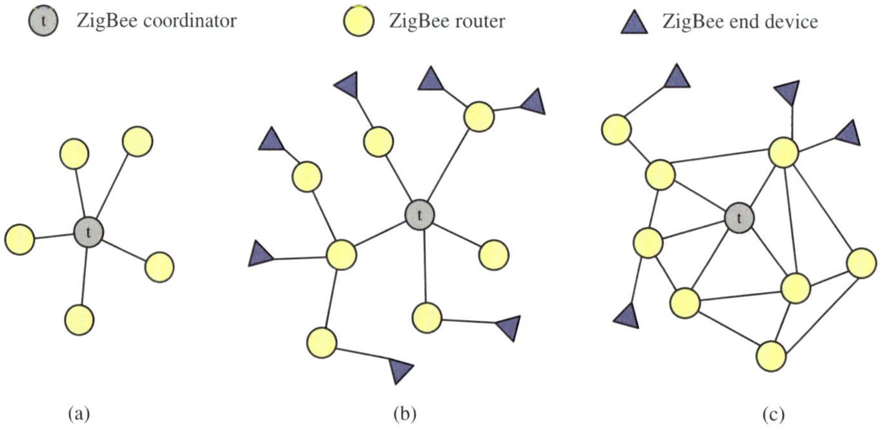

Fig. 9.2. ZigBee network topologies: (a) star, (b) tree, and (c) mesh.

and controlling the network. A star network has a coordinator with devices directly connecting to the coordinator. For tree and mesh networks, devices can communicate with each other in a multihop fashion. The network is formed by one ZigBee coordinator and multiple *ZigBee routers*. A device can join a network as an *end devices* by the associating with the ZigBee coordinator or a ZigBee router.

ZigBee defines a distributed address assignment mechanism. A device is said to join a network successfully if it can obtain a network address from the coordinator or a router. Before forming a network, the coordinator determines the maximum number of children of a router (Cm), the maximum number of child routers of a router (Rm), and the depth of the network (Lm). Note that a child of a router can be a router or an end device, so $Cm \geq Rm$. ZigBee specifies a distributed address assignment using parameters Cm, Rm, and Lm to calculate nodes' network addresses. While these parameters facilitate address assignment, they may sometimes prohibit a node from joining a network. A node is called an *orphan node* when it can not associate with the network but there are still unused address spaces remaining. This situation is called the *orphan problem*. For example, in Fig. 9.3(a), the router-capable device A has two potential parents B and C. But, router A cannot associate to router B or C because B and C have reached their maximum capacity of $Cm = 2$ children. So, A becomes an orphan node. Figure 9.3(b)

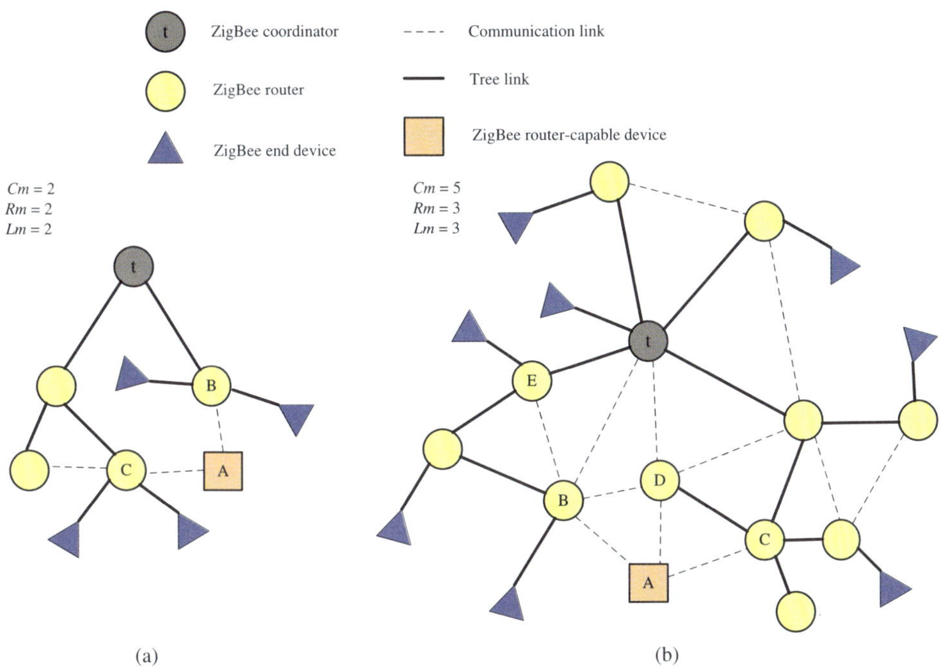

Fig. 9.3. The example of orphan problem in ZigBee networks.

shows a more complicated example. The router-capable device A has three potential parents B, C, and D. Router B and D cannot accept A as their child because they have reached the maximum depth of $Lm = 3$. Router C also cannot accept A as its child because C has reached its maximum capacity of $Rm = 3$ children routers. Hence, A becomes an orphan node. However, if routers can connect their children intelligently, the orphan problem can be relieved. In Fig. 9.3(b), if router B is connected to router E, then router B has remaining capacity to accept A. Then, every node can join to the network. Figure 9.3 are small-scale example. In large-scale networks, the orphan problem could be more serious. The new version ZigBee standard, ZigBee Pro, proposes a stochastic mechanism to avoid the orphan problem. However, the stochastic mechanism needs to address a new problem, the duplicate address detection problem.

In the rest of this chapter, we will review the network formation procedure of ZigBee 1.0 in Sec. 9.2. Section 9.3 discusses the orphan problem. Section 9.4 introduces a solution of the orphan problem. Finally, Sec. 9.5 concludes this chapter.

9.2. ZigBee Network Formation

According to ZigBee/IEEE 802.15.4 standards,[11,17] a ZigBee network is formed by the following procedures. A network should start from a PAN coordinator. Devices that are coordinator-capable and do not currently join a network can be a candidate of a ZigBee coordinator. A device that desires to be a coordinator will scan all channels to find a suitable one. After selecting a channel, this device broadcasts a beacon containing a PAN identifier to initialize a PAN. Every coordinator-capable which do not join to a network can be a PAN coordinator. Hence, several different PANs can coexist at the same time.

Devices can join a PAN by performing the association procedures and specifying its role, as a ZigBee router or a ZigBee end device. A device should first scan channels to find a list of available PANs. After scanning all channels, the device can choose a suitable one from the list of available PANs to join. By listening the beacon broadcast by a PAN coordinator or coordinator, a device can send association request to the beacon sender. If the device hears multiple beacons, it chooses the beacon sender with the smallest hop count to the coordinator. On reception of the association request, the beacon sender will reply an acknowledgment to the device. Note that the acknowledgment to an association request does not mean that the device has associated with the beacon sender successfully. The coordinator will determine whether its current resources are sufficient to accept the device. The device has to wait for a decision from the coordinator. If current resources of coordinator are sufficient, the coordinator will allocate a 16-bit short address to the device. The association response is sent to the device by appending the device's address in beacon frames to indicate that the association result is successful. On receiving the beacon frame, the device sends a data request to the coordinator to

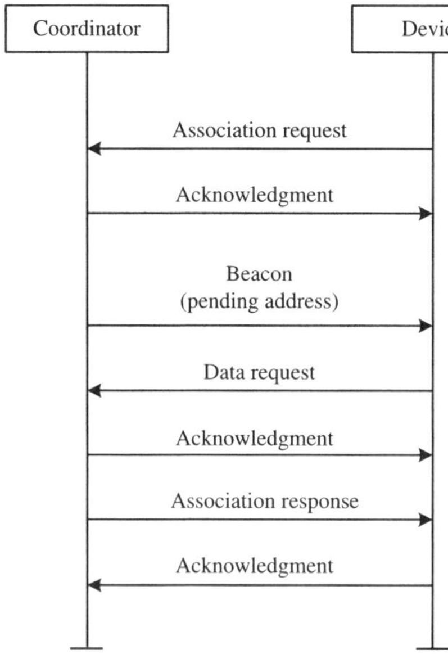

Fig. 9.4. The association procedure in IEEE 802.15.4.

retrieve the association results. Then, the coordinator sends an acknowledgment following by a association response. Finally, the device sends an acknowledgment to confirm its receipt. This short address received from the coordinator is the network address of the device. Figure 9.4 shows the steps of the association procedure.

In ZigBee, network addresses are assigned to devices by a distributed address assignment scheme. The coordinator determines Cm, Rm, and Lm. The coordinator and each router can have at most Rm child routers and at least $Cm - Rm$ child end devices. Devices' addresses are assigned in a top-down manner. For the coordinator, the whole address space is logically partitioned into $Rm + 1$ blocks. The first Rm blocks are to be assigned to the coordinator's child routers and the last block is reserved for the coordinator's own child end devices. From Cm, Rm, and Lm, each node computes a parameter called $Cskip$ to derive the starting addresses of its children's address pools. The $Cskip$ for the coordinator or a router in depth d is defined as:

$$Cskip(d) = \begin{cases} 1 + Cm \times (Lm - d - 1), & \text{if } Rm = 1, \quad (9.1a) \\ \dfrac{1 + Cm - Rm - Cm \times Rm^{Lm-d-1}}{1 - Rm}, & \text{otherwise.} \quad (9.1b) \end{cases}$$

The coordinator is said to be at depth 0, and a node is at depth $d + 1$ if its parent is at depth d. The subtree at depth $d + 1$ will contain no more than $Cskip(d)$ nodes. To further understand Eq. (9.1b), consider a node x at depth d and its child y. The maximum number of children of node y is Cm, of which no more than Rm are routers. So, y has at most $Cm \times Rm$ grandchildren and $Cm \times Rm^2$ grand grandchildren. Therefore, the size of the subtree rooted at y is bounded by

$$Cskip(d) = 1 + Cm + Cm \times Rm + Cm \times Rm^2 + \cdots + Cm \times Rm^{Lm-d-2}. \tag{9.2}$$

Since the depth of subtree rooted at y is at most $Lm - d - 1$, we can derive that

$$\begin{aligned} \text{Eq. (9.2)} &= 1 + Cm \times (1 + Rm + Rm^2 + \cdots + Rm^{Lm-d-2}) \\ &= 1 + Cm \times (1 - Rm^{Lm-d-1})/(1 - Rm) \\ &= \text{Eq. (9.1b)}. \end{aligned}$$

Address assignment begins from the ZigBee coordinator by assigning address 0 to itself. If a parent node at depth d has an address A_{parent}, the nth child router is assigned to address $A_{parent} + (n-1) \times Cskip(d) + 1$ and nth child end device is assigned to address $A_{parent} + Rm \times Cskip(d) + n$.

Figure 9.5 shows a small example, assuming that the whole address space is 21. The address of coordinator t is 0. By Eq. (9.1b) the $Cskip$ of t is $(1 + 5 - 3 - 5 \times$

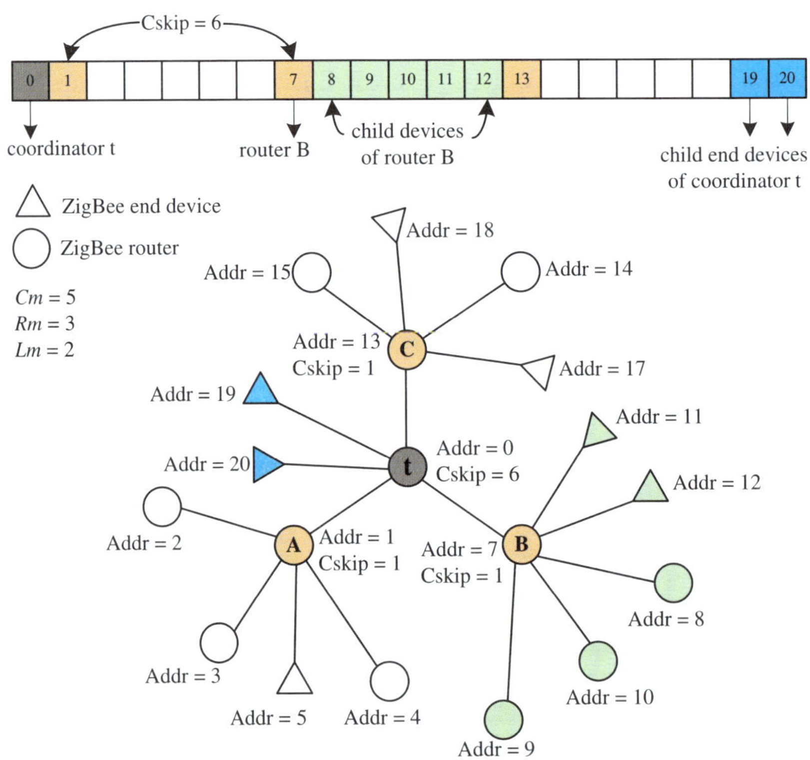

Fig. 9.5. An small-scale ZigBee address assignment example.

$3^{2-0-1})/(1-3) = 6$. So the reserved address spaces for t's three child routers is 6. Router A, B, and C, will be assigned to address 1, 7, and 13, respectively. The last two addresses, 19 and 20, are allocated to t's two child end devices. The address space for router B's child nodes are from 8 to 12.

Assuming a full-scale address space, Fig. 9.6 shows an example with $Cm = 6$, $Rm = 4$, and $Lm = 3$. In Fig. 9.6(a), the depth and address of the coordinator t are both 0. By Eq. (9.1b), the $Cskip$ of the coordinator is $(1+6-4-6\times 4^{3-0-1})/(1-4) = -93/-3 = 31$. So child routers of the t will receive addresses of $0+(1-1)\times 31+1 = 1$, $0+(2-1)\times 31+1 = 32$, and $0+(3-1)\times 31+1 = 63$. The two child end devices are assigned to address $0+4\times 31+1 = 125$ and $0+4\times 31+2 = 126$. Fig. 9.6(b) shows the address assignment and parameters of t's children. The $Cskip$

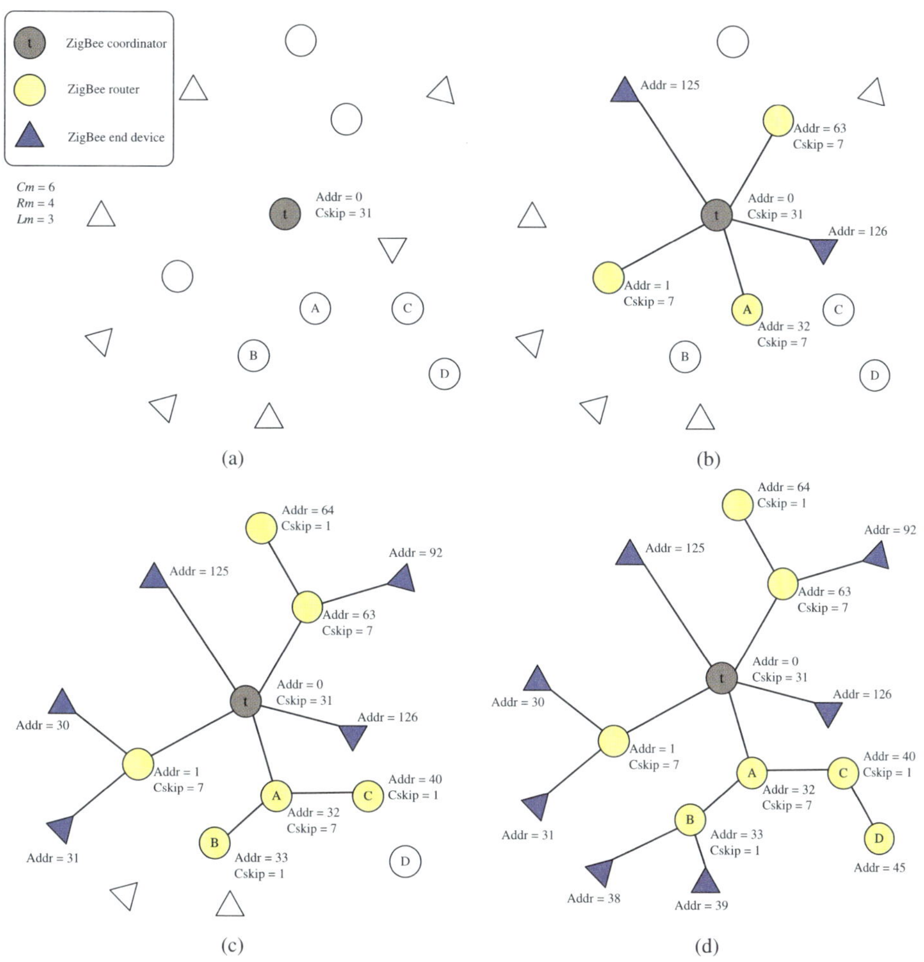

Fig. 9.6. A full-scale ZigBee address assignment example.

value of nodes of depth $d = 1$ is $(1 + 6 - 4 - 6 \times 4^{3-1-1})/(1 - 4) = -21/-3 = 7$. Fig. 9.6(c) shows the addresses of nodes of depth $d = 2$. Fig. 9.6(d) shows the final result of the assignment. Note that the maximum network address capacity is $2^{16} = 65536$. So the coordinator can not arbitrarily choose its Cm, Rm, and Lm.

9.3. The Orphan Problem

By the above formation rules, some devices may not be able to join the network even if there are remaining address spaces. The earlier Fig. 9.3(b) already shows a small-scale example. In large-scale network, we need a systematical solution to reduce the number of orphan nodes. For example, if we set $Cm = Rm$, a router at depth d serving as a leaf node implies a loss of $(1 - Rm^{Lm-d+1})/(1 - Rm)$ address spaces. Therefore, how to avoid this situation is a critical issue.

Given a sensor network, the orphan problem can be divided into two subproblems, the *Bounded-Degree-and-Depth Tree Formation* (*BDDTF*) problem and the *End Devices Maximum Matching* (*EDMM*) problem. The first subproblem only considers the router-capable devices in the sensor network. The network can be modeled as a graph $G_r = (V_r, E_r)$, where V_r consists of all router-capable devices and the coordinator t and E_r contains all symmetric communication links between nodes in V_r. Given parameters Cm, Rm, and Lm such that $Cm \geq Rm$, the goal of BDDTF problem is to assign the parent-child relationships to nodes such that as many nodes in V_r can join the network as possible. The objective is to construct a tree T rooted at t from the graph G_r such that T can satisfy the ZigBee tree definition in terms of the out-degree of each node. The *Degree-Constrained Spanning Tree* (*DCST*) problem can be reduced to a special case of the BDDTF problem. It has been proved that the DCST problem is a NP-complete problem.[18] Hence, the BDDTF problem is also a NP-complete problem. The details of the proof can be found in the work.[19]

After connecting routers, the backbone network is already constructed. Then, the second EDMM subproblem will connect non-router-capable devices to the tree T constructed earlier such that the ZigBee definition is followed. The goal is to connect as many end devices to the backbone as possible. According to Ref. 18 the EDMM problem can be translated to a maximum matching problem in a bipartite graph as follows.

From tree T, we can construct a graph $G_d = (\{\hat{V}_r \cup V_e\}, E_d)$, where $\hat{V}_r$ contains all routers excluding the ones at depth Lm, V_e contains all end devices, and E_d contains all symmetric communication links between $\hat{V}_r$ and V_e. For example, Fig. 9.7(a) shows the original tree T and Fig. 9.7(b) shows the corresponding graph G_d. Note that three routers at depth 2 are not included in G_d because they can not accept more children. Next, we will translate graph G_d into a bipartite graph $G_b = (\{\hat{V}_{br} \cup V_{be}\}, E_{bd})$.

(1) Depending on its current connections, a vertex $v \in \hat{V}_r$ may accept $C_v \geq (Cm - Rm)$ or even more end devices. The latter happens when a router has not

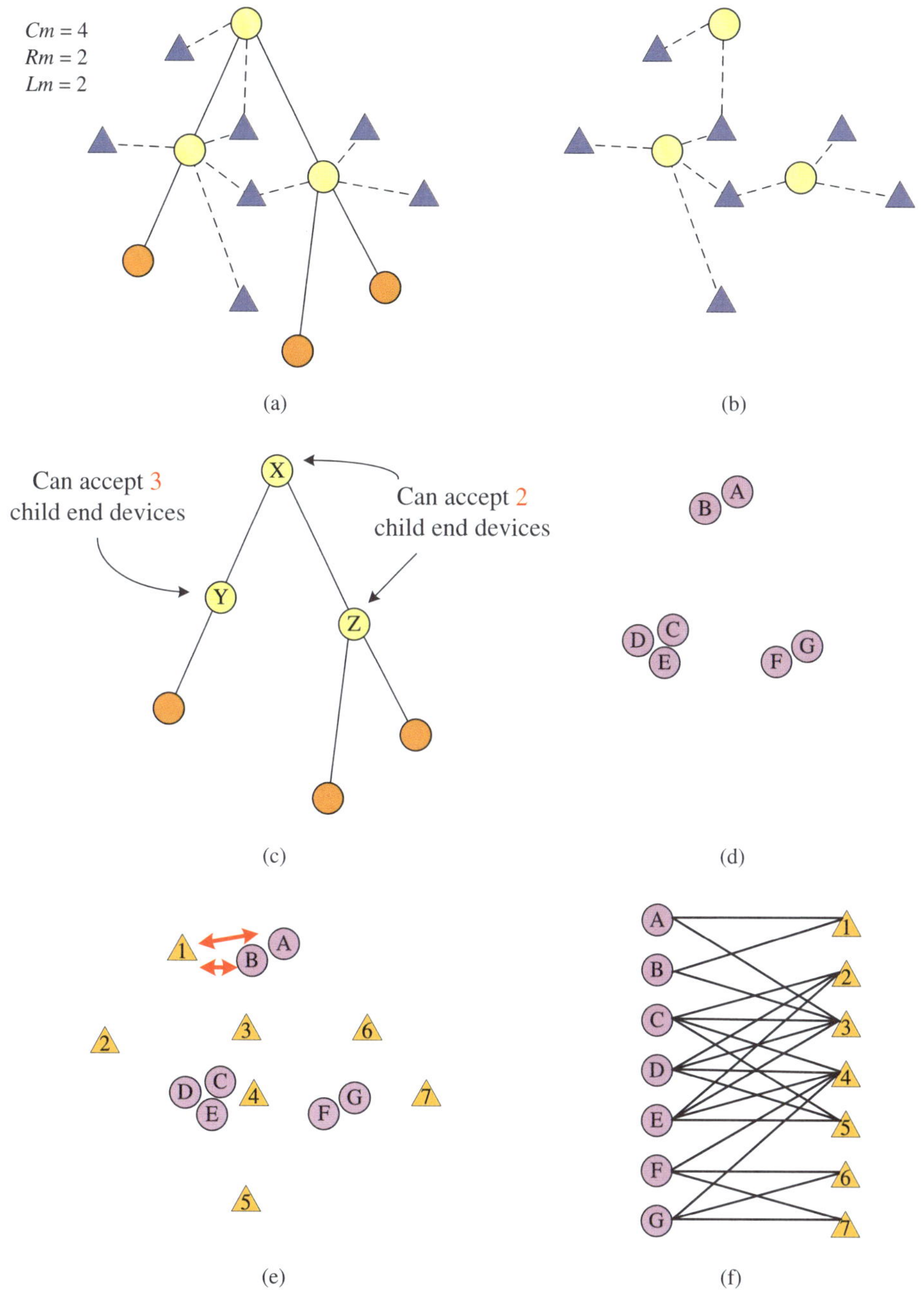

Fig. 9.7. (a) The original tree T, (b) the graph $G_d = (\{\hat{V}_r \cup V_e\}, E_d)$, (c) the tree T excluding end devices, (d) the graph $\hat{V}_{br}$, (e) the graph $\hat{V}_{br} \cup V_{be}$ and (f) the final result of the graph $G_b = (\{\hat{V}_{br} \cup V_{be}\}, E_{bd})$.

consumed all its capacity on child routers. For example, in Fig. 9.7(c), routers X, Y, and Z can accept 2, 3, and 2 more child end devices, respectively. Therefore, we generate 2, 3, and 2 vertices for nodes X, Y, and Z, respectively, and put these new nodes in $\hat{V}_{br}$. Figure 9.7(d) shows the vertex set $\hat{V}_{br}$.

(2) From each vertex $u \in V_e$, generate a vertex u in V_{be}. Figure 9.7(e) shows the vertex set $\hat{V}_{br} \cup V_{be}$, where A and B are generated from X, C, D, and E are generated from Y, and F and G are generated from Z.

(3) From each edge (v, u) in E_d, where $v \in \hat{V}_{br}$ and $u \in V_{be}$, connect each of the vertices corresponding to v with the vertex u. These edges form the set E_{bd}. For example, in Fig. 9.7(e), vertices A and B each has an edge to vertex 1.

$G_b = (\{\hat{V}_{br} \cup V_{be}\}, E_{bd})$ is a bipartite graph with edges connecting vertices in $\hat{V}_{br}$ and vertices in V_{be}. Figure 9.7(f) shows the final result of the above example. Since each vertex in $\hat{V}_r$ is connected to at most one vertex in V_e, this translates the EDMM problem to the maximum matching problem.

9.4. A Solution to the Orphan Problem

As mentioned above, the orphan problem can be divided into two subproblems. Since the first BDDTF problem is a NP-complete problem, we will present a centralized heuristic algorithm to solve it. The second EDMM problem can be solved by any algorithm for the maximum matching problem.

9.4.1. *Span-and-Prune*

Span-and-Prune is a centralized algorithm to solve the BDDTF problem. In this algorithm, BFS trees will be repeatedly generated from the network. Some nodes will be truncated from each tree if the tree is not conformed to the ZigBee definition. The truncation is done based on nodes' *association priorities* in the tree.

Given a BFS tree T in network, the association priorities of nodes are defined as below:

- A node x has a higher priority than another node y if the subtree rooted at x in T has more nodes than the subtree rooted at y.
- If the subtrees rooted at nodes x and y have the same number of nodes, the one with less potential parents has a higher priority. A node regards a neighbor as a potential parent if this neighbor has a smaller hop count distance to the root in T than itself.

The above definitions are based on the considerations of address space utilization. The first rule is so defined because node x may have a better utilization. The second rule is so defined because a node with less potential parents may encounter difficulty to attach to the network. Figure 9.8 shows an example. If $Rm = 3$, the coordinator t will choose nodes A, C, and D as its child routers because they have larger subtrees.

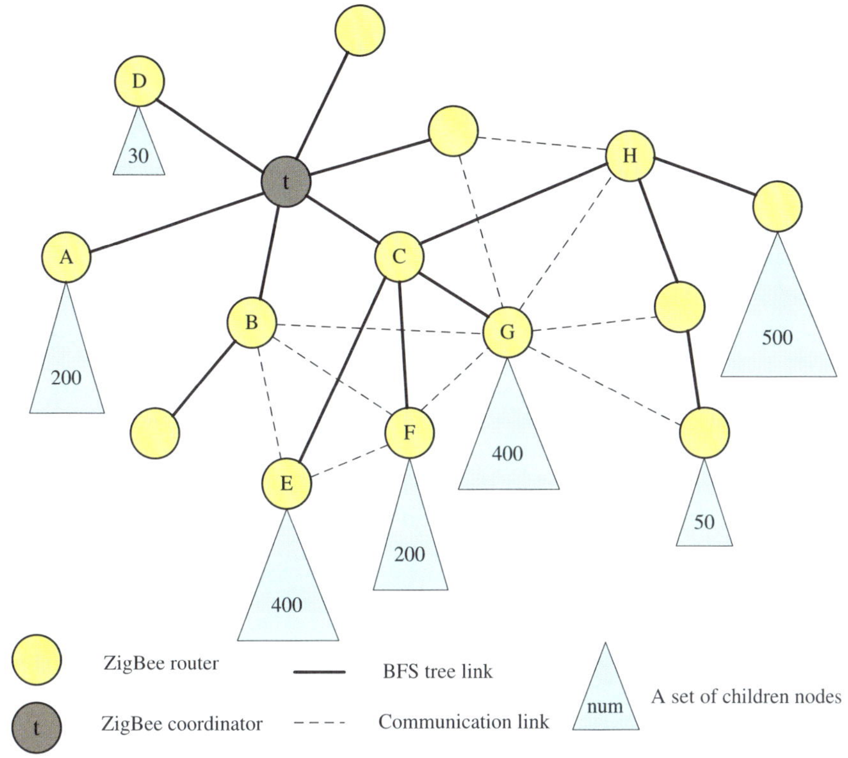

Fig. 9.8. An example of priority assignment.

Similarly, router C will choose E, G, and H as its child routers. However, if $Rm = 2$, the coordinator t will choose A and C as its child routers. Further, router C will choose E and H as its child routers. Node that G is not selected because it has more potential parents than E and thus has a higher probability to be connected in later stages of the formation.

Given a graph $G_r = (V_r, E_r)$, the goal of Span-and-Prune algorithm is to find a tree $T = (V_T, E_T)$ from G_r conforming to the ZigBee tree definition. The algorithm consists of a sequence of iterations. Initially, T contains only the coordinator t. Then in each iteration, there are two phases: *Span* and *Prune*. In the Span phase, the algorithm picks a node in T, say x, and span from x a subtree T' to include as many nodes not yet in T as possible. Then, the algorithm attaches T' to T to form a larger tree. However, the new tree may not satisfy the ZigBee definition. So in the Prune phase, some of the newly added nodes in T' may be trimmed. The resulting tree is then passed to the next iteration for another Span and Prune phases. This is repeated until no more nodes can be added. Each node in the network will be spanned at most once. To keep track of the nodes yet to be spanned, a queue Q will be maintained. The details of the algorithm is presented below.

(1) Initially, let queue Q contains only one node t. Let the depth of t to zero. Also, let the initial tree T contain only t, i.e., $T = (t, \emptyset)$.
(2) (Span Phase) Check if Q is empty. If so, the algorithm is terminated and T is the final ZigBee tree. Otherwise, dequeue a node x from queue Q, i.e., $x = \mathit{dequeue}(Q)$, and construct a spanning tree T' from x as follows. Assuming the depth of x in T to be $\mathit{depth}(x)$, x spans a subtree rooted from itself with height not exceeding $Lm - \mathit{depth}(x)$ in G_r in a breadth-first manner by including as many nodes in $V_r - V_T \cup \{x\}$ as possible. Let the resulting tree be T'.
(3) (Prune Phase) Attach T' to T by joining node x. Still, name the new tree T. Since some of the nodes in T' may violate the Rm parameter, the algorithm traverses nodes in T' from x in a breadth-first manner to trim T.

   (a) When visiting a node, say y, set y as "traversed" and check the number of children of y. If y has more than Rm children, y computes the association priority of their priorities based on T (refer to the definitions of nodes' association priorities in a tree given in the beginning of this section). Only the Rm highest prioritized children will remain in T, and the other children will be pruned from T.
   (b) When each node, say y', that is pruned in step 3(a) or 3(b), let $\mathit{tree}(y')$ be the pruned subtree rooted at y'. Since $\mathit{tree}(y')$ is pruned, the algorithm will try to attach y' to another node n in T if n satisfies the following conditions: (1) n is neighboring to y' but not a descendant of y', (2) n is not traversed yet, and (3) $\mathit{depth}(n) + 1 + \mathit{height}(\mathit{tree}(y')) \leq Lm$. If so, the subtree $\mathit{tree}(y')$ will be connected to node n. If there are multiple such candidates, the one with a lower depth is connected first. If no such node n can be found, y prunes all its children. Then for each pruned child, we recursively perform this step 3(b) to try to reconnect it to T. This is repeated until no further reconnection is possible.

(4) After the above pruning, call the resulting tree T. For nodes that are newly added into T in step 3, insert them into queue Q in such a way that nodes with lower depth values are inserted first (these nodes will go through Span and Prune phases again). Then, go back to step 2.

To summarize, step 3(a) is to prune those nodes violating the Rm constraint. In order to allow more vertices to join the network, step 3(b) tries to recursively reconnect those pruned subtrees back to T. Step 4 prepares newly joining nodes in Q for possible spanning in step 2.

Figure 9.9 illustrates a step-by-step example. Figure 9.9(a) shows the graph G_r with parameters $Rm = 3$ and $Lm = 3$. Initially, the tree T only contains t. Figure 9.9(b) shows the result after forming a BFS tree T' rooted at t. At this time, some nodes may violate the Rm constraint. Then, start to prune some nodes from the lower depth nodes. From Fig. 9.9(b), we can observe that node t has more than 3 child routers. Compare the association priorities of t's 5 child nodes. In this

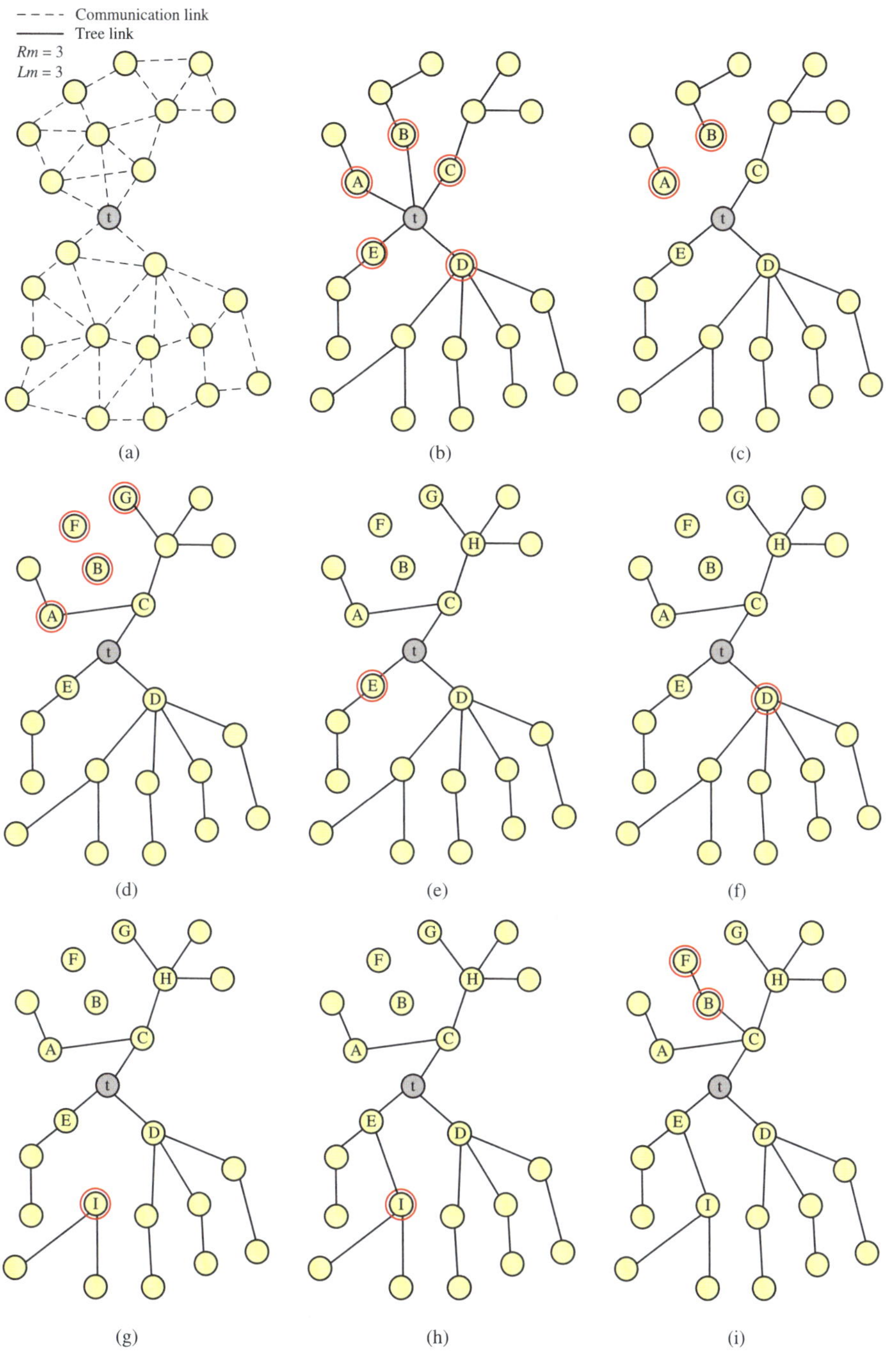

Fig. 9.9. An example of the Span-and-Prune algorithm.

example, router A and B have lower association priorities and will be pruned. This is because that the subtree rooted at A and B are smaller. When pruning by t, router A can reconnect to C. But, router B can not find any parent to reconnect to. If reconnecting to A or C, it will violate the rule in step 3(b)(3). As a result, router B prunes its child node, as shown in Fig. 9.9(d). Router F, the child of B, tries to reconnect to a new parent but also fail. Then, router F prunes its child node G. Luckily, as shown in Fig. 9.9(e), router G can reconnect to a new parent H. At this time, router F and B leave the T and have to wait for the opportunity to rejoin T in later iterations. After checking t, the algorithm keeps on checking other nodes. As shown in Fig. 9.9(e), router E needs not to prune an child. Next, check router D, as shown in Fig. 9.9(f). Router D will prune its child I because I has more potential parents than other child. In this example, I has 3 potential parent, but D's other children have only two. The result is shown in Fig. 9.9(g). Then, router I can reconnect to E, as shown in Fig. 9.9(h). After checking all the nodes spanned by t, the first iteration ends. In the second iteration, the algorithm starts span phase from router C. Then, router B can connect to C and F can connect to B. Fig. 9.9(i) shows the final result of this example, where no orphan node exists. The final tree T conforms the ZigBee specification.

9.4.2. *Connecting end devices*

After connecting routers in the BDDTF problem, we can obtain a bipartite graph $G_b = (\{\hat{V}_{br} \cup V_{be}\}, E_{bd})$, as defined in Sec. 9.3. The goal is to connect as many end devices to the routers in tree T as possible, which can be translated as a bipartite maximum matching problem. So the EDMM problem can be solved by applying a bipartite maximum matching algorithm[20] on G_b. Since an optimal solution exists, with the given G_b, the number of orphan end devices can be minimized. Figure 9.10(a) shows the graph G_b in Sec. 9.3. Figure 9.10(b) shows the result of

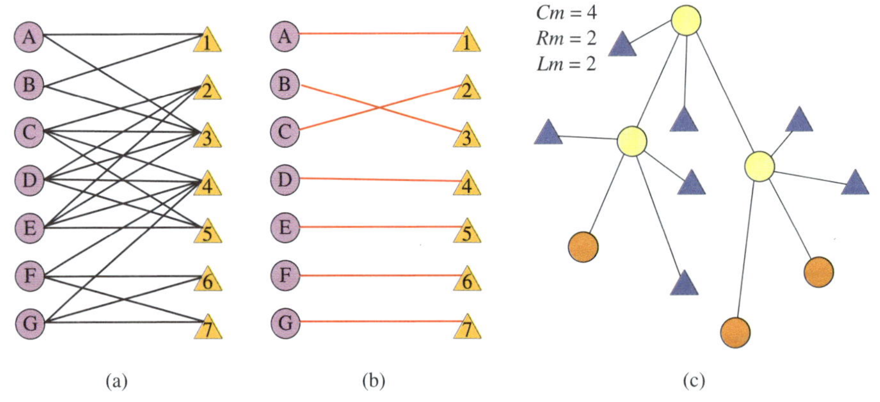

Fig. 9.10. An example of the EDMM problem.

applying bipartite maximum matching algorithm to this graph. Each end device can associate to a parent router. The result tree is shown in Fig. 9.10(c).

9.5. Conclusion

This chapter introduces the network formation (orphan) problem in ZigBee networks. There could be a misconception that the network formation problem can be trivially solved by enlarging Cm, Rm, or Lm. In practice, devices' capabilities and application demands should be carefully deliberated before doing so. Larger Cm or Rm imposes more memory space requirement on routers. A larger Lm may induce longer network delay. Also, enlarging these values incurs longer address space (ZigBee specifies a 16-bit address space). Besides, in theory, it can not be guaranteed that there are no orphan devices with any given Cm, Rm, and Lm. Therefore, orphans are an inherent problem given the Cm, Rm, and Lm constraints. So, this chapter presents a network formation strategy to relieve the orphan problem.

To avoid the orphan problem, the ZigBee Pro specification proposes a stochastic address assignment scheme. In this assignment, a parent node simply decide random addresses for its child devices. The probability that two nodes getting the same address is very low (roughly around 2^{-16}). But such assignment can not guarantee the uniqueness of addresses. ZigBee Pro defines a procedure to resolve address conflicts. When a device discovers an address conflict, it floods the information to the whole network. The nodes with conflicted address choose new random addresses. Obviously, this scheme causes packet overheads. The new version standard or related researches may solve the problem in the future.

References

1. M. A. Batalin, G. S. Sukhatme and M. Hattig, Mobile robot navigation using a sensor network, *Proc. of IEEE Int'l Conference on Robotics and Automation*, (2004).
2. M.-S. Pan, C.-H. Tsai and Y.-C. Tseng, Emergency guiding and monitoring applications in indoor 3D environments by wireless sensor networks, *International Journal of Sensor Networks (IJSNet)*, **1**(1/2), 2–10 (2006).
3. M.-S. Pan and L.-W. Yeh and Y.-A. Chen and Y.-H. Lin and Y.-C. Tseng, A WSN-based Intelligent Light Control System Considering User Activities and Profiles, *IEEE Sensors Journal*, 8(10), 1710–1721, (2008). (to appear).
4. X. Wang, J. S. Dong, C. Chin, S. Hettiarachchi and D. Zhang, Semantic space: An infrastructure for smart spaces, (2004).
5. Terrestrial ecology observing systems, http://research.cens.ucla.edu/areas/2007/Terrestrial/.
6. R. Szewczyk, A. Mainwaring, J. Polastre, J. Anderson and D. Culler. An analysis of a large scale habitat monitoring application. *Proc. of ACM Int'l Conference on Embedded Networked Sensor Systems (SenSys)*, (2004).
7. Micaz mote, http://www.xbow.com/Products/productdetails.aspx?sid=164.
8. Tmote sky, http://www.moteiv.com/products/tmotesky.php.
9. Dust Network Inc, http://www.dustnetworks.com/flash-index.shtml.

10. ZigBee alliance, http://www.zigbee.org/.
11. ZigBee Specification, ZigBee specification, v. 1.0, (2004).
12. ZigBee Specification, ZigBee specification, v 1.1, ZigBee document 064112 (2006).
13. ZigBee Specification, ZigBee specification, ZigBee document 07819 (2007).
14. Chipcon corporation, http://www.chipcon.com/.
15. Ember corporation, http://www.ember.com/.
16. Jennic — wireless microcontrollers, http://www.jennic.com/.
17. IEEE Std 802.15.4, IEEE standard for information technology — telecommunications and information exchange between systems — local and metropolitan area networks specific requirements part 15.4: Wireless medium access control (MAC) and physical layer (PHY) specifications for low-rate wireless personal area networks (LR-WPANs), (2003).
18. M. R. Garey and D. S. Johnson, *Computers and Intractability: A Guide to the Theory of NP-Completeness*, W. H. Freeman Company (1979).
19. M.-S. Pan and Y.-C. Tseng, The orphan problem in zigbee-based wireless sensor networks, *ACM/IEEE Int'l Symp. on Modeling, Analysis and Simulation of Wireless and Mobile Systems* (*MSWiM*), (2007).
20. T. H. Cormen, C. E. Leiserson and R. L. Rivest, *Introduction to Algorithms*, MIT Press (2001).

Chapter 10

The Latest Researches on Dominating Problems in Wireless Sensor Network

Xiaofeng Gao*, Feng Zou†, Donghyun Kim‡ and Ding-Zhu Du§

Department of Computer Science
University of Texas at Dallas
800 W. Campbell Road, Richardson
TX 75080 USA
**xxg052000@utdallas.edu*
†fxz063000@utdallas.edu
‡dhk051000@utdallas.edu
§dzdu@utdallas.edu

This chapter discusses the latest researches on dominating problems in wireless sensor networks, especially focusing on approximation techniques to deal with various dominating set problems. According to the property of wireless sensor network, our problem models are built on special kinds of communication graphs: *unit disk graph*, *disk graph*, *unit ball graph* etc. Besides, we introduce different types of methodology used for approximation algorithms to solve dominating problems, including the investigation of complexity strategies. Our survey also includes the latest research topics including dominating problems with weight assignment, dominating problems under directed graph, connected dominating set problems in three dimensional space, k-connected m-dominating set problem, weakly connected dominating set problem, etc.

10.1. Introduction

A wireless sensor network (WSN) is a kind of wireless network which consists of spatially distributed autonomous devices using sensors to cooperatively monitor physical or environmental conditions[1] (such as temperature, sound, vibration, pressure, motion or pollutants, at different locations). The development of wireless sensor networks was originally motivated by military applications such as battlefield surveillance. Later, wireless sensor networks are used in many civilian application areas, including healthcare applications, environment and habitat monitoring, home automation, and traffic control.[2,3] In computer science and telecommunications,

This work is supported in part by National Science Foundation under grant CCF-9208913 and CCF-0728851.

wireless sensor network is an active research area with numerous workshops and conferences arranged each year.

Sensor networks are usually formed by one or more base stations and a large number of inexpensive nodes, each of which is typically equipped with a radio transceiver or other wireless communications device, a small microcontroller, and an energy source, usually a battery. The main task of a sensor network is to collect, process, and deliver sensing data including physical parameters and events to a central base station where the collected information may be used for various purposes. However, the size and cost constraints on sensor nodes result in corresponding constraints on resources such as energy, memory, computational speed and bandwidth. For instance, due to limited radio range and battery power constraint, most of the nodes cannot communicate directly with a base station, but rather rely on their peers to forward messages to and from base stations,[4] meaning that each sensor supports a multi-hop routing algorithm (several nodes may forward data packets to the base station).

Compared with traditional computer networks, wireless sensor networks (similar as other types of wireless network) lack the physical network infrastructure of a hierarchical structure, resulting in the difficulty to achieve scalability and efficiency.[4] (e.g., all routing and network management functions must be performed by ordinary nodes). To improve the performance of WSN and increase efficiency, we usually select a virtual network infrastructure to organize ordinary nodes into a hierarchy.[5,6] The construction of this infrastructure is the primary application of *Connected Dominating Set* (CDS)[7] in wireless networks. The routing protocols rely on such infrastructure are called backbone-based routing[5] or spine-based routing.[8] The main advantage is that it simplifies the routing process to the one in a smaller subnetwork generated from the connected dominating set. This means that only gateway hosts need to keep routing information. As long as changes in network topology do not affect this subnetwork, there is no need to recalculate routing tables.[9] As a consequence, it is desirable to find a *Minimum Connected Dominating Set* (MCDS) of a given set of nodes. In our survey, we are aiming at introducing different designs or algorithms to select a MCDS under various circumstance, especially latest researches on weight version, 3-dimensional space and directed graphs.

In this chapter, we model these ad hoc and sensor networks by communication graphs, where each vertex (or node) represent a communication device equipped with wireless transceivers or radios, and each edge (or link) gives the communication relation between the two devices it connects. Since different networks have their own characteristics, we will use different graphs to represent their topological properties. The detailed definition for each type of graph will be shown in the next section. Besides, since we mainly focus on the selection of the base stations in wireless sensor networks, in our graph we assume that the topology of each network will not change during a period of time.

The following sections are organized as follows. In Sec. 10.2, we will introduce the commonly used network models and graphs to describe different wireless networks. Besides, we will also list the classification of algorithms and the definition of complexity as preliminaries. In Sec. 10.3, we will list the definition of several types of CDS problems, including other related combinatorial optimization problems. In Sec. 10.4 we are going to survey algorithms for MCDS problem and some theoretical analysis. In Sec. 10.5 we plan to discuss CDS problem under weight version, and show the corresponding methodology to design algorithms. In Sec. 10.6 we will propose latest researches on CDS problems in directed graphs. In Sec. 10.7 we will list other types of CDS problem, including the design of protocols and analysis. Finally, in Sec. 10.8 we will conclude this chapter and give a summary for the latest research on dominating problem in wireless sensor networks. Besides, some open questions are discussed in this part.

10.2. Network Models and Preliminaries

As mentioned above, people usually use communication graphs to model wireless sensor networks. In this section, we will introduce several types of network models that may used to describe our problems. Each geometrical graph has its own properties, and can be used under special circumstances to represent networks in the real world. In the second part of this section, some basic concepts of the complexity and approximation is introduced as preliminaries for this chapter.

10.2.1. *Network models*

Since wireless sensor network has its specific characteristics, in the communication graphs, we usually use disks to represent a sensor (or base station) in 2-dimensional Euclidean space. The center of each disk represents the position of the sensor, and the disk represents the transmission range for the corresponding sensor. To simplify the algorithm design process, we firstly assume that each node has the same transmission range, and set the radius of this range as unit length 1. As a consequence, if one node can send data to another node, then the receiver can reply messages to the sender. We set the rule that if two node can transfer data to each other, then there exist an edge between them in the communication graph. Then it comes the definition of *unit disk graph.*[10]

Definition 10.1 (Unit Disk Graph). Given an undirected graph $G = (V, E), G$ is called a ***Unit Disk Graph*** if for each vertex $v \in V, v$ is the center of a disk with unit radius 1, and there exists an edge $(v_1, v_2) \in E$ means that the distance between vertices v_1 and v_2 is less than or equal to 1. Say, $dist(v_1, v_2) \leq 1$.

Figure 10.1 is an example of *Unit Disk Graph* for wireless sensor network. However, due to the complexity of environment, the equipment difference, and sensor

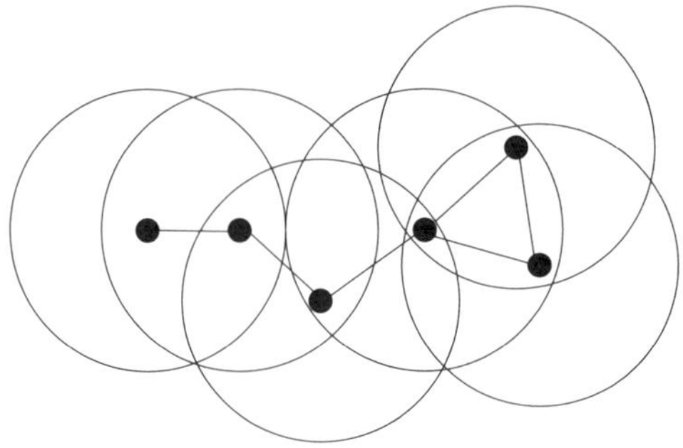

Fig. 10.1. Unit Disk Graph model for wireless sensor network.

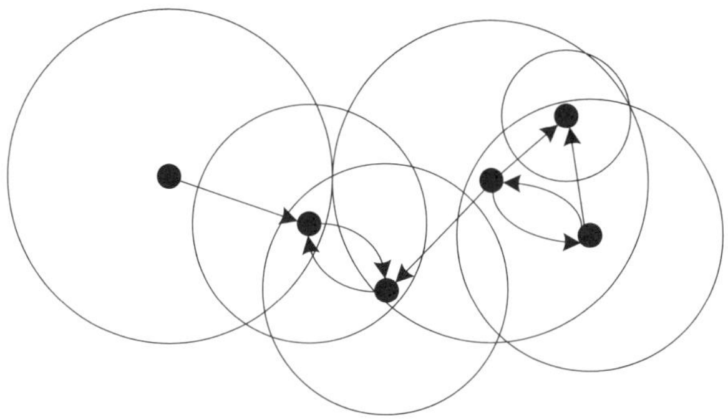

Fig. 10.2. Disk Graph model for wireless sensor network.

type variations, the transmission ranges of all nodes are not necessarily equal. In such condition, we use *disk graph* to represent the wireless sensor networks, where each disk still denotes a sensor, and the radius of this disk denotes the radius of transmission range for the corresponding sensor. Besides, an arc from one node to another means that the first node can transfer data to the second node, but not vice versa. The following is the formal definition of *disk graph*.

Definition 10.2 (Disk Graph). Given a directed graph $G = (V, A), G$ is called a ***Disk Graph*** if for each vertex $v \in V, v$ is the center for a disk with arbitrary radius r, and if there exist an arc $(v_1, v_2) \in A$, then v_2 lays within v_1's transmission range. Say, $dist(v_1, v_2) \leq r_1$.

Figure 10.2 is another example of *disk graph* for wireless sensor network. If we consider data processing problems for wireless network under complicated environment, e.g., mountainous areas, out-space or underwater space, we need to model the topology under 3-dimensional Euclidean space. Similar as *unit disk graph*, we assume that each node has the same transmission range. As a conclusion, the related graph is called *Unit Ball Graph* (UBG).

Definition 10.3 (Unit Ball Graph). Given an undirected graph $G = (V, E)$ in 3-dimensional space, G is called a ***Unit Ball Graph*** if for each vertex $v \in V$, v is the center of a ball with unit radius 1, and each edge $(v_1, v_2) \in E$ means that the distance between vertices v_1 and v_2 in 3-dimensional space is less than or equal to 1. Say, $dist(v_1, v_2) \leq 1$.

In an UBG, every vertex corresponds to a center of a ball in the space, and the distance between two points is the Euclidean distance. The ball represents the transmission range (or the space it could cover) of the corresponding equipment in the wireless networks.

If we want to design algorithms under more accurate topologies, we can use more general graph like *geometric intersection graph.*[11] Actually, UDG, DG and UBG are all special types of intersection graph. In our paper, we are mainly focusing on dominating problems under these three types of graphs.

Some papers refer our definitions as *Containment Model*,[12] which means only if one node lays within another node's transmission range, we will have an edge between these two nodes in the communication graph. To represent it formally, given a graph $G = (V, E)$, for each node $v \in V$, let $A(v)$ denote the area covered by v's transmitter, then $(u, v) \in E \Leftrightarrow u \in A(v)$ or $v \in A(u)$. Some researchers use other version of definitions to define UDG, say, the *Intersection Model.* The main difference is that they assume if two node's transmission ranges have intersection, then there exist an edge in communication graph between these two nodes. More specifically, $(u, v) \in E \Leftrightarrow A(u) \cap A(v) \neq \emptyset$. Actually, these two kinds of definitions are equivalent. We can easily transfer one to another during implementations. To keep consistence, in this survey we use containment model as our network models.

10.2.2. *Centralized and distributed algorithms*

The approximation algorithms we proposed here are either *centralized* or *distributed.*[13] A centralized algorithm solves a problem from global point of view. We usually know the topology and the required information in advance and use *approximation ratio* (will introduce later) to evaluate the performance of such algorithms. Centralized algorithms have theoretical significance in designing and analyzing approximations for wireless sensor networks. It is usually considered as "watershed" to classify different optimization problems.

On the contrary, a distributed algorithm solves a problem from local point of view. Each sensor will run distinct copy of the algorithm and they transfer messages to each other to communicate the process. Such kind of algorithm becomes more and more important in wireless sensor network because we do not need to collect information beforehand. Besides, if the network changes, distributed algorithms can adjust the result easier. They has practical significance for wireless sensor networks. However, the performance of these algorithms are more difficult to evaluate. Besides the approximation ratio, researchers also use *message complexity* and *time complexity* to exhibit the performance of distributed algorithms. Most of the designers test their distributed algorithms with numerical examples.

Compared with distributed algorithms, the centralized algorithms for the same problem usually have better approximation ratio, but worse time complexity. In this survey, we will list important algorithms for dominating and coverage problems in the literature, either centralized or distributed, and mostly focus on their performance analysis.

10.2.3. *Complexity and approximability*

Garey and Johnson[14] proved that finding minimum size dominating set in a given graph is NP-hard. Therefore, the most commonly used algorithm to solve such kind of problems is approximation algorithm. It is desirable to introduce some basic classification of approximation and the techniques to analyze complexity and approximability.

Firstly, we introduce the definition of *NPO* class for optimization problems.[15]

Let $\mathcal{P}$ be an optimization problem, $\mathcal{I}$ be the set of its instance, $\mathcal{S}(x)$ be the set of its feasible solution, $p(|x|)$ be a polynomial running time bound for x. For an instance $x \in \mathcal{I}$ together with a feasible solution $y \in \mathcal{S}(x)$, there is an objective function measure $f(x, y) \in \mathcal{N}$ of that solution.

Definition 10.4 (NPO Class). *NPO* is a class of problems in which each problem $\mathcal{P}$ satisfies:

(1) For every $x \in \mathcal{I}$ and $y \in \mathcal{S}(x)$, we have $|y| \leq p(|x|)$ for some polynomial p;
(2) $\forall x, y$ with $|y| \leq p(|x|)$, the decision question whether $y \in \mathcal{S}(x)$ can be determined within polynomial time; and
(3) given $x \in \mathcal{S}(x)$ and $y \in \mathcal{S}(x)$, the objective function $f(x, y)$ is computable in polynomial time.

The class *PO* refers to all optimization problems in *NPO* which have algorithms that can find the optimal solution within polynomial time.

Definition 10.5 (Approximation Ratio).[16] Let Π be an *NPO* problem. For any instance $x \in \mathcal{I}$, let $opt(x)$ be the cost for optimal solution of x. Then the approximation ratio for any feasible solution $y \in \mathcal{S}(x)$ is:

$$R(x, y) = \max\left\{\frac{f(x, y)}{opt(x)}, \frac{opt(x)}{f(x, y)}\right\}.$$

The first fraction is used to measure minimization, while the second fraction is used to measure maximization.

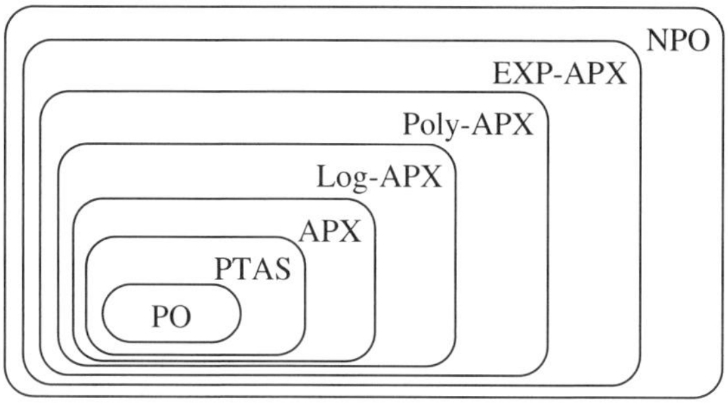

Fig. 10.3. Relationship among complexity classes.

Definition 10.6 ($r(n)$-approximation Algorithm). Let Π be an *NPO* problem, and $\mathcal{A}$ be an algorithm. For every instance $x \in \mathcal{I}, \mathcal{A}$ will return a feasible solution $\mathcal{A}(x) \in \mathcal{S}(x)$. Given a function r: $\mathcal{N} \mapsto [1, \infty]$, then the algorithm $\mathcal{A}$ is an $r(n)$-***approximation algorithm*** if for every instance $x \in \mathcal{I}$, $R(x, A(x)) \leq r(|x|)$. If there exists an $r(n)$-approximate algorithm for Π, we say that Π is approximable within $r(n)$.

Next, we will introduce the class *PTAS*.

Definition 10.7 (PTAS).[17] PTAS is the class of *NPO* problems that admit a ***Polynomial-Time Approximation Scheme***, which includes a family $\{\mathcal{A}_\varepsilon\}_{\varepsilon>0}$ of $(1+\varepsilon)$-approximation algorithms, and for each fixed $\varepsilon > 0, \mathcal{A}_\varepsilon$ runs in polynomial time in the input size.

An algorithm which has a constant approximation ratio is called a *constant-factor approximation*. The class *APX* is the collection of *NPO* problems which is approximable with constant $\alpha > 1$ (in polynomial time). Beyond *APX*, we have another three classes named *Log-APX*,[18] which is the class of problems approximable within ratios that are logarithms of the size of the instance; *Poly-APX*,[19] which is the class of graph-problems approximable within ratios of the maximum degree Δ of the input graph; and *EXP-APX*, which is the class of problems approximable within ratios that are exponent of the size of the instance. The majority of the problems we discussed here belong to *APX*, while some distributed algorithms solves these problems by *Poly-APX* approximations. Figure 10.3 gives the relationships among those complexity classes for optimization problems discussed in our paper.

10.3. Dominating Problem Related Concepts

In this section, we lists definitions for various dominating problems and some related problems. Actually, researchers always design algorithms for CDS problem in two steps. The first step is to select a *dominating set*, and the second step is to connect this dominating set. Therefore, our definition includes some related problems like *Maximal Independent Set* problem, *Steiner Tree* problem, *Spanning Tree* problem, etc. Besides, we are trying to give definitions for different variation of CDS problems, which will be introduced in the later section of our survey.

10.3.1. *Original dominating set problem*

The original concept of dominating problem can be tracked back from 1850,[20] when a popular problem spread among chess enthusiasts in Europe. This problem can be described as "Determine the minimum number of queens on the chessboard such that every little square can be either attacked or occupied by a queen". Later this problem was formulated as dominating set of a graph. The formal definition can be shown as follows.

Definition 10.8 (Dominating Set). Given a UDG $G = (V, E)$, a subset $D \subseteq V$ is called a ***Dominating Set*** of G if for each vertex $v \in V$, either $v \in D$, or there exist an edge $(u, v) \in E$ and $u \in D$.

Due to the invention of wireless network, people gradually found that dominating set can be modeled as the base station to improve the performance of routing protocols. Since an effective network requires that each node can send messages to all the network, and receive data from any other nodes, the *connected dominating set* (CDS) has more practical significance. The definition of CDS is listed as following:

Definition 10.9 (Connected Dominating Set). Given a UDG $G = (V, E)$, a subset $C \subseteq V$ is called a ***Connected Dominating Set*** of G if

(1) C is a *dominating set*, and
(2) the subgraph induced by C (denote as $G[C]$) is connected.

Therefore, a big problem in the theoretical community is to find good approximation of *minimum connected dominating set* (MCDS) with small approximation ratio.

Problem 10.1 (Minimum Connected Dominating Set). *Given a UDG $G = (V, E)$, find a Connected Dominating Set C with minimum cardinality,* (*or minimum number of nodes in C, represent as* $\min |C|$). *This problem can be written as MCDS.*

10.3.2. *Dominating problem under weight version*

When consider constructing base station for wireless sensor networks, the cost, energy consuming and power for each station is not necessarily the same. As a result, we assign each node a weight in the communication graph to represent these differences. Then we have another type of dominating problem: *minimum weight connected dominating set* problem (MWCDS).

Problem 10.2 (Minimum Weight Connected Dominating Set). *Given a UDG $G = (V, E, W)$, where V is the set of disks, E is the set of edges and W is the set of weight assigned to each disks. The problem of Minimum Weight Connected Dominating Set is to find a Connected Dominating Set C, and the sum of the weight for nodes in C is minimum.*

Usually researchers use partition[21] and shifting policy[22,23] to solve MWCDS. They also design algorithms by two steps. Firstly select a *Minimum Weight Dominating Set* (MWDS), then connect this set by some greedy algorithm. The detailed discussion can be referred from Sec. 10.5.

10.3.3. *Dominating problem in directed graphs*

In practice, the transmission ranges of all nodes in the network are not necessarily equal. In this case, we can use *disk graph* to model the communication graph. Then we modify our definition of *connected dominating set* into the following definition:

Definition 10.10 (Strongly Connected Dominating Set). Given a DG $G = (V, A)$, a subset $C \subseteq V$ is called a ***Strongly Connected Dominating Set*** of G if

(1) C is a *dominating set*, and
(2) the subgraph induces by C (denote as $G[C]$) is strongly connected.

Here strongly connected means for any nodes $u, v \in V$, there exists a path from u to v in $G[C]$, and also exists a path from v to u in $G[C]$. The two paths may have different intermediate nodes.

Similarly, we can define *minimum weight strongly connected dominating set* (MWSCDS) by assigning weight to each node in DG.

10.3.4. *Other related problems*

We list a number of definitions from graph theory in this subsection. These definitions are always used in the construction of algorithms to find MCDS, which may be mentioned in this chapter later:

Definition 10.11 (Maximal Independent Set). Given a graph $G = (V, E)$, a subset $M \subseteq V$ is called an ***Independent Set*** if we select any two nodes $u, v \in M$, there doesn't exist an edge $(u, v) \in E$. M is a ***Maximal Independent Set*** (MIS) if we insert any node from $V \backslash M$ into M, then the undated M will not be an independent set any more.

Actually, each MIS is a *Dominating Set* (DS). Besides, finding a MIS for a graph is easier than finding a DS. Therefore, researchers always construct an approximation to select MIS, then use different strategies to connect them into a CDS.

Definition 10.12 (Steiner Tree). [24] Given a graph $G = (V, E)$, a selected subset $S \subseteq V$, a ***Steiner Tree*** is a tree in G includes all vertices in S.

If we already has a DS for graph $G = (V, E)$, then connect this DS into a CDS is equivalent to finding a Steiner Tree for G, where the selected subset S is the DS.

Definition 10.13 (Spanning Tree). Given a graph $G = (V, E)$, a ***Spanning Tree*** is a tree composed of all the vertices and some (or perhaps all) of the edges of G.

Finding a MCDS in G is also equivalent to the problem of finding a spanning tree T with maximum number of leaves in G, and the non-leaf nodes in T form a minimum connected dominating set.

10.4. Algorithms for MCDS Problem

Garey and Johnson[14] proved that MCDS is NP-hard in general graphs by a reduction from the *Set Cover* Problem. Lund[25] and Feige[26] showed that for any fixed number $0 < \varepsilon < 1$, there is no polynomial time algorithm with performance ratio $\leq (1-\varepsilon)H(\Delta)$ unless $NP \subset DTIME[n^{O(\log\log n)}]$, where Δ is the maximum degree of the input graph and H is the harmonic function. Baker[22] proposed a polynomial time approximation scheme (PTAS) for planar graphs.

For unit disk graphs, Clark[27] proved that *minimum dominating set* (MDS) remains NP-hard in UDG. Lichtenstein[28] showed that MCDS is NP-hard in UDG. Many prior works provided constant-factor approximation for MCDS in UDG.[29–35] Cheng *et al.*[36] and Hunt *et al.*[37] gave PTAS for computing a MCDS in UDG.

In this section we are dealing with algorithms to select MCDS problem under UDG graphs. We are trying to list these methodologies through the way people constructing the algorithms. Note that although PTAS has better approximation ratio, algorithms with constant-factor approximation ratio may have smaller time or message complexity, which can be widely used in implementation.

10.4.1. *MIS and MCDS*

A majorities of works use *Maximal Independent Set* (MIS) to compute MCDS. It is well known that each MIS for graph G is a dominating set in graph theory, so we only need to connect a MIS to form a MCDS.

Compared with CDS, MIS is much easier to construct. Therefore, people usually construct the approximation for CDS with two steps. The first step is to find a MIS, and the second step is to make this MIS connected. As a result, the performance of these approximations highly depends on the relationship between the size of MIS and the size of MCDS in graph G. Let $mis(G)$ be the size of selected MIS, $connect(G)$ be the size of disks that are used to connect this MIS, and $mcds(G)$ be the size of minimum CDS. Then, the approximation ratio for such algorithm is

$$\frac{mis(G) + connect(G)}{mcds(G)} = \frac{mis(G)}{mcds(G)} + \frac{connect(G)}{mcds(G)}.$$

$\frac{mis(G)}{mcds(G)}$ is also called the theoretical bound to approximate CDS.

For selecting MIS part, Wan *et al.*[38] constructed a distributed algorithm and proved that selecting a MIS in graph G can have size $mis(G) \leq 4 \cdot mcds(G) + 1$. Later, Wu and her cooperators[39] improved this result into $mis(G) \leq 3.8 \cdot mcds(G) + 1.2$. Funke *et al.*[40] discussed the relation between $mis(G)$ and $mcds(G)$ and gave a theorem saying that $mis(G) \leq 3.453 \cdot mcds(G) + 8.291$, but the proof lack evidences. Li and Gao[41] improved the proof and gave a better bound as $mis(G) \leq 3.399 \cdot mcds(G) + 4.874$. Let's introduce the basic ideas for each algorithm separately.

Wan's Algorithm. Wan and Alzoubi *et al.*[29,38,42] constructed two distributed algorithms to select a CDS with size at most $8opt + 1$. At the beginning, they construct an arbitrary rooted spanning tree T by the distributed leader-election algorithm.[42]

The first distributed algorithm has two phases. The first phase assigned a rank number to each node, while the second phase constructed a MIS by a color-marking process.

Phase 1: Each node maintains four local variables: x_1, the number of neighbors whose levels have not been identified; x_2, the number of children who haven't reported the completion; *levellist*, the levels of its neighbors; and y, the number of lower-ranked neighbors.

- *Initialize*: set $(x_1, x_2, levellist, y)$ for each node i as ($|i$'s neighbor$|$, $|i$'s children$|$, $\emptyset$, 0). Here $|i$'s neighbor$|$ means the number of i's neighbor.
- *LEVEL message*: After T has constructed, the root r broadcast a LEVEL message with its level 0. Each receiver who receives a LEVEL message will record sender's ID and level to *levellist* and then decrement x_1 by 1. If the sender is its parent in T, this receiver sets its own level to its next child level (1 + its level), then rebroadcast a LEVEL message with its level.
- *LEVEL-COMPLETE message*: When node i receives a LEVEL message, then if $x_1 = 0$, let y be the number of lower-ranked neighbors calculated from *levellist*; if $x_2 = 0$, and its own level has been determined, reply a LEVEL-COMPLETE message to its parent.

  When node i receives a LEVEL-COMPLETE message, decrement x_2 by 1. After that, if x_2 remains 0 and $i \neq r$, transfer LEVEL-COMPLETE message to its parent and resets x_2 to the number of children.
- *Terminate*: When local variable $x_2 = 0$ at root r, reset x_2 as the number of its children and the algorithm terminate.

Phase 2: Each node has a local list named *blacklist* to record the IDs of its black neighbors. (*blacklist* can only contain less than 5 nodes, which will be proved later).

- *Initialize*: The root r mark itself and broadcast a BLACK message. Each node will be marked with white color.
- *Receiver*: When receiving a BLACK message, node i add sender's ID to its *blacklist*. If i's color is white, it colors itself as gray and broadcasts a GRAY message including its level. When receiving a GRAY message, if the sender's rank is lower than itself, a white node decrements y by 1; if $y = 0$ after update, it marks itself as black and broads a BLACK message.

  When a leaf node is marked with either gray or black, it transmit a MARK-COMPLETE message to its parent. When receiving a MARK-COMPLETE message, a node decrements x_2 by 1. If $x_2 = 0$ after update and $i \neq r$, i will transmit MARK-COMPLETE message to its parent.
- *Terminate*: When root r's local variable $x_2 = 0$, the algorithm will terminate. At this time all the nodes have been marked with either gray or black. Now we will have a MIS as a result.

Next, they connects the nodes in the MIS to form a CDS. The algorithm can be shown as follows:

- *Initialize*: The root joins the CDS and then broadcast an INVITE message.
- *Receiver*: When a black node receives an INVITE message for the first time, it JOIN the dominating tree, and then it will initiate an INVITE message. When a gray node receives an INVITE message for the first time, it will transmit it to its black neighbor in the lower level, and the two nodes will JOIN the dominating tree together.
- *Terminate*: When all black nodes join the CDS, the algorithm will terminate.

This algorithm has time complexity $O(n)$ and message complexity $O(n\log(n))$. The constructed CDS has size no more than $8opt + 1$.

Analysis: The approximation ratio analysis is heavily based on the geometrical constraint that "a node is adjacent to at most five independent neighbors".[34] As a consequence, the size of an arbitrary MIS will be no more than five times the number of nodes in the optimal MIS set. This result can be proved briefly as follows:

Theorem 10.1. *The size of any MIS in a UDG G ($mis(G)$) is at most $4 \cdot mcds(G) + 1$.*

Proof. Let M be an MIS of V, and T be a spanning tree of MCDS. We order nodes in T by $v_1, v_2, \ldots, v_{mcds(G)}$. Let $M_1 \subset M$ be the set of neighbor nodes for v_1. Similarly, let M_i be the set of neighbor nodes for v_i. Since v_1 has at most five independent neighbors, $|M_1| \leq 5$. Besides, for any $2 \leq i \leq opt$, at least one node in

$v_1, v_2, \ldots, v_{mcds(G)}$ is adjacent to v_i. Therefore, M_i can only lie in the shadow as a sector of at most $\frac{2\pi}{3}$ (which can be shown in Fig. 10.4). As a result, $|M_i| \leq 4$. Then we have

$$|M| = \sum_{i=1}^{mcds(G)} |M_i| \leq 5 + 4(mcds(G) - 1) = 4 \cdot mcds(G) + 1.$$

□

For the second algorithm connecting a dominating tree, it inserts some additional nodes to MIS, and finally the whole algorithm has an approximation factor of at most 8. Actually, this boundary becomes a theoretical bound to evaluate the performance for a branch of algorithms in the literature.[30,35,38,43]

Wu's Contribution. From Theorem 10.1, we can see that no matter which algorithm we used to select MIS, the theoretical bound for MIS and MCDS remains the same. Therefore, the relationship between MIS and MCDS mostly depend on the geometrical property in UDG. According to this, Wu and her cooperators[39] improve this bound into $mis(G) \leq 3.8 \cdot mcds(G) + 1.2$. They firstly defined a *unit arc-triangle abc*, which is a unit triangle *abc* with edge length 1, together with three arcs with radius 1 and center a, b, c respectively. (see Fig. 10.5)

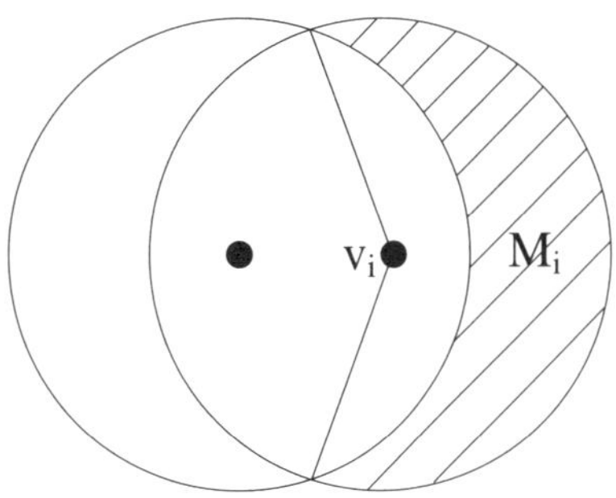

Fig. 10.4. Relation between M_i and v_i.

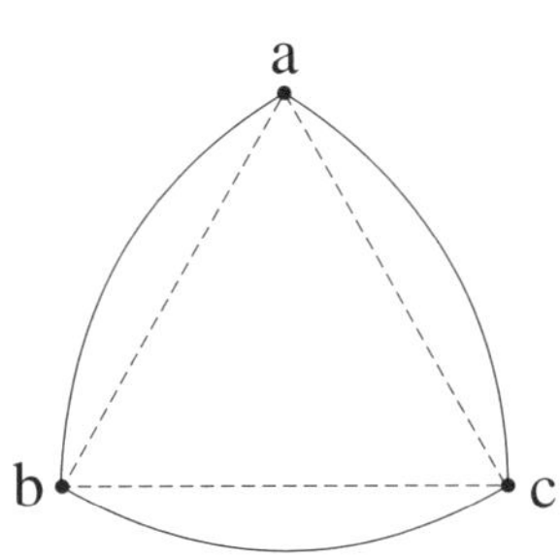

Fig. 10.5. Unit arc-triangle *abc*.

It is easy to prove that this unit arc-triangle abc cannot contain two independent vertices, since any two independent vertices should have distance greater than 1. Next, Wu proved the following lemma with the help of this triangle, which is the crucial part of the whole work.

Lemma 10.1. *The neighbor area of two adjacent vertices contains at most eight independent nodes.*

The main idea to prove this lemma is using contradiction. From Theorem 10.1, it is trivial that the area covered by two adjacent vertices will contain at most 9 independent nodes. Now consider two adjacent node u and v. Let $N(u)$ and $N(v)$ denote the two disks with center u, v, respectively. Let I denotes the independent set in this area. Firstly prove that the intersection area $A = N(u) \cap N(v)$ has only 1 vertex in I. Then either $N(u) \backslash A$ or $N(v) \backslash A$ may contain at most 4 vertices in I. Next, using unit arc-triangle, they showed that if fix a vertice within A, then it is impossible to have 4 vertices in both $N(u) \backslash A$ and $N(v) \backslash A$. There must exist two vertices that lie too close to each other, which is against the constraint of independent set. Figure 10.6 gives a simple example for this proof.

Then they selected a spanning tree for graph G, rebuilt it from the root. Once adding a node, from lemma 10.1 they finally proved $mis(G) \leq 3.8 \cdot mcds(G) + 1.2$ by induction.

Funke's Distributed Algorithm. Funke *et al.*[40] gave a distributed algorithm to compute MCDS in UDG with approximation ratio less than 7. The basic idea of their algorithm is also to select a MIS and connect it. They mentioned a new method to evaluate the ratio of $mis(G)$ and $mcds(G)$. Firstly, let's list their distribute algorithm:

Each node may have five colors. *black* means the node belongs to MIS; *blue* means the node is adjacent to a node in MIS; *gray* means the node is in $V \backslash$MIS; *red* means the node is a neighbor to gray or blue node; and *white* represents other conditions except the above four.

- *Initialize*: One node is colored *red*, the rest are colored *white*.
- *Apply Phase*: Each *red* node sends an APPLY-MSG with its ID.

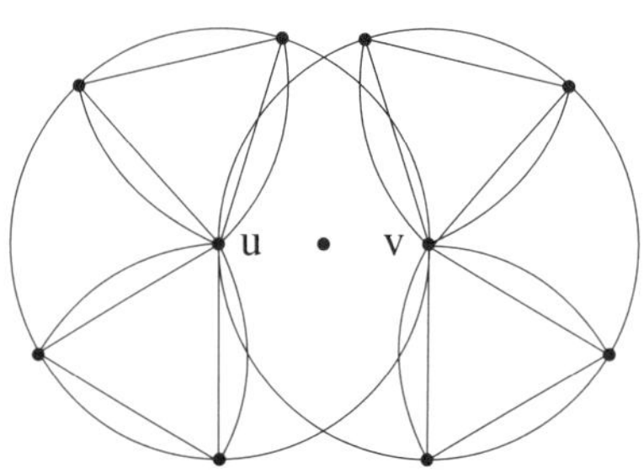

Fig. 10.6. Contradiction to prove lemma 10.1.

- *Confirm Phase*: If a *red* node receives an APPLY-MSG with larger ID, colors itself *black* and sends a CONFIRM-MSG with its ID and its parent's ID. Each *blue* node that receives a CONFIRM-MSG with parent ID equal to its own ID, colors itself *gray*.
- *Update Phase*: Each *red* or *white* node receiving one or more CONFIRM-MSG colors itself *blue* and sends an UPDATE-MSG with its ID. Each *white* node that receives an UPDATE-MSG from node i colors itself *red* and sets its parent as i.

The *black* nodes form a independent set and the *gray* nodes connect them as a CDS. In this article, the author said that the rough upper bound of $mis(G)$ and $mcds(G)$ in a UDG G should be $mis(G) \leq 3.748 \cdot mcds(G) + 5.252$.

Theorem 10.2. *The rough bound for $mis(G)$ and $mcds(G)$ is $mis(G) \leq 3.748 \cdot mcds(G) + 5.252$.*

Proof. Given an UDG $G = (V, E)$, let M be the set of disks forming MCDS. If we increase the radius of disks in M from 1 to 1.5, and decrease the radius of the rest disks in $V \backslash M$ from 1 to 0.5, then we can construct a new graph G'. It is easy to know that all the disks in V are located inside the area formed by M. (For disks in M, obviously they are located inside themselves, and for disks in $V \backslash M$, e.g., v_1, since M is a MCDS, there exist a disk $v_2 \in M$ dominating v_2. Therefore $dist(v_1, v_2) \leq 1$. Besides, the radius of v_1 is 0.5, while the radius of v_2 is 1.5, so v_1 must locate inside v_2's disk.)

If we select a MIS for G, then based on the definition of UDG, the distance between any two disks from MIS should be greater than 1. And since the radius of disks in $V \backslash M$ for G' is 0.5, any of two disks from MIS will not intersect each other. (To simply the conception, we can consider the radius of the disks in both MIS and M as 0.5) Then we can get the conclusion that the sum of maximum area for MIS should be less than the area of MCDS, which is a rough bound for $\frac{mis(G)}{mcds(G)}$.

Say, consider two adjacent vertices u, v in MCDS (also see Fig. 10.4), the maximum number of MIS should be $N(u) \cup N(v)/area(i)$, where $area(i)$ is the area of disk with radius 0.5. Therefore, if we mimic the growth of a spanning tree for MCDS, then the maximum number of MIS should be less than the total areas induced from M divide the area for a small disk with radius 0.5, which is $mis(G) \leq 3.748 \cdot mcds(G) + 5.252$. □

Li's Theorem. Later, Li and Gao[41] proved by Voronoi Division[44] and CDS's geometrical properties that $mis(G) \leq 3.453 \cdot mcds(G) + 4.839$. Here, after Voronoi Division, the minimum size of one Voronoi cell should be a heptagon cell with one side cut by a boundary arc from MCDS (refer to Fig. 10.7).

They further applied Euler's Formula to show a better bound as $mis(G) \leq 3.399 \cdot mcds(G) + 4.874$, if there are no holes in the area constructed by the MCDS. If there exist some holes, then a round bound is calculated as $mis(G) \leq 3.478 \cdot mcds(G) + 4.874$.

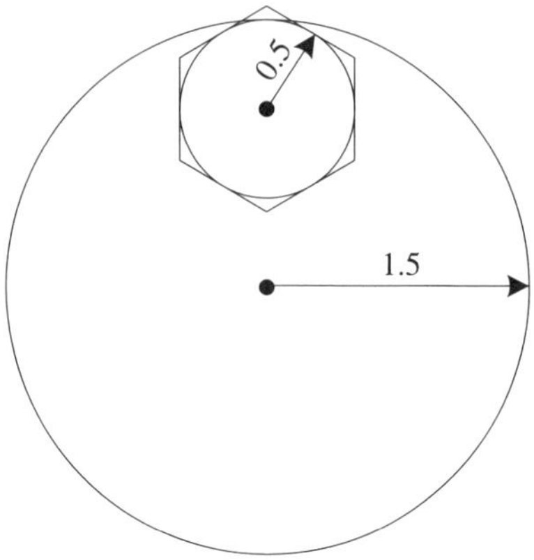

Fig. 10.7. Smallest Voronoi cell.

After selecting a MIS, researchers use different strategies to connect this set into a CDS. They commonly use *Steiner Tree*, *Spanning Tree* or other greedy heuristics, the following subsection give some milestones to connect a dominating set in the literature.

10.4.2. *Steiner tree and greedy algorithm*

As mentioned in Sec. 10.3, Steiner Tree construction is commonly used to connect a dominating set into a CDS. Blum's survey[4] gave a detailed introduction about this topic. The typical and classical algorithm is Guha and Khuller's second algorithm in Ref.[45] They modified Klein and Ravi's concept[46] of "spider decomposition" into "branch-spiders". Its distributed implementations[5,8] applies a spanning tree to approximate the computation of Steiner points. Min[35] improved the Steiner Tree algorithm by *Steiner tree with minimum number of Steiner nodes* (ST-MSN).[47–49] His algorithm contains two phases. The first phase constructs a MIS and color it as *black* (the rest nodes are colored with *gray*). In the second phase a gray node is colored as black if it is adjacent to at least three connected black components. If no node satisfies this condition, a gray node which is adjacent to at least two connected black components will be colored as black. His algorithm has performance ratio 6.8 in UDG. It can be extended into a distributed algorithm.

In Guha's work,[45] they also proposed a greedy algorithm selecting CDS within one step. In this approach, a CDS is formed by growing the tree T with root r. r is the node with maximum node degree in this graph. Next, v with maximum number of neighbors (not in T) is selected. Repeat this step and construct a spanning tree. The non-leaf node of this spanning tree is a CDS actually.

10.4.3. *PTAS*

Cheng *et al.*[36] gave a polynomial time approximation scheme (PTAS) for CDS in UDG, which is a really important work with theoretical significance. Firstly, we need to have an arbitrary constant factor approximation to calculate CDS in advance. Then the main process is listed as follows:

For a given UDG $G = (V, E)$, where $|V| = n$, assume that all the disks are located in a square plane $Q = \{(x, y)|0 \leq x \leq q, 0 \leq y \leq q\}$, where q is related to n. Divide Q into squares each with side length $m \times m$. Let $p = \lfloor \frac{q}{m} \rfloor + 1$. Widen Q into a bigger region $\widetilde{Q} = \{(x, y)| -m \leq x \leq pm, -m \leq y \leq pm\}$ (see Fig. 10.8).

Name this partition as $P(0)$, and denote by $P(a)$ the partition obtained from $P(0)$ by shifting it such that the left-bottom corner of $P(a)$ is at $(a - m, a - m)$, for $a = 0, 1, \ldots, m - 1$.

For each square e, define the *Inner* area I_e and *Boundary* area B_e (see Fig. 10.9). If $e = \{(x, y)|im \leq x \leq (i + 1)m, jm \leq y \leq (j + 1)m\}$,

$$I_e = \{(x, y)|im + h \leq x \leq (i + 1)m - h, jm + h \leq y \leq (j + 1)m - h\},$$

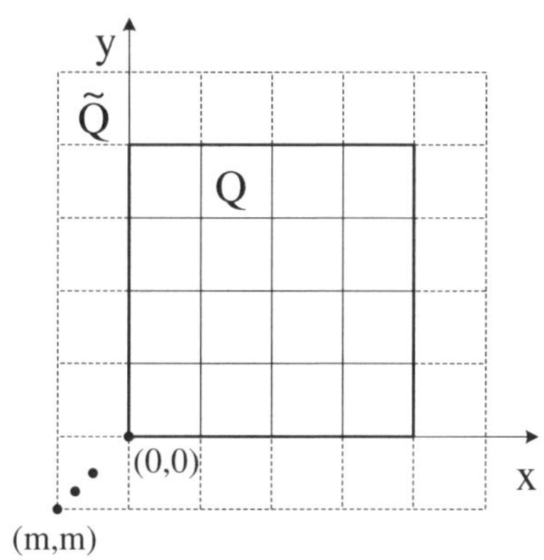

Fig. 10.8. Partition for Graph G.

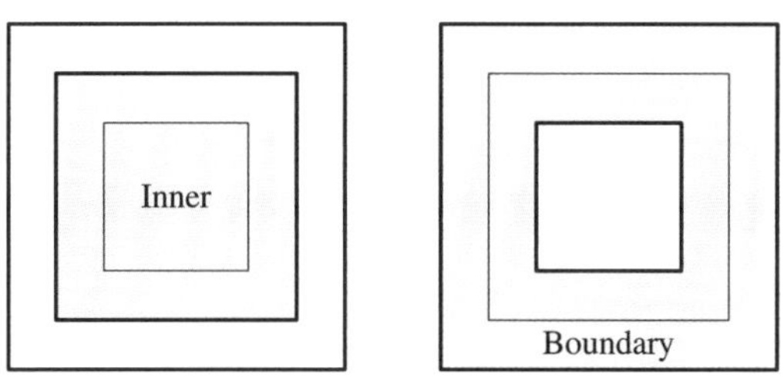

Fig. 10.9. Inner region and boundary region for a square.

$$B_e = e - \{(x,y)|im + (h+1) \le x \le (i+1)m - (h+1), jm + (h+1) \le y \le (j+1)m - (h+1)\}.$$

For each component of the inner area, compute a minimum CDS. To dominate nodes not in the inner area, use a constant-approximation algorithm to compute a CDS of G, and union those CDS which belong to the "boundary area" of the partition into the above CDS's. The overlap of inner area and boundary area ensures the connectivity of the output. The shifting strategy is used to select a partition such that the number of vertices to calculate CDS falling into the boundary area of this partition is small enough relative to ε. Actually, this algorithm has approximation ratio $(1+\frac{1}{s})$ for MCDS in UDG, running in time $n^{O((s \log s)^2)}$.

10.5. Algorithms for MWCDS Problem

If we consider the difference for the capability of wireless sensor network, the cost, energy consuming and power for node is not necessarily the same (e.g., assigning small weight to the sensors with large remaining battery life). Thus, we need to assign each node a weight. Then we have another type of dominating problem: *minimum weight connected dominating set* problem (MWCDS).[50]

Garey and Johnson[14] proved the emphminimum weight dominating set (MWDS) is NP-hard in general graph. Vazirani[51] proved that the algorithms for MWDS can be achieved with $O(\log n)$ by reduction to the weighted set cover problem. The best known approximation algorithm for MWCDS in general graph also has time complexity $O(\log n)$.[45]

In UDG, a lot of researchers provided PTAS for MCDS,[36,37] but these strategies are heavily relied on the fact that within a $k \times k$ square, the optimal dominating set for unit disks has size no more than $O(k^2)$, which can be enumerate by exhaustive search within polynomial time. However, in the weighted version, there is no such property to bound the size of optimal solution, as the optimal solution may contain a large number of disks with small weight. Leeuwen[52] has presented asymptotic fully polynomial time approximation schemes (achieving ratio $1+\varepsilon$ only for sufficiently large inputs) for MDS and MCDS in UDG with bounded density.

Wang and Li[50] gave the first distributed algorithms for MWDS and MWCDS in UDG with approximation ratio $O(\min\{\log \Delta, \sigma\})$, where Δ is the maximum degree of the graph and σ is the ratio of maximum weight to the minimum weight of a disk. Ambühl[53] constructed the first constant-factor approximation for MWDS and MWCDS with approximation ratio 72 and 89, respectively. Later, Gao[54] and Huang *et al.*[55] gave a $(6+\varepsilon)$-approximation for MWDS and $(10+\varepsilon)$-approximation for MWCDS. Zou[56] modified Huang's algorithm with approximation ratio $(9.875+\rho)$.

Ambühl's Constant-Factor Approximation. The core of Ambühl's Algorithm[53] are partition strategy and a dynamic algorithm. Firstly, they divided the place into small squares, each with size $\mu \times \mu$. Next, they gave a 2-approximation for each small square by using a dynamic problem twice. The following is an important lemma used in several constant-factor approximation, and its proof is a construction of dynamic algorithm.

Lemma 10.2. *Consider a set P of points lying inside a horizontal strip and a set $\mathcal{D}$ of disks with radius one and with centers either above or below the strip (Fig. 10.10). Give each disk with a nonnegative weight. Suppose the union of all disks covers P. Then the minimum weight subset of disks covering P can be computed in time $O(m^4 n)$ where $n = |P|$ and $m = |\mathcal{D}|$.*

The proof for this lemma is constructive. It gives a polynomial time algorithm by dynamic programming. It says that as long as the set of centers P in a horizontal strip can be dominated by a set of centers D above and/or below the strip, then an optimal subset of D dominating P can be found in polynomial time.

After selection for each square, Ambühl analyzed the geometrical relation between surrounded disks and a square, and finally combining the solution of each square, forming a result with size no more than $72opt$. Then they connected the selected DS with idea of node-weight Steiner Tree problem,[45] which as approximation ratio 17.

Huang's Algorithm. Unlike Ambühl, Huang[55] firstly selected DS strip by strip, then combined these subsolution together, finally applied shifting policy to form the final result. His heuristics can find a DS with approximation ratio $(6 + \varepsilon)$.

At the beginning, Given a UDG G containing n disks in the plane. Let $\mu < \sqrt{2}$ be a real number which is sufficiently close to $\sqrt{2}$, say $\mu = 1.4$. Partition the area into squares with side length μ. Then for each square select a pseudo "sandglass" range which could be covered by disks from the upper square or lower square (see Fig. 10.11). Using lemma 10.2, we could select optimal solution for sandglasses of small square in a strip.

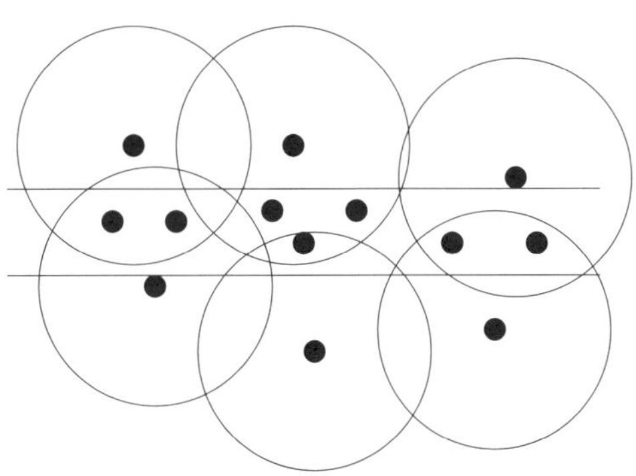

Fig. 10.10. A covering problem about a strip.

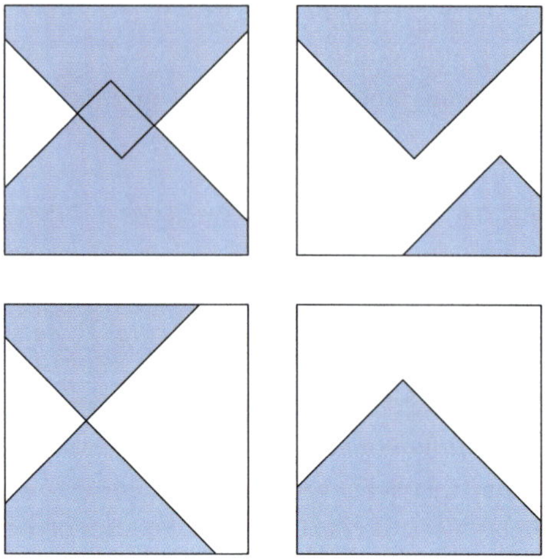

Fig. 10.11. Examples for pseudo sandglass.

Let S_{ij} denote square lies at $\{(x,y)|i\mu \leq x < (i+1)\mu, j\mu \leq y < (j+1)\mu\}$. Let K be a sufficiently large number, and name $K \times K$ squares a block Q. We firstly use dynamic programming to calculate MWDS in $K \times K$ squares.

Algorithm: Calculate MWDS in $K \times K$ Squares

Step 1 For each S_{ij}, choose its sandglass or randomly select a $d \in S_{ij}$.

Step 2 If $d \in S_{ij}$ is selected, then remove d and all disks dominated by d.

Step 3 For each strip $\cup_{j=1}^{K} S_{ij}$ from $i = 1$ to K, calculate dominating set for the union of disks in the sandglasses.

Step 4 For each strip $\cup_{i=1}^{K} S_{ij}$ from $j = 1$ to K, calculate dominating set for the remaining disks not covered by Step 3.

The Union of disks chosen in the above steps form a WDS for $K \times K$ squares.

Next, they select MWDS for the whole region. Using shifting policy, each time they move the partition two squares right and two squares up to its original position, then repeat this step until the new partition superposes the original one. After calculation, Huang proved that his algorithm is a $(6+\varepsilon)$-approximation for MWDS.

To connect MWDS, they also used the concept of node-weighted Steiner tree and the characteristics of independent set. By inserting additional nodes each step into MWDS, they finally constructed a MWCDS with $(10+\varepsilon)$-approximations.

10.6. Algorithms for MSCDS Problem

It is desirable to study *minimum strongly connected dominating set* problem (MSCDS), since in practice, the transmission of every sensor may not be the same.

At this time the corresponding communication graph is *disk graph* (DG). It is trivial that MSCDS is NP-hard in DG since MCDS is NP-hard in UDG.[57]

Thai's Contribution. Thai[58] studied MSCDS in disk graphs with a constraint that each disk i should have a transmission range $r_i \in [r_{min}, r_{max}]$. Besides, all the edges in the network are bidirectional (an edge (u, v) is bidirectional if both (u, v) and (v, u) are in E). Her algorithm has two phases. The first phase is to select a MIS in this graph, and the second phase is to connect this MIS set. Let $k = \frac{r_{max}}{r_{min}}$, and assume in the graph, every node is adjacent to at most K independent nodes. The performance of her algorithm is a constant factor $(K + 2 + \ln K)$, where

$$K = \begin{cases} 5 & \text{if } k = 1 \\ 6(3\lceil \log_2 k \rceil + 2) & \text{otherwise.} \end{cases}$$

Later, Thai and Wang *et al.*[59] extended her algorithms such that it can be used under more general circumstance. The main discussion still relies on the relationship between MIS and MSCDS. They proved that in the general disk graph, the largest number of independent nodes that each node could adjacent to is

$$K = \begin{cases} 5 & \text{if } k = 1 \\ 10 \left\lfloor \dfrac{\ln k}{\ln(2\cos(\pi/5))} \right\rfloor & \text{otherwise.} \end{cases}$$

They presented two different algorithms to select MIS in DG. The first one is similar to Wan's work,[38] while the second one is a greedy algorithm selecting the biggest disks in the graph each round. Finally, they applied a Steiner Tree algorithm to connect the MIS into a MSCDS.

Wu's Pruning Algorithm. Wu *et al.*[60] proposed a centralized algorithm to find CDS in general graphs. This algorithm can be shortly described as follows:

Initially all the vertices are unmarked. They exchange their neighborhood information to their adjacent neighbors. Therefore every node will have the information of their 2-hop neighbor after sharing the information. Then mark the vertex as a dominator which has two unconnected neighbors. After this process the set of marked vertices form a CDS, but with a lot of redundant nodes. To prune these nodes, they provided two principles based on the neighborhood subset coverage. A vertex u can be pruned from CDS if

- there exists a node v with high ID number such that u's closed neighbor set is a subset of v's closed neighbor set; or
- two of u's connected neighbors in CDS with higher IDs can cover all of u's neighbor.

They then extended their work to DG.[20] Since there may exist some unidirectional links in DG (an unidirectional link $(u, v) \in A$ implies (v, u) is not existing

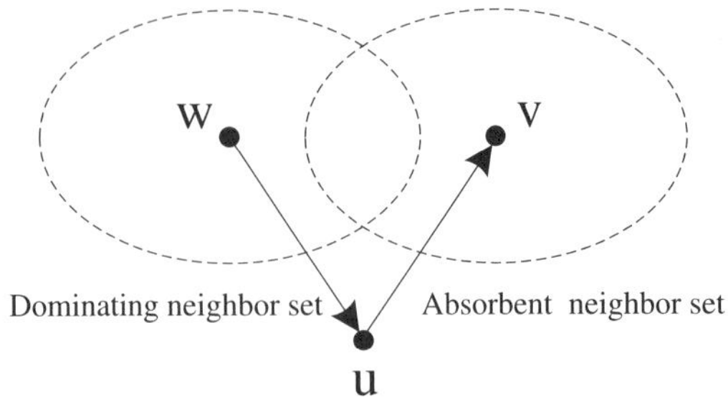

Fig. 10.12. Dominating and absorbent set for u.

in A), they modified their neighbor set into an absorbent neighbor set in terms of the directions of the connected edges. Figure 10.12 denotes the dominating and absorbent set of node u. In this case, the objective is to find a set which is both dominating and absorbent for a given directed graph.

The original marking process is modified as follows: when there exists a node w in a node u's dominating set and there exists another node v in u's absorbent set which can only be connected via u, add u into the dominating and absorbent set. Similar post-process principles are used to prune redundant nodes in the resulted dominating and absorbent set.

This algorithm has time complexity of $O(\Delta^3)$ and message complexity of $\Theta(m)$, where Δ is the maximum degree of nodes in this graph.

Li's Broadcasting Tree Algorithm. In directed graph, there also exists CDS problem under weight version. Some researchers consider weight as *power* to achieve energy-effective approximations.[61,62] We name this problem as *minimum weight strongly connected dominating set* problem (MWSCDS). Li and her co-authors[63] proved that this problem is NP-hard and gave three approximation algorithms. Their main idea is to find a broadcasting tree $\overrightarrow{T}$ from root to the other vertices, and then find another reverse broadcasting tree $\overleftarrow{T}$ which considers the incoming edges as the "message transferring" edges. Finally combining the two trees together as $S = \overrightarrow{T} \cup \overleftarrow{T}$, it is easy to prove that S is our required CDS. One of their algorithms has approximation ratio $2(1+\ln(n-1))$, where n is the number of nodes in the graph.

10.7. New Categories for Dominating Problems

Recently, researchers are interested in MCDS and MWCDS problems under different constraints. E.g., consider the fault-tolerance and robustness of the virtual backbone; build up wireless sensor network under mountainous or underwater place; select base level communication networks to form basic hierarchy, etc. We briefly list several new categories as follows.

10.7.1. *MCDS in 3-dimensional space*

When considers complex geographic area, it is not sufficient to model communication graph in 2-dimensional space, e.g., under-water sensor systems, outer-space sensor systems, laptop in a multi-layer building. Therefore, we use *unit ball graph* (UBG) to represent the model in 3-dimensional space, which is more reasonable to reflect real-life wireless network. (to simply discuss, we assume that each node has almost the same transmission range.) Actually, since UDG is a special case of UBG, the minimum independent set, minimum vertex cover, minimum dominating set and minimum connected dominating set problems are all known to be NP-hard.

Butenko[64] provided the first constant factor approximation scheme for MCDS problem in UBG. The main idea is to select a MIS in UBG, and then connect it through intermediate vertices to guarantee connectivity. The approximation ratio for this algorithm is 22. Zhong *et al.*[65] proposed another similar algorithm to select CDS. They also separated the algorithm into two phases. The first phase selects MIS in UBG, while the second phase connect them as a tree. But they further discussed the performance by using the geographic characteristics. As a result, they proved that the algorithm is a 16-approximation, with message complexity $O(n\Delta)$ and time complexity $O(n)$. Hansen *et al.*[66] defined a *random unit ball graph* and compared the performance of two closely related CDS algorithms. A random UBG is formed from n random points in an $l_n \times l_n \times l_n$ cube, and both of the two algorithms[20,67] has size $\Theta(l_n^3)$.

Zhang and her cooperator[68] proposed the first PTAS for CDS in UBG. She simulated Cheng's proof by partition process.[36] However, Cheng's proof depends on a geometrical property which holds in 2-dimensional space but no longer true in the 3-dimensional space. Zhang divided the space into lots of small cubes, and defined the "boundary" and "inner" area for each cube. By shifting policy, she presented an algorithm to select CDS and proved that it is a PTAS. The time complexity of this algorithm is $n^{O(1/\varepsilon^2)}$. Besides, this solution can be extended to k-dimensional space for any $k \geq 1$.

10.7.2. *k-Connected m-dominating problem*

If the network is prone to failures and nodes may have mobility and turn on and off frequently, it is difficult to achieve a robust and stable routing protocol. To satisfy the requirement of fault tolerance and routing flexibility for wireless network, scientists defined a new problem named *k-connected m-dominating problem* (kmCDS).[69] Here k-connectivity guarantees that between any two nodes in CDS there exist at least k different paths. m-domination takes care of fault tolerance and robustness, which means that any nodes which doesn't belong to CDS should have at least m adjacent neighbors from CDS.

The regular CDS problem can be judged as 1-connected 1-dominating problem. Wu[69] proposed a distributed kmCDS algorithm for general constants k and m with low message complexity. She also gave a centralized algorithm with a constant factor approximation ratio. Dai[70] showed three K-CDS protocols. The first one is a probabilistic approach which is based on K-Gossip algorithm.[17] The second one is a deterministic approach from K-coverage problem. The last one is a color-based algorithm dividing the whole network into k-disjoint subsets based on coloring process. Wang *et al.*[71] proposed a centralized 64-approximation algorithm to construct a 2-connected virtual backbone in wireless ad hoc network. Shang[72] proposed three centralized algorithms. The first one is dealing with 1mCDS, the second one selects 2mCDS and the third one can construct kmCDS, where $3 \leq k \leq m$. Thai[73] gave a centralized algorithm, but it requires the graph to be $\max(k, m)$ connected.

10.7.3. *Weakly connected dominating set*

Actually, the concept of *Weakly Connected Dominating Set* (Weakly CDS) is mostly used for clusterheads and clustering methodology. The definition can be shown as follows:

Definition 10.14 (Weakly Connected Dominating Set). Given a CDG $G = (V, E)$, a subset $C \subseteq V$ is called a ***Weakly Connected Dominating Set*** of G if

(1) C is a *dominating set*, and
(2) the subgraph weakly induced by C (denoted as $N[C]$) is connected. Actually, $N[C]$ is the subgraph induced by C and its neighborhood.

We divide the graph into several clusters by Weakly CDS such that each cluster member is within radio range of at least one clusterhead. There are two approaches to do this. The first one is to cluster node geographically if nodal location information is known. The second one is to cluster the node base on the graph topology. Ephremides[74] gave the first algorithm to calculate Weakly CDS by electing each node's neighbor with the lowest ID as their clusterhead. Chen and Liestman[75] proposed a series of approximations to computing Weakly CDS used to cluster mobile ad hoc networks. Nodes learn about their current neighbors' ID through periodic beacons. Whenever a node with a lower ID moves into range of a clusterhead, it becomes the new clusterhead. Gerla[76] reduced the number of clusters by highest connectivity clustering.

10.8. Conclusion and Discussion

In this chapter, we are aiming at the latest researches on dominating problems in wireless sensor networks. Since wireless network lacks physical infrastructures (i.e., base stations) or centralized administrations (i.e., mobile switching centers), selecting a virtual backbone has significant importance. A *Connected Dominating Set* (CDS) fixes this requirement and thus becomes an crucial combinatorial concept in the construction of wireless networks. Finding a *Minimum Connected Dominating Set* is currently an attractive topic in this field.

According to the special property of wireless sensor networks, people often use *unit disk graph* (UDG), *disk graph* (DG) etc., to represent the communication graph of such networks. Since finding MCDS is NP-hard in both general graph and UDG, researchers constructed various approximation algorithms to select a feasible solution which may be very close to the optimal solution. Some algorithms are really time-consuming. Thus people use distributed algorithms to reduce the complexity, but the result sometimes is not as good as those selected from centralized algorithms, in most cases.

Usually, finding a *Maximal Independent Set* (MIS) is much easier than finding a CDS in graph theory. Besides, it is well known that a MIS is also *Dominating Set*. Thus the majorities of works dealing with CDS problems are trying to find a MIS and then connect it. The relationship between MIS and CDS has been analyzed thoroughly in the literature. However, a branch of works did select a CDS directly by *Steiner Tree* problem or *Spanning Tree* problem, etc.

Due to the speedy development of wireless networks, people gradually extend their attention to different variations of CDS problems. In recent years, several research groups got big achievements for related dominating problems. We now have constant-factor heuristics to solve MCDS problem under weight version, PTAS to find CDS in three-dimensional space, Log-APX approximation to construct CDS with bounded diameters, and a lots of researches on d-hop CDS, k-Connected m-Dominating problems.

However, we still have a lot of things to do in the future. For instance, does there exist a PTAS to construct *Minimum Weight Connected Dominating Set* (MWCDS) in UDG? How about *Minimum Weight Strongly Connected Dominating Set* in DG? Furthermore, for many variations of dominating problem, there's no detailed theoretical discussion about the approximation performance of the existing heuristics. Many works only have numerical experiments under some special conditions to show the robustness of their algorithms. These topics are all worth considering as future works.

References

1. R. Kay and F. Mattern, The design space of wireless sensor networks, *IEEE Wireless Communications*, **11**(6), 54–61 (2004).
2. G. T. Huang, Casting the wireless sensor net, *Technology Review*, 50–56 (2003).
3. H. Salem and N. Mohamed, Middleware challenges and approaches for wireless sensor networks, *IEEE Distributed Systems Online*, **7**(3), art. no. 0603-03001 (2006).
4. J. Blum, M. Ding, A. Thaeler and X. Z. Cheng, Connected dominating set in sensor networks and MANETs, *Handbook of Combinatorial Optimization*, 329–369 (2004).

5. B. Das, E. Sivakumar and V. Bhargavan, Routing in ad-hoc networks using a virtual backbone, *Proceedings of the 6th International Conference on Computer Communications and Networks(IC&N '97)*, 1–20 (1997).
6. R. Sivakumar, B. Das and V. Bharghavan, An improved spine-based infrastructure for routing in ad hoc networks, *Proceedings of the 3rd IEEE Symposium on Computers and Communications (ISCC'98)* (1998).
7. T. W. Haynes, S. T. Hedetniemi and P. J. Slater, *Fundamentals of Domination in Graphs*, A Series of Monographs and Textbooks, Marcel Dekker, Inc. (1998).
8. B. Das, E. Sivakumar and V. Bhargavan, Routing in ad-hoc networks using a spine, *IEEE International Conference on Computers and Communications Networks'97* (1997).
9. J. Wu and H. Li, A dominating-set-based routing scheme in ad hoc wireless networks, *Proceedings of the Third International Workshop Discrete Algorithms and Methods for Mobile Computing and Communications (DIALM'99)* (1999).
10. M. L. Huson and A. Sen, Broadcast scheduling algorithms for radio networks, *Military Communications Conference, IEEE MILCOM '95*, (2), 647–651 (1995).
11. T. A. McKee and F. R. McMorris, *Topics in Intersection Graph Theory*, Philadelphia: Society for Industrial and Applied Mathematics (SIAM Monographs on Discrete Mathematics and Applications, No. 2) (1999).
12. T. Nieberg, Wireless sensor networks: Graph topologies and local clustering, *ASCI Springschool on Wireless Sensor Networks*, (2008).
13. H. Attiya and J. Welch, *Distributed Computing: Fundamentals, Simulations, and Advanced Topics*, Wiley-Interscience (2004).
14. M. R. Garey and D. S. Johnson, *Computer and Interactablity: A Guide to the Theory of NP-Completeness*, Fressman, San Francisco (1978).
15. P. Crescenzi and V. Kann (eds.), *A Compendium of NP Optimization Problems*, from http://www.nada.kth.se/~viggo/problemlist/.
16. T. Nieberg, *Independent and Dominating Sets in Wireless Communication Graphs*, Doctorial Thesis in University of Twente Repository (2006).
17. G. Ausiello, P. Crescenzi, G. Gambosi, V. Kann, A. Marchetti-Spaccamela and M. Protasi, *Complexity and Approximation: Combinatorial Optimization Problems and Their Approximability Properties*, Springer-Verlag Berlin, Heidelberg (1999).
18. B. Escoffier and V. Th. Paschos, Completeness in approximation classes beyond APX, *Theoretical Computer Science*, **359**(1), 369–377 (2006).
19. C. Bazgan, B. Escoffier and V. Th. Paschos, *Poly-APX and PTAS-Completeness in Standard and Differential Approximation*, Springer Berlin, Heidelberg (2004).
20. J. Wu, Extended dominating-set-based routing in ad hoc wireless networks with unidirectional links, *IEEE Transactions on Parallel and Distributed Systems*, **13**(9), 866–881 (2002).
21. D. Z. Du and F. Hsu (eds.), *Combinatorial Network Theory (Applied Optimization)*, Kluwer Academic Publishers (1995).
22. B. S. Baker, Approximation Algorithms for NP-complete Problems on Planar Graphs, *Journal of ACM*, **41**, 153–180 (1994). Extended abstract published in the proceedings of FOCS'83, 265–273 (1983).
23. D. S. Hochbaum and W. Maass, Approximation schemes for covering and packing problems in image processing and VLSI, *Journal of the ACM*, **32**(1), 130–136 (1985).
24. F. K. Hwang, D. S. Richards and P. Winter, *The Steiner Tree Problem*, Elsevier, North-Holland (Annals of Discrete Mathematics, Vol. 53) (1992).

25. C. Lund and M. Yannakakis, On the hardness of approximating minimization problems, *Journal of the ACM*, **41**(5), 960–981 (1994).
26. U. Feige, A threshold of $\ln n$ for approximating set cover, *Proceedings of the 28th ACM Symposium on Theory of Computing*, ACM, 314–318 (1996).
27. B. N. Clark, C. J. Colbourn and D. S. Johnson, Unit disk graphs, *Discrete Mathematics*, **86**, 165–177 (1990).
28. D. Lichtenstein, Planar formulae and their uses, *SIAM Journal on Computing*, **11**(2), 329–343 (1982).
29. K. M. Alzoubi, P. J. Wan and O. Frieder, New distributed algorithm for connected dominating set in wireless ad hoc networks, *Proceedings of the 35th Hawaii International Conference on System Sciences*, Big Island, Hawaii (2002).
30. M. Cadei, X. Cheng and D. Z. Du, Connected domination in ad hoc wireless networks, *Proceedings of the 6th International Conference on Computer Science and Informatics* (2002).
31. B. Gao, Y. H. Yang and H. Y. Ma, An efficient approximation scheme for minimum connected dominating set in wireless ad hoc networks, *IEEE Vehicular Technology Conference No. 60*, Los Angeles CA (2004).
32. B. Han and W. J. Jia, Design and analysis of connected dominating set formation for topology control in wireless ad hoc networks, *Proceedings of 14th International Conference on Computer Communications and Networks* (*ICCCN 2005*), 7–12 (2005).
33. B. Han, H. H. Fu, L. D. Lin and W. J. Jia, Efficient construction of connected dominating set in wireless ad hoc networks, *Proceedings of First IEEE International Conference on Mobile Ad Hoc and Sensor Systems*, Florida (2004).
34. M. V. Marathe, H. Breu, H. B. Hunt III, S. S. Ravi and D. J. Rosenkrantz, Simple heuristics for unit disk graphs, *Networks*, **25**, 59–68 (1995).
35. M. Min, H. W. Du, X. H. Jia, C. X. Huang, S. Ch. Huang and W. L. Wu, Improving construction for connected dominating set with steiner tree in wireless sensor networks, *Journal of Global Optimization*, **35**, 111–119 (2006).
36. X. Cheng, X. Huang, D. Li, W. Wu and D. Z. Du, Polynomial-time approximation scheme for minimum connected dominating set in ad hoc wireless networks, *Networks*, **42**(4), 202–208 (2003).
37. H. B. Hunt III, M. V. Marathe, V. Radhakrishnan, S. S. Ravi, D. J. Rosenkrantz and R. E. Stearns, NC-Approximation Schemesfor NP- and PSPACE-hard Problems for Geometric Graphs, *Journal of Algorithms*, **26**(2), 238–274 (1998).
38. P. J. Wan, K. M. Alzoubi and O. Frieder, Distributed construction of connected dominating set in wireless ad hoc networks, *Proceedings of the Third ACM Internat. Workshop on Discrete Algorithms and Methods for Mobile Computing and Communications*, 7–14 (1999).
39. W. L. Wu, H. W. Du, X. H. Jia, Y. S. Li and S. Ch. Huang, Minimum connected dominating sets and maximal independent sets in unit disk graphs, *Theortical Computer Science*, **352**, 1–7 (2006).
40. S. Funke, A. Kesselman and U. Meyer, A simple improved distributed algorithm for minimum CDS in unit disk graphs, *ACM Transactions on Sensor Networks*, **2**(3), 444–453 (2006).
41. X. Y. Li, X. F. Gao and W. L. Wu, A better theoretical bound to approximate connected dominating set in unit disk graph, *The 3rd International Conference on Wireless Algorithms, Systems and Applications* (*WASA 2008*), October 26–28 (2008).

42. K. M. Alzoubi, P. J. Wang and O. Frieder, Distributed heuristics for connected dominating sets in wireless ad hoc networks, *Journal of Communications and Networks*, **4**(1), (2002).
43. Y. S. Li, M. T. Thai, F. Wang, C. W. Yi, P. J. Wan and D. Z. Du, On greedy construction of connected dominating sets in wireless networks, *Wireless Communications and Mobile Computing*, **5**, 927–932 (2005).
44. G. M. Voronoi, Nouvelles applications des paramètres continus à la théorie des formes quadratiques. deuxième Mémoire: Recherches sur les parallélloèdres primitifs. *J. Reine Angew. Math.*, **134**, 198–287 (1908).
45. S. Guha and S. Khuller, Improved methods for approximating node weighted steiner trees and connected dominating sets, *Information and Computation*, **150**(1), 57–74, (1999).
46. P. Klein and R. Ravi, A nearly best-possible approximation algorithm for node-weighted steiner trees, *Journal of Algorithms*, **19**, 104–115 (1995).
47. D. Chen, D. Z. Du, X. Hu, G. H. Lin, L. Wang and G. Xue, Approximations for Steiner trees with minimum number of steiner points, *Journal of Global Optimization*, **18**, 17–33 (2000).
48. D. Z. Du, L. Wang and B. Xu, The euclidean bottleneck steiner tree and steiner tree with minimum number of steiner points, *The 7th Annual International Computing and Combinatorics Conference* (*COCOON 2001*), 509–518 (2001).
49. G. H. Lin and G. L. Xue, Steiner tree problem with minimum number of steiner points and bounded edge-length, *Information Processing Letters*, **69**, 53–57 (1999).
50. Y. Wang and X. Y. Li, Distributed low-cost backbone formation for wireless ad-hoc networks, *Proceedings of the 6th ACM International Symposium on Mobile Ad Hoc Networking and Computing* (*MobiHoc 2005*) 2–15 (2005).
51. V. V. Vazirani, *Approximation Algorithms*, Springer (2001).
52. E. J. van Leeuwen, Approximation algorithms for unit disk graphs, *Proceedings of the 31st International Workshop on Graph-Theoretic Concepts in Computer Science* (*WG'05*), LNCS **3787**, 351–361 (2005).
53. C. Ambühl, T. Erlebach, M. Mihal'ák and M. Nunkesser, Constant-factor approximation for minimum weight (Connected) dominating sets in unit disk graphs, book chapter in *Approximation, Randomization, and Combinatorial Optimization. Algorithms and Techniques, Proceedings of the 9th International Workshop on Approximation Algorithms for Combinatorial Optimization Problems* (*APPROX 2006*) and *10th International Workshop on Randomization and Computation* (*RANDOM 2006*), Springer Berlin/Heidelberg, 3–14 (2006).
54. X. F. Gao, Y. C. Huang, Z. Zhang and W. L. Wu, $(6+\varepsilon)$-approximation for minimum weight dominating set in unit disk graphs, *The 14th Annual International Computing and Combinatorics Conference* (*COCOON 2008*), Dalian, China, June 27–29 (2008).
55. Y. C. Huang, X. F. Gao, Z. Zhang and W. L. Wu, A better constant-factor approximation for weighted dominating set in unit disk graph, to be appeared in *Journal of Combinatorial Optimization* (2008).
56. F. Zou, X. Y. Li, D. H. Kim and W. L. Wu, Two constant approximation algorithms for node-weighted steiner tree in unit disk graphs, to be appeared in *The 2nd Annual International Conference on Combinatorial Optimization and Applications* (*COCOA 2008*), St. John's, Newfoundland, Canada, August 21–24 (2008).
57. A. D. Amis, R. Prakash, T. H. P. Vuong and D. T. Huynh, Max-min D-cluster formation in wireless ad hoc networks, *Proceedings of INFORCOM*, 32–41 (2001).

58. M. T. Thai and D. Z. Du, Connected dominating sets in disk graphs with bidirectional links, *IEEE Communications Letters*, **10**(33), 138–140 (2006).
59. M. T. Thai, F. Wang, D. Liu, S. W. Zhu and D. Z. Du, Connected dominating sets in wireless networks with different transmission ranges, *IEEE Transactions on Mobile Computing*, **6**(7), 721–730 (2007).
60. J. Wu, and H. Li, On calculating connected dominating set for efficient routing in ad hoc wireless networks, *Proceedings of the 3rd International Workshop on Discrete Algorithms and Methods for Mobile Computing and Communications*, 7–14 (1999).
61. J. Wu, M. Gao and I. Stojmenovic, On calculating power-aware connected dominating sets for efficient routing in ad hoc wireless networks, *Proceedings of International Conference on Parallel Processing* (*ICPP*), 346–356 (2001).
62. J. Wu, F. Dai, M. Gao and I. Stojmenovic, On calculating power-aware connected dominating sets for efficient routing in ad hoc wireless networks, *Journal of Communications and Networks*, **5**(2), 169–178 (2002).
63. D. Y. Li, H. W. Du, P. J. Wan, X. F. Gao, Z. Zhao and W. L. Wu, Minimum power strongly connected dominating sets in wireless networks, *The 2008 International Conference on Wireless Networks* (*ICWN'08*), Las Vegas, Nevada, USA, July 14–17 (2008).
64. S. Butenko and O. Ursulenko, *On Minimum Connected Dominating Set Problem in Unit Ball Graphs*, from http://ie.tamu.edu/people/faculty/butenko/papers (2007).
65. X. F. Zhong and J. Wang, Connected dominating set in 3-dimensional space for ad hoc network, *Proceedings of Wireless Communications and Networking Conference,* (*WCNC 2007*), 3609–3612 (2007).
66. J. C. Hansen and E. Schmutz, Comparison of two CDS algorithms on random unit ball graphs, *ALENEX/ANALCO 2005*, Vancouver, BC, Canada (2005).
67. F. Dai and J. Wu, Performance Analysis of broadcast protocols in ad hoc networks based on self pruning, *IEEE Transaction on Parallel and Distributed Systems*, **15**(11) (2004).
68. Z. Zhang, X. F. Gao, W. L. Wu and D. Z. Du, PTAS for minimum connected dominating set in unit ball graph, *The 3rd International Conference on Wireless Algorithms, Systems and Applications* (*WASA 2008*), October 26–28 (2008).
69. Y. W. Wu, F. Wang, M. T. Thai and Y. S. Li, Constructing k-connected m-dominating sets in wireless sensor networks, *Military Communications Conference* (*MILCOM 2007*), Orlando, FL, October 29–31 (2007).
70. F. Dai and J. Wu, On constructing k-connected k-dominating set in wireless network, *IEEE International Parallel and Distributed Processing Symposium* (2005).
71. F. Wang, M. T. Thai and D. Z. Du, 2-connected virtual backbone in wireless network, *IEEE Transactions on Wireless Communications* (2007).
72. W. Shang, F. Yao, P. J. Wan and X. Hu, Algorithms for minimum m-connected k-dominating set problem, *The 2nd Annual International Conference on Combinatorial Optimization and Applications* (*COCOA 2008*) (2007).
73. M. T. Thai, N. Zhang, R. Tiwari and X. Xu, On approximation algorithms of k-connected m-dominating sets in disk graphs, *Theoretical Computer Science* (2007).
74. A. Ephremides, J. Wieselthier and D. Baker, A design concept for reliable mobile radio networks with frequence hopping signaling, *Proceedings of the IEEE*, **75**, 56–73 (1987).
75. Y. Chen and A. Liestman, Approximating minimum size weakly-connected dominating sets for clustering mobile ad hoc networks, *ACM MobiHoc*, (2002).

76. M. Gerla and J. T. Tsai, Multicluster, mobile, multimedia, radio network, *ACM/Baltzer Journal on Wireless Networks*, **1**, 255–265 (1995).

The following references are not cited in the text

53. S. Meguerdichian, F. Koushanfar, M. Potkonjak and M. Srivastava, Coverage problems in wireless ad-hoc sensor networks, *IEEE Infocom 2001*, **3**, 1380–1387 (2001).

Part IV

Architecture, Design and Testbed

Chapter 11

Elements of Sensornet Testbed Design

Divya Sakamuri
Ford Motor Company
dsakamuri@gmail.com

Hongwei Zhang
Department of Computer Science
Wayne State University
hzhang@cs.wayne.edu

High fidelity experimental facilities play an important role in evaluating new sensornet protocols. In this chapter we will discuss the important elements of designing and implementing high fidelity sensornet testbeds, and we present in detail the elements of NetEye — a testbed with desirable features such as high-fidelity wireless environment, cost-effective hardware, web interface, and software tools to enable users to run potentially complex experiments. For instance, we will examine in detail the hardware details, software systems, and implementation (e.g., interference control) of NetEye.

11.1. Introduction

The research of wireless sensor networks (which we refer to as *sensornets* hereafter) has become prosperous in recent years because of their potential applications in important domains, such as environmental monitoring, surveillance, and disaster recovery. Wireless, sensor network scenarios are expected to grow rapidly at the edge of the Internet. These systems will also be increasingly used in pervasive computing applications where the Internet enables monitoring and interaction with every aspect of the physical world. Over the past few decades, the Internet has evolved into a global network supporting a variety of computing and telecommunication applications. In the future the Internet must also respond to the many emerging requirements such as those posed by wireless sensor networks.

In order to help build the next generation Internet which will include wireless and sensor network devices, researchers need a vehicle to drive their next ideas. Researchers are investigating next generation network architecture and protocols, but they need a facility to evaluate them. The evaluation can be done using analytical modeling, simulation or high-fidelity measurements.

Analytical modeling provides insights into the effects of various parameters and their interactions. In spite of its flexibility, analytical modeling is used somewhat less often in sensornet research compared to simulation or measurements. This is partly due to the complexity and tractability of analytical modeling. Another disadvantage of analytical modeling is its often simplified mathematical assumptions which may not capture all the complex behaviors of sensornets.

Simulation is a replication of reality. When applied to the study of research design, simulations can serve as a suitable substitute for constructing and understanding field research. Simulations are easier to set up than physical experiments, are easy to repeat and modify, and are highly portable. Nonetheless, most existing simulators are unable to model many essential characteristics of the "real world." because of their simplifying assumptions. Therefore, Simulations with simplified assumptions may not produce accurate results.

In view of the limitations of simulated environments, accordingly, wireless and sensor network experimental facilities are very important to the research community. When building high-fidelity experimental facilities, the following characteristics are desirable:

- Realistic environments which are not too sterile;
- Simple programming and experimental interface;
- Flexible, comprehensive experiment control;
- Scale in terms of devices;
- Mix of devices providing heterogeneity.

In the following sections we will discuss in detail the design issues, the architecture, and the implementation of sensornet testbeds that embody the above characteristics.

11.2. Design Issues for Wireless and Sensor Network Testbeds

To meet the goals of any deployment, proper design is the key factor. The testbed design should be done in such a way that the users can rely on the results of the facility. To obtain accurate results, the testbed should provide a controlled, realistic environment. Moreover, the testbed should be easy to use.

The deployment of a testbed with self-forming networks of wireless devices and sensor network devices requires a lot of design issues to be considered, among which are the following issues:

- Interference control
- Topology control
- Resource management
- Health monitoring necessity and requirements
- Provision of user tools
- Provision of administrative tools

11.2.1. *Interference control*

For testbeds to accurately generate results, an interference controlled environment is necessary. The wireless network devices are referred to by IEEE as 802.11 devices and the wireless sensor network devices as 802.15.4. One of the important concerns when building a wireless sensor network testbed is its coexistence with other wireless networks. Coexistence can be said to be "the ability of one system to perform a certain task in a given shared environment where other systems may or may not be using same set of rules". There will be many scenarios when different radios will operate in the same place and same time explosively growing the Industrial, Scientific and Medical (ISM) band usage. 802.15.4 radios share the 2.4 GHz ISB band with lots of other wireless devices like 802.11, Bluetooth headsets, 2.4 GHz cordless phones, microwaves, etc.

In some testbeds, deployment of both wireless and wireless sensor networks may be necessary. In such a situation 802.15.4 networks and 802.11 networks should operate simultaneously. Although the unlicensed ISB bands do not require strict coordination between the deployed devices, they do not permit all forms of behavior between the devices. The devices might interfere with each other and there could be loss of data and performance degradation.

To understand the potential problem, the available channels and RF spectrums for the 802.11 and 802.15.4 standards are shown in the following table and figure.

There are 11 channels in 802.11 with only 3 non-overlapping channels. Each channel has a 22 MHz frequency range. There are 16 channels in 802.15.4 with a 3 MHz frequency range and each channel is 5 MHz apart.

Table 11.1. 2.4 GHz ISM band (IEEE 802.15.4 and IEEE 802.11 channels).

	IEEE 802.11		IEEE 802.15.4	
	Ch.	Freq. (GHz)	Ch.	Freq. (GHz)
2.4 GHz ISM Band	1	2.401–2.423	11	2.405
	2	2.404–2.428	12	2.410
	3	2.411–2.433	13	2.415
	4	2.416–2.438	14	2.420
	5	2.421–2.443	15	2.425
	6	2.426–2.448	16	2.430
	7	2.431–2.453	17	2.435
	8	2.436–2.458	18	2.440
	9	2.441–2.463	19	2.445
	10	2.446–2.468	20	2.450
	11	2.451–2.473	21	2.455
			22	2.460
			23	2.465
			24	2.470
			25	2.475
			26	2.480

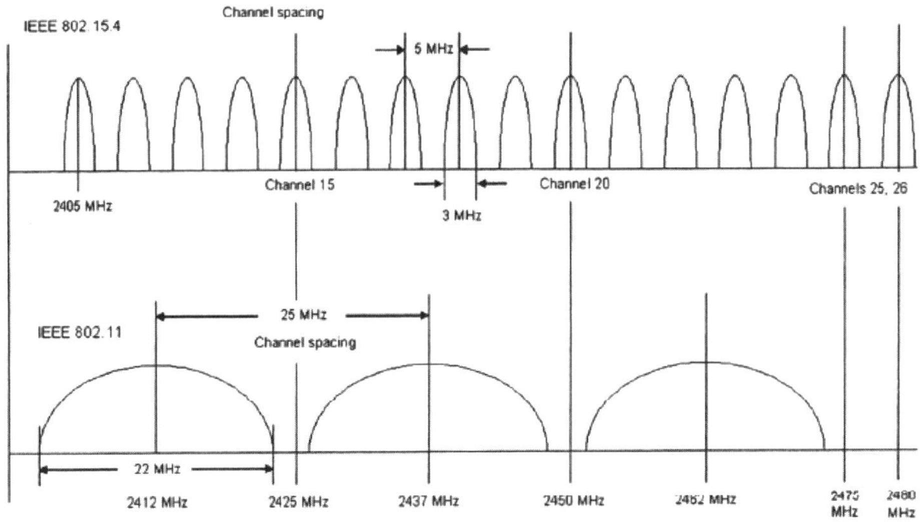

Fig. 11.1. RF channel spectrum of IEEE 801.15.4/ZigBee and IEEE 802.11b/WiFi.

Since the RF channels in 802.11 and 802.15.4 overlap there is a cause for concern. Even the beacon packets from the 802.11 access point cause considerable interference. To reduce the amount of interference from 802.11 devices, a channel on 802.15.4 that does not interfere with any 802.11 channel should be used.

From Fig. 11.1, we can observe the RF spectrum of channels 15–24 of 802.15.4 overlap with the channels 1–11 of 802.11. This shows that channels 25 and 26 in the 802.15.4 standard are interference free from any channels of the 802.11.

11.2.2. *Topology control*

A few of the important topology design considerations are to choose which place to use, which equipment to use, how the devices should be placed on the chosen equipment, etc.

Once the sensor and wireless devices are chosen according to the requirements the physical and radio properties of the devices should be studied. The equipment to place these devices should be selected appropriately. For example wood can be chosen to place the devices as it will not conduct. The sensor devices will have large transmission ranges indoors. Experiments should be done appropriately to set the transmission range to form a multi-hop network. Attenuator can be used to reduce the communications over large range.

11.2.3. *Resource management*

Resource allocation and management is a key factor for any shared computing and communication infrastructure. Resource allocation should provide fairness, efficiency, and reasonable performance for each scheduled task while honoring federated control. The challenge is to schedule all the tasks contending to use the nodes at the particular time. Some services using the testbed need guaranteed allocation of resources but some services may need just best-effort service model.

The shared testbed can either perform strict space sharing where individual jobs control a subset of nodes or best-effort scheduling where individual jobs receive resources inversely proportional to the number of currently competing jobs. The amount of resources that can be reserved by an application, the relative priority of best-effort applications, and the proportion of global resources subject to admission control are all matters of the resource allocation policy implemented in a particular testbed.

One of the important tasks of the resource allocation mechanism implemented is to allow efficient usage of the resources available. It should be ensured that the users only acquire only as much resources as they truly need and for only the period of time they really need them. Renewing of the resource privileges every few minutes should be implemented to ensure the resources usage efficiently.

Resource allocation algorithms implemented in the shared system, like a testbed should satisfy the following requirements:

(a) *Heterogeneous user base*
The testbed can be used for a simple network experiment or a complex system architecture research. The resource allocation algorithm should provide some baseline guarantee of the resource availability to both kinds of users.

(b) *Policy implementation*
The resource allocation should implement a appropriate policy to guarantee resources to the individual users and applications. The policy can either share equal resources for all the users or allocate more resources to certain type of users. If the first type is implemented then many of the resources will be wasted if the resources are not being used by them in a given particular time. The second method lacks fairness; a normal user may or may not get the resources he wants to use.

(c) *Resource isolation*
Once the policy mentioned in the above section is implemented, there should be resource isolation. Virtualization is one technique that can be used to provide isolation. Resource allocation and isolation are enforced on a per node basis.

(d) *Security and authentication*
Security is a primary requirement for any resource allocation infrastructure. Users must have a secure mechanism for authenticating themselves to the system and for receiving the resources that they are entitled to. Users should not be allowed to consume more than their allocated share of resources denying other users from using the system.

(e) *Separation of policy and mechanism*
Following two kinds of policies, best effort or guaranteed allocation, there should not be any fixed constraint on which user gets which resources, priorities of the jobs, etc. Basic mandatory classes of resource principles and the capabilities types should be defined which will take care that the resources are allocated within the authorized usage limits.

(f) *Providing proper incentives*
The enabled resource allocation policies should ensure user commitment to the continued maintenance and growth of the infrastructure and promote user consumption of only as many resources as they require, especially during times of peak demand.

11.2.4. *Health monitoring necessity and requirements*

A health monitoring service should be considered important while designing a wireless and sensor network testbed. The testbed will contain lots of hardware devices. It is natural for faults to occur in the middle of the experiment affecting the quality of the data. The fault can be due to the relatively unreliable wireless sensor network devices, software faults, or incorrect configuration of the devices. The faults can be categorized as follows:

(a) *Device failure*
Device failure, which the name itself suggests may be due to hardware failure or software fault that fails the device completely. There will be many hardware devices that might fail. The failure might be in the wireless sensor device, wireless device, etc. It depends on the deployed devices in the particular testbed.

(b) *Software defects*
Software defects and errors might corrupt a device or a network interface. This might be due to a bug in the code or using wrongly configured software.

(c) *Fault on the network interface*
Communication between the devices might also fail due to driver failure, an unplugged Ethernet cable, detached cards, etc. A situation where all the network interfaces fail, resulting in a detached forest of devices, is also a possible. These faults are important to be diagnosed for both the users and the administrators of the testbed.

There are several important requirements to be considered while developing a health monitoring service since both the administrators and users use this tool. The requirements are as follows:

(a) *Correctness and reliability*
The monitoring results obtained should be correct. Incorrect data leads to misuse of the testbed facility. The status of each and every resource in the network

should be reliably obtained. The monitoring service should be reliable in the manner that it should not be affected by the experiments scheduled on the testbed or the communication procedures. If this happens then the monitoring results might be incorrect.

(b) *Efficiency*
The monitoring application should be efficient. This means it should not consume lots of time and lots of testbed resources. It should be efficient enough to monitor using less time, few messages, and fewer resources.

(c) *Independent and adaptable*
A testbed runs with lots of hardware devices. Hardware devices do not last forever; they might be replaced due to several reasons. The health monitoring code should be independent of all such changes and should adapt to any replacements on the testbed. It should be adaptable even when the network devices, interfaces, and the configuration changes with very little effort.

(d) *Availability*
Monitored results should be available to the users and administrators in real time. To accommodate this requirement, health monitoring code should be automated to run periodically or it should be flexible to even run on demand. The results should be displayed on the GUI for the users and the administrators.

(e) *Handling heterogeneity*
A wireless and wireless sensor network testbeds may have many different devices with different capabilities and limitations. The health monitoring application should be capable enough to monitor the status of different hardware components like wireless devices, sensor network devices, Ethernets, embedded Linux systems, etc.

11.2.5. *Provision of user tools*

The kind of user tools to be provided to the user using the testbed is another important design decision to be made. The tools should be very user friendly, flexible for the use; and provide the user with full control on his experiment. A graphical user interface should be provided to each user for easy access and control of his experiments. The interface should also be remotely available. Ideally, the sensor network testbed GUI should have the necessary tools to perform the following operations:

(a) *Tool for registering as a new user*
New users should be able to register into the testbed for doing their experiments. The users should be given a form to fill in and the administrator should check the accuracy of the information. Once the validation of the user information is done, he should be given access to the testbed with appropriate privileges. This method provides an easy way for both the users and administrators.

(b) *Tool for scheduling an experiment*
The user, once provided authentication, should be able to schedule the nodes for his experiment. The nodes should be assigned according to the resource allocation algorithm implemented in the testbed. The algorithm can either be best-effort access or guaranteed access to the nodes. The user can select the start time for his experiment and also the duration to run his program.

(c) *Tool for knowing the job status*
The user will always want to know the status of his scheduled experiment. The status should be communicated to the user through a GUI interface. This increases the user trust on the deployed testbed. Also implementing the necessary security mechanisms (the user should view only his jobs) is appropriate.

(d) *Tool for canceling the experiment*
The testbed design should be done in such a way that it should save the resources whenever possible. There should be a provision to cancel the scheduled experiment at any moment. This saves lots of resources if the user has scheduled a wrong experiment, or on the wrong nodes that he does not want to use. Another advantage is if the user has specified a wrong duration, say 100 minutes instead of 10 minutes, it is not a good idea to wait for 100 minutes when the user really does not want to.

(e) *Tool for injection of real time data*
The user might want to inject the data into the wireless or sensor devices when necessary. It might be any time during the experiment (real time). A GUI interface should allow the user to inject his data into the appropriate nodes when necessary. This injection should be abstract enough not to interfere with other nodes running different experiments and the data logging facility.

(f) *Tool for monitoring the health status of the nodes*
To provide the user with up-to-date information about the nodes, a health monitoring service is necessary. If the user checks the health of the node often while the job is in process he can determine the quality and correctness of the output data. If the node is up and running before the job and after the job too, then if is less likely that the produced result is not correct. If the node is running before the job and if it fails in the middle and still gives some results, the users will know the result is not accurate. Through the health monitoring tool, users can also know the job statistics on a particular testbed.

(g) *Provision to collect the results*
The job of a testbed is not done with experiment scheduling, resource allocating, health monitoring, etc. It has to provide the results to the users for analysis. A GUI should provide the user with the link to collect his experimental data, errors if any to analyze.

With all the above facilities provided and running, a testbed provides a realistic, flexible, easy to use environment to the users. Such testbed provisioning is of high importance to the research community as it eliminates most of the disadvantages of simulated environments.

11.2.6. *Provision of administrative tools*

Administrative tools are necessary for maintenance of the testbed. Different kinds of administrative tools can be developed according to the requirements. The following explained administrative tools are very important in any testbed.

(a) *Creating New Users*
Only the administrators should have privileges to create new users. Administrators should have a handy tool to add the user into the system. This helps to reduce the manual work of the administrators.

(b) *Health Monitoring as an Administrative Tool*
The health monitor serves both as an administrator as well as a user tool. For administrators it is to help maintain the testbed. Through this service, administrators will easily know the nodes that are down and fixing the node will be easier. This way because the administrators do not have to go and check each node manually in such a large facility.

11.3. Survey of Existing Testbeds

The setting up of different wired, wireless and sensor network testbeds is growing in fast pace. A few of the important testbeds in United States are listed in the following table:

11.3.1. *Kansei*

The Kansei Testbed at Ohio State University was developed to provide sensing at scale. The Kansei testbed consists of stationary array with 210 nodes (XSM and

Table 11.2. Testbeds detail chart.

Testbed name	Year	Establishment
Kansei	2004	The Ohio State University
Motelab	2004	Harvard University
SensorNet	2005	Intel Berkeley Research Labs
Orbit	2005	Rutgers(WINLAB), Columbia, and Princeton, Lucent Bell Labs, IBM Research and Thomson
Emulab	2002	University of Utah
Planetlab	2002	Berkeley, Intel Research, MIT, Washington, Rice, Princeton, Columbia, Duke, Utah, HP

Stargates) on a rectangular 15 × 14 rectangular bench with 3 feet spacing, 150 TMote sky nodes for mobility, 50 Trio motes in a portable array that duplicates the sensors in a stationary array for at-scale high fidelity sensing, and 5 robotic mobile nodes.

The objectives of the Kansei testbed include

- Provision of heterogeneous hardware infrastructure for wireless and sensor network experiments. Stargates are used as wireless network devices and TMote sky nodes are used as sensor nodes.
- A time accurate hybrid simulation engine for simulation that is designed to simulate large-scale experiments with an emphasis on high fidelity on timing, application, radio and sensing environments and complements the prior work on simulation.
- High fidelity sensor data generation and real-time data and event injection on the fly, which enables dynamic experiments with the mobile nodes where the user can change the input processes in real time.
- Software components to support complex multi-tier experiments utilizing real hardware resources, and data generation and simulation engines.

In the Kansei testbed a user can define the topology and schedule a job through the remote web interface. There is provision for data storage, data analysis, remote access, and high fidelity sensor data generation and injection. Easy data retrieval is another added advantage in the Kansei Testbed. The Kansei Testbed includes a cluster of PCs for running visualizations, compute-intensive analysis, high-fidelity sensor data generation, hybrid simulation, and diagnostic analysis. One of the PCs, called Director is a remotely accessible multi-user framework provides the services. It provides services for experiment scheduling, deployment, monitoring and management for all array platforms like motes and stargates, creation and management of testbed configurations, system administrative services for managing the testbeds, and it contains tools for data injection, and logging of all array platforms and tools for hybrid simulation. "Chowkidar" which means watchman, is Kansei's health monitoring tool. Periodically the health-monitoring service runs automatically giving important data about the testbed devices.

Health monitoring serves both users and the administrators. For users monitoring this data helps in analyzing the real time data if any node is corrupted or producing error, etc. For the administrators it helps in detecting if the node or device is not working and helps in knowing the reason why it happened. The software is developed in PHP, Perl, and MySQL as the backend.

11.3.2. *Motelab*

The objective of the Motelab testbed at Harvard is to meet the challenge of deploying, developing, and debugging applications on realistic environments on a large scale. Recently, they have deployed 190 TMote Sky sensor "motes" with T1 MSP430 processors running at 8 MHz, with 10 KB of RAM, 1 Mb Flash Memory, and a Chipcon CC2420 radio. The CC2420 radio operates at 2.4 GHz and has an indoor range of approximately 100 meters. The motes are powered from wall power. The motes run the TinyOS operating system and are programmed in NesC language. The mote provides two TCP ports, one for reprogramming and one for data logging. The functionality of Motelab includes create, edit and schedule a job, programming the node, and logging the data through a central server. Users access the testbed using the web browser to set up or schedule jobs and download data.

The different software components of the motelab are

- Web interface for job creation, scheduling, and data collection.
- MySQL database backend for storing the collected data.
- DBLogger, a Java program to parse the generated data. It will be started at the beginning of every job. It connects to the data logging port of emote and its main job is to collect the data.
- Job Daemon, a Perl script job running as a cron job is responsible to set up experiments, which involves reprogramming nodes and starting other necessary system components like DBLogger and tears them down when finished, and dumping the data from the MySQL database into a format suitable for download.

Resource scheduling in motelab is done through defining the user quota, which facilitates sharing the lab between multiple uses. The quota does not control how much total access the user will have on the lab. It limits the number of outstanding jobs the user can post to the lab at once. Motelab also provides direct access to the nodes serial port over a TCP/IP connection. This helps in monitoring and injecting the data to the motes via its serial port. An important service motelab avails is power measurement. Since the sensor network developers become aware of power as a design constraint this feature is developed. A networked Keithley Digital Multimeter is attached to a node and it will sample continuously at 250 Hz, it bursts at 3000 Hz, and this value is displayed on the main page of the web interface.

There are two different ways to use motelab. One is batch use where a user can schedule a batch of jobs and does not have to worry about them till he gets the data. Other is real time use, where the user can interact directly with their job by attaching to the exposed per-node serial forwarder or accessing the MySQL database. Motelab has a connectivity daemon, which is kind of health monitoring tool. It is used to collect the information about the nodes and graphically represent the connectivity on the Maps pages. The administrators can run it periodically when the lab is available. A Java program that runs during the job connects directly to active nodes and uses this connection to tell them when to send messages and when to listen. A Perl script accesses the database tables and calculates the packet losses and updates the connectivity information between the pair of nodes.

11.3.3. *SensorNet*

SensorNet is a testbed by Intel Berkeley Research. It has 150 MicaZ motes with CC2420 802.15.4 radios. A canonical testbed incorporates a collection of compute and sensing nodes that are coupled together by an out-of-band communication channel and a power supply. This channel provides for remote control, reprogramming and data collection independent of a node's wireless capabilities. The power supply eliminates the need to replace batteries, reducing the physical maintenance needs of the testbed.

The current testbed resource allocation algorithm has the following shortcomings:

- Inability of meeting real user demands on a large system.
- Either lack or have inadequate mechanisms for resolving contention among competing users during peak times of demand. This system often requires direct system administrator intervention to resolve conflicts.
- They provide limited mechanisms for expressing resource. So the user cannot express desired resources and their associated constraints.
- This affects the efficient utilization of the underlying resources by limiting the system's ability to make intelligent allocations for multiple users.

To address user contention Intel Research Berkeley has developed tool "Mirage" for allocation of resources. It applies microeconomic approach to arbitrate among competing users. Users will be given virtual currency to request for the resources. A combinatorial auction is then run periodically to determine which bids are allocated resources based on supply and demand while aiming to maximize aggregate utility. A combinatorial auction is periodically run to determine which user bids are allocated resources based on supply and demand. Any user who ever spends more currency on particular resources is the winner. The aim is to maximize the aggregate utility of the resources on the testbed.

11.3.4. *Orbit*

Orbit is an open-access research testbed for next generation wireless networks. The Orbit testbed consists of an indoor radio grid emulator for controlled experimentation and an outdoor field trial network for end-user evaluations in real-world settings. It consists of 20×20 802.11 radio nodes with 1 m spacing in the indoor testbed and a mix of 3G and 802.11 nodes in the outdoor testbed which spans over a region of 5 Km wide and 2 km long space.

The design objectives of the Orbit testbed at Winlab, Rutgers include

- Scalability in terms of the number of wireless nodes.
- Reproducibility of experiments which can be repeated in similar environments for similar results.

- Open-access flexibility giving the researcher high-level control over protocols and software used on the testbed.
- Extensive measurement capability at all layers providing cross layer experimental possibility.
- Access to the testbed remotely through a web interface.

11.3.5. *Emulab*

Emulab at the University of Utah has a wide range of environments developing, debugging, and evaluating the systems. They call it universally available "Internet in the room" to provide balance between control and realism. The main design goal of Emulab is to provide penalty free accessibility of the nodes that is hundred percent configurable. The other goals are scalability and flexibility. Emulab contains 160 end nodes and 40 core nodes (PC650/800) which are wired, a few 802.11a/b/g nodes, 25 Mica2 motes for wireless sensor networks, 6 Garcia motes for mobility.

There are different experimental environmental facilities in Emulab like the following:

- Emulation — An emulated experiment allows specifying an arbitrary topology and gives controllable, predictable and repeatable environments giving full control of the nodes.
- Live Internet experimentation — Using PlanetLab, Emulab provided a full featured environment to run the applications at hundreds of sites around the world.
- An 802.11 wireless environment for wireless applications.
- Software Defined Radio — It gives control over layer 1 of a wireless network. Everything from signal processing and up is done in software.
- A sensor network facility for sensor applications.
- A mobile sensor Network facility for sensor applications involving mobility.
- Simulation — Using the ns-2 emulation facility simulated environment can interact with real networks.

Emulab provides services through provisioning of web-based tools to remotely configure reserve and control machines, to define error models, latency, bandwidth, and packet ordering. It provides high speed network processor chips. Emulab also has non-intrusion instrumentation for security. Emulab network testbed software provides the first remotely-accessible mobile wireless and sensor testbed. This testbed is robust. Robots carry motes and single board computers through a fixed indoor field of sensor-equipped motes, all running the user's selected software. In real-time, interactively or driven by a script, remote users can position the robots, control all the computers and network interfaces, run arbitrary programs, and log data.

Emulab provides simple path planning, a vision-based tracking system accurate to 1 cm, live maps, and webcams. Precise positioning and automation allow quick and painless evaluation of location and mobility effects on wireless protocols, location algorithms, and sensor-driven applications.

11.3.6. *PlanetLab*

PlanetLab works as a global platform for designing and evaluating network services. PlanetLab is the first testbed that is distributed across the world with 834 nodes at 408 sites. Planet Lab's design evolved incrementally based on experience gained from supporting a live user community called experience-driven design, and the design decisions made with conflicting requirements called conflict-driven design.

The design objectives in PlanetLab include

- Immediate availability to researchers to do their experiments. It is achieved by spreading the nodes all across the world and implementing a fair resource allocation algorithm.
- Global platform that supports both short term experiments and long running services. The services run continuously and support real client workload.
- Autonomy and decentralized control is achieved through distribution of control to different organizations who contributed to PlanetLab and thus reducing the centralized control.
- Scalability to support many users with minimal resources by promoting efficient resource sharing.
- Distributed virtualization, which means running a service as a slice in every node which acts as an individual system. The user does not even know that he is just using a part of the resources; it seems all the resources are allocated to him through this service.
- Unbundled management services used in the PlanetLab testbed has three arguments, namely
    - To allow the system to more easily evolve;
    - To permit third-party developers to build alternative services, enabling a software bazaar, rather than rely on a single development team with limited resources and creativity; and
    - To permit decentralized control over PlanetLab resources, and ultimately, over its evolution.

11.3.7. *Physical parameter comparison of different testbeds*

Each testbed discussed so far has a different level of design detail according to the goal and requirements. Table 11.3 provides the comparison chart of different testbeds with respect to different physical parameters like the type, node type, radio type, scale and field.

Table 11.3. Physical parameter comparison table for different testbeds.

Parameter	Kansei	MoteLab	SensorNet	Orbit	Emulab	PlanetLab
Type	Wireless, wireless sensor	Wireless sensor	Wireless sensor	Wireless	Wired, Wireless, Wireless sensor and Mobile	Wired networks
Node type	XSM, Stargates TMote sky, robotic mobile nodes	TelosB, Mica2 motes, MIB-600 motes	Sensor motes	802.11 nodes, 3G cellular	Pc(600/850) nodes, 802.11X nodes, mica2 motes, robotic nodes	Wired nodes
Radio type	802.15.4	802.15.4	802.15.4	802.11	802.11/ 802.15.4	—
Scale	1500	190	150	400	250	846
Field	Indoor/ Outdoor	Indoor	Indoor	Indoor	Indoor	Distributed

Table 11.4. Design parameter comparison of different testbed.

Design	Kansei	Motelab	SensorNet	Orbit	Emulab	PlanetLab
Topology design	3 ft wood tables, 20 db antenna	Multiple floors	—	Indoor 20×20 nodes with 1m space.	Multiple floors	Across the world
Resource allocation	FCFS, best-effort	FCFS with user quota, best-effort	Auction model	FCFS, best-effort	FCFS	Best-effort and guaranteed
Health monitoring	Chowkidar	Connectivity graphs	—	Script	Slice, sliver mechanism	Health Monitoring service
Tools	Select topology, Schedule, Upload, manage, retrieve	Select topology, Schedule, upload, manage, retrieve	No user tools for data logging and automated reprogramming	Schedule Ruby script to upload and select nodes, orbit commands	Ns2 script to select topology, schedule, run and terminate the experiment. Results through email	Scripts to schedule program

11.3.8. *Design parameter comparison of different testbeds*

Table 11.4 provides the comparison chart of different testbeds with respect to different design parameters like the topology, resource allocation, health monitoring, and available tools.

11.4. NetEye

The NetEye testbed at Wayne State University is deployed to facilitate research on wireless and wireless sensing applications at scale. The NetEye testbed consists of a controlled indoor environment with a set of sensor nodes and wireless nodes deployed permanently. This topic helps the reader to understand the implementation of the design issues in greater detail.

The NetEye testbed provides a web interface to create and schedule a job on the testbed while automated reprogramming of the sensor devices and storing the experimental data on the server. NetEye has the following features:

- It motivates application deployment by providing access to a large scale, fixed sensor network.
- Through automatic storage and logging of data, it accelerates the debugging and development of an application.
- NetEye provides a web interface allowing both local and remote users to easily access the testbed.
- The resource scheduling mechanism used in NetEye ensures a fair share of resources to its users.
- NetEye consists of heterogeneous hardware for computations, data storage, and to support complex experimentation.
- It provides real-time data and event injection on the fly.
- Software components in NetEye support multi-tier complex experiments.

11.4.1. *Interference control in NetEye*

The NetEye testbed has both wireless and wireless sensor network devices. The NetEye testbed deals with the issue of coexistence between wireless and sensor networks thus providing an interference controlled environment. The wireless network devices are referred to by IEEE as 802.11 devices and the Wireless Sensor Network devices as 802.15.4 radio devices. Both these devices share the 2.4 GHz ISB band. So there is a chance that the packets from one device can be interrupted by the other and the packets may be lost. More details about considering this as an important design issue are explained in Sec. 2.

In NetEye this issue is taken seriously since the testbed setup itself contains both wireless and wireless sensor devices. There are many access points around the NetEye testbed set up, so definitely there is a need to find an interference free channel for 802.15.4 radio devices. There are 11 channels in 802.11 with only 3 non-overlapping channels. Each channel has a 22 MHz frequency range. There are 16 channels in 802.15.4 with 3 MHz frequency range and each channel is 5 MHz apart.

To measure the environmental noise, a TinyOS application, written in the NesC language that samples RF energy at 1 KHz by reading the RSSI register of the CC2420 radio is used. The register contains the average Received Signal Strength

Indicator (RSSI) over the past 8 symbol periods (125 microseconds). The application logs this data to flash for a fixed period of time (2 minute period with one sample for a millisecond). The data is collected on the PC through UART (serial port).

Noise is sampled on different radio channels in a variety of environments; including the NetEye embedded testbed lab at Wayne State University which has six access points from the surrounding areas, Undergraduate library at Wayne State University where there is heavy usage of 802.11, Deroy apartments where there is no access point present but some peer-to-peer networks exist and an outdoor quiet area in Richmond where neither access points nor peer-to-peer networks exists.

To find the difference on how just the existence of the 802.11 access point without heavy usage and with heavy usage changes the interference levels on 802.15.4, an experiment is conducted to collect RSSI values while downloading a large HTTP file.

Table 2.1 in Chapter 2 shows the RF spectrum of available channels for 802.11 and 802.15.4. According to the table it seems like channels 25 and 26 of 802.15.4 do not interfere with any channels of 802.11.

Following experiments are done to determine the interference channel to provide the controlled environment:

- Channel 11 set in 802.15.4 when channel 1 is set in 802.11 network
- Channel 16 set in 802.15.4 when channel 6 is set in 802.11 network
- Channel 17 set in 802.15.4 when channel 6 is set in 802.11 network
- Channel 21 set in 802.15.4 when channel 11 is set in 802.11 network
- Channel 22 set in 802.15.4 when channel 11 is set in 802.11 network
- Channel 26 set in 802.15.4 when channel 1 is set in 802.11 network
- Channel 26 set in 802.15.4 when channel 6 is set in 802.11 network
- Channel 26 set in 802.15.4 when channel 11 is set in 802.11 network

The following tables show the measured RSSI values at different areas at different times. The median and confidence intervals (95%) for 5000 samples are represented in the tables and the box plots are used to represent the overlapping and non-overlapping confidence intervals.

11.4.1.1. *NetEye Embedded Lab*

NetEye Embedded Lab is at Wayne State University and is the place where the testbed is set up. The room has few access points around. The values when Channel 26 is set in 802.15.4 and channels 1, 6, 11 are set in 802.11 are measured and they are stable with standard deviation almost less than 1. Channels 11, 17, and 21 in 802.15.4 have non-overlapping confidence intervals (CI) compared to channel 26 when corresponding interfering channels are set in 802.11.

The box plot below shows the non-overlapping confidence intervals between the interfering and non-interfering channels. The dark gray line represents the median and the notches represent the confidence intervals.

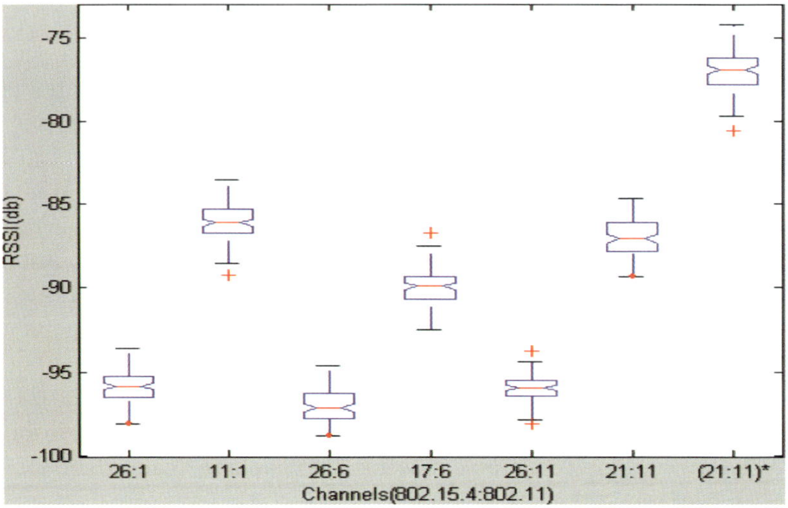

Fig. 11.2. Boxplot showing median and 95% CI-NetEye Embedded lab.

The first column is when channel 26 (non-interfering) is set in 802.15.4 and column 2 is when channel 11 (interfering) is set in 802.15.4 when channel 1 is set in 802.11. The RSSI values do not overlap showing the significantly different values. Likewise other values need to be compared. The last column (21:11)* shows the different non-overlapping performance compared to 21:11. This is when a large file is being downloaded and the values are significantly different.

11.4.1.2. *Undergraduate library at Wayne State University*

The Undergraduate library at Wayne State University has a heavy usage of 802.11 network. The box plot below shows the non-overlapping confidence intervals between the interfering and non-interfering channels. The red line represents the median and the notches represent the confidence intervals. The first column is when channel 26 (non-interfering) is set in 802.15.4 and column 2 is when channel 11 (interfering) is set in 802.15.4 when channel 1 is set in 802.11. The RSSI values do not overlap showing the significantly different values. Likewise column 26:6 and 17:6 show non-overlapping values. Columns 26:11 and 21:11show non-overlapping CI values.

11.4.1.3. *Deroy apartments*

The apartments in Wayne State University does not have any access points but have a few peer-peer networks. The box plot below shows the overlapping confidence intervals between all the channels. The red line represents the median and the notches represent the confidence intervals. The first column is when channel 26 (non-interfering) is set in 802.15.4 and column second is when channel 11 (interfering) is

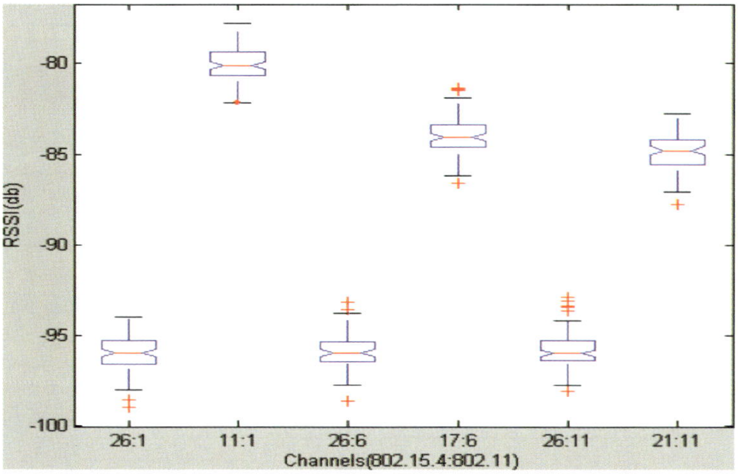

Fig. 11.3. Boxplot showing median and 95% CI-Undergraduate Library.

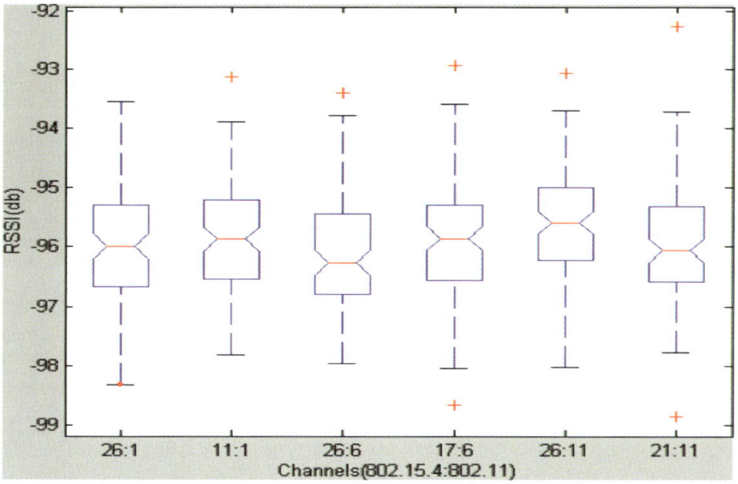

Fig. 11.4. Boxplot showing median and 95% CI-Deroy apartments.

set in 802.15.4 when channel 1 is set in 802.11. The RSSI values do overlap showing the values are in the same range. Likewise column 26:6 and 17:6 show overlapping values. Columns 26:11 and 21:11 show non overlapping CI values because of the existence of peer-peer networks.

11.4.1.4. *Quite area in Richmond*

There are no access points and peer-to-peer networks and the mean values are high, with much less standard deviation. The values at different confidence intervals are

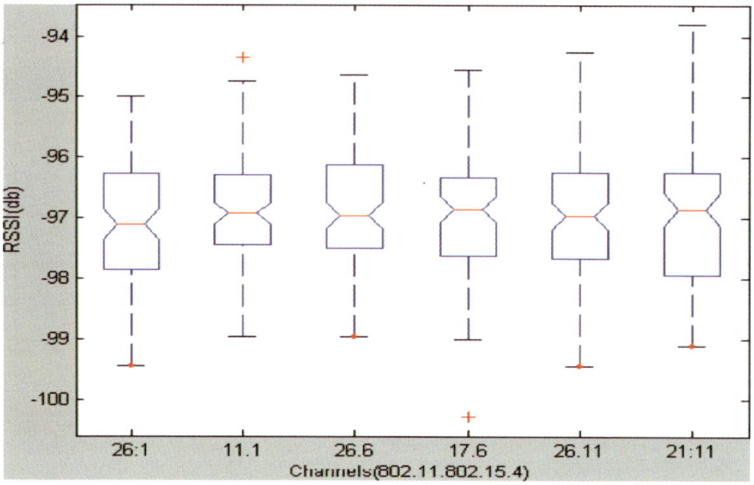

Fig. 11.5. Boxplot showing median and 95% CI-Richmond.

also almost in the same range. The box plot below shows the overlapping confidence intervals between all the channels. The red line represents the median and the notches represent the confidence intervals. The first column is when channel 26 (non-interfering) is set in 802.15.4 and column second is when channel 11 (interfering) is set in 802.15.4 when channel 1 is set in 802.11. The RSSI values do overlap showing the values are in the same range. Likewise column 26:6 and 17:6 show overlapping values. Columns 26:11 and 21:11 show overlapping CI values because of the non-existence of access points and peer-peer networks.

11.4.2. *Results*

With a different set of experiments done at different times and different places, it can be concluded that channel 26 set in sensor devices provides the interference free environment even in the presence of access points. It is not affected by any channel at 802.11 networks. It provides necessary abstraction even in the presence of wireless network. This is a very important study for setting up a sensor testbed since if the interfering channel is set it will be affected even by the beacon packets from the access points and there is high possibility to provide less accurate results to the user.

11.4.3. *Elements of NetEye*

The block diagram below shows all the elements of NetEye. The elements include hardware and software components.

The details of all the elements of the NetEye testbed are as follows.

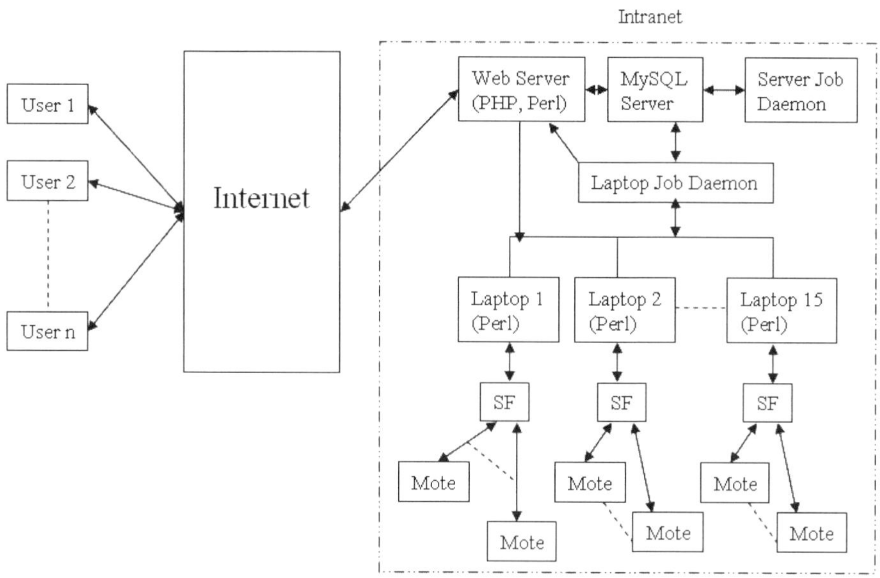

Fig. 11.6. Elements of NetEye.

11.4.3.1. *Hardware components*

NetEye consists of a fixed array of wireless and sensor nodes. The wireless nodes are Dell Vostro 1400 laptops with a Intel dual core processor, 1 GB RAM, and 80 GB hard disk. The operating system on the laptops is Linux Fedora core 8. There are 15 laptops arranged on 15 wooden benches. The benches are 1 foot apart column wise. Proper ventilation and air conditioning facilities are provided for the laptops as these will be used on a 24/7 basis.

The NetEye testbed has 130 "TelosB motes" connected to the laptops. The motes are connected through the USB interface. There are 6 to 12 motes connected to the laptops depending on the topology design. The design is based on providing a multi-hop network. The design is also optimized to reduce the number of USB hubs and cables used. There are 21 USB hubs connecting 130 motes to the laptops. TelosB is a 802.15.4 compliant device designed by UC Berkeley and manufactured by Crossbow Solutions. It has a T1 MSP430 microcontroller, 2.4 GHz Chipcon CC2420 radio, 4 MHz 8 bit CPU, 128 KB instruction memory, 4 KB RAM, and a USB interface.

Motes run TinyOS 2.0.2, which is a lightweight event-based operating system that implements the networking stack and communication with the sensors, and provides the programming environment for this platform. Each mote accommodates a light sensor and has a customized onboard facility to hold a 3 db RF attenuator. The spacing between the motes is 2 feet. Since the sensors are low power radio devices the TelosB motes use the power from the laptops which inturn use wall power.

Laptops in each column are connected through a Gigabit Ethernet switch to an Ethernet back-channel network that provides high-bandwidth connectivity to and from the nodes for management commands, data injection and extraction. The NetEye server connects to join the local Ethernet back channel network and it also has another Ethernet card through which it connects to the Internet. The NetEye server provides remote access to the users for creating, editing, and scheduling the job.

11.4.3.2. *Topology control in NetEye*

Topology control is one of the important design issues for setting up a testbed. The topology setup in NetEye supports multi-hop transmission between the motes.

In the NetEye testbed wooden benches are used to hold the laptops and the motes since wood is a bad conductor. Another advantage is it does not interfere much with the signal propagation. The benches are 5 feet high in order to reduce the ground effect.

Channel 26 is set on the sensor nodes to avoid interference with any channels on wireless networks. The radio characteristics of the sensor networks are measured in the NetEye testbed. The experiments are done to select the minimum power level and to obtain reliable packet delivery in a multi-hop network. In the indoor environment the transmission ranges will be high. To deal with this a 3 db attenuator attached to each TelosB mote is used.

To achieve a multi-hop network a NesC program that broadcasts 10000 packets is scheduled on one of the nodes. All the other nodes are scheduled with a receiver program. The data is collected from all the nodes and the packets received are counted to know the Packet Delivery Rate (PDR). The experiments are done using different Power Levels (PL) and between different distant nodes. The graph below shows the Packet Delivery Rate at different power levels and at different distances.

Power levels 1 and 2 has very low delivery rate. Power level 3 can be considered since it offers reliable packet delivery rate up to 6 hops. Power levels 4, 5, and 6 have very high transmission ranges even with the attenuator.

The actual network connectivity in the network depends on the power level adopted on the motes. The following box plots show the variation of packet delivery rate as a function of distance, when the power level is 2, 3, and 6.

From Fig. 11.8, we see that the network is sparse at power level 2, where most nodes can talk to a limited number of nodes. Figure 11.9 shows at power 6 level the density is fairly high; almost any two nodes can talk to each other with high probability. Figure 11.8 also shows at power level 3, a node can reach many nodes in the network, and some links are reliable while some are not. Thus power level 3 gives a typical multi-hop network (about 6 hops).

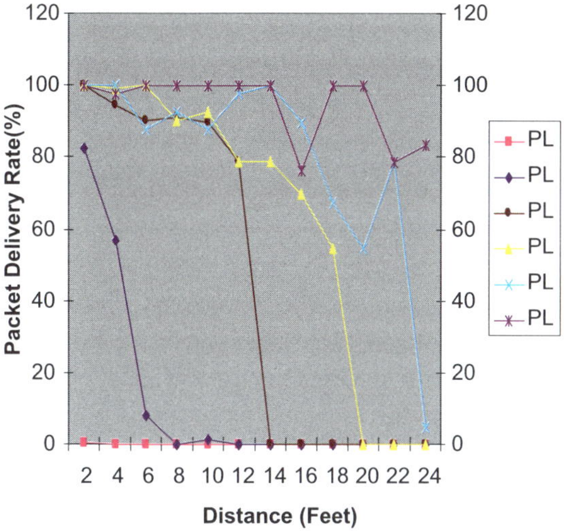

Fig. 11.7. PDR versus Distance-At different power levels at channel 26.

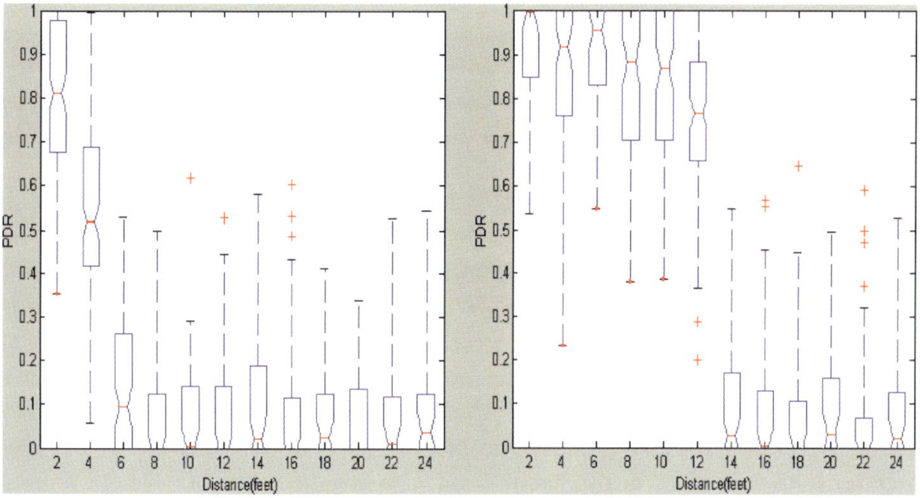

Fig. 11.8. Boxplot for PDR versus Distance at power level 2 and power level 3.

11.4.3.3. *NetEye server*

The NetEye server is a remotely accessible framework for wireless sensor network applications. A user experiment is referred to as a job. NetEye server provides the following services:

- Web interface for experiment scheduling a job, deployment, and monitoring the fixed array platform.
- Resource scheduling for the user jobs to support multiple user jobs.

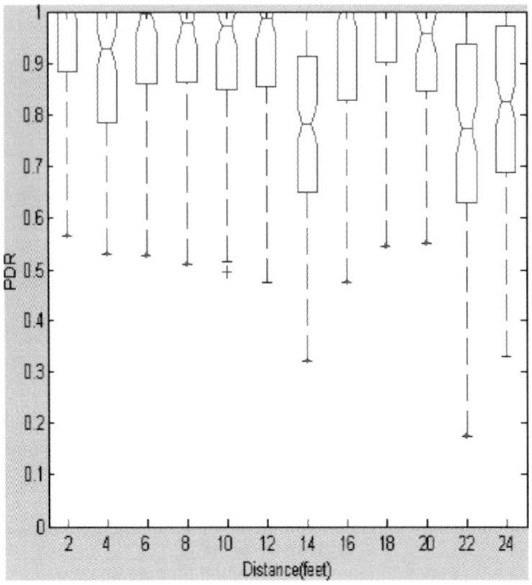

Fig. 11.9. Boxplot for PDR versus Distance at power level 6.

The job specified by the users consists of one or more files like sensor network executables, scripts, support files etc., which should be programmed to run on the specific set of resources for a specified interval of time. The status of the jobs may be monitored during execution. On the successful completion of the jobs, output must be retrieved.

The NetEye server also handles the resource allocation mechanism according to the need and availability of the node which is FCFS scheduling. The NetEye server provides the set of services for optimized resource allocation for gathering the status of the NetEye testbed. The NetEye server collects the availability information from each of the laptop, which act as an interface between the server and the sensor nodes, considers the next job requirement, and allocates the appropriate resources for the job.

The NetEye server also implements the core set of system utilities. It includes tools for data injection, health monitoring, and logging of data. System administrative services are also part of the NetEye server. These services include user management for creation and deletion of users, assigning access privileges to the users, and platform administration like restarting a node, etc.

The NetEye server exposes these services for scheduling, managing, creating jobs etc, through a web interface using a web server. The NetEye server implementation is independent of specific hardware and platform.

11.4.3.3.1. NetEye server implementation:

The NetEye server implementation is done in a way that if the sensor node has to be deployed a component on the server will be invoked, which in turn invokes a component in the laptop to which the node is connected. All the components in the NetEye server are hierarchical and is independent. The main NetEye server runs on Linux (which also runs the Apache webserver for the web interface).

Testbed scheduling, administration, management, and experimentation are implemented in a multi threaded daemon that uses scripts and utilities written as PERL modules and which encapsulate testbed services. PHP modules implement the web-accessible testbed services, such as job-creation, storage of experiment data, and a testbed health monitoring page. A MySQL database provides persistence for storing job configurations and user reservations. Data generated by jobs are stored on the server database and may be retrieved by links through the web interface. Data injection is done by an Injector Manager component on the server and the implementation is socket programming in the C language.

11.4.3.4. *Integration between NetEye server and motes (Laptops)*

The laptops serve as integration points and interface the motes with the server. They also, in turn, acts as wireless network devices.

It provides the channels for:

- Data collection: The laptop collects the experimental data from the motes attached to it and sends it to server.
- Local data storage: The laptop stores the local information about the motes and locally stores the data from the nodes during the running of the experiment.
- Transfer of data like the executable files, injection files, and output files between the server and motes.
- Local node information: The laptop collects the local node information. The health monitor service contacts each laptop to collect the health status of the nodes.
- Data injection: Each laptop has an injector for injecting events to applications running on it, as well as to serve as a bridge that injects events into the application on the mote. Each mote application has a receptor component that receives injections and takes appropriate actions.

11.4.3.4.1. Integration point (Laptop) implementation:

The laptops also run on the Linux operating system. They have the local MySQL database. The laptops act as clients to the MySQL server set up on the NetEye server. In the database the local health information of the nodes, the jobs scheduled on the particular nodes attached to the laptop etc, are stored. The duration and start time of a particular job are pushed on to the laptop by the server if the node attached to it is selected for a particular job. Reprogramming the nodes and collecting the data from the nodes is done through daemons (written in Shell and Perl).

Each laptop has an injector which is invoked by the Injector Manager from the server for injecting events to applications on fly. Each mote application has a receptor component that receives injections and takes appropriate actions. The injector code in the laptops is in C the language. TinyOS is installed on the each laptop to handle programming motes attached to it.

11.4.3.5. *Software components*

NetEye consists of several different software components for providing the necessary functionality and services on the testbed.

The main components are:

(a) *Web interface*
PHP generated pages are used for the user interface for job creation, scheduling, and data collection. Administrators also have an interface to control the testbed functionality. After logging users have the access to the following functionality:

- Home page
- Topology page
- Schedule tier-1 jobs page
- Schedule tier-2 jobs page
- Select node-group page
- Manage Tier-1 jobs page
- Manage Tier-2 jobs page
- Health monitor page
- Help and instructions page

(b) *MySQL Database*
MySQL database is used to store all the information necessary for running the testbed. There are two categories of information stored:

- Data related to the jobs: The JID, information of the user who scheduled the job, scheduled time, start time of the job, duration, information about the input files, status of the jobs, and the links for output retrieval are stored in this database.
- Testbed status data: The health status of each node, the work status of the node, etc. are stored in this database.

(c) *Job Daemon*
Perl and Shell scripts run as cron jobs for setting up, running, and tearing down the jobs. The job daemon also does reprogramming of the nodes and starts necessary services like the serial forwarder and serial listener to get the data to the PC for a particular job. After the specified duration the job daemon tears the jobs down, kills processes which were running during the jobs, and puts the output data back to the server and updates the databases with the links.

NetEye provides the following functionality through different software components.

11.4.3.5.1. New user:

A new user can easily register into the NetEye testbed. A user can run his 802.11 experiments as well 802.15.4 experiments on NetEye testbed. The user has to just fill in the new registration form available on the web interface of NetEye, answering a few simple questions.

As soon as the account is available for the user, a login and password will be provided to the user through the email he has specified in the registration form. A login directory will be created for the user at the start when he registers, which will contain all the input files and output files for the jobs specified by the user. Different users can have input files with the same names. The aspect of creating directories for individual users helps in preventing the user files from being overwritten with one another.

The New User form is implemented in PHP. As the user registers an automated mail is sent to the administrator stating the user's interest in registration. An account will be created for the user through the automated administrative tools with appropriate user privileges. A directory will be created automatically (written in Perl script) on the server for the user to store user input files and output files.

11.4.3.5.2. Topology selection:

Each user is provided with the topology of the testbed from which he can select a subset of nodes he wanted for the experiment. A user-friendly interface is provided for the user to select the nodes remotely.

The user has two options while selecting the topology:

- The user is given the option to name the selected nodes if he wants. This is stored in the database for reusing rather than selecting it every time if he wants to use the same set of nodes. This is available in the creating node group web page in the NetEye web interface.
- If he does not want the option of naming the nodes he can directly select them and use them. This is available in scheduling tier-1 job web page in the NetEye web interface.

The graphical selection tool is provided in the form of a grid of 10×13 for topology selection where a click will select the appropriate nodes for the user. This tool is implemented in Javascript and PHP.

11.4.3.5.3. Schedule jobs:

NetEye users can schedule jobs through a web interface. The user can specify the start time of the job, the nodes selected for the experiment, and the duration time for the experiment. The user can upload the executable that needs to be programmed on the selected nodes.

The user can schedule the other jobs simultaneously and if the resources are available those will be allocated; otherwise the job will be in the pending state. In tier-2 jobs the user can upload support files along with the executable. The support files should be in zipped format.

The Schedule Job web page is in PHP. As the jobs are scheduled an entry will be made into the MySQL database about the job information like JID, start time, duration etc.

11.4.3.5.4. Upload files:

For the users to run their experiments users can upload their executables through the web interface. Once the file is uploaded it will be stored in the user directory, which is created during user registration. These will be copied to the appropriate laptops through the secured copy protocol according to the user node selection. The selected nodes will be programmed with the uploaded file.

For the ease of the users, the files uploaded by them will be stored and the user can select from the stored files as well. The user can select from only the files he has uploaded and not from other's files. This facility serves two purposes:

- If the user has to run the same experiment at different times, he does not have to upload them again, he can just select from the existing files.
- If the user does not have his executable files available to him at a particular moment when he wishes to run his experiment, he can upload them earlier and use them when he wants to run the experiment.

For tier-2 jobs there is a possibility that he can upload support files along with his executable all in zipped format. Both the executable and support files will be uploaded in one directory, so that those can be used easily whenever needed. The schedule web page will link the upload web page and is in PHP. The user files will be uploaded into the directory through a PHP program but the secured copy protocol is implemented in Perl to copy the files to the laptops. The uploaded files are stored in the database on the server for further usage.

11.4.3.5.5. Resource management in NetEye:

In any shared computing and communication infrastructure resource allocation plays an important role. The NetEye testbed will be shared by many users and each user should get a fair share of resources.

FCFS resource allocation is used in the NetEye testbed. The user is provided with the topology of the testbed from which he can select a subset of nodes he wants for the experiment. A user-friendly interface is provided for the user to select the nodes remotely. The user is also allowed to specify the start time if he wants to, otherwise the current time will be taken as the start time for his experiments. A few services running as daemons on the individual laptops collect availability information of all the nodes and send it to the server. The server stores all the information in the MySQL database and the resource allocator uses the information from the database to check the availability and allocates the resources to the user. If not the user's job will be put in the pending list and will be allocated with the resources once they are available. The allocation is based on the start time as the priority.

After the specified duration of a particular job, a module that will be running as the daemon will tear down the job and free the resources for further usage. After the duration, the daemon tears down the job and notifies the server. The resources are made available for further usage.

There are different tables in MySQL database which hold the state information about all the nodes in the facility. Job daemons (written in Perl) collect state information about the nodes from the database tables. They are responsible for setting up the jobs, tearing down the jobs after the duration, and updating the status of the nodes in the database. A local database is maintained in each laptop, which acts as a client to the NetEye server. The database holds the local information about the availability of the nodes and updates it to the server.

11.4.3.5.6. Manage jobs:

The user can manage his jobs through the web interface remotely. There will be some sensitive information about the user and he might not want others to collect his data. For security reasons and providing confidentiality the user can view just his jobs.

The Manage jobs interface shows the user details about his job including the Job ID, the input file, start time, duration, and the status of the job. A link to the output directory is also provided in the Manage jobs interface. A cancel job option is provided on this web page if the user wishes to cancel his job. The status of the jobs will always be shown to the user through the Manage jobs webpage. There will be a different status for each job depending on the availability of the nodes. The different statuses for a given job are as follows:

- Pending: The job has been entered in the database, but the resources requested are not yet allocated.
- Reserved: The resources for the particular job are allocated.
- Running: The motes are programmed and the job is running.
- Finished: The job is finished and the packaging module on the server is preparing for the output.
- Completed: The output link is available to the user and he can download from the provided link.

The web page for manage jobs is implemented in PHP. The job information and the status of the job is picked from the MySQL database and displayed to the user. The output link provision is also done in PHP once the job is finished.

11.4.3.5.7. Cancel jobs:

If the user mistakenly schedules a job it should be corrected by canceling the job. It is useful for both the user as well as the resource providers. For the user it is useful because he does not have to waste time waiting for job that he does not want to complete or if he wants to schedule a different job on the same nodes he does not have to wait till resources get free. For the providers wastage of resources is reduced.

In NetEye the user is given the option to cancel a job if he does not want it or he has mistakenly scheduled it. This option is provided on the Manage Jobs webpage for the remote users. No output will be provided to the user. The job will be torn down and the resources will be freed for further usage.

The cancel job option is provided on the Manage Jobs web page which is in PHP. For canceling the job there are daemons running on the server as well on the laptops (written in Perl). Once the user cancels a job, then the information will be updated in the database by the daemon running on the server which will be picked up by the daemon running on the particular laptop to which the node is attached. This daemon will kill all the necessary processes like serial forwarder, listen tool, etc. to tear down the job and update it to the database on the server.

11.4.3.5.8. Programming the motes:

The user can upload the executable to program on the selected nodes. The users also have an option to select an already uploaded file for programming. For security reasons he can just use the files he has uploaded earlier. Programming the nodes is done using shell script. A daemon running on the individual laptops checks if the nodes are allocated to the particular job scheduled and it calls this shell script to program on the motes.

The users have two options while programming the motes:

- If the user does not select the injection service, just the Java listen tool will start running and collect the data from the motes through serial port. The user has to take care to write his code to send the data through the UART.
- If the user selects the injection service, a serial forwarder (one instance for each mote), an injection tool, and a listen tool listening to the serial forwarder will be opened. The program running on the mote should have a receptor component to read the data from the serial port. The data is written to the serial port using the serial forwarder.

11.4.3.5.9. Killing a job:

The user processes for a particular job have to be killed after the scheduled duration or if the user cancels the job. If the jobs are not properly killed it will hamper the resource availability on the testbed.

A shell script will be called by a Perl daemon to kill the processes running by the job after the duration or on the selection of the cancel option. The script will collect the processes ID's and kill the listen tool, serial forwarder, and the injection tool to free the resources.

11.4.3.5.10. Data retrieval:

The user can easily retrieve his experimental data using the link provided on the web page. The output will be in zipped format. The user can just download his data with a simple click. The user can't either see or download other's data for security reasons.

The directory created for the user will be used to store his experimental data. Each output file is named with the Job ID to prevent it from being overwritten by other files. The Java listen tool and the serial forwarder tool are used to collect experimental data. Once the duration of a job is completed, a secured copy protocol is used by each laptop to push the data to the server. The data thus obtained is zipped on the server by the packaging module written in Perl and the link is provided to the user.

11.4.3.5.11. NetEye injection:

NetEye provides a service of real-time data injection. Users can inject traces of data to the nodes through a web interface option. If the user selects this option a tool called Injection Manager on the server will be invoked to send the traces to the selected nodes through a set of dedicated ports. The user has to upload a file that contains the injection traces. The format should be such that the first field should contain the IP address of the laptop to which the mote is attached and the second field is the port number of the mote.

The port number can be obtained from the node ID itself. For example node "A0" means it is the mote attached to port 0 of Machine A. The IP address of the laptop to which the mote is attached can be obtained through the topology web page. The last field should be the time interval between each injection. There will be 6 bytes of data between the port number and time interval. Through this facility the user can pipe the output of one job to the other job on the fly. It is also possible for the user to send some input traces to the nodes for running a particular job if need be in real time.

The injection option is provided to the user on the Schedule Job web page. If the user selects it he is given an option to upload a file that contains the injection traces. The PHP script checks if the option is selected and updates it to the database on the server. A daemon on the server will invoke the injection manager tool (written in the C language) and send the data through the socket to the individual laptop to which the node is attached. A daemon running on the individual laptops will check the database if the injection is selected for a particular job. If it is a serial forwarder (tool provided by TinyOS), a injection tool (written in C language) and a listen tool (provided by TinyOS) will be invoked.

There will be different instances of serial forwarders and injection tools running on different ports. The ports are selected as per the USB port to which the mote is attached. The injection tools will listen to the port to which the server sends the data and inject the data to the serial forwarder. The serial forwarder will in turn send the data to the serial port. The mote application that the user specifies should have a receptor component which will read from the UART and take appropriate actions.

11.4.3.5.12. Health monitoring:

Health monitoring is one of the important services in any testbed for both users and administrators. Remote users can check the health status of the nodes on the testbed. The health monitoring daemon uses an executable to periodically run on all the available nodes to monitor its health status. Through this facility a user knows the following details about the testbed:

- Number of Tier-1 nodes up
- Number of Tier-1 nodes down
- Number of Tier-2 nodes up
- Number of Tier-2 nodes down
- Number of Tier-1 nodes busy
- Number of Tier-1 nodes free
- Number of Tier-2 nodes busy
- Number of Tier-2 nodes free
- Number of Tier-1 jobs running
- Number of Tier-1 jobs pending
- Number of Tier-2 jobs running
- Number of Tier-2 jobs pending
- List of nodes that are down

Through this information a user knows which nodes are not available and cannot be used for scheduling. The administrators can identify the broken nodes for fixing them easily through this service; otherwise the administrator has to check each and every node manually for its health status.

A health monitor daemon (written in Perl) runs periodically on all the available nodes to determine if the nodes are up and running. A NesC module is run on the nodes automatically and the data is collected to the laptop through the Java listen tool. The data collected to the laptop is checked for correctness if the mote has generated an AM type 99 message. If it is of type 99 then a Perl daemon script running on the laptop accesses the database table on the server and updates that the motes attached to is up and running; otherwise it updates the corresponding mote as down. The server receives the health information from all the laptops about the motes attached to it. Finally a PHP module collects the information from the MySQL database dynamically and displays the information to the user.

11.4.3.5.13. Administrative tool to add new users:

The NetEye testbed also provides an administrative tool to add users and allow access privileges to them. Once the user registers using the registration form an automated email will be sent to the admin. After checking the authenticity of the information the administrator will add the user into the database. Appropriate access rights are given to the user by the administration. The default is a normal user who can use the testbed for scheduling, data retrieval, etc. The normal user won't have rights to view other's data. This admin tool is provided on the web interface and can only be seen if logged in as admin. The code uses PHP and MySQL database.

11.5. Concluding Remarks

We have discussed the important elements of sensornet testbed design, and we have presented in detail the design and implementation of the NetEye testbed. The design issues and the implementation details presented in this chapter will be useful for researchers who are interested in building their own testbeds.

Future work on NetEye includes increasing the scale and upgrading to accommodate mobile robots. Other areas of future work include integrating NetEye with the Global Environment for Network Innovations (GENI), which will consist of a global wired network with programmable, virtualized network elements along with edge wireless access deployments intended to support experimentation with mobile computing devices, embedded sensors, etc.

As a part of this effort, NetEye will participate in the Kansei Consortium (which includes organizations such as The Ohio State University and Los Alamos National Lab) to deliver a prototype of GENI-fied infrastructure for wireless sensor network experimentation. Each testbed site will offer multiple types of sensornet platforms and operate autonomously. The prototype will also include a number of researcher client tools and researcher portal services. It will provide publicly available support for programmability, virtualization, and slice-based experimentation.

References

1. D. Raychaudhuri and M. Gerla, (eds.), *New Architectures and Disruptive Technologies for the Future Internet: The Wireless, Mobile and Sensor Network Perspective*, NSF WMPG Workshop Report, (August 2005).
2. J. Evans, D. Raychaudhuri and S. Paul, *Overview of Wireless, Mobile and Sensor Networks in GENI*, GENI Design Document 06-14, Wireless Working Group, (September 2006).
3. S. Paul, *Requirements Document for Management and Control of GENI Wireless Networks*, GENI Design Document 06-15, Wireless Working Group, (September 2006).
4. T. Anderson and A. Vahdat. (eds), *GENI Distributed Services*, GENI Design Document 06-24, Distributed Working Group, (September 2006).
5. E. Ertin, A. Arora, R. Ramnath, M. Nesterenko, V. Naik, S. Bapat, V. Kulathumani, M. Sridharan, H. Zhang and H. Cao, Kansei: A testbed for sensing at scale, *Proceedings of the 5th IEEE International Conference on Information Processing in Sensor Networks* (*ISPN 2006*), (April 2006).

6. S. Bapat, W. Leal, T. Kwon, P. Wei and A. Arora, Chowkidar: A Health Monitor for Wireless Sensor Network Testbeds. *Proceedings of the 3rd IEEE International Conference on Testbeds and Research Infrastructure for the Development of Networks and communities* (TridentCom 2007), (May 2007).
7. D. Raychaudhuri, I. Seskar, M. Ott, S. Ganu, K. Ramachandran, H. Kremo, R. Siracusa, H. Liu and M. Singh, Overview of the ORBIT radio grid testbed for evaluation of next-generation wireless network protocols, *Proceedings of 1st IEEE International Conference on Testbeds and Research Infrastructure for the Development of Networks and communities* (TridentCom 2005), (February 2005).
8. G. Werner-Allen, P. Swieskowski and M. Welsh, MoteLab: A Wireless Sensor Network Testbed, *Proceedings of the 4th IEEE International Symposium on Information Processing in Sensor Networks* (ISPN 2005), (April 2005).
9. B. N. Chun, P. Buonadonna, A. AuYoungz, C. Ngy, D. C. Parkesy, J. Shneidmany, A. C. Snoerenz and A. Vahdatz, Mirage: A microeconomic resource allocation system for sensornet testbeds, *Proceedings of the 2nd IEEE Workshop on Embedded Networked Sensors* (EmNetS-II), (May 2005).
10. D. Johnson, T. Stack, R. Fish, D. M. Flickinger, L. Stoller, R. Ricci and J. Lepreau, Mobile Emulab: A robotic wireless and sensor network testbed, *Proceedings of 25th IEEE International Conference on Computer Communications* (INFOCOM 2006), (April 2006).
11. http://www.emulab.net/.
12. L. Peterson, A. Bavier, M. E. Fiuczynski and S. Muir, Experiences Building PlanetLab, *Proceedings of the 7th conference on USENIX Symposium on Operating Systems Design and Implementation* (7), (2006).
13. A. Bavier, M. Bowman, B. Chun, D. Culler, S. Karlin, S. Muir, L. Peterson, T. Roscoe, T. Spalink and M. Wawrzoniak, Operating system support for planetary-scale network services, *Proceedings of the 1st conference on Symposium on Networked Systems Design and Implementation* (1), (2004).
14. L. Peterson, PlanetLab-A blueprint for introducing disruptive technology into the internet, *Proceedings of ACM HotNets-1Workshop, Princeton*, New Jersey, USA, (October 2002).
15. http://www.xbow.com.
16. C. Won, J.-H. Youn, H. Ali, H. Sharif and J. Deogun, Adaptive radio channel allocation for supporting coexistence of 802.15.4 and 802.11b, *Proceedings of 2005 IEEE 62nd Vehicular Technology Conference* (VTC-2005-Fall), (September 2005).

Chapter 12

Time Reversal for Ultra-Wideband Communications: Architecture and Test-Bed

N. Guo, R. C. Qiu, Q. Zhang, B. M. Sadler*, Z. Hu, P. Zhang, Y. Song and C. Zhou

Wireless Networking Systems Laboratory
Department of Electrical and Computer Engineering
Center for Manufacturing Research
Tennessee Technological University
Cookeville, TN 38505, USA

This chapter presents a wideband radio system design concept that takes advantage of rich multipath propagation. Depending upon the channel information, each pair of transmitter and receiver in the system chooses a transmit waveform that is optimal in some sense. The transmitters are capable of waveform level preprocessing, while the receivers can be rather simple since they do not need special means (like a RAKE combiner) to capture dispersed energy over time, and even equalizers may not be necessary. In particular, the channel impulse response (CIR) can be utilized to provide physical-layer security enhancement thanks to the spatial focusing property of time reversal preprocessing. This design concept is especially attractive to wireless sensor networks (WSN) because (1) low-complexity and low-cost receivers are strongly demanded for any WSN, (2) security is vulnerable in WSNs and enhancement at physical layer is extremely desirable, and (3) deploying WSNs in harsh and scattering radio frequency (RF) environments is quite meaningful and necessary. A few realistic radio channels are studied based on experimental data, aiming at best designing the preprocessing systems. In addition, design and implementation work of an experimental time reversal radio test-bed is reported, verifying the concept of preprocessing plus simple receivers.

12.1. Background

Recent advances in miniaturization, low-power electronics and wireless communications, stimulated by increasing demands for automation in home and industrial areas, have triggered tremendous interests in the wireless sensor network (WSN)

*US Army Research Laboratory, AMSRD-ARL-CI-CN, 2800 Powder Mill Road, Adelphi, MD 20783.

research, development and deployment. There are many challenges in WSN design, and some of the challenges are due to tough constraints and conditions posed by specific applications and environments. Examples of these constraints and conditions include power consumption, node simplicity, node cost, non-line-of-sight propagation, severe multipath, and low signal leakage, etc.

Mainly due to potentially low implementation complexity, suboptimal reception strategies, such as transmitted reference (TR)[1–8] and its variants[9–13] as well as energy detection,[14–17] have gotten increasing attention for complexity and cost constrained wideband applications. These schemes may be enhanced to handle multipath and inter-symbol interference (ISI) at the cost of complexity. One philosophy to simplify the receivers without sacrificing overall performance is to shift part of receiver-side functions to the transmitter side, which is meaningful for a centralized network where one powerful central station communicates with a large number of nodes. Preprocessing at the transmitter can be viewed as a performance enhancement to the system where the receivers are simple but perform relatively poorly.

Sensor nodes are often deployed in open areas, thus more vulnerable than those in a wired network in terms of security. The WSN security is still an open field and most proposed security approaches are based on encryption and authentication mechanisms. In other words, majority of them are implemented at the layers above the physical layers.

In this chapter, a wideband radio system design concept that takes advantage of scattering propagation environments is provided. Depending upon the channel information, each pair of transmitter and receiver in the system chooses a transmit waveform that is optimal in some sense. An example is the use of time reversal preprocessing (pre-filtering) at the transmitter to focus the signal at the receiver.[18–28] In such a system with time reversal preprocessing, the receivers can be very simple, because they do not need special means (like a RAKE combiner) to capture dispersed energy over time, and even equalizers may not be necessary. In particular, the channel impulse response (CIR) can be utilized to provide physical-layer security enhancement thanks to the spatial focusing property of time reversal preprocessing.[25,29,30]

12.2. Suboptimal Schemes Using Low-Complexity Receivers

The functions of a receiver in a communication system include energy capture and demodulation. It is well known that, in terms of maximum signal-to-noise (SNR) ratio at the decision stage, the best reception strategy over an additive white Gaussian noise (AWGN) channel is to match the received data symbol waveform at the receiver. When the channel is frequency selective (due to multipath propagation), the matching process should take into account the multipath channel characteristics. RAKE receiver is such a matching based reception technique that is able to handle multipath distortion.

To demodulate the data, an optimal receiver employs a local template as a reference to correlate with the incoming information-embedded signal, where the template is a piece of received reference symbol waveform. Of course, the condition for optimal reception is that the demodulation reference can be accurately set. Practically the template is obtained from channel estimation. However, in selective fading environments, such as home and machinery areas, multipath turns to rich as the signal bandwidth increases. For instance, in the ultra-wide bandwidth (UWB) scenario, up to a hundred of resolvable paths may be observed from the CIR. This means a RAKE receiver has to contain a large number of fingers to achieve acceptable performance, implying a high-complexity, power hungry and expensive solution. Alternatively, orthogonal frequency division modulation (OFDM) is also an efficient means for optimum performance in frequency selective (multipath) channel cases. An OFDM scheme divides a frequency band into a large number of non-frequency-selective subbands and transmits data over these subbands in a parallel basis. Both of RAKE receiver and OFDM can handle multipath very well, but they are not cheap and low-power-consumption solutions, thus they may not be suitable for WSN applications. Motivated by the need for simple wireless receivers with satisfactory performances, a number of old-fashion reception techniques have regained popularity.[4,5,9–17] These suboptimal schemes do not require channel estimation at all and are not quite sensitive to timing error.

Transmitted reference (TR) is a communication scheme with the reference symbols being transmitted along with the data symbols. In order to eliminate the requirement for channel estimation at the receiver, both the message and the reference are transmitted through two dedicated subchannels separated by time or frequency, where the channel separation is small enough to ensure coherence between the two subchannels. The information bits may be modulated in pulse position modulation (PPM) or antipodal format. The received up-to-date reference signal is directly used to demodulate the data. Figure 12.1 describes the time-separated TR scheme. The core of the receiver in a time-separated TR system is a delay line device followed by a correlator. The simplicity is achieved at the cost of performance penalty in the following two aspects. First of all, half of the total transmit power is spending in transmitting the reference. Secondly, the received reference signal is "dirty" — noise polluted, which results in a non-Gaussian cross-noise term in addition to a Gaussian noise term in the correlator's output. The non-Gaussian noise is much stronger than the Gaussian noise, leading to significant performance degradation. Aiming at improving the original TR scheme, a number of TR variants have been proposed.

A straight-forward way to reduce the overhead is to reduce percentage of reference symbols, i.e., only one referenced symbol is transmitted for a block of data symbols (called stored reference in Ref. 31), implying that a piece of received reference waveform is stored at the receiver and serves as a reference for demodulating multiple data symbols. However, the waveform storage can be very expensive. To remove the overhead completely, the reference can be provided through differentially

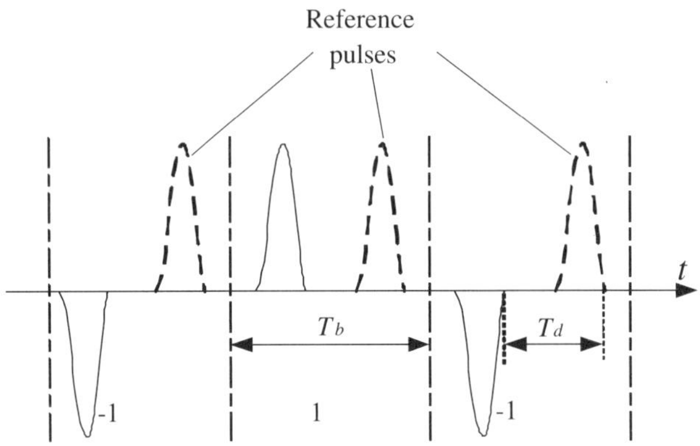

(a) Transmitted pulses.

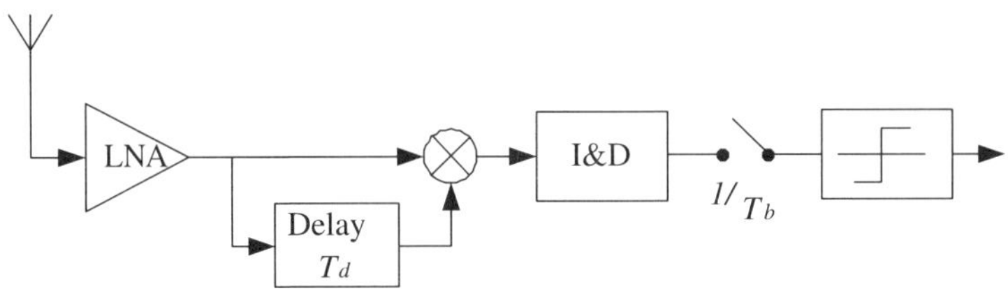

(b) Receiver structure.

Fig. 12.1. Time-separated TR scheme.

encoding, so that a modulated data bit can be demodulated by using the previous symbol as reference. This differentially encoded TR is called autocorrelation demodulation in Simon's book[32] and DTR in the paper by Chao and Scholtz.[10] By eliminating the dedicated reference transmission, the energy efficiency is improved by about 3 dB.[10]

The template noise level may be suppressed by averaging (or accumulating) over a few received reference symbols.[33] Averaging can be applied to DTR receivers too if decision feedback is utilized.[11] However, implementing the averaging function at waveform level requires storing multiple received symbol waveforms, which is not cheap for either analog or digital approaches.

Alternatively, performance may be improved by resorting to multi-symbol detection combined with DTR.[12,13,32] Incoming received raw symbols are grouped into blocks of L consecutive symbols, without overlap between any two consecutive blocks. The received raw symbols are processed using differential demodulation to obtain multiple decision statistics for joint decision. A DTR based multi-symbol detection receiver structure is given in Fig. 12.2, and refer to the paper[12] for details.

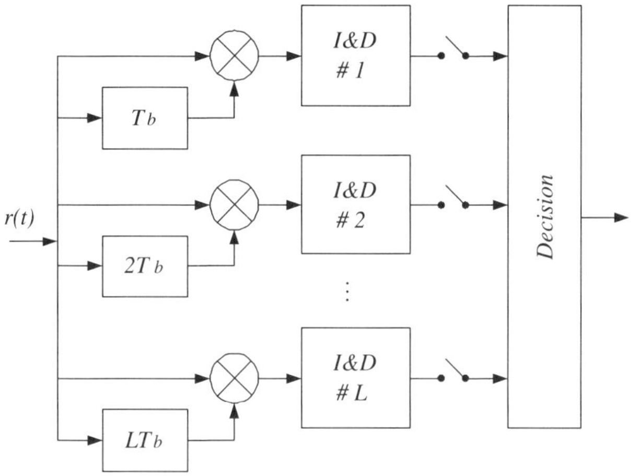

Fig. 12.2. A DTR based multi-symbol detection receiver structure.

Note that there is a drawback in all schemes of time-separated TR and its variants: expensive and bulky delay elements are required at the receivers. This huge disadvantage prevents the time-separated TR schemes from being widely accepted. Without using any delay device, a frequency-separated TR can provide the reference at the cost of frequency expansion.[6–8] One of proposed frequency-separated TR scheme is called slightly frequency-shifted reference (FSR) technique[6] suitable for low data rate applications, and implementing an FSR receiver is quite easy.

Different from the template-correlation schemes mentioned above, another family of suboptimal reception schemes includes energy (square-law) detector and envelop detector. With either of the detectors, both on-off keying (OOK) and pulse position modulation (PPM) can be adopted as modulation schemes. One problem with these two unipodal modulation schemes is that they cause spectral spikes due to non-zero mean of the symbol values. Scrambling encoding can remove the spectral spikes and time hopping (TH) may be considered for both multiple user access and spectral spike reduction. The receiver uses an integrator to accumulate signal energy. For better performance the signal can be weighted prior to integration and there must be a best weighting function depending on the signal waveform and the noise level.[34–38] In fact, implementation of weighting function is not of low complexity and this contradicts the philosophy of low-complexity receiver design. A relatively simpler weighting method is a gating function which is equivalent to the use of a proper integration interval.[17,28,39,40] A practical implementation of a smart integrator is to control the integrator's on-duration. Denoted by R_b the symbol rate and consider a received symbol waveform with most of the energy concentrated in an interval T_I. If $T_I < T_b = 1/R_b$, then integrating over the interval T_I outperforms integrating over the interval T_b, since both gather almost the same amount of signal energy but the latter gathers more noise.

All of the discussed suboptimal schemes are of low-complexity in the sense that no channel estimation is required and they are less sensitive to timing error. A common shortcoming is that they are not able to work with typical linear equalization techniques, thus they are not suitable for applications where ISI exists apparently. Unlike linear receiver, the equivalent discrete channels of some suboptimal schemes behave nonlinearly, where an equivalent discrete-time channel has data input at one end and it outputs decision statistic plus noise at the other end.[17,28,41,42] For both DTR and energy detection, their equivalent discrete channels can be modeled as[17,28]

$$z_k = \vec{d}_k^T C \vec{d}_k + \eta_k, \tag{12.1}$$

where subscript k is a symbol timing index, z_k is the decision statistic, $\vec{d}_k$ is a data vector whose dimension covers the ISI length in symbol, C is a matrix determined by the channel, and η_k is a noise term. This means that the signal part in the output of the equivalent discrete channel, i.e., $\vec{d}_k^T C \vec{d}_k \stackrel{def}{=} S_k$, is a nonlinear function of data vector $\vec{d}_k$. As a matter of fact, the equivalent discrete channel represented by $S_k = \vec{d}_k^T C \vec{d}_k$ is a special case of second-order Volterra model.[41,43] In general, z_k contains a desired signal and a nonlinear inter-symbol-interference (ISI) component that cannot be well handled by normal linear equalization techniques. This fact suggests the use of some waveform level channel shortening techniques.

12.3. Waveform Preprocessing

Modern communication systems rely on analog and digital signal processing to combat various impairments such as noise, channel fading (flat and frequency-selective fading), and interferences. For a given environment, a global optimum system under some sort of criterion delivers the best performance. By "global" we mean joint transmitter-receiver optimization. However, most existing work on the joint transmitter-receiver optimization is at symbol-rate level.[44–49] It can be expected that by breaking the symbol-rate constraint and allowing continuous-time or fractional-symbol-level processing, the performance can be improved further. In other words, given a communication channel, we prefer to design a set of transmit waveforms as well as a receiver with proper structure and algorithm, such that the system achieves some sort of optimum under some conditions and constraints. The signal processing goals could be capacity-reaching, maximum SNR, and minimum mean square error (MMSE), etc. In most wireless communication scenarios the channel characteristics are time-varying and up-to-date channel information is only available at the receivers. This is why traditionally signal processing efforts are focused on the receiver side.

It is reasonable to consider single-carrier pulse-based radio links for WSN applications, since they have potential to be of low-complexity if major receiver-side linear processing functions are shifted to the transmitter side. It is well known that low probability of interception and low probability of detection (LPI/LPD) can be easily achieved using pulse-based signaling. Also, a narrow-pulse-based single-carrier system can be used for ranging or penetration radar purposes.

A unique issue associated with wireless communications is frequency-selective fading caused by multipath propagation. As for interferences in radio systems, ISI and inter-user interference (IUI) are typically concerned. Listed below are some receiver-based schemes to handle noise, multipath impact and interferences.

- Matched filter (MF): it is placed at the receiver and matches the given transmit symbol (or chip) waveform; for AWGN noise, it maximizes the SNR at the peak of the MF's output.
- RAKE receiver: a family of technique to collect the signal energy dispersed over multipath components; an ideal RAKE receiver actually matches the overall received waveform; when major paths are resolvable, a practical RAKE receiver structure can be a combination of a regular chip-level MF and a multipath combiner functioning as a finite impulse response (FIR) filter; a RAKE receiver operates at fractional-symbol (or fractional-chip) rate.
- Equalization: a symbol-rate discrete-time processing to remove or reduce ISI; an equalizer is placed at the receiver, usually taking symbol-rate samples from the MF's output as its input.
- (Receiver-based) multi-user detection: this is a broad range of techniques that remove or reduce IUI; the multi-user detection operates at symbol-rate.

When channel and/or multi-user information is available at the transmitter, it seems no strong reason not to use it. Recently, transmitter based signal processing, or preprocessing, has received increasing attention. Preprocessing can be time-reversal pre-filtering (or pre-RAKE), pre-equalization, multi-user precoding, or some processing for a set of compromised goals. Preprocessing can be used along in a transmitter-centric system where traditional receiver-based signal processing is shifted to the transmitters to simplify the receivers. It can also works with receiver-based signal processing to achieve joint transmitter-receiver optimization.

Our special interest is on preprocessing at fractional-symbol rate (or simply, waveform preprocessing), in conjunction with a suboptimal receiver. Below are two examples of symbol waveforms.

- Pulse shaping: it uses a transmitter-side filter to create a transmit waveform that has desired roll-off spectrum; traditional pulse shapes include raised cosine and truncated sin functions, etc.
- Maximum-SNR transmit waveform: a transmit symbol waveform to achieve the maximum SNR at the MF's output; it is an eigenfunction of the CIR autocorrelation (implying the CIR has to be known first); and a homogeneous Fredholm integral equation needs to solved for the eigenfunction with the strongest channel gain.[50,51]

The transmit waveform optimization problem can be further stated in detail as follows. It is well known that the optimum receiver matches the whole symbol waveform distorted by the channel, not the transmitted symbol waveform. However, from system optimization point of view, such a waveform matching alone is not enough. We can further maximize SNR at the receiver by carefully designing the transmitted waveform.[50,51]

Given the channel impulse response $h(t)$ and fixed transmitted power P_t, we wish to achieve the maximum SNR at the receive by jointly designing the transmitted waveform and a good receiver. This problem has been discussed in Ref. 50 for communication over troposcatter channels and in Ref. 51 for radar detection.

Assuming the transmitted pulse $p(t)$ (to be optimized) is confined to the symmetric time interval $[-T/2, T/2]$. The energy of transmitted pulse is then

$$E_p = \int_{-T/2}^{T/2} |p(t)|^2 dt. \tag{12.2}$$

It follows from detection theory that the best receiver is still a MF matched to the received waveform $p(t) * h(t)$, where $h(t)$ is the CIR and "$*$" denotes convolution operation. The (maximum) SNR at the output of such a MF is given by.

$$SNR = 2E_y/N_0, \tag{12.3}$$

where $E_y = \int_{-T/2}^{T/2} |p(t) * h(t)|^2 dt$ is the received signal energy. The problem is then reduced to find the optimum $p(t)$ such that E_y is maximized, under the constraint of fixed E_p.

It has been shown in Refs. 52 (p. 125) and 51 that the optimum $p(t)$ can be obtained by solving the following homogeneous Fredholm integral equation

$$\mu_n \phi_n(t) = \int_{-T/2}^{T/2} \kappa(t-\tau)\phi_n(\tau)\, d\tau, \tag{12.4}$$

and let $p(t) = \phi_0(t)$, where $\phi_0(t)$ is the eigenfunctions corresponding to the maximum eigenvalue μ_0 and the kernel $\kappa(t)$ is the autocorrelation of the CIR: $\kappa(t) = h(t) * h(-t)$. When convolved with the kernel over the interval $[-T/2, T/2]$, pulse waveform $\phi_0(t)$ reproduces itself, scaled by a constant μ_0. With optimum $p(t) = \phi_0(t)$ we achieve the maximum SNR

$$SNR = 2\mu_0 E_p/N_0. \tag{12.5}$$

It is worth noting that this maximum-SNR waveform may lead to severe ISI if the duration of $p(t) = \phi_0(t)$ exceeds the symbol duration, which is one reason preventing the scheme from being widely applicable.

A transmitter capable of general waveform synthesizing or arbitrary waveform generating would be the ultimate goal of preprocessing. A digital FIR filter based waveform generator would be flexible and become more and more feasible as the

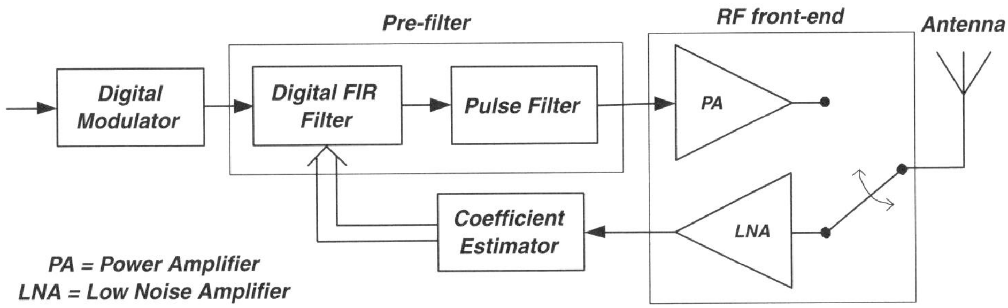

Fig. 12.3. A conceptual transmitter structure capable of preprocessing (in the RF front-end frequency up- and down-conversion may be used to shift the signal frequency).

semiconductor technology advances. A common structure of this type of waveform generators is a digital FIR filter followed by an analog interpolating or shaping filter as illustrated in Fig. 12.3. However, for any digital implementation, sampling rate as well as quantization resolution are limited. From a perspective of implementation, trade-off between performance and feasibility or cost must be made. Time reversal with mono-bit or ternary quantization and sub-Nyquist rate sampling has been proved working satisfactorily, according to computer simulation and test-bed based experiment.[25,28] The practical limitations should be considered in the performance optimization.

12.4. Time Reversal Enabled Physical Layer Security and SDMA

In addition to a performance enhancement method, preprocessing can be an enabling technique as well. For example, a transmitter equipped with a time-reversal pre-filter bank followed by multiple antennas can not only focus signal temporally at the receiver, but also focus signal spatially at the intended location (the receiver). Figure 12.4 shows a MISO (multiple input antennas and single

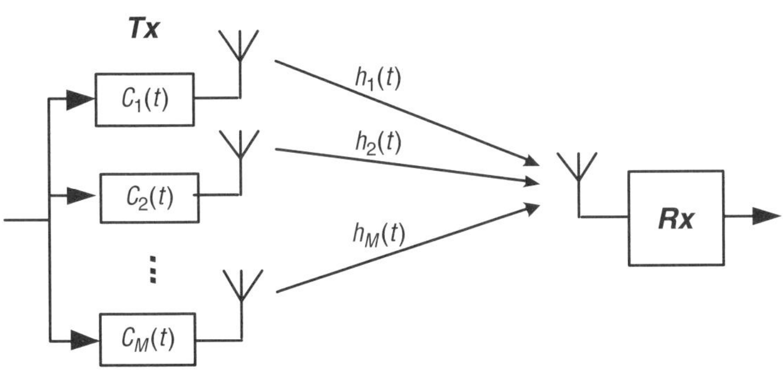

Fig. 12.4. MISO configuration.

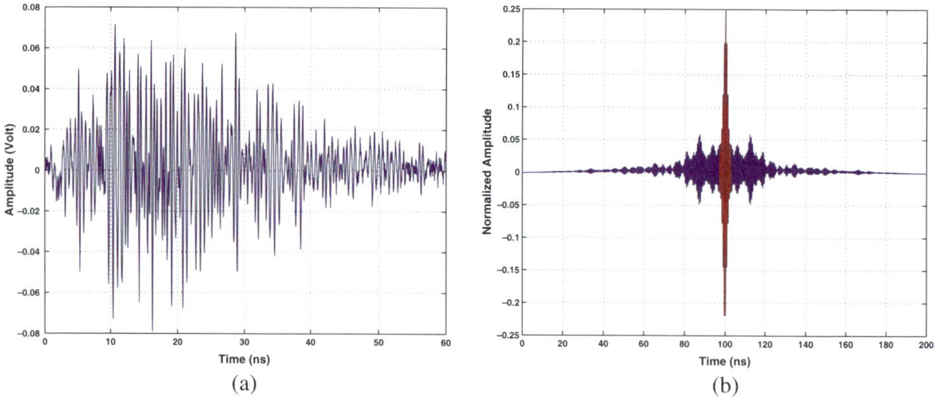

Fig. 12.5. Waveforms at the receive antenna's output. (a) Figure caption for figure 2a. (b) MISO time reversal (4 antenna elements at the transmitter; the main lobe shape is about the same as the transmit pulse shape).

output antenna) preprocessing configuration. The temporal focusing is illustrated in Fig. 12.5, assuming a MISO configuration with four transmit antennas and a practical waveform generator. The spatial focusing mechanism of a MISO time-reversal scheme can be explained in the following way. The pre-filtered signals travel from the transmit antennas to different locations, and at the intended location they are transformed to temporally condensed signals and their main lobes add up coherently; while at any location other than the intended one, the signals originating from different transmit antennas are widely-spread in time and have no similarity at all, thus together they appear to be a piece of noise-like waveform. Apparently, MIMO (multiple input antennas and multiple output antenna) will work too, where the multiple receive antennas can provide diversity or data multiplexing. The spatial focusing property of multi-antenna time-reversal preprocessing can be used for spatial division multiple access (SDMA)[23,28] or prevention of information leakage/interception.[25]

Physical-layer security is extremely desired for security vulnerable wireless sensors networks. It has been proved that channel randomness and reciprocity can be used to establish secure keys against eavesdropping.[29,30,53] Without using sophisticated procedure to achieve information-theoretic security, a simpler scheme to be proposed can add some level of security too. The time-reversal pre-filter's impulse response (ideally a time reversed CIR) can be viewed as a location based security key,[25] and this key can be obtained through reverse channel sounding thanks to channel reciprocity. The transmitted signal from a single antenna is temporally condensed at an intended location, while it is widely dispersed in time at other locations, which can be directly turned into location-based security enhancement at some circumstances.

To test capability of low probability of interception (LPI), suppose that there is a smart intercept receiver attempting to demodulate the signal sent to the intended receiver, assuming the interceptor employs the same type of receiver and knows all parameters (including data rate and timing information, etc.) used by the intended receiver, except its pre-filter's setting. Simply consider a SISO (single input antenna and single output antenna) DTR-time-reversal scheme in a multipath environment with excess delay spread much greater than the symbol duration T_b. Here a relatively simple FIR pre-filter is employed: it uses mono-bit coefficients and operates at the Nyquist rate. Its coefficients are generated by sampling a truncated CIR and then taking the signs from the samples. Location-based security enhancement in an office area is demonstrated in Fig. 12.6 in terms of BER performance for a set of intercept locations, where the intended receiver integrates over the main lobe of width T_I while the intercept receiver integrates over the whole symbol duration T_b, E_b/N_0 is measured at the intended receiver, and both the intended and intercept receivers are about 6 m apart from the transmitter. Surprisingly, even just several tens of centimeters away from the intended receiver, although the interceptor has known all critical parameters, due to severe ISI, it has very little chance to understand what it is listening to, which means security has been greatly enhanced without using any traditional encryption method. More important, the "security key" is

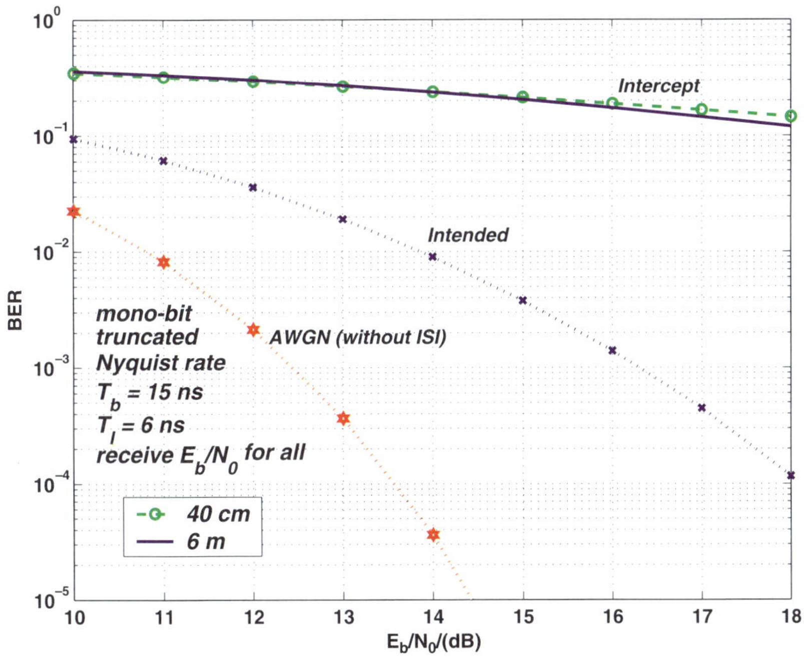

Fig. 12.6. Demonstration of location-based security taking advantage of ISI.

obtained at the physical layer based on the scattering nature, without consuming additional radio resource. In this example the intended receiver suffers from some ISI impact, but it can be reduced if some countermeasure is taken.

If equipped with multiple transmit antennas, the transmitted energy would truly focus at the intended location, achieving prevention of information leakage from an electromagnetic (EM) radiation point of view.

Another interesting feature of time reversal is its SDMA enabling. Note that the temporal/spatial focusing mechanism is not able to remove ISI and IUI completely. According to some indoor experiments, an SDMA multiuser system solely based on time reversal can suffer from strong IUI because of cross-correlations between the radio links, and even increasing the number of transmit antennas cannot fully solve the problem.[28] For demonstration purpose, consider a rather simple time-reversal SDMA system using pulse based DTR scheme. If time reversal combined with pulsed signaling, a pulse train would appear at the intended receiver. Shrinking the integration window to capture the signal peaks at the receiver could result in a lowered SNR, but it reduces the IUI impact as well, since the signal to interference ratio around a signal peak is higher. Overall speaking, a narrow integration window may lead to a higher SINR (Signal to Interference plus Noise Ratio) and better performance, if the impact of IUI is much more significant than that of the background noise. For simplicity, assume the receiver samples the signal at peak instants, without integrating the signal over a main-lobe interval. To reduce the IUI impact further, a stage of decorrelation precoding (of course, other types of multi-user precoding can be considered too) is added to the transmitter to remove the IUI at the instants of signal peaks.

Shown in Fig. 12.7 are a set of simulation results for multi-user schemes with different settings, where by default the pre-filter is significantly simplified (mono-bit time reversal), "ideal" refers to an ideal pre-filter, and "pre-decorr" refers to decorrelation precoding at the transmitter and sampling peaks at the receivers. The BER performance is mainly affected by the accuracy of pre-filtering, ISI, IUI as well as integration window size T_I. Two integration window sizes are considered here: $T_I = 6\,\text{ns}$ (default) and $T_I = 0.1\,\text{ns}$ (for peak capturing method). Based on these trials we have the following observations: (1) the mono-bit time-reversal scheme without precoding performs worst as expected; (2) the peak-sampling scheme yields improved performance; (3) decorrelation precoding combined with peak sampling improves the performance further and leads to more than 1.5 dB gain over the the mono-bit time-reversal scheme; and (4) in the ideal time-reversal scenario, applying decorrelation precoding plus peak sampling does not provide additional gain.

Time reversal combined with MISO is feasible, since the identical timing clock is shared by the multiple waveform generators. The system is especially promising when the number of antennas is large, say 16, 64, 128. The large number of antennas can be integrated into one antenna system.

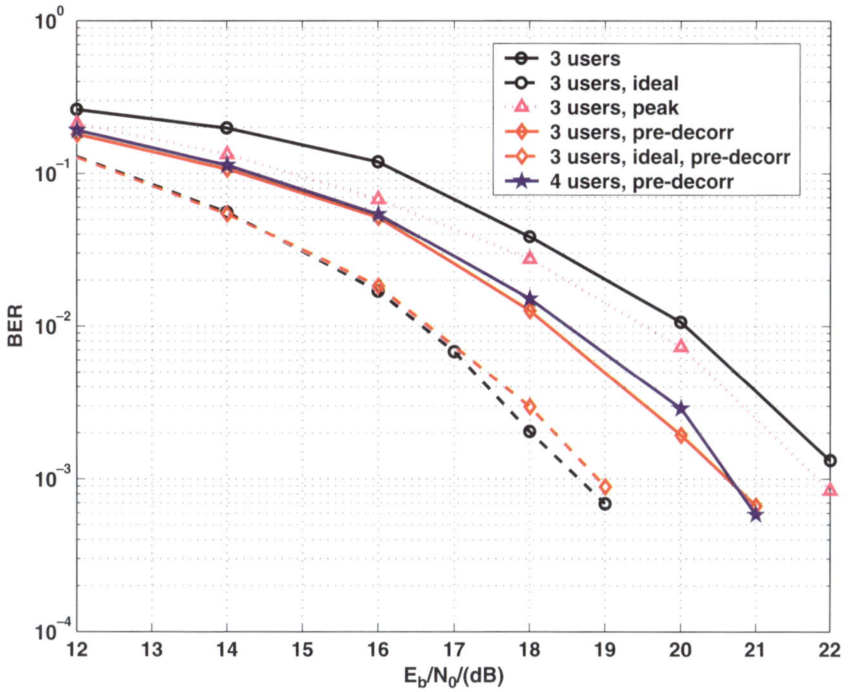

Fig. 12.7. Multi-user performance of a time-reversal-enabled SDMA system ($T_b = 50\,\text{ns}$).

When time reversal combined with MIMO is used, the timing clock synchronization is hard to achieve at the receiver since the focused waveforms are too sharp to be aligned with each other.

Due to the same reason of timing clock, time reversal is hard to be used in the spatially distributed network. Some preliminary work has been reported.[54,55] The spatial aspects of multiple antennas need more investigation in the framework of time reversal.

12.5. Channel Characteristics and Case Study

Well understanding channel characteristics in a particular environment is an essence to design a high performance communication system for the corresponding environment. In this section, different channel characteristics will be introduced and then four cases of channel analysis will be presented in detail.

12.5.1. *Channel characteristics*

The channel characteristics are a set of basic information and distinguishing properties of the communication channel, including CIR, transfer function, channel energy, path loss, channel reciprocity, temporal focusing, and channel capacity, etc. The channel transfer function is simply a Fourier transform of the CIR, thus either of them can be derived from another by taking Fourier transform or inverse Fourier transform.

12.5.1.1. *Time domain measurement of channel impulse response (CIR)*

The CIR is a time domain characteristic and it can be represented using the well-known tapped delay line (TDL) model. Time domain channel sounding is straight forward to get the CIR. In a time domain channel sounding experiment, the transmitter sends a pulse train through a transmit antenna to sound the channel and the waveform is picked up by a receive antenna and recorded as measurement data. One difficulty in time domain channel sounding is to generate sounding pulses that contain most signal energy in the frequency band of interest and are easy to be captured and processed. A digital sampling oscilloscope (DSO) is typically used to capture the waveform and store the data, where the sampling rate have to be sufficiently high to capture the details. The CIR in tap delay line model can be estimated from the received noisy waveform using "CLEAN", a matching pursuit algorithm.

12.5.1.2. *Frequency domain measurement of channel transfer function*

A channel transfer function gives the complex gain of the channel at different frequencies, thus frequency domain channel sounding is recommended to get channel transfer function directly. With a vector network analyzer (VNA), a frequency domain channel sounding setup would be quite easy. The VNA functions as both a transmitter and a receiver; it sweeps a set of sinusoid signals within the predetermined frequency band and generates the S-parameters containing the complex transfer function. Frequency domain channel sounding can cover wide range of frequencies, as far as the sweep time is much less than the channel coherent time. One disadvantage in a VNA based high frequency measurement is that the transmission range is limited due to large attenuation of the connecting cables. Because the frequency range is limited for a VNA, a rectangular spectral window is automatically posed. However, the spectral window may be reshaped to take into account any specific filter effect.

12.5.1.3. *Channel energy*

The energy of the channel is defined as

$$E_h = \int_0^{T_h} h^2(t)dt, \tag{12.6}$$

where $h(t)$ is CIR and T_h is its support.

12.5.1.4. *Path loss*

The received power is given by

$$P_r = P_t - PL + G_t + G_r, \tag{12.7}$$

where P_r and P_t are the receive and transmit powers in dBm, respectively; G_r and G_t are the receive and transmit antenna gains in dBi, respectively; and *PL* is the path loss in dB.

The path loss between a pair of antennas is the reduction in power density of an electromagnetic wave as it propagates through space. It takes into account many physics effects including free-space path "loss", refraction, diffraction, reflection and absorption. Path loss is environment dependent and it is a function of frequency and distance. Practically path loss can be calculated using formula

$$PL(d, f) = PL(d_0, f) + 10n(f)\log_{10}\left(\frac{d}{d_0}\right), \tag{12.8}$$

where $n(f)$ is the path loss exponent, f is the frequency of interest, d is the distance between the transmitter and the receiver, and d_0 is the reference distance. $n(f)$ is equal to 2 for propagation in free-space. A path loss exponent greater than 2 means the propagation environment is relatively lossy, while a tunnel or a hallway act as a waveguide, resulting in a path loss exponent less than 2.

12.5.1.5. *Channel reciprocity*

A real-time CIR is the key information to achieve the optimum performance in a wireless communication system, and channel sounding and estimation are required to generate the up-to-date CIR. Channel reciprocity refers to similarity of a pair of opposite-direction channels between two sites, where both the effect of propagation media and the effect of circuits at the two ends are taken into account. Perfect channel reciprocity can benefit a two-way wireless communication system, because channel sounding and estimation based on one link can be used for both forward link and reverse link. However, in reality, the channel reciprocity is not always obvious since there are many unpredictable nonlinear physics phenomena associated with the media and the circuits. This motivates experimental validation of channel reciprocity.

12.5.1.6. *Relative temporal focusing as a function of locations*

As mentioned before, pre-filtering (i.e., time reversal) can make the effective CIR temporally focusing and spatial focusing can be achieved using a bank of pre-filters followed by an array of antennas. Considering here a time reversal pre-filtering system with a single transmitter using a time reversed CIR as the pre-filter coefficients. Let the intended receiver location be represented by $\mathbf{r}_0$ and the unintended receiver location by $\mathbf{r}_i$. Correspondingly, denote $h(\mathbf{r}_0, t)$ and $h(\mathbf{r}_i, t)$ the CIRs for the locations $\mathbf{r}_0$ and $\mathbf{r}_i$, respectively. Relative temporal focusing at any location $\mathbf{r}_i$ with respect to the intended location $\mathbf{r}_0$ can be characterized by a metric $D(\mathbf{r}_0, \mathbf{r}_i)$ called directivity, which is defined as

$$D(\mathbf{r}_0, \mathbf{r}_i) = \frac{max|R_{hh}(\mathbf{r}_0, \mathbf{r}_i, t)|^2}{max|R_{hh}(\mathbf{r}_0, \mathbf{r}_0, t)|^2}, \tag{12.9}$$

where $R_{hh}(\mathbf{r}_0, \mathbf{r}_0, t)$ is a CIR autocorrelation for the intended receiver and $R_{hh}(\mathbf{r}_0, \mathbf{r}_i, t)$ is a crosscorrelation of the two CIRs. $R_{hh}(\mathbf{r}_0, \mathbf{r}_0, t)$ and $R_{hh}(\mathbf{r}_0, \mathbf{r}_i, t)$ are given by

$$R_{hh}(\mathbf{r}_0, \mathbf{r}_0, t) = h(\mathbf{r}_0, -t) * h(\mathbf{r}_0, t), \tag{12.10}$$

$$R_{hh}(\mathbf{r}_0, \mathbf{r}_i, t) = h(\mathbf{r}_0, -t) * h(\mathbf{r}_i, t). \tag{12.11}$$

12.5.1.7. *Theoretical spectral efficiency*

To evaluate the overall effects of the channel and different spectrum-shaping schemes, spectral efficiencies are calculated. The spectrum-shaping schemes to consider include water filling, time reversal, channel inverse and constant power spectrum density (PSD). A zero-mean band-limited Gaussian random data source which has maximum entropy is used for all different spectrum-shaping schemes. For the sake of simplicity, we further assume the data source has a flat in-band spectrum. When the water-filling spectral shape is applied, the spectral efficiency reached the maximum, i.e., the channel capacity. Channel capacity is an important channel characteristic and can be served as a performance bound to guide system design.

Figure 12.8 shows the block diagram of a SISO system, where the input signal $a(t)$ is a band-limited white Gaussian random process with zero mean, bandwidth W and unit one-sided PSD, $x(t)$ is the spectrum-shaping pre-filter, $s(t)$ is the transmit signal, $h(t)$ represents CIR, $n(t)$ is the additive white Gaussian noise with one-sided PSD N_0, and $r(t)$ represents the received signal. Their Fourier transforms are denoted by $A(f)$, $X(f)$, $S(t)$, $H(f)$, $N(f)$ and $R(f)$, respectively. Assume the support of $A(f)$ is $[f_0, f_1]$, so that $W = f_1 - f_0$.

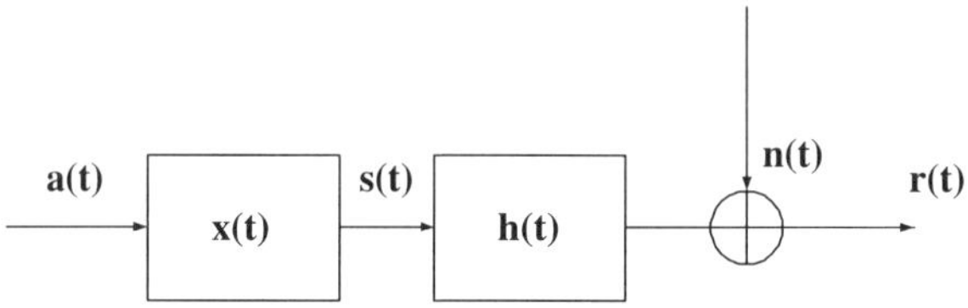

Fig. 12.8. Block diagram of a SISO system.

The transmitted power is

$$P = \int_{f_0}^{f_1} R_S(f)df, \tag{12.12}$$

where $R_S(f)$ is the one-sided PSD of the transmitted signal $S(t)$,[56] and it is given by

$$R_S(f) = |X(f)|^2. \tag{12.13}$$

The noise power at the receiver is expressed as

$$N = N_0(f_1 - f_0). \tag{12.14}$$

The SNR at the transmitter, denoted by ρ, is

$$\rho = \frac{P}{N}. \tag{12.15}$$

Denoting R the transmit bit rate, the spectral efficiency in bits/s/Hz can be expressed as

$$\frac{R}{W} = \frac{\int_{f_0}^{f_1} \log_2 (1 + \frac{R_S(f)|H(f)|^2}{N_0})df}{f_1 - f_0}. \tag{12.16}$$

When water filling is used to form the spectrum-shaping pre-filter, we have

$$R_S(f) = \left(\mu - \frac{N_0}{|H(f)|^2}\right)^+ \tag{12.17}$$

where $(x)^+ = \max[0, x]$, the constant μ is the water level chosen to satisfy the power constraint with equality

$$\int_{f_0}^{f_1} R_S(f)df = P, \tag{12.18}$$

and the spectral efficiency reaches the maximum, i.e., the channel capacity

$$\frac{C}{W} = \frac{\int_{f_0}^{f_1} \left(\log_2 (\frac{\mu|H(f)|^2}{N_0})\right)^+ df}{f_1 - f_0}. \tag{12.19}$$

When time reversal is used, it follows that

$$X(f) = \sqrt{\frac{P}{\int_{f_0}^{f_1} |H(f)|^2 df}} H^*(f), \tag{12.20}$$

where * means complex conjugate and the spectral efficiency is

$$\frac{R}{W} = \frac{\displaystyle\int_{f_0}^{f_1} \log_2 \left(1 + \frac{\rho(f_1 - f_0)|H(f)|^4}{\displaystyle\int_{f_0}^{f_1} |H(f)|^2 df}\right) df}{f_1 - f_0}. \tag{12.21}$$

For channel inverse is used, we have

$$X(f) = \frac{\sqrt{\frac{P}{\int_{f_0}^{f_1} \frac{1}{|H(f)|^2} df}}}{H(f)} \tag{12.22}$$

and

$$\frac{R}{W} = \log_2 \left(1 + \frac{\rho(f_1 - f_0)}{\int_{f_0}^{f_1} \frac{1}{|H(f)|^2} df} \right). \tag{12.23}$$

Finally, if the transmitted signal has the constant PSD from f_0 to f_1, then

$$R_S(f) = \frac{P}{(f_1 - f_0)}, \tag{12.24}$$

and

$$\frac{R}{W} = \frac{\int_{f_0}^{f_1} \log_2 (1 + \rho|H(f)|^2) df}{f_1 - f_0}. \tag{12.25}$$

12.5.2. *Case study*

Four different cases of channel analysis are presented. The first two cases are about the channel reciprocity in a car engine compartment and an office environment, respectively. The third case analyzes the channel characteristics in a rectangular metal cavity. Finally, in the case four, some measurement results conducted inside a manufacturing plant are provided.

12.5.2.1. *Case 1: Channel reciprocity in a car engine compartment*

A pair of omni-directional antennas were placed in the car engine compartment. The antenna locations are labeled in Fig. 12.9. Figure 12.10 illustrates channel reciprocity between the forward link A-G and the reverse link G-A, where link A-G corresponds to transmission from antenna A to antenna G, and link G-A corresponds to a reverse transmission. Two received waveforms measured in the forward and reverse links almost coincide with each other. The correlation between these two waveforms is as high as about 0.98, so that channel reciprocity can be declared from the engineering point of view. The bottom plot in Fig. 12.10 shows a closer look of the upper plot. It was found that whether the engine was on or off, no difference could be observed from measurement. Moreover, similar results were obtained for different pairs of antenna locations.

Although time-domain measurement was used, the same conclusion can be expected for frequency-domain validation.

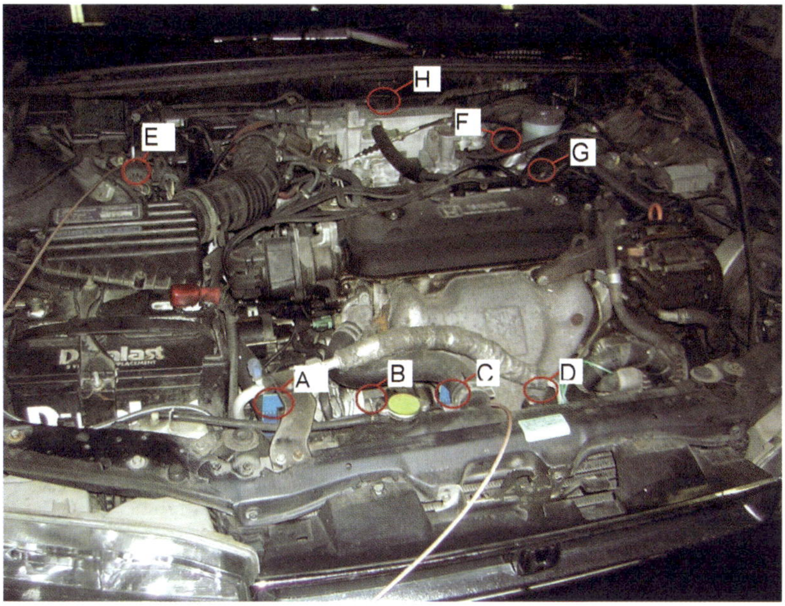

Fig. 12.9. Display of a car engine compartment.

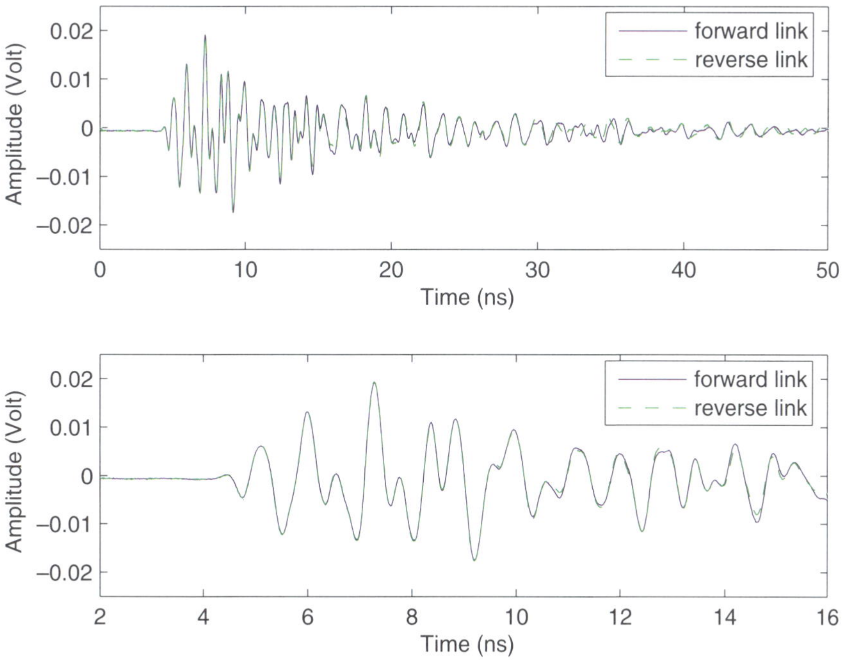

Fig. 12.10. Channel reciprocity validation in a car engine compartment.

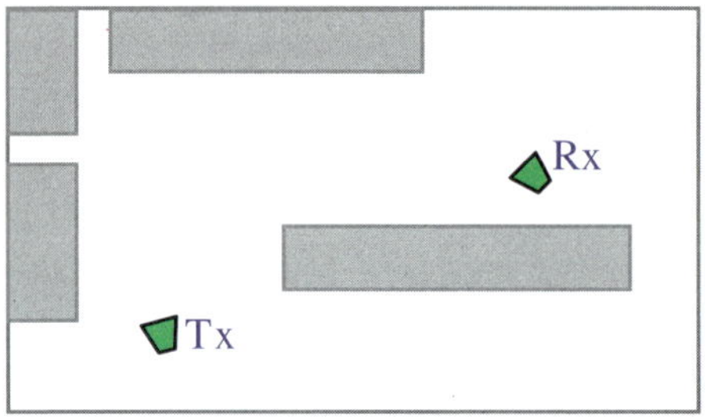

Fig. 12.11. Skeleton of an office environment and antenna placement.

12.5.2.2. *Case 2: Channel reciprocity in an office environment*

The time domain channel sounding was conducted in a lab/office area in Tennessee Technological University. It is a typical indoor area with wooden and metallic furnitures (chairs, desks, bookshelves and cabinets). Directional horn antennas were used. A skeleton of the measurement environment is shown in Fig. 12.11 and antenna separation is about 6 m. No LOS was available during the measurement.

The antenna locations for the forward link are shown in Fig. 12.11. Both received waveforms for the forward link and the reverse link are presented in Fig. 12.12, and the two waveforms agree with each other very well. The correlation between these two waveforms is about 0.98. The bottom plot in Fig. 12.12 shows a closer look of the waveform with the arrival time from 10 ns to 36 ns.

12.5.2.3. *Case 3: Channel characteristics in a metal cavity*

Study of communications inside a metal cavity holds huge importance because the cavity can be viewed as an emulation of different confined metal environments like intra ship, intra vehicle, intra engine, and so on. In this case, wide-band channel characteristics in such an environment are analyzed, which will help us know this type of channels better. Frequency domain channel sounding was performed inside a rectangular metal cavity by using a VNA. The dimension of the cavity is 16 feet by 8 feet by 8 feet, and the surface material of the cavity is aluminum. The channel sounding setup is illustrated in Fig. 12.13. Omni-directional antennas were used, with the transmit antenna being fixed and the receive antenna sliding along the horizontal central line in the cavity. The distance between transmitter antenna and receiver antenna varied from 0.5 m to 4 m in a step of 0.5 m. Table 12.1 lists the main parameters for this experiment. Measurement were also performed in an office and a hallway for comparison purpose.

Channel transfer functions and the corresponding passband CIRs for the three different environments are depicted in Fig. 12.14. In all the cases, the distance between the transmitter antenna and the receiver antenna is about 4 m. It is observed that the delay spread of channel is about 800 ns in the cavity, while in the

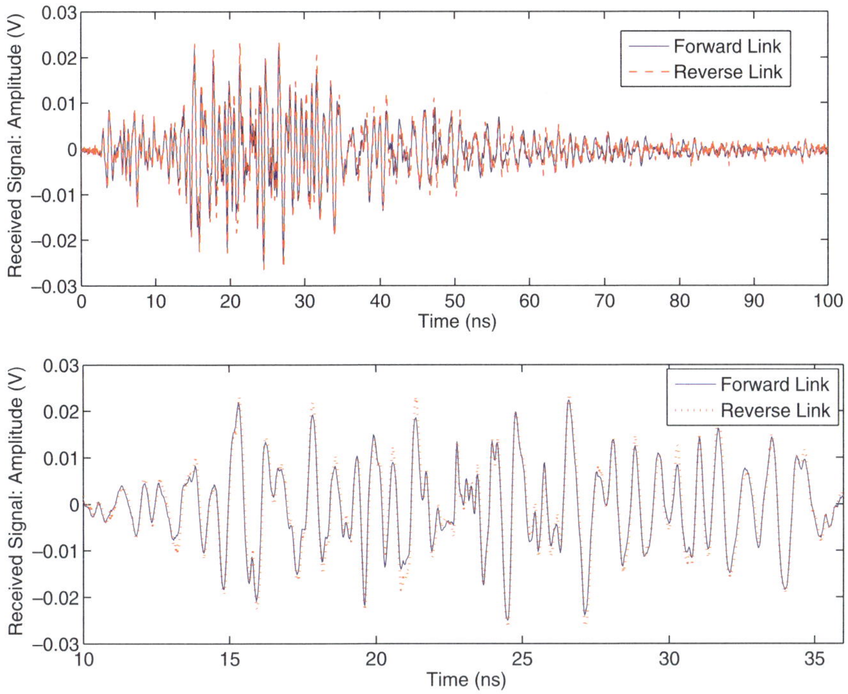

Fig. 12.12. Comparison of the received waveforms of the two links in an office environment.

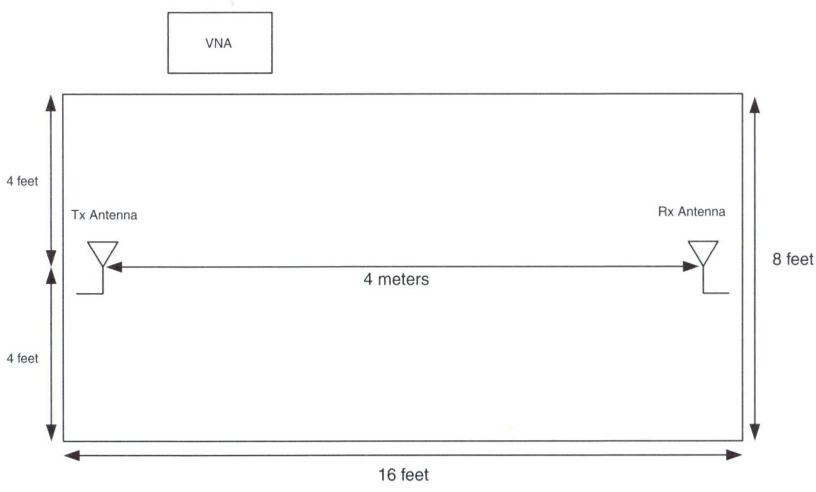

Fig. 12.13. Setup for channel sounding in rectangular metal cavity.

Table 12.1. Measurement parameters setup.

Parameter	Value
Frequency band	3 GHz–10 GHz
Number of points	7001
Transmission power	10 dBm
Frequency step	1 MHz
Antenna polarization	vertical
Number of averaging	128
Antenna height	1.35 m

office and the hallway they are less than 200 ns. The in-cavity CIR with large delay spread consists of a large number of multipaths which does not appear in the office and the hallway.

Channel energy comparison is shown in Fig. 12.15. It is can be seen that the channel energy in the cavity is much higher than those in the office and the hallway. For example, when the distance between the antennas is 3 m, the channel energy in the cavity is nearly 20 dB higher than those in the other two environments. Moreover, the channel energy in the cavity is very stable as the antenna separation changes, but the channel energies in the office or the hallway drop apparently as the antenna separation increases from 0.5 m to 3 m.

For analyzing temporal focusing versus locations, the transmit antenna was fixed on the horizontal central line, and the receive antenna was moved along a line that is 4 m away from the transmit antenna and perpendicular with the horizontal central line. As shown in Fig. 12.16, 18 receive antenna locations with 3-cm separation were tested. In evaluation we consider the first location $\mathbf{r}_0$ as the intended receiver and all others ($\mathbf{r}_i$, $i = 1, 2, \ldots, 17$) as the unintended receivers. The received waveform autocorrelation $R_{hh}(\mathbf{r}_0, \mathbf{r}_0, t)$ between the transmitter and the intended receiver is presented in Fig. 12.17(a), and the crosscorrelation $R_{hh}(\mathbf{r}_0, \mathbf{r}_1, t)$ between the transmitter and the unintended receiver at location $\mathbf{r}_1$ is presented in Fig. 12.17(b).

The directivity in the cavity is calculated by using Eq. (12.9) and shown in Fig. 12.18. It is observed that the directivity drops by almost 20 dB when the unintended receiver is only 3 cm away from the intended receiver, which implies that communication security inside a metal cavity can be enhanced by taking advantage of the rich scattering property.

Finally, spectral efficiencies are calculated based on the measured data. Figure 12.19 shows spectral efficiencies in the cavity for different spectrum-shaping schemes. Among the four spectrum-shaping schemes, water filling, as expected, gives the maximum spectral efficiency (actually, the channel capacity), while channel inverse gives the minimum. At low transmit SNR time reversal performs better than constant PSD, but the spectral efficiency of constant PSD approaches that of water filling at high transmit SNR. Figure 12.20 shows spectral efficiencies of

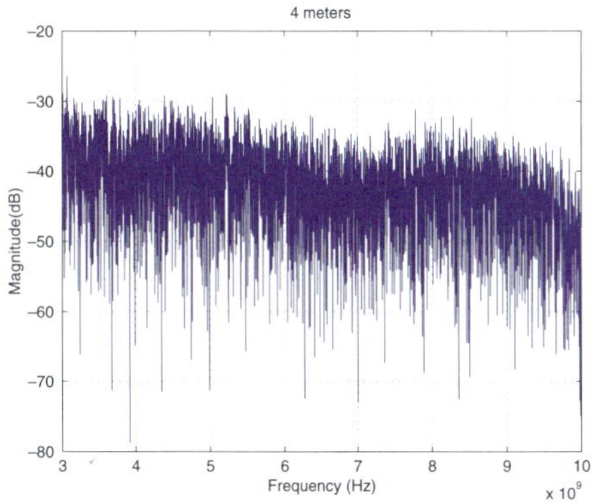

(a) Channel transfer function in cavity.

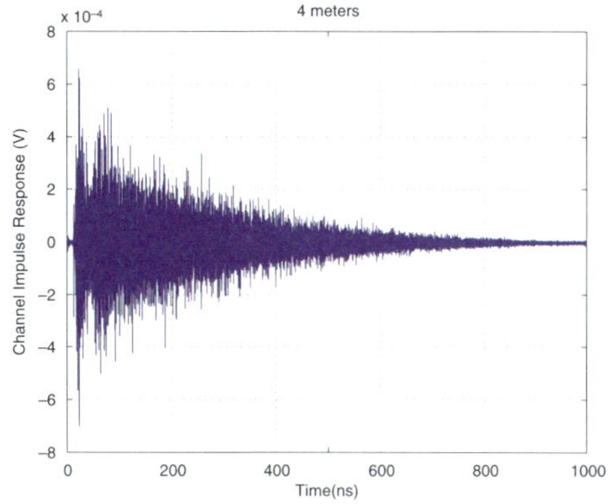

(b) The passband CIR in cavity.

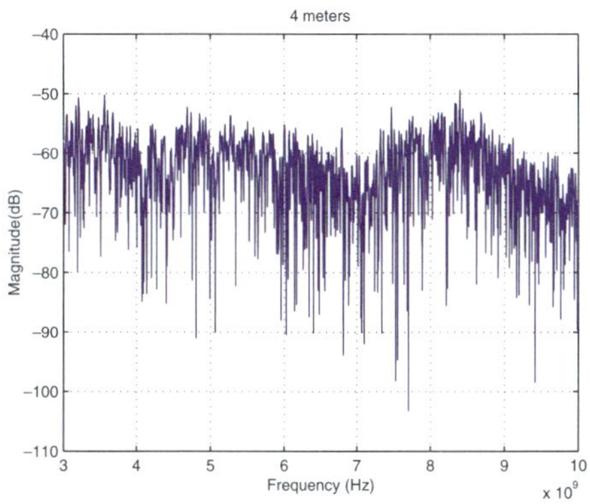

(c) Channel transfer function in office.

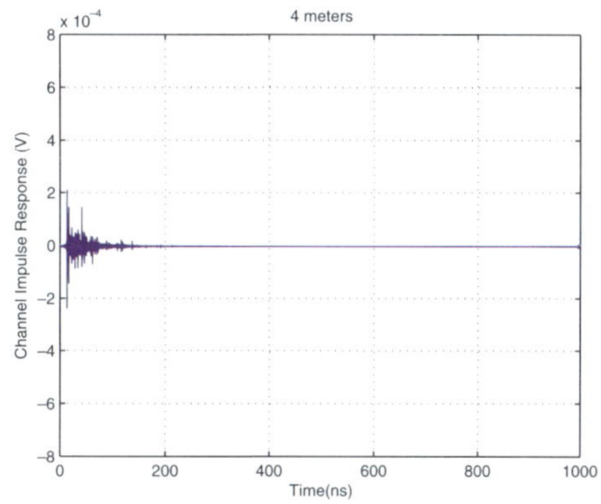

(d) The passband CIR in office.

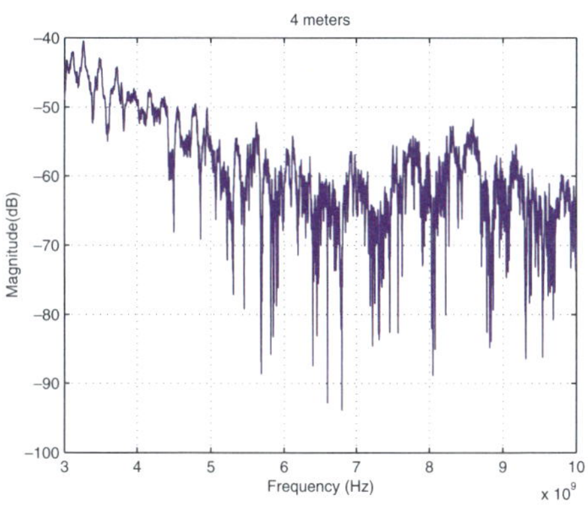

(e) Channel transfer function in hallway.

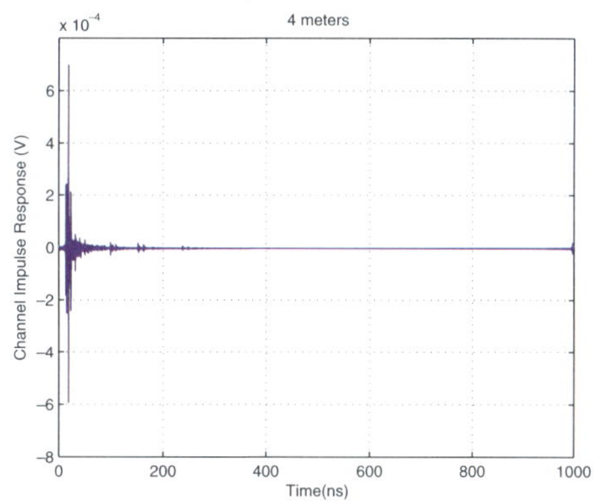

(f) The passband CIR hallway.

Fig. 12.14. Channel transfer function and the corresponding passband CIR in different environments.

water filling (i.e., channel capacities) in the cavity, the office and the hallway when water filling is used. The channel capacity in the cavity is much higher than those in the other two environments, suggesting that confined metal environments have potential to support very high data rate transmission.

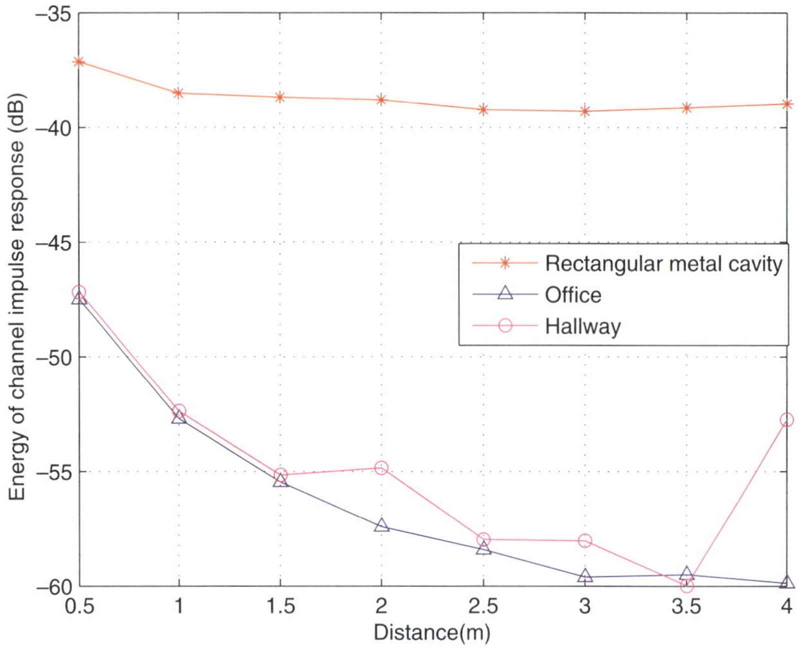

Fig. 12.15. Energy of channel in rectangular metal cavity, office and hallway environments.

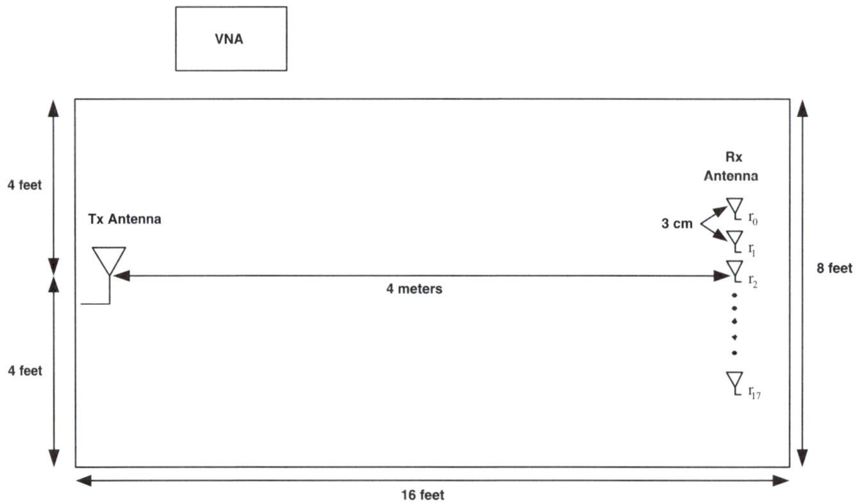

Fig. 12.16. Setup for analyzing relative temporal focusing.

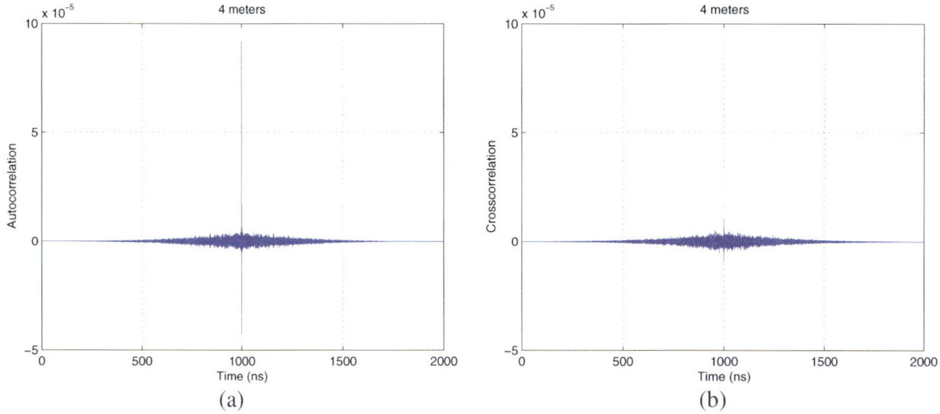

Fig. 12.17. Received waveform correlations for different receiver locations. (a) Waveform autocorrelation of the intended receiver and (b) waveform crosscorrelation between the intended receiver and the unintended receiver at r_1.

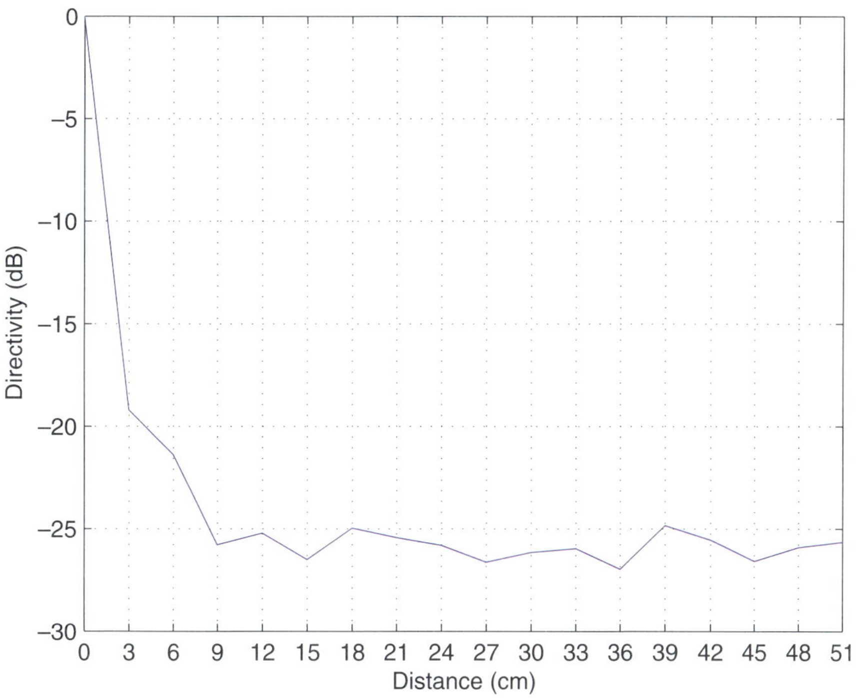

Fig. 12.18. Directivity in the rectangular metal cavity.

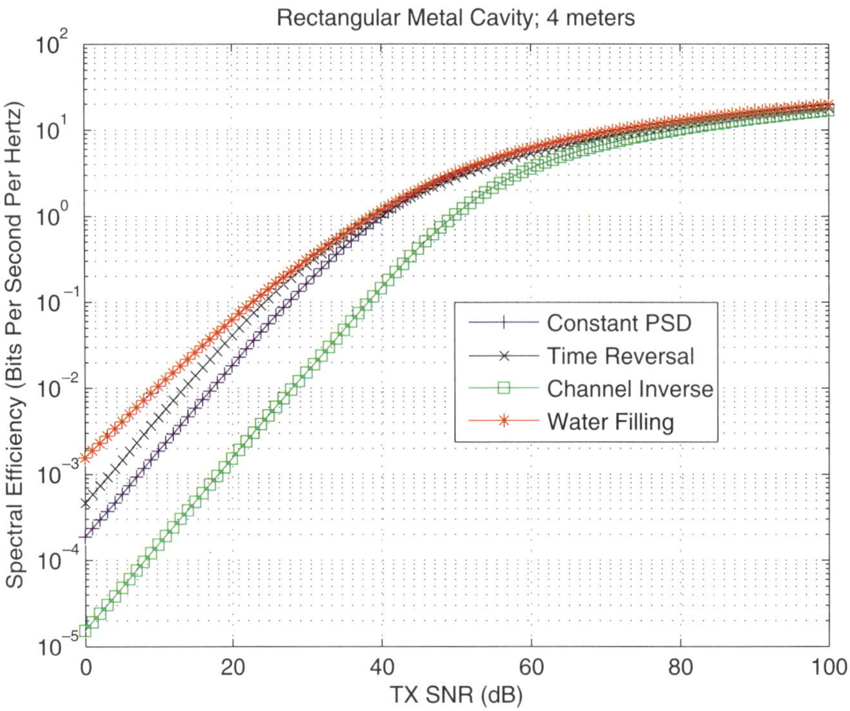

Fig. 12.19. Spectral efficiencies of different pre-filtering in the cavity.

12.5.2.4. *Case 4: Radio channel measurements in a manufacturing plant*

An industry environment like a in-building manufacturing area is a very complex environment for the electromagnetic wave propagation. Due to its complexity, it is hard to evaluate the channel using some prediction models which require enormous number of geometric information about the environment. It seems that measurement is the only way to study channel characteristics in such type of environments. In this case study, path loss exponent n is calculated based on the measurement data collected inside a manufacturing plant. As for transmit-receive antenna pairs, several combinations, including Omni-Omni, Omni-Horn and Horn-Horn were tested. An omni-directional antenna has wide coverage angle at the penalty of short transmission range, while a horn antenna can transmit far but has a narrow coverage angle. The mentioned three antenna combinations can fit different applications and requirements. Path loss exponents for different measurement areas are calculated and listed in Table 12.2. Figure 12.21 shows the received waveform captured directly by a DSO when antennas were placed along a production line. The impression is that the signal envelop decays slowly, and the delay spread is in the order of microsecond.

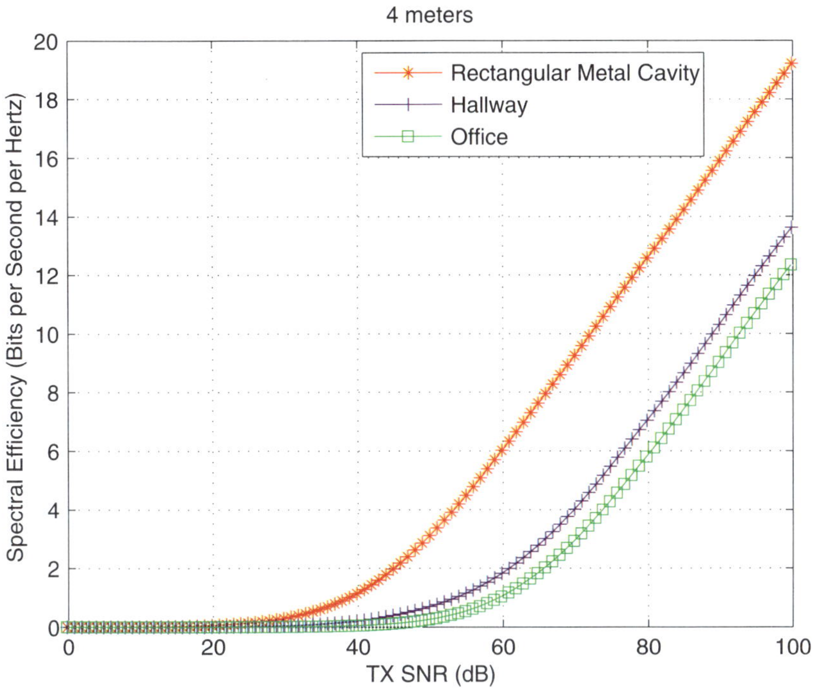

Fig. 12.20. Spectral efficiencies of water filling (i.e., channel capacities) in different environments.

Table 12.2. Path loss exponents for different measurement areas.

Environment	Antenna distance	Path loss exponent
Beside the product line (LOS)	25 m	1.68
Chassis area (NLOS)	30 m	2.26
Crosslane (NOLS)	33 m	2.51
Along the product line (NLOS)	60 m	2.10
Dense area (NLOS)	68 m	2.33

12.6. A Reference Example of Time Reversal Radio Test-Bed

The work of radio system design is to provide an efficient solution under some theoretical and practical criteria. A top-down design flow covers many aspects ranging from a very high level design to detailed implementations. A number of issues need to be considered: frequency band, architecture, data rate, modulation, synchronization, coexistence, interference, dynamic range, and many implementation issues. As for the system with preprocessing for wideband applications like UWB, one of the major challenges is in the waveform generator. Specifically, it is about how to choose a proper sampling rate as well as quantization resolution, and how to efficiently implement the algorithm. Based on our indoor experiments in UWB band, a

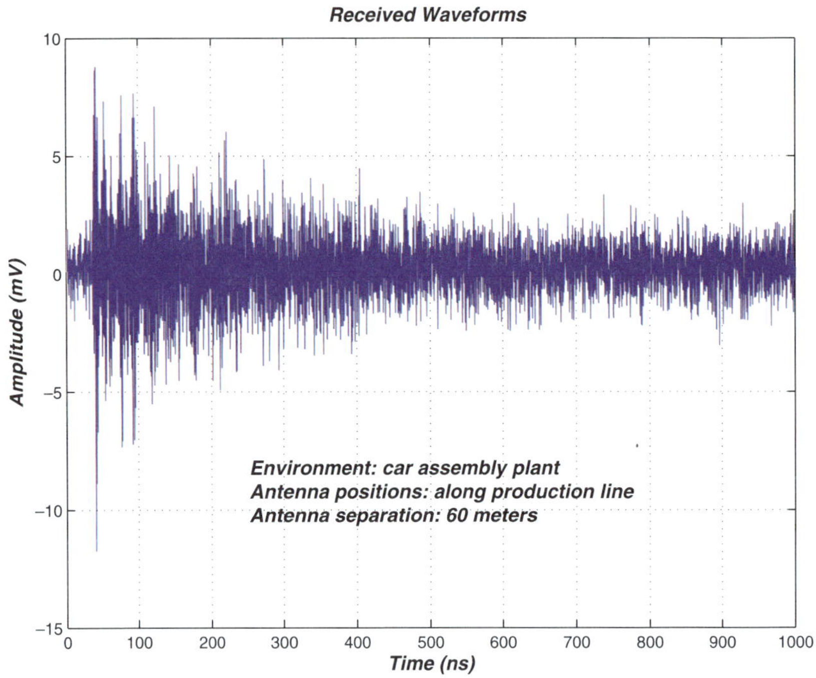

Fig. 12.21. The received waveform when the antennas are along the product line.

reduced-complexity pre-filter can function very well and implementing time-reversal preprocessing for microwave-band communications is feasible. A reference example of time reversal radio test-bed is presented in the following.

12.6.1. *Design considerations*

We adopt pulse based signaling and transmitter-side processing as system design guideline. Although direct pulse (carrier less) transmission can largely reduce complexity of transmitter RF front-end, it is not a good choice for multi-purpose radio testbed mainly because of its inflexibility. As a matter of fact, a modulated pulse is not only easy to generate but also more flexible: the center frequency is controlled by a local oscillator and the spectral shape is governed by the baseband pulse. Conceptual testbed architecture is shown in Fig. 12.22, where all baseband and control functions are implemented using FPGAs. Following an FIR filter (implemented in the FPGA), the digital-to-analog converter (DAC) outputs desired analog waveforms. The simple receiver philosophy is reflected in this testbed with on/off keying (OOK) or binary pulse position modulation (2-PPM) and diode based non-coherent detector at the receiver. At the receiver, demodulation is done in digital domain,

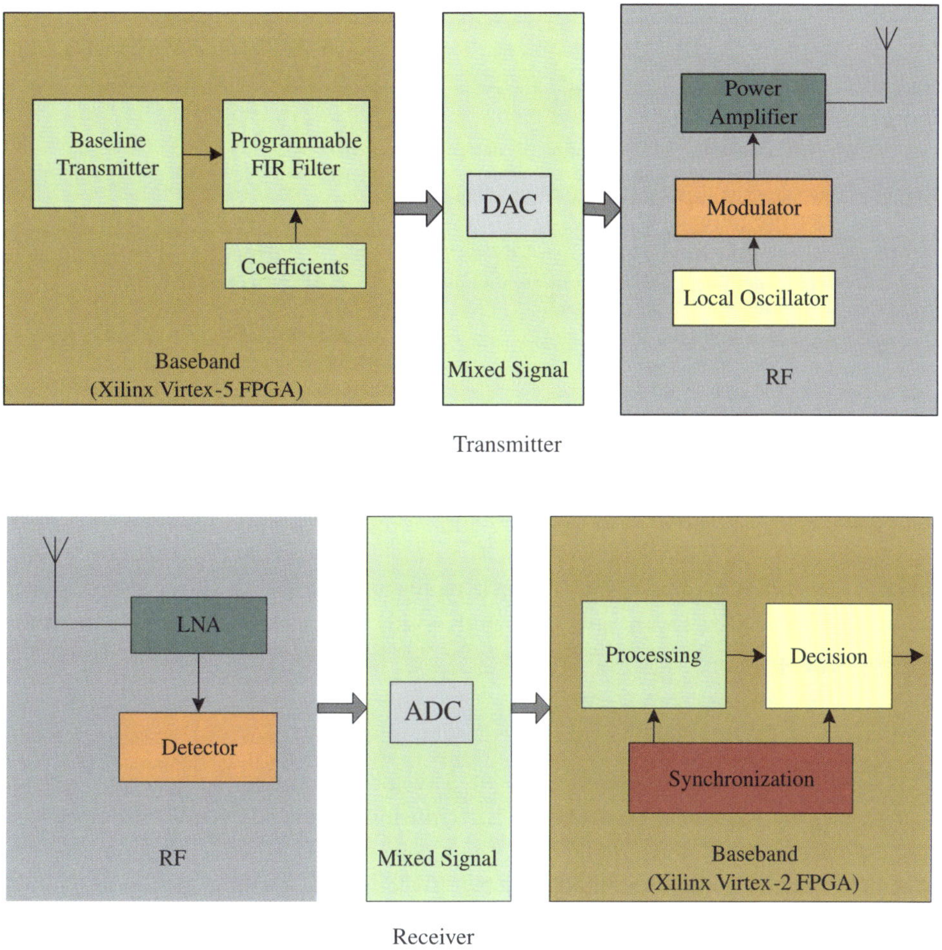

Fig. 12.22. Overall test-bed architecture.

so that algorithms and parameters can be adjusted easily. Of course, the analog-to-digital converter (ADC) is power hungry and it may be replaced by some customized circuits or commercially available products in the future.

12.6.1.1. *Link budget estimation*

The link budget estimation shown in Table 12.3 is based on the following conditions: (1) free space propagation, and (2) OOK modulation with equi-probable transmission of "0" and "1" bits. The transmitted power used here is estimated considering the actual components used in the transmitter. Spectrum measurement shows that the estimated transmitted PSD is closed to the measured result. The actual transmission range depends on the propagation environments. Path loss is

Table 12.3. A link budget example.

Bit rate	6.25 Mb/s
Minimum required SNR per bit	$E_b/N_{0,\min} = 16\,\text{dB}$
Center frequency	4 GHz
Transmitter antenna gain	3.5 dBi
Receiver antenna gain	3.5 dBi
Distance between the two antennas	15 meters
Receiver noise figure	6 dB
Implementation loss	4 dB
Transmitted power (input to antenna)	−16.45 dBm (0.0227 mW)
Bandwidth (approximately)	800 MHz
EIRP spectral density	−41.98 dBm/MHz
Path loss at 1 m	44.48 dB
Path loss at 3 m	54.03 dB
Total path loss	68.00 dB
Received power	−77.45 dBm
Link margin	2.59 dB
Proposed minimal receiver sensitivity	−80.04 dBm

much larger in a none-line-of-sight (NLOS) environment and the large delay spread would introduce ISI. Extra path loss and/or ISI can shorten transmission range significantly.

12.6.1.2. *Calibration phase*

This testbed has programmable transmit waveform function. To generate desired waveforms, the waveform generator at the transmitter has to be calibrated prior to regular data transmission. In addition, the receiver needs to set a proper amplification gain and decisions thresholds priorly. Tasks in the calibration phase include channel sounding, channel estimation, FIR filter coefficient optimization, determining thc amplification gain, and choosing the thresholds. In reality, the channel information can be obtained at either the transmitter or the receiver, but in either cases a feedback channel and some handshaking procedure are necessary. Considering limited sampling rate and resolution, there exist a best set of filter coefficients under some criterion. There have been intensive work on channel sounding and estimation, and many proposed methods can be considered. we sound the channel using lab instruments, estimate the channel and optimize the coefficients in an off-line manner. The amplification gain and thresholds are set manually.

12.6.1.3. *Energy collection*

A direct consequence of a high-bandwidth UWB signal is ultra fine multipath delay resolution in multipath propagation environments. Theoretically, to efficiently capture the signal energy dispersed over a large number of individual paths, either a

RAKE receiver scheme or an OFDM scheme can provide high performance, given perfect synchronization and channel estimation. Realistically, a RAKE receiver with tens of fingers is infeasible, and both schemes mentioned above are financially improper for low-cost low-data-rate applications. There is a huge potential market for these lower-end applications, such as sensor networks. In response to this need, several suboptimal receiver schemes, including TR and energy detection using a square law detector, have regained popularity in the UWB community. Although both TR and energy detection suffer from performance penalty, they have no need for sophisticated channel estimation and precise synchronization, which significantly reduces receiver complexity and cost. OOK modulation and energy detection is indeed a reasonable combination. Received signal energy can be captured easily using a square law or diode detector followed by an integrator, and OOK works fine if the data symbol boundary is roughly known and inter-symbol-interference (ISI) is negligible. Pulse position modulation (PPM) is another popular modulation for pulse based wide band systems, and high order PPM or called M-ary PPM is promising to work with channel coding to achieve wide range of scalability.

A conceptual diagram of energy detector based receiver is shown in Fig. 12.23, where an integrator following the detector accumulates the signal energy. The integration window size is a key parameter that affects performance. Since the integrator captures both the signal energy and the harmful noise energy, a smart way of energy capture is to weight the incoming signal before integration, which is at the cost of higher complexity. A simpler way is to integrate the incoming signal over a proper integration window. Instead of using fancy integrators, we rely on the waveform generator at the transmitter to focus signal energy and set the integration window to a fixed size that is much smaller than a typical delay spread in a NLOS environment.

12.6.1.4. *Synchronization and state transition*

We have designed a 3-stage synchronization method that is of lower complexity than traditional direct correlation based methods. Here are functions of the three stages: stage 1 for signal-arrival detection (or coarse synchronization), stage 2 for chip synchronization, and stage 3 for frame synchronization. The main advantages of this 3-stage approach include: (1) the stage 1 provides coarse timing quickly and

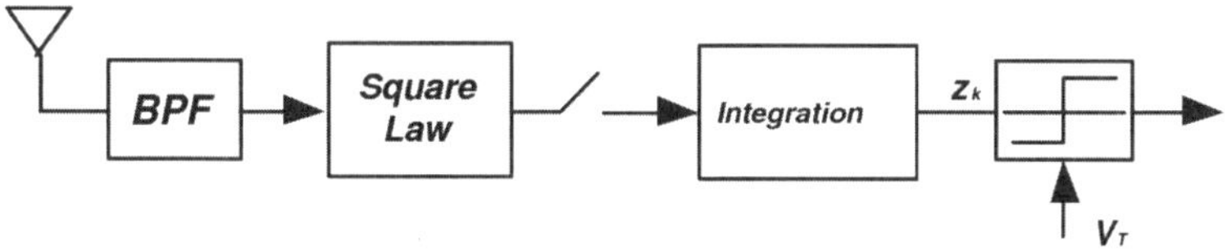

Fig. 12.23. Conceptual diagram of energy detector based receiver.

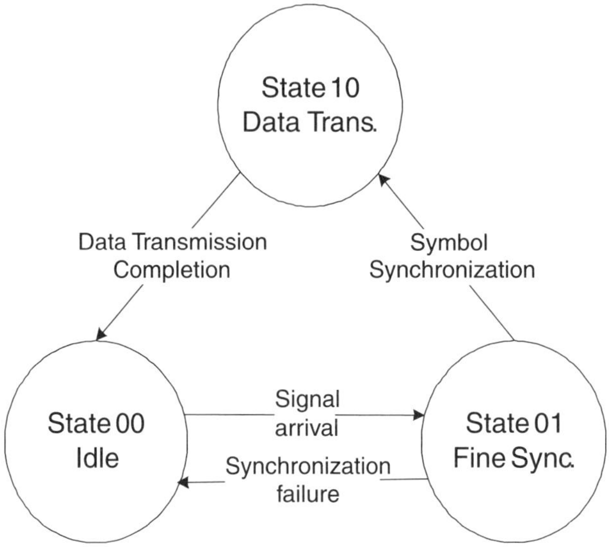

Fig. 12.24. State transition diagram.

reduces search space; and (2) hard decision is made after stage 2, so that the stage 3 deals with mono-bit sequence, resulting in less computation and lower complexity. To shorted the overall synchronization time further, parallel chip level processing is employed at the cost of more FPGA resources occupation.

The receiver has three working state and the state transition diagram is given in Fig. 12.24. Starting with the idle state, if the receiver detects "Signal arrival", the system goes to the fine synchronization state; if synchronization succeeds, the system enters into the data transmission state, demodulates the data and goes back to the original idle state after demodulation. On the other hand, if synchronization failed, the system returns back to the idle state. These state transitions are executed by the finite state machine (FSM) implemented in FPGA.

12.6.2. *Implementation*

12.6.2.1. *Transmitter*

Design of Waveform Generator

A symbol waveform can include multiple pulses to reduce peak power while keeping enough symbol energy (in this design a symbol contains one data bit). Scrambling coding is necessary to remove DC component and reduce the spectral spikes in the modulated signal. In typical indoor environments, delay spread is in the order of tens of nanoseconds, and inter-pulse-interference (IPI) is inevitable as the pulse repetition rate reaches the level of tens of MHz. A waveform generator is placed at the transmitter to focus the received signal in time and reduce the ISI impact.

OOK and PPM are two modulation schemes that are suitable for non-coherent detection. For higher data rates, a 2-PPM symbol duration has to be double of an OOK symbol duration to avoid IPI. However, finding a proper threshold for OOK demodulation at unknown level of background noise is challenging, but threshold selection is not necessary for 2-PPM scheme if using differential energy detection.

Time reversal waveforms have been used to test the system and verify the performance. In a time reversal system, the transmit chip waveform is the time-reversed version of the CIR, which is environment dependent. The waveform generator in the transmitter has to be programmable to match the instant CIR. Studies have shown that the received signal concentrates a large percentage of the total energy in a short period of time, enabling the use of some simple receiver that have little toleration to IPI and ISI.

In the transmitter, the baseband waveform generator consists of a pre-filter module implemented in Xilinx Virtex-5 FPGA, a DAC supporting Gsps sampling rate, and the corresponding connection buses. The pre-filter is a pair of FIR filters with programmable coefficients able to quadrature sequences.

On the market there are not many DAC and ADC products supporting Gsps sampling rates. Top concerns in selecting them include multiplexing or demultiplexing features, reconfigurability and dual-channel. The DAC chip used in the testbed supports dual-channel, 14-bit resolution, and sampling clock rate up to 1.0 Gsps. It also features 2:1 (or 28:14) multiplexing, waveform memories, low voltage differential signal (LVDS) interface and configurability. Although the high speed digital interface standard LVDS has been used in the transmitter, the connection between the FPGA and the DAC is actually a bottleneck that limits the speed. This fact suggests that to increase the speed further, higher ratio multiplexing, shorter connection and maybe some other efforts have to be considered.

Transmitter RF Front-End

We mainly rely on off-the-shelf products for RF front-ends in the transmitter. The transmitter RF front-ends is illustrated in Fig. 12.25. The baseband signal from the DAC is up-converted to a bandpass signal by the modulator, and after passing through the power amplifier, finally the amplified bandpass signal radiates from the antenna.

Reconfigurability and wide frequency range are preferred for the local oscillator (LO). A quadrature type of modulator (or up-converter) is needed to handle complex signals. Baseband bandwidth and input LO frequency range of a modulator (or up-converter) are particularly important to generate wideband signals. The power amplifier has to be of wide bandwidth and there are many choices. A variable attenuator may be used with the power amplifier in order not to break the FCC emission power ruling.

One common issue in RF implementation is carrier leakage rejection. Although the modulator has very good carrier isolation (say, $-37\,\text{dBm}$), there are some other

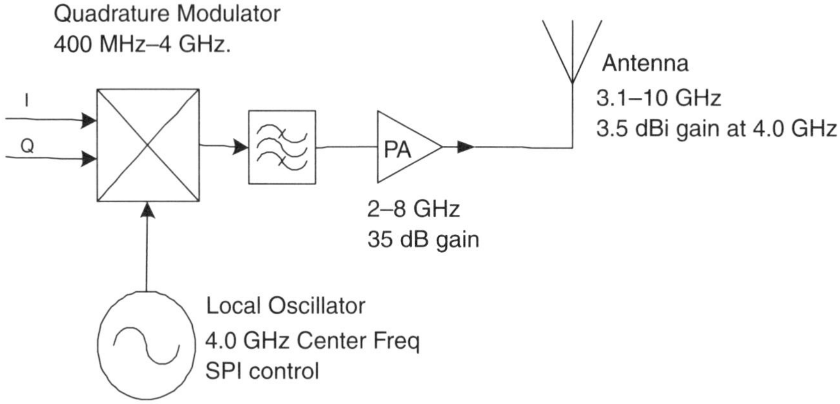

Fig. 12.25. The diagram of transmitter RF front-ends.

paths that the carrier can pass to the output port. Also, unbalanced bias between the two differential input ends of a modulator (or up-converter) makes carrier contribution at the output. Conventional RF decoupling techniques can reduce carrier leakage. In addition, a narrow band notch filter at the carrier frequency may be employed to suppress the output carrier frequency.

System Control

All system control tasks are taken cared by the FPGAs. Configuring some devices such as DAC and local oscillator (LO) is part of system control. The serial peripheral interface (SPI) bus is a simple and flexible interface standard that allows one master device to communicate with one or multiple slave devices, and it can support data rates up to tens of Mbps. In the transmitter, the LO is connected to the FPGA via an SPI bus with the FPGA serving as the SPI master and the LO as the SPI slave. It shows that SPI bus protocol is efficient and can increase system's flexibility. The system control flow chart in the transmitter side is presented in Fig. 12.26.

12.6.2.2. *Receiver*

Front-End Amplification

Requirements for receiver front-end amplification include low noise figure (<4 dB), enough gain (max. gain >60 dB) and proper dynamic range (>30 dB), considering medium range indoor communications. A combined amplifier is built by concatenating a low noise amplifier (LNA) module with ultra low noise figure, a variable attenuator and a gain block.

ADC and its Interface to FPGA

An 8-bit monolithic bipolar ADC with sampling rate up to 1.5 Gbps has been selected. The variable sampling rate is achieved by controlling the output frequency

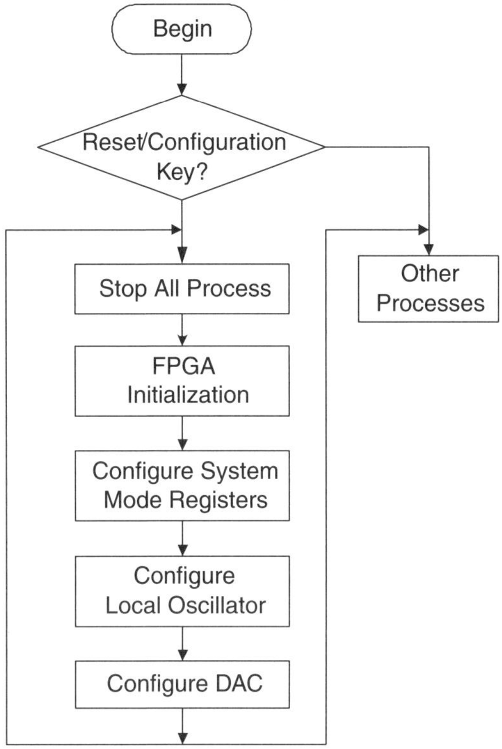

Fig. 12.26. System control flow for the transmitter.

of the clock source. The ADC features an on-chip, selectable 8:16 output demultiplexer. A double-data-rate (DDR) interface implemented in FPGA connects the ADC to the FPGA. Although the maximal resolution is 8 bits, lower resolution can be chosen in signal processing.

In the receiver of the radio testbed, the ADC employs a fully differential 8 bits quantizer and a unique encoding scheme to limit metastable states, with no error exceeding 1 LSB max. To facilitate a lower rate digital interface, the ADC features an on-chip, selectable 8:16 positive-referenced emitter-coupled logic (PECL) compatible output demultiplexer that reduces the output data rate to one-half the sampling clock rate.

An ADC-FPGA interface has been carefully designed to support a sampling rate of 800 Msps in the receiver. A single-data-rate (SDR) interface with a FIFO memory is implemented in FPGA to receive data from the ADC.

In designing the high-speed interface between ADC (or DAC) and FPGA, signal integrity has become a critical issue. Many signal integrity problems are electromagnetic phenomena in nature. There are two concerns for signal integrity: the timing and the quality of the signal. Signal timing mainly depends on the delay caused by the physical length and the material of each segment along a signal propagating path. Signal waveform distortions can be caused by reflection, cross talk, and power/ground noise.

An important parameter is the characteristic impedance Z_0 defined as the voltage-to-current ratio at any point along the transmission line. If the far end is terminated with resistance $R = Z_0$ over the entire frequency band, impedance matching is perfect and the forward propagating wave is fully absorbed by the load. On the other hand, an impedance mismatched load would cause reflecting wave traveling back to the source, and it may be reflected again if the source is impedance mismatched, resulting in rings on top of the original waveform. Such ringing has a serious impact on signal integrity, reduces noise/interference toleration margins, and even leads to malfunction. A way to avoid reflections and ensure signal integrity is a proper termination. Most high-speed data interface standards (such as LVDS) require load-end termination for impedance matching but do not require source/driver-end termination. For better result, double-end termination at both ends of the connection bus has been adopted. It can be observed in Fig. 12.27 that the signal swing is reduced significantly with the presence of the proposed termination.

FPGA Based Receiver Processing

The receiver Verilog coding is more complicated than the transmitter's because much more digital signal processing algorithms need to be implemented in the receiver. In addition, parallel chip level processing is employed for fast acquisition, at the cost of more FPGA resources occupation.

The routed FPGA design shown in Fig. 12.28 is observed using the software Xilinx FPGA editor. The blue/light area indicates the occupied logic resources. The target FPGA device in the receiver is one of the Virtex II platform. The detailed logic utilization for the transmitter and receiver is shown in Table 12.4. It can be seen that more resources are utilized in the receiver.

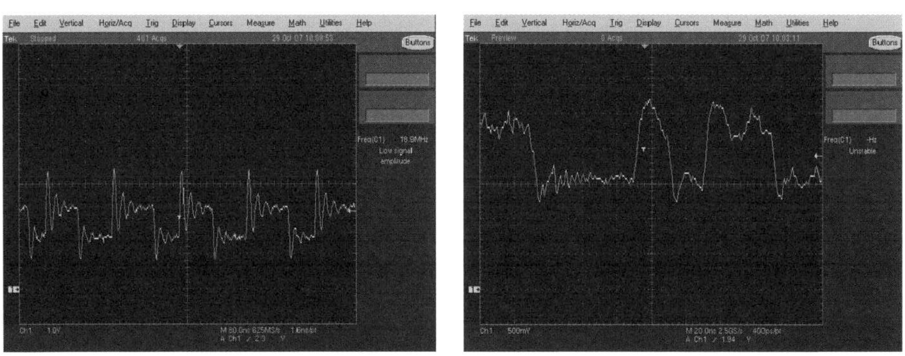

(a) Data waveform with load-end termination only. (b) Data waveform with double-end termination.

Fig. 12.27. Impact of termination on high-speed data transmission.

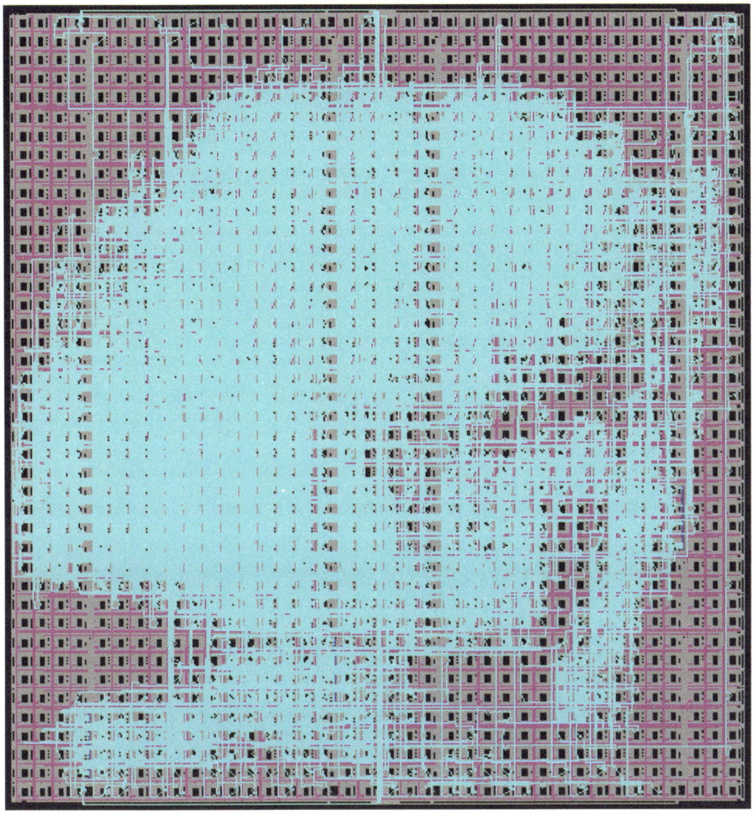

Fig. 12.28. Routed FPGA design for the receiver.

Table 12.4. Device utilization summary.

	Transmitter	Receiver
Number of slice flip flops	495	1533
Number of 4 input LUTs	573	2250
Number of occupied slices	331	1813
Total number of 4 input LUTs	642	2635
Number of bonded IOBs	48	52
Number of DCMs	0	2
Number of PLL/ADVs	1	0
Number of BlockRAM/FIFO	1	0
Total equivalent gate count for the design	146795	376714

12.6.3. *System test and results*

The functionalities of the time reversal testbed and the temporal focusing property can be verified through experiment. A packet with a given data payload is transmitted repeatedly. The transmit and receive antennas are placed in a non-line-of-sight

(NLOS) manner. At the receiver, if the demodulated sequence matches to the transmitted sequence, then we can say the system is working properly. Moreover, waveform level temporal focusing can be observed at the receiver using an oscilloscope.

12.6.3.1. *Preparing the experiment*

In addition to the testbed, below is a list of instruments used in the experiment, and each of them must be calibrated well before use.

- Vector Network Analyzer (VNA)
- Spectrum Analyzer (SA)
- Logic Analyzer (LA)
- Digital Phosphor Oscilloscope (DPO)

Time reversal template (coefficients of the FIR pre-filter) preparation is a major task in the experiment. Specifically, the CIR has to be estimated and converted into a fixed-point sequence, and then load the sequence to the coefficient memory. In a real system, we need to implement channel sounding and estimation functions to provide the transmitter with the template. However, for the sake of time reversal functionality verification, with help of lab instruments, we can obtain the template off line and load it to the memory in advance.

12.6.3.2. *Environment and system setup*

According to time reversal theory, the environment should be as complex as possible, so that rich multipath can be obtained. According to this philosophy, our system test is performed in a typical non-line-of-sight (NLOS), three-compartment office environment (Fig. 12.29). Transmit antenna and receive antenna are located in compartment A and compartment B, as can be seen from Fig. 12.29. There are wood and metal shelves, desks and chairs, computers and electronic equipments in the office. These furnitures reflect signals and cause multipath propagation. These antennas are omni-directional and the line-of-sight between is blocked by the wall and furnitures. This setup ensures plenty of multipaths.

Note that the transmitted signal is a passband signal while the time reversal template is a baseband signal. There are different ways to prepare the template and the frequency domain channel sounding method has been adopted. The passband channel transfer function is measured using a VNA. As shown in Fig. 12.30, the frequency sweeps from 3.5 GHz to 4.5 GHz with 1 MHz resolution, covering the frequency band of the transmitted signal. In reality the measured passband channel transfer function is always associated with a known spectral window. If $h(t)$ is the CIR for the frequency range of interest, the equivalent baseband CIR would

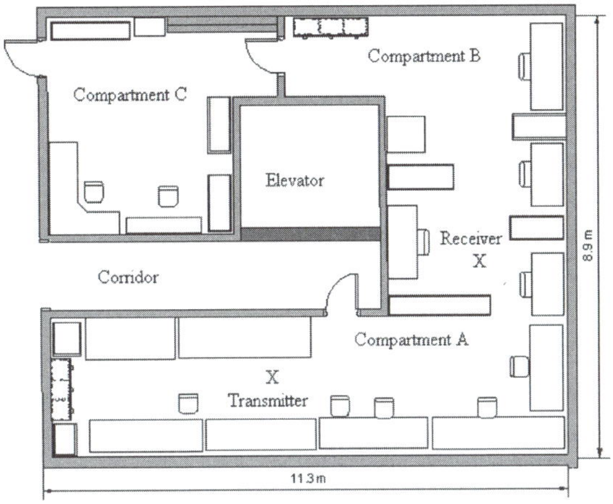

(a) Office layout.

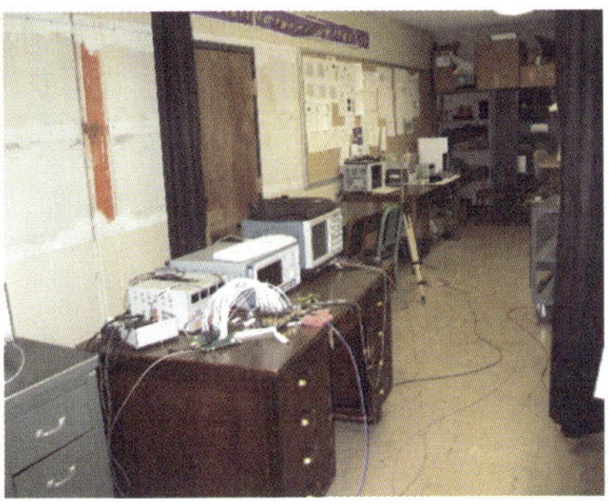

(b) Compartment A.

(c) Compartment B.

Fig. 12.29. Office environment.

be $h'(t) = h(t)e^{-j\omega_c t}$, where ω_c is the center frequency. To estimate $h'(t)$, the measured passband channel transfer function is down-converted, then apply inverse Fourier transform (IFT) to the baseband channel transfer function to obtain a filtered baseband CIR, and finally the baseband CIR $h'(t)$ can be estimated using some deconvolution algorithm like CLEAN to remove the filter effect. The filter effect is due to the spectral window and the filter is an IFT of the known spectral window. Depicted in Fig. 12.31 is the magnitude of the filtered baseband CIR based on measurement.

$h'(-t)$ would be an ideal baseband time reversal template, but it cannot be accurately generated due to the practical limitations. What have been tested is a ternary-quantized real-number baseband template with sampling rate 500 Msps.

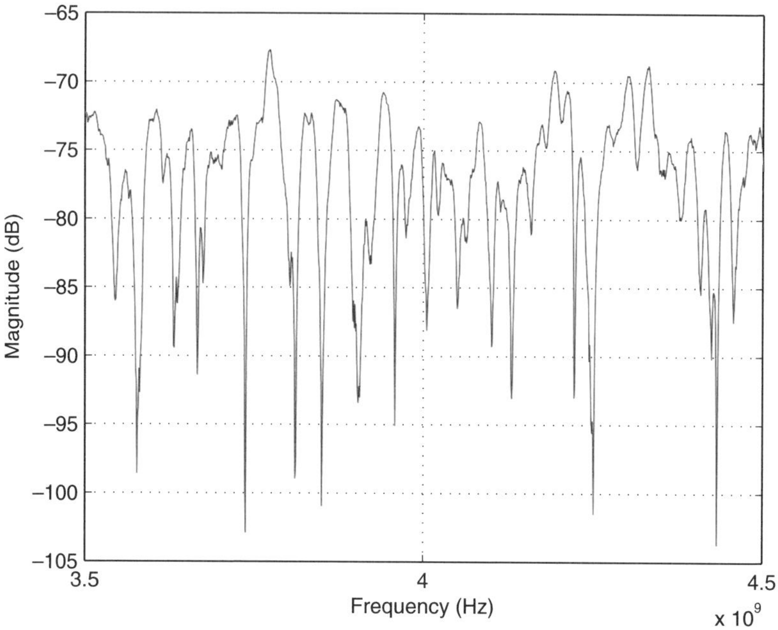

Fig. 12.30. Rectangle-windowed channel transfer function measured by a VNA; frequency sweeps from 3.5 GHz to 4.5 GHz with 1 MHz resolution.

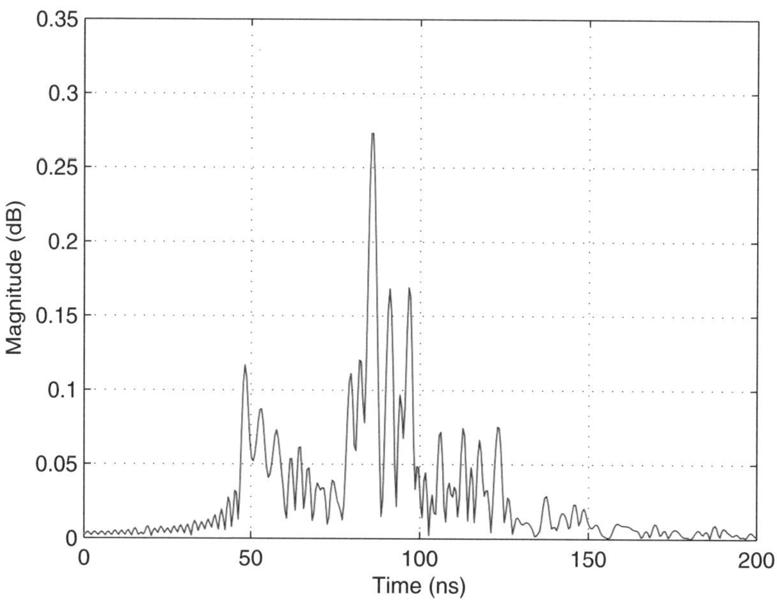

Fig. 12.31. Magnitude of the filtered baseband CIR based on measurement.

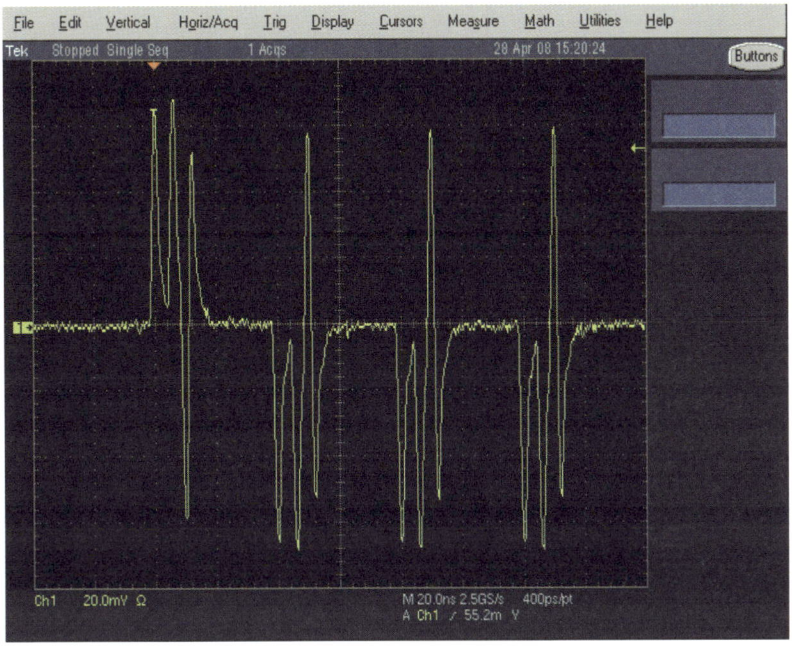

Fig. 12.32. Baseband time reversal waveform after scrambling.

This template was optimized under maximum correlation criterion. Figure 12.32 is a piece of baseband signal corresponding to four scrambled chips, captured at the waveform generator's output by a Tektronix TDS 7104 DPO. Since the approximate baseband time reversal template contains four 2-ns pulses, each chip comprises four 2-ns pulses. Figure 12.33 is the spectrum of the modulated waveform captured at the transmitter by a Rohde & Schwarz Spectrum Analyzer FSEM20. The center frequency is about 4 GHz and the 10 dB bandwidth is about 800 MHz.

At the receiver side the DPO is used to monitor the detector's output as well as the demodulated bit stream, and one could tell if the system is running properly simply by observing the demodulated bit stream.

12.6.3.3. *Experimental results*

During the first demonstration,[57] a given pseudo-random (PN) sequence was transmitted periodically at bit rate 6.25 Mbps. Figure 12.34 shows the system test observations. The top trace is the transmitted baseband waveform, the middle trace is the detector output, and the bottom trace is the demodulated bit stream. In order to observe the signals more conveniently, the scales for top trace, middle trace and bottom trace are set to 50 mV/div, 100 mV/div, and 5 V/div, respectively. The top

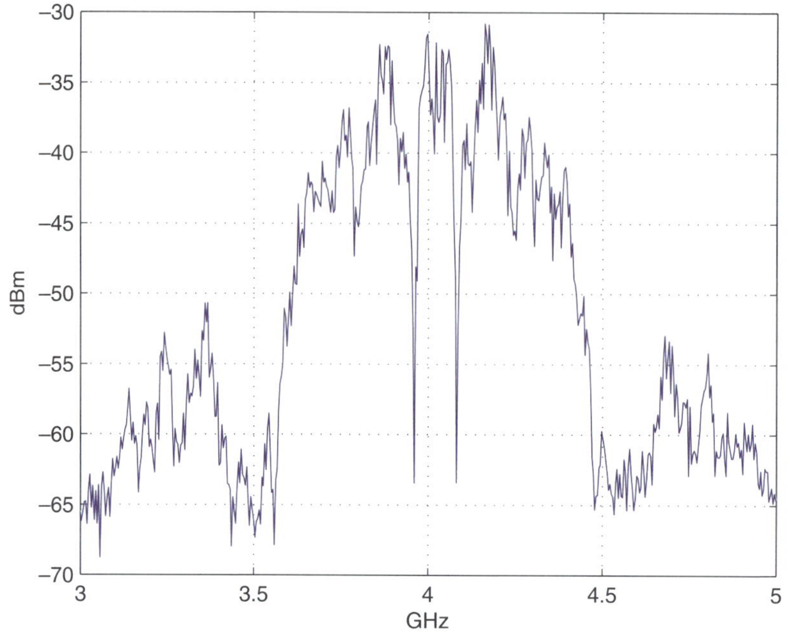

Fig. 12.33. Spectrum of time reversal waveform after modulation.

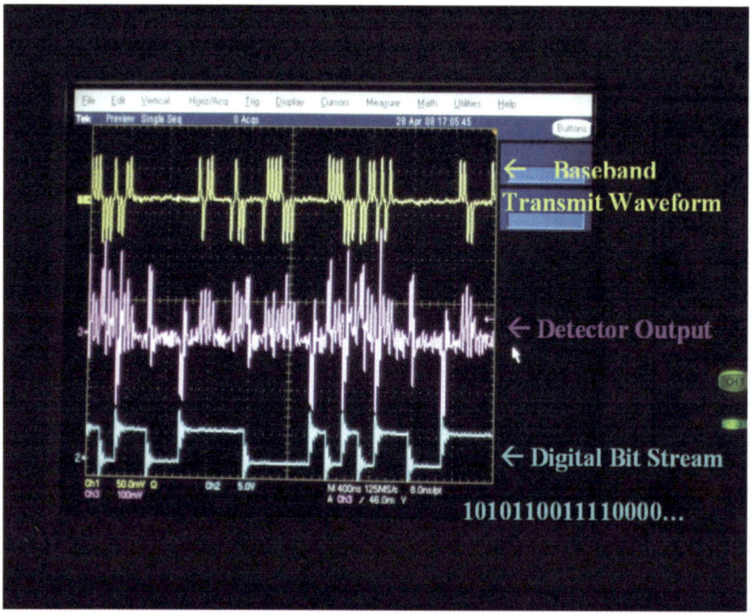

Fig. 12.34. System test result.

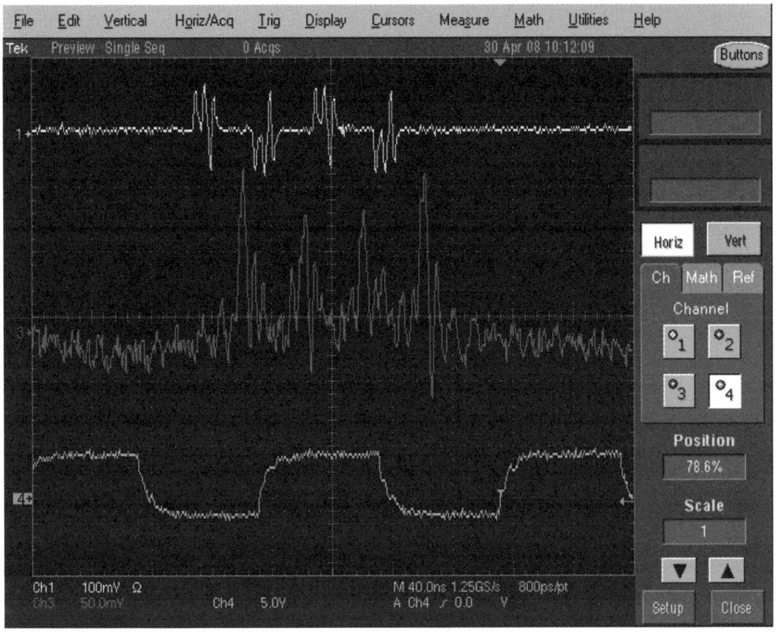

Fig. 12.35. Temporal focusing property of time reversal.

trace is simply a zoom-out version of Fig. 12.32. Although there are some interferences observed on both the middle and the bottom trace, distinguishable peaks can be seen on the middle trace and the PN sequence can be read clearly from the bottom trace.

A close-up of the middle trace is shown in Fig. 12.35. The top trace is the baseband transmitted waveform, the middle trace is the received waveform at the detector's output, and the bottom trace is a data clock running at 6.25 MHz, the same as the data rate. Temporal focusing property can be observed from the middle trace. Four pulses are transmitted in each chip period, while in the detector's output there is only one strong peak in each chip period, because the four separated pulses arrived at the receiver at the same time after traveling through different paths and add up constructively. Although the mainlobe is dominant, some sidelobes are noticeable, suggesting that either the waveform generator needs to be refined, or other signal processing techniques should be combined.

12.7. Conclusions

High-resolution of ultra-wideband pulses leads to rich multipath. Fading is secondary for UWB systems. The channel is reciprocal for a long period of time — much longer than its narrow-band counterpart. The central idea presented in this chapter is to take advantage of this reciprocity to focus multipath pulses at the receiver — through waveform preprocessing at the transmitter. This scheme allows to use simple receivers and enables spatial division multiplexing access (SDMA) and additional physical layer security.

The principles and design philosophy, along with an example of experimental time reversal test-bed, have been introduced. Waveform level preprocessing with fractional symbol sampling is a general pre-filtering process at the transmitter for different optimum criteria. Some traditional receiver based processing functions can be taken care of by preprocessing, so that suboptimal reception schemes such as transmitter-reference and square law detector can be used without significantly sacrificing overall performance. Preprocessing paired with simple receivers are especially attractive to wireless sensor network (WSN) applications where strict constraints are posed. In addition to performance enhancement, preprocessing also features SDMA or physical layer security enhancement without consuming extra radio resources. Knowing the characteristics of scattering channels is the key to best design a preprocessing system, which motivates our experiment based investigation on a few realistic radio channels. The concept of preprocessing plus simple receivers has been demonstrated using a time reversal radio test-bed working in microwave band in the indoor environment.

For future work, security and anti-jamming capabilities are enhanced by channel reciprocity. This line of thought needs further research. The availability of five GHz digital-to-analog converter (DAC) makes this direction feasible. Compressed sensing provides a revolutionary approach to handle waveforms of much wider bandwidth.[58] Transient UWB pulses are compressible.[59] Information theory can be used for secrecy. Ultra-wideband sensing and networking can be integrated into one radio. This radio must have the ability to access spectrum dynamically — cognitive radio and cognitive radar.[60] As a result, wideband (e.g., multi-GHz) spectrum sensing is needed — but an open problem.

Acknowledgment

This work is funded by the Office of Naval Research through a contract (N00014-07-1-0529), National Science Foundation through two awards (ECS-0622125) and (ECCS-0821658), the Army Research Laboratory and the Army Research Office through a STIR contract (W911NF-06-1-0349) and a DURIP contract (W911NF-05-1-0111), and ONR Summer Faculty Fellowship Program Award. The NSF International Research and Education in Engineering (IREE) program has sponsored Qiu's visit at Lund University, Sweden.

The authors wants to thank their sponsors Santanu K. Das (ONR), and Robert Ulman (ARO) for inspiration and vision. The Director of Center for Manufacturing Research (CMR) at TTU (Kenneth Currie) and the chair of ECE (Stephen Parke) at TTU has provided the authors with good support for carrying out this research. P. K. Rajan is helpful in many discussions.

References

1. J. R. Pierce and A. L. Hopper, Nonsynchronous time division with holding and with random sampling, *Proc. IRE*, 1079–1088 (1952).
2. C. K. Rushforth, Transmitted-reference techniques for random or unknown channels, *IEEE Trans. Inform. Theory*, 39–42 (1964).
3. G. D. Hingorani and J. C. Hancock, A transmitted reference system for communication in random or unknown channels, *IEEE Trans. Commun. Tech.*, **13**, 293–301 (1965).
4. N. Stralen, A. Dentinger, K. Welles II, R. Gaus, R. Hoctor and H. Tomlinson, Delayed hopped transmitted reference experimental results, *Proc. IEEE Conf. on Ultra Wideband Systems and Technologies*, Baltimore, Maryland, 93–98 (2002).
5. J. D. Choi and W. S. Stark, Performance of ultra-wideband communications with suboptimal receivers in multipath channels, *IEEE J. Select. Areas Commun.*, **20**, 1754–1766 (2002).
6. D. L. Goeckel and Q. Zhang, Slightly frequency-shifted reference ultra-wideband (UWB) radio: TR-UWB without the delay element, *Proc. IEEE Milcom'05*, **5**, 3029–3035 (2005).
7. D. L. Goeckel, J. Mehlman and J. Burkhart, A class of ultra wideband (UWB) systems with simple receivers, *Proc. IEEE Milcom'07*, **5**, 1–7 (2007).
8. H. Liu, A. F. Molisch, S. Zhao, D. Goeckel and P. Orlikt, Hybrid coherent and frequency-shifted-reference ultrawideband radio, *Proc. IEEE Globecom'07*, 4106–4111, Washington, DC (2007).
9. M. Ho, V. Somayazulu, J. Foerster and S. Roy, A differential detector for an ultra-wideband communications system, *Proc. 55th IEEE Veh. Tech. Conf.*, **4**, 1896–1900 (2002).
10. Y. Chao and R. A. Scholtz, Optimal and suboptimal receivers for Ultra-wideband transmitted reference systems, *Proc. IEEE Globecom'03*, 759–763 (2003).
11. S. Zhao, H. Liu and Z. Tian, A decision feedback autocorrelation receiver for pulsed ultra-wideband systems, *Proc. IEEE Rawcon'04*, (2004).
12. N. Guo and R. C. Qiu, Improved autocorrelation demodulation receivers based on multiple-symbol detection for UWB communications, *IEEE Trans. Wireless Commun.*, **5**, 2026–2031 (2006).
13. V. Lottici and Z. Tian, Multiple symbol differential detection for UWB communications, *IEEE Trans. Wireless Commun.*, **7**, 1656–1666 (2008).
14. Y. Souilmi and R. Knopp, On the achievable rates of ultra-wideband PPM with non-coherent detection in multipath environments, *Proc. IEEE ICC'03*, **5**, 3530–3534 (2003).
15. M. Weisenhorn and W. Hirt, Robust noncoherent receiver exploiting UWB channel properties, *Proc. IEEE UWBST'04*, Kyoto, Japan, 156–160 (2004).
16. S. Paquelet, L. Aubert and B. Uguen, An impulse radio asynchronous transceiver for high data rates, *Proc. IEEE UWBST'04*, Kyoto, Japan, 1–5 (2004). *IEEE Commun. Lett.*, **10**, 655–657 (2006).
17. N. Guo, J. Zhang, R. Qiu and S. Mo, UWB MISO time reversal with energy detector receiver over ISI channels, *Proc. IEEE CCNC'07*, Las Vegas, NV (2007).
18. M. Fink, Time reversal of ultrasonic fields — Part I: Basic principles, *IEEE Trans. Ultrason., Ferroelec. Frequency Control*, **39**(5), 555–566 (1992).
19. T. Strohmer, M. Emami, J. Hansen, G. Pananicolaou and A. J. Paulraj, Application of time-reversal with MMSE equalizer to UWB communications, *Proc. Globecom'04*, Dallas, TX, 3123–3127 (2004).

20. P. Kyristi, G. G. Pananicolaou, P. Eggers and A. Oprea, MISO time reversal and delay spread compression for FWA channels at 5 GHz, *IEEE Ant. and Wireless Prop. Lett.*, **3**, 96–99 (2004).
21. H. T. Nguyen, J. B. Andersen and G. F. Pedersen, The potential use of time reversal techniques in multiple element antenna systems, *IEEE Com. Lett.*, **9**, 40–42 (2005).
22. H. T. Nguyen, J. B. Andersen, G. F. Pedersen, P. Kyritsi and P. C. F. Eggers, Time reversal in wireless communications: A measurement-based investigation, *IEEE Trans. Wireless Commun.*, **5**, 2242–2252 (2006).
23. H. T. Nguyen, I. Z. Kovcs and P. C. F. Eggers, A time reversal transmission approach for multiuser UWB communications, *IEEE Trans. Ant. Prop.*, **54**, 3216–3224 (2006).
24. A. E. Akogun, R. C. Qiu and N. Guo, Demonstrating time reversal in ultra-wideband communications using time domain measurements, *Proc. 51st International Instrumentation Symposium*, Knoxville, TN, May 8–12 (2005).
25. N. Guo, R. C. Qiu and B. M. Sadler, An Ultra-wideband autocorrelation demodulation scheme with low-complexity time reversal enhancement, *Proc. IEEE MILCOM'05*, **5**, 3066–3072, Atlantic City, NJ (2005).
26. R. C. Qiu, C. Zhou, N. Guo, and J. Q. Zhang, Time reversal with MISO for ultra-wideband communications: Experimental results, *IEEE Antenna and Wireless Propagation Letters*, **5**, 269–273 (2006).
27. N. Guo, J. Zhang and R. Qiu, UWB MISO time reversal with energy detector receiver over ISI channels, *Proc. IEEE CCNC'07.*
28. N. Guo, B. M. Sadler and R. C. Qiu, Reduced-complexity UWB time reversal techniques and experimental results, *IEEE Trans. Wireless Commun.*, **6**, 4221–4226 (2007).
29. R. Wilson, D. Tse and R. A. Scholtz, Channel identification: secret sharing using reciprocity in ultrawideband channels, *IEEE Trans. Inf. Forensics and Security*, **2**, 364–375 (2007).
30. M. Bloch, J. Barros, M. R. D. Rodrigues and S. W. McLaughlin, Wireless information-theoretic security, *IEEE Trans. Inf. Theory*, **54**, 2515–2534 (2008).
31. R. A. Scholtz, The origins of spread spectrum communications, *IEEE Trans. Commun.*, **30**, 822–854 (1982).
32. M. K. Simon, S. M. Hincdi and W. C. Lindscy, *Digital Communication Tcchniqucs — Signal Design and Detection*, Englewood Cliffs, NJ, Prentice Hall (1994).
33. L. Yang and G. B. Giannakis, Optimal pilot waveform assisted modulation for ultra-wideband communications, *IEEE Trans. Wireless Commun.*, **3**, 1236–1249 (2004).
34. J. Romme and G. Durisi, Transmit reference impulse radio systems using weighted correlation, *Proc. 2004 IEEE Conf. on Ultra Wideband Systems and Technologies*, Tyoko, Japan, 141–145 (2004).
35. Y. Chao and R. A. Scholtz, Weighted correlation receivers for ultra-wideband transmitted reference systems, *Proc. IEEE Globecom'04*, **1**, 66–70 (2004).
36. J. Romme and K. Witrisal, Transmit reference UWB systems using weighted autocorrelation receivers, *TEEE Trans. Microwave Theory and Tech.*, **54**, 1754–1761 (2006).
37. Z. Tian and B. Sadler, Weighted energy detection of ultra-wideband signals, *Proc. 2005 IEEE 6th Workshop on Signal Processing Advances in Wireless Communications*, 1068–1072 (2005).
38. J. Wu, H. Xiang and Z. Tian, Weighted noncoherent receivers for UWB PPM signals, *IEEE Commun. Lett.*, **10**, 655–657 (2006).

39. S. Franz and U. Mitra, Integration interval optimization and performance analysis for UWB transmitted reference systems, *Proc. 2004 IEEE Conf. on Ultra Wideband Systems and Technologies*, Tyoko, Japan, 26–30 (2004).
40. Y.-L. Chao, Optimal integration time for UWB transmitted reference correlation receivers, *Proc. 38th Asilomar conf. on Signals, Systems and Computers*, **1**, 647–651 (2004).
41. K. Witrisal, G. Leus, M. Pausini and C. Krall, Equivalent system model and equalization of differential impulse radio UWB systems, *IEEE J. Select. Areas Commun.*, **23**, 1851–1862 (2005).
42. M. Pausini, G. J. M. Janssen and K. Witrisal, Performance enhancement of differential UWB autocorrelation receivers under ISI, *IEEE J. Select. Areas Commun.*, **24**, 815–821 (2006).
43. A. V. Oppenheim and R. W. Schafer, *Discrete-Time Signal Processing*, 2nd ed, Upper Saddle River, New Jersey: Prentice Hall Inc. (1999).
44. J. Yang and S. Roy, Joint transmitter-receiver optimization for multi-input multi-output systems with decision feedback, *IEEE Trans. Inf. Theory*, **40**, 1334–1347 (1994).
45. J. Yang and S. Roy, On joint transmitter and receiver optimization for multiple-input-multiple-output (MIMO) transmission systems, *IEEE Trans. Commun.*, **42**, 3221–3231 (1994).
46. H. Sampath, P. Stoica and A. Paulraj, Generalized linear precoder and decoder design for MIMO channels using the weighted MMSE criterion, *IEEE Trans. Commun.*, **49**, 2198–2206 (2001).
47. A. Scaglione, P. Stoica, S. Barbarossa, G. B. Giannakis and H. Sampath, Optimal designs for space-time linear precoders and decoders, *IEEE Trans. Signal Proc.* [*see also IEEE Trans. Acoustics, Speech, and Signal Proce*] **50**, 1051–1064 (2002).
48. D. P. Palomar and M. A. Lagunas, Joint transmit-receive space-time equalization in spatially correlated MIMO channels: a beamforming approach, *IEEE J. Select. Areas Commun.*, **21**, 730–743 (2003).
49. D. P. Palomar, M. A. Lagunas and J. M. Cioffi, Optimum linear joint transmit-receive processing for MIMO channels with QoS constraints, *IEEE Trans. Signal Proc.* [*see also IEEE Trans. Acoustics, Speech, and Signal Proce*] **52**, 1179–1197 (2004).
50. J. W. Matthews, Eigenvalues and troposcatter multipath analysis, *IEEE J. Select. Areas Commun.*, **10**, 497–505 (1992).
51. M. R. Bell, Information theory and radar waveform design, *IEEE Trans. Inf. Theory*, **39**, 1578–1597 (1993).
52. H. L. Van Trees, *Detection, Estimation, and Modulation Theory, Part I*, New York: Wiley (1968).
53. R. Ahlswede and I. Csiszar, Common randomness in information theory and cryptography. I. Secret sharing, *IEEE Trans. Inf. Theory*, **39**, 1121–1132 (1993).
54. M. Calderon and R. C. Qiu, *Time Reversal for Ultra-Wideband (UWBR)Sensor Networking*, Tech. Rep., Final Report to Army Research Office, Grant no. W911NF-06-1-0349, 151 pages, TTU, Cookeville, TN (2007).
55. R. C. Qiu *et al.*, *Ultra-Wideband Communications Systems and Testbed*, Final Report to Army Research Office Grant no. W911NF-05-01-0111 (DURIP), Tennessee Tech. University, Cookeville, TN, July 2007, 240p.
56. R. G. Gallager, *Information Theory and Reliable Communication*, John Wiley & Sons, Inc. (1968).

57. R. C. Qiu *et al.*, *Time-Reversal Based Range Extension Technique for Ultra-Wideband (UWB) Sensors and Applications in Tactical Communications and Networking* (Quarterly) Technical Report to Office of Naval Research (ONR) Contract No. N00014-07-1-0529, Tennessee Tech University, Cookeville, TN (April 2008), 69p.
58. R. C. Qiu, *Underwater Acoustic Sensor Networks, Physics-Based Channel Models and Fundamental Limits*, Auerbach Publications, Taylor & Francis Group (2008).
59. R. C. Qiu, *Ultra-Wideband Wireless Communication: Physical and Information-Theoretical Limits.* Course Reader for ECE 7750 and ECE 7970, Tennessee Technological University, http://iweb.tntech.edu/rqiu (March 2008).
60. S. Haykin, Cognitive radar, *IEEE Signal Processing Magazine*, 30–40 (2006).

The following references are not cited in the text

26. F. Edbauer, Bit error rate of binary and quaternary DPSK signals with multiple differential feedback detection, *IEEE Trans. Commun.*, **40**, 457–460 (1992).

Chapter 13

Design of Self-Organizing Sensor Networks Using Percolation Theory

R. R. Brooks

Holcombe Department of Electrical and Computer Engineering
Clemson University, P.O. Box 340915, Clemson
SC 29634-0915, USA
rrb@acm.org

Sensor networks are deployed in, and react with, chaotic environments. Designing the network using peer-to-peer self-organization primitives allows the system to adapt autonomously to changes in the environment. This paper summarizes work in applying percolation theory and random graph formalisms to the design and implementation of sensor networks. Issues with surveillance applications and system security are highlighted in our discussion.

13.1. Introduction

Sensor networks can be viewed at many levels of abstraction. Effective systems must adapt at each level. These networks are composed of a large number of autonomous devices. At the highest level of abstraction, all devices must work in a coordinated manner as a single entity. User interests vary dynamically. Top-down control must insure that tasks performed by the network fulfill operational requirements. Specific regions and/or target types will be of interest part of the time, but not at others. Connectivity maintenance requires a high degree of coordination.

Bottom-up self-organization needs to guarantee system ability to adapt to unforeseen events. The environment varies dynamically. Weather, wind, and noise change effective sensing ranges unpredictably.[1] All nodes have finite energy resources and eventually cease to function. Radio communications can be jammed. These factors require bottom-up reaction and reconfiguration in a fully autonomous mode.

Sensor networks are distributed amorphous computing environments, consisting of a large number of nodes and communications links, subject to intermittent failure, likely destruction, and limited power resources.[2] Human configuration and control of the entire system is futile. Humans steer the network by declaring general interests. Translating higher-level tactical objectives into low-level activities is an ill-posed problem. Efficient resolution of this problem in a chaotic network of failure prone nodes will require bottom-up emergent control *push* interacting with the user's *pull*.

It is important to decentralize the system without sacrificing robustness and accuracy. Top-down control is need driven and deliberative. Bottom-up control is reactive and geared towards maintaining an orderly substrate on top of an underlying chaotic environment. The goal is to produce deliberative adaptation of the network to overcome the complexity inherent in real environments.

This chapter looks at applying percolation and random graph theory to the design of robust sensor networks. Robustness is created by allowing the networks to adapt autonomously. We will show how this adaptation can be predicted and supported by using techniques derived from random graph and percolation theories.

The rest of this chapter is organized as follows. Section 2 provides the essential background for this work. It discusses percolation theory, random graph theory, self-organization of sensor networks, and power consumption. Section 3 describes probabilistic connectivity matrices, what they are and how they can be used to analyze sensor networks. In Sec. 4, we explain how to use percolation theory and random graph theory to design sensor networks. We consider surveillance and security applications. The paper concludes by discussing insights in Sec. 6.

13.2. Background

We now present the technical background assumed by the rest of this chapter.[3] Percolation theory is the branch of physics that deals with fluid flow through random media.[4] In this case, the sensor network is the random medium that information flows through. Random graph theory is the branch of mathematics that deals with stochastically generated graph structures.[5] We concentrate on the commonalities of these two fields of study.

Traditionally, the tuple [V, E] defines a graph. V(E) is a set of vertices (edges). Each edge e is defined by (i, j) where i and j are the two vertices connected by e. Unless specified otherwise, we consider only undirected graphs where $(i, j) = (j, i)$. Directed graphs (di-graphs) exist where $(i, j) \neq (j, i)$. An edge (i, j) is incident on vertices i and j. We do not consider multi-graphs where multiple edges connect the same end-points. The terms vertex and node will be used interchangeably. Similarly, edge and link are used synonymously.

The degree of a node is the number of edges incident on the node. For directed graphs, there are also the concepts of in-degree (out-degree) for the number of edges leaving (joining) the node. A graph is called regular, when all nodes in the graph have the same degree.

We will also provide a general discussion of self-organization. This discussion will look at the system both from the bottom-up and the top-down. This section will conclude with a discussion of power consumption issues. Power consumption is an important consideration, since it will define the operating limits of many sensor networks.

13.2.1. *Percolation theory*

Percolation theory studies flow through random media.[4] Commonly, the random media is modeled as a regular tessellation of a d dimensional space where vertices are points connecting edges. It is also possible to consider arbitrary graphs. Two different models exist; site (bond) percolation is where vertices (edges) are either occupied or empty. We discuss only bond percolation, note that it is possible to create dual graphs to convert site (bond) percolation problems to bond (site) problems. These graphs can be considered models of wireless networks with a cellular infrastructure.

As an example, we will consider a rectangular tessellation of a 2-dimensional space. This model requires three parameters: x the number of nodes in a row, y the number of nodes in a column, and p the probability of an edge being occupied. Note that n, the total number of nodes, is equal to xy. Our method is only valid for finite problems. We assume that physical systems will always be finite. The properties of infinite tessellations are also known.[6]

13.2.2. *Random graph theory*

Random graphs are graphs that are stochastically constructed. Several classes of random graphs have been proposed. The first class we discuss in detail is the Erdös-Rényi random graph.[5] These graphs are defined by the number of nodes n and a uniform probability p of an edge existing between any two nodes. Let's use E for $|E|$ the number of edges in the graph. Since the degree of a node is the result of multiple Bernoulli trials with probability p, the degree of an Erdös-Rényi random graph follows a Bernoulli distribution. As the graph scales, the number of nodes n approaches infinity, and the degree distribution asymptotically converges to a Poisson distribution.

The expected number of hops between any two nodes in this graph grows proportionally to the log of the number of nodes.[7] Note that Erdös-Rényi graphs do not necessarily form a single connected component. When $E - n/2 \ll -n^{2/3}$ the graph is sub-critical and almost certainly not connected. A phase change occurs in the critical phase where $E = n/2 + \mathrm{O}(n^{2/3})$ and in the supercritical phase where $E - n/2 \gg -n^{2/3}$ a single giant component becomes almost certain. When $E = n \log n/2 + \mathrm{O}_p(n)$ the graph is fully connected.[8] The expected number of edges for an Erdös–Rényi graph is $n(n-1)p/2)$.

The second graph class considered is the family of "small world" graphs.[9] They have two characteristics: (i) a small expected value for the number of hops between any two nodes, and (ii) significant clustering among the nodes. The rate of increase of the number of hops between nodes for these graphs is roughly equivalent to that of Erdös-Rényi graphs.[9]

For example small-world (SW) graphs, we use the *connected caveman model*.[9] To construct connected caveman graphs, use this procedure:

- Construct a set of complete sub-graphs.
- In each sub-graph, one edge is removed and replaced with an edge connecting the sub-graph to the next one; forming a cycle reminiscent of a "string of pearls."
- A fixed number of edges in the system are replaced with random edges.

The connected caveman SW model has three parameters: (i) n the number of nodes in the graph, (ii) c the number of nodes in each sub-graph, and (iii) e the number of edges rewired.

The node degree distribution in this model is nearly constant. The mean node degree value is c (the number of nodes in the complete subgraph) minus one. Variance around the mean is caused by two sets of Bernoulli trials: (i) the probability an edge connected to the vertex is chosen to create the "string of pearls" raising (or reducing) the node degree by one, and (ii) the likelihood of an edge attached to the vertex being re-wired.

This graph structure is discussed because: (i) the small expected number of hops between nodes is attractive for sensor network applications, (ii) it is a structure that can be easily maintained as a distributed system, and (iii) it has a partially deterministic structure.

The third graph class is the scale-free model. It comes from empirical analysis of real-world systems, such as e-mail traffic, the World Wide Web, and disease propagation.[7] In scale-free graphs the node degree distribution varies as an inverse power law (i.e., $\mathrm{P}[d] \propto d^{-\gamma}$). They are called scale-free because the power law structure implies nodes existing with non-zero probability at all possible scales. The expected number of hops for scale-free networks is smaller than the expected number of hops for Erdös–Rényi and small-world graphs.[7] Scale-free (SF) graphs are defined by two parameters: number of nodes n, and scaling factor γ. Empirical analysis done by different research groups at different times find the Internet's γ parameter value ranging from 2.1 to 2.5).[7] Of the random graph classes discussed, node degree variance in this class is the largest.

Scale-free networks are discussed for several reasons: (i) they appear in existing systems like the Internet and are of use for large-scale wired networks, (ii) the small number of expected hops between nodes is attractive, (iii) studies indicate that their structure has unique dependability properties,[10] and (iv) epidemiological studies using this model indicate that there may be parallels between biological pathogen propagation and computer virus propagation.[11] An algorithm constructs these graphs using positive feedback and producing graphs with $\gamma \approx 3$.[12] Barabási's use of positive feedback plausibly explains how SF systems emerge and why they are wide-spread. The majority of nodes have degree one or two, but there exist a small number of hub nodes with a very large degree. Erdös–Rényi and small world graphs have an almost flat architecture with node degree clustered about the mean. The hub nodes dominate the topology of the scale free graphs. The ranked embedding illustrates that it is extremely unlikely that a node would be many hops away from a major hub.

Scale-free networks provide good statistical descriptions of large, evolving, wired networks with no centralized control. Wireless networks are also of importance. In particular *ad hoc* wireless networks, which have no fixed infrastructure, are suited to analysis as a type of random graph.[13] A fixed radius model for random graphs is used to analyze phase change problems in ad hoc network design.

The model[13] places nodes at random in a limited two-dimensional region. Two uniform random variables provide a node's x and y coordinates. Two nodes in proximity to each other have a very high probability of being able to communicate. For this reason, they calculate the distance r between all pairs of nodes. If r is less than a given threshold, then an edge exists between the two nodes. In their work, many similarities are found between this graph class and the graphs studied by Erdös and Rényi. Their analysis looks at finding phase transitions for constraint satisfaction problems. These graphs differ from Erdös–Rényi graphs in that they have significant clustering, like the small world graph class. We create an edge with probability one when the distance between two nodes is less than the threshold value. We allow the probability to be set to any value in the range $[0...1]$.

We construct range-limited graphs from the following parameters:

- n — the number of nodes
- $\max\_x(\max\_y)$ — the size of the region in the $x(y)$ direction
- r — the maximum distance between nodes where connections are possible
- p — probability that an edge exists connecting two nodes within the range

Construction of range-limited random graphs proceeds in two steps: (i) sort the nodes by either their x (or possibly y) coordinate and use order statistics to find the expected values of that coordinate, (ii) determine probabilities for edges existing between nodes based on these expected values.

13.2.3. *Self-organization*

This discussion is based on initial work.[14] Scalable top-down control requires a hierarchical topology. Flat organizations need direct communication with all participating nodes. Once the number of components surpasses a critical value, the communications overhead becomes untenable. Similarly, the latency imposed by the volume of information that users must process in a large flat hierarchy makes decisions from higher levels obsolete by the time they can be formulated.

Within a hierarchy, each layer has its own responsibilities and information requirements. The top level provides general guidance. Each level in the hierarchy accepts commands from the higher level, refines them to fit local constraints, creates more detailed instructions, and distributes them to lower levels. Events occurring at lower levels are relayed to higher levels, which extract relevant information for their superiors thereby reducing the volume of data. Higher-level instructions should not be overly restrictive to allow freedom for quick reaction as needed.

The role of an individual node may vary over time. For example, if a supervisory node fails it should be possible to elect a replacement. We have implemented a more sophisticated approach for sensor network tasking in the DARPA SenseIT program.[15] Mobile code is used to overcome storage constraints that are ubiquitous in embedded systems. Nodes are initially configured with behaviors they are most likely to need. As needs change, programs are downloaded and storage reclaimed. In many ways, the local software configuration is managed like a local cache. We have implemented polymorphism and distributed dynamic linking to support this in networks of heterogeneous nodes. Control roles in the DEDs hierarchy may change to better suit environmental conditions.

Equally important is the system's ability to respond autonomously to perceived changes in its operational environment. Self-configuration and adaptability are essential, since the nodes must adapt to maintain three separate hierarchies:

- *Control hierarchy* — The control hierarchy must be able to morph and re-emerge, since connectivity may be broken at any point in the hierarchy.
- *Sensor coverage* — Changes in the environment (such as fog) or failures in the sensor network can result in the occlusion, or loss of coverage, of regions of interest. It may be necessary to reassign sensors or move nodes to re-establish coverage.
- *Network connectivity* — In addition to observing regions of interest, the network must report events to data consumers. To respond to jamming, or low battery power, network configuration must be flexible. Multiple routes within the network should be maintained. It may be necessary for nodes to reposition themselves autonomously.

Since connectivity can be broken at any point in the hierarchy, self-organization must be supported to allow the hierarchy to re-emerge. Candidate approaches to self-organization have been derived by researchers in artificial life studying insect colony coordination,[16] in physics studying quantum optics,[17] and chemistry studying non-equilibrium thermodynamics.[18]

Each node defines its local behaviors in response to an uncontrollable and frequently hostile environment. Tasks are performed in a distributed environment requiring coordination among multiple nodes. Communication may be corrupted with noise. Components are prone to failure. As network size increases, the probability of all components functioning at a given time decreases exponentially. Nonlinear interactions exist between failure modes. Under these conditions, efficient operation cannot rely on static plans. Van Creveld has defined five characteristics hierarchical systems need to adapt to this type of chaotic environment[19,20]:

- Decision thresholds far down in the hierarchy.
- Self-contained units at a low level.
- Bottom-up and top-down information circulation.
- Informal communications.
- Commanders seek to supplement routine reports.

Organizations using this approach have been successful in market economies, war, and law enforcement.[21] Our approach is influenced by and is consistent with these points. Each entity is self-contained and makes as many decisions as possible locally. Operational information and data travel in both directions in the hierarchy. The final two points imply informal activities that are difficult to implement in automated systems. In this section, we discuss local decisions made far down in the hierarchy to counteract the chaotic environment. Self-organization needs to occur to allow the system to adapt quickly to arbitrary unforeseen events.

The distributed control architecture can be modeled as a network of interacting automata. This is an abstraction of distributed systems that is a modification of Cellular Automata.[22] A cellular automata (CA) is a synchronously interacting set of elements (network nodes) defined as abstract machines. A CA is defined by:

- d the dimension of the automata
- r the radius of an element of the automata
- δ the transition rule of the automata
- s the set of states of an element of the automata

An element's (node's) behavior is a function of its internal state and those of neighboring nodes as defined by δ. Wolfram's study of CA[23] found four qualitative classes of CA:

- Stable — where all elements eventually evolve to the same state.
- Periodic — where the global system evolves into regular structures.
- Chaotic — where no discernible structure emerges and the system remains in a constant state of flux.
- Interesting — where no global stable regime occurs but areas of local stability emerge spontaneously.

Chaotic regimes are clearly undesirable. Stable and periodic regimes are desirable but in some conditions may be inflexible and incapable of adapting to a changing environment. The interesting regime allows for spontaneous adaptation. It has been hypothesized that the ideal state for adaptation is stability on the edge of chaos,[24] where chaos supports a quick search through new regimes when stability is no longer possible.

The communications and sensing coverage constructs are just as important as the control hierarchy. Since they depend both on system state and node position, they cannot be adequately modeled using a pure CA approach. The model of free agents in a cellular space[25] allows agents to migrate between elements in a CA environment. The behaviors of agents and CA elements influence each other. In our approach, agents are sensing platforms that may or may not be mobile. CA elements are grid points defining surveillance regions. Surveillance targets can also be modeled as agents. In this way, we can study self-organization regimes for sensor coverage and maintenance of communication connectivity. We currently plan on only studying first order effects. It may in fact be possible to study interactions between control hierarchy, sensor coverage and communications connectivity maintenance, but this depends on the results of the modeling thrust.

Many theories exist for self-organization and spontaneous emergence of order.[16,17,22,24,26] Those based on thermodynamic models[17,18] are likely to be untenable, since they are based on models defined by sets of differential equations. It is unlikely that we will be able to derive suitable sets of equations to adequately represent general circumstances. Some artificial life constructs[16,22] are based on a few basic interactions among multiple participants:

- Positive feedback — includes recruitment and reinforcement of behaviors.
- Negative feedback — counterbalances positive feedback to stabilize the system.
- Amplification of fluctuations — randomness and fluctuations are crucial to system adaptation.
- Multiple interactions — simple behaviors at the microscopic level can provide intelligent adaptations at the macroscopic level.

13.2.4. *Power consumption*

This section summarizes some findings from a previous paper.[27] Sensor networks rely on battery power. Research into the use of ambient energy sources[28] to power sensor networks and comes to the unfortunate conclusion that, although promising, this is not currently feasible. Reliance on limited, non-renewable battery energy resources means that, to achieve a reasonable network lifetime, all aspects of sensor networks must be energy efficient.

Some publications posit that computation power needs will decrease until negligible, and wireless communications energy will dominate the energy consumption by sensor networks.[29,30] This logic combines Moore's law stating that feature sizes halve every 18 months with the fact that smaller feature sizes require less power. Unfortunately, this ignores important factors: (i) leakage energy consumption grows as feature size decreases, and (ii) Moore's law also states that clock rates increase at the rate feature sizes shrink. Faster clock rates require more energy. Realistic energy models for sensor networks will have to account for all aspects of node behavior.

From the power consumption analysis[31]:

- For most commercial ARM8 processor instructions, the energy required is $4.3 * 10^{-12}$ joules per bit. Multiplication requires $31.9 * 10^{-12}$ joules per bit.
- Berkeley smart dust prototypes consume $\sim 0.05 * 10^{-12}$ joules per bit for most instructions (multiplication not supported).
- Radio frequency ground communications require 10^{-7} joules per bit for 0–50 meters, and $50 * 10^{-6}$ joules per bit for 1–10 kilometers.

The mote and radio figures are lower bounds, based on research prototypes. Commercial products are unlikely to reach these levels of efficiency in the near future:

- Per bit energy consumption for multiply instructions on commercial processors is in the range 48 (MC68328 DragonBall) to 0.84 (SA-110 StrongARM)$*10^{-12}$ joules per bit.[32]
- Communications require from $\sim 40 * 10^{-6}$ joules (GSM cellular phone) to $1 * 10^{-7}$ joules (Bluetooth for 10 s of meters) per bit.[31]
- Reception energy needs for GSM are $2 * 10^{-6}$ joules per bit, and 10^{-7} joules per bit for Bluetooth.[31]

Energy needs for communications are proportional to $r^{-\alpha}$ where r is range. The α exponent is in the range 2 to 5. A value of 3.5 is reasonable for many applications.[33] For commercial and prototype systems, transmitting one bit for one hop is on the order 10^5 times more expensive than computing one instruction on one bit.

Transmission energy[6,31] is supposed to be the dominant drain on sensor networks when per hop communication is over 10 meters. This claim is based on applications with minimal on-board computation. The two examples[31] only sample data, do analog-to-digital conversion, execute a filter, and transmit data. The other example does a least squares estimate of vehicle velocity from five data samples. This amounts to executing one very small matrix multiplication. For nodes with minimal to no local data processing, communications energy consumption is certain to dominate computation energy requirements.

Our empirical tests indicate that, for many classes of sensor network applications, computation dominates energy consumption. Beamforming and CPA based tracking approaches have been compared.[34–36] The beamforming approach was found to be more accurate, while requiring $\sim 10^3$ times more energy. Communications energy requirements were calculated from the bluetooth energy per bit. Computation energy was measured on an AMD Athlon 4 mobile processor. Communication was responsible for less than 20% of the total energy drain. Both applications used embedded Linux. Beamforming is computation intensive, performing cross-correlation over multiple time series to estimate signal direction of arrival. The CPA based approach requires minimal computation. This study of representative sensor network applications supports the view that power awareness must consider computation and communication.

13.3. Probabilistic Connectivity Matrices

Additional information on the analytical tools discussed here can be found.[3,37] We represent a graph by its the connectivity matrix. The connectivity matrix M is a square matrix where each element $m(i, j)$ is 1(0) if there is (not) an edge connecting vertices i and j. For undirected graphs this matrix is symmetric.

As a matter of convention, the diagonal of the matrix can consist of either zero's or one's. One's are frequently used, based on the simple assertion that each vertex is connected to itself. We use the convention where the diagonal is filled with zeros.

A *walk* of length z is an ordered list of z edges $((i_0, j_0), (i_1, j_1), \ldots, (i_z, j_z))$, where each vertex j_a is the same as vertex i_{a+1}. A *path* of length z is a walk where all i_a are unique. If j_z is the same as i_0, the path is a *cycle*.

A useful property of connectivity matrices is the fact that element $m^z(i, j)$ of the power z of graph G's connectivity matrix M (i.e., M^z) is the number of walks of length z from vertex i to vertex j that exist on G.[38] This can be verified using the definition of matrix multiplication and the definition of the connectivity matrix. It is possible to find the connected components in a graph using iterative computation of M^z. After each exponentiation:

- Set all non-zero elements of the M to one, giving C^1.
- Set C^{i+1} to C^iC^1
- Set all non-zero elements of C^{i+1} to 1.
- Set C^{i+1} to the inclusive or of C^{i+1} and C^i.
- Stop when C^{i+1} is equal to C^i.

Each row of C^i has a one in the element corresponding to each node in the same connected component. The number of distinct rows is the number of connected components.

13.3.1. *Definitions*

Definition. The *probabilistic connectivity matrix* of an n node random graph is an n-by-n matrix where each element (j, k) is the Bernoulli probability an edge exists between nodes j and k. By convention we set elements where $j = k$ to zero. The probabilistic connectivity matrix construct translates random graph classes into an equivalent set of probabilities for the existence of edges between two given nodes.

For an Erdös-Rényi graph each element (j, k), where $j \neq k$, has the same value p.

For range limited graphs, element (j, k), where $j \neq k$, of the probabilistic connectivity matrix has value:

$$p(2c - c^2), \tag{13.1}$$

where c is a constant defined as:

$$c = r^2 - \left(\frac{j}{n+1} - \frac{k}{n+1}\right)^2 \quad (13.2)$$

when

$$r^2 \geq \left(\frac{j}{n+1} - \frac{k}{n+1}\right)^2 \quad (13.3)$$

and otherwise zero.

The small world connectivity matrix is constructed by essentially using the algorithm that creates a graph instance. For the connected caveman model example:

- Create an n by n matrix
- Populate the diagonal of the matrix with c-by-c blocks of value one. If n is not a multiple of c, the last block will be n mod c by n mod c. This matrix is block diagonal.
- Set diagonal values to zero.
- Connect the fully connected components. For all blocks: Block starting address j and last address $k = j + c$. Set elements $(k-1, k)$ and $(k, k-1)$ to zero. Set elements $(k+1, k)$ and $(k, k+1)$ to zero. Set element $(n-1, n)$ and $(n, n-1)$ to zero, and $(1, n)$ and $(n, 1)$ to one.
- Count the zeroes and ones in the matrix excluding the diagonal. The probability of gaining a connection by the rewiring step becomes $2e/$(number of zeroes). The probability of losing a connection by the rewiring step becomes $2e/$(number of ones).
- For all elements of the matrix except diagonals (which remain zero), if the element is one (zero) subtract (add) the probability of losing (gaining) a connection.

Creating a probabilistic connectivity matrix for scale-free graphs is challenging. Scale-free graphs are characterized by n the number of nodes and γ the scaling factor. The first step is to compute the probability distribution for node degree d. Remember $P[d] \propto d^{-\gamma}$. We compute the probability distribution, by finding a constant factor for all probabilities to sum to 1. Set:

$$P[d] = bd^{-\gamma}. \quad (13.4)$$

Since node degree ranges from 1 to $n-1$:

$$1 = \sum_{d=1}^{n-1} bd^{-\gamma} \quad (13.5)$$

$$b = 1 \Big/ \sum_{d=1}^{n-1} d^{-\gamma} \quad (13.6)$$

We now have a closed form solution for the node degree probability distribution.

The next step is to determine how many edges are incident on each node. Construct a vector v of $n-1$ elements, whose values range from 0 to 1. Each element k of the vector contains the value:

$$v[k] = \sum_{d=1}^{k-1} bd^{-\gamma}. \tag{13.7}$$

Vector element $v[0]$ has the value zero and element $v[n-1]$ has the value one. Each element represents the probability of a node existing of degree less than or equal to k.

Each row of the probabilistic connectivity matrix represents the expected behavior of $1/n$th of the nodes of the class under consideration. We now construct a vector v' of n elements, the value of $v'[k]$ states how many edges are incident on node k. Set $v'[k]$ to the index of the largest element of v whose value is less than or equal to k/n.[a]

The elements of the connectivity matrix are probabilities of connections between individual nodes. These values are computed using the insight that scale-free networks result from positive feedback.[12] Nodes are more likely to connect to other nodes with many connections. The value of each matrix element (k, i) is therefore:

$$P[k, i] = \frac{v''[i]v'[k]}{\sum_{m \neq k} v'[m]}. \tag{13.8}$$

The likelihood of choosing another node i to receive a given edge from the current node k is the degree of i divided by the sum of the degrees of all nodes except k. Summing these factors would give a total probability of one for the row. Since k has degree $v'[k]$ these probabilities are multiplied by $v'[k]$, so that the total of the probabilities for the row is k. This finishes the derivation of Eq. (13.8).

We modify the values of Eq. (13.8) in two ways. Since node degrees have an exponential distribution, the values of the bottom rows are often much larger than the other degrees. The result of (13.8) for values of k and l close to n can be greater than one. To avoid having elements of the matrix with values greater than one (i.e., probability greater than one), we compute the matrix elements in a double loop starting with k (outer loop) and i (inner loop) set to $n-1$. The values of k and i are decremented from $n-1$ to zero. If the value of Eq. (13.8) is greater than one then the corresponding element is set to one and the value copied from $v'[k]$ for computing row k is decremented by one. This keeps all matrix elements in the range zero to one, so that they represent probabilities.

The other modification of element values that deviates from (13.8) forces the matrix to be symmetric. When computing a row k and $k < n-1$, all elements for

[a]It would also be possible to use the mean, or a weighted average of the index values that point to elements in the range $(k-1)/n$ to k/n. Since Eq. (13.8) can give values greater than one, constraining matrix element values to the range $[0\ldots1]$ flattens the degree distribution. Using the maximum index value counteracts this tendency.

$i > k$ are set to be the same as the values computed for element (i, k). If the value of element (i, k) is one, the value copied from $v'[k]$ is again decremented. In some cases this may force the sum of row k to deviate from $v'[k]$. If the deviation is significant enough, the resulting connectivity matrix may only have a degree distribution that approximates the scaling factor γ.

As an example of percolation theory, we construct probabilistic transition matrices for a rectangular tessellation of a 2-dimensional space. This model requires three parameters: x the number of nodes in a row, y the number of nodes in a column, and p the probability of an edge being occupied. Note that n, the total number of nodes, is equal to xy. The matrix construction method is only valid for finite problems. Once the matrix has been constructed, however, scaling analysis can be performed to consider infinite ranges.

Excluding edge effects in this tessellation, each node (i, j) has four immediate neighbors: $(i+1, j)$, $(i, j+1)$, $(i-1, j)$, and $(i, j-1)$. Each vertex is assigned the unique row position $(i+(j-1)y)$ in the connectivity matrix. (This assumes that $i(j)$ ranges from 0 to $x(y)$ and makes the matrix row major. Readers that are dogmatic about C or FORTRAN can change these conventions at will.[39]) Vertices outside the range $([1 \ldots x], [1 \ldots y])$ are ignored, since they are out of bounds. In the connectivity matrix all positions are set to 0, except that for each node (i, j) the positions in its row $(i+(j-1)y)$ that correspond to its neighbors:

$$i - 1 + jy,\ i + 1 + jy,\ i + (j-1)y,\ i + (j+1)y \tag{13.9}$$

are set to p.

13.3.2. *Uses*

Applications of the probabilistic connectivity matrix representation are mainly derived from the fact that each element l_{ij} of a connectivity matrix L raised to the power k expresses the number of walks from node i to node j. Since our matrix is probabilistic instead of computing the number of paths using matrix multiplication, we compute the probability that a path exists using a similar approach. A walk from i to j of 2 hops exists when there is an intermediate node m with edges from i to m and m to j. In this case, the probability of this path existing is the product of elements $l_{l,m}$ and $l_{m,j}$ of the probabilistic connection matrix. The total probability of the path existing is computed by calculating the inclusive or for all intermediate nodes. A convenient way of computing this is computing the complement of the probability that all paths do not exist:

$$l_{ij}^{h} = 1 - \prod_{k=1}^{n} (1 - l_{ik}^{h-1} l_{kj}). \tag{13.10}$$

This can be implemented by taking a standard matrix multiplication implementation and replacing the summation of products in the inner loop with Eq. (26). Note that we constrain diagonal values to remain zero.

The probability a path of two hops exists between nodes j and k $(j \neq k)$ in a random graph is:

$$1 - \prod_{l=0}^{n-1} (1 - (j,l)(l,k)), \tag{13.11}$$

where (j,l) and (l,k) are elements of the probabilistic connectivity matrix.

By definition, connectivity matrices are square with the numbers of rows and columns both equal to the number of vertices in the graph (n). Each element (j,k) is the probability of an edge existing between nodes j and k. Since we consider only non-directed graphs, (j,k) should equal (k,j). Note:

- The sum of each row (column) of the probabilistic connectivity matrix M provides the expected degree of every node in G.
- M is a probabilistic connectivity matrix of random graph class G. We define *rpm*-graphs (*r*egular *p*robability *m*atrix) graphs as graph classes where each node has equivalent probabilities of being connected to other nodes. If a graph class defines *rpm*-graphs, all nodes in G are equivalent and every row (column) is a permutation of every other row (column).
- For an *rpm*-graph class G, the value of the eigenvalue with the largest magnitude of its associated connectivity matrix is the expected degree of each node in G.

Empirical evidence shows that the Internet is a scale-free network with a scaling factor close to 2.5.[7] The resiliency of the Internet to random failures and intentional attacks has been analyzed using a scale-free model.[10] Simulations show that the Internet would remain connected even if over 90% of the nodes fail at random, but that the network would no longer be connected if only 15% of the best-connected hub nodes should fail. In this section, we show how this problem can be approached analytically. The techniques given here allow an analytical approach to the same problem:

- Construct a matrix that describes the network under consideration.
- The effect of losing a given percentage of hub nodes can be estimated by setting all elements in the bottom j rows and left j columns to zero, where j/n approximates the desired percentage.
- Compute C^2 and see whether the probabilities increase or decrease. If they decrease, the network will partition.
- Find the percentage where the network partitions.

Many graph properties follow a 0–1 law. The property either appears with probability 0 or probability 1 in a random graph class, depending on the parameters that define the class. Frequently an abrupt phase transition exists between these two phases.[5,13] The parameter value where the phase transition occurs is referred to as the critical point. The connectivity matrices defined in this paper can be useful for identifying critical points and phase transitions.

For Erdös-Rényi graphs of n nodes and probability p of an edge existing between any two nodes, the critical point for the property of graph connectivity occurs when $P = 1 - (1 - P^2)^{n-1}$. When $P > 1 - (1 - P^2)^{n-1}$, the graph will tend to not to be connected. When $P < 1 - (1 - P^2)^{n-1}$, the graph will tend to be connected.

13.4. Applications

We now discuss a number of applications of these ideas.

13.4.1. *Surveillance networks*

Consider a surveillance network charged with reporting when a member of a class of objects (*targets*) traverses a given surveillance domain (*terrain*). Reports are sent to a user community that we assume, for the sake of discussion, is external to the terrain. The network will be viable as long as it assures that: (i) an object traversing the terrain is detected (with acceptable error rates), and (ii) the user community is alerted.[27]

This criterion is a tautology: the network is viable as long as it performs its mission. To date, the implications of this tautology have been overlooked. For example, the following methods of determining network viability do not fit the criterion:

- *Network connectivity* — If full network connectivity is needed, the sensor network is a giant serial system. Network availability will fall exponentially with the number of sensor nodes (n), and thus large networks will have an unacceptable mean time to failure. For networks with any redundancy, some nodes can be isolated from the network without compromising its application.
- *Sensing coverage* — refers to placing nodes so that sensor detection regions have little overlap, but the system monitors the entire terrain. Since sensing ranges and coverage regions are unpredictable, problems with this "cookie cutter" approach are well known, and often due to environmental influence. Real-world approaches consider distributed surveillance as a tracking problem using sensors with finite space and time sampling rates. Coverage approaches ignore sensor errors, background noise, and occlusion. In addition, coverage analysis creates a serial system, which fails when any component fails. Once again, we have a serial system where dependability falls exponentially with network size.

Network connectivity ignores sensing issues. Sensing coverage ignores wireless communications issues.

We propose a network viability criterion that is a direct consequence of the network model,[13] where nodes with a fixed communications range are placed at random in the terrain. Simulations show that ad hoc networks with range limited communications exhibit phase change phenomena like those found in random graph and percolation theories.

In these models, network behavior has two phases. In the first phase, the probability of connection between nodes is small and the network has a large number of isolated components. As connection probability grows, the expected size of the largest component grows logarithmically. In the second phase, the network is dominated by a unique giant component that contains most of the system nodes. There are still isolated holes in the network. The size of the largest hole shrinks logarithmically as connection probability increases. The transition between these two phases is extremely steep. For random graphs, the curve of the maximum component size versus edge probability takes the form $e^{-e^{-c}}$. In percolation theory, the inflection point of this curve is referred to as the percolation threshold.

Percolation theory has established these properties for systems with a giant component[4]:

- For systems above the percolation threshold, a path exists that connects the terrain's external boundaries.
- At the percolation threshold, property 1 is self-similar over scales.

Consider sensor networks with nodes either randomly placed, in a regular tessellation, or a weighted combination of the two. Sensor nodes are vertices in a random graph structure. Edges between vertices represent either an active communications link, or detection of a target passing between nodes. In practice, the edge probability distribution is the minimum of the two likelihoods.

Above the phase change (percolation threshold) a single giant component connects most of the sensor nodes ($\mathrm{O}(n)$). It has at least one path connecting all the terrain's external boundaries (property 1). This property is true for subsets of the system across scales (property 2). Thus, for a sensor network with a giant component, targets traversing the network will be detected by at least one node that can report the detection to the user community. Therefore, the network fulfills our viability criterion.

This shows the network is viable while it has a giant component. In our simulation, we infer the loss of the giant component from the loss of property 1. When there is no path between the terrain's external boundaries, the giant component is fractured. Consider the worst-case scenarios for networks with initial configurations above the percolation threshold:

- A target entering the network cannot be detected and/or reported while in a hole. Since the largest hole above the percolation threshold is $\mathrm{O}(\log n)$, this is the upper limit of the target's ability to avoid detection in the initial network configuration.
- As nodes lose power: (i) maximum hole size grows logarithmically, (ii) the network becomes sparse, and (iii) the network approaches the percolation threshold. As long as we are above the percolation threshold property 1 holds and a target has to pass through a graph edge to traverse the terrain. Once it does so, a

node connected to the giant component detects the target and notifies the user community. Property 2 says that property 1 holds for regions inside the terrain up to the percolation threshold.

13.4.2. *Clone detection*

We have a statistical approach for detecting cloning attacks in networks whose security guarantees are based on random key predistribution.[40] In random key predistribution, before deployment each node is equipped with a key-ring of k keys chosen at random from the same large pool of P keys. Given k and P, there is a well defined probability that any two nodes will share at least one cryptographic key and use symmetric key cryptography to communicate. After deployment, nodes find their common keys and can communicate securely.

Each node uses its keys as an authentication token. We analyze statistics on how often keys are used for authentication to determine which keys are being used by cloned nodes. Note that node authentication occurs only during network initialization. In this paper key usage refers only to the node authentication process, it does not refer to the number of times a key is used to encrypt or decrypt individual packets in the sensor network.

Each node constructs a Bloom filter of the keys it has in common with its neighbors (i.e., the neighbor's authentication credentials). This Bloom filter is securely transmitted to a server that records key usage data. The use of Bloom filters significantly reduces the traffic volume and provides greater security since keys are not sent over the network. The server creates a key usage histogram from the Bloom filters.

Keys whose use exceeds the threshold value are thought to be used by clones and are ostracized from the network. The key detection protocol succeeds in removing all cloned keys from the network when a high false positive rate α is allowed.

13.4.3. *Key server choice*

Keyservers maintain the security of the multicast region by controlling group formation and membership. Using our approach, there is the threat that network security could be compromised if malicious nodes collude to be chosen as keyservers. They could then undermine the keyserver election scheme and skew the process to favor the election of malicious nodes. In this section, we describe how we avert this possibility by using a secure selection scheme.[25]

The selection scheme ensures that all nodes have an equal chance of becoming keyserver. When selecting the keyservers, each node:

- Generates a random number n.
- Calculates a hash value from the number $h(n)$. Any hashing algorithm ranging from modulo arithmetic to SHA1 could be used.

- Broadcasts the hash value to participating nodes. This commits the node to its number without revealing its value.
- Waits an agreed upon time-out period for every participating node to broadcast its hash value.
- Broadcasts a list of all nodes that have transmitted hash values.
- Matches the lists it receives to its local list and requests a hash value from any missing node.
- Waits an agreed upon time-out period, then broadcasts its random number.
- Verifies random numbers against pre-committed hash values to ensure integrity.

The keyserver is then chosen using agreed-upon criteria based on these random numbers. For example, the node whose id satisfies (13.12) becomes the keyserver.

$$\mathrm{Mod}\left(\left(\sum_{i=1}^{n} r_i\right), n\right) + 1, \tag{13.12}$$

where r_i is the pseudo random number generated by node i of the n nodes participating in the selection process. Note that collusion to foil this approach to favor any given node effectively requires the cooperation of all participating nodes.

13.4.4. *Key management*

We construct the key tree by using a two-pass protocol,[41,42] where phase (i) creates an initial tree and phase (ii) groups nodes to assign tree nodes to sets of physical sensor nodes. Phase (i) constructs initial tree T_{bd} which is used to construct T_b in Phase (ii)

- Initialize T_{bd} by making the keyserver the root node. It is both root and leaf at this point.
- Each node not in the tree T_{bd}, that is one hop from a leaf node, becomes its child.
- Repeat step 2, $(h - 1)$ times where h is the maximum number of hops from the keyserver to any sensor node in the multicast group.

Phase (ii) construct binary key tree T_b from initial tree T_{bd}. (We will illustrate this phase with an example shown in Fig. 13.16.)

- Assign any leaf node of the tree T_{bd} as n_t.
- Count number of siblings of n_t (*child nodes of its parent node*).
- if (even) group parent with n_t group all siblings into pairs.
- if (odd) do not group parent node group all siblings and n_t into pairs.
- Remove nodes that were grouped in step 2 from consideration and repeat steps 1 and 2 until all nodes are grouped.
- Fuse grouped nodes into single nodes, reconstruct a balanced tree of the fused nodes and repeat steps 1, 2 and 3.

- Repeat step 4 until only one node exists in the initial tree. Construct the key tree according to the grouping of nodes at every iteration in step 4.

13.4.5. *Byzantine agreement*

In a Byzantine attack, a compromised node forwards manipulated information to cripple the decisions of legitimate nodes and, in certain cases, also to influence the result. Assume that a cloned node C reports incorrect information about its key usage by transmitting randomly generated Bloom filters. In this case, when a keyserver has to calculate the key usage statistics, it will discard the extreme τ values after sorting as in the Byzantine agreement protocol. False information from malicious nodes thus gets thrown out. In short, if the opinion of a liar has to count then he ought to speak the truth.

Consider a network of N nodes scattered randomly on unit area. Let c of the n nodes be adversaries. The probability that an illegitimate node gets selected as the keyserver is same as any other node in the network, i.e., c/n. If we pick k nodes at random as keyservers, the expected number of cloned keyservers is $(c{\cdot}k)/n$. According to the group agreement protocol in Sec. 9.1, to secure the network against a Byzantine attack, we have to introduce redundancy in the network. To tolerate c clones in the entire network, we have to select $\max\{(3c * k)/n + 1, k\}$ keyservers.

13.4.6. *Sybil attack*

The Sybil attack[43,44] is an attack on a network where one compromised node acts as multiple nodes (i.e., has multiple identities.) For example, multiple Sybil identities can drain resources from legitimate nodes by sending spurious traffic. Alternatively, Sybil nodes can skew voting algorithms, like Byzantine Agreement. Sybil attacks are known to affect routing, data aggregation and detection of cloned nodes in sensor networks. Our approach counteracts these attacks, since they make it easier for compromised nodes to be identified.

We select k nodes out of N nodes distributed randomly in a square field of area A as keyservers. Hence, the density of keyservers in the field is k/A. In the case of a Sybil attack, a compromised keyserver reports the existence of multiple keyservers. This leads to an increase in the density of reported keyservers. We have a prior threshold on the density of keyservers in the sensor network. Since the keyservers are selected at random, their density should remain within a predictable variance from the mean. A Sybil attack will increase keyserver density when the multicast region is contained entirely in the field. Alternatively, compromised keyservers can report a concave region outside the regular field to create Sybil nodes without changing the node distribution. To counter this, it is advisable to restrict deployments to predefined regions.

The key usage statistics will also support the detection of the Sybil nodes. Since the Sybil nodes require its keys to be used multiple times, they quickly fall into the category of suspicious cloned nodes that will be ostracized by the network.

13.5. Conclusions

This chapter discusses briefly percolation theory and random graph theory. We then introduced the idea of probabilistic connectivity matrices and show how to use these matrices to predict phase changes in sensor networks. This was followed by discussing a number of applications we found for this approach. This includes:

- Determining when surveillance networks stop working,
- Detecting cloned sensor nodes,
- Autonomous management of cryptographic keys by sensor networks,
- Detecting Byzantine attacks on sensor networks, and
- Detecting Sybil attacks on sensor networks.

Acknowledgments

The author would like to acknowledge the inputs of Hemanth Siddulgari, Brijesh Pillai, Matthew Pirretti, Prashanth Govindaraju, Suresh Rai, S. S. Iyengar and Steve Racunas in the research this work is based on.

References

1. D. C. Swanson, *Signal Processing for Intelligent Sensor Systems*. Dekker, San Francisco (2000).
2. R. R. Brooks and S. S. Iyengar, *Multi-Sensor Fusion: Fundamentals and Applications with Software*, Prentice Hall (1998).
3. R. R. Brooks, Random networks and percolation theory, Chapter 49 of *Distributed Sensor Networks*, (eds.) S. S. Iyengar and R. R. Brooks, 907–947, Taylor & Francis, Boca Raton, FLA (2005).
4. D. Stauffer and A. Aharony, *Introduction to Percolation Theory*, Taylor & Francis, London (1992).
5. B. Bollobás, *Random Graphs*, Cambridge University Press, Cambridge, UK (2001).
6. J. M. Rabaey, J. Ammer, T. Karalar, S. Li, B. Otis, M. Sheets and T. Tuan, PicoRadios for wireless sensor networks: The next challenge in ultra-low-power design, *Proceedings of the International Solid-State Circuits Conference*, San Francisco, CA (February 3–7, 2002).
7. R. Albert and A.-L. Barabási, Statistical mechanics of complex networks, arXiv:cond-mat/0106096v1 (June 2001).
8. S. Janson, T. Luczak and A. Rucinski, *Random Graphs*, John Wiley & Sons, New York (2000).
9. D. J. Watts, *Small Worlds*, Princeton University Press, Princeton, NJ (1999).
10. R. Albert, H. Jeong and A.-L. Barabási, Error and attack tolerance of complex networks, *Nature*, **406**, 378–382 (July 27, 2000).

11. R. Pastor-Satorras and A. Vespignani, Epidemic spreading in scale-free networks, *Physical Review Letters*, **86**(14), 3200–3203 (2 April 2001).
12. A.-L. Barabási and R. Albert, Emergence of scaling in random networks, *Science*, **286**, 509–512 (15 October 1999).
13. B. Krishnamachari, S. B. Wicker and R. Bejar, Phase transition phenomena in wireless ad-hoc networks, *Symposium on Ad-Hoc Wireless Networks, GlobeCom2001*, San Antonio, Texas (November 2001). http://www.krishnamachari.net/papers/phaseTransitionWirelessNetworks.pdf
14. R. R. Brooks, Need for self-configuration, Chapter 44 of *Distributed Sensor Networks*, (eds.) S. S. Iyengar and R. R. Brooks, 847–854, Taylor & Francis, Boca Raton, FLA (2005).
15. R. R. Brooks, *et al.* Reactive sensor networks: Mobile code support for autonomous sensor networks, *Distributed Autonomous Robotic Systems DARS 2000*. Springer-Verlag (October 2000).
16. E. Bonabeau, G. Theraulaz, J-L. Deneubourg, S. Aron and S. Camazine, Self-organization in social insects, *Working Papers of the Satna Fe Institute 1997*. http://www.santafe.edu/sfi/publications/Working-Papers/97-04-032.txt (1997).
17. H. Haken, *Synergetics*, Springer-Verlag, Berlin (1983).
18. G. Nicolis and I. Prigogine, *Self-Organization in Non-Equilibrium Systems*, Wiley, New York (1977).
19. M. L. van Crefeld, *Command in War*, Harvard University Press, Cambridge, MA (1986).
20. T. Czerwinski, *Coping with the Bounds: Speculations on Nonlinearity in Military Affairs*, National Defense University, Washington, DC (1998).
21. A. K. Cebrowski and J. J. Garsta, Network-centric warfare: Its origin and future, *Proceedings of the Naval Institute* (1998). http://www.usni.org/Proceedings/Articles98/PROcebrowski.htm.
22. C. Adami, *Introduction to Artificial Life*, Springer-Verlag, New York (1998).
23. S. Wolfram, *Cellular Automata and Complexity*, Addison-Wesley, Reading, MA (1994).
24. S. Kaufmann, *The Origins of Order*, Oxford University Press, New York (1993).
25. M. Pirretti, R. R. Brooks, N. Vijaykrishnan and M. Kandemir, The sleep deprivation attack in wireless sensor networks, *International Journal of Distributed Sensor Networks*, **2**(3) 267–288 (2006).
26. R. R. Brooks, Stigmergy — An Intelligence Metric for Emergent Distributed Behaviors, *NIST Workshop on Performance Metrics for Intelligent Systems*, Gaithersburg, MD (August 2000).
27. R. R. Brooks and H. Siddulgari, Adaptive optimizations for surveillance network longevity, *International Journal of Distributed Sensor Networks*, Accepted for Publication (2006).
28. S. Roundy, P. K. Wright and J. M. Rabaey, *Energy Scavenging for Wireless Sensor Networks*, Kluwer Academic Publishers, Amsterdam (2004).
29. I. F. Akyildiz, W. Su, Y. Sankarasubramaniam and E. Cayirci, A survey on sensor networks, *IEEE Communications*, **40**(8), 102–114 (2002).
30. G. J. Pottie and W. J. Kaiser, Wireless integrated network sensors, *Communications of* he *ACM*, **43**(5), 51–58 (May 2000). http://portal.acm.org/citation.cfm?doid=332833.332838
31. L. Doherty, B. A. Warneke, B. E. Boser and K. S. J. pister, Energy and performance considerations for smart dust, *International Journal of Parallel and Distributed systems and Networks*, **4**(3), 121–133 (2001).

32. D. W. Carman, P. S. Kraus and B. J. Matt, *Constraints and Approaches for Distributed Sensor Network Security (Final)*, NAI Labs Technical Report #00-010 (1 September, 2000).
33. F. Zhao and L. J. Guibas, *Wireless Sensor Networks: An Information Processing Approach*, Morgan Kaufmann, San Francisco (2004).
34. E. Slavin, R. R. Brooks and E. Keller, A comparison of tracking algorithms using beamforming and CPA methods with an emphasis on resource consumption vs. performance, *PSU/ARL ESP MURI Technical Report* (2002).
35. S. Phoha and R. Brooks, *Emergent Surveillance Plexus MURI Annual Report*, The Pennsylvania State University Applied Research Laboratory, *Report 1*, Defense Advanced Research Projects Agency and Army Research Office (March 2002).
36. S. Phoha and R. Brooks, *Emergent Surveillance Plexus MURI Annual Report*, The Pennsylvania State University Applied Research Laboratory, *Report 2*, Defense Advanced Research Projects Agency and Army Research Office (March 2003).
37. R. R. Brooks, B. Pillai, S. Rai and S. Racunas, Mobile network analysis using probabilistic connectivity matrices, *IEEE Transactions on Systems Man and Cybernetics*, Part C: Applications and Reviews, **37**(4), 694–702 (2007).
38. D. M. Cvetkovic, M. Doob and H. Sachs, *Spectra of Graphs*, Academic Press, NY (1979).
39. W. H. Press, S. A. Teukolsky, W. T. Vetterling and B. P. Flannery, *Numerical Recipes in FORTRAN*, Cambridge University Press, Cambridge, UK (1992).
40. R. R. Brooks, P. Y. Govindaraju, M. Pirretti, N. Vijaykrishnan and M. Kandemir, On the detection of clones in sensor networks using random key predistribution, *IEEE Transactions on System Man and Cybernetics*, Part C: Applications and Reviews, **57**(6), (in press) (2007).
41. R. R. Brooks, B. J. Pillai, M. C. Weigele and M. G. Pirretti, Multicast encryption infrastructure for security in sensor networks, *International Journal of Distributed Sensor Networks*, Accepted for Publication (2006).
42. R. R. Brooks, B. J. Pillai, M. C. Weigele and M. G. Pirretti, Optimal layout of multicast groups using network embedded multicast security in *ad hoc* sensor networks, *International Journal of Distributed Sensor Networks*, Accepted for Publication (2006).
43. J. R. Doucear, The Sybil attack, Proc. of the IPTPS02 Workshop, Cambridge, MA (USA) (March 2002).
44. A. J. Menezes, P. C. van Oorschot and A. A. Vanstone, Handbook of applied cryptography. CRC Press, Boca Raton, FLA (1996).

The following references are not cited in the text

45. R. R. Brooks, S. Phoha and E. Peluso, Stability and controllability analysis of fuzzy petri net JFACC models, *DARPA-JFACC Symposium on Advances in Enterprise Control* (1999).
46. R. A. DeCarlo, M. S. Brancky, S. Pettersson and B. Lennartson, Perspectives and results on the stability and stabilizability of hybrid systems, *Proceedings of the IEEE*, **88**(7), 1069–1082 (July 2000).
47. M. Dorigo, V. Maniezzo and A. Colorni, The ant system: Optimization by a colony of cooperating agents. *IEEE Transactions on Systems, Man, and Cybernetics-Part B*, **26**(1), 29–41 (1996).

48. J. E. Hopcroft and J. D. Ullman, *Introduction to Automata Theory, Languages, and Computation.* Addison-Wesley, Reading, MA (1979).
49. S. Phoha, R. R. Brooks and E. Peluso, A constructivist theory for distributed intelligent control of complex dynamic systems, *Symposium on Advances in Enterprise Control*, San Diego (1999).
50. Pillai, B. (MS) *Network Embedded Support for Sensor Network Security* (May 2006).
51. J. Portugali, *Self-Organization and the City.* Springer-Verlag, Berlin (2000).
52. K. Rudie and W. M. Wonham, Think globally, act locally: Decentralized supervisory control, *IEEE Transactions on Automatic Control*, **37**(11), 1692–1708 (1992).
53. K. Zhou, J. C. Doyle and K. Glover, *Robust and Optimal Control*, Prentice Hall PTR, Upper Saddle River, NJ (1996).

Chapter 14

Performance of Bridging Algorithms in IEEE 802.15.3 Multi-Piconet Networks

Jelena Mišić, Muhi Ahmed Ibne Khair
and Vojislav B. Mišić
University of Manitoba
Winnipeg, Manitoba, Canada

In this chapter, we introduce the bridging problem from the viewpoint of the recent IEEE 802.15.3 high data rate WPAN, and present alternative solutions that are possible in 802.15.3 networks. Then, we investigate the performance of a network with two piconets interconnected in a parent-child manner and linked through a bridge device which operates in a master-slave fashion. We have designed an adaptive bandwidth allocation algorithm for bridge down link CTA allocation, and examined the impact of the value of the smoothing constant and threshold hysteresis on the throughput, blocking probability, and average queue size for the downlink queue at the bridge.

14.1. Introduction

The IEEE 802.15.3 standard for high data rate Wireless Personal Area Networks (HR-WPANs) is designed to fulfill the requirements of high data rate suitable for multimedia applications whilst ensuring low end-to-end delay.[1] Devices in 802.15.3 networks are organized in small networks called piconets, each of which is formed, controlled, and maintained by a single dedicated device referred to as the piconet coordinator (PNC). However, there are many applications in which a multi-piconet network must be used: for example, small scale mesh networks[2] could be implemented using 802.15.3 standard. 802.15.3 networks can also be used in multimedia sensor networks, where their high data rate ensures reliable transmission of still images or video feeds from the sensors, e.g., in surveillance or military applications.

The 802.15.3 standard provides the basic piconet interconnection capability in the form of parent-child piconet topology, in which the time on the working channel is shared among the two piconets. However, the standards does not give much guidance as to the actual algorithm for topology construction, not does it provide the algorithms for bandwidth allocation which is needed to achieve the desired performance levels of a multi-piconet network.

In this chapter, we investigate the performance of a two-piconet network in a parent-child topology where the child piconet coordinator acts as the master-slave bridge to allow communication between the two piconets. We describe two adaptive algorithms for bandwidth allocation and examine their performance through extensive simulation. We show that the second algorithm provides much better performance despite its relative computational simplicity.

The chapter is organized as follows. In Sec. 14.2 we describe the major characteristics of the 802.15.3 standard, and highlight the way in which multi-piconet operation may be achieved in Sec. 14.3. In Sec. 14.6, we examine the performance of fixed bandwidth allocation and describe an adaptive algorithm with symmetrical thresholds, which is then modified to include hysteresis in Sec. 14.7. Finally, Sec. 14.8 concludes the chapter and provides some directions for future research.

14.2. Operation of 802.15.3 Networks

The IEEE 802.15.3 standard describes the requirements for physical (PHY) and medium access control (MAC) layer protocols for a high data rate wireless personal area network. Its high data rate and low latency make it suitable for multimedia applications, but also ensure easy reconfigurability and high resilience to interference, since it operates in the unlicensed Industrial, Scientific, and Medical (ISM) band at 2.4 GHz. (Note that this band is shared with a number of other communication technologies such as 802.11 b/g WLANs, 802.15.1 Bluetooth piconets, 802.15.4 low data rate WPANs, and others.)

An 802.15.3 network is formed in an ad hoc fashion: upon discovering a free channel, the PNC capable device starts the piconet by simply transmitting period beacon frames; other devices that detect those frames then request admission, or association (as it is referred to in the 802.15.3 standard). The coordinator duties include transmission of periodic beacon frames for synchronization, admission of new devices to the piconet, as well as allocation of dedicated time periods to allow unhindered packet transmission by the requesting device.

Time in an 802.15.3 piconet is structured in superframes delimited by successive beacon frame transmissions from the piconet coordinator. Each superframe contains three distinct parts: the beacon frame, the contention access period (CAP), and the channel time allocation period (CTAP), as shown in Fig. 14.1. During the Contention Access Period, devices compete with each other for access; a form of CSMA-CA algorithm is used. This period is used to send requests for CTAs (defined below) and other administrative information, but it can also be used for transmission of smaller amounts of asynchronous data.

The Channel Time Allocation Period contains a number of individual sub-periods (referred to as Channel Time Allocation, or CTA) which are allocated by the piconet coordinator upon explicit requests by the devices that have data to transmit. Requests for CTAs are sent during the Contention Access Period; as such, they are

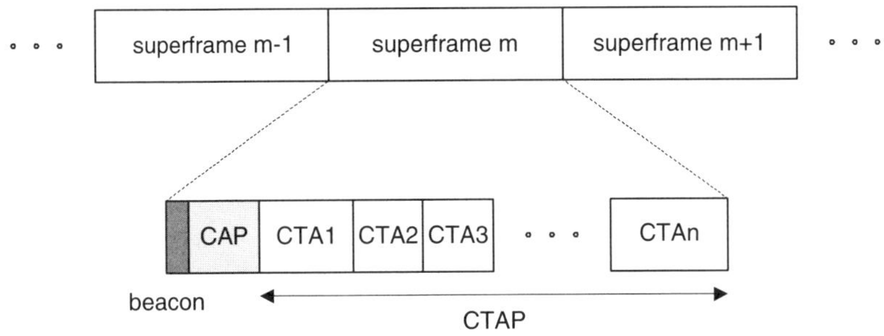

Fig. 14.1. Superframe structure in an 802.15.3 network.

subject to collision with similar requests from other devices. The decision to grant the allocation request or not rests exclusively with the piconet coordinator, which announces its decision in the next beacon frame; CTA allocation may be temporary or may last until explicit deallocation by the piconet coordinator. Once a device is allocated a CTA, other devices may not use it, and contention-free access is guaranteed. Special CTAs known as Management Channel Time Allocation (MCTA) are used for communication and dissemination of administrative information between the piconet coordinator and its devices.

Unlike other WPANs such as Bluetooth and 802.15.4, direct device-to-device communication is possible in an 802.15.3 piconet. In case the communicating devices are not within the transmission range of each other, the piconet coordinator (which, by default, must be able to communicate with both) may be involved as an intermediary, leading in effect to multi-hop intra-piconet communication. It is worth noting that problems of this nature may be alleviated by adjusting the transmission power, but also by making use of the adaptive data rate facility provided by the 802.15.3 standard. Namely, if transmission at the full data rate of 55 Mbps suffers from too many errors because the signal-to-noise-plus-interference ratio (SINR) is too low, different modulation schemes with lower data rate may be used to give additional resilience. This problem and its solutions, however, are beyond the scope of the present chapter.

Reliable data transfer in 802.15.3 networks is achieved by utilizing acknowledgments and retransmission of non-acknowledged packets. The standard defines three acknowledgment modes:

- no acknowledgment (No-ACK) is typically used for delay sensitive but loss tolerant traffic such as multimedia (typically transferred through UDP or some similar protocol);
- immediate acknowledgment (Imm-ACK) means that each packet is immediately acknowledged with a small packet sent back to the sender of the original packet; and

- delayed acknowledgment (Dly-ACK), where an acknowledgment packet is sent after successfully receiving a batch of successive data packets; obviously, this allows for higher throughput due to reduced acknowledgment overhead — but the application requirements must tolerate the delay incurred in this case, and some means of selective retransmission must be employed to maintain efficiency.

14.3. Interconnecting IEEE 802.15.3 Piconets

The 802.15.3 standard contains provisions for the coexistence of multiple piconets in the same (or partially overlapping) physical space. Since the data rate is high, up to 55 Mbps, the channel width is large and there are, in fact, only five channels available in the ISM band for use of 802.15.3 networks. If 802.11-compatible WLAN (or, perhaps, several of them) is/are present in the vicinity, the number of available channels is reduced to only three in order to prevent excessive interference between the networks adhering to two standards. As a result, the formation of multiple piconets must utilize time division multiplexing, rather than the frequency division one, as is the case with Bluetooth. Namely, a piconet can allocate a special CTA during which another piconet can operate. There are two types of such piconets: a child piconet and a neighbor piconet.

A child piconet is the one in which the piconet coordinator is a member of the parent piconet, as shown in Fig. 14.2(a). It is formed when a PNC-capable device which is a member of the parent piconet sends a request to the parent piconet coordinator, asking for a special CTA known as a private CTA. Regular CTA requests include the device addresses of both the sender and the receiver; a request for a private CTA is distinguished by virtue of containing the same device address as both the sending and the receiving node. When the parent piconet coordinator allocates the required CTA, the child piconet coordinator may begin sending beacon frames of its own within that CTA, and thus may form another piconet which operates on the same channel as the parent piconet, but is independent from it. The private CTA is, effectively, the active portion of the superframe of the child piconet. The child superframe consists, then, of this private CTA which can be used for communication between child piconet coordinator (PNC) and its devices (DEVs); the remainder of the parent superframe is reserved time — it can't be used for communication in the child piconet. Figure 14.2(b) shows the communication patterns in this topology.

The timing relationship of superframes in parent and child piconets is shown in Fig. 14.2(b), where the top part corresponds to the parent piconet and the bottom part to the child piconet. Note that the distinction is logical rather than physical, since the piconets share the same RF channel.

A given piconet can have multiple child piconets, and a child piconet may have another child of its own. Obviously, the available channel time is shared between those piconets, at the expense of decreased throughput and increased delay; but the effective transmission range may be increased.

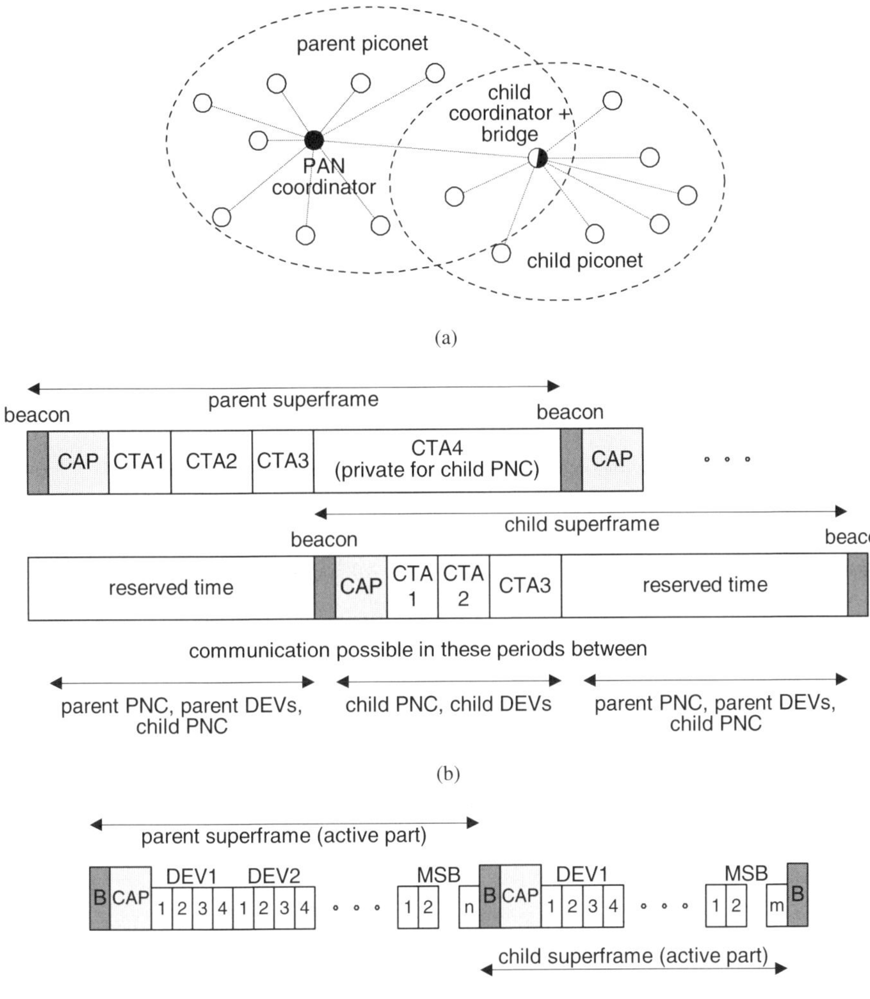

Fig. 14.2. Parent-child interconnection. (a) Topology. (b) Communication patterns. (c) Superframe structure. MSB denotes the CTA allocated to the MS bridge.

Challenges. As can be seen from the discussion above, the main challenge in forming a multi-piconet network that uses the same RF channel — i.e., a complex network in which *all* piconets are related through parent-child relationships — is to develop a network-wide distributed scheduling algorithm that will allocate channel time to all devices in an efficient and fair manner. Since time division multiplexing among each parent-child piconet pair is used, we need not worry about collisions between transmissions originating from different piconets in the network which plague MAC protocols based on CSMA-CA such as 802.15.4:[3] transmissions during allocated CTAs are guaranteed to be conflict-free. However, transmission scheduling and bandwidth allocation pose significant difficulties, in particular when multiple piconets are connected. It is worth noting that the problem of optimal scheduling in a multi-piconet Bluetooth environment (which also uses TDMA) has been shown to be NP-complete.[4]

The need to wait until the appropriate active portion of the superframe incurs some additional delays besides the usual transmission delay and access delay in the outbound queue of the source device; furthermore, the bridge device operates its own queues (one for each direction of the traffic) and these can also add delay to the total packet transmission time. Further problems arise from the finite size of various device buffers which packets have to pass on their route from the source node in one piconet, to the destination node in another one. Once these buffers are full, newly arrived packets will be rejected, which leads to packet losses or, if acknowledgments are used, more frequent retransmissions. In the latter case, efficiency is reduced, and the probability of overflowing other buffers earlier in the packet route increases, thus causing rapid performance degradation. If reliable transfer is needed, the possibility of packet blocking necessitates the use of Imm-ACK or Dly-ACK acknowledgment policy. In addition, we must devise an efficient and fair algorithm to partition the available channel time between the piconets, taking into account the traffic intensity both within the piconets and between them.

Using different RF channels. Multi-piconet networks can also be created using a different scenario, in which several multi-piconet networks operate in the same physical space but on different RF channels. While *physical* conflicts between transmissions originating from different multi-piconet networks are still absent by virtue of frequency division multiplexing, *scheduling* conflicts between the piconets will be the main source of complexity, as the device that wants to act as a bridge must alternatively synchronize with piconets that operate according to entirely unrelated schedules. This precludes the use of Master-Slave bridges to interconnect such piconets. Namely, the Master-Slave bridges must not abstain from their duties as the PNCs in their respective piconets for prolonged periods of time. As a result, piconets operating on different RF channels favor interconnection through Slave-Slave bridges, i.e., devices that act as ordinary nodes in each of the piconets they belong to. As such devices have no coordinator duties, their absence from a given piconet will not cause any problems there. In fact, their absence might even go unnoticed if there happens to be no traffic directed to such devices during that time interval.

Neighbor piconets. The 802.15.3 standard also provides the concept of the neighbor piconet, which is intended to enable an 802.15.3 piconet to coexist with another network that may or may not use the 802.15.3 communication protocols; for example, an 802.11 WLAN in which one of the devices is 802.15.3-capable. A PNC-capable device that wants to form a neighbor piconet will first associate with the parent piconet, but not as an ordinary piconet member; the parent piconet coordinator may reject the association request if it does not support neighbor piconets. If the request is granted, the device then requests a private CTA from the coordinator of the parent piconet. Once a private CTA is allocated, the neighbor piconet can begin to operate. The neighbor piconet coordinator may exchange commands with the parent piconet coordinator, but no data exchange is allowed. In other words, the neighbor piconet is simply a means to share the channel time between the two networks. Since, unlike the child piconet, data communications between the two piconets are not possible, this mechanism is unsuitable for the creation of multi-piconet networks.

14.4. Implementing Multi-Piconet Networks with 802.15.3

In this Section we will first explain the interconnection (bridging) mechanism, followed by our proposed scheduling algorithm for channel time allocation in a multi-piconet network. The superframe structure of our MAC protocol follows the IEEE 802.15.3 MAC superframe and the channel time allocation is based on TDMA, during the guaranteed access period, and CSMA/CA, during the contention period.

Two common approaches, namely the Master-Slave bridge and the Slave-Slave bridge are used for piconet interconnection in different networks. In the case of a Master-Slave bridge, Fig. 14.3(a), the bridge device is the PNC for Piconet 2 and a normal member of Piconet 1. In the case of a Slave-Slave bridge, Fig. 14.3(b), the bridge device is an ordinary member (DEV) in both piconets. We can combine both types of bridges in a multi-piconet environment in order to cover larger areas. The choice of the type of interconnection depends on location of the bridge device within the network. The interconnection will be established through a Master-Slave bridge if a PNC-capable device is located in such a way that it can easily control one piconet and participate in the other one. On the other hand, the Slave-Slave bridge can be used if no suitable PNC-capable device can be found, or if the two piconets operate on different RF channels, possibly because the traffic volume is too high to be serviced with half the available bandwidth.

Operation of the Master-Slave bridge. The bridge establishes a connection between a parent and a child piconet where the bridge device acts as the PNC of the child piconet. The bridge device maintains two queues to temporarily store, and subsequently deliver, the traffic in both directions. As can be seen from Fig. 14.2(b), the superframe duration is the same for both parent and child piconets; in fact, the child superframe is simply a private CTA from the parent superframe. The only setup operation needed in this case is for the child piconet PNC to request a private CTA as explained above. Once such a CTA is allocated by the parent piconet PNC, the child piconet PNC simply begins to send beacons at the beginning of the

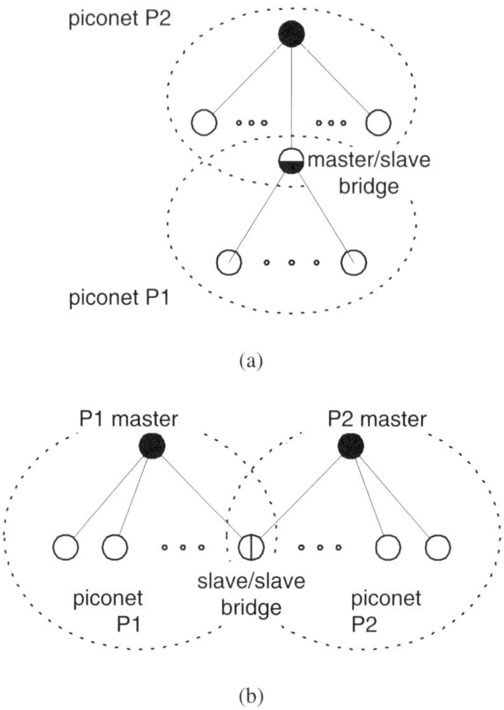

Fig. 14.3. Bridge topologies for multi-piconet networks. (a) Master-Slave (MS) bridge interconnection. (b) Slave-Slave (SS) bridge interconnection.

CTA, which is also the beginning of its own superframe. Devices that need to send data to the other piconet can simply request their own CTAs from their respective PNCs.

Operation of the Slave-Slave bridge. A device that is already associated with a piconet can detect the presence of a new piconet by receiving a beacon sent by its PNC, or a control packet with a piconet identification number (PNCID) that is different from the existing one. Whenever a prospective bridge device detects the presence of two piconets within its transmission range, it initiates the connection establishment algorithm (Algorithm 14.1). First, the device waits for the MCTA period or CAP period to send a request command for bridging. Then it will use the four-way handshake (RTS-CTS-DATA-ACK) to send the request command, piggybacking its current scheduling information to the neighbor PNC. The neighbor PNC adjusts its scheduling information based on the received scheduling information from its neighbor piconet. If the PNC is a Master-Slave bridge in its own right, it will request a private CTA from its parent PNC, trying to accommodate the demands of the bridge device. The bridge requirements are, simply, that the neighboring child piconets obtain channel time for transmission (i.e., private CTAs) without interfering with each other. A positive response from the parent PNC establishes the connection between the child piconets. After the connection establishment, the bridge device needs to maintain a table that keeps track of the scheduled times of activity in each piconet. The PNCID uniquely identifies each record in the table and helps the bridge device switch in a timely fashion between different piconets.

Algorithm 14.1 The Slave-Slave bridge connection.

1: scan presence of overlapped coverage
2: **if** scan == positive **then**
3: send join-request to neighbor PNC using four way handshaking protocol
4: receive feedback from neighbor PNC
5: update scheduling table with PNCID and received scheduling information
6: **end if**

Channel Scheduling. The channel time scheduling of the network under consideration will be based on average queue size of the devices. The queue size of an ordinary device (i.e., not a PNC or a bridge device) primarily depends on packet arrival rate of that device. The queue size for a bridge device is based on the incoming packet queue sizes from neighbor piconets and outgoing packet queue sizes to the neighbor piconets. The bridge device will use the average of these two queues size to determine its channel time requirement. The devices send requests for channel time based on the average queue size to their respective PNCs. The PNC uses Algorithm 14.2 based on the request from the bridge in question. In case of a request from a bridge device, the PNC schedules channel time and a private CTA (for the child piconet) in such a way that there will be no overlap of channel time between the two adjacent piconets.

A representative topology that employs both types of bridge interconnection is shown in Fig. 14.4. In this network, the parent piconets P1 and P2 are located beyond each other's transmission ranges and, thus, can operate on the same RF channel. However, the presence of two child piconets that can hear each other — they are, in fact, interconnected — presents a challenge for scheduling. In order to resolve this, the two parent piconets P1 and P2 will assign channel time for their children in different time slots, based on the scheduling information they exchanged during connection establishment. Let us consider time slots in the superframe in Fig. 14.4. The time slots represented by P1/P2 (or P2/P1) imply that P1 and P2 can communicate at the same time. On the other hand, when a child piconet is operating, no other piconet in its range can talk. In this case we can assume that a single superframe (actually two superframes from two different parent piconets) are divided into four time slots. Within each time slot, the devices will have guaranteed channel time and contention period. There are also MCTAs in each time slot during which a new node can join or a bridge can establish a connection.

There is a chance of conflict during the MCTA period as the new devices do not have any knowledge of the current scheduling information resulting in the hidden terminal problem. We will use the four way handshaking protocol to resolve this problem.

Algorithm 14.2 Scheduling of channel time.

```
if request command from Master-Slave bridge then
   assign private CTA anywhere in the superframe
end if
if request command from Slave-Slave bridge then
   check piggyback data for neighbor scheduling information
   if no scheduling information then
      request for scheduling information
   end if
end if
scheduling information received
calculate required channel time based on average queue size
determine private CTA position
assign private CTA and channel time
```

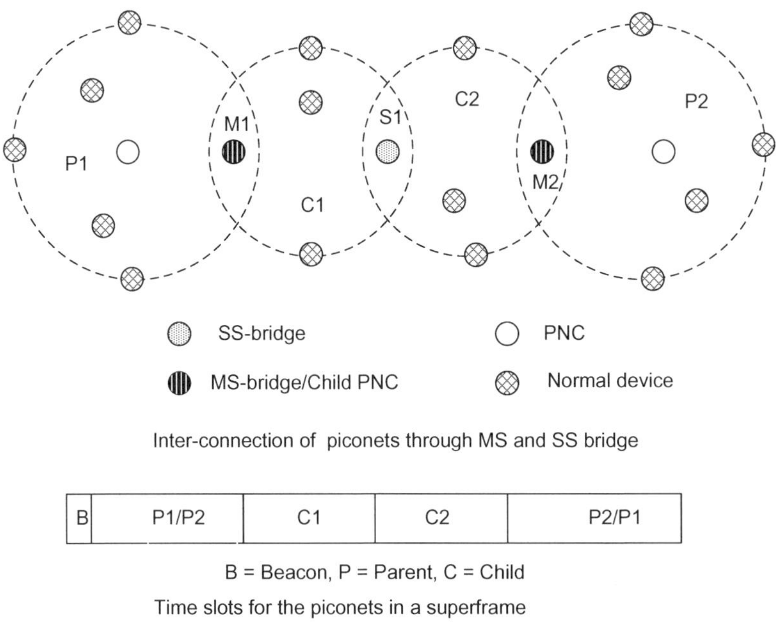

Fig. 14.4. A multi-piconet structure that employs both types of bridge interconnection.

14.5. Related Work

The MAC protocols for wireless multi-piconet networks are different from the traditional wireless MACs in terms of self organization, distributed nature, multi-hop, and mobility. Multi-piconet networks can be designed with a single RF channel or multiple RF channels. For simplicity, we will focus on a single channel network with a parent-child interconnection.

Multi-piconet networks have often been developed using the IEEE 802.11 DCF MAC protocol, and most of the research work in this area was based on using the features of 802.11 MAC protocol, possibly slightly modified to improve network performance. Bicket *et al.*[5] have evaluated the performance of 802.11 b networks; their experiments have shown that an ad hoc network implemented using 802.11 b technology can achieve sustained throughput of around 630 Kbps, significantly below the supported data rate of 11 Mbps. Similarly, Yamada *et al.*[6] have identified two problems of 802.11 b based networks: limited throughput and degradation of fairness. To solve these problems they have introduced two new control packets, namely Invite-to-Send (ITS) and Copied CTS (CCTS). The use of ITS and CCTS packets has brought some improvements in throughput, but at the cost of increased control overhead and delay. Also, the overhead due to ITS and CCTS packets and end-to-end packet delay will increase with the network load. However, in an 802.15.3 network, data communications are accomplished using dedicated time periods, hence there is no need to introduce additional control packets such as ITS and CCTS.

MACA was developed to solve the hidden and exposed terminal problems of traditional CSMA[7] protocols. In MACA, the sender and receiver exchange RTS and CTS control packets before sending a data packet to avoid collisions. Fullmer and Garcia-Luna-Aceves[8] describe the scenario where MACA fails to avoid collisions due to hidden terminals. MACA may also make a device wait for a long period to access the medium because its use of the BEB[a] algorithm.[7]

To overcome the problems of MACA, a new solution was proposed by Bharghavan *et al.* called Media Access Protocol for Wireless LANs (MACAW).[9] Basically MACAW is a modification of the BEB algorithm in MACA. It introduces acknowledgment and data-sending (DS) control packets producing the RTS-CTS-DS-DATA-ACK sequence for data transfer. The IEEE 802.11 standard[10] has been developed by adopting the CSMA and MACAW with further modifications to support wireless LANs.

However, neither IEEE 802.11 MAC nor MACAW provide support for real time data transfers because of the absence of guaranteed time slots. Therefore, Lin and Gerla[11] proposed an enhanced version of MACA called MACA with Piggybacked

[a]In Binary Exponential Backoff (BEB), a device doubles the size of its backoff window if a collision is detected.

Reservation (MACA/PR) to support real-time traffic. The MACA/PR protocol is a contention based protocol with a reservation mechanism. It has been designed to support multimedia data in multihop mobile wireless network providing guaranteed bandwidth through reservation. Every node keeps the reservation information of sending and receiving windows of all the neighbor nodes in a table, which is refreshed after every successful RTS-CTS-DATA-ACK (known as four way handshaking protocol) cycle. The RTS and CTS packets are exchanged for the first packet in the transfer of a series of real-time data packets. The reservation information for the next data packet is piggybacked with the prior data packet and the receiver confirms this reservation in the acknowledgment control packet.

The limitation of MACA/PR is that it requires help from the network layer routing protocol. However, MACA/PR has better performance in terms of latency, packet loss, mobility, and bandwidth share than both asynchronous packet radio network (PRNET[b]) and synchronous TDMA based MACs. The use of fixed reserved time slots in MACA/PR can result in wastage of bandwidth. Manoj and Ram Murthy[12] have proposed a modification to the reservation mechanism of MACA/PR to prevent bandwidth wastage. In the modified scheme, the reserved slots can be placed at any position in the superframe and unused resources (channel time) are released after a successful transmission.

We note that the 802.15.3 MAC uses TDMA based channel allocation to provide guaranteed time slots for data transfer. However, the piggybacked reservation information of MACA/PR can be employed together with the TDMA based MAC to support real-time data transfer along with best-effort traffic in 802.15.3 based multi-piconet networks.

Xiao[13] has performed a detailed performance evaluation of the IEEE 802.15.3[1] and IEEE 802.15.3a[14] standards through simulation and mathematical analysis. He has also done a throughput analysis of the 802.11[10] protocol, which uses backoff with counter freezing during inactive portions of the superframe. The freezing and backoff techniques are essentially the same in the 802.11 and 802.15.3 MACs, except that different ways of calculating the backoff time are utilized. The backoff and freezing have an impact on the performance of the network; especially the backoff has a direct impact on the delay parameter. Large backoff windows can result in longer delays. On the other hand, small backoff windows may increase the probability of collisions. Xiao used the backoff procedures defined in the 802.11 and 802.15.3 MAC specifications; this work gives us performance of the protocol in terms of throughput over various payload sizes, but the performance of reliable transmission in error-prone wireless network during contention period needs more study.

[b]In a PRNET, the devices use the same channel and share it dynamically.

14.6. Fixed versus Adaptive CTA Allocation

To investigate the performance of an 802.15.3 network formed by two piconets interconnected with a MS bridge, we have built a simulator using the object oriented Petri Net engine Artifex by RSoftDesign, Inc.[15] In the topology considered, the parent piconet consisted of nine devices, while the child piconet consisted of five devices (not counting either coordinator). The child piconet coordinator is also the bridge toward the parent piconet. Each of the ordinary nodes in either piconet has Poisson traffic with a specified packet arrival rate, with packets of 1,200 bytes each (chosen to correspond to an average IP packet size). Packet destinations are randomly selected within the same piconet with the total probability of P_l, and in the other piconet with the probability of $1 - P_l$. For convenience, we refer to the traffic from the parent to child piconet as downlink traffic, and the traffic in the opposite direction as uplink traffic. The structure of the superframe is shown in Fig. 14.2(c). Each of the ordinary devices is allocated a CTA sufficient for four packets, while the bridge device is allocated an additional CTA with b packet slots for inter-piconet traffic; this holds for both parent and child piconet superframes. In this manner, the total superframe duration is close to the maximum value of 65.535 ms prescribed by the standard.[1]

The total run length of our simulation is 100 seconds, after the initial warm up period of 6 seconds. We have varied the packet arrival rate from 10 to 50 packets/s, while the locality probability was varied from 0.65 to 0.9. The size of the downlink queue at the bridge was fixed at 100 packets. Measured bridge throughput is shown in Fig. 14.5 as a function of packet arrival rate (in packets per second per node) and locality probability P_l. The number of packet slots in the CTA allocated to bridge downlink traffic (which, in Fig. 14.2(c), corresponds to the MSB period in child piconet superframe) has been varied from $b = 3$ to 7. As can be seen, higher bandwidth allocation results in higher throughput and reduced blocking probability at the bridge; but at the same time, it takes some time away either at the expense of CTAs allocated to other devices. Higher bandwidth may also be wasted if there is no traffic.

A much better solution would be to allocate the bandwidth to the bridge in an adaptive manner. This, however, is complicated by the essentially random character of inter-piconet traffic due to Poisson packet arrivals. To smooth those fluctuations, we apply a simple transformation known as exponentially weighted moving average, or EWMA.[16] In this approach, the bandwidth allocated by the bridge is determined on the basis of exponentially smoothed value of bridge downlink queue size, which is recalculated at each new packet arrival as

$$\overline{Q}_{i+1} = \alpha Q_{i+1} + (1 - \alpha)\overline{Q}_i, \qquad (14.1)$$

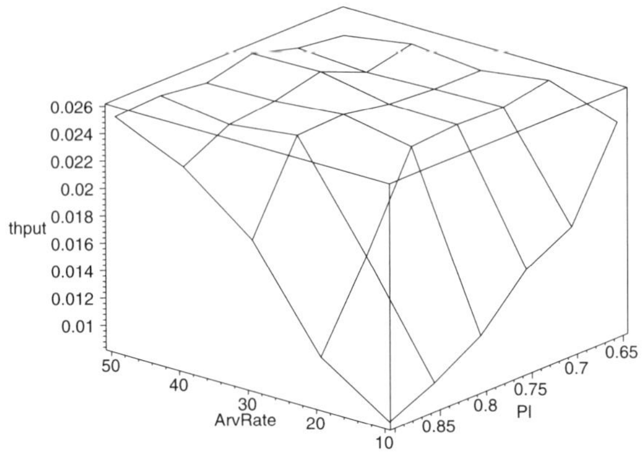

(a)

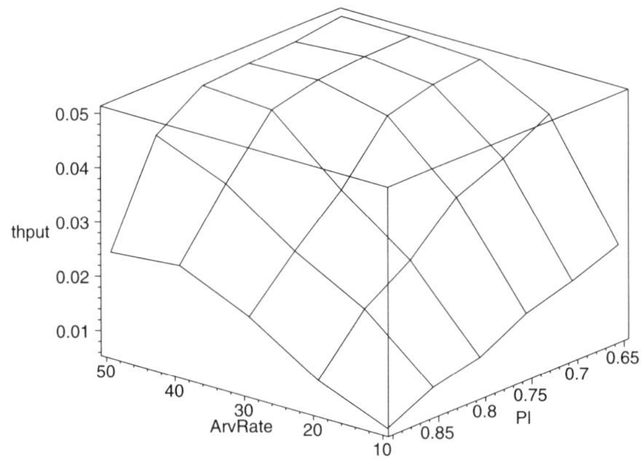

(b)

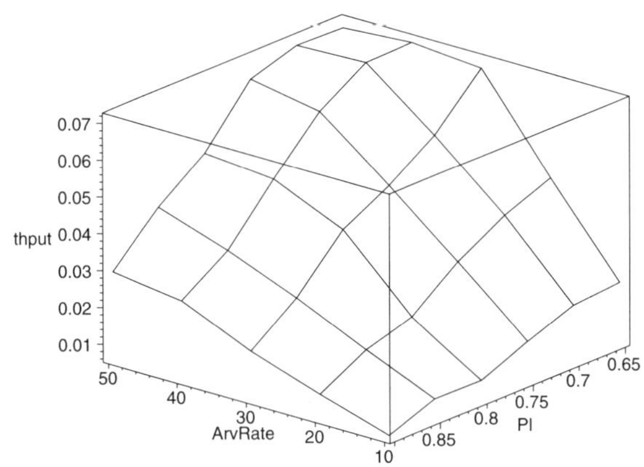

(c)

Fig. 14.5. Bridge throughput under fixed bandwidth allocation. (a) Throughput at $b = 3$. (b) Throughput at $b = 5$. (c) Throughput at $b = 7$.

where Q and $\overline{Q}$ denote the instantaneous and smoothed bridge downlink queue size, while the index refers to the time instant of packet arrival. The level of smoothing depends primarily on the smoothing constant α: the higher its value, the more weight is assigned to most recent reading. The actual bandwidth allocation follows Algorithm 14.3. Changes may be explicitly requested by the bridge and granted by the coordinator of the child piconet; alternatively, the bridge can just report the instantaneous queue size in each superframe, and the coordinator can use the algorithm to calculate the required bandwidth allocation itself.

Algorithm 14.3 Adaptive CTA allocation for down link.

1: Q_{i+1} measured and/or reported by the bridge
2: $\overline{Q}_{i+1} = \alpha Q_{i+1} + (1-\alpha)\overline{Q}_i$
3: CTAforDLqueue $= (\overline{Q}_{i+1} - q_0) \mod \Delta q + b_0$

Measured results for bridge throughput are shown in the diagrams in the left hand column of Fig. 14.6, for different values of the smoothing constant α; we have set $b_0 = 3$, $q_0 = \Delta q = 20$. As can be seen, the adaptive algorithm manages to maintain the throughput at values close to the one obtained under fixed bandwidth allocation with $b = 5$. On the basis of these measurements, it seems that the value $\alpha = 0.5$ would be the best choice for the smoothing constant, although the differences are rather small.

Unfortunately, exponential smoothing does not solve all problems, as can be seen from the diagrams of blocking probability, shown in the right hand column of Fig. 14.6, which demonstrate that this parameter is not significantly affected by the choice of the smoothing constant α. Namely, as soon as a packet leaves the downlink queue, the allocation will be adjusted downward, and the queue will take longer to empty. As a result, the amount of bandwidth allocated to the bridge is still too sensitive to the average downlink queue size, and benefits of adaptivity are not fully realized.

14.7. Adaptive CTA with Threshold Hysteresis

In order to correct this, we have introduced a small amount of hysteresis into the adaptive bandwidth allocation algorithm. Namely, the thresholds for allocation adjustment will differ, depending on the direction of the adjustment, and upward adjustments will have higher thresholds than their downward counterparts. In this manner, when a sufficient number of packets arrive to the downlink queue, the bandwidth allocation will remain high until the bulk of the increase is processed, i.e., delivered to their respective destinations. The modified algorithm is shown as Algorithm 14.4.

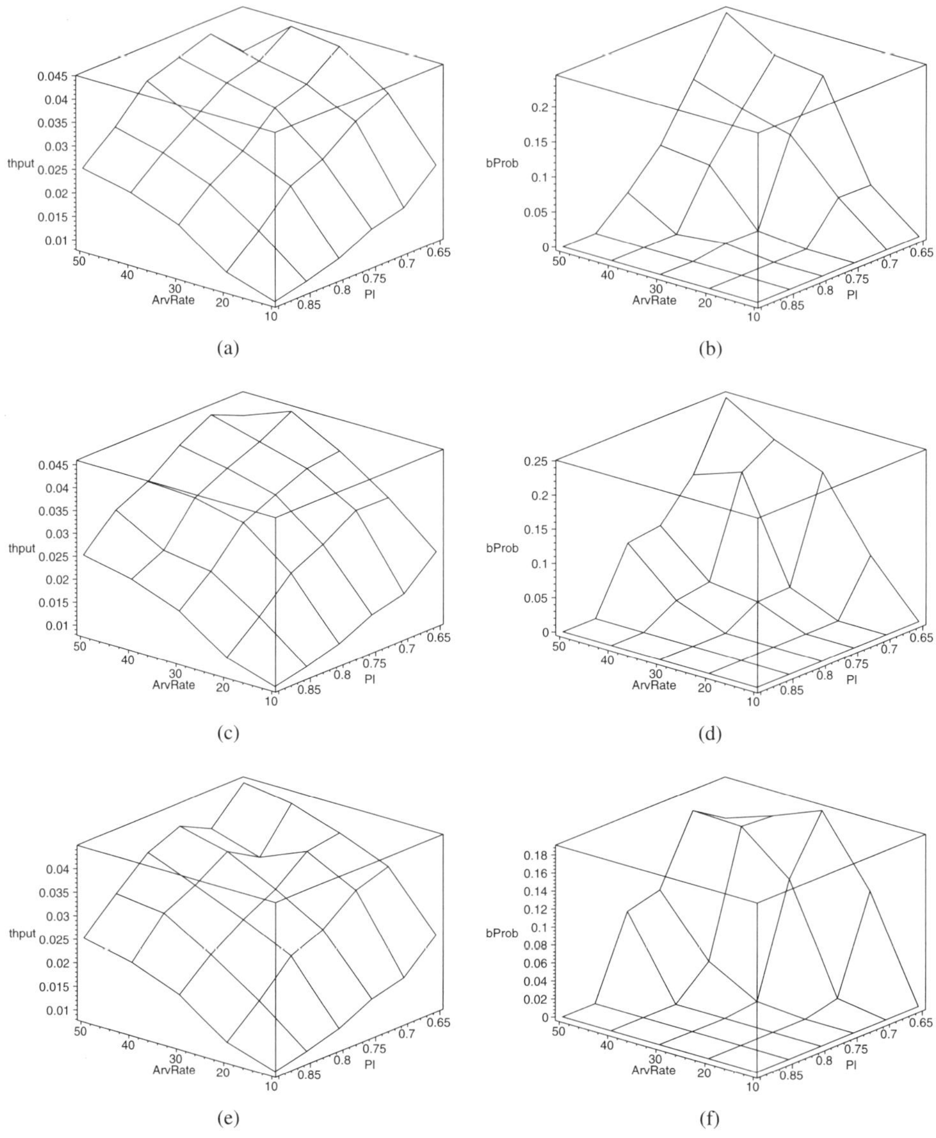

Fig. 14.6. Bridge throughput and blocking probability under adaptive bandwidth allocation. (a) Throughput, $\alpha = 0.3$. (b) Blocking probability, $\alpha = 0.3$. (c) Throughput, $\alpha = 0.5$. (d) Blocking probability, $\alpha = 0.5$. (e) Throughput, $\alpha = 0.7$. (f) Blocking probability, $\alpha = 0.7$.

Algorithm 14.4 Adaptive CTA allocation with hysteresis threshold for downlink.

Q_{i+1} measured and/or reported by the bridge
$\overline{Q}_{i+1} = \alpha Q_{i+1} + (1-\alpha)\overline{Q}_i$
if $\overline{Q}_{i+1} > \overline{Q}_i$ **then**
    CTAforDLqueue $= (\overline{Q}_{i+1} - q_0) \mod \Delta q + b_0$
else
    CTAforDLqueue $= (\overline{Q}_{i+1} - (q_0 - \chi)) \mod \Delta q + b_0$
end if

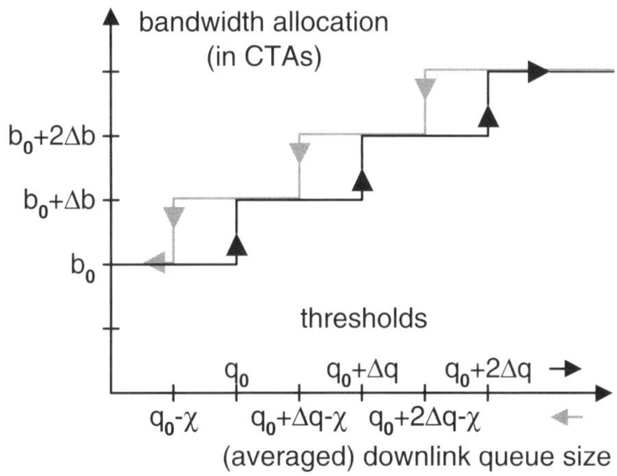

Fig. 14.7. Adaptive CTA allocation with hysteresis.

The dependency between the bandwidth allocation and average queue size in the adaptive algorithm with hysteresis can be graphically depicted as in Fig. 14.7.

The measured results, including throughput, blocking probability at the bridge, and average downlink queue size, are shown in Fig. 14.8. For illustration, we have shown these results for three values of the smoothing constant α.

Finally, Fig. 14.9 shows the corresponding throughput and blocking probability. As can be seen, throughput shows a marked improvement in the case $\alpha = 0.5$, being close to the value achieved under fixed bandwidth allocation with $b = 7$, Fig. 14.5(c). Furthermore, blocking probability is much lower than for other values of α, and it remains lower in a wider range of values of packet arrival rate and locality probability. Similar observation can be made for the average downlink queue size at the bridge, which in the most part of the observed range stays well below the maximum size of 100 packets. This confirms the validity of the adaptive bandwidth allocation approach.

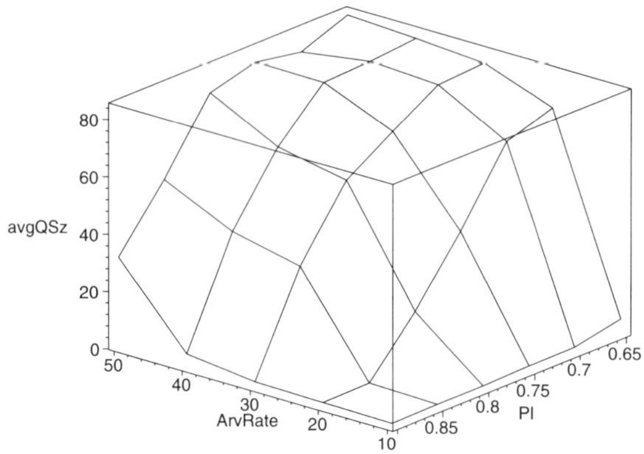

(a)

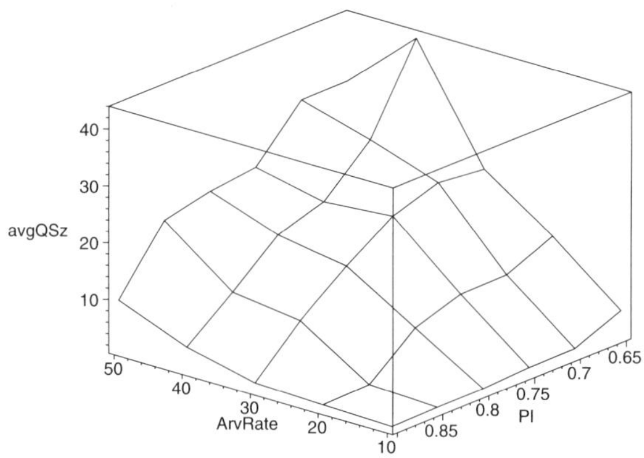

(b)

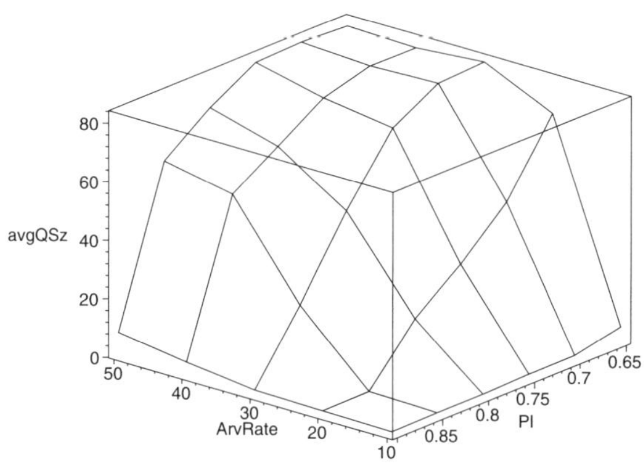

(c)

Fig. 14.8. Average queue size under adaptive algorithm with hysteresis. (a) Average queue size at $\alpha = 0.3$. (b) Average queue size at $\alpha = 0.5$. (c) Average queue size at $\alpha = 0.7$.

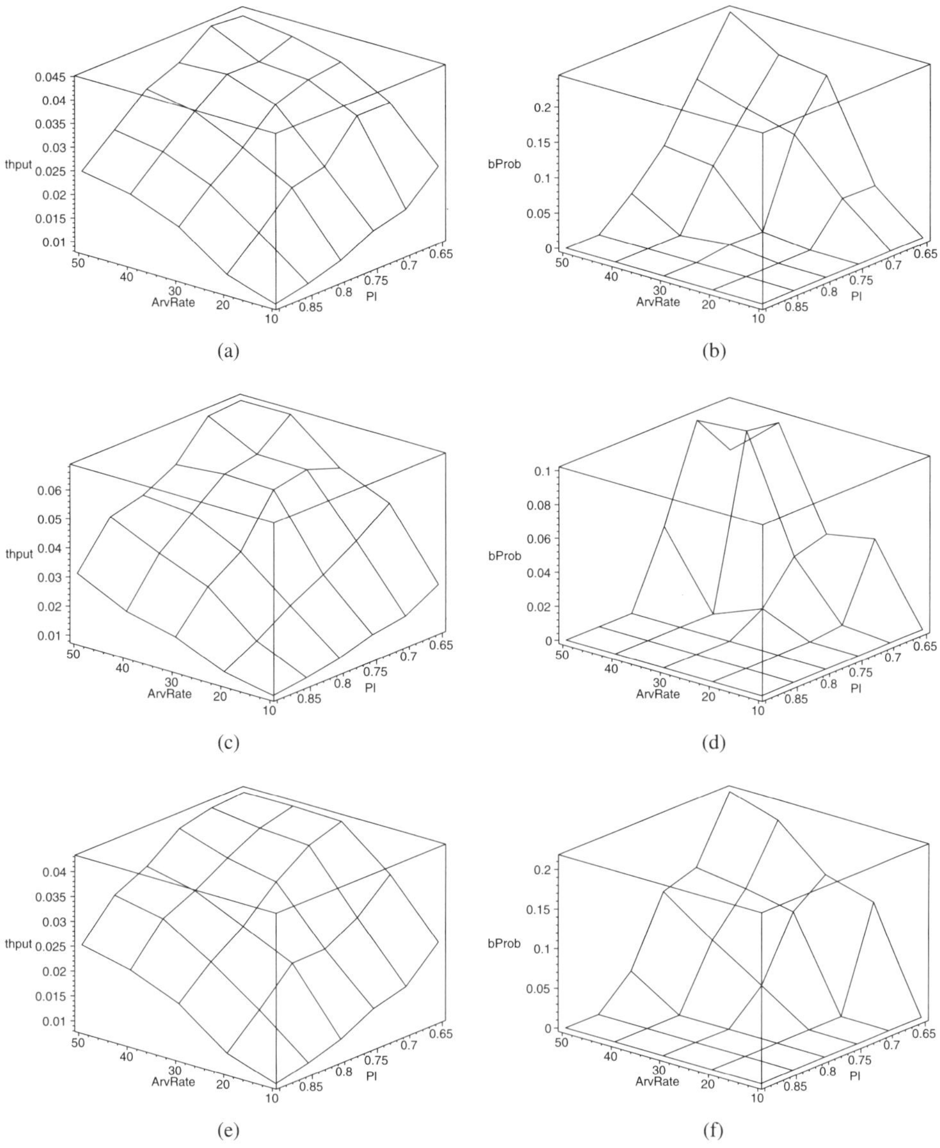

Fig. 14.9. Performance of adaptive algorithm with hysteresis. (a) Throughput at $\alpha = 0.7$. (b) Blocking probability at $\alpha = 0.7$. (c) Throughput at $\alpha = 0.5$. (d) Blocking probability at $\alpha = 0.5$. (e) Throughput at $\alpha = 0.3$. (f) Blocking probability at $\alpha = 0.3$.

14.8. Conclusion

In this chapter, we have considered the performance of a two-piconet network built upon the recent IEEE 802.15.3 high data rate WPAN standard. The parent and child piconets are interconnected through a Master-Slave bridge which also acts as the coordinator of the child piconet. We have shown that an adaptive algorithm for allocating downlink bandwidth to the bridge, utilizing threshold hysteresis, can easily outperform any fixed bandwidth allocation algorithm. Further work will focus on extensions to control the bandwidth allocation for uplink traffic, as well as that of ordinary nodes in the network.

References

1. Standard for part 15.3: Wireless medium access control (MAC) and physical layer (PHY) specifications for high rate wireless personal area networks (WPAN), IEEE standard 802.15.3, IEEE, New York, NY (2003).
2. I. F. Akyildiz, X. Wang and W. Wang, Wireless mesh networks: A survey, *Computer Networks*, **47**(0), 445–487 (March 2005).
3. J. Mišić and V. B. Mišić, *Wireless Personal Area Networks: Performance, Interconnections and Security with IEEE 802.15.4*, John Wiley and Sons, New York, NY (2008).
4. N. Johansson, U. Körner and L. Tassiulas, A distributed scheduling algorithm for a Bluetooth scatternet, *Proceedings of the International Teletraffic Congress — ITC-17*, 61–72, Salvador de Bahia, Brazil (2001).
5. J. Bicket, D. Aguayo, S. Biswas and R. Morris, Architecture and evaluation of an unplanned 802.11b mesh network, *11th ACM International Conference on Mobile Computing and Networking*, **1**, 31–42, Cologne, Germany (2005).
6. A. Yamada, A. Fujiwara and Y. Matsumoto, Enhancement of mesh network oriented IEEE 802.11 MAC protocol, *10th Asia-Pacific Conference on Communications and 5th International Symposium on Multi-Dimensional Mobile Communications*, **1**, 142–146, Kanagawa, Japan (2004).
7. C. Ram Murthy and B. Manoj, *Ad Hoc Wireless Networks, Architecture and Protocols*, Prentice Hall, Upper Saddle River, NJ (2004).
8. C. L. Fullmer and J. J. Garcia-Luna-Aceves, Floor acquisition multiple access (FAMA) for packet-radioi networks, *ACM SIGCOMM '95*, 262–273, Cambridge, MA (1995).
9. V. Bharghavan, A. Demers, S. Shenker and L. Zhang, MACAW: a media access protocol for wireless LAN's, *ACM SIGCOMM '94*, 212–225, London, UK (1994).
10. Standard for wireless LAN medium access control (MAC) and physical layer (PHY) specifications, IEEE standard 802.11, IEEE, New York, NY (1997).
11. C. R. Lin and M. Gerla, MACA/PR: An asynchronous multimedia multihop wireless network, *IEEE INFOCOM '97*, 118–125, Kobe, Japan (1997).
12. B. S. Manoj and C. S. Ram Murthy, Real-time support for ad hoc wireless networks, *IEEE ICON '02*, 335–340, Grand Copthorne Waterfront, Singapore (2002).
13. Y. Xiao, MAC layer issues and throughput analysis for the IEEE 802.15.3a UWB, *Dynamics of Continuous, Discrete and Impulsive Systems, Series B: Applications & Algorithms*, **12**, 443–462 (2005).
14. *IEEE 802.15 WPAN high rate alternative PHY Task Group 3a (TG3a)*. (Available online at http://www.ieee802.org/15/pub/TG3a.html, August 2006).
15. *Artifex v.4.4.2*, RSoft Design, Inc., San Jose, CA (2003).
16. S. Delurgio, *Forecasting — Principles, and Application*, McGraw-Hill/Irwin, New York (1998).

Part V

Security

Chapter 15

Security Trends and Challenges in Wireless Sensor Networks

S. A. V. Satya Murty*, P. Gireesan Namboothiri[†]
and Krishna M. Sivalingam[†,‡]

**Indira Gandhi Center for Atomic Research, Kalpakkam, India*

[†]*Indian Institute of Technology Madras, Chennai, India*

[‡]*University of Maryland, Baltimore County*
Baltimore, MD, USA

[‡]*krishna.sivalingam@ieee.org*

This chapter provides an overview of security issues in Wireless Sensor Networks (WSN). If first describes the security requirements followed by common attacks and threats in such networks. Then, some of the important security mechanisms such as encryption/decryption, key management and distribution are presented. This is followed by description of implementations of security mechanisms available in current generation WSN operating systems such as TinyOS.

15.1. Introduction

Recent Advances in Sensor Technology, Data Processing and Wireless Communications have enabled the development and large scale deployment of low cost, low power, multi-functional sensor nodes that are small in size and communicate continuously.[1–3] These nodes typically consist of one or more hardware sensors, analog to digital converter, and a CPU/microcontroller with small amount of memory and communication system. These sensor nodes are often densely deployed either inside the phenomenon or very close to it. The current generation sensors have serious hardware constraints due to limited power, limited memory and limited computation capabilities. Wireless sensor networks (WSN) are created by networking several hundreds of such sensor nodes to form a large scale network. The networking of sensors provides several advantages over stand-alone sensors, such as collaborative sensing, redundancy and fault tolerant operation. Figure 15.1 presents an example sensor network consisting of sensor nodes and a base station.

[‡]Corresponding author.

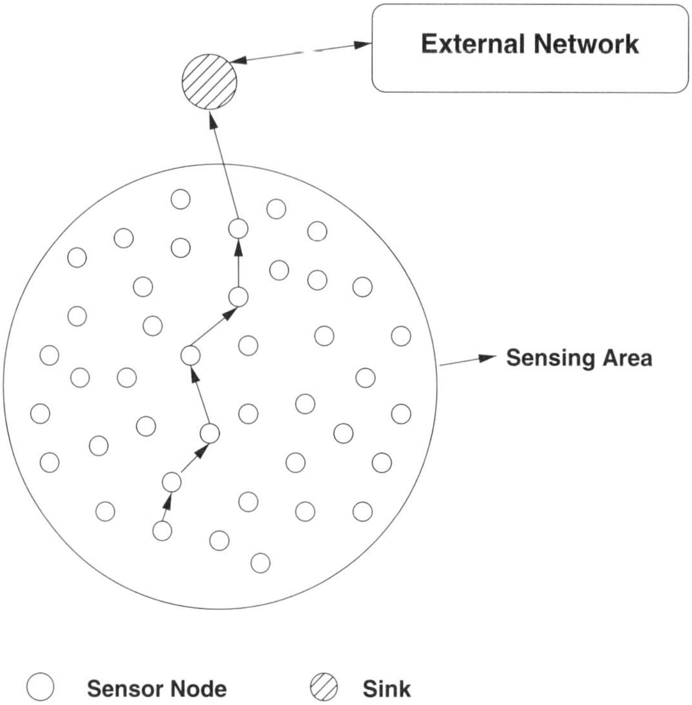

Fig. 15.1. An example sensor network.

Development of wireless sensor networks was originally inspired by defense applications. But applications in several domains have been studied over the past several years. Some of the common applications are: military target detection, classification and tracking for surveillance, for monitoring self forces, equipment and ammunition etc., nuclear, biological and chemical attack detection, structural health monitoring, flood warning and detection, water and air pollution monitoring, wildlife tracking, etc. As could be seen from some of these applications, the data that wireless sensor networks carry could be of very sensitive nature. Further, the sensor nodes can be situated in unattended locations leading to destruction by hostile action. Hence, security of data communications is very essential in wireless sensor networks. Due to the system constraints, providing secured communication in WSNs is a challenging task, as will be described later.[4–11]

15.2. Requirements and Challenges

This section presents an overview of the basics of network security requirements and specific challenges in sensor networks.

15.2.1. *Security requirements*

Network security is broadly defined as protection of confidentiality, integrity and availability of network assets and services from associated threats and vulnerabilities.

Confidentiality is required to ensure that sensitive information is well protected and not revealed to unauthorized persons. Maintaining confidentiality is much more difficult in wireless sensor networks because the information traveling between the sensor nodes or between the sensor node and the base station is communicated in a wireless mode. So, any adversary having the appropriate equipment may eavesdrop on the communication. By eavesdropping, the adversary could overhear the critical information that is sensed and the routing information. Based on the sensitivity of the data stolen, the damage could be severe.

In some cases, the sensor nodes could be compromised because they are in an unattended area. Compromised nodes are a big threat to confidentiality since the adversary could steal critical data stored on the nodes such as cryptographic keys that are used to encrypt information or contents of memory or the information collected.

Authentication techniques verify the identity of the participants in the communication, distinguishing legitimate users from intruders. In the case of sensor networks, it is essential for each sensor node and base station to have the ability to verify that the data received was actually sent by a trusted sender and not by an adversary.

When the information is transmitted from one node to another node or node to the base station, there is a danger that the information could be altered by an adversary in between. Thus, the integrity of the data is very important. Integrity controls must be implemented to ensure that information will not be altered in any way.

Another related issue is that of *freshness*. One of the common attacks in networks is the message replay attack, where an adversary may capture messages exchanged between nodes and replay them later to cause confusion to network. The data freshness objective ensures that messages are fresh, meaning that they obey message ordering and have not been reused. To achieve freshness, the network protocols must be designed in a way to identify duplicate packets and discard them.

Another key requirement is that of *Availability*. The network should be robust and tolerate various attacks and node failures so that it continues to be functional despite compromised and failed nodes.

Secure localization is also an important requirement in WSNs. Since the information flow in WSN is data centric rather than address centric, the nodes should be able to determine their locations in order to support accurate monitoring and tracking applications.[12] The locationing system should be robust and secure so that inaccurate location information is not used to make network decisions. Similarly, secure time synchronization mechanisms are needed to ensure that the network nodes maintain accurate time information that other networking and security mechanisms will depend upon.[13]

15.2.2. *Challenges in sensor networks*

The sensor nodes' resource constraints pose a major obstacle to the implementation of the traditional computer security techniques in a wireless sensor network. The unreliable communication channel and unattended operation make the security defences even harder. Further more, due to inherent unattended feature of wireless sensor networks, the physical attacks to sensors play an important role in the operation of wireless sensor networks.

The important aspects of WSN are categorized into four major categories,[14] as explained below.

A WSN has many constraints compared to a traditional computer network. Due to these constraints, it is difficult to directly deploy the existing security approaches to the area of WSN. Therefore, to develop useful security mechanisms while borrowing the ideas from the current security techniques, it is necessary to know and understand these constraints first.

All security implementations require certain amount of resources including processing power, memory, energy etc. The processing power available in the current generation sensor nodes is quite limited. For instance, the Crossbow TelosB mote's processor clock frequency (as of October 2008) is 4 MHz. Hence, implementing high end security encryption and decryption mechanisms is difficult and time consuming. A sensor node is also typically equipped with a small amount of memory and storage space (e.g., 1 MB of Flash RAM for data storage and 128 KB of RAM in Crossbow MICAz mote). In order to build an effective security mechanism, it is thus necessary to limit the code size of the security algorithm.

Energy is the biggest constraint to wireless sensor capabilities; current generation sensor nodes are often equipped with two AA batteries. We assume that once the sensor nodes are deployed in a sensor network, they cannot be easily replaced (high operating cost) or recharged (high cost of manual replacement, especially in remote terrain). Therefore, the battery charge taken to the field must be conserved to extend the life of the individual sensor node and entire sensor network. The impact that security has on the life span of the sensor (i.e., its battery life) needs to be carefully studied. The extra power consumed by sensor nodes due to the security is related to the processing power required for security functions. (e.g., encryption, decryption, signing the data and verifying signatures), energy required to transmit the security related data or overhead (initialization vectors needed for encryption/decryption), the energy required to store security parameters in a secured manner (encryption key storage).

Unreliable communication is another deterrent to sensor security. The security of the network relies heavily on the defined protocol, which in turn depends on the communication. Normally, the packet based routing of the sensor network is connectionless and thus inherently unreliable. Packets may get damaged due to channel errors or dropped at highly congested nodes. The result is lost or missing packets. Further more the unreliable wireless communication channel also results in damaged packets. Higher channel error rate also forces software developer to devote resources to error handling. Even if the channel is reliable, the communication may still be unreliable due to the broadcast nature of WSN and the possible transmission collisions.

The multi hop routing, network congestion and in-node processing can lead to greater latency in the network, thus making it difficult to achieve synchronization among sensor nodes. The synchronization issues can be critical to sensor security where security mechanism relies on critical event reports and cryptographic key distribution.

Depending on the function of the WSN, the sensor nodes may be left unattended for long period of time. It may result in exposure to Physical Attacks, node compromises, malfunctioning and other issues. Remote Management of Sensor Networks makes it virtually impossible to detect physical tampering and physical maintenance issues. Perhaps the most extreme example for this is a sensor node used for remote reconnaissance missions behind enemy lines. In such a case, the node may not have any physical contact with friendly forces once deployed.

Wireless sensor networks are often designed as distributed networks without a central management point. However, if designed incorrectly, the network organization can become difficult, inefficient and fragile, and thus vulnerable to security attacks.

This section summarized the challenges and obstacles involved in implementing security mechanisms in WSNs. Security can be achieved in WSNs using two different approaches. In the proactive or preventive approach, confidentiality, integrity and authentication is provided using the standard cryptography techniques of encryption, signatures, and hash functions. In the reactive approach, possible attacks on the system are studied and defense mechansims are developed to protect against such attacks.

In the following sections, we will first describe research done on the proactive approaches; and then describe research done on reactive approaches.

15.3. Symmetric Encryption Techniques

One of the proactive measures implemented for satisfying security requirements and protecting the wireless sensor networks from attacks is encryption. Wireless sensor networks are unique in this aspect due to the constraints imposed in terms of low processing power, memory and energy. In WSNs, symmetric encryption mechanisms have been used predominantly due to their lower cost, compared to asymmetric mechanisms. The advantage of Symmetric Ciphers is their simplicity and the ease of efficient implementations using hardware modules. Hardware for symmetric encryption schemes supporting Counter (CTR), Cipher Block Chaining (CBC), and CBC-MAC modes are commonly used in variety of applications. However, in recent work, it has been shown that it is also possible to effectively use asymmetric encryption techniques, such as those based on Elliptic Curve Cryptography (ECC), in WSNs.[15,16]

We will discuss issues related to symmetric encryption in this section. One important aspect of using symmetric encryption in wireless sensor networks is key management. Key Management issues are not unique to wireless sensor networks. They have been studied even in the wired networks. Normally, key establishment is done using one of the many public key protocols such as the Diffie-Hellman Public key protocol.

Most of the popular Internet related security techniques are unsuitable in low power wireless sensor networks, because they use asymmetric cryptography also called public key cryptography. In this case, two keys which are mathematically related are maintained. One of them is called public key which is made public and the other key is called private key which is known to the owner only. Data is encrypted with the public key and decrypted with the corresponding private key. The problem with the asymmetric encryption in a wireless sensor network is the computation overhead put on the individual nodes in the sensor network. Thus symmetric encryption has been often the choice for applications that can not afford the computational complexity of asymmetric encryption. Symmetric key encryption schemes use a single shared key for both encrypting and decrypting data. Some common examples of symmetric cryptography are Data Encryption Standard (DES), 3DES, AES and RC5.

One major handicap of symmetric encryption is the key exchange problem. The communicating hosts need to know the shared key before they communicate securely. Distributing a shared key securely to communicating hosts is an important issue as pre-distributing the key between the communicating hosts is not always feasible.

In the next section, a summary of some of the seminal works in key management in sensor networks is presented.

15.3.1. *Key management for symmetric encryption*

Key management refers to operations including generation of keys, secure transmission of keys, generation of transport key (session key) and revocation of compromised keys. Most of the key management implementation works in phases. Key pre-distribution phase is done while deployment. A transport key (session key) generation phase is used to create an agreed session key for each transmission session.

This is to improve security by preventing cryptanalysis of captured ciphers. If there are multiple hops between source node and destination then path key establishment phase is used to protect the transmission path. Based on deployment structure, the key distribution mechanisms can be classified as pairwise, group based and hierarchical.

The various pre-distribution based key management techniques developed for wireless sensor networks can be classified into two types: probabilistic and deterministic schemes.

- **Probabilistic schemes:** In this scheme, a set of keys are pre-distributed to each sensor node with the assumption that any given pair of nodes will share a common key with a certain (presumably high) probability. The desired probability to achieve a given network connectivity can be determined from system parameters such as network size, memory capacity of sensor node, etc. The various schemes in this category[17–22] focus mainly on the different ways to set up shared keys (also called pairwise keys) between sensor nodes.
- **Deterministic schemes:** In this scheme, there are typically no offline steps such as key pre-distribution. The only keys that might be pre-distributed are the individual keys that each sensor shares with the base station. Other keys such as pairwise keys shared between nodes or group keys are established after deployment. The different schemes that fall under this category include.[23–26]

15.3.2. *Probabilistic schemes*

This section describes in the detail some of the various probabilistic schemes proposed for key management in WSNs. In this discussion, let n denote the number of nodes in the network.

15.3.2.1. *Basic key pre-distribution scheme*

This scheme[17] is based on probabilistic key sharing among the nodes of a random graph. Each sensor node is allocated a *key ring* before it is deployed, where the key ring consists of keys randomly drawn from a large pool of keys. The basic idea is that a given sensor node will share a common key with other sensor nodes with some probability. This scheme requires storage of fewer keys ($\ll n$) as compared to key sharing between every pair of nodes ($n - 1$), where n is the number of nodes in the network, but has similar security properties. The details of the scheme are as follows:

Key distribution: This refers to the manner in which keys are pre-distributed, shared keys are discovered and then established as cryptographic keys for encryption. Key distribution consists of three phases:

- Key pre-distribution: Initially a large pool of keys is generated along with identifiers for each key. The pool (denoted as P) contains 2^{17} to 2^{20} keys. From the

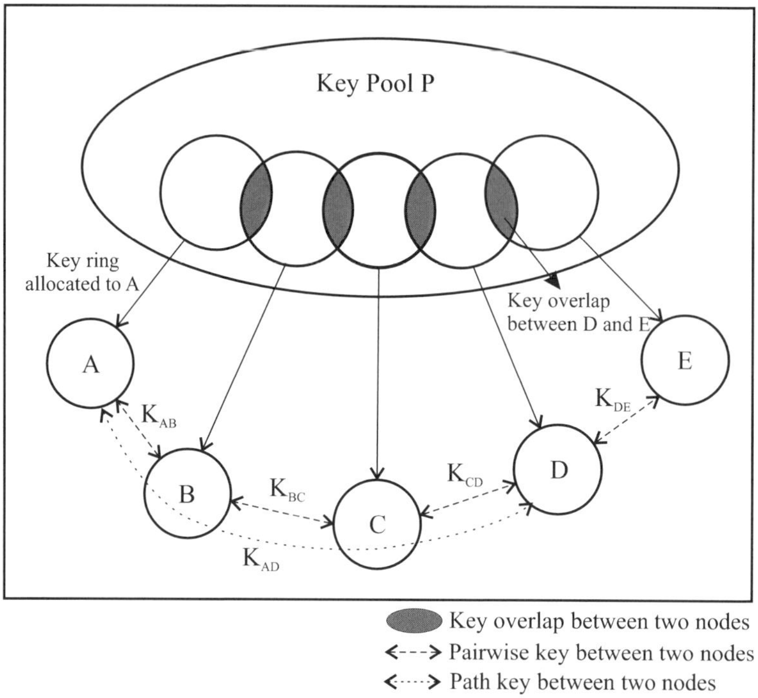

Fig. 15.2. Key distribution in the basic probabilistic key pre-distribution scheme.

key pool P, m keys are randomly drawn without replacement and assigned to a sensor node, forming its key ring. Figure 15.2 shows the allocation of key rings to sensor nodes, where the shaded part represents the overlap between key rings allocated to any two sensor nodes. This step is repeated for all the nodes to be deployed. The key ring is loaded into the memory of each sensor. For each sensor node, its identifier and the key identifiers of its associated key ring are stored on a trusted node, called the **controller**.

- Shared-key discovery: This phase occurs at the time of sensor network initialization. Each node discovers the nodes with which it shares a common key by broadcasting the list of key identifiers in its key ring and then establishing the common key as a pairwise key. This phase establishes the sensor network and its topology since a link exists between two sensor nodes only if they share a common key.
- Path-key establishment: As keys are randomly selected, a shared key may not exist between a pair of nodes after the shared-key discovery phase. However, if there exist other nodes through which a multi-hop path exists between the pair of nodes, then a key can be established between this node-pair. Such a key is called a *path key*. Referring to Fig. 15.2, node A can establish a path-key with node D since there exists a multi-hop path between A and D through nodes B and C.

Revocation: Whenever a sensor node is compromised by an adversary, the entire key ring allocated to that node must be revoked. Due to random drawing of keys from the pool, the keys that must be revoked would also be present in key rings allocated to other sensor nodes. Thus, it is necessary to remove the keys from the entire network and not just the key ring of compromised sensor. In order to achieve this, the controller broadcasts a revocation message containing a list of the identifiers of keys to be revoked. This revocation may lead to removal of certain links in the sensor network, and the shared-key discovery and path-key establishment protocols may have to be re-executed.

Re-keying: This is performed to replace the expired keys and is achieved by the sensor node by running the revocation algorithm explained above for its own key ring.

Since the topology of the sensor network depends on the existence of links between sensor nodes after execution of the shared-key discovery and the path-key establishment protocols, it is critical to select appropriate values for the key pool P and the key ring m such that the sensor network is connected. Random-graph theory can be used to derive values for the expected degree d of a node and probability p such that a link exists between two nodes. The limited memory of a sensor node also places a upper bound on the size m of key ring stored on each node. On the other hand, a small value of m would disconnect the sensor network. Similarly, a multi-link path key may be established between pair of nodes even if they are in wireless range of each other. Hence appropriate values of parameters such as pool size P, key ring size m, degree d and probability p must be chosen to ensure that the scheme works as desired.

15.3.2.2. *q-composite random key pre-distribution scheme*

The basic key pre-distribution scheme has been extended using multiple key matching in Ref. 19. This scheme proposes that two sensor nodes should share at least q keys ($q > 1$) from their respective key rings instead of just a single key, as in the basic scheme. The motivation behind sharing of q keys is that any adversary needs to break all of them in order to compromise a link between the nodes. As the amount of key overlap (q) increases, the network becomes more resilient against node capture. However to facilitate key overlap, size of the key pool has to be reduced drastically. Thus by compromising a single node, the adversary can obtain a large sample of the key pool as compared to the basic scheme. This tradeoff makes it necessary to find the optimal amount of key overlap, which ensures that an adversary cannot break links between non-compromised nodes. Additionally, the compromise of a single node should not provide the adversary with enough knowledge about the key pool. Critical design parameters are size of the key pool P, the value of q given the probability p of two nodes sharing q keys and the number of keys m that could be stored on a sensor node.

15.3.2.3. *Multi-path key reinforcement scheme*

This scheme proposed in Ref. 19 can be used to secure an established link between two sensor nodes by re-establishing the link key through multiple paths. The basic idea is that after a link key has been established between two sensor nodes after the key setup phase, that key will be updated by the co-ordination of other nodes over multiple disjoint paths between the two nodes. A sensor node u that wants to update its link key with another node v has to know all the disjoint paths between itself and v. Node u then generates random values for each disjoint path, and routes them to node v. After v receives all the random values, both u and v can combine the initial link key and the random values in some manner to come up with an updated link key. (The simplest way to combine all values is to perform bit-wise exclusive or.)

The advantage of the scheme is that an adversary cannot break the updated link key unless it is able to successfully eavesdrop all the disjoint paths between the two nodes, which is harder than eavesdropping the only link between two sensor nodes. However, finding multiple disjoint paths between two nodes is expensive in terms of communication overhead and it is suggested to limit the scheme to paths of not more than 2 hops. With increased network overhead, the scheme can be used with the basic key pre-distribution scheme to provide sufficient security of the link keys.

15.3.2.4. *Random pairwise keys scheme*

The most ideal pairwise key pre-distribution scheme is the one in which each node shares a key with all other nodes in the network. Clearly, this scheme is infeasible due to the large storage overhead of keys per sensor node. However, it is often unnecessary to store all $n-1$ keys on each sensor node. If the network is modeled as a random graph then a value for the probability p for which the graph is connected can be expressed in terms of the number of nodes n and the storage size of keys m on the sensor node. Thus each node needs to store only np pairwise keys in order to ensure a connected sensor network as compared to $n-1$ keys in the ideal pairwise scheme. This scheme, called random pairwise keys scheme, is proposed in Ref. 19. Each sensor node, having key storage capacity of m, is pre-loaded with np pairwise keys in its key ring (i.e., $m = np$). After deployment, neighboring nodes search for each other's IDs in their key rings and establish pairwise keys.

The random pairwise scheme is perfectly resilient against node capture because all the keys in the network are unique. Thus, compromise of any sensor node does not reveal any information about link keys between other non-compromised nodes. Additionally node-to-node authentication can be achieved if each sensor node stores the ID of the sensor node along with the key it shares with that node. This is because the key is unique and no other node in the network can have the same key. This scheme can be extended for multiple hops.

15.3.2.5. *Node ID based indexing scheme*

Another variant of the basic key pre-distribution scheme has been proposed in Ref. 21. In this scheme, a pseudo-random generator is used to generate indexes of the keys that will be assigned to a sensor node. The generator is initialized with a seed that depends on the sensor node (such as its ID) and is thus publicly known. Therefore, knowledge of a sensor node's ID allows computation of indexes of the keys to be assigned to that node. Thus, by exchanging lists of key indexes, two sensor nodes can discover shared keys and subsequently establish a pairwise key to secure the channel between them. This leads to an efficient shared-key discovery protocol. Only the key indexes are revealed, no information about the actual keys is revealed. Finally, the use of pseudo-random key assignment also provides the desirable property of implicit node to node authentication. A disadvantage is that it involves additional storage overhead of the index of each key along with the actual keys.

15.3.2.6. *PIKE scheme*

In Ref. 22, sensor nodes are used as trusted intermediaries to set up the shared keys–this scheme is called PIKE: Peer Intermediaries for Key Establishment. In this approach, the network node IDs are represented in the form (x, y), where $x, y \in \{0, 1, 2, \ldots, \sqrt(n) - 1\}$. Every node is pre-deployed with a total of $2\sqrt(n) - 1$ keys, with each key shared with exactly one node from the sets (i, y) $\forall i \in \{0, 1, 2, \ldots, \sqrt(n) - 1\}$ and (x, j) $\forall j \in \{0, 1, 2, \ldots, \sqrt(n) - 1\}$. The idea is that any two nodes A and B can find a node that shares pairwise keys with A and B. Mechanisms for locating such intermediaries based on different heuristics is presented in Ref. 22.

15.3.2.7. *Polynomial-based key pre-distribution*

A general framework for pairwise key pre-distribution in sensor networks which is based on the polynomial-based key pre-distribution protocol is presented in Ref. 20. A bivariate t-degree polynomial $f(x, y)$ over F_q (q is a large prime number) has the property that $f(x, y) = f(y, x)$. If two sensor nodes u and v wish to establish a common key $f(u, v)$, node u computes $f(u, v)$ by evaluating $f(u, y)$ at point v and node v computes key $f(v, u)$ by evaluating $f(v, y)$ at point u. Thus from the property of bivariate polynomials, $f(u, v) = f(v, u)$ and the two sensor nodes can establish a pairwise key.

The general framework consists of a pool of bivariate t-degree polynomials. In order to establish pairwise keys, two nodes should have polynomial shares on the same bivariate polynomial. Two instantiations of this framework are:

Random subset assignment: In this scheme, polynomials are randomly chosen from a pool F of polynomials and their polynomial shares are assigned to the sensor nodes. This is similar to assigning a key ring to each sensor node in the basic key pre-distribution scheme. Subsequent to random assignment of the subset of polynomials to the sensor nodes, polynomial shares are discovered using techniques similar to shared-key discovery. Additionally path-key establishment can be carried out to establish pairwise keys with other sensor nodes which do not have polynomial shares on the same polynomial. It has been shown that if no more than t shares on the same polynomial are disclosed, no pairwise keys constructed using this polynomial between any two non-compromised sensor nodes will be disclosed.

Grid-based key pre-distribution: This scheme works by creating a grid and assigning sensor nodes to intersection points of rows and columns in the grid. A grid of size $m \times m$ is constructed, where the number of sensor nodes in network can be at most m^2. A set of $2m$ polynomials $\{f_i^c(x,y), f_i^r(x,y)\}_{i=0,\ldots,m-1}$ is also constructed, where c and r stand for column and row respectively. Thus, each row i is associated with $f_i^r(x,y)$ where $i = 0$ to $m-1$ and similarly each column j is associated with $f_j^c(x,y)$ where $j = 0$ to $m-1$. Each sensor node is assigned to a unique intersection point (i,j) in the grid and allocated polynomial shares of $f_i^r(x,y)$ and $f_j^c(x,y)$. Depending on this information, each sensor node can perform share discovery and path discovery to establish pairwise keys. Each sensor node has two polynomial shares. Each bivariate polynomial (assigned to either the row or the column) is shared by m different sensor nodes. Thus, $2(m-1)$ pairwise keys can be established directly by each sensor node with other sensor nodes.

15.3.2.8. *Blom's mechanism based scheme*

In Ref. 18, a key distribution framework that is based on Blom's key pre-distribution scheme[27] is presented.

In Blom's scheme, a symmetric matrix $Kn \times n$ stores all pairwise keys of a group of n nodes. Element k_{ij} is the key of node i used to secure its connection with node j. K = (DG)TG, where $D_{(\lambda+1)\times(\lambda+1)}$ is a symmetric matrix and $G_{(\lambda+1)\times}n$ is called the public matrix. (DG)T is also called secret matrix. Each node i stores the ith row of secret matrix and the ith column of public matrix G. After deployment, each pair of nodes i and j can individually compute a pairwise key by exchanging their columns in plaintext because the key is the dot product of their own row and the column of the other's. Their rows are always kept secret.

The basic Blom's scheme requires nodes to store $\lambda + 1$ keys, where $\lambda \ll n$, the number of nodes. It guarantees that any two nodes can always generate a pairwise key. Communication security between two non-compromised nodes is guaranteed as long as the number of compromised nodes is less than or equal to λ. The work presented in Ref. 18 extends this concept to multiple (ω) key spaces and requiring each node to store λ keys for some $\tau, 2 \leq \tau < \omega$ key spaces. This scheme ensures that two nodes can obtain a pairwise key with a high probability. The scheme can be extended by using multiple-hop paths to allow two nodes that do not directly share a key to securely communicate with each other.

15.3.3. *Deterministic schemes*

This section describes in detail the various deterministic schemes proposed for key management in WSNs.

15.3.3.1. *Secure pebblenets*

A scheme based on a global key called Traffic Encryption Key (TEK) is presented for sensor networks termed as pebblenets.[23] A pebblenet is defined as a large ad-hoc network of pebbles (i.e., sensors) which are resource constrained and of limited size. Each pebble is equipped with a group identity key, which allows it to be a part of the network and participate in key management. The pebbles are assumed to be tamper resistant, so node capture by an adversary does not reveal the group identity key.

The TEK is shared by all the nodes and is periodically refreshed. TEK generation and distribution requires selection of a key manager to perform these tasks. The paper presents techniques to select a key manager from among all the sensors in a dynamic and distributed manner. The protocol consists of two phases. In the first phase, a secure cluster-head selection protocol is executed so that the network is partitioned into clusters, consisting of a cluster-head and ordinary nodes. The method used for formation of clusters and selection of cluster-head is based on a weighted policy, where each pebble has a weight depending on parameters like mobility, remaining battery power, etc. Nodes with the highest weight among each group of nodes (i.e., the cluster) become cluster-heads. Cluster-heads subsequently organize themselves into a backbone. In the second phase, a subset of cluster-heads is selected, from which a new key manager is elected for the next round of TEK generation and distribution. The new TEK is generated and broadcast to all the cluster-heads which subsequently send it to the remaining nodes in their cluster. The frequency of TEK re-keying (i.e., generation and distribution) depends on the level of security desired in the network.

Thus, the secure pebblenets scheme is based on using a single, deterministic global key that is periodically changed.

15.3.3.2. *Localized encryption and authentication protocol (LEAP)*

LEAP[24] is a key management protocol for sensor networks that classifies communication in a sensor network into different types and establishes keys to secure each type of communication. The protocol is designed to support optimization of in-network processing and restrict the security impact of node compromise only to the neighbors of the compromised node. Instead of the single-key model described above, four types of keys are established: an individual key shared with the base station, a pairwise key shared with another sensor node, a cluster key shared with multiple neighboring nodes and a group key which is shared by all the nodes in the network. The motivation for this protocol is that different keying mechanisms are needed to secure different types of communication. For example, the key used to secure communication between the base station and an individual sensor should be different from the key used to secure communication between a pair of sensors and the key used to encrypt broadcast messages.

The individual key shared between each sensor node and the base station is pre-loaded into the node before deployment. After the initial deployment, sensors discover their immediate neighboring sensors and establish pairwise keys with them. It involves the exchange of master secrets derived from each others' node identifiers. Referring to Fig. 15.3, node V computes its pairwise key with node W as $K_{VW} = f_{K_W}(V)$, where f is a pseudo-random function. The key K_W is a master key which is derived as $K_W = f_{K_I}(W)$, where K_I is an initial key loaded into each node. A critical assumption is that this process of key establishment is completed within a certain time limit, which is less than the time taken by an adversary to compromise a sensor node.

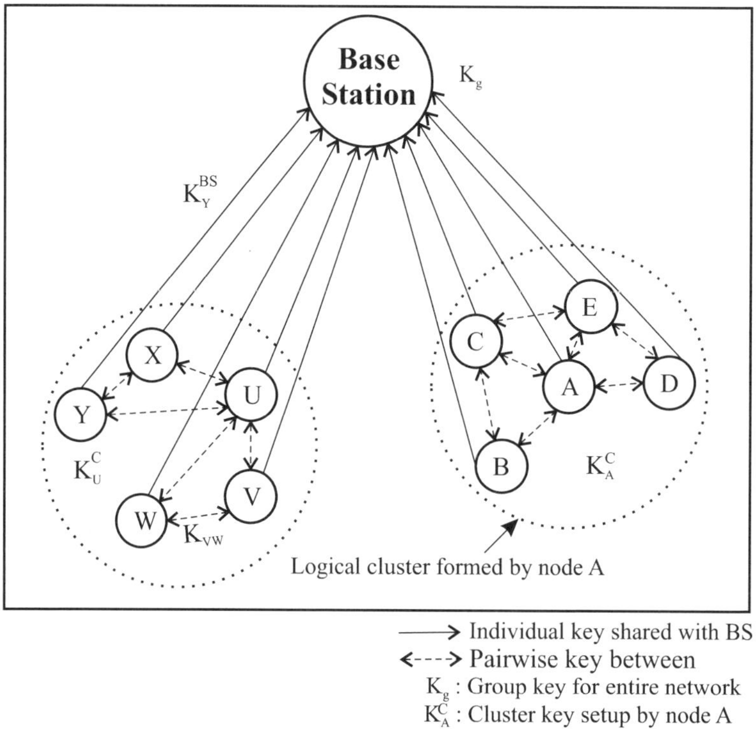

Fig. 15.3. The LEAP deterministic key management scheme.

The motivation behind establishment of the cluster keys is that it will enable in-network processing techniques like data aggregation and passive participation. This is possible when the messages are encrypted using a locally shared key so that neighboring nodes are able to decrypt the messages so as to enable data aggregation (e.g., MAX operation) or passive participation (detect neighboring malfunctioning or compromised nodes). In order to establish a cluster key between neighboring sensor nodes, a node A generates a random key K_A^C, encrypts it with the pairwise key it shares with each of its neighbors and transmits the encrypted random key to each neighbor. Each node can then decrypt and establish the random key as a cluster key. Figure 15.3 shows the cluster key formed by node A. Finally, the group key is distributed in a hop-by-hop fashion. The base station sends the new group key to its neighbors by encrypting it with the cluster key it shares with them. Each neighbor in turn decrypts the group key and encrypts it with cluster key it shares with its neighbors. This process continues recursively until all the nodes receive the new group key. One limitation of this method of group key distribution is that it involves substantial overhead in key encryption and decryption at each hop.

15.3.3.3. *KeEs*

The KeEs protocol presented in Ref. 25 provides key management to achieve confidentiality and group-level authentication in order to protect the WSN against passive adversaries. For this scheme to work, the sensor nodes are assumed to be tamper resistant as in pebblenets. The scheme consists of two phases: key generation and key synchronization. The decision to trigger key generation and key synchronization is based on two approaches: centralized, where the base station invokes the command to generate and update the session key; and distributed, where a system parameter μ controls the time-out for key generation and synchronization.

Key Generation: Each sensor node is deployed with two random seeds. In this phase, each sensor node autonomously generates the session key through a unique combination of the initial random seeds. The session key is similar to a network-wide key known only to the uncompromised sensor nodes in the network. This session key is used by all the nodes for encryption and authentication. The trigger to generate the session key is given by a base station in the centralized approach. The distributed approach assumes that each sensor node's local clock is loosely synchronized with the clocks of other sensor nodes since it is not always possible to achieve an exact time synchronization between the WSN nodes. The session key is re-keyed (or re-generated) after μ clock ticks.

Key Synchronization: In the centralized approach, each sensor node receives a re-key command from the base station instructing it to update the session key. Thus, each sensor node performs re-keying in a unique manner and a new session key is established. In the distributed approach, each sensor node generates new session key according to its local time-out. Apart from the time-out parameter, other factors to be considered are the difference δ between clocks of any two sensor nodes and the maximum communication time Δ required for the transmission and reception of a message. Thus, a mathematical expression can be derived from μ, δ and Δ which gives the number of session keys each sensor node should store in order to decrypt any incoming message.

The advantage of the distributed approach for key synchronization is that there is very little communication overhead since each node generates and updates its session key autonomously without communicating with other sensors. The KeEs protocol provides forward secrecy, i.e., subsequent keys cannot be recovered by an adversary having old session keys and backward secrecy, i.e., previous session keys cannot be recovered by the adversary from the current key.

15.3.3.4. *EYES security architecture 1 (ESA1)*

A key management architecture called EYES Security Architecture 1 (ESA1) has been proposed in Ref. 26 for the *EYES* research project on sensor networks.[28] The sensor network is organized as a collection of clusters which are of two types: supervised and unsupervised. Each supervised cluster has a designated supervisor node. The supervisor nodes are assumed to be tamper resistant and more resource rich than other sensors. The unsupervised cluster only consists of ordinary sensor nodes. Due to the heterogeneous nature of the nodes, two security realms are possible:

- *Supervised realm*: This is the supervised cluster consisting of the supervisor node and the sensor nodes. This realm supports node-to-node communication using intra-supervised cluster keying and inter-supervised cluster keying for ensuring confidentiality and authentication.
- *Unsupervised realm*: This only consists of unsupervised nodes and supports group communication within a single unsupervised cluster using intra-unsupervised cluster keying.

Communication between unsupervised and supervised realm is realized through unsupervised-to-supervised cluster keying.

Key Deployment: In supervised clusters, the supervisor node is equipped with the keys of all the supervised nodes in the cluster. Thus each node shares its private key with only the supervisor node. There is also a backup cluster key known by all the nodes used in the event of supervisor failure. To be part of a supervised cluster, a node has to share its private key with the supervisor and possess the cluster key. In the unsupervised cluster, every node shares the same cluster key. There are no supervisors present to ensure confidentiality and authentication. To be part of an unsupervised cluster, a node only needs to possess the cluster key.

Key refreshment: In order to maintain the freshness of keys used for encryptions, the keys need to be refreshed. The decision to re-key is triggered when the number of encrypted messages with a particular key reaches a specified threshold.

Key establishment: As the network is divided into clusters, different types of keying mechanisms exist for establishing keys within a single cluster and within multiple clusters.

- *Intra-Supervised cluster keying*: This mechanism is used to establish a session key between two sensor nodes belonging to the same cluster with the help of the supervisor node. A node A, that wants to establish a session key with another node B, first authenticates itself with the supervisor S by sending a nonce for freshness and a MAC of nonce concatenated with node B's ID. After round of message transfers between S, A and B, the session key K_{AB} is established between nodes A and B.
- *Inter-Supervised cluster keying*: This mechanism is used to establish a session key between two sensor nodes belonging to different supervised clusters. Both the supervisor nodes play a role in key establishment.
- *Intra-Unsupervised cluster keying*: In the unsupervised clusters, all the nodes directly use the cluster key to derive the session and MAC keys.
- *Unsupervised-to-Supervised cluster keying*: A complicated situation arises when a node in an unsupervised cluster wants to establish a key with a supervised node in a supervised cluster. An idea of visitor certificates is employed where the unsupervised node has to submit its visitor certificate to the supervisor of a supervised node.

15.3.4. *Recent research on key management*

This section presents recent research on key management in sensor networks. A comprehensive survey may also be found in Ref. 29.

15.3.4.1. *SLIMCAST [Secure Level Key Infrastructure for Multicast and Group Communication]*

SLIMCAST uses geographic routing with cluster based key management.[30] A multicast tree is formed for communication between member nodes. This tree will consist of actively participating nodes as well as forwarding nodes which are included to ensure connectivity. Each level in the tree will consist of a parent node with all participating and forwarding child nodes (that is within one hop). A level key is established only between participating nodes (and not forwarding nodes). Thus, key updates needed due to joining/leaving action of a new node will be handled within that level.

The protocol provides support for localized joining, secure data multicasting, in-network processing and data aggregation (for both 1 → N and N → 1 aggregation), secure on demand joining/leaving and periodic joining.

The major overhead in SLIMCAST is the encryption required per hop, which is higher compared to traditional aggregation protocols such as Star and Logical Key Hierarchy protocol (LKH). The level based structure enables better adaptation to node compromises since only level nodes are updated. The protocol is scalable allowing dynamic addition of large number of nodes with low update costs.

15.3.4.2. *Robust algorithm for group key management*

The algorithm presented in Ref. 31 extends the basic Blom's scheme for group key management. Based on the assumption that deployment knowledge is available, the algorithm partitions the sensor field into grids. The recommended grid structure is hexagonal because it approximates the circle better. A group is created with n nodes where $n = \frac{N}{t}$, where t is the total number of groups and N is the total sensors deployed. The center of the grid is taken as the deployment point. The communication can be viewed as either inter- or intra-group. Each group is named by the relative position in the deployment plane starting from $(1, 1)$ for upper left grid.

Every group is preloaded with a common matrix G and a private matrix A. Any two nodes in same group compute their shared key by selecting a row from G and column from A. One more private matrix used in this scheme is matrix B which is same size that of A. The B matrix for a group is generated by selecting a set of groups, called basic groups, and assigning distinct B matrices to each. For non-basic groups, the B matrix is obtained from neighboring basic groups. By carefully choosing the assignment scheme, it can ensure that neighboring groups always share a common matrix.

Every pair of neighboring nodes exchanges their group index, the indices of the B matrix from which they picked the rows and their column of G. If two neighboring nodes i and j have the same group index, they compute the pairwise key individually from their respective row of matrix A and the column of matrix G received from the other. If they share several B matrices, they can select one of the shared matrices and compute pairwise keys from the row of matrix B and column of G received from the other. If this is not possible, nodes i and j use multi hop communication to transmit messages.

15.3.4.3. *Clustering based keys*

An algorithm based on clustered deployment and consisting of two type of keys, Inter- and Intra-Cluster keys, is presented in Ref. 32. The former keys are used to secure communication between two or more groups and the latter keys are used for secure communication within each group. The system uses dynamic key management scheme for eliminating storage of too many keys and for better security. The hierarchy consists of three levels: level 1 consist of group of nodes; level 2 consist of cluster heads (CH) for each group and level 3 consist of Head of Cluster Heads (HCH). A unique ID is given to each node, each cluster head and each group of clusters. The ID generation for individual nodes is done by the cluster head, while the ID generation for cluster heads and the clusters is done by the HCH. Figure 15.4 illustrates the basic cluster organization.

Thus, secure group communication (SGC) system is used in this case. There are many different cryptographic protocols proposed for achieving SGC. One of them is the Tree based Group Diffie-Hellman problem (TGDH).[33] It extends the Diffie-Hellman concepts to compute a group key, by dynamically forming a tree of group elements. Diffie-Hellman key exchange works on the idea that the Computational Diffie-Hellman (CDH) problem is hard. That is, given a group $\boldsymbol{G}$, element g uniform in $\boldsymbol{G}$ and x, y uniform in $\boldsymbol{Z}_p$, the CDH problem states that it is hard to compute g^{xy} given (g, g^x, g^y).

Figure 15.5 presents an example tree structure to illustrate the principle of TGDH. TGDH is based on the Discrete Logarithmic Problem (DLP). Each leaf node i generates a random number a_i that is set equal to $K_i = a_i$ which is the private share of that node; and a blind key $BK_i = g^{K_i} \mod p$ where g and p are public parameters. The leaf node broadcasts this value to all its members. A non-leaf node x which has leaf nodes i and j calculates its private key share as $K_x = g^{BK_i BK_j} \mod p$. The public key share of the non-leaf node is computed as $BK_x = g^{K_x} \mod p$. This BK value is then broadcast to the members. This step continues till the root node computes and broadcasts its value. The value computed by the root node will be treated as the key for the entire group.

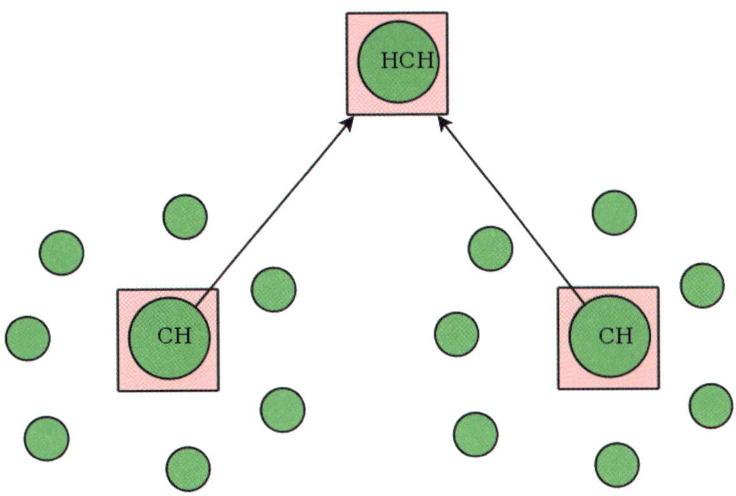

Fig. 15.4. Clustering based key management.

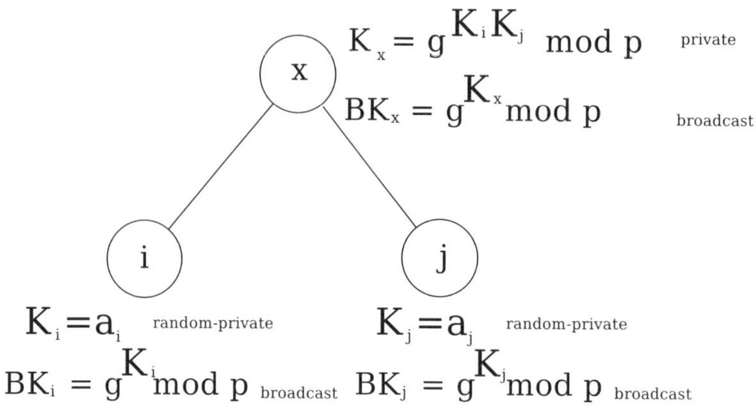

Fig. 15.5. Tree based Group Diffie-Hellman (TGDH) exchange.

Thus, the multi-party Diffie-Hellman problem with TGDH is used to compute the group key. Pre-deployed symmetric key systems are used to broadcast the partial keys from each nodes.

The energy overhead of group key computation is much lower compared to that of the SPIN protocol. The routing algorithms tested are directed diffusion and AODV, that are available in TinyOS. The optimum number of partial keys is shown to be 15 for 25 node groups, where each group has 50 nodes.

15.3.4.4. *SHELL*

In Ref. 34, a hierarchical and distributed approach for key management called SHELL is presented. The methodology used is Exclusion Based System (EBS) for re-keying in large networks and provides collusion resistance. An EBS is defined as a collection Γ of subsets of the set of members. An EBS Γ of dimension $(N; k; m)$ represents a situation in a secure group where there are N members numbered 1 through N, and where a key server holds a distinct key for each subset in Γ. Each subset of Γ corresponds to a key; the elements of a subset $A \in \Gamma$ are the nodes that have that key. Furthermore, for each $t \in [1, N]$, there are m elements in Γ whose union is $[1, N] - \{t\}$. From this, it follows that the key server can evict any member t, rekey, and let all remaining members know the replacement keys for the k keys they are entitled to know. This is done by multicasting m messages encrypted by the keys corresponding to the m elements in Γ whose union is $[1, N] - \{t\}$. Each new key is encrypted by its predecessor in order to limit decipherability only to the appropriate members.

In SHELL, the individual nodes report to a cluster head that is also called a gateway. The next level in the hierarchy has command nodes that communicate with gateways. The nodes are classified as sensing nodes that sense events and as relaying nodes that relay the data from a sensing node to the gateway using multi-hop transmission. The normal nodes use short-haul (short range) communication to transmit data to the gateway nodes; and gateways use long-haul transmission to reach the command node.

Each sensor node has a preloaded discovery key K_{sg}, a one-way hash function to recompute K_{sg}, and two preloaded keys (Ks_{ch} and Ks_{key}) for initial key distribution. The protocol assumes that a node can store $\boldsymbol{K}$ administrative keys and $\boldsymbol{c}$ communication keys. Each *gateway* can communicate with at least two other gateways. Every gateway forms an EBS matrix and generates communication key for its own cluster. It generates the administrative keys for other clusters, refreshes *data keys* after setting up the network and detects compromised nodes. The *command node* keeps track of the key pool of valid keys and IDs over an area. It authenticates the gateway and sensor nodes. It also periodically initiates key renewal for communication between gateways and for communication in each cluster.

This protocol is shown to be highly scalable because of the low overhead of EBS, even with increasing number of nodes. Further, collusions can be prevented with pre-deployment knowledge.

15.3.4.5. *LDK algorithm*

A Location Dependent Key Management (LDK) algorithm is presented in Ref. 35 The nodes are classified as normal nodes and as anchor nodes, the latter considered as *tamper proof.* All nodes use a common hash algorithm. Some of the nodes are assumed to have capability to communicate in different power levels. Each node is assumed to be within the maximum transmission range of an anchor node. With these assumptions, LDK allows nodes to be added dynamically. In the pre-deployment phase, a common key is loaded in each node along with R keys out of total P keys, where R $\leq$ P. In the initiation phase, the anchor nodes transmit a *beacon* at each power level. The beacon message consists of a nonce encrypted using the key $\boldsymbol{K}$ and the authentication code. Each normal node receives more than one beacon message. The nodes decrypt this message, retrieve the key updates and calculate the *derived key ring.* The number of keys in the derived key ring equals the number of beacons times the size of original key ring. Then, the R keys in original key ring along with common key $\boldsymbol{K}$ are deleted. In the communication phase, sensor nodes setup secure links among themselves. A pair of neighboring sensor nodes set up a secure link using a key obtained by hashing all the common keys if the number of common keys in the derived ring is greater than a threshold. Figure 15.6 explains the concept using three beacon nodes.

The advantage of LDK is that it supports dynamic node addition. For a set of 200 AN and 500 motes, the number of optimal power levels of anchor nodes is shown to be two; with a threshold value of 3. In this scheme, the transmission range of AN

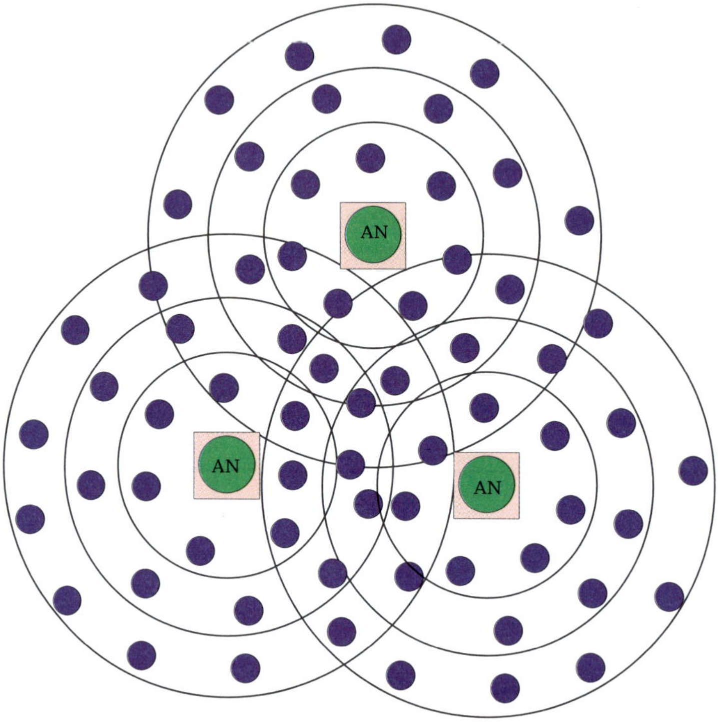

Fig. 15.6. Location dependent key management that uses a set of beacon nodes to transmit partial key information.

nodes should be much larger than that of motes for reducing key compromise due to node capture.

15.4. Public Key Cryptography in Sensor Networks

In recent years, there has been work on the application of public key cryptography (PKC) to wireless sensor networks. Initially, PKC was considered to be very expensive for implementation given the resource limitations of sensor nodes. However, recent research based on Elliptic Curve Cryptography (ECC)[16,36] is providing crucial evidence to support the claim that ECC can be used in WSNs.

15.4.1. *Elliptic curve cryptography*

Elliptic Curve Cryptography (ECC) was originally conceived in 1980s and hence since been developed over the past two decades.[37] ECC is based on the theory of elliptic curves over finite fields. The computational difficulty of Elliptic curve cryptographic schemes is similar to the discrete logarithm schemes used in modular arithmetic. The main advantage of ECC is that it offers considerably greater security for a given key size. For example, the equivalent key size of RSA is 1024 bits for an ECC key size of 163 bits for a given level of security. If the key size is smaller, faster cryptographic operations are possible. The security and practicality of a given asymmetric cryptosystem relies upon the difference in difficulty between performing a given cryptography operation and its inverse. The difference in difficulty between the forward and the inverse operation in a given system is a function of the key length used. Now that the processing power available to attack the cryptosystem is higher, longer key lengths are required. However, the processing power required for forward operation is much lesser than that is required for the reverse operation. Thus, Elliptic Curve Cryptography (ECC) offers better computing advantages over the other asymmetric cryptosystems such as RSA.

In Ref. 38, a hybrid key establishment scheme that makes use of the difference in computational and energy constraints between the sensor node and the base station is presented. In this scheme, the major cryptographic burden is on the base station where the resources are greater. On the sensor node side, symmetric key operations are used in place of their asymmetric algorithms. The sensor and the base station authenticate using elliptic curve cryptography.

Some of the early work on implementing ECC on sensor class devices has been presented in Ref. 36. The implementation was done on Atmel Atmega128 (8 MHz) chipset and Chipcon CC1010 (14 MHz) chipset, for 160, 192 and 224 bit keys. A number of optimizations were done, including Pseudo-Mersenne primes with an exponent size of $e = 2^{16} + 1$. The ECC implementation was compared to RSA (RSA-1024 and RSA-2048) implementations optimized using Chinese Reminder Theorem, Montgomery multiplication and Optimized Squaring. A hybrid multiplication method was introduced that was used by both ECC and RSA algorithms.

Subsequently, an experiments analysis of energy consumed for ECC systems was reported in Ref. 16. The experiments were done using a system with a Chipcon CC1000 wireless transceiver and Atmel Atmega128L controller (4 MHz). Programming was done in nesC and C languages, along with assembly code to implement RSA and standardized ECC over finite fields ($GF(p)$). For data rate of 12.4 Kbps, the energy spent to transmit and receive one byte was 59.2 μJ and 28.6 μJ respectively. The energy for random number generation was not considered in this calculation.

The main assumption is that the network was administrated by single organization, which reduces many parameters in negotiation phase in a Public Key Infrastructure (PKI) system. An abbreviated X.509 certificate containing only unique device id, public key and signature were used. This reduced the size of traditional RSA 1024-bit certificates from 700 bytes to 262 bytes and ECC-160 from 530 to 86 bytes approximately. The packet sizes were 41 bytes out of which the header was 9 bytes.

The main results from this analysis are summarized next. For ECDSA the energy is estimated by measuring energy for elliptic curve point multiplication and integer inversion. Very small amount of energy is spent for hashing, integer addition and multiplication. One RSA-1024 sign operation takes 5132 bytes whereas ECDSA-160 takes only 385 bytes. The key generation in RSA is also time consuming because of operations on large primes.

The typical results for signing and verification using RSA-1024 was 304 mJ and 11.9 mJ respectively. For RSA-2048, the corresponding values were 2302.7 mJ and 53.7 mJ. For key exchange using RSA-1024, the client and server operations respectively consumed 15.4 mJ and 304 mJ. For RSA-2048, the corresponding values were 57.2 mJ for the client and 2302.7 for the server.

For ECDSA-160, the system consumed 22.82 mJ for signing and 45.09 mJ for verification, while key exchange consumed 22.3 mJ by the client and server. This is because computation involves only random number generation and calculation of corresponding public key using ECDH. Similar values for ECDSA-224 were 61.54 mJ for signing, 121.98 mJ for verification, and 60.4 mJ for key exchange. The total energy for RSA/ECC will be sum of energy spent for computation and communication costs. For RSA-1024, this was 397.7 mJ for client and 390.3 mJ for the server, whereas for ECC-160 this was 93.7 and 93.9 respectively for the client and server, approximately 75% lower than of RSA.

Further, the time and memory consumed for ECC was much lower than that of RSA. ECC-160 multiplication takes 1.61 seconds consuming 282 bytes of data memory whereas RSA-1024 private key modular exponentiation takes nearly 22 seconds consuming 930 bytes of data memory.

The above results were fundamental in showing that ECC based cryptography is indeed suitable for motes than RSA, given that no other optimization is used in RSA. More details can be found in Ref. 36.

15.4.2. *Cryptographic reductions*

In order to support ECC in Wireless Sensor Networks, there are several needed cryptographic reductions. Some of these are summarized below.

Barret and Montgomery Reductions. Barret and Montgomery reductions are methods to replace division operations that are more complex to calculate with less expensive operations.

Barret reduction finds $z \mod p$ for given positive integers z and p. The quotient z/p is estimated using less expensive operations involving powers of a suitably chosen base b. A modulus-dependent quantity b^{2k}/p must be calculated, making the algorithm suitable for the case that many reductions are performed with single modulus.

Montgomery operations are similar to Barret reduction, but used to calculate modular exponentiation. It is not efficient for single multiplication.

Projective coordinate system. A standard model of a projective plane, consisting of the classes $X = [x] = [x1, x2, x3]$ of points of R modulo non-zero multiplicative constants. A system of projective coordinates results from a projective base, which is a system of four points of the plane $\{A, B, C, D\}$ represented by corresponding vectors $\{[a], [b], [c], [d]\}$ of R3, such that:

(1) $\{a, b, c\}$ build a basis of R3 and
(2) $d = a + b + c$

The projective base defines a projective coordinate system in which we write $X = u[a] + v[b] + w[c]$, where $\{u, v, w\}$ is defined modulo a non-zero multiplicative constant, and resulting from the corresponding representation of $[x] = X$, through the basis vectors: $x = ua + vb + wc$. We write this as: $X = uA + vB + wC$. $\{u, v, w\}$ are the projective coordinates of X with respect to the system $\{A, B, C, D\}$. In particular, points $\{A, B, C, D\}$ have the respective coordinates $\{(1, 0, 0), (0, 1, 0), (0, 0, 1), (1, 1, 1)\}$. $\{A, B, C\}$ are often called the basis points of the projective coordinate system. D is called the coordinator of the system.

Non Adjunctive Form (NAF). A Non Adjunctive Form of a positive integer k is an expression $k = \sum_i k_i 2^i$; where $k_i \in \{0, +/-1\}$, $k_{l-1} \neq 0$ and no two consecutive digits k_i are nonzero. The length of NAF is l.

15.5. Practical Cryptosystem Implementations in WSNs

Implementations of cryptographic mechanisms are available for the TinyOS platform,[39] the most widely used OS in current generation motes.

TinySec, a part of the TinyOS distribution, is a link layer security library supporting symmetric cryptography.[5] The package provides facilities for message authentication and encryption. TinySec-AE provides authentication and encryption, while TinySec-Auth provides only authentication. RC5 and Skipjack are the underlying block ciphers used in TinySec which work in CBC-MAC mode for providing authentication and encryption. When compiling applications, the user needs to specify TINYSEC = true for enabling the encryption library.

The HIGHT scheme,[40] designed for lightweight 8-bit computing devices, has been added to TinySec and supports 64-bit block length and 128-bit key length.[41] A comparison of the three schemes is listed in Table 15.1.

Table 15.1. Table comparing Skipjack, RC5 and HIGHT.

Algorithm	Key Size (bits)	Block Size (bits)	Rounds
Skipjack	0-2040	32/64/128	0-255
RC5	80	64	32
HIGHT	128	64	32

Table 15.2. Comparison of reductions in public key cryptosystems implemented in TinyOS.

Algorithm	Reductions Used	Key Size (bits)
TinyECC	Barret, Hybrid Multiplication, Hybrid Squaring, Projective Coordinates, Shamir's trick for Signature verification, Pseudo Mersenne Primes for curve specific optimization	128, 160, 192
ECC Wang and Li	Projective Coordinate System for curve point operations, Non Adjunctive Forms and Sliding window, Pseudo Mersenne Primes	160
RSA Wang and Li	Montgomery reductions, Chinese Reminder Theorem	1024

Regarding public key cryptosystems, ECC and RSA have been ported to TinyOS with suitable reductions to support low power operation. Table 15.2 summarizes the reductions used and performance gain for three such implementations.[42,43]

A related comprehensive survey of cryptographic implementations for sensor networks may be found in Ref. 44.

15.6. WSN Attacks and Threats

The above sections described techniques to protect data using mechanisms providing confidentiality, integrity and related security goals. However, as in wired networks, weaknesses and vulnerabilities exist in the network despite the best available cryptosystems. Such weaknesses are often the target of malicious users to launch attacks on the system. In this section, we first describe the types of attackers and then the different types of attacks.[45]

As in any network security scenario, the attacker can be either *an outsider or insider* using *passive, active or both* attacks. An outsider has to use brute force or other methods to get more information about the network. The insider has more knowledge about the network, its architecture, protocols used. In passive attacks, the adversary only monitor the packets without tampering or dropping the packets. In active attacks, the adversary may drop or tamper packets, or may not follow the designed protocols. Attackers can also be classified as *Mote class* or *Laptop class*. In the mote class attacker model, the adversary uses nodes similar to sensor nodes deployed, whereas the latter class attacker uses far more powerful devices with significantly higher computing and energy resources.

We next describe the different type of attacks that are possible in a WSN. Since Sensor Networks are used for sensitive and important applications, denial of service (DoS) attacks can be expected and counter measures need to be planned in the network design. A Denial of Service attack is defined as any event that reduces or prevents a system to perform its intended function. This is usually done by exploiting the software vulnerabilities, resource exhaustion, etc. Sensor Networks designed to work in harsh environments should be designed to continue functioning even in the presence of failures, due to such DoS attacks. The system should be designed to be robust such that it can prevent some classes of DoS attacks. Fault tolerance may mitigate even node subversions and efficient protocols will prevent adversaries' efforts to waste resources.

At the physical node level, *Physical Tampering* of sensor nodes is a highly potent form of attack. An adversary can physically tamper the nodes, interrogate them, compromise them or destroy them. It is impractical to control the access to thousands of nodes spread over a region of kilometers. When the nodes are compromised the adversary can replace a sensor, change the hardware or steal the sensitive information like cryptographic keys to gain better access to higher levels of communication. One defence is to design the sensor nodes such that their physical packaging is tamper proof. The nodes can also be designed to react to tampering in fail safe manner, i.e., the node can erase the cryptographic keys or the entire memory when the adversary is trying to tamper the node. Other traditional defenses could be hiding the nodes or camouflaging them behind some other objects. In most systems, however, the base stations and gateways nodes are assumed to be trusted. If a base station is compromised, it is assumed that entire network data is compromised.

At the networking level, each layer of the network architecture is vulnerable to different types of DoS attacks and has different solutions for its defense.[46] There are some attacks which cut across multiple layers or exploit interactions between them.

15.6.1. *Physical layer*

Sensor networks mostly use wireless communications for transmission and reception. Some of the common physical layer attacks are described below.

Jamming is a well known attack in wireless communications. It is the process of an adversary transmitting data at the same time on the same radio frequency which the network nodes are using. An adversary can disrupt the entire network with a very small number of randomly distributed jamming nodes. For single frequency networks, this attack is simple and effective.

The affected node can identify jamming from the failure of its neighbors by sensing the presence of constant carrier energy and a lack of response. Constant jamming completely impedes communication, where as sporadic jamming can cause intermittent disruption. The standard defense against jamming is to use spread spectrum communications. Spread spectrum uses two techniques: Frequency hopping and direct sequence spread spectrum. If the system uses frequency hopping, the jammer also has to follow the precise hopping sequence or jam a wide section of the band. Direct sequence technique is commonly used in mobile phone networks. Both these techniques require greater abilities and have design complexities.

If the attacker continuously jams the entire network, it results in a denial of service attack. The sensor nodes should be able to overcome this problem. One way is to switch to a lower duty cycle and conserve as much energy as possible. Periodically, the nodes can verify and check whether jamming has ended and if so transmit the data and if not go back to sleep mode. If the jamming is intermittent, the nodes can prioritize their traffic and send the important information to the base station. Nodes should cooperate to send that type of prioritized traffic.

In a large scale deployment, the attacker is less likely to succeed in jamming the entire network. In such a scenario, the nodes surrounding the affected region can cooperatively map and report the DoS attack boundary to the base station and reroute the traffic along this boundary to the base station. To the surrounding nodes, the region appears to suffer complete or intermittent failure.

15.6.2. *MAC/Link layer*

The adversary can launch attacks at the MAC/link layers through collision, exhaustion, unfairness, etc.

Since the wireless sensor nodes work in broadcast mode, the attacker can create a collision in one octet of transmission to corrupt the entire packet transmitted. A corrupted ACK control message could initiate exponential backoff in some MAC protocols. The amount of energy the attacker needs to induce collision is very small. To verify and correct variable levels of corruption in message, error correcting codes are used. However, the malicious nodes can corrupt more data than the network can correct. Also, these error correcting codes would be a overhead in the form of processing and communication. The network can identify the malicious collisions through collision detection, but no complete solution exists. A malicious node can also intentionally and repeatedly deny access to the channel by spending very little energy, similar to jamming attacks.

An adversary can also exhaust the energy of the sensor nodes by creating conditions of repeated retransmissions by triggering an unusually late collision. A self sacrificing node could exploit the interactive nature of the MAC layer protocols in an interrogation attack. The node could repeatedly send a Request-To-Send (RTS) packet expecting the targeted node to send a Clear-To Send (CTS) response. Such continuous transmission would eventually exhaust the energy resources of both sides. To overcome this problem, rate limiting could be one solution in which the network ignores requests in excess of predefined number.

Intermittent application of these attacks or abusing a cooperative MAC layer priority scheme will eventually lead to a form of denial of service called unfairness. This attack may not completely prevent legitimate access but cause degradation of service. This may affect the real time users to miss their target deadlines. One solution against this threat is to use small frames so that an individual node can acquire the channel only for a short time. However, this approach may contribute to increased overheads.

15.6.3. *Network and routing layer*

In large scale deployments of sensor network, messages get transmitted over many hops before reaching their destination. So, most of the sensor nodes act as routers for through traffic. This adds to the vulnerabilities that may be experienced in network layer.

Most of the attacks against sensor nodes in the network layer fall in one of these categories:

Spoofed, altered or replayed routing information: In this attack, the routing information exchanged between the nodes is targeted. By spoofing, altering or replaying the routing information, the attackers will be able to create routing loops, attract or repel network traffic, extend or shorten source routes, generate false error messages, segment the network, increase the latency.

Black hole attack: In multi hop wireless sensor networks, the sensor nodes act as routers to relay messages from their children to their parents and eventually to a base station. In the black hole attack, the attacker drops all the packets coming from their children nodes. In order to remain unnoticed, the attacker node keeps sending self generated packets only. Thus the adversary node may look normal to their parent. The administrator will not be able to make out the cause for some sensor nodes not responding. The administrator may even think that the nodes have failed or there is no path for these nodes to the base station.

As shown in Fig. 15.7, the adversary node n3 does not forward any messages from its children nodes n4 and n5 to the parent node n1. In order to remain unnoticed adversary node generates messages and transmits its self generated messages to parent node n1.

Sink hole attack: The effect of black hole attack is limited by the number of children nodes. The sink hole attack is an advanced version of the black hole attack in which the attacker tries to attract more neighbors by advertising wrong routing

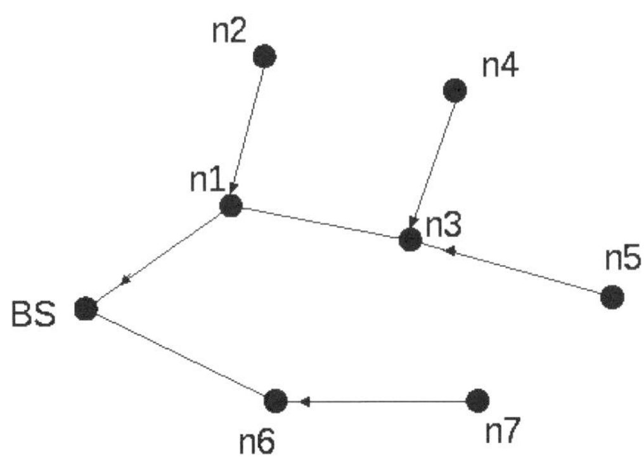

Fig. 15.7. An example to illustrate the black hole attack.

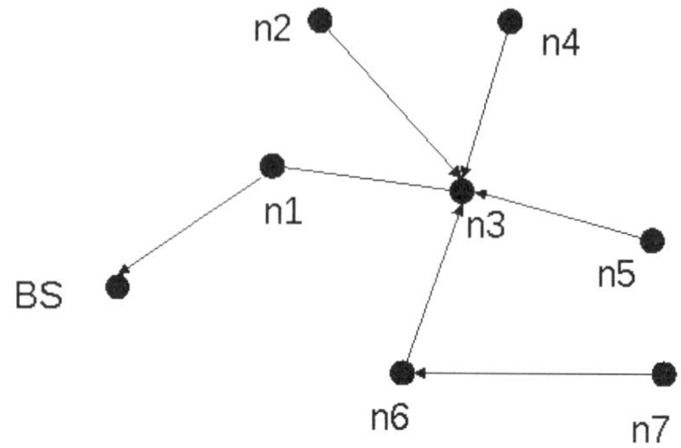

Fig. 15.8. An example to illustrate the sink hole attack.

information. This includes its (pretended) ability to transmit the data to the base station in lesser number of hops. This makes the attacker capable of affecting a large number of nodes.

As illustrated in Fig. 15.8, the node n3 is the adversary node which advertises one hop count route to the base station. As a result, the nodes n6 and n2 try to route their data through n3. Now, the distance from the affected nodes to the base station has increased and node n3 may drop the packets from some of the nodes causing a denial of service attack.

Selective forwarding attack: Multi hop networks are based on the assumption that every node which receives the packets faithfully forwards them to the base station.

The selective forwarding attack is cleverer than the previous two attacks. In this attack, the attacker selectively drops some packets. The selection of dropped packets is based on some predefined criterion such as source address, contents or completely random, to avoid detection.

As shown in Fig. 15.9, the attacker node n3 forwards all packets except the ones it receives from n5. As a result, the attacker causes denial of service attack on node

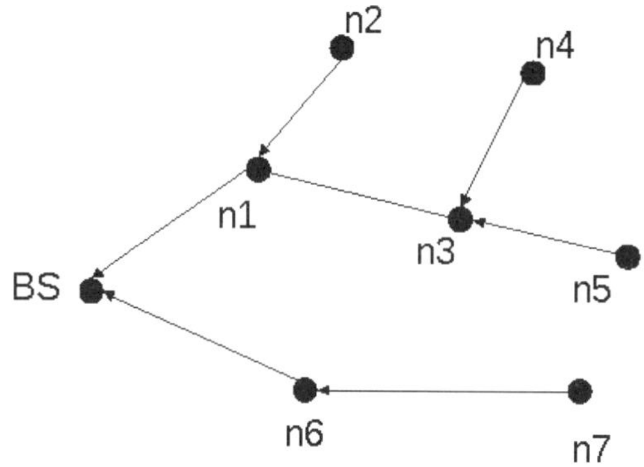

Fig. 15.9. An example to illustrate the selective forwarding attack.

n5, while remaining normal for other children nodes such as n4. The administrator will think that node n5 is faulty and hence not sending any packets.

Misdirection attack: In the sensor networks, it is assumed that every node forwards the packets to the base station (or sink) along the shortest path. In this misdirection attack, the adversary routes the packets from its neighbors to other distant nodes instead of forwarding along the shortest path. The main objective of the adversary is to increase the latency or preventing some packets from reaching the base station. To remain unnoticed, the attacker keeps sending its own messages to its legitimate forwarding node. This type of attack is more damaging in densely deployed networks.

As shown in Fig. 15.10, the adversary node n5 does not forward the packets to its legitimate forwarding node n4; instead, it sends them to distant nodes n12 or n13. In this attack, the attacker can cause a route loop that causes its children to change their path and select another node as their parent. For example, if node n5 routes packets of node n6 to n12 or n13, it results in a route loop. Thus in this situation, the node n6 has to change its parent from n5 to n4 to avoid infinite loops. This sort of attacks are very difficult for the nodes to detect.

Sybil attack: In this attack, a malicious node in the sensor network impersonates other nodes or claims false identities.[47] In the worst case, the adversary generates an arbitrary number of additional node identities, using only one physical node. The Sybil node can get its identity in two ways. It can create a new identity for itself or take the identity from a legitimate node. The malicious node's additional identities are known as Sybil nodes. Sybil attack is performed by the Sybil nodes by communicating directly with the legitimate nodes. When a legitimate node sends a radio message to Sybil node, one of the malicious identities listens to the message. Similarly, the messages sent from Sybil nodes to the legitimate nodes are actually sent from one of the malicious devices. In the indirect communication mode, the

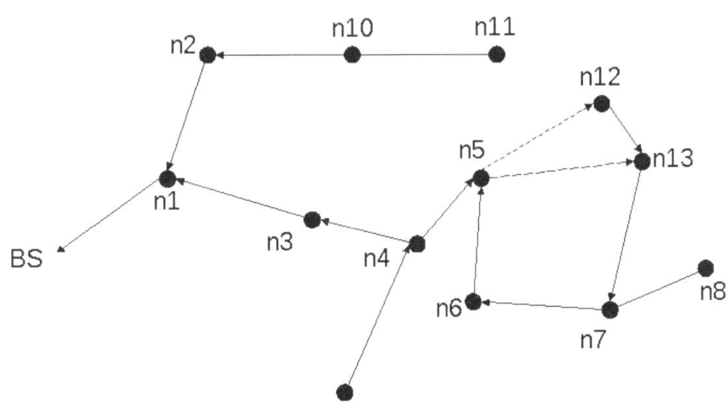

Fig. 15.10. An example to illustrate the misdirection attack.

legitimate nodes will not be able to communicate directly with the Sybil nodes. Instead, the messages are routed through some malicious devices.

In some cases, the adversary can create a serious attack by trying to have all his Sybil identities communicate in the network at the same time. In some other cases, the adversary may present large number of identities over a period of time, while acting as a smaller number of identities at any given instant of time.

In the known attacks, Sybil attacks can defeat replication and fragmentation mechanisms in peer to peer storage systems. The same problem can exist in distributed storage in wireless sensor networks. If the sensor network is designed to replicate or fragment data across several nodes, it may be actually storing data in Sybil identities generated by the same adversary node.

The Sybil attacks can also seriously affect routing algorithms in sensor networks. One weak mechanism is multi-path routing where routes looking like disjoint could in fact go through a single adversary node presenting multiple Sybil identities. Another vulnerable mechanism is geographic routing, i.e., a routing principle that relies on geographic position information. In wireless sensor networks, one node sends a message to the geographic location of the destination instead of using the network address. For this, the node can determine its own location and the source is aware of the location of the destination. When geographic routing is used, a Sybil node, by virtue of having more than one set of coordinates, could appear to be present in more than one place at once.

Sybil attacks also affect data aggregation, voting, fair resource allocation, misbehavior detection protocols. Efficient query protocols compute aggregates of sensor readings with in the network and transmit the aggregated value to conserve the energy. In the Sybil attack, the malicious node may contribute many readings, resulting in an erroneous data aggregate. Wireless Sensor networks use voting for a number of tasks to take a decision. The Sybil attack could contribute many votes through its malicious node resulting in a wrong decision. In the fair resource allocation, the network resources are allocated on a per node basis. The Sybil attack can be used to allow a malicious node to obtain an unfair share of the resources. In misbehavior detection, the wireless sensor network can be designed to detect a particular type of misbehavior. It is likely that such behavior detector has some false positives. Hence, it may not take any action until it observes repeated offenses by the same node. In Sybil attack, the malicious node will indicate different nodes to be misbehaving differently thus going undetected.

The defense against Sybil attack is to validate the identity of each node. This can be done in two ways: Direct validation in which a node directly tests whether another node is valid; Indirect validation in which the nodes that have been already verified are permitted to validate other nodes.

Radio resource testing is one of the approaches being used for direct validation. This approach relies on the assumption that any physical node has only one radio. It is also assumed that radio is incapable of simultaneously sending or receiving on more than one channel. For example, consider that a node wants to verify that none of its neighbors are Sybil nodes. It can assign each of its neighbors a different channel to broadcast some message on. Then, it can randomly choose a channel on which to listen. If the neighbor that was assigned that channel is legitimate, it should hear the message. By repeating the test sufficient number of times, the Sybil nodes can be identified with high probability.

Another way to prevent Sybil attacks is to perform identity registration. There is a difference between peer to peer networks and wireless sensor networks in that in wireless sensor networks there could be a trusted central authority managing the network, thereby knowing the deployed nodes. The central authority will also be able to disseminate that information securely to the network. To identify the Sybil attacks, a node can poll the network and compare the results to the registered deployment. To avoid the Sybil attack, any node can check the list of known good identities to validate another node as legitimate.

Random key pre distribution is another technique that can be used to defend against the Sybil attack. Other defenses include registration, position verification and code attestation.

Position verification techniques can also be used. In this case, it is assumed that the sensor network is immobile once deployed. In this method, the network verifies the physical position of each node. Sybil nodes can be detected using this approach because they will appear to be at the same position as the adversary node that generates them.

Remote code attestation is another technique that is used to defend against Sybil attack. The basic principle is to use the fact that the code running on malicious node will be different from that on a legitimate node. Therefore, by verifying the memory content of the node, it could be ascertained whether it is a legitimate node or a malicious node.

Worm hole Attack: In a worm hole attack, an attacker connects two distant points in the network using a low latency link. The link is normally established through long range wireless communications. Once the worm hole link is established, the adversary convinces the nodes who are normally multiple hops away from a base station that they are only one or two hops away from the base station through the worm hole. This will lead to a sink hole, as the adversary on the other side of the worm hole link can artificially provide a lower hop route to the base station. This will create a situation where all the traffic in the surrounding area will be drawn through the worm hole. This will always be true when the end point of the worm hole link is relatively far from a base station. The current solutions for worm hole attacks are limited in large sensor networks.

HELLO flood attack: In sensor networks, many protocols require nodes to broadcast HELLO packets to announce themselves to their neighbors and the node that has received such a packet will assume that it is within normal range of the sender.

A laptop class attacker broadcasting routing information with high transmission power could make the nodes believe that the attacker is its neighbor. An adversary advertising a very high quality route to the base station to every node in the network could cause a large number of nodes to attempt to use this route. But these nodes which are far away from the adversary will be sending packets to nowhere. The network will be left in a state of confusion. An adversary does not necessarily need to construct legitimate traffic in order to use the HELLO flood attack. It can simply rebroadcast overhead packets with sufficiently large radio power to be received by every node in the network. HELLO floods can also be treated as one way broadcast worm holes.

Acknowledgment spoofing attack: If the protocol uses link layer acknowledgments, they can be forged. This results in adversary creating an impression that a disabled node is alive or a weak link appear to be strong.

In summary, there are several types of attacks possible in sensor networks. At present, only some of these attacks can be handled in a satisfactory manner. There have been several proposals that identify vulnerabilities and some heuristices approach to handle these, a survey of which is available in Refs. 7, 8 and 11 An exhaustive description of all these approaches is beyond the scope of this chapter.

15.7. Other Issues

This section highlights other related issues in WSN security, such as secure aggregation and intrusion detection systems.

15.7.1. *Secure aggregation*

A important security related challenge with regard to data gathering in sensor networks is that of secure aggregation. In a wireless sensor network, each sensor node collects/senses data and transmits it to the base station via the intermediate nodes. To reduce the amount of data being transmitted, the data is aggregated at some nodes. If one of the intermediate nodes is compromised, the node can modify, forge or even discard the messages. It can even transmit false aggregation values. The encryption process can also interfere with aggregation. If we encrypt messages with a unique key that is shared only between that node and the base station, it poses a problem for the intermediate nodes, as it needs to understand and process the received data to perform aggregation. One solution could be having the same key on every device to enable encryption. But any adversary who acquires the key from a single node would then take control of the whole sensor network.

In Ref. 48, a light weight security mechanism is designed to effectively find out any anomalous behavior such as modifying the message, dropping the message or transmitting false aggregated value. It is based on the concept of delayed aggregation and delayed authentication. In the delayed aggregation, instead of aggregating messages at the very next hop, node messages are transmitted unchanged to the next node and then aggregated. This will increase transmission costs but guarantees the integrity of data assuming that two consecutive nodes are not compromised. In the delayed authentication scheme, instead of trying to authenticate messages right away, they are authenticated after a time delay. This requires the authentic keys to be symmetric keys and they are conveyed to the authenticator nodes after a time delay.

There has been a fair amount of work on secure aggregation in recent years. Some of the related work on secure aggregation in sensor networks is available in Refs. 49 to 52.

15.7.2. *Intrusion detection systems for WSNs*

Intrusion Detection Systems (IDS), as the name implies, are systems that detect any intrusions into the network by an attacker. Intrusion Detection Systems are well studied and developed for wired networks. But these systems are mainly designed for perimeter security. These systems cannot be mapped directly to wireless sensor networks. This is mainly due to the resource constraints posed by wireless sensor networks. Also wired networks are more organized networks in the sense that the complete data traveling in the network can be made available for monitoring at a point.

Traditionally Intrusion Detection Systems are developed around two concepts, viz., Anomaly based Intrusion Detection (AID) and Misuse based Intrusion Detection (MID). Anomaly based Intrusion Detection is primarily based on the assumption that intruders demonstrate abnormal patterns of behavior when compared to that of legitimate nodes and detect the intrusion based on this unusual behavior. This is done first by developing a profile of behavior of the network in normal conditions. The intrusion detection system is then evaluated against this profile to detect any intrusions. The advantage of this system is that the normal behavior can be accurately characterized, then this method would detect any previously unknown attacks. This is particularly advantageous in the wireless sensor networks where it is difficult to define the signature. But the disadvantage with this system is that it is susceptible for false positives.

In Misuse Intrusion Detection Systems, the system maintains a database of intrusion signatures. This is similar to the intrusion detection systems implemented in wired networks. By constantly comparing the system activity against these signatures, any intrusion by the adversary in to the network can be detected. The advantages of this technique are that it is less prone to false positives and requires less computational power of the sensor node. But the disadvantage is that only known attacks can be detected and any new attack can not be found. Also, generating the signature database is difficult.

Intrusion Detection Systems have been classified into two types, viz, Host based and network based. In the host based intrusion detection system, the intrusions are detected based on the OS audit trails, system call audit trails, logs etc. In the network based intrusion detection system, the intrusions are found completely on the packets that have been captured from the network.

Since WSNs can be used in many important applications like defense, health etc., the security of the data being transmitted is very important. Also the timeliness or correctness of the data being transmitted to the base station from the sensor nodes is equally important for the person concerned to take timely and correct decision. Hence, the wireless sensor networks shall be secured to ensure that packets are not obstructed by any adversary. But because of the various constraints posed by Wireless Sensor Networks, security is not a trivial issue and intrusions do take place. In Ref. 53, an Intrusion Tolerant Routing Protocol for Wireless Sensor Networks (INSENS) is presented. It has a characteristic that any single compromised mode can affect only a localized portion of the network and cannot affect the entire sensor network. The objective of intrusion tolerance for secure wireless sensor networks is to provide protection against two types of attacks, viz., denial of service attacks that flood data packets in the entire network and routing attacks that transmit wrong control packets containing false routing information within the network.

Intrusion tolerance can be designed to take advantage of the asymmetric architecture of the wireless sensor network. The base station acts as a gateway providing uplink between the wireless network and wired network. Base station also has more computing power, memory, bandwidth than the sensor nodes. INSENS routing system adheres to the following design principles. It places limitations on the type of communication to avoid denial of service type flooding attacks. The individual sensor nodes are not permitted to broadcast to the entire sensor network. Only the base station is permitted to broadcast to the other nodes in the network. Base station is authenticated via one way hashes, so that individual sensor nodes cannot spoof the base station and then flood the network. For unicast packets, the sensor node has to communicate through the base station which acts as a packet filter to prevent denial of service through a single node. INSENS is also designed to be resilient to distributed denial of service attacks. This is because multiple nodes will not be able to broadcast to the entire sensor network. Also, the control routing information has to be authenticated to avoid advertisement of the false routing data. Hence, the base station always receives correct partial knowledge of the topology. Although the base station may not receive the complete topology information, due to localized intrusions, the base station will be able to construct the picture of the network correctly. To take care of the resource constraints of the sensor nodes, symmetric key cryptography is chosen for confidentiality and authentication between base station and each of the sensor nodes. Base station is selected as the central point for computation and distribution of routing tables. Redundant multiple routing is built in to INSENS to achieve secure routing and avoid the problem of compromised nodes. The network paths are disjointly designed so that even if an intruder takes down a single node or path, other path exist to forward the message to the correct destination.

The overall design of INSENS is based on three principles: use of redundancy to tolerate intrusions without any need for detecting compromised nodes; all compute intensive operations are carried out in the base station and reducing the role of sensor nodes in building routing tables; the scope of the effects by intruders is reduced by limiting flooding and using relevant authentication schemes.

More recent work on this topic can be found in Refs. 54 to 57.

15.8. Conclusions

This chapter presented a survey of security in wireless sensor networks. The various system limitations and challenges, the types of security attacks, and security requirements were discussed. A survey of key management techniques for symmetric key encryption techniques was presented. The recent developments in public key encryption based WSN security mechanisms were also highlighted. The chapter concluded with an overview of practical implementations of security mechanisms in current generation devices (such as Crossbow Motes) and operating systems (such as TinyOS).

Acknowledgments

The authors are pleased to acknowledge the assistance and discussions with Shantanu Prasade and Sasikanth Avancha.

References

1. C. Raghavendra, K. Sivalingam and T. Znati, Eds., *Wireless Sensor Networks*, Springer Publishers, Boston, MA (2004).
2. H. Karl and A. Willig, *Protocols and Architectures for Wireless Sensor Networks*, John Wiley and Sons (2005).
3. A. Swami, Q. Zhao and Y.-W. Hong and L. Tong, *Wireless Sensor Networks: Signal Processing and Communications Perspectives*, John Wiley and Sons (2007).
4. S. Avancha, J. Undercoffer, A. Joshi and J. Pinkston, Security for wireless sensor networks, (eds.) C. S. Raghavendra, K. M. Sivalingam and T. Znati, *Wireless Sensor Networks*, Chapter 12, Kluwer Academic Publishers, Boston, MA (2004).
5. C. Karlof, N. Sastry and D. Wagner, TinySec: a link layer security architecture for wireless sensor networks, *Proceedings of the ACM International Conference on Embedded Networked Sensor Systems (SenSys)*, 162–175, New York, NY, USA (2004). ACM. ISBN 1-58113-879-2. doi: http://doi.acm.org/10.1145/1031495.1031515.
6. H. Chan and A. Perrig, Security and privacy in sensor networks, *IEEE Computer*, **36**(10), 103–105 (2003).

7. D. Djenouri, L. Khelladi and A. N. Badache, A survey of security issues in mobile ad hoc and sensor networks, *IEEE Communications Surveys and Tutorials*, **7**(4), 2–28 (2005), ISSN 1553-877X.
8. Y. Wang, G. Attebury and B. Ramamurthy, A survey of security issues in wireless sensor networks, *IEEE Communications Surveys and Tutorials*, **8**(2), 2–23 (2006), ISSN 1553-877X. doi: 10.1109/COMST.2006.315852.
9. Y. Xiao, *Security in Sensor Networks*, CRC Press (2006).
10. D. Liu and P. Ning, *Security for Wireless Sensor Networks*, Springer (2007).
11. Y. Zhou, Y. Fang and Y. Zhang, Securing wireless sensor networks: a survey, *IEEE Communications Surveys and Tutorials*, **10**(3), 6–28 (2008), ISSN 1553-877X. doi: 10.1109/COMST.2008.4625802.
12. K. Ravichandran and K. M. Sivalingam, Secure localization in sensor networks, In (ed.) Y. Xiao, *Security in Sensor Networks* **2006**, Chapter 12, CRC Press, 291–310.
13. R. Poovendran, C. Wang and S. Roy, *Secure Localization and Time Synchronization for Wireless Sensor and Ad Hoc Networks*, Springer (2006).
14. J. P. Walters, Z. Liang, W. Shi and V. Chaudhary, Wireless sensor network security: A survey, (ed.) Y. Xiao, *Security in Distributed, Grid, and Pervasive Computing*, chapter 17, CRC Press (2006).
15. B. Arazi, I. Elhanany, O. Arazi and H. Qi, Revisiting public-key cryptography for wireless sensor networks, *Computer*, **38**(11), 103–105 (2005), ISSN 0018-9162. doi: http://dx.doi.org/10.1109/MC.2005.388.
16. A. S. Wander, N. Gura, H. Eberle, V. Gupta and S. C. Shantz, Energy analysis of public-key cryptography for wireless sensor networks, *Proceedings of the Third IEEE International Conference on Pervasive Computing and Communications (PERCOM)*, 324–328, Washington, DC (2005), ISBN 0-7695-2299-8, doi: http://dx.doi.org/10.1109/PERCOM.2005.18.
17. L. Eschenauer and V. Gligor, A key-management scheme for distributed sensor networks, *ACM Conference on Computer and Communications Security*, 41–47, Washington, DC (2002).
18. W. Du, J. Deng, Y. S. Han, P. Varshney, J. Katz and A. Khalili, A pairwise key predistribution scheme for wireless sensor networks, *ACM Transactions on Information and System Security* (2005).
19. H. Chan, A. Perrig and D. Song. Random key predistribution schemes for sensor networks, *IEEE Symposium on Security and Privacy*, Oakland, CA (2003).
20. D. Liu and P. Ning, Establishing pairwise keys in distributed sensor networks, *Proc. of ACM Conference on Computer and Communications Security*, Washington, DC (2003).
21. R. D. Pietro, L. V. Mancini and A. Mei, Random key assignment for secure wireless sensor networks, *ACM Workshop on Security of Ad Hoc and Sensor Networks*, 62–71, Washington, DC (2003).
22. H. Chan and A. Perrig, PIKE: Peer intermediaries for key establishment in sensor networks, *Proc. IEEE INFOCOM*, Miami, FL (2005).
23. S. Basagni, K. Herrin, D. Bruschi and E. Rosti, Secure pebblenets, *Proc. ACM MobiHoc*, 156–163, Long Beach, CA (2001).
24. S. Zhu, S. Setia and S. Jajodia, LEAP: Efficient security mechanisms for large-scale distributed sensor networks, *Proc. of ACM Conference on Computer and Communications Security*, 62–72, Washington, DC (2003).
25. R. D. Pietro, L. V. Mancini and S. Jajodia, Providing secrecy in key management protocols for large wireless sensor networks, *Elsevier Ad Hoc Networks Journal* (2003).

26. Y. W. Law, R. Corin and P. H. H. S. Etalle, A formally verified decentralized key management architecture for wireless sensor networks, *Proc. of IFIP TC6/WG6.8 Conference on Personal Wireless Communications* (*PWC*), Venice, Italy (2003).
27. R. Blom, An optimal class of symmetric key generation systems, *Proc. EUROCRYPT '84*, 335–338, Paris, France (1984).
28. P. J. M. Havinga, S. Etalle, H. Karl, M. Z. C. Petrioli, H. Kip and T. Lentsch, EYES: energy efficient sensor networks, *Proc. IFIP TC6/WG6.8 Conference on Personal Wireless Communications* (*PWC*), **LNCS 2775**, 198–201, Venice, Italy (2003).
29. S. A. Camtepe and B. Yener, *Key Distribution Mechanisms for Wireless Sensor Networks: A Survey*, Technical Report TR-05-07, Rensselaer Polytechnic Institute (2005).
30. J.-H. Huang, J. Buckingham and R. Han, A level key infrastructure for secure and efficient group communication in wireless sensor network, *Proceedings of the First International Conference on Security and Privacy for Emerging Areas in Communications Networks* (*SECURECOMM*), 249–260, Washington, DC, USA (2005). IEEE Computer Society. ISBN 0-7695-2369-2. doi: http://dx.doi.org/10.1109/SECURECOMM.2005.3.
31. Z. Yu and Y. Guan, A robust group-based key management scheme for wireless sensor networks, *Proc. of IEEE Wireless Communications and Networking Conference* (*WCNC*), **4**, 1915–1920 (March, 2005). doi: 10.1109/WCNC.2005.1424812.
32. B. Panja, S. K. Madria and B. Bhargava, Energy and communication efficient group key management protocol for hierarchical sensor networks, *Proceedings of the IEEE International Conference on Sensor Networks, Ubiquitous and Trustworthy Computing* (*SUTC*), 384–393, Washington, DC, USA, (2006). IEEE Computer Society. ISBN 0-7695-2553-9-01. doi: http://dx.doi.org/10.1109/SUTC.2006.63.
33. Y. Kim, A. Perrig and G. Tsudik, Tree-based group key agreement, *ACM Transactions on Information Systems Security*, **7**(1), 60–96 (2004), ISSN 1094-9224. doi: http://doi.acm.org/10.1145/984334.984337.
34. M. F. Younis, K. Ghumman and M. Eltoweissy, Location-aware combinatorial key management scheme for clustered sensor networks, *IEEE Transactions on Parallel and Distributed Systems*, **17**(8), 865–882 (2006), ISSN 1045-9219. doi: http://doi.ieeecomputersociety.org/10.1109/TPDS.2006.106.
35. F. Anjum, Location dependent key management using random key-predistribution in sensor networks, *Proceedings of the 5th ACM Workshop on Wireless security (WiSe)*, 21–30, New York, NY, USA (2006), ACM. ISBN 1-59593-557-6. doi: http://doi.acm.org/10.1145/1161289.1161293.
36. N. Gura, A. Patel, A. Wander, H. Eberleand and S. C. Shantz, Comparing Elliptic Curve Cryptography and RSA on 8-bit CPUs, *Proc. of International Conference on Cryptographic Hardware and Embedded Systems* (*CHES*), 119–132 (2004).
37. H. Cohen, G. Frey, R. Avanzi, C. Doche, T. Lange, K. Nguyen and F. V. (Editors), *Handbook of Elliptic and Hyperelliptic Curve Cryptography*, Chapman and Hall/CRC (2005).
38. www.certicom.com, *Elliptic Curve Cryptography* (*ECC*) *Tutorial*. http://www.certicom.com/index.php/ecc-tutorial (2004).
39. TinyOS Team, Tinyos community forum: An open-source os for the networked sensor regime, http://www.tinyos.net (2008).
40. D. Hong, J. Sung, S. Hong, J. Lim, S. Lee, B.-S. Koo, C. Lee, D. Chang, J. Lee, K. Jeong, H. Kim, J. Kim and S. Chee, Hight: A new block cipher suitable for low-resource device, *Cryptographic Hardware and Embedded Systems* (*CHES*), 46–59 (2006). doi: http://dx.doi.org/10.1007/11894063_4.

41. W. K. Koo, H. Lee, Y. H. Kim and D. H. Lee, Implementation and analysis of new lightweight cryptographic algorithm suitable for wireless sensor networks, *International Conference on Information Security and Assurance, (ISA)*, 73–76 (April 2008), doi: 10.1109/ISA.2008.53.
42. A. Liu and P. Ning, Tinyecc: A configurable library for elliptic curve cryptography in wireless sensor networks, *IEEE International Conference on Information Processing in Sensor Networks (IPSN)*, 245–256 (2008), doi: 10.1109/IPSN.2008.47.
43. H. Wang and Q. Li, Efficient implementation of public key cryptosystems on Mote sensors (short paper), *Proc. International Conference on Information and Communications Security (ICICS)*, 519–528 (Raleigh, NC) (2006).
44. R. Roman, C. Alcaraz and J. Lopez, A survey of cryptographic primitives and implementations for hardware-constrained sensor network nodes, *ACM/Baltzer Mobile Networks and Applications*, **12**(4) 231–244 (2007), ISSN 1383-469X. doi: http://dx.doi.org/10.1007/s11036-007-0024-2.
45. C. Karlof and D. Wagner, Secure routing in wireless sensor networks: Attacks and countermeasures, *Proc. of First IEEE International Workshop on Sensor Network Protocols and Applications*, Anchorage, AL (2003).
46. A. D. Wood and J. D. Stankovic, Denial of service in sensor networks, *IEEE Computer*, pp. 54–62 (2002).
47. J. Newsome, E. Shi, D. Song and A. Perrig, The sybil attack in sensor networks: analysis & defenses, *Proceedings of the 3rd International Symposium on Information Processing in Sensor Networks (ISPN)*, 259–268, New York, NY, USA (2004), ACM. ISBN 1-58113-846-6. doi: http://doi.acm.org/10.1145/984622.984660.
48. L. Hu and D. Evans, Secure aggregation for wireless networks, *Workshop on Security and Assurance in Ad hoc Networks*, 384, Washington, DC, USA (2003). IEEE Computer Society. ISBN 0-7695-1873-7.
49. B. Przydatek, D. Song and A. Perrig, SIA: Secure information aggregation in sensor networks, *ACM SenSys*, Los Angeles, CA (2003).
50. H. Chan, A. Perrig and D. Song, Secure hierarchical in-network aggregation in sensor networks, *Proceedings of the 13th ACM Conference on Computer and Communications Security (CCS)*, 278–287, New York, NY, USA (2006). ACM, ISBN 1-59593-518-5. doi: http://doi.acm.org/10.1145/1180405.1180440.
51. H. Yu, Dos-resilient secure aggregation queries in sensor networks, *PODC '07: Proceedings of the Twenty-Sixth Annual ACM Symposium on Principles of Distributed Computing*, 394–395, New York, NY, USA (2007), ACM, ISBN 978-1-59593-616-5. doi: http://doi.acm.org/10.1145/1281100.1281190.
52. K. B. Frikken and I. Joseph A. Dougherty, An efficient integrity-preserving scheme for hierarchical sensor aggregation, *Proceedings of the First ACM Conference on Wireless Network Security (WiSec)*, 68–76, New York, NY, USA (2008), ACM, ISBN 978-1-59593-814-5. doi: http://doi.acm.org/10.1145/1352533.1352546.
53. J. Deng, R. Han and S. Mishra, INSENS: Intrusion-tolerant routing in wireless sensor networks, *Computer Communications*, **29**(2), 216–230 (2006).
54. A. Agah, S. K. Das, K. Basu and M. Asadi, Intrusion detection in sensor networks: A non-cooperative game approach, *IEEE International Symposium on Network Computing and Applications*, 343–346 (2004), doi: http://doi.ieeecomputersociety.org/10.1109/NCA.2004.1347798.
55. V. Bhuse and A. Gupta, Anomaly intrusion detection in wireless sensor networks, *Journal on High Speed Networks*, **15**(1), 33–51 (2006), ISSN 0926-6801.

56. R. Roman, J. Zhou and J. Lopez, Applying intrusion detection systems to wireless sensor networks, *IEEE Consumer Communications and Networking Conference* (*CCNC*), 640–644 (2006).
57. Z. Yu and J. Tsai, A framework of machine learning based intrusion detection for wireless sensor networks, *IEEE International Conference on Sensor Networks, Ubiquitous and Trustworthy Computing* (*SUTC*), 272–279 (2008), doi: 10.1109/SUTC.2008.39.

Chapter 16

CBKE: Chord-Based Key Establishment Schemes for Wireless Sensor Networks

Zhijie Jerry Shi, Bing Wang and Fan Zhang

Department of Computer Science and Engineering
University of Connecticut, Storrs, CT 06269

Because of limited resources at sensor nodes, sensor networks typically adopt symmetric-key algorithms to provide security functions such as protecting communications between nodes. In order to use symmetric-key algorithms, two nodes need to establish a secret session key first. In this chapter, we describe a novel chord-based key establishment (CBKE) protocol that allows any pair of nodes in a sensor network to establish a secret session key. CBKE is a generalized deterministic key establishment scheme that provides great flexibility for balancing memory overhead, reliability, and communication cost. We also analyze the properties of CBKE and explore the performance trade-offs using simulation.

16.1. Introduction

As wireless sensor networks are adopted in more and more applications, the security of sensor networks becomes increasingly important because sensor nodes are deployed in the field and communicate through wireless channels, thus vulnerable to attacks of many kinds. Like in many other systems, security goals in wireless sensor networks are achieved through cryptographic algorithms. Major types of cryptographic algorithms to provide confidentiality include symmetric-key and public-key algorithms. Typically, sensor networks adopt symmetric-key algorithms since public-key algorithms are computationally expensive while sensor nodes have limited computational capability and battery energy. To use symmetric-key algorithms, two sensor nodes need to agree on a secret key first. This process is called *key establishment* (or *key exchange*). While public-key algorithms are used to perform key establishment in systems that have more resources, it is desirable to perform

---

A preliminary version of this chapter appeared in Ref. 1. This research was supported by National Science Foundation CAREER awards 0644188 and 0746841, and the University of Connecticut Large Grant.

key establishment in sensor networks with symmetric-key algorithms only, for the same reasons described earlier.

In the past several years, key establishment in sensor networks has attracted a lot of attention (see Ref. 2 for a survey). In this chapter, we focus on *pairwise* key establishment that allows any two nodes in the network to agree on a secret key, since pairwise communications are the most common cases in sensor networks.[3,a] Existing pairwise key establishment schemes can be broadly classified into the following five major categories: *trusted-server-based schemes, random key pre-distribution schemes, deterministic key pre-distribution schemes, location-based schemes, and in-situ schemes.* Trusted-server-based schemes (e.g., Ref. 4) use a trusted server as an arbiter to establish pairwise keys between two nodes. Random key pre-distribution schemes (e.g., Refs. 5 and 6) preload a set of keys chosen from a global key pool into each node. Two neighboring nodes share a common key with a certain probability. Two nodes not presharing a key establish keys by finding a path in the induced key-sharing graph (where two nodes are connected if they share a key). The performance of random key pre-distribution schemes can be improved by using multiple key spaces (e.g., Refs. 7 and 8) or by regulating the nodes that share each seed.[9] Deterministic key pre-distribution schemes pre-distribute keys in a deterministic manner. One extreme form of deterministic key pre-distribution is full pairwise key pre-distribution in which every pair of nodes share a unique key and each node has to store as many keys in its memory as the number of nodes in the network. The other extreme is that all nodes preload a single key. PIKE[10] is between these two extremes. It considers the node ID space as a logical grid. Any two nodes in the same row or column preshare a unique key; nodes not presharing a key establish keys through intermediate nodes. Location-based schemes (e.g., Refs. 11–13) take advantage of location information to improve key establishment. In *in-situ* schemes,[14–16] instead of preloading keys, sensors compute keys after deployment to adapt to the post-deployment network topology.

Several other types of key establishment schemes are proposed recently. For example, Teymorian *et al.* propose a cellular automata based scheme that allows sensors to establish pairwise keys during any stage of the network operation;[17] Zhang *et al.* propose a random perturbation-based pairwise key establishment scheme that utilizes multiple perturbed polynomials to establish keys between any pair of nodes directly.[3]

In this chapter, we study a novel chord-based key establishment (CBKE) protocol for pairwise key establishment. CBKE is a deterministic key pre-distribution scheme. It is very flexible and achieves a wide range of performance trade-offs among memory overhead, reliability, and communication cost. As we shall see, existing deterministic key distribution schemes, including full pairwise pre-distribution,

---

[a]Key establishment in sensor networks can also be group-based (for multicast as in Refs. 11, 12, 18) or network-based (for broadcast as in Refs. 19 and 20).

single network-wide key scheme, and PIKE, are special cases of CBKE. By choosing parameters properly, CBKE can meet various design goals. For example, in networks that have a large number of nodes and require low memory overhead, CBKE can reduce the number of preloaded keys to $\log_2 N + 1$, where N is the number of nodes in a network.

The rest of the chapter is organized as follows. Section 16.2 describes the CBKE scheme. We discuss its properties in Sec. 16.3 and study performance trade-offs in Sec. 16.4. We then examine the security of CBKE in Sec. 16.5. After discussing several improvements in Sec. 16.6, we conclude the chapter in Sec. 16.7.

16.2. Chord-Based Key Establishment Scheme

In this section, we first describe the basic CBKE and then extend it to a generalized scheme.

16.2.1. *Basic CBKE scheme*

Since CBKE employs deterministic key pre-distribution, we start with the key pre-distribution process. We then describe the key establishment process and a mechanism to improve reliability.

16.2.1.1. *Key pre-distribution in basic CBKE*

Consider a sensor network of N nodes. Node i is assigned an ID of i, $i = 0, \ldots, N-1$. For simplicity, we assume $N = 2^m$. So each ID is represented with m bits. Inspired by Ref. 21, we consider that these nodes are arranged in a circle in the order of their ID, which increases in a clockwise direction. The *distance* between two nodes is defined as the length of the shorter path along the circle from one node to the other. This shorter path can be either clockwise or counterclockwise. Let $D(i,j)$ denote the distance between nodes i and j. It can be computed as $D(i,j) = \min(i-j, j-i)$.[b] When preloading keys, we let node i preshare a key with nodes $i \pm 2^0, i \pm 2^1, \ldots, i \pm 2^{m-2}, i + 2^{m-1}$. That is, nodes i and j preshare a key if and only if the distance between them is a power of two, i.e., $D(i,j) = 2^x$ for some $x \in \{0, \ldots, m-1\}$. Let $K_{i,j}$ denote the key preshared by nodes i and j. Then $K_{i,j} = K_{j,i}$. On the circle, we connect two nodes with a chord if they preshare a key. During key establishment, a session key is forwarded along the chords from a source to a destination. So we name our scheme a *Chord-based Key Establishment* (CBKE) scheme.

With the above key pre-distribution, each node shares a unique key with $2m-1 = 2\log_2 N - 1$ nodes. The number of preloaded keys on each node can be reduced to $m+1$, using the method proposed in Ref. 22.

---

[b]All computations involving node IDs are modulo N. For simplicity, we do not indicate it explicitly.

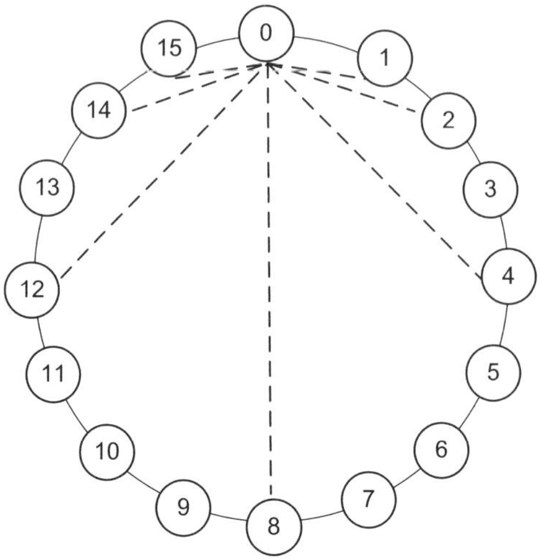

Fig. 16.1. An illustration of key pre-distribution in CBKE ($N = 16$).

Figure 16.1 shows an example of key pre-distribution for a network of 16 nodes, in which node 0 preshares keys with nodes 1, 2, 4, 8, 12, 14 and 15. In the figure, node 0 is connected with each of these nodes with a chord.

16.2.1.2. *Key establishment in basic CBKE*

Suppose that a source node s wants to establish a session key with a destination node d. For this purpose, s first generates a random key r. The key establishment process is basically forwarding the key to d through a secure path (i.e., along chords in the circle); s confirms the success of key establishment if it receives an ACK message from d that is encrypted with r. Let $k = D(s, d)$, k_i denote bit i[c] in the binary representation of k, and $H(k)$ be the *Hamming weight* of k (i.e., the number of 1's in k's binary representation). Since nodes s and d are not the same, $k \neq 0$ and $H(k) > 0$. We now describe the key establishment process, as summarized in Fig. 16.2.

Node s finds a node n_1 that is closer to d and preshares a key with s. In particular, s randomly selects u such that $k_u = 1$ and computes $n_1 = s \pm 2^u$. The operation, + or −, depends on whether the shorter path from s to d is clockwise or counterclockwise. If it is clockwise, + is performed. Otherwise, − is performed. Since k has $H(k)$ 1 bits and s may select any of these 1's, s has $H(k)$ different choices for n_1. We refer to these nodes, which can be selected by s to forward the session key, as *descendants* of s. It is clear that n_1 is closer to d than s because

[c]We adopt the little-endian convention in this chapter. So bit 0 is the least significant bit, i.e., the right most bit.

At the source node s:
Generate a session key r
$k = D(s,d) = (k_{m-1}, \ldots, k_0)_2$
Randomly choose u such that $k_u = 1$
if s is closer to d clockwise
  Compute $n_1 = s + 2^u$
else
  Compute $n_1 = s - 2^u$
Encrypt (r, d) using key K_{s,n_1}
Send the encrypted message to node n_1

At an intermediate node or the destination node n_i:
Decrypt the received message to recover (r, d)
if $(n_i \neq d)$ { // Not the destination
  $k = D(n_i, d) = (k_{m-1}, \ldots, k_0)_2$
  Randomly choose u such that $k_u = 1$
  if n_i is closer to d clockwise
    Compute $n_{i+1} = n_i + 2^u$
  else
    Compute $n_{i+1} = n_i - 2^u$
  Encrypt (r, d) using key $K_{n_i,n_{i+1}}$
  Send the encrypted message to node n_{i+1}
}
else { // At the destination
  Generate a random value ρ
  Encrypt (s, d, ρ) with r
  Send the encrypted (s, d, ρ) to s
}

Fig. 16.2. Basic CBKE scheme: node s establishes a session key with node d.

$D(n_1, d) = D(s, d) - 2^u < D(s, d)$. After n_1 is selected, s sends (r, d) to n_1. The message is encrypted with K_{s,n_1}, which is the key preshared by s and n_1.

After n_1 receives the encrypted message from s, it recovers r and d with K_{s,n_1}. If n_1 is not the destination node, it selects one of its descendants n_2 and forwards (r, d) to it. If n_2 is not d either, it will repeat the process. Since the session key r gets closer to d after each hop, it will arrive at d when all the bits in the distance k are changed to 0.

Once d receives r, it sends an ACK message to s. The ACK message can be (s, d, ρ) encrypted with r, where ρ is a random value generated by d. If s can retrieve s and d with r from the ACK message, it assumes that d has received r successfully. Then it can start a secure communication session with d.

We refer to a path along which a session key is forwarded securely from s to d as a *logical path*. On a logical path, a node and its descendant form a *logical hop* since they are not necessarily neighboring nodes in the physical network. Two nodes on

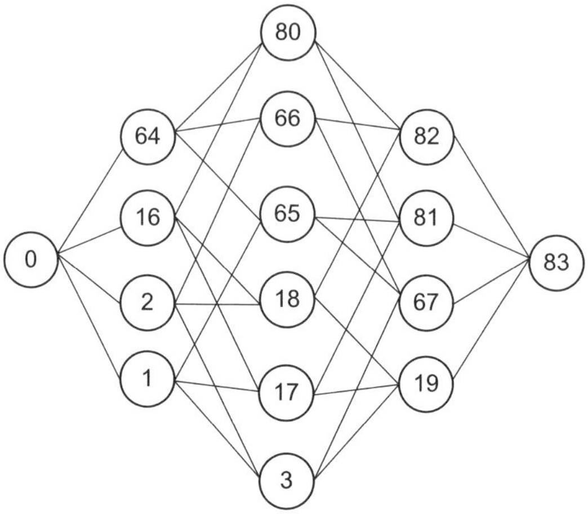

Fig. 16.3. Logical paths from source 0 to destination 83.

a logical hop preshare a key, which is used to protect key forwarding messages. A logical path is only used for key forwarding — the ACK message is sent directly from d to s; after the session key is established, the secure communications between s and d also take a direct path.

We illustrate the basic scheme with an example shown in Fig. 16.3. Suppose $N = 256$ and node 0 wants to send a session key r to node 83. The distance between the two nodes is $k = D(0, 83) = 83 = 01010011_2$. Since $H(k) = 4$, node 0 has four descendants: nodes $64 = 0 + 2^6$, $16 = 0 + 2^4$, $2 = 0 + 2^1$, and $1 = 0 + 2^0$, where the exponents 6, 4, 1, and 0 are the position of 1's in k. Node 0 randomly picks one of the descendants, say node 64, and forwards r and the destination ID 83 to it. The message is protected with key $K_{0,64}$. After receiving and decrypting the message, node 64 finds out that it is not the destination. It then forwards the message to one of its descendants (nodes 65, 66, and 80). This process continues until node 83 receives r.

16.2.1.3. *Utilizing multiple logical paths*

In the basic CBKE scheme shown in Fig. 16.2, a session key is forwarded along a single logical path from s to d. A single path, however, does not provide sufficient reliability for key establishment if nodes may fail. As we see in Fig. 16.3, many logical paths can be utilized to forward a key from s to d. Forwarding a session key simultaneously through multiple logical paths improves reliability. The key can reach the destination node even if all but one logical path are broken.

We introduce a parameter l to our basic scheme and allow a node to forward a session key to l descendants simultaneously. In particular, a node n_i forwards the session key to $\min(l, H(D(n_i, d))$ descendants simultaneously. The message to each of the l descendants is protected by the unique key preshared by n_i and its descendants. A descendant may receive the same session key multiple times due to the overlaps among logical paths, but it only forwards the key once.

When $l = 1$, only a single logical path is used to forward the session key from s to d, as illustrated in Fig. 16.2. When not restricting l, i.e., a node forwards the key to all its descendants, CBKE works in the *flooding* mode. There is a clear trade-off in choosing l: a large l improves the reliability of key establishment while increasing communication cost. We will explore the trade-offs in Sec. 16.4.

We again use the example in Fig. 16.3 to illustrate forwarding along multiple paths. Suppose $l = 2$. Each node forwards the session key to up to two descendants. Source node 0 randomly chooses two nodes from its four descendants, nodes 64, 16, 2, and 1. Suppose nodes 64 and 16 are selected. Node 0 forwards the session key to these two nodes simultaneously. The message to node 64 is encrypted with $K_{0,64}$ and the message to node 16 is encrypted with $K_{0,16}$. After receiving the (encrypted) session key, node 64 chooses two descendants from nodes 65, 66 and 80. Nodes 16 also chooses two of its descendants randomly. Note that node 80 is a descendant for both nodes 64 and 16. It may receive the session key twice, but it only forwards the key once. Since the session key is forwarded along multiple paths, it can reach the destination node 83 even if some nodes (e.g., node 16) fail.

To reduce communication cost, multiple logical paths can be utilized in a different way. They do not have to be involved in forwarding simultaneously. Instead they can be utilized in series or in a combination of parallel and series. The source node s can keep trying to forward a session key to d with a certain l that incurs less communication cost (e.g., $l = 1$ or $l = 2$) until the key is successfully sent or a predetermined number of trials is reached. When $l = 1$, the multiple logical paths are tried in series. Since each time the descendants involved in forwarding are randomly chosen, it is very likely that different logical paths are taken at different times. This method can achieve similar reliability as trying multiple logical paths simultaneously with a larger l. However, it requires other mechanisms such as acknowledgment messages or time-out to detect failed attempts.

16.2.2. *Generalized CBKE scheme*

In the basic CBKE scheme, we consider k as a binary number and change a 1 bit to 0 after each logical hop when forwarding the session key from s to d. We can generalize the scheme by representing k as a radix 2^b number, where $b \geq 1$, and changing a non-zero digit of k to 0 when forwarding the session key to d. In the generalized CBKE scheme, $H(k)$ represents the number of non-zero digits in k.

Key pre-distribution. When the radix is 2^b, k can be represented with g digits $(k_{g-1}, k_{g-2}, \ldots, k_1, k_0)$, where $g = \lceil m/b \rceil$. Each digit k_i, $i = 0, \ldots, g-1$, has 2^b different values. Two nodes preshare a key if their distance is $a \times 2^{ib}$, where $0 <$

Table 16.1. Nodes presharing a key with node 0 ($N = 256, b = 2$).

Distance to node 0	Node IDs	Group
$0001_4 = 1$	1 and 255	
$0002_4 = 2$	2 and 254	1
$0003_4 = 3$	3 and 253	
$0010_4 = 4$	4 and 252	
$0020_4 = 8$	8 and 248	2
$0030_4 = 12$	12 and 244	
$0100_4 = 16$	16 and 240	
$0200_4 = 32$	32 and 224	3
$0300_4 = 48$	48 and 208	
$1000_4 = 64$	64 and 192	4
$2000_4 = 128$	128	

$a < 2^b$ and $0 \le i < g$. In other words, if the distance between two nodes has only one non-zero digit, they preshare a key.

Because k has g digits and each digit has $2^b - 1$ non-zero values, a node needs to establish a unique key with $2 \times (2^b - 1) \times (g - 1) + (2^b - 1)$ nodes. Using the method proposed in Ref.[22] each node needs to store $(2^b - 1) \times g + 1 = (2^b - 1) \times \lceil m/b \rceil + 1$ keys.

We use an example to illustrate key pre-distribution in the generalized CBKE scheme. Suppose $N = 256$ and $b = 2$. The distance between two nodes can be represented with a 4-digit radix-4 number. Node 0 preshares a unique key with 21 nodes, which are listed in Table 16.1. In the table, we use a subscript 4 to indicate radix-4 numbers. We also group the nodes according to the position of the non-zero digit in their distance to node 0. In general, the nodes presharing a key with a particular node can be divided into g groups as k has g digits.

Key establishment. The key establishment process in the generalized CBKE is similar to the process in the basic CBKE, which is shown in Fig. 16.2. The only difference is that at each hop, a node n_i randomly selects a non-zero digit k_u in $k = D(n_i, d)$ and compute $n_{i+1} = n_i \pm k_u \times 2^{bu}$. Similarly, + is performed if n_i is closer to d clockwise. Otherwise, − is performed. After each logical hop, one of the non-zero digits in k is changed to 0. Consequently, a logical path has at most g hops. On average, the larger b is, the shorter logical paths we have.

As in the basic CBKE scheme, we can use l to control the number of descendants to which a node may forward a session key. Also, the multiple paths can be utilized in parallel, in series, or in a combination of both.

We use the example in Fig. 16.4 to illustrate the generalized CBKE scheme. Suppose $N = 256$, $b = 2$, $l = 1$, and node 0 wants to send a session key r to node 83. The distance between the two nodes is $k = D(0, 83) = 83 = 1103_4$. Since k has three non-zero digits, $H(k) = 3$. Node 0 has three descendants: nodes 3, 16,

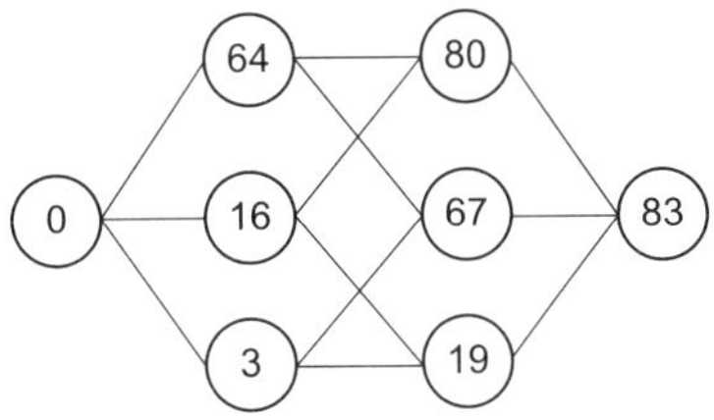

Fig. 16.4. Logical paths from source 0 to destination 83 ($b = 2$).

and 64. It randomly picks one of the descendants, say node 3, as the next node on the logical path. After node 3 receives r, it selects either node 67 or node 19 as the next node, which then forwards r to node 83. Because of the larger radix, a logical path now has only three hops, instead of four hops in the case shown in Fig. 16.3.

Relationship to existing deterministic schemes. We remark that several existing deterministic schemes are special cases of CBKE. The full pairwise scheme is CBKE with $b = m$, where each pair of nodes preshare a unique key. PIKE[10] is essentially a CBKE scheme with $b = m/2$, where each node prestores $O(\sqrt{N})$ keys and each logical path contains two logical hops. When nodes in a group share the same key, CBKE with $b = m$ has a single group and all nodes share the same key, which becomes the single-key predistribution scheme.

16.3. Properties of CBKE Schemes

We next describe several properties of the CBKE schemes. Recall that $k = D(s, d)$, where s is the source node and d is the destination node. We consider k as a radix 2^b number and $H(k)$ is the number of non-zero digits in k.

Memory overhead. As mentioned earlier, the number of preloaded keys into each node is $(2^b - 1) \times \lceil m/b \rceil + 1$, where m is the number of bits required to represent a node ID. Hence the memory overhead increases with b.

Length of a logical path. When the session key is forwarded from s to d, the number of non-zero digits in k is reduced by one after each logical hop. Eventually the distance becomes 0 at d. Therefore, a logical path from s to d has $H(k)$ logical hops. The expectation of $H(k)$ is roughly

$$\left\lfloor \frac{m-1}{b} \right\rfloor \times \frac{2^b - 1}{2^b} + \frac{2^a - 1}{2^a}, \tag{16.1}$$

where $a = (m - 1) \bmod b$. This is can be explained as follows. For a randomly chosen source-destination pair, their distance is uniformly distributed in $[1, 2^{m-1}]$. Consider all the numbers from 0 to $2^{m-1} - 1$. They can be represented by $(m-1)$ bits. We divide $(m - 1)$ bits in groups of b bits (since the radix is 2^b). Then for each b bits in a group, the expected Hamming weight is $(1 - 1/2^b)$ since the Hamming weight is not 1 only when all these b bits are zero, which happens with the probability of $1/2^b$. Since there are $\lfloor \frac{m-1}{b} \rfloor$ groups, we obtain the first term in Eq. (16.1). The second term in (16.1) represents the expected Hamming weight of the a bits that are not included in the groups. The above does not consider the distance of 2^{m-1}. When considering it, we obtain the exact formula for the expectation of $H(k)$,

$$E(H(k)) = \frac{(\lfloor \frac{m-1}{b} \rfloor \times \frac{2^b-1}{2^b} + \frac{2^a-1}{2^a}) \times 2^m + 1}{2^m - 1}. \tag{16.2}$$

We can see that (16.1) provides a close approximation to (16.2) for relatively large m. Observe from the above that, on average, $H(k)$ and hence the length of logical paths decrease with b. When $b = 1$, the average number of hops is about $(m-1)/2$. It reduces to approximately $3(m-1)/8$ when $b = 2$, and to approximately 2 when $b = m/2$.

Number of logical paths and hops. There are more than one logical path from s to d if $H(k) > 1$. We now compute the total number of logical paths that can be used for key establishment. Let S denote the set of nodes that may participate in forwarding and S_i denote the set of nodes in S whose distance to s has i non-zero digits, $i = 0, \ldots, H(k)$. In particular, $S_0 = \{s\}, S_{H(k)} = \{d\}$. Starting from S_0, the session key is forwarded to a node in S_1, and then to a node in S_2, and so on. Consider a node $n_i \in S_i$. We have $D(n_i, d) = H(k) - i$. Therefore, node n_i has $H(k) - i$ descendants, all of which are in S_{i+1}. Node n_i has $(H(k) - i)$ choices when selecting a descendant in S_{i+1}. For example, s has $H(k)$ choices, and a node in S_1 has $H(k) - 1$ choices. Hence, the total number of logical paths from s to d is

$$\prod_{i=0}^{H(k)-1} (H(k) - i) = H(k)!. \tag{16.3}$$

The number of nodes in set S_i is $\binom{H(k)}{i}$ because i out of $H(k)$ non-zero digits in k have changed to 0 for a node in S_i. Combining with the previous observation that each node in S_i has $H(k) - i$ different ways to reach nodes in S_{i+1}, we obtain the total number of logical hops that may be used in forwarding as

$$\sum_{i=0}^{H(k)-1} (H(k) - i)\binom{H(k)}{i} = H(k)2^{H(k)-1}. \tag{16.4}$$

We now look at some examples. In Fig. 16.3, $b = 1$, $S_0 = \{0\}$, $S_1 = \{1, 2, 16, 64\}$, $S_2 = \{3, 17, 18, 65, 66, 80\}$, $S_3 = \{19, 67, 81, 82\}$, and $S_4 = \{83\}$. Each logical path from node 0 to node 83 contains $H(k) = H(01010011_2) = 4$ logical hops. The total number of logical paths from node 0 to node 83 is $H(k)! = 4! = 24$. The total number of logical hops is $H(k)2^{H(k)-1} = 4 \times 2^3 = 32$. In Fig. 16.4, $b = 2$, $S_0 = \{0\}$, $S_1 = \{3, 16, 64\}$, $S_2 = \{19, 67, 80\}$, and $S_3 = \{83\}$. Each logical path from node 0 to node 83 has $H(k) = H(1103_4) = 3$ logical hops. The total number of logical paths from node 0 to node 83 is $H(k)! = 3! = 6$. The total number of logical hops is $H(k)2^{H(k)-1} = 3 \times 2^2 = 12$.

Summary. In summary, when b increases, the memory overhead increases, while, on average, the length of a logical path and the total number of logical paths decrease. If we assume that nodes in a network are uniformly distributed and node failures are also uniformly random, then each logical hop contains a similar number of physical hops and has a similar probability to break. Therefore, on average, a shorter logical path incurs less communication cost and provides better reliability. However, when a logical path is short, the total number of logical paths from a source to a destination is also small, which limits the number of logical paths that can be used for key establishment, and hence limits the degree of reliability that can be achieved. In Sec. 16.4, we will study how the choice of b affects communication cost and reliability in detail.

16.4. Performance Trade-Offs

In this section, we explore how the choices of b and l affect the *memory overhead*, *reliability*, and *communication cost* of CBKE. The memory overhead is the number of keys that are preloaded into a sensor node. The reliability is the probability that a pair of nodes can establish a session key successfully when nodes may fail. The communication cost is the average number of messages transmitted in the network for a key establishment. In the following, simulation results are obtained using a simulator that we developed.

We assume a network of $N = 4096$ nodes ($m = 12$) and each node has a fixed physical position. The transmission range of a node is one unit and the node density is 20 nodes per square unit. We adopt GPSR[23] as the routing protocol in the physical network. So every node knows the position of the destination node and its neighboring nodes. We set b and l to a wide range of settings: $b = 1, 2, \ldots, 6$, and $l = 1, 2, 3$ and unlimited (i.e., in the flooding mode). Note that when $b = 6$, CBKE is similar to PIKE.[10]

We first compare the memory overhead for different choices of b. As we discussed in Sec. 16.2.2, the number of preshared keys on each node is $(2^b - 1) \times \lceil m/b \rceil + 1$, which increases with b. In particular, when $b = 1$, the number of preshared keys is $O(\log_2 N)$; when $b = m/2$, the number of preshared keys is $O(\sqrt{N})$. Figure 16.5 plots the memory overhead for various values of b. We observe that, as b increases from 1 to 6, the number of preloaded keys first increases gradually and then increases sharply. Therefore, when memory is a stringent constraint, it is desirable to choose smaller values of b.

We now consider the average number of logical hops. Figure 16.6 plots the average number of hops for all combinations of source and destination pairs versus b. As expected, the average number of hops decreases as b increases. Since the nodes are uniformly randomly deployed, the lengths of logical paths reflects the lengths of physical paths, and hence communication costs. To confirm this, we randomly choose $10,000$ pairs of nodes in the network and establish keys for each pair. We

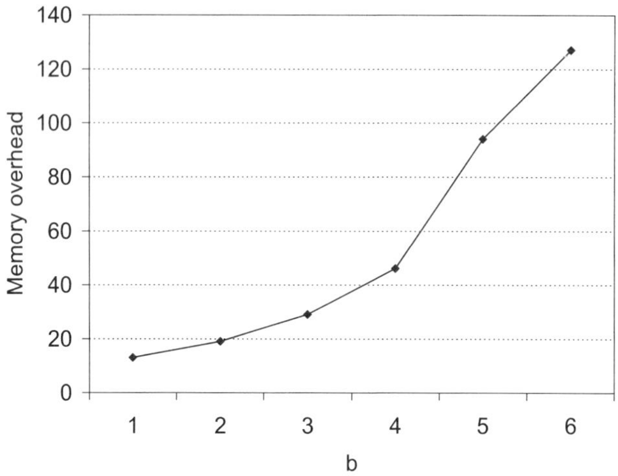

Fig. 16.5. Memory overhead, $m = 12$.

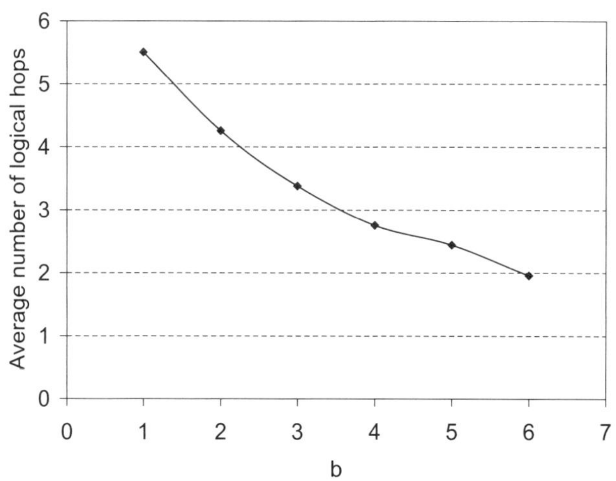

Fig. 16.6. Average number of logical hops, $m = 12$.

then obtain the average communication cost when b increases from 1 to 6. The communication cost matches the results in Fig. 16.6 (scaled up by the average length of a logical hop).

We now explore how the values of b and l affect the reliability and communication cost of CBKE. We set node failure rate, p, to values between 0.1 and 0.5, with an increment of 0.1. For each value of p, we randomly choose 10,000 pairs of alive nodes in the network and establish keys for each pair. We then obtain the average reliability and communication cost over all the pairs.

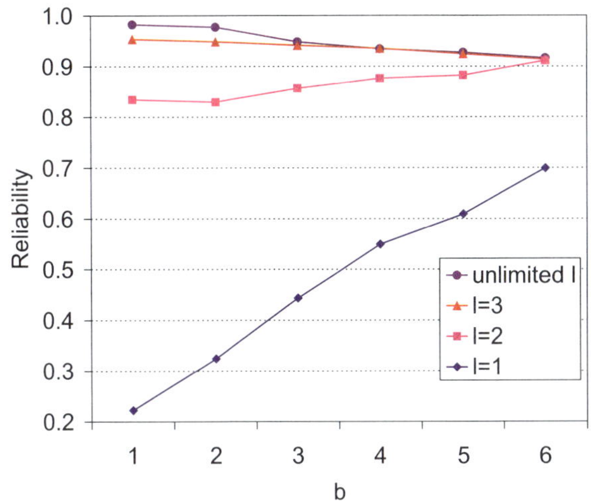

Fig. 16.7. Reliability of CBKE, $p = 0.3$, $m = 12$.

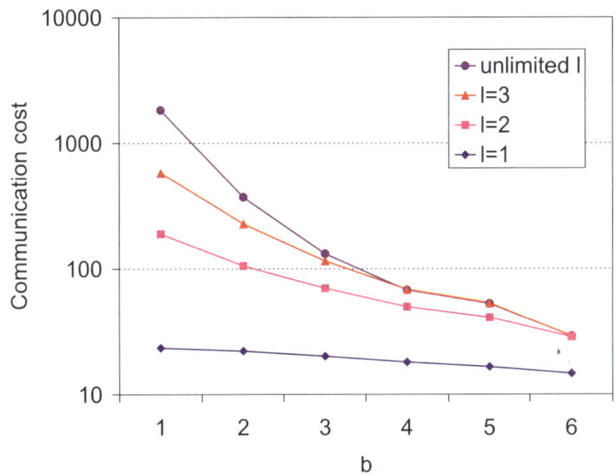

Fig. 16.8. Communication cost of CBKE, $p = 0.3$, $m = 12$.

Figures 16.7 and 16.8 plot the average reliability and communication cost for $p = 0.3$. We observe that when $l = 1$, the average reliability increases significantly with b. This is because larger values of b lead to shorter logical paths and thus to higher probabilities of successful key establishments. As l increases from 1 to 2, the average reliability for all values of b increases significantly, indicating the effectiveness of using multiple paths to increase reliability. When $l = 3$, we observe that the average reliability decreases with b. This is because when $l = 3$, more logical paths can be utilized for key establishment for small values of b and hence result in good reliability. As b increases, the number of logical paths that can be utilized for key establishment decreases significantly. Although each logical path is more likely to be successful, the overall reliability decreases because of the small number of logical paths. When not limiting l, we observe a similar trend as when $l = 3$. In Fig. 16.8, as expected, we observe that the average communication cost decreases with b since the average length of a logical path decreases as b increases. Furthermore, as l increases, the average communication cost may increase significantly, especially when b is small, since a much larger number of logical hops are involved.

We observe similar trends in reliability and communication cost for other values of p ($0.1, 0.2, 0.4$, and 0.5). In general, the average reliability increases with b for small values of l, and decreases with b for large values of l; the highest reliability is achieved when $b = 1$ and not limiting l, at the price of the highest communication cost.

In summary, we see a clear trade-off in memory overhead, reliability, and communication cost when choosing different values of b and l in CBKE. The best choices of the parameters depends on the constraints of a specific setting. For instance, one may determine b and l to achieve the highest reliability for certain constraints of memory overhead and communication cost. By tuning the parameters of b and l, CBKE provides a wide range of performance trade-offs among memory overhead, reliability, and communication cost.

16.5. Security of CBKE

We now analyze the security of CBKE. Under a *passive* attack model where attackers only passively monitor the communications in the sensor networks, CBKE is secure. This is because when a session key is forwarded along a logical path, it is protected with the shared key between two nodes on every hop, and hence cannot be revealed through passive monitoring. Under an *active* attack model where attackers are capable of compromising sensor nodes and then retrieve the information stored on those nodes (including preshared keys), CBKE can become insecure. This is because a session key is known by all intermediate nodes along a logical path (an intermediate node needs to decrypt the protected session key with the shared key on the previous hop and then encrypt it with the shared key on the next hop). Therefore, if an attacker compromises an intermediate node, it can potentially obtain the session key, and decrypt all the messages protected by this session key. We next analyze the security of CBKE assuming an active attack model where a session key and thus the communication channel between a source and destination are compromised if any node on the logical path is compromised.

Assume the logical path from the source node s to the destination d has $H(k)$ hops, where $H(k)$ is the number of non-zero digits in k, and k is the distance between s and d. We also assume that both s and d are secure, and the probability of other nodes being compromised is p_s. Then the probability of the session key

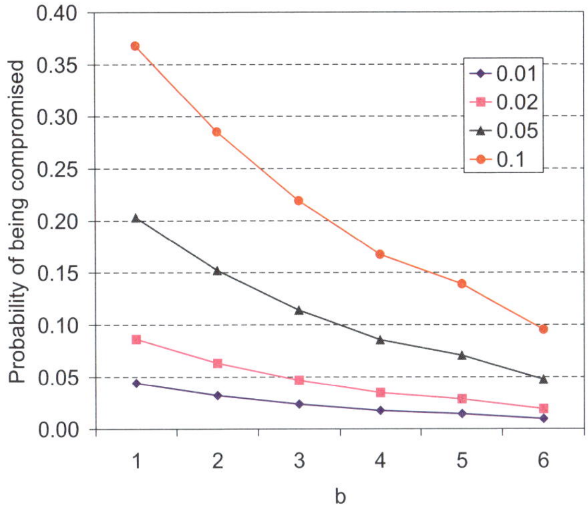

Fig. 16.9. Security of CBKE, $m = 12$, $l = 1$.

being compromised is $1 - (1 - p_s)^{H(k)-1}$ (since there are $H(k) - 1$ intermediate nodes). It is clear that as $H(k)$ decreases, the probability that a session key is compromised decreases. Adopting a larger radix decreases $H(k)$ and thus improves security. This can be seen in Fig. 16.9, which illustrates how the radix affects the security of CBKE with $m = 12$ and $l = 1$. This figure shows the probabilities of the channel between s and d being compromised for four choices of p_s: 0.01, 0.02, 0.05 and 0.1. A point in the figure represents an average probability when k is uniformly randomly chosen from 1 to 2^{m-1} (i.e., s and d are chosen randomly). We can see clearly from the figure that increasing b results in less vulnerability or better security. Intuitively, the less nodes participate in the key establishment process, the less likely the key and the channel are compromised.

For a fixed radix, the security of CBKE can be improved as follows. Source node s sends multiple secret values to d through multiple disjoint paths, one value on one path, and an attacker needs to know all the values to construct the session key. To minimize the communication and energy overhead, we look at the case that s sends two secret values to d over two disjoint path. In particular, one value is sent through the clockwise path and the other through the counterclockwise path. Both s and d can construct the session key by exclusive or-ing the two values. Since the two paths are disjoint, none of the intermediate nodes knows both secret values. Even if an adversary compromises one or more nodes on one path, he cannot construct the session key. Assume that the clockwise distance from s to d is k. The counterclockwise distance from s to d is $N-k$, where $N = 2^m$ is the total number of nodes in the networks. Assume that both s and d are secure, and the probability of other nodes being compromised is p_s. Then the probability of the session key being

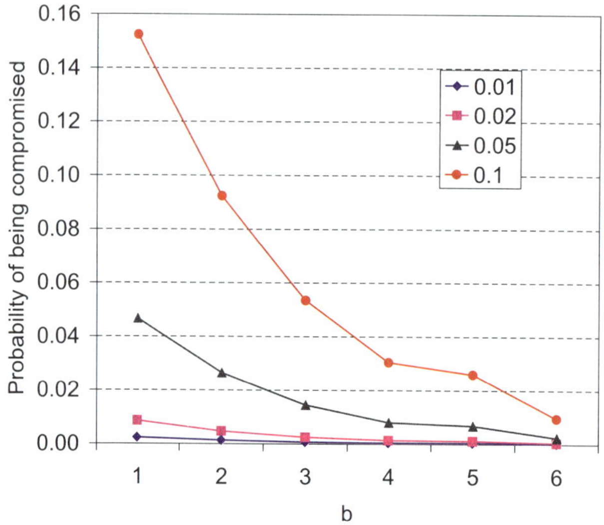

Fig. 16.10. Security of CBKE when sending two secrets through two disjoint paths, $m = 12$.

compromised is $(1-(1-p_s)^{H(k)-1})(1-(1-p_s)^{H(N-k)-1})$. We now reexamine the example illustrated in Fig. 16.9, in which $m = 12$ and $l = 1$. Figure 16.10 shows the security of CBKE when using two disjoint paths. We again consider four choices of p_s: 0.01, 0.02, 0.05, and 0.1. A point in the figure represents an average probability that the channel between s and d is compromised when k is uniformly randomly chosen from 1 to 2^{m-1} (i.e., s and d are chosen randomly). We see from these two figures that the security of CBKE is improved significantly by forwarding secrets through two disjoint paths. For example, when $p_s = 0.1$ and $b = 1$, the probability of compromising the session key reduces from 0.368 (single-path) to 0.152 (two-path). When $p_s = 0.1$ and $b = 6$, the probability of compromising the key decreases from 0.095 (single-path) to 0.010 (two-path).

This improvement, however, comes at a cost. First, sending multiple secrets incurs large communication and energy overhead as more packets are forwarded from a source to a destination. In the case the source sends out two secret values, the communication cost is doubled on average. Secondly, sending multiple secrets reduces reliability. When one of the multiple paths fails to deliver the secret to the destination, the destination cannot construct the session key and thus cannot establish a secure communication channel with the source.

16.6. Further Improvements to CBKE

CBKE can be further improved, especially under specific configurations. We discuss a few of them here.

16.6.1. *Forwarding paths*

In CBKE, the total number of logical paths from s to d is $H(k)!$. For relatively small $H(k)$ (e.g., $H(k) = 1$ or 2), $H(k)!$ logical paths may not provide sufficient amount of path redundancy. More logical paths can be utilized if one chooses additional intermediate nodes. For instance, suppose $s = 0$, $d = 6$, $m = 4$, and $b = 1$. The current CBKE scheme provides only two paths: $(0, 2, 6)$ or $(0, 4, 6)$. If both nodes 2 and 4 fail, the session key cannot be forwarded to node 6. However, it can be done through additional paths such as $(0, 8, 6)$ and $(0, 1, 5, 6)$.

One way to choose additional forwarding paths is by representing the distance between a source and a destination using non-adjacent form (NAF). NAF is a signed-digit representation that does not allow adjacent non-zero digits. For instance, in the example above, the distance 6 can be represented in its NAF of $(1, 0, -1, 0)_{NAF}$, which provides two additional forwarding paths: $(0, 8, 6)$ and $(0, 14, 6)$. One advantage of using NAF is that the distance thus represented may have a smaller Hamming weight, leading to a shorter logical path from a source to a destination. For instance, consider source 0 and destination 7. In regular binary form, the distance from the source to the destination, 7, has Hamming weight of 3, and hence the number of logical hops is 3. In NAF, the Hamming weight reduces to 2 (the NAF of 7 is $(1, 0, 0, -1)_{NAF}$), and hence the number of logical hops reduces to 2. When m is large and $b = 1$, the average number of hops between two nodes reduces from $(m - 1)/2$ (in regular binary form) to about $(m - 1)/3$ when using NAF (since the Hamming weight of an integer using NAF is one third of the number of bits in the integer[24]). The binary NAF provides even shorter logical paths compared to the case of $b = 2$ (in regular form), in which the average number of hops is about $3(m - 1)/8$ (see Sec. 16.3).

16.6.2. *Partial deployment*

So far, we have assumed that the number of nodes in the network is a power of the radix selected. In a real deployment, the assumption may not be true. Nodes deployed in a sensor network may not take all the IDs in the ID space. We will refer to this scenario as *partial deployment*. Since some IDs are not present in the network, they cannot participate in the key forwarding as expected. A simple approach is to consider these IDs belong to failed nodes and use a trial-and-error strategy. This approach, however, has large communication overhead. It will be more efficient to let the nodes be aware of undeployed IDs and take this into account when deciding forwarding paths. We next describe a scheme for partial deployment. For simplicity, we take the case of $b = 1$ as an example; our scheme also applies to other radices. Note that when $b = m/2$, CBKE is similar to PIKE. For this specific case, the partial deployment problem is also discussed in Ref. 10.

Let us assume we represent an ID with m bits. In the case of partial deployment, we deploy IDs in the order that is specified by a counter. This counter starts with 0.

It is similar to a binary counter, but it adds one to the most significant bit (MSB) and propagates the carry from MSB to the least significant bit (LSB). We next use $m = 4$ as an example to illustrate this deployment order. The first node deployed has ID 0. Adding one to the MSB, the second node to be deployed is hence $1000_2 = 8$. Again adding one to the MSB and propagating the carry from MSB to LSB, the third node to deployed is hence $0100_2 = 4$. Afterwards, node $1100_2 = 12$ is deployed, followed by $0010_2 = 2$, $1010_2 = 10$, $0110_2 = 6$, $1110_2 = 14$, $0001_2 = 1$, $1001_2 = 9$, $0101_2 = 5$, $1101_2 = 13$, $0011_2 = 3$, $1011_2 = 11$, $0111_2 = 7$, and $1111_2 = 15$. We can see, in this deployment order, a newly deployed ID preshares a unique key with at least two IDs that have already been deployed (if more than two IDs have been deployed).

Suppose we have deployed N nodes and $N < 2^m$. Given any two nodes, we look at how to find a logical path between them such that the logical path consists of deployed nodes only. If $N = 2^x$ and $x < m$, the lower $(m-x)$ bits of all the deployed IDs are 0. We can therefore consider the deployed nodes as having ID lengths of x (i.e., ignore the lower $(m - x)$ bits since they are 0) and take the normal CBKE forwarding strategy. The number of hops on a logical path is no more than $x - 1$. If $2^x < N < 2^{x+1}$, the lower $(m - x - 1)$ bits of all the deployed IDs are 0. We classify the IDs into two groups, P_x and Q_x, depending on whether bit $(m - x - 1)$ is 0 or 1.[d] All the IDs in P_x have bit $(m-x-1)$ as 0; all the IDs in Q_x have bit $(m-x-1)$ as 1. There are 2^x IDs in P_x, represented as $v \times 2^{m-x}$ where $v = 0, 1, 2, \ldots, 2^x - 1$ (since their lower $(m - x)$ bits are 0). There are $(N - 2^x)$ nodes in Q_x, having the form of $v \times 2^{m-x} + 2^{m-x-1}$ and $v \in [0, 2^x - 1]$. Suppose that the source node is s and the destination is d. We consider the following four cases:

- Both s and d are in P_x. Node s can take the normal forwarding strategy. The longest path has $x - 1$ logical hops.
- Node s is in P_x and d is in Q_x. Suppose d's ID is $v_d \times 2^{m-x} + 2^{m-x-1}$. Node s can first send the key to one node in P_x that preshare a key with d (e.g., node $v_d \times 2^{m-x}$). That node then forwards the session key to d. The longest path in this case consists of x logical hops.
- Node s is in Q_x and d is in P_x. This case is similar to the one above. Node s first sends the session key to a node in P_x that preshares a key with it. That node then forwards the key to d. The longest path in this case has x logical hops.
- Both s and d are in Q_x. We next show that there exists a logical path between s and d that involves only the nodes in Q_x. We consider only the $N-2^x$ nodes in Q_x (i.e., we ignore the nodes in P_x). Let $N_1 = N - 2^x$. Suppose $2^{x_1} \leq N_1 < 2^{x_1+1}$. Since all the IDs in Q_x have the same lower $(m - x)$ bits, we only need to consider the upper x bits. Our problem of finding a logical path reduces to one

[d]Recall that we refer to the lowest bit (the right most bit) as bit 0, the second lowest bit as bit 1, the third lowest bit as bit 2, and so on.

that considers a smaller number of nodes (i.e., the number of nodes reduces from N to N_1) and a smaller ID space (from x bits to x_1 bits). In this new problem, we repeat the process as in the original problem until the relationship of s and d falls into one of the three earlier cases, and we are done. The logical path therefore only contains nodes in Q_x, and the longest path consists of no more than x_1 logical hops ($x_1 < x$).

To summarize, for any value of N, we can always find a logical path between any two nodes and the logical path consists of only deployed nodes. Although we take $b = 1$ as an example to illustrate the method that handles partial deployment, it can be adopted for handling other radices when $b > 1$.

16.7. Conclusions

In this chapter, we have discussed CBKE, a pairwise key establishment protocol for large-scale sensor networks. The scheme provides more flexibility than previously proposed deterministic key exchange protocols to balance memory overhead, reliability, and communication cost. We also evaluated the trade-offs using simulation. Last, we analyzed the security of CBKE, and proposed further improvement to CBKE.

References

1. F. Zhang, Z. Shi and B. Wang, Chord-based key establishment schemes for sensor networks, *Proceedings of ITNG*, 731–737, Las Vegas, NV (April 2008).
2. S. A. Çamtepe and B. Yener, *Key Distribution Mechanisms for Wireless Sensor Networks: A Survey*, Technical Report TR-05-07, Computer Science Department, Rensselaer Polytechnic Institute (March 2005).
3. W. Zhang, M. Tran, S. Zhu and G. Cao, A random perturbation-based scheme for pairwise key establishment in sensor networks, *ACM MobiHoc*, Montreal, QC, Canada (September 2007).
4. A. Perrig, R. Szewczyk, V. Wen, D. Culler and J. D. Tygar, SPINS: Security protocols for sensor networks, *MobiCom*, 189–199 (July 2001).
5. L. Eschenauer and V. Gligor, A key management scheme for distributed sensor networks, *ACM Conference on Computer and Communication Security* (*CCS*), 41–47 (November 2002).
6. A. P. H. Chan and D. Song, Random key predistribution schemes for sensor networks, *IEEE Symposium on Security and Privacy*, 197–213 (May 2003).
7. W. Du, J. Deng, Y. S. Han and P. K. Varshney, A pairwise key pre-distribution scheme for wireless sensor networks, *ACM Conference on Computer and Communication Security* (*CCS*), 42–51, New York, NY (October 2003).
8. D. Liu and P. Ning, Establishing pairwise keys in distributed sensor networks, *ACM Conference on Computer and Communication Security* (*CCS*), 52–61, New York, NY (October 2003).

9. P. Tague and R. Poovendran, A canonical seed assignment model for key predistribution in wireless sensor networks, *ACM Transactions on Sensor Networks*, **3**(4) (October 2007).
10. H. Chan and A. Perrig, PIKE: Peer intermediaries for key establishment in sensor networks, *IEEE INFOCOM* (March 2005).
11. L. Zhou, J. Ni and C. V. Ravishankar, Efficient key establishment for group-based wireless sensor networks, *Proc. of ACM Workshop on Wireless Security* (*WiSe*) (September 2005).
12. D. Liu, P. Ning and W. Du, Group based key pre-distribution in wireless sensor networks, *Proc. of ACM Workshop on Wireless Security* (*WiSe*) (September 2005).
13. W. Du, J. Deng, Y. S. Han, S. Chen and P. Varshney, A key management scheme for wireless sensor networks using deployment knowledge, *Proc. IEEE INFOCOM*, Hong Kong (March 2004).
14. F. Liu and X. Cheng, A self-configured key establishment scheme for large-scale sensor networks, *Proc. of IEEE International Conference on Mobile Ad-hoc and Sensor Systems* (*MASS*) (October 2006).
15. L. Ma, X. Cheng, F. Liu, J. Rivera and F. An, iPAK: An *in-situ* pairwise key bootstrapping scheme for wireless sensor networks, *IEEE Transactions on Parallel and Distributed Systems* (*TPDS*), **18**(8), 1174–1184 (August 2007).
16. F. Liu and X. Cheng, LKE: A self-configuring scheme for location-aware key establishment in wireless sensor networks, *IEEE Transactions on Wireless Communications* (*TWC*), **7**(1), 224–232 (January 2008).
17. A. Y. Teymorian, L. Ma and X. Cheng, CAB: A cellular automata-based key management scheme for wireless sensor networks, *Military Communications Conference* (*MILCOM*) (October 2007).
18. S. Zhu, S. Setia and S. Jajodia, Leap: Efficient security mechanisms for large-scale distributed sensor networks, *ACM Transactions on Sensor Networks* (*TOSN*), **2**(4), 500–528 (November 2006).
19. D. Liu and P. Ning, Efficient distribution of key chain commitments for broadcast authentication in distributed sensor networks, *Proc. of the 10th Annual Network and Distributed System Security Symposium*, 263–276 (February 2003).
20. D. Liu and P. Ning, Multilevel μ-TESLA: Broadcast authentication for distributed sensor networks, *ACM Transactions on Embedded Computing Systems* (*TECS*), **3**(4), 800–836 (November 2004).
21. I. Stoica, R. Morris, D. L. Nowell, D. R. Karger, M. F. Kaashoek, F. Dabek and H. Balakrishnan, Chord: A scalable peer-to-peer lookup protocol for internet applications, *SIGCOMM*, 149–160, San Diego, CA (August 2001).
22. S. I. Huang, Adaptive random key distribution schemes for wireless sensor networks, *Proceedings of the International Workshop on Advanced Developments in Software and Systems Security* (December 2003).
23. B. Karp and H. T. Kung, GPSR: greedy perimeter stateless routing for wireless networks, *MobiCom*, 243–254 (August 2000).
24. G. Reitwiesner, Binary arithmetic, *Advances in Computers*, **1**, 231–308 (1960).

Chapter 17

Key Management in Wireless Sensor Networks with Multiple Base Stations

Yong Wang*, Byrav Ramamurthy† and Yuyan Xue‡

Department of Computer Science and Engineering
University of Nebraska-Lincoln
Lincoln, NE 68588-0115 USA
**ywang@cse.unl.edu*
†byrav@cse.unl.edu
‡yxue@cse.unl.edu

Most of the proposed key management protocols for wireless sensor networks (WSNs) in the literature assume that a single base station is used and that the base station is trustworthy. However, there are applications in which multiple base stations are used and the security of the base stations must be considered. This chapter investigates key management in wireless sensor networks with multiple base stations. It includes two parts: the first part introduces the current key management protocols in the literature; the second part presents a key management protocol, mKeying, for wireless sensor networks which include multiple base stations. mKeying includes two schemes, a key distribution scheme, mKeyDist, supporting multiple base stations in the network, and a key revocation scheme, mKeyRev, used to efficiently remove the compromised nodes from the network. Our analyses show that the proposed protocol is efficient and secure against the compromise of the base stations and the sensor nodes.

17.1. Introduction

Wireless sensor networks (WSNs) are promising solutions for many applications and security is an essential problem for WSNs. Among all security issues in WSNs, key management is a core mechanism to ensure the security of network services and applications in WSNs.

Most of existing works in the literature consider a WSN with a single base station. However, as the size of the sensor network grows, the distances between

*Yong Wang is currently with Calient Networks.

the base station and the associated sensor nodes also become larger. The increase in the distances may result in the following changes:

- The performance of the network degrades due to the increase in the packet loss as the size of the network grows.
- The lifetimes of the sensor nodes are reduced due to the high energy consumption involved in query-flooding and data-retrieval between the sensor nodes and the single base station.
- The lifetime of the sensor network is shortened dramatically because the energy of the sensor nodes close to the base station is exhausted quickly.

The deployment of multiple base stations in a sensor network is a promising solution.[1–3] By allowing multiple base stations in a sensor field, we can reduce the distances between the sensor nodes and the base stations, and thus reduce the energy consumption in sensor nodes and improve the performance of the sensor network.

In this chapter, we consider a WSN with multiple base stations. We consider the situations in which both the base stations and the sensor nodes could be compromised. Since the base stations are usually resource-rich devices, we assume that the base stations can communicate with each other directly using high speed wireless links. The base stations can work cooperatively in data acquisition in the network. To detect a compromised base station or a sensor node, intrusion detection techniques are involved. We assume that there are some methods to detect a compromised base station or sensor node in the network.

A key management protocol designed for a WSN with multiple base stations must satisfy the following requirements:

(1) The base stations and the sensor nodes can authenticate the messages from each other.
(2) The capture or compromise of any base stations should not affect the security of the sensor network.
(3) The capture or compromise of any sensor nodes should not affect the security of the sensor network.
(4) The capture or compromise of both a base station and sensor nodes should not affect the security of the sensor network.

This chapter investigates key management in wireless sensor networks with multiple base stations. It includes two parts: the first part introduces the current key management protocols in the literature; the second part presents a key management protocol, mKeying, for wireless sensor networks which include multiple base stations. mKeying includes two schemes, a key distribution scheme, mKeyDist, supporting multiple base stations in the network, and a key revocation scheme, mKeyRev, used to efficiently remove the compromised nodes from the network.

17.2. Key Management Protocols in WSNs

Key management is a core mechanism to ensure the security of network services and applications in WSNs. The goal of key management is to establish required keys between sensor nodes which must exchange data. Key management includes two aspects: key distribution and key revocation. Key distribution refers to the task of distributing secret keys between sensor nodes to provide communication secrecy and authenticity. Key revocation refers to the task of securely removing keys which are known to be compromised. Due to the constraints on sensor nodes, key management schemes in WSNs have many differences with the schemes in ad hoc networks.

WSNs suffer from many constraints on sensor nodes, including low computation capability, small memory, limited energy resources, etc. These constraints make the use of public key cryptography nearly impossible in sensor networks.[4] Thus, most proposed key management schemes are based on symmetric key cryptography. Further, a straight pairwise private key sharing scheme between every pair of nodes is also impractical in WSNs. A pairwise private key sharing scheme requires pre-distribution and storage of $n - 1$ keys in each node where n is the number of nodes in a sensor network. Due to the large amount of memory required, pairwise schemes are not viable when the network size is large. Moreover, most key pairs would be unusable since direct communication is possible only among neighboring nodes. This scheme is also not flexible for node addition and revocation.

In the remainder of this section, we first introduce key distribution protocols. Then, we discuss key revocation protocols. Another investigation of key management mechanisms for WSNs can be found in the paper by Camtepe and Yener.[5]

17.2.1. *Key distribution protocols*

Figure 17.1 shows a taxonomy of key distribution protocols in WSNs. According to the network structure, the protocols can be divided into centralized key distribution schemes and distributed key distribution schemes. According to the probability of key sharing between a pair of sensor nodes, the protocols can be divided into probabilistic key distribution schemes and deterministic key distribution schemes.

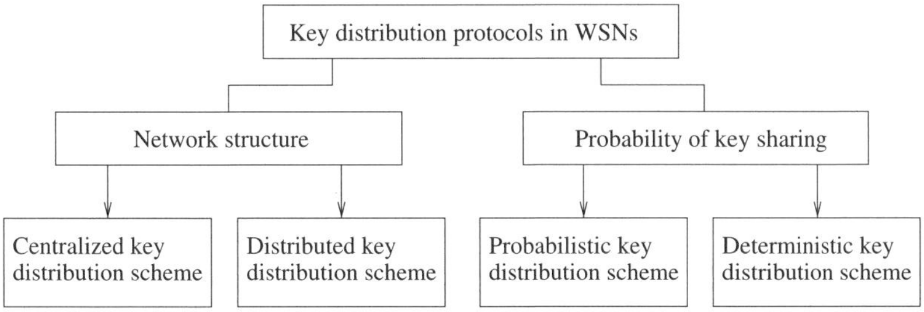

Fig. 17.1. Key distribution protocols in WSNs: a taxonomy.

In this section, we present a detailed overview of the main key distribution protocols in WSNs. We start with key distribution protocols based on network structure.

17.2.1.1. *Network structure based key distribution protocols*

The underlying network structure plays a significant role in the operation of key management protocols. According to the structure, the protocols can be divided into two categories: centralized key distribution schemes and distributed key distribution schemes.

Centralized key distribution schemes. In a centralized key distribution scheme, there is only one entity, which is often called a key distribution center (KDC), controlling the generation, regeneration and distribution of keys. The only proposed centralized key distribution scheme for WSNs in current literature is the LKHW scheme, which is based on Logical Key Hierarchy (LKH).[6] In this scheme, the base station is treated as a KDC and all keys are logically distributed in a tree rooted at the base station.

The central controller does not have to rely on any auxiliary entity to perform access control and key distribution. However, with only one managing entity, the central server is a single point of failure. The entire network and its security will be affected if there is a problem with the controller. During the time when the controller is not working, the network becomes vulnerable as keys are not generated, regenerated and distributed. Furthermore, the network may become too large to be managed by a single entity, thus affecting scalability.

Distributed key distribution schemes. In the distributed key distribution approaches, different controllers are used to manage key generation, regeneration and distribution, minimizing the risk of failure and allowing for better scalability. In this approach, more entities are allowed to fail before the whole network is affected.

Most proposed key management schemes are distributed schemes. These schemes also fall into deterministic and probabilistic categories which are discussed in detail in the following subsection.

17.2.1.2. *Key distribution protocols based on the probability of key sharing*

Next, we present the key management protocols based on the probability of key sharing between a pair of sensor nodes. We first discuss deterministic approaches and then discuss probabilistic approaches.

Deterministic approaches. Zhu *et al.* proposed a key management protocol, Localized Encryption and Authentication Protocol (LEAP), for sensor networks.[7] LEAP supports the establishment of four types of keys for each sensor node:

- an individual key shared with the base station (pre-distributed).
- a group key that is shared by all the nodes in the network (pre-distributed).

- pairwise keys shared with immediate neighboring nodes.
- a cluster key shared with multiple neighboring nodes.

The pairwise keys shared with immediate neighboring nodes are used to protect peer to peer communication while the cluster key is used for local broadcast. The pairwise keys can be setup as follows: in the key pre-distribution stage, each sensor node is loaded with an initial key K_I and each node A generates a master key $K_A = f_{K_I}(A)$ where f is a pseudo-random function. Then, in the neighbor discovery stage, A broadcasts a HELLO message and expects an acknowledgment from neighboring nodes, e.g., node B:

$$A \rightarrow * : A$$

$$B \rightarrow A : B, MAC(K_B, A|B).$$

Node A computes its pairwise key with B, $K_{A,B} = f_{K_B}(A)$ and node B knows A, K_B and can also compute $K_{A,B}$ in the same way. Then, $K_{A,B}$ serves as their pairwise key.

Cluster key establishment follows the pairwise key establishment phase. Suppose node A wants to establish a cluster key with all its immediate neighbors $B_1, B_2, \ldots, B_m$. Node A first generates a random key K_A^c, then encrypts this key with the pairwise key shared with each neighbor, and finally transmits the encrypted key to each neighbor B_i where $1 \leq i \leq m$.

$$A \rightarrow B_i : (K_A^c)_{K_{AB_i}}.$$

LEAP uses unicast for key exchange. Notice that most of the proposed security protocols were based on point-to-point handshaking procedures to negotiate session keys. Lai *et al.* proposed a BROadcast Session Key (BROSK) negotiation protocol.[8] BROSK assumes a master key is shared by all nodes in the network. To establish a session key K with its neighbors, such as node B, a sensor node A broadcasts a key negotiation message:

$$A \rightarrow * : ID_A|N_A, MAC(K, ID_A|N_A)$$

$$B \rightarrow * : ID_B|N_B, MAC(K, ID_B|N_B).$$

A and B will receive the broadcast message. They can verify the message using the master key K and both A and B can calculate the shared session key:

$$K_{A,B} = MAC(K, N_A|N_B).$$

BROSK therefore establishes pairwise session keys between every two neighboring nodes. It is both scalable and energy efficient.

Camtepe and Yener proposed a deterministic key distribution schemes for WSNs using Combinatorial Design Theory.[9] The Combinatorial Design Theory based pairwise key pre-distribution (CDTKeying) scheme is based on block design techniques in combinatorial design theory. It employs symmetric and generalized quadrangle design techniques. The scheme uses a finite projective plane of order n (for prime power n) to generate a symmetric design with parameters $n^2+n+1, n+1, 1$. The design supports n^2+n+1 nodes, and uses a key-pool of size n^2+n+1. It generates n^2+n+1 key-chains of size $n+1$ where every pair of key-chains has exactly one key in common, and every key appears in exactly $n+1$ key-chains. After the deployment, every pair of nodes finds exactly one common key. Thus, the probability of key sharing among a pair of sensor nodes is 1. The disadvantage of this solution is that the parameter n has to be a prime power, thus indicating that not all network sizes can be supported for a fixed key-chain size.

Lee and Stinson proposed two combinatorial design theory based deterministic schemes: ID-based one-way function scheme (IOS) and deterministic multiple space Blom's scheme (DMBS).[10] They further discussed the use of combinatorial set systems in the design of deterministic key pre-distribution schemes for WSNs.[11]

Probabilistic approaches. Most proposed key distribution schemes in WSNs are probabilistic and distributed schemes.

Eschenauer and Gligor introduced a key pre-distribution scheme for sensor networks which relies on probabilistic key sharing among the nodes of a random graph.[12] The scheme consists of three phases: key pre-distribution, shared-key discovery, and path key establishment. In the key pre-distribution phase, each sensor is equipped with a key ring held in the memory. The key ring consists of k keys which are randomly drawn from a large pool of P keys. The association information of the key identifiers in the key ring and sensor identifier is also stored at the base station. Further, the authors assumed that each sensor shares a pairwise key with the base station. In the shared key discovery phase, each sensor discovers its neighbors within wireless communication range with which it shares keys. Two methods to accomplish this are suggested.[12] The simplest method is for each node to broadcast a list of identifiers of the keys in their key ring in plain text allowing neighboring nodes to check whether they share a key. However, the adversary may observe the key-sharing patterns among sensors in this way. The second method uses the challenge-response technique to hide key-sharing patterns among nodes from an adversary. For every K_i on a key ring, each node could broadcast a list $\alpha, E_{K_i}(\alpha), i = 1, \ldots, k$ where α is a challenge. The decryption of $E_{K_i}(\alpha)$ with the proper key by a recipient would reveal the challenge and establish a shared key with the broadcasting node. This method requires the challenge α be well known in the sensor network allowing the recipient with the proper key to discover the challenge.

Finally, in the path-key establishment phase, a path-key is assigned for those sensor nodes within wireless communication range and not sharing a key but connected by two or more links at the end of the second phase. If a node is compromised, the base station can send a message to all other sensors to revoke the compromised node's key ring. Re-keying follows the same procedure as revocation. The messages from base station are signed by the pairwise key shared by base station and sensor nodes and thus it is ensured that no adversary can forge a base station. If a node is compromised, the attacker has a probability of approximately k/P to attack successfully any link. Because $k \ll P$, it only affects a small number of sensor nodes.

Inspired by the work by Eschenauer and Gligor,[12] which we call the basic random key scheme in the following section, additional random key pre-distribution schemes have been proposed in other studies.[13–18]

In the basic random key scheme, any two neighboring nodes need to find a single common key from their key rings to establish a secure link in the key-setup phase. However, Chan *et al.* observed that increasing the amount of key overlap in the key ring can increase the resilience of the network against node capture.[13] Thus, they proposed a q-composite keying scheme. It is required to share at least q common keys in the key setup phase to build a secure link between any two neighboring nodes. Further, they introduced a key update phase to enhance the basic random key scheme. Suppose A has a secure link to B after key setup phase and the secure key is k from the key pool P. Because k may be residing in the key ring memory of some other nodes in the network, the security of the link between A and B is jeopardized if any of those nodes are captured. Thus, it is better to update the communication key between A and B instead of using a key in the key pool. To address the problem, they presented a multipath key reinforcement for the key update. Assume there are j disjoint paths between A and B. A generates j random values $v_1, v_2, \ldots, v_j$ and then routes each random value along a different path to B. When B has received all j keys, the new link key can be computed by both A and B as:

$$k' = k \oplus v_1 \oplus v_2 \oplus \cdots \oplus v_j.$$

The adversary has to eavesdrop on all j paths if he/she wants to reconstruct the communication key. This security enhancement comes at the cost of more communication overhead needed to find multiple disjoint paths. Further, Chan *et al.* also developed a random-pairwise keys scheme for node-to-node authentication.

Blundo *et al.* presented a polynomial-based key pre-distribution protocol for group key pre-distribution.[19] The proposed scheme can also be adapted to sensor networks. The key setup server randomly generates a bivariate t-degree polynomial $f(x, y) = \sum_{i,j=0}^{t} a_{ij}x^i y^j$ over a finite field F_q where q is a prime number that is large enough to accommodate a cryptographic key such that it has the property of $f(x, y) = f(y, x)$. For each sensor i, the setup server computes a polynomial share of $f(x, y)$, that is, $f(i, y)$. For any two sensor nodes i and j, node i can compute the common key $f(i, j)$ by evaluating $f(i, y)$ at point j, and node j can compute the same key $f(j, i) = f(i, j)$ by evaluating $f(j, y)$ at point i. In this approach, each sensor node i needs to store a t-degree polynomial $f(i, x)$, which occupies $(t + 1) \log q$ storage space. This scheme is unconditionally secure and t-collusion resistant. However, the storage cost for a polynomial share is exponential in terms of the group size, making it prohibitive in sensor networks.

Inspired by the work by Eschenauer *et al.*,[12,13,19] Liu and Ning proposed a polynomial pool-based key pre-distribution scheme.[14] The scheme includes three phases: setup, direct key establishment and path key establishment. In the setup phase, the setup server randomly generates a set F of bivariate t-degree polynomials over the finite field F_q. For each sensor node, the setup server picks a subset of polynomials $F_i \subseteq F$ and assigns the polynomial shares of these polynomials to node i. In the direct key establishment stage, the sensor nodes find a shared polynomial with other sensor nodes and then establish a pairwise key using the polynomial-based key pre-distribution scheme proposed by Blundo.[19] The path key establishment phase is similar to that in the basic random key scheme. Further, the proposed framework allows for the study of multiple instantiations of possible pairwise key establishment schemes. Two of the possible instantiations, the key pre-distribution scheme based on random subset assignment and the grid-based key pre-distribution scheme, are also presented and analyzed in the chapter.

Similar to the work by Liu and Ning,[14] Du *et al.* presented another pairwise key pre-distribution scheme[16] which uses Blom's method.[20] The key difference between Liu's work[14] and Du's work[16] is that Liu's scheme[14] is based on a set of bivariate t-degree polynomials while Du's scheme[16] is based on Blom's method. The proposed scheme allows any pair of nodes in a network to be able to find a pairwise secret key. As long as no more than λ nodes are compromised, the network is perfectly secure (which is called the λ-secure property). To use Blom's method, during the pre-deployment phase, the base station first constructs a $(\lambda + 1) \times N$ matrix G over a finite field $GF(q)$, where N is the size of the network and G is considered to be public information. Then the base station creates a random $(\lambda + 1) \times (\lambda + 1)$ symmetric matrix D over $GF(q)$, and computes a $N \times (\lambda + 1)$ matrix $A = (D \cdot G)^T$, where $(D \cdot G)^T$ is the transpose of $D \cdot G$. Matrix D needs to be kept secret, and should not be disclosed to adversaries. It is easy to verify that $A \cdot G$ is a symmetric matrix.

$$A \cdot G = (D \cdot G)^T \cdot G = G^T \cdot D^T \cdot G = G^T \cdot D \cdot G = (A \cdot G)^T.$$

Thus, we know $K_{ij} = K_{ji}$. The idea is to use K_{ij} (or K_{ji}) as the pairwise key between node i and node j. To carry out the above computation, in the pre-distribution phase, for any sensor $k = 1, \ldots, N$:

- Store the kth row of matrix A at node k.
- Store the kth column of matrix G at node k.

Therefore, when nodes i and j need to find the pairwise key between them, they first exchange their columns of G, and then compute K_{ij} and K_{ji} respectively using their private rows of A.

In Du's proposed scheme,[16] each sensor node is loaded with G and τ distinct D matrices drawn from a large pool of ω symmetric matrices $D_1, \ldots, D_\omega$ of size

$(\lambda + 1) \times (\lambda + 1)$. For each D_i, calculate the matrix $A_i = (D_i \cdot G)^T$ and store the j-th row of A_i at this node. After deployment, each node needs to discover whether it shares any space with neighbors. If they find out that they have a common space, the nodes can follow Blom's method to build a pairwise key. The scheme is scalable and flexible.[16] Moreover, it is substantially more resilient against node capture as compared to Liu's scheme.[14]

Hwang *et al.* extended the basic random key scheme and proposed a cluster key grouping scheme.[18] They further analyzed the tradeoffs involved between energy, memory and security robustness.

Notice that location information helps to avoid unnecessary key assignments and thus improve the performance of sensor networks, such as connectivity, memory usage, and network resilience against node capture. Taking this into account, two random key pre-distribution schemes were proposed.[17,21] Although the presented schemes show improved performance, the deployment information, such as location, is required when sensors are deployed.

The above-mentioned schemes are classified and compared in Table 17.1.

17.2.2. *Key revocation protocols*

Key revocation refers to the task of securely removing keys which are known to be compromised. To detect a compromised sensor, intrusion detection techniques are employed. Intrusion detection is out of the scope of this work. We assume that there are some methods[22–24] for a base station to detect a compromised sensor node. Another issue which must be considered is reconfiguration. The topology of the WSN needs to be rebuilt after the compromised sensors are removed. Sensors might be re-deployed to replace those compromised sensors. The rest of the section reviews several known key revocation schemes in WSNs.

Recent work conducted on key revocation for WSNs include the schemes proposed by Eschenauer *et al.*[12,13,25–27] and no other schemes have been reported to date. These key revocation schemes can be divided into two categories: the centralized key revocation schemes[12,26,27] and the distributed key revocation schemes.[13,25] We discuss these in turn below.

17.2.2.1. *Centralized key revocation scheme*

In centralized key revocation scheme, a centralized authority (base station) is used to revoke compromised sensors.[12] Eschenauer and Gligor presented a key management scheme for WSNs, which also includes a centralized key revocation scheme (referred to as EsRev scheme in the remainder of the chapter).[12] In case a sensor node is compromised, the base station can send a message to all other sensors to revoke the compromised node's key ring. The revocation scheme can be divided into three phases: signature key distribution, key revocation and link reconfiguration.

Table 17.1. Classification and comparison of key distribution schemes in WSNs.

	Protocol	Ref.	Theory	Master key	Pairwise key	Path key	Cluster key	Scalability	Resiliency	Processing load	Comm. load	Storage load
I	All pairwise	—	n/a	n/a	Yes	No	No	Low	Low	Low	Low	High
	LEAP	7	n/a	Yes	Yes	Yes	Yes	Good	Low	Low	Low	Low
	BROSK	8	n/a	Yes	Yes	No	No	Good	Low	Low	Low	Low
	LKHW	6	LKH	Yes	Yes	No	Yes	Limited	Low	Low	Low	Low
	CDTKeying	9	Combinatorial	n/a	Yes	No	No	Good	Good	Medium	Medium	High
	IOS & DMBS	10	Combinatorial	n/a	Yes	No	No	Good	Good	Medium	Medium	High
II	Basic random key	12	Random graph	n/a	Yes	Yes	No	Good	Good	Medium	Medium	High
	q-composite	13	Random graph	n/a	Yes	Yes	No	Good	Good	Medium	Medium	High
	Polynomial based	14	t-degree polynomial & random graph	n/a	Yes	Yes	No	Good	Good	Medium	Medium	High
	Blom based	16	Blom's method & random graph	n/a	Yes	Yes	No	Good	Good	Medium	Medium	High
	Deployment knowledge based	17	Random graph	n/a	Yes	Yes	No	Good	Good	Medium	Medium	Medium
	Cluster key grouping	18	Random graph	n/a	Yes	Yes	No	Good	Good	Medium	Medium	High
	Location based	21	Random graph	n/a	Yes	Yes	No	Good	Good	Medium	Medium	Medium

Note: Category I denotes deterministic approaches and category II denotes probabilistic approaches. Master key is the key shared by all the nodes in the network. Pairwise key is the key shared between two neighboring nodes. Path key denotes the key shared between any two nodes which need exchange data but does not share a pairwise key. Cluster key denotes the common key shared by all cluster members.

In the signature key distribution phase, the base station generates a signature key K_e and unicasts it to each node by encrypting it with a pairwise key K^{ci} shared by the base station with the ith sensor node.

In the key revocation phase, the base station broadcasts a single message containing a list of key identifiers for the key ring to be revoked signed by the signature key. Each sensor verifiers the signature of the key revocation message, locates those identifiers in its key ring, and removes the corresponding keys.

Once the keys are removed from the key rings, some links may disappear, and the affected nodes need to reconfigure those links by restarting the shared-key discovery, and possibly the path-key establishment, phases.

EsRev scheme requires n unicast messages and one broadcast message to revoke a compromised sensor node. In a large scale sensor network, distributing the signature key might be a problem. Pre-distributing the signature key might be possible; however, once the signature key is compromised, the adversary could use the signature key to duplicate the revocation messages from the base station.

Zhang *et al.* proposed a location-based revocation scheme utilizing multiple revocation messages.[27] When the revocation area is large or complicated, the revocation area can be divided into sub-areas. For each sub-area, a revocation message is sent to a certain node within that area using GPSR protocol,[28] and then the revocation message is multicasted to the remaining sub-area. The revocation message includes the identifier of the sensor nodes to be revoked and the scope of the revocation area. On receiving the message, for each node, if it has received the message before or is outside of the revocation area, the message is dropped. If the sensor node is within the revocation area indicated by the revocation message, the sensor node records the identifier of the revoked sensor node, and rebroadcast the message to its neighboring nodes. The revocation scheme, referred to as the GPSRRev scheme, is also a centralized key revocation scheme.

17.2.2.2. *Distributed key revocation scheme*

In a distributed key revocation scheme, no centralized authority is used. Chan *et al.* proposed a distributed key revocation scheme for sensor networks[13] and further investigated this scheme.[25] In this distributed key revocation scheme, a vote is cast and collected among sensor nodes. If the vote tally against a sensor node exceeds a specified threshold, the sensor node will be revoked. Chan's scheme depends on the secret sharing scheme.[29] The distributed key revocation scheme is described below.

The revocation timeline is divided into sessions. Each sensor has at most s_{total} revocation sessions against any target nodes (compromised nodes). Before the sensor network is deployed, the setup server generates a t degree random polynomial $q_{A_s}(x) = a_0 + a_1 x + \cdots + a_{t-1} x^{t-1}$ for each session s on sensor node A. For each node B of A's participants (a participant of A is a sensor which shares a key with node A), the setup server loads the revocation vote $(q_{B_s}(x_{AB_s}), x_{AB_s})$ from A against B on node A. This revocation vote is encrypted by a mask $Mask_{AB_s}$ that B gives to A. That is, the preloaded data on A against B is $E_{Mask_{AB_s}}(q_{B_s}(x_{AB_s}), x_{AB_s})$. For each vote, the setup server also loads the $\log m$ authentication hash values for the Merkle tree with leaves $(q_{B_s}(x_{iB_s}), x_{iB_s})$ for each node i in B's participants (a total of m leaves). The root R_B of the Merkle tree is also loaded on A. Finally, the setup server loads $H^2 q_{B_s}$, which is the hash of the hash of the revocation polynomial of B on A. This will allow nonlocal participants (a nonlocal participant of B is a sensor node which shares a key with B but multi-hops (> 1) away from B) to verify the authenticity of a revocation decision against B.

In the beginning of each session, the masks are exchanged among neighboring nodes. The purpose of the mask key is to ensure that each node is only able to revoke sensors within its immediate neighborhood.

Each revocation session is divided into three states: pending, active and completed. The pending state indicates that there is no voting occurs in the current session. When the first vote of the session is cast and received by A, A changes its state to active. The active state lasts for exactly Δ_s time for each node, after which the node transitions to the completed state for this session, and starts the pending state for the next session.

When A votes against B during the revocation session s, it decrypts the vote using B's mask key $Mask_{AB_s}$ and broadcasts $(q_{B_s}(x_{AB_s}), x_{AB_s})$ along with the $\log m$ Merkle authentication values. This is a local neighborhood broadcast. The broadcast only needs to go far enough to ensure complete dissemination in the neighborhood of B. The node receiving the vote verifies the authenticity of the vote using the Merkle authentication values. The node will disseminate the broadcast if the verification is successful. When A casts a vote on B, it will vote both in the current session and on the next session. Voting on the next session occurs immediately upon completion of the current session.

When A's state for the session has transited to completed state, it counts the number of votes it has received when it was in the active state. If A has at least t revocation votes, then A can use these t points to compute the random t-degree polynomial q_{B_s} using the secret sharing scheme.[29] From this, A computes the hash of the polynomial, Hq_{B_s}. This value is then broadcasted through the entire network. All participants of B receiving this value can verify it by computing the hash of the received value. If the verification is successful, the keys shared with B will be revoked.

Note that Chan's scheme, referred to as DistRev scheme, is built on some simplifying assumptions; for example, each node knows its neighboring nodes before deployment. It is hard to satisfy these requirements.

Compared with the centralized key revocation schemes, the distributed key revocation schemes are faster because they require local broadcast and avoid a single point of failure. However, the distributed key revocation schemes are also more complex than the centralized key revocation schemes and, hence, more prone to design error since compromised sensor nodes can participate in the revocation protocol and attempt to block or circumvent it. In addition, it is also possible to compromise enough nodes to sabotage the distributed key revocation scheme. For more detailed information about the distributed key revocation scheme, please refer to the work by Chan *et al.*[13,25]

As discussed before, many key management protocols have been specifically designed for WSNs, however, most of the proposed key management protocols consider a single base station in the WSN and assume that the base station is trustworthy. In consideration of multiple base stations and their security, none of the current proposed key management protocols can be directly used. For example, most proposed key management protocols assume that each sensor node is preloaded with a master key, shared by all nodes in the sensor network, or a pairwise key, shared with the base station.[12] A simple clone of a base station to multiple base stations indicates that all the base stations use the same master key or the same key set of pairwise keys. Several issues arise under such assumptions. First, the base station can authenticate the messages from the sensor nodes; however, the sensor nodes cannot authenticate the messages from the base stations. Second, once a base station is captured or compromised, the master key and the whole pairwise key set are exposed. As a result, any adversaries with this key set can utilize the WSN without incurring any cost to deploy the sensor network.

A few papers discussed multiple base stations in the literature.[1,2,30] However, most of the papers focus on how to save energy and improve network lifetime by using multiple base stations in the network. None of these works discussed key management issues. In the paper by Zhang *et al.*,[27] the authors considered a sensor network with multiple mobile base stations and proposed some schemes to restrict a mobile base station without impeding its capability to carry out any authorized operations for an assigned task. However, the proposed revocation schemes were based on local multicast and may be not scalable to large sensor networks.

Next, we present our proposed key management protocol, mKeying, for the WSNs with multiple base stations.

17.3. mKeying: A Key Management Protocol for WSNs with Multiple Base Stations

In this section, we present a key management protocol, mKeying, for WSNs with multiple base stations. We assume that there are at most m base stations and n sensors in the network ($m \ll n$). The base stations are deliberately distributed in the field to ensure that each sensor node can be reached by at least γ ($\gamma < m$) base stations within one hop of communication range. The base stations and the sensor nodes are identified by globally unique numbers called *base station identifier* and *sensor identifier* respectively. There is no overlapping between the base station identifier space and the sensor identifier space.

mKeying includes two schemes, a key distribution scheme, mKeyDist, and a key revocation scheme, mKeyRev. In the remainder of this section, we first motivate and present an overview of the mKeying protocol. Then, we introduce security model and demonstrate broadcast authentication, key distribution, revocation, and bootstrap processes using the mKeying protocol.

17.3.1. *mKeying overview*

Our proposed key management protocol supports the establishment of five types of keys for each sensor node — *pairwise key*, *individual key*, *session key*, *encryption key* and *message authentication code (MAC) key*.

Pairwise key: Each sensor shares a pairwise key with each of its immediate neighbors. The pairwise key is used to generate the encryption key and the MAC key to ensure data confidentiality and authentication.

Individual key: Each node has a unique key shared pairwise with the base station. This key is used for the base station to authenticate individual sensor node.

Session key: This is a global key shared by all nodes in the network. The need for the session key is motivated by the key revocation scheme. We present an efficient key revocation scheme, KeyRev, for a WSN with single base station using a globally distributed session key.[26] In this paper, we extend the KeyRev scheme to support multiple base stations in the network (Sec. 17.3.5).

Encryption key and message authentication code key: The encryption key and the MAC key are used to ensure the security of the communication in a sensor network. The encryption key and the MAC key are derived from the pairwise key and the session key (Sec. 17.3.4).

17.3.2. *Security model*

In literature, most research studies assume that the base station is trustworthy and consider only the compromise of the sensor nodes. However, due to the hostile environments in the deployment area, it is necessary to consider the security of the base stations as well. In this chapter, we consider the situations in which both the base stations and the sensors can be compromised.

17.3.3. *Broadcast authentication*

We limit the capability of broadcasting authentication messages only to the base stations. We adopt the practical broadcast authentication protocol proposed by Liu *et al.*[31] to support multiple base stations in the WSNs. Note that the broadcast authentication protocol for WSNs with multiple base stations must be properly designed. A simple clone of $\mu TESLA$ instance for each mobile base stations does not work. Two schemes were proposed: a basic approach and a special instantiation for long-lived senders. We use the second one.[31]

17.3.4. *mKeyDist, key distribution scheme*

17.3.4.1. *Pairwise key and individual key*

The pairwise key and the individual key can be set up using Blundo's theory.[19]

Before sensor nodes are distributed, the setup server randomly generates a bivariate t-degree polynomial

$$f(x,y) = \sum_{i,j=0}^{t} a_{ij}x^i y^j$$

over a finite field F_q where q is a prime number that is large enough to accommodate a cryptographic key such that it has the property of $f(x,y) = f(y,x)$. For each sensor i, the setup server computes a polynomial share of $f(x,y)$, that is, $f(i,y)$, and loads the single-variate polynomial $f(i,y)$ to the sensor i. For any two sensor nodes i and j, node i can compute the common key $f(i,j)$ by evaluating $f(i,y)$ at point j, and node j can compute the same key $f(j,i) = f(i,j)$ by evaluating $f(j,y)$ at point i. Thus, both the sensor i and the sensor j can find the shared pairwise key.

For example, let the setup server generate a bivariate 2-degree polynomial $f(x,y) = x^2 + 3xy + y^2$. Sensors 5 and 6 are loaded with a single-variate 2-degree polynomial $f(5,y) = y^2 + 15y + 25$ and $f(6,y) = y^2 + 18y + 36$ respectively. When sensors 5 and 6 exchange their identifiers, sensors 5 calculates $f(5,6) = 6^2 + 15 * 6 + 25 = 151$ and sensors 6 calculates $f(6,5) = 5^2 + 18 * 5 + 36 = 151$. Both of them can calculate the same pairwise key 151.

The individual key can be set up in the same way. Before the base stations are deployed, each base station j is loaded with a single-variate polynomial $f(j,y)$. By exchanging the identifiers between a base station and a sensor node, both the base station and the sensor node can find the shared individual key.

17.3.4.2. *Session key*

The session key is a global key shared by all the nodes. We propose to use distributed key schemes such as secure group communication schemes to generate a group key among the base stations first. Then, the session key can be derived from the group key and dynamically distributed to the sensor nodes. The secure group communication schemes are out of the scope of this chapter. Please refer to Ref. 32 for details.

Let K_g be the group key generated by the secure group communication scheme, the session key K_s^i in ith session can be derived from the group key using a pseudo-random function $\mathcal{G}$:

$$K_s^i = \mathcal{G}(K_g, i).$$

The distribution of session key is based on the personal key share distribution scheme.[33] Let K_s^i be the current session key in the ith session, the session key distribution process is described below:

(1) Secret share distribution: In the pre-distribution stage, the setup server randomly picks m $2t$-degree masking polynomial, $h_j(x) = h_{j,0}+h_{j,1}x+\cdots+h_{j,2t}x^{2t}$, $1 \leq j \leq m$, over F_q. Each sensor s_u is preloaded with the personal secret, $S_u = \{h_j(u)|1 \leq j \leq m\}$. Each base station b_j gets the polynomial $h_j(x)$.
(2) Distinct share broadcast: Given a set of revoked sensor nodes, $R = \{r_1, r_2, \ldots, r_w\}$, $w \leq t$, the base station b_j randomly picks a t-degree polynomial $p_j(x)$ and constructs $q_j(x) = K_s^i - p_j(x)$. Then, the base station distributes the shares of t-degree polynomial $p_j(x)$ and $q_j(x)$ to non-revoked sensors via the following broadcast message:

$$\begin{aligned} M = &\{R\} \\ &\cup \{P_j(x) = g(x)p_j(x) + h_j(x)\} \\ &\cup \{Q_j(x) = g(x)q_j(x) + h_j(x)\}, \end{aligned} \tag{17.1}$$

where the revocation polynomial $g(x)$ is constructed as

$$g(x) = (x - r_1)(x - r_2)\cdots(x - r_w).$$

The broadcast authentication is ensured by the scheme in Ref. 31.
(3) Session key recovery: If any non-revoked sensor nodes s_u receives such a broadcast message, it evaluates the polynomial $P_j(x)$ and $Q_j(x)$ at point u and gets $P_j(u) = g(u)p_j(u) + h_j(u)$ and $Q_j(u) = g(u)q_j(u) + h_j(u)$. Because s_u knows $h_j(u)$ and $g_j(u) \neq 0$, it can compute $p_j(u) = \frac{P_j(u)-h_j(u)}{g(u)}$ and $q_j(u) = \frac{Q_j(u)-h_j(u)}{g(u)}$. s_u finally can compute the new session key $K_s^i = p_j(u) + q_j(u)$. The revoked sensors cannot recover the session key because $g(x) = 0$.

A sensor node can recover multiple copies of the session key since each sensor node can be reached by at least γ base stations. A session key is only accepted when the sensor node restores at least γ copies of the session key.

17.3.4.3. *Encryption key and message authentication code key*

Let $K_{A,B}$ denote the pairwise key shared between the sensor A and the sensor B, and K_s^i be the current session key. The encryption key K_{encr} and the message authentication code (MAC) key K_{mac} are calculated as follows:[26]

$$K_{encr} = \mathcal{F}(MAC(K_{A,B}, K_s^i), 1)$$
$$K_{mac} = \mathcal{F}(MAC(K_{A,B}, K_s^i), 2),$$

where $\mathcal{F}(K, x)$ is a pseudo-random function and x is an integer 1 or 2 for generating K_{encr} or K_{mac} respectively.

The complete message A sends to B is:

$$A \rightarrow B : \{M|T_s\}_{K_{encr}}, MAC(K_{mac}, \{M|T_s\}_{K_{encr}}), \tag{17.2}$$

where M is the message, and T_s is the timestamp when sending the message. The sensor B can calculate the same K_{encr} and K_{mac} with the sensor A. Thus, B can authenticate and decrypt the message.

17.3.5. *mKeyRev, key revocation scheme*

We consider three situations in the key revocation process: the compromise of a base station, the compromise of a sensor node, and the compromise of both a base station and a sensor node. We assume that each sensor maintains a list: *node revocation list* (*NRL*). A *NRL* includes all the entity (base station or sensor node) identifiers which have been revoked in the network. The revocation list is empty initially and will be populated as the time goes by. The revocation list is checked for any incoming and outgoing messages to ensure that only the valid entities are involved in the network.

Case 1: When a base station is compromised, the compromised base station needs to be removed from the network. Since the security of the communication is ensured by the encryption key and the MAC key which are both bound up with the session key, the compromised base station can be removed from the network if it cannot reveal the next session key. To do this, the compromised base station will be forced to leave the group and a new group key is generated. Thus, when the new session key is distributed to the network, the compromised base station will be removed from the network.

Since a sensor node accepts a session key only when it can restore at least γ ($\gamma < m$) session keys for the same session from the distinct share broadcast messages (Eq. (17.1)), an attacker must compromise γ base stations to start the revocation attack.

Case 2: If a sensor node is found to be compromised, the compromised sensor can be removed using the session key distribution scheme. After the compromised sensor identifier is added to the revocation list, the revoked sensor cannot recover the new session key since $g(x) = 0$ and thus the revoked sensor cannot reveal the new encryption keys and the MAC keys. Although the compromised sensor still has the pairwise keys with its neighboring nodes, it cannot decrypt any messages and authenticate itself in the network.

Since the capability of broadcasting authentication messages is limited to the base stations only (ensured by the scheme by Liu *et al.*[31]), a compromised sensor node cannot start the revocation attack either.

Case 3: In case that both a base station and a sensor node are compromised, the base station needs to be revoked first, followed by the revocation of the sensor node. The detail steps are described in Case 1 and Case 2.

17.3.6. *Bootstrap*

To bootstrap a WSN using mKeying, pre-distributed key materials are required to be loaded on the sensor nodes before they are deployed. These pre-distributed key materials include the polynomials used to set up the pairwise key, the secret shares to recover the session key, and the required materials for broadcast authentication.[31] After the sensor nodes are deployed, the pairwise keys are set up first, followed by the distribution of the session key. Then, the encryption keys and the MAC keys can be set up on the fly.

17.4. Security and Performance Analysis

In this section we first discuss the security of the protocol. Then, we analyze the computation, communication costs and storage requirement of mKeying protocol.

17.4.1. *Security analysis*

Our proposed key management protocol — mKeying, satisfies the following properties:

Property 1. Only the authorized sensors can communicate in the network. The communication among the sensors is ensured by the encryption key K_{encr} and the MAC key K_{mac} as shown in Eq. (17.2). Unauthorized sensors (outside attackers) cannot participate the communication without proper assigned key materials.

Property 2. The session key distribution process is secure. The distribution of session key is based on the personal key share distribution scheme.[33] A revoked sensor cannot recover the session key because $g(x) = 0$. Since the broadcast authentication is ensured by Liu's scheme,[31] an outside attacker cannot masquerade a base station disseminating a session key and start a revocation attack either.

Property 3. The key revocation scheme is secure inspite of not removing the pre-distributed key materials at a compromised sensor node. Although, without removing the pre-distributed key materials, the compromised sensor could reveal the pairwise keys, the adversaries cannot figure out the encryption key K_{encr} and MAC key K_{mac} if the session key is updated. In the worst case, an adversary might use chosen plaintext attack to crack the session key, however, the attack itself is also time consuming. As long as the session key lifetime is less than the session key cracking time, the proposed key revocation scheme is secure.

17.4.2. *Performance analysis*

Because base stations are usually regarded as resource-rich nodes, we focus on the performance of sensor nodes:

17.4.2.1. *Computation cost*

There are five different types of keys in our proposed protocol. To calculate the pairwise key, the individual key, and the session key, polynomial evaluation is required. The computation of polynomial evaluation is efficient. The calculation of the encryption key and the MAC key is based on a pseudo-random function. Thus, the key distribution scheme is efficient in computation.

17.4.2.2. *Communication cost*

Since the setup of the pairwise key and the individual key does not involve any extra message exchanges among the sensor nodes and the base stations (the base station identifier and the sensor identifier can be send along with a message between the sensor node and the base station), we focus on the distribution of the session key. The session key is distributed to the network using broadcasting message in one round. The maximum size of the broadcast message in bits is decided by $S = (5t + 2)\log q$. Assume B indicate the transmission rate of the base stations, L be the maximum range between the base stations and the sensor nodes. The session key distribution time can be calculated as:

$$t_s = \frac{S}{B} + \frac{L}{3 * 10^8} \approx \frac{(5t+2)\log q}{B}.$$

(the propagation delay is very small compared with the transmission time). In case a sensor node is compromised, no extra messages are required to remove the compromised sensor node.

17.4.2.3. *Storage requirement*

Let d represent the number of neighboring nodes around a sensor and m be the number of the base stations. Each sensor node need d storage units for the pairwise keys, m storage units for the individual keys, and three storage units for the session key, the encryption key and the MAC key. In addition, to calculate the pairwise key and the individual key, each sensor need $t + 1$ storage units for the t-degree polynomial and each sensor has also to be loaded with m secret shares to recover the session key. Thus, the total storage units of keys required for each sensor is $2m + d + t + 4$.

17.5. Simulations and Discussion

The proposed key distribution scheme, mKeyDist, does not require any extra message exchanges among the sensor nodes and the base stations. Thus, the key distribution scheme does not add any extra communication overhead. In this section, we focus on the performance of the key revocation scheme, mKeyRev. We evaluated the performance of the mKeyRev scheme in SENSIM, a component-based discrete-event simulator for sensor networks. We consider two sensor network experimental settings: a small-scale sensor network with 100 nodes uniformly dispersed in a field with dimension 100 m × 100 m and a large-scale sensor network with 1000 nodes uniformly dispersed in a field with dimension 2000 m × 2000 m. In both the networks, we assume each sensor node can be reached by at least four base stations ($\gamma = 4$).

We compare the mKeyRev scheme with the centralized key revocation scheme, EsRev scheme[12] and the GPSR-based revocation scheme, GPSRRev scheme.[27] Both of the schemes, EsRev scheme and GPSRRev scheme, are designed for single-base-station WSNs. For these two schemes, we assume the base station is located at the center of field. We further assume that the sensor filed in the GPSRRev scheme is divided into four subareas.

The evaluation metrics include the key revocation time and the average energy consumption per node to revoke a compromised sensor in the network. The key revocation time is the time duration from when the key revocation protocol starts until all the uncompromised sensor nodes receive the key revocation message. We consider the mKeyRev scheme operating on a finite field F_q, where q is a 56-bit integer. The polynomial degree t in the mKeyRev scheme is set to four. We use the simulator parameters that represent the Mica2 Mote radio characteristics. For each test, we randomly select one sensor to be revoked and run the simulation ten times. The average value is measured.

Tables 17.2 and 17.3 show the key revocation time and the average energy consumption to revoke a compromised sensor node in the two sensor networks. As the tables show, the GPSRRev and the mKeyRev schemes are much better than the EsRev scheme in both the key revocation time and the average energy consumption per node. The GPSRRev scheme is better than the mKeyRev scheme in the key revocation time in the small-scale sensor network; however, the mKeyRev scheme

Table 17.2. Key revocation time.

Scheme	100-node WSN Time (seconds)	1000-node WSN Time (seconds)
EsRev	49.63	496.06
GPSRRev	1.02	4.04
mKeyRev	2.36	2.48

Table 17.3. Average energy consumption to revoke a compromised sensor.

Scheme	100-node WSN Energy (Joules)	1000-node WSN Energy (Joules)
EsRev	0.71	7.14
GPSRRev	0.19	0.29
mKeyRev	0.04	0.04

is better than the GPSRRev scheme in the large-scale sensor network. Further, in both of the networks, the mKeyRev scheme consumes less energy than the EsRev and the GPSRRev schemes. Note that the key revocation time and the average energy consumption to revoke a single sensor node by using mKeyRev scheme have only a slight difference between the 100-node sensor network and the 1000-node sensor network. It indicates that the mKeyRev scheme is scalable to large-scale sensor networks. The good performance of the mKeyRev scheme is due to the efficient session key distribution scheme shown in Sec. 17.3.4. The mKeyRev scheme is the best in overall performance for removing a compromised sensor node in the network.

Notice that the proposed protocol requires a session key to be distributed to the network during each session. The duration of the session time could be set and adjusted dynamically according to the application to reduce the background traffic in the sensor network. In addition, a few papers have been proposed to address the key management issues in heterogeneous sensor networks which can also be used to improve the performance of the sensor network when the size of the network grows.[34,35] We are confident that our proposed protocol can also be applied to heterogeneous sensor networks.

17.6. Conclusions and Summary

In this chapter, we discuss the current key management protocols in the literature and present a key management protocol, mKeying, for wireless sensor networks with multiple base stations. mKeying includes two schemes, mKeyDist and mKeyRev. Unlike most existing key management protocols for wireless sensor networks which assume that a single base station is used and the base station is trustworthy, the mKeying protocol supports multiple base stations and considers the situations in which both the base stations and the sensor nodes can be compromised. Our analyses show that the proposed protocol is efficient and secure against the compromise of the base stations and the sensor nodes. We assume that an appropriate routing protocol is used to support multiple base stations in the network. Further investigations include the security issues related to data acquisition and the routing issues arising in supporting multiple base stations.

References

1. S. R. Gandham, M. Dawande, R. Prakash and S. Venkatesan, Energy efficient schemes for wireless sensor networks with multiple mobile base stations, *Proceeding of IEEE Global Telecommunications Conference*, **1**, 377–381 (December 2003).
2. E. I. Oyman and C. Ersoy, Multiple sink network design problem in large scale wireless sensor networks, *Proceeding of the IEEE International Conference on Communications*, 3663–3667 (June 2004).
3. Y. Wang, *Key Management Protocols in Hybrid Wireless Sensor Networks*, PhD thesis, University of Nebraska-Lincoln (September 2007).
4. Y. Wang, G. Attebury and B. Ramamurthy, A survey of security issues in wireless sensor networks, *IEEE Communications Surveys and Tutorials.* **8**(2), (2006).
5. S. A. Camtepe and B. Yener, *Key Distribution Mechanisms for Wireless Sensor Networks: A Survey*, Technical Report TR-05-07, Computer Science Department at RPI (2005).
6. R. D. Pietro, L. V. Mancini, Y. W. Law, S. Etalle and P. J. M. Havinga, LKHW: A directed Diffusion-Based secure multicast scheme for wireless sensor networks, *ICPPW'03: Proceedings of the 32nd International Conference on Parallel Processing Workshops*, 397–406, IEEE Computer Society Press (2003).
7. S. Zhu, S. Setia and S. Jajodia, LEAP: Efficient security mechanisms for large-scale distributed sensor networks, *CCS'03: Proceedings of the 10th ACM conference on Computer and Communications Security*, 62–72, New York, NY, USA (2003). ACM Press. ISBN 1-58113-738-9.
8. B. Lai, S. Kim and I. Verbauwhede, Scalable session key construction protocols for wireless sensor networks, *IEEE Workshop on Large Scale Real Time and Embedded Systems* (2002).
9. S. A. Cametepe and B. Yener, Combinatorial design of key distribution mechanisms for wireless sensor networks, *Proceedings of 9th European Symposium on Research Computer Security*, Sophia Antipolis, France (2004).
10. J. Lee and D. R. Stinson, Deterministic key predistribution schemes for distributed sensor networks, *Proceedings of Selected Areas in Cryptography*, 294–307 (2004).
11. J. Lee and D. R. Stinson, A combinatorial approach to key predistribution for distributed sensor networks, *Proceedings of the IEEE Wireless Communication and Networking Conference* (2005).
12. L. Eschenauer and V. D. Gligor, A key-management scheme for distributed sensor networks, *CCS'02: Proceedings of the 9th ACM conference on Computer and communications security*, 41–47, New York, NY, USA, (2002), ACM Press. ISBN 1-58113-612-9.
13. H. Chan, A. Perrig and D. Song, Random key predistribution schemes for sensor networks, *Proceedings of IEEE Symposium on Security and Privacy*, Oakland, CA, USA (May 2003).
14. D. Liu and P. Ning, Establishing pairwise keys in distributed sensor networks, *CCS'03: Proceedings of the 10th ACM Conference on Computer and Communications security*, 52–61, New York, NY, USA (2003), ACM Press. ISBN 1-58113-738-9.
15. R. D. Pietro, L. V. Mancini and A. Mei, Random key-assignment for secure wireless sensor networks, *SASN'03: Proceedings of the 1st ACM Workshop on Security of Ad Hoc and Sensor Networks*, 62–71, New York, NY, USA, (2003). ACM Press, ISBN 1-58113-783-4.
16. W. Du, J. Deng, Y. S. Han and P. K. Varshney, A pairwise key pre-distribution scheme for wireless sensor networks, *CCS'03: Proceedings of the 10th ACM conference*

on Computer and communications security, 42–51, New York, NY, USA (2003). ACM Press. ISBN 1-58113-738-9.
17. W. Du, J. Deng, Y. S. Han, S. Chen and P. K. Varshney, A key management scheme for wireless sensor networks using deployment knowledge, *Proceedings of IEEE INFOCOM*, 586–597 (2004).
18. D. D. Hwang, B. Lai and I. Verbauwhede, Energy-memory-security tradeoffs in distributed sensor networks, *Proceedings of 3rd International Conference on Ad-Hoc Networks and Wireless*, 70–81 (July 2004).
19. C. Blundo, A. D. Santis, A. Herzberg, S. Kutten, U. Vaccaro and M. Yung, Perfectly-secure key distribution for dynamic conferences, *CRYPTO '92: Proceedings of the 12th Annual International Cryptology Conference on Advances in Cryptology*, 471–486, London, UK (1993), Springer-Verlag, ISBN 3-540-57340-2.
20. R. Blom, An optimal class of symmetric key generation systems, *Proceedings of the EUROCRYPT 84 Workshop on Advances in Cryptology: Theory and Application of Cryptographic Techniques*, 335–338, New York, NY, USA (1985), Springer-Verlag New York, Inc. ISBN 0-387-16076-0.
21. D. Liu and P. Ning, Location-based pairwise key establishments for static sensor networks, *Proceedings of the ACM Workshop on Security in Ad Hoc and Sensor Networks* (October 2003).
22. S. Zhu, S. Setia, S. Jajodia and P. Ning, An interleaved hop-by-hop authentication scheme for filtering of injected false data in sensor networks, *Proceedings of IEEE Symposium on Security and Privacy*, 259–271, Oakland, CA, USA (May 2004).
23. F. Ye, H. Luo, S. Lu and L. Zhang, Statistical en-route filtering of injected false data in sensor networks, *Proceedings of IEEE INFOCOM* (2004).
24. G. Wang, W. Zhang, C. Cao and T. L. Porta, On supporting distributed collaboration in sensor networks, *Proceedings of MILCOM* (2003).
25. H. Chan, V. Gligor, A. Perrig and G. Muralidharan, On the distribution and revocation of cryptographic keys in sensor networks, *IEEE Transactions on Dependable and Secure Computing*, **2**(3), 233–247 (2005).
26. Y. Wang, B. Ramamurthy and X. Zou, KeyRev: An efficient key revocation scheme for wireless sensor networks, *ICC '07: Proceedings of IEEE International Conference on Communications*, Glasgow, Scotland, UK (June 2007).
27. W. Zhang, H. Song, S. Zhu and G. Cao, Least privilege and privilege deprivation: towards tolerating mobile sink compromises in wireless sensor networks, *MobiHoc '05: Proceedings of the 6th ACM International Symposium on Mobile Ad Hoc Networking and Computing*, 378–389, New York, NY, USA (2005), ACM Press. ISBN 1-59593-004-3. doi: http://doi.acm.org/10.1145/1062689.1062737.
28. B. Karp and H. T. Kung, GPSR: greedy perimeter stateless routing for wireless networks, In *MobiCom '00: Proceedings of the 6th Annual International Conference on Mobile Computing and Networking*, 243–254, New York, NY, USA (2000), ACM Press, ISBN 1-58113-197-6. doi: http://doi.acm.org/10.1145/345910.345953.
29. A. Shamir, How to share a secret, *Commun. ACM.* **22**(11), 612–613 (1979), ISSN 0001-0782. doi: http://doi.acm.org/10.1145/359168.359176.
30. A. Das and D. Dutta, Data acquisition in multiple-sink sensor networks, *SIGMOBILE Mob. Comput. Commun. Rev.* **9**(3), 82–85 (2005), ISSN 1559-1662. doi: http://doi.acm.org/10.1145/1094549.1094561.
31. D. Liu, P. Ning, S. Zhu and S. Jajodia, Practical broadcast authentication in sensor networks, *MobiQuitous '05: Proceedings of the 2nd Annual International Conference on Mobile and Ubiquitous Systems: Networking and Services*, 118–129, San Diego, CA, USA (July 2005).

32. X. Zou, B. Ramamurthy and S. S. Magliveras, *Secure Group Communications Over Data Networks*, Springer (2005).
33. D. Liu, P. Ning and K. Sun, Efficient self-healing group key distribution with revocation capability, *CCS '03: Proceedings of the 10th ACM conference on Computer and communications security*, 231–240, New York, NY, USA (2003), ACM Press, ISBN 1-58113-738-9, doi: http://doi.acm.org/10.1145/948109.948141.
34. P. Traynor, H. Choi, G. Cao, S. Zhu and T. L. Porta, Establishing pair-wise keys in heterogeneous sensor networks, *Proceedings of IEEE INFOCOM* (2006).
35. P. Traynor, R. Kumar, H. B. Saad, G. Cao and T. L. Porta, LIGER: Implementing efficient hybrid security mechanisms for heterogeneous sensor networks, *ACM MobiSys*, Uppsala, Sweden (2006).

Chapter 18

Performances of Key Management Schemes in Wireless Sensor Networks

Boushra Maala*, Hatem Bettahar† and Abdelmadjid Bouabdallah‡

Compiegne University of Technology
Computer Science Department
Heudiasyc lab. France
**balkubei@hds.utc.fr*
†hbettaha@hds.utc.fr
‡bouabdal@hds.utc.fr

Key management in wireless sensor networks (WSN) is a challenging problem because of the limited resources of sensor nodes and their vulnerability against physical attacks. Several key management schemes have been proposed in order to secure the communications within the network. In this chapter, we evaluate the performances of the key management schemes in terms of key storage overhead as well as in terms of resistance degree against node capture.

18.1. Introduction

Wireless Sensor Networks (WSN) are widely used in different domains. They constitute an inexpensive, practical, and flexible solution for a variety of monitoring, detection and control applications.[1,2] In the military domain, WSN may be used for friendly forces monitoring, battlefield surveillance and biological attack detection. They also can be used in the environment domain for forest fire monitoring and agriculture monitoring. In addition, we can cite patient physiological data monitoring application in the health domain. For all such applications, communication security is an important requirement. The achievement of this requirement is a challenging task because of the "fragile nature" of WSN. Indeed, WSN have a set of characteristics which complicates the implementation of traditional security

*PhD student.
†An assistant professor and a member of the RO team (Algorithms for Networking and Optimization) at the Heudiasyc lab. (UMR-CNRS 5699) in the UTC, France.
‡Professor and the leader of the Networking and Optimization Research Group (ARO) of the Heudiasyc Lab. (UMR CNRS 6599) in the UTC, France.

and key management solutions. First of all, the wireless nature of communications in WSN, makes it easier for attackers to intercept all transmitted packets. Second, WSN are constrained by the limited resources of the sensors, this includes memory, processing capacity, transmission bandwidth, and energy. Due to these limitations, it is difficult to implement complicated security solutions in WSN. Third, in many cases, a large number of sensors are needed to be deployed in a hostile environment, which makes it very hard to have a continuous control on sensors (i.e., to update software, to change batteries) once they are in place. Finally, WSN are vulnerable to physical attackers. An attacker can capture one or more sensors and reveal all stored security information (stored keys) which enables him to compromise a part of the WSN communications. For all these reasons, an efficient key management scheme should be implemented in the sensor before its deployment.

This scheme should provide the following requirements:

- Low processing/energy consumption.
- Low memory usage.
- High attack resistance level.

Some requirements are conflicting, and it is hard to provide them at once. During these last years, several key management schemes have been proposed in the literature.[3–12] However, as we will explain in the following section most of these proposals do not respect the totality of these requirements. As an example, the solution which uses a unique master key for all sensor nodes in the network[13] satisfies only the two first requirements (low processing, low storage), but it makes the network highly vulnerable to physical attacks.

In order to evaluate the proposed key management schemes, we define two evaluation metrics, which are key storage overhead metric and resistance degree metric.

The goal of this performance evaluation is to help the user to apply the suitable key management scheme with respect to the requirements of the deployed applications. In military applications, due to the high security importance of the collected information, the resistance degree against capture node is the most important metric. Thus, the user must apply a key management scheme with a high resistance degree. While, in agriculture monitoring applications, since the security of collected information is not a critical need, and the deployed sensors may be simple sensors (low computation capacity and low memory size), the user can apply a key management scheme with low key storage overhead.

The rest of this chapter is organized as follows: In Sec. 18.2, we present and classify the key management schemes proposed in the literature. In Sec. 18.3 we define the evaluation metrics: key storage overhead and resistance degree against node capture. Then, in Sec. 18.4, we evaluate the performance of the key management schemes in terms of key storage overhead and resistance degree. We conclude the chapter in Sec. 18.5.

18.2. Classification of Key Management Schemes in WSN

These last years, several solutions have been proposed for key management in WSN. As shown in Fig. 18.1, we can classify these solutions into four categories: *Master Key technique, Pair-Wise Key Technique, Key-Pool Technique* and *Combined Technique.*

18.2.1. *Master key technique*

This technique is based on a unique shared key, which is pre-distributed for all sensors in the network. This shared key is used to generate session keys between any two sensors. The basic version of the Master Key Technique is presented in Broadcast session key negotiation protocol (BROSK).[11] In Ref. 9, authors proposed

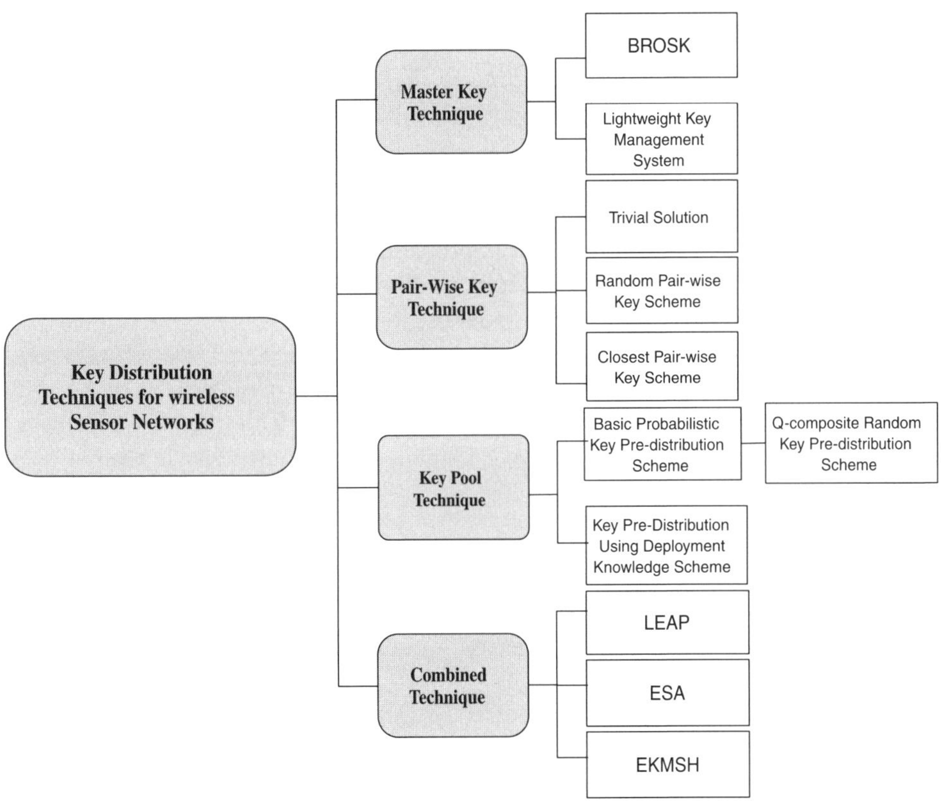

Fig. 18.1. Key distribution schemes.

to organize the sensor network in several sub-groups and to use a separate shared key within each sub-group. A different key will be used to communicate between sub-groups.

The Master Key Technique is scalable and may be applied in large WSN. It is also efficient in terms of key storage overhead, since each sensor will have to store only the unique master key. However, this leads to a very weak resistance degree against node capture, since the capture of a unique node will compromise all communications in the network.

18.2.2. *Pair-wise key technique*

In this technique, as shown in Fig. 18.2, a separate pair-wise key is pre-distributed to each pair of nodes in the network. These pair-wise keys will be used to independently secure communications between each two nodes. In the basic version of this technique, called the *trivial solution*,[13] each node should store exactly $(N-1)$ pair-wise keys; one key with each other sensor in the network. This basic version offers a high level of resistance against node capture attack. However it suffers from an important memory consumption for key storage. It is a non scalable solution, and may only be used in small or medium WSN. In order to enhance the scalability of this technique, several solutions have been proposed to reduce the number of stored keys by each sensor.

In *Random pair-wise key scheme*,[8] authors proposed to use only $Np = N{\cdot}p$ keys instead of $(N-1)$ keys for each node, where p is the probability that two nodes in the network are connected. By adapting the probability p to the WSN characteristics, we can reduce the number of stored keys, and hence the scalability, while keeping a good level of connectivity between nodes.

Another enhancement solution is the *Closest pair-wise pre-distribution keys scheme*.[12] This solution restricts the number of keys stored by a node to only C keys $(C < N)$, where C is the number of "closest" neighborhood. Choosing to share keys with neighbors will guarantee a high level of connectivity in the network.

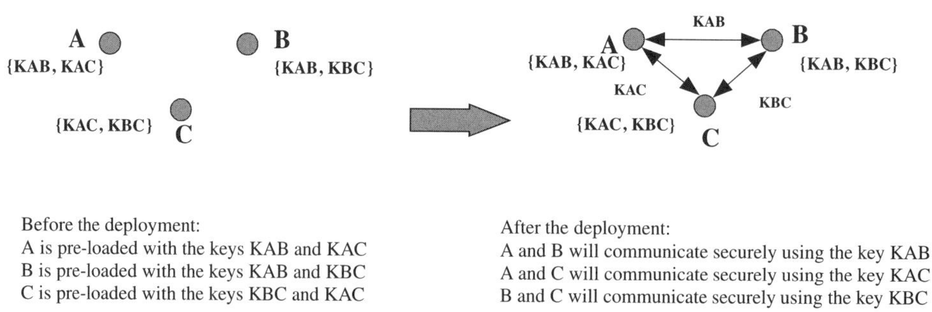

Fig. 18.2. Pair-wise technique.

However, in order to apply this scheme we need to predict the future localization of each node in the network, which is not always possible.

18.2.3. *Key pool technique*

As illustrated in Fig. 18.3, this technique uses a key pool composed of a large number of keys (KP keys). Each node in the WSN randomly selects, and stores, a subset of k keys from this pool. This process is done off-line. When the WSN is deployed, nodes begin exchanging messages containing the identifiers of their own keys, in order to discover if they have a common key. If two nodes notice that they have a common shared key, they will be able to establish a secure channel. This basic version of Key Pool technique is presented in the *basic probabilistic key pre-distribution scheme*.[10] The random key distribution, using a unique pool, helps to establish a high network connectivity. However, this basic version is not resistant against node capture because the attacker will reveal k keys, and each one of these keys may be used to compromise one or more channels in the WSN.

In Ref. 8, Chan *et al.* proposed to modify this basic version by using q common keys ($q > 1$) instead of just one in order to establish a secure channel between two nodes. By increasing the amount of key overlap required for secure channel setup, the network resistance against node capture is reinforced.

Authors in Ref. 14 proposed to enhance the overall performances of the two previous schemes by using *deployment knowledge* whenever it is available. With such knowledge, each node only needs to carry a fraction of the k keys required by the two previous schemes. In fact, a node will need only to store the keys that will be shared with its neighbors.

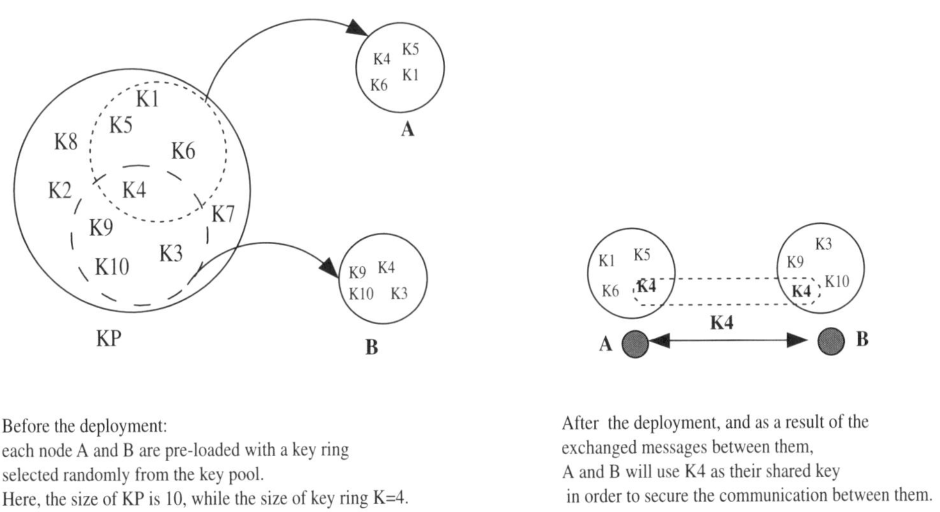

Fig. 18.3. Key pool technique.

18.2.4. *Combined technique*

Some recent works propose to organize the WSN into different regions (domains, clusters) and to apply an adequate different key distribution technique inside each region. Clustering the WSN may be based on security considerations such as in ESA,[15] on location and neighborhood knowledge such as in LEAP[16] or on a logical hierarchy organization such as in EKMSH.[17]

In *ESA* (*Eyes Security Architecture*),[15] the WSN is divided into two types of clusters: supervised and unsupervised clusters. A supervised cluster consists of a supervisor node and a group of supervised nodes, while an unsupervised cluster consists only of unsupervised nodes having no security requirements. For supervised clusters, a combination of the pair-wise key and the master key techniques is used. Each supervised node stores two keys, a pairwise key used to secure the communication with its supervisor, and a cluster key used, as a backup key, to ensure the communication inside the cluster in case of supervisor failure. In addition to all shared keys with its supervised nodes in the cluster, each supervisor node stores a domain key which is used to secure the communications between all supervisors. For unsupervised nodes, no keys are distributed. The main contribution of this proposal is the classification of sensors into supervised and unsupervised clusters. This classification may be applied in some particular applications and may contribute in decreasing the key management overhead in the network.

In *LEAP* (*Localized Encryption and Authentication Protocol*),[16] each sensor node stores four types of keys: (1) An individual key shared with the base station. This key is used to secure communication between the node and the base station. (2) Pairwise keys shared with its immediate neighbors. These keys are used to secure communications that require privacy or source authentication. (3) A cluster key shared with multiple neighbors. This key is mainly used for securing locally broadcast messages. (4) A global group key that is shared by all the nodes in the network. This key is used by the base station to encrypt messages that are broadcasted to the whole group.

Even though the use of different keys to secure different types of communication channels in the WSN may increase the overall efficiency of the communications, it leads to a very low resistance degree.

Recently, authors in Ref. 17 proposed a combined key management scheme for hierarchical WSN (military organizations). In this scheme, sensors are organized into a set of groups placed in different levels of a tree structure. A master key is used to secure communications within each group. Communications between groups in different levels are secured using pair-wise technique. In this scheme, each sensor should store its *group key*, an *uplevel pair-wise key* shared with its parent (its commander), a *downlevel group key* which is the group key of the group commanded by this sensor (child group), and finally a set of individual *downlevel pair-wise keys* shared with each sensor in this child group.

Table 18.1. Comparison between different key distribution schemes in WSN where: ++ excellent, + good, - medium, - - bad

Technique	Scheme	Scalability	Resistance	Key connectivity
Master key	BROSK[11]	++	- -	++
	Lightweight key management system[9]	+	-	++
Pair-wise	Trivial solution[13]	- -	++	++
	Random pair-wise key scheme[8]	-	++	+
	Closest pair-wise key scheme[12]	+	++	+
Key pool	Basic probabilistic scheme[10]	+	+	-
	Q-composite random scheme[8]	-	++	- -
	Using deployment knowledge[14]	+	+	+
Combined	ESA[15]	+	-	+
	LEAP[16]	++	- -	++
	EKMSH[17]	++	- -	++

Performances of key distribution schemes: Table 18.1 gives an idea on the performances of all the schemes presented above in terms of scalability, node capture resistance and key connectivity. A detailed study of the resistance as well as key storage performances is presented in Sec. 18.5.

18.3. Evaluation Metrics

In this chapter, we evaluate the performance of key management schemes based on two metrics: Key Storage Overhead (KSO) and Resistance Degree (RD).

(1) Key Storage Overhead (KSO):
Since the limited available memory in a sensor node is one of the most important constraints in designing a key management scheme. We define Key Storage Overhead (KSO) metric as the average number of keys stored by each sensor in the WSN.

(2) Resistance Degree against node capture (RD):
As an attacker may compromise one or more nodes in the network, and reveals their keys, he will capable to compromise all communication secured using these keys. To evaluate the impact of attack, we define the Resistance Degree metric (RD) as the ratio of non-compromised links (over the total network links) when one sensor node of the network is compromised:

$$RD = 1 - \frac{N_{CL}}{N_{TL}}, \tag{18.1}$$

where N_{CL} is the number of compromised links when one node is compromised, and N_{TL} is the total number of available secured links in the network. A link between two sensor nodes is considered as compromised if the associated encryption key is revealed. A scheme with a good resistance degree against node capture will have $RD \approx 1$ meaning that capturing one sensor node will not compromise any secured channel in the WSN. This is the case of pair-wise schemes. In contrast, a scheme with a very bad resistance degree against node capture will have $RD \approx 0$ meaning that capturing one sensor node will compromise all secured channels in the WSN. This is the case of Master key schemes.

18.4. Performance Evaluation and Comparison

In this section, we evaluate the performances of the key management schemes based on the evaluation metrics KSO and RD.

18.4.1. *Key storage overhead evaluation*

In this paragraph, we calculate the key storage overhead for each technique, then we compare all the schemes in terms of KSO using an example of a WSN with 600 nodes. Results for the considered example are summarized in Table 18.3.

18.4.1.1. *Calculating the key storage overhead* (KSO)

Hereafter, we calculate the key storage overhead for each technique and resume the results in Table 18.2.

Master key technique: As explained in the related works section, in the basic scheme of this technique (BROSK[11]), each node needs to store only one key so $KSO = 1$. In the Lightweight key management system scheme,[9] the network is organized into g sub-groups and each node needs to store one key to identify the

Table 18.2. Key storage overhead (Z: number of supervised clusters, m: number of neighbors and d: depth of the tree structure).

Technique	Scheme	Node type	KSO
Master key	BROSK[11]	all nodes	1
	Lightweight key management system[9]	each node	$2 + (g - 1)$
Pair-wise	Trivial solution[13]	all nodes	$N - 1$
	Closest pair-wise key scheme[12]	all nodes	C
	Random pair-wise key scheme[8]	all nodes	$N{\cdot}p$
Key pool	Basic probabilistic scheme[10]	all nodes	k
	Q-composite random scheme[8]	all nodes	k
	Using deployment knowledge[14]	all nodes	$\leq k$
Combined	LEAP[16]	all nodes	$2{\cdot}m + 3$
	ESA[15]	supervised nodes	2
		supervisor nodes	$\frac{N}{2 \cdot Z} + 1$
	EKMSH[17]	leaf nodes	2
		root node	$\log_d(N) + 1$
		intermediate nodes	$\log_d(N) + 3$

Table 18.3. Key storage overhead in a 600 nodes WSN.

Technique	Scheme	KSO per node
Master key	BROSK[11]	1
	Lightweight key management system[9]	11
Pair-wise	Trivial solution[13]	599
	Closest pair-wise key scheme[12]	200
	Random pair-wise key scheme ($p = 0.33$)[8]	198
Key pool	All schemes[8,10,14]	40
Combined	LEAP[16]	135
	ESA[15]	4
	EKMSH[17]	4

nodes in its sub-group, one key to communicate with nodes within its sub-group, and one key to communicate with each other sub-group, so $KSO = 2 + (g - 1)$.

Pair-wise technique: In the trivial scheme,[13] each node should store $(N - 1)$ pair-wise keys to communicate securely with other nodes in the network. So $KSO = N - 1$. With the C closest pair-wise scheme,[12] each node needs to store only C pair-wise keys depending on the memory size of the sensor node. So $KSO = C$. Finally, in the Random pair-wise scheme,[8] each node must store $N{\cdot}p$ pair-wise keys in order to achieve an overall connectivity probability p. So, $KSO = N{\cdot}p$.

Key pool technique: In the basic and Q-composite schemes,[8,10] each node should store a key ring of size k to establish secure communications with other nodes in the network. So $KSO = k$. Furthermore, by using the deployment knowledge scheme,[14] the maximum size of the key ring stored by each node is k. So we can write $KSO \leq k$.

Combined technique: In LEAP,[16] each node must store four types of keys: an individual key used to communicate with the base station, pair-wise keys with each one of its immediate neighbors, a cluster key used for broadcast communications within its neighbors, and a group key which is a shared key with its neighbors. In addition, the node should store the cluster keys of all its neighbors. So, in LEAP, $KSO = 2.m + 3$, where m is the average number of neighbors.

In ESA,[15] each supervised node stores two keys: a unique key for the pair-wise communication with its supervisor node, and a cluster rescue key used to communicate within the cluster whenever the supervisor node is not available. Each supervisor node stores all pair-wise keys of all supervised nodes within its cluster, and a domain key which is used to communicate with other supervisor nodes of the same domain. So $KSO = 2$ for each supervised node, and $KSO = \frac{N}{2 \cdot Z} + 1$ for each supervisor node, where Z is the number of supervised clusters.

In EKMSH scheme,[17] if we consider the case of a complete tree of depth d, each group will have approximately $\log_d(N)$ nodes. Each leaf node stores two keys:

a group key used within its group, and a pair-wise key shared with its commander. So $KSO = 2$ for leaf nodes. The root node stores all pair-wise keys of its children as well as their group key, so $KSO = \log_d(N) + 1$ for the root node. Finally, an intermediate node must store all pair-wise keys shared with its children, children group key, its group key and its pair-wise key shared with its commander. So $KSO = \log_d(N) + 3$ for an intermediate node. Table 18.2 resumes the results of key storage overhead performances calculated above.

18.4.1.2. *Comparison in terms of key storage overhead* (*KSO*)

In order to fairly compare the different schemes, we consider an example of WSN with 600 nodes ($N = 600$). For each scheme we apply a set of assumptions that leads to a WSN with similar characteristics. These assumptions are separately detailed for each scheme. For schemes with more than one type of nodes (this is the case of ESA and EKMSH), we will calculate an overall KSO average among all nodes. Furthermore, in some schemes we need additional deployment information about the WSN. We will consider that the sensor nodes are uniformly distributed on a square grid with area X^2 with $X = 400$ meters. Each sensor has a communication range of $\Pi \cdot r^2$ with $r = 75$ meters.

Master key technique: In BROSK,[11] each node stores only one key, so $KSO = 1$. For Lightweight key management system,[9] we suppose that the 600 nodes are organized into 10 sub-groups ($g = 10$). So, $KSO = 11$.

Pair-wise technique: For the trivial scheme $KSO = 599$. For the closest pair-wise scheme, we consider sensors with a memory capacity of 200 keys ($C = 200$). So $KSO = 200$. Finally for the Random pair-wise scheme, we consider a connectivity probability of 33% ($p = 0.33$) so $KSO = 198$.

Key pool technique: For this technique,[8,10,14] $KSO = k$, where k is the size of the key ring for each node. The k keys are randomly chosen from a global key pool of KP keys ($k \ll KP$). Using results in Ref. 10, the probability that two nodes are connected is $p = \frac{\ln(N)}{N} + \frac{11.5}{N}$, and the probability of sharing a key between two nodes in a neighborhood is $p' = \frac{n'}{m-1}$ where $n' = p * (N-1)$ is the expected degree of a node, and m is the number of neighbors. Using the above assumptions about the nodes distribution, we can deduce the number of neighbors: $m = \frac{N \cdot \Pi \cdot r^2}{X^2}$. The probability p' can also be written as $p' = 1 - \frac{(1-\frac{k}{KP})^{2(KP-k+0.5)}}{(1-\frac{2k}{KP})^{(KP-2k+0.5)}}$. Using these two forms of p', we can deduce the size of the key ring, k, as function of N. Let us, finally consider a key pool size of 5,000 keys ($KP = 5{,}000$). By applying all these considerations, we obtain the following values: $p = 0.0298$, $n' = 18$ nodes, $m = 66$ nodes, $p' = 0.2769$ and $k = 40$ keys. As a conclusion $KSO = 40$ for the key pool technique.

Table 18.4. RD: Resistance Degree performances against node capture.

Technique	Scheme	RD
Master key	BROSK[11]/ Lightweight key management system[9]	0
Pair-wise	Trivial solution[13]	$1-\frac{2}{N}$
	Random pair-wise key scheme[8]	$1-\frac{2p}{N-1}$
	Closest pair-wise key scheme[12]	$1-\frac{2c}{N(N-1)}$
Key pool	Basic probabilistic scheme[10]	$1-\frac{k}{KP}$
	Q-composite random scheme[8]	$1-\frac{k!(KP-q)!}{(k-q)!KP!}$
Combined	LEAP[16]	$1-\frac{N+2\cdot m+1}{N\cdot(1+\frac{N-1}{2}+m)}$
	ESA[15]	$1-\frac{2\cdot N+2\cdot Z^2-4\cdot Z}{N^2+2\cdot N\cdot Z^2-4\cdot Z}$
	EKMSH[17]	$1-\frac{2\cdot(\log_d(N))^2+2}{N\cdot(\log_d(N)+1)-2}$

Combined technique: In LEAP,[16] $KSO = 2.m + 3$ where m is the number of neighbors. By taking into consideration the same assumptions as for key pool technique, we have $m = 66$ nodes. So $KSO = 135$ keys. In ESA,[15] there are two types of nodes, supervised and unsupervised. In order to calculate the average KSO, we consider that half of the nodes (300) in the WSN are supervised and the other half (300) are unsupervised nodes. The supervised nodes are organized into 5 clusters ($Z = 5$). Considering these assumptions, we will have 295 supervised nodes storing 2 keys each and 5 supervisor storing 61 keys each. The average number of stored key in ESA is $KSO = 4$ keys. Note that unsupervised nodes are not considered. In EKMSH,[17] we have three types of nodes: leaf nodes, intermediate nodes and a root node. In order to calculate the average KSO, we suppose that the WSN is organized in a complete binary tree with depth $d = \frac{\log_{10}(N+1)}{\log_{10}(2)}$, and having 2^{d-1} leaf nodes. So, for our 600 nodes WSN, we will have 300 leaf nodes storing 2 keys each, 299 intermediate nodes storing 6 keys each and one root node storing 4 keys. Hence the average number of keys storage per node of the WSN is $KSO = 4$ keys, which is equivalent to that of ESA.

Table 18.3 summarizes all key storage overhead values calculated above. As a conclusion, we can notice that the basic master key technique is the best one in terms of key storage overhead, while the pair-wise technique is the worst.

18.4.2. *Resistance degree evaluation*

In the following, we first calculate the resistance degree (RD) for each technique and resume the results in Table 18.4. Then, as for the Key Storage Overhead (KSO), we compare all the schemes in terms of RD using an example of a WSN with 600 nodes. Results for the considered example are summarized in Fig. 18.4.

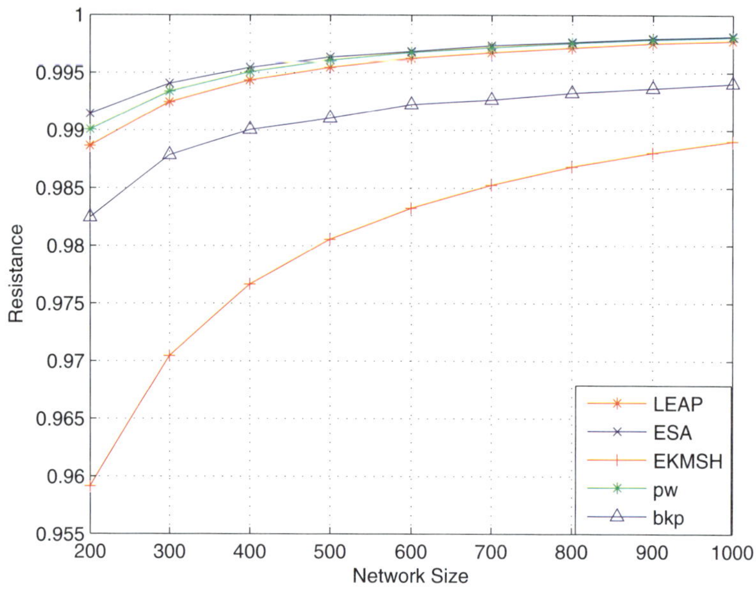

Fig. 18.4. Resistance Degree evaluation (with $r = 75$, $X = 500$, $Z = 5$, $d = 3$).

18.4.2.1. *Calculating the resistance degree* (RD)

Master key technique: Using this technique,[9,11] all nodes store and use a unique master key. So compromising a node in the WSN will reveal this unique shared key and compromise all secured channels in the network. The resistance degree is therefore equal to zero: $RD = 0$. This is the worst scheme in terms of resistance against node capture.

Pair-wise technique: In the trivial pair-wise scheme,[13] each node has $N_{CL} = (N - 1)$ secure links which will be compromised if the node is captured. For the closest pair-wise scheme[12] $N_{CL} = C$, and for the Random pair-wise scheme[8] $N_{CL} = N{\cdot}p$. The total number of links in the network is $N_{TL} = \frac{N(N-1)}{2}$ links. As a conclusion, $RD = 1 - \frac{2}{N}$ for the trivial solution, $RD = 1 - \frac{2c}{N(N-1)}$ for the closest pair-wise scheme, and $RD = 1 - \frac{2p}{N-1}$ for the random pair-wise scheme. For all these schemes RD tends to 1 for large networks ($N \gg 1$). Therefore, Pair-Wise Technique is very resistant against node capture.

Key pool technique: In the Basic scheme,[10] each node stores a key ring of a size k randomly chosen from a key pool of size KP. A captured sensor will, then, reveal k keys from KP possible keys. So $RD = 1 - \frac{k}{KP}$. This is considered as a good resistance degree, since the key pool is generated and used off-line and can then have a very large size. For the Q-composite scheme,[8] the resistance degree can be written as $RD = 1 - \frac{k!(KP-q)!}{(k-q)!KP!}$. Where q is the number of keys needed to generate the shared key between any two nodes.

Combined technique: In LEAP,[16] each sensor node has four types of secured channels: one channel with the base station, m channels to communicate with its m neighbors in the cluster using the shared key (broadcast channel), m channels using individual pair-wise keys with its m neighbors and N channels to communicate with all network nodes. Then, the number of compromised channels when one node is compromised is $N_{CL} = N + 2{\cdot}m + 1$. In order to calculate the resistance degree, we need to calculate the total number of communication channels in the network. Indeed, there are N channels between the base station and all nodes in the network, $\frac{N(N-1)}{2}$ channels between each two nodes using the same group key, $\frac{N \cdot m}{2}$ channels using cluster key within neighbors, and $\frac{N.m}{2}$ channels within neighbors using pair-wise keys. So, $N_{TL} = N{\cdot}(1 + \frac{N-1}{2} + m)$. We can, then, calculate the resistance degree as $RD = 1 - \frac{N+2\cdot m+1}{N\cdot(1+\frac{N-1}{2}+m)}$.

For ESA,[15] we suppose that half of sensors $(\frac{N}{2})$ are supervised and the other half $(\frac{N}{2})$ are unsupervised. We also suppose that there are Z supervised clusters. Since, the unsupervised nodes are supposed to be without security requirements, they are not considered in the resistance degree computation. We also neglect the backup key within a cluster because it is used only in very rare cases where the supervisor node is out of service. With these assumptions, there are $\frac{N}{2 \cdot Z}$ pair-wise channels between the supervisor node and its cluster nodes and Z channels using a domain key within supervisor nodes in the network. Since, there are Z supervised clusters in the network, the total number of secured channels in the network is $N_{TL} = \frac{N}{2} + Z^2$. Whenever a supervisor node is compromised, there will be $(\frac{N}{2 \cdot Z} + (Z-1))$ revealed keys. However, compromising a normal node will reveal only 1 key. Having Z supervisor nodes and $\frac{N}{2} - Z$ normal nodes, the average number of compromised channels when one node is compromised is $N_{CL} = \frac{N+Z^2-2\cdot Z}{\frac{N}{2}}$. Then we can compute the resistance degree as $RD = 1 - \frac{2.N+2\cdot Z^2-4\cdot Z}{N^2+2\cdot N\cdot Z^2-4\cdot Z}$.

For EKMSH,[17] we limit the computation of RD to intermediate nodes only. Whenever an intermediate node is compromised, the following channels will be revealed: $\frac{\log_d(N)(\log_d(N)-1)}{2}$ channels inside its cluster due to the use of the group key, $\frac{\log_d(N)(\log_d(N)-1)}{2}$ channels inside its children cluster because it stores their group key, $\log_d(N)$ pair-wise channels with its children, and one pair-wise channel with its commander. Thus, $N_{CL}=(\log_d(N))^2 + 1$. The total number of channels is $N_{TL} = N \cdot \frac{\log_d(N)+1}{2} - 1$. Then, $RD = 1 - \frac{2\cdot(\log_d(N))^2+2}{N\cdot(\log_d(N)+1)-2}$.

We notice here that all channels in such hierarchical organization do not have the same importance, for example a secured channel between two commanders is more important than a simple secured channel between two soldiers. In order to take into account such nuance we need a more precise resistance calculation model. Table 18.4 resumes the resistance degree performances calculated above.

18.4.2.2. *Comparison in terms of Resistance Degree* (*RD*)

In order to compare the different schemes in terms of the resistance degree, we plotted the *RD* performances calculated in the previous section.

In Fig. 18.4 we plotted the Resistance Degree of the following schemes: the Trivial pair-wise protocol (Trivial PW), the Basic key pool protocol (Basic KP) and the combined technique schemes: LEAP, ESA and EKMSH. We varied the WSN size from 200 to 1000 nodes. We notice that the resistance degree of the Trivial pair-wise scheme is better than the remainder schemes except the ESA scheme, but we must always remember that in ESA scheme, the security requirements are applied on only the half of the nodes in the network. We can also see that the EKMSH scheme is the scheme with the worst resistance degree, while the resistance degree of Basic key pool scheme is worst than the pair-wise technique.

18.5. Conclusion

WSN applications are going to be widely used in different domains: military, agriculture, health and so on. Several key management schemes are proposed in order to secure the communications among the nodes. All these schemes aim to answer the requirements and the specifications of WSN. Therefore, it is important to evaluate the performances of the different proposed schemes, in order to select the scheme which is suitable to be applied for the deployed application.

In this chapter, we have classified the key management schemes proposed in the literature based on their key distribution paradigm, into four techniques: The Master key technique, the Pair-wise key technique, the Key pool technique and the Combined technique. Then, we have evaluated their performances based on two important metrics which are Key Storage Overhead and Resistance Degree against node capture.

Our analysis has brought interesting conclusion: the Master key technique has the best key storage overhead metric, and a very weak resistance degree against node capture, so it is suitable for the applications where the security level of information is not very important, or for the applications deployed within friendly environments, also, it is very useful for WSN with sensor nodes of low capacities (memory, energy, computation capacity...). While, the Pair-wise technique has a high resistance degree against node capture, but it suffers from an important key storage overhead. So, it is very interesting to apply it for the applications deployed within hostile environments, but for an WSN with a small size. The Key pool technique can be considered as the medium solution between all techniques. It can be used for different applications because of its good performance in terms of resistance degree against node capture, and its reasonable key storage overhead. Also, the

Combined technique gives a medium performance in terms of resistance degree and key storage overhead, but we must always remember that in combined technique the WSN is organized into regions (clusters or domains), and an adequate different key distribution technique inside each region.

References

1. N. Xu, A survey of sensor network applications, *IEEE Communication Magazine*, **40**(8), 102–114 (2002).
2. J. L. Hill, *System Architecture for Wireless Sensor Networks.* PhD thesis, Dissertation, University of California, Berkeley (May 2003).
3. J. Lee and D. Stinson, Deterministic key pre-distribution schemes for distributed sensor networks, *Proc. of 11th International Workshop, SAC 2004*, 294–307, Waterloo, Canada (August 2004).
4. R. Pietro, L. Mancini and A. Mei, Random key-assignment for secure wireless sensor networks, *SASN '03: Proceedings of the 1st ACM Workshop on Security of Ad Hoc and Sensor Networks*, 62–71, Fairfax, Virginia, USA (2003).
5. S. Camtepe and B. Yener, Combinatorial design of key distribution mechanisms for wireless sensor networks, *Proc. of the 9th European Symposium on Research Computer Security*, 293–308 (September 2004).
6. R. Blom, An optimal class of symmetric key generation systems, *EUROCRYPT 84 Workshop on Advances in Cryptology: Theory and Application of Cryptographic Techniques*, 335–338, USA (December 1985).
7. C. Blundo, A. Santis, A. Herzberg, S. Kutten, U. Vaccaro and M. Yung, Perfectly secure key distribution for dynamic conferences, *Inf. Comput.*, **146**(1), 1–23 (1998).
8. H. Chan, A. Perrig and D. Song, Random key predistribution schemes for sensor networks, *IEEE Symposium on Security and Privacy*, 197–213, Berkeley, California (May 2003).
9. B. Dutertre, J. Cheung and S. Levy, *Lightweight Key Management in Wireless Sensor Networks by Leveraging Initial Trust*, Computing Science Technical Report SRI-SDL-04-02, System Design Laboratory, SRI International (April 2004).
10. L. Eschenauer and V. Gligor, A key-management scheme for distributed sensor networks. In *CCS '02: Proceedings of the 9th ACM Conference on Computer and Communications Security*, 41–47, Washington, DC, USA (November 2002).
11. B. Lai, S. Kim and I. Verbauwhede, Scalable session key construction protocol for wireless sensor networks, *Proc. IEEE Workshop on Large Scale Real Time and Embedded Systems (LARTES)*, Austin, Texas (December 2002).
12. D. Liu and P. Ning, Location-based pairwise key establishments for static sensor networks, *SASN'03: Proceedings of the 1st ACM Workshop on Security of Ad Hoc and Sensor Networks*, 72–82, Fairfax, Virginia, USA (2003).
13. S. Camtepe and B. Yener, *Key Distribution Mechanisms for Wireless Sensor Networks: A Survey*, Technical Report TR-05-07, Rensselaer Polytechnic Institute, Computer Science Department (March 2005).
14. W. Du, J. Deng, Y. Han, S. Chen and P. Varshney, A key management scheme for wireless sensor networks using deployment knowledge, *Proc. of IEEE INFOCOM'04*, 586–597, Hongkong, China (March 2004).

15. Y. Law, R. Corin, S. Etalle and P. Hartel, A formally verified decentralized key management for wireless sensor networks, *Proc. of the 4th IFIP TC6/WG6.8 International Conference on Personal Wireless Communications* (*PWC*), 27–39, Venice, Italy (2003).
16. S. Zhu, S. Setia and S. Jajodia, Leap: Efficient security mechanisms for large-scale distributed sensor networks, *Proc. of 10th ACM Conference on Computer and Communications Security* (*CCS'03*), 62–72, Washington, DC, USA (October 2003).
17. X. Chen and J. Drissi, An efficient key management scheme in hierarchical sensor networks, *Proc. of 2nd IEEE International Conference on Mobile Ad hoc and Sensor Systems Conference* (November 2005).

Chapter 19

Trust Establishment in Wireless Sensor Networks

Chun-Fai Law and Yu-Kwong Kwok*

MTR Corporation, Hong Kong
Colorado State University
Fort Collins, CO 80526, USA
**Ricky.Kwok@colostate.edu*

Trust establishment has long been a challenging problem in Wireless Sensor Networks (WSNs) due to high security requirements and strict resource constraints in WSNs. Recent approaches based on randomized key pre-distribution schemes mainly focus on key allocations supported by the pre-deployment estimations of the post-deployment information items. Unfortunately, such information items may be unavailable or may change over time. The performance of the resulting network may be unstable and unable to react to the change of topology due to sensor node dynamics.

We first present a detailed survey of recently proposed techniques for trust establishment in WSNs. Then, we introduce our novel key redistribution framework that exploits the key mobility concept, designed based on adaptability to post-deployment contexts. We show that our framework can be applied to most existing key pre-distribution schemes (both key-based and polynomial-based) to further improve their performance. To fight against node capture attacks, we also proposed a recovering scheme, namely, *node replenishment scheme*, to replace the compromised links and the functions of the compromised region. Analytical and simulation results indicate that our proposed work are practical and able to improve the performance of a WSN significantly with a small amount of additional resources.

19.1. Introduction

Wireless Sensor Networks (WSNs)[1] have gained remarkable attention after recent advancements of electronic and wireless technologies. A WSN usually consists of ultra small autonomous devices called sensor nodes, which are battery powered, limited in memory storage and computational power. In a typical application scenario, sensors cooperatively monitor physical and environmental conditions and then transmit collected data to a sink node or base station via wireless links for

*Corresponding author.

further analysis. For instance, in a military scenario, WSNs are deployed in a large scale with well over 10,000 nodes[2–4] for gathering a large volume of target recognition data. Smart Dust,[5] WINS,[6] and μAmps[7] are well known examples of WSN research projects.

The development of WSNs was originally motivated by the military sensing and tracking arena, such as battlefield surveillance. When sensor nodes are deployed in hostile areas, security becomes extremely important as nodes are subjected to different kind of threats.[8–12] Nodes may be captured and the communications among them may be eavesdropped or altered. Therefore, messages transmitted between sensor nodes must be encrypted using various cryptographic protection schemes to guard against different types of malicious attacks. Hence, *trust establishment* is one of the most critical components to set up a secure communication environment in a WSN based information system.[13]

Although many traditional trust establishment schemes have been proposed, a WSN is unique due to its distributed and resource-constrained properties. Some methods such as using a master key or pairwise private sharing of keys are proposed,[13] but they are either too insecure or impractical[14] for WSNs. Currently, many trust establishment schemes have been developed for wireless sensor networks.[13,15] Among them, key pre-distribution schemes are widely considered as practicable solutions in WSNs.[2,4,13,16–18] A typical key pre-distribution scheme works by having keys distributed to all nodes prior to deployment. Eschenauer *et al.*[4] pioneered this field of research by proposing a randomized key pre-distribution scheme, which relies on probabilistic key sharing among nodes using random graph theory.[19]

Unfortunately, as detailed in our survey in this chapter, most key pre-distribution schemes can only achieve a certain level of connectivity and are unable to improve the resource utilization after deployment. Specifically, the connectivity of a trust establishment scheme is characterized by a probability which is limited by the amount of usable resources such as memory. Obviously, providing more resources is undesirable as the sensor nodes are very tiny and subjected to attacks in hostile areas.

In this chapter, we aim at addressing the key allocation problems and repairing a WSN in the post-deployment phase. We exploit the idea of key redistribution to provide better key utilization, without using additional deployment knowledge. The key redistribution mechanisms increase the link formation based on the existing neighboring keys. Specifically, a group of nodes share the memory loading to achieve higher connectivity and lower security risk. Performance evaluation illustrates that our proposed approach exhibits significant enhancements over existing approaches and even outperforms the classic scheme using deployment knowledge. We also propose a novel node replenishment scheme to repair a compromised WSN. Under this node replenishment scheme, additional nodes carrying old and new keys are replenished to the original WSN. Link replacement is then carried out to replace those compromised links by the new ones. Simulation results indicate that our proposed schemes are practical and able to improve the network performance of a compromised WSN significantly with a small amount of additional resources.

The rest of the chapter is organized as follows. In Section 19.2, we give a brief introduction of Wireless Sensor Networks. Section 19.3 overviews popular trust establishment schemes in WSNs and Sec. 19.4 discusses several enhancement techniques of WSNs. We introduce our new "Node-key Mobility" concept in Sec. 19.5 and present two corresponding schemes, namely *key redistribution* in Sec. 19.6 and *node replenishment* in Sec. 19.7, respectively. In Sec. 19.8, we evaluate the performance of the proposed schemes analytically with extensive simulations. The chapter is concluded in Sec. 19.9 with highlights for future works.

19.2. Characteristics of Wireless Sensor Networks

Wireless Sensor Networks (WSNs) are often regarded as a kind of Mobile Ad-hoc Networks (MANETs). In order to make sensor nodes cheaper and smaller so as to facilitate large scale deployment, heavyweight and computation intensive programs are not expected to be executed on the tiny sensor devices. These limitations make the design of trust establishment schemes in WSNs highly challenging. A brief summary of the constraints is described below:

(1) *Energy limitation*: Sensor devices are usually small in size and battery-powered. The limited supply of power restricts the computational and communication capabilities of sensor nodes. Indeed, an effective energy conservation scheme is vital for maximizing the lifetime of operation from a single node to the entire network.[20] Nowadays, a typical sensor node can operate for a week (under full operation) to several months.
(2) *Memory storage limitation*: Due to the small size, sensor nodes are equipped with limited amount of memory. Apart from storing key materials, it is still necessary to store the key management program and many other applications for operation. For instance, a popular sensor device, namely Berkeley MICA2 Mote,[21] has only 128 KBytes program memory.
(3) *Vulnerability to attacks*: As WSNs are usually deployed in hostile environments, nodes are exposed to physical attacks by the potential adversaries. In most practical scenarios, it is possible for the attackers to compromise a node physically and take full control of the node without being detected. This is often called "node capture attack".
(4) *Lack of post-deployment knowledge*: Without deployment knowledge, such as location information, the distribution of sensor nodes may follow a randomly scattered pattern. Therefore, the network topology is hard to be determined *a priori* so that the optimization of trust establishment is very difficult.

In general, the major barrier for enhancing security in WSNs is their weak computational and communication capabilities. These inherent properties make traditional cryptographic protocols, such as Diffie-Hellman key agreement[22] and RSA signature[23] techniques, undesirable when compared to the symmetric key approaches[24] in terms of energy and computational requirements. These public key schemes are either too computation intensive or too large to fit in the resource-constrained sensor nodes. As a result, a trust establishment scheme using symmetric keys is our main focus in this chapter.

19.3. Survey of Recently Proposed Trust Establishment Schemes

In this section, we present a detailed survey of the key pre-distribution techniques in WSNs. Although symmetric key-based schemes are our focus in this chapter, asymmetric key-based approaches are also discussed as they are emerging in this area and considered as future alternative for advanced sensor equipment.

19.3.1. *Symmetric key-based approaches*

Generally, these schemes are further divided into two categories: *deterministic* and *probabilistic* key pre-distribution schemes.

19.3.1.1. *Deterministic key pre-distribution schemes*

A deterministic scheme assigns keys to each node intentionally so that these keys are used for specific purposes. Since each key is selected carefully, it is expected that the number of keys stored for each node will not be large; otherwise, the cost of key assignment will be very high if the network is deployed in a large scale. Thus, this scheme usually focuses on the communication between a fixed number of entities such as node-to-base station, node-to-gateway, and gateway-to-base station. A simple example is the master key approach in which each node communicates with a single common key.[13]

Jolly *et al.*[25] proposed a lightweight key management protocol. They observed that sensor-to-sensor secure communication is not always necessary in some applications. Thus, very few keys (typically two) are enough to establish secure connections between nodes and base station as well as cluster gateways. Since there is no sensor-to-sensor communication, the first key is used to talk with the base station while the second one is used to talk with the cluster gateway. These two keys can be computed efficiently and distributed to sensor nodes before deployment. Their objective is to provide a cost-effective key infrastructure to secure the sensor network. However, their design requires a centralized key server and the re-keying[a] process suggested is inefficient due to the large amount of message exchanges (i.e., a large overhead).

[a]Re-keying refers to the process of replacing an old key with a new one.

Based on a trusted intermediary node and the underlying routing protocol, Chan *et al.*[16] introduced a class of key establishment protocols, called Peer Intermediaries for Key Establishment (PIKE). By assuming the existence of routing information, PIKE uses a third node C located somewhere in the network to act as a trusted intermediary between two nodes A and B. The trusted entity shares a common key with both node A and node B so that the key establishment protocols can be securely routed through node C to perform connection establishment. The objectives of PIKE are to provide a uniform communication pattern for key establishment and reduce the communication and memory overheads when the network size increases. However, the dependence on the underlying routing protocol makes this scheme less attractive and it is hard to adapt to topology changes. It is noted that PIKE is considered as a deterministic key pre-distribution scheme because any two nodes are guaranteed to be able to set up a key.

19.3.1.2. *Probabilistic key pre-distribution schemes*

Eschenauer *et al.*[4] proposed a random key pre-distribution scheme (referred to as *basic scheme* in this chapter) in 2002. Based on random graph theory,[19] the *basic scheme* relies on probabilistic key sharing among nodes and uses a simple shared key discovery protocol and path key establishment for the connection setup process. This scheme assumes that the sensor network forms a random graph and keys are installed in nodes prior to deployment. Each sensor node installs a random set of keys from the key pool. Any two neighbors are connected if they are able to find a common key.

The principle of key pre-distribution is widely adopted in many key management schemes in WSNs. One of the major reasons is that it can provide an acceptable level of security on the resource-constrained sensor nodes. After the pioneering work of the random key pre-distribution scheme proposed by Eschenauer *et al.*,[4] many enhancements on the *basic scheme* have been proposed. In the following, we briefly discuss several typical trust establishment schemes which enhance the *basic scheme* in different ways.

Chan *et al.*[2] proposed a q-composite key pre-distribution scheme in which q common keys ($q > 1$) are required to establish a single secure link between two neighboring nodes. This scheme achieves better security under small scale attack (when the fraction of compromised nodes is less than 0.5%) while increasing the vulnerability when the number of compromised nodes increases. They also proposed a *random pairwise scheme* which can be regarded as a randomized version of the pairwise scheme. In the pairwise scheme, each sensor node has $n-1$ keys which are privately shared with another node in the network. To reduce the memory storage, the random pairwise scheme only picks a subset of keys from those $n-1$ keys. Thus, the memory usage of the sensor node is reduced but the network connectivity is also decreased. The random pairwise scheme provides full resilience against node capture attack as even when some nodes are compromised, the remainder of the network remains fully secure. However, due to the limited memory storage of sensors, each node can only hold a limited amount of unique keys. The number of key stored cannot scale well with the increasing network size. As a result, the maximum network size supported is smaller than that of the *basic scheme*.

Based on the known attack probabilities[b] in different regions, Chan *et al.*'s scheme[26] targets at enhancing the overall network resilience.[c] Their scheme adjusts the number of distinct keys stored in a sensor node depending on the attack probability of the region they are going to be deployed. If a node is going to be deployed in a region with a higher attack probability, fewer keys will be assigned to it and vice versa. In this case, the adversaries have a higher probability to attack a node with fewer keys stored, and therefore the number of keys exposed to the adversaries after each attack is smaller. It is clear that there are two drawbacks in this approach. Firstly, a certain extent of connectivity is sacrificed. Secondly, additional information on a known and fixed attack probability is required to be known before deployment. Nevertheless, the authors showed that there is a substantial improvement in network resilience.

Du *et al.*[17] proposed a random key pre-distribution method built on the Blom key pre-distribution scheme[27] to improve network resilience. Blom's original scheme uses a single key space to allow any pair of nodes to compute a secret key. Each node is required to store $\lambda + 1$ keys and the scheme guarantees that as long as no more than λ nodes are compromised, all the links between non-compromised nodes remain secure. Du *et al.* extended this idea to multiple key spaces instead of a single one. Two nodes share a pairwise key only if they hold a common key space. Their scheme keeps the λ-secure property but relaxes the memory requirement. Consequently, the network formed results in a *connected* graph with a probability instead of a guaranteed *complete* graph by Blom's scheme. Later, Du *et al.*[3] tried to reduce the memory usage using the deployment knowledge (e.g., location) while achieving the same level of connectivity. However, such a piece of knowledge is not always available, especially in a hostile area and dynamic network environment. Specifically, offline estimation of the node distribution after deployment is generally considered as unrealistic and inaccurate under these situations.

Liu *et al.*[28] proposed a polynomial pool-based pairwise key pre-distribution scheme. Instead of deploying keys, their scheme uses bivariate t-degree polynomials $f(x,y) = \sum_{i,j=0}^{t} a_{ij}x^i y^j$, such that $f(x,y) = f(y,x)$, to compute the pairwise communication keys between nodes. For each node i, the setup server computes a polynomial share $f(i,y)$, which is derived from the polynomial function $f(x,y)$, and installs $f(i,y)$ into node i prior to deployment. Based on the property of bivariate

---

[b]Attack probability refers to the probability that a node within a certain region will be captured.
[c]Network resilience generally refers to the ability of a network to resist being affected by some attacks.

polynomial, two nodes i and j are able to establish a secure connection if they can compute the same key $f(i,j) = f(j,i)$. This polynomial pool-based scheme is based on the basic polynomial-based key pre-distribution proposed by Blundo *et al.*[29] Two nodes are able to establish a secure connection only if they share at least one polynomial function in common by exchanging polynomial function IDs. An attacker requires to capture at least $t+1$ polynomial shares in order to retrieve the original t-degree polynomial function. This scheme shows a significant enhancement of network resilience as long as the number of nodes captured is under a certain threshold, i.e., t in this case. It is interesting to note that this scheme is equivalent to Du *et al.*'s pairwise key pre-distribution scheme discussed above.

Eltoweissy *et al.*[30] developed a protocol for dynamic re-keying in the post-deployment phase. Under the long life cycle assumption, re-keying is necessary in the addition or revocation[d] of nodes. By doing so, node capture attacks can no longer further compromise the rest of the network. When some nodes are suspected to be compromised, the base station sends the re-keying instruction(s) to the cluster controllers[e] to trigger the corresponding re-keying operations. The drawbacks are that their approach requires the coordination among a base station and the cluster controllers. In addition, there is an assumption that the compromised nodes can be detected accurately by the base station.

Based on the design objectives (or constraints consideration) of the above schemes, we summarize this comparison in Table 19.1.

19.3.2. *Asymmetric key-based approaches*

It is well known that public key cryptosystems are in general more versatile than the symmetric cryptography. They can provide more functions such as digital signature and key exchange. However, they are computationally expensive and undesirable to be implemented in the resource-constrained sensor networks. With advancement of sensor network technologies in recent years, implementation of

Table 19.1. Comparison of popular symmetric trust establishment schemes in WSNs.

Scheme	Energy awareness	Memory consumption	Network resilience	Network connectivity	Additional requirement
Eschenauer[4]	Average	High	Poor	Average	None
Jolly[25]	Very good	Very low	Poor	N/A	None
Chan[26]	Good	High	Good	Average	Attack probabilities
Du[3]	Good	Low	Average	Good	Location information
Liu[28]	Average	High	Good	Average	None
Eltoweissy[30]	Average	Low	Good	Average	None

[d]Node revocation is used to remove some detected misbehaving nodes.
[e]A cluster controller is responsible for organizing and managing a particular cluster of nodes.

asymmetric cryptographic protocols in resource-constrained sensor devices becomes possible. In this section, we review several public key cryptosystems for trust establishment systems in WSNs.

Watro *et al.*[31] proposed a set of public key based protocols, called TinyPK, to support authentication and key agreement between a sensor network and a commonly trusted third party outside the sensor network. They exploited the efficiency of the public operations in RSA[23] cryptosystems with the characteristic that the public operations are very fast compared to other public key technology computations by explicitly choosing some small indices as public keys. Their protocols are specially designed such that the computationally expensive operations are placed on the third parties whenever possible. However, some basic functions, such as revocation of compromised private keys, are not supported. Using their protocols, they demonstrated that the RSA[23] and Diffie-Hellman key agreement techniques[22] can be deployed in existing sensor network devices.

As for energy-efficient cryptosystems, there are some other options proposed, such as the XTR public key system,[32] and Elliptic Curve Cryptography (ECC).[33,34] Among them, ECC receives most attentions. ECC operates on groups of points over elliptic curves. Its security stems from the hardness of elliptic curve discrete logarithm problem (ECDLP). To solve the integer factorization problem of RSA, there are sub-exponential algorithms. However, only exponential algorithms are known for solving the ECDLP. This is the reason why ECC can achieve the same level of security with smaller key sizes. In the future, it is believed that ECC will dominate the area of developing public key cryptosystems in WSNs.[35]

Malan *et al.*[36] presented a public key infrastructure (PKI) based on ECC to be executed on the MICA2 Mote. They argued that by carefully implementing the multiplication of points on elliptic curves, PKI for secret keys' distribution is tractable on the MICA2 platform. In fact, ECC is believed to offer security computationally equivalent to that of RSA with significantly smaller key size. For instance, a 163-bit ECC key is computationally equivalent to a 768-bit RSA key.[37] ECC offers an alternative solution to make public key cryptography become feasible on lower power sensor devices.

19.4. Survey of WSN Resilience Enhancement Techniques

In this section, we overview a number of enhancement techniques in WSNs which are used to strengthen the network resilience or to recover a compromised WSN.

To prevent physical node capture attacks, the most effective technique is to install a tamper-resistance hardware[38,39] to every sensor node. With the incorporation of the tamper-resistance hardware, a sensor node is nearly impossible to be compromised by an attacker. However, this technique is generally considered as impractical due to the high cost and large size of the tamper-resistance hardware. In view of this, Alarifi *et al.*[40] proposed to use a code diversifying technique. They proposed to use different memory locations to store sensitive information for different nodes. Even if an attacker cracks a sensor node by using the node capture attack suggested in Ref. 41 and figures out the location of the sensitive information in the memory of that particular node, the memory location information cannot be used to crack the sensitive information of other nodes in the network. This technique can greatly lengthen the time the attacker needs to compromise a node. Unfortunately, an attacker can still compromise the whole network if he is given enough time.

Currently, most of the proposed work suggested that a compromised node has to be isolated from other network components after it is detected. However, Strasser and Vogt[42] suggested that this isolation approach is a waste of resource because a compromised node can still function normally after it is recovered. They discussed some guidelines for node recovery and proposed a method to reprogram the compromised nodes. As a result, the recovered nodes can be restarted in a "clean" state. However, in Ref. 42, they also admitted that this recovery mechanism is quite complicated and they argued that it is worthwhile to do so.

Yang *et al.*[43] and Chatzigiannakis *et al.*[44] proposed the concept of node redeployment. Their schemes try to redeploy the nodes in the network after they are deployed so as to extend the lifetime, delivery ratio, etc. This idea is similar to our node replenishment idea proposed in Sec. 19.7. However, our work focuses on the feasibility and the effectiveness of the use of node replenishment to replace the functions of the compromised nodes and repair some of the compromised links by link replacement strategy whenever possible.

Corke *et al.*[45] suggested to replenish additional nodes to repair the connectivity using a flying robot. They observed that a WSN may be disconnected due to random large scale deployment. They proposed an algorithm to determine the gaps where the helicopter can drop additional nodes at. This idea is very similar to our node replenishment scheme too except that it is not applied to a compromised WSN for recovering nodes and links.

19.5. Node-Key Mobility

In Sec. 19.3, it is observed that many key management schemes follow the "static-key-static-node" model. In Fig. 19.1, we extend the mobility concept from the nodes to the keys. Specifically, we allow the pre-distributed keys to move after deployment and it is so-called the "dynamic-key-static-node" model. Moreover, for a compromised WSN, we propose a node replenishment scheme, which is presented in Sec. 19.7, based on the key mobility idea.

19.6. Proposed Key Redistribution Framework

Our proposed general key redistribution framework introduces an additional key redistribution phase as illustrated in Fig. 19.2. This phase consists of three

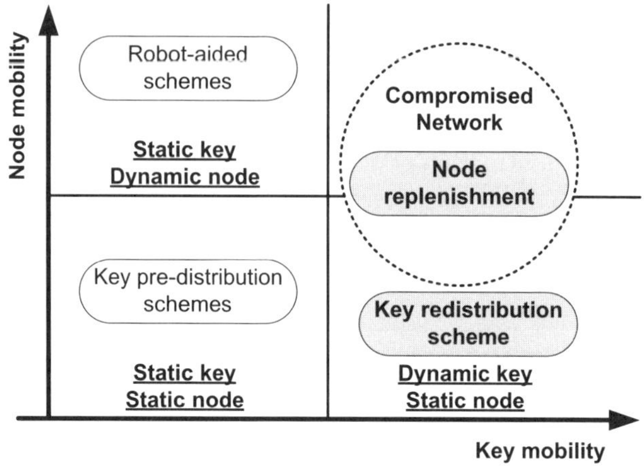

Fig. 19.1. Trust establishment model in WSNs.

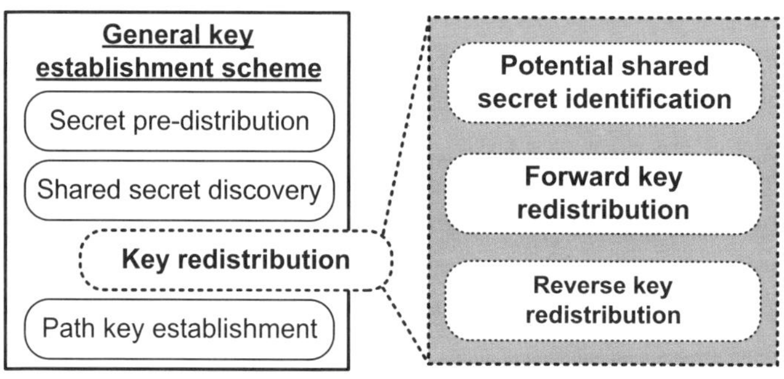

Fig. 19.2. General framework for key redistribution.

sub-phases: *potential shared secret identification*, *forward key redistribution*, and *reverse key redistribution*. The key redistribution framework is presented as pseudocode in Algorithm 19.1.

19.6.1. *Potential shared secret identification*

At the end of shared secret discovery phase, each node has received lists of secret identifiers, $list_{Sid}$, broadcast from its neighbors. These lists are used to identify the secrets, such as keys or polynomials, distributed from the setup server. By intersecting $list_{Sid}$ of the connected neighbors and that of the unconnected neighbors, a node stores the common secret identifiers in a *commonSet*. These common identifiers represent the *potential shared secrets*, which are used to redistribute keys securely via encrypted links from the connected neighbors.

Algorithm 19.1. Key redistribution framework

```
L_c ← lists of connected neighbors
L_u ← lists of unconnected neighbors
node_id = an identifier representing a specific node
self = an identifier representing the original node
for i ∈ L_u do
   /* potential shared secret identification */
   commonSet = {} /* store the potential shared secrets. (default = empty).*/
   for j ∈ L_c do
      sharedSecrets = intersect(secret(i), secret(j))
      commonSet = union(commonSet, sharedSecrets)
   end for
   /* forward key redistribution */
   request = rearrange(commonSet) /* to reduce the number of trials */
   reply = broadcast(request) /* broadcast the request and wait for reply */
   if reply(key, node_id) == successful then
      redistribute(key, node_id → self)
      /* node with ID = node_id then delete that key */
   else
      /* reverse key redistribution */
      send(unusedKey, self → node_id)
      encryptedKey = received(node_id → self)
      forward(encryptedKey, self → i)
   end if
end for
```

19.6.2. *Forward key redistribution*

The *potential shared secrets* identified in the previous stage refer to the secrets that exist in current connected neighbors and they can be used to connect to the unconnected neighbors. However, these secrets may not be available for redistribution in all situations. For instance, a secret is revoked or deleted. Thus, a node needs to negotiate with those connected neighbors which contain certain selected *potential shared secrets* and waits for their replies. Multiple requests on the same secret are handled on a first-come-first-served basis. This stage will terminate if the node successfully gets the keys or all the *potential shared secrets* are tried. In the first case, the connected neighbors will delete the corresponding keys for security purpose. For the latter case, another method known as *reverse key redistribution* is proposed and will be discussed subsequently.

19.6.3. *Reverse key redistribution*

When all the potential shared secret requests are failed, a node can resort to creating a new key for connection establishment with the aid of a potential shared secret k_{common}. An unused key is picked randomly and sent to one of its connected neighbors which contains the selected *potential shared secret*. The selected connected neighbor computes a new communication key and delivers the resultant key to the original node and the unconnected neighbor. This method does not require the original node to know k_{common} for decryption and allows redistributing new assigned key securely to the unconnected neighbor. The direction of redistribution is reversed as the key is moving towards the connected neighbor.

Throughout the key redistribution phase, any unconnected neighbor which is able to find at least one *potential shared secret* in the connected neighbors is then linked.

19.6.4. *Integration with key-based pre-distribution schemes*

In random key pre-distribution schemes, such as Ref. 4, a key is regarded as a secret. The goal of our scheme is to redistribute keys from connected neighbors to reach unconnected nodes. In contrast to those schemes which require pre-deployment knowledge, e.g., Ref. 3, our scheme solely bases on the information received from the connected neighbors. This makes our scheme able to be easily integrated with many existing random key pre-distribution schemes. Now let us describe the key-based redistribution as an integration to the *basic scheme*[4]:

(1) **Potential common keys identification**
At the end of the shared key discovery phase, each node has received lists of key identifiers, $list_{Kid}$, broadcast from its neighbors. By intersecting $lists_{Kid}$ of the connected and that of the unconnected neighbors, a node is able to determine all *potential common keys* and redistribute them securely via encrypted links from the connected neighbors.

(2) **Forward key redistribution**
The *potential common keys* identified in the previous stage refer to the keys that exist in current connected neighbors and they can be used to connect to the unconnected neighbors. However, these keys may not be suitable for redistribution in all situations. Thus, a node needs to send a request to those connected neighbors which contain certain selected *potential common keys* and waits for their replies. In the case that the key cannot be used for redistribution (e.g., the key is currently in use in the connected neighbors), the node will try to request for the next selected *potential common key*. The selection preference is based on ascending order of the keys in the key occurrence pattern. As shown in Algorithm 19.1, a node tries to rearrange the sequence before sending out the request.

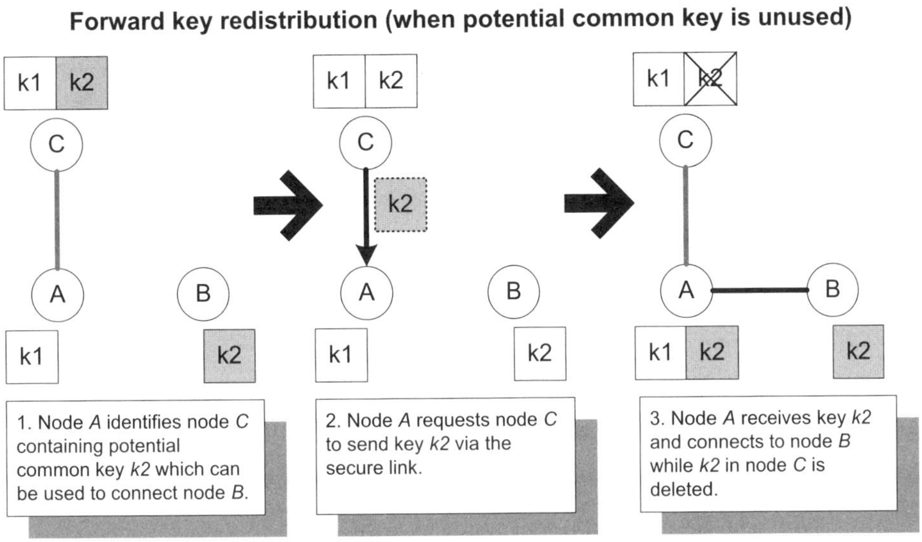

Fig. 19.3. Forward key redistribution (key-based scheme).

The objective of the rearrangement is to reduce the number of trials based on the observation that two connected neighbors will have certain probability to be neighborhood themselves. Specifically, the smaller the number of occurrence of the keys, the higher will be the chance of successfully getting the key for redistribution. This stage will terminate if the node successfully gets the key or all the *potential common keys* are tried. In the first case, the key redistribution phase can be regarded as completed. The ownership of the key is transferred to the requesting node and the original owner is required to delete the key for security purpose.

A simple example is shown in Fig. 19.3 to illustrate the above processes. For the latter case, another method known as *reverse key redistribution* is proposed.

(3) Reverse key redistribution

When all the potential common key requests are failed, a node can only resort to creating a new key for connection establishment with the aid of a potential common key k_{common}. Using the concept from the q-composite key scheme,[2] an unused key k_{unused} is sent to a connected neighbor, which has the required k_{common}, to generate a new communication key $k_{new} = hash(k_{common}||k_{unused})$ in which keys are hashed in some canonical order. As shown in Fig. 19.4, the $k_{new} = Hash(k2||k3)$ is encrypted using $k_{common} = k2$ in the connected neighbor and then securely delivered to the target node either directly or backward through the original node. This method does not require the original node to know k_{common} for decryption and allows redistributing new assigned key

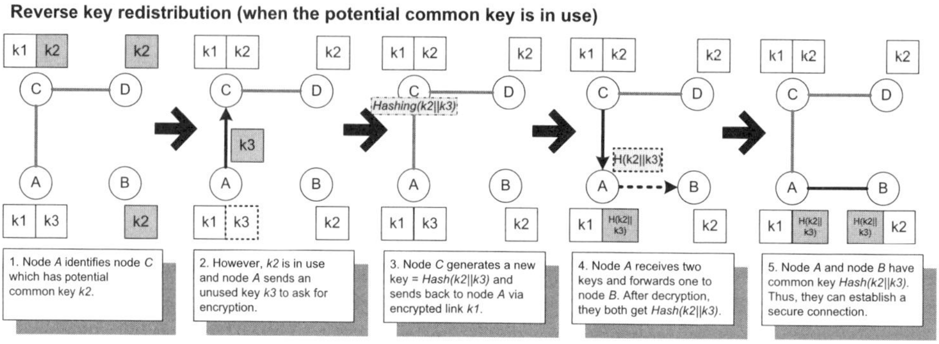

Fig. 19.4. Reverse key redistribution (key-based scheme).

securely to the unconnected neighbor. The direction of redistribution is reversed as the key is moving towards the connected neighbor.

19.6.5. *Integration with polynomial-based pre-distribution schemes*

In this section, we first review the polynomial based key pre-distribution scheme (referred to as *polynomial scheme*)[28] and then present our proposed polynomial-based redistribution scheme. As shown in Fig. 19.2, the polynomial-based redistribution scheme is similar to the key-based one except that it does not have the last sub-phase (i.e., the reverse key redistribution). The last sub-phase is skipped due to overlapping with the path key establishment phase.

The *polynomial scheme* deploys polynomials instead of keys. We use the Random Subset Assignment Scheme (RS),[28] which is an instantiation of the *polynomial scheme*, for illustration in this chapter. It is divided into three phases:

- *Subset assignment*: Initially, a setup server randomly generates a pool of s bivariate t-degree polynomials over a finite field F_q. Each sensor node randomly picks a subset of s' polynomials from the pool and is assigned the IDs of these s' polynomials.
- *Polynomial share discovery*: To establish a connection, a polynomial share discovery phase is carried out. If two nodes share the same polynomial, they are said to share the same secret and are able to generate a pairwise communication key.
- *Path discovery*: When two nodes fail to establish a direct link, they can start the path key establishment phase. If the source node is able to find a path to the destination node, a pairwise key can be exchanged via the secure path. Given the network is connected, there is always a path between any two nodes.

The *polynomial scheme* is considered more general and secure. Many new trust establishment schemes, e.g., Ref. 30, have adopted this approach. Therefore, redistribution of key polynomials is highly demanding for improving the network performance. Let us describe the polynomial-based redistribution as an integration to the Random Subset Assignment Scheme (RS)[28]:

(1) Potential polynomial share identification
At the end of the polynomial share discovery phase, a node has recognized its neighbors and their lists of polynomial IDs, $list_{Pid}$. By intersecting $list_{Pid}$ of its connected neighbors and that of unconnected neighbors, the node can determine all *potential polynomial shares*. This identification process is computationally efficient because only the polynomial IDs are used in comparison.

(2) Forward key redistribution
In polynomial-based redistribution, a node requests only the pairwise communication keys, but not the polynomials, in order to establish secure connections. This is the main difference compared to the key-based redistribution. Once a *potential polynomial share* is identified, a node needs to send a request to those connected neighbors which contain certain selected *potential polynomial shares* and waits for their replies. If the requesting polynomial share is not in use, then a communication key is computed and redistributed to the requesting node. Otherwise, the node will try to request for the next selected *potential polynomial share*. Since the number of polynomials stored in a node is relatively small (usually less than 10, as shown in Ref. 28), it may not be necessary to apply the rearrangement algorithm to reduce the number of trials as proposed in Sec. 19.6.4.

The polynomial-based redistribution does not require deletion of any polynomial. Our proposed mechanism only redistributes communication keys, not the polynomial itself. Our task is to ensure that there is no duplication of communication key existing in the network. Each node must mark down all the polynomial shares used for generation of communication keys, in either the polynomial share discovery or in the redistribution phase. Specifically, every polynomial can only generate one unique communication key.

Figure 19.5 illustrates a simple example for polynomial-based forward key redistribution with 3 nodes. Node A finds that its connected neighbor, node C, contains the common polynomial $p2$, which can be used to connect node B. Instead of redistributing the whole polynomial $p2$, node A sends a request to node C for generating a new key k using polynomial $p2$ with $nodeID = B$, i.e., $k = p2(C, B)$. The new key k is transmitted to node A through the secure direct link. Due to the characteristic of bivariate polynomial, node B only needs the ID of node C in order to produce the same key k. Finally, node A and node B contain the same key k and they can establish a connection.

In Fig. 19.6, when there is a link between node B and node C, the consequence of redistribution is degenerated to path discovery. Initially, node A discovers

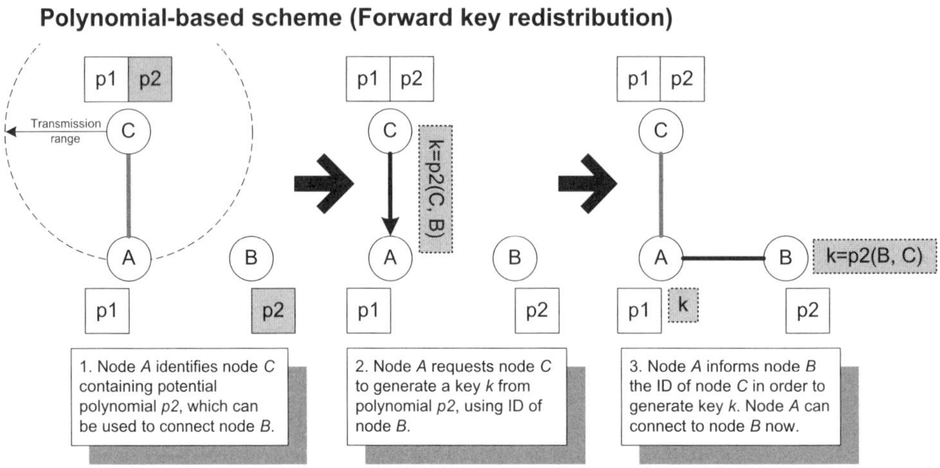

Fig. 19.5. Polynomial-based forward key redistribution.

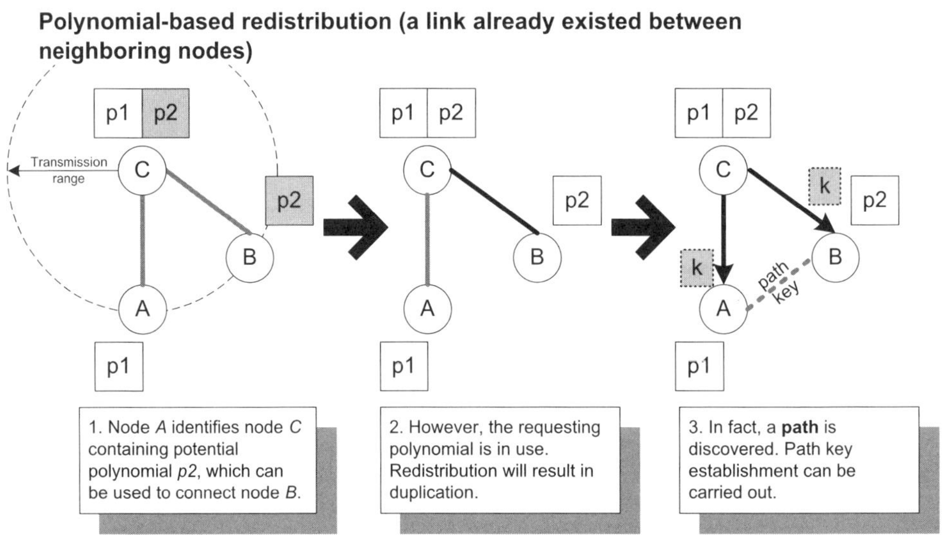

Fig. 19.6. Polynomial-based reverse key redistribution (degenerated to path discovery).

node C containing the polynomial $p2$ which is useful to connect node B. At this moment, node A has no knowledge about the direct link between node B and node C. It sends a request to node C for generation of key k using node B's ID. However, node C recognizes that the requested key, $k = p2(C, B)$, is already existed or generated before. Further duplication will result in poor security. Therefore, the request for generation of key k is failed. In fact, this implies that node C discovers a path from node A to node B via itself. Path key establishment can then be taken place.

19.7. Proposed Node Replenishment Scheme

When a node is captured, an attacker can readily get the sensitive information stored inside the captured node. Such sensitive information involves encryption keys and keys related data. It is a waste of resources if the network is completely abandoned due to a fraction of nodes being captured, as most parts of the network (and possibly most nodes) are still functioning. This motivates our novel design of schemes for recovering the compromised links by a *link replacement strategy* and recovering the functions of compromised nodes by a *node replenishment strategy.*

Specifically, to tackle the issue of compromised keys, which also affects the parts of the network outside the compromised region, we propose a link replacement strategy. The main idea of this strategy is to do *key rollover* to help replacing the old keys which are originally used to secure the links. On the other hand, to tackle the issue of compromised nodes, we propose to make use of the knowledge of the attack pattern to estimate the most effective region to replenish the nodes into the network. These two ideas will be elaborated in detail in Secs. 19.7.1 and 19.7.2, respectively.

19.7.1. *Link replacement strategy*

The main idea of link replacement strategy is to do key rollover, so that some of the compromised links can be recovered. In the following section, we discuss the link replacement procedures in detail.

19.7.1.1. *Link replacement procedures*

Suppose there are three nodes A, B, and C as shown in Fig. 19.7. The links AB, BC, and AC are secured by keys K_c, K_a, and K_b, respectively. To perform *key rollover*, the following procedures are carried out:

(1) Choose a link in which the key used to secure the link would like to be replaced. In the figure, the link BC is chosen and we need to replace key K_a with another key $K_{a''}$.
(2) The sensor node opposite to the chosen link is responsible to generate a secret and send the generated secret to the adjacent nodes of the chosen link securely through the links. From Fig. 19.7, node A is responsible to generate a secret $K_{a'}$ and send $K_{a'}$ to node B and node C through the links AB and AC which are secured by keys K_c and K_b, respectively.
(3) The two nodes adjacent to the chosen link generate the new key of the chosen link independently. New key can be generated by hashing the original key with

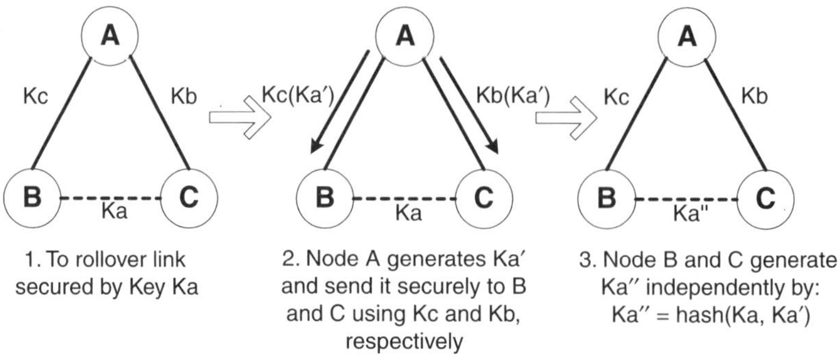

Fig. 19.7. Link replacement procedures.

that of the new secret received. Refer to the figure, nodes B and C generate the same new key $K_{a''} = hash(K_a, k_{a'})$. From now onwards, $K_{a''}$ is used to secure the link BC.

(4) The remaining two keys K_b and K_c used to secure the links AC and AB, respectively, can be replaced by following the same procedures described above.

19.7.2. *Node replenishment strategy*

The main idea of the node replenishment strategy is to replace the functions of the compromised nodes as well as the dead nodes in a WSN by deploying some new nodes into the network. Before applying the node replenishment strategy, there are several issues to be considered:

(1) Firstly, where should we deploy the new nodes?
(2) Secondly, how can a newly deployed node interact with the existing old nodes which have already been deployed in the network?
(3) Thirdly, how can newly deployed nodes interact among themselves?

In this section, we describe our node replenishment strategy in detail and explain how this strategy can tackle the above issues.

- *Where should the new nodes be deployed?*
  With the assumption that the attack pattern and the attack region can be detected, it is possible to limit the target region for node replenishment to a rectangle as shown in Fig. 19.8. The rectangular area can be easily derived with the knowledge of the attack pattern and the compromised nodes' locations. The new nodes can then be randomly distributed in the target region.
- *How can the newly deployed nodes interact with the existing nodes in the network?*
  Basically, the key pool of the newly deployed nodes contains both new generated keys and the old keys. To connect the existing nodes in the network, only the

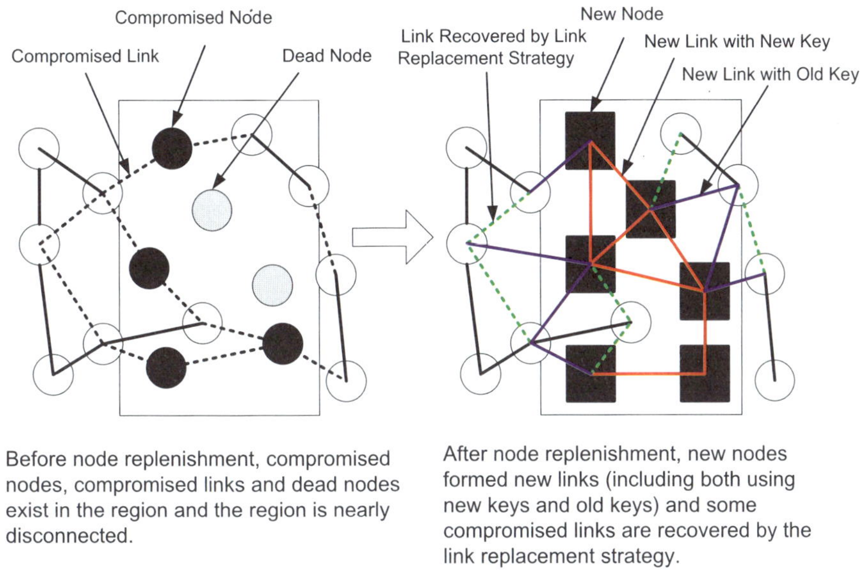

Fig. 19.8. Node replenishment strategy.

old keys can be used. It is possible for a newly deployed node to connect to the normal existing nodes as shown in Fig. 19.8 or the compromised nodes which are not shown in the figure.

— If a newly deployed node connects to a normal node, it is possible for the newly established link to be secure or compromised. The probability of the existence of a secure (or a compromised link) depends on the ratio of the compromised links in the region. As a result, it will not affect the ratio of compromised links in the region. However, as discussed in Sec. 19.7.1, link replacement strategy will be performed together with the link addition process. In this sense, the addition of the new link can help reduce the ratio of compromised links in the region.

— If a newly deployed node connects to a compromised node, the newly established links are supposed to be compromised. This will increase the ratio of the compromised links in the region. However, we assume that within a rectangle region, the amount of compromised nodes are small. As a result, the increase in the compromised links ratio due to this reason is expected to be acceptable.

- *How can the newly deployed nodes interact themselves?*

A newly deployed node can only use newly generated keys in the key pool to connect other newly deployed nodes in the region. The reason is that the newly generated keys do not exist in the existing nodes, so it is not easy for an attacker to compromise these new keys before new nodes are deployed. In other words, all the new links formed and secured by new keys are normal links according to this rationale. However, another related issue arises due to the separation of the newly generated keys and existing old keys in the key pool of the newly deployed nodes. Specifically, with a fixed key ring size m (the newly deployed nodes are supposed to have the same key ring size with that of the existing nodes), what should be the appropriate ratio between the new keys and the old keys?

— The ratio between new keys and old keys determines the number of new links formed between new nodes themselves and that between new nodes and old nodes. The higher this ratio, the larger the number of new links formed between new nodes. These links are resilient to the previously captured nodes. However, the higher this ratio, the smaller amount of links formed between the new nodes and old nodes. This contradicts our original idea of extending the lifetime of the existing network. We believe that finding an optimal ratio is an important research problem, which is outside the scope of the present chapter. In the following, we assume that this ratio is 1:1.

19.8. Performance Evaluation

19.8.1. *System configuration*

Simulations are performed in MATLAB with the parameters shown in Table 19.2.

This configuration is to simulate the deployment of a large sensor network with 10,000 nodes. It is widely adopted in other research work (e.g., Refs. 2 to 4). Under the random deployment pattern, the average number of neighbors for each node is about 48.

Our key redistribution framework can be applied to different networks with different configurations. In fact, the scalability of the framework is based on the scalability of the underlying probabilistic key pre-distribution scheme. When there are at least one connected neighbor and at least one unconnected neighbor, key redistribution mechanisms can be started.

Table 19.2. Simulation parameters.

Definition	Default	Range
The number of nodes, n	10,000	>1000
The size of key pool, $\|S\|$	100,000	>10,000
The size of polynomial pool, s	43	
The deployment region	$1000\,\text{m} \times 1000\,\text{m}$	
The wireless transmission range for each node, R	40 m	
The key ring size, m	100	10–200

19.8.2. *Connectivity of key redistribution framework*

Since our key redistribution framework critically depends on the number of connected neighbors after the shared secret discovery phase, we first examine at the local connectivity estimated in the *basic scheme*.[4] The probability that any two neighboring nodes share at least a common key is: $p_{local} = 1 - \Pr$ [two nodes do not share any key], and thus:

$$p_{local} = 1 - \frac{\left(1 - \frac{m}{|S|}\right)^{2(|S|-m+\frac{1}{2})}}{\left(1 - \frac{2m}{|S|}\right)^{(|S|-2m+\frac{1}{2})}}. \tag{19.1}$$

After the sharing key discovery phase, keys from connected neighbors are redistributed to further increase connectivity. Although those keys are distributed in different nodes, they are accessible through secure links as if from a single storage. Key ring of a particular node is combined with that of the connected neighbors virtually. Given the expected node degree d, we can compute the expected number of connected neighbors d_{conn} before redistribution:

$$d_{conn} = p_{local} \times d. \tag{19.2}$$

When there exists at least one connected and one unconnected neighbors (i.e., $0 < d_{conn} < d$), key redistribution can take place. The local connectivity between a node and one of its unconnected neighbors is now computed as follows. For any node, there are $\binom{|S|}{m}$ ways to pick m keys from the key pool of size $|S|$. Beside the triggering sensor node and its unconnected neighbor, d_{conn} neighbors are also involved in the key redistribution process. Hence, the total number of ways for those involved nodes to pick m keys is $\binom{|S|}{m}^{d_{conn}+2}$. Now, assuming keys of unconnected neighbor are drawn out of the key pool $|S|$ without replacement, the number of possible key rings is $\binom{|S|}{m}$. Then, keys for the remaining nodes (the sensor node itself and its connected neighbors) must be picked from the remaining $(|S| - m)$ keys from the key pool. There are $\binom{|S|-m}{m}^{d_{conn}+1}$ ways to do this.

Let p'_{local} be the probability that a node and one of its unconnected neighbors share at least a common key after the first key redistribution, which is calculated as:

$$p'_{local} = 1 - \left[\frac{\binom{|S|-m}{m}}{\binom{|S|}{m}}\right]^{d_{conn}+1}, \tag{19.3}$$

where $d_{conn} < d$.

The equation can be further simplified by using Stirling's approximation for $n!$ to obtain:

$$p'_{local} = 1 - \left(\frac{\left(1 - \frac{m}{|S|}\right)^{2(|S|-m+\frac{1}{2})}}{\left(1 - \frac{2m}{|S|}\right)^{(|S|-2m+\frac{1}{2})}} \right)^{d_{conn}+1} . \tag{19.4}$$

For the polynomial-based redistribution, we use the same approach and p'_{local} follows that:

$$p'_{local} = 1 - \left(\prod_{i=0}^{s'-1} \frac{s - s' - i}{s} \right)^{d_{conn}+1} . \tag{19.5}$$

Based on the configuration settings in Sec. 19.8.1, Fig. 19.9 shows the analytical and simulation results of local connectivity estimated by the key-based redistribution scheme and the basic scheme using Eq. (19.4). With increasing storage of secrets, the initial connectivity p_{local} rises slowly, resulting in more connected neighbors. However, the improvement of connectivity p'_{local} is at a much faster rate than p_{local} because a set of secret shares are accessible once an additional neighbor

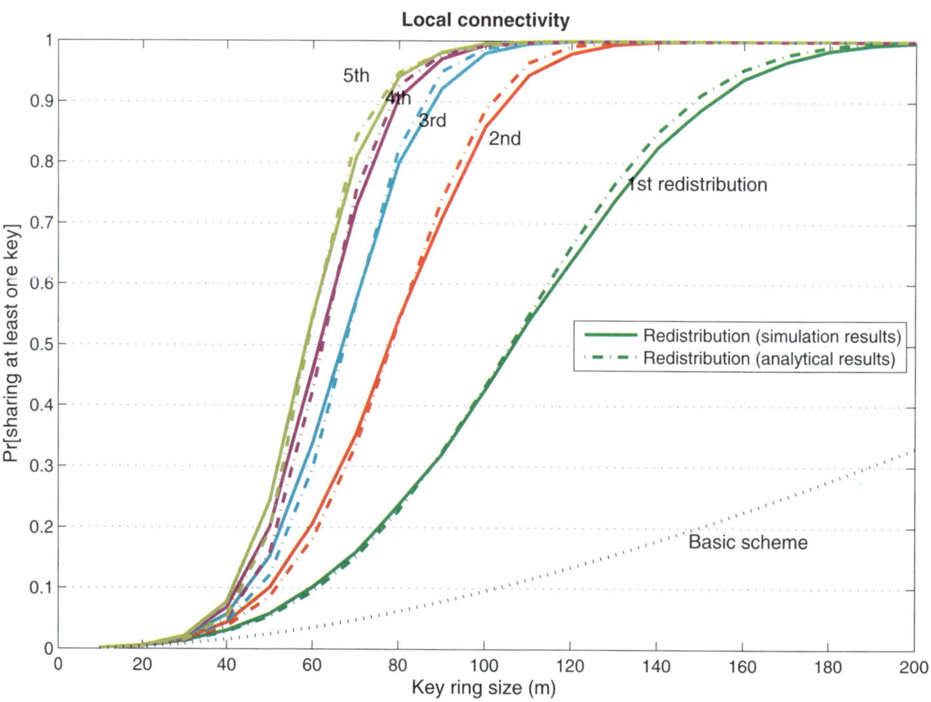

Fig. 19.9. Probability of sharing at least one key between two neighboring nodes.

joins. For polynomial-based redistribution, we use Eq. (19.5) to estimate the local connectivity, and both the analytical and simulation results are shown in Fig. 19.12.

19.8.3. *Security analysis of key redistribution framework*

To evaluate the resilience of our framework against node capture attack, we measure the fraction of communication links compromised when x nodes are captured. Let K be the key for securing a link between two nodes which are not compromised. Given a node (other than these two nodes) is captured, the probability that K is not compromised is $\left(1 - \frac{m}{|S|}\right)$. When x nodes are compromised, the probability that K is still not compromised is $\left(1 - \frac{m}{|S|}\right)^x$. So, the expected fraction of total keys/links compromised in the *basic scheme* can be estimated as:

$$f_{comp}(m) = 1 - \left(1 - \frac{m}{|S|}\right)^x, \tag{19.6}$$

where x is the number of nodes compromised. In addition, from the q-composite scheme[2] with $q = 2$, the expected fraction of total keys compromised is calculated as $(f_{comp}(m))^2$.

In our key-based redistribution, the total secure links of a node actually consist of l_{pre} links from the pre-distribution phase and l_{rev} links from the reverse key redistribution phase. These l_{rev} links are special because they are made secure by hashing two keys. When a node is captured, m keys are exposed. They can be used to compromise links which are made secure by a single key in the network (*Type I*[f]). Meanwhile, they can also be used to compromise links which are protected by hashing two keys (*Type II*).

The probabilities that a link belongs to *Type I* and *Type II* are $\frac{l_{pre}}{l_{pre}+l_{rev}}$ and $\frac{l_{rev}}{l_{pre}+l_{rev}}$, respectively, and the expected fraction of total links compromised is estimated as:

$$\Pr[\text{Type I}](f_{comp}(m)) + \Pr[\text{Type II}](f_{comp}(m))^2. \tag{19.7}$$

In the polynomial-based redistribution, the calculation is different depending on the key generation method during the path key establishment phase. In this chapter, we assume that a path key is computed using the polynomial in the intermediate node. The path key is compromised only if the corresponding polynomial is revealed. The property of the polynomial-based scheme ensures that when $x \leq t$, none of the polynomials can be compromised and thus, the network is perfectly secure. When $x > t$, the probability of a particular polynomial being compromised is (as shown

[f]Forward key redistribution will not affect the overall key distribution patterns.

in Ref. 28):

$$f_{comp}(s') = 1 - \sum_{i=0}^{t} \frac{x!}{(x-i)!i!} \left(\frac{s'}{s}\right)^{i} \left(1 - \frac{s'}{s}\right)^{x-i}. \tag{19.8}$$

As our redistribution scheme avoids duplication of communication keys, it follows the estimation of fraction of compromised links in Eq. (19.8) but with a smaller value of s'. Therefore, our polynomial-based redistribution scheme is still t-collusion resistant.

19.8.4. *Security analysis of link replacement strategy*

We present our security analysis on the replacement procedure by considering the following cases:

- **Case (1): None of the link is compromised.**
  In this case, since all three links are still secured, the key replacement strategy simply does key rollover on the keys which have not been compromised yet. As a result, there is no change in the number of the compromised links in the network.
- **Case (2): Either one of the three links is compromised.**
  In this case, the only compromised link is recovered to a normal link. This case involves two subcases:
  - In the first sub-case, the chosen link is a normal link and the newly generated secret must pass through the compromised link. Since the transmission of a secret through a compromised link is supposed to be leaked out, it is reasonable to assume that the attacker knows the newly generated secret used to do key rollover. However, since the original key is still secured, hashing the original key with a leaked secret will still lead to a secure new key.
  - In the second sub-case, the chosen link is a compromised link and the secret passes through two normal links. Since the secret passes through two normal links, it is reasonable to assume that the attacker does not know the newly generated secret. As a result, hashing a secure secret and a compromised key will result in a secure new key. By doing so, the compromised link is replaced by a normal link.
- **Case (3): Two or more links are compromised.**
  In this case, since two or more links are compromised, the secret generated must pass through the compromised link. As a result, the newly generated key will remain in the same status as that of the original key, i.e., if the original key is a compromised key, then the new key is also a compromised key and vice versa.

To summarize, there are three different cases for the link replacement strategy. Two cases have no effect to the total number of the compromised links in the network, while one case will actually reduce the total number of the compromised

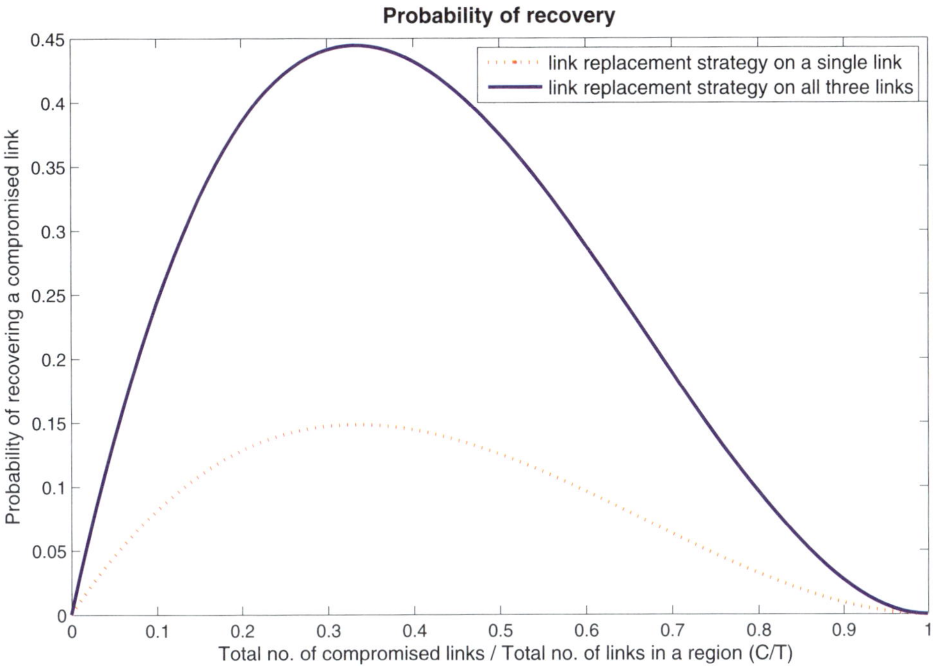

Fig. 19.10. Probability of recovery ratio of compromised links in a region.

links. More importantly, we are interested in determining the probability of having the case of reducing the total number of the compromised links in the network whenever a triangle structure (similar to the one in Fig. 19.7) exists.

Suppose the total number of the compromised links is C, the total number of links is T. With these two parameters, we can assume that a link has a probability of $\frac{C}{T}$ to be compromised. With the existence of a triangle structure, the probability of the existence of *Case* (2) discussed above is given below:

$$Pr[Case(2)] = 3 \times \left(\frac{C}{T}\right) \times \left(1 - \frac{C}{T}\right)^2. \tag{19.9}$$

Figure 19.10 shows the results of Eq. (19.9) when only one of the three links is undergoing link replacement strategy and when all the three links are undergoing link replacement strategy. The results show that our replacement strategy performs reasonably well (around 40% improvement) in the case where there are about 30% to 40% compromised links in region under consideration.

19.8.5. *Security analysis of node replenishment strategy*

By deploying new nodes in the compromised region, new links can be formed with three different cases. Afterwards, link replacement strategy can be applied. In this

Table 19.3. Notation.

Symbol	Description
N_r	Number of nodes in the region
N_c	Number of compromised nodes in the region
N_n	Number of new nodes in the region
C_r	Number of compromised links in the region
C_n	Number of compromised links after link addition
$C_{n'}$	Number of compromised links after link addition and link replacement
T_r	Number of links in the region
T_n	Number of links after link addition
$T_{n'}$	Number of links after link addition and link replacement
p_o	Secure connectivity ratio using old keys
p_n	Secure connectivity ratio using new keys
d	Expected number of neighbors (Degree) after the node replenishment

section, we mathematically show the effect of the node replenishment strategy to the network resilience in the compromised region. Table 19.3 lists the notation used in this section.

Equation (19.10) illustrates the compromised links ratio in the region after the link addition process is completed. Obviously, the total number of new links formed depends critically on the number of old keys and new keys in the newly deployed node. The second term in the denominator represents the newly established links to the old nodes, while the third term represents the newly established links within the new nodes. On the other hand, if a new node connects to a compromised node, the new link formed is also compromised. The number of compromised links formed in this case is represented by the second term in the numerator in Eq. (19.10). If a new node connects to a normal node, there is a probability $\frac{C_r}{T_r}$ that the new link formed has already been compromised. The number of compromised links formed due to this case is represented by the third term in Eq. (19.10). However, there is no compromised link formed if a new node connects to a new node.

$$\frac{C_n}{T_n} = \frac{C_r + (p_o \times d \times N_n)\left(\frac{N_c}{N_r+N_n} + \frac{N_r-N_c}{N_r+N_n} \times \frac{C_r}{T_r}\right)}{T_r + \left(\left(p_o \times \frac{N_r}{N_r+N_n}\right) + \left(p_n \times \frac{N_n}{N_r+N_n}\right)\right) \times d \times N_n}. \tag{19.10}$$

After new links are formed with both new nodes and existing nodes (no matter compromised or not), new compromised links ratio $\frac{C_n}{T_n}$ is formed based on Eq. (19.10). At this stage, the link replacement strategy discussed in Sec. 19.7.1 will then be performed. By applying Eq. (19.9) and Eq. (19.10), the compromised links ratio in the region after the whole node replenishment process can be estimated by Eq. (19.11).

$$\frac{C_{n'}}{T_{n'}} = (1 - Pr[Case(2)] \times \frac{C_n}{T_n}. \tag{19.11}$$

19.8.6. *Simulation results*

19.8.6.1. *Local connectivity*

We compare our simulation results with the *basic scheme*[4] and the scheme using deployment knowledge.[3] We also integrated our key redistribution framework into the deployment knowledge scheme to evaluate portability and performance. The combined scheme is also investigated and the result is plotted in the same graph. Figure 19.11 illustrates the local connectivity, i.e., the probability of sharing a key between two nodes against various key ring size m.

First of all, our simulation results match well with the analytical results presented in Sec. 19.8.2 in which the key-based redistribution schemes improve the connectivity with increasing number of connected nodes. Given $|S| = 100,000$, the connectivity rises sharply when p_{local} is around 0.1–0.3. To reach $p = 0.5$, our scheme requires $m = 106$, the basic scheme needs $m = 263$, while Du's approach only needs $m = 67$. However, at high connectivity, i.e., $p'_{local} > 0.8$, our scheme outperforms both approaches. By using the idea of key redistribution, the performance gain comes from the adequate supply of keys from connected neighbors. This is similar to obtaining sub-key pools in Du's scheme via the established secure links. When p_{local} further increases, our scheme achieves the maximum connectivity.

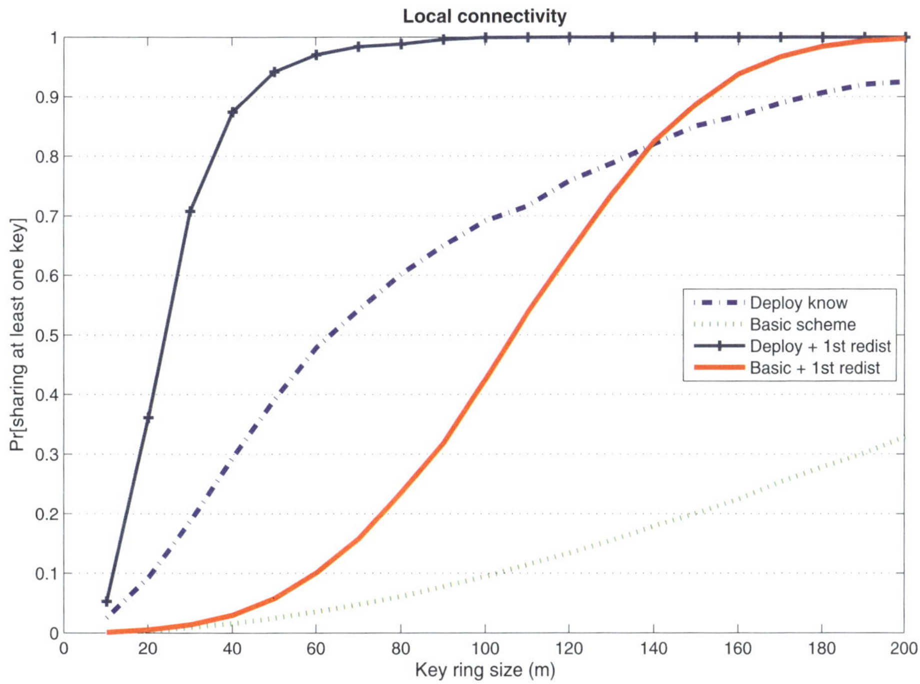

Fig. 19.11. Local connectivity.

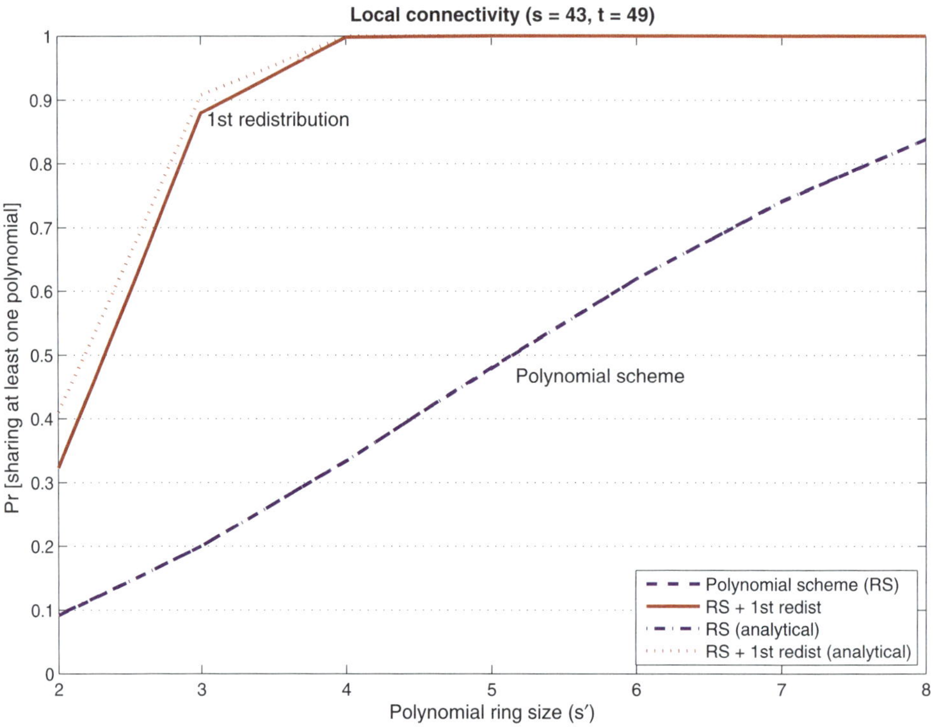

Fig. 19.12. Probability of sharing at least one polynomial between two neighboring nodes.

In the combined deployment knowledge and key redistribution scheme, the plot demonstrates the portability of our algorithm. The curve of combined scheme shows that the connectivity can be greatly increased with much fewer keys. This is highly important to memory-constrained sensor devices.

Figure 19.12 shows similar results for the polynomial-based redistribution. Since the polynomial pool size is much smaller than the key pool size, the chance to find a potential shared secret is much higher which results in great improvement after a single iteration. Nevertheless, both plots show that it is possible for our key redistribution framework to boost the connectivity up to 1. This indicates that all the isolated components are finally rejoined and the network becomes fully connected.

19.8.6.2. *Network resilience*

From Fig. 19.13, we note that the network resilience of our key-based redistribution scheme is better than that of the *basic scheme* and approaches that of the scheme using deployment knowledge. However, our scheme does not rely on any deployment knowledge and thus, requires larger key ring size m to achieve certain

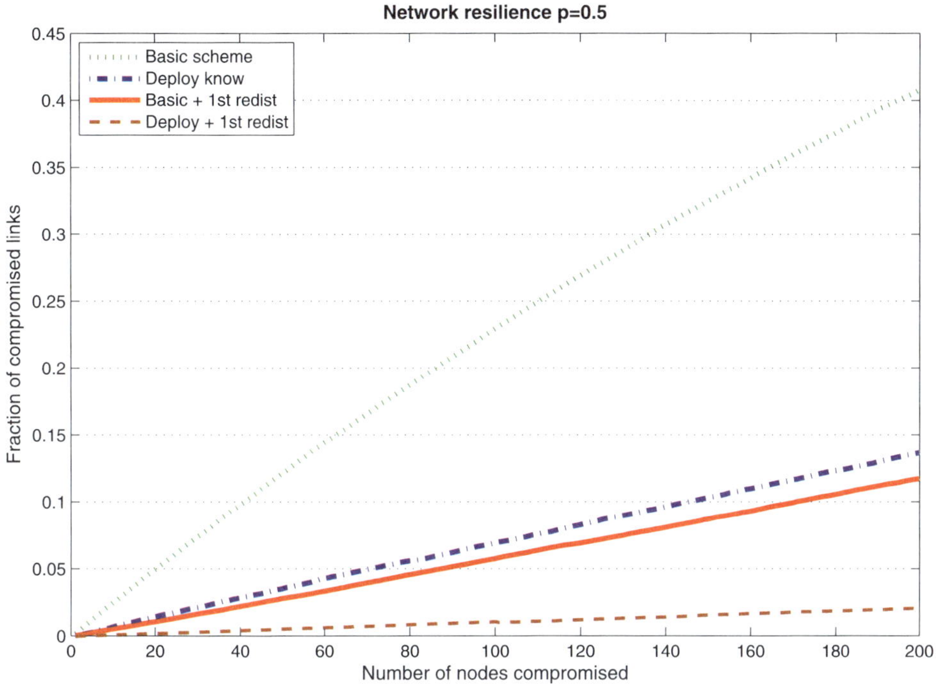

Fig. 19.13. Network resilience of key-based redistribution at $p = 0.5$.

level of connectivity. In the case of high connectivity, our approach achieves better resilience than that of both schemes. The reason is that the larger the number of links created by the redistribution process, the higher the chance of them to be secured by hashing two keys. For example, with $p = 0.5$, only 87 out of 106 keys are used to secure 20% of the links, but the remaining 19 redistributed keys are used to secure 80% of the links of the network which are locally concentrated. These 19 redistributed keys are hashed keys so that they can only be revealed when the two corresponding keys are compromised. Therefore, they can achieve higher security compared to the original pre-distributed keys.

Figure 19.14 illustrates the enhancement of network resilience over the polynomial scheme. To maintain a connectivity of 0.5, our polynomial-based redistribution scheme only requires $s' = 3$ polynomials while the original scheme (RS) needs $s' = 5$ polynomials. More importantly, the perfectly secure threshold improves from $x = 300$ to $x = 450$. The reason is that fewer secrets are exposed in each compromise and hence more nodes are needed to be captured. Comparing the key-based approaches (shown together in the same figure), our scheme even outperforms the basic scheme due to the reduction of key ring size and the protection of *Type II* links.

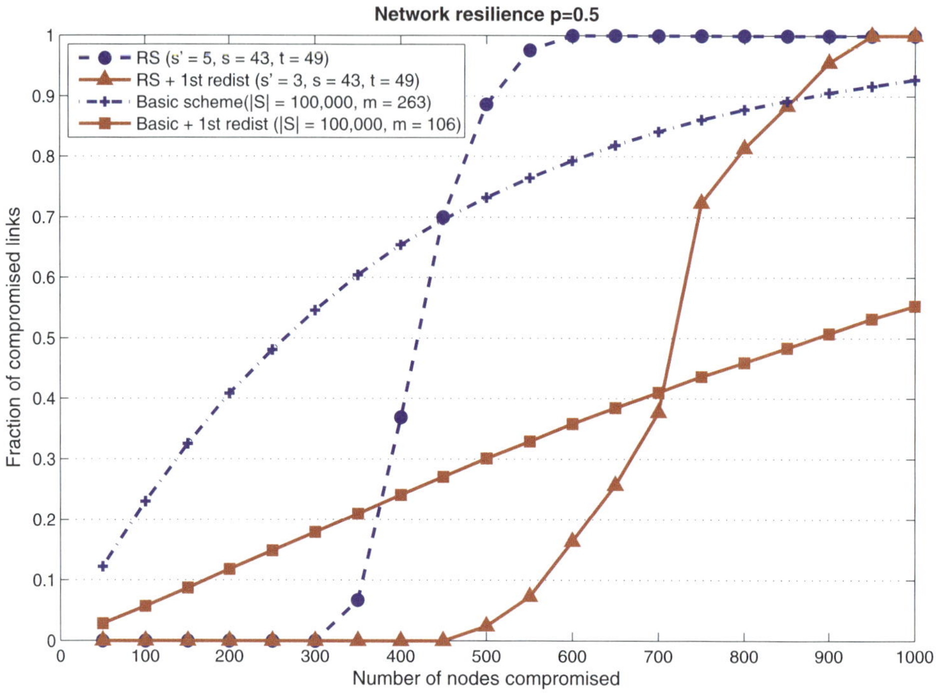

Fig. 19.14. Network resilience of polynomial-based redistribution at $p = 0.5$.

Table 19.4. Performance of node replenishment applied to the basic scheme.

Replenishment interval	No. of nodes added	Improvement of network resilience
50	77	0%
100	195	4.72%
150	296	7.93%

19.8.7. *Node replenishment applied to the basic scheme*

To study the effect of node replenishment, we measure the network resilience of a trust establishment scheme before and after adding new nodes on the *basic scheme*. In Table 19.4, 77, 195, 296 nodes are newly added in the compromised region upon 50, 100, 150 nodes are compromised, respectively. We can see that when more nodes are compromised, we need to deploy more new nodes as the compromised region is larger. Figure 19.15 illustrates the change of network resilience at different attack intervals. For example, at 100 compromised nodes, 195 nodes are replenished in order to replace certain number of compromised links. After link replacement, the network resilience is improved by 4.72%.

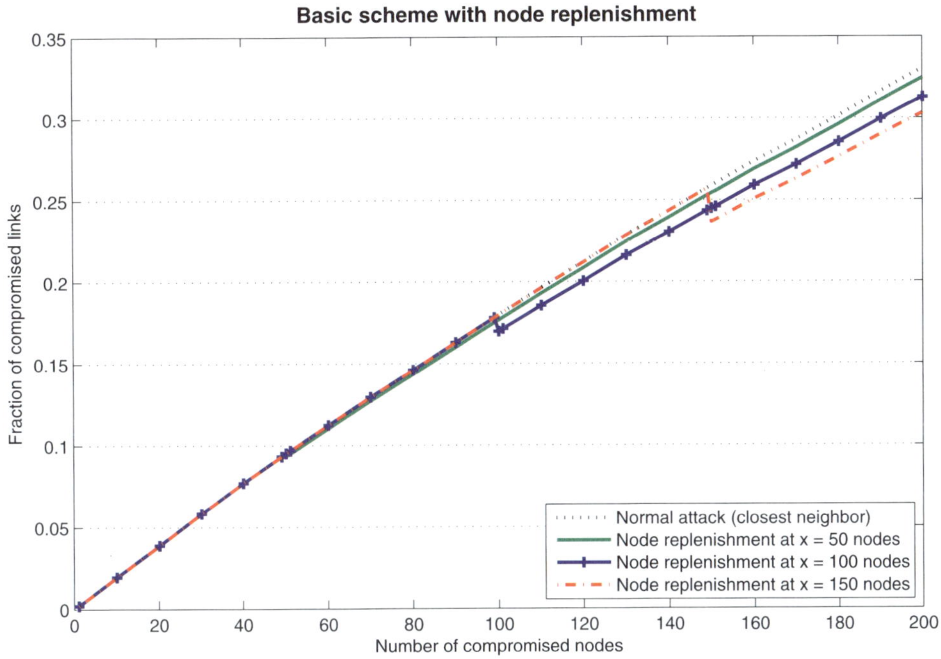

Fig. 19.15. Performance of node replenishment applied to the basic scheme.

19.8.8. *Node replenishment applied to the deployment knowledge scheme*

Our proposed node replenishment strategy can be applied to the deployment knowledge scheme.[3] Figure 19.16 shows the change of network resilience as a measure of node replenishment. We can see that there is a sharp change of the fraction of compromised links when new nodes are replenished in the compromised region. However, as shown in Table 19.5, the percentage of improvement is less significant than that from the *basic scheme*. This is because the nodes in the vicinity of the compromised area may contain keys from the same sub key pool. Consequently, the link replacement continues to use those compromised keys for message encryption. As a result, the new links are already compromised before they are used to replace the old ones.

19.8.9. *Node replenishment applied to both schemes in a region*

In the previous sections, we considered the network resilience in the whole network after the node replenishment. In this section, we specifically investigate the network resilience in the region where new nodes are deployed by comparing the simulation results with that of the analytical results.

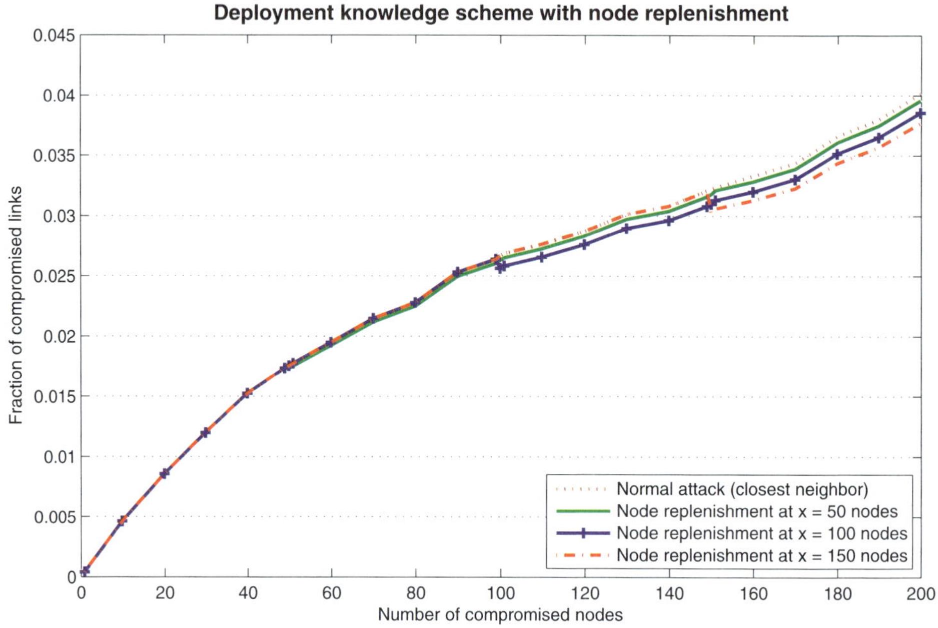

Fig. 19.16. Performance of node replenishment applied to the deployment knowledge scheme.

Table 19.5. Performance of node replenishment applied to the deployment knowledge scheme.

Replenishment interval	No. of nodes added	Improvement of network resilience
50	64	0%
100	168	2.87%
150	243	5.45%

In our simulations, we only consider the time durations before and after new nodes are deployed when 100 nodes are compromised and neglect the links connected to the compromised nodes.[g] For the *basic scheme*, we use the following settings for analytical calculations: $p_o = 0.0952$, $p_n = 0.995$, $d = 83$, $N_r = 195$ and $N_n = 195$. For the *deployment knowledge scheme*, we use the following settings for analytical calculations: $p_o = 0.418$, $p_n = 0.273$, $d = 85$, $N_r = 168$ and $N_n = 168$.

Table 19.6 illustrates the simulation and mathematical analysis results on both *basic scheme* and *deployment knowledge scheme*. Both sets of results indicate that the node replenishment schemes can achieve significant improvement in the region in

[g]The terms considering the connection to the compromised nodes in Eq. (19.10) are removed in these analytic results.

Table 19.6. Performance of the node replenishment in the target region.

	Basic scheme		
Description	Original	Simulation	Analytical
Compromised Links	154	144	203
Total Links	911	9393	9338
Compromised Ratio	0.169	0.0153	0.0217
Improvement	*N/A*	10.0%	7.79%
	Deployment knowledge scheme		
Compromised Links	462	565	607
Total Links	931	3265	4087
Compromised Ratio	0.496	0.1730	0.1485
Improvement	*N/A*	1.87%	2.34%

which the improvement in *basic scheme* is larger than that of *deployment knowledge scheme*.

19.9. Concluding Remarks

In this chapter, we first provide a detailed survey of contemporary trust establishment techniques in WSNs. We describe potential drawbacks of these existing techniques. To improve the performance of WSNs in the post-deployment phase, we have proposed a general key redistribution framework and a node replenishment scheme for WSNs. It is observed that existing probabilistic key pre-distribution schemes usually assume the static-key-static-node model. To increase the connectivity, excess unused keys are always pre-installed in sensor nodes to boost the probability. This results in inefficient resource memory usage and vulnerability to node capture attack.

Our approach makes use of secrets or keys from neighbors connected after the key setup phase to reach unconnected nodes. Two instantiations, namely key-based and polynomial-based redistribution schemes are presented to demonstrate the portability for integration with prior schemes.[4,28] Analytical and simulation results show significant improvements achieved by our schemes, including connectivity and resilience.

Due to vulnerability of node capture attack, we propose a novel recovery scheme — *Node Replenishment Scheme*. It includes a Link Replacement Strategy which is based on key rollover to recover some of the compromised links in the network. At the same time, the Node Replenishment Scheme can also replace the functions of the compromised nodes and the dead nodes in the compromised region.

In our study, we assume that it is possible to detect the compromised region based on the characteristics of the node capture attack pattern. However, how this can be done in practice remains as one of the most challenging future work.

References

1. I. F. Akyildiz, S. Weilian, Y. Sankarasubramaniam and E. Cayirci, A survey on sensor networks, *IEEE Communications Magazine*, **40**(8), 102–114 (August 2002).
2. H. Chan, A. Perrig and D. Song, Random key predistribution schemes for sensor networks, *IEEE Symposium on Security and Privacy*, 197–213 (May 2003).
3. W. Du, J. Deng, Y. S. Han, S. Chen and P. K. Varshney. A key management scheme for wireless sensor networks using deployment knowledge. In *INFOCOM 2004*, **1**, 586–597 (March 2004).
4. L. Eschenauer and V. D. Gligor, A key-management scheme for distributed sensor networks, *The 9th ACM Conference on Computer and Communications Security*, 41–47 (November 2002).
5. Smart Dust Project, http://robotics.eecs.berkeley.edu/~pister/smartdust/ (2008).
6. WINS Project, http://www.janet.ucla.edu/wins/ (2008).
7. μAmps Project, http://www-mtl.mit.edu/researchgroups/icsystems/uamps/ (2008).
8. H. Fu, S. Kawamura, M. Zhang and L. Zhang, Replication attack on random key pre-distribution schemes for wireless sensor networks, *The 6th Annual IEEE SMC Information Assurance Workshop*, 134–141 (June 2005).
9. J. Newsome, E. Shi, D. Song and A. Perrig, The sybil attack in sensor networks: analysis & defenses, *The 3rd International Symposium on Information Processing in Sensor Networks*, 259–268 (April 2004).
10. B. Parno, A. Perrig and V. Gligor, Distributed detection of node replication attacks in sensor networks, *IEEE Symposium on Security and Privacy*, 49–63 (May 2005).
11. W. Wang and B. Bhargava, Visualization of wormholes in sensor networks, *ACM Workshop on Wireless Security*, 51–60 (October 2004).
12. A. D. Wood and J. A. Stankovic, Denial of service in sensor networks, *IEEE Computer Magazine*, **35**(10), 54–62 (October 2002).
13. Y.-K. Kwok, Key management in wireless sensor networks, *Security in Distributed and Networking Systems*, Yang Xiao and Yi Pan (eds.), World Scientific Publishing Co. (2007).
14. H. Chan, V. D. Gligor, A. Perrig and G. Muralidharan, On the distribution and revocation of cryptographic keys in sensor networks, *IEEE Transactions on Dependable and Secure Computing*, **2**(3), 233–247 (September 2005).
15. R. Anderson, H. Chan and A. Perrig, Key infection: smart trust for smart dust, *ICNP 2004*, 206–215 (October 2004).
16. H. Chan and A. Perrig, PIKE: Peer intermediaries for key establishment in sensor networks, *INFOCOM 2005*, **1**, 524–535 (March 2005).
17. W. Du, J. Deng, Y. S. Han, P. K. Varshney, J. Katz and A. Khalili, A pairwise key predistribution scheme for wireless sensor networks, *ACM Transactions on Information and System Security*, **8**(2), 228–258 (May 2005).
18. D. Liu and P. Ning, Location-based pairwise key establishments for static sensor networks, *The 1st ACM Workshop on Security of Ad Hoc and Sensor Networks*, 72–82 (October 2003).
19. P. Erdös and A. Rényi, On the evolution of random graph, *Publ. Math. Inst. Hung. Acad. Sci.*, **5**, 17–61 (1960).
20. V. Raghunathan, S. Ganeriwal and M. Srivastava, Emerging techniques for long lived wireless sensor networks, *IEEE Communications Magazine*, **44**(4), 108–114 (April 2006).

21. Crossbox Technology, http://www.xbow.com/ (2008).
22. W. Diffie and M. Hellman, New directions in cryptography, *IEEE Transactions on Information Theory*, **22**, 644–654 (November 1976).
23. R. L. Rivest, A. Shamir and L. Adleman, A method for obtaining digital signatures and public-key cryptosystems, *Communications of the ACM*, **21**, 120–126 (February 1978).
24. A. Perrig, R. Szewczyk, J. D. Tygar, V. Wen and D. E. Culler, SPINS: Security protocols for sensor networks, *Wireless Networks*, **8**(5), 521–534 (September 2002).
25. G. Jolly, M. C. Kuscu, P. Kokate and M. Younis, A low-energy key management protocol for wireless sensor networks, *The 8th IEEE International Symposium on Computers and Communication*, **1**, 335–340 (June 2003).
26. S.-P. Chan, R. Poovendran and M.-T. Sun, A key management scheme in distributed sensor networks using attack probabilities, *GLOBECOM 2005*, **2**, 1007–1011 (December 2005).
27. R. Blom, An optimal class of symmetric key generation systems, *EUROCRYPT Workshop on Advances in Cryptology*, 335–338 (April 1984).
28. D. Liu, P. Ning and R. Li, Establishing pairwise keys in distributed sensor networks, *ACM Transactions on Information and System Security*, **8**(1), 41–77 (February 2005).
29. C. Blundo, A. D. Santis, A. Herzberg, S. Kutten, U. Vaccaro and M. Yung, Perfectly secure key distribution for dynamic conferences, *CRYPTO 1992*, **740**, 471–486 (August 1992).
30. M. Eltoweissy, M. Moharrum and R. Mukkamala, Dynamic key management in sensor networks, *IEEE Communications Magazine*, **44**(4), 122–130 (April 2006).
31. R. Watro, D. Kong, S. Cuti, C. Gardiner, C. Lynn and P. Kruus, TinyPK: Securing sensor networks with public key technology, *The 2nd ACM Workshop on Security of Ad Hoc and Sensor Networks*, 59–64 (October 2004).
32. A. K. Lenstra and E. R. Verheul, The XTR public key system, *The 20th Annual International Cryptology Conference on Advances in Cryptology*, 1–19 (August 2000).
33. N. Koblitz, Elliptic curve cryptosystems, *Mathematics of Computation*, **48**(177), 203–209 (January 1987).
34. V. S. Miller, Use of elliptic curves in cryptography, *Lecture Notes in Computer Science: Advances in Cryptology*, **218**, 417–426 (August 1985).
35. N. Gura, A. Patel, A. Wander, H. Eberle and S. C. Shantz, Comparing elliptic curve cryptography and rsa on 8-bit cpus, *Workshop on Cryptographic Hardware and Embedded Systems*, 119–132 (August 2004).
36. D. J. Malan, M. Welsh and M. D. Smith, A public-key infrastructure for key distribution in tinyos based on elliptic curve cryptography, *The 1st Annual IEEE Communications Society Conference on Sensor and Ad Hoc Communications and Networks*, 71–80 (October 2004).
37. K. Lorincz, D. J. Malan, T. R. Fulford-Jones, A. Nawoj, A. Clavel, V. Shnayder, G. Mainland, M. Welsh and S. Moulton, Sensor networks for emergency response: Challenges and opportunities, *IEEE Pervasive Computing*, **3**(4), 16–23 (October 2004).
38. R. Anderson and M. Kuhn, Tamper resistance: A cautionary note, *The 2nd USENIX Workshop on Electronic Commerce*, **2**, 1–11 (November 1996).
39. F. Stajano and R. Anderson, The resurrecting duckling: Security issues for ad-hoc wireless networks, *The 7th International Workshop on Security Protocols*, 172–194 (April 1999).

40. A. Alarifi and W. Du, Diversify sensor nodes to improve resilience against node compromise, *The 4th ACM Workshop on Security of Ad Hoc and Sensor Networks*, 101 112 (October 2006).
41. C. Hartung, J. Balasalle and R. Han, *Node Compromise in Sensor Networks: The Need for Secure Systems*, Technical Report CU-CS-990-05, Department of Computer Science, University of Colorado at Boulder (January 2005).
42. M. Strasser and H. Vogt, Autonomous and distributed node recovery in wireless sensor networks, *The 4th ACM Workshop on Security of Ad Hoc and Sensor Networks*, 113–122 (October 2006).
43. Y. Yang and M. Cardei, Movement-assisted sensor redeployment scheme for network lifetime increase, *The 10th ACM Symposium on Modeling, Analysis, and Simulation of Wireless and Mobile Systems*, 13–20 (October 2007).
44. I. Chatzigiannakis, A. Kinalis and S. Nikoletseasm, An adaptive power conservation scheme for heterogeneous wireless sensor networks with node redeployment, *The 17th Annual ACM Symposium on Parallelism in Algorithms and Architectures*, 96–105 (July 2005).
45. P. Corke, S. Hrabar, R. Peterson, D. Rus, S. Saripalli and G. Sukhatme, Deployment and connectivity repair of a sensor net with a flying robot, M. Ang and O. Khatib (eds.) *Experimental Robotics IX: 9th International Symposium on Experimental Robotics (ISER'04)*, 333–342 (June 2006).

Chapter 20

Detection of Compromised Wireless Sensor Nodes

Min Song

Electrical and Computer Engineering Department
Old Dominion University, Norfolk, VA 23529, USA
msong@odu.edu

Gregory E. Patrick

Astute Informatics, Inc.
Chesapeake, VA 23321, USA
gregory.e.patrick@gmail.com

George Hsieh

Department of Computer Science
Norfolk State University
Norfolk, VA 23504, USA
ghsieh@nsu.edu

In wireless sensor networks, an adversary may deploy malicious nodes into the network or physically obtain legitimate nodes, reprogram and redeploy them into the network to launch various attacks. These nodes are collectively called compromised nodes. They can undermine the network security by launching various attacks at various layers. In this chapter, we analyze the unique features of wireless sensor networks and present the challenges of compromised nodes detection. We classify the techniques for detecting compromised nodes into authentication-based and behavior-based methods. The state-of-the-art detection techniques are briefly surveyed. Finally, we describe the details of one specific technique based on data transmission quality and its performance.

20.1. Introduction

A wireless sensor node, also called *mote*, is a computational device that has sensing device, processor, transceiver, memory, and power supply. The sensing devices sense the environment and gather the data that represent the physical conditions being monitored. The sensor readings are sent to the local processor for preliminary processing and then sent to the base station in a multi-hop wireless communication manner for further processing. Motes are programmed with the appropriate operating parameters and security credentials before deployed. The programming interface is either a direct serial connection or a USB connection. The operating system and other programs stored in the program memory dictate all operations of the mote. In order to obtain detailed and integrated data, a large number of sensor nodes are generally distributed over the area interested. To form a network, each node initiates a simple neighbor discovery protocol by broadcasting its credentials, e.g., node ID and cryptographic information. More detailed information on wireless sensors and sensor networks can be found in Ref. 1.

Wireless sensors have a variety of applications, including battlefield surveillance,[2] environmental monitoring,[3] medical applications,[4] and space applications.[5] Security is critical for many of these applications. Battlefield surveillance, for example, requires all information be authentic in order to ensure that there is indeed a target present in the battlefield. Unfortunately, an adversary may deploy malicious motes into the network or physically obtain legitimate motes, reprogram and redeploy them into the network to either launch various attacks and/or collect data on behalf of it. These nodes are collectively called compromised nodes (C-Nodes). They can undermine the network security by launching various attacks at various layers.

At the physical layer, an attacker may physically tamper with legitimate nodes (L-Nodes) to obtain the credentials. According to an experimental study,[6] it only took less one minute to extract all information stored onboard the mote's EEPROM, Flash, and SRAM. Once the credentials are in hand, an adversary could clone the node by loading the node's credentials onto multiple L-Nodes and surreptitiously insert them at strategic locations within the network.[7] Using these replicated nodes, the adversary can inject false data and suppress L-Nodes. At the data link layer, C-Nodes may starve the L-Nodes by occupying the communication channel continuously. At the network layer, C-Nodes can launch various attacks including routing attack, deny of service (DoS) attack, and wormhole attack. A C-Node performs routing attacks by dropping, altering, and/or filtering routing messages. In DoS attacks, a C-Node makes a node or a group of nodes unavailable to the rest of the network. For the wormhole attack, multiple C-Nodes pretend to be one node and cause other nodes to have incorrect topology knowledge of the network. At the application layer, a C-Node may launch data attacks. To initiate a data attack, C-Nodes alter data, filter data or report false data to trigger false alarms.[8] If there is no effective method to identify the C-Nodes, they can be used to attack other network elements, compromise data integrity, or leak information. Therefore, detecting C-Nodes is one of the most critical security issues for wireless sensor networks.

The remainder of this article is organized as follows. In Sec. 2, we first present the challenges of C-Nodes detection. Section 3 surveys the literature on the state-of-the-art techniques on C-Nodes detection. In Sec. 4, we describe the details of one specific technique based on data transmission quality and its performance. Finally, Sec. 5 provides the concluding remarks.

20.2. Challenges of C-Node Detection

In recent years, significant research effort has been devoted to detecting malicious nodes in wired networks and traditional wireless networks. However, these solutions are not effective in sensor network environments. This is because wireless sensor networks have unique characteristics and thus present unique challenges on C-Nodes detection. These challenges include resource constraint, unattended operation, difficulty in distinguishing between compromised and faulty nodes, and the fact that no node in the network can be trusted.

First, wireless sensor nodes are designed with the goals of (1) being small in order to be utilized in different environments; and (2) being relatively cheap so that they can be massively deployed. Consequently, they are severely constrained in computation capability, memory capacity, communication bandwidth and range, and power supply lifetime. The well-known MicaZ OEM motes[9] come with a processor running at less than 10 MIPS, 128 KB program flash memory, 4 KB RAM, 4 KB EEPROM, and non-rechargeable 2X AA batteries. The data rate of the communication channel is less than 250 Kbps. Furthermore, a good portion of the memory is already used for the code required to perform the core control, sensing, data processing, and communication functions. All additional code for add-on features, such as security, must fit within the remaining available memory space. Thus, for any security measures to be viable for the wireless sensor networks, they must be designed and implemented to operate within the severe resource constraints of these networks.[10,11]

Secondly, the nature of unattended operation makes the network maintenance impossible. As a result, sensor networks are typically deployed with high density and redundancy. While this makes it easier to fulfill the task, it also brings challenges to C-Nodes detection. For instance, given that N nodes are initially deployed, it is quite normal that there exist $N - m + k$ nodes functioning in the network after some time, where m is the number of nodes died and k is the number of new nodes added to the network by an adversary. Without an appropriate C-Nodes detection scheme, the network itself cannot tell the difference between the $N - m$ nodes and k nodes.

Third, sensors are prone to failures and thus may provide inaccurate information from time to time. It is hard to distinguish C-Nodes from faulty nodes or temporarily underperforming nodes, given the dynamic and unpredictable environment. For instance, it is quite possible that a mote underperforms just because of some legitimate factors in the network. These factors include collision or interference, volatile radio connectivity, asymmetric communications, hardware crash, and environment disturbance. The aforementioned unattended operation and harsh environment make the problem even more challenging. A solid C-Nodes detection algorithm must be robust and fault-tolerant.

The last challenge lies in the fact that no node can be trusted in sensor networks, since any mote could be captured or controlled by the adversary. For this reason, even if an alert from mote i against mote j is observed, no definite conclusion can be made from this single alert, because node i itself might be compromised while node j is innocent. Keep in mind that C-Nodes have incentives to vote against L-Nodes, so that the votes of the L-Nodes could be discredited at the base station. Therefore, a certain fraction of motes in an area should participate in the decision-making process and agree on an observation.[12]

Given these unique characteristics of sensor networks, special attention must be paid when designing C-Nodes detection techniques. Before surveying the literature, we present the performance metrics for C-Nodes detection schemes.

- *Detection rate.* This can be measured by the ratio of the number of C-Nodes detected to the total number of C-Nodes present in the network.
- *False positive.* This is the number of L-Nodes that are marked as C-Nodes.
- *Computational cost.* This can be measured by the algorithm complexity or the time to reach a decision.
- *Communication overhead.* This can be measured by the number of control messages exchanged in the network in order to reach a decision.

20.3. Techniques on C-Nodes Detection

The techniques for detecting C-Nodes can generally be classified into two categories: authentication-based schemes and behavior-based schemes. The basic idea of authentication-based schemes is to confirm the authenticity of a node by verifying its key information. Thus the way keys are established plays a critical role. A strong keying scheme helps to prevent C-Nodes from joining the network. On the other hand, the concept behind behavior-based schemes is to determine the authenticity of a node based on its behavior. The fundamental assumption is that the behavior of C-Nodes must be different from that of L-Nodes. Compared to the authentication-based schemes, the behavior-based schemes take a passive approach to detect C-Nodes. Next, we provide more detailed analysis on these schemes.

20.3.1. *Authentication-based schemes*

The simplest keying scheme is to use a single network-wide key during the network lifetime. Apparently, this scheme is unacceptable because of its single point of failure. Advanced keying schemes include using multiple keys and relying on trusted third party.

In the multiple-keying scheme, each pair of nodes keeps multiple keys for communications.[13–15] In the key setup phase, nodes exchange their keys by local broadcasting. Each node then keeps a hash table to indicate its common keys with neighbors. Before a node communicates with another node, both nodes select a common key to authenticate each other. This scheme improves the network resiliency against node captures. If the network uses a key pre-distribution scheme, a node's ID could correspond to the set of secret keys it shares with its neighbors.[7] In this system, an adversary gains little advantage by claiming to posses an ID without actually holding the appropriate keys.

Another totally different keying scheme is to rely on trusted third party.[16] In most cases, the trusted party is the base station. Prior to the network deployment, a unique symmetric key is generated for each node in the network. The key is stored in the node's memory and can be used to authenticate and secure communications between the node and the base station. The base station keeps a database of all node keys. A comprehensive study on keying schemes in wireless sensor networks can be found in Ref. 17.

It is worth mentioning that regardless of which keying scheme is used, some level of reliable transport is assumed before the keys are actually established. Moreover, it is possible that an adversary can crack the keys by brute-force search or reverse engineering of chips or programs on motes. If the instruction level source code is available, it may take less than one minute to locate the storage position of keys or find the keying schema. Even when the key information is not available, sensors might be compromised too, i.e., the chip is hacked. Thus, compromised nodes remain a problem, even when authentication-based schemes are deployed.

20.3.2. *Behavior-based schemes*

Behavior-based schemes typically run three independent procedures: behavior measuring, decision making, and responding. Next, we will describe each of these procedures.

20.3.2.1. *Behavior measuring*

A sensor node's behavior can be defined as the way it operates and its response to network events. Based on this definition, there are five types of behaviors that can be measured for the purpose of C-Nodes detection.

The first type of behavior is the Tx/Rx power.[18] Generally, a sensor network is configured to operate at a consistent Tx/Rx power level. If a node's power level significantly deviates from others, this node is likely a C-Node. Another parameter of this type is the received signal strength.[19] A message transmission is considered suspicious if its signal strength is incompatible with its originator's geographical position. To detect anomaly, the signal strength of a reception is compared with its expected value which is calculated using geographical information and the preconfigured Tx/Rx specification.

The second type of behavior is distance.[20] For a stationary sensor network, the distance between any two nodes should remain roughly constant. A node is considered a C-Node if the difference between the actual distance and the expected one exceeds a threshold. Here the distance can be measured via packet arrival time,[21] the time difference of packet arrival, the angle of signal arrival, or the received signal strength.

The third type of behavior is location information. To measure this type of behavior, each sensor first obtains its location using a localization scheme. Then sensors verify whether the derived locations are correct or not. A node is considered a C-Node if the difference between the derived location and the actual location is greater than a threshold. The protocol presented in Ref. 7 has each node broadcast its location claim, along with a signature authenticating the claim. Each of the neighboring nodes probabilistically forwards the claim to a randomly selected set of nodes called witness. If any witness receives two different location claims from the same node ID, it can revoke the replicated one.

The fourth type of behavior is neighborhood information. The reason to consider neighborhood information as one type of behavior is that each node in the network can be uniquely characterized by its neighborhood information. One novel scheme for detecting clone attacks is for each sensor node to compute a social fingerprint by extracting the neighborhood characteristics, and to verify the legitimacy of the originator for each message by checking the enclosed fingerprint.[22] Before deployment, each sensor node is preloaded with a codeword. Then a node can compute its social fingerprint based on the code-words collected from its neighborhood. Each sensor node should also compute the fingerprints for the nodes in its neighborhood, and store them for later verification purpose. Whenever a sensor node sends a message to the base station, it should include its fingerprint as well. Then the neighboring nodes can verify the legitimacy of the source node by comparing the enclosed fingerprint with their own record.

The fifth type of behavior is the node's response to network events. With the assumption that the code running on C-Nodes will be at least one line different to the code running on L-Nodes, software-based attestation schemes have been developed for C-Nodes detection.[23] These schemes are based on a pseudorandom noise generation mechanism and a lightweight block-based pseudorandom memory traversal algorithm. The basic idea is that each mote is loaded with pseudorandom noise in its unused program memory before deployment. If more than half of the neighbors agree to attest one specific node, they collaborate to verify the integrity of the code running on this node in a distributed manner. In particular, each node is distributed with and keeps a challenge as well as the corresponding response. During an attestation, each neighbor sends the challenge and waits for the response from the attested node. The attested node is considered compromised, if the received response is different from the local one. To make the detection process more interesting,

Shaneck *et al.* proposed remote software attestation by sending a piece of attestation code to a sensor node.[24] To defend node collusions while incurring a small overhead, a Random Block Memory Traversal scheme is proposed in Ref. 25. When a high-end sensor wants to challenge a low-end sensor, it generates a random number indicating the start memory address and the block size. The low-end sensor then calculates a checksum over each block. The final output is the XOR of all the checksums.

Other types of node behavior can also be found in the literature, such as the number of packets dropped, the traffic/flow distribution, etc. To make the characterization more accurate, a node's behavior can be measured from multiple aspects.[26] Each sensor node monitors the behavior of its immediate neighbors, and conducts the inspection based on multiple aspects of node behavior. A neighbor is suspected to be an internal adversary if its behavior is "extreme" compared with those from the same neighborhood. The comparison is done by considering all aspects simultaneously.

20.3.2.2. *Decision making*

The decision making process can be conducted in a centralized or distributed manner. In centralized decision-making schemes, the base station is believed to be a trusted entity by all the nodes in the network. It gathers information from the entire network and makes the final decision whether a node is compromised or not. The decision is then accepted by the network. As such, the fundamental assumption is that the base station is an uncompromised node throughout the network lifetime. In distributed decision-making schemes, the decision of whether a node is compromised or not can be made locally across the network, i.e., conceptually any node in the network can make a decision based on the local information.

One notable centralized decision-making scheme was presented in Ref. 27. The authors introduced a concept of inferred graph and established an observer model. An observer O_1 will raise the alert about observer O_2 when the amount of abnormal behaviors of O_2 exceeds an expected threshold. As a result, (O_1, O_2) becomes a suspicious pair. The base station then establishes an inferred graph for them. Eventually, the base station partitions all nodes in the inferred graph into two subsets, one for suspicious nodes and the other for unsuspicious nodes. Nodes belong to the intersection of the two subnets are believed to be compromised nodes.

Recall that wireless sensor networks usually consist of a large number of sensor nodes and one base station that collects all the data and then relays the information to the outer network. At some point, the base station can easily become the performance bottleneck. The centralized decision-making scheme further adds burden to the base station. Thus it is challenging to make decisions in a timely manner. Additionally, the nodes close to the base station are subject to an undue level of communication burden that may shorten the network's lifetime. Two techniques are developed to alleviate this situation. The first one is to deploy few more base stations into the network to gather the regional information. These add-on base stations may also conduct preliminary processing and then send the mined information to the base station. While these add-on base stations improve the detection performance, they also bring new risky-point to the network. The second technique is to divide the network into multiple clusters. Each cluster has a head to handle the information collection. Like the add-on base stations, cluster heads may also perform preliminary processing and send the aggregated information to the base station. Since the cluster heads involve the additional computing load, an efficient algorithm is needed to elect new heads from time to time. Thus, it is possible that a C-Node becomes the head before it is detected. Should this occur, an L-Node might be maliciously marked as a C-Node.

In some cases, the add-on base station and cluster heads may perform the decision-making functionality and leave the central base station to prove the decision. However, if the add-on base stations or cluster heads themselves get compromised, the adversary can gain the control of the entire network or cluster.

In distributed decision-making schemes, the decision can be made by any node. In particular, every node observes the behavior of its neighboring nodes. Once node i suspects node j, node i will call for the attention of all neighboring nodes by issuing a voting request. Using a voting scheme, neighbors can reach a consensus on the legitimacy of node j. One of the voting schemes is called majority rule. In this scheme, node j will be marked as a C-Node if a majority of the votes are against it. Unfortunately, this decision is valid only if the number of nodes participating in the vote is larger than the number of nodes that can be compromised. As we mentioned early, no node can be trusted in sensor networks. With the majority rule, if node i itself is a C-Node and a majority of the neighboring nodes are C-Nodes, then node j will be flagged as a C-Node even though it is an L-Node. Therefore, one of the design requirements for voting-based schemes is that the voting scheme performs well even when local majorities are formed by C-Nodes.

Due to the dynamic network traffic load and poor network connection, a legitimate node j might temporarily exhibit abnormal behavior. In this case, a simple voting scheme may label it as a C-Node. For this reason, some decision-making schemes combine the advantages of the centralized and distributed schemes.[21] In these schemes, once node i finishes the voting process on node j, it sends the result to the base station for the final proof. Only if the base station concurs with the decision can node i broadcast the result to the network.

20.3.2.3. *Responding*

Once a C-Node is detected, it should be isolated from the network. The rest of the nodes can take appropriate actions, including changing their routing and neighboring information, and updating the cryptographic keys.

20.4. DTQ-Based C-Nodes Detection

In this section, we introduce one scheme for C-Nodes detection. The novelty of this scheme is that a node's communication quality is measured by other nodes, instead of itself, using the Data Transmission Quality (DTQ) function. The DTQ function is defined in a way such that it remains roughly constant or changes smoothly for L-Nodes, while it keeps decreasing noticeably for C-Nodes. More detailed information about this scheme can be found in Ref. 28.

20.4.1. *Network model*

The entire sensor network is divided into multiple groups. Nodes are aware of their group information. The authenticity of a node is only determined by the nodes in the same group. A group may split into subgroups, and multiple groups may merge into a super group. Packets may traverse different groups. Thus, there are two types of flows in terms of groups: inbound flows and outbound flows. For the purpose of C-Nodes detection, only the outbound flows are of our interest. The process of detecting C-Nodes can be divided into two steps. First, it needs to determine whether a group has a C-Node. Should a C-Node exist in the group then the second step is to locate it.

20.4.2. *The DTQ function*

We introduce the Data Transmission Quality (DTQ) function to measure a node's communication quality. Each node maintains a DTQ table that stores the DTQ values of other nodes that are in the same group and are along the communication path. Each entry in the DTQ table also contains time stamp information to indicate the time when the DTQ value was updated. The DTQ values change according to both long-term and short-term data transmission statistics, and are updated after each data burst ends. There are four variables in the DTQ function, as described below.

- E: the energy cost of transmitting one data burst. It can be the physical cost of electrical energy or equivalently the number of instructions executed.
- D: the packets that have been successfully transmitted. In a data burst, the source node keeps all the E and D values of other nodes along the path and updates them by adding the latest E and D values.
- p: the probability of successful transmission when sensors work normally. The reason for this variable is because a successful transmission depends not only on the sensor network itself, but also on the environment.
- $STB()$: the stability of a sensor node. It measures how fast the transmission quality changes in a period of time. As a statistical function of data transmission

history, we define the $STB()$ function as follows,

$$STB() = \begin{cases} \left[\dfrac{S(d,u)}{L(d,u)}\right]^{a} = \left[\dfrac{\sum_{i=1}^{n/m} \dfrac{d_i}{u_i}}{\sum_{j=1}^{n} \dfrac{d_j}{u_j}}\right]^{a} & \text{if } \left[\dfrac{\sum_{i=1}^{n/m} \dfrac{d_i}{u_i}}{\sum_{j=1}^{n} \dfrac{d_j}{u_j}}\right] < 1 \\ \left[\dfrac{S(d,u)}{L(d,u)}\right]^{1/a} = \left[\dfrac{\sum_{i=1}^{n/m} \dfrac{d_k}{t_i}}{\sum_{j=1}^{n} \dfrac{d_j}{t_j}}\right]^{1/a} & \text{if } \left[\dfrac{\sum_{i=1}^{n/m} \dfrac{d_i}{t_i}}{\sum_{j=1}^{n} \dfrac{d_j}{t_j}}\right] > 1 \end{cases}, \tag{20.1}$$

where d_i and u_i represent the bytes successfully transmitted and the bytes attempted to be transmitted, respectively, when sending the ith data burst; $\alpha > 1$; n is a positive integer, which defines how many historical data are kept; m is a positive integer, and $n\%m = 0$. Therefore, we can know the recent $1/m$ part of DTQ trends during the past n data bursts. The quotient of $S(d,u)/L(d,u)$ reflects the quality trends in recent data transmissions. If $S(d,u)/L(d,u) > 1$, it indicates that the data transmission quality is increasing; otherwise, the recent data transmission quality is decreasing.

The DTQ function is defined as follows,

$$DTQ = k\frac{D}{E} \cdot STB() \cdot \frac{1}{p}, \tag{20.2}$$

where $k > 0$.

In Eq. (20.2), D/E reflects how many packets a node successfully transmits in a unit energy. If a C-Node selectively forwards data, drops packets, or sends data to incorrect routing path, its D/E value decreases. The $STB()$ function measures the stability of performance. Notice that the instantaneous increase of stability does not help to increase the DTQ value. However, the decrease of stability quickly decreases the DTQ value. When environment factors influence data transmissions, the $1/p$ reduces the environmental impact to the measurement of DTQ values. Ideally, it should totally eliminate the environmental impact.

20.4.3. *Operations*

We consider two scenarios: intra-group communications and inter-group communications. In the first scenario, the sender and receiver belong to the same group. In this case, the receiver sends an ACK packet to the sender after it has received all the data. In the second scenario, the sender and receiver belong to different groups. In this case, only the first node in each group sends an ACK packet to the fist node in the upstream group. When receiving an ACK packet, a node updates the

DTQ values of all nodes along the path. If an ACK packet is not received or the ACK indicates that data have been altered, the DTQ values of all involving nodes decrease. On the other hand, if the ACK packet shows the data transmission is successful, the DTQ values of all nodes along the path remains roughly constant or changes smoothly. Whenever a node updates its DTQ table, it refreshes the overall quality of all nodes along the path. If attacks occur, the sender or the first node at each group decreases the DTQ values of all nodes along the path. The next step is to locate the attacking node within the group. This is done by a voting procedure.

Let N_{DTQ} be the set of nodes listed in a DTQ table, $|N_{DTQ}|$ be the number of nodes, q_i be the DTQ value for node i. We define a threshold per group as follows,

$$Th = r\frac{1}{|N_{DTQ}|}\sum_{i \in N_{DTQ}} q_i, \tag{20.3}$$

where $0 < r < 1$.

If a node finds one or multiple DTQ values are below the threshold, the node believes that there might be a C-Node present in its group. In such a case, the node broadcast a message to other nodes in the group to initiate a voting procedure. The voting result will determine the authenticity of the suspicious node.

In the process of group voting, DTQ values with recent time stamps are more important than that with old time stamps. Thus simply comparing the number of nodes that vote for and against a suspicious node may not be accurate. For this reason, we define a variable w as the weight of DTQ values. Assuming there are n nodes vote to determine the authenticity of node m. Let q_{im} be the DTQ value of node m in the DTQ table of node i, w_{im} be the weight of q_{im}, we define the voting result as,

$$V_m = \sum_{i=1}^{n} w_{im} q_{im} v_{im}, \tag{20.4}$$

where $v_{im} = 1$, if node i votes for node m, and $v_{im} = -1$, if node i votes against node m.

If $V \ll 0$, the group believes that node m is a C-Node. Node m will then be dismissed from the group. All nodes within the group will remove node m from their DTQ table and routing table.

If $V \gg 0$, the group believes that node m is an L-Node and the nodes that voted against m need to update their DTQ values of node m. Suppose the ratio of FOR-vote and AGAINST-vote is $f{:}a$, then the nodes voted against node m update their DTQ values as follows,

$$q_m = q_m \times \left(1 + \frac{f}{f+a}\right). \tag{20.5}$$

If $V \approx 0$, there is no coherent point of view because $f{:}a \approx 1{:}1$. In such a case, the group will split itself into two subgroups: FOR-group (including node m) and

AGAINST-group. In our later simulations, we define $V \approx 0$ if

$$V < \frac{1}{10} \sum_{i=1}^{n} w_i q_i. \tag{20.6}$$

20.4.4. *Simulations and analysis*

We have developed a simulator to evaluate the DTQ-based C-Nodes detection scheme. The network configuration is as follows. All nodes are static and homogenous. Traffic follows Poisson distribution. The path length complies with uniform distribution. For the convenience of simulation, we use the total attempts of transmitting outbound data to measure E. So D/E is the probability of successful data transmission. In the STB() function, $\alpha = 4$. Initially there are 150 nodes equally divided into five groups. Each group has 1–5 C-Nodes performing data alter attacks. The p complies with uniform distribution with a range of $[0.7, 1)$.

Our first simulation is about the detection rate versus group size. During the simulation, L-Nodes randomly become C-Nodes and then begin to attack the network until they are detected. Once a C-Node is detected and eliminated, a new C-Node is generated. However, the percentage of C-Nodes in the network is always less than 15%. Figure 20.1 illustrates the detection rate under different group size and p values. It can be seen that the group size impacts the detection rate negatively. The reason is that a larger group size brings fewer groups in a network,

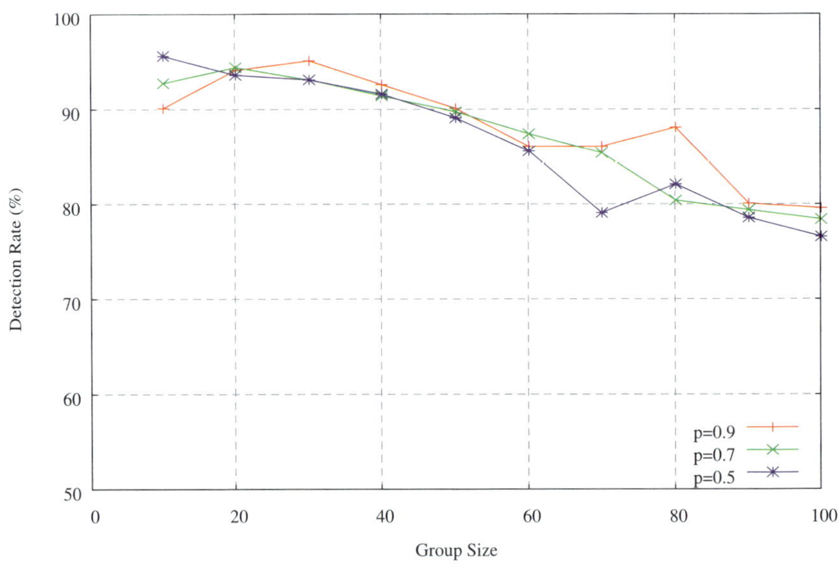

Fig. 20.1. Detection rate versus group size.

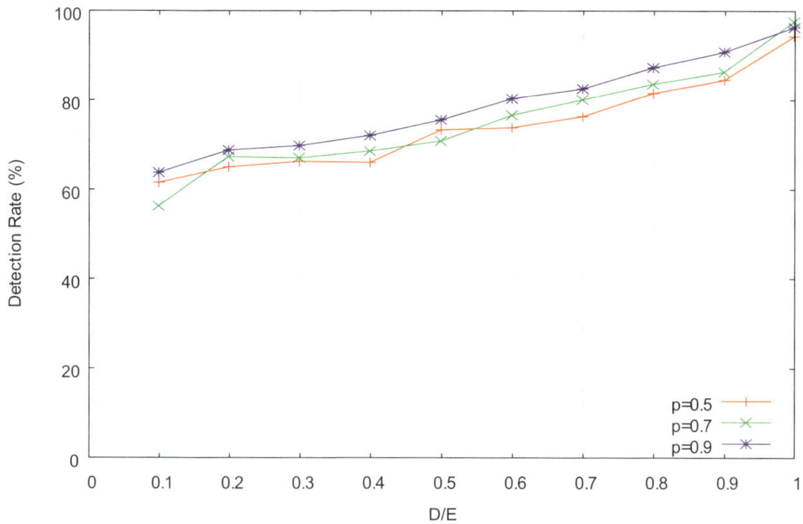

Fig. 20.2. Detection rate versus D/E value.

and then fewer ACK packets are referable. Moreover, a larger group size leads to a longer path, and thus more L-Nodes are involved. Therefore, with the increase of the number of nodes in a group, the detection rate slightly decreases. Figure 20.1 also shows that p reduces the environmental impact effectively.

If the group size keeps constant, the detection rate changes based on the value of D/E. Our early discussion suggests that D/E reflects the transmission success ratio. With the increase of D/E, the detection rate increases linearly. Figure 20.2 shows the impact of D/E to detection rate under different p values.

Notice that not all voting results can identify C-Nodes correctly, because L-Nodes might be polluted by C-Nodes. Figure 20.3 shows the relation between false positive rate and the C-Node percentage. In this simulation, two types of voting methods are used. In the Pick-One method, the network only judges the most suspicious node. If the voting result shows the suspicious node is compromised, then other nodes whose DTQ values lower than the threshold are reset to average value. In the Pick-All method, all nodes that have exceeded the threshold are voted. The Pick-One method gives the innocent victims opportunities to restore their DTQ values; thus it yields much better performance on false positive than the Pick-All method.

Figure 20.3 also shows that although most C-Nodes can be detected, the false positive rate become significant if more than 10–15% nodes are compromised in the network. However, from the comparison of the two series, it shows that the nodes with lowest DTQ values usually are not false positives. Consequently, false positive rate could be lower if we decrease the threshold value in Pick-All method.

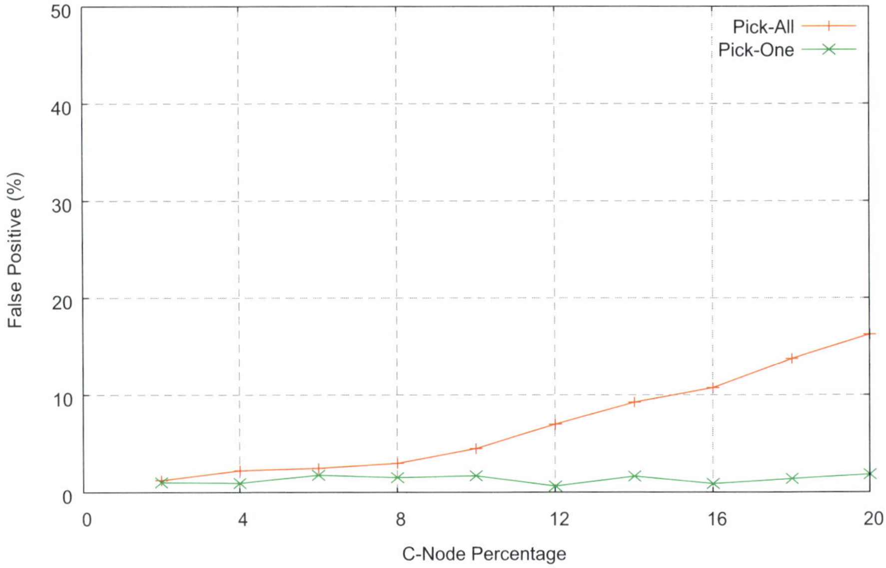

Fig. 20.3. False positive rate versus C-Node percentage.

20.5. Conclusions

We have analyzed the unique features of wireless sensor networks and presented the challenges in designing compromised nodes detection schemes. These challenges include resource constraint, unattended operation, difficulty in distinguishing between compromised and faulty nodes, and the fact that no node in the network can be trusted. The techniques for detecting compromised nodes are classified into two categories: authentication-based and behavior-based. The basic idea of authentication-based schemes is to confirm the authenticity of a node by verifying its key information. The concept behind behavior-based schemes is to determine the authenticity of a node based on its behavior. The fundamental assumption in this case is that the behavior of compromised nodes must be different from that of legitimate nodes. Behavior-based schemes typically run three independent procedures: behavior measuring, decision making, and responding. The pros and cons of each scheme are also analyzed. In this article, we also described one specific technique on C-Nodes detection. The novelty of this technique is that a node's communication quality is measured by other nodes using the Data Transmission Quality (DTQ) function. The novel property of the DTQ function is that it remains roughly constant or changes smoothly for L-Nodes, while it keeps decreasing noticeably for C-Nodes. The performance of the DTQ-based detection technique was also presented.

References

1. F. Akyildiz, W. Su, Y. Sankarasubramaniam and E. Cayiric, A survey on sensor networks, *IEEE Communication Magazine*, **20**(8), 102–114 (2002).
2. T. Bokareva *et al.*, Wireless sensor networks for battlefield surveillance, *Proceedings of the Land Warfare Conference* (2006).
3. S. N. Simic and S. Sastry, Distributed environmental monitoring using random sensor networks, *Proceedings of the 2nd International Workshop on Information Processing in Sensor Networks*, 582–592 (2003).
4. J. A. Stankovic *et al.*, Wireless sensor networks for in-home healthcare: Potential and challenges, *Proceedings of High Confidence Medical Device Software and Systems Workshop* (2005).
5. S. Shetty *et al.*, Wireless sensor payload design for sounding rocket, *Proceedings of the ISCA 22nd International Conference Computers and their Applications*, 295–300 (2007).
6. C. Hartung, J. Balasalle and R. Han, *Node Compromise in Sensor Networks: The Need for Secure Systems*, Technical report CU-CS-990-05.
7. B. Parno, A. Perrig and V. Gligor, Distributed detection of node replication attacks in sensor networks, *Proceedings of the 2005 IEEE Symposium on Security and Privacy*, 49–63 (2005).
8. S. Zhu, S. Setia, S. Jajodia and P. Ning, An interleaved hop-by-hop authentication scheme for filtering of injected false data in sensor networks, *ACM Transactions on Sensor Networks*, **3**(3), Article No. 14 (2007).
9. URL: http://www.xbow.com/Products/productdetails.aspx?sid=191.
10. K. Romer and F. Mattern, The design space of wireless sensor networks, *IEEE Wireless Communications*, **11**(6), 54–61 (2004).
11. C. Karlof and D. Wagner, Secure routing in wireless sensor networks: Attacks and countermeasures, *Proceedings of the 1st IEEE International Workshop on Sensor Network Protocols and Applications*, 113–127 (2003).
12. K. Ioannis, T. Dimitriou and F. C. Freiling, Towards intrusion detection in wireless sensor networks, *Proceedings of the 13th European Wireless Conference* (April 2007).
13. L. Eschenauer and V. D. Gligor, A key management scheme for distributed sensor networks, *Proceedings of the 9th ACM Conference on Computer and Communication Security*, 41–47 (2002).
14. H. Chan, A. Perrig and D. Song, Random key predistribution schemes for sensor networks, *Proceedings of IEEE Symposium on Security and Privacy*, 197–213 (May 2003).
15. S. Zhu, S. Setia, G. Mason and S. Jajodia, LEAP: Efficient security mechanisms for large-scale distributed sensor networks, *Proceedings of the 10th ACM Conference on Computer and Communications Security*, 62–72 (2003).
16. A. Perrig *et al.*, SPINS: Security protocols for sensor networks, *Proceedings of the 7th ACM/IEEE Mobicom*, 521–534 (2001).
17. H. Chan, A. Perrig and D. Song, Key distribution techniques for sensor networks, Chapter 13 of *Wireless Sensor Networks*, (eds.) C. S. Raghavendra, Krishna M. Sivalingam and T. F. Znati, Kluwer Academic, 2004, ISBN:1402078838.
18. I. Onat and I. A. Miri, An intrusion detection system for wireless sensor networks, *Proceedings of IEEE International Conference on Wireless and Mobile Computing, Networking and Communications*, 253–259 (2005).

19. W. R. P. Junior *et al.*, Malicious node detection in wireless sensor networks, *Parallel and Distributed Processing Symposium*, 24b (2004).
20. H. Song, L. Xie, S. Zhu and G. Cao, Sensor node compromise detection: The location perspective, *Proceedings of the 2007 International Conference on Wireless Communications and Mobile Computing*, 242–247 (2007).
21. M. Mathews, M. Song, S. Shetty and R. McKenzie, An anomaly-based algorithm to detect compromised nodes in wireless sensor networks, *International Journal of Computer and Information Science*, **9**(1), 11–20 (2008).
22. K. Xing, F. Liu, X. Cheng and D. H. Du, Real-time detection of clone attacks in wireless sensor networks, *Proceedings of ICDCS 2008*, 3–10 (June 2008).
23. Y. Yang, X. Wang, S. Zhu and G. Cao, Distributed software-based attestation for node compromise detection in sensor networks, *Proceedings of the 26th IEEE International Symposium on Reliable Distributed Systems*, 219–230 (2007).
24. M. Shaneck, K. Mahadevan, V. Kher and Y. Kim, Remote software-based attestation for wireless sensors, *Lecture Notes in Computer Science*, DOI: 10.1007/11601494, 27–41 (2005).
25. X. Du, Detection of compromised sensor nodes in heterogeneous sensor networks, *Proceedings of IEEE ICC*, 1446–1450 (May 2008).
26. F. Liu, X. Cheng and D. Chen, Insider attacker detection in wireless sensor networks, *Proceedings of IEEE INFOCOM*, 1937–1945 (May 2007).
27. Q. Zhang, T. Yu and P. Ning, A framework for identifying compromised nodes in sensor networks, *ACM Transactions on Information and System Security*, **11**(3), Article number 12 (March 2008).
28. T. Li, M. Song and M. Alam, Compromised sensor nodes detection: A quantitative approach, *Proceedings of the 28th International Conference on Distributed Computing Systems — the 1st International Workshop on Wireless Security and Privacy*, 352–357 (June 2008).

Chapter 21

SWAT: A Decentralized Self-Healing Mechanism for Wormhole Attacks in Wireless Sensor Networks

Chonho Lee* and Junichi Suzuki†

Department of Computer Science
University of Massachusetts, Boston
**chonho@cs.umb.edu*
†jxs@cs.umb.edu

This paper proposes and evaluates a decentralized self-healing mechanism that detects and recovers from wormhole attacks in wireless multi-hop sensor networks. Upon detecting a wormhole attack, the proposed mechanism, called SWAT, identifies the locations of malicious nodes (or wormhole nodes), isolates them from the network and recovers the routing structure distorted by them. SWAT is the first mechanism that performs both wormhole node isolation and routing structure recovery against wormhole attacks. Unlike many other wormhole detection mechanisms, SWAT does not require any extra networking facilities (e.g., timing analysis and localization facilities) as well as special hardware (e.g., GPS). Instead, it uses network connectivity information only in a decentralized manner. Simulation results show that SWAT yields 100% wormhole attack detection, 0% false detection, 100% wormhole node isolation and 0% false isolation in dense networks. The results also show that SWAT outperforms multi-path routing mechanisms in terms of control overhead and power consumption and outperforms another connectivity-based detection mechanism in terms of false isolation rate and recovery efficiency.

21.1. Introduction

The wormhole attack is one of the most severe security threats in wireless multi-hop sensor networks.[1–3] In this attack, two malicious nodes, called *wormhole nodes*, are strategically placed at distant points in the network, and they are connected in one hop via wireless out-of-band link or wired link called a *wormhole link*. Through this link, wormhole nodes make far apart nodes believe they are close with each other. Taking advantage of this deceptive belief, one wormhole node attracts data packets from its neighboring nodes (called *affected* nodes), tunnels them through a wormhole link and replays them at the other wormhole node.

A major impact of wormhole attacks is that wormhole nodes collude to distort routing structure and take a full control of the data traffic through a wormhole link.

Wormhole attacks can disrupt any mechanisms that rely on topological proximity. For example, connectivity-based localization mechanisms fail such that far apart nodes are localized nearby. This can result in a critical failure in wireless sensor networks because location information is always important in many protocols and applications. Wormhole nodes can also degrade the latency of data delivery from individual nodes to the base station and increase power consumption of nodes by imposing extra node-to-node data transmissions when one wormhole node attracts packets near the base station and replays them at the other that is far from the base station.

Another major impact of wormhole attacks is that wormhole nodes can easily perform secondary (passive and active) attacks anytime. For example, wormhole nodes may eavesdrop, delay, modify or selectively drop incoming packets. They may also impose extra routing structure reconstruction, thereby increasing power consumption of nodes, by turning off a wormhole link periodically.

A challenging issue of wormhole attacks is that attackers do not need to know the cryptographic measures used in the network and posses cryptographic keys. Wormhole attacks cannot be defeated even if the network retains confidentiality and authenticity because wormhole nodes do not create extra packets but simply replay packets that already exist in the network. As far as wormhole nodes are passive, they are invisible.

This paper proposes and evaluates a decentralized self-healing mechanism that detects and recovers from wormhole attacks. Upon detecting a wormhole attack, the proposed mechanism, called SWAT,[a] isolates wormhole nodes from the network by eliminating links connected to them, and recovers the routing structure distorted by the wormhole nodes. SWAT is the first mechanism that performs both wormhole node isolation and routing structure recovery against wormhole attacks. With scalability in mind, SWAT is designed as a decentralized in-network detection mechanism that uses network connectivity information only. Simulation results show that SWAT yields 100% wormhole attack detection, 0% false detection, 100% wormhole node isolation and 0% false isolation in dense networks. The results also show that SWAT outperforms multi-path routing mechanisms in terms of control overhead and power consumption and outperforms another connectivity-based detection mechanism in terms of false isolation rate and recovery efficiency.

This paper is organized as follows. Section 21.2 overviews wormhole attacks. Section 21.3 compares SWAT with existing work. Section 21.4 describes the self-healing process and design rationales of SWAT. Section 21.5 shows a series of simulation results to obtain the performance implications of SWAT and compare SWAT with other wormhole detection mechanisms. Section 21.6 concludes this paper with some discussion on future work.

[a]Self-healing mechanism against Wormhole Attacks.

21.2. Preliminaries: Wormhole Attacks

The wormhole attack was first identified in wireless ad-hoc networks by Hu *et al.*,[4] and it was first discussed in the context of wireless sensor networks by Karlof *et al.*[5] Figure 21.1 shows example wormhole attacks. Figure 21.1(a) shows a normal, undistorted tree-based routing structure. Figures 21.1(b) and (c) show two routing structures distorted under wormhole attacks. A number shown in each node (circle) indicates the topological distance (hop count) to the base station.

In Fig. 21.1(b), a wormhole node, M2, attracts packets from its neighboring (shaded) nodes and forwards them to the other wormhole node, M1. Using a wormhole link, M1 and M2 make their neighboring nodes believe that they are close. For example, the node B believes that the node C is a direct neighbor. As a result, B forwards packets to the base station through M2, rather than A, because the routing path through M2 is the shortest toward the base station. This way, M2 distorts its

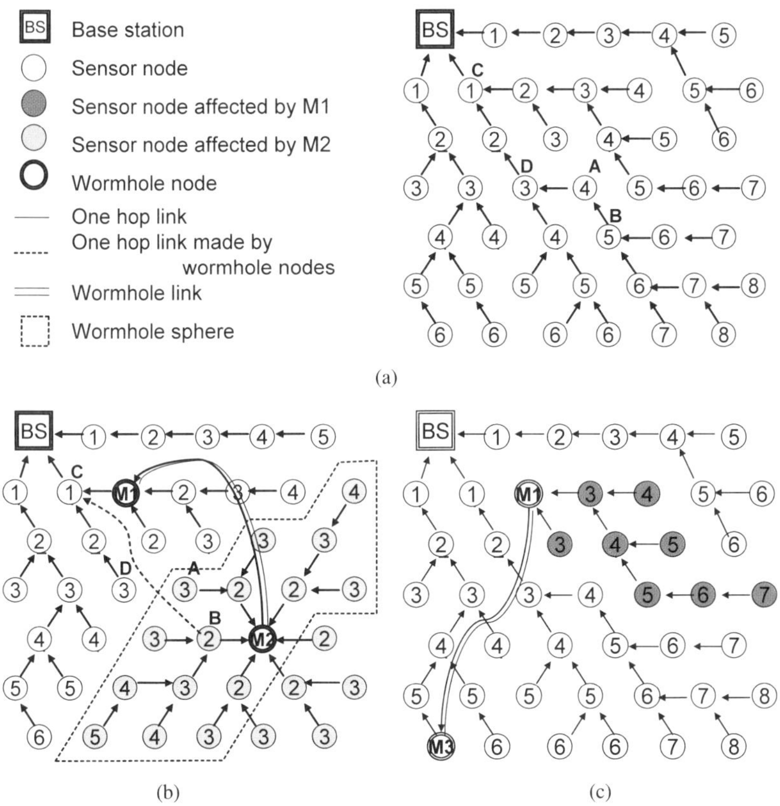

Fig. 21.1. Example wormhole attacks. (a) Normal, undistorted routing structure, (b) routing structure distorted by M1 and M2 (wormhole nodes) and (c) routing structure distorted by M1 and M3 (wormhole nodes).

surrounding routing structure. A wormhole attack in Fig. 21.1(b) forms a *wormhole sphere*, which is a set of affected nodes that change their routing paths due to a wormhole attack. For example, in Fig. 21.1(a), the node B points the node A as its parent node in its routing path; however, due to a wormhole attack, B changes its parent node from A to M2 in Fig. 21.1(b). Thus, B is included in a wormhole sphere. When a wormhole is formed, the network is topologically separated. For example, the node A is no longer connected to the node D due to a wormhole attack. (See Figs. 21.1(a) and (b).) This link loss contributes to a network separation. A set of nodes that separate the network at the edge of a wormhole sphere is called *edge nodes*. The node A is an edge node of a wormhole sphere.

In Fig. 21.1(c), a wormhole node, M1, receives packets from eight (shaded) nodes in its subtree and forwards them to the other wormhole node, M3. M1 distorts routing structure by diverting incoming packets. This packet diversion incurs a higher number of node-to-node packet transmissions toward the base station, thereby imposing higher power consumption of nodes.

21.3. Related Work

Hu *et al.* propose the notions of geographical and temporal leashes.[6] A geographical leash ensures that a packet receiver exists within a certain range (e.g., transmission range) from a packet sender. When a node receives an out-of-range packet, it eliminates the packet under the assumption that the packet arrived through a wormhole link. This detection method requires each node to know its precise location. Several variations of geographical leashes have been proposed by Capkun *et al.*,[7] Wang *et al.*[8] Hu *et al.*,[9] and Sastry *et al.*[10] These mechanisms require each node to equip an extra device such as a GPS receiver, directional antenna or ultrasound transceiver in order to obtain its location information.

A temporal leash ensures that a packet receiver receives packets from their senders within a certain time bound. When a node receives an out-of-date packet, it eliminates the packet under the assumption that the packet arrived through a wormhole link. This detection method requires nodes to perform precise clock synchronization and timing analysis on the order of hundred nanoseconds to a few milliseconds.[11,12] Zhen *et al.* propose a similar approach that measures packet round-trip time between a node and its neighbors in order to examine whether each neighbor is a physical neighbor or not.[13] Unlike the detection methods based on geographical and temporal leashes, SWAT does not require any extra networking facilities (e.g., time synchronization, timing analysis and localization facilities) as well as special hardware devices such as GPS receivers. This can contribute to reduce the costs to deploy large-scale WSNs, which deploy a large number of nodes.

Poovendran *et al.*,[14] Lazos *et al.*[15] and Khalil *et al.*[16] propose device-free detection mechanisms. They assume special nodes, such as anchor, locator and guard nodes, which need to be always uncompromised. The special nodes know their locations and localize their neighboring nodes. Using the location information, individual or special nodes detect and eliminate the packets transmitted via wormhole links. In contrast, SWAT does not require any special nodes and does not rely on location information. Instead, it uses network connectivity information only.

Phuong *et al.* propose a detection method that leverages network traffic information.[17] Each node monitors the number of incoming/outgoing packets, and detects a wormhole attack by identifying an imbalance or a dramatic change of traffic volume based on a CUSUM (Cumulative Sum) algorithm. In this method, each node is required to utilize a large amount of memory space to keep traffic record for a certain time period. In contrast, SWAT uses network connectivity information and requires less memory space.

Vajda *et al.*[18] propose a detection method using network connectivity information. The base station periodically examines the number of direct neighbors of each node and statistically determines a wormhole attack under the assumption that nodes have a higher number of neighboring nodes around wormhole nodes. This centralized method does not scale well in large-scale WSNs. The more often the base station collects connectivity information from individual nodes, the higher power consumption they need to incur. The less often the base station collects connectivity information, the longer delay it detects wormhole attacks. Unlike this method, SWAT is designed as a decentralized in-network detection method.

Hou *et al.* discuss a decentralized detection method using connectivity information.[19] They claim that every node should always have an alternative path to each of its direct neighbor nodes in addition to a direct (one-hop) path. Each node seeks such alternative paths to its direct neighbors and alerts if they are not found. The control overhead of this method is quite expensive because each node keeps flooding control packets. In SWAT, each node does not always keep flooding control packets, thereby retaining lower control overhead.

Wang *et al.*[20] and Xu *et al.*[21] propose other detection methods using connectivity information. Both methods obtain the topological distance (hop count) from each node to the base station, and construct a distance map for all pairs of nodes by using multi-dimensional scaling techniques. Based on the distance map, the base station[20] or each node[21] detects a wormhole attack by identifying the routing structure distorted by wormhole nodes. These methods are computationally expensive; its computational complexity is $O(N^3)$ where N is the number of direct neighbors of each node. In contrast, SWAT maintains lower computational complexity ($O(N^2)$).

All of the aforementioned methods can detect wormhole attacks; however, they cannot identify the locations of wormhole nodes and neutralize them by isolating them from the network. In contrast, SWAT inherently considers and performs wormhole node isolation by eliminating the links connected to them so that no more packets will be transmitted via wormhole link in the future.

Maheshwari *et al.* propose a decentralized detection method that is most similar to SWAT.[22] This method leverages connectivity information to isolate wormhole nodes from the network. Although it is more computationally efficient than any other decentralized detection methods including SWAT, it cannot pinpoint the locations of wormhole nodes. As a result, it isolates several normal, uncompromised nodes around wormhole nodes in order to guarantee isolating all wormhole nodes. Unlike this method, SWAT is designed to minimize false isolation. In addition, it recovers the routing structure distorted by wormhole nodes. Maheshwari *et al.* do not consider routing structure recovery.

21.4. SWAT: The Proposed Self-Healing Mechanism

SWAT performs its self-healing process in two phases: *detection* and *recovery* phases. In the detection phase, SWAT detects a wormhole attack and identifies the locations of wormhole nodes. In the recovery phase, SWAT isolates wormhole nodes from the network and recovers distorted routing structure.

SWAT operates under a few assumptions. First, sensor nodes are uniformly and densely deployed in an observation area, and each node has the same transmission range. Second, the base station constructs a routing tree structure by propagating a control packet to individual nodes on a hop-by-hop basis. (Fig. 21.1(a) shows an example routing tree.) Based on the routing tree, each node forwards incoming data packets to its next hop (parent) node. Third, each node maintains a neighbor list that contains the connectivity information on physical neighbor nodes in one and two hops away. For each neighbor node, the list maintains its node ID, its parent node ID and the hop count to the base station. In order to obtain and update the neighbor information, each node exchanges its direct neighbor's information with the direct neighbors.

21.4.1. *Detection phase*

In the detection phase, SWAT detects a wormhole attack and identifies the locations of wormhole nodes. Using its neighbor list, each node monitors the network connectivity with physical neighbor nodes that are one and two hops away. When a node finds any connectivity anomaly with them, it produces a control packet, called *danger signal*. A danger signal indicates the existence of a wormhole attack. Danger signals are used to locate wormhole nodes and trigger the next phase, recovery phase, which isolates wormhole nodes and recovers distorted routing structure. There are three types of danger signals: *DS1*, *DS2* and *DS3*. Each of DS1 and DS2 signals indicates that a node is connected to a wormhole node. A DS3 indicates that a node exists at the edge of a wormhole sphere.

A DS1 indicates a connectivity anomaly between a normal (uncompromised) node and a wormhole node. Using its neighbor list, every node examines how many nodes each of its physical direct neighbors is connected to. Given an assumption that nodes are uniformly deployed in an observation area, each node should maintain the same number of physical direct neighbors. However, when a node is connected to a wormhole node, it is likely the node has a higher number of physical direct neighbors. For example, in Fig. 21.2, wormhole nodes M1 and M2 make the node A have 11 direct neighbors, although it should have six direct neighbors as B does. Therefore, a node produces a DS1 when it finds a neighboring node who has a less number of direct neighbors than it does. When a DS1 is produced on a node, it stays on the node.

Similar to DS1, a DS2 also indicates a connectivity anomaly between a normal (uncompromised) node and a wormhole node. Using its neighbor list, each node counts the number of two-hops-away physical neighbors whose parent node is same as its own. It is likely the number grows under a wormhole attack. For example, Fig. 21.3(a) shows a normal, undistorted routing tree. In this example, the node C shares its parent node (B) with only one two-hops-away node (E). However, under a wormhole attack (Fig. 21.3(b)), five two-hops-away nodes, including E, F and A,

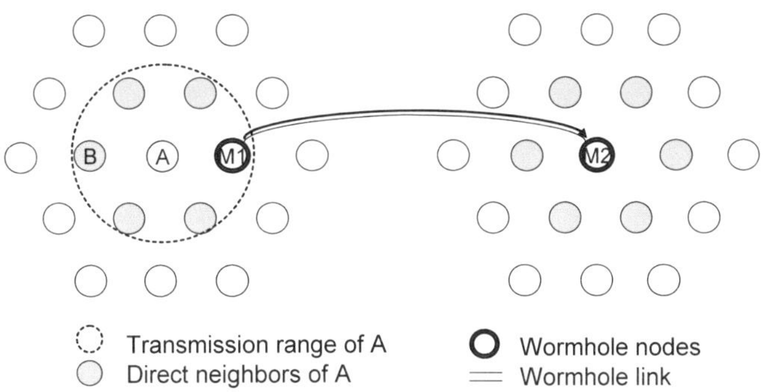

Fig. 21.2. An example case where a DS1 is produced.

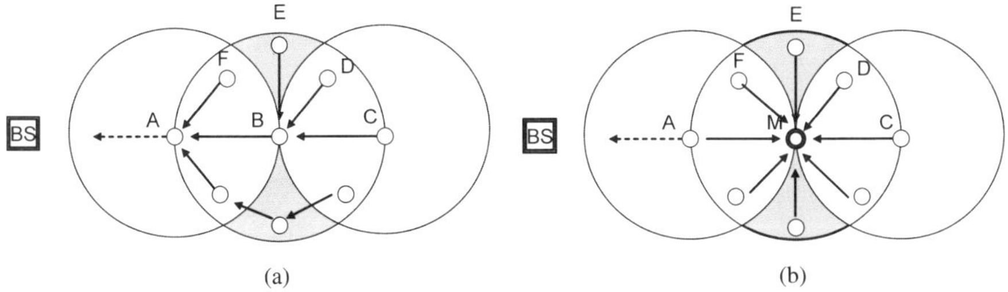

Fig. 21.3. An example case where a DS2 is produced. (a) No wormhole attack and (b) under a wormhole attack.

point the node M as its parent as C does. Therefore, when the number of two-hops-away neighboring nodes that point the same parent node exceeds a threshold Th_2, a node produces a DS2. The produced DS2 stays on the node.

The DS2 production depends on the value of Th_2 and network density, which is measured as the number of physical direct neighbor nodes of each node. If both values are low, a node may produce a false positive DS2. In Fig. 21.3(a), the node C can share its parent with the nodes in shaded areas (e.g., the node E) and may produce a false positive DS2. Therefore, Th_2 needs to be configured so that it can minimize false positive DS2 production. For example, when the number of physical direct neighbors of each node is four (Fig. 21.4(a)), there can exist up to two two-hops-away nodes (B and D) that share the parent with the node C. If there are more than two such nodes, it is likely the node C is connected with a wormhole node. Therefore, the value of 2 is used for Th_2 when the number of direct neighbors of each node is four. When the number of physical direct neighbors of each node is five, there can exist up to three two-hops-away nodes (B, D and E) that share the parent with the node C (Fig. 21.4(b)). If there are more than three such nodes, it is likely the node C is connected with a wormhole node. Therefore, the value of 3 is used for Th_2 when the number of physical direct neighbors of each node is five.

A DS3 indicates that a node exists at the edge of a wormhole sphere. Using a neighbor list, each node examines the following condition, and if it is satisfied, the node produces a DS3.

$$\frac{n_{hc}}{N} > Th_3. \tag{21.1}$$

n_{hc} denotes the number of physical direct neighbor nodes that have the same hop count to the base station. N denotes the total number of physical direct neighbor nodes. Without wormhole attacks (Fig. 21.5(a)), each node has physical direct neighbors whose hop counts are in $[hc - 1,\ hc + 1]$, where hc is its own hop count to the base station. For example, the node B is two hops away to the base station, and A and C (B's direct neighbors) are one and three hops

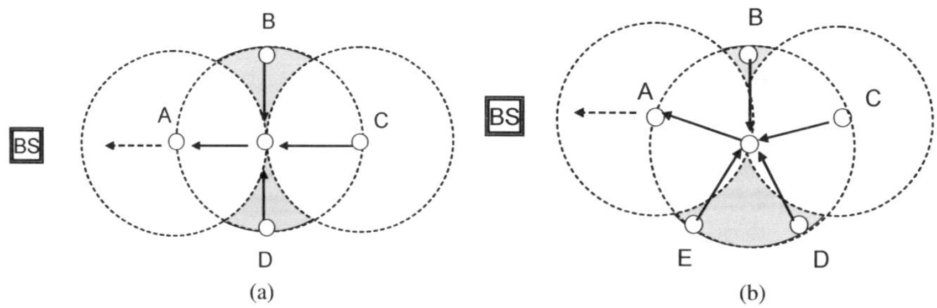

Fig. 21.4. Two-hops-away neighboring nodes in different degrees of network density. (a) The number of neighboring nodes = 4 and (b) the number of neighboring nodes = 5.

away, respectively. In contrast, when a wormhole sphere is formed by a wormhole attack, it is likely n_{hc} grows around the wormhole sphere's edge. For example, in Fig. 21.5(b), the wormhole node M2 attracts packets from its neighboring nodes and forwards them to M1; the edge of a wormhole sphere exists around the node A. In this case, the number of nodes that are three hops away to the base station becomes larger within A's transmission range. (Note that the area S3's size is larger in Fig. 21.5(b) than Fig. 21.5(a).) Therefore, when $\frac{n_{hc}}{N}$ exceeds a threshold, Th_3, on a node, the node produces a DS3. When a DS3 is produced on a node, it is sent to the nodes between the node and its hc-hops-away parent node. The propagated DS3 stays on each node between its originator node to its hc-hops-away parent node.

A proper value of Th_3 is determined by analyzing the maximum size of an area where nodes have the same hop counts to the base station. Figure 21.6 focuses on the S3 area around the node A in Fig. 21.5(a). The size of $S3$ is maximized when $x = 0$; i.e., $Z = R$ where R is A's transmission range. It is approximately 1.913 R^2

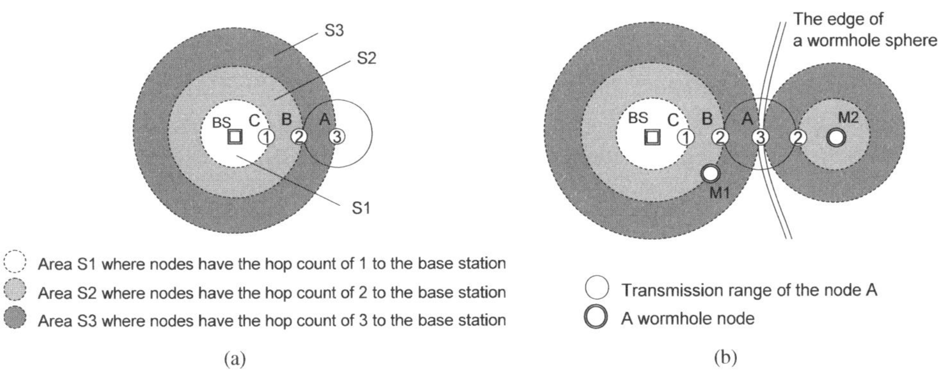

Fig. 21.5. An example case where a DS3 is produced. (a) No wormhole attack and (b) under a wormhole attack.

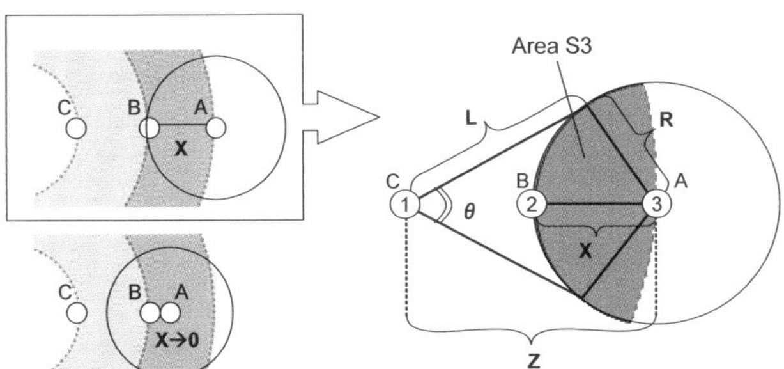

Fig. 21.6. Size of an area where nodes have the same hop counts to the base station.

as derived below.

$$\begin{aligned} Area(S) &= \int_R^{2R} ArcLength(L,\theta)dL \\ &= \int_R^{2R} L\cdot\theta dL \\ &= \int_R^{2R} 2L\cos^{-1}\left(\frac{L^2+Z^2-R^2}{2LZ}\right)dL \\ &= \int_R^{2R} 2L\cos^{-1}\left(\frac{L}{2R}\right)dL \approx 1.913R^2. \end{aligned}$$

Given the maximum size of $S3$ under no wormhole attacks, $Area(S)/\pi R^2 \approx 0.6$ is used for Th_3.

21.4.2. *Recovery phase*

In the recovery phase, SWAT isolates wormhole nodes from the network and recovers distorted routing structure. This recovery process is executed with three types of control packets, called *recovery packets*: *RCV1*, *RCV2*, and *RCV3*. RCV1 and RCV2 are designed to isolate wormhole nodes from the network by removing links connected to them. RCV3 is designed to recover the routing structures distorted in wormhole spheres.

Each recovery packet is produced on a node when a certain combination of danger signals (i.e., DS1, DS2 and DS3) is available on the node. In other words, danger signals trigger the production of recovery packets. Of eight possible combinations of three types of danger signals, SWAT considers four combinations to produce recovery packets. (See Table 21.1.) Each combination (or each node state) is represented as a sequence of three binary numbers. The value of 1 means that a corresponding danger signal is available, and the value of 0 means that it is not available. For example, (1, 1, 1) denotes that all of DS1 and DS2 and DS3 signals are available

Table 21.1. Production of recovery packets.

The state of a node (DS1, DS2, DS3)	Produced recovery packet(s)
(1, 1, 0)	RCV1
(1, 0, 0)	RCV1
(1, 1, 1)	RCV2 and RCV3
(0, 1, 1)	RCV2 and RCV3
(1, 0, 1)	None
(0, 1, 0)	None
(0, 0, 1)	None
(0, 0, 0)	None

on a node. In this case, a RCV2 and a RCV3 are produced. In (1, 0, 1), (0, 1, 0) and (0, 0, 1), no recovery packets are produced in order to minimize the chances to trigger the recovery phase with potential false positive danger signals.

An RCV1 isolates a wormhole node from the network. An RCV1 is produced when a node is in the (1, 1, 0) or (1, 0, 0) state (Table 21.1). Once an RCV1 is produced on a node, it is broadcasted to the node's physical direct neighbors. When a node receives an RCV1, it removes the RCV1's sender node from its neighbor list. If the RCV1 sender is its parent node, it selects a new parent node from its neighbor list. The new parent node must not be the RCV1 receiver's child node. Figure 21.7 shows an example of the recovery phase with RCV1 packets. In this example, the node B believes that its parent is the node F due to the wormhole link between M1 and M2. When B receives an RCV1 packet(s) from a shaded node(s) out of its physical direct neighbors (e.g., D, F, G and I), it removes those nodes from its neighbor list. (Note that those shaded nodes can be in the (1, 1, 0) or (1, 0, 0) state.) B selects the new parent from its neighbor list; in this example, B selects E. This way, B avoids to connect with a wormhole node (M1) so that it will never send packets to M1 in the future. Similarly, in Fig. 21.7, the node G believes its parent is the node A due to a wormhole link. Upon receiving an RCV1 packet(s) from some of its physical direct neighbors including I, F, A, B and D, G removes those nodes from its neighbor list and selects another node (J) as the new parent. Through this process, G detours incoming packets to J rather than sending them to a wormhole node (M2). In Fig. 21.7, wormhole nodes (M1 and M2) are isolated when both A and G perform the recovery phase with RCV1 packets.

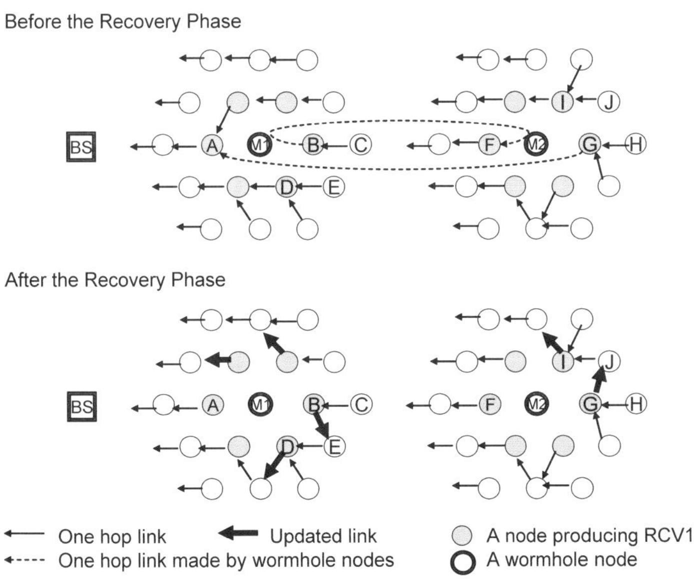

Fig. 21.7. An example of the recovery phase with RCV1 packets.

Similar to an RCV1, an RCV2 isolates a wormhole node from the network. It is specifically designed to isolate a wormhole node that forms a wormhole sphere (e.g., M2 in Fig. 21.1(b)). It is produced when a node is in the (1, 1, 1) or (0, 1, 1) state. Once an RCV2 is produced on a node, it is broadcasted with the hops-to-live count of two toward the nodes that are physically two hops away. When a node receives an RCV2, it removes a link to its parent node and selects the RCV2's sender node as the new parent. Figure 21.8 shows an example of the recovery phase with RCV2 packets. In this example, a wormhole node, M, attracts packets from its physical direct neighbors, and the node F broadcasts an RCV2 packet. Upon receiving the RCV2 packet, the nodes A and E change their parent from M to F. They broadcast the RCV2 again to D and G; then D and G changes their parents to E and A, respectively. The wormhole node M is isolated when all of its physical direct neighbors perform the recovery phase with RCV2 packets.

An RCV3 recovers the routing structure distorted in a wormhole sphere. It is produced when a node is in the (1, 1, 1) or (0, 1, 1) state. Once a node produces an RCV3, it sends the RCV3 to its child nodes and changes its parent node to one of the child nodes. If a node does not have any child node when receiving an RCV3, the node discards the RCV3 and selects one of its physical direct neighbors as its parent node. Figure 21.9 shows an example of the recovery phase with RCV3 packets. In

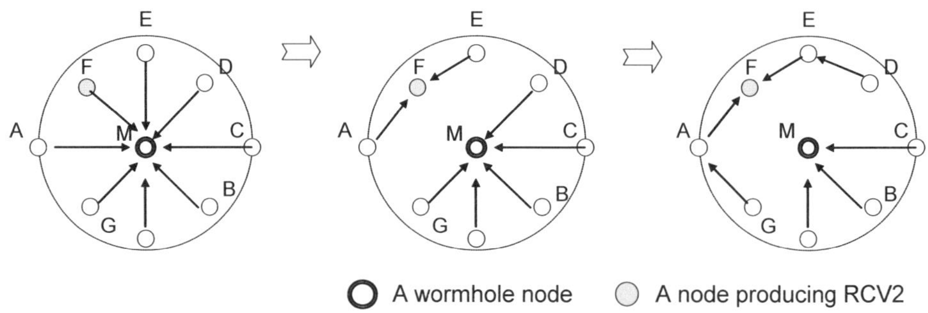

Fig. 21.8. An example of the recovery phase with RCV2 packets.

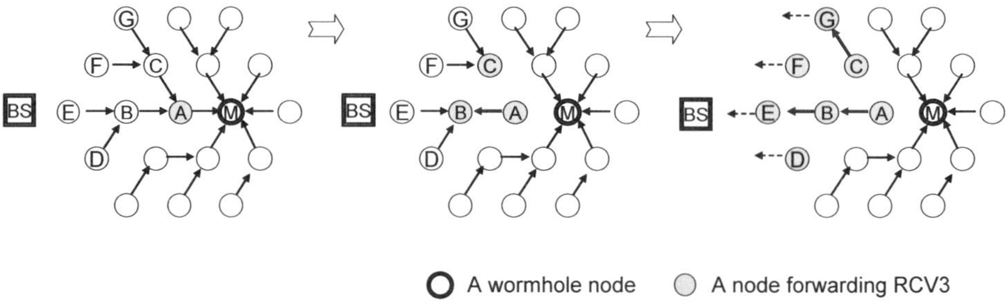

Fig. 21.9. An example of the recovery phase with RCV3 packets.

this example, a wormhole node, M, attracts packets from its neighboring nodes, and the node A produces an RCV3. A sends the RCV3 to B and C, and change its parent from M to B. When B receives the RCV3 from A, it forwards it to E and D, and it changes its parent from A to E. When C receives the RCV3 from A, it forwards it to F and G, and it changes its parent from A to G. Since F and G exist on the edge of a wormhole, they do not have child nodes. Therefore, they discard incoming RCV3 packets and selects one of its physical direct neighbors as its parent node. The wormhole node M is isolated when all of its neighboring nodes perform the recovery phase with RCV3 packets.

21.5. Simulation Results

This section shows a series of simulation results to evaluate SWAT. SWAT is implemented on TinyOS and simulated in the TOSSIM simulator.[23] In this simulation work, 100 sensor nodes are located in a 10×10 grid topology where the number of physical direct neighbors of each node is eight (Fig. 21.10). Node IDs are numbered from 0 to 99 from the left-top corner to the right-bottom corner. The base station is located at the left-top corner (the node 0), and two wormhole links are simulated between wormhole nodes (the nodes 22 and 77, and the nodes 22 and 90) are considered. At the beginning of a simulation, a routing tree is constructed, and the nodes 22 and 77 form a wormhole sphere as shown in Fig. 21.1(b). The node 77 attracts data packets from its neighboring nodes and forwards them to the node 22, which in turn forwards them to the node 90. Each node periodically transmits data packets (sensor reading) every 100 seconds. Thus, in average, the base station receives one data packet per second.

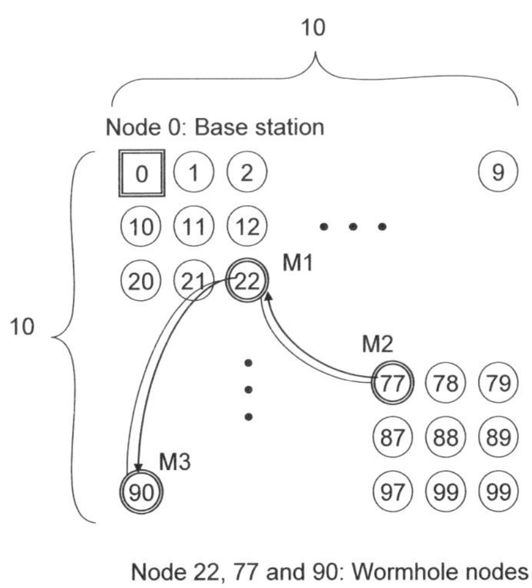

Fig. 21.10. Simulated network.

21.5.1. *Performance implications of SWAT*

Figure 21.11 shows the number of data packets that the base station receives every 15 seconds. (The base station is supposed to receive 15 data packets every 15 seconds.) Due to wormhole nodes, some packets are transmitted to the base station via wormhole links, and others are not. As Fig. 21.11 shows, more than half (9 to 11) packets are transmitted via wormhole links. This means that more than half nodes in the network are affected by wormhole nodes. When SWAT starts its self-healing process at the 60th second, it detects and isolates wormhole nodes immediately; the number of data packets transmitted via wormhole links drops to zero. Accordingly, the route recovery phase is successfully executed by the 120th second; all of 15 data packets are transmitted to the base station by avoiding wormhole nodes. Figure 21.11 also shows control overhead in the detection and recovery phases (gray bars). It is measured by the number of node-to-node transmissions of control packets (danger signals and recovery packets). The total number of control packet transmissions is 101 from the 60th to 120th second. The authors of the paper believe that quick wormhole detection and routing structure recovery compensate for this control overhead.

Figure 21.12 shows how SWAT self-heals a routing structure distorted by wormhole nodes. Figure 21.12(a) shows a routing structure under a wormhole attack at the 15th second. The nodes 22, 77 and 90 are wormhole nodes as shown in Fig. 21.10. Each arrow indicates a routing path across nodes. The node 77 forms a wormhole sphere, and the network is topologically separated. In contrast, Fig. 21.12(b) shows a routing structure recovered by SWAT (at the 150th second). Each thick arrow

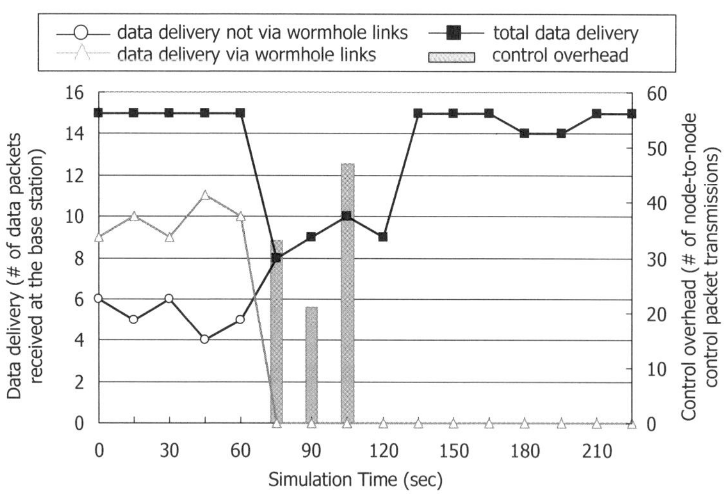

Fig. 21.11. Data delivery and control overhead.

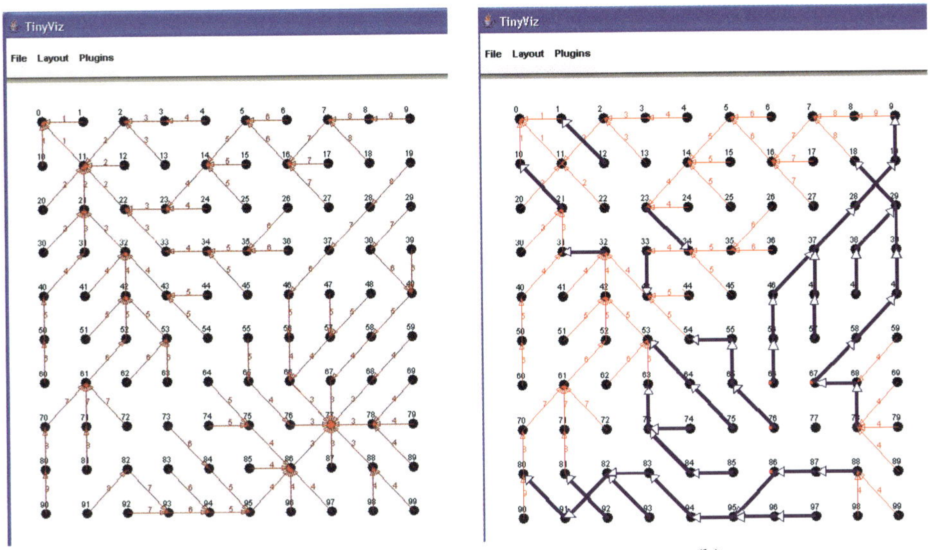

(a) (b)

Fig. 21.12. Recovery of a distorted routing structure. (a) Distorted routing structure and (b) recovered routing structure.

denotes a routing path that SWAT changes in its recovery phase. All three wormhole nodes are successfully isolated; no nodes possess links to wormhole nodes.

Figure 21.13 shows power consumption of control packets in the detection and recovery process. It is measured with power current in mA because the same voltage is used in all nodes. The simulated power current used in the sleep, listening and broadcast states are 5 mA, 10 mA and 25 mA, respectively, as reported by Shnayder *et al.*[24] The X-Y coordinate represents the network; each cell denotes a node. Figure 21.13(a) shows that power consumption is higher around wormhole nodes (the nodes 22, 77, and 90) due to producing DS1 signals and broadcasting RCV1 packets. Figure 21.13(b) shows that the nodes around the wormhole node 77 consume a higher amount of power than others by producing DS2 signals and broadcasting RCV2 packets. As described in Sec. 21.4.1, DS2 is specifically designed to detect the wormhole nodes that form wormhole spheres. Figure 21.13(c) shows the power consumption due to DS3 signals and RCV3 packets. Figures 21.13(d) and 21.13(e) show the amount of power spent for DS3 signals and RCV3 packets, respectively. These figures illustrate that DS3 signals are propagated from the edge of a wormhole sphere and DCV3 packets are transmitted throughout the wormhole sphere. As Fig. 21.13 demonstrates, the control packets of SWAT works well as they are designed.

Figure 21.14 shows how many nodes die over time by running out of power with and without SWAT. As discussed in Secs. 21.1 and 21.2, wormhole attacks can shorten the network's lifetime due to packet diversion. Under a wormhole attack, the

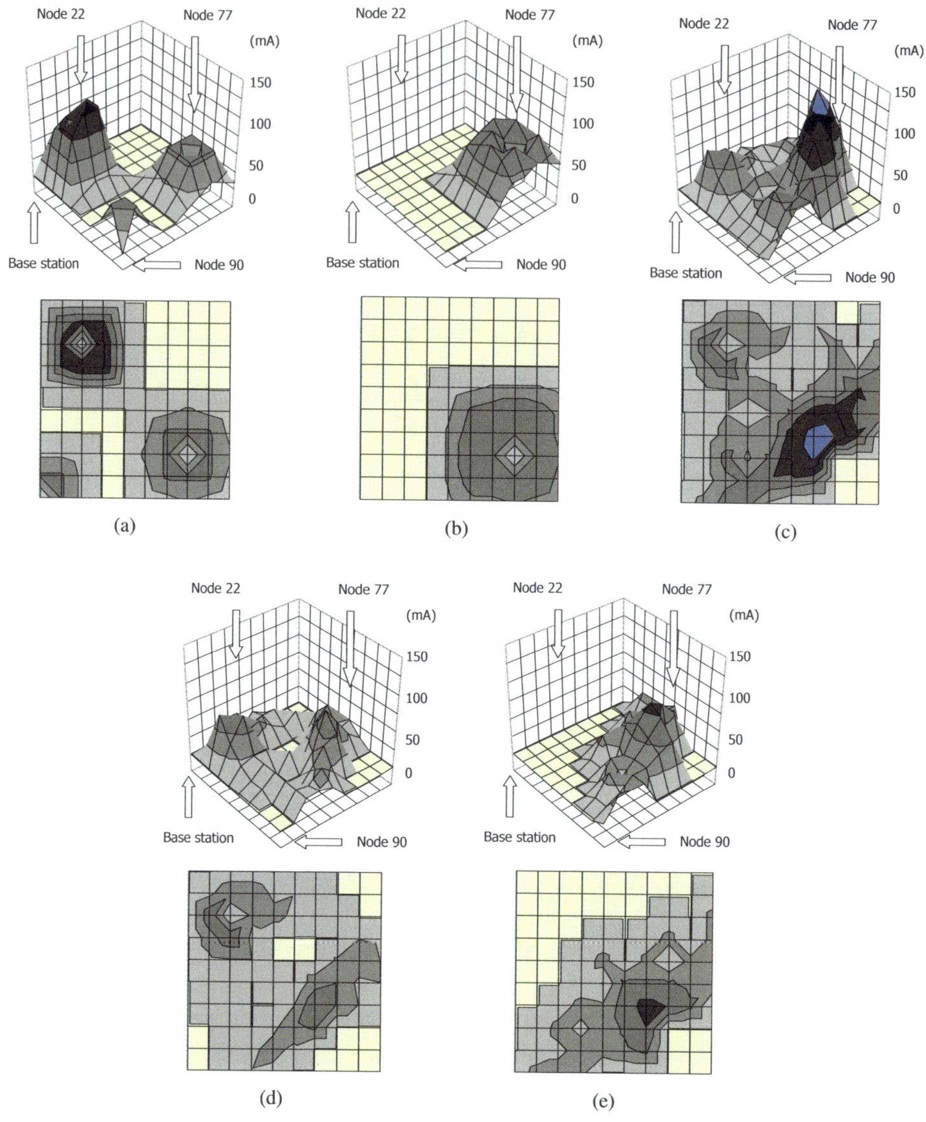

Fig. 21.13. Power consumption of control packets in the detection and recovery phases. (a) DS1 and RCV1, (b) DS2 and RCV2, (c) DS3 and RCV3, (d) for DS3 and (e) for RCV3.

first dead node is observed at the 440th second, and 51 of 100 nodes are dead at the 600th second. In contrast, using SWAT, the first dead node is observed at the 480th second, and 40 nodes are dead at the 600th second. SWAT successfully expands the network's lifetime by eliminating unnecessary power consumption imposed by wormhole nodes. Figure 21.14 also demonstrates that this benefit compensates well for the power consumption of SWAT shown in Fig. 21.13.

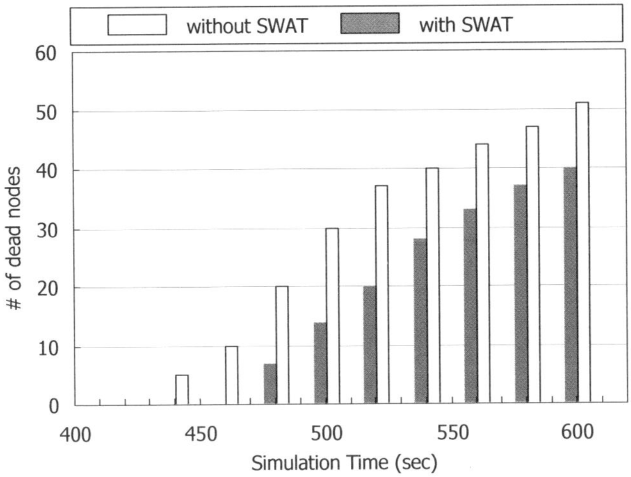

Fig. 21.14. Network lifetime with and without SWAT.

Table 21.2. False isolation in different degrees of network density.

Network density	4	6	8	10	12
False isolation	5	2	1	0	0
Total control overhead	76	89	101	112	115

Table 21.3. Memory footprint in a MICA2 mote.

		RAM(KB)	ROM(KB)
	Detection module		2.0
SWAT	Recovery module		2.5
	House keeping module		7.4
	Total	1.6	11.9
Blink		0.04	1.6

Table 21.2 illustrates false isolation in different degrees of network density. False isolation is measured as the number of normal, uncompromised nodes that SWAT incorrectly identify as wormhole nodes and isolate. Network density is represented as the number of physical direct neighbor nodes of each node. As shown in Table 21.2, false isolation decreases as network density grows. In the network density of 10 and 12, no false isolation occurs. However, control overhead (the number of node-to-node control packet transmissions) increases as network density grows.

Table 21.3 shows the memory footprint of SWAT in a MICA2 mote, and compares it with the footprint of Blink (an example program in TinyOS), which periodically turns on and off an LED. The total memory footprint of SWAT is 1.6 KB in

RAM and 11.9 KB in ROM. Of the total ROM footprint, the wormhole detection module occupies 2.0 KB and the recovery module occupies 2.5 KB. The housekeeping module includes neighbor list maintenance and routing tree construction as well as the standard control component in TinyOS, which is responsible of packet transmission and timer control. SWAT is implemented lightweight; it consumes only a small portion of the capacity of a MICA2 mote. (A MICA2 mote has 4 KB in RAM 128 KB in ROM.) SWAT can also run on a smaller-scale mote, for example, TelosB, which has 48 KB ROM.

21.5.2. *Performance comparison with other mechanisms*

This section compares SWAT with other wormhole detection mechanisms: flooding-based multipath routing mechanisms (MULTI1[25] and MULTI2[26]) and a connectivity information based mechanism (CONNECT[22]). In MULTI1, each node replicates every incoming data packet and transmits the replicated packets through multiple routing paths toward the base station. In MULTI2, each node reactively discovers multiple paths to the base station per incoming data packet, selects one of them that does not go through wormhole links, and transmits a packet to the selected path. Routing path selection is performed with a statistical analysis method. CONNECT is discussed in Sec. 21.2.

Figure 21.15 compares data delivery and control overhead in SWAT, MULTI1, MULTI2 and CONNECT. Figure 21.15(a) is same as Fig. 21.11. Compared with MULTI1 and MULTI2, SWAT is much less expensive in terms of control overhead. SWAT does not always generate control packets (i.e., danger signals and recovery packets), but generates them only during the detection and recovery phases. Sacrificing control overhead, MULTI1 and MULTI2 guarantee that the base station always receives 15 data packets without using wormhole links. SWAT does not provide this guarantee; however, it performs routing structure recovery so that the base station can receive 15 data packets without using wormhole links.

Both SWAT and CONNECT perform wormhole attack detection and wormhole node isolation quickly; the number of data packets transmitted via wormhole links drops rapidly from the 60th to the 70th second. After wormhole node isolation, SWAT recovers distorted routing structure in order to increase the number of data packets that the base station receives. It does not increase in CONNECT because CONNECT does not consider routing structure recovery as discussed in Sec. 21.2. In terms of control overhead, CONNECT outperforms SWAT. It does not require to transmit control packets across nodes.

Figure 21.16 shows the total power consumption from the 60th to 120th second in SWAT, MULTI1, MULTI2 and CONNECT. Figure 21.16(a) indicates that, in SWAT, the nodes around wormhole nodes spent more powers than the other nodes in order to generate/transmit danger signals and recovery packets. SWAT does not impose unaffected nodes to consume power. Figure 21.16(b) shows all nodes

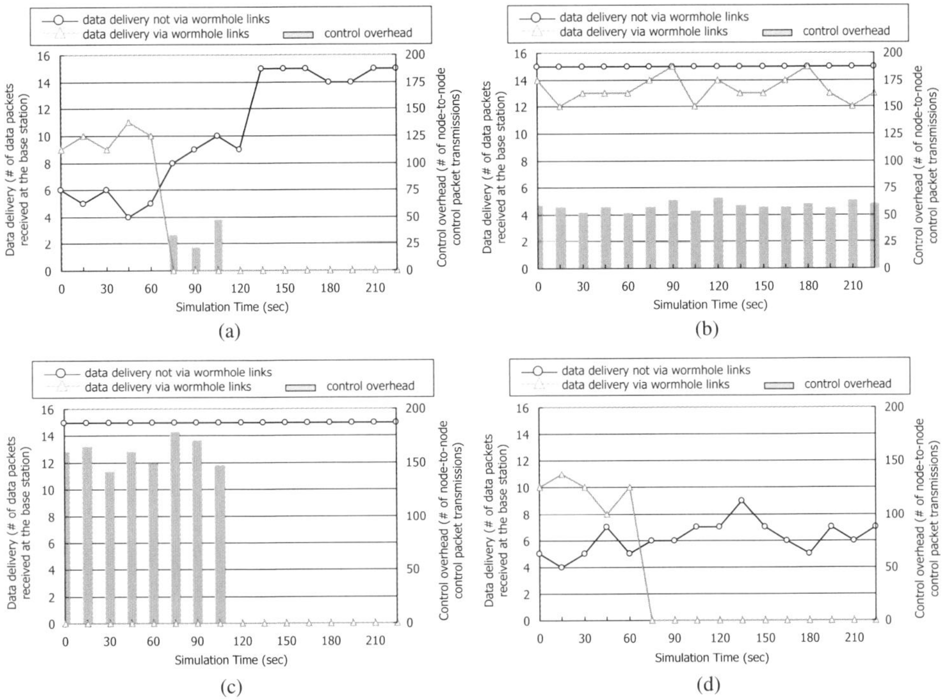

Fig. 21.15. Data delivery and control overhead in SWAT and other related mechanisms. (a) SWAT, (b) MULTI1, (c) MULTI2 and (d) CONNECT.

consume a very similar amount of power in MULTI1. Figure 21.16(c) shows the nodes around the base station consume more power than the other nodes. Power consumption in MULTI1 and MULTI2 are quite high due to their high control overhead shown in Fig. 21.15. Both mechanisms incur unnecessary power consumption to unaffected nodes. Power consumption in CONNECT is very low because it does not require to transmit control packets across nodes (Fig. 21.15).

Table 21.4 shows the false detection and isolation in SWAT and CONNECT. False detection is measured as the number of normal, uncompromised nodes that are incorrectly identified as wormhole nodes. False isolation is measured as the number of normal, uncompromised nodes that are incorrectly isolated from the network. As discussed in Sec. 21.5.1, false detection and isolation decrease in SWAT as network density (the number of physical direct neighbors of each node) grows. In CONNECT, false isolation increases as network density grows, although false detection remains zero. In the network density of 12, CONNECT incorrectly isolates more than 30% nodes (36 nodes) in the network. As described in Sec. 21.2, CONNECT cannot pinpoint the locations of wormhole nodes and isolates several normal, uncompromised nodes around wormhole nodes.

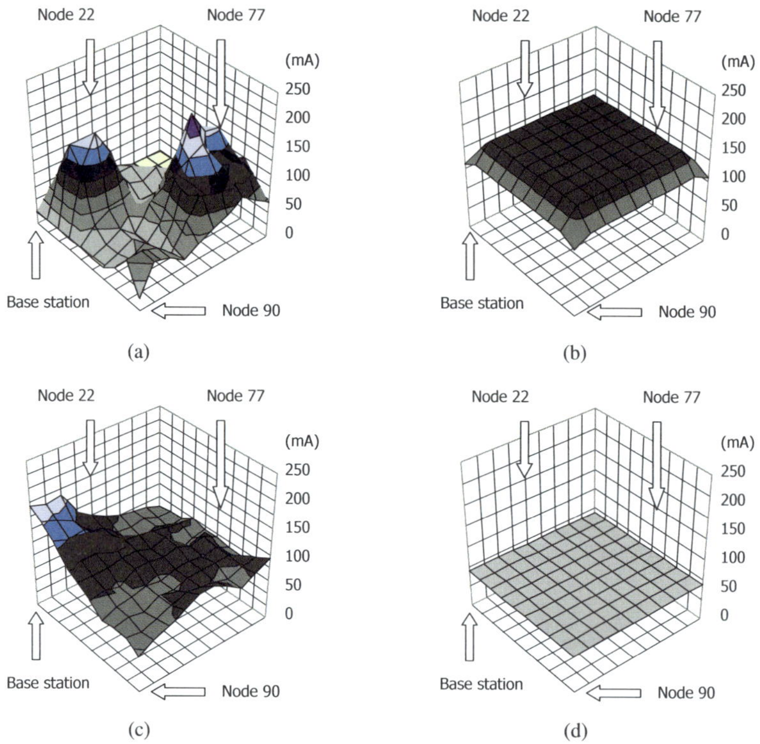

Fig. 21.16. Total power consumptions in SWAT and other related mechanisms. (a) SWAT, (b) MULTI1, (c) MULTI2 and (d) CONNECT.

Table 21.4. False detection and false isolation in different degrees of network density.

		Network density				
		4	6	8	10	12
SWAT	False detection	5	2	1	0	0
	False isolation	5	2	1	0	0
CONNECT	False detection	0	0	0	0	0
	False isolation	12	18	24	30	36

21.6. Conclusion

This paper proposes and evaluates a decentralized self-healing mechanism, SWAT, which detects and recovers from wormhole attacks in wireless sensor networks. Upon detecting a wormhole attack, SWAT identifies the locations of wormhole nodes, isolates them from the network and recovers the routing structure distorted by them. SWAT is the first mechanism that performs both wormhole node isolation and routing structure recovery against wormhole attacks. Unlike many other wormhole detection mechanisms, SWAT does not require any extra networking facilities (e.g., timing analysis and localization facilities) as well as special hardware (e.g., GPS). Instead, it uses network connectivity information only in a decentralized manner. Simulation results show that SWAT yields 100% wormhole attack detection, 0% false detection, 100% wormhole node isolation and 0% false isolation in dense networks. The results also show that SWAT outperforms multi-path routing mechanisms in terms of control overhead and power consumption and outperforms another connectivity-based detection mechanism in terms of false isolation rate and recovery efficiency. SWAT is implemented lightweight so that it can operate on resource-limited sensor nodes such as MICA2 and TelosB nodes.

Future research directions are to make SWAT more robust against a wider range of network topology, network density and node mobility configurations. Moreover, SWAT will be empirically evaluated with real sensor nodes.

References

1. A. Perrig, J. Stankovic and D. Wagner, Security in wireless sensor networks, *Communications of the ACM*, **47**(6), (June 2004).
2. H. Alzaid, S. Abanmi, S. Kanhere and C. Chou, *Detecting Wormhole Attacks in Wireless Sensor Networks*, Technical report, Department of Computer Science and Engineering, University of New South Wales (October 2006).
3. M. A. Gorlatova, *Review of Existing Wormhole Attack Discovery Techniques*, Technical report, School of Information Technology and Engineering, University of Ottawa (August 2006).
4. Y. Hu, A. Perrig and D. Johnson, *Wormhole Detection in Wireless Ad Hoc Network*, Technical report, Department of Computer Science, Rice University (June 2002).
5. C. Karlof and D. Wagner, Secure routing in sensor networks: Attacks and countermeasures, *Proc. of 1st IEEE International Workshop on Sensor Network Protocols and Applications* (May 2003).
6. Y. Hu, A. Perrig and D. Johnson, Packet leashes: A defence against wormhole attacks in wireless networks, *Proc. of the 22nd IEEE International Conference on Computer Communications*, 1976–1986 (April 2003).
7. S. Capkun, L. Buttyan and J. Hubaux, Sector: Secure tracking of node encounters in multi-hop wireless networks, *Proc. of the First ACM Workshop on Security of Ad Hoc and Sensor Networks*, 21–32 (October 2003).
8. X. Wang and J. Wong, An end-to-end detection of wormhole attack in wireless ad-hoc networks, *Proc. of the 31st Annual International Computer Software and Applications Conference*, 39–48 (July 2007).
9. L. Hu and D. Evans, Using directional antennas to prevent wormhole attacks, *In Network and Distributed System Security Symposium* (February 2004).
10. N. Sastry, U. Shankar and D. Wagner, Secure verification of location claims, *Proc. of the ACM Workshop on Wireless Security* (September 2003).
11. D. L. Mills, *A Computer-Controlled Loran-C Receiver for Precision Timekeeping*, Technical report, Department of Electrical and Computer Engineering, University of Delaware (March 1992).

12. D. L. Mills, *A Precision Radio Clock for WWV Transmissions*, Technical report, Department of Electrical and Computer Engineering, University of Delaware (August 1997).
13. J. Zhen and S. Srinivas, Preventing replay attacks for secure routing in ad hoc. networks, *Proc. of the Second International Conference on ADHOC Networks and Wireless* (October 2003).
14. R. Poovendran and L. Lazos, A graph theoretic framework for preventing the wormhole attack in wireless ad hoc networks, *ACM Journal of Wireless Networks*, **13**(1), 27–59 (January 2005).
15. L. Lazos and R. Poovendran, Serloc: Secure range-independent localization for wireless sensor networks workshop on wireless security archive, *Proc. of the Third ACM Workshop on Wireless Security* (October 2004).
16. I. Khalil, S. Bagchi and N. B. Shroff, Liteworp: A lightweight countermeasure for the wormhole attack in multihop wireless network, *Proc. of International Conference on Dependable Systems and Networks* (October 2005).
17. T. Phuong, L. Hung, S. Cho, Y. Lee and S. Lee, An anomaly detection algorithm for detecting attacks in wireless sensor networks, *Proc. of the Fourth IEEE Intelligence and Security Informatics Conference* (May 2006).
18. I. Vajda, L. Buttyan and L. Dora, Statistical wormhole detection in sensor networks, *Proc. of the Second European Workshop: Security and Privacy in Ad-hoc and Sensor Networks* (July 2005).
19. Y. Hou, C. Chen and B. Jeng, Distributed detection of wormholes and critical links in wireless sensor networks, *Proc. of the Third International Conference on Intelligent Information Hiding and Multimedia Signal Processing*, 639–642 (November 2007).
20. W. Wang and A. Lu, Interactive wormhole detection and evaluation, *Information Visualization*, **6**(1), 3–17 (January 2007).
21. Y. Xu, G. Chen, J. Ford and F. Makedon, Distributed wormhole attack detection in wireless sensor networks, *Proc. of the First Annual IFIP Working Group 11.10 International Conference on Critical Infrastructure Protection* (March 2007).
22. R. Maheshwari, J. Gao and S. R. Das, Detecting wormhole attacks in wireless networks using connectivity information, *Proc. of the Twenty-sixth IEEE International Conference on Computer Communications*, 107–115 (May 2007).
23. P. Levis, N. Lee, M. Welsh and D. Culler, Tossim: Accurate and scalable simulation of entire tinyos applications, *Proc. of the First ACM Conference on Embedded Networked Sensor Systems* (November 2003).
24. V. Shnayder, M. Hempstead, B. Chen, G. Werner-Allen and M. Welsh, Simulating the power consumption of large scale sensor network applications, *Proc. of the Second ACM Conference on Embedded Networked Sensor Systems* (November 2004).
25. S. Berton, H. Yin, C. Lin and M. G. Secure, Disjoint, multipath source routing protocol for mobile ad-hoc networks, *Proc. of the Fifth International Conference on Grid and Cooperative Computing* (October 2006).
26. L. Qian, N. Song and X. Li, Detection of wormhole attacks in multi-path routed wireless ad hoc networks: A statistical analysis approach, *Journal of Network and Computer Application*, **30**(1), 308–330 (January 2007).

Part VI

Localization and Location Discovery

Chapter 22

Node Localization in Wireless Sensor Networks

Ziguo Zhong*, Jaehoon Jeong, Ting Zhu, Shuo Guo and Tian He†

Department of Computer Science and Engineering
The University of Minnesota
200 Union Street SE, Minneapolis, MN 55455
**zhong@cs.umn.edu*
†tianhe@cs.umn.edu

Sensor node localization is one of the most challenging problems in the wireless sensor network field. Although many excellent works have been done for the sensor node positioning issue, it is still an open problem. This chapter tries to give an comprehensive introduction about the sensor node localization in WSN. Starting from the method taxonomy based on the feature of those localization solutions, all three categories including (i) ranging-based, (ii) ranging-free and (iii) event-driven localization are discussed. In addition, the basic ideas for thirteen well-known sensor node localization papers belonging to diverse categories are discussed for giving solid examples. At the end of the chapter, all techniques are summarized, compared and commented.

22.1. Introduction

The geographical location information of each sensor node in the network is critical for many applications,[1,2] such as battle field detection,[3,4] animal habitat monitoring,[5,6] environment data collection[4,7,8] and etc. This is because users need to know not only what happened, but also where interested events happened. For example, in the battle field detection application scenario, the knowledge of where the enemy comes from can be much more critical than only knowing the appearance of the enemy. In addition, some routing protocols[9–11] are built under the assumption that geographic parameters of sensor nodes are available for routing table building. However, sensor node localization is in fact still one of the challenging open problems, because of extremely demanding requirements for low cost, tiny size and high energy efficiency at the sensor node side. For instance, due to cost and energy issues, GPS, which is the most widely used technique in localization, can hardly be applicable for every sensor node in the networks.

Many excellent ideas[12–53] have been proposed for addressing node positioning in sensor networks. Most of them can be categorized into three classes: (i) range-based localization,[15–33] (ii) range-free localization,[34–47] and (iii) event-driven localization.[48–53]

Range-based localization approaches are built on top of distance or angle measurements among sensor nodes in the networks. Range-based methods either are costly for using per-node ranging hardware, or requiring careful in-field calibration and environment profiling.[36,41,54,55]

Range-free sensor node localization does not need any forms of ranging. Instead, the location of each node is estimated based on the knowledge of proximity to the anchor/beacom nodes whose location information is known.[35–37] Range-free localization methods normally have low accuracy, highly depending on the density and distribution of the anchor nodes.

Event-driven localization makes use of localization events which are generated and propagate across the area where sensor networks are deployed. With known time-spatial relationship embedded in the event distribution, the location of each sensor node can be obtained by mapping the time of event detection with the event position at that time instance. Since sensor nodes only need to detect the events and report the detections, event-driven approaches apply an asymmetric system architecture[49] which significantly reduces the cost and energy consumption at the resource constrained sensor node side.

In the following sections of this chapter, typical solutions for the three categories of localization methods will be briefly introduced, followed by a comparison summary.

22.2. Ranging-Based Localization

Range-based localization systems, such as GPS,[56] Cricket,[18] AHLoS,[21] AOA,[25] Robust Quadrilaterals[57] and Sweeps,[28] have been put into research and practical usage for a relatively long time comparing with ranging-free and event-driven localization systems. The methodology of range-based localization is trying to do ranging among in-field sensor nodes. Namely, ranging-based localization is based on fine-grained point-to-point distance or angle estimation for identifying per-node location. After obtaining ranging results, e.g., distance or angle measurements, geographical calculations can be applied for computing the final position of each target sensor node.

In the following subsections, four types of ranging-based sensor node localization approaches are explained, which are (i) signal strength based ranging, (ii) angle triangulation, (iii) TOA(time of arrival)/TDOA(time difference of arrival) based ranging, and (iv) other ranging methods.

Signal strength based ranging[16,57–62] is a commonly used technique for localization. According to the received signal strength and the signal propagation model, the distance between the transmitter and the receiver can be estimated. As a typical example, RADAR[16](Radar: An In-building RF-based User Location and Tracking System) is an early but famous work for localizing the sensor nodes based on radio RSSI (Receive Signal Strength Indicator) measurements.

Angle triangulation[19,25–27] need node pair angle measurements rather than distance measurement. Giving the bearing measurements, triangulation techniques can be used for coordinates computation. AOA[25] (Ad Hoc Positioning Systems (APS) using AOA) is an good example for systems using angle triangulation.

The basic idea for TOA/TDOA[63–65] based method is to estimate the distance between the signal transmitter and the receiver through the signal time-of-fly measurements, given the signal propagation speed. Cricket[18] (The Cricket Location-Support System) applies TDOA (Time Difference of Arrival) techniques and achieves good system accurate.

The paper Doppler[66] (Tracking mobile nodes using RF Doppler shifts) estimates the velocity (movement vector) of the mobile target sensor node according to doppler effects.

In fact, the measurements of signal strength (RSSI), time delay (TOA/TDOA) and velocity speed are only different formats/modalities for distance estimation. After obtaining distance or angle measurements, which are equivalent in geometry, the position parameters can be calculated by geographic computation, which are actually independent with specific ranging methodology.

22.2.1. *Radar: An in-building RF-based user location and tracking system*[16]

RADAR[16] is an indoor localization and tracking systemRF signal strength is used to indicate the distance between the sender and the receiver. This distance information is used to locate the mobile host by triangulation.

Multiple base stations are placed in this system to provide overlapping coverage in the desired area. Every base station periodically broadcasts beacon messages. The mobile device records the base stations' signal strength and sends this information back to base station. Base station estimates the mobile device's location based on the empirical measurements and signal propagation model so as to provide location-aware services and applications.

This procedure can be reversed in a system with more number of base stations than mobile hosts. As shown in Fig. 22.1, three base stations are deployed in different places, the mobile host periodically broadcasts beacons and the base stations record the signal strength information. Since RADAR does not assume the symmetry of signal strength, the above two approaches won't affect the accuracy of the location and tracking.

During the empirical measurement experiment, the information of signal strength and signal to noise ratio are recorded for four different directions at

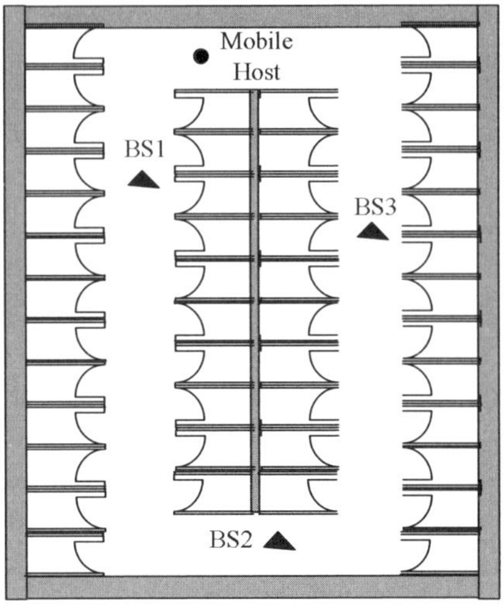

Fig. 22.1. The RADAR system overview.

seventy distinct physical locations. These information can be represented in the form (x, y, d, ss_i, snr_i), where $i \in \{1, 2, 3\}$ corresponding to the three base stations. Sample mean is used to summarize multiple signal strength samples from a base station.

Two approaches are proposed to determine the best match of the location and orientation of the mobile host for a given set of signal strength measurements. One is the empirical method, which uses the location and signal strength data during the off-line empirical measurement. The other method is the signal propagation modeling, which considers the effects of obstacles or walls between the transmitter and the receiver.

In order to estimate the mobile host's location, RADAR uses the *Euclidean distance* to measure the distance between the observed set of signal strength measurements and the recorded signal strength at a set of locations, then choose the one with the minimum distance.

By using the empirical method, the RADAR system can estimate the mobile host's location with very high accuracy. The median distance error is from 2 to 3 meters. But it requires to construct the signal strength data set for the physical environment that the system is deployed. Moreover, when the location of a base station or the physical environment is changed, the data collection process needs to be done again. While the signal propagation modeling approach can address this issue. Although it is not as accurate as the empirical method, it does not need detailed empirical measurements, which makes it easier to be deployed.

The indoor environment changes dynamically, various number of people inside the building could also affect the RF signal strength. So more sophisticated method needs be investigated to improve the system robustness and accuracy. One approach is to record multiple sets of signal strength at different times of the day, then the base stations can perform the matching for the newly received signal strength with those pre-recorded data sets.

The design of RADAR provides an indoor localization and tracking system. Unlike the infrared wireless networks approach, RADAR provides ubiquitous coverage with high accuracy. Both the empirically-determined and theoretically-computed signal strength information is used to triangulate the mobile host's coordinates.

22.2.2. *Ad hoc positioning systems (APS) using AOA*[37]

AOA[25] is a method to determine the orientation and position of all the nodes inside the ad-hoc network. It is under the assumption that each node has angle of arrival (AOA) measurement capability, which requires either an antenna array, or several ultrasound receivers.

Figure 22.2 illustrates how AOA works. Assume node A, B, and C already know their coordinates, node D needs to identify its own location. If node D knows node A, B, and C's coordinates together with the angles $\widehat{BDA}$, $\widehat{ADC}$, and $\widehat{CDB}$, it can calculate its position using triangulation.

In ad-hoc networks, some nodes may be far away from the landmarks. They can only communicate with their immediate neighbors. Orientation forwarding scheme is proposed to propagate the orientation to these nodes. Here orientation means radial, bearing, or both. The term *bearing* refers to the measured angle respect to the other object. Orientation forwarding scheme works as follows: First, the nodes that are immediate neighbors of the landmarks get their bearing/radials directly from the landmarks. Then for the nodes that are not the landmarks' immediate neighbors, they will use the method shown in Fig. 22.3 to get their own orientation. The thick black arrow represents the heading of the node. Here we assume that node A, B and C are neighbors of each other. B and C already know their bearings

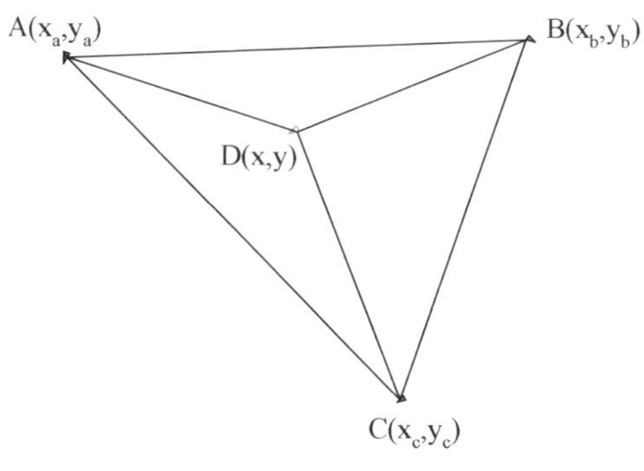

Fig. 22.2. Positioning by triangulation.

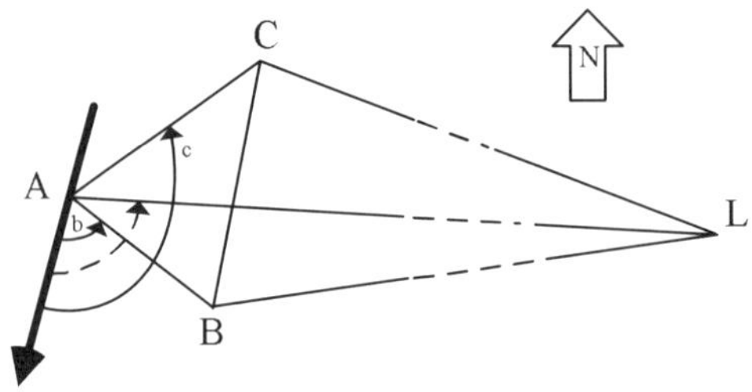

Fig. 22.3. Node A infers its bearing to L.

respect to landmark L, which is far away from B and C. If node A knows its bearings to B and C (angles $\hat{b}$ and $\hat{c}$), then A can calculate all the angles in triangles $\triangle ABC$ and $\triangle BCL$. Furthermore, A can get its bearing with respect to L as $\hat{c} + \widehat{LAC}$. After A getting its orientation, A will propagate this information to its neighbors that have not got their orientations.

Using the orientation forwarding scheme, measurement errors also get propagated. Two methods can be used for reducing the error propagation. One is to use the TTL scheme for the distance vector packets, the other is to use a threshold value to eliminate triangles that have small angles.

The design of AOA provides a method for the nodes to infer their absolute coordinates and absolute orientations in an ad hoc network by communicating with their immediate neighbors. It does not require any additional infrastructure. Since AOA uses localized communication protocol, it is scalable to very large networks. The error propagated during orientation forwarding is a major issue that affect the accuracy of the nodes' position and orientation.

22.2.3. *The Cricket location-support system*[18]

Cricket[18] is a location-support system for indoor location dependent applications. The beacon nodes periodically sends out combined RF and ultrasound signals. Based on the time difference of arrival between the RF and ultrasound signals at the receiver side, the receiver can calculate its own location. It achieves five design goals: user privacy, decentralized administration, network heterogeneity, low cost, and portion-of-a-room granularity.

The idea of using the signal time-of-flight for distance measurement is intuitive, however in order to make the system work well, there are a lot of issues need to be addressed. First of all, the system is designed to be a decentralized beacon network. Due to being lack of coordination, the RF transmissions from different beacons may collide with each other. This issue is addressed by introducing randomness during the time of beacon transmission.

Since the ultrasonic signals sent out by different beacons are the same, the receiver may perform false correlation between the RF signal and the neighboring beacon's ultrasound. The second challenge is to minimize the RF and ultrasonic interference among neighboring beacons. Two methods are used to address this issue. One is to select proper system parameters to reduce the incorrect correlation, the other is to use listener inference algorithms, which includes three simple algorithms: Majority, MinMean, and MinMode.

In order to ensure the listeners to make the correct judgement of their locations, it's important to place a beacon in an appropriate location. Figure 22.4 shows that the listener in Room B may think it is in Room A, since the beacon in Room A is closer to the listener. Centralized solution may overcome this issue, but it needs the listener provides its own information, which may expose the user privacy.

Figure 22.5 shows a simple engineering solution, which preserves the user privacy and suitable for the autonomously managed environment. The beacon is placed in a location that has fixed distance to the physical or virtual boundary that demarcate two spaces. Such placement ensures the listener to make correct choice when the listener's distance from the boundary is larger than 1 foot.

Comparing to other location-tracking systems such as Bat,[29] Active Badge,[67] and RADAR,[16] Cricket provides location-support service. It preserves user privacy.

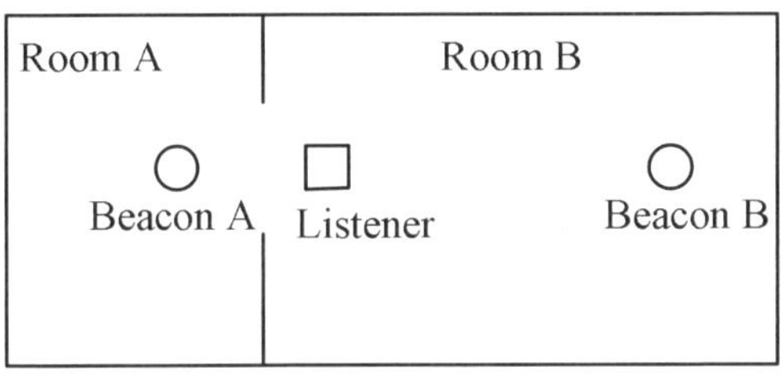

Fig. 22.4. Wrong positioning of beacons.

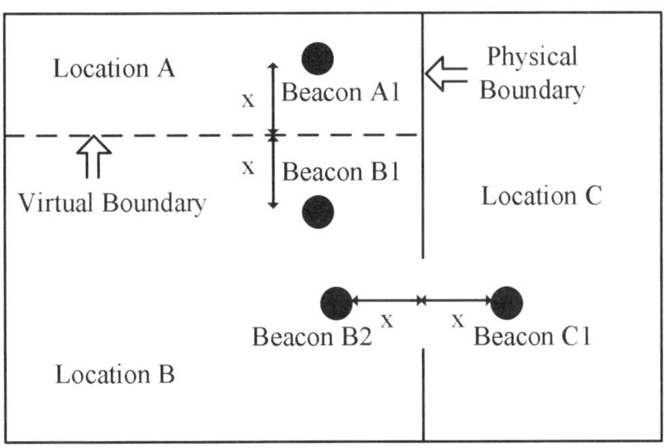

Fig. 22.5. Correct positioning of beacons.

Its decentralized approach makes the system easier to be managed. It also has a lot of other advantages, such as network heterogeneity, easy to deploy, and low cost. Each component only costs $10. Since it uses time difference of arrival method to localize the mobile host, the speed of the tracked mobile host can not be very fast. Moreover, it can not identify the orientation of the tracked device.

22.2.4. *Tracking mobile nodes using RF doppler shifts*[66]

Doppler Shift Localization[66] is a ranging-based localization for mobile nodes (i.e., tracking) in sensor networks. The main idea of Doppler Shift Localization is to use the RF Doppler shifts at stationary anchor nodes (called infrastructure nodes) for the estimation of the location and velocity of a mobile node. In order to mitigate the measurement error and deal with abrupt motion change, Doppler Shift Localization adopts the combination of Constrained Non-linear Least Squares (CNLS) and Extended Kalman Filter (EKF).[66] Figure 22.6 shows the mobile node localization based on the RF Doppler Shift measurement. As shown in Fig. 22.6(a), a mobile node T and an anchor node A transmit RF signals of frequencies f_t and f_a, respectively. Six anchor nodes from S_1 to S_6 measures the Doppler shift of the interference signal of the frequencies f_t and f_a at their RF receiver. The arrow from each anchor node indicates the vector for the relative speed of S_i and T. With the Doppler shifts and relative speeds of these anchor nodes along with the moving node's speed, Doppler Shift Localization can localize the location of the mobile node according to its movement. Figure 22.6(b) shows the estimation of the velocity at each anchor node after the mobile node moves further. The magnitude of the Doppler shifts measured by S_i depends of the relative speed of S_i and T, which can be calculated by projecting the mobile node's velocity $\overrightarrow{v}$ on the line $\overline{TS_i}$. The length of the projected vectors is determined by both the velocity vector $\overrightarrow{v}$ and

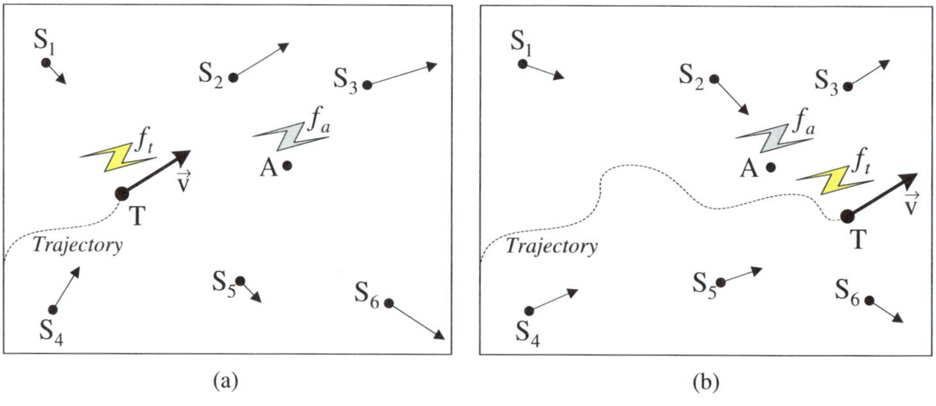

Fig. 22.6. Mobile node localization based on doppler shift measurement.

the location of T. Thus, the velocity vectors at anchor nodes are different between Figs. 22.6(a) and 22.6(b).

Doppler Shift Localization has the following assumptions: (i) The tracked node cooperates with the tracking system for trivial detection; (ii) The locations of the infrastructure nodes are known as stationary anchor nodes; and (iii) The tracked node and the infrastructure nodes are time-synchronized at an relatively accurate level, such as a few microseconds.

Doppler Shift Localization consists of three phases: (i) Coordination phase; (ii) Measurement Phase; and (iii) Tracking Phase. During the *coordination phase*, infrastructure nodes are notified to take part in the mobile node tracking in a certain region. They are time-synchronized to allow for the data fusion for the tracking. During the *measurement phase*, the ranging measurement is performed for the Doppler shifts and relative speeds at the anchor nodes which are low-cost sensors, such as Mica2 motes. During the *tracking phase*, the estimation of the location and velocity of the mobile node is performed based on an Extended Kalman Filter (EKF). When an abrupt change of motion is detected, the Kalman filter state is updated through the Constrained Non-linear Least Squares (CNLS) optimization with the last collected measurements.

Measuring Doppler shifts is a key function in the Doppler Shift Localization. The low sampling rate due to the sensor hardware limitation decreases the frequency of the interference signal, leading to the smaller Doppler shift. Thus, in order to reduce the inaccuracy caused by this smaller Doppler shift, the Doppler Shift Localization proposes a *radio interferometry* to indirectly analyze high frequency radio signals with low-cost sensors.[66] As shown in Fig. 22.6(a), the mobile node T transmits an unmodulated sine wave at frequency f_t and an anchor node A transmits a sine wave at frequency f_a, such that $f_t > f_a$. These two signals interfere with each other and become an interference signal with an envelope frequency of $f_t - f_a$. The signal transmitted by T will be Doppler shifted by Δf_t^i at each anchor node S_i. The measured envelope frequency f_i of the interference signal at S_i is $f_i = f_t - f_a + \Delta f_t^i$ such that Δf_t^i is the Doppler shift and the magnitude of Δf_t^i depends on the relative speed of S_i and T. Due to measurement errors for f_i, the Doppler Shift Localization estimates the location and speed vector of the mobile node by a *non-linear optimization* method called Constrained Non-linear Least Squares (CNLS).

The Doppler Shift Localization provides the tracking more accurate than a simple Extended Kalman Filter (EKF). The EKF provides the good tracking when the mobile node moves at a constant speed without any change of its direction. However, when the mobile node changes its speed and direction dramatically, EKF does not work well. Therefore, the Doppler Shift Localization updates the Kalman filter state for the mobile node tracking using only EKF. On the other hand, when the abrupt change of the movement (called *maneuver*) is detected, a new Kalman filter state is calculated by the CNLS optimization and is used to update the Kalman filter state at EKF. This EKF-CNLS algorithm improves the tracking accuracy by as much as 50% of the regular EKF.

The Doppler Shift Localization can provide more accurate localization of products in a warehouse than passive RFID system providing only the proximity to a reader. Another advantage of the Doppler Shift Localization can easily support the multiple target tracking. The multiple target tracking is possible by letting each tracked node transmit the RF signal at a unique frequency. Therefore, the Doppler Shift Localization is an efficient, indoor/outdoor localization scheme for a cooperative mobile node, transmitting an RF signal for localization.

22.2.5. *Remarks for ranging-based localization*

As it shows in previous sections, AOA and Cricket systems both need special additional hardware such as ultrasound/infrared transmitter/receiver for ranging purpose. Per-node ranging device is costly and energy hungry. Therefore, as in the RADAR and Doppler systems, many range-based methods tried to eliminate expensive or energy hungry ranging devices by assuming and using RSSI[16,20,24,41,68] with noise filtering and many other advanced algorithms[22,69–73] for mitigating errors brought about by multi-path fading, background interference and irregular signal propagation. However, recent empirical study[20,55,74,75] concluded that unless careful calibration and environment profiling can be accomplished, radio ranging irregularity[36,41,55,75] is detrimental to the system accuracy.

In addition, ranging signals generated by sensor nodes have a very limited effective range because of energy and form factor concerns. For example, ultrasound signals usually effectively propagate 20–30 feet using an on-board transmitter.[18] Consequently, these range-based solutions require an undesirably high deployment density.

All in all, constraints on the cost, energy and hardware footprint of each sensor node make these range-based methods undesirable for massive outdoor deployment.

22.3. Ranging-Free Localization

Range-free solutions[34–38,41] try to estimate the location of each sensor node based on the information of geographic proximity to the anchor nodes whose positions are known. In those solutions, sensor nodes estimate their locations according to the known position information of the surrounding anchor nodes. Different anchor combinations help to narrow the location area where a normal node possibly be located. Anchor-based approaches normally demand high and uniformly distributed anchor density in the network so as to achieve good positioning accuracy. In reality, it is highly appreciated to use as few anchor nodes as possible in order to reduce system cost. Different from some early IR or magnetic sensor based systems,[67,76–79] newly proposed methods get rid of additional proximity sensing hardware, while only RF is used.

In the following, five ranging-free sensor node localization approaches are briefly introduced, which are Centroid[35](GPS-Less Low Cost Outdoor Localization for Very Small Devices), APIT[36] (Rang-free Localization Schemes in large-scale Sensor Networks), Connectivity-MDS[41] (Localization from Mere Connectivity), APS[37] (Ad-hoc Positioning Systems), and Waling GPS[80] (Walking GPS: A practical Solution for Localization in Manually Deployed Wireless Sensor Networks).

Centroid and APIT both make use of the proximity information with surrounding stationary position know sensor nodes (anchor or beacon nodes). Connectivity-MDS computes an optimal estimation of the relative node topology based on mere connectivity info among sensor nodes. APS estimates the geographic distance among sensor nodes using number of communication hops[42,43] (DV-Hop), and Walking GPS illustrates a simple but effective localization method: using mobile beacons.[59–61,81–83]

22.3.1. *GPS-less low cost outdoor localization for very small devices*[35]

Centroid[35] is an early work for sensor node localization. The idea proposed in this paper is very straight forward. The target sensor node selects k neighboring anchor nodes (k is a variable) with most reliable communication link quality. Then the location of the target sensor node is calculated as the gravity center of all the selected k anchor nodes, as shown by the following equation.

$$(X_{est}, Y_{est}) = \left(\frac{X_1 + X_2 + \cdots + X_k}{k}, \frac{Y_1 + Y_2 + \cdots + Y_k}{k}\right).$$

22.3.2. *Ranging-free localization schemes in large-scale sensor networks*[36]

This paper, namely APIT,[36] presents a ranging-free localization for large scale sensor networks. The main idea of APIT is to perform sensor location estimation by isolating the target area into *triangular regions* among beacon nodes.

Figure 22.7 shows the area-based APIT algorithm. A sensor node receives beacon messages from the beacon nodes that are anchors. The sensor makes all possible triangles with three anchors among all of the perceived anchors. As shown in Fig. 22.7, the maximum overlapping area for the sensor node is computed at first; this intersection area is considered as the possible area where the sensor node is located. APIT then decides the center of gravity of this intersection area as the position of the sensor node.

APIT has the following assumptions: (i) Anchor nodes with location information are deployed along with non-anchor nodes; (ii) the node density is relatively high

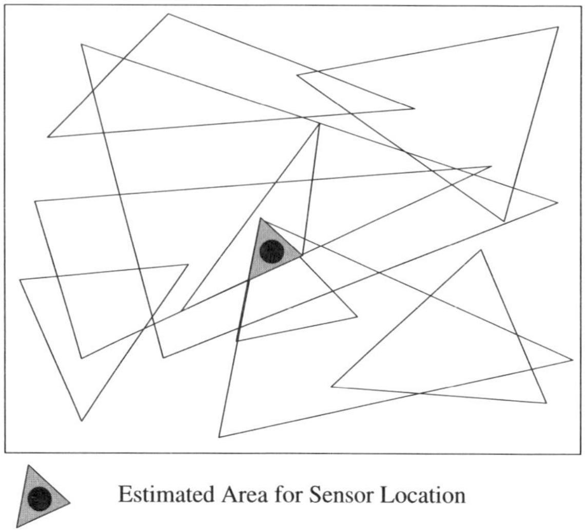

Fig. 22.7. Area-based APIT localization.

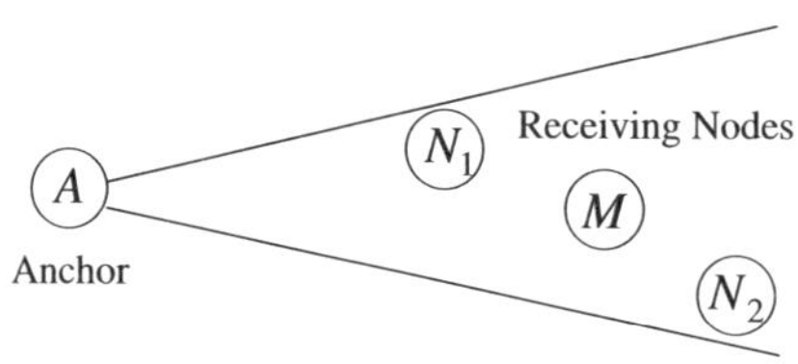

Fig. 22.8. Departure test for measuring the relative distance.

with connectivity above 6; and (iii) the beacon signal strength attenuates monotonically as the distance between the anchor and the non-anchor increases.

APIT consists of three steps: (i) the Departure Test; (ii) the Approximate Point-In-Triangulation Test (APIT); and (iii) APIT Aggregation. The *departure test* is to check whether a node is further away from an anchor than a neighbor. Figure 22.8 shows the departure test. This test is based on the observation that the received beacon signal strength at a node is monotonically decreasing according to the distance from an anchor. In Fig. 22.8, node M has weaker signal strength for the beacon from anchor A than neighbor N_1, but it has stronger signal strength than neighbor N_2. The *APIT test* determines whether a node is inside the triangle for three anchors or not. Figure 22.9 shows the *APIT test*;[36] if node M has no neighbor simultaneously *further from/closer to* all three anchors A, B and C consisting of a triangle, M is assumed to be inside triangle $\triangle ABC$. Otherwise, M is assumed to be outside this triangle. Figure 22.9(a) illustrates an example that M is inside $\triangle ABC$ and Fig. 22.9(b) illustrates an example that M is outside $\triangle ABC$.

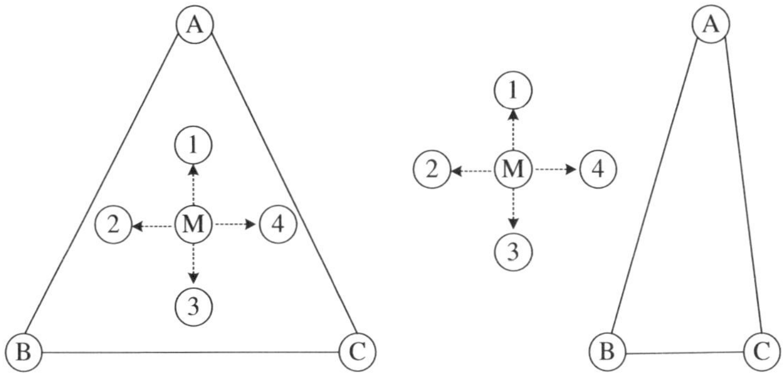

(a) Inside Case (b) Outside Case

Fig. 22.9. APIT test for checking the node's position for anchor triangle.

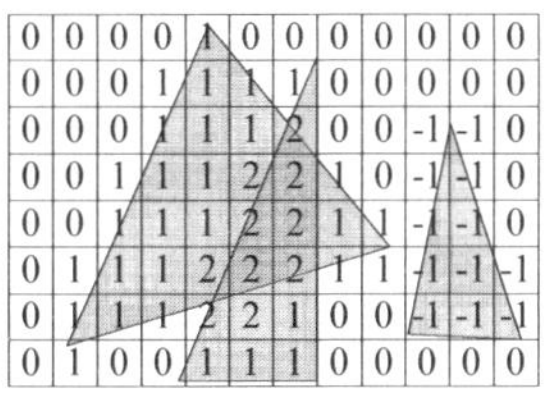

Fig. 22.10. APIT aggregation based on scan for determining the maximum overlapping area.

APIT can make mistake in this APIT test due to both the *edge effect* of node M and the *irregular placement* of neighbors. This problem requires a more robust APIT test. APIT provides a more robust APIT test through the aggregation of multiple APIT tests; this APIT test is called *APIT aggregation*. Figure 22.10 shows the APIT aggregation based on a grid SCAN algorithm; for each APIT inside decision, the values of the grid regions are incremented, but for each APIT outside decision, those of the grid regions are decremented. For all of the possible triangles, the APIT test is performed for each grid region and then the maximum overlapping area is obtained. As shown in Fig. 22.10, the aggregated area of grid regions with value 2 is the maximum overlapping area. Finally, we can determine the sensor's location with the center of gravity for this maximum overlapping area.

APIT targets at the localization of a static sensor network with high node density. The trade-off exists between the node density and the localization accuracy. Through the aggregated decisions based on this high node density, APIT can provide the good estimation for node location even under the noisy environment for individual APIT test. In order to reduce the cost of the anchor deployment, APIT can use a single moving anchor advertising the beacons at different locations. Therefore, APIT is a range-free localization appropriate to a dense sensor network allowing the coarse accuracy in node location.

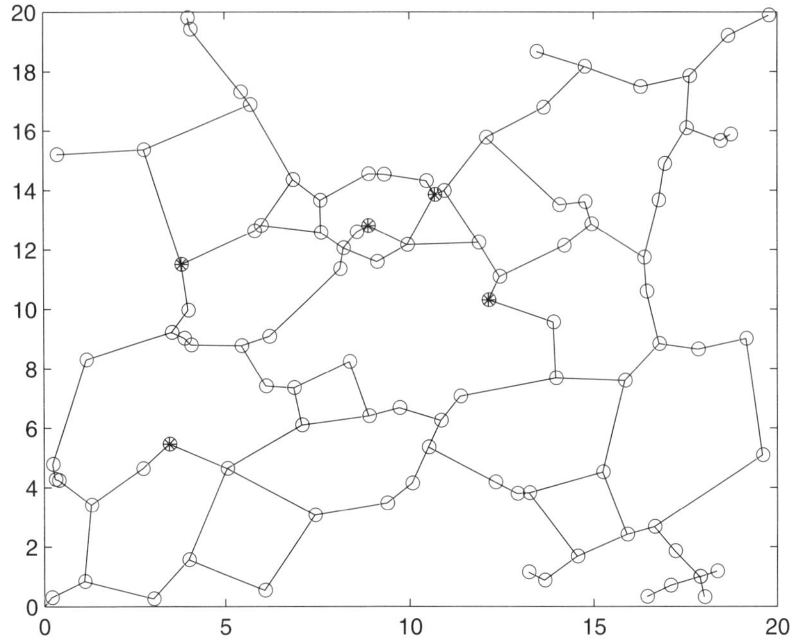

Fig. 22.11. Original graph.

22.3.3. *Localization from mere connectivity*[39]

Localization from Mere Connectivity[39] (Connectivity-MDS) is a centralized algorithm that derives the locations of sensor nodes using only connectivity information. Localization from mere connectivity is based on the classical metric multidimensional scaling (MDS), a data analysis technique from mathematical psychology. It works well when there are very few anchor nodes, without constraints on where those anchor nodes are located. Connectivity-MDS can also make use of additional information such as estimated distance between each pair of nodes when it is available.

In Connectivity-MDS, the network is represented by an undirected graph with vertices V and edges E. If estimated distances between neighboring nodes are available, entries in E are associated with such information. Otherwise E only provides connectivity information and consists of only 1s and 0s. As shown in Fig. 22.11 where a hundred nodes are placed randomly in a 20×20 field, the all-pairs shortest path matrix P can be computed using E, either by Dijkstra's or Floyd's algorithm.

The relative graph in Fig. 22.12 is then obtained by applying classical MDS to P. In classical MDS, P is firstly converted into a double centered matrix B:

$$B = -\frac{1}{2}\left(I - \frac{1}{N}U\right) P^2 \left(I - \frac{1}{N}\right) U,$$

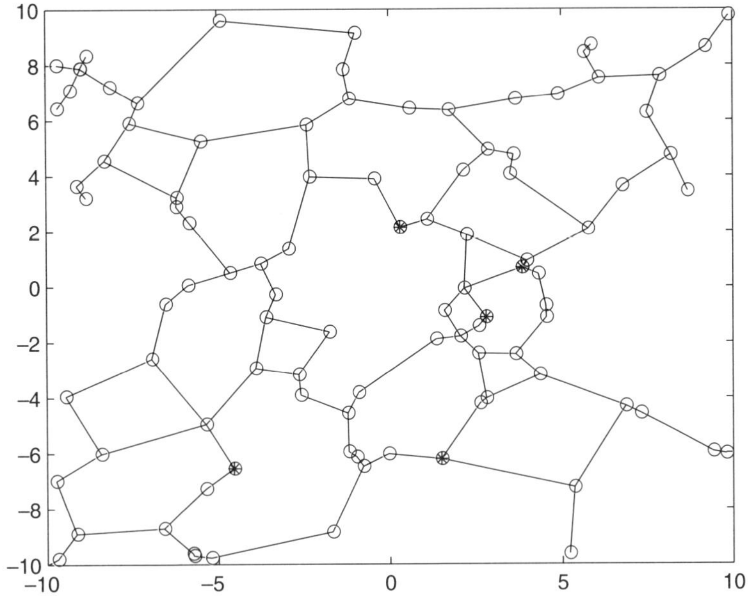

Fig. 22.12. Relative graph.

where N is the number of nodes and U is a $N \times N$ matrix with all 1s. Then the coordinates of the nodes X is computed by taking the Singular Value Decomposition (SVD) of B:

$$\begin{aligned} B &= VAV^T \\ X &= VA^{\frac{1}{2}} \end{aligned} .$$

From Fig. 22.12, the relative graph is shifted and rotated compared with the original graph. With the known location of the anchor nodes (the solid dots in the figure), the relative graph can be finally transformed to the final graph.

The complexity of Connectivity-MDS is $O(n^3)$. Since it requires very few anchor nodes which are not necessarily well-deployed, it is a promising localization algorithm. However, it has certain limitations. It requires global information of the network since it is centralized. One way to solve this problem might be dividing the network into several sub-networks with three or more anchors within each sub-network. By putting all patches together the final locations of all nodes can be derived. Another drawback is that the performance degrades when the number of anchor nodes is large. One possible solution is to use more advanced MDS algorithm such as anchor point method.

22.3.4. *Ad-hoc positioning systems*[37]

In APS,[37] a distributed, hop by hop algorithm named Ad-hoc Positioning System (APS) is proposed to locate sensor nodes within the network. Using the similar idea

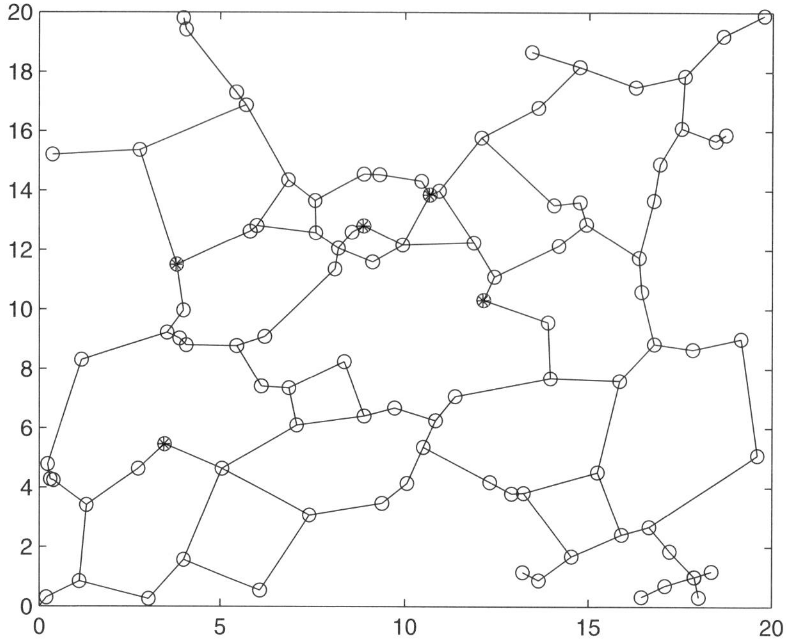

Fig. 22.13. Final absolute graph.

as GPS, APS requires a number of anchor nodes with known location information. Each node estimates its distance to at least three of those anchor nodes by communicating only with its neighbors, and computes its own position by solving linear systems iteratively.

In the paper, three methods are proposed to estimate the distance from a node to an anchor node: "DV-hop", "DV-Distance" and "Euclidean" propagation methods.

"DV-hop" works for isotropic network where the properties of the network are the same in all directions, thus distance between node pair is proportional to communication hop count. In "DV-hop", each node maintains a table with the positions of each local anchor and the least number of hops from each anchor to itself. By exchanging tables with its neighbors, the positions of all local anchor nodes are available in the table, as well as the number of hops away from each anchor. Then each anchor node computes the average number of hops in each direction and distribute such information by controlled flooding, where a node only reads and forwards its first message and ignores all subsequences. An example is shown in Fig. 22.14. In this figure, A_1, A_2 and A_3 are three anchor nodes. A_1 is 2 hops away from A_2 and 5 hops away from A_3 so that it computes the average size of each hop as $\frac{40m+105m}{2+5} = 20.7m$. Similarly, A_2 and A_3 computes the average size of each hop as $\frac{40m+60m}{2+3} = 20m$ and $\frac{60m+105m}{3+5} = 20.6m$. All anchors then distribute their estimation to the nodes within the network. Suppose node B receives A_3's result

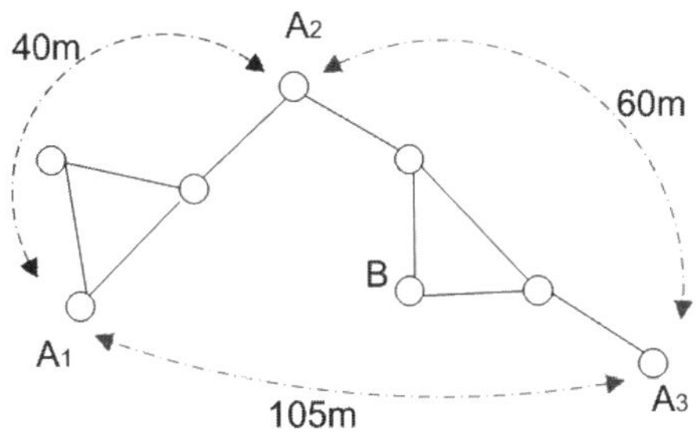

Fig. 22.14. The idea of DV-Hop.

first, which is $20.6m$. Using this information, B can finally compute its distance from all anchor nodes in its table.

The second method, "DV-Distance", has the similar idea but measures distance between neighboring nodes directly and propagates distance information in meters instead of in hops. It benefits from the fact that hop count is not necessarily proportional to the real distance. However, it is more sensitive to measurement errors.

The third method, "Euclidean" works well when the topology is non-isotropic. It propagates true Euclidean distance to the anchor node and works only when a node has at least two neighbor nodes that have already had the estimation of distance from a anchor and their distance is also known. By applying Pithagora's generalized theorem a node can finally estimate its distance from this anchor.

After the distances from several anchors becoming available, a node starts to use the GPS triangulation method to compute its own position. It starts with an initial estimated position and computes the position correction based on the comparison between the distance table and the distance from its current estimated position to all anchors. In each iteration, a linear system is solved by any least square method such as Householder method. The process stops when the position correction is below a certain threshold.

APS has several advantages. First, it is distributed, thus requires no global information and special infrastructure. Second, the propagation methods only require a node to communicate with its immediate neighbors, hence have a low signaling complexity and energy consumption.

22.3.5. *Walking GPS: A practical solution for localization in manually deployed wireless sensor networks*[80]

Walking GPS[80] is a practical and cost effective solution for manually deployed wireless sensor networks. In walking GPS, the deployer (either a person or a vehicle) is equipped with a GPS device which periodically sends broadcasting messages with its current location information. Sensor nodes can then infer their current positions by receiving these messages.

The Walking GPS system consists of two components: the GPS Mote and the Sensor Mote. The GPS Mote receives its global GPS coordinates from the GPS device and transforms the global GPS coordinates into local coordinates in order to reduce overhead. The sending power is limited to ensure that only the nearest sensor mote receives the broadcasting message. The sending frequency is also associated with the deployment rate. The Sensor Mote, on the other hand, receives local coordinates from the GPS Mote and infer its location information from the message. If, for some reason, a Sensor Mote does not have its own position, it will query for its neighbors' positions and computes its own position by the GPS triangulation procedure.

The walking GPS supports two types of mote deployment. The first type is that each sensor mote is turned on right before its deployment, and the second deployment type is that sensor motes are turned on all the time. For the first type, sensor motes only read the first received message and find their own positions. For the second one, sensor motes should infer their deployment time from the RSSI value of received messages.

From extensive experiments, walking GPS is shown to work very well in manually deployed wireless sensor networks: all sensor motes are shown to be able to locate themselves with an average error within $2m$. However, it works only when the sensor motes are deployed manually, which limits its use in many applications.

22.3.6. *Remarks for ranging-free localization*

Ranging-free localization methods eliminate per-node ranging hardware, which reduces the overall system cost. The above five ranging-free methods illustrate three types of ranging-free approaches: (i) anchor proximity; (ii) radio connectivity; and (iii) mobile beacon. For anchor proximity based methods, normally a considerable number of anchor nodes is needed for achieving good system accuracy. Radio connectivity based solutions could be affected by the notorious fact of radio irregularity. Mobile beacon is an easy and practical solution, however, it is not applicable in many prohibitive environments where per-node manual deployment is not possible. Overall speaking, ranging-free methods are cheaper than ranging-based methods but with lower system accuracy or limited application scenarios.

22.4. Event-Driven Localization

Event-driven localization brings in localization events which are generated and propagate across the area where sensor networks are deployed. According to the pre-known time-spatial relationship embedded in the event distribution,[48,49] and the sequential detection of the event in the time domain[52,84] or in the space domain,[50] the location of each sensor node can be estimated.

In the following, four event-driven sensor node localization methods are summarized, which are SpotLight[49] (Spotlight: A High Accuracy, Low-Cost Localization System for Wireless Sensor Networks), MSP[52] (MSP: Multi-Sequence Positioning of Wireless Sensor Nodes), Uncontrolled Events[84] (Sensor Node Localization Using Uncontrolled Events), and Stardust[50] (StarDust: A Flexible Architecture for Passive Localization in Wireless Sensor Networks).

SpotLight, MSP and Uncontrolled Events forms three generations of event-driven localization solutions from preciously controlled event distribution to uncontrolled event distribution. All of the above three methods depend on the time-domain sequential detection of the localization events at the sensor node side. Stardust pinpoints the sensor nodes by processing the image of node's reaction to the flashing localization event.

22.4.1. *Spotlight: A high accuracy, low-cost localization system for wireless sensor networks*[49]

The top level idea of the Spotlight system is to remove all the expensive and energy depletion functions for the localization from the resource constrained sensor node to an external specific localization focused entity the spotlight device. As shown in Fig. 22.15, the localization device generates some from of localization events according to certain well defined "Event Function", and then it receives the detection report from the sensor nodes. According to the time-spacial relationship embedded in the "Event Function", the spotlight device is able to get the location information

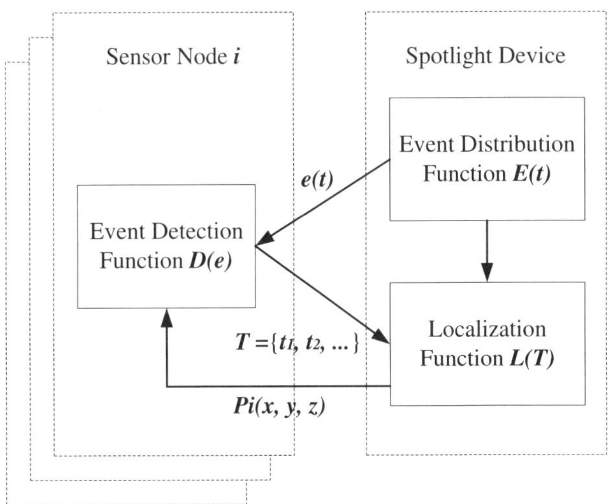

Fig. 22.15. The basic idea of Spotlight system

of each node. This location info is then feedback to those nodes, so that every node in the network obtains its location.

The asymmetric structure of the spotlight system achieves the goal of low cost of each node, which actually determines the whole cost of the network. The powerful computing capability and abundant energy supply of the spotlight device realizes the configurable high accuracy of the localization. However, in the SpotLight System, the event distribution needs to be both accurate as to time and precise about the space, which adds system cost and results in slow localization speed. Precise event distribution is difficult to achieve without careful calibration, especially when the event-generating devices require certain mechanical maneuver.

22.4.2. *MSP: Multi-sequence positioning of wireless sensor nodes*[52]

MSP[52] brings in anchor nodes for event-driven localization. Without depending on rigid time-spatial relationship carried by the localization event distribution, MSP obtains possible location area of each sensor node by processing multiple one-dimensional *node sequences* within which relative position information along the event propagation direction is embedded.

Figure 22.16 illustrates how the algorithm works. MSP works by extracting relative location information from multiple simple one-dimensional orderings of nodes.

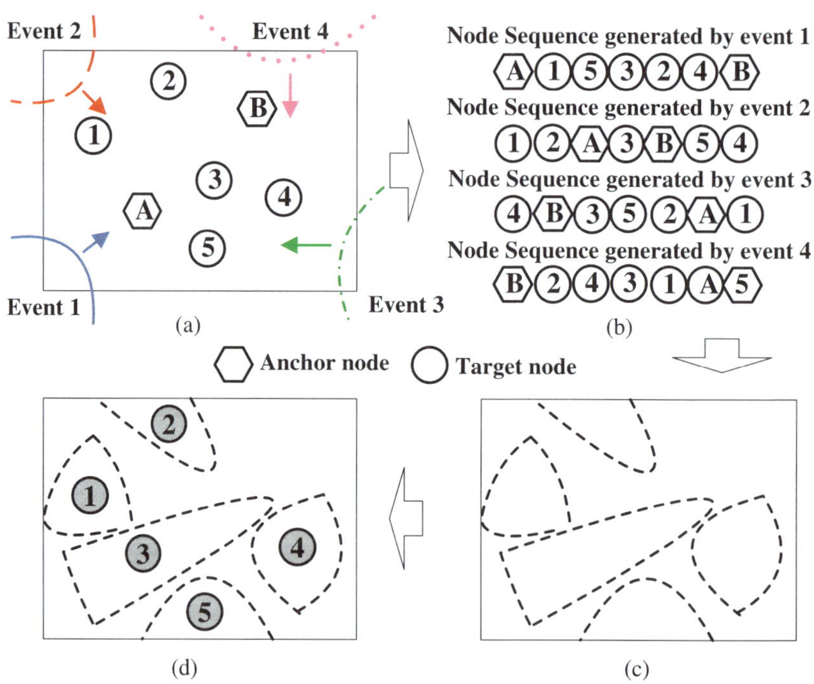

Fig. 22.16. The MSP system overview.

Figure 22.16(a) shows a layout of a sensor network with anchor nodes and target nodes. Target nodes are defined as the nodes to be localized. Briefly, the MSP system works as follows. First, events are generated one at a time in the network area (e.g., ultrasound propagations from different locations, laser scans with diverse angles). As each event propagates, as shown in Fig. 22.16(a), each node detects it at some particular time instance. For a single event, we call the ordering of nodes, which is based on the sequential detection of the event, a *node sequence*. Each node sequence includes both the targets and the anchors as shown in Fig. 22.16(b). Second, a multi-sequence processing algorithm helps to narrow the possible location of each node to a small area (Fig. 22.16(c)). Finally, a distribution-based estimation method estimates the exact location of each sensor node, as shown in Fig. 22.16(d).

In MSP, each localization event generates one node sequence and each node sequence gives out an partition of the whole area. The whole area can be divided into $O(N^2d^2)$ parts with N anchors and d events. Therefore, with sufficient events and anchors, accurate positioning is achievable. Figure 22.17 shows an example of two nodes sequences created by straight line scan events. Anchor nodes (location

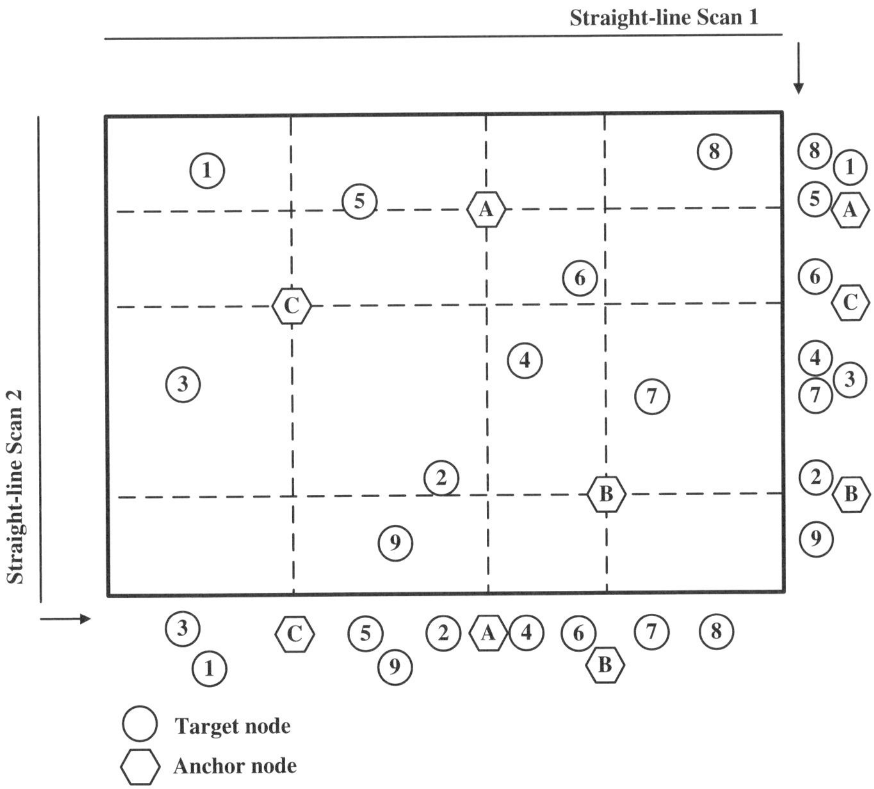

Fig. 22.17. Node sequence and map partition.

pre-known) in two node sequences split the area into 16 small parts, and each target node (needs to be localized) gets its location area according to its ranking in the node sequence.

Several improvements concerning node sequence processing are proposed in the MSP paper, such as Sequence-Based MSP, Iterative MSP, Distribution-Based Estimation and Adaptive MSP, all of which works together enhances the accuracy of the localization results.

The design of MSP provides a trade off between the physical cost (anchors) and soft cost (localization event). So only a few number of anchor nodes are necessary. In addition, the requirement for accurate event distribution control is removed. However, the setup of MSP assumes that accurate control of the event generation is available, e.g., straight-line scan with certain angle. Therefore, MSP is actually a hybrid solution combining anchors and semi-controlled localization events.

22.4.3. *Sensor node localization using uncontrolled events*[84]

The setup of MSP assumes that accurate control of the event generation is available, e.g., straight-line scan with certain angle. In a practical system, control over event generation could be costly and hard. Uncontrolled events proposed a sensor node localization system design based on totally uncontrolled events. This solution eliminates the control over event generation and event distribution. Therefore, it could significantly improve the flexibility and convenience for system deployment.

There are two levels of control over the localization events: (i) control of how to generate the event, e.g., a straight-line laser beam scan event at certain angle. This type of control is named as control of *event generation parameter*; (ii) control over event propagation, e.g., keep constant scan line-speed, which is called control of *event distribution*. For randomly generated events, neither of the above controls is possible, and in reality, both levels of control could be hard and costly to achieve.

The basic idea for localization using uncontrolled events is to estimate the event generation parameter using anchors in the field, and then shrink the possible location area of each normal node according to the estimated event parameter. In brief, as it is shown in Fig. 22.18, the system works as follows. First, certain type of events are generated in the network, e.g., straight-line laser beam scan with uncontrolled angle, direction and speed. As each event propagates, sensor nodes detect the event sequentially at different time instances, which naturally gives out an ordering of in-the-field nodes called *node sequence*. For example, as shown in Fig. 22.18(a), a top-down scan event generates node sequence (3 A 1 6 4 8 C 2 B 7 5). Here we use uppercase letters (e.g., A, B, C) denote anchor nodes and numbers (e.g., 1, 2, 3) denote normal nodes. Second, node sequences processing algorithms try to estimate the event generation parameter, e.g., possible scan angle range, by processing ordered anchor subsequences which can be extracted directly from node sequences

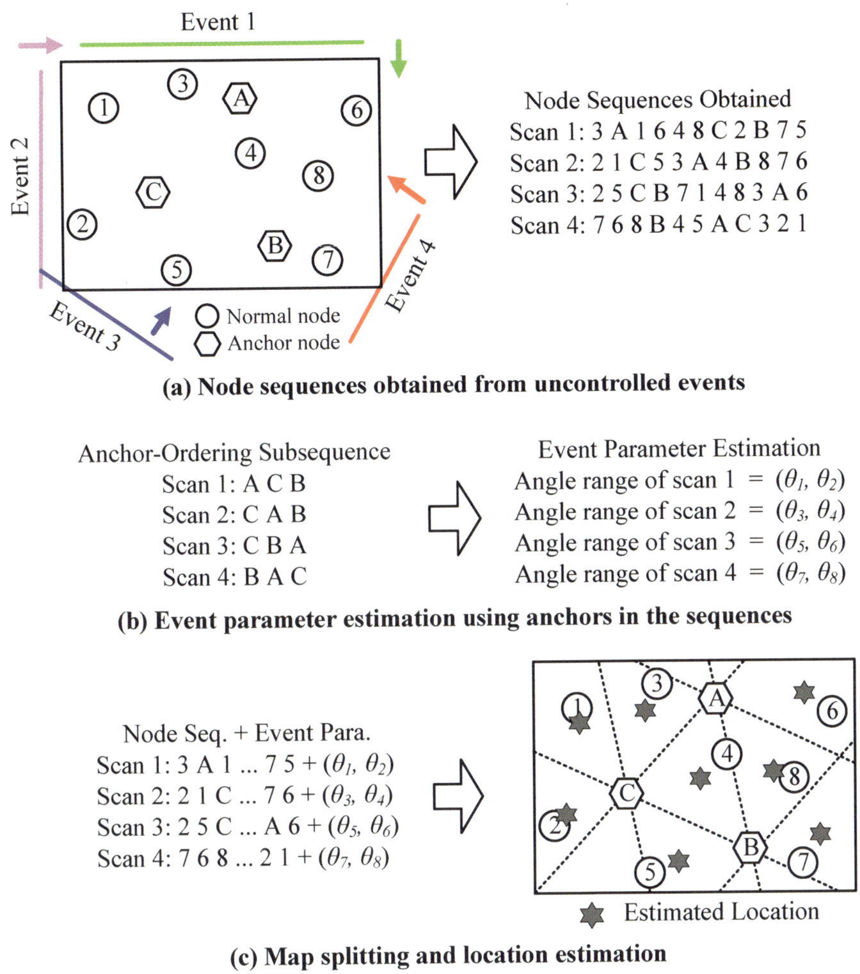

(a) Node sequences obtained from uncontrolled events

(b) Event parameter estimation using anchors in the sequences

(c) Map splitting and location estimation

Fig. 22.18. System overview.

as shown in Fig. 22.18(b). Third, processing a node sequence with its corresponding estimated event generation parameter, the whole map can be divided into lots of small parts. Each normal sensor node obtains a possible location area, which is composed of different single or multiple parts, according to their ranks in the node sequence. With multiple events, final location area of a normal node could be shrunk dramatically by extracting the joint region of the possible location areas given by all the node sequences. Thus the estimated position could be got from a relatively small location area to achieve good localization accuracy (Fig. 22.18(c)).

As the third generation of the event-driven localization method, sensor node localization using only randomly generated events provides excellent system flexibility while adding no extra cost at the resource constrained sensor node side.

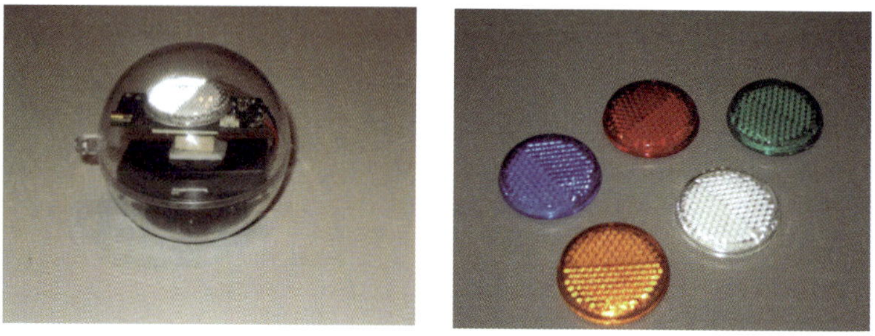

(a) (b)

Fig. 22.19. CCR and sensor nodes.

In addition, localization using uncontrolled events provides a nice potential option of achieving node positioning through natural ambient events.

22.4.4. *StarDust: A flexible architecture for passive localization in wireless sensor networks*[50]

StarDust,[50] which works much faster than all of the above three event-driven localization approaches, uses label relaxation algorithms to match *light spots* reflected by corner-cube retro-reflectors (CCR), shown in Fig. 22.19, with the sensor nodes using various kinds of constraints. Label relaxation algorithms converges only when a sufficient number of robust constraints are obtained. Due to the environmental impact on the optical event and the RF connectivity constraints, however, StarDust is less accurate than Spotlight.

Figure 22.19 shows the CCR and the sensor node used in the StarDust system. CCR can reflect the light back to its coming direction. Figure 22.20 illustrates an example of the system implementation of StarDust. Figure 22.20(a) shows an stadium in which sensor nodes are deployed. In Fig. 22.20(b), when a flashing light spot is generated to illuminate the area with sensor nodes, which is shown more clear in Fig. 22.20(c), we take a picture of this area. By computer image processing, a result shown in Fig. 22.20(d) can be obtained. This figure indicates that the locations of each sensor nodes can be determined.

Although in the paper StarDust, multiple effective solutions are provided for differentiating the sensor node in the image shown in Fig. 22.20(d), it is still a challenging problem in some scenarios.

22.4.5. *Remarks for event-driven localization*

Comparing with ranging-based and ranging-free localization methods, event-driven localization methods can achieve tradeoff between system accuracy and system flexibility, between "hard cost" (number of anchor nodes) and "soft cost" (number of localization events). As an relatively new kind of method, event-driven sensor node

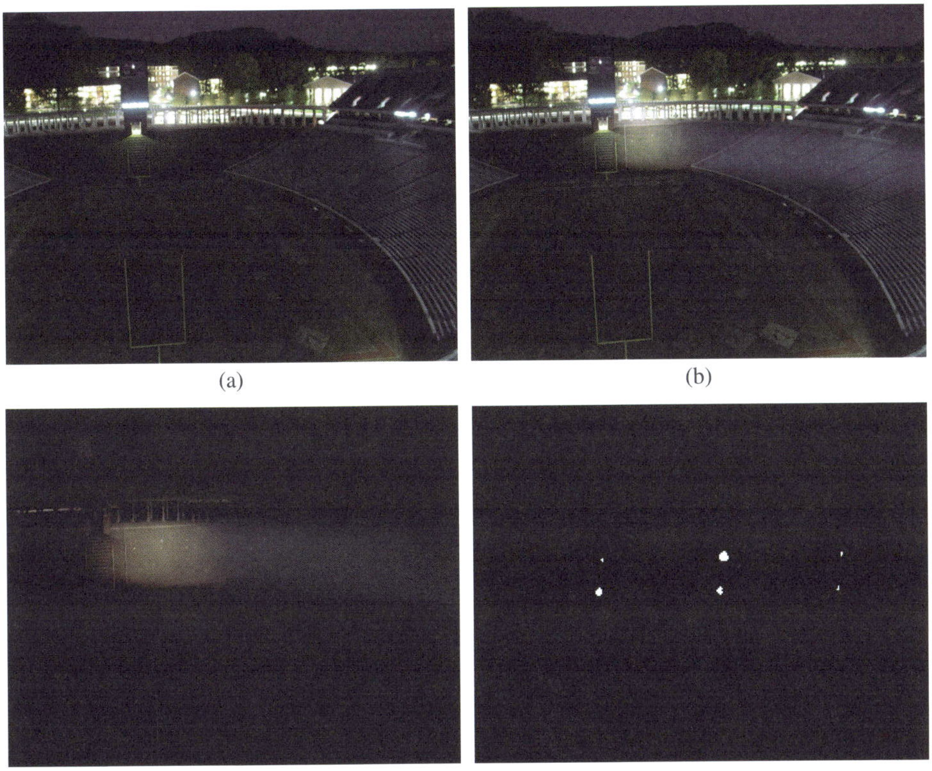

(a) (b) (c) (d)

Fig. 22.20. StarDust example system.

localization is now attracting more and more attention from the researchers and considered as the promising solution with good system flexibility.

22.5. Chapter Summary

Localizing the sensor nodes randomly deployed in the network is still an open and challenging problem in the WSN field. It is an open problem because there is not a single solution which could achieve desirable features including good accuracy, low cost, fast speed, high confidence and etc, simultaneously for all applications. It is a challenging problem because of the extremely limited resource and cost constraints at the sensor node side. This chapter introduces one kind of taxonomy for the sensor node localization methods. However, there are other approaches not belonging to any of the three classes, or crossing multiple categories. Nevertheless, any solution itself is always an issue about tradeoff between system cost and localization performance including accuracy, speed, and etc.

References

1. D. Culler, D. Estrin and M. Srivastava, Overview of sensor networks, *IEEE Computer Magazine*, **37**(8) (2004).
2. M. Gaynor, S. Moulton, M. Welsh, A. Rowan, E. LaCombe and J. Wynne, Wireless sensor network applications, *AMCIS '04* (2004).
3. A. Arora, P. Dutta, S. Bapat, V. Kulathumani, H. Zhang, V. Naik, V. Mittal, H. Cao, M. Demirbas, M. Gouda, Y. Choi, T. Herman, S. Kulkarni, U. Arumugam, M. Nesterenko, A. Vora and M. Miyashita, A line in the sand: A wireless sensor network for target detection, classification, and tracking, *Comput. Netw.* **46**(5), 605–634 (2004). ISSN 1389-1286. http://dx.doi.org/10.1016/j.comnet.2004.06.007.
4. T. He, S. Krishnamurthy, L. Luo, T. Yan, L. Gu, R. Stoleru, G. Zhou, Q. Cao, P. Vicaire, J. A. Stankovic, T. F. Abdelzaher, J. Hui and B. Krogh, VigilNet: An integrated sensor network system for energy-efficient surveillance, *ACM Transactions on Sensor Networks*, **2**(1) (2006).
5. A. Cerpa, J. Elson, D. Estrin, L. Girod, M. Hamilton and J. Zhao, Habitat monitoring: Application driver for wireless communications technology, *Proceedings of the 2001 ACM SIGCOMM Workshop on Data Communications in Latin America and the Caribbean* (2001).
6. A. Mainwaring, J. Polastre, R. Szewczyk, D. Culler and J. Anderson, Wireless sensor networks for hatitat monitoring, *WSNA '02*, Atlanta, Georgia (September 2002).
7. G. Werner-Allen, J. Johnson, M. Ruiz, J. Lees and M. Welsh, Monitoring volcanic eruptions with a wireless sensor network, *EWSN '05* (2005).
8. A. Terzis, A. Anandarajah, K. Morre and I.-J. Wang, Slip Surface Localization in Wireless Sensor Networks for Landslide Prediction. In *IPSN '06* (2006).
9. B. Karp and H. T. Kung, GPSR: Greedy perimeter stateless routing for wireless networks, *MobiCom '00* (2000).
10. Y. J. Kim, R. Govindan, B. Karp and S. Shenker, Geographic routing made practical, *NSDI'05* (2005).
11. C. Intanagonwiwat, R. Govindan and D. Estrin, Directed diffusion: A scalable and robust communication paradigm for sensor networks, *Proceedings of the Sixth Annual Internatioanl Conference on Mobile Computing and Networking*, Boston, MA (August 2000).
12. J. Hightower and G. Borriello, Location systems for ubiquitous computing, *IEEE Computer*, **34**(8), 56–77 (August 2001).
13. L. Girod, V. Bychkovskiy and J. E. D. Estrin, Locating tiny sensors in time and space: A case study, *Internal Conference on Computer Design(ICCD)*, Freibury, Germany (September 2002).
14. K. Langendoen and N. Reijers, Distributed localization in wireless sensor networks, a comparative study, *Computer Networks*, **43** (2003).
15. D. Moore, J. Leonard, D. Rus and S. Teller, Robust distributed network localization with noisy range measurements, *SenSys '04* (2004).
16. P. Bahl and V. N. Padmanabhan, Radar: An in-building RF-based user location and tracking system, *InfoCom '00* (2000).
17. A. Harter, A. Hopper, P. Steggles, A. Ward and P. Webster, The anatomy of a context-aware application, *Proc. ACM MOBICOM '99*, Seattle, Washington (1999).
18. N. B. Priyantha, A. Chakraborty and H. Balakrishnan, The cricket location-support system, *MobiCom '00* (2000).
19. K. Chintalapudi, R. Govindan, G. Sukhatme and A. Dhariwal, Ad-hoc localization using ranging and sectoring, *InfoCom '04* (2004).

20. C. D. Whitehouse, The design of calamari: An ad-hoc localization system for sensor networks, *Master Degree Project Report, University of California at Berkeley* (2002).
21. A. Savvides, C. C. Han and M. B. Strivastava, Dynamic fine-grained localization in ad-hoc networks of sensors, *MobiCom '01* (2001).
22. A. Savvides, H. Park and M. Srivastava, The bits and flops of the N-hop multilateration primitive for node localization problems, *Proc. WSNA '02*, Atlanta, GA (September 2002).
23. J. Hightower, G. Boriello and R. Want, SpotON: An indoor 3D location sensing technology based on RF signal strength, *University of Washington CSE Report 2000-02-02* (February 2000).
24. K. Yedavalli, B. Krishnamachari, S. Ravula and B. Srinivasan, Ecolocation: A sequence based technique for RF-only localization in wireless sensor networks, *IPSN '05* (2005).
25. D. Niculescu and B. Nath, Ad hoc positioning system (APS) using AOA, *InfoCom '03* (2003).
26. D. Niculescu and B. Nath, Vor base stations for indoor 802.11 positioning, *MobiCom '04: Proceedings of the 10th annual international conference on Mobile computing and networking*, 58–69, New York, NY, USA, (2004). ACM. ISBN 1-58113-868-7. http://doi.acm.org/10.1145/1023720.1023727.
27. J. Bruck, J. Gao and A. A. Jiang, Localization and routing in sensor networks by local angle information, *MobiHoc '05* (2005).
28. D. K. Goldenberg, P. Bihler, M. Gao, J. Fang, B. D. O. Anderson, A. S. Morse and Y. R. Yang, Localization in sparse networks using sweeps, *MobiCom '06* (2006).
29. A. Ward, A. Jones and A. Hopper, A new location technique for the active office, *IEEE Personal Communications*, **4**(5), 42–47 (October 1999).
30. J. Albowicz, A. chen and L. Zhang, Recursive position estimation in sensor networks, *Proceedings of the 9th International Conference on Network Protocols* (*ICNP*), 35–41, Riverside, CA (November 2000).
31. P. Biswas, T. C. Liang, K. C. Tho, T. C. Wang and Y. Ye, Semidefinite programming approaches to sensor network localization with noisy distance measurements, *IEEE Transactions on Automation Science and Engineering*, **3**(4), 360–371 (October 2006).
32. J. Beutel, *Geolocation in a Picoradio Environment*, Master's thesis, University of California, Berkeley, USA (1999).
33. Y. Kwon, K. Mechitov, S. Sundresh, W. Kim and G. Agha, Resilient localization for sensor networks in outdoor environments, *ICDCS '05*, 643–652 (2005).
34. L. Lazos and R. Poovendran, SeRLoc: Secure range-independent localization for wireless sensor networks, *WiSe '04* (2004).
35. N. Bulusu, J. Heidemann and D. Estrin, GPS-less Low cost outdoor localization for very small devices, *IEEE Personal Communications Magazine*, **7**(4) (August 2000).
36. T. He, C. Huang, B. M. Blum, J. A. Stankovic and T. Abdelzaher, Range-free localization schemes in large-scale sensor networks, *ACM MobiCom'03* (2003).
37. D. Niculescu and B. Nath, Ad-hoc positioning systems, *In Proceedings of IEEE GlobeCom* (2001).
38. A. Baggio and K. Langendoen, Monte-Carlo localization for mobile wireless sensor networks, *MSN '06* (2006).
39. X. Ji and H. Zha, Sensor positioning in wireless ad-hoc sensor networks with multidimensional scaling, *InfoCom '04* (2004).
40. Y. Shang and W. Ruml, Improved MDS-Based localization, *InfoCom '04* (2004).
41. Y. Shang, W. Ruml, Y. Zhang and M. P. J. Fromherz, Localization from mere connectivity, *MobiHoc '03* (2003).

42. D. Niculescu and B. Nath, DV based positioning in ad hoc networks, *Journal of Telecommunication Systems*, **22**(4), 267–280 (2003).
43. R. Nagpal, Organizing a global coordinate system from local information on an amorphous Computer, *A.I. Memo 1666*, MIT A.I. Laboratory (1999).
44. R. Nagpal, H. Shrobe and J. Bachrach, Organizing a global coordinate system from local information on an ad hoc sensor network, *IPSN '03*, Palo Alto, CA (2003).
45. C. Wang and L. Xiao, Locating sensors in concave environments, *IEEE InfoCom '06*, Barcelona, Spain (April 2006).
46. L. Doherty, K. S. J. Pister and L. E. Ghaoui, Convex position estimation in wireless sensor networks, *InfoCom '01* (2001).
47. S. Simić and S. Sastry, *Distributed Localization in Wireless Ad Hoc Networks*. Tech. Rep. UCB/ERL M02/26, EECS Department, University of California, Berkeley (2002).
48. K. Römer, The lighthouse location system for smart dust, *MobiSys '03* (2003).
49. R. Stoleru, T. He, J. A. Stankovic and D. Luebke, A high-accuracy, low-cost localization system for wireless sensor networks, *Sensys'05* (2005).
50. R. Stoleru, P. Vicaire, T. He and J. A. Stankovic, Stardust: A flexible architecture for passive localization in wireless sensor networks, *Sensys'06* (2006).
51. A. Nasipuri and R. E. Najjar, Experimental evaluation of an angle based indoor localization system, *WiNMee '06* (2006).
52. Z. Zhong and T. He, MSP: Multi-sequence positioning of wireless sensor nodes, *Sensys'07* (2007).
53. Z. Zhong and T. He, Sensor node localization using uncontrolled events, *IEEE ICDCS '08* (2008).
54. D. Ganesan, B. Krishnamachari, A. Woo, D. Culler, D. Estrin and S. Wicker, Complex behavior at scale: An experimental study of low-power wireless sensor networks, *Technical Report UCLA/CSD-TR 02-0013* (2002).
55. K. Whitehouse, C. Karlof, A. Woo, F. Jiang and D. Culler, The effects of ranging noise on multihop localization: An empirical study, *IPSN '05* (2005).
56. B. H. Wellenhoff, H. Lichtenegger and J. Collins, *Global Positions System: Theory and Practice, 4th Edition* (Springer-Verlag 1997).
57. D. Moore, J. Leonard, D. Rus and S. Teller, Robust distributed network localization with noise range measurements, *Proceedings of the 2nd International Conference on Embedded Networked Sensor Systems (SenSys '04)*, 50–61 (2004).
58. K. Lorincz and M. Welsh, MoteTrack: A robust, decentralized approach to RF-based location tracking, *Proceedings of Int. Workshop on Location and Context-Awareness* (2005).
59. P. N. Pathirana, N. Bulusu, A. V. Savkin and S. K. Jha, Node localization using mobile robots in delay-tolerant sensor networks, *IEEE Transactions on Mobile Computing*, **4**(3), 285–296 (May–June 2005).
60. R. Peng and M. L. Sichitiu, Localization of wireless sensor networks with a mobile beacon, *MASS '04*, Fort Lauderadale, FL (October 2004).
61. N. B. Priyantha, H. Balakrishnan, E. D. Demaine and S. Teller, Mobile-assisted localization in wireless sensor networks, *InfoCom '05*, Miami, FL (March 2005).
62. P. Corke, R. Peterson and D. Rus, Networked robots: Flying robot navigation using a sensor net, *ISSR '03* (2003).
63. J. Werb and C. Lanzl, Designing a positioning system for finding things and people indoors, *IEEE Spectrum*, **35**(9), 71–78 (September 1998).
64. L. Girod, *Development and Characterization of an Acoustic Rangefinder*, Tech. Rep. 00-728, University of Southern California (April 2000).

65. M. Broxton, J. Lifton and J. Paradiso, Localizing a sensor network via collaborative processing of global sitmuli, *EWSN '05* (2005).
66. B. Kusy, A. Ledeczi and X. Koutsoukos, Tracking mobile nodes using RF doppler shifts, *Sensys'07* (2007).
67. R. Want, A. Hopper, V. Falcao and J. Gibbons, The active badge location systems, *ACM Transactions on Information Systems*, **40**(1), 91–102 (1992).
68. K. Srinivasan and P. Levis, RSSI is under appreciated, *EmNets '06* (2006).
69. L. Girod and D. Estrin, Robust range estimation using acoustic and multimodal sensing, *Proceedings of IROS '01*, Maui, Hawaii (October 2001).
70. C. Savarese, J. Rabay and K. Langendoen, Robust positioning algorithms for distributed ad-hoc wireless sensor networks, *USENIX Technical Annual Conference*, Monterey, CA (June 2002).
71. R. Peng and M. L. Sichitiu, Robust probabilistic constraint-based localization for wireless sensor networks, *SECON '05*, Santa Clara, CA (September 2005).
72. K. Whitehouse and D. Culler, Calibration as parameter estimation in sensor networks, *1st ACM International Workshop on Wireless Sensor Networks and Application*, Atlanta, GA (September 2002).
73. D. Niculescu and B. Nath, Error characteristics of ad hoc positioning systems (APS), *MobiHoc '04* (2004).
74. K. Whitehouse, C. Karlof and D. Culler, A practical evaluation of radio signal strength for ranging-based localization, *SIGMOBILE Mob. Comput. Commun. Rev.* **11**(1) (2007).
75. E. Elnahrawy, X. Li and R. Martin. The limits of localization using RSSI, *SECON '04* (2004).
76. A. Harter and A. Hopper, A distributed location system for the active office, *IEEE Network* (January 1994).
77. R. Azuma, Tracking requirements for augmented reality, *Communications of the ACM*, **36**(7), 50–51 (July 1993).
78. http://www.ascension-tech.com.
79. R. Azuma, Tracking requirements for augmented reality, *Communications of the ACM*, **36**(7), 50–55 (July 1993).
80. R. Stoleru, T. He and J. A. Stankovic, Walking GPS: A practical solution for localization in manually deployed wireless sensor networks, *In EmNetS-I* (2004).
81. P. Dutta and S. Bergbreiter, *Mobiloc: Mobility Enhanced Localization*, Technical report, The Ohio State University, University of California, Berkeley (2003).
82. A. Galstyan, B. Krishnamachari, K. Lerman and S. Pattem, Distributed online localization in sensor networks using a moving target, *IPSN '04*, Berkeley, California (April 2004).
83. K. F. Ssu, C. H. Ou and H. C. Jiau, Localization with mobile anchor points in wireless sensor networks, *IEEE Transactions on Vehicular Technology*, 1187–1197 (May 2005).
84. Z. Zhong, D. Wang and T. He, Sensor node localization using uncontrolled events, *IEEE ICDCS '08* (2008).

Chapter 23

Distributed Location Service by Using Quorum Methods for Large Scale Wireless Sensor Networks

Dandan Liu*

Computer School, WuHan University, China
liudd2004@hotmail.com

Xiaohua Jia

Computer Science, City Univ. HK and Computer School WuHan Univ., China
csjia@cityu.edu.hk

Ivan Stojmenovic

SITE, University of Ottawa, Canada and EECE Univ. Birmingham, UK
Ivan@site.uottawa.ca

Location service provides position of mobile destination to source node, which is essential for geographic (or location assisted) routing algorithms in wireless sensor networks. This chapter first presents a brief review and analysis of traditional solutions on location service, where only local knowledge is required. The techniques reviewed include flooding based and hashing based schemes. Next, the chapter investigates the distributed location service which applies quorum methods. Basic quorum takes the row-column approaches so that the overhead of each routing task, including location service, can be controlled at $O(\sqrt{n})$, where n is the number of nodes in the networks. A connected dominating set can be established as backbone for quorum construction. As each location update and search works upon the backbone, the overhead can be further reduced. Moreover, if the quorum system adopts a hierarchical structure, both update and search operation can be restricted within the level as low as possible. We mainly focus on the representative research works that presented algorithms and approaches to create the quorum system for location service.

*Corresponding author.

23.1. Introduction

23.1.1. *Background*

Advances in hardware and wireless network technologies have created low-cost, low-power and multifunctional sensor devices (called sensor nodes). A Wireless Sensor Network (WSN)[1] consists of many tiny sensor nodes deployed across a physical space, providing functions of data sensing, information processing and communication. Similar to ad hoc wireless networks, WSNs do not have wired network infrastructure. Sensor nodes communicate with each other via radio signals, which are broadcast in nature. The communication between nodes that are not within each other's transmission range relies on the relay by intermediate nodes. The WSNs can be applied in a wide range of our daily applications, such as environment or habitat monitoring, target surveillance and object tracking, traffic monitoring and traffic control, and so on.[2] Many of these applications require hundreds of thousands of these tiny wireless nodes spread over very large areas. The increase in scale along with the limited capabilities of the wireless nodes pose new challenges for routing in such networks.

The location based routing protocols has recently emerged as an important approach to address the scalability and energy efficiency for large-scale networks. They utilize the location information of nodes to forward packets and can achieve better energy efficiency than the topology-based methods. Each node can determine its own location through the use of GPS or some collaborative location protocols.[3] The main challenge of geographic routing protocols is the design of an efficient location service system, which has two main operations: location update and location retrieval. In WSNs, sensor nodes are static and route reports on event discovery to a special node (base station or actuator) that can be mobile. Because of frequent mobility, the location of the destination should be identified before reports transmission could be accomplished. Mobile nodes should register their current position with location service. When a source node has no information about the location of a desired communication recipient, it contacts the service and requests that information. Thereafter the routes between source and destination can be established.

However, there are several challenges to design and implement an efficient location service for the resource constrained WSNs. First, the system is limited by the energy capacity of WSNs. Sensors are powered by batteries and it may not be possible to recharge or replace them in many applications. The system operations must be energy efficient. Second, the system is limited by the bandwidth capacity of sensor nodes. The interactions (i.e., communications) among the sensors must be kept minimal. Third, sensor nodes do not have global topology information and they, sometimes, even do not have global identifiers. Each sensor node only knows its own and its neighbors' positions, and its operations must be based on its local information.

23.1.2. *Quorum method*

Quorum method was originally used in consistency control for data replicas in distributed database system. Replication of data is the key technology for high availability and fault tolerance in a distributed system. Upon receiving a request to perform an operation on a particular data, the server is responsible for cooperating with other servers that have copies of the data. Different replication schemes involve different number of servers for the successful accomplishment of an operation. For example, in the traditional read-any/write-all scheme, a writing request must be finished by all servers in the system, so that a read operation can be performed by any single server. However, this scheme is not reliable because failure in any one of the servers will cause the failure of write operation, and the failure of data accessing. Quorum consensus method aims at reducing the number of servers taking part in data operation. A quorum is a subgroup of servers whose size enables them to make decisions. For example, if having majority is the criterion, a quorum must consist at least $n/2$ servers cooperating to carry out operations, where n is the total number of servers in the system.

Quorum method was early used by Gifford[4] to develope a file replication scheme in which a number of "votes" is assigned to each physical copy at a replica manager of a single logical file. In each transaction, a read quorum of R votes must be collected to proceed with read operation, and a write quorum of W votes must be collected to perform write operation. The R and W are set as:

W > half the total votes
R + W > total number of votes for the group.

This ensures that there is at least a common copy involved in operation between any pair of a read quorum and a write quorum or two write quorums. There is always a subset of the representatives of a file whose votes total to W. Thus, any read quorum is guaranteed to get a current copy, which is determined by the version numbers.

Quorum method has been also used in preventing transactions in different partitions of networks from producing inconsistent results.[5] It requires that an update operation on a logical object should be completed successfully within a quorum. Without enough members to form a quorum, operations can not be performed and therefore avoid conflicting results.

The reliability and performance characteristics of the quorum method can be controlled by appropriately adjusting R and W. In general situation comparing to the file replication scheme,[4] each physical copy at a single server can be regarded as being assigned with the same number of votes, say 1. Thus, W and R mean the number of nodes composing each quorum. There is tradeoff between the overhead consumption in write operation and read operation. The performance of write operation improves as W decreases, and similarly for reads by decreasing R. The choice of R and W depends on the ratio of read to write, the cost of read and write, and the desired reliability and performance in an application.

In Ref. 6, the number of nodes within a quorum was reduced to approximately $\sqrt{n}$. That is, n servers in the system can be partitioned conceptually into $\sqrt{n}$ rows and $\sqrt{n}$ columns. Each column and row serves as a quorum; all of the quorums form a quorum system. There is always a server located in the intersection of each pair of row and column. Comparing with the $O(n)$ servers involved for accessing data in traditional read-any/write-all or read-all/write-one replica schemes, and the $O(n/2)$ servers involved in having majority criterion schemes, quorum method has significantly reduced the communication overhead to $O(\sqrt{n})$ and achieves significant energy savings.

23.1.3. *Overview of the chapter*

There are many existing localized protocols for location updates,[7] while a survey on position based routing can be found in Refs. 8 and 9. Authors[10] give performance comparison among several location services. In this chapter we will first briefly review the flooding based and hashing based approaches, and then focus on the description of quorum-related methods.

Location services can be divided into flooding-based and rendezvous-based approaches. Flooding based location services can be further classified according to the area that the flooding takes place, which includes full area, requested zone and hierarchical zone. All of them suffer from the flooding-related problems, such as heavy overhead, message implosion, etc. In Sec. 23.2 we will illustrate the typical flooding based location service.

Recently, lots of protocols are proposed in a novel fashion, called rendezvous based protocols. The basic idea in this kind of protocols is that all nodes in the network agree with a mapping. When nodes are going to send out location updates, they choose a subset of available nodes. If nodes need to find some other nodes, they sent out location queries to a potentially different subset of nodes. Different protocols are designed to make sure that the intersection of two subsets is not empty. There are two different approaches for performing the mapping, hashing-based and quorum-based approaches.[10] Hashing based methods include flat and hierarchical strategies, which differ at whether a hierarchy of recursively defined subareas are applied. Section 23.3 will explain this kind of methods and analyze their disadvantages.

The other approach, quorum based one, is a scalable and energy efficient method and has several advantages. Therefore, in the following sections, we will focus on illustrating this kind of method. Quorum based method can be further divided into flat, backbone based and hierarchical strategies. Specifically, Sec. 23.4 introduces the basic row-column location services. The quorum system in this section is constructed based upon a flat network topology. By adjusting the parameters of quorum system, the location service can be utilized in different applications with different requirements. Several relevant quorum based location services are also introduced.

We will introduce a connected dominating set (DS) and quorum based location service in Sec. 23.5. Backbones created by dominant nodes are small size, do not have parameters, and preserve network connectivity without the help of other nodes. Location updates and destination searches are restricted to backbone nodes. The method preserves the main advantage of basic quorum-based method originally proposed in Ref. 11 and handling efficiently group mobility scenario with low overhead.

Section 23.6 will illustrate a hierarchical quorum based location service. It uses hierarchical rings as the update and search quorums and guarantees the search operation will return the most up to date location information of a node.

We provide some advices for practitioners in Sec. 23.7, and conclude this chapter in Sec. 23.8.

23.2. Flooding Based Location Service

23.2.1. *Full area*

The simplest protocol to disseminate location in WSNs is by flooding: the source node sends its current location to all of its neighbors, and each of its neighbors stores and sends a copy of the updated location to its neighbors. Such a straightforward protocol is stateless, and it disseminates the update quickly in a network. However, the message cost of flooding is heavy. A node always sends the update to its neighbors regardless of whether or not they have already received the same update from another node. Another drawback of flooding method is the message implosion. When the update is sent to a node with high degree, many copies of the data start floating around the network. Some nodes would eventually be jammed by the incoming packets. References 12 and 13 are typical work of proactive and reactive protocols for information (i.e., location or other data) dissemination in WSNs.

23.2.2. *Requested zone*

A distance routing effect algorithm for mobility (DREAM) is described in Ref. 14. The source or any intermediate node A calculates the direction of destination D and, based on the mobility information about D, chooses an angular range. The message m is forwarded to all neighbors whose direction belongs to the selected range. The range is determined by the tangents from A to the circle centered at D and with radius equal to a maximal possible movement of D since the last location update. The area containing the circle and two tangents is referred as the request zone in

Ref. 15. Ko and Vaidya[15] described, independently, an almost identical algorithm, called LAR scheme 1, and a few modifications of it. The modifications in Ref. 15 include sending route requests before the message itself.[16] Recovery procedures, based on partial or full flooding, to start flooding if the given algorithm fails to find the route within a timeout interval, are proposed by both papers.[14,15] Reference 15 also proposed the LAR scheme 2. In this scheme, the source or each intermediate node A will forward the message to all nodes that are closer to the destination than A is. Wu and Harms[17] proposed to improve LAR algorithm in location update part. In Ref. 17, any two neighboring nodes periodically exchange full routing table (information about all nodes in the network).

The definition of the request zone[14,15] was modified in Ref. 18 in order to provide uniform framework with the corresponding notions in GEDIR and MFR methods. It[18] discusses the V-GEDIR, CH-MFR and R-DIR methods, in which m is forwarded to exactly those neighbors which may be best choices for a possible position of destination (using the appropriate criterion). The request zone in R-DIR method[18] may include one or two neighbors that are outside of angular range, because they can have the closest direction for the tangents to the circle. In VGEDIR method, these neighbors are determined by intersecting the Voronoi diagram of neighbors with the circle (or rectangle) of possible positions of destination, while the portion of the convex hull of neighboring nodes is analogously used in the CH-MFR method.

23.2.3. *Hierarchical zone*

Amouris *et al.*[19] presented a position based multi-zone routing protocol for wide area mobile ad-hoc networks. Their algorithm is based on location updates within circles of increasing radii. Each node floods its update within circle of radii $r, 2r, 4r, 8r, \ldots$ (each subsequent circle has twice larger radius than previous one). Whenever a given node A moves outside one ith circle with radius $2^i r$, node A floods the update packet throughout the $(i+1)$th circle with radius $2^{i+1}r$. At the same time, a new ith circle is defined to be centered at current node location. Later, the data forwarding can follow these circles of last updates. Source nodes will send message toward the last reported location of destination (using the DIR method), which since the last report has moved within the circle of some radius. As routing message moves closer to destination, the information about position of destination becomes more precise, and nodes are able to send message toward center of circles with twice smaller radius than previously, until the node is eventually reached.

In this method, the approach of flooding within each hierarchical circle still may cause many problems such as high energy cost and signal collision. In addition, the radius of larger circles may encompass almost all nodes of the network, and the routing paths discovered by the algorithm do not have near optimal hop counts (which may be important in quality of service applications). But, if the path quality is important, one can consider this algorithm only as the destination search step in the second phase of the location service.

23.3. Hashing Based Location Services

In hashing based protocols, each node chooses its location server via a hashing function, either in the node identifier space or in the location space. The group composed by all location servers plays the similar role as write quorum. The size of quorum is closely related to the location servers selection. Recall that either in the traditional read-one/write-all scheme, or in the scheme of having majority criterion, the expression $R + W > n$ should be abided where R is the size of read quorum, W is the size of write quorum, and n is the total number of nodes. Differently, in hashing based method, only a subset of n nodes inside the network are selected as the location servers. Later, location update and retrieval occur in these location servers. The availability of this method lies in the common knowledge of hash function for producing the intersection. Hashing based protocols can be further divided into flat hashing and hierarchical hashing.

23.3.1. *Flat protocols*

In the flat hashing based protocols (such as Refs. 20–23), each node calculates for itself a home region, which may consist of one or more nodes within a fixed location area in the network. The selection of such home region follows a uniform and well-known hash function. This home region, acting as location servers, will store the location update and reply to corresponding queries for that node. The number of location servers for each node is independent of the total number of nodes n, but the energy consumption on these $O(1)$ servers is comparatively high, which may cause some other problems such as bottleneck in networks.

A typical example is Ref. 21, in which a home region scheme was introduced for maintaining location information of mobile nodes. Each node is associated with a home region. The home region is a circle centered at the initial position of that node, which is known to others in the network, with certain preset radius. All nodes that are currently located inside the region are home agents for that node. When the node changes its location, it sends update information to its home agents; and when other nodes want to route messages to it, they send location inquiry toward the same region of agents. The agents take the responsibility of both write and read operation.

Reference 24 proposed a similar home agent based protocol for maintaining location information of mobile nodes. Different from the one used in Ref. 21, the system has only one home agent shared by all sensor nodes. The home can be a real node, or a geographic region with a number of sensors. It serves the same purpose as rendezvous nodes in the quorum based system. This protocol can be easily extended to a distributed version of home agent method by using a hash table. Obviously, Refs. 21 and 24 will impose heavy communication load on the home agents and the nodes close to them[25] proposes also to use multiple home regions, but distributed uniformly over the area in which the nodes move about.

23.3.2. *Hierarchical protocols*

In the hierarchical hashing based protocols (such as Refs. 26–30), networks are divided into several hierarchical grids. One or more nodes in each level are designated as location servers for each node, so that location updates and queries only need to traverse up or down the hierarchy to find them. Because the height of the hierarchy is $O(\log n)$, effectively each node's location is disseminated to $O(\log n)$ location servers.

The typical work that applies hierarchical hashing-based method is GLS,[28] which performs hashing in the node identifier space, instead of the geographic location space. The field is first partitioned into a hierarchy of grids with squares of increasing size. An order-i square is part of only one order-$(i+1)$ square. Nodes will update to order-$(i+1)$ square when it leaves its previous order-i square and the expire-time for the location is based on the time taken to travel order-i square. It selects three location servers in each level of the grid hierarchy. To perform a request, source searches the servers by traveling up and down the hierarchies, using the same hash function. Figure 23.1 demonstrated an example of location service by using GLS protocol. Node D selects three location servers in each hierarchy, and updates its current location to them. For example, node A which is the location server in D's order-4 square receives the updated location of D. When node S searches D, it will first find node B as the best node (least ID greater than D) in S's order-2 square, and forward the query to B. Next, B will similarly find node A as the best node in S's order-3 square and forward the query to A. Since node A has the matched

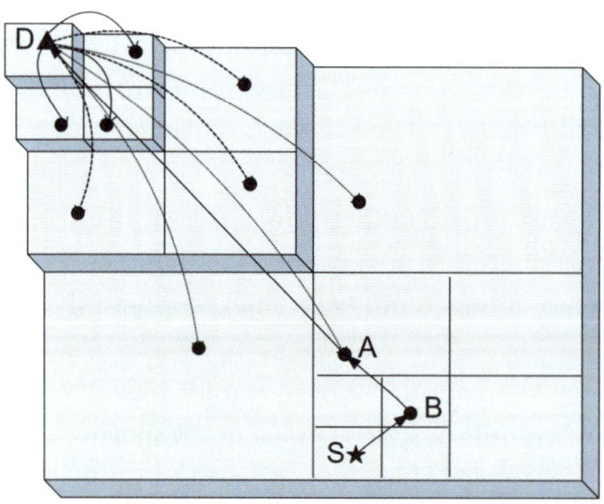

Fig. 23.1. Location update and search in GLS protocol.

information about D, it can directly send the query to node D, and the query is finished.

However, there are some problems in this grid based hierarchical protocol. Firstly, as it hashes the node ID space, some consistency needs to be handled, e.g., when nodes cross grid boundaries. In addition, it suffers the "gridding effect". If source and destination are near the boundaries of two high-order sibling squares, even though they are very close to each other, they still may have to travel many steps up the common hierarchy containing both nodes, which defeats the purpose of using hierarchy for query locality.[10] Finally, the bootstrapping issue is much complicated. The location servers should be updated in a recursive way. This will consume significant energy and operating time.

Another similar work DLSP[29] introduces a distributed location service protocol (DLSP) for wireless sensor networks. Similar to GLS, DLSP is built on a hierarchical grid structure. The differences are that DLSP selects eight servers in each level of the hierarchy, and the update is triggered by the expire-time or exceeding the movement threshold. In addition, the location obtained from the server may become outdated and the query will not be able to find the destination D within a single round if D moves too fast. As a result, the node closest to the last reported location will start a new round when it receives the query, instead of using a forward pointer as in GLS. The authors also propose an optimization DLSP-SN to reduce the update overhead, and an improvement DLSP-ASN for delivering continuous data streams.

23.4. Quorum Based Location Service

In recent years, many protocols are proposed in a novel fashion, called quorum based protocols. They do not apply any sort of flooding strategy for message dissemination, and there is no need to create or maintain location tables for all nodes in the network. The quorum based approaches are more appropriate to be applied for location service in WSN environments, thus we focus on this issue in the following sections.

Query and update strategies in regular networks (based on square, hexagonal and triangular tessellations) were previously employed for location management in cellular networks.[31–33] Authors in Ref. 34 have discussed several methods on how to generate quorum systems. Given a set S of n servers, a quorum system is a set of mutually disjoint subsets of S whose union is S. When one of servers requires information from the other, it suffices to query one server from each quorum. It is possible to form quorums of size approximately $n^{1/2}$.[6] Each column serves as a quorum. Thus each node (i, j) (located in ith row and jth column) replicates its data to all servers (i', j) in its column. To extract the information from server (i, j), server (i', j') may inquire within its i'th row, and the server (i', j) will provide requested information. Variations of this scheme are used in fixed networks, where the set of queried servers contains at least one server that belonged to the quorum that received the latest update. Hence, each query returns the latest value of the queried data.

To apply quorum method for location service in ad hoc networks, mobile nodes should occasionally intelligently update their current location information to a subset of nodes in the network to form an update quorum. When a node wants to communicate with another node whose current location is unknown, it makes a query to a subset of nodes, which form a search quorum. Common node in both update and search quorums provides the location information to the querying node as desired. However, in the WSNs, randomly deployed sensor nodes do not stay in the same "column", and the distributed information may easily disperse due to node movement. Moreover, it is not clear what the "column" is, and how all the nodes in a column, once defined, will receive latest updates. Consequently, some basic desirable properties of quorum based systems may not hold, such as row and column intersections, mutual disjointness of columns, and others. Thus it is a challenge design algorithms for collecting appropriate members for matching quorums to produce rendezvous with small cost.

23.4.1. *Flat protocols*

The representative work on the flat quorum based location service include papers.[11,35,36] The basic idea is that when a node needs to update its location information, it propagates its location information in both north and south directions to reach the north and south boundaries of the network. All nodes that receive the update packet form a north-south column. When a querying node wants the position of the destination node, it first checks whether the location recorded in its database is outdated. If so, the node propagates its search packet in both east and west directions to reach the boundaries. All nodes involved form an east-west row. For example in Fig. 23.2, the trajectory of moving node D is $D_1 \Rightarrow D_2 \Rightarrow D_3$. When D is at D_3, it starts update procedure. All black nodes receive the latest location of D, and all gray nodes receive the query and take the responsibility to provide the

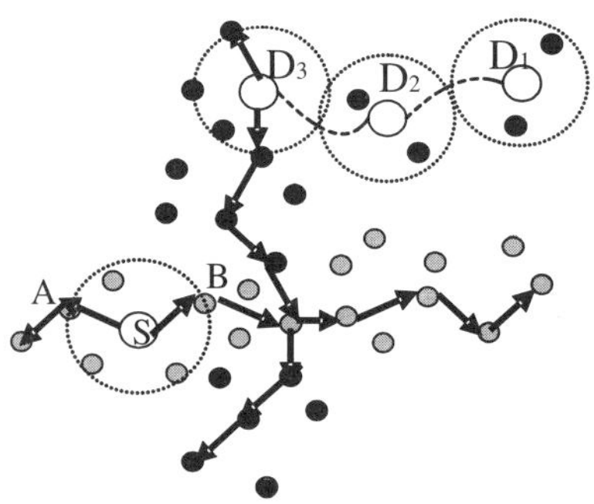

Fig. 23.2. Quorum construction.

best information if they have. The search packet is bound to obtain the required location from a rendezvous node between a pair of column and row quorums.

In this location service, the overhead of each quorum task is $O(\sqrt{n})$, where n is the number of nodes in the network. The advantage of this method compared to existing solutions is that nodes can announce and find their locations without any sort of flooding or broadcasting throughout the whole network. Also, the method uses relative positions of nodes and thus is suitable for use when all nodes move in the same direction.

There are several other issues need to be dealt with in this flat quorum based protocols:

A) Update Interval

Distance-based updates (based on absolute distance traveled since last update) and movement-based updates (based on the velocities of nodes) can be used to calculate the interval of update quorum construction. However, authors in Ref. 37 claimed that these two criteria may have limited usefulness in ad-hoc networks (such location updates are used in Refs. 14 and 15). For instance, nodes may move within a small circle, causing unnecessary location updates. They concluded experimentally that the best strategy is to update when a certain pre-specified number of links incident on a node have been established or broken since the last update.

Based on this scheme, the update quorum construction adopts the following method. Each node uses a counter to count the number of previously made changes in edge existence (the number of created or broken edges with neighboring nodes). The availability of geographic position information enables nodes to estimate the connection time with other nodes, as proposed in Refs. 38 and 39. When the counter reaches a fixed threshold value e, location update is initiated, and e is reset to 0.

For example in Fig. 23.2, node D first moves from position D_1 to D_2. Since the edge change of D does not reach the threshold e, there is no update and D only transmits to its direct neighbors. When node moves to position D_3, the edge change reaches e. Therefore, D begins the update to form the update quorum.

B) Implementation

The frequent problem with the scheme is that the northernmost node as determined by the northward update may be only locally northernmost. A "horizontal" destination search can miss such a node, which can remain "below" it. To overcome this problem, each locally northernmost node may switch to FACE mode[40] until another node, more northern, is found on a face. Such node may return back to regular upward move. The switch between regular and face modes can be repeated a few times. The process terminates when the first edge of the outer face in the same *face_time* is about to be repeated. The FACE algorithm can be improved by applying a short-cut scheme.[41] The final result will be that all nodes at the outer face of the network will receive location update. Reference 36 provides a theorem to prove that the method guarantees that "horizontal" destination search and "vertical" location update will intersect at one of nodes on the outer face. The drawback is that these nodes will have more traffic demands.

C) Variants of Quorum Based Location Service

Note that if both update and search quorum constructions, one towards the east and one towards the west, continuing traversing the outer boundary, the communication overhead will be double with respect to a version that will only follow one direction. The overhead can also be reduced if only one of search or update follows the outer boundary, while the other is not needed at all. In fact, different applications have different requirements on communication overhead, success rate or other metrics. Therefore, in order to be better utilized in various application, several variants of quorum based location service can be considered. They differ by whether greedy only or greedy-face-greedy (GFG) method is applied, or one or two directions are selected. The denotations are taken from the article.[36]

(1) CR
Applying greedy only routing, location update is performed along north-south direction to form a "column", and search is performed along east-west direction to form a "row". The rendezvous occur at the cross point of the "column" and "row". The energy consumption is the least compared to the other three variants. But this variant will have low success rate when the WSN has void area or the nodes are mobile.

(2) CRCR
Applying greedy only routing, location update is performed along both north-south and east-west directions. The shape of the update quorum is like a cross "+". Location search does the similar operation. Then there will be two sets of rendezvous between the two cross, which increases the success rate.

(3) CFRF
Applying GFG method, update and search packets are transmitted along north-south and east-west directions, respectively. Since face routing is used in both updating and searching, quorums can be extended to reach the extreme points of the network. Thus the rendezvous between update and search quorums is guaranteed. The drawback is that the communication overhead is quite large as perimeter nodes are involved in transmissions in four directions.

(4) CFRF(N)
The only difference from the variant CFRF is that updating is along north only direction, and search is along east only direction. Compared to the variant CFRF, location search is also guaranteed as the face routing is utilized, while the overhead is reduced because the perimeter traversal is restricted to two directions.

23.4.2. *Other flat quorum based protocols*

After the technical report version of the quorum based location service presented in Sec. 1.4.1,[35] a number of other relevant articles on location service were published in literature. The basic row-column quorum based location service presented was named in several subsequent articles (e.g., Ref. 42) as XYLS protocol.

The following location services differ at the distribution of location servers.

A) line

An application of quorum-based protocol is given in Ref. 43 as follows. "Generalizing an idea presented in Ref. 35, a replacement scheme using trajectories is as follows: possible destinations (servers S) advertise their position along arbitrary lines and clients C will replace their flooding phase with a query along another arbitrary line which will eventually intersect the desired destinations line. The intersection node then notifies the client about the angle correction needed to contact the server directly. In order to guarantee that the server and client lines intersect inside the circle with diameter CS, it is in fact necessary for the nodes each to send in four cardinal directions."

B) zone

Melamed, Keidar and Barel[44] describe Octopus location service scheme. Octopus divided the network area into horizontal and vertical strips. Specifically, the location update protocol is initiated by each strip's end nodes. The end node broadcasting a STRIP_UPDATE packet to direction d will include in the packet all its neighbors that are in the same strip. Upon receiving the packet, a node will update its own database according to the packet. If it is also designated as the packet target and is not the strip's end node, then it similarly appends to the packet all its neighbors that reside in the same strip. The propagation of STRIP_UPDATE packet completes when it reaches the end node in the other side of the strip. Therefore, the location of each node will be stored at all the nodes residing in its horizontal and vertical strips. For example in Fig. 23.3, node A, B, C and D are end nodes in the strips. According to the scheme, they will send STRIP_UPDATE packet towards each direction (the direction of the big arrow in Fig. 23.3). After the aggregation in update procedure (the small arrows in Fig. 23.3), each node, e.g., M, will receive the location information of all nodes within the horizontal and vertical strips.

This protocol aggregates updates, thus the number of messages is reduced. Nevertheless, each message becomes longer and therefore overhead reduction is questionable. Another difference with quorum based system described in Refs. 11 and 35 is the division into grids and propagation within grids. However, in low-density scenarios, this reduces the change of propagating in desired directions. Third, the movement of individual nodes to new grids may still require individual location updates. Finally, in Octopus, the parameter of strip width ω should be carefully

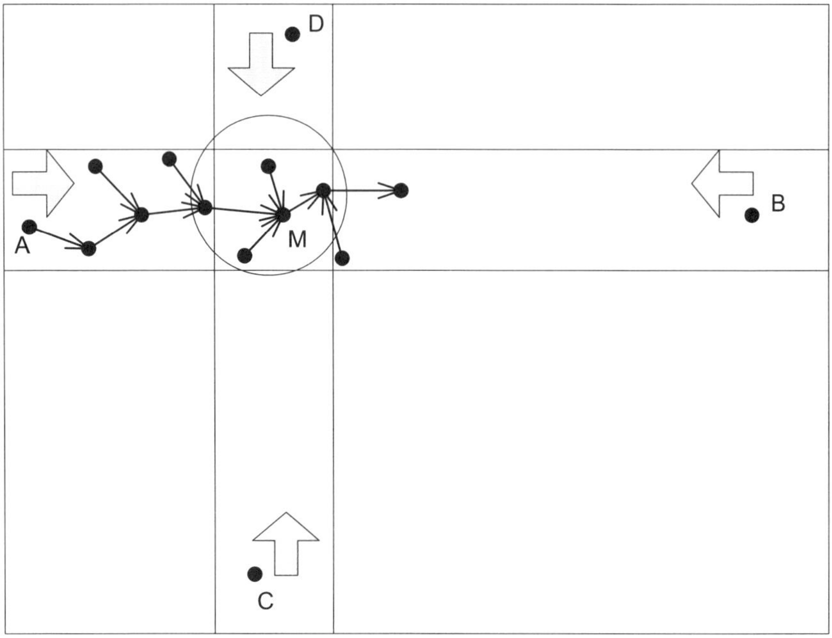

Fig. 23.3. Quorum construction by Octopus.

tuned. As presented in Ref. 44, setting $\omega = R$ can reduce the per node packet and byte complexities while it does not reduce the reliability compared to choosing $\omega \leq \frac{\sqrt{3}}{2}R$.

Jiang and Ling[42] proposed SEEKER location service also based on aggregate updates, which integrates a group of position updates. Network is divided into grids. Position updates are aggregated and forwarded in the east and west directions. Location queries are sent in north and south directions. The whole process of location update and location queries by SEEKER is similar to that of Octopus.

Li and Santoro[45] proposed a distributed zone-based sensor relocation protocol, ZONER, for mobile sensor networks on the basis the quorum based technique. ZONER is able to effectively discover previously-deployed redundant sensors without being concerned with obstacles or network ununiformity, and it relocates them in a shifting way to replace failed nonredundant ones without changing network topology. In ZONER, each redundant node registers itself with all the non-redundant nodes inside a vertical registration zone across the entire network; when a node fails, its specified neighbors inquiry all the non-redundant nodes inside a bounded horizontal request zone for redundant nodes; because the request zone intersects with a number of registration zones, the non-redundant nodes in the intersection areas can provide the requester with redundant node information. Face routing[40] is applied similarly as in this article to deal with void areas.

C) Spiral shape

Authors in Ref. 46 proposed an adaptive location management (ALM) model for mobile ad hoc networks. First, each node defines its origin by a well-known hash function, that is $H(id) = o(u, v)$. Later, from the predefined origin, each node creates a set of location servers based on Archimedean spiral formula $R = a\theta$. That is, the centers c of location servers are defined every θ degree as the spiral curve winds itself around the nodes's origin. All nodes located within the disk $< c, r >$ record the location information of the node. Both the distribution of location servers and the destination search follow an Archimedean spiral. ALM combines two notions: mobility rate and distance in order to adapt dynamically the key parameters of the location management procedures. The fuzzy logic concept is utilized to deal with imprecise and uncertain information since mobile ad hoc networks are dynamic in nature. ALM also provides sufficient redundancy of location information through the network to avoid single points of failure.

D) Comb-needle

Liu, Huang and Zhang[47] gave a generalization of basic quorum bases strategy. Their comb-needle discovery support model resembles an ancient method: use a comb to help find a needle in sands or a haystack. Each sensor node advertises its DATA message to $2l$ of its vertical neighbors (the route of the DATA forms a vertical needle with length $2l$). A querying node disseminates its request first vertically to the entire field (forming the comb-backbone) and then fans out horizontally from the comb-backbone at the gap s between the comb-teeth. The route of the request forms a vertical comb with gap s between the teeth (Fig. 23.4). When $s \leq 2l$, the request message is bound to meet the DATA message. The advantage of the comb-needle model is that parameters s and l can be adjusted depending on frequencies of events and queries in the system in a dynamical way so that the message cost

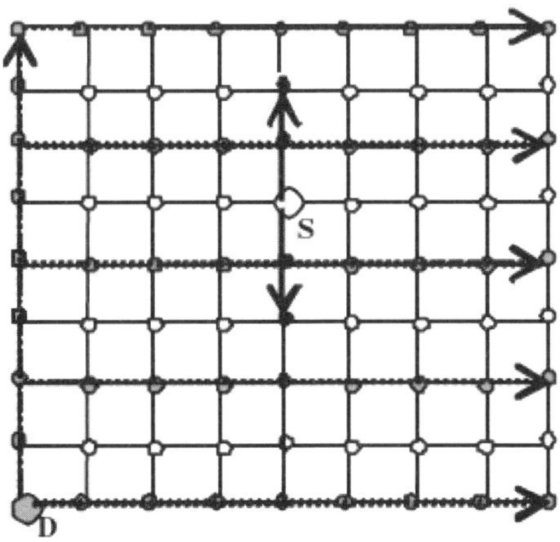

Fig. 23.4. Comb and needle.

can be reduced. However, in an irregular network, the request messages can hardly follow a comb shape, and the comb may miss the needle (i.e., the success rate of a request finding its matched data is poor). This problem will be even more severe in the presence of "void area" in the network.

Besides the difference in the distribution of location servers, some protocols proposed to modify the operation of location search. The main location management proposals have, as a common characteristic, two distinct phases: the location search of the position of a destination node and the data transmission toward that node. The authors in Ref. 48 proposed to send the initial packets of a flow to learn the position of their destination instead of adopting a dedicated query packet. Since such scheme will introduce some new tradeoffs, Ref. 48 also proposed an adaptive mechanism to provide a source with indications on which scheme to adopt at an individual case basis. The cost depends on certain conditions, including the size of packets, the size of the flow to be transmitted, and so on. At the longterm, as each cooperative node seeks to adopt the lowest cost scheme for each transmission, they claim that the methods can achieve overall performance enhancement of the location management as well as a reduction in the battery consumption of nodes.

23.5. Backbone and Quorum Based Location Service

One of observed drawbacks of the flat quorum based (row-column) location service is the performance in large scale and/or dense networks, as too many nodes become involved in processing requests, and outer faces contain too many short edges. Some articles had proposed to apply backbone scheme for quorum construction. Quorum based location service then continues mainly on the backbone nodes. Other nodes may be used to connect backbone nodes. The main advantage is that the overhead caused by location updates was controlled by restricting them within the backbone. There are mainly three strategies for creating backbones. They are cluster, grid and connected dominating set methods, respectively.

23.5.1. *Cluster as the backbone*

Haas and Liang[34,49,50] proposed a variant of quorum based distributed mobility management scheme. First, virtual backbone is initiated and maintained.[50] Two "neighboring" backbone nodes may be up to $2r+1$ hops away. A distributed scheme for initiating is based on selecting, repeatedly, a node with maximal number of unassigned r hop neighbors as backbone nodes, and assigning all its r hop neighbors to that node. We observe that this is, in fact, a well-known clustering algorithm[51] generalized to r hops. The maintenance of cluster structure is known to require significant communication overhead (for instance, local changes may cause global updates by chain effect).[52,53] Nodes in virtual backbone are database servers for location information. They define a quorum system, which is a set of subsets such that any two subsets intersect in small number of preferably constant number t of databases. Each subset then has the same size k. In Ref. 34 the choice of subsets is uniform and is performed by applying a centralized balanced incomplete block design algorithm. The selection of these subsets at random was discussed in Ref. 49. When a node moves, it updates its location with one subset containing the nearest backbone node. Each source node then queries the subset containing its nearest backbone for the location of destination, and uses that location to route the message.

The routing algorithm is not discussed in Refs. 34, 49 and 50. It can be easily observed that location updates, destination searches are not local, and that they involve routing between backbone nodes. Thus backbone nodes must exchange their location information in order to perform their duties. It is not clear whether subset querying or backbone node communication can be done more efficiently than by flooding all nodes. Taking the entire overhead into account, it is not clear whether the whole routing algorithm will perform better than a simple flooding algorithm, with redundant retransmissions eliminated (roughly half nodes suffice to retransmit to achieve reliable flooding).[54] The flooding based routing algorithm does not require any location updates, requires no quorum based structure for its maintenance (which, in turn, relies on flooding anyway), and does not require communication overhead for its own backbone structure, which is dominating set as defined in Refs. 53 and 54.

23.5.2. *Grid as the backbone*

Zhang, Zhao and Labrador[55] introduced the Anchor Location Service (ALS), a grid-based location service designed for large-scale wireless sensor networks. A global grid structure is first built as the backbone, the node nearest to the grid points is assigned as grid node. Each sink selects the nearest grid node as its sink agent to distribute its location information. Then the sink agent selects some special grid nodes as its location servers (anchors) and builds an anchor system. The anchor selection process is achieved by means of propagating anchor setup messages by the sink along four orthogonal directions (North, South, East and West). Intermediate nodes between two neighboring grid nodes will relay the setup messages and only the recruited anchors store and retrieve the active sink location. During the location search, the source node queries the anchor system to obtain the latest location of the sink agent. In addition, Ref. 55 also introduced a sink agent chain to keep track of the sink if it moves.

However, using grid as the backbone for quorum system has some drawbacks. First, grid leaders alone do not preserve network connectivity.[56] Thus update and search messages should be sometimes relayed by other nodes, which then do not store necessary information. If the intersection of row and column is at such node, the destination information is not found because it was not stored there. Thus the overall design has additional problems to be studied. Second, the choice of square size α for partitioning is a parameter to be tuned. In ALS, if α is large, the space will be divided into fewer grids, each of which will take more area. Thus the message exchange within each grid will be large. Moreover, since fewer grid nodes are selected, the location information can only be stored at fewer servers, which will reduce the rate for successful destination search. But if α is small, since the setup packets have to go through each grid node along the direction even if multiple grid nodes are within transmission radius, more grid nodes will be selected as anchors, which leads to more hops for update or search routing. Next, nodes need to learn exact grid boundaries they belong to, which requires additional overhead and adds to imprecision problems. Further, grid leader selection requires each node to send and receive additional messages. To select grid leaders, every node must compare its location with location of nearby candidates, and the "winner" must announce its decision.

23.5.3. *Dominating set as the backbone*

Liu, Jia and Stojmenovic[57] proposed to apply a different backbone concept which does not have drawbacks listed above. It is based on connected dominating set (DS) construction.[56,58–60] A connected dominating set (DS) is first created as backbone for quorum construction. Each node decides whether or not it is a dominating node by a self-pruning scheme.[56,58–60] All the location update and destination search operations are made upon the nodes that belong to the constructed DS.

This method is adaptive to group movement scenarios, since all decisions are made based on relative rather than absolute coordinates. Nodes react to topological changes rather than to change in their absolute coordinates. For instance, when all nodes move in a certain direction synchronously then DS based solution does not require any messages and updates (relative network structure remains unchanged). If they are aware of planned movement then even "hello" messages are not required (until a deviation from planned movement occurs). This then does not change DS set and invokes no backbone maintenance messages. Thus using DS as the backbone for quorum based location service preserves the main advantage of basic quorum based method originally proposed in Ref. 35, and handles efficiently group mobility scenario with low overhead. Additionally, DS and quorum based approach handles location service and routing around void areas and preserves path rather than flooding based searches. The DS based location service includes two operations: backbone establishment and its implementation.

A) Dominating Set Establishment

A Connected Dominating Set (DS) is first constructed on network G. Nodes exchange 1-hop neighbor information through HELLO messages periodically. Each node decides whether or not it is dominant based on its key. To achieve a better performance, the key of a node u can be configured as follows: $Key(u) = \{degree(u), energy(u), id(u)\}$. This means that nodes with higher neighbor degree have a larger probability to be selected as dominant. In static sensor networks, the construction of DS is done at the beginning and is maintained only when sensors change activity status from sleeping to active and vice versa (periodically, every ΔT time). However, mobility imposes more challenges for maintaining such backbone structure. There are two ways to construct DS as the backbone:[57]

(1) Dynamic backbone maintenance with additional inform messages. Dominating nodes send notice to neighbors and invoke the backbone maintenance mechanism only when current topology change counters are over.
(2) Periodic backbone maintenance with beacon messages. DS is constructed each ΔT time and according to periodic hello message.

The selection of optimal maintenance interval ΔT is tricky, as it depends on local and global mobility and stability. The status change may occur long before ΔT expires. Therefore the article[57] opted for additional local reevaluation based on creation and breakage of links of considered node with current backbone nodes. The topology change counter $BThre$ is first fixed. Whenever a dominating node oversees a change in its backbone status that is over the $BThre$, neighbors are informed by a message. The node as well as all its direct neighbors updates their backbone status immediately. Link status evaluations can be made any time appropriate information is available, such as observing topological change based on direction and speed of movement, or reception of message from neighbor with piggybacked position information, or a round of hello messages.

B) Implementation

After selecting (or self-selecting) backbone nodes, the details of quorum based location service become identical to its original scheme, as elaborated in Ref. 35. The difference is that only backbone nodes participate. Figure 23.5 gives an example

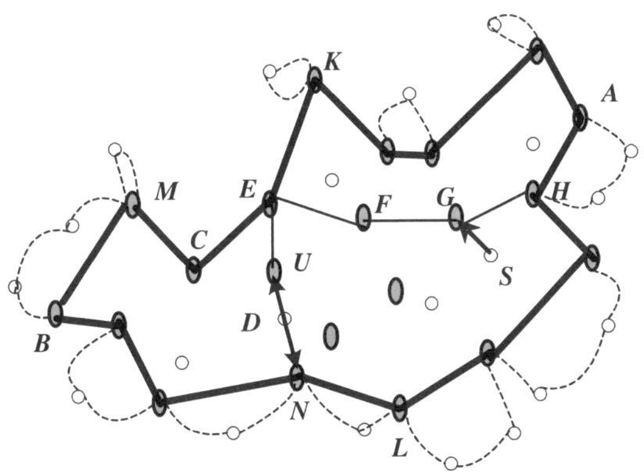

Fig. 23.5. Update and search with or without backbone nodes.

to illustrate this point, showing path with and without applying backbone enhancement. In Fig. 23.5, all solid nodes indicate backbone nodes, and all hollow nodes including source S and destination D indicate regular nodes. Consider the update procedure as an example. According to the DS based quorum location service, the location update by D is forwarded along the "column" $DNL - DUEK$ (indicated by bold lines). The "column" is constructed by applying the greedy mode in north-south direction until reaching the border of the network. As the face routing is adopted, the column end nodes L and K will switch to the boundary mode, and continue to extend their update following GFG algorithm. Since only backbone nodes are considered as candidates for forwarding, the update packets will traverse the outer boundary of DS as indicated by the "heavy" bold lines in the figure, and all the solid nodes along the line will be recruited as location servers.

As a comparison, the route of the inefficient face routing in the original quorum system presented in Ref. 11 is also shown in Fig. 23.5 (in short dash curve). Since all nodes can participate in the forwarding, the overall system overhead will be considerable large. Thus using backbone as an enhancement for quorum construction can significantly reduce the consumption caused by perimeter transmission (the route in heavy bold line compared with the short dash curve). It can also improve the storage usage of the network, as fewer nodes need to record the information.

23.6. Hierarchical Quorum Based Location Service

As wireless sensor networks (WSN) are getting deeper into all levels of human lives and applied in a wider range of our daily applications, many applications require more and more sensors deployed in a super large scale. The topological changes become more frequent, and the energy consumption becomes faster. The increase in scale along with the limited capabilities of the wireless nodes poses new challenges for location service in such networks.

Hierarchical methods are effective ways to handle location service in large scale networks. In this section, we present a novel location service by applying hierarchical quorum method. Nodes are assumed to be deployed in the Euclidean plane. Each node knows its own and the direct neighbors' locations (e.g., their coordinates), which can be easily obtained by GPS (or other positioning service) and probing (or hello) message exchanges. This location service combines the concept of quorum method with a hierarchical ring structure. It follows the "distance effect": the mobile node sends updates to multiple nodes at each hierarchy. The higher hierarchy the nodes are, the less frequently they will be updated.

23.6.1. *Location update*

A set of geographic rings R_i^k centered at C_i^k where $(k = 0, 1, 2, \ldots)$ are defined for each node. The kth routing ring is a geographic circle with radius $r(k)$ that suffice

$r(k+1) = 2r(k)$. The ring that has a larger radius is referred to with a higher hierarchy. The R_i^0 ring is called the core ring for node and the center C_i^0 is always the immediate location of the node.

The update scheme can be described as follow. Let L_i be the current location of node i. When i is about to leave one of its rings, say $R_i^k (k > 0)$, it redefines R_i^h (for all $0 < h \leq k$) to be centered at current location L_i and sends update to the new ring R_i^k. Specifically, each node maintains a table for all its rings. The ring table holds the currently defined centers C_i^k of each hierarchy k. When node's current location L_i relative to C_i^k for some k changes by more than $r(k)$, (i.e., $d(L_i, C_i^k) \geq r(k)$), a set of new update rings R_i^h are redefined so that $C_i^h \leftarrow L_i$ (for all $0 < h \leq k$). Upon the redefinition of the new ring R_i^k, an update packet, including the current location L_i, the timestamp and the expire-time, is sent out to R_i^k. Therefore, all nodes on R_i^k know the location of destinations is at L_i.

23.6.2. *Location search*

Upon receiving the request from application to locate a destination node D, the source node S first checks the location information of D in its local database. If the query can not be satisfied locally, a query, generated by S, is transmitted along the 0th searching ring. All the nodes on the ring are required to provide the up to date information if they have. However, if there is no information provided, the search comes to the one level up ring of the current one. That is, the query is transmitted to the 1th ring. Consequently, the search will be extended to higher and higher hierarchies until reaching the ring of certain level from which an available information can be obtained. Once the search meets with one ring of destination, the strategy turns to the second phase. The search will follow the ring where the intersection occurs until it gets better information. But if there is no such information, the search will turn to the center of the current ring.

The specific process is explained in Fig. 23.6. The trajectory of moving node i is $P_0 \Rightarrow P_1 \Rightarrow P_2$. According to the update scheme, when node i is at P_2, the set of rings for i is updated to R_i^1, R_i^2, R_i^3 respectively. The intersection between R_i^3 and R_i^2 is denoted as Q_2, and similarly the intersection of R_i^2 and R_i^1 is Q_3 in the figure. Source S is trying to locate node i which has moved to position P_2. At the beginning of the search, S tries to find the information from its local tables, which collect the information from the core ring R_S^0. Unluckily, the query can not obtain the required data since there is no intersection with any R_i^k $(k = 0, 1, 2, 3)$. Therefore, the search is extended to the higher hierarchy R_S^1 where two intersections, Q_0 and Q_1 between R_S^1 and R_i^3 exist (Fig. 23.6). Since the information from Q_0 and Q_1 has the same time stamp, the search will choose either one to start the second phase.

Suppose the second phase of search starts from the intersection Q_1, and the direction of ring traversal is clockwise. The search then will follow the ring R_i^3 (oriented along the direction of the arrow in Fig. 23.6) until it gets better information

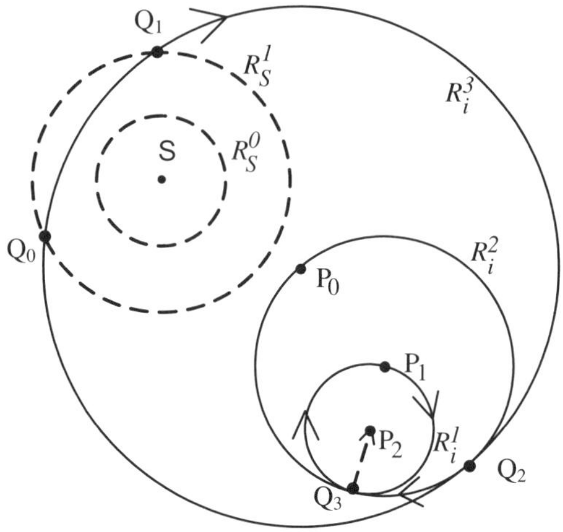

Fig. 23.6. Search route.

from Q_2. Note that the location information recorded on the ring is always its center. Therefore, the expected location of i acquired from Q_2 is the center of R_i^2, i.e., P_1. Clearly, the position P_1 is newer than P_0. As a result, the search changes to the newer ring R_i^2, and traverses the ring until it gets better information from Q_3. Similarly, as P_2 is newer than P_1, the search changes to the newer ring R_i^1. After it traverses the ring, the best information it can obtained is still position P_2. Therefore, the search will directly be forwarded towards this most up to date location, and find the destination there finally.

23.7. Thoughts for Practitioners

Quorum method is widely utilized in location service and routing in wireless sensor networks. To improve energy efficiency and shorten communication latency, cross-layer design could be adopted for specific applications of WSNs. For example, improved performance can be obtained by jointly considering physical layer issues and network layer issues. Based on different applications, techniques and algorithms that are introduced in this chapter could be employed.

However, there is trade-off between success rate of destination search and energy efficiency. The increase in success rate may lead to the increase of overhead and delay of operation. There are some parameters on quorum construction that can be determined to optimize the performance of the services. They can be analyzed and determined depending on task of networks and objective of applications. For example, if the operation of search is more frequent than the update, then the face routing stated in the chapter should be adopted only by location updates, to decrease the energy consumption.

23.8. Conclusions and Direction for Future Research

The goal of this chapter is to investigate current research work on quorum based location service. Thus we focus on studying and analyzing the quorum related methods. The quorum based methods include basic quorum, dominating set based quorum and hierarchical quorum, respectively. In addition, as a comparison, we also briefly review the traditional flooding and hashing based methods for location service.

Although quorum based location service in wireless sensor networks has been well studied, there are challenges for future research. Most existing solutions for efficient update and search are usually designed for idealized networks with no signal interference, packet loss, and so on. This is because in order to confirm the basic claims and expectations, make the simulation repeatable, and make the verification independent, a basic simulation setup is needed. However, more realism requires more complex assumptions, and more detailed corresponding simulations. This includes adding medium access layer to analyze the impact of message collisions. More details on simulations, with the view of matching assumptions and simulation model and making their parallel advance, can be found in Ref. 61.

In addition, most existing protocols are designed for lossless networks where all sensor nodes are assumed to have the same energy status. In future work, protocols should address the bottleneck problem: how to balance resources among sensors (e.g., saving more energy for more resource-constrained sensors) so that the overall system lifetime is maximized.

References

1. D. Culler, D. Estrin and M. Srivastava, Overview of sensor networks, *Computer*, **37**(8), 41–49 (2004).
2. K. Martinez, J. K. Hart and R. Ong, Sensor network applications, *Computer*, **37**(8), 50–56 (2004).
3. J. Bachrach and C. Taylor, *Localization in sensor networks*, (ed.) I. Stojmenovic, *Handbook of Sensor Networks: Algorithms and Architectures*, 277–310. Wiley (2005).
4. D. K. Gifford, Weighted voting for replicated data, *Proc. 7th Symposium on Operating Systems Principles*, 150–162. ACM (1979).
5. G. Coulouris, J. Dollimore and T. Kindberg, *Distributed Systems: Concepts and Design, Edition 3* (Addison-Wesley 2005).
6. M. Maekawa, A $n^{1/2}$ algorithm for mutual exclusion in decentralized systems, *ACM Transactions on Computer Systems*, **3**(2), 145–159 (1985).
7. I. Stojmenovic, *Location Updates for Efficient Routing in Wireless Networks*, *Handbook on Wireless Networks and Mobile Computing*, 451–471, Wiley (2002).
8. S. Giordano and I. Stojmenovic, *Position Based Routing Algorithms for Ad Hoc Networks: A Taxonomy*, (eds.) X. X. Cheng, Huang and D. Du, *Ad Hoc Wireless Networking*, 103–136. Kluwer (2004).
9. I. Stojmenovic, Position based routing in ad hoc networks, *IEEE Communications Magazine*, **40**(7), 128–134 (2002).

10. S. M. Das, H. Pucha and Y. C. Hu, Performance comparison of scalable location services for geographic ad hoc routing, *Proc. IEEE INFOCOM*, **2**, 1228–1239 (2005).
11. D. Liu, I. Stojmenovic and X. Jia, A scalable quorum based location service in ad hoc and sensor networks, *Proc. IEEE MASS*, 489–492 (2006).
12. W. R. Heinzelman, J. Kulit and H. Balakrishnan, Adaptive protocols for information dissemination in wireless sensor networks, *Proc. 5th ACM MOBICOM*, 174–185 (1999).
13. C. Intanagonwiwat, R. Govindan and D. Estrin, Directed diffusion: a scalable and robust communication paradigm for sensor networks, *Proc. 6th ACM MOBICOM*, 56–67 (2000).
14. S. Basagni, I. Chlamtac, V. Syrotiuk and B. Woodward, A distance routing effect algorithm for mobility (dream), *Proc. 4th ACM MOBICOM*, 76–84 (1998).
15. Y. Ko and N. Vaidya, Location-aided routing (lar) in mobile ad hoc networks, *Proc. 4th ACM MOBICOM*, 66–75 (1998).
16. D. Johnson and D. Maltz, *Dynamic Source Routing in Ad Hoc Wireless Networks*, (eds.) T. Imielinski and H. Korth, *Mobile Computing*, 153–181. Kluwer (1996).
17. K. Wu and J. Harms, Location trace aided routing in mobile ad hoc networks, *Proc. IEEE ICCCN*, 354–359, Las Vegas (2000).
18. I. Stojmenovic, A. Ruhil and D. Lobiyal, Voronoi diagram and convex hull based geocasting and routing in wireless networks, *Wireless Communications and Mobile Computing*, **6**(2), 247–258 (2006).
19. K. Amouris, S. Papavassiliou and M. Li, A position based multi-zone routing protocol for wide area mobile ad-hoc networks, *Proc. 49th IEEE Vehicular Technology Conference*, 1365–1369 (1999).
20. L. Blazevic, L. Buttyan, S. Capkun, S. Giordano, J.-P. Hubaux and J.-Y. Le Boudec, Self-organization in mobile ad hoc networks: The approach of terminodes, *IEEE Communications Magazine*, **39**(6), 166–175 (2001).
21. I. Stojmenovic, Home agent based location update and destination search schemes in ad hoc wireless networks, (eds.) A. Zemliak and N. Mastorakis, *Advances in Information Science and Soft Computing*, 6–11. WSEAS Press (2002).
22. S. Woo and S. Singh, Scalable routing protocol for ad hoc networks, *Wireless Networks*, **7**(5), 513–529 (2001).
23. S. Giordano and M. Hami, *Mobility Management: The Virtual Home Region*, Technical Report SSC/037, EPFL (1999).
24. D. Liu, X. Hu and X. Jia, Energy efficient information dissemination protocols by negotiation for wireless sensor networks, *Computer Communications*, **29**(11), 2136–2149 (2006).
25. C. Cheng, H. Lemberg, S. Philip, E. D. Berg and T. Zhang, Slalom: A scalable location management scheme for large mobile ad-hoc networks, *Proc. IEEE WCMC*, **2**, 574–578 (2002).
26. R. Morris, J. Jannotti, F. Kaashoek, J. Li and D. Decouto, Carnet: A scalable ad hoc wireless network system, *Proc. 9th ACM SIGOPS European Workshop*, 61–65 (2000).
27. G. Pei and M. Gerla, Mobility management for hierarchical wireless networks, *Mobile Networks and Applications*, **6**(4), 331–337 (2001).
28. J. Li, J. Jannotti, D. S. J. D. Couto, D. R. Karger and R. Morris, A scalable location service for geographic ad hoc routing, *Proc. 6th ACM MOBICOM*, 120–130 (2000).
29. Z. Chen, M.-G. Cho and K. G. Shin, Design of location service for a hybrid network of mobile actors and static sensors, *Proc. 27th IEEE Int. Real-Time Systems Symposium*, 202–211 (2006).

30. Y. Xue, B. Li and K. Nahrstedt, A scalable location management scheme in mobile ad-hoc networks, *Proc. IEEE LCN*, 102 (2001).
31. G. Krishnamurthy, A. Azizoglu and A. Somani, Optimal location management algorithms for mobile networks, *Proc. 4th ACM MOBICOM*, 223–232 (1998).
32. R. Prakash, Z. Haas and M. Singhal, *Load Balanced Location Management for Mobile Systems Using Dynamic Hashing and Quorums*, Technical Report TR-UTDCS-05-97, The University of Texas at Dallas (1997).
33. R. Prakash and M. Singhal, A dynamic approach to location management in mobile computing systems, *Proc. 8th Int. Conf. on Software Eng. & Knowledge Eng. SEKE96*, 488–495 (1996).
34. Z. J. Haas and B. Liang, Ad hoc mobility management with uniform quorum systems, *IEEE/ACM Transactions on Netwoking*, **7**(2), 228–240 (1999).
35. I. Stojmenovic, *A Scalable Quorum Based Location Update Scheme for Routing in Ad Hoc Wireless Networks*, Technical Report TR-99-09, SITE, University, Ottawa, (1999).
36. I. Stojmenovic, D. Liu and X. Jia, A scalable quorum-based location service in ad hoc and sensor networks, *Int. J. Communication Networks and Distributed Systems*, **1**(1), 71–94 (2008).
37. G. Karumanchi, S. Muralidharan and R. Prakash, Information dissemination in partitionable mobile ad hoc networks, *Proc. IEEE Symposium on Reliable Distributed Systems*, 488–495 (1999).
38. I. Stojmenovic, M. Russell and B. Vukojevic, Depth first search and location based localized routing and qos routing in wireless networks, *Proc. IEEE Int. Conf. on Parallel Processing*, 173–180 (2000).
39. W. Su, S. Lee and M. Gerla, Mobility prediction in wireless networks, *Proc. IEEE MILCOM*, 491–495 (2000).
40. P. Bose, P. Morin, I. Stojmenovic and J. Urrutia, Routing with guaranteed delivery in ad hoc wireless networks, *ACM/Kluwer Wireless Networks*, **7**(6), 609–616 (2001).
41. S. Datta, I. Stojmenovic and J. Wu, Internal nodes and shortcut based routing with guaranteed delivery in wireless networks, *Cluster Computing*, **5**(2), 169–178 (2002).
42. J.-R. Jiang and W.-J. Ling, *Seeker: An Adaptive and Scalable Location Service for Mobile Ad Hoc Networks*, Master's thesis, National Central University, Taiwan, China (2007).
43. D. Niculescu and B. Nath, Trajectory based forwarding and its applications, *Proc. 9th ACM MOBICOM*, 260–272 (2003).
44. R. Melamed, I. Keidar and Y. Barel, Octopus: A fault-tolerant and efficient ad-hoc routing protocol, *Proc. 24th IEEE Symposium on Reliable Distributed Systems (SRDS 2005)*, 39–49 (2005).
45. X. Li and N. Santoro, Zoner: A zone-based sensor relocation protocol for mobile sensor networks, *Proc. 6th IEEE Int. Workshop on Wireless Local Networks (WLN)*, 923–930 (2006).
46. N. Nikaein and C. Bonnet, Alm — adaptive location management incorporating fuzzy logic for mobile ad hoc networks, *Proc. MedHocNet*, Italy (2002).
47. X. Liu, Q. Huang and Y. Zhang, Balancing push and pull for efficient information discovery in large-scale sensor networks, *IEEE Transactions on Mobile Computing*, **6**(3), 241–151 (2007).
48. A. Ziviani, S. Fdida, J. de Rezende and O. Duarte, Enhancing location management in mobile ad hoc networks, *Proc. MedHocNet*, Italy (2002).

49. Z. Haas and B. Liang, Ad-hoc mobility management with randomized database groups, *Proc. IEEE ICC*, 489–492 (1999).
50. B. Liang and Z. Haas, Virtual backbone generation and maintenance in ad hoc network mobility management, *Proc. IEEE INFOCOM*, **3**, 1293–1302 (2000).
51. C. Lin and M. Gerla, Adaptive clustering for mobile wireless networks, *IEEE J. Selected Areas in Communications*, **15**(7), 1265–1275 (1997).
52. M. Gerla, T. Kwon and G. Pei, On demand routing in large ad hoc wireless networks with passive clustering, *Proc. IEEE WCNC*, **1**, 100–105 (2000).
53. J. Wu and H. Li, On calculating connected dominating set for efficient routing in ad hoc wireless networks, *Proc. 3rd Int. Workshop on Discrete Algorithms and Methods for Mobile Computing and Communications*, 7–14 (1999).
54. I. Stojmenovic, M. Seddigh and J. Zunic, Dominating sets and neighbor elimination based broadcasting algorithms in wireless networks, *IEEE Transactions on Parallel and Distributed Systems*, **13**(1), 14–25 (2002).
55. R. Zhang, H. Zhao and M. Labrador, A scalable and energy efficient sink location service for large-scale wireless sensor networks, *Ad Hoc and Sensor Wireless Networks Journal*, **4**(4), 289–320 (2007).
56. D. Simplot-Ryl, I. Stojmenovic and J. Wu, *Energy Efficient Backbone Construction, Broadcasting, and Area Coverage in Sensor Networks*, (ed.) I. Stojmenovic, *Handbook of Sensor Networks: Algorithms and Architectures*, 343–379, Wiley (2005).
57. D. Liu, X. Jia and I. Stojmenovic, Quorum and connected dominating sets based location service in wireless ad hoc, sensor and actuator networks, *Computer Communications*, **30**(18), 3627–3643 (2007).
58. J. Carle and D. Simplot-Ryl, Energy efficient area monitoring for sensor networks, *IEEE Computer*, **37**(2), 40–46 (2004).
59. F. Dai and J. Wu, An extended localized algorithm for connected dominating set formation in ad hoc wireless networks, *IEEE Transactions on Parallel and Distributed Systems*, **15**(10), 908–920 (2004).
60. F. Ingelrest, D. Simplot-Ryl and I. Stojmenovic, Smaller connected dominating sets in ad hoc and sensor networks based on coverage by two-hop neighbors, *Proc. 2nd IEEE Int. Conf. on Communication System Software and Middleware (COMSWARE)*, 1–8 (2007).
61. I. Stojmenovic, Simulations in wireless sensor and ad hoc networks: Matching and advancing models, metrics and solutions, *IEEE Communications Magazine*, **46**(12), 102–107 (2008).

Part VII

Energy Efficiency

Chapter 24

Energy Considerations for MAC Protocols in Wireless Sensor Networks

Feng Shu*, Taka Sakurai†, Hai L. Vu‡ and Moshe Zukerman§

*Stichting IMEC Nederland, P.O. Box 8550
5605 KN Eindhoven, The Netherlands
fshu@ieee.org

†ARC Special Research Centre for Ultra Broadband Information Networks
Department of Electrical and Electronic Engineering
The University of Melbourne, Australia

‡Centre for Advanced Internet Architectures, Faculty of I.C.T.
Swinburne University of Technology
P.O. Box 218, VIC 3122, Australia

§Electronic Engineering Department, City University of Hong Kong

We begin with a survey of energy-saving techniques proposed in the medium access control (MAC) layer, and then develop a framework to minimize energy consumption in wireless sensor networks. While satisfying a range of quality of service requirements, such as the packet transmission success rate and maximum delay constraint, we optimally choose the lengths of periods in which sensors are active and inactive, such that the *energy consumption per unit time* in the entire network is minimized. We first use our framework to optimize the values of the MAC attributes *macBeaconOrder* and *macSuperframeOrder* in an IEEE 802.15.4 beacon-enabled star network. Then we consider a much simpler protocol, which we call "select-and-transmit" (S&T), and the same framework is applied to find the optimal lengths of the active and inactive portions.

24.1. Introduction

A sensor network is a collection of nodes with sensing, computing and communication capabilities that continuously observe and collect information on the entities or phenomena of interest in the physical world.[1] Initial research on sensor networks was driven by defense applications and can be dated back to the 1970s.[2] In these early sensor networks (e.g., a radar network used for air traffic control), the sensor nodes are usually large, expensive, and have unconstrained power supply.

Recent advances in microelectromechanical (MEMS) technology, wireless networking and low-power processors have enabled the development of wireless sensor networks (WSNs) which typically consist of a large number of diminutive, cheap, and usually battery-powered microsensors. These sensor nodes can be scattered on the ground, in the air, under water, on human bodies, and in vehicles or buildings. Applications envisioned for WSNs include military sensing, surveillance systems, healthcare systems, industrial and manufacturing automation, distributed robotics, and environment monitoring.[2–5]

Networked microsensor technology has been predicted to be one of the most important technologies for the 21st century, and it could revolutionize spatial information collection and drastically enhance our understanding of the physical environment.[6] On the other hand, it also poses new technical challenges in data processing, energy efficiency, network control and routing, collaborative information processing, sensor management, network security, and other fields.[7,8] In response to the opportunities and challenges, there has recently been a surge in research interest in sensor networks. The IEEE 802.15.4 standard[9] has been defined and the Zigbee Alliance has been set up to promote low-power low-rate wireless personal area networks. Many WSN research groups (e.g., SmartDust,[10] PicoRadio,[11] and WiseNet[12]) have been established. Hardware and software products for WSNs manufactured by companies like Chipcon, Crossbow and Ember are now commercially available.

One of the main challenges for a WSN is its need for an unprecedented system lifetime without human intervention. In many application scenarios, a deployed WSN is targeted to operate autonomously for several years.[12] A typical sensor node is comprised of a few components such as one or more sensing units for measurement, a microprocessor and a small amount of memory for computing and data storage, and a short range radio for wireless communication.[5] Each of these components consumes energy when a sensor node works. Unlike the traditional wireless devices that are typically mains-powered or powered by rechargeable batteries, low-cost and disposable WSN sensor nodes are constrained by limited on-board batteries that usually cannot be replaced or recharged. As a result, it is necessary to minimize energy consumption at all levels of a WSN system.

In recent years, tremendous research efforts have been devoted to the area of low-power design for WSNs. Heinzelman *et al.*[13] introduced a clustering protocol architecture called low-energy adaptive clustering hierarchy (LEACH). It randomly rotates the cluster head positions among all the nodes in the network to evenly distribute the energy load of cluster head operation and, as a result, maximizes the network lifetime. Estrin *et al.*[14,15] proposed a data-centric routing protocol called directed diffusion, where a sensing task is disseminated throughout the network as a task of interest and the data of the events that match the interest are transmitted along multiple gradient paths. A survey of routing protocols for WSNs can be found in Ref. 16. Ye *et al.*[17] identified the major sources of energy waste and proposed a medium access control (MAC) protocol for sensor networks where a low duty cycle is used to allow nodes to spend most of their time asleep. Data aggregation techniques were introduced to perform in-network filtering to combine the redundant messages from highly correlated sources that detect common phenomena.[18,19] In the physical layer, energy-harvesting technologies that exploit solar, vibration, wind or other sources of energy were proposed to supplement power supply for sensor nodes.[20]

It is recognized that MAC protocols play a crucial role in meeting the stringent requirement of energy consumption in sensor networks.[12,21] In this chapter, we restrict our attention to performance improvements for energy efficiency in the MAC layer. Given the low energy consumption requirement of sensor networks, simplicity has been an important objective in the design of MAC protocols including the IEEE 802.15.4 MAC. A question that may be posed is whether further simplification can be made to the MAC protocol. We consider here a simpler protocol, "select-and-transmit" (S&T), which resembles the first step of the slotted ALOHA protocol;[22] in this scheme, a sensor node chooses a transmission slot uniformly in an equally slotted period without using carrier sensing. We compare the S&T MAC protocol with the IEEE 802.15.4 MAC in terms of energy consumption over a wide range of scenarios. In this way, we challenge the IEEE 802.15.4 MAC and perhaps identify scenarios and applications where the standard may not be the best option.

Furthermore, we propose a new framework to minimize energy consumption for WSNs that operate using low duty cycles and are laid out in a single-hop star topology. Given user-specific quality of service (QoS) requirements (e.g., packet delivery ratio and maximum delay constraints), we optimize the active and inactive time periods of sensor nodes such that the energy consumption per unit time in the entire network is minimized. The S&T MAC protocol and the IEEE 802.15.4 MAC are examined under this energy optimization framework.

The remainder of this chapter is organized as follows. In Sec. 24.2, we briefly review the energy saving techniques proposed in the MAC layer for WSNs. The S&T MAC scheme and its analysis are presented in Sec. 24.3. In Sec. 24.4, we describe the energy models and the energy optimization framework for both the S&T MAC and the IEEE 802.15.4 MAC. Numerical results and discussion are presented in Sec. 24.5.

24.2. MAC Layer Energy Saving Techniques

The primary design goal of WSN MAC protocols is to meet the stringent requirement of energy efficiency. Traditional performance metrics (e.g., throughput, delay and fairness) for data networks become secondary in WSNs and are usually traded for energy cost.[23]

The major sources of energy waste in WSNs have been identified as idle listening, collisions, overhearing, protocol overhead and overemitting.[17,24] Idle listening refers to the listening performed by nodes for receiving possible traffic that is in fact not sent, and it would occur in many sensor network applications where traffic load is low. Packet collisions also deteriorate the energy efficiency of a WSN. When a transmitted packet is involved in a collision, it would be discarded and possibly retransmitted. Another source of energy waste is overhearing, which means that a node receives packets that are actually not destined for itself. Moreover, protocol overhead consumes energy when control packets are exchanged in the network. The last primary reason for energy waste is overemitting, which occurs when a node sends a message but its intended receiving node is not ready. In the following, we briefly review the existing WSN protocols that use various strategies to eliminate or mitigate the aforementioned causes of energy waste.

24.2.1. *Fixed allocation protocols*

Collisions, idle listening and overhearing can be avoided by using fixed allocation schemes. Sohrabi *et al.*[25] introduced a distributed protocol called self-organization medium access control for sensor networks (SMACS). This protocol enables nodes to discover their neighbors and build communication schedules without centralized control. Nodes transmit packets using TDMA schedules and randomly choose frequencies (or frequency hopping sequences) to allow concurrent transmissions.

Pei and Chien[26] proposed a power aware clustered TDMA (PACT) MAC protocol which uses passive clustering to rotate the duties of being the communication backbone nodes based on battery energy levels. In PACT, each frame consists of control mini-slots and data slots. In the beginning of a frame, every node turns on its radio to confirm the allocation of the TDMA data slots by exchanging control packets in the control mini-slots. It then shuts down the radio during the slots where it does not transmit or receive packets.

Some other TDMA-based MAC protocols for WSNs can be found in Refs. 27 to 29. These protocols are inherently free of collision and idle-listening, but they suffer from increased protocol overhead, packet delay and system complexity. In addition, it is inefficient to use static slot assignments in dynamic network environments where the number of active nodes are constantly varying.

24.2.2. *Random access protocols*

In a random access MAC protocol, backlogged nodes contend for the medium to transmit packets, and thus it is more flexible and requires less central control compared to a fixed allocation scheme. Ye *et al.*[17] proposed Sensor MAC (S-MAC), which uses CSMA-CA for channel access. As depicted in Fig. 24.1, S-MAC operates using low duty cycles, and each node chooses a sleep schedule and shares it with its neighbors before a listen-sleep cycle starts. Nodes that have common sleep schedules form virtual clusters to reduce control overhead. In S-MAC, nodes only stay awake if involved in communication tasks. To reduce delay, S-MAC uses a technique called adaptive listening, in which a node who overhears its neighbor's transmission will wake up for a short period at the end of the transmission in case it is

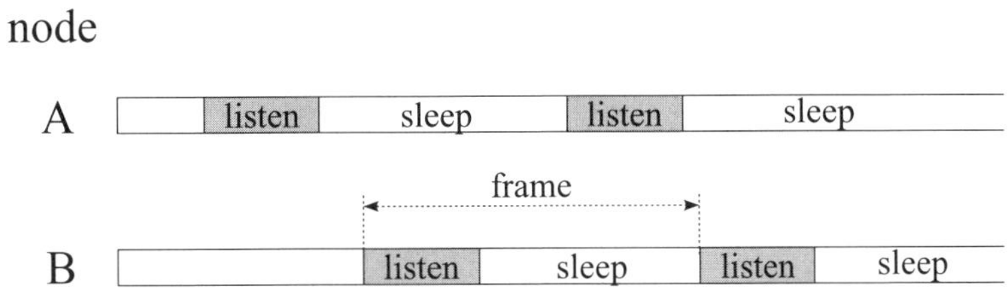

Fig. 24.1. S-MAC duty cycle.

the next hop for the packet. S-MAC also introduces a message-passing technique, in which long messages are fragmented into many small fragments and transmitted in a burst, and only RTS/CTS exchange is used. The length of the time period to transmit all the fragments and their ACK packets is included in the duration field of RTS/CTS packets. Nodes that hear these RTS/CTS packets will go to sleep until the transmission is finished.

One of the challenges of using S-MAC in a real sensor network is to appropriately determine a sleep schedule, especially under varying traffic loads. The timeout MAC (T-MAC) was introduced by van Dam and Langendoen[30] to adaptively choose a duty cycle. In T-MAC, if a node does not detect any activation event for an empirically determined time threshold *TA*, it assumes that no neighboring nodes want to communicate with it, and goes to sleep. When a node overhears an RTS/CTS message indicating that other nodes will commence transmitting, it temporarily turns off its radio. The node wakes up again at the end of the transmission and starts a new time-out. The advantage of T-MAC is that it dynamically adjusts itself to network traffic fluctuations. However, the aggressive turn-to-sleep policy may cause an early sleep phenomenon where a node goes to sleep when a neighbor node still has messages for it.

Lin *et al.*[31] proposed a dynamic sensor-MAC (DSMAC) by adjusting duty cycles to varying traffic conditions to achieve a good trade-off between energy consumption and packet delay. In DSMAC, all nodes use a common basic service duty cycle at the beginning. When a node sends a packet, the one-hop delay of the packet (the time difference between the arrival of a packet and its departure) is piggybacked. If the receiver node notices that the packet delay is intolerable, it makes a decision to double the duty cycle by reducing the length of the sleep period. In the synchronization period of the next cycle, the new duty cycle is announced, and a node will adopt it provided its queue is non-empty and the battery level is above a certain threshold.

Polastre *et al.*[32] introduced a CSMA-based protocol called Berkeley MAC (B-MAC) which provides configurable interfaces of system services for performance optimization. In B-MAC, clear channel assessment is performed by using a weighted moving average of samples for effective collision avoidance. Instead of using exponential backoffs, B-MAC includes a configurable linear backoff mechanism to minimize

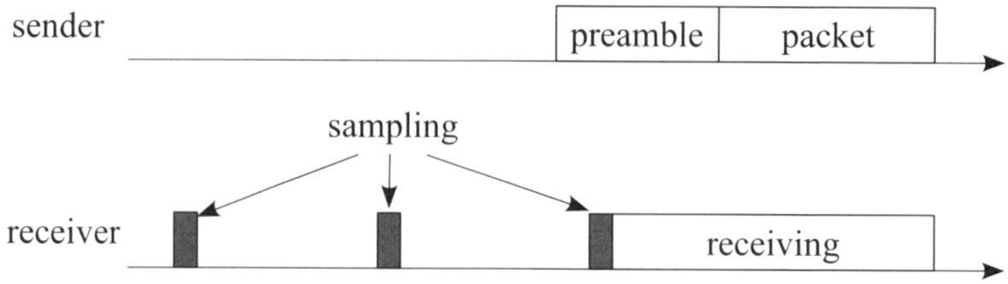

Fig. 24.2. Preamble sampling technique.

packet delay. Furthermore, an adaptive low power listening technique is employed to reduce duty cycles and minimize idle listening.

El-Hoiydi *et al.*[33] developed the wireless sensor MAC (WiseMAC) protocol that uses a preamble sampling technique. Preamble sampling is based on a carrier sense technique that effectively shifts the energy cost from the receiver to the senders. As illustrated in Fig. 24.2, a sender node transmits a wake-up preamble followed by the backlogged message. In WiseMAC, all nodes in the network perform channel sampling periodically with independent sampling offsets. If the channel is detected busy, it continues to listen and receives data. To reduce the energy consumption caused by unnecessarily long preambles, the authors introduced a scheme where sampling schedules are shared among direct neighbors by piggybacking schedules into acknowledgment frames. Consequently, a sender node can transmit a minimized wake-up preamble just before the sampling moment of the intended receiver to minimize energy consumption.

Wake-up-frame (WUF)[34] is another approach which is based on the preamble sampling technique. A WUF frame is composed of multiple short WUFs (SWUFs), each of which includes the destination address and the position of the current SWUF in the whole WUF. When a node wakes up, it starts to listen to the preamble. As long as it receives a complete SWUF, it knows the destination address of the pending data. If the data is not intended for itself, the node immediately goes back to sleep to avoid overhearing. If the node is the destination, it reads the position of the SWUF and may decide to sleep until the data come. In this way, the unnecessary waiting time is drastically reduced. The authors extended their approach by combing WUF and the WiseMAC to obtain a further optimized low-power MAC.[35]

Lu *et al.*[36] designed the data gathering MAC (DMAC) protocol to achieve very low packet delay without compromising energy efficiency. As shown in Fig. 24.3, a hierarchical node-to-sink data gathering tree is formed in DMAC. The protocol operates using a low duty cycle, and each cycle is divided into receiving, sending and sleep periods. The main design feature of DMAC is that it uses a staggered wake-up schedule such that packets can be transmitted continuously from nodes to sink along a multihop path (see Fig. 24.3). In a receiving state, a node receives packets from its leaf nodes which contend for the medium based on a CSMA protocol.

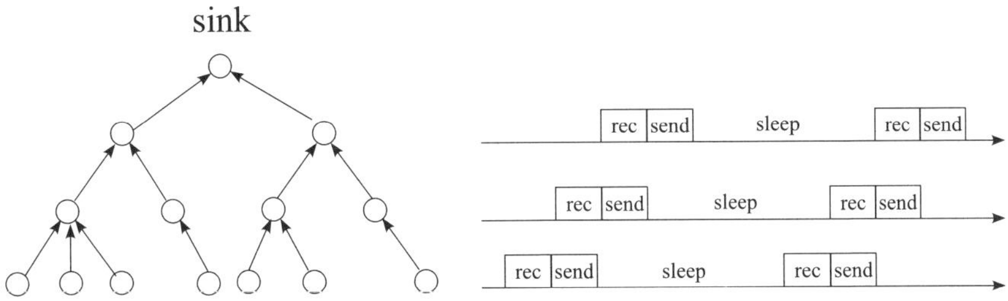

Fig. 24.3. DMAC in data gathering tree (adapted from Ref. 36).

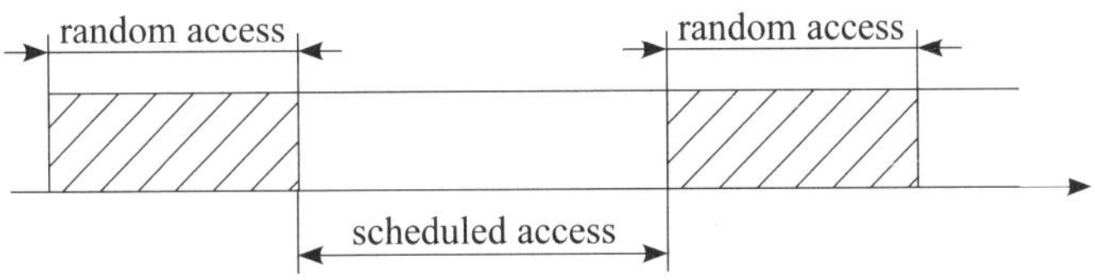

Fig. 24.4. Slot organization in TRAMA.

Park *et al.*[37] proposed an asynchronous MAC protocol called fine-grained wakeup request MAC (FG-MAC) in which a low power listening techniques is used. FG-MAC reduces power consumption by minimizing the wakeup duration and avoiding collisions. The methods of fine-grained wakeup transmission with long acknowledgment and collision avoidance with random length preambles are proposed for energy efficiency.

Despite the flexibility and low protocol overhead, random access MAC protocols may suffer from collisions, idle listening, and long packet delay under high contention levels.

24.2.3. *Hybrid TDMA/CSMA protocols*

A few hybrid MAC protocols that combine the strengths of TDMA and random access have been proposed. Rajendran[38] developed the traffic-adaptive MAC (TRAMA) protocol for energy-efficient and collision-free channel access in WSNs. In TRAMA, time is divided into random access and scheduled access periods, as depicted in Fig. 24.4. In the random access period, nodes transmit signaling packets, establish two-hop topology information among neighboring nodes, and exchange transmission schedules. As a result, backlogged nodes are allocated dedicated slots in the scheduled access periods for data transmission.

Rhee *et al.*[39] introduced a hybrid MAC protocol, called Zebra MAC (Z-MAC), which operates adaptively to the contention level of the network. In Z-MAC, a time slot is assigned to an owner node of the slot, and the other nodes that can also use the slot are called non-owners of the slot. Unlike fixed slot assignment in TDMA, CSMA-based random access is used for data transmission in Z-MAC. The owner node of a slot has the priority to access the slot by using a smaller initial contention window than those of the non-owner nodes. When the contention level is high, the owner nodes have prioritized channel access to their slots to avoid collisions so that Z-MAC behaves like TDMA. Under low contention, however, the protocol operates like CSMA because the owner node of a slot may not have data to transmit and the non-owner nodes can contend for the use of the slot. In this way, the Z-MAC protocol is able to dynamically switch between TDMA and CSMA depending on the traffic load.

24.2.4. *Other protocols*

Some other WSN MAC protocols that use distinct energy saving techniques from the aforementioned protocols were also proposed. Schurgers *et al.*[40] developed the sparse topology and energy management (STEM) protocol, in which a low-power secondary paging channel is used for transmitting wake-up signals. Upon receiving a wake-up signal, a node turns on its primary radio for data transmission. The authors show that the protocol is especially suitable for networks having sporadic traffic.

Tay *et al.*[41] proposed a CSMA/p^* protocol that uses optimal channel access probabilities for CSMA to minimize the probability of collision. The same authors empirically chose a non-uniform probability distribution for channel access and developed the Sift protocol that is a suboptimal version of CSMA/p^* in the case of unknown network size.[42]

Recently, researchers have proposed cross-layer techniques to minimize energy consumption in WSNs. For instance, Jurdak *et al.*[43] introduced a cross-layer framework where a flexible cost function at the routing layer and adaptive duty cycles at the MAC layer are used to adapt a node's behavior to its local state. Cui *et al.*[44] considered the joint design of the physical, MAC and routing layers by solving convex optimization problems.

24.3. S&T MAC Scheme

In this section, we describe the S&T MAC scheme. We also derive the probability that at least k out of n nodes successfully transmit their packets under the S&T MAC. This is a new solution to a problem that bears some similarity to certain occupancy problems.[45]

24.3.1. *Protocol description*

The network scenario we consider, similar to that defined in IEEE 802.15.4, is a beacon-enabled star-topology network where one node is designated as the network

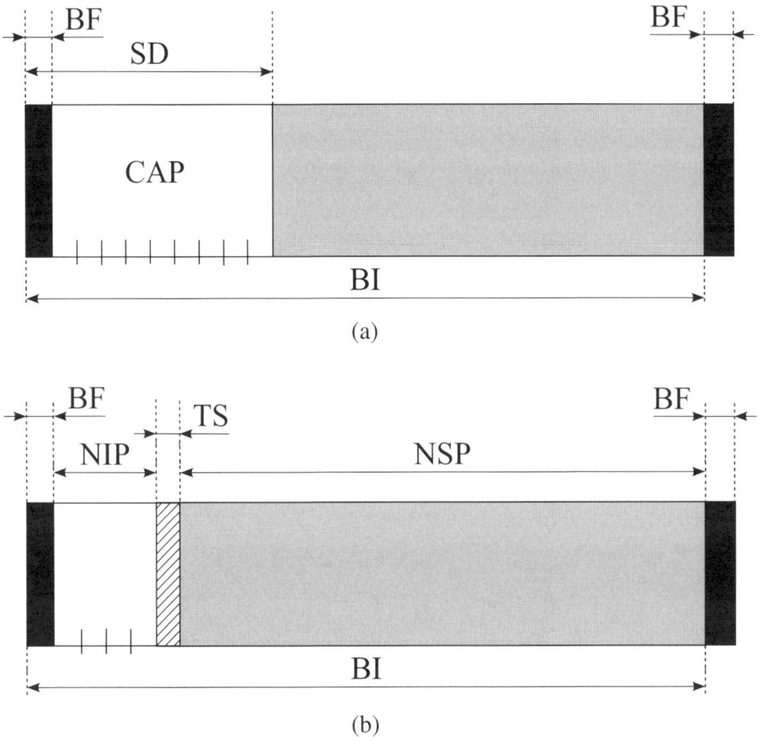

Fig. 24.5. S&T MAC superframe structures. (a) Network coordinator superframe and (b) sensor node superframe.

coordinator. As shown in Fig. 24.5(a), in the S&T superframe structure, we divide the superframe duration (SD) into coarse slots such that each slot is sufficient to transmit one packet. The slot size can be slightly increased if acknowledgment frames are required after the successful reception of the data by the coordinator.

In the S&T MAC, a backlogged node wakes up at the beginning of a beacon interval (BI), listens to the beacon frame (BF), and then chooses a slot for transmission in the contention access period (CAP) according to a uniform distribution, i.e., if TS denotes the index of the chosen slot, then $TS = i$, $i = 1, 2, \ldots, T$, with probability $1/T$. (Note that we call $i = 1$ the slot immediately after the BF.) Let T_{bn}, T and T_{bi} denote the lengths (all measured in number of slots) of BF, CAP and BI, respectively.

After waiting for a node idle period (NIP), T_{nip}, which equals $TS - 1$ slots, the node transmits its packet and then goes back to sleep for a node sleep period (NSP), T_{nsp}, until the end of the current BI. If two or more nodes select the same slot, a collision results. The superframe structure for the nodes is illustrated in Fig. 24.5(b).

24.3.2. *Protocol analysis*

Because a node chooses a transmission slot uniformly in T, the mean of T_{nip} in the S&T MAC is given by

$$E[T_{nip}] = \frac{T-1}{2}. \tag{24.1}$$

We can also compute the mean of the node sleep period T_{nsp} as follows:

$$\begin{aligned} E[T_{nsp}] &= T_{bi} - T_{bn} - E[T_{nip}] - 1 \\ &= T_{bi} - T_{bn} - \frac{T+1}{2}. \end{aligned} \tag{24.2}$$

The occurrence of at least one collision in S&T MAC, p_c, is given by

$$\begin{aligned} p_c &= 1 - P(\text{no collision}) \\ &= 1 - \binom{T}{n} \Big/ T^n, \end{aligned} \tag{24.3}$$

where n denotes the number of contending nodes. As depicted in Fig. 24.6, the probability of at least one collision is almost unavoidable in S&T MAC, even when n is small and T is big. This is obviously undesirable for most of the traditional data networks, in which QoS requirements such as low loss rate and high throughput need to be met.

However, as discussed in Ref. 46, a considerable packet loss may still be tolerable in the context of sensor networks. This is because multiple nodes may be deployed in the same geographic area for fault-tolerance and reliability, and so it is highly possible that many nodes will sense the same events. In order to deliver the

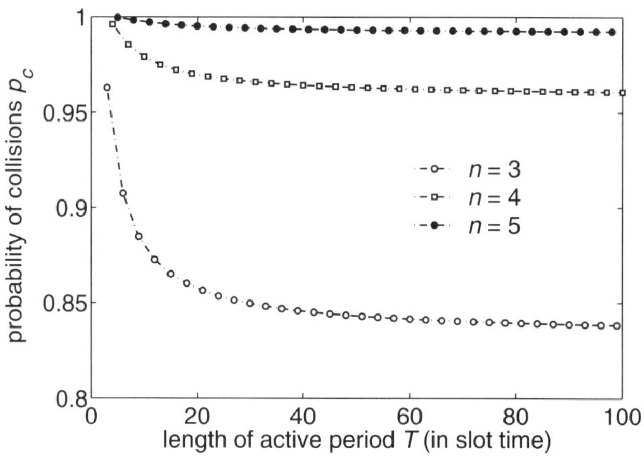

Fig. 24.6. Probability of collision.

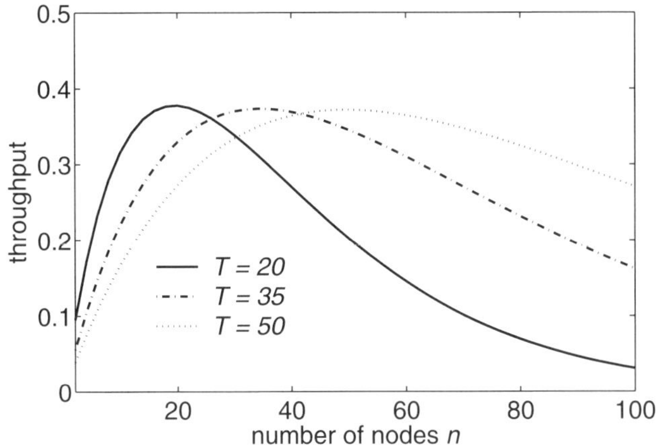

Fig. 24.7. Throughput.

information of an event to the coordinator, only one (or a few more for reliability) out of the nodes that observe the event is required to successfully report the event.[41]

At this point, we digress slightly to mention an interesting fact concerning the throughput of the protocol. According to the results in Exercise 3.4,[47] the expected number of slots with exactly one packet is given by

$$n_s = n\left(1 - \frac{1}{T}\right)^{n-1}. \tag{24.4}$$

Let S be the normalized throughput which is defined as follows:

$$S = \frac{n_s}{T}. \tag{24.5}$$

Figure 24.7 shows the throughput for different scenarios. It can be observed that when the number of slots is equal to the number of nodes, i.e., $n = T$, the throughput is maximized.

We now derive the probability that at least k out of n nodes successfully transmit their packets (i.e., without collisions) in a given T using the S&T MAC scheme. This is in fact equivalent to a generalized birthday problem pertaining to the probability that at least k out of n people have different birthdays. Let P_k denote the probability that *exactly* k out of n nodes are successful. The following result holds.

Lemma 24.1. (a) *If* $n \leq T$,

$$P_n = \frac{T!}{T^n(T-n)!}. \tag{24.6}$$

(b) *If* $0 \leq k \leq n-2$ *and* $k < T$,

$$P_k = \frac{1}{T^n} \times \sum_{w=k}^{\min(n,T)} \binom{n}{w}\binom{T}{w}\binom{w}{k} w!\,(-1)^{w-k}(T-w)^{n-w}. \tag{24.7}$$

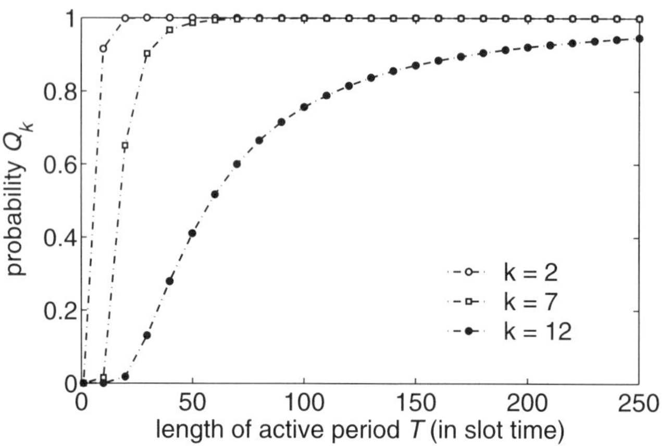

Fig. 24.8. Probability Q_k versus length of active period T. $n = 15$.

Proof. See the Appendix in Ref. 48. □

We define Q_k to be the probability that *at least* k out of n nodes are successful. It follows from Lemma 24.1 that for $1 \leq k \leq n-2$ and $k < T$:

$$Q_k = 1 - \sum_{j=0}^{k-1} P_j, \tag{24.8}$$

where P_j is given by (24.7). Note that when $k = n-1$, P_k is equal to P_n, i.e., the probability of $n-1$ successes out of n nodes is the same as the probability that all of the n nodes are successful. This is because the last node cannot collide with itself.

Figure 24.8 demonstrates that when k is relatively small compared to n, the probability Q_k can be made to quickly converge to 1 through a modest increase in T, while a much larger T is required for the same effect if k is large. A large active period T is undesirable since it corresponds to high energy consumption. These results suggest that the S&T MAC is most likely to be a competitive MAC solution for scenarios where only a small proportion of the packets are needed to report some event (e.g., event-driven workload[41]). It should be noted that the S&T MAC has the advantage of simplicity; it entails only a small number of operations which may facilitate the reduction of energy consumption for computation and possibly lead to simplification of hardware design.

24.4. Energy Optimization Framework

In this section, we first describe the energy models and then formulate optimization problems which minimize the energy consumption per unit time of the whole network. We then apply the energy optimization framework to the S&T MAC and the IEEE 802.15.4 MAC.

Consider N to be a random variable representing the number of backlogged nodes at the beginning of a BI, and let n denote an outcome of N. We also allow the requirement for the number of successful packets k to vary as a function of n, and we capture this dependence through the notation $k(n)$. In addition, we introduce the following notation.

- N_{all} : number of nodes (excluding the coordinator) in the network.
- p_N : probability mass function of N.
- D_{max} : maximum delay constraint, [s].
- $W_{k(n)}$: probability of at least k successes out of n nodes for the IEEE 802.15.4 MAC.
- $Q_{k(n)}$: probability of at least k successes out of n nodes for the S&T MAC.
- $\eta_{k(n)}$: a user-specific QoS requirement for $W_{k(n)}$ and $Q_{k(n)}$.
- S_{bn} : slot duration for the BF, for the IEEE 802.15.4 MAC, [s].
- S_{sd} : length of SD in the IEEE 802.15.4 MAC, [s].
- S_{bi} : length of BI in the IEEE 802.15.4 MAC, [s].
- S_{nip} : average node idle time spent in backoff state, for the IEEE 802.15.4 MAC, [s].
- S_{nsp} : average node sleep time, for the IEEE 802.15.4 MAC, [s].
- m_{cca} : average number of CCA operations performed in one BI, for the IEEE 802.15.4 MAC.
- m_{tx} : average number of packet transmissions in one BI, for the IEEE 802.15.4 MAC.
- t_{slot} : slot size, for the S&T MAC, [s].
- P_{active} : average coordinator power consumption during SD, [mW].
- P_{idle} : node power consumption in idle period, [mW].
- P_{sleep} : node power consumption in sleep period, [mW].
- E_{sum}^{std} : overall energy consumption in one BI, for the IEEE 802.15.4 MAC, [mJ].
- $E_{sum}^{s\&t}$: overall energy consumption in one BI, for the S&T MAC, [mJ].
- E_0 : node energy consumption to wake up and listen to the BF, [mJ].
- E_t : node energy consumption to transmit a packet, [mJ].
- E_{cca} : energy consumption to perform a CCA operation, [mJ].

24.4.1. *Energy models*

A typical sensor node consumes energy when it carries out different operations such as computation, data storage, radio communication, etc. In our energy models, we only investigate the energy consumption of the radio unit, which is highly relevant

Table 24.1. Electrical specifications.

Parameter	Value
Voltage (V)	3
Transmit current (mA)	20
Receive current (mA)	15
Idle current (mA)	10
Average current for active coordinator (mA)	16
Sleep current (mA)	0.03
Initialize radio and time (mA, s)	6, 3.5×10^{-4}
Turn on radio and time (mA, s)	1, 1.3×10^{-3}
Sleep to RX and time (mA, s)	15, 2.5×10^{-4}

to the design of MAC protocols. A sensor node usually supports four modes of operation (e.g., the Chipcon CC1000 transceiver[49]):

- sleep, in which a node operates under a very low power consumption and its radio is completely turned off;
- idle, in which a node temporarily turns off some circuitries, and its radio unit operates in a low power mode and can be immediately turned on by receiving a corresponding command;
- transmit, in which a node transmits data;
- receive, in which a node receives data;

In addition, we also consider the energy consumption when a node turns on its radio, switches between transmitting and receiving states, and samples the channel to determine the channel status. In our energy models, we use the same electrical specifications as in Ref. 32, and they are summarized in Table 24.1.

In the following, we apply the energy models to the S&T MAC scheme and the IEEE 802.15.4 MAC. For simplicity, we do not use acknowledgments for both of the two MAC schemes and assume an ideal channel such that every transmitted packet that does not suffer a collision is successfully received.

24.4.1.1. *S&T MAC*

In the S&T MAC, the overall energy consumption in a network during one BI consists of a few components. Firstly, the network coordinator is active for $T_{bn} + T$ slots and inactive for $T_{bi} - T_{bn} - T$ slots. Secondly, every node spends energy E_0 in waking up and listening to the BF. When a node wakes up, it switches from sleep mode to receive mode and turns on its radio. Thirdly, the backlogged nodes transmit their packets by randomly selecting slots in T. Therefore, a backlogged node on average spends T_{nip} in the backoff state and goes back to sleep for T_{nsp}, i.e., the rest of the current BI. Finally, non-backlogged nodes immediately go to sleep after the BF and expend $P_{sleep}(T_{bi} - T_{bn})$ amount of energy.

Therefore, given that there are N_{all} nodes in a network and n of them are backlogged, the overall energy consumption in one BI for the S&T MAC, $E^{s\&t}_{sum}$,

can be given by

$$E_{sum}^{s\&t}(n) = \underbrace{(P_{active}(T_{bn} + T) + P_{sleep}(T_{bi} - T_{bn} - T))\, t_{slot}}_{for\ coordinator} + \underbrace{N_{all}E_0}_{for\ all\ nodes}$$
$$+ \underbrace{n(P_{idle}E[T_{nip}]t_{slot} + E_t + P_{sleep}E[T_{nsp}]t_{slot})}_{for\ backlogged\ nodes}$$
$$+ \underbrace{(N_{all} - n)P_{sleep}(T_{bi} - T_{bn})t_{slot}}_{for\ non\text{-}backlogged\ nodes}. \tag{24.9}$$

24.4.1.2. *IEEE 802.15.4 MAC*

Similarly, the following four components contribute to the overall energy consumption of an IEEE 802.15.4 network in one BI. The first part is from the fact that the network coordinator is active for S_{sd} and inactive for $(S_{bi} - S_{sd})$. Secondly, each node in the network consumes E_0 in waking up and listening to the BF. Moreover, the backlogged nodes perform, on average, m_{cca} CCA operations in one BI and m_{tx} of the nodes eventually transmit their packets using the slotted CSMA-CA mechanism. The CCA mode we choose for our energy model is "carrier sense only", in which a busy medium is reported only when a signal with the modulation and spreading characteristics of 802.15.4 is detected.[9] A backlogged node on average spends S_{nip} in the backoff state and goes back to sleep for S_{nsp}, i.e., the rest of the current BI. Finally, non-backlogged nodes consume $P_{sleep}(S_{bi} - S_{bn})$ amount of energy in one BI.

In summary, the overall energy consumption in a BI for the IEEE 802.15.4 MAC, E_{sum}^{std}, is given by:

$$E_{sum}^{std}(n) = \underbrace{P_{active}S_{sd} + P_{sleep}(S_{bi} - S_{sd})}_{for\ coordinator} + \underbrace{N_{all}E_0}_{for\ all\ nodes}$$
$$+ \underbrace{m_{cca}E_{cca} + m_{tx}E_t + n(P_{idle}S_{nip} + P_{sleep}S_{nsp})}_{for\ backlogged\ nodes}$$
$$+ \underbrace{(N_{all} - n)P_{sleep}(S_{bi} - S_{bn})}_{for\ non\text{-}backlogged\ nodes}. \tag{24.10}$$

Note that there are two major differences between the energy consumption models of the two MAC schemes. Firstly, a S&T node does not perform carrier sensing before transmission. Secondly, in the standard, a backlogged node may not have a chance to transmit its packet before the end of the current CAP, while in S&T MAC, every backlogged node transmits its packet.

24.4.2. *Energy consumption optimization*

In sensor networks, there is an inherent trade-off between energy efficiency and other performance metrics such as average packet delay and packet delivery ratio.

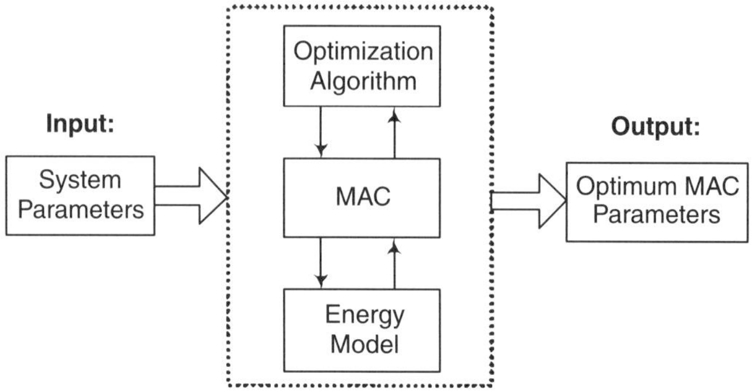

Fig. 24.9. Energy minimization framework.

To minimize energy consumption, sensor networks usually operate with extremely low duty cycles (e.g., 1% or 0.1%) such that sensor nodes are allowed to spend most of their time sleeping. In the existing MAC protocols for WSNs, duty cycles are either empirically decided (e.g., as in S-MAC[17]) or adaptive only to traffic loads (e.g., as in T-MAC[30] and DSMAC[31]). The solution to the problem of optimal duty cycles while satisfying a range of user-specific QoS constraints still remains unaddressed.

In this work, we present an energy optimization framework which minimizes energy consumption in sensor networks and attains the flexibility to incorporate various QoS requirements. Figure 24.9 shows the general structure of the proposed framework. Given the system parameters such as the traffic models and the user-specific QoS parameters, we design duty cycle optimization algorithms that interact with the underlying MAC protocol and energy models. Our aim is to minimize the expectation of the overall energy consumption per unit time. To this end, we describe the generic optimization problem as follows:

Objective function: *minimize: expected unit time energy consumption*
Decision variables: *sensor active and inactive time periods in one cycle*
Constraints: *packet delivery ratio and maximum packet delay.*

Taking the expectation of the overall energy consumption per unit time in one BI, we now formulate the energy optimization problem for the S&T MAC as follows:

$$\begin{aligned} \min : \ & \frac{1}{T_{bi}\ t_{slot}} \sum_{n=0}^{N_{all}} p_N(n)\ E_{sum}^{s\&t}(n) \\ s.t. \quad & Q_{k(n)} \geq \eta_{k(n)} \\ & (T_{bi} + T)t_{slot} \leq D_{max} \\ & T \geq k(n) \\ & T_{bi} \geq T + T_{bn}, \end{aligned} \tag{24.11}$$

where $n = 0, 1, \ldots, N_{all}$. Here the decision variables are T and T_{bi}. The first constraint is to satisfy that at least k out of n nodes are successful with probability no less than $\eta_{k(n)}$, and the second constraint is to meet the maximum delay requirement. The third constraint is to set a lower bound for T, which must be greater than or equal to the number of the required successful nodes $k(n)$. The fourth constraint shows that the length of a SD is no longer than that of a BI.

Similarly, the optimization problem for the IEEE 802.15.4 MAC is formulated as follows:

$$\begin{aligned} \min : \ & \frac{1}{S_{bi}} \sum_{n=0}^{N_{all}} p_N(n)\ E_{sum}^{std}(n) \\ s.t.\ \ & W_{k(n)} \geq \eta_{k(n)} \\ & S_{bi} + S_{sd} - S_{bn} \leq D_{max} \\ & 0 \leq SO \leq BO \leq 14, \end{aligned} \tag{24.12}$$

where $n = 0, 1, \ldots, N_{all}$. The decision variables are SO and BO. Note that S_{sd} and S_{bi} are one-to-one functions of SO and BO, respectively. Again, the first and the second constraints are packet delivery ratio and maximum packet delay, respectively. The worst case packet delay we consider is equal to $S_{bi} + S_{sd} - S_{bn}$, which will be explained in the traffic model in the next section. The third constraint $0 \leq SO \leq BO \leq 14$ is defined in the standard.

24.5. Numerical Evaluation

In this section, we first describe the traffic model we used and define three different scenarios to evaluate the performance of the proposed energy optimization framework. We then solve the energy optimization problems for the S&T MAC and IEEE 802.15.4 MAC and present the numerical results.

24.5.1. *Traffic model*

In the scenarios we consider, a node becomes backlogged if during the previous BI (including the sleep time) one or more packets have been generated for transmission. The random variable N representing the number of backlogged nodes at the beginning of a BI is generally distributed and this distribution is denoted as $p_N(n)$, where n denotes an outcome of N.

We make the observation that if more than one packet is in the transmission buffer, it is possible for users to make choices regarding the order of transmission and whether redundant packets can be dropped. In particular, if packets awaiting transmission contain information on the same event, only the latest is relevant, and it is sensible to discard the old ones. In our setup, we assume that when a node generates a new packet, it will be accommodated into the transmission buffer if the buffer is empty. When there is already a packet in the node's buffer, the action taken depends on the status of the node. If the node is active, it means the buffered packet is attempting to transmit, so the new packet will wait to transmit in the next BI. If the node is sleeping, the new packet will replace the old one, which will be discarded.

Furthermore, since duty cycles of sensor networks are usually very low, we assume that a packet which is generated in the previous BI will be discarded if it fails to be transmitted in the current SD. This explains the worst case delay constraints we used for the optimization problems for both MAC schemes.

24.5.2. *Scenario definition*

As mentioned in Sec. 24.4, k is defined as a function of n. To evaluate the energy consumption performance for the two MAC protocols, we define a generic function $k(n) = \min(\alpha_1 n, \alpha_2 N_{all})$, where $\alpha_1, \alpha_2 \in (0, 1)$ and $\alpha_1 \geq \alpha_2$. This function typically allows k to increase proportionally with n until it hits the upper bound $\alpha_2 N_{all}$ when n is close to N_{all}.

Three scenarios with different values of α_1 and α_2 are defined for evaluation, as shown in Table 24.2. In Scenario A, we are interested in the successful transmission of a very small proportion of the packets. Applications consistent with these scenarios could be event-driven sensor networks (refer to Ref. 41 for detailed examples). Conversely, in Scenario C most of the packets need to be transmitted successfully. Scenario B corresponds to an intermediate case.

24.5.3. *Results and discussion*

We adopted the electrical specifications used in Ref. 32 (reproduced in Table 24.1), which are based on the CC1000 transceiver.[49] We assume that the transmit and receive power levels are constant and the same for all nodes. Some other system parameters are shown in Table 24.3. We also used the specifications of the various frequency bands (i.e., the frequency bands of 868 MHz, 915 MHz and 2.4 GHz) defined in IEEE 802.15.4.[9] Note that the slot sizes we used in S&T MAC are 0.01 s, 0.005 s, and 0.001 s corresponding to the frequency bands 868 MHz, 915 MHz and 2.4 GHz, respectively.

We chose Poisson processes for packet generation of the nodes, which means that for each node, the probability to become backlogged at the beginning of a BI

Table 24.2. Evaluation scenarios.

Scenario	α_1	α_2
A	0.2	0.1
B	0.5	0.4
C	0.8	0.7

Table 24.3. Other system parameters.

Parameter	Value
Data packet size (PHY) (bytes)	25
Beacon frame size (bytes)	25
Maximum packet delay (s)	5
Average packet arrival rate (packets/s)	0.5
QoS requirement $\eta_k(n)$	0.90
Number of slots for BF in S&T MAC, T_{bn}	1
Slot duration for S&T MAC	variable

is given by

$$p_{nd} = 1 - e^{-\lambda t}, \tag{24.13}$$

where λ is the average packet arrival rate and $t = T_{bi}\ t_{slot}$ for the S&T MAC and $t = S_{bi}$ for IEEE 802.15.4 MAC. Given a network with N_{all} sensor nodes, the probability mass function of N is given by

$$p_N(n) = \binom{N_{all}}{n} p_{nd}^n (1 - p_{nd})^{N_{all}-n}. \tag{24.14}$$

We implemented a simulator for the IEEE 802.15.4 MAC in the C++ programming language. For each set of parameters (i.e., SO, BO, n and N_{all}), we ran a simulation to obtain the packet delivery ratio $W_{k(n)}$ and all the parameters required to compute the energy consumption based on (24.10). We have repeated the process a sufficient number of times such that the radius of the 95% confidence interval based on student-t distribution is within 5% of the energy consumption value. For the S&T MAC, given a set of values of T, T_{bi}, n and N_{all}, we have the analytical results (24.1) and (24.3) for the two parameters required for the energy consumption computation, and therefore no simulations were required.

Since T, T_{bi}, SO and BO are all integer-valued and their ranges are limited by D_{max}, we were able to use exhaustive search to solve the optimization problems. For the case of the S&T MAC, we used the analytical result for $Q_{k(n)}$ (24.8) to exclude cases that violate the constraint $Q_{k(n)} \geq \eta_{k(n)}$. We used the GNU Multiple Precision (GMP) arithmetic library to compute factorials for large numbers.[50]

Figures 24.10–24.12 illustrate the performance comparisons of the minimal energy consumption for the S&T MAC and the IEEE 802.15.4 MAC in various frequency bands and scenarios. Results for the 915 MHz frequency band are not shown because they are similar to the results for the 868 MHz frequency band.

It can be observed that the energy consumption is significantly reduced when high data rate is used. For relatively small k in Scenario A and B, the energy consumption of the two MAC schemes are comparable. In fact, the S&T MAC has lower energy consumption than the standard in Scenario A when the frequency band is 2.4 GHz.

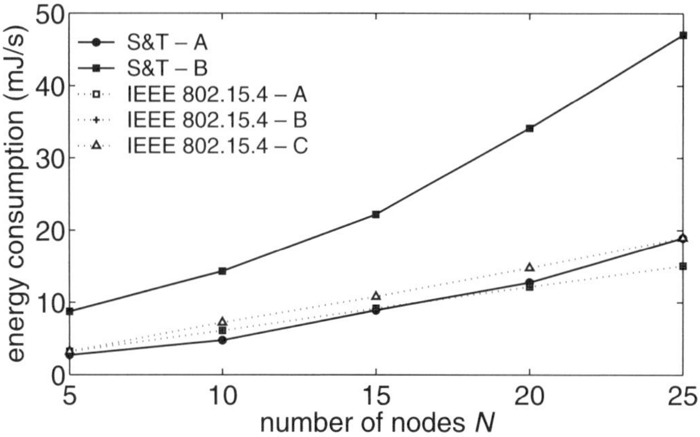

Fig. 24.10. Minimal energy comparison between S&T MAC and IEEE 802.15.4 MAC in the 868 MHz frequency band.

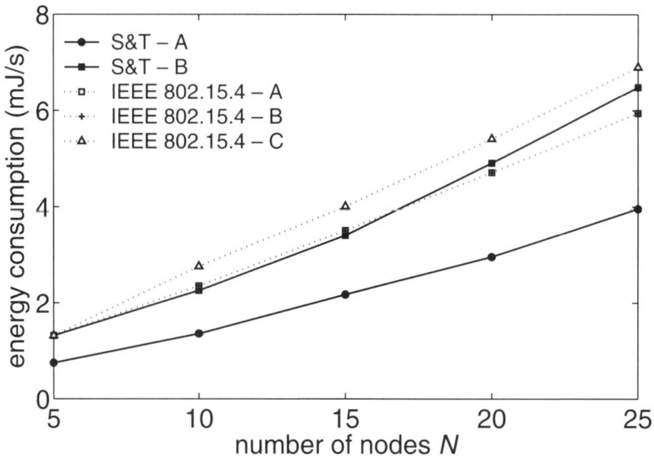

Fig. 24.11. Minimal energy comparison between S&T MAC and IEEE 802.15.4 MAC in the 2.4 GHz frequency band.

However, in Scenario C where k is relatively large, the standard can still maintain a low level of energy consumption, while the energy of the S&T MAC increases dramatically, as depicted separately in Fig. 24.12. This is because when k is relatively large, the length of CAP, T, needs to be large (and thus the node idle period T_{nip} is greatly increased), as shown in Fig. 24.8. The optimal solutions for the two MAC schemes are listed in Table 24.4.

We also discovered by simulation that the energy consumption of the 802.15.4 MAC under our proposed energy minimization framework does not benefit from the

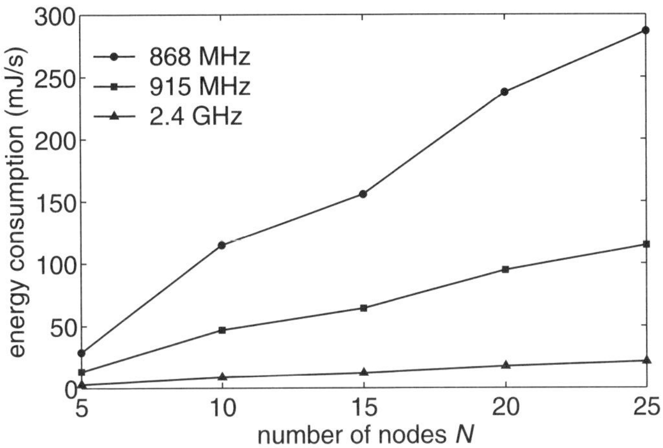

Fig. 24.12. Minimal energy consumption of the S&T MAC in Scenario C.

Table 24.4. Optimal solutions for 802.15.4 MAC and S&T MAC in different frequency bands.

		Scenario A				Scenario B				Scenario C			
		802.15.4		S&T		802.15.4		S&T		802.15.4		S&T	
Band	N_{all}	SO	BO	T	T_{bi}	SO	BO	T	T_{bi}	SO	BO	T	T_{bi}
	5	0	6	6	492	0	6	30	468	0	6	97	401
	10	0	6	6	492	0	6	30	468	1	6	202	296
868 MHz	15	0	6	10	448	0	6	34	464	1	6	202	296
	20	0	6	11	487	0	6	41	457	1	6	230	286
	25	0	6	15	483	0	6	47	451	1	6	230	286
	5	0	7	6	992	0	7	30	968	0	7	97	901
	10	0	7	6	992	0	7	30	968	1	7	202	796
915 MHz	15	0	7	10	998	0	7	34	964	1	7	202	796
	20	0	7	11	987	0	7	41	957	1	7	230	768
	25	0	7	15	983	0	7	47	951	1	7	230	768
	5	0	7	6	4992	0	7	30	4968	0	7	97	4901
	10	0	7	6	4992	0	7	30	4968	1	7	202	4796
2.4 GHz	15	0	7	10	4998	0	7	34	4964	1	7	202	4796
	20	0	7	11	4987	0	7	41	4957	1	7	230	4768
	25	0	7	15	4983	0	7	47	4951	1	7	230	4768

use of the battery life extension mode. Figure 24.13 compares the energy consumption between the battery life extension mode and the regular mode for the standard operating at 2.4 GHz. Similar results were found for the other frequency bands. The energy consumption remains virtually unchanged when k is small as in Scenario A and B. In Scenario C, while the battery life extension mode shows minor advantage for low traffic load, it performs even worse than the regular mode when the node

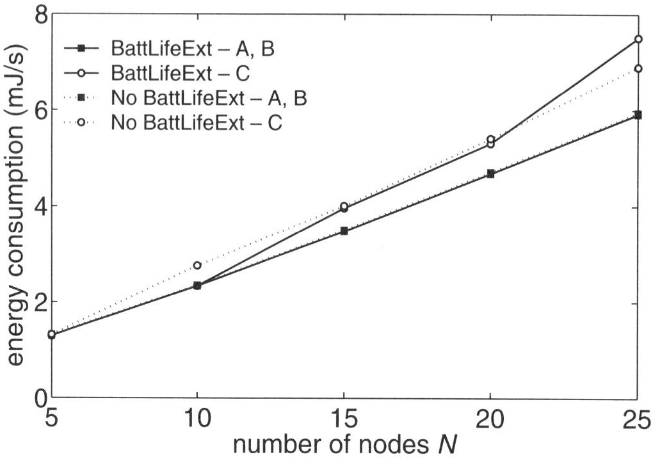

Fig. 24.13. Battery life extension mode and regular mode of 802.15.4 in 2.4 GHz frequency band.

Table 24.5. 802.15.4 battery life extension mode.

N_{all}	SO	BO
5	0	7
10	0	7
15	1	7
20	1	7
25	2	7

population becomes large. This is because in the battery life extension mode, the *backoff exponent BE* starts from 2 and thus it has a smaller backoff range than the regular mode, while the maximum number of backoffs, *macMaxCSMABackoffs*, remains the same. When the traffic load increases, there is more contention and more nodes will reach *macMaxCSMABackoffs* and give up transmission. In order to meet the proportion of successful packet transmissions, the SD must be increased, which results in an increase in energy consumption. This is verified by the results in Table 24.5. For example, when N_{all} is equal to 25 in the 2.4 GHz frequency band with Scenario C, the optimal SO becomes 2 ($SO = 1$ is no longer a feasible solution), whereas in the regular mode, the optimal SO remains at 1 (see Table 24.4).

24.6. Conclusions

In this chapter, we focused on the problem of energy optimization in WSNs. We presented a brief literature review for MAC protocols which use various techniques to reduce energy consumption in WSNs. Given the low energy consumption requirement of sensor networks, simplicity has been an important feature in the design of MAC protocols, including the IEEE 802.15.4 MAC. We considered a simpler protocol, called S&T MAC, in which a sensor node chooses a transmission slot uniformly in an equally slotted period without using carrier sensing. We also derived the probability that at least k out of n nodes successfully transmit their packets under the S&T MAC, which is a new solution to a problem similar to certain occupancy problems.

Sensor networks usually operate with low duty cycles to minimize energy consumption. We presented an energy optimization framework which minimizes energy consumption per unit time of the entire network by optimizing the active and sleep periods, and attains the flexibility to incorporate various QoS requirements, such as packet delivery ratio and maximum packet delay. More specifically, we formulated duty cycle optimization problems that interact with the underlying MAC protocol and energy models when the system parameters such as the traffic models and the user-specific QoS parameters are given.

We then applied the framework to the S&T MAC and IEEE 802.15.4 MAC. Using the same QoS requirements, our results showed that, in most cases, the standard has better performance than the S&T MAC in terms of energy consumption. For scenarios where the packet delivery ratio is low, the S&T MAC has comparable (in some cases even better) performance than the IEEE 802.15.4 MAC. Although the energy efficiency of the S&T MAC has no obvious advantage in most cases compared to the IEEE 802.15.4 MAC, the simplicity of its operations, as discussed in Sec. 4.3.2, might be an appealing feature for many sensor network applications where the system complexity is desirably kept as low as possible. We have also shown that the battery life extension mode of the standard under our energy minimization framework is no more energy efficient than the regular mode.

Acknowledgments

This work was supported by the National ICT Australia (NICTA) and the Australian Research Council (ARC). F. Shu was supported by NICTA Victoria Laboratory. T. Sakurai and M. Zukerman are with the ARC Special Research Centre for Ultra-Broadband Information Networks (CUBIN).

References

1. C. S. Raghavendra, K. Sivalingam and T. Znati, *Wireless Sensor Networks*. Kluwer Academic Publishers (2004).
2. C. Y. Chong and S. P. Kumar, Sensor networks: evolution, opportunities, and challenges, *Proc. IEEE*, **91**(8), 1247–1256 (2003).
3. I. F. Akyildiz, S. Weilian, Y. Sankarasubramaniam and E. Cayirci, A survey on sensor networks, *IEEE Communications Magazine*, **40**(8), 102–114 (2002).

4. J. D. H. Callaway, *Wireless Sensor Networks: Architectures and Protocols.* Auerbach Publications (2003).
5. M. Tubaishat and S. Madria, Sensor networks: An overview, *IEEE Potentials*, **22**(2), 20–23 (2003).
6. 21 ideas for the 21st century, *Business Week*, 78–167 (1999).
7. A. J. Goldsmith and S. B. Wicker, Design challenges for energy-constrained ad hoc wireless networks, *IEEE Wireless Communications*, **9**(4), 8–27 (2002).
8. N. Bulusu and S. Jha, *Wireless Sensor Networks: A Systems Perspective*, Artech House (2005).
9. IEEE 802.15.4, Wireless medium access control (MAC) and physical layer (PHY) specifications for low rate wireless personal area networks (LR-WPANS). Standard, IEEE (2003).
10. J. M. Kahn, R. H. Katz and K. S. J. Pisterb, Next century challenges: Mobile networking for "smart dust", *Proc. Annual ACM/IEEE International Conference on Mobile Computing and Networking* (*MobiCom*), 271–278, New York, NY, USA, ACM Press (1999).
11. J. M. Rabaey, M. J. Ammer, J. L. da Silva, D. Patel and S. Roundy, PicoRadio supports ad hoc ultra-low power wireless networking, *IEEE Computer*, **33**(7), 42–48 (July 2000).
12. C. C. Enz, A. El-Hoiydi, J. D. Decotignie and V. Peiris, WiseNET: An ultralow-power wireless sensor network solution, *IEEE Computer*. **37**(8), 62–70 (2004).
13. W. Heinzelman, A. Chandrakasan and H. Balakrishnan, An application-specific protocol architecture for wireless microsensor networks, *IEEE Transactions on Wireless Communications*, **1**(4), 660–670 (2002).
14. D. Estrin, R. Govindan, J. Heidemann and S. Kumar, Next century challenges: Scalable coordination in sensor networks, *Proc. of the ACM/IEEE International Conference on Mobile Computing and Networking* (*MobiCom*), 263–270, Seattle, Washington, USA, ACM (1999).
15. C. Intanagonwiwat, R. Govindan, D. Estrin, J. Heidemann and F. Silva, Directed diffusion for wireless sensor networking, *IEEE/ACM Trans. Networking*, **11**(1), 2–16 (2003).
16. J. N. Al-Karaki and A. E. Kamal, Routing techniques in wireless sensor networks: A survey, *IEEE Wireless Communications*. **11**(6), 6–28 (2004).
17. W. Ye, J. Heidemann and D. Estrin, Medium access control with coordinated adaptive sleeping for wireless sensor networks, *IEEE/ACM Trans. Networking*, **12**(3), 493–506 (June 2004).
18. L. Krishnamachari, D. Estrin and S. Wicker, The impact of data aggregation in wireless sensor networks, *Proc. of International Conference on Distributed Computing Systems* (*ICDCS*), 575–578 (July 2002).
19. K. Dasgupta, K. Kalpakis and P. Namjoshi, An efficient clustering-based heuristic for data gathering and aggregation in sensor networks, *Proc. of IEEE Wireless Communications and Networking* (*WCNC*), pp. 1948–1953 (2003).
20. A. Kansal and M. B. Srivastava, An environmental energy harvesting framework for sensor networks, *Proc. of the International Symposium on Low Power Electronics and Design* (*ISLPED*), 481–486 (2003).
21. F. Shu, *Analysis and Optimization of MAC Protocols for Wireless Networks*, PhD thesis, The University of Melbourne, Australia, http://eprints.infodiv.unimelb.edu.au/archive/00003857 (2007).
22. L. Roberts, ALOHA packet system with and without slots and capture, *Comput. Commun. Rev.*, **5**(2), 28–42 (1975).

23. M. Ali, U. Saif, A. Dunkels, T. Voigt, K. Romer, K. Langendoen, J. Polastre and Z. A. Uzmi, Medium access control issues in sensor networks, *ACM SIGCOMM Computer Communication Review*, **36**(2), 33–36 (2006).
24. I. Demirkol, C. Ersoy and F. Alagoz, MAC protocols for wireless sensor networks: A survey, *IEEE Communications Magazine*, **44**(4), 115–121 (2006).
25. K. Sohrabi, J. Gao, V. Ailawadhi and G. J. Pottie, Protocols for self-organization of a wireless sensor network, *IEEE Personal Commun.*, **7**(5), 16–27 (2000).
26. G. Pei and C. Chien, Low power TDMA in large wireless sensor networks, *Proc. of IEEE Military Communications Conference (MILCOM)*, **1**, 347–351 (2001).
27. S. Chatterjea, L. F. W. van Hoesel and P. J. M. Havinga, AI-LMAC: An adaptive, information-centric and lightweight mac protocol for wireless sensor networks. *Proc. of Intelligent Sensors, Sensor Networks and Information Processing Conference (ISSNIP)*, 381–388 (2004).
28. L. F. W. van Hoesel, T. Nieberg, H. J. Kip and P. J. M. Havinga, Advantages of a TDMA based, energy-efficient, self-organizing MAC protocol for WSNs, *Proc. of IEEE Vehicular Technology Conference (VTC), Spring*, **3**, 1598–1602 (2004).
29. J. Li and G. Y. Lazarou, A bit-map-assisted energy-efficient MAC scheme for wireless sensor networks, *Proc. of the International Symposium on Information Processing in Sensor Networks (IPSN)*, 55–60 (2004).
30. T. van Dam and K. Langendoen, An adaptive energy-efficient MAC protocol for wireless sensor networks, *Proc. of ACM Conference on Embedded Networked Sensor Systems (SenSys)*, 171–180 (2003).
31. P. Lin, C. Qiao and X. Wang, Medium access control with a dynamic duty cycle for sensor networks, *Proc. IEEE Wireless Communications and Networking Conference (WCNC)*, **3**, 1534–1539 (2004).
32. J. Polastre, J. Hill and D. Culler, Versatile low power media access for wireless sensor networks, *Proc. ACM Conference on Embedded Networked Sensor Systems (SenSys)*, 95–107 (2004).
33. A. El-Hoiydi and J.-D. Decotignie, WiseMAC: An ultra low power MAC protocol for the downlink of infrastructure wireless sensor networks, *Proc. International Symposium on Computers and Communications (ISCC)*, **1**, 244–251 (June 2004).
34. X. Shi, G. Stromberg, Y. Gsottberger and T. Sturm, Wake-up-frame scheme for ultra low power wireless transceivers, *Proc. IEEE Global Telecommunications Conference (GLOBECOM)*, **6**, 3619–3623 (2004).
35. X. Shi and G. Stromberg, SyncWUF: An ultra low-power MAC protocol for wireless sensor networks, *IEEE Transactions on Mobile Computing*, **6**, 115–125 (2007).
36. G. Lu, B. Krishnamachari and C. S. Raghavendra, An adaptive energy-efficient and low-latency MAC for data gathering in wireless sensor networks, *Proc. International Parallel and Distributed Processing Symposium (IPDPS)*, 224–231 (2004).
37. T. R. Park, M. J. Lee and J. Park, FG-MAC: Fine-grained wakeup request MAC for wireless sensor networks, *IEEE Commun. Lett.*, **11**(12), 1022–1024 (2007).
38. V. Rajendran, K. Obraczka and J. J. Garcia-Luna-Aceves, Energy-efficient, collision-free medium access control for wireless sensor networks, *Wireless Networking*, **12**(1), 63–78 (2006).
39. I. Rhee, A. Warrier, M. Aia and J. Min, Z-MAC: A hybrid MAC for wireless sensor networks, *Proc. 3rd international conference on Embedded networked sensor systems (SenSys)*, 90–101 (2005).
40. C. Schurgers, V. Tsiatsis, S. Ganeriwal and M. Srivastava, Optimizing sensor networks in the energy-latency-density design space, *IEEE Transactions on Mobile Computing*, **1**(1), 70–80 (2002).

41. Y. C. Tay, K. Jamieson and H. Balakrishnan, Collision-minimizing CSMA and its applications to wireless sensor networks, *IEEE J. Select. Areas Commun.*, **22**(6), 1048–1057 (2004).
42. K. Jamieson, H. Balakrishnan and Y. Tay, *Sift: A MAC Protocol for Event-Driven Wireless Sensor Networks*, Technical Report Tech. Rep. 894, MIT Lab Comput. Sci. [Online]. Available: http://www.chipcon.com/.
43. R. Jurdak, P. Baldi and C. V. Lopes, Adaptive low power listening for wireless sensor networks, *IEEE Transactions on Mobile Computing*, **6**(8), 988–1004 (2007).
44. S. Cui, R. Madan, A. J. Goldsmith and S. Lall, Cross-layer energy and delay optimization in small-scale sensor networks, *IEEE Transactions on Wireless Communications*, **6**(10) 3688–3699, (2007).
45. W. Feller, *An Introduction to Probability Theory and Its Applications.* John Wiley & Sons Inc., (1968). 3rd Edition, Volume I.
46. F. Shu, T. Sakurai, M. Zukerman and H. L. Vu, Packet loss analysis of the IEEE 802.15.4 MAC without acknowledgments, *IEEE Commun. Lett.*, **11**(1), 79–81 (2007).
47. N. L. Johnson and S. Kotz, *Urn Models and Their Application.* John Wiley & Sons, Inc., (1977).
48. F. Shu, T. Sakurai, H. L. Vu and M. Zukerman, Does a WSN MAC based on uniform access without re-attempts have merits? *Proc. IEEE Region 10 International Conference (TENCON)*, (2006).
49. Chipcon, Chipcon Transceiver CC1000 Data Sheet v2.2. [Online]. (2004). Available: http://www.chipcon.com/.
50. The GNU Multiple Precision Arithmetic Library. [Online]. Available: http://www.swox.com/gmp/.

Chapter 25

Energy Efficient Approach to Dynamic Clustering in Sensor Networks Using Genetic Algorithm

Rahul Khanna

Intel Corporation, 2111 NE 25th Ave.
Hillsboro, OR 97124, USA
rahul.khanna@intel.com

Huaping Liu

School of EECS, Oregon State University
Corvallis, OR 97331, USA
hliu@eecs.oregonstate.edu

Hsiao-Hwa Chen

Department of Engineering Science
National Cheng Kung University, Taiwan
hshwchen@ieee.org

This chapter discusses a mechanism of clustering multi-hop sensor networks with a goal to generate optimal number of sensor-clusters in a secure and power efficient manner. It uses genetic algorithm (GA) to adaptively create various components such as cluster-members, cluster-heads, and routing agents. The allocation of these components is then used to evaluate the average fitness of the system based on the sequence of communication links towards the sink. It is expected to minimize the power consumption of the sensor system while maximizing the sensor objectives (coverage and exposure). Runtime evaluation of the system can support changing dynamics, related to coverage, task requirements, failures, incremental redeployment and reconfiguration.

25.1. Introduction

Low-cost integration and miniaturization of micro-sensors[1–5] have generated significant interest in the area of disposable sensors. These are motion capable, randomly deployed, infrastructure-less, data-centric sensors equipped with data processing capabilities and sensory circuits that cannot be charged (or rarely charged) or replaced. These sensors are constrained in energy, bandwidth, storage, and processing-capabilities and find their uses in the areas of homeland-security, disaster-recovery, target-identification, reconnaissance, medical applications, defense applications,[6] and intrusion-detection, etc. Deployment of such network can be done, for example, by dropping a large number of disposable sensor nodes in a random fashion. The ultimate goal is to develop a long-lasting sensor network containing nodes with non-renewal and limited energy resource. Sensors process the sensory data and transmit to the target (sink) in a secure manner. Network layer adapts to the changing connectivity due to failure of some nodes and new nodes powering up. It sets up the energy-efficient route that transmits the non-redundant data from source to the sink in order to maximize the battery (and sensor's) life. In case of mobile sensors, locomotion can be exploited to reduce the communication overhead (maximize the battery and sensor's life) by relocating these sensors at an optimal position.

This chapter introduces a novel concept of adaptive clustering. In general, clustering of a network to minimize the distance is an NP-hard problem.[7,8] The mechanism discussed in this chapter is an energy-efficient sensor-network design using an evolutionary algorithm[9] that divides the randomly deployed sensors into an optimal number of independent clusters with cluster-head and optimal route. Genetic algorithm (GA) is such algorithm that mimics the natural evolution proposed by Charles Darwin in 1858. GA has been successfully applied to a wide range of combination problems. They are particularly useful in applications involving design and optimization, where there are large numbers of variables and where procedural algorithms are either non-existent or extremely complicated.

Cluster infrastructure consists of member nodes, cluster-heads and a route to the sink. Cluster-head collects the data from those sensors that belong to its cluster, fuses the collected data and sends them to the sink in a compressed manner via the most cost-effective route in single or multiple hops. It is assumed that while the sensors may be deployed in a non-hospitable environment, the sink is a stationary component that is located at a safe location. The goal is to discover clustered topology, optimal locality with optimal routes to the sink. For problems such as these, where there are several, often conflicting, objectives, multiple objective genetic algorithm (MOGA) could be used. MOGA evolves a set of solutions (the population) towards the Pareto-optimal front, where trade-off analysis can be performed to select a suitable solution. In this scenario, GA algorithms are designed with multiple objectives: (1) discover the optimal clusters with cluster members and cluster head, (2) discover low-cost path to the sink using one or more hops (3) further maximize the coverage by moving (or re-orienting) sensors (once deployed) at the expense of battery life, (4) enable security attributes adaptively based on observed data integrity and battery usage (due to deployment in hostile environment), and (5) tune parameters of proactive mechanisms like dynamic power scaling (DPS) and dynamic transmission scaling (DTS) to optimize battery power.

Energy dissipation of the sensor node is the sum of sensor transceiver and micro computations. Dynamic voltage and frequency scaling (DVFS)[10,11] is a key technique in exploiting the hardware characteristics of processors to reduce energy dissipation by lowering the supply voltage and operating frequency. Since performance is needed only for a small fraction of the time, the DVFS algorithm enables energy savings while providing the peak computation power in general-purpose systems by optimizing performance and battery life. The proactive scheme predicts the future work requirements and sets up the power states according to the dynamic policy with parameters related to minimum work, and maximum deferment. These policies support data bursts, runtime constraints and optimal power states.

The chromosome of the GA defines all the building blocks to a solution of the problem at hand in a form that is suitable for the genetic operators and the fitness function. Adequate chromosome representation and resolution of objectives towards greater fitness help generate optimal parameters related to (a) resolving routing imbalances, (b) allocating sensors optimally for various functions, (c) resolving load imbalances, (d) reducing overhead traffic, (e) positioning sensors to avoid shadowing effect, redundant usage, sub-optimal clustering, (f) migrating load, and (g) enabling security attributes for secure communication. In the context of secure mobile sensor clustering, four chromosome representations are described: sensor node, route, locomotion and security attributes.

Mobility provides an ability to re-position (or self-repair) the sensor (nodes, routers, cluster-heads) strategically so as to maximize the overall objective (cluster membership, security overhead, and routes) with an extra degree of freedom. However, motion costs battery life and therefore sensors cannot be moved very frequently. Therefore, an efficient dynamic re-positioning and security uses long-range prediction based on historical trends or generational improvement over a period of time with the primary goal of maximizing the coverage in a resource constrained environment.

Data security provides a unified and efficient scheme for maximum reliability and privacy. The reliable functioning of the sensor objectives depend on the secure communications between various functional elements (nodes and sink). This requires identifying compromised or falsely added nodes, secure re-deployment/addition of nodes, and preventing passive listening by a malicious intruder using elements of authentication, integrity, privacy (or confidentiality), and anti-playback. All communications need to be secure to avoid data intercept, analysis and alteration by an intruder who can device methods to reduce the effectiveness of the sensor network. This must be done in a manner such that time required to circumvent the security measures using brute-force methods takes longer than the life of the network.

25.2. Related Work and Motivation

Work related to mobile sensor networks include dynamic approaches where sensor nodes are deployed one at a time, with each node making use of data gathered from previously deployed nodes to determine its optimal deployment location,[12] potential fields to reduce deployment time,[13] self-organization strategies and algorithms for responsive adaptation of sensor nodes to coverage of a field with multiple dynamically changing contexts,[14] optimal deployment of sensors toward critical region to ensure quality of the readings of the value of interest.[15] Work related to sensor security include a solution using simple symmetric cryptographic algorithms.[16,17] Asymmetric cryptographic algorithms are not suitable for providing security on wireless sensor networks due to limited computation, power, and storage resources available on sensor nodes. Although most of the schemes described above are promising, they do not deal with the sensor networks holistically that require optimization of the competing objectives (clustering, positioning, routing and security) for a high energy efficiency.

Work related to power optimization includes dynamic voltage scaling (DVS) methodology that inserts additional information into the communication channel to guide the selection of proper voltages for data decryption (encryption) and processing in order to reduce the total computational energy consumption,[18] real-time DVS (RT-DVS) that modifies the OS's real-time scheduler, and task management service to provide significant energy savings while maintaining real-time deadline guarantees,[11] PowerTOSSIM that proposes efficient emulation of the sensor node hardware platform coupled with careful instrumentation of the power states, which generates an event-driven simulator directly from TinyOS code and emits power state transitions,[19] Bult *et al.* present advances in low-power systems spanning network design, through power management, low power mixed signal circuits, and highly integrated RF network interfaces,[20] Xing *et al.* present that significant energy reduction can be achieved by jointly optimizing the transmission power and sleep time of nodes based on the network workload.[21] DVFS is an important power optimization feature in Intel and AMD class of micro-processors that provide multiple performance states using voltage and frequency scaling. ARM's intelligent energy manager (IEM) voltage and frequency scaling reduces system-level power and energy consumption by as much as 15 to 20%.

25.3. Genetic Algorithm

Genetic algorithm[9] is a stochastic search technique that resembles the natural evolution proposed by Charles Darwin in 1858. GA has been successfully applied to a wide range of combination problems. They are particularly useful in applications involving design and optimization, where there are large numbers of variables and where procedural algorithms are either non-existent or extremely complicated.

While there are well established identification techniques[22] for linear models, the same can not be said about nonlinear ones. The potential of GA as global optimizers permits undertaking complex optimization problems and therefore allows for greater degrees of freedom in the selection of the models structure. This helps in identification of non-linear model parameters allowing the *a priori* use of the physical knowledge of the process. Genetic algorithms, with their many potential solutions approach, can search multiple points simultaneously and, therefore, can avoid being caught in a local optimum when a global optimum is sought.

Genetic algorithms are based on the principals of natural selection, where each possible solution (a set of power equation coefficients) is represented as a binary string (chromosomes) and an associated fitness measure. Successive solutions are built as a part of evolutionary process where one set of selected individual solutions give rise to another set of solutions for the next generation. Individuals with high fitness measure are more likely to be selected into the mating pool with an assumption that they will produce a fitter solution in the next generation (next run). Solutions with the weaker fitness measures are naturally discarded. We use roulette-wheel selection to simulate natural selection, where solutions with a higher functional fitness are less likely to be eliminated, while there exists a chance that they may be. There also exists a small likelihood that some weaker solutions may survive the selection process as it may include some component (genes) that may prove useful following the crossover process. Mathematically, the likelihood of selecting a potential solution is given by:

$$p_i = \frac{F_i}{\sum_{j=0}^{N} F_j}, \tag{25.1}$$

where P_i is the likelihood that a specific solution is going to be selected for mating pool, F_i represents the functional fitness of the candidate solution and N is the total number of potential solutions in a population.

Genetic algorithms have proved to be useful in cases where the search space is large, complex and not well understood with almost no domain knowledge. They can handle large number of variables with arbitrary constraints and multiple objectives. We use GA due to its potential of handling a large number of variables that not only share the non-linear relationship to the battery power, but also share a certain degree of correlation with each other. Mathematical solutions to such problem can be extremely complex and easily converge to a local optimal solution or no solution at all. GA has advantages over traditional optimization approach **(can "due to the fact that it" be replaced by "since the latter"?)** can never reach an optimal solution. Depending upon the complexity of workload relationship to the utilization of several active components in a system, the solution search space could involve large number of variables with high dimensionality. These variables tend to be noisy and discontinuous with little or no information about the corresponding interactions between their respective components. The problem is further aggravated by the fact that hardware/software based power/thermal optimization functions kick in autonomously, making the complete solution highly non-linear.

25.3.1. *Clustering solution*

The system consists of an initialization module and an adaptation module. The initialization module helps code gene for each sensor. This gene contains the identification of each sensor and any other specific information. This information may be related to sensor objectivity, next-hop, cluster-domain, etc. The initialization module also initiates temporary clusters of the sensors with a domain identification and cluster-heads. The adaptation module is responsible for cluster adaptation and load adaptation. Cluster adaptation is responsible for creating accurate cluster boundaries due to addition, deletion, or modified sensor objectives. Load adaptation is responsible for creating optimal routes from cluster-heads to the sink. Adaptation modules are governed by a fitness function that is specific to the network objective in a load-balanced network. It prevents the flow of redundant information while maximizing the network bandwidth usage and battery life.

It is interesting to note that two competing objectives are required to create an energy-efficient sensor network. While cluster membership will keep on changing because of dead or depleted nodes, routes to sink will keep on changing to avoid high-cost paths (like multiple clusters using the same cluster-head to route the data to the sink). Therefore, we use multi-objective genetic algorithms.[23] While simple GA converges to a single solution, MOGA evolves a set of solutions (the population) towards the Pareto-optimal front where trade-off analysis can be performed to select a suitable solution.

25.3.2. *Genetic algorithm components*

The process of genetic algorithm takes place in the sink (or a similar centralized identity). This algorithm repeats itself upon multiple triggers. These triggers are related to battery alert, deteriorating route fitness alert or periodic actions based on fixed timers. Once the optimal fitness is achieved, the corresponding chromosome representation to that fitness is committed and the sensors are instructed to assume the new functions by relinquishing the old functions.

(a) **Initial population:** Initial chromosomes strings are seeded partially randomly using a random number generator (RNG) and partially using population of previous samples. This population is coded with a gene structure.
(b) **Evaluation:** Each chromosome string is evaluated for the fitness using the fitness function. A fitness function includes and correctly represent all or at least the most important factors that affect the performance of the system. The major issue in developing a fitness function is the decision on which factors are the most important ones.

(c) **Reproduction:** Reproduction is a process in which individual strings are copied according to their fitness function values, which also means that individuals with larger fitness value will have a higher probability of contributing an offspring in the next generation. The algorithm uses the standard weighted roulette wheel method to select n individuals for reproduction to the mating pool. The chromosome with the highest fitness value represents a better chromosome to take part in reproduction. N chromosomes will again be reproduced from the n chromosomes selected for reproduction using a crossover probability. During reproduction, we choose multiple cross-over points. Cross-over points and the locations are calculated using an RNG. As in this example, two chromosome strings having three random cross-over points will create a resultant chromosome after cross-over as below:

Parents:
100 000 001 100 001 100 100 100 001 100 **100 001 100 100 100 000 001** 100 100 001 010 010 010 010 010
100 010 010 100 100 010 100 010 001 001 **001 001 010 001 001 000 100** 010 001 100 010 000 001 100 010

Children:
100 000 001 100 001 **010 100 010 001 001** 100 001 100 100 100 000 001 **010 001 100 010 000 001 100 010**
100 010 010 100 100 **100 100 100 001 100** 001 001 010 001 001 000 100 **100 100 001 010 010 010 010 010**

(d) **Mutation:** Newly reproduced N chromosomes are transferred to the mutation pool. The mutation operator mutates chromosome in the mutation pool according to mutation probability which will make it adaptive. We will choose a maximum mutation probability p_m. In any generation, mutation probability will be inversely proportional to the average fitness of the standard number of population in any generation. Therefore

$$p_g = p_m \left(1 - N \frac{\text{Fitness}_{\text{avg}}}{\text{Fitness}_{\text{total}}}\right). \tag{25.2}$$

Mutation function uses function flip (toss of a coin) to decide whether to invert the bit or not.

(e) **Selection:** Finally N chromosomes are chosen out of $2N$ chromosomes according to their fitness values. These chromosomes are carried over to the next generation. $2N$ chromosomes consist of N parent chromosomes and N children.

25.4. Chromosome Representation

The chromosome of the GA contains all the building blocks to a solution of the problem at hand in a form that is suitable for the genetic operators and the fitness function. It is also mentioned by name "string". It represents a set of parameters that defines a proposed solution to the problem that the genetic algorithm is trying to solve.

25.4.1. *Cluster node representation*

Each individual sensor node in a cluster network is represented by a 3-bit binary number called "gene". These three-bit genes, which define the feature of the node, are called "allele" and are represented as follows:

000 - Node Inactive (powered off).
001 - Node chosen as Cluster-Head (CH).
010 - Node chosen as Inter-Cluster Router (ICR).
100 - Node chosen as Sensor (NS).

Each cluster is represented by a cluster-head, and cluster-members are represented by inactive/active sensors and inter-cluster routers. Cluster-head is responsible for data-fusion from various node-sensors and inter-cluster router is responsible for routing cluster data (from cluster-head) to the sink.

For example, in a 25-node system, the number of bits required to represent the complete system would be $3 \times 25 = 75$. Therefore, the size of the string would be 60-bits. For the scenario shown in Fig. 25.1, this string lies as follows:

100 000 001 100 001 100 100 100 001 100 100 001 100 100 100 000 001 100 100 001
010 010 010 010 010

Each chromosome is evaluated for the fitness using the TNF function (defined in Sec. 25.5) for node selection. Upon completion of the GA algorithm, a function is assigned to each node. Once the functions are assigned, each type of nodes then performs the following functions:

25.4.1.1. *Inter-cluster routers (ICR)*

Each router starts listening to "sink" or "Lx router" and finds out the next-hop energy requirements to the sink and/or Lx routers that it can listen to by exchanging data and bounds checking. Additionally, it exchanges a conflict-free proximity unique ID (PUID) with other neighboring routers (Sec. 25.10). Individual router temporarily designates itself as Lx based on the next hop it sends the data to, where $x = 0, 1, 2, \ldots$ represents the number of hops between the sink and itself. $L(x)$ can send data to only an $L(x - 1)$ that is closer to the sink. Each router then sends the neighboring routers (and/or sink) information to the sink using the temporary router.

Upon cost-analysis using a parallel GA algorithm, the sink will designate a primary and fail-over path to each router and send this information using the node

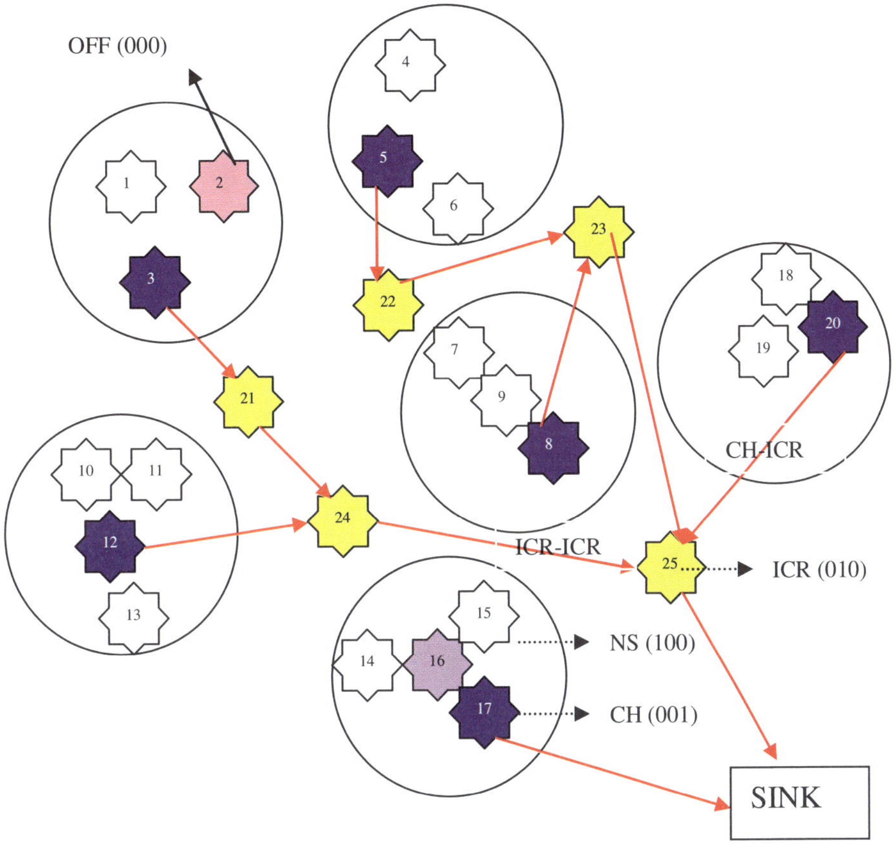

Fig. 25.1. Sensor node clustering. Each node is assigned function as a result of genetic algorithm and the resulting chromosome structure. For the example below, chromosome structure is 100 000 001 100 001 100 100 100 001 100 100 001 100 100 100 000 001 100 100 001 010 010 010 010 010.

it received that information from. This is a periodic process that repeats at a predefined interval. Lx routers will update its next-hop information by replacing the temporary next-hop with that provided by the sink. Lx routers will receive this information periodically from the sink. It starts advertising (router advertisement) its presence with the cost of using this path at regular intervals. This cost is evaluated using the following metrics:

(i) Average data flowing through this router (dynamic)
(ii) Energy requirements to reach next hop (static).

Average cost of using the next-hop (static) Lx routers will trigger an attention message when the battery reaches an attention state (battery condition in quantized steps). This attention message is carried to the sink using the current path. The sink will use this message as a trigger point for re-configuration and running a new instance of node-selection genetic algorithm. In the new instance, the failing node is permanently marked "Powered Off (000b)".

25.4.1.2. *Sensor-nodes (NS)*

Each sensor node starts listening to the available cluster-heads (CH advertisement) and calculates the cost of communicating with the available cluster-heads. Individual sensor attaches to a cluster-head based on the calculated cost and become the part of that cluster. This step also involves receiving the unique PUID from the cluster-head (Sec. 25.10). The sensor then updates the chosen cluster-head with the sensor data. These data include the NS-CH cost of all available cluster-heads it evaluated.

Sensor node triggers an attention message when the battery reaches an attention state (battery condition in quantized steps). This attention message is carried to the sink using the elected cluster-head. Sink will use this message as a trigger point to re-configuration and running a new instance of node-selection genetic algorithm.

25.4.1.3. *Cluster-head (CH)*

Each cluster-head starts CH advertisement to invite nodes (NS) and sends the NS-inter-cluster-router (NS-ICR) data received from the sensors to the sink. Individual cluster-head listens to the router advertisement and selects the low-cost router (ICR) en-route to the sink. This step also involves receiving the unique PUID from the ICR (Sec. 25.10).

These cluster-heads can participate in data fusion. The resulting information is then communicated to the sink using the selected router. Sink returns the application unique ID (AUID) (Sec. 25.10) to the cluster-head during the setup (or re-initialization) phase.

25.4.1.4. *Sink*

Sink is an entity where all the event data collection and dissemination take place. This information is then processed for sensor related functions. Sink also receives the statistical and status information from routers and cluster-heads. This information is processed in the following manner:

(a) It collects the information regarding valid router-router (ICR-ICR) communication. This information includes energy requirements for communication and the corresponding globally unique identification number (GUID).
(b) It evaluates the average data that pass through each router by processing the data received by the sink (from SN).
(c) It evaluates the cost of NS-CH communication for all valid links. This information is passed by the cluster-head during the setup operation.

(d) It allocates an application specific AUID (Sec. 25.10) to the cluster-head to uniquely identify the message trace.
(e) Listens to any alert message (battery conditions).
(f) Performs a GA to evaluate the optimal route using the fitness function based on parameters obtained in step (a) and step (b). This is triggered based on periodicity or an alert event.
(g) Performs a GA to designate functional unit to each node using the fitness function based on the parameters obtained in step (c). This is triggered based on alert event.

25.4.2. *Route representation*

Route-selection GA uses a different chromosome structure (Fig. 25.2) than that used in node-selection GA. Characteristics of route-selection chromosomes are given as follows: Each node (CH and ICR) is represented by $\log_2(N)$ bits, where N is the maximum number of ICR nodes that can be reached by this node. Hence an individual in this case is represented by a string that consists of all such nodes with representation to the next ICR. For example, (0010) (0010) (001) (010) represents R12, R22, R31, R42 connections, where Rxy are the yth route of the xth node.

Route selection is similar to the node selection with the following exceptions and an extra trigger point. This algorithm repeats itself at a regular interval to ascertain the acceptable thresholds of route-loads during the constant usage of the sensor system. Each chromosome is evaluated for the fitness using the TRF function (for route selection) as defined in Sec. 25.6. Route-selection GA keeps on making attempts to achieve the most cost-effective path for a given topology (as selected in node-selection) in which there can be multiple paths. At certain point certain fitness threshold is reached beyond which further conversion to higher fitness may

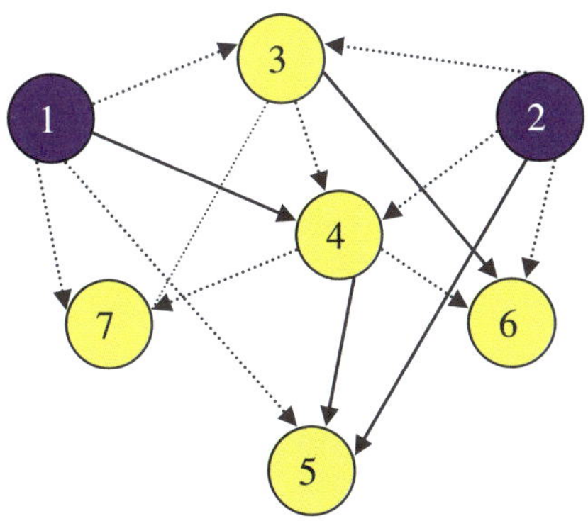

Fig. 25.2. Chromosome structure of the route. For example, for nodes 1, 2, 3, 4, chromosome string is represented by (0010) (0010) (001) (010); for node 1, route 2 is selected that connects to ICR 4; for node 2, route 2 is selected that connects to ICR 5; for node 3, route 1 is selected that connects to ICR 6.

not be possible. This condition can happen due to battery condition and bad node assignments. This will cause a node-reassignment alert, which in turn will cause the node-selection GA to run again with changed conditions. In general scheme of things, the route selection can sometimes act as a resisting factor for the node-selection. While nodes may have been assigned the functions based on a high fitness factor, it may not be suitable for routing the packets in a multi-hop system. This will cause a re-configuration (running route selection GA) again until both objectives reach an acceptable convergence point. This is a dynamic process and keeps on repeating over the life-time of the system.

25.4.3. *Motion vector representation*

This section describes the representation of the vector movement of a sensor. The GA executes in the sink where it triggers upon battery alert, deteriorating route fitness alert, or periodic action. Upon reaching optimal fitness, the deployment corresponding to that fitness is committed and the sensors are instructed to assume the new positions by relinquishing the old positions.

Chromosome string is formed using each individual sensor node's motion vector represented by a 7-bit binary number called "gene" as shown in Fig. 25.3. The

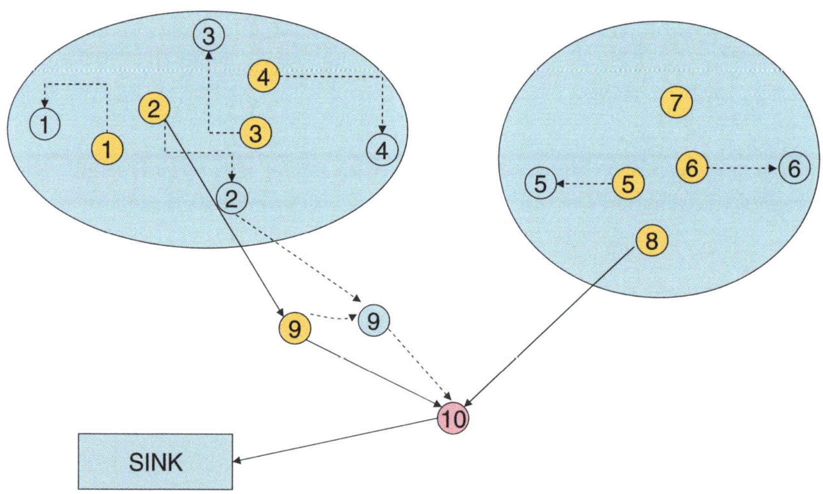

(0100001 1100000 1011000 0010111) (1110001 0011100 1000000 1010101) (0010001) (0000000)
(1110001 0110001 0001101 1010011) (1010001 0010100 1000000 1010101) (0010001) (0000000)
(0110000 0110000 1011000 0010111) (1110001 0011100 1000000 1010101) (0010001) (0000000)
(1 2 3 4) (5 6 7 8) (9) (10)

Fig. 25.3. Node re-positioning as a result of genetic algorithm. In this example, nodes 1, 2 undergo 3 replacements; nodes 3, 4 undergo 2 replacements; nodes 5, 6, 9 are replaced only once. Other nodes do not move.

chromosome string hierarchy can be defined as

$$((\widehat{\theta}x\theta x\widehat{S}xS)_1(\widehat{\theta}x\theta x\widehat{S}xS)_2(\widehat{\theta}x\theta x\widehat{S}xS)_3\ldots)_1\ldots$$
$$((\widehat{\theta}x\theta x\widehat{S}xS)_1(\widehat{\theta}x\theta x\widehat{S}xS)_2(\widehat{\theta}x\theta x\widehat{S}xS)_3\ldots)_n$$

where $(\widehat{\theta}x\theta x\widehat{S}xS)_i$ represents the motion vector with the following properties:

(1) $(\widehat{\theta}\theta)$ represents $0°(00)$, $90°(01)$, $180°(10)$, $270°(11)$ angular movement
(2) $(\widehat{S}S)$ represents the number of finite steps the sensor travels in the direction given by angular movement
(3) Sensor is moved only if one of the x values is 1.

Each chromosome is evaluated for the fitness using the TNMF function (for node locomotion) as defined in Sec. 25.9.

25.4.4. *Security attribute representation*

In this section we design the genetic algorithm for enabling security attributes (authentication and encryption) on nodes. These nodes are represented with a chromosome string (Fig. 25.4) that is formed using each individual sensor node's security

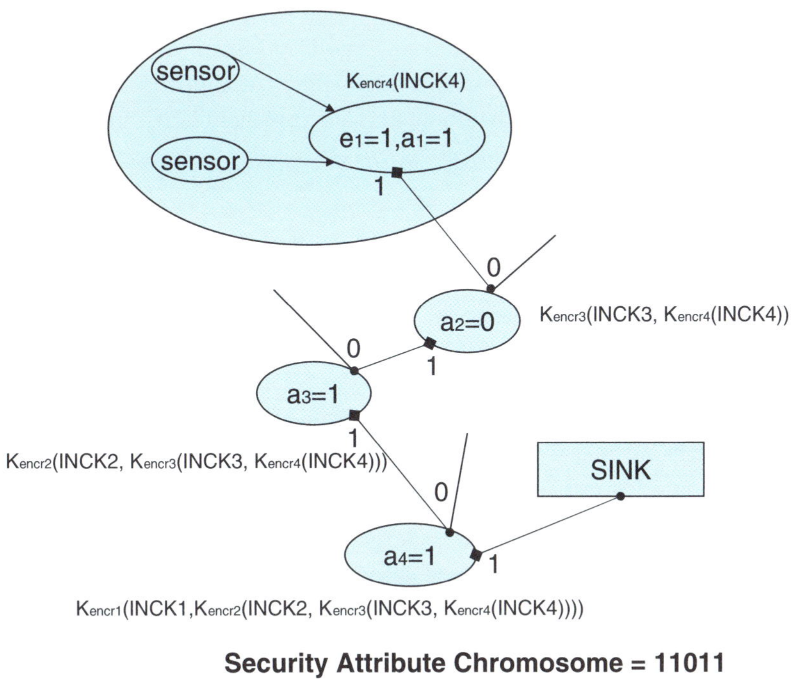

Fig. 25.4. Sink mediates the INCK keys at ICR and CH ports. These keys enable the authentication based on security attribute chromosome generated by genetic algorithm (GA). For example, node 2 does not require message authentication at port 0, but requires at port 1. $\mathrm{INCK}^1_{\mathrm{mac2}} = \mathrm{INCK}^0_{\mathrm{mac3}}$.

policy represented by a 2-bit binary number and defined as

$$(e_1 a_1 a_2 \cdots a_N)_1 (e_1 a_1 a_2 \cdots a_N)_2 \cdots (e_1 a_1 a_2 \cdots a_N)_R,$$

where $(e_1 a_1 a_2 \cdots a_N)_i$ represents the security attributes $(e_1, a_1, \ldots, a_n)$ on node n of route i, and e_1 and a_n represent the encryption bit and authentication bit, respectively. It should be noted that the first node is always a CH where data encryption can optionally take place by setting $e_1 = 1$.

Each chromosome is evaluated for the fitness using the SNF function (for secure attribute selection) as defined in Sec. 25.8.1. Security settings compete with node-selection or locomotion. Nodes are assigned functions or locations based on the corresponding fitness factors, which may be suboptimal for securing the packets due to battery conditions. This triggers re-configuration until all objectives reach an acceptable convergence. Like node/route selection, and mobility estimation, this is a dynamic process that repeats over system's life-time.

25.5. Node Selection Fitness Function

The node selection fitness function is a weighted function that measures the quality or performance of a solution based on functional assignment to the sensor nodes (Sec. 25.4). This function is maximized by the GA system in the process of evolutionary optimization. It helps in re-assignment of the functional aspect of the sensor node, when the fitness falls under certain threshold. This fitness function is comprised of the following components:

25.5.1. *Coverage fitness (CF)*

A sensor node has an objective to maximize the blanket coverage and the total detection area. In many applications of sensor networks, the number of neighboring nodes plays an important role. If the network is to be connected, the number of neighbors of each node needs to grow at $\Theta(\log n)$, where n is the number of nodes in the network.[24] Based on the density of deployment ρ, each node will have at least K neighbors and optimal isotropic communication range (R_c) with its neighbors (sensor nodes and cluster-heads).[25] CF fitness depends on the percentage of nodes that have at least K neighbors:

$$\mathrm{CF} = \sum_i \min\left(1, \frac{N_i}{K}\right), \tag{25.3}$$

where N_i is the number of fully connected sensor nodes in cluster i.

Sensor coverage efficiency can be improved by re-positioning the sensor node such that its data transmission is uniformly optimized by fusion, elimination, or compression methods. This is further improved by optimizing the quality of sensing for a given SNR.

25.5.2. *Cluster-head fitness (CHF)*

Sensor nodes connected to each cluster-head should be uniformly distributed. This prevents cluster-head overloading. CHF defines the fitness based on the uniformity of the sensor nodes and cluster-heads:

$$\mathrm{CHF} = 1 - \min\left(1, \frac{1}{N} \cdot \left(\sum_{n} \frac{|\rho_n - \rho|}{\rho}\right)\right), \tag{25.4}$$

where n is the cluster-head number, N is the number of cluster-heads in the system, ρ_n is the number of nodes attached to this cluster-head, and ρ is the average number of nodes per cluster in a system calculated as

$$\rho = \frac{\text{Total Sensor Nodes}}{\text{Total Cluster-Heads}}. \tag{25.5}$$

Any cluster consisting of more than ρ sensor nodes will be penalized. Mobility aids in improving the uniformity of sensor nodes and cluster-heads by rewarding the migration of sensor nodes between cluster-heads with low CHF. Migration helps to achieve higher CHF if sensor migration is from high-density clusters to those with lower density.

25.5.3. *Node communication fitness (NCF)*

A node needs power p to communicate with another node that is d distance away. The power required to communicate with the cluster-head can be computed using the path loss expressed as[26]

$$PL(d) = PL_0 + 10\mu \log_{10}\left(\frac{d}{d_0}\right) + S, \tag{25.6}$$

where d is the distance between the sensors, d_0 is a reference distance typically chosen as $1m$ for sensor networks, PL_0 is the path loss at the reference distance d_0, μ is the path loss exponent, typical in the range of $2 \sim 4$, and S is a zero-mean Gaussian random variable that gives the deviation in path loss from its average value.

For example, sensor nodes calculate these values p by responding to CH advertisements that it can listen to during setup operation. These values are then sent to the sink via a temporary low-cost path chosen by the sensor node during the setup phase. The NCF function is obtained as

$$\mathrm{NCF} = 1 - \min\left(1, \frac{1}{N} \cdot \sum_{i}\sum_{j}\left(\max\left(0, \frac{p_{ij} - p_t}{p_t}\right)\right)\right), \tag{25.7}$$

where p_{ij} represents inter-node communication energy relationship (as measured by individual sensor node), p_t represents energy threshold, and N is the number of sensor-nodes in the system.

25.5.4. *Battery status fitness (BF)*

Anytime sensor-node communicates with the cluster-head or cluster-head communicates with inter-cluster router, there is a penalty paid in terms of battery usage. Battery is also consumed during the sensing operation or other related functions. Each node alerts the sink about its battery status (Q) when it crosses the quantized limit (or thresholds). These thresholds will be used to penalize the use of those nodes for operations that consume more battery power. Penalty for using the node with a low battery capacity depends upon the type of node and its usage. For example, a node with low battery capacity will have a greater penalty for inter-cluster routers than the cluster-head. Similarly cluster-head will have a greater penalty than the sensor-node. Therefore, penalty suffered by each node depends upon the battery status and the type of node assignment. The battery status fitness function is expressed as

$$\mathrm{BF} = 1 - F(Q, \text{Node Type}), \tag{25.8}$$

where $F(\cdot)$ is the penalty with $0 \leq F(Q, \text{Node Type}) \leq 1$. Mobility provides an opportunity to exchange the functional assignments between nodes with variable residual energy. Sensor movement is rewarded on ICRs and CHs with lower battery and router load fitness because node movement influences the router's load as a result of re-balancing of the battery capacity by exchanging functional objectives. Realistically, it is only practical to exchange roles when the nodes are within the communication range and possess enough battery capacity to support the required functions.

25.5.5. *Router load fitness (RLF)*

Inter-cluster routers participate in routing the traffic originating from cluster-heads or other ICR to the sink. Routers are penalized if they cater to more than the average number of CH and ICR. This avoids overloading routers. The RLF function is expressed as

$$\mathrm{RLF} = 1 - \frac{1}{N} \cdot \sum_{n} \frac{|\varrho - \varrho_n|}{\varrho}, \tag{25.9}$$

where n is the ICR index, N is the number of ICR in this system, and ϱ and ϱ_n are given as

$$\varrho = \frac{\text{Total(CH + ICR)}}{\text{Total ICR}}, \tag{25.10a}$$

$$\varrho_n = \text{Connected CH} + \text{ICRCost}_n, \tag{25.10b}$$

where ICRCost_n (nth ICR) is updated as a result of GA function (part of MOGA) that evaluates the *cost of using* a router using route selection fitness function (Sec. 25.6). RLF can be further improved by the movement of the cluster-head and inter-cluster routers with lower router load fitness. Movement of the CH and ICR can help attain higher RLF due to exchanging roles with another functional node (cluster-head, sensor node). This can help maintain the existing topology by exchanging the nodes with higher battery capacity for router purposes (and exchanging the functional objectives).

25.5.6. *Sensor effector fitness (SEF)*

Transmitting and receiving bits wirelessly is the most energy consuming operation done by the nodes. SEF measures the power consumed due to sensory action of clusters with the net effect to re-arrange the sensor nodes. The goal is to uniformly optimize the sensor data by fusion, elimination or compression methods. This amounts to re-clustering operation that matches sensor nodes to the cluster-heads by aggregating (or eliminating) identical or duplicate packets from multiple nodes. Energy savings are realized due to reduced transmission overhead as a result of eliminating large amount of redundant data. Other elimination methods include transitioning the sensor operation to a low-duty-cycle state using a leaky bucket heuristics or eliminating the duplicate paths and turning off the sensors with high degree of redundancy or simply re-clustering.

Additional energy conservation can be achieved as a result of data compression by either fusing or reducing the correlated information. Within the cluster, this operation is performed by the cluster-head that also updates the sensor node's spatial or temporal policy parameters. Across the cluster, this is done by reducing the amount of bits that must be sent by each cluster, thereby significantly extending their lifetime.[27] Mechanisms such as *Slepian-Wolf distributed source coding*[28] can compress the content at the original sources in a distributed manner (Fig. 25.5) without explicit routing-based aggregation. This operation is performed using the sink mediation where it identifies the extent of correlation and updates the CH with new NS policy coding parameters. CH then applies these coding parameters to the respective NS in the associated cluster. This operation is performed using a pre-determined update timer to avoid excessive transmissions from the sink while helping to adapt to the changing correlations. Higher inter-cluster correlations introduce extra communication overhead for mediated traffic.

It is possible with certain probability that sensors belonging to the different clusters may have high correlation. This can cause redundant information to traverse through CH and ICR to the sink. The degree of correlation is calculated by analyzing the historical data from the sensor node. This analysis is done in spatial, temporal or spatio-temporal domain. Such analysis will rank the sensor based on the power usage for sensory functions. NS power usage depends on the following factors:

(a) Degree of correlation within local sensors
(b) Degree of correlation between cluster-heads carrying the fused data

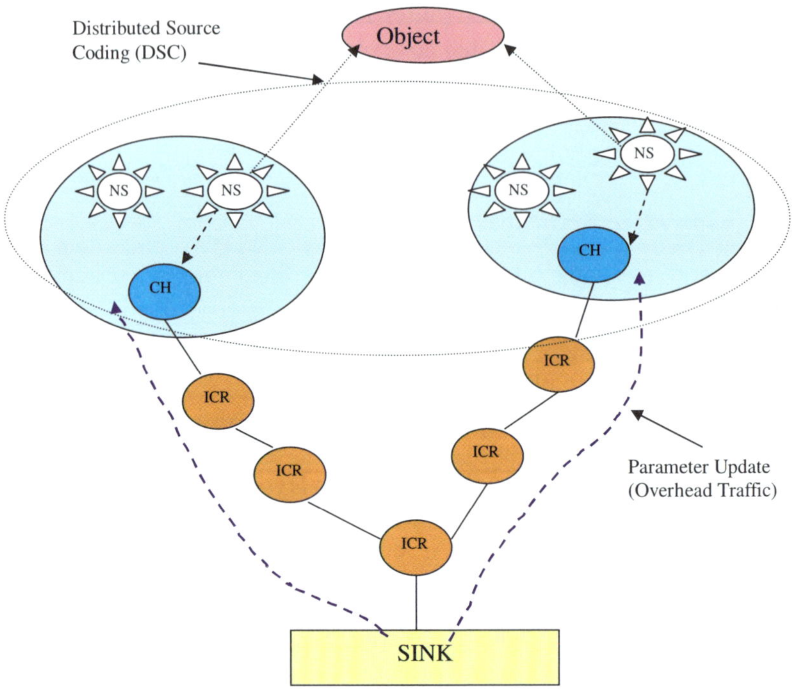

Fig. 25.5. An example of distributed source coding (DSC), where an object is monitored from two sensor nodes encapsulated across different clusters. Coding parameters are exchanged with the help of the sink that also monitors the correlation between packets arriving from different clusters. This also introduces the transmission overhead on intermediate routers and cluster-heads.

(c) Compression credit that reduces the redundancy in the information with some overhead. This overhead is calculated by measuring the extra information carried as side-bands or additional communication required to convey the compression parameters to the NS. Various compression schemes are addressed in Refs. 29 and 30.

Average energy consumption per cluster can be optimized by exploiting the redundancy between various sensors in spatial, temporal or spatio-temporal dimensions and uniformly distributing among clusters. For example, a cluster allocated on the blind side of the sensory environment may not have much use as a sensor node. Sensors in that clusters may very well belong to a different clusters and be used as a Cluster-Head or an Inter-Cluster-Router (ICR).

$$\begin{aligned}\mathrm{SEF} &= \lambda_1\left(1-\frac{1}{N}\cdot\left(\sum_j \min\left(1,\frac{|\sum_i(E_{ij})-E_{\mathrm{avg}}|}{E_{\mathrm{avg}}}\right)\right)\right)\\ &\quad+\lambda_2\left(1-\frac{1}{M}\cdot\left(\sum_j\sum_i\left(\frac{I_{ij}H_{ij}}{H_{\max}}\right)\right)\right), \qquad (25.11)\end{aligned}$$

where E_{ij} is the average sensory power consumption of the ith sensor node in jth cluster, E_{avg} is the average sensory power consumed by all clusters, N and M are the total number of clusters and sensor nodes, respectively, H_{ij} is the number of hops between jth cluster and the sink, $H_{\max}$ is the maximum number of hops possible in the sensor network, $I_{ij} = 1$, if sensor node i of cluster j is correlated with another sensor node in a different cluster, and $I_{ij} = 0$, otherwise. λ_1 and λ_2, which satisfy $\lambda_1 + \lambda_2 = 0.5$, are the contributions to the SEF fitness due to sensory power consumption and overhead traffic, respectively.

25.5.7. *Total node fitness (TNF)*

TNF is the final fitness that is evaluated in the GA algorithm for the appropriate node assignment. It is described by

$$\text{TNF} = \alpha_1\text{CHF} + \alpha_2\text{NCF} + \alpha_3\text{BF} + \alpha_4\text{RFL} + \alpha_5\text{SEF} + \alpha_6\text{CF}, \qquad (25.12)$$

where $\alpha_1 + \alpha_2 + \alpha_3 + \alpha_4 + \alpha_5 + \alpha_6 = 1$ and α_i depends upon the relative significance of the component. These values can be made adaptive using an external heuristics.

25.6. Route Selection Fitness Function

This function plays an important role in generating balanced routes according to node allocation using GA based on node fitness function. During the setup operation, both cluster-heads and inter-cluster-routers start transmitting the data on the most cost effective ICR. Although it is not guaranteed that the setup connection will remain cost-effective over a period of time. GA predicts the optimal route topology based on the cost of using an ICR for the next sampling period. CH and ICR are updated with this information during each sampling period. Route fitness function takes into account the traffic patterns, battery capacity, and transmission energy. Sink is able to predict the optimal topology because of the following properties:

(a) It is aware of the static routes that are either formed during the setup operations or updated during GA operations during a sampling period. This will help GA evaluate the average load on each router (since destination of all communication is the sink).
(b) It is aware of the amount of data (bits) received from each cluster which then traverse through a static routes as in (a).
(c) Each ICR updates the sink of its battery capacity as soon as it crosses a threshold value.
(d) It is aware of the energy-cost of transmission to its nearest neighbors. This is proportional to the distance between ICH and its next hop (or sink). This information is sent by the router during the setup phase.

Based on the predicted optimal route fitness, the sink will update the cost of using this ICR for the next sampling period. The total route fitness (TRF) is given by:

$$\mathrm{TRF} = \mathrm{BF} + \mathrm{NCF} + \frac{1}{N} \cdot \sum_{k} \frac{\max(\mathrm{ICR}(j,k)) - \mathrm{Curr}(\mathrm{ICR}(j,k))}{\mathrm{ICR}(j,k)}. \quad (25.13)$$

$$\begin{aligned}
\mathrm{ICR}(j,k) &= \text{Average bit-rate handled by ICR } j \text{ that can} \\
&\quad\ \text{communicate with node } k \text{ (CH or ICR)} \\
\max(\mathrm{ICR}(j,k)) &= \text{ICR with the highest bit-rate that can be} \\
&\quad\ \text{communicated by node } k \\
\mathrm{Curr}(\mathrm{ICR}(j,k)) &= \text{Current ICR that has been designated to} \\
&\quad\ \text{communicate with node } k \\
N &= \text{Total number of nodes (CH and ICR)} \\
BF &= \text{Battery fitness of the router in question} \\
\mathrm{NCF} &= \text{Node (CH-ICR or ICR-ICR) communication fitness} \\
\mathrm{ICRCost}_n &= 1 - \frac{1}{M} \cdot \sum_{k} \frac{\max(\mathrm{ICR}(j,k)) - \mathrm{ICR}(j=n,k)}{\max(\mathrm{ICR}(j,k))},
\end{aligned}$$

where k = all the nodes that can communicate with ICR n. For example, in Fig. 25.6, for ICR-2, $k = \{$CH1, CH2, CH3, ICR1, ICR3$\}$, M equals the total number of k nodes that can communicate with ICR n; for ICR-2, $M = 5$.

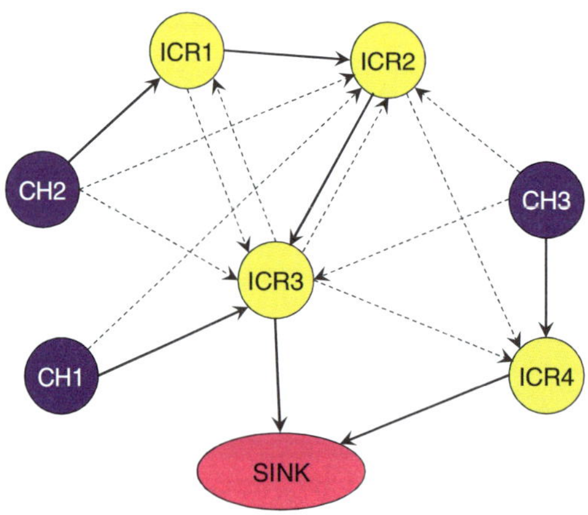

Fig. 25.6. Sample output of the route-selection GA. Thick lines represent the low-cost selected route. Dotted lines represent other possible routes, but with higher relative cost (lower fitness). As the system conditions change, low-cost routes can become high-cost routes and vice versa. There is a high likelihood that ICR 3 may turn out to be a high-cost path if CH 2 becomes highly active.

25.7. Power Optimization Fitness

Power scaling optimizes the functional blocks of the sensors for a given quality-of-service (QoS) as perceived by the sink. QoS policy is defined as a function of (i) security attributes, (ii) importance and accuracy of sensor data (packet priority), and (iii) maximum node-sink delay (sensor data, control data, etc.). QoS policies along with quantifiable observations (workloads, data arrival patterns, battery levels, node stability) adjust the power-scaling parameters of the functional blocks of the node to enhance QoS compliance. For a given functional block, these parameters assume static conditions within a tunable observation period (T_{obs}).

25.7.1. *Power optimization components*

The following sections define various functional blocks **(of ..., power optimization procedure)** and corresponding controls. Three major functional blocks that contribute to power-optimization are memory, micro-controller, and wireless subsystem.

25.7.1.1. *Memory buffer subsystem*

Memory subsystem comprises of transmit/receive buffer (TRB), transmission request queue (TRQ), performance counters (PC), and tunable registers (TR) (Fig. 25.7). Memory buffer is divided into multiple blocks with independent power control applied according to anticipated demand. Data received by the receive buffer is processed for further action (authentication, header manipulation, etc.) before committing to the TRQ. Once in TRQ, data is transmitted to the next hop upon inactivity timer expiration or reaching burst threshold. Number of active memory blocks, observation timer, inactivity timer and burst thresholds are estimated based on QoS policies, sink feedback, and activity trends as measured by performance counters. Performance counters measure the mean number of packet arrivals/serviced and IDC for packet arrivals[31] (index of dispersion for count). IDC is defined as the variance of the number of packet arrivals divided by the mean number of packet arrivals in an interval of length t. It provides a measure of fluctuation of the receiving rate over a given interval, which reflects considerable burstness in the received packets. Burstness can be an indication of packet loss and buffer occupancy. TRQ schedules transmit requests according to the maximum transmission rate, optimal transmission window (OTW) (burst size), and QoS requirements relative to delay tolerances. For burst size less than the OTW, TRQ defers the transmit request for a duration equal to the inactivity interval threshold (η_k^j) for jth node at time t given by

$$\eta_t^j = \eta_{t-1}^j + \frac{\eta_{\min}}{N} \sum_i \beta_i^j(\text{mem}), \tag{25.14}$$

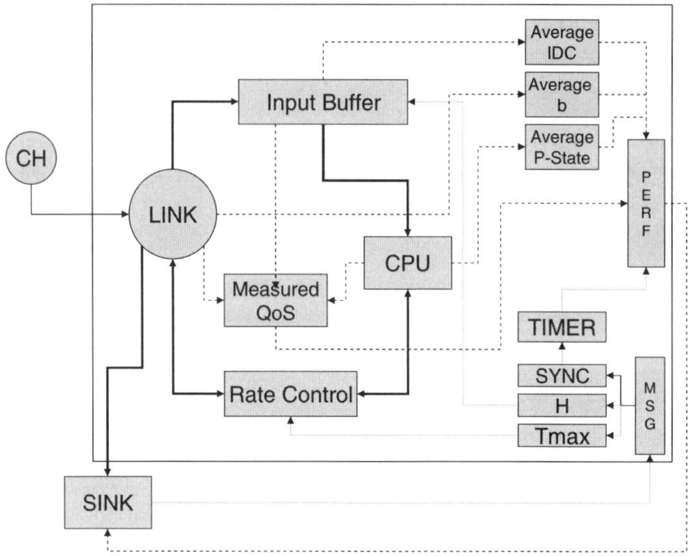

Fig. 25.7. Performance counters monitor CPU power, modulation power and QoS compliance. It transmits the performance data upon timer trigger. Sink uses this data to generate performance targets for nodes. Rate controller uses this data to distribute delay targets to CPU, link and buffer control.

where β_i^j represents the memory sub-system QoS quantity as defined in Sec. 25.7.3. It is calculated based on delay compliance between predicted and actual delay experienced by the data packets towards the sink. OTW is updated as a result of control message sent by the target node.

25.7.1.2. *Micro controller (μC) subsystem*

Micro controller is an integral component of the sensor node and plays an influential role in power conservation. Operations performed by micro-controllers are related to message handling, security protocols, event handling and performance monitoring. Major functions include message parsing, data manipulation, data/performance sampling, encryption, decryption, authentication, PIN assertions, timers and interrupt assertions.

Processor's dynamic power dissipation is proportional to capacitance, clock frequency, and the square of supply voltage ($P \propto C_L.V_{dd}^2 \cdot f$). This implies that to accumulate the same amount of computation, using lower voltage will consume less energy in longer time because the power level is much lower.[18] We use discrete performance states using voltage scaling represented by P_i, where i is the state number. For X discrete states, P_0 is the highest-power/least-latency state, whereas P_X is the performance state.

Since, upon packet arrival, we are uncertain about computational requirements, any unused cycles allotted would eventually be wasted due to idling for extra processor cycles. DVS algorithm avoids wasting cycles by reducing the operating frequency and ensuring that deadline guarantees are not violated by doing so.[11] Based on the QoS requirements of each message and its respective security attributes, P-state ceiling is set for the period of tunable interval (T_{obs}). The ceiling is adjusted according to the delay targets of the ICR or CH nodes.

$$P_t^j = \min(X, P_{t-1}^j) + \frac{\gamma}{N}\sum_i \beta_i^j(\text{cpu}), \tag{25.15}$$

where X is the maximum number of discrete performance states (P-states), γ is the scaling factor ranging between 1 and 2, and $\beta_i^j(\text{cpu})$ is the QoS compliance factor (Sec. 25.7.3). CPU state of node j is incremented or decremented according to QoS compliance of all CH packets passing through it.

25.7.1.3. *Wireless link subsystem*

The transmission time decreases as bit rate increases; is the amount of data to be transmitted is fixed, an increase in bit rate results in a reduced duty-cycle. When the radio switches from the sleep mode to the transmission mode, not only a high exit latency can make it difficult to achieve the required duty-cycle (<1%), but also a significant amount of power is consumed for starting up the transmitter.[32] Therefore optimal tuning is needed to avoid reactive response to an idle slot during transmission. The tuning element consists of predicting idle (T_{off}) time between data bursts. The receiver circuit is turned OFF during that period and turned ON ahead of the idle time expiration using exponential averaging algorithm.

Power savings are also realized by running micro-controller at the optimal P-state and radio at optimal frequency, which spreads the computations in time and transmits the data in a quick burst. This requires decoupling between computational and transmission rate, where each can run at its optimal point using rate-matching between computational processing and data transmission. Since the instantaneous traffic load is mostly lower than the peak value, transmissions can be slowed down, to the optimal operating point. Similar to DVS [Sec. 25.7.1.2], which uses voltage adaptation for an effective CPU power management, dynamic modulation scaling adapts the modulation level to match the instantaneous traffic.

We will use M-ary quadrature amplitude modulation (M-QAM) as the adaptive multilevel modulation scheme because of its lower symbol error probability and bit energy consumption than M-ary phase-shift keying (M-PSK) for a given signal-to-noise ratio (SNR). Sensor node adjusts constellation size (b) and symbol rate (R_s) to reduce the overall energy. Schurgers *et al.*[33] define the following expression for minimizing energy required to transmit one bit by choosing the correct values of b and R_s:

$$E_{\text{bit}} = \left[C_S \cdot (2^b - 1) + C_E + C_R \cdot \frac{R_{S\_\max}}{R_S}\right]\frac{1}{b}, \tag{25.16}$$

where C_E and C_R are functional components that incorporate electronic circuitry for filtering, up-converting and modulating. Parts of the circuitry operates at frequencies proportional to instantaneous symbol rate (R_S), while other parts operate at frequencies proportional to the maximum symbol rate ($R_{S\_\max}$). C_S represents the function of target performance that is weakly dependent upon b. Since high value of R_S results in minimizing delay and energy transmitted per bit, it is logical to maximize this value to $R_{S\_\max}$. Hence, the constellation size b is the only option required for tradeoff between energy and delay. b_t^i is initially set to the maximum for the ith node at time t and tuned dynamically according to the sink feedback and QoS targets. Similar to η [Eq. (25.14)], this parameter is tuned as a function of target and measured QoS.

25.7.2. *Coordinated tuning*

This section discusses the aspects of coordinated tuning and fitness function (Fig. 25.7). While tuning is necessary to maximize the performance/energy ratio of given set of nodes for a given topology (clustering, routing, etc.) and QoS, fitness function is required to optimize the sensor network topology to achieve the target performance/energy ratio for the entire network with optimal battery utilization. GA utilizes the optimal operating points and performance feedback of the nodes of the instantaneous topology to calculate the output of the fitness function which influences the cluster formation/placement, membership, functional attributes, and routing decisions.

Coordinated tuning is necessary for identifying the operating point in order to maximize the performance of the node with respect to energy consumed. Performance is measured using a QoS function that is dependent upon communication delay, messaging priority, etc. Router node j estimates the QoS error for cluster head packet i (ξ_i^j) using:

$$\xi_i^j(x) = \frac{T_i^j(x) - D_i^j(x)}{D_i^j(x)}, \tag{25.17}$$

$$D_i^j(x) = \phi_x \cdot \max(\epsilon, (1 - Qp_i)) \cdot T_{i_{\max}}^j, \quad 0 \le Qp_i \le 1, \tag{25.18}$$

where T_i^j represents the processing delay for packet i on ICR j, Qp_i is the priority of ith packet, $T_{i_{\max}}^j$ is the maximum delay allowed for ith packet on jth ICR and ϕ_x is the delay contribution factor due to processing element x =(Memory ϕ_{IIT}, CPU ϕ_p, Link ϕ_b). Each processing element measures QoS compliance by calculating the differential between measured ($T_i^j(x)$) and expected delay ($D_i^j(x)$). It scales the ϕ_x parameters accordingly to reduce the QoS error. Periodically, sink sends the SYNC-sink message containing new parameters ($T_{i_{\max}}^j$, Qp_i for all member nodes ($R(i)$) of route catering CH i. Each ICR and CH node implements the closed-loop-control function that minimizes the ξ_i^j by tuning inactivity interval threshold (η^j) [Eq. (25.14)], CPU P-state ceiling (P^j) [Eq. (25.15)] and modulation scaling parameter (b^j) [Eq. (25.16)]. Each of these components contribute partially to the maximum allowed delay $T^j_{i\,\max}$ thereby operate within its QoS bounds.

While early arrivals can cause a bursty traffic and memory pressures, late arrivals can cause performance issues. To avoid that situation, ϕ_x is tuned by monitoring the transmit buffer for a period of programmed interval (T_{obs}). For high bandwidth cases, we limit the transmit buffer utilization to 70%. This is done by first reducing the modulation delay factor ϕ_b to minimum bounds, then increasing the CPU delay factor ϕ_{cpu} and finally increasing memory delay factor ϕ_{IIT}. For low utilization case, we reduce the CPU delay factor first, followed by modulation delay factor and finally memory.

25.7.3. *Power scaling fitness function (PSFF)*

This section defines a new fitness function that rewards the uniformity of the power states and QoS compliance within an established route. This function also penalizes a disproportionate allocation of power-states with respect to other routes as well as non-optimal provisioning of memory buffer. Elements of fitness function are described as follows:

(1) **QoS Fitness (ω_i^1)** is defined as degree to which routes are compliant with respect to allocated delay budget. A route i is considered compliant (β_i) if the measured delay (D_i) falls within $\pm\delta$% of target delay (T_i). Over-compliance as well as under-compliance are both penalized though with a non-uniform penalty factor ($\widetilde{\lambda}$, λ). QoS fitness is written as

$$\omega_i^1 = 1 - \frac{\sum_j (\widetilde{\lambda}|\max(0, \beta_i^j - \delta)| + \lambda|\min(0, \beta_i^j + \delta)|)}{N}, \tag{25.19}$$

$$\beta_i^j(x) = \max\big(-1, \min\big(1, \xi_i^j(x)\big)\big), \tag{25.20}$$

where $\xi_i^j(x)$ represents QoS error for ith packet (route) on jth node.

(2) **Buffer Optimization (ω_i^2)** is the measure of effective memory utilization. Packets from different sources (CH and ICR) arrive at different times and are statistically multiplexed into the common buffer. These packets can have variable rates depending upon sampling variances and QoS. Buffer occupancy is dependent upon service times of the CPU and wireless subsystem, which is optimized as a part of tuning process. It penalizes non-optimal provisioning of the memory blocks that can cause over allocation or reactive switching between memory power-states. Furthermore, inadequate buffer between CPU and transmit logic can cause coupling between CPU processing and transmission rates. Buffer optimization is written as

$$\omega_i^2 = 1 - \frac{\sum_j \min(1, |B^j_{i\_\text{prid}}/B^j_{i\_\text{act}} - 1|)}{N}, \tag{25.21}$$

where $B^j_{i\_\text{prid}}$ is the predicted buffer size based on exponential averaged quantity and $B^j_{i\_\text{act}}$ is the actual buffer size required.

(3) **Uniform Power-State Distribution (ω^3_i)** penalizes the routes that consume disproportionate amount of power as compared to average power utilization by other routes. It uses average P-state residency $(\overline{P^j_i})$ [Eq. (25.15)] and average modulation scaling $(\overline{b^j_i})$ [Eq. (25.16)] as the measure of power consumption by a node j. As described above, one of the many reasons for non-uniform distribution is heterogeneous message priorities, variable rates and security attributes. Uniform power-state distribution is written as

$$\omega^3_i = 1 - \frac{\sum_j \min\left(2, \left(|\overline{P} - \overline{P^j_i}| + |\overline{b} - \overline{b^j_i}|\right)\right)}{2N}. \tag{25.22}$$

Overall PSFF fitness function of route i is the weighted sum of all contributing elements. While TNF (Sec. 25.5.7) incorporates communication energy as a part of NCF, it lacks the energy contribution due to other components like micro-controller and wireless logic. We modify that equation by adding PSFF contribution as:

$$\text{PSFF}_i = \mu_1\omega^1_i + \mu_2\omega^2_i + \mu_3\omega^3_i, \tag{25.23}$$

$$\text{TNF} = \alpha_1\text{CHF} + \alpha_2\text{NCF} + \alpha_3\text{BF} + \alpha_4\text{RFL} + \alpha_5\text{SEF} + \alpha_6\text{CF} + \alpha_7\text{PSFF}, \tag{25.24}$$

where $\alpha_1 + \alpha_2 + \alpha_3 + \alpha_4 + \alpha_5 + \alpha_6 + \alpha_7 = 1$ and α_i depends upon the relative significance of the component. These values can be made adaptive using an external heuristics.

25.8. Secure Communication Fitness

In our security model, the sink is considered a trusted component that establishes a necessary trust relationship for secure forwarding of data between various node types. Nodes closest to the sink form the most trusted relationships. Farther nodes build the hierarchy of trust starting from the sink which is apparent from the predetermined routing decisions that are created during setup and later during reconfiguration. Ingredients of security architecture create a trust relationship between various node-types for the reasons related command/message execution, data forwarding, etc. Any authentication is mediated through sink and components of the trusted routing hierarchy. To achieve a power efficient authentication we employ certain elements of secure network encryption protocol (SNEP).[17] Encryption portion of the protocol is executed between first-initiator (FI) and the sink with other components in the hierarchy acting as an authenticated (or un-authenticated) pass-through. First initiator is a cluster-head or an ICR that either initiates a command or participates in data fusion for delivery to sink. Elements of security are:

(1) **Master Key (MK)** derives keys for symmetric encryption (K_{encr}), message authentication (K_{auth}), and generates pseudo-random numbers (K_{rand}).[17] The derived keys can be changed randomly upon request by the sink. The master key is shared between a node and the sink *a priori* and used for exclusive node-sink messaging. A pseudo-random number is generated using a derived key K_{rand} and a counter C. This number is inserted in the message before encryption to avoid plain-text attacks.

$$K_{\text{rand}}^{n+1} = \text{MAC}(K_{\text{rand}}, C^n). \tag{25.25}$$

(2) **Inter-Node Communication Key (INCK)** is the sink-mediated shared key between two nodes that authenticates (INCK_{mac}) the messages between them. Since the sink is aware of the routing hierarchy, it encapsulates an INCK=$\{(\text{INCK}_{\text{mac}}^0), (\text{INCK}_{\text{mac}}^1)\}$ for each ICR (or CH) that takes part in authentication. Each node decrypts the encapsulated packet using its K_{encr} (derived from the master key) and extracts its INCK. $\text{INCK}_{\text{mac}}^0$ and $\text{INCK}_{\text{mac}}^1$ are the MAC keys used at ports 0 and 1, respectively.

(3) **Encryption and Authentication** Similar to the SPIN protocol,[17] we use counter-mode block cypher for encryption/decryption and CBC-MAC[34] for authentication. The counter-mode block cypher requires a shared counter between a node and the sink which is incremented on each block. Since it is a stream-cipher, the message length is the same as the plain text and hence a lower communication overhead. While some routers can be used as pass-through, other routers enforce admission control using MAC based authentication. Sink can change the authentication requirements of ICR and CH depending on energy requirements and perceived security threat as measured by the battery quantization levels and the number of bad packets.

Battery limitations and computational overhead prevent us from maintaining the same threat levels by employing encryption and authentication mechanisms on all nodes. Ideal enabling reduces the computational overhead while maintaining the adequate security levels by identifying the strategic nodes. Strategic nodes are optimally enabled for security by evaluating the battery status, network traffic, malformed or retries on a specific route and number of nodes in a single route handling authentication. For the purpose of GA, we evaluate a fitness function that competes for the optimal enablement of the security ingredients on the sensor nodes.

25.8.1. *Secure node fitness* (*SNF*)

SNF rewards the security enabling on nodes based on the perceived threat involving data integrity for secure communication. Sink keeps track of all the ill-formed packets received on a particular route. While routes (CH $\rightarrow$ sink) are penalized for carrying malformed and retried packets, they are rewarded for enabling authentication on routers (ICR) and encryption on cluster-heads. Additional penalty is awarded if the authentication is enabled disproportional to threat level quantized to M levels. While system can react proportionally to the perceived threat, it may not be enabled in an energy efficient manner. SNF rewards energy efficient enablement of security attributes that are measured against battery quantization levels and rate of battery usage. Sink uses hysteresis to compute the battery usage that is indicative of data communication, average number of connecting nodes, and locomotion, etc.

$$\mathrm{SNF} = 1 - \frac{1}{2R}\sum_{i=1}^{R}\left(\left|\frac{\theta_i}{M} - \frac{\lambda_1 K_i}{N} - \lambda_2\right| + \sum_{n=1}^{N}\frac{I_i^n F_i^n(Q,\psi)}{N}\right), \qquad (25.26)$$

where $\lambda_1 + \lambda_2 = 1$ with λ_2 being the reward contribution due to encryption of the first initiator (FI), R is the total number of routes, θ_i is the threat level of route i as calculated by sink, K_i is the number of nodes (ICR(s) and CH) that are enabled for authentication and encryption in route i, N is the total number of nodes (ICR(s) and CH) in route i, $I_i^n = 1$ (else 0) if node n in route i is enabled for authentication, and $F_i^n(.)$ is penalty for enabling admission control on node i on route j that has battery level at Q and rate of battery usage at ψ. This approach adapts the security attributes proportional to the perceived threat and in a manner that promotes efficient battery usage and minimizes the effects of aberrant nodes.

25.9. Mobility Fitness

Mobility allows the nodes to seek out power optimization, request data fusion from other nodes to perform cooperative sensing, seek out repair, and locate data portals from which to report. But mobility comes with a price as locomotion is costly in terms of node size and power consumption. An optimal locomotion strategy is achieved by sensor node's ability to monitor its own power as well as its interaction with environmental dynamics. Locomotion is employed to maximize the fitness by rearranging its position to achieve the optimality of the parameters defined in the following sections.

25.9.1. *Coverage uniformity fitness (CUF)*

CUF expresses the coverage improvement by filling the coverage holes and maximizing the detection area using sensor movement. This is done by re-balancing the communication distances between member nodes of the cluster. Closely placed nodes are rewarded for moving away while farther nodes are rewarded for moving toward each other to attain coverage equilibrium. When the distances between nodes become optimal, the distance to the farthest neighboring node and the required transmission power are minimized which helps maximize the NCF. CUF is expressed as

$$\mathrm{CUF} = 1 - \frac{1}{2M}\sum_{j}\left(\min\left(1, \frac{|d_j^{\min} - \overline{d_j}|}{\overline{d_j}}\right) + \min\left(1, \frac{|e_j^{\min} - \overline{e_j}|}{\overline{e_j}}\right)\right), \qquad (25.27)$$

where M is the number of clusters, $d_j^{\min}$, $\overline{d_j}$ are, respectively, the minimum and mean communication distances between nodes in cluster j, and $e_j^{\min}$ and $\overline{e_j}$ are, respectively, the minimum and mean communication distances between nodes and cluster-head in cluster j.

Uniformly distributed sensor nodes spend energy more evenly than nodes with an irregular topology. GA exploits the sensor motion ability by positioning the sensors in a manner to increase the coverage, reduce the inter-node interference, and minimize the power required to communicate.

25.9.2. *Node motion fitness (NMF)*

The average distance traveled by a node is related to its movement at the expense of battery life. So, the expected distance is an important estimate of energy required for nodes with limited energy supply. Hence it is desired to stabilize the motion characteristics while achieving the overall system objectives (coverage and longer network life). These characteristics are related to motion frequency and oscillations.

(1) *Motion Frequency* measures an average movement of the sensor in a given amount of time bounded by a threshold which is a function of the battery life defined by battery fitness. Larger movements of sensors with limited battery life is penalized which makes it highly prohibitive to achieve locomotion as the system ages.
(2) *Location Stability* measures an inability of nodes to attain stable position due to competitive objectives. Nodes are penalized for having excessive movement or un-sustained oscillations.

The node motion fitness is expressed as

$$\text{NMF} = \frac{1}{2}\left((1 - F_i(Q, \text{distance})) + (1 - \phi_i(n))\right), \tag{25.28}$$

where $\phi_i(n)$ is the ith sensor node's penalty measure for visiting the same location for n times ($0 \leq \phi_i(n) \leq 1$), $F_i(\cdot)$ is the ith sensor node's penalty with $0 \leq F_i(Q, \text{Node Type}) \leq 1$, Q is the battery status represented in quantized steps, *distance* is the estimated distance traveled by the node which is estimated indirectly using energy-based localization based on multiple energy reading at different known sensor locations.

The signal energy measured on the ith sensor over a time interval t, denoted by $y_i(t)$, can be expressed as

$$y_i(t) = \frac{G_i.S(t)}{|\boldsymbol{r}(t) - \boldsymbol{r}_i|^{\alpha}} + \epsilon_i(t), \tag{25.29}$$

where G_i is the gain factor of the ith sensor, α ($\approx$2) is an energy-decay factor, and $\epsilon_i(t)$ is the cumulative effects of the modeling error of the parameters, $S(t)$ denotes the energy emitted by the target at time t, $\boldsymbol{r}(t)$ is a $D \times 1$ vector denoting the coordinates of the target at time t, $\boldsymbol{r}_i$ is a $D \times 1$ vector denoting the cartesian coordinates of the ith stationary sensor.

The total fitness associated with node movement is given by total node motion fitness

$$\text{TNMF} = \alpha_1\text{CUF} + \alpha_2\text{NMF}, \tag{25.30}$$

where $\alpha_1 + \alpha_2 = 1$ and individual weight is dependent upon implementation. Mobility generates a better distribution of energy among various functional nodes attributed to an extra degree of freedom that relocates the node strategically to achieve better battery utilization (fitness). This also reduces frequent re-clustering because now the roles are exchanged by just exchanging the positions while maintaining fitness parameters in equilibrium.

25.10. Naming Convention

Naming convention is an important ingredient of the sensor network system architecture. An optimal naming convention will reduce the messaging overhead as well as facilitate collaborative signal processing. Each sensor supports three types of naming conventions:

(a) *Globally Unique Sensor ID* (GUID) is the uniquely identifiable node identification number that is hard-coded in the sensor hardware. This ID is used during the setup phase (or re-initialization phase).

(b) *Proximity Unique ID* (PUID) is the unique identification of the nodes contained within the neighborhood of a cluster (NS ID, CH ID, and ICR ID). This ID is used among the neighboring nodes for link-layer data exchange and collaborative signal processing. These IDs are allocated dynamically in the following manner:

   (i) ICR(s) self-allocate its own PUID during the setup (or re-initialization) phase that involves negotiation between the neighboring ICR(s). This ID is used for ICR-ICR link-layer forwarding and not contained in the message header.

   (ii) CH(s) receives its PUID from ICR(s) during the CH-ICR binding operation (Sec. 25.4.1.3). This ID is used for CH-ICR link-layer forwarding and not contained in the message header.

   (iii) NS(s) receives its PUID from CH(s) during the NS-CH binding operation (Sec. 25.4.1.2). This ID is used for NS-CH link-layer forwarding. This ID can optionally be carried in the message header when the message flows through the ICR.

(c) *Application Unique ID* (AUID) is allocated by the sink to the cluster-head for message identification. This ID enables the sink to uniquely identify the origin of the message up to the node level. This is a data-layer ID that is carried in the message header and filled in by the cluster-head. This ID is for application use only, and system topology has no visibility into its construction or usage. AUID can be attribute-named data that can enable in-network processing with filters, supporting data aggregation, nested queries and similar techniques that are critical to reduce network traffic and conserve energy.[35]

The addressing in this manner reduces the overhead due to addressing bits during the message transmission. This method is scalable to the size of the network. Smaller networks with fewer nodes will use less addressing bits than the larger networks.

25.11. Overhead Traffic

The GA used to perform *Node Function Selection*, *Route Selection*, *Security Attribute Selection* and *Node Repositioning* is targeted with many competitive objectives running at the sink. It is important to note that the sink builds up the *Node Database* tree by snooping the routed data and the setup-data (initialization step) consisting of node ID, transmission distance (to ICR and other neighboring nodes), associated CH and routes to the sink (primary and fail-over routes). This data is further evaluated at the sink for the creation of additional data-points consisting of various fitness categories defined in Secs. 25.5, 25.6, 25.8.1, and 25.9. While most of the fitness data can be indirectly inferred from the regular data (normal data and setup data), battery loss due to coverage cannot be measured using this method. Moreover, changes in the associations and designations require extra messaging between sink and nodes. Hence various sources of the overhead traffic are:

(i) Setup Messaging — This is mandatory messaging (Sec. 25.4) required for initial setup of the network. These messages are exchanged once during initialization-step and in extreme cases can also be triggered by sink.
(ii) Sink Alert Messaging — This message is performed when sink determines the need for new allocations for nodes and routes as a result of performing GA.
(iii) Node Alert Messaging — This messaging is initiated by the nodes towards sink, in order to identify critical information. Currently, this messaging is used for alerting when:
   (a) Battery levels falls below the thresholds.
   (b) A fail-over route is chosen for future routings. Each ICR identifies itself (starting with the failed over ICR).
(iv) Node Battery Status — The node battery status data flow through the pre-established path using the extra bits in the SN messaging data. Three extra bits in the header gives eight quantization levels.
(v) Correlation Data Timer — This timer updates the spatial or temporal correlation parameters of the sensor nodes that compresses the overall data in a distributed coding.[28] An update has to traverse through all the ICR(s) en-route

to the co-operating nodes residing in different clusters. This is a low duty-cycle operation that can adapt to the changing environment thus limiting the expenditure involved in update overhead.

(vi) Closed Loop Feedback — Sink provides feedback data (SYNC-sink message) related to target delay, QoS and security attributes that is used for power and security optimization.

As described, most of the overhead traffic is caused during the setup-operation. A small percentage of messages also flow as Alerts and messages between source and sink. Most of the cost of indirect inference and GA execution is pushed to the sink. As a result, cost of overhead-traffic on the nodes is greatly reduced. Increase in the number of nodes (large networks) shows a longer delay in *Initialization Setup* and *Message Propagation*. Longer delays are mitigated by sub-dividing a large network into smaller domains with identifiable boundaries.

25.12. Sensor Construction

A self-organization mechanism using a contention-free time-division multiple access (TDMA) medium access protocol can be used for sensor networks.[36] During the setup phase, nodes interact in a random access manner. As the clusters are formed during the setup phase or re-clustering event (upon GA trigger), incremental TDMA schedules are formed for sensor nodes, cluster-heads, and inter-cluster-routers. Re-clustering as a result of GA evaluation (and the corresponding alert) will modify the existing TDMA schedules to accommodate the newly formed clusters. Incremental determination of the TDMA schedules is based on the known range limitations on the radio where certain nodes are expected to be outside the region of radio interference with the current node. At the same time, as a result of distributed scheduling, some nodes with similar schedules may interfere with each other. This can be remedied by using multiple channels or spreading codes, that will reduce the overhead due to transmission management. Typical sensors used in this scenario have the following characteristics:

(a) Transmitter — Transmits the data at various power levels. It should have the ability to quickly enter and exit from one power-state to another.

(b) Receiver — Receives the data targeted toward it. It additionally comprises of a low-power listening engine. Sensor radio consumes almost the same energy as when transmitting, searching for the next packet. To reduce energy consumption during the non-transmitting periods, energy-aware protocols are used. These protocols involve extra transmission overhead in terms of extra attention bits and reduced sampling of the radio channel. As defined in Sec. 25.7.1.3, this component is also responsible for predicting the idle time during which receiver circuit is turned off. Idle period prediction can be done using a simple exponential averaging mechanism.

(c) Power control — Controls the power to be transmitted according to the function assigned.
(d) Function control — Performs the protocol actions related to the function. These actions are related to identification, advertising, power-control, performing bindings and associations with other nodes, and sensing, etc.
(e) Test control — Performs the test functions. Test control is transparent to the function control and does not interfere with its working. This control is required to simulate a future topology while not interfering with the current one. GA will make use of this function to evaluate the fitness before committing this topology to all nodes.
(f) Alert generation — Generates an alert action to the sink upon any critical/warning or quantized event (like battery depletion). Alert data are used by the sink in the evaluation of the fitness parameters.
(g) Memory — Limited memory is required to collect the data payload related to sensing, test-data, or route-queues. A buffer overflow can cause the packets to be dropped. A temporary overflow memory allocation can be received from the neighboring node that belongs to the same cluster. Such allocation can be expensive as it comes at the cost of transmission overhead.
(h) Adaptive duty cycling — All ICR nodes put themselves in a low-duty-cycle state when they are not required to transmit any data through them. A Wake-on-Wireless (WoW) signal[37] can wake a sensor from the low-power state to the high-power state.

These characteristics are required for proper functioning of the self-organizing sensor network using genetic algorithms. Most of these characteristics are related to the functional adaptation of the sensor based on function allocation by the sink without interrupting the sensing operation.

25.13. Summary

This chapter presents an approach to design a self-organizing network based on genetic algorithms. Sensors that are placed at random are assigned functions (sensing node, cluster-head, router, or inactive-node) based upon the results of GA. The

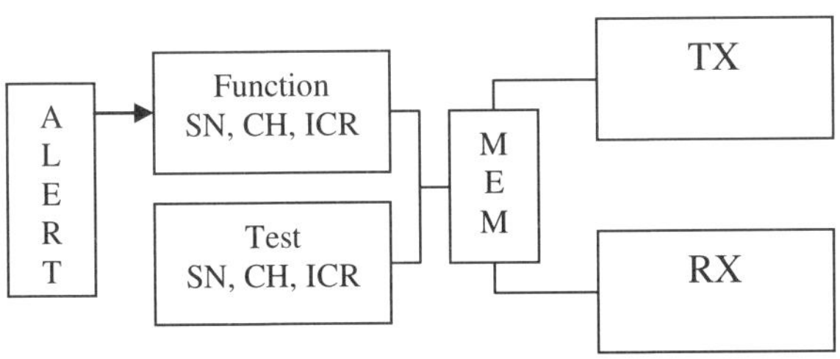

Fig. 25.8. Illustration of sensor construction.

GA approach optimizes the network to maximize energy usage along with battery conservation with route optimization. To fulfil the needs of secure communication, a novel approach of adapting the security attributes proportional to the perceived threat is presented that promotes efficient battery usage and minimizes the effects of aberrant nodes. To further maximizes coverage and network life, this approach exploits mobility and dynamic power scaling, which optimally relocates the sensor node and tunes its components (memory, CPU and Wireless Link) that optimizes node assignments, route and security attributes. This leads to a better distribution of energy among various functional nodes attributed to an extra degree of freedom that relocates the node strategically to achieve better battery utilization (fitness). It also reduces frequent re-clustering because now the roles are exchanged by just exchanging the positions while maintaining fitness parameters in equilibrium and fewer nodes reach their functional thresholds. It is found that a dynamic deployment significantly outperforms the static one with a 15–20% reduction in the number of lost nodes. While nodes are lost exponentially in static deployment case, they die gradually in clusters for the dynamic deployment case due to better distribution of the total energy. In a multi-hop network, heterogeneous traffic flows are multiplexed into an ICR, which causes variations in the resource consumption. Re-clustering with power scaling fitness function bias reduces such variations and enhances the QoS compliance (up to 20%) with guaranteed delays and 5–8% improvement in the number of nodes with a valid route to sink.

References

1. I. F. Akyildiz, W. Su, Y. Sankarasubramaniam and E. Cayirci, Wireless sensor networks: A survey, *Computer Networks*, **38**, 393–422 (2002).
2. K. Akkaya and M. Younis, A Survey on routing protocols for wirelsss sensor networks, *Ad Hoc Networks*, **3**, 325–349 (2005).
3. R. Min, M. Bhardwaj, S.-H. Cho, E. Shih, A. Sinha, A. Wang and A. Chandrakasan, Low power wireless sensor networks, *Proc. Int. Conf. VLSI Design*, Bangalore, India (2001).
4. J. M. Rabaey, M. J. Ammer, J. L. da Silva, Jr., D. Patel and S. Roundy, PicoRadio supports ad hoc ultra low power wireless networking, *IEEE Computer*, **33**, 42–48 (2000).
5. R. H. Katz, J. M. Kahn and K. S. J. Pister, Mobile networking for smart dust, *Proc. 5th Annual ACM/IEEE Int. Conf. Mobile Computing and Networking (MobiCom'99)*, Seattle, WA (1999).
6. H. O. Marcy, J. R. Agre, C. Chien, L. P. Clare, N. Romanov and A. Twarowski, Wireless sensor networks for area monitoring and integrated vehicle health management applications, *Proc. AIAA Guidance, Navigation, and Control Conf.*, Portland, OR, USA (1999).
7. P. Pardalos and H. Wolkowicz, Quadratic assignments and related problems, *DIMACS Series in Discrete Mathematics and Theoretical Computer Science*, **16** (1994).
8. D. Fudenberg and J. Tirole, *Game Theory*. MIT Press (1991).

9. D. Goldberg, *Genetic Algorithm in Search, Optimization and Machine Learning.* Addison-Wesley Publishing Company, Inc. (1989).
10. K. Govil, E. Chan and H. Wassermann, Comparing algorithms for dynamic speed-setting of a low-power CPU, *Proc. Int. Conf. MobiCom'95*, Berkeley, California, USA (1995).
11. P. Pillai and K. G. Shin, Real-time dynamic voltage scaling for low-power embedded operating systems, *Proc. 18th ACM Symp. Operating Systems Principles*, Banff, Alberta, Canada (2001).
12. A. Howard, M. J. Mataric and G. S. Sukhatme, An incremental self-deployment algorithm for mobile sensor network, *Autonomous Robots*, **13**, 113–126 (2002).
13. A. Howard, M. J. Mataric and G. S. Sukhatme, Mobile sensor network deployment using potential fields: A distributed, scalable solution to the area coverage problem, *DARS'02* (2002).
14. S. Y. Wu, C. H. Liu and C. K. Tzeng, Self-organization for dynamic context coverage in capability-constrained mobile sensor networks, *Proc. IEEE SUTC'06* (2006).
15. G. Trajcevski, P. Scheuerman and H. Bronnimann, Mission-critical management of mobile sensors (or, How to Guide a Flock of Sensors), *Proc. 1st Workshop DMSN*, Toronto, Canada (2004).
16. H. Cam, S. Ozdemir, D. Muthuavinashiappan and P. Nair, Energy efficient security protocol for wireless sensor networks, *Proc. IEEE*, 2981–2984 (2003).
17. A. Perrig, R. Szewczyk, V. Wen, D. Culler and J. D. Tygar, SPINS: Security protocols for wireless sensor networks, *Proc. ACM Mobile Comp. and Network* (2001).
18. L. Yuan and G. Qu, Design space exploration for energy-efficient secure sensor network, *Proc. IEEE Int. Conf. Application-Specific Systems, Architectures, and Processors* (2002).
19. V. Shnayder, M. Hempstead, B. Chen, G. W. Allen and M. Welsh, Simulating the power consumption of large-scale sensor network applications, *Proc. Int. Conf. Embedded Networked Sensor Systems*, Baltimore, MD, USA (2004).
20. K. Bult, A. Burstein, *et al.*, Low power systems for wireless microsensors, *Proc. 1996 Int. Symp. Low Power Electronics and Design*, Monterey, California, USA (1996).
21. G. Xing, C. Lu, Y. Zhang, Q. Huang and R. Pless, Minimum power configuration in wireless sensor networks, *Proc. 6th ACM Int. Symp. Mobile Ad Hoc Networking and Computing*, Urbana-Champaign, IL, USA, 25–27 (2005).
22. L. Pronzalo and E. Walter, *Identification of Parametric Models from Experimental Data.* Springer-Verlag (1997).
23. J. Horn, J. N. Nafpliotis and D. Goldberg, A niched Pareto genetic algorithm for multiobjective optimization: Evolutionary Computation, *Proc. 1st IEEE Conf. Computational Intelligence*, 82–87 (1994).
24. F. Xue and P. R. Kumar, The number of neighbors needed for connectivity of wireless networks, *Wireless Networks*, **10**(2), 169–181 (2004).
25. S. Poduri and G. S. Sukhatme, Constrained coverage for mobile sensor networks, *Proc. IEEE Int. Conf. Robotics and Automation*, New Orleans, LA, USA, 165–172 (2004).
26. Q. Li, J. Aslam and D. Rus, Hierarchical power aware routing in sensor networks, *Proc. DIMACS Workshop on Pervasive Networking* (2001).
27. J. Chou, D. Petrovic and K. Ramchandran, Tracking and exploiting correlations in dense sensor networks, *Proc. 36th Asilomar Conf. Signals, Systems and Computers* (2002).
28. T. M. Cover and J. A. Thomas, *Elements of Information Theory.* John Wiley (1991).

29. S. Goel and T. Imielinski, Prediction-based monitoring in sensor networks: Taking lessons from MPEG, *ACM Computer Communication Review*, **31**, 82–98 (2001).
30. S. Lindsey and C. S. Raghavendra, PEGASIS: Power-efficient Gathering in sensor information systems, *Proc. Aerospace Conf.* (2002).
31. R. Gusella, Characterizing the variability of arrival processes with indexes of dispersion, *IEEE J. Select. Areas Commun.*, **9**(2), 203–211 (1991).
32. A. Wang, S. Cho, C. Sodini and A. Chandrakasan, Energy-efficient modulation and MAC for asymmetric microsensor systems, *Proc. ISLPED* (2001).
33. C. Schurgers, O. Aberthorne and M. B. Srivastava, Modulation scaling for energy aware communication systems, *Proc. Int. Symp. Low Power Electronics and Design*, Huntington Beach, CA, USA, 96–99 (2001).
34. US National Institute of Standards and Technology (NIST), DES model of operation, *Federal Information Processing Standards Publication*, **81** (FIPS PUB 81).
35. J. Heidemann, F. Silva, C. Intanagonwiwat, R. Govindan, D. Estrin and D. Ganesan, Building efficient wireless sensor networks with low-level naming, *Proc. ACM Symp. Operating Systems Principles*, Chateau Lake Louise, Banff, Alberta, Canada, 146–159 (2001).
36. K. Sohrabi and G. J. Pottie, Performance of a novel self-organization for wireless ad-hoc sensor networks, *Proc. IEEE Veh. Technol. Conf.* (1999).
37. E. Shih, P. Bahl and M. Sinclair, Wake on wireless: An event driven energy saving strategy for battery operated devices, *Proc. ACM/IEEE Int. Conf. Mobile Computing and Networking (Mobicom)*, Atlanta, GA (2002).

Part VIII

Multimedia Sensor Networks

Chapter 26

Information Collection and Storage in Wireless Multimedia Sensor Network

Yuehhua Lee*, Kui Wu* and Jiming Chen†

**Computer Science Department*
University of Victoria

†College of Information Science and Engineering
Zhejiang University

Sensors are small autonomous devices with wireless communication and sensing capabilities. The miniaturization of sensors makes them very limited in energy supply, communication bandwidth, storage space, and computational power. The rationale behind using tiny sensors includes the ease of deployment in a large scale, and the non-trivial aggregate processing power if many tiny sensors are networked and cooperate together. With the state-of-the-art electronic engineering technology, we are able to push sensor technology from processing simple information such as temperature and humidity readings to processing video and audio data. Such development, however, poses many research and engineering challenges. The commercial applications of wireless multimedia sensor systems are still in infancy due to many unsolved problems. Instead of covering all aspects of wireless multimedia sensor networks, this chapter focuses on the research issues and recent progress on information collection and storage in such networks.

26.1. Introduction

A sensor node is a small autonomous device which is normally equipped with a micro-controller, a wireless transceiver, memory, and sensing devices. When many small sensor nodes are networked and work together with wireless communication, they form a wireless sensor network (WSN). In the past decade, WSN technology has headed toward a new era. The applications of conventional sensor networks normally relate to monitoring scalar physical measurement like temperature, humidity, and light intensity in a monitoring area. The simple readings are insufficient to describe complex physical world, for instance the flow of traffic or a car accident, and as such the broader adoption of WSN technology are subject to the breakthrough in sensor engineering. Fortunately, with state-of-the-art MicroElectroMechanical Systems (MEMS) technology, we are now able to embed inexpensive cameras and microphones as part of the sensing devices and empower the sensor nodes to capture multimedia information. When a WSN is of such capability, it is called a wireless multimedia sensor network (WMSN).

The rise of WMSNs is exciting. This new type of networks opens the door to many interesting applications involving multimedia content and has attracted substantial academic research and industrial development in recent years. The ability of capturing and processing multimedia information also makes existing system more powerful. Listed below are several practical systems that can benefit from WMSN technology:

- **Intelligent Transportation System (ITS)** When the government officers discovered that building more freeways only attracted more automobiles and caused higher traffic congestion in the late 20th century, they sought help from management means. The ITS is one of the major trends among the modern transportation management systems. The conventional sensor technology is a key factor of ITS in the past. Nowadays, WMSN technology plays a more important role in ITS. Camera sensors can help the traffic management in a variety of ways. To list a few, camera sensors can capture the image of a speeding automobile and inform the authority to issue a ticket; A WMSN can detect a car accident and inform the control center; It can also observe traffic congestion and adjust the length of time of the green light.
- **Parking space finder** A WMSN can be used to identify whether a parking lot is occupied or not. By a simple query, the network can tell a driver the nearest available parking lot.
- **Civil surveillance** Since the closed-circuit surveillance cameras became available, surveillance systems were widely used in residential districts, galleries, and many different sites to ensure security. The multimedia sensors make the surveillance more flexible and easier. For example, multiple wireless multimedia sensors can dynamically adjust the field of view (FOV) of a pan/tilt/zoom (PTZ) camera to eliminate any blind spots. The real-time video can be sent to security personnel at different locations. Moreover, the sensors can trigger the alarm automatically when an intruder is detected.
- **Medical caretaker** A WMSN may help elders or patients of chronic diseases who convalesce at home. When any emergency occurs, the medical personnel is able to see the on-the-spot videos and provide quick help. The sensors are also to identify simple accidents and react automatically. For example, a fall detection system is developed at the Yale University[1] to decrease the possibility that the patients get unconscious and are not able to trigger the alarm or call the hospital by themselves.
- **Wildlife monitoring and battlefield surveillance** Wildlife habitat and battlefield surveillance are two classical applications with wireless sensor networks. With the help of multimedia sensors, the biologists can collect more information

such as animal sound or motion. The military can classify the enemies more precisely and take proper reaction.

- **Nursery room** A WMSN may detect any anomaly in a nursery room by collectively analyzing multiple sources, such as abnormal cries, high fever, and coughs. Moreover, the parents may see their baby closely via the camera whenever an anomaly is detected and alarms are raised.

The WMSNs share many features with the conventional wireless sensor networks, including strict energy constraint, low bandwidth, unreliable wireless links, small storage space, and low computation capability. Required to support multimedia processing, WMSNs have distinct characteristics and pose more research and development challenges:

(1) The energy required by cameras on the sensor node is comparable to that required by wireless transmission, which is the most energy-consumption part of the sensor. That is, any sensor scheduling algorithms need to consider not only wireless transmission but also the coordination of cameras.
(2) The bandwidth of WMSNs is generally too small to transmit multimedia streams in realtime. We need new protocols and new encoding methods to satisfy the Quality of Service (QoS) of multimedia streaming.
(3) The multimedia content is several order of magnitude larger than the scaler data (e.g., temperature readings). The scarce storage resource becomes more intensive and requires new management schemes.
(4) Multimedia processing methods often have high computational complexity, and the micro-controllers on the sensors are hard to execute complex methods. We need new, low-complexity algorithms to process multimedia data.
(5) Multimedia sensors usually have a sensing model largely different from conventional ones. Much research uses a circular region to approximate the sensing coverage of a sensor. This assumption, however, does not hold for video sensors because the camera covers a conoid region instead of a circle. Besides, if a multimedia sensor uses PTZ camera, it can change its sensing region. As the result, many protocols and algorithms using the circular sensing coverage model cannot apply to WMSNs.

The above challenges require existing algorithms for wireless sensor networks to be improved to support the multimedia data. In this chapter, we introduce recent research closely related to information processing over WMSNs, particularly on multimedia collection and storage. Regarding multimedia collection, Sec. 26.2 introduces several algorithms to achieve quality multimedia data streaming, and Sec. 26.3 discusses the camera scheduling problem. Regarding information storage, Sec. 26.4 includes new designs for the storage management of multimedia sensor networks. We summarize the chapter in Sec. 26.5.

26.2. Collection of Multimedia Streams

Multimedia streaming requires high bandwidth which is hard to guarantee in wireless sensor networks. Although substantial research efforts have been devoted to compressing multimedia data and reducing bandwidth overhead, most existing algorithms cannot be used directly to WMSNs due to their high computational complexity. Algorithms for multimedia streaming suitable for wireless sensor networks should incur only simple calculations and small memory space to fit the capability of a mote-level sensor node. In the following, we introduce two simple compression algorithms: a Piecewise Linear Approximation (PLA) method for audio compression and distributed source coding for video compression. We also introduce an ultra low-power image sensor that uses address-event data representation to compress video streams without any video encoding scheme.

26.2.1. *Audio streaming*

Acoustic information is preferred in many applications of sensor networks due to its simplicity compared to video streams. In some harsh situations such as underwater environment, video streaming is unnecessary or technically very difficult. For example, biologists are more interested in animals sounds, such as whales' song, than the visual information, which is the dark ocean that cannot be captured easily by normal camera lens. Although the audio information are one-dimensional data stream, the required bandwidth may still exceed the limit of sensor nodes. For example, in order to record human voice with high quality, at least we need to sample at 8 KHz and 16 bits per sample. The required bandwidth is 128 kbps, much larger than the 38 kbps that a MICA2[2] mote can support. Normal compression approaches, e.g., Fourier transform, discrete cosine transform, and wavelets, are hard to apply because they require sophisticated mathematical operations which are not supported by sensors.

An audio stream is a one-dimensional time series $X = \{x_1, \ldots, x_n\}$ and can be properly compressed by Piecewise Linear Approximation (PLA). The well-known approach of PLA is the linear regression which finds a set of m segments $\hat{X} = \{s_1, s_2, \ldots, s_m\}$ $(m < n)$ that minimizes the approximation error. The approximation error is defined as the maximal error between X and $\tilde{X}$ at any time index, that is, $\max_{i=1}^{n}\{|x_i - \tilde{x}_i|\}$, where $\tilde{x}_i$ is the point on one of the line segments in $\hat{X}$ approximating x_i. Unlike linear regression, the on-line algorithm introduced here is actually a variation of PLA, which finds the minimum number of segments within a given bound on the approximation error. This is to guarantee that the quality of audio data recovered from the line segments meets a given requirement.

Soroush *et al.* overcame both bandwidth and computation difficulties with simple PLA-based online algorithms that compress and transmit audio streams in resource-constrained sensor networks.[3] The algorithm runs in linear time and requires only constant memory space while achieving about 80% bandwidth reduction for audio streams with audio quality acceptable for most applications. In the following we introduce two algorithms designed in Ref. 3 suitable for audio streaming over WMSNs.

26.2.1.1. *Optimal PLA for audio streaming*

A line segment s can be represented by its slope m and its left endpoint (i, y_i), where i is the time index and y_i is the value at time i. For two points (samples) (i, x_i) and $(j, x_j)(i < j)$, a line segment s can be used to approximate (i, x_i) and (j, x_j) within an error bound ϵ if and only if:

- The y_i is within the error bound of x_i, i.e., $(x_i - \epsilon) \leq y_i \leq (x_i + \epsilon)$.
- The slope m is between $\frac{(x_j+\epsilon)-y_i}{j-i}$ and $\frac{(x_j-\epsilon)-y_i}{j-i}$.

If we use m and y_i as the two axes of a coordinate system, we can see that every point in the shadowed parallelogram of Fig. 26.1 represents a valid line segment approximating points (i, x_i) and $(j, x_j)(i < j)$. We call this shadowed parallelogram the $i \to j$ parallelogram. Reversely, if a line segment can approximate points (i, x_i) and $(j, x_j)(i < j)$, such a line segment must reside in the $i \to j$ parallelogram shown in Fig. 26.1. Clearly, if we assume there are $l(l > 0)$ points between time i and time j, we can construct $l + 1$ parallelograms, i.e., $i \to i+1, i \to i+2, \ldots, i \to j$. If the $l+1$ parallelograms have a common intersection area, we are certain that there exists a line segment approximating all points from time i to time j, inclusively.

According to the above observation, the on-line algorithm in Ref. 3 begins with the first two points and computes their parallelogram according to above criteria. When a new data comes in, the algorithm computes the parallelogram of the first point and the new point. Once the parallelogram is constructed, the points, except the first point, *are dropped to save memory space*. If the two parallelograms has

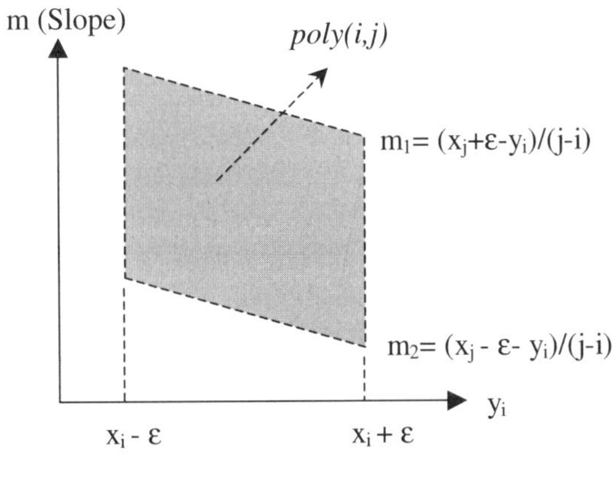

Fig. 26.1. Polygon.[3]

intersection, the algorithm records the intersection and keeps on going to check the next incoming point. The operation repeats until the intersection of all parallelograms between the first point and the newest point becomes empty, in which case the algorithm outputs a line segment to approximate all points seen so far, excluding the last point. Since a point in the intersection of parallelograms represents a valid line segment, the output line segment can be determined by a point randomly selected from the last non-empty intersection of parallelograms. The algorithm restarts with the last point as the next starting point.

Note that checking whether or not a new parallelogram intersects with previous intersection is a hard problem, because the number of edges of the intersection is two times the number of parallelograms in the worst case. We, however, can take advantage of the special features of the created parallelograms: Each parallelogram has two vertical edges and the horizontal width of all parallelograms is the same. Furthermore, the absolute slope of the upper and lower edges becomes smaller and smaller as time goes.

Figure 26.2 shows how the algorithm exploits those properties to check intersection. It excludes the case that a parallelogram fully falls within the previous parallelograms, because this is a very simple to handle without calculating and recording any intersection points. Figure 26.2(a) is the upper part of a parallelogram. Figure 26.2(b) shows that if two parallelograms intersect, their slope edges $\overline{AB}$ and $\overline{CD}$ must intersect. Line $\overline{FG}$ represents the upper slope edge of the third parallelogram. If all three parallelograms intersect with one another, $\overline{FG}$ must intersect either $\overline{CE}$, $\overline{EB}$, or the right vertical edge beneath B. Furthermore, if $\overline{FG}$ intersect $\overline{CE}$ or $\overline{EB}$, $\overline{FG}$ must intersect $\overline{CB}$. Therefore, we only need to keep track of the vertical lines as well as the line connecting the upper left point and the lower right point. The lower part of Fig. 26.2(b) has similar property. The algorithm only stores the vertical lines and the line connecting the lower left point and the upper right point. In total, four edges are enough to verify if the intersection is empty. In Fig. 26.2(a) and (b),

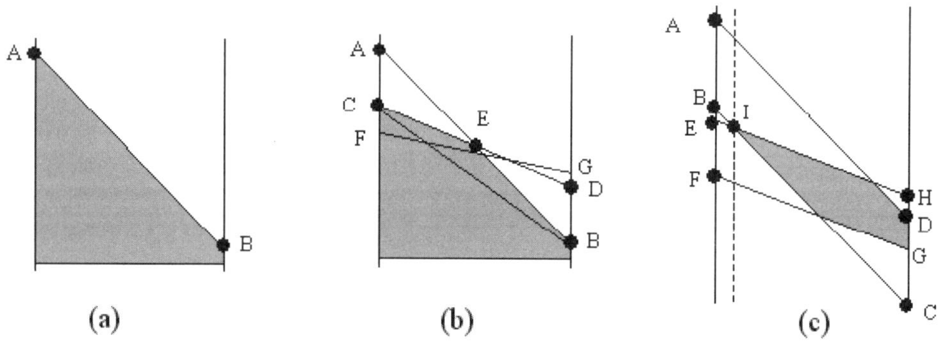

Fig. 26.2. An approach to check the intersection of polygons.[3]

the two vertical lines remains constant to make the algorithm easy to understand. Figure 26.2(c) shows a special case which the left vertical edge becomes a point.

It is easy to see that both computing the parallelograms for new coming points and updating the intersection only require constant time and constant memory space. Because the algorithm always moves ahead to check new incoming data and *never* revisits previously processed points, also because the algorithm only records the intersection of parallelograms and discards the actual data once processed, the time complexity and space complexity for total n points are $O(n)$ and $O(1)$, respectively. It has been proven that this algorithm is optimal in the sense that the number of output line segments is minimum.[3]

26.2.1.2. *PLAZA*

Another simple, fast online algorithm, called PLAZA (Piecewise Linear Approximation with Zoning Angle), is proposed in Ref. 3 for audio streaming with tiny sensors. Although PLAZA is not optimal in the number of line segments used for approximation, it is light in computation and very effective in audio compression as shown in Ref. 3.

PLAZA builds on the simple observation: Given an error bound ϵ and two points (i, x_i) and (k, x_k) $(i < k)$, we can construct a *zoning angle* from (i, x_i) to (k, x_k), denoted by $\theta^{\epsilon}_{(i,k)}$ and defined as the angle that has (i, x_i) as the end-point, $((i, x_i), (k, x_k))$ as the bisector, and has a degree of $2 \arctan \frac{\epsilon}{|x_i x_k|}$, where $|x_i x_k| = \sqrt{(k-i)^2 + (x_k - x_i)^2}$. An example of zoning angle $\theta^{\epsilon}_{(i,k)}$ is shown in Fig. 26.3(a). Clearly, the zoning angle defines a zone that includes all potential line segments that approximate x_i and x_k and use x_i as the start point. Equivalently, if a line segment with start point x_i can be used to approximate x_i and x_k, it must fall within the zoning angle $\theta^{\epsilon}_{(i,k)}$.

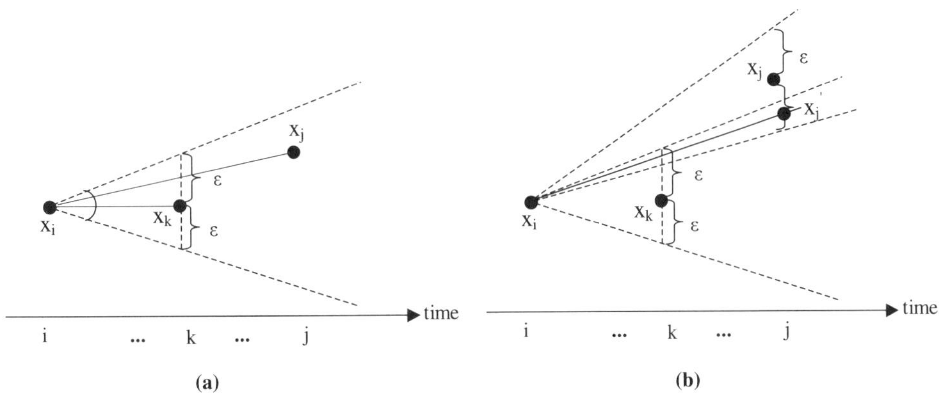

Fig. 26.3. An example of zoning angle.[3]

Based on the above observation, PLAZA works as follows. Starting from a point x_i, for each new incoming point, $x_k (k = i+1, i+2, \ldots)$, PLAZA builds the zoning angle $\theta^{\epsilon}_{(i,k)}$ and calculates the intersection of zoning angles, $\cap_{k=i+1,i+1,\ldots}\theta^{\epsilon}_{(i,k)}$, as shown in Fig. 26.3(b). This process repeats until the intersection of the zoning angles becomes empty, in which case PLAZA outputs a line segment and restarts from the last point.

Algorithm PLAZA scans each point in a data stream only once and stores only the intersection of zoning angle in main memory, the algorithm clearly has linear time complexity and constant space complexity. It incurs very simple computation, because only two major operations are required: constructing the zoning angle and calculating the intersection of zoning angles.

26.2.2. *Video streaming*

26.2.2.1. *Address-event image sensor*

Compared to audio streaming, video streaming is more challenging due to the larger bandwidth requirement and higher complexity in video data. The main difficulties of dealing with video streams in sensor networks include:

(1) The traditional CMOS cameras on sensor nodes consume too much energy to operate, depleting battery power quickly.
(2) Transmitting a video stream requires high bandwidth which normal sensor networks cannot provide.
(3) The micro-controller of a sensor node cannot accomplish complex video encoding.

Much research has been done in the past decade to overcome the above technical difficulties. A typical example is the low-power image sensors, called ALOHAim1 and ALOHAim2 (Fig. 26.5) designed by Culurciello *et al.* at Yale University.[4–7] The

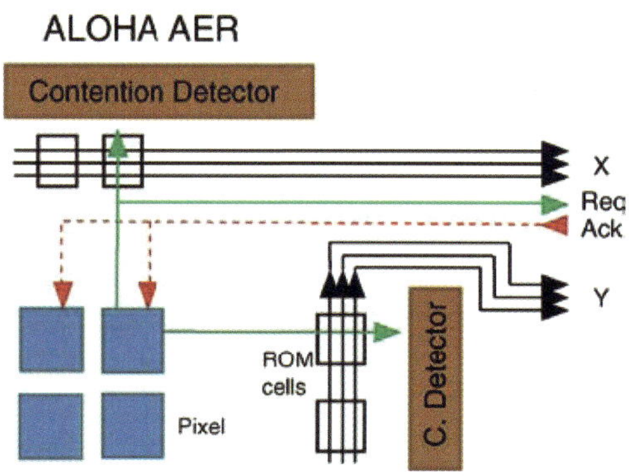

Fig. 26.4. The architecture of ARE image sensor circuit.[6]

Fig. 26.5. An ALOHA image sensor with MICA2 sensor node.[6]

ALOHAim1 and ALOHAim2 both employ Address-Event Representation (AER) of information to decrease the energy consumption in capturing images. In the normal CMOS cameras, each pixel reports its value or voltage periodically and sequentially. Such behavior is undesirable because the sensor blindly collects all information, some of which may not be useful. In the AER architecture, each pixel has a threshold, a pixel reports a fix value only if the change of light intensity cross the threshold. Thus, the sensor saves much energy because its pixels only report when necessary. The power consumption is several magnitudes smaller than other off-the-shelf products. It is claimed that ALOHAim2 sensors may run up to 4.5 years using 2 AA batteries and thus work perfectly for WMSN applications.[7]

The architecture of the ALOHA sensors is shown in Fig. 26.4. The ROM cells around pixels can output the address (X-Y coordinate) of any pixel. When a pixel collects enough light, the pixel triggers the ROM. The pixel value and the address will be sent to the bus. The contention detectors near the ROM cells are responsible for coping with the situation that multiple pixels access the ROM simultaneously. The design of the contention detector circuit is one of the major differences between ALOHAim1 and ALOHAim2. The ALOHAim2 uses a digital contention detector, and saves more energy than ALOHAim1, which uses an analog contention detector. Table 26.1 compares the specifications of both image sensors.

When using an AER image sensor to capture videos, we can further apply the concept of AER to compress the video. Because each event represents a change in light intensity, the AER method eliminates much redundancy by nature. Moreover, the sensor nodes can simply drop a certain ratio of incoming events to decrease bandwidth cost further. Therefore, the AER image sensor node gains considerable advantages by avoiding the computation-intensive video encoding algorithms. A final note is that the main purpose of an AER image sensor and that of a normal camera are quite different. The AER image sensors are normally used to examine the motion of objects, while the conventional cameras are good at taking a snapshot

Table 26.1. The specifications of ALOHAim1 and ALOHAim2 image sensors.[6]

Item	ALOHAim1	ALOHAim2
Technology	0.6 μm 3M CMOS	0.6 μm 3M CMOS
Array size	32 × 32	64 × 64
Pixel size	32.7 × 29.7 μm	32.7 × 29.7 μm
Fill factor	6.5%	6.5%
Sensor core size	1.2 × 1.2 mm	2.4 × 2.4 mm
Bandwidth	8.13 μHz to 10 MHz(Pixel) 8.33 mHz to 10 MHz(Array)	8.13 μHz to 5 MHz(Pixel) 8.33 mHz to 5 MHz(Array)
Throughput	110 M bps	220 M bps
Dynamic range	241 dB(pixel)/181 dB (array)	235 dB(pixel)/175 dB (array)
Sensitivity	1.7×10^3(array) 2.8×10^9(pixel)	5.6×10^5(array) 9.1×10^{11}(pixel)
FPN	4.36%	4.36%
Max FPS	4.88 K	2.44 K
Digital power	115 μW at 3.3 V	5.75 μW at 2.35 V
Analog power	680 μW at 3.3 V	3.9 nW at 2.35 V

of objects. When AER image sensors are used to capture video streams, the end-user normally only see a set of light spots describing the motion and the shape of objects at the base station. Such property serves well in many applications such as a fall detection system.[1]

26.2.2.2. *Distributed source coding*

Video content requires very complex encoder, e.g., the MPEG part 10, which is hard to implement on sensor nodes. Some researchers use lower video resolution to mitigate the encoding complexity and reduce bandwidth cost. Thanks to Wyner and Ziv who found that the burden of coding can be pushed at the decoder side if the information of data is available.[8] Such a coding scheme is named distributed source coding. It is clear that distributed source coding matches perfectly for wireless sensor networks because it is usually the case that the encoders are low-level devices (i.e., sensors) but the decoders are powerful devices (e.g., desktop computers) in such networks.

Below we briefly introduce the preliminary concept of distributed source coding using the Slepian-Wolf code.[9] Other practical distributed source codes can be found in Refs. 8–10. Suppose that binary strings X and Y are both 3-bit long and the Hamming distance of X and Y is at most 1. Then, if the decoder knows Y, the Slepian-Wolf code can represent X using 2 bits only. This is done by arranging the possible outcomes of X into 4 sets: $Z_{00} = \{000, 111\}$, $Z_{01} = \{010, 101\}$, $Z_{10} = \{100, 011\}$, and $Z_{11} = \{001, 110\}$. Within each set, the Hamming distance of every codeword is 3. Hence, if the decoder knows Y as well as which set X belongs to, the decoder can find X by checking the Hamming distance between Y and the codeword. If the Hamming distance is not larger than 1, that codeword is the answer of X. The

Slepian-Wolf code uses syndromes $s = XH^T$ to identify the set where $H = \begin{bmatrix} 1 & 0 & 1 \\ 0 & 1 & 1 \end{bmatrix}$ is the parity-check matrix. In general, the decoder receives s and Y. It finds all X satisfying $s = XH^T$ and checks the Hamming distance of Y and each X. The one whose Hamming distance to Y is no larger than 1 is the source data. In the above example, assume that $X = (010)$ and $Y = (110)$. We have $s = XH^T = 01$. Then Y and s will be transmitted to the decoder. The decoder knows from s that X belongs to the set Z_{01}. The one whose Hamming distance to Y is smallest in Z_{01} is 010, which is the source data.

We can observe from the above example that the encoding is much simpler than the decoding, confirming the property of distributed source coding. In image compression, distributed source coding can exploit the correlation between two images which have overlapping area. For video compression, a key frame or previous frame can be used to compress the current frame.[8]

26.3. Camera Scheduling Problem

In the previous section, we discuss the problem of audio streaming and video streaming without considering detailed application context. That is, we only consider how we can get the information from each individual sensor and how sensors can cooperatively transmit information at the coding level. In this section, we move up to the application layer and introduce how information can be searched for in the physical world. When video information is involved, searching for relevant video information from the physical world is called the camera scheduling problem.

When we use a PTZ camera to monitor multiple objects, we need to decide (1) which object the camera should observe, and (2) how much time the camera should stay on each object. The objective is to identify or observe as many objects as possible. This problem rises when a commercial PTZ camera is used in a wireless multimedia surveillance network. Since the sensor node has full control of its camera, a good camera scheduling algorithm helps the surveillance system to achieve better coverage.

26.3.1. *Single camera*

In Ref. 11, Costello *et al.* discuss how an active PTZ camera monitors multiple people in the monitoring area. They design a scheme with heterogeneous cameras to observe as many people as possible. One camera has wide field of view and low resolution. It transmits videos to estimate the path of each person in the monitoring area. Another camera is a PTZ camera and has higher resolution. The PTZ camera is in charge of capturing clear images of individuals for a face recognition system. The scheduling problem is to decide the sequence of observing each individual and the amount of time spent on each individual.

Costello *et al.* also point out that recognizing a person and switching to another target cannot be done instantly. Therefore, when monitoring an individual, the camera must stay with the current target for a small amount of time. The length of time is determined by the underlying face recognition system and the traffic in the monitoring area. If the time is too short, the system cannot identify the target. Moreover, the camera will pan, tilt, and zoom all the time, wasting a lot of energy.

Costello's scheduling method puts the people in different class of priority. A static and a non-static algorithms are proposed and tested in Ref. 11. With the static algorithm, the system observes the people with high-priority class first. For the people within the same class, the algorithm uses *random*, *first-in-fist-serve*, and *earliest deadline first* policies to decide the ordering of each person being observed. The deadline to tracking a person is the estimated time when the person leaves the monitoring area. The non-static algorithm uses the *current min-loss throughput optimal* policy. Each person is assigned a weight. When a person leaves without being observed, the assigned weight to this people is lost. The goal is to minimize such the total weighted loss.[12] According to the simulation, the static algorithm with the earliest deadline first observes the most number of people at least once in a given time. On the other hand, the *current min-loss throughput optimal* policy has the best performance if we count the number of people that are observed multiple times.

26.3.2. *Multiple cameras*

In Ref. 13, Qureshi and Terzopoulos extend Costello's work to multiple PTZ-cameras. They also remark that the modeling of the camera scheduling problem should address the following characteristics. First, a camera should not be locked by its subject. It should be able to switch to another subject even though it does not record long enough to identify the subject. Second, the arrive times of pedestrians are unknown. Thus, the camera scheduling algorithm should be an on-line algorithm.

According to the above characteristics, Qureshi and Terzopoulos develop a weighted round robin algorithm to schedule multiple cameras. Pedestrians are arranged into multiple queue of different priority. When the first pedestrian of a queue is popped, the highest weight is given to a camera that is the best to observe the pedestrian.[13] The weight is decided by two factors: the distance and the rotation angle. If the distant between the camera and the pedestrian is short, the camera should have a large weight. If the camera only needs to pan a small angle to monitor the pedestrian, the camera should also have a high weight. In order to achieve load balancing, the weight of free cameras should be set to infinity. In order to prevent a subject from locking a camera, the weight changes dynamically and the system puts an upper limit on the time that a camera monitors a subject. This weighted round robin algorithm is tested with different configurations.[13] The conclusion is that the above mentioned algorithm performs very well when we allow (1) preemption (i.e., the camera may switch subject at any time), (2) multiple observation (i.e., each pedestrian can be observed multiple times), and (3) multi-class (i.e., the pedestrians are arranged into multiple queues of different priority).

26.4. Multimedia Storage

26.4.1. *Multi-fidelity storage system*

Even though the memory modules are fairly small and inexpensive nowadays, sensor nodes usually have very small storage space, not enough to store multimedia content. The storage space of current sensor nodes varies from several kBs (Crossbow mica2) to few GBs (Microsoft SensCam).[2,15] Table 26.2 provides brief information on memory size of several broadly-used sensors. The multimedia data can quickly drain all the storage space of the above products. Since many WMSN applications need to store a large number of audio and video streams, building an effective and efficient storage manage scheme is a crucial issue for the success of WMSNs. Many storage management approaches of conventional wireless sensor networks can be applied to WMSNs as well. Such approaches normally aim to minimize the energy consumption and bandwidth overhead or aim to maintain a distributed database with fast and efficient data retrieval.[16,17] In this section, we introduce the storage management schemes as well as algorithms specifically designed for multimedia data.

The idea of Pillai's *multi-fidelity storage system*(MFS)[14] comes from the observation that *not all objects and events are of the same level of interests or importance.* For example, some applications such as face recognition systems for criminal investigation require high resolution videos, while a healthcare or smart alarm system may only need a low resolution gray scale videos. Even for the same application, different objects may have different importance and thus require different concerns. Figure 26.6 shows the architecture of the multi-fidelity storage system. The multimedia streams are gathered by a variety of multimedia sensors. According to the different policies of different applications, the storage management algorithm degrades the original multimedia stream to a proper format of smaller size. The *transforms* are a group of APIs that convert one multimedia format to another, for example, from bitmap format to JPEG format. Pillai's MFS system can support dynamic policies. An application may set an expiration time for each policy. Moreover, each policy can change over time. By specifying a time parameter, the policy can store new incoming streams in a high-quality format and degrade to a low-quality format to save storage space as time goes. The MFS system, however, cannot convert the

Table 26.2. The storage space of well-known sensor nodes.

Sensor node	SenseCam	Mica2	Imote2	IRIS	XYZ	Stargate
Storage	1 GB	512 KB	64 MB	512 KB	256 KB	32 MB

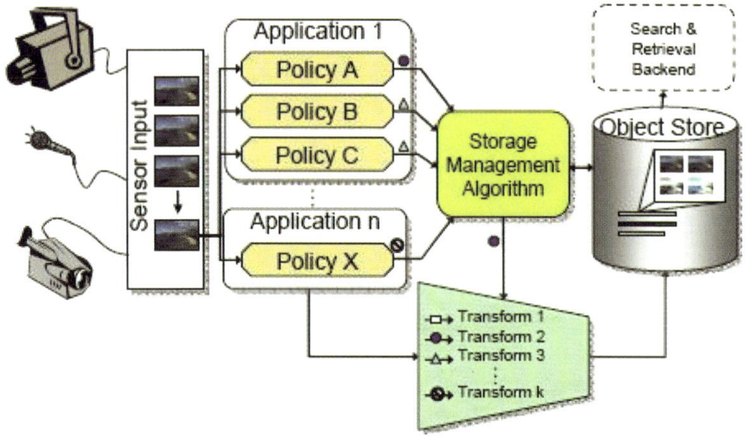

Fig. 26.6. The architecture of Multi-Fidelity Storage.[14]

data from low fidelity to high fidelity because of the lossy compression methods it uses.

When multiple policies conflict against one another, the MFS system handles the conflicts in two ways: (1) If the system has plenty of space, the MFS system may save different formats of the same data in the storage. (2) If the storage space is scarce, the MFS system stores the *minimum covering set* of all policies. A *covering set* is a set of data formats, where all policies can be satisfied by applying proper *transforms* on a format in the covering set. For example, the raw multimedia stream is a *covering set* of all policies. If one application requires true color video and another application requires only gray-scale video, the system will store the video with true color. The MFS system chooses the covering set which occupies minimum storage space to satisfy multiple policies.

When the storage space is exhausted, the MFS system deletes data in a *fair-share* manner. The key idea is to assign a cost value to each object, policy, and application. The cost values of objects and policies are set to the amount of space they occupy after proper transformation. And the cost of applications is the total size of their covering set. When the MFS system has to delete data, it applies the following steps to select objects to remove:

(1) Let A be the application of the highest cost.
(2) Let $P \in A$ be the policy of the highest cost.
(3) Let $O \in P$ be the object of the highest cost and delete O.
(4) Update cost values and covering sets.

The above rules make each application and each policy suffer roughly the same loss after deletion and occupy a fair share of storage space in the long run.

26.4.2. *IRISnet data management scheme*

IRISnet[18] is a well-known architecture for global-scale multimedia sensor networks. It has a neat and practical scheme to manage the huge amount of data all over such a large-scale network. The data management in IRISnet is enforced by a software entity called OA (*Organizing Agent*), which supports distributed data storage and querying by using XML (Extensible Markup Language) and Xpath (XML Path Language), respectively.[19,20] Because the OAs are computational-intensive, IRISnet runs the OAs on PC-level nodes instead of sensor motes. Similar design can also be seen in Ref. 21 where the storage management is done in powerful *storage hubs*.

At the very beginning, the OA establishes a logical *hierarchy* of data and forms a distributed database in the IRISnet. The mapping of the data hierarchy and the physical locations of data is also managed by the OA. In order to manage the database efficiently, the IRISnet defines data ownership, which dictates who owns what part of data, and data storage, which describes the actual data stored at each site. It also defines **IDable** nodes and two types of information, **local information** and **local ID information**, which are described below.

(1) Initially, each node is assigned an additional **id_s** which is unique among its siblings of the same *element name* (The *element name* is an ordinary attribute of a node). If the 2-tuple (element name, **id_s**) of a node N is unique among its siblings and the parent of N is **IDable**, then N is said to be **IDable**. The root node is set to be an **IDable** node. The pair (element name, **id_s**) is used as N's ID.
(2) The **local information** of an **IDable node** N includes all information of N, N's **non-IDable** children and their descendants.
(3) The **local ID information** of any node includes the ID of that node and the IDs of its **IDable** children.

The IRISnet uses the above definitions to partition the logical hierarchy and determines the responsibility of each OA. In each OA, the *status* attribute of a node N describes the relationship between the OA and N.

(1) If the *status* is *owned*, the OA has the local information of the N and local ID information of N's ancestors. Moreover, the OA is responsible for answering any query about N.
(2) If the *status* is *complete*, the OA has the same information above. This may happen when the OA cache N's information.
(3) If the *status* is *ID-complete*, the OA knows the local ID information of N and N's ancestors.
(4) If the *status* is *incomplete*, the OA knows N's ID only.

There are two important features of the OAs. One is that when a Xpath query is injected into the network, the IRISnet sends the query down to the *lowest common ancestor* in the data hierarchy. This feature enables the parallel execution and avoids many unnecessary in-network executions. The purpose of finding the lowest common ancestor is to create a DNS-style name service in the IRISnet. Since each **IDable** node has unique ID among its siblings and has a **IDable** parent node, each **IDable** node is uniquely identified by the concatenation of IDs from the root. The concatenated string can be a domain name, and we can take advantage of a parser to extract the DNS of the lowest common ancestor from the Xpath query.

The second key feature is the caching method. When a query is executed in the network, each OA may store the results passed by. Thus, the subsequent queries can be answered quickly if partial or whole answer of the subsequent queries is in the cache. In Ref. 19, a QEG (Query-Evaluate-Gather) scheme is proposed to make use of caching. The OA that receives a Xpath query should generate a XSLT (eXtensible Stylesheet Language Translations) program from the Xpath query and use XSLT in the QEG scheme. The basic steps of QEG include:

(1) The OA identifies the target node of the query, the element name of target, and other relevant information.
(2) Based on the status of the target node, the OA decides whether the local information is in the answer.
(3) A sub-query should be sent to proper descendant to find the rest of the answer. The OA returns when it gather all responds from all sub queries.

Note that passing the query directly to the target node or lowest common ancestor may cause some additional executions in the network. The QEG scheme improves the IRISnet database by discovering (1) whether the local cache contains answers, and (2) where is the rest of the answer.

26.5. Concluding Notes

As an emerging area, WMSNs have plentiful new applications as well as meliorate many conventional sensor network applications. Interesting new research problems and technical challenges arise in every aspect and worth more attention from the research community. Instead of introducing all research problems, this chapter focuses on the challenges and recent progress on information collection and storage in WMSNs. Generally speaking, algorithms for conventional sensor networks involving only scalar data like temperature readings are usually not suitable for WMSNs due to the high bandwidth requirement and the high coding complexity of multimedia data. As the first step, effective methods should be found to collect multimedia information from WMSNs. For this, this chapter introduces two lightweight algorithms for audio streaming and special video cameras suitable for capturing the motion of objects. Distributed source coding is briefly introduced as a useful coding scheme for WMSNs. The chapter then talks about the camera scheduling problem, which aims to effectively obtain useful video information from different application contexts. Once multimedia data is collected, we need new approaches for effective data storage and management. To this end, this chapter introduces two data storage systems: multi-fidelity storage system (MFS) and IRISnet data management system.

References

1. Z. M. Fu, E. Culurciello, P. Lichtsteiner and T. Delbruck, Fall detection using an address-event temporal contrast vision sensor, *Proceedings of IEEE International Symposium on Circuits and Systems (ISCAS)*, Seattle, USA (May 2008).
2. *MICA2 Mote Datasheet.* Crossbow technology. http://www.xbow.com/products/Product_pdf_files/Wireless_pdf/MICA2_Datasheet.pdf.
3. E. Soroush, K. Wu and J. Pei, Fast and quality-guaranteed data streaming in resource-constrained sensor networks, *Proceedings of the 9th ACM International Symposium on Mobile Ad Hoc Networking and Computing (MobiHoc'08)*, Hong Kong, China (May 2008).
4. E. Culurciello, R. Etienne-Cummings and K. A. Boahen, A biomorphic digital image sensor, *IEEE Journal of Solid-State Circuits*, **38**, 281–294 (February 2003).
5. E. Culurciello and R. Etienne-Cummings, Second generation of high dynamic range, arbitrated digital imager, *Proceedings of 2004 IEEE International Symposium on Circuits and Systems*, Vancouver, Canada (May 2004).
6. E. Culurciello and A. G. Andreou, CMOS image sensors for sensor networks, *Analog Integrated Circuits and Signal Processing*, **49**, 39–51 (October 2006).
7. E. Park, E. Culurciello and A. Savvides, Address-event video streaming over wireless sensor networks, *Proceedings of IEEE International Symposium on Circuits and Systems (ISCAS 2007)*, New Orleans, US (May 2007).
8. B. Girod, A. Aaron, S. Rane and D. Rebollo-Monedero, Distributed video coding, *Proceedings of IEEE* (January 2005).
9. Z. Xiong, A. D. Liveris and S. Cheng, Distributed source coding for sensor networks, *IEEE Signal Processing Magazine*, **21**, 80–94 (2004).
10. S. Pradhan and K. Ramchandran, Distributed source coding using syndromes (discus): Design and construction, *IEEE Transactions on Information Theory*, **49**, 626–643 (2003).
11. C. J. Costello, C. P. Diehl, A. Banerjee and H. Fisher, Scheduling an active camera to observe people, *Proceedings of the ACM 2nd International Workshop on Video Surveillance and Sensor Networks* (2004).
12. R. L. Givan, E. K. P. Chong and H. S. Chang, Scheduling multiclass packet streams to minimize weighted loss, *Queueing Systems*, **41**, 241–270 (2002).
13. F. Z. Qureshil and D. Terzopoulos, Surveillance camera scheduling: A virtual vision approach, *Multimedia Systems*, **12**, 269–283 (2006).
14. P. Pillai, Y. Ke and J. Campbell, Multi-fidelity storage, *Proceedings of the ACM 2nd International Workshop on Video Surveillance and Sensor Networks* (2004).
15. *Introduction to SenseCam.* Microsoft Sensors and Devices group. http://research.microsoft.com/sendev/projects/sensecam/default.htm.
16. R. Biswas, K. Chowdhury and D. Agrawal, Data-centric attribute allocation and retrieval (dcaar) scheme for wireless sensor networks, *Proceedings of IEEE*

International Conference on Mobile Adhoc and Sensor Systems, Washington, DC, USA (November 2005).
17. D. Ganesan, B. Greenstein, D. Estrin, J. Heidemann and R. Govindan, Multiresolution storage and search in sensor networks, *ACM Transactions on Storage* (*TOS*), **1**, 277–315 (August 2005).
18. J. Campbell, P. B. Gibbons, S. Nath, P. Pillai, S. Seshan and R. Sukthankar, Irisnet: An internet-scale architecture for multimedia sensors, *Proceedings of the 13th Annual ACM International Conference on Multimedia*, Singapore (2005).
19. A. Deshpande, S. Nath, P. B. Gibbons and S. Seshan, Cache-and-query for wide area sensor databases, *Proceedings of ACM SIGMOD* (2003).
20. S. Chen, P. B. Gibbons and S. Nath, Database-centric programming for wide-area sensor systems, *Proceedings of IEEE International Conference of Distributed Computing in Sensor Systems* (2005).
21. I. F. Akyildiz, T. Melodia and K. R. Chowdhury, A survey on wireless multimedia sensor networks, *Computer Networks*, **51**, 921–960 (March 2007).

Chapter 27

Secure Image Transmissions in Wireless Multimedia Sensor Networks

Wei Wang*, Dongming Peng†, Honggang Wang‡
and Hamid Sharif§

Department of Computer and Electronics Engineering
University of Nebraska – Lincoln, NE, USA
**wwang@unlnotes.unl.edu*
†dpeng@unlnotes.unl.edu
‡hwang@unlnotes.unl.edu
§hsharif@unlnotes.unl.edu

Hsiao-Hwa Chen

Department of Engineering Science
National Cheng Kung University, Taiwan, ROC
hshwchen@ieee.org

The strong need for secure wireless multimedia services such as privacy and confidentiality, integrity and authenticity, has driven the development of an emerging research area in low cost wireless multimedia sensor networks. However, traditional security (encryption/authentication) techniques cannot be directly applied to secure multimedia over wireless sensor networks due to the inborn challenges such as limited energy, computing and bandwidth resources, as well as the error prone wireless channel which provides an open media vulnerable to malicious interception and packet injection attacks. This chapter presents an overview of the state-of-the-art research progresses for resource-quality-driven secure multimedia (using digital image as an illustrative example) over wireless sensor networks. The existing security techniques for multimedia services and their applications to secure wireless multimedia sensor networks are reviewed. Furthermore, frontier researches on digital image selective encryption and image stream authentication and their optimizations within energy-constrained wireless sensor networks are reviewed and discussed in depth. Finally, the interactive encryption/authentication and cross layer resource allocation schemes are investigated and advocated to achieve energy efficiency, multimedia security and media quality jointly.

27.1. Introduction

Nowadays Wireless Multimedia Sensor Networks (WMSN)[1] have been applied to many areas such as battlefield assistance, disaster relief, healthcare, telemedicine, etc. In many sensitive scenarios including military, homeland security, and medical applications, the content security of multimedia data collection and streaming has become a major concern. It has formidable research challenges due to extremely limited energy on battery cells, low computation and memory capacity in hardware, and limited bandwidth resources on radio transceivers, etc. Furthermore, the open wireless environment in WMSN is extremely vulnerable to malicious attacks including packet interception/injection, eavesdropping, content modification, etc. In addition, multimedia data is usually bulk-sized and content sensitive, while the encryption/decryption and signing/verification operations are very slow due to the computation complexity. Finally, in the error-prone wireless channel bit/symbol errors and packet/frame losses are inevitable because of environmental noises and interferences, which may significantly impact the end-to-end encrypted/authenticated media quality.

Multimedia encryption[2–9] and stream authentication[10–15] have been proposed to deal with these aforementioned challenges brought by the bandwidth intensive but loss tolerant multimedia streaming, limited energy and computation capabilities, and time-consuming encryption/signing algorithms. However, multimedia privacy/integrity and Quality of Service (QoS) still form a challenging gap between current researches and the application need. There is a serious lack in joint consideration of QoS and multimedia encryption/authentication — the information encryption and authentication are designed primarily in application layer while the network QoS scheduling algorithms are commonly designed in low layers of the protocol stacks. Some of our recent researches[16–19] have shown the advantage and energy-quality gain of joint consideration of application media security and low layer resource allocation and QoS scheduling in WMSN. In this chapter, we will systematically review and analyze the research gap between multimedia security and QoS scheduling, discuss and advocate the joint encryption/authentication and resource allocation design.

This chapter is organized as follows. In Sec. 27.2, we review the current researches regarding multimedia encryption and multimedia stream authentication, and their applications to WMSN. In Sec. 27.3, we discuss both the design of multimedia selective encryption and network resource allocation to provide multimedia confidentiality in WMSN. In Sec. 27.4, we discuss the joint design of multimedia stream authentication and network resource allocation to provide multimedia integrity in WMSN. In Sec. 27.5, we draw conclusion and show the outlook in this research area.

This chapter presents a systematic overview and conceptual tutorial on secure image transmissions in wireless multimedia sensor networks. For more technical details please refer to the publications in reference list, especially those in Refs. 16–19, 25 and 27.

27.2. Review of Related Works

In multimedia confidentiality/privacy protection field, many approaches have been proposed to encrypt multimedia content. Those approaches can be categorized into two types: multimedia selective encryption and secret entropy coding.

The selective encryption based multimedia ciphering approaches can provide fast encryption performance using strong block cipher because it only encrypts a very tiny but important portion of the media stream. It is computationally infeasible to crack or recover the secret ciphered data without the knowledge of the decoded encrypted data and the cipher key. In a recent research,[6] the frequency domain Discrete Cosine Transform (DCT) coefficients were judiciously selected to hide the semantic meaning of the video streams. The research in Ref. 20 applied block & motion vector secret shuffling and permutation to achieve content privacy. Some other approaches emphasized on compression domain selective encryption, for example, the research in Ref. 8 proposed effective media content confidentiality by partially encrypting the Quad-tree and SPITH stream structure; some other research in Ref. 21 advocated the ciphering the content important and significant bit-planes.

The secret entropy coding based approaches were also designed to integrate multimedia encryption and multimedia compression together without losing the compression performance. The researches in Refs. 5, 22 and 23 proposed Multiple Huffman Table (MHT) based secret entropy encryption. They combined encryption processes and the last stage of the compression processes — entropy coding — using multiple entropy coding tables (e.g., Huffman tables) alternately in a secret and pseudo-random order. Relatively high content confidentiality and unaffected compression efficiency were both achieved by those approaches. However, recent research work published in Ref. 9 presented chosen plaintext attacks on the basic MHT schemes and the enhanced methods with random bit insertion. Other similar research works on secret entropy coding applied pseudo-randomized or interval splitting based Arithmetic Coding[7,24] to achieve content privacy.

In multimedia integrity/authenticity protection field, stream authentication has been recently proposed to authenticate multimedia content in a packet-by-packet basis adaptive to lossy wireless channels where symbol errors and frame losses are inevitable. Recent research in Ref. 10 considered stream level authentication bit-budget allocation by Unequal Authentication Protection (UAP), which unequally protects JPEG packets by allocating different crypto-hash tags to different packets to achieve an optimal authentication results. Another recent article in Ref. 11 addressed the optimized content aware authentication problem for JPEG2000 image delivery over lossy networks. By effectively computing an authentication graph adaptive to the channel environment, authentication image quality was optimized within the given authentication bit-budget. Other similar researches regarding stream authentication were found in Refs. 12–15 and 26.

Stream authentication scheme aims to verify as many packets as possible, while selective encryption tries to encrypt data as little as possible by controlling the most important part of the streaming media. Because selective encryption and stream authentication both change the correlation and involve extra inter-dependency among different parts in the final encrypted/signed image bit streams, the traditional Unequal Error Protection (UEP) based QoS Scheduling is not desirable to these new secure image delivery paradigms especially in WMSN. Furthermore, most of those works are either delay-constrained or rate-constrained distortion optimization for general wireless networks. However, they can not be directly applied to WMSN due to the high priority of energy efficiency requirement. Thus, the new challenges include; how to consider multimedia content security in WMSN resource allocation, and how to energy-efficiently transmit selectively encrypted images and stream authenticated images over WMSN.

27.3. Confidentiality/Privacy Solutions for Wireless Multimedia Sensor Networks

Joint design of selective encryption and network resource allocation (QoS scheduling) is an important step to achieve secure multimedia streaming over wireless sensor networks. Exploiting the interaction between selective encryption and QoS scheduling are major research challenges. In this section, we discuss an effective position based selective encryption scheme suitable for UEP, as well as an efficient privacy oriented resource allocation scheme providing image privacy, image quality and energy efficiency simultaneously.[16–18]

27.3.1. *Position-based digital image selective encryption*

The position based selective encryption schemes were originally proposed in Refs. 16–18 to achieve efficient encryption which is suitable for UEP based transmission in WMSN. The natural digital images convey semantic information through the positions and locations of image pixels of various magnitude values. Most commonly used image coding algorithms such as wavelet based image compression schemes exploit shape and position information of the regions as well as the lighting information in regions.[18,25,27] Thus encryption on shape and position information bits leads to extremely high difficulty of reconstructing the image content, even transmitting with the pixel magnitudes values in unprotected plain-text.[18] For readers' convenience, we re-explain the concepts and methodologies in position based selective encryption as follows. The original discussion can be referred to[16–18] as well as the foundations of position based UEP in Refs. 25 and 27.

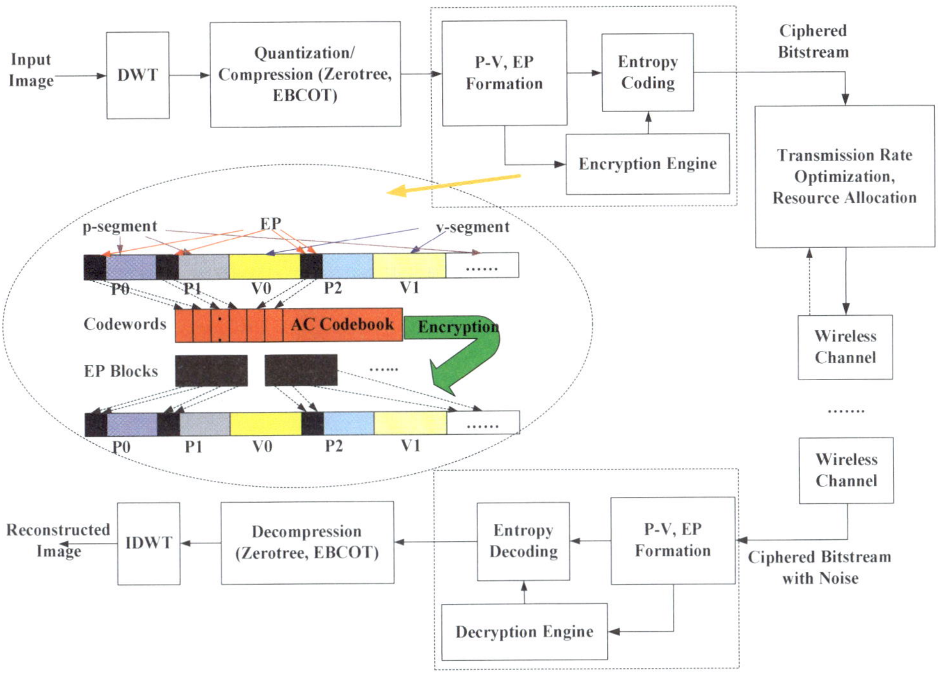

Fig. 27.1. Position based selective encryption and privacy oriented resource allocation framework. Figure Sources: Refs. 16 and 18.

The designing methodology of the position based selective encryption and corresponding resource allocation are illustrated in Fig. 27.1. The locations of perception-significant large value wavelet coefficients are determined by the clustering model of the perception-insignificant small value coefficients, which is translated into bit-stream structure after compression.[18,25] If the current coding coefficient is in the highest two resolution levels in the wavelet matrix, the coded symbol is marked as Paramount Skeleton (PS),[18] which contains the root information of wavelet decomposition trees. The very beginning of PS symbols marked as the Encrypted Processions (EP) are encrypted, where the length of EP in each PS can be flexibly configured by users.[18] Because run-length coding and arithmetic coding can effectively propagate any single bit/symbol error to the rest of the encrypted code stream due to compression dependency, the tiny part of EP tightly controls the skeleton of PS and PS controls structure of p-segment.[18] Furthermore, the bit-stream structure information only resides in p-segments[25] rather than v-segments,[25] thus selective encryption is only applied to p-segments rather than v-segments.[16,18]

In Fig. 27.2, we show an illustrative example of the position based selective encryption performance, which has already been reported in our previous published works,[16,18] where a $64 * 64$-pixel image with wavelet based compression algorithms applied is encrypted using strong block based Advanced Encryption Standard

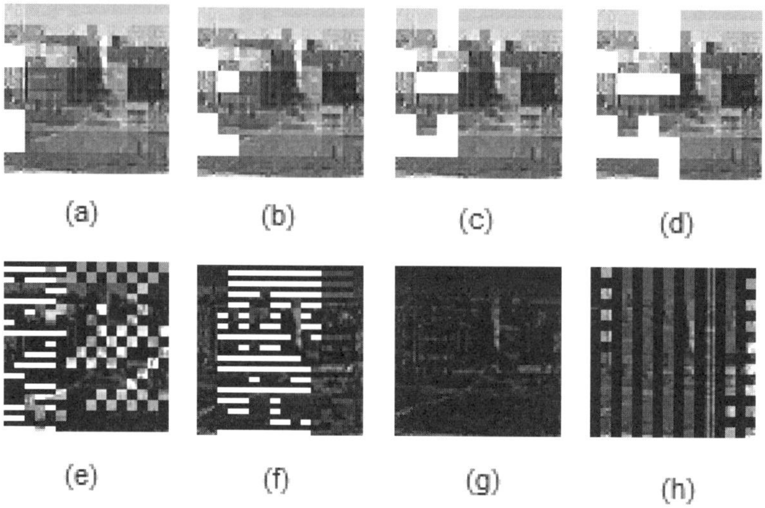

Fig. 27.2. Blindly decoded images without key for position based selective encryption and sub-band selection encryption for image "building". (a)–(d) sub-band selection encryption encrypting 1 to 4 AES blocks respectively. (e)–(h) Position based selective encryption encrypting 1 to 4 AES blocks respectively. Figure Sources: Refs. 16 and 18.

(AES) encryption algorithm on those crucial skeleton parts. For comparison, the effects of other popular selective encryption approaches such as frequency sub-band selective encryption are also illustrated. Because of the compression inter-packet dependency of the image bit stream and the high computational complexity of encryption/decryption operations, it is unnecessary to encrypt the whole image bit stream.[18] Instead, selecting a small portion of the "crucial EP information" can still achieve desirable perception privacy and confidentiality.[16,18] In the conventional frequency selectively encryption approaches, low frequency wavelet or DCT coefficients with high magnitude concentration can also be encrypted effectively. But in the latter approaches, the magnitude concentration privacy will not necessarily lead to perception privacy because the decoding of the whole picture does not necessarily rely on the decoding of those encrypted coefficients.[16,18]

27.3.2. *Privacy oriented resource allocation*

Although selective encryption does not change the length of the bit stream, it brings extra inter-packet dependency overhead which must be considered in the UEP based network resource allocation. In our previous research works of Refs. 16 and 18, the privacy oriented resource allocation schemes were proposed to achieve image privacy, image quality and energy efficiency simultaneously.

The image packets in the compressed bit stream have different perception importance, e.g., p-segments and v-segments,[25] which deserve unequal communication error protection, and the unequal protection leads to different delivery quality performances and energy consumption overheads. Furthermore, the EP information tightly controlling the structure of p-segments is encrypted.[18] Without the EP information the image bit stream can hardly be reconstructed, thus ciphered parts of the EP information deserve more communication protection than plain-text p-segments and v-segments.[18] Let $\varepsilon[\Delta D]$ denote the expected distortion reduction (i.e., quality) of the decrypted and reconstructed image, $\{BER(i), M_{\max}(i), R(i), \text{etc}\}$ denote the resource allocation strategies including desirable BER and power control, link layer retransmission limit, physical layer transmission data rate, etc,[25,27] the overall privacy oriented resource allocation can be formulated as the following equations[18]:

$$\underset{i\in\{EP\}\cup\{p-segment\}\cup\{v-segment\}}{\{BER(i), M_{\max}(i), R(i), etc\}} = \arg\max\{\varepsilon[\Delta D]\}. \tag{27.1}$$

Subject to the total energy consumption constraint[18]:

$$\sum_i E(i) \le E_{\max}. \tag{27.2}$$

Referring to the existing packet dependency dictated by the image compression algorithm and the extra packet dependency brought by the selective encryption, the expected decrypted image quality can be quantitatively analyzed as described in Refs. 16 and 18, which is also illustrated in Eq. (27.3) here. For each image packet, a distortion reduction value Δd is associated with it denoting the importance of that packet. Besides the distortion reduction associated to each image packet, the packet loss ratio g of a specific packet, the decoding dependency determined by the compression algorithms (i.e., p-segment and v-segment dependency[25]) and the extra packet dependency (i.e., each p-segment is tightly controlled by a couple of ciphered EP blocks listed in the set B) determined by the selective schemes should also be considered in the privacy oriented resource allocation framework.[16,18]

$$\begin{aligned}\varepsilon[\Delta D] &= \sum_{i=0}^{N-1}\left(\left(\sum_{j=0}^{i}\Delta d_p(j)\right)\cdot g_p(i+1)\cdot\prod_{j=0}^{i}\left((1-g_p(j))\cdot\prod_{k|j\in B_k}(1-g_B(k))\right)\right)\\ &\quad+\sum_{i=0}^{N-2}\left(\left(\sum_{j=0}^{i}\Delta d_v(j)\right)\cdot\prod_{j=0}^{i}(1-g_v(j))\right.\\ &\quad\left.\times g_p(i+1)\cdot\prod_{j=0}^{i+1}\left((1-g_p(j))\cdot\prod_{k|j\in B_k}(1-g_B(k))\right)\right)\end{aligned} \tag{27.3}$$

Experimental performance study in Ref. 18 also supported the privacy oriented resource allocation, which is also shown in Fig. 27.3 here. The EP blocks in the cipher stream is much more important than the p-segments and v-segments in the plain-text stream; if the packets containing EP blocks are erased by the error-prone

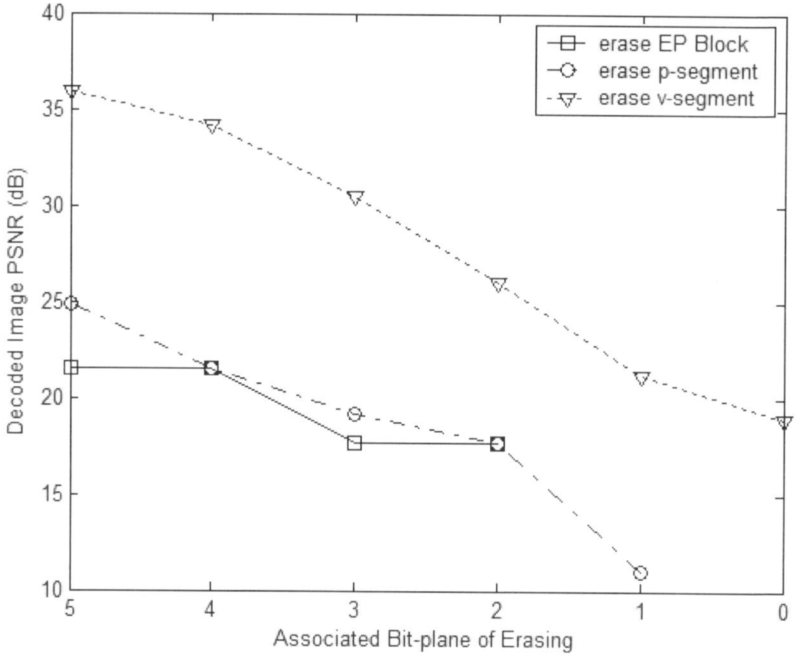

Fig. 27.3. Decoded images quality with erased image packets in the selective encryption applied "building image". Different packets in the bit stream show significantly different perception importance. Figure Sources: Ref. 18.

wireless channel, the decrypted and decoded image quality is very low even if the p-segments and v-segments packets are transmitted and received correctly. Thus EP blocks in the cipher streams deserve more protection than the other two types of packets.[16,18] In the other two types of packets, p-segments show more perception relevance than v-segments.[16,18,25,27]

27.4. Integrity/Authenticity Solutions for Wireless Multimedia Sensor Networks

Joint consideration of image stream authentication and network resource allocation is another important step to achieve secure multimedia streaming over wireless sensor networks. The seamless integration and interactive design of stream authentication and resource scheduling are the major research challenges in this research area. In this section, we review a simple stream authentication scheme suitable for UEP in WMSN, as well as an effective and energy inexpensive authentication aware resource allocation scheme providing image integrity, image quality and energy efficiency simultaneously.[19] The methodology and analysis discussed in this section were originally published in Ref. 19.

27.4.1. *Robust and efficient image stream authentication*

Stream authentication has recently been advocated in literature to perform multimedia integrity protection for its advantages of adaptability to wireless channels and non-ambiguity verification of each packet.[10–14,19,26] Traditional watermark based content authentication has been widely applied to integrity and copyright protection. However, watermarks are embedded before compression in the middle frequency of the transform domain coefficients, lacking the adaptability to time-varying wireless channel conditions. Furthermore, allocating authentication resources on middle frequency coefficients is on the contrary of UEP concept.[19] In addition, watermark based authentication offers integrity with ambiguity and is difficult to use mathematical provable statements about the system security,[26] and the level of security is considerably less than stream authentication.[26] Finally, watermark based authentication often involves energy and computation intensive error concealment schemes which is impractical for low cost wireless devices such as wireless sensor nodes.[11,12,19]

Digital signatures and crypto-hash links are typically applied to stream authentication for authenticating each packet transmitted in the wireless channel, thus each packet can be authenticated without ambiguity.[10–12] The extra overhead brought by the stream authentication are two folds, the extra rate (or authentication tag size) associated to crypto-hash attached to each image packet, and the extra inter-packet dependency of these crypto-hash links.[26] Thus, designing a stream authentication scheme for image bit streams is equivalent to designing a hash graph among the image packets with minimum extra rate and dependency overhead, while suitable for communication resource allocation.[10–12]

Designing a complete and accurately optimized authentication hash graph is computational intensive which is not suitable for online authentication of low cost WMSN, because there are typically a large number of packets in the compressed image bit stream.[19] For the stream authentication in WMSN, authentication graph design should perform reasonable simplification by considering the existing inter-packet dependency determined by the compression algorithms. For example, as shown in Fig. 27.4, which was originally presented in our recent research,[19] to apply crypto-hash stream authentication to a multi-layer JPEG2000 compressed bit stream, the hash dependency among the layers are assigned the same as the JPEG2000 inter-layer dependency. Research in Ref. 11 also utilized similar approach to follow the compression dependency, which is naturally compatible to the rate-distortion theory.[11] Thus, each high layer packet associates its authentication dependency to the previous packet in the previous layer, and no extra inter-packet dependency is involved in this scheme. The authentication hash assignment for layer 0 packets can be further simplified to support the online stream authentication in WMSN. Besides the signature packets, all the other packets in layer 0 are classified into the same QoS level, and the authentication hash association of each packet

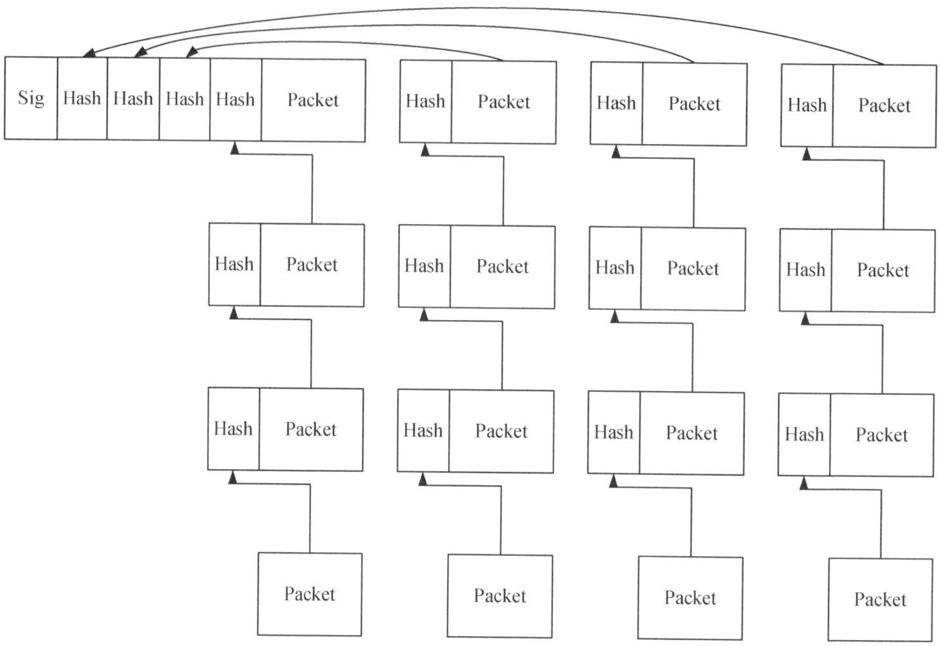

Fig. 27.4. Simplified authentication hash link assignment for multi-layer JPEG2000 based bit stream structure. Figure Sources: Ref. 19.

is assigned to the root signature packet.[19] By means of this non-trivial simplification, the authentication complexity is significantly reduced without incurring too much additional overhead. The only additional dependency overhead is on the signature packet, without which the whole bit stream is useless. However, the following authentication aware resource allocation can desirably compensate this disadvantage by allocating more communication resources on the signature root packet.

27.4.2. *Authentication aware resource allocation*

In the image stream authentication systems, the authenticated image is defined as the image reconstructed exclusively from the authenticated image packets.[19,26] Thus, the purpose of the cross layer authentication aware resource allocation design is to provide optimized "authenticated image quality" given the total energy budget. Because the packets in the compressed and authenticated bit stream have significant different perception importance, and authentication aware resource allocation in energy constrained WMSN becomes an important issue. In this view, the important packets critical to the verification and decoding of subsequent packets are more important than the others, and those important packet should be transmitted with more energy overhead to achieve a better packet delivery performance; for the packets that are not critical to the decoding and verification of other packets, packet delivery performance becomes less important and significant energy saving can be achieved by UEP based resource allocation.

As discussed in details in Ref. 19, in the L layer JPEG2000 bit stream, by optimally allocating authentication dependency $a_{l,i}$ and network resources including expected packet error rate $\varsigma_{l,i}$ as well as energy consumption budget $E_{l,i}$ of each packet, for a given Lagrange multiplier λ tuning the overall energy-quality tradeoff, the cross layer problem can be formulated as the following equations.[19]

$$\underset{l\in\{0,1\cdots L-1\},i\in\{0,1\cdots N_l-1\}}{\{a_{l,i},\varsigma_{l,i},E_{l,i}\}} = \arg\max\{\varepsilon[\Delta D]-\lambda E\}. \tag{27.4}$$

To solve the optimization problem of the authentication aware resource allocation, the expected total distortion reduction $\varepsilon[\Delta D]$ and the total energy consumption E need to be expressed in close forms given the inter-packet compression and authentication dependency. In a similar approach to the research work discussed in Ref. 19, here we use $\Delta D_{l,i}$ to denote the distortion reduction of the ith image packet in layer l, and $\theta_{l,i}$ to denote the successful packet delivery probability, and $v(a_{l,i})$ to denote the verification probability of that packet according to the hash chain allocation assignment scheme $a_{l,i}$. The close form authenticated image quality expectation can be expressed as follows.[19]

$$\varepsilon[\Delta D] = \sum_{l=0}^{L-1}\sum_{i=0}^{N_l-1}\Delta D_{l,i}\theta_{l,i}v(a_{l,i}). \tag{27.5}$$

And the total energy consumption can also be expressed as follows[19]:

$$E_{tot} = \sum_{l=0}^{L-1}\sum_{i=0}^{N_l-1}E_{l,i}. \tag{27.6}$$

Thus given the close form of the expression of authenticated image quality and total energy consumption, the optimization problem can be straightforwardly solved by multiple interactive searches described in Refs. 11 and 28, or QoS level categorized simplification solution described in Ref. 19. Overall, the stream authentication and resource allocation are reciprocal in WMSN. Stream authentication may involve extra rate and dependency overhead, thus the design of an optimized stream authentication scheme needs consideration of the existing packet dependency and resource allocation advantages; on the other hand, flexible authentication aware network resource allocation can effectively protect the important packets in the authenticated bit stream, while significantly reduce the stream authentication complexity.

27.5. Conclusions and Outlook

The conventional multimedia encryption and authentication technologies cannot be directly applied to WMSN due to the extremely limited energy, computing and communication resources. However there is a strong need for secure WMSN since the open and error prone wireless channel is extremely vulnerable to malicious eavesdropping and alteration attacks. In this chapter, we have provided a research overview of the recent progresses for wireless secure multimedia over sensor networks. Firstly, we surveyed the existing security schemes for multimedia encryption-authentication and the challenges to directly apply secure multimedia in wireless sensor networks. In addition, we have reviewed and summarized some cutting edge researches regarding digital image selective encryption and image stream authentication. We have also discussed their application methodologies to energy-constrained WMSN. Finally, the privacy oriented and authentication aware cross layer resource allocation schemes have also been discussed and advocated to achieve energy efficiency, media security and media quality in secure WMSN.

Acknowledgments

The researches[16–19,25,27] discussed in this chapter were supported in part by US National Science Foundation grant No. 0707944 for wireless sensor networks research and Taiwan National Science Council research grants NSC96-2221-E-006-345 and NSC96-2221-E-006-346.

References

1. I. Akyildiz, T. Melodia and K. Chowdhury, A survey on wireless multimedia sensor networks, *Elsevier J. Comput. Netw.*, **51**(4), 921–960 (2007).
2. T. Lookabaugh and D. C. Sicker, Selective encryption for consumer applications, *IEEE Commun. Mag.*, **42**(5), 124–129 (2004).
3. W. Puech, J. Rodrigues and A. Bors, Analysis and cryptanalysis of a selective encryption method for JPEG images, *Proc. IEEE International Workshop on Image Analysis for Multimedia Interactive Services*, 77–77 (2007).
4. M. Kankanhalli and T. Guan, Compressed domain scrambler/descrambler for digital video, *IEEE Trans. Consum. Electron.*, **48**(2), 356–365 (2002).
5. C.-P. Wu and C. J. Kuo, Design of integrated multimedia compression and encryption systems, *IEEE Trans. Multimedia*, **7**(5), 828–839 (2005).
6. L. Tang, Methods for encrypting and decrypting MPEG video data efficiently, *Proc. Int. Conf. ACM Multimedia*, 219–229 (1996).
7. M. Grangetto, E. Magli and G. Olmo, Multimedia selective encryption by means of randomized arithmetic coding, *IEEE Trans. Multimedia*, **8**(5), 905–917 (2006).
8. H. Cheng and X. Li, Partial encryption of compressed images and videos, *IEEE Trans. on Signal Process.*, **48**(8), 2439–2451 (2000).
9. O. Au, J. Zhou, Y. Chen and Z. Liang, Security analysis of multimedia encryption schemes based on multiple Huffman table, *IEEE Signal Process. Letters*, **14**(3), 201–204 (2007).
10. Z. Li, Q. Sun, Y. Lian and C. W. Chen, Joint source-channel-authentication resource allocation and unequal authenticity protection for multimedia over wireless networks, *IEEE Trans. Multimedia*, **9**(4), 837–850 (2007).

11. Z. Zhang, Q. Sun, W. Wong, J. Apostolopoulos and S. Wee, An optimized content-aware authentication scheme for streaming JPEG-2000 images over lossy networks, *IEEE Trans. Multimedia*, **9**(2), 320–331 (2007).
12. Z. Zhang, Q. Sun, W. Wong, J. Apostolopoulos and S. Wee, Rate-distortion-authenticaion optimized streaming of authenticated video, *IEEE Trans. Circuit Systems for Video Technol.*, **17**(5), 544–557 (2007).
13. Q. Sun and S. Chang, A secure and robust digital signature scheme for JPEG2000 image authentication, *IEEE Trans. Multimedia*, **7**(3), 480–494 (2005).
14. D. Skraparlis, Design of an efficient authentication method for modern image and video, *IEEE Trans. Consumer Electronics*, **49**(2), 417–426 (2003).
15. C. Tzeng and W. Tsai, A new approach to authentication of binary images for multimedia communication with distortion reduction and security enhancement, *IEEE Commun. Letters*, **7**(9), 443–445 (2003).
16. W. Wang, D. Peng, H. Wang and H. Sharif, A cross layer resource allocation scheme for secure image delivery in wireless sensor networks, *Proc. ACM International Wireless Communications and Mobile Computing Conference (IWCMC)*, 152–157 (2007).
17. W. Wang, D. Peng, H. Wang and H. Sharif, An adaptive approach for image encryption and secure transmission over multirate wireless sensor networks, *Special Issue on Distributed Systems of Sensors and Applications, Wireless Communications and Mobile Computing Journal (WCMC)*, John Wiley & Sons (2008).
18. W. Wang, D. Peng, H. Wang, H. Sharif and H. H. Chen, Energy-constrained quality optimization for secure image transmission in wireless sensor networks, *Special Issue on Multimedia Transmission over Emerging Wireless Technologies (MTWT), Hindawi Advances in Multimedia Journal* (2007).
19. W. Wang, D. Peng, H. Wang, H. Sharif and H. H. Chen, Energy-distortion-authentication optimized resource allocation for secure wireless image streaming, *Proc. IEEE Wireless Communications and Networking Conference (WCNC)* (2008).
20. W. Zeng and S. Lei, Efficient frequency domain selective scrambling of digital video, *IEEE Trans. Multimedia*, **5**(1), 118–129 (2003).
21. M. P. H. Schmit and A. Uhl, Selective bitplane encryption for secure transmission of image data in mobile environments, *Proc. The 5th Nordic Signal Processing Symposium* (2002).
22. C.-P. Wu and C. J. Kuo, Fast encryption methods for audiovisual data confidentiality, *Proc. SPIE Int. Symp. Information Technologies 2000*, Boston, MA, 284–295 (2000).
23. C.-P. Wu and C. J. Kuo, Efficient multimedia encryption via entropy codec design, *Proc. SPIE Security and Watermarking of Multimedia Content III*, **4314** (2001).
24. J. Wen, H. Kim and J. D. Villasenor, Binary arithmetic coding with key-based interval splitting, *IEEE Signal Process. Lett.*, **13**, 69–72 (2006).
25. W. Wang, D. Peng, H. Wang, H. Sharif and H. H. Chen, Energy-constrained distortion reduction optimization for wavelet-based coded image transmission in wireless sensor networks, *IEEE Transactions on Multimedia (TMM)*, Accepted.
26. Q. Sun, J. Apostolopoulos, C.-W. Chen and S.-F. Chang, Quality-optimized and secure end-to-end authentication for media delivery, *IEEE Proceedings*, **96**(1), 97–110 (2008).
27. W. Wang, D. Peng, H. Wang, H. Sharif and H. H. Chen, Optimal image component transmissions in multirate wireless sensor networks, *Proc. IEEE Global Communications Conference (GLOBECOM)* (2007).
28. P. Chou and Z. Miao, Rate-distortion optimized streaming of packetized media, *IEEE Trans. Multimedia.*, **8**(2), 390–404 (2006).

Part IX

Monitoring and Detection

Chapter 28

Environmental Monitoring Sensor Network Design and Deployment

R. R. Brooks* and Sampada Karandikar†

Holcombe Department of Electrical and Computer Engineering
Clemson University, P.O. Box 340915
Clemson, SC 29634-0915, USA
**rrb@clemson.edu*
†skarand@clemson.edu

C. Post‡ and S. Esswein

Forestry Department, Clemson University
P.O. Box 340915, Clemson, SC 29634-0915, USA
‡cpost@clemson.edu

We present our experiences designing and implementing two environmental monitoring sensor networks. One network monitored the turbidity of stream water in an area undergoing development. The other network collected hydrology data from a reservoir. Each network was designed and implemented by computer engineering undergraduates during one semester. These interdisciplinary design projects provided the students with a chance to apply their acquired knowledge in an interdisciplinary setting.

28.1. Introduction

The Clemson University Holcombe Department of Electrical and Computer Engineering curriculum requires all undergraduates to complete a capstone project. This chapter discusses the capstone projects for Spring 2006 and Spring 2008.

During those semesters, the students designed and implemented sensor networks for monitoring the environment. These projects were made possible by the intersecting research interests of Dr. Post and Dr. Brooks. Dr. Post of Clemson's Department of Forestry and Natural resources has an active research agenda focused on integrating sensor networks with Geographic Information Systems technologies. Dr. Brooks of Clemson University's Holcombe Department of Electrical and Computer Engineering has been active in distributed sensing research since 1993. His experience includes implementing and testing prototype sensor networks for DARPA and ONR.

Although challenging, these projects have many desirable characteristics. Instead of being abstract academic exercises, these projects fulfill a real need. The students have a client for their work. The client is an engineering layman. Students interact with the client, find the client's needs, create a design that fulfills those needs, and show that the finished product works to the client's satisfaction.

The finished product also requires mastery of many technologies that dominate today's market:

- Embedded processors collect data,
- Wireless networks disseminate information, and
- Web technologies aggregate, process and display data.

28.2. Project Framework

The course starts with a meeting where the problem domain is presented. The students then have two weeks to develop a system specifications document and architecture. The specifications document must state in quantifiable terms the success criteria are for the system.

The architecture document decomposes the system into a set of components that can be implemented in parallel. The class divides itself into groups. Each group implements a single component. Once the specifications and architecture documents are complete, the class presents their plans to the instructor. The instructor:

- Modifies the specifications document until consensus is reached. This document becomes a contract. The class must implement the system so that the specifications are satisfied. If the system does not function satisfactorily, the entire class fails the course.
- Points out potential problems in the system architecture. The students have the final say in the system architecture and are free to ignore the instructor's advice. For example, the architecture is often a star structure with a central component coordinating all activities. Star architectures place an unfair integration burden on students working on the central component. It is difficult to field this type of system within our time constraints.

The specifications and architectures document become a contract between the class and the instructor. Example milestones, deliverables, etc. are given in Table 28.1.

The class self-organizes itself into groups. Each group is in charge of implementing a system component. The groups interact to define the applications programming interfaces (APIs) that will be used to integrate the system. Each group implements "stub code" that is used for testing its own component. Note that

Table 28.1. Milestones and credit for milestones.

Item	Responsible	Deliverable	Due date	% grade
Participation in system planning and development	Individual	Oral and written	Ongoing	10
System specifications document — states higher level functionality expected by the system. Document needs to be officially accepted by Dr. Brooks and Dr. Post.	Class	PDF document	1/16/2008	5
System architecture document — This higher level document states all system components. It states the class members that are responsible for implementing the component. It includes a higher level description of the deliverables for each group. The semantics of each component are given. A Gant chart is provided for each component showing the implementation timeline for that component.	Class	PDF document	1/16/2008	5
Component API document — Header file must document the format of all system calls provided by the component. An English description of the semantics of all system calls must be provided. UML document stating all the use-cases for the component needs to be provided, as well as stub code that will be used to test the software component for compliance.	Group	PDF document. C/C++ header files. UML diagrams in soft and hard copy.	2/8/2008	10
Component test document and demonstration — Students must show component fulfilling all use/cases. The demonstration will use the test stub code delivered with the component API document.	Group	PDF document, live demonstration, C/C++ code, statistical analysis as appropriate	3/7/2008	15

(Continued)

Table 28.1. (*Continued*)

Item	Responsible	Deliverable	Due date	% grade
Final Documentation — Includes system architecture, implementation plans, test plans, testing results, and description of prototype demonstration. (discussion of global issues, contemporary issues, societal issues, ethical and security aspects of the system, environmental impact, and understanding of lifelong learning is worth 20% of this grade).	Class	PDF document, C/C++ code, statistical analysis as appropriate	4/18/2008 (9:00 AM)	20
Jury evaluation dry run	Class	Live demonstration, oral presentation, supporting material	4/22/2008	5
Peer evaluation	Individual	Each student fills out a form evaluating their peers	4/25/2008	10
Jury evaluation	Class	Live demonstration, oral presentation, supporting material	04/25/2008 (preliminary)	20
Total				100

the stub code has minimal functionality and mimics the other group's side of the interface. In this way, each group can work independently to implement its own component. Once the components are ready, the full system can be implemented and field tests are performed.

Students are given as much freedom as possible in system design and implementation. This allows them to try new ways of doing things and find their own style of working. We specifically allow them to make mistakes. They are held accountable. The final system must work. We find that allowing them the freedom to make mistakes while under faculty supervision helps them in their career development.

The faculty supervisor meets weekly with each group to monitor and assess progress. We have found the student peer evaluations invaluable in determining the final grades. Every student has the option of providing input. The grades are normalized to prevent grade inflation. The final product is presented to a jury panel of industry representatives and university faculty.

We now present the two environmental monitoring applications that we have implemented: stream turbidity and reservoir hydrology monitoring.

28.3. Stream Turbidity

As a part of a forestry research program, a sensor network was constructed to collect water turbidity information at regular intervals. Turbidity is the cloudiness of a fluid caused by the presence of suspended particles. It is of interest when land development occurs, since it indicates erosion. Turbidity information was transferred via a data communications network to a host on campus. That host used standard tools for data analysis (i.e., excel, matlab, etc.)

The individual nodes were Berkeley motes embedded processors that have wireless communications. These nodes are extremely power efficient. Unfortunately, they are little beyond the research prototype stage. They use the tiny OS operating system and the Ness-C programming language. Although these software components are built on top of the C programming language, they have a large number of nonstandard constructs. Although these constructs are meant to enable efficient real-time programming, they have a reputation of being extremely difficult to learn. Dr. Post had two graduate students working on the project that have mastered use of these software components. One of those students, Pinky Tejwani, was an ECE M.S. student who provided help to students enrolled in the course.

The individual nodes were connected to home made sensors that returned an analog value documenting the degree of turbidity of the water. The Forestry Department had some software components implemented that were relevant to this project. Students were encouraged to leverage as much legacy code as possible.

Although the motes have wireless communications, they were not able to transmit data directly to the Clemson University campus. Students had to develop a system that collects data from the motes network at regular time intervals and relay the data to a host connected to the Internet. A number of alternative approaches existed, including the use of prepaid cell phones. As a part of this project, students had to implement this relay interface. Analysis of the architecture had to show the solution to be both cost effective and sustainable. A major issue for these networks is the fact that all system nodes rely on battery power. This guarantees that the system will fail eventually. Being parsimonious with system resources delays this eventuality.

In addition to relaying sensor data from the field to campus, the network had to be self-aware. Regular updates on network health had to be sent to campus. The workstation receiving the sensor data had to maintain a database of network health information. A network administrator had to be able to quickly verify that the network was operational and diagnose any current or imminent network failures.

Some form of data verification was needed to certify that the data was adequately secure and not modified by unauthorized parties. It is not possible to fully guarantee data security without compromising the systems ability to run for a long period of time. The proposed design had to explicitly quantify this tradeoff.

The project included using the network to collect data for the Forestry Department. The Forestry personnel provided us with a laydown for the nodes at the desired site. Students had to configure the software to support the laydown and show that the system ran autonomously for a reasonable period of time. The students also had to demonstrate the system's ability to diagnose and inform the administrator of some classes of network failure.

28.3.1. *System architecture and specifications*

Figure 28.1 shows a schematic of the system. We now present the systems specifications that were developed.

The mote system shall:

- Operate environmental sensors and periodically record their values
- Keep track of mote system health and report it along with sensor data
- Communicate with the relay system over a ZigBee/802.15.4 radio link
- Respond to requests for enumeration and sensor data from the relay system
- Relay messages from other mote systems
- Apply data integrity mechanisms on transmitted data
- Implement power conservation measures to extend unattended deployment time
- Attempt to communicate with nearby relay systems upon initialization

The relay system shall:

- Communicate with the mote system over a ZigBee/802.15.4 radio link
- Communicate with the root system over a long-range communications link
- Respond to requests for enumeration from the root system
- Relay messages from mote systems to the root system
- Keep track of relay system health and report it along with mote system data
- Arbitrate communications between the mote and relay systems to minimize collisions
- Implement power conservation measures to extend unattended deployment time
- Keep track of system health
- Attempt to communicate with nearby mote systems upon initialization
- Attempt to communicate with the root system upon initialization
- Have the capability to broadcast to all mote systems within range

The relay system shall not:

- Process data from mote systems
- Modify data received from mote systems

The root system shall:

- Be a fixed-installation with access to network and power infrastructure
- Communicate with the relay systems over a long-range communications link
- Continuously monitor the long-range communications link
- Process data from the mote systems received via the relay systems
- Store all data into the database after processing, along with data integrity metrics

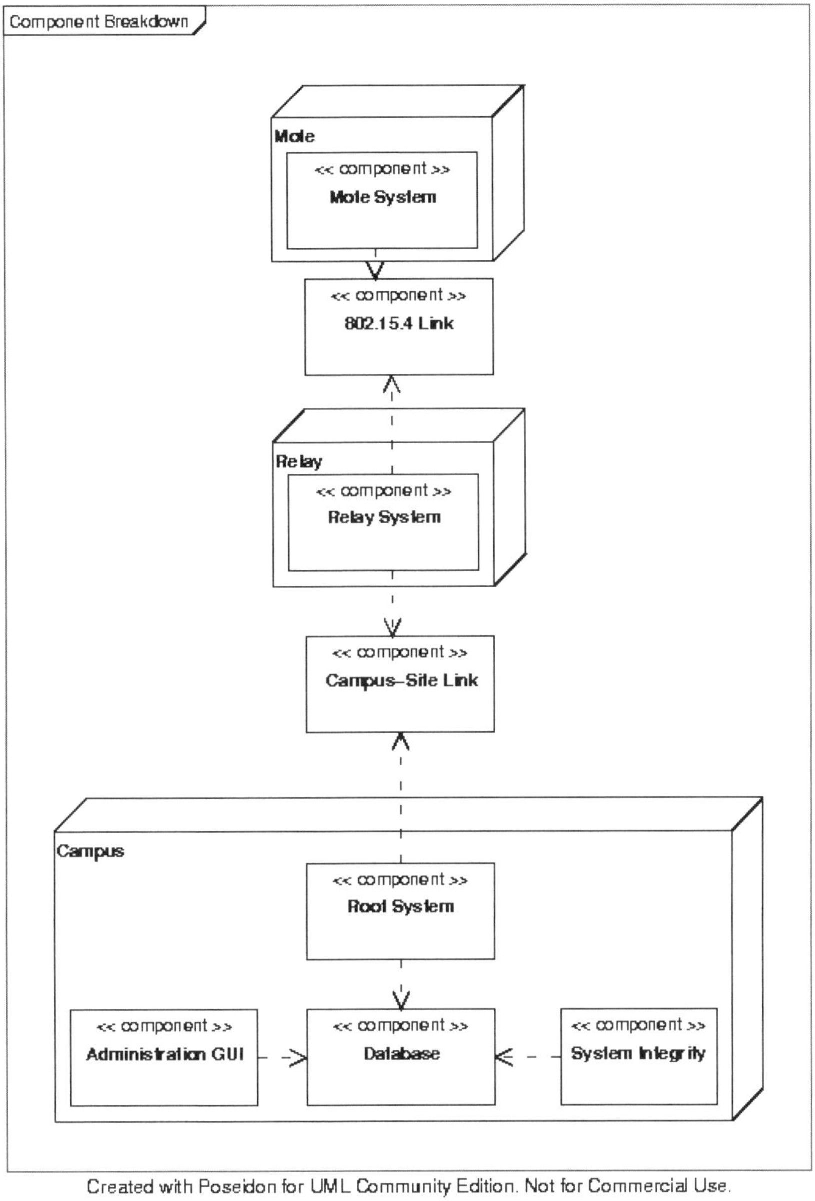

Fig. 28.1. Architecture of the stream turbidity monitoring system.

- Forward communications sent from the administration GUI to the relay systems
- Continuously listen for communications from the administration GUI
- Have the capability to broadcast to all relay systems

The root system shall:

- Provide a mechanism to specify a mote and its coordinates
- Provide a mechanism to specify a relay and its coordinates
- Provide a mechanism for viewing system health
- Provide a mechanism for exporting data to an external format
- Utilize authorization mechanisms to prevent unauthorized use
- Communicate with the database and root systems
- Store all information about the system in the database

The database shall:

- Provide long-term storage for data in a secure format
- Communicate with the root system and the administration GUI
- Prevent access to unauthorized users

Miscellaneous components:

- The system shall provide data integrity, integrated elsewhere into this specification, to provide the system administrators an indication of the validity of data measurements in relation to network health.
- The system shall keep track of statistics indicating the health of each node.
- The system shall implement physical security measures on the relays to reduce the possibility of tampering and theft of equipment.

The ZigBee/802.15.4 link shall:

- Interface between the mote systems and the relay systems
- Ensure protocol compatibility between the mote systems and relay systems
- Provide broadcast as well as point-to-point communication capabilities

The ZigBee/802.15.4 link shall not:

- Provide encryption

The campus-site link shall:

- Interface between the relay systems and the root system
- Ensure protocol compatibility between the relay systems and the root system
- Provide broadcast as well as directed root-to-relay communication capabilities

The campus link shall not:

- Provide encryption

28.3.2. *Implementation details*

This section provides details about the system implementation. We discuss the architecture shown in Fig. 28.1 divided into three segments. The server system includes the database, GUI, and system integrity components. The relay system describes the network communications between the sensor nodes and the server. Finally, the sensor nodes subsection describes the data collection system.

28.3.2.1. *Server*

Figure 28.2 shows sample screenshots from the system user interface. The root system is installed on the same server as the rest of the on-campus software and has

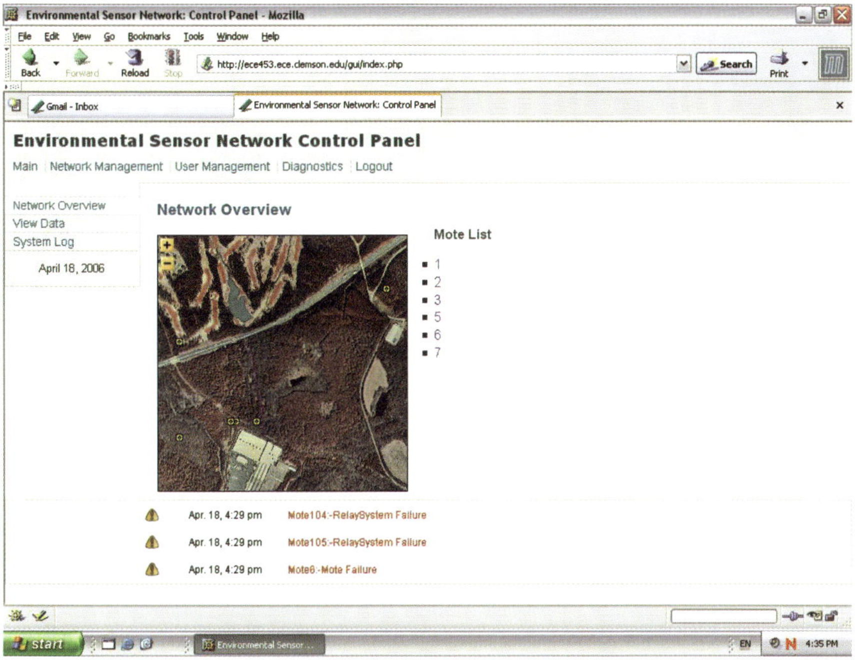

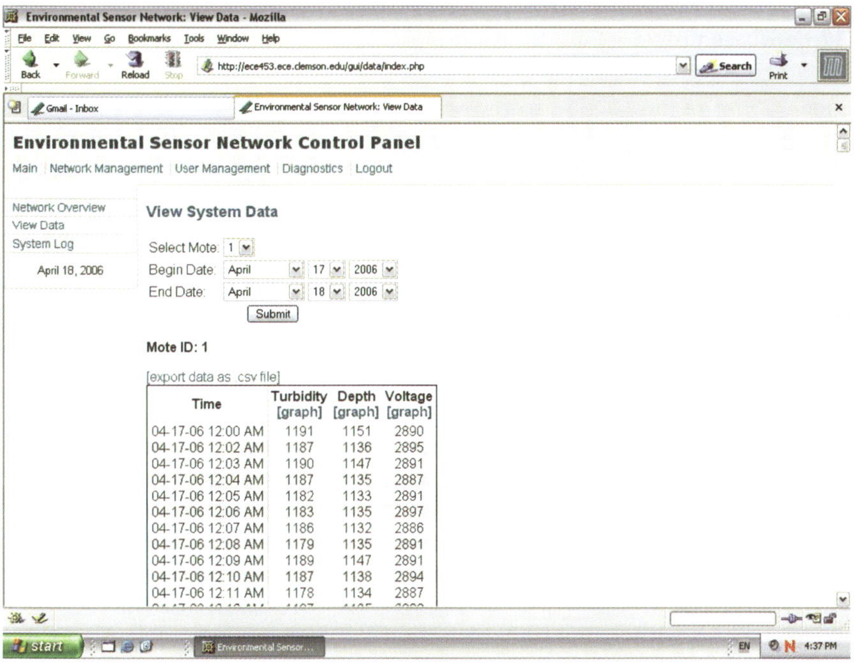

Fig. 28.2. GUI screenshots.

three major subsystems. Relay i/o is responsible for arbitrating communications with deployed relay systems and interpreting received data. The database interface manages communication with the database and allows the insertion of received sensor data. The core component links the relay i/o and database interface and decompresses and processes received sensor data into a format readable by the database. As data packets are inserted in the database using predefined SQL queries, a conversion is performed on the associated timestamps in an effort to compensate for the inaccuracy of the mote clocks.

This interface was the most visible part of the server. The administration GUI provides the user with the ability to set up, configure, and monitor the entire sensor network. The GUI also provides basic tools for displaying and exporting collected data. It is implemented in on a Linux server running the Apache webserver. The server has a reserved DCHP entry and a static DNS entry in Clemson's network for ease of access. An interactive map of the deployed sensor network is also provided. The GUI web pages use a combination of HTML, CSS, PHP, Javascript, and Python. HTML is used for text markup, CSS (cascading style sheets) for page layout, and PHP for server side scripting. The interactive map is composed of two parts: a client-side Javascript component and a server-side Python script. The server side script combines data from a static map and the database using mapscript. The client side script makes requests to the server as information is needed, allowing for a fully interactive display.

The database provides long-term storage for sensor data. A SQL-based database was chosen to ensure security, encapsulation, and compatibility between the system components that require access to the sensor data. MySQL was selected over a proprietary file format to ease development and integration due to the variety of interfaces available almost every major language has bindings or libraries for MySQL.

System integrity encompasses the overall quality of the entire system - including hardware, software, and collected data. It monitors the health of the field equipment, ensures the validity of sensor data, and provides procedures for detecting and mitigating errors at all levels. Data integrity tested and problems are reported via alerts and errors abnormalities are detected. This functionality is implemented as a library of functions run on incoming data.

28.3.2.2. *Relay*

Figure 28.3 shows the interior of a relay node. The relay system is composed of five major subsystems. All of which, except for the data management subsystem, run in separate threads to ease the timing constraints imposed by the associated hardware interfaces. The systems run on AMD Geode GX-based single-board computers using motes with standard base-station software for communication with the deployed sensor motes and MultiTech MultiModem EDGE cellphone modems for communication with the root system via the Internet.

Fig. 28.3. Relay nodes.

We used a DTRI DT166, AMD Geode GX2-based embedded system. This system has both low power characteristics and the USB host controller required to connect our external devices — the base station mote and cellular modem. The systems have 128 MB of RAM and a 64 MB Flash disk for storage. We are running a custom Linux distribution from a ramdisk loaded at startup from the Flash disk. Using a ramdisk and disallowing writes to the Flash disk at runtime ensure system longevity and reduce the chance of hardware failure. For the link from the relay systems to the on-campus server, we use MultiTech MultiModem EDGE USB cellphone modems. These modems provide a TCP/IP stack, reducing the implementation overhead in both the relay and root systems. It is USB bus-powered and can be powered down on command to conserve power.

The relay system hardware is housed in NEMA 4x waterproof enclosures. In addition to the computer and modem, appropriate power supplies and batteries were chosen to allow for unattended deployment times ranging from 1 week to 1 month, depending on transmission intervals and power utilization. The standard antennas included with the cellular modems provide more than adequate performance, but it was determined that fairly large antennas would be required for the base station motes to ensure sufficient range and sensitivity. The HyperGain HG2412U 12 dBi omnidirectional (vertical) 802.11b/g base station was selected because the 802.15.4 radios on the motes operate on the same ISM frequency band as standard wireless ethernet.

On the software side, the relay system consists of the core, mote i/o, root i/o, data management, and health monitoring subsystems. The Core subsystem manages all of the different components of the Relay System and is responsible for system startup and thread generation. It acts as a crossbar switch between the mote i/o, root i/o, health monitoring, and data management subsystems. At regular intervals, a set of data is pulled from data management, built into a convenient packet format, and sent to root i/o for transmission. The health monitoring subsystem is responsible for monitoring the system battery voltage and the signal strength reported by the cellphone modem.

The data management subsystem stores sensor readings received from motes as well as internal health monitoring packets. Each mote has a corresponding queue that used as temporary storage while received data packets are waiting to be transmitted to the server on campus.

The mote i/o subsystem provides an interface between the USB-connected base-station mote and the core subsystem. It implements the relay side of the mote-relay network protocol. The mote i/o thread installs a SIGALRM timer to provide an accurate reference clock for the network protocol. The thread also thread maintains a set of protocol state machines, one for each associated mote. The state machine instances themselves handle the actual network protocol, providing a level of modularity allowing the number of motes associated with each relay and the actual protocol used over the mote-relay link to be changed easily. As data packets are received and validated, they are passed to the Core component.

The mote i/o subsystem is needed to process the traffic between the motes and the rest of the Relay System. It accommodates the asynchronous nature of communicating with the motes and provides a layer of abstraction. This abstraction allows the other components of the relay to concern themselves with data received from the associated motes and not the underlying protocol and any errors that may occur in transmission.

The root i/o subsystem is responsible for managing the cellphone modem. It is needed to abstract the interface with the cellphone modem and manage the asynchronous nature of its operation. The cellphone modem incorporates a minimal TCP/IP stack, which reduces the protocol complexity necessary, but increases the intricacy of the modem interface. Data compression is used on this link to reduce the cost of deployment since the pre-paid cellular data plans chosen charge by the kilobyte.

28.3.2.3. *Sensor nodes*

Figure 28.4 shows sensor nodes under preparation. The sensor nodes consist of a field-deployed network of motes and their associated sensors. The chosen mote platform was moteiv TMote Sky, so mote-level development was done in NesC, a heavily customized derivative of C, in the TinyOS environment. Both NesC and TinyOS are open-source projects developed by moteiv to support their products. Aside from the motes themselves, a turbidity sensor and a pressure transducer are part of the deployed sensor package. These sensors are connected to a custom-designed power supply board controlled by a digital i/o signal from the associated mote, thus increasing the sensors' expected battery lifetime considerably.

A robust communications protocol and packet format were developed to allow reliable communications between the mote and relay systems. The protocol uses a "stop-and-wait" system similar to that of a basic implementation of TCP/IP with send and receive window sizes of 1 packet. The packet format carried by this protocol makes efficient use of the small packet size dictated by TinyOS and incorporates all data fields needed to provide reliable communication.

In addition to an implementation of the network protocol, several other software components are required on the motes themselves. A buffering system was developed to allow the motes to queue up a series of sensor measurements for batch transmission. In addition, code to actually read the sensors attached to the analog to digital converters is needed, as well as software for controlling the digital i/o for the sensor power supply.

A ruggedized housing for each sensor package and its associated mote was developed as well. The housing consists of a sealed PVC tube with sensors mounted

Fig. 28.4. Preparation of sensor nodes.

Fig. 28.5. Deployment of a relay node.

through the bottom endcap and the mote mounted in top endcap. The sensor end is submerged in the stream while the end with the mote end is held high out of the water to protect it from moisture and increase radio range.

28.3.3. *Deployment*

The system had two deployments. A test deployment was executed on a small farm adjacent to the Clemson University campus. That test run for less than a week. It allowed for debugging the system.

Fig. 28.6. Sensor node creation.

A longer deployment was done at the construction site of the Clemson University International Center for Automotive research in Greenville, SC. It ran successfully for over two weeks. It stopped running due to the batteries losing power.

The only portion of the system that needed to be modified was the relay system. For some reason, the cell phone modem would enter an undefined state in the middle of the night. This problem had not occurred during the test deployment. This problem was overcome by scheduling a system reboot each night.

28.3.4. *Lessons learned*

The deployment was considered a success. The system worked reliably. In fact, the students were able to implement many things that the instructors were expecting to fail.

The hardware worked well. The relay nodes used more power than wished for. We decided to use more energy efficient hardware in the enxt iteration.

28.4. Issaqueena Reservoir

In Spring 2008, a campus wide initiative was started at Clemson University to develop an improved environmental monitoring infrastructure. Dr. Post and

Fig. 28.7. Sensor node deployment.

Dr. Brooks decided to use the same approach as in 2006 to create an initial prototype.

The Issaqueena Reservoir was picked as a deployment site for a hydrology sensor network to collect sensor information at regular intervals. This information needed to be transferred via a data communications network to a host on campus that uses standard tools for data analysis (i.e., excel, matlab, etc.)

The class was to build sensor nodes that collect information as to the volume of water entering the reservoir and the volume of water exiting the reservoir over the dam separating the reservoir from Lake Hartwell. The sensing modes for measuring water entering the reservoir are well defined. A new technology was needed for measuring the volume of water leaving the lake over the dam. The students also needed to be certain that these nodes have sufficient power to function adequately over long periods of time.

The sensing modes for water entering the reservoir were established in coordination with Dr. John Hains of Biological sciences and Dr. Larry Murdoch of Geological Sciences at Clemson University. The class was in charge of proposing configuration alternatives and determining their cost.

Some of the node hardware was well defined. Dr. Post and his student Mr. Esswein were using programmable wireless devices for communications. The exact hardware configurations had need to be established early in the project.

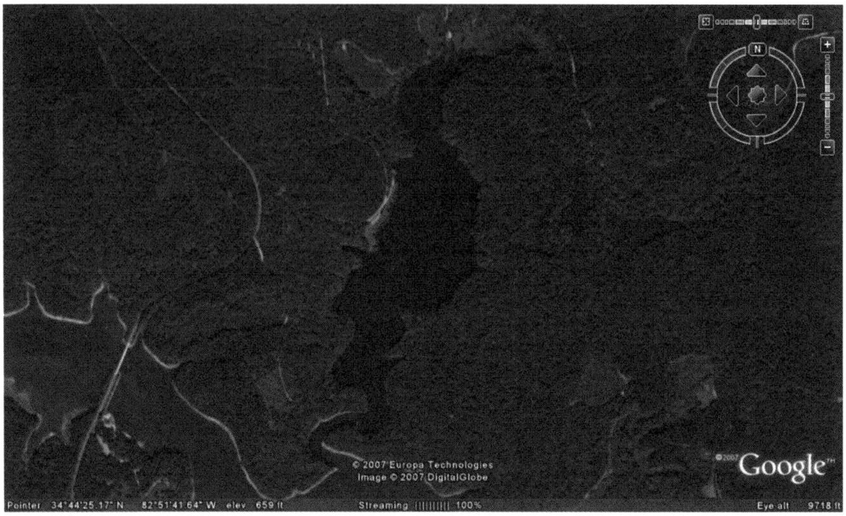

Fig. 28.8. Issaqueena Reservoir.

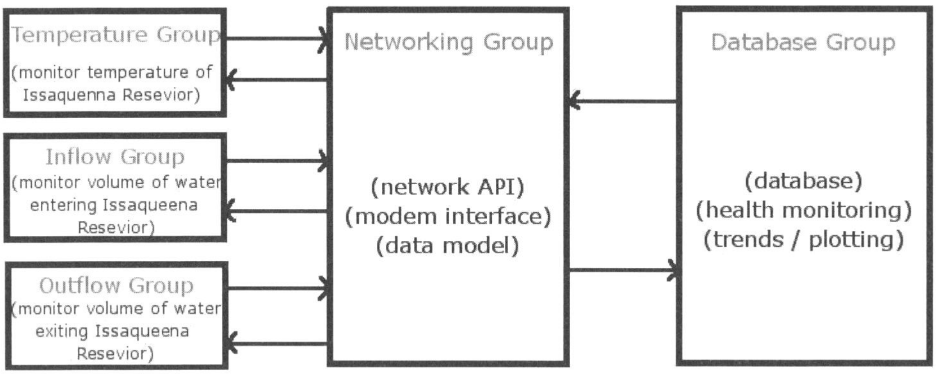

Fig. 28.9. System architecture.

Students came up with a small number of alternatives and advised the research team about the pros and cons of each design choice. One possible problem was the possibility of passersby tampering with the nodes. We needed to find ways of either hardening or camouflaging the nodes to minimize these problems.

We also implemented a health monitoring system for the network. The ability to diagnose reasons for problems, and possibly correct software issues remotely was desired.

Finally, an interface allowed our data to be read into appropriate data analysis tools, such as Matlab and/or Octave. A small number of analysis macros will be constructed that allow data to be tracked in real time, identify trends, estimate signal to noise ratio of the data, and plot graphs.

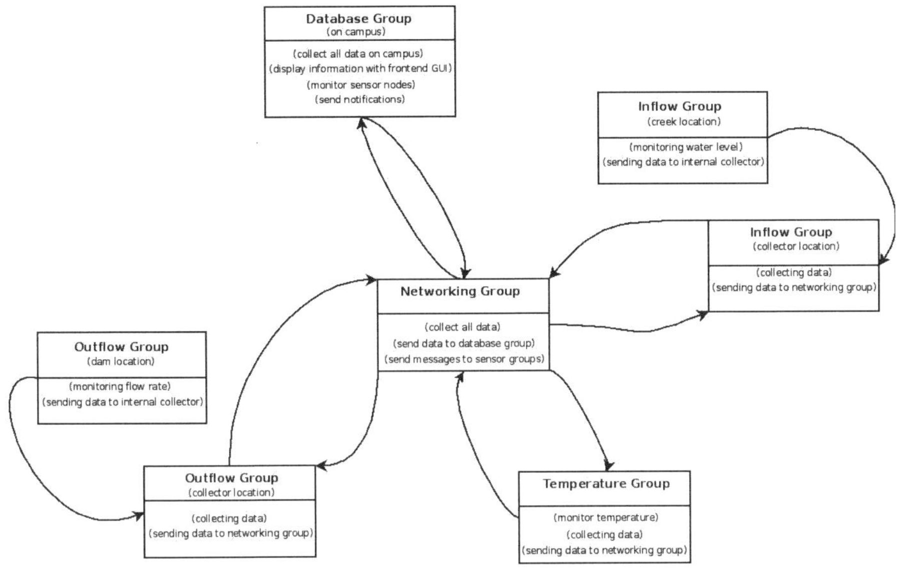

Fig. 28.10. Higher level design.

Part of the project included field testing the system. Tests illustrated all the features that were developed, including health monitoring.

28.4.1. *Architecture*

The goal was to create a fault-tolerant, tamper-resistant environmental sensor network so that temperature and water flow in and out of the Lake Hartwell Dam can be measured and analyzed. This project architecture had five component groups: temperature sensors, water inflow sensors, water outflow sensors, networking, and data storage/analysis.

The network monitored the inflow into the reservoir and the outflow over the dam at a maximum time interval on the order of seconds. The temperatures at several depths at various points were measured. These sensors communicated wirelessly with a central modem, which passed data in a standardized format (NetCDF) over the distributed publisher/subscriber network. Subscribers of this sensor network included a persistent database for long-term data storage and various data analysis tools such as MATLAB, Octave, and/or R. These data analysis tools will track trends, plot data points, and detect malfunctioning sensor nodes. The sensor nodes, network, and data components support health monitoring information and remote repair and/or reset commands (receiving, transmitting, and sending, respectively). The sensor network could function on the order of weeks without battery replacements. The onfield sensor and network hardware were reasonably resistant to tampering by hunters and other interlopers, either unintending or malicious.

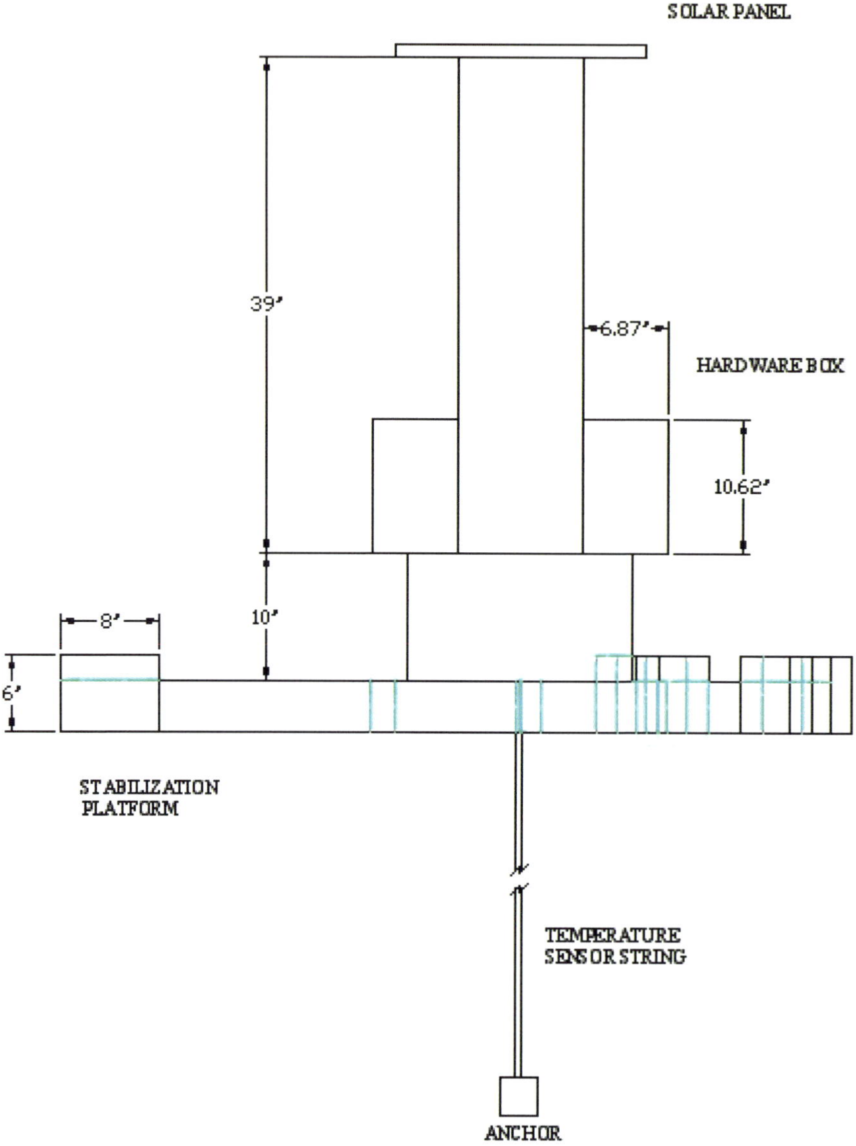

Fig. 28.11. Buoy design.

28.4.2. *Implementation details*

We now discuss the implementation details of the system. Each component is discussed in turn. During this project, the hardware choices varied over the semester. Some of the original choices were found to not adequately meet the system requirements. We will discuss only the final implementation.

28.4.2.1. *Temperature sensors*

To read the temperature of the water in the middle of Issaqueena Lake, a buoy system was needed. The requirements for the buoy required that the temperature be read from the surface of the lake to the bottom. The exact specification for the spacing of the temperature sensors varied during the course of the project, as did the desired number of sensing positions.

A NexSens TS110 temperature string was custom manufactured for the project with sensors at the exact depths needed. The sensor contained inside the strings are Programmable Resolution 1 Wire Digital Thermometers which run on a 1 Wire bus. The sensors were each calibrated to be accurate to 0.1 degree and are capable of running in "parasitic power mode" where they do not require an external power source and can receive power over the bus.

Due to power restraints on board the buoy, a small, low-power embedded computer was needed to read the temperature sensors, store the data, and send the data to a remote base station. Three computer systems were considered: the WebDT LX166 thin client, the GumStix verdex XL6P embedded computer system, and the Java SunSPOT embedded computer system.

The GumStix was chosen due to its extremely low power consumption, built in serial ports (on the console expansion board), and the fact that it can run Linux. Using the GumStix allowed for full programmability of the hardware on the buoy. The sensors could be read at a user defined interval, stored, and then relayed on to the remote station. To communicate with the remote station, a Digi Xbee RF Modem was used. The modem was connected directly to a RS232 on the GumStix.

Since the ideal design would allow the buoy to be self sufficient for an extended period of time, a large enough battery and a large solar panel were needed to power the buoy. The battery had to be able to power the buoy continuously for a few days without losing power in case bad weather prevented the solar panel from charging the battery. A 12 V, 12 mAh lead acid battery was used in conjunction with a 20 W solar panel and charge controller.

The height of the buoy and the base allowed for easy mounting of the hardware and the attachment of the anchor. To protect the hardware from water, pollen, and other foreign substance, two waterproof plastic cases were attached to the sides of the buoy. One for all the electronics and the other for the battery and solar charge controller. Finally, to ensure maximum stability and to provide extra buoyancy, a wooden frame was constructed out of 2×4's and Styrofoam in which the buoy sat.

The raw analog data from the pressure transducers was converted to a digital format at a pre-determined sample rate using a custom built analog-to-digital (A/D) board. Once this data was in digital form, it was transmitted to a second location for data collection.

Fig. 28.12. Outflow sensors on the dam.

The second location contained two Digi Xbee Pro RF modules and a Gumstix computer. For data collection, one Xbee and the Gumstix computer was used.

28.4.2.2. *Outflow sensors*

The amount of water leaving the reservoir was measured by finding how much water was flowing over the dam. Sensors on the dam relayed information to a second location. An Xbee at location two rccived data from the Xbee at the dam.

It was determined that the best method for measuring flow rate over the dam was based on an empirical formula for flow rate over a broad-crested weir. The flow rate depends on the weir coefficient, the length of the weir, L, and the head of water over the dam. The weir coefficient and length of the weir (the dam) are constant (1.704 m1/2/s and 30.5308 m respectively); therefore, the remaining variable, H, should be monitored to determine the flow rate.

Monitoring the height of the water over the dam was accomplished using four Level Master Schaevitz pressure transducers placed near the crest of the dam. The pressure transducers output a variable analog signal based on how much water is above the sensor. This information can be used to determine the amount of water flowing over the dam.

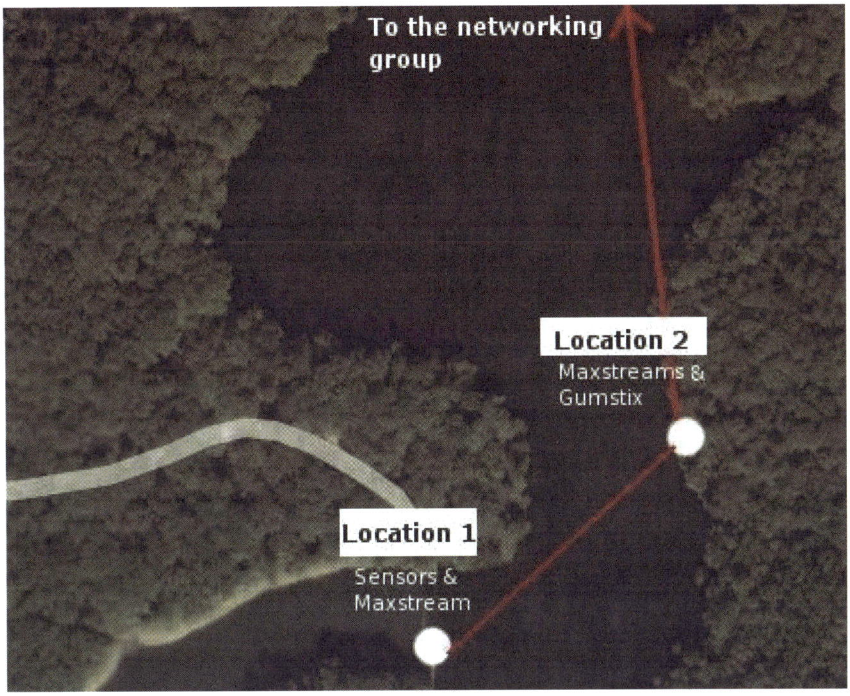

Fig. 28.13. Outflow information relay.

Hardware placement was a key issue for the outflow group. First, it was important that all hardware be tamper-resistant. Therefore, all hardware at location one was placed on the inside of a fenced area on the dam structure. The hardware enclosure and pressure sensor enclosure were bolted to the dam. Second, placement of the pressure sensors was important for several different reasons. First, the sensors needed to be partially submerged, so it was important that these sensors not present a danger to any recreational swimmers. Also, the sensors needed to be placed some distance away from the dam crest in order to provide accurate results. Considering these two issues, the pressure sensors were placed in an enclosure and bolted to the side structure of the dam.

Once data was received, the Gumstix computer parsed the data for the pressure sensor values and ran computations on these values to determine flow rate. After the flow rate was calculated, this information, along with a timestamp, was written to a file.

28.4.2.3. *Inflow sensors*

The inflow sensors measured the volume of water entering the reservoir by measuring the depth of water at the main streams entering the system. Data sampling was done at a number of points.

Fig. 28.14. Inflow sensor node.

The GumStix verdex XL6P processor was used primarily due to its low power requirements. It also provided RS-232 ports. We used 12 V-12 Ah sealed lead acid batteries. These provide sufficient voltage and amperage to run both the modems and GumStix. However, the GumStix requires a 5V input and so the voltage must be stepped down using a voltage reduction kit.

The AquaRod sensors are powered with a 3.6 V lithium battery. Our system utilizes the AquaRod water level and temperature logger. For the purposes of this project, only the water level measurement capabilities were of any concern. These sensors are capacitance based and therefore are better for use in an outdoor environment than standard pressure transducers. They are accurate up to 1/100 of a foot which is more than accurate enough for our purposes.

All water depth data retrieved from an AquaRod sensor is fed into a method which uses this depth measurement along with specific parameters based on the stream conditions at the sensor location to calculate the volumetric flow via Manning's Equation.

In this specific situation, sensor depth measurements are made in millimeters and flow is calculated in cubic meters per second. This calculated data is buffered into an array and the time at which the sensor reading took place is stored. Once five sensor reading and calculation cycles have been completed, a NetCDF file is prepared which contains the flow data and the times at which the readings were

Fig. 28.15. Network relay.

made. This file is then converted into a byte array and transmitted to the networking central data collector.

We use a Gumstix microcomputer running a custom Linux 2.6 build. The Verdex XL6P board is built around a Marvell PXA270 600 MHz processor and provides 128 MB RAM and 32 MB Flash. We chose the Gumstix microcomputer for our application based on three reasons: low power, programming simplicity, and helpful documentation. The maximum power consumption of the Gumstix assembly is around 1 W (200 mA at 4.5 V) and typical usage is much less; this is on the order of a tenth the power needed by an alternative AMD Geode box. Power consumption is important since the device is running off a marine battery. The Gumstix was simple to configure with our custom Linux build. Also, the serial and Ethernet ports natively supported our modems.

28.4.2.4. *Network system*

Data from all of the sensor groups were aggregated at a central position and then relayed to campus. For the link between our collector and the sensor groups' nodes, we use an 802.15.4 ZigBee radio to receive packets from the distributed sensor groups — inflow, outflow, and temperature.

We use a Digi Connect WAN modem for the backhaul link from the collector to the campus database server. Dr. Post and the forestry department maintain the monthly service contract through AT&T for the modem. The plan includes unlimited data transmission/reception and a static IP address. The cellular modem allows for an extremely reliable backhaul link as GPRS reception and power is the only requirement. Solar power was used to recharge the battery and lengthen the effective deployment time.

28.4.2.5. *Database*

The Data Handling Group was responsible for maintaining the Publish-Subscribe network which the Networking Group to transmit sensor data to the server on campus.

The group was also responsible for maintaining the server, as well as the software on it, and the related website. The purpose of the website is to allow end-users remote access to monitor the data received from the sensors in the field, as well as send remote resets and alter the sampling frequencies, as needed.

Special software used in setting up the user interface included:

- ActiveMQ — the "backbone" of the Publish-Subscriber network
- DotNetNuke (DNN) — website framework
- Tomcat — interacts with the website to provide connectivity to the Publish-Subscribe network for the remote reset and sensor frequency forms
- GoogleMap — provides sensor locations for easy monitoring on the website factors (listed below), and by analyzing the relative benefits that each of those choices demonstrated.

With the DNN framework intact a way to pull the Data from a database was needed. DNN lacks an easy way to connect to custom databases for data display. There are multiple ways to go about doing this, two popular ways are ReportGrid and ListX. ReportGrid is a easy to use way of displaying data grids, very fast. ListX is a slightly more robust implementation which allows for scripting. ListX was the choice due to the ability of ListX to be easily configured, scripted, and exported. ListXs' ability to output to Excel format made it a great choice for the project and really separated it from the competition.

A custom server application named "Susie" integrates the messaging server and the database. Susie exports a client API that is used by the networking group to communicate with the database group over their cell modem. The Susie server application parses incoming data messages in NetCDF format and imports them nto the database. Susie server came about because of a need to get data from the messaging server to the database.

The Publish-Subscribe network which connects the Networking Group to the Data Handling Group is Java-based, implementing the ActiveMQ technology developed by Apache. The Networking Group publishes messages containing the NetCDF files which are then collected by the Susie server.

The Susie server application is the central component of the Susie architecture. It runs on the same hardware as the database and messaging server. It bridges these two components by parsing NetCDF data messages and importing them to the database for use by software running on the web server.

The server application is also responsible for responding to sensor error notifications. In the event of a sensor error it will notify interested parties via email. These steps ensure that the faulty sensor will be replaced as soon as possible.

Once the data has been parsed, the website, using DotNetNuke, executes a series of queries, depending on the current page, and displays the current statistics of the sensors, sensor health, or an overview of the entire system. Through the website, an end-user also has the capability to reset sensors remotely, as well as altering the frequency at which sensors are sampling. At present, it isn't possible to reset an individual sensor, only groups: inflow, outflow, and temperature. Similarly, since all the temperature sensors are on a single string, their sampling frequency is controlled as a single unit.

28.4.3. *Deployment*

The system was deployed and tested on the reservoir. It reliably transferred data to campus. Further development is being performed by additional research groups. Extensions will include a dedicated communications link and possibly live video feeds.

28.4.4. *Lessons learned*

The students were able to apply their hardware and software implementation skills on this project. Many students were surprised by the difficulty of integration and collaboration across groups. That is a major selling point for implementing capstone projects using this approach. Many students lack the soft skills of communication when they graduate with an engineering degree. We hope that this experience helps them in adjusting to their future career.

Some other students felt that deployment problems could have been reduced by doing more planning in advance. On the other hand, they blamed most of the deployment problems on hardware and software not acting as expected during integration and field test. Again, we feel that these insights are useful to young engineers.

28.5. Conclusions

This chapter provided an overview of two sensor networks that we have implemented for environmental monitoring. Both projects were successfully designed, implemented, and tested during one semester. These projects are challenging for computer engineering students, but are very worthwhile. The students are forced to collaborate outside their discipline and produce products for an external customer. We also have found the course design to be very beneficial to the students. Designing APIs and integrating individual components into a larger product are important skills for their profession.

Acknowledgments

The authors would like to thank the students who took the Clemson University ECE453 Software Practicum course in Spring 2006 and Spring 2008. This chapter documents the work they performed. This work would not have been possible without the support of Dr. Gene Eidson of the Clemson University Restoration Institute. Dr.s K. C. Wang of the Clemson ECE Department, Dr. John Hains of the Clemson Biological Sciences Department, and Dr. Larry Murdoch of the Clemson Geosciences Department were very helpful and provided needed guidance to the students. We would also like to thank Dr. Badr of the State of South Carolina Department of Natural Resources, Kelly Waller of Intel Corporation, Dr. Wang, Dr. Hains, Phil Lyles, and Samuel Hoover for serving on the jury for this course.

Chapter 29

Distributed Edge Detection with Error Resilience for Wireless Sensor Networks

S. Selvakennedy

School of Information Technologies J12
University of Sydney, NSW 2006, Australia
s.kennedy@usyd.edu.au

Many sensor network-based monitoring applications are becoming feasible, as fundamental data collection and network protocols are becoming efficient in handling simple sense-and-send function. As the resources of sensor nodes expand, these nodes are capable of performing more complex functions. Moreover, the need to realize the complete loop of sense-control-actuate similar to the wired sensing facility demands for more in-network processing to enable any meaningful in-network control. One such useful primitive function for many applications is edge or boundary detection of a phenomenon. In this chapter, we define edge detection, and then, extend a distributed edge detection algorithm using basic geometry rules to handle isolated sensor errors. This algorithm is then benchmarked against one of the best localized edge detection scheme. It is found that our algorithm readily outperformed its counterpart in dealing with both convex as well as non-convex regions.

29.1. Introduction

The disruptive idea of integrating a microcontroller, miniature sensors and a radio interface has generated immense interest in the ad hoc wireless network research community as well as from the industry. These sensor nodes are typically stationary due to their unique application needs, substantially more resource constrained and more densely deployed than mobile ad hoc networks. Due to the portability and self-configurability of wireless sensor networks (WSNs), they are found to be useful in various application domains, both for civil and military purposes. Typically, these applications entail simple sensing and relaying physical characteristics of interest back to a sink for processing and storage. However, in some applications, latency and energy constraints call for more in-network processing and *in situ* response generation. Recently, there have been some proposals to introduce more *intelligence* into the network itself in the form of data aggregation/compression function that is informed of the spatial and/or temporal correlations.[1,2] This is inline with the rapid advance of the hardware especially the node's processing capacity according to Moore's Law.

With the foreseeable increase of in-network processing, it may also facilitate in the provision of automated response through suitable controllers and actuators to complete the sense-control-actuate loop as in the traditional control systems. A generic sensor-to-actuator coordination model for an event-driven application is proposed in Ref. 3. Accomplishing such a feedback loop mostly requires application-specific knowledge and data semantic processing against statistical processing, for instance, as required for data aggregation. Even though such semantic processing notionally requires application-specific knowledge, there are certain primitive functions that may be applied across many application domains. For instance, the notion of an event spanning across an area, instead of occurring at specific points, is readily envisaged in numerous applications such as monitoring seismic disturbances, contaminant flows, chemical concentrations as well as events occurring in a relatively shorter time span like fire emergencies. For these applications, basic primitives like the extent of the *event region*, the number of nodes on the *event boundary* and the *event epicenter* might be useful for characterizing the phenomenon for suitable feedback generation by the controllers and actuators. In any emergency applications involving humans where the latency involved in the identification of an event to the response generation could result in a life or death outcome, it is paramount to determine the perimeter of the phenomenon as early as possible. If available, this might facilitate a real-time response generation, such as activating the appropriate sprinklers for tackling fire before emergency squads arrive at the scene.

For such real-time needs, it might only be feasible to accomplish such processing within the network itself in a distributed manner through collaborative processing. In case where the phenomenon spans a large area, enumerating all sensors within its region to a designated node for further higher-level processing before initiating a response is likely to miss the application's response deadline. A more scalable solution might entail identifying just the nodes on the event boundary, whereby the associated geometry of the event could subsequently be deduced. Accordingly, the controller (i.e., one of the sensor nodes) could then activate the appropriate actuators to generate the required response. Such an event processing primitive is useful in the previously highlighted scenarios. The primitive for detecting nodes on the event boundary is likened to *edge detection* as in image processing by Cintalapudi and Govindan,[4] and congruously termed *boundary estimation* by Nowak and Mitra[5] in their pioneering efforts.

An edge detection algorithm tests whether a node lies on or near an edge of an application-defined event of interest using some neighborhood information. There are two factors that could limit the estimation performance, namely sensor node spatial density and the noise in the readings. Since edge detection is a well-known primitive in image processing with efficient algorithms available for centralized processing, they could be naturally applied towards sensor data. Liu *et al.*[6] presented a centralized scheme based on Hough transforms to detect and track events. This transformation maps a non-local phenomenon to a point in the dual-space and the locations of the sensor nodes to a set of lines that partitions the dual space. Such a transformation reduces the detection problem to finding and tracking the point bounded by these lines. In Ref. 7, a generalized hierarchical architecture based on wavelet transforms is proposed for multi-resolution querying of regularly-placed sensor nodes. This architecture is demonstrated to be useful for queries involving non-local phenomenon such as edges that span beyond a node's radio range. Inspired by Ref. 7, Nowak and Mitra[5] presented a multi-hierarchical scheme for estimating the boundary of a large-scale phenomenon by sharing of lower dimensional statistics (against sharing all readings) with ancestral nodes within the hierarchy and pruning of irrelevant branches. Even though this scheme is shown to achieve optimal error-energy tradeoff, the model did not consider the cost of forming and maintaining such a hierarchical structure.

In Ref. 4, three localized algorithms are proposed based on ideas in statistical thresholding, image processing and pattern recognition. The statistical scheme involves testing a Boolean function of neighbor values against a predefined application threshold. In their second scheme, they applied the Prewit filter algorithm from image processing by computing the gradients in x and y directions. If the composite gradient is larger than a threshold, an edge node is declared. The final scheme is based on the pattern recognition classifier (PR-Classifier), which aims to classify nodes into a bipartite set of similar and dissimilar values. The partition is validated against a *partition validity measure*.[8] A successful partition implies the presence of an edge. It is found that PR-Classifier performed the best as it explicitly encodes the notion of location of the nodes in its estimation, and it does not require a threshold to influence its performance. Using a similar approach to Prewit filtering as above, Devaguptapu and Krishnamachari[9] demonstrated that an image-processing based scheme is amenable for edge detection but it is highly sensitive to node density and nodes' radio range. For an optimal performance, all the above schemes require neighborhood information greater than immediate neighbors. Moreover, it is unclear how these approaches would perform against irregular event geometries. In Ref. 10, we proposed a localized edge detection scheme based on basic geometric rules and trigonometry. As it uses one-hop neighborhood information, its message overhead is just linear in number of neighbors. It depends on a simple *tangent fitting* process.

In this chapter, we extend this algorithm to be resilient against random isolated measurement errors, which may be due to faulty equipment and they are likely to be uncorrelated.[11] Unlike other localized algorithms, our approach is applicable to convex as well as non-convex regions irrespective of the event area. To highlight its performance gain, it is compared against the best localized edge detection from Ref. 4. We find our proposal readily outperformed PR-Classifier over a broad range of operating conditions and scenarios in terms of accuracy, energy budget as well as robustness against random errors.

The rest of the chapter is organized as follows. In Sec. 2, our relevant terminology and system assumptions are defined. The details of the proposed algorithm are then given in Sec. 3. The mechanisms used to improve its robustness against isolated errors are also explained there along with the benchmark PR-Classifier algorithm. The results from our extensive simulations are presented and discussed in Sec. 4, followed by some concluding remarks in Sec. 5.

29.2. Assumptions and Terminology Definition

Based on the adopted application, sensor nodes can be carefully deployed in a grid-like topology or randomly dispersed on a plane due to terrain inaccessibility. The main requirement for our purpose is that each node knows its location perhaps using some kind of localization technique.[12] Although we assumed a node location is specified by (x, y), our proposed algorithm is readily applicable in a 3D space.

The notion of event edge is defined in Ref. 4. Just for completeness and ease of exposition of the proposed algorithm later, we highlight the core definitions and concepts here. The initial step in event edge detection is for the nodes to discover which sensor readings are *interesting*. We assume that the range of interest is pre-defined by the application, or may be learnt by monitoring the normal conditions over time such that they can recognize interesting event readings.[13] Accordingly, a reasonable data threshold is defined at each sensor node that enables it to ascertain whether its reading corresponds to an event. However, it is still possible for the nodes with faulty sensors to report an event when they are outside the affected region. Similarly, a sensor node within the event region may report a non-event reading. Such reporting is said to contradict the *ground truth*. To counter such problems, we may resort to use a probabilistic mechanism to isolate uncorrelated faults, say using the Bayesian algorithm presented in Ref. 11. In our case, this however entails dual broadcasts by each node with an *interesting* value (i.e., one for announcement of its reading, and the next for announcing its confidence), resulting in significant overhead. Instead, it is more energy efficient if the edge detection algorithm itself exhibits sufficient robustness against such errors. The latter approach is adopted here to minimize the overhead of our event processing algorithm, while exhibiting error resilience.

As all considered events here span an area, nodes located within this region are termed *affected* nodes. Otherwise, they are *unaffected* nodes. The edge of a phenomenon is the imaginary boundary between these sets, i.e., the set of all points (x, y) where the sets intersect. This is the *ideal edge*, and represents the ground truth that bounds the event region. However, due to the deployment artifact and finite limit of the sensor node density, this edge could only be approximated. In one such approximation, a sensor node may declare itself to be on an event edge, if it is closer to the ideal edge than any of its neighbors, as shown in Fig. 29.1. All shaded nodes represent affected nodes and the numbered nodes are the edge nodes. Even though node 4 is not on the ideal edge, it is the nearest node to this

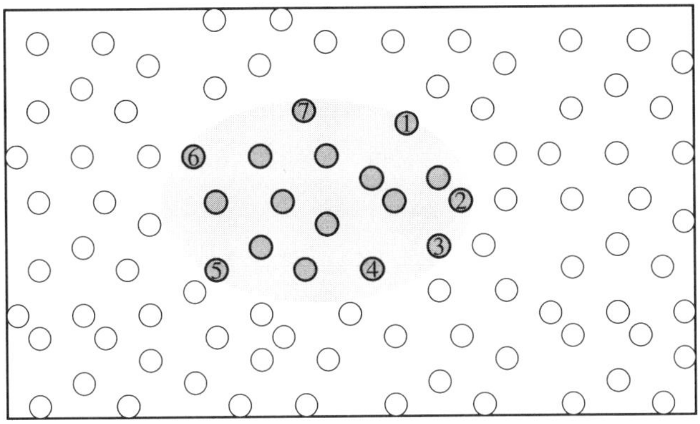

Fig. 29.1. The shaded area represents an event region of affected nodes. The edge nodes are numbered, and the other affected nodes are in the interior.

edge than its neighbors. In this example, the edge node set forms a convex region encapsulating all other affected nodes. We initially exploit the notion of convexity of some special class of event regions to perform efficient edge detection. However, to ensure the effectiveness of our proposal against non-convex regions, we further introduce additional rules based on some statistical properties as explained further, which simultaneously handles sensor errors.

29.3. Localized Edge Detection

When an event of interest breaks out on the monitored terrain, some nodes sensing within the affected region capture the phenomenon. However, to be able to draw a conclusive view of the event, those affected nodes should exchange their information with the neighbors to discover the extent of the event. Even though the sink could readily compute this information with complete network knowledge, some applications might have stringent latency requirement or reporting needs that discounts any offline processing idea. Moreover, more energy savings could be realized if we could trade off between communication and in-network processing. In the following subsections, two localized edge detection algorithms are described. The first is the proposed T-Fit algorithm based on simple geometric principles, whereas the latter is the pattern recognition-based algorithm reported to be the best in Ref. 4. Also, we suggest some improvements to the latter algorithm using additional rules to reduce its time complexity, besides being presented for the sake of completeness and clarity to aid the comparative arguments drawn later in the results section.

29.3.1. *The T-Fit algorithm*

As stated before, the proposed algorithm utilizes a form of tangent fitting to perform the edge test. Before a tangent segment is drawn, it is necessary to identify two farthest nodes from the neighborhood. In order to detect nodes on the edge of the

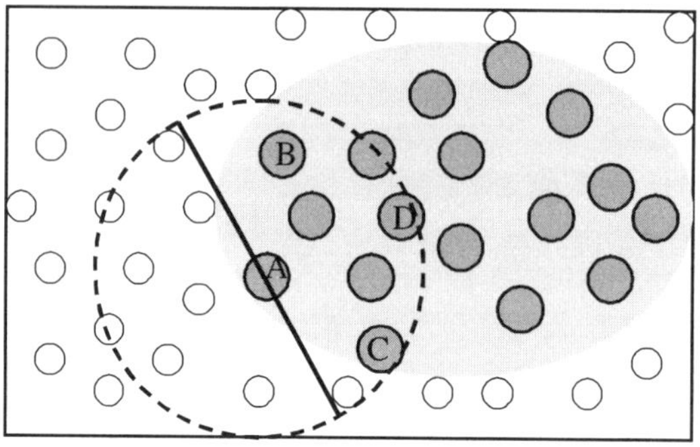

Fig. 29.2. A convex event-affected region is shown as a shaded area with affected nodes. Dashed circle centered at node A represents its radio range. A tangent segment is drawn on node A parallel to its farthest affected neighbors of B and C. From this tangent-fit test, node A is an edge node.

affected region, each affected node broadcasts an urgent message upon detecting an event after some random backoff. From these messages, the nodes gather the extent of the event coverage by populating its neighbor table. Based on this neighborhood information, an affected node classifies its affected neighbors into four quadrants on a Cartesian coordinate system with the current node as the origin. The node is on the boundary of a convex region, if the tangent drawn parallel to its farthest two nodes borders the rest of the affected neighbors. More specifically, the node is an edge node, if the angle between itself as the vertex and its farthest two neighbors is smaller than π radian, as shown in Fig. 29.2. Even though the radio range of node A is drawn as a perfect circle in this figure, it is only for visual convenience. T-Fit does not demand isotropic communications. Any resulting neighborhood from imperfect radio propagation can be used to identify the equivalent nodes B and C to represent the tangent.

As the nodes are classified into four quadrants, if the affected neighbors are only populated in two quadrants, such a node is highly likely to be on the boundary, like node A in Fig. 29.2. However, if the neighbors are populated in all four quadrants, such a node is surely not on the boundary, like node D. When the neighboring nodes are populated in either one or three quadrants, more careful considerations are required. The former situation might represent an isolated erroneous sensor reading, whereas the latter might imply an edge node if the neighbors are inside the tangent. To clarify our solution for the first case, Fig. 29.3 depicts a situation where a convex region has a valid edge node in A whose neighbors are only populated in one quadrant. As such, as long as a node has a certain number of affected nodes as neighbors, it is deemed eligible as an edge. To determine such a *necessary* condition, we resorted to some empirical evaluations, as described in the next subsection. Even though this condition may not be *sufficient* in all cases, it is found to perform extremely well against numerous scenarios as demonstrated later.

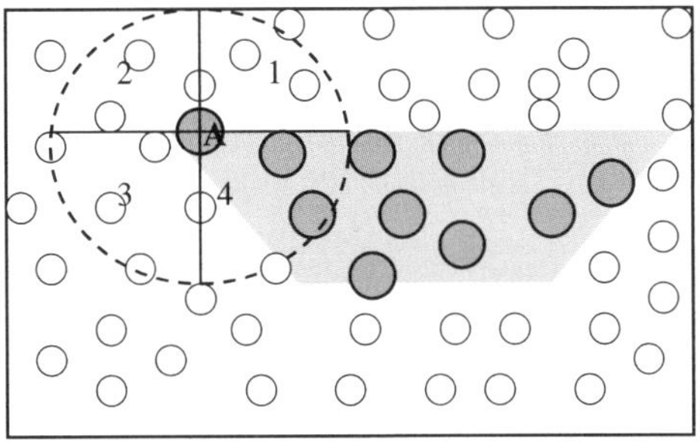

Fig. 29.3. A convex trapezoidal region that may have been bounded by a non-natural artifact. Node A is a valid edge node with all its affected neighbors populated only in the fourth quadrant.

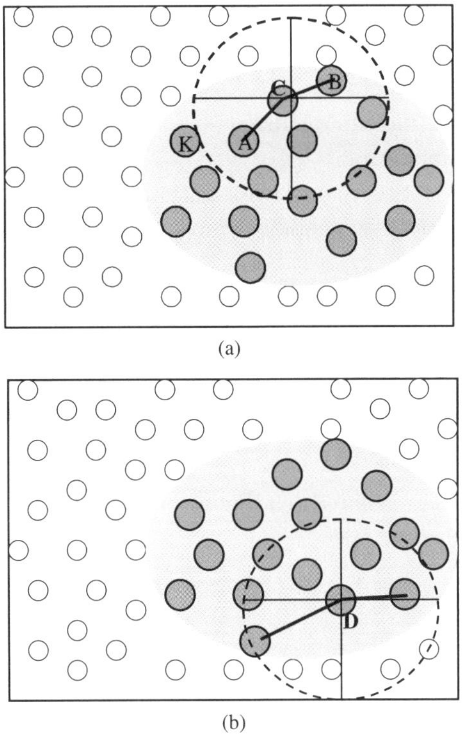

Fig. 29.4. Tangent-fit test for edge detection on nodes C and D with their affected neighboring nodes populated in three quadrants $\{1, 3, 4\}$ and $\{1, 2, 3\}$, respectively. (a) Node C is on edge as the angle is lesser than π radian; (b) Node D is not on the edge.

For the latter case where neighbors are populated in exactly three quadrants, we need to determine the node's farthest two affected nodes across diagonal quadrants. If the angle between these nodes is smaller than π radian, it is on the edge as depicted in Fig. 29.4(a). At first glance, it might appear odd that node C is deemed an edge node. One might think that if a tangent is drawn parallel to nodes B-K, node C might have failed the edge test. However, as previously stated, this is a localized algorithm that considers only direct neighbors, and node K is outside node C's radio range. In Fig. 29.4(b), a node that failed the edge test is depicted. To compute the angle in the tangent-test, a node has to determine its specific quadrant combination. There are four possible combinations, namely sets $\{1,2,3\}$, $\{1,3,4\}$, $\{1,2,4\}$ and $\{2,3,4\}$. Using basic trigonometry, we could then determine the angle between these nodes. The complete T-Fit algorithm is given in Algorithm 1.

Algorithm 29.1 The T-Fit Edge Detection Algorithm

```
// classify all affected neighbors into 4 quadrants with current as origin
for (all affected neighbors, n_i) {
        // compute slope from current node
        Compute slope to n_i
        Classify n_i into its quadrant
        if (n_i in quadrant j) {
                // Store some information
                Increase neighbor count in quadrant j
                Check n_i if it is the smallest or largest slope to current node
        }
}
// the next step needs improvement for error resilience (see later)
Store how many quadrants has affected neighbors → quadsAffected
// perform edge test
if (quadsAffected = 0) {
        Node has an isolated reading error
        onBoundary = false
}
else if (quadsAffected < 3)
        // need to isolate cases 1 and 2 (see later)
        onBoundary = true
else if (quadsAffected == 3) {
        Compute angle among 3 nodes from sets of non-empty quadrants
        if (angle < PI)
                onBoundary = true
}
else {
        // has neighbors in all quadrants
        onBoundary = false
}
```

From Algorithm 1, it is obvious that this algorithm has time complexity as well as message overhead in linear of number of affected nodes, and in the worst case, both are linear in number of direct neighbors. For the resource-constrained sensors, these are highly desirable properties. To improve T-Fit against sensor errors, we introduce some necessary rules further without affecting its time or space complexities.

29.3.2. *Error resilience of T-Fit*

Due to the expected long unattended operation of sensor nodes, it is possible that some sensors may gradually exhibit inaccurate readings. Some sensing hardware may lose calibration or completely fail. Moreover, during the neighbor exchange of event announcements, some of these messages may be lost due to collisions on the shared wireless channel. Thus, it is critical for any event processing algorithm to anticipate such errors and still function correctly. In order to understand the influence of neighbors, it would be useful to obtain some statistical properties of both edge and non-edge nodes in error-free environments. These tests might assist in devising some necessary conditions prior to edge test in T-Fit.

Accordingly, we performed certain empirical evaluations on different event geometries to capture relevant statistical properties based on the neighborhood information for edge detection. In these empirical tests, we specifically gathered the affected neighbor node distribution both for edge and non-edge nodes in an error-free environment. For this purpose, the monitored terrain is $100\,\text{m} \times 100\,\text{m}$ with 350 nodes uniformly randomly distributed. Each node has a 15-m radio range. Figure 29.5(a) depicts the neighbor distribution for a 30-m radius circular event region, whereas Fig. 29.5(b) shows this distribution for a rectangular $40\,\text{m} \times 80\,\text{m}$ event region. The x-axis of both graphs represents the affected node ids, ordered initially as non-edge and edge nodes, and then further sorted according to their neighbor percentages in ascending order. In both figures, it is visually obvious that internal nodes have more affected neighbors than the edge nodes, consistent with the intuition. More interestingly, even for the edge nodes bounding different event geometries, there is a minimum percentage of affected neighbors that qualifies these edge nodes. For instance, edge nodes with the minimum percentages in both figures [nodes with id 204 in Fig. 29.5(a) and 247 in Fig. 29.5(b)] have at least 30% affected neighbors. Since this property is implicitly related to radio range, it naturally varies with node degree. This fact can be adopted into the T-Fit algorithm as a *necessary qualification condition* before the edge test is performed. Thus, we chose to use 20% as minimum qualification threshold. Under uniform node deployment, this implies a threshold of 5% per quadrant, which is used to guard against spurious errors and aimed to reduce false identifications.

Based on the above analysis, we improved the robustness of T-Fit in two parts of the algorithm. Firstly, during the neighbor classification process (lines 2–13 of Algorithm 1), we store the count of affected neighbors in each quadrant. If the

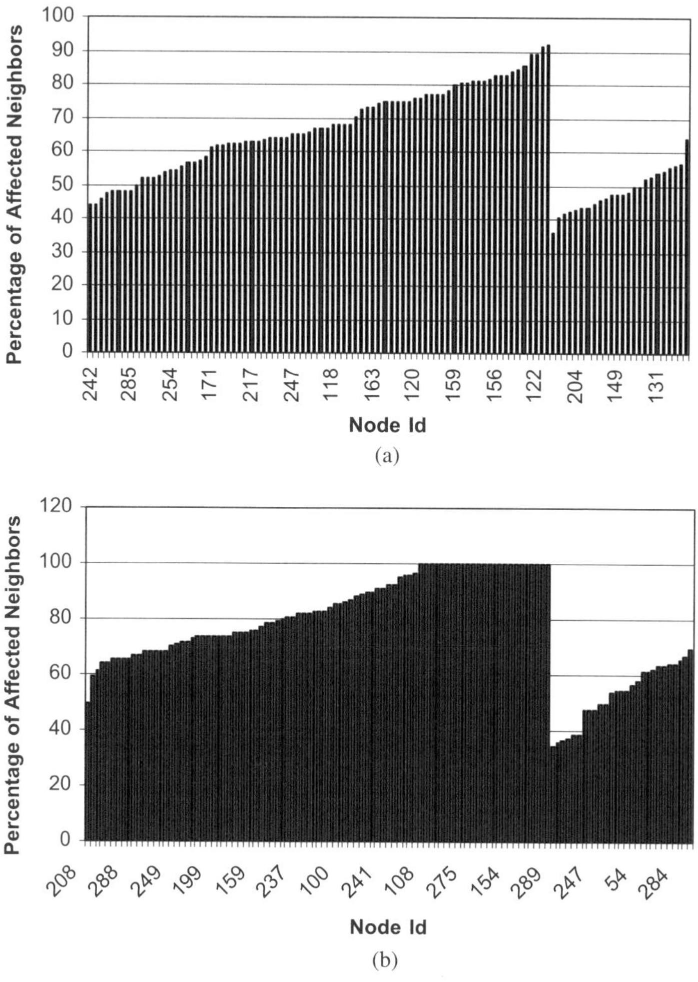

Fig. 29.5. Percentage of affected neighbor distribution against node Id: (a) circular region and (b) rectangular region.

count of a quadrant is lesser than the above 5% threshold, its effect is disregarded in the second part of T-Fit (lines 15–29 of Algorithm 1). Based on the same scenario as above, we performed simulations to test and verify the effect of this rule for a 5% independent sensor error probability. Figure 29.6 depicts T-Fit's performance before and after the inclusion of the rule. A shaded node with square bound implies a detected edge node. A node with any dashed border (round or square) is an erroneous node. It is clearly evident how this simple rule has substantially increased the number of identified edge nodes to correctly bound the actual affected region, as depicted in Fig. 29.6(b). Furthermore, the number of false positives is also reduced.

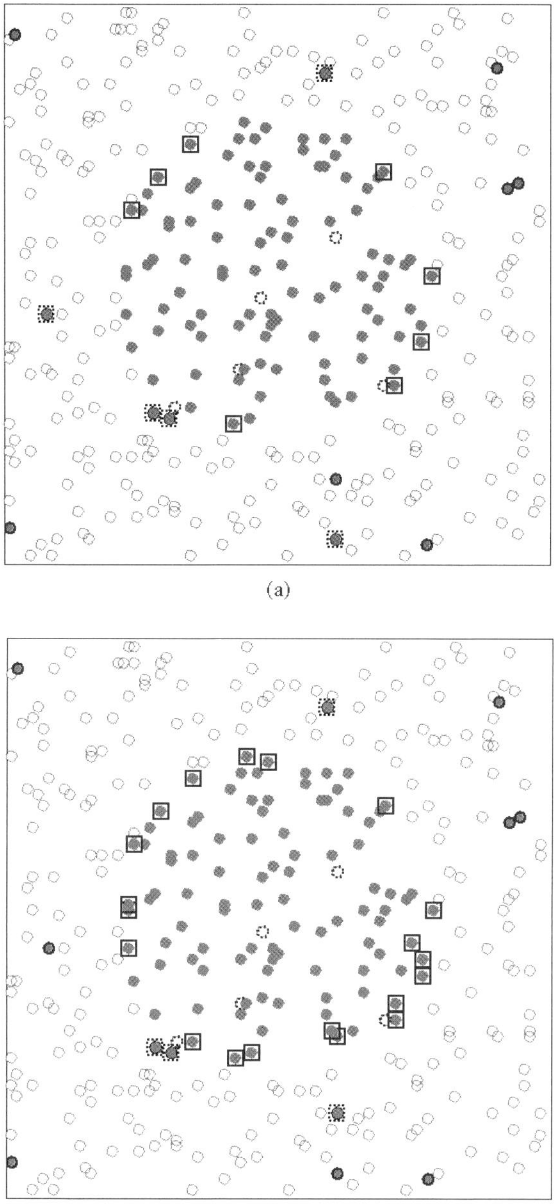

(a)

(b)

Fig. 29.6. Visualizations of circular event regions with 30-m radius. The shaded nodes indicate the presence of an event correctly (without brim) or erroneously (with black brim). The edge nodes are bounded with a square. Any dashed brim indicates a sensor reading that contradicts ground truth, and a dashed square bound represents an edge node with conflicting reading to ground truth. (a) Original T-Fit and (b) improved T-Fit.

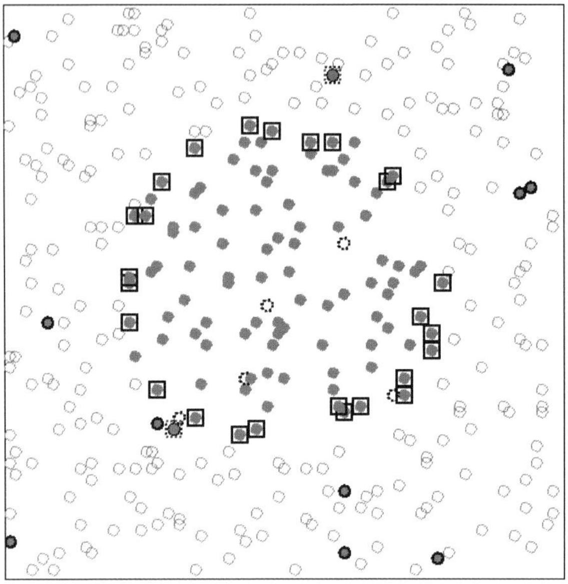

Fig. 29.7. Visualization of the improved T-Fit of a circular 30-m radius event region.

After the neighbor classification process in T-Fit, the edge test is performed based on the number of affected quadrants. The second improvement involves when less than three quadrants are affected (lines 19–20). Due to the possibility of a clump of errors, we now consider the scenarios of one and two quadrants separately. When only neighbors from one quadrant are involved, this node is definitely on the edge. For the latter case, a further rule is used to ensure only consecutive quadrants are considered for edge qualification. This rule is employed to overcome a clump of sensor errors in a neighborhood from generating false positives. For instance, if a node's affected neighbors are in quadrants 0 and 1, then this node is an edge node. However, if a node's neighbors are in non consecutive quadrants, say quadrants 1 and 3, due to spurious errors, this node is quite unlikely to be on the event edge. It is also highly likely that its own reading is inconsistent with the ground truth. Figure 29.7 depicts T-Fit's performance after the incorporation of all identified rules to counter sensor errors. For all subsequent performance evaluations, this improved T-Fit is adopted.

29.3.3. *The PR-Classifier algorithm*

In Ref. 4, it is demonstrated that the following classifier algorithm adopted from the pattern recognition literature achieved the best performance for diverse tested scenarios against statistical as well as image processing algorithms. As such, this algorithm would be an ideal benchmark for our algorithm. We will term it

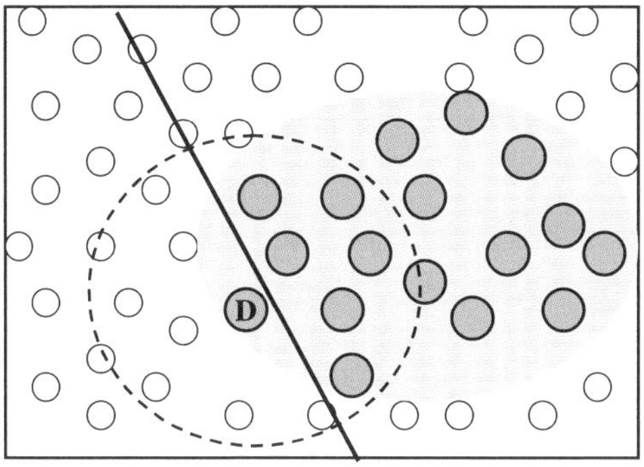

Fig. 29.8. An event-affected region is shown as a shaded area. Dashed circle centered at node D represents its probe range, is generally larger than the radio range. The line drawn on node D represents the best partition using linear classification. Even though node D appears outside the line, it is still within the tolerance range for a valid edge.

PR-Classifier. A classifier-based approach relies on the information provided by all neighbors irrespective whether they are affected or otherwise (if a neighbor does not send an urgent notification, it is deemed unaffected). Based on this information, the classifier attempts to partition data into two classes. The appropriateness of this classification may be assessed by a partition validity measure.[8] A valid partition implies the presence of an edge. In Ref. 4, a linear classifier is used to simplify the exploration of its parametric space. According to this classifier, if the valid partitioning line is within certain tolerance distance from the current reference node, this node is deemed an edge. Figure 29.8 depicts such an edge detection using PR-Classifier.

PR-Classifier aims to find a line that maximizes the number of sensors with like event-predicate values on each side of the line. Let s_r be the sensor performing edge detection. Let $L(m, c)$ be the line specifying the classifier. The classifier score J_s is defined as[4]:

$$J_{s_r}(m, c) = \left| \sum_{\forall s \in PA_{s_r}} V_s SN(mx_s + y_s + c) \right|, \tag{29.1}$$

$$SN(x) = \begin{cases} -1 & \text{if } x < 0 \\ 0 & \text{if } x = 0 \\ 1 & \text{if } x > 0 \end{cases},$$

where V_s is the event predicate (1 if detected event, otherwise -1) and PA_s is the probe region (R) of sensor s. Based on the findings in Ref. 4, the best probe range is twice the radio range. To obtain two-hop neighbors readings, we could either rely on an *any-to-any* routing protocol, limited flooding or use a higher transmit power level, if available. Typically, any-to-any routing protocol is not used in WSNs as the most common communication pattern is sensor to the sink. The latter two approaches have similar energy consequences but the last approach is slightly easier to implement. Thus, we adopt the final strategy for the collection of the readings from within the probe range. To find the optimal line based on J_s, the y-axis intersection is sampled in region $c \in [s_r \cdot y - R, s_r \cdot y + R]$ and the line slope m [which is $\tan(\theta)$] sampled in region $\theta \in [0, \pi]$. Sampling for c is modified here to reduce the sampling space without sacrificing accuracy. The J_s score is evaluated at all these sample lines, and the line with the highest value is chosen at the partitioning line. Sensor s_r is deemed a valid edge node if it lies within the selected tolerance radius (t), $(m^* x_s + y_s + c^*)/\mathrm{SQRT}(m^* + 1) \leq t$, where m^* and c^* are the optimal values from the sampling process. The PR-Classifier algorithm is accordingly summarized next as Algorithm 2. This implementation adopts better sampling range and some additional rules compared to the original specification in Ref. 4.

From Algorithm 2, it is evident that PR-Classifier should have a worse time complexity than T-Fit. Firstly, even though the sampling spaces of c and θ are reduced compared to the original specification in Ref. 4, they are still large constants (say k and m). Moreover, due to its use of two-hop neighbors, the number of nodes to process is quadratic in node degree D. This results in $O(kmD^2)$. Similarly, its message complexity is $O(D^2)$ due to its probe range. To investigate the performance of the above algorithms, we developed discrete-event simulators in C++. The results of the simulations and their analyses are given further.

29.4. Results and Discussions

Extensive simulations are performed to quantify the performance of the T-Fit algorithm as well as to benchmark against PR-Classifier. In most cases, there are 350 sensor nodes distributed randomly in a square $M \times M$ region with $M = 100\,\mathrm{m}$. To quantify the energy efficiency of these algorithms, the transceiver energy parameters are set as: $E_{\mathrm{elec}} = 50\,\mathrm{nJ/bit}$ and $\varepsilon_{\mathrm{fs}} = 10\,\mathrm{pJ/bit/m^2}$.[14] The data message size is fixed at 30 bytes. Initially, the radio range is fixed at 15 m. Unless otherwise stated, all the following investigations adopt these values as their system parameters. For the purpose of simulating errors in some scenarios, we chose to use the *bit-flipping* technique as in Ref. 4, where with some probability a reading is inverted from a non-event to an event value and vice-versa. For all simulation results in this paper, each experiment is repeated 10 times and a 95% confidence interval is obtained. Most variations are within 20% of the sample average values.

For ease of exposition, different sets of results are presented in the following order:

- Visualization of the detected edge nodes;
- The impact of non-convex event geometry;
- The impact of node density;

Algorithm 29.2 The PR-Classifier Algorithm

```
for (θ ∈ [0, π]) {
        m = tan(θ)
        for (c ∈ [s_r · y − R, s_r · y + R]) {
                for (all neighbors s in probe range) {
                // classify all nghs with respect to this line
                        if (line is neither vertical of horizontal)
                                d = m x_s + y_s + c
                        else if (line is vertical)
                                d = x_s − c
                        else
                        // horizontal line, c is x-axis intersection
                                d = y_s + c
                        if (d < 0)
                                SN = −1
                        else if (d > 0)
                                SN = 1.0
                        if (s is an affected node)
                                J_s+ = SN
                        else
                                J_s+ = −SN
                }
                if (|J_s| is the best score so far)
                // store best line
                        maxScore = |J_s|
        }
}
if (best line is not vertical)
        if ( (m* x_{s_r} + y_{s_r} + c*) / sqrt(m^2 + 1) ≤ t )
                onBoundary = true;
else
// a vertical line, use slightly different test

        if (x_s − c* ≤ t)
                onBoundary = true
```

- The impact of event region size;
- The impact of sensor reading errors.

These are the performance metrics utilized in our investigations:

- *Mean distance to boundary*: This metric represents the average distance of the identified edge nodes to the ideal event edge.
- *Total energy*: This metric represents the energy dissipated by all sensors handling message exchanges in the edge detection algorithms.

29.4.1. *Network visualizations*

For ease of comprehension and appreciation of subsequent comparative results, a set of results are identified and visualized here. For the initial set of visualizations, the event region is assumed to be circular with a 35-m radius. Figure 29.9 depicts the visualization for T-Fit with affected nodes shaded and the identified edge nodes further bounded by a square. In this visualization, it is clearly visible how T-Fit is able to correctly identify the boundary of the event as one could visually trail the edge nodes. Such accurate edge detection would assist many applications highlighted in the Introduction section to monitor the perimeter of a phenomenon of interest. To visualize the performance of T-Fit in the presence of sensor reading errors, Fig. 29.10

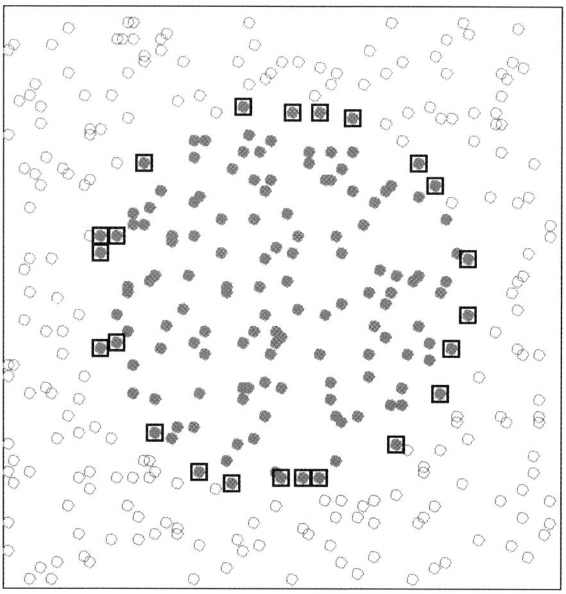

Fig. 29.9. Visualization of T-Fit for a network with 350 nodes at 15-m radio range of a circular event region with 35-m radius. The affected nodes are shaded, and the edge nodes are bounded by a square.

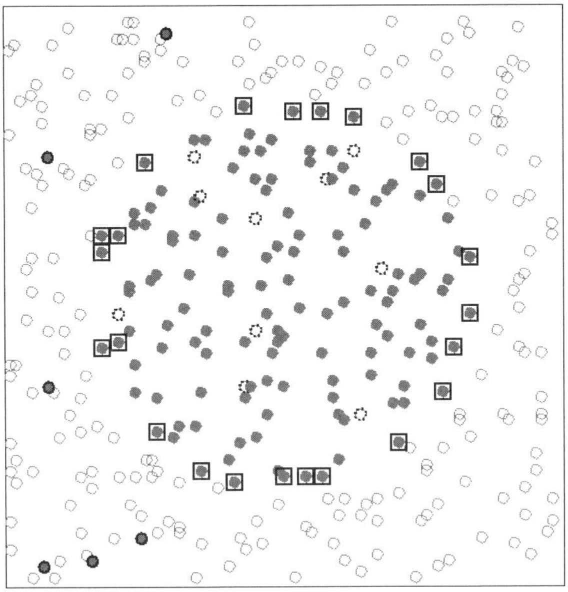

Fig. 29.10. Visualization of T-Fit for a network with 350 nodes at 15-m radio range of a circular event region with 35-m radius. Sensor readings may exhibit erroneous behavior with probability 0.05. The shaded nodes indicate the presence of an event correctly (without brim) or erroneously (with black brim). The edge nodes are bounded with a square. Any dashed brim indicates a sensor reading that contradicts ground truth, and a dashed square bound represent an edge node with conflicting reading to ground truth.

depicts the network for the same scenario as Fig. 29.9. However, it is assumed that a sensor node may exhibit reading error against the ground truth, and this error probability is set to 5%. It is evident that T-Fit is highly resilient against isolated errors by successfully identifying all valid edge nodes as in the error-free environment (Fig. 29.9). T-Fit is robust against most errors, but whenever the fault is too close to the real event region, it is not able to differentiate them (Fig. 29.7). In the latter case, it may not even be necessary to isolate them, as they are located quite near to the boundary anyway.

Figure 29.11 depicts the visualization for PR-Classifier with the affected nodes shaded and the identified edge nodes further bounded by a square. For this algorithm, its tolerance radius is set to 2 m to be comparable to T-Fit. A larger range would result in a *thicker* edge to be detected. In this visualization, it is clearly visible how PR-Classifier approximates the boundary more loosely due to its fuzzy-like classification behavior. Some of the nodes that are even nearer to the virtual boundary are left out. This may not be ideal for some applications, especially when it borders a dangerous event outbreak, like a chemical spill, that needs to be strictly inclusive. To visually depict PR-Classifier's performance in the presence of reading errors, the error probability is set to 5% as before. However, at a 2-m tolerance radius,

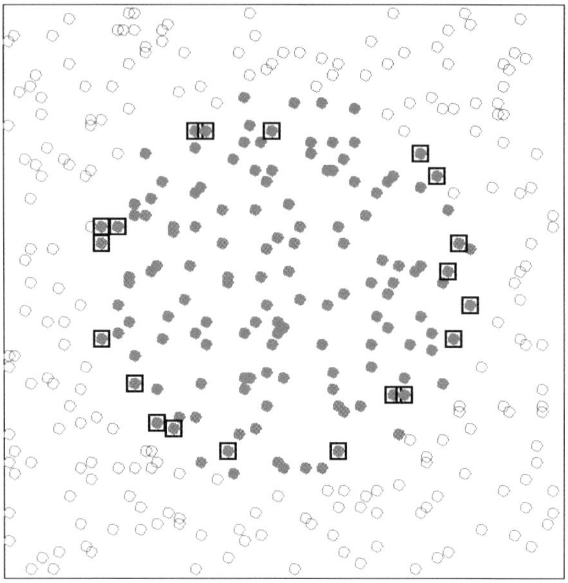

Fig. 29.11. Visualization of PR-Classifier for a network with 350 nodes at 15-m radio range of a circular event region with 35-m radius. A tolerance radius of 2 m is used to coincide with T-Fit.

PR-Classifier is unable to perform predictably. Instead, a 3-m tolerance radius is adopted. Figure 29.12 presents this visualization. This time its fuzzy classification behavior actually has had a positive effect on its outcome. Due to this classification nature, the faulty readings affected the classifier score to its benefit than in an error-free network, and as such, PR-Classifier is quite robust against these errors.

To understand the effectiveness of the above algorithms against other convex regions, we investigated their performance against rectangular event regions. For this study, two different areas are used to represent a small and a large event. Figure 29.13 depicts the edge nodes identified by our T-Fit algorithm. As this algorithm is designed for a general convex region, it is able to identify the appropriate edge nodes in both cases with a clear boundary visible from the selected edge nodes. Clearly, there are no other affected nodes lying outside of the imaginary boundary formed by these edge nodes.

As for PR-Classifier, it performs contrastingly for different sized regions for the same scenario as above. In Fig. 29.14(a), this algorithm is not able to approximate the boundary acceptably with more than 10% of the valid edge nodes are left unidentified for this smaller region. On the contrary, for a larger region [Fig. 29.14(b)] with respect to radio range, PR-Classifier performs better. If one trails the identified edge nodes, the boundary approximates more of an elliptical region instead of a rectangular one. This is clearly an artifact of its classification, whereby it requires both affected and unaffected nodes to influence the partitioning. In any case, there are

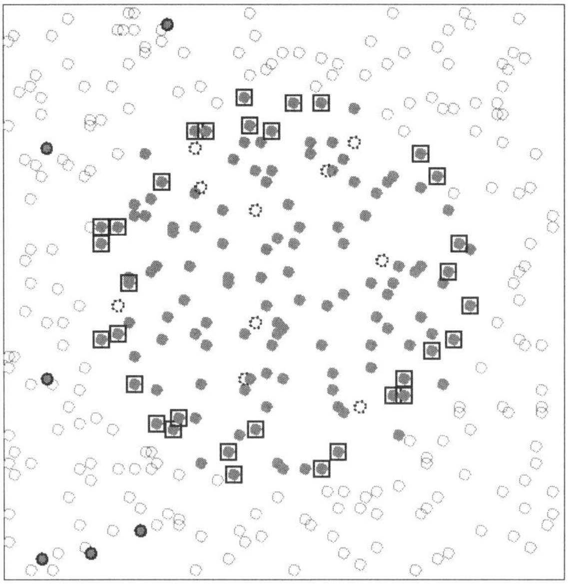

Fig. 29.12. Visualization of PR-Classifier for a network with 350 nodes at 15-m radio range of a circular event region with 35-m radius. Sensor readings may exhibit erroneous behavior with probability 0.05.

certain nodes that are even closer to the ideal edge, but left unidentified in its edge test as before. Thus, this algorithm is mostly suitable for large regions, whereas T-Fit is applicable in most scenarios.

29.4.2. *Impact of non-convex event geometry*

The initial design of T-Fit exploited the property of convex regions to improve its detection accuracy. However, this could have limited its usefulness against irregular or non-convex regions. Accordingly, T-Fit was extended as described in Sec. 29.3. Since such non-convex event geometries may be prevalent in many natural settings, it is imperative for an edge detection algorithm to perform accurately even in such environments. To simulate a non-convex region, we simply partially overlapped two convex shapes, namely two circular events with 20-m radius each. All other parameters are selected as indicated earlier. Figure 29.15 depicts the detection outcomes of both T-Fit and PR-Classifier, respectively. Even though T-Fit is not specifically designed for such geometries, it performed surprisingly accurately compared against its counterpart. We can quite readily trail the edge nodes in Fig. 29.15(a) to identify the boundary. Even though this would not have been possible with a strict tangent test, the introduction of the additional resilience rules has significantly improved its detection accuracy. As for PR-Classifier's behavior, it is consistent with the previous rectangular region test (Fig. 29.14) and similar argument applies.

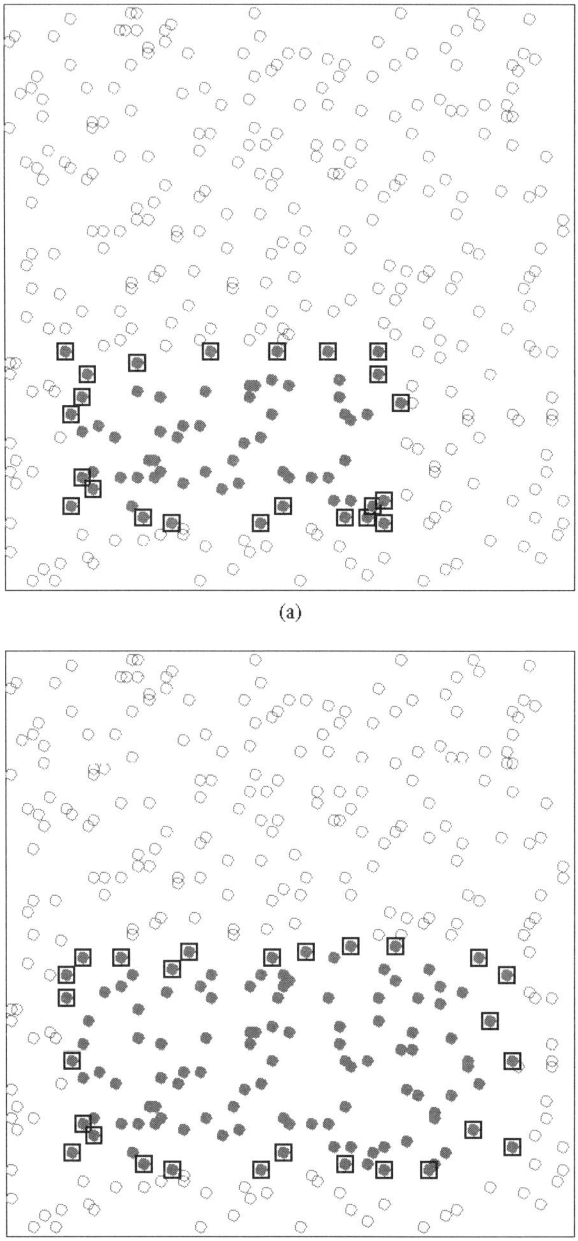

(a)

(b)

Fig. 29.13. Visualization of T-Fit for networks with 350 nodes at 15-m radio range of rectangular event regions. (a) 60 m × 30 m and (b) 80 m × 40 m.

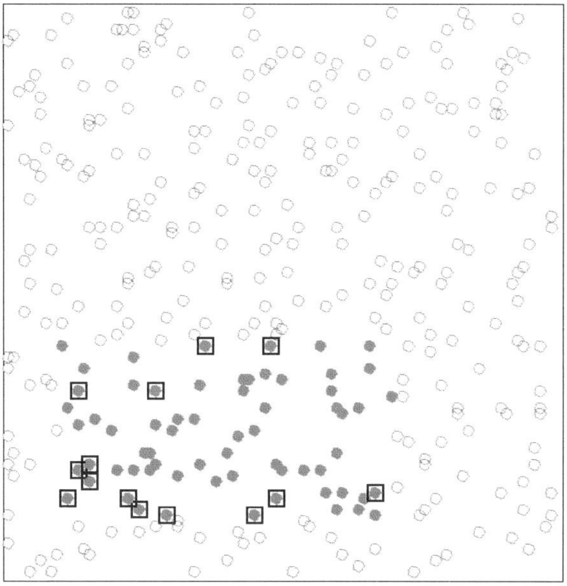

(a)

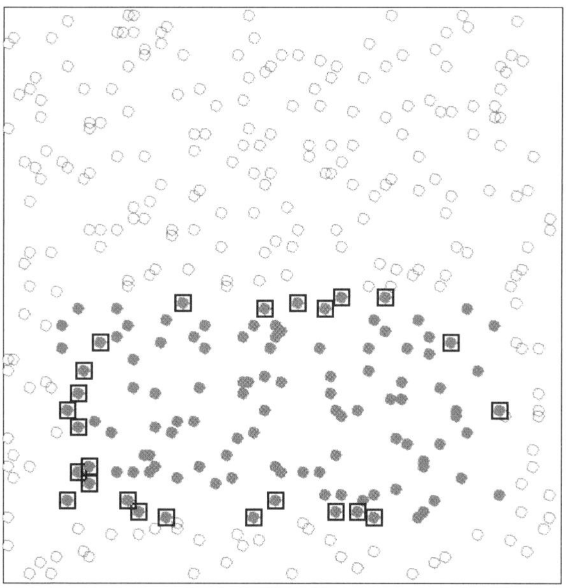

(b)

Fig. 29.14. Visualization of PR-Classifier for networks with 350 nodes at 15-m radio range of rectangular event regions. The tolerance radius is 3 m: (a) 60 m × 30 m and (b) 80 m × 40 m.

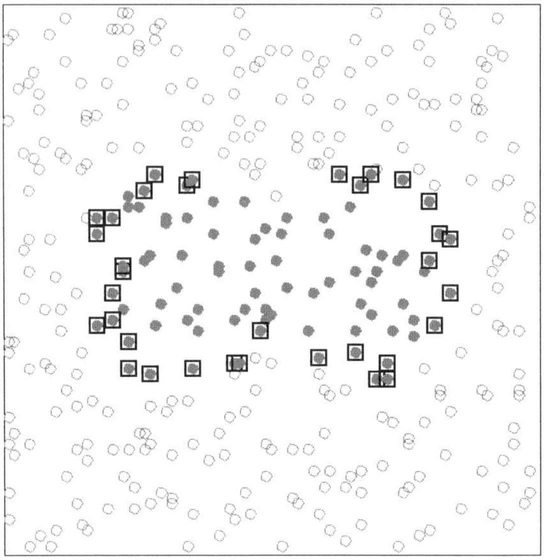

(a)

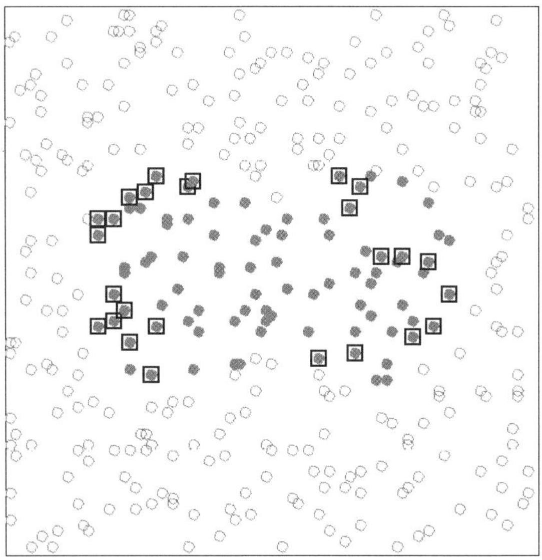

(b)

Fig. 29.15. Visualization of non-convex affected regions for networks with 350 nodes at 15-m radio range: (a) T-Fit and (b) PR-Classifier.

29.4.3. *Impact of node density*

For the rest of the results presented in this paper, the performance is obtained for circular event regions only. The resultant performance evaluations are however still

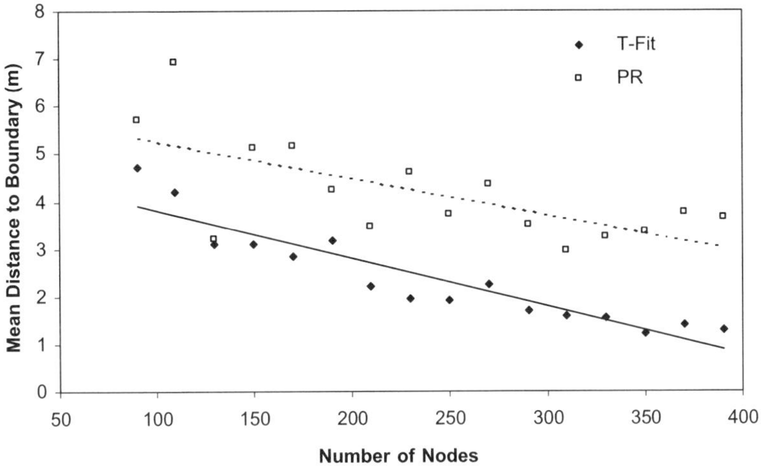

Fig. 29.16. Mean distance to event boundary against number of nodes for a 35-m circular event area and nodes with 15-m radio range.

representative of their general behavior. In this study, we examined the influence of node density on the edge detection behavior in terms of both accuracy and energy usage. For the same monitored terrain area, we varied the number of sensors in range [80, 400]. In Fig. 29.16, the mean distance of edge nodes is plotted for both algorithms. As expected, both algorithms' accuracy improved with density and the rate is almost similar. However, T-Fit achieves 40% higher accuracy on average against PR-Classifier. T-Fit almost surely identifies the nodes farthest from an event's epicenter as edges, whereas PR-Classifier may some time identifies a thick edge with many nodes within the tolerance range of the border, even when a short tolerance is used. To appreciate the energy usage behavior of both algorithms, Fig. 29.17 depicts the total energy usage plot for the same scenario. Since PR-Classifier requires two-hop neighborhood information for its best performance, its energy usage increases nearly in quadratic to number of nodes whereas it is only linear for T-Fit. This is consistent with the message overhead analysis of PR-Classifier given earlier. Thus, it is clearly evident that not only T-Fit is able to achieve higher accuracy, but it is also able to be energy efficient simultaneously meeting most needs of typical WSN applications.

29.4.4. *Impact of event area*

In this study, we examined the influence of event region size on the edge detection behavior in terms of both accuracy and energy usage. For the same monitored terrain area, we varied the event radius in range [18, 50]. An upper range limit of 50-m radius is chosen for the 100 m × 100 m terrain as any larger radius would blanket the whole terrain and the edge detection behavior would be nearly invariant.

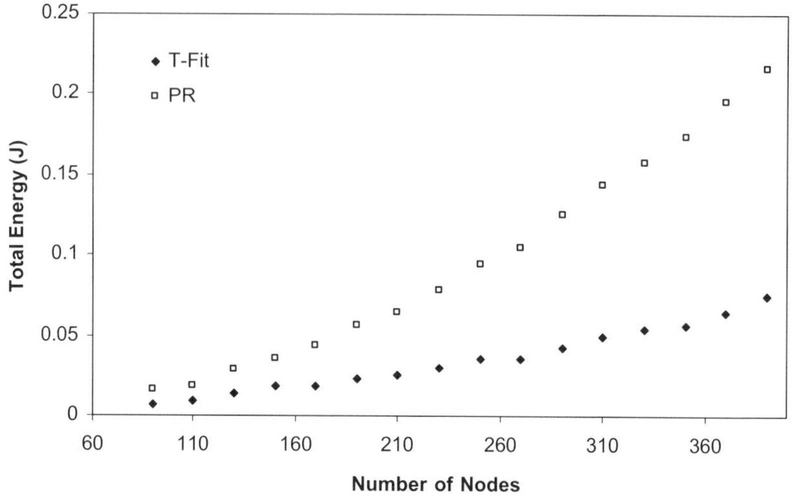

Fig. 29.17. Total energy dissipation against number of nodes for a 35-m circular event area and nodes with 15-m radio range.

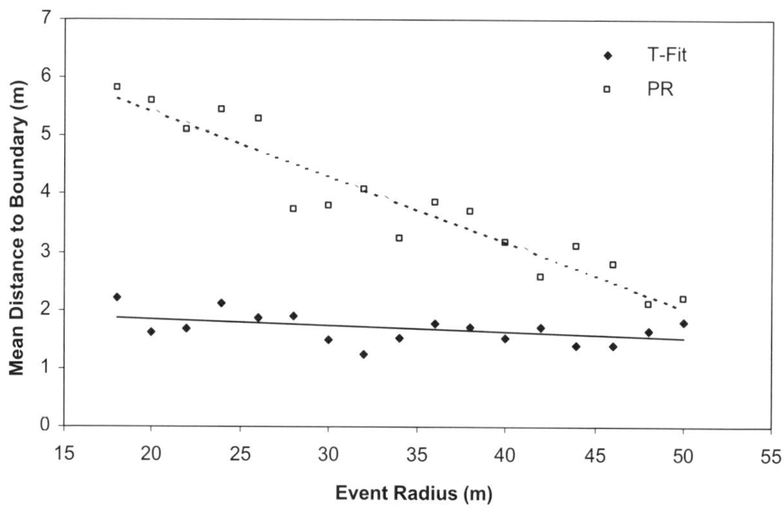

Fig. 29.18. Mean distance to event boundary against affected circular event radius for a network with 350 nodes at 15-m radio range.

In Fig. 29.18, the mean distance of edge nodes is plotted for both algorithms. Due to T-Fit's edge node identification nature, its accuracy is rather stable as the node density is fixed. It maintains the detection accuracy at around 2 m of the ideal edge. On the contrary, PR-Classifier's performance improves with the event area

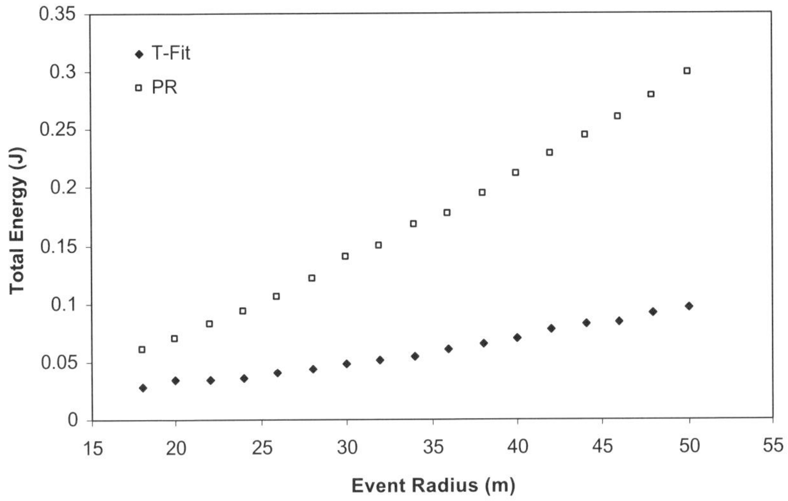

Fig. 29.19. Total energy dissipation against affected circular event radius for a network with 350 nodes at 15-m radio range.

consistent with our earlier observation. The energy dissipation behavior for the same scenario is depicted in Fig. 29.19. Similar performance as in Fig. 29.17 is seen, and similar argument applies even here.

29.4.5. *Impact of sensor reading error*

In this final set of experiments, we investigated the impact of independent sensor reading errors on both algorithms. For the same monitored terrain area and node density, we varied the event radius in range [20, 50]. In Fig. 29.20, the mean distance of edge nodes is plotted for both algorithms. As a base performance, we also included T-Fit's curve on mean distance for an error-free network (using the diamond marker). This base curve assists us in seeing the influence of errors on both algorithms. It is obvious that T-Fit performed significantly better than PR-Classifier for smaller and medium event areas. This observation is consistent with the previous results. For large event sizes, performance of both algorithms seems to converge. This is mainly due to the coverage of the event that is now almost as big as the terrain itself, where almost all nodes are affected! Naturally, both algorithms could only identify the nodes close to the terrain boundary as the edge nodes, as there are few unaffected nodes left.

To demonstrate their robustness against variable sensor errors, we varied the error probability in range [0.01, 0.05]. For this scenario, the affected circular event region area is fixed at 35-m radius. In Fig. 29.21, it is evident that T-Fit readily outperformed its competition by approximating the event edge around 2-m closer

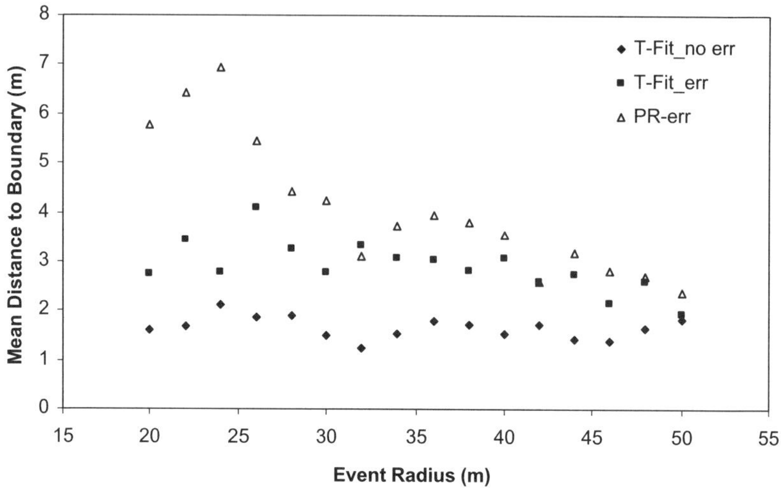

Fig. 29.20. Mean distance to event boundary against event radius for circular event regions and a network with 350 nodes at 15-m radio range. Sensor reading error is at probability 0.05.

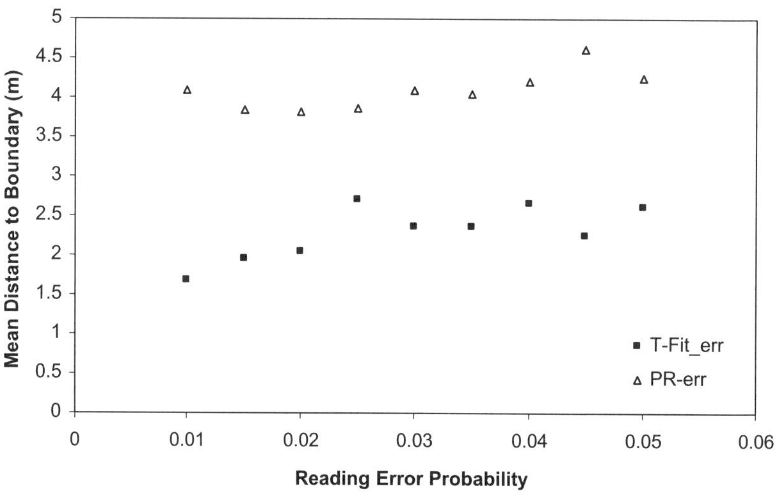

Fig. 29.21. Mean distance to event boundary against sensor error probability for a circular event region and a network with 350 nodes at 15-m radio range.

to the ground truth than the other approach. T-Fit is clearly more resilient against such independent errors. This is mainly due to the additional rules introduced after the classification step, which would disregard isolated event readings based on the adopted threshold against spurious sensor errors. As such, its robustness will be another plus-point for its adoption into WSNs.

29.5. Conclusions

As wireless sensor networks evolve from a simple sense-and-send technology towards more intelligent in-network processing, there are now more applications that could benefit from them. For certain applications whereby there is a need to respond swiftly towards a phenomenon of interest, it is also attractive to provide automated in-network actuation to minimize human intervention, which is likely to be the main source of delay. One of the identified primitive functions that should be located within the network is edge or boundary detection. Even though edge detection can be readily accomplished at the sink with the complete network knowledge probably using well-known image-processing algorithms, it is not trivial to perform them in-network in a localized manner.

In this chapter, we introduced an energy-efficient edge detection algorithm based on simple geometry. Initially, the algorithm uses tangent-fitting to identify edge nodes. However, a strict tangent test alone would fail in other scenarios such as when dealing with irregular event geometries as well as sensor errors. Therefore, T-Fit is further fitted with some qualifying conditions based on certain statistical and geometry properties to be robust in these scenarios. It is then benchmarked against one of the best localized algorithms in the literature. In addition, we also suggested further improvements towards the benchmark algorithm itself. Using extensive simulations, it is demonstrated that T-Fit readily outperformed its competition in terms of accuracy, robustness as well as energy efficiency. It performed equally well against different convex and non-convex regions. Moreover, its worst-case time and space complexities are just linear in number of neighbors.

As a primitive function, we believe this algorithm could readily be used by more complex or higher-level primitives or by the applications themselves. Some higher-level primitives that may benefit employing this edge detection technique are event area computation and event center localization. The feasibility of such an extension is left for further work.

Acknowledgments

This work was supported in part by grant ARC Discovery Project DP0664782.

References

1. R. Cristescu, B. Beferull-Lozano and M. Vetterli, *INFOCOM*, 2571–2582 (2004).
2. H. Gupta, V. Navda and S. R. Das *et al.*, *MobiHoc*, Urbana-Champaign, IL, USA, 402–413 (2005).
3. T. Melodia, D. Pompili and V. C. Gungor *et al.*, *6th ACM International Symposium on Mobile Ad Hoc Networking and Computing*, Urbana-Champaign, IL, USA, 99–110 (2005).

4. K. K. Chintalapudi and R. Govindan, *IEEE International Workshop on Sensor Network Protocols and Applications*, Anchorage, AK, USA, 59–70 (2003).
5. R. Nowak and U. Mitra, *Information Processing in Sensor Networks*, Palo Alto, CA, USA, 80–95 (2003).
6. J. Liu, P. Cheung and F. Zhao *et al.*, *1st ACM International Workshop on Wireless Sensor Networks and Applications*, Atlanta, GA, USA, 131–139 (2002).
7. D. Ganesan, D. Estrin and J. Heidemann, *ACM SIGCOMM Computer Communication Review*, **33**(1), 143–148 (2003).
8. R. O. Duda, P. E. Hart and D. G. Stork, *Pattern Classification*, 2nd ed., John Wiley and Sons (2000).
9. D. Devaguptapu and B. Krishnamachari, *SPIE Aerosense*, Orlando, FL, USA, 247–256 (2003).
10. S. Selvakennedy, *Mobile Ad-hoc and Sensor Networks*, LCNS, Springer, Berlin/Heidelberg, **4325**, 588–599 (2006).
11. B. Krishnamachari and S. Iyengar, *IEEE Transactions on Computers*, **53**(3), 241–250 (2004).
12. D. Niculescu, *IEEE Network*, **18**, 24–29 (2004).
13. R. A. Maxion, *Emergent Computation* (1991).
14. W. B. Heinzelman, A. P. Chandrakasan and H. Balakrishnan, *IEEE Transactions on Wireless Communications*, **1**(4), 660–670 (2002).

Chapter 30

Enabling Periodic Monitoring Applications in Wireless Sensor Networks: Design and Analysis of an Efficient MAC Protocol

Miguel A. Erazo*, Yi Qian†, Kejie Lu† and Domingo Rodriguez†

**School of Computer and Information Sciences*
Florida International University, Miami, FL 33199

†Department of Electrical and Computer Engineering
University of Puerto Rico at Mayagüez, Mayagüez, PR 00681

In this chapter, we present a new medium access control (MAC) protocol for wireless sensor networks with periodic monitoring applications. In particular, we design a listen-sleep time schedule for sensor nodes, and we propose a path establishment algorithm for route selection. To evaluate the performance of the proposed protocol, we conduct detailed analysis and simulations. Numerical results show that, compared to existing MAC protocols, our new protocol can significantly reduce energy consumption, average packet delay, and packet loss due to collisions.

30.1. Introduction

Wireless sensor networks (WSNs) consist of battery-operated sensor devices with computing, data processing, and communication components. In the past few years, extensive research has been conducted in this area due to the wide range of applications of WSNs. Amongst a variety of challenges in WSN design and implementation, energy conservation is one of the most critical issues since batteries are the only energy source to power the sensor nodes.

Similar to other shared-medium networks, *medium access control* (MAC) protocols enable the successful operation of the WSN. In general, the MAC protocol in a WSN must achieve two goals. The first is the creation of the network infrastructure. Since thousands of sensor nodes are densely scattered in a sensor field, the MAC scheme must efficiently establish communication links for data transfer. This forms the basic infrastructure needed for wireless communication hop by hop and gives the sensor network self-organizing ability. The second objective is to fairly and efficiently share communication resources between sensor nodes.

In the literature, several MAC protocols for WSNs have been proposed with a goal of increasing the network lifetime by conserving energy. Instead of investigating the MAC for a general WSN scenario, our goal in this book chapter is to develop a new MAC protocol for WSNs for periodic monitoring, e.g., environmental monitoring. In our scheme, the *Base Station* (BS) starts and maintains synchronization. After nodes are synchronized, they only wake up on specific times when a sample of a variable is taken.

The main contributions of this book chapter are design and analysis of a new MAC protocol for WSNs. In particular:

- We design a staggered listen-sleep time schedule with which nodes only turn on their radios when a sample is taken with the objective of consuming the least possible amount of energy.
- We propose an algorithm to make sure that only one specific route (path) is active at a time. With this, we intend to lower delay, collisions and energy consumption for sensor nodes.
- We propose a simple and unique synchronization in the whole network.
- Finally, we compare the proposed new MAC performance with some of the previous MAC protocols in terms of energy consumption, delay and packet loss in simulations. We show that our new protocol reduces delay and collisions dramatically.

In the remainder of the chapter, a brief survey of related works is presented in Sec. 30.2. The description of our protocol is in Sec. 30.3. Performance analysis and simulation results are presented in Sec. 30.4. Finally, the conclusions are given in Sec. 30.5.

30.2. Related Work

In the literature, many protocols have been proposed for WSNs. Most of them aim to achieve low energy consumption in transmitting packets between nodes. These protocols also have the goals of low delay and minimum packet loss.

Ye *et al.*[1] proposed S-MAC for WSN. S-MAC uses a few novel techniques to reduce energy consumption and support self-configuration. First, nodes form *virtual clusters* based on common sleep schedules to reduce control overhead and enable traffic-adaptive wake-up. Second, S-MAC uses in-channel signaling to avoid overhearing unnecessary traffic. Finally, S-MAC applies *message passing* to reduce contention latency.

Ye *et al.*[2] introduced SCP-MAC, which uses *Scheduled Channel Polling* (SCP) to achieve more energy savings than other protocols that use coordinated transmissions and listen periods. The contributions of SCP-MAC are the ultra low duty cycles it achieves and its capability to adapt to variable traffic loads. Dam *et al.*[3] proposed T-MAC, a contention-based MAC protocol for WSNs. Lu *et al.*[4] proposed D-MAC, a protocol whose objective is to achieve very low latency.

Mainwaring *et al.*[5] provided an in-depth study of applying WSNs to real-world habitat monitoring. A set of system design requirements are developed that cover the hardware design of the nodes, the design of the sensor network, and the capabilities for remote data access and management.

In our previous work,[6] we proposed SEA-MAC for WSN specialized for environmental monitoring applications. SEA-MAC focused on reducing energy consumption in environmental monitoring applications. Compared to S-MAC,[1] SEA-MAC reduces the *duty cycle* (DC) of nodes, and thus lowers drastically idle listening.

In this book chapter, we propose a new MAC protocol to achieve even lower energy consumption for periodic monitoring applications. Our protocol takes advantage of the fact that the traffic pattern is periodic to achieve low energy consumption levels. Furthermore, our approach focuses on reducing packet delay and collisions.

30.3. Protocol Design Overview

30.3.1. *Overview of proposed protocol*

In,[7] Boukerche *et al.* described 3 types of applications for WSN: (1) Critical conditions monitoring, e.g., fire incident, (2) Periodic monitoring, e.g., sensing temperature every minute, and (3) Query-based application scenarios. In this book chapter, we focus on the second type of applications, namely periodic monitoring. For such applications, we assume that it is desirable to sample physical variables periodically. In this way, we know in advance how many samples must be taken in an interval of time and the specific instants when they are taken. In our protocol, nodes periodically wake up when a sample is taken. In this way, nodes save a lot of energy in avoiding idle listening between two consecutive samples.

The objectives of the design of our new MAC protocol are the following: first, lower energy consumption by reducing duty cycle; second, reduce delay and collisions; and finally, make synchronization simpler and unique in the whole network.

In a wide-area large-scale network, it is likely that packets experience a huge delay, particularly when nodes are far away from the closest sink or base station. For online monitoring, it is desirable the delay to be as low as possible. For that purpose, we propose a staggered wakeup schedule which is similar to that proposed in Ref. 4. In our scheme, nodes on a path wake up sequentially to forward a packet to the next hop, so sleep delay is reduced. Also, we did not use the *ready-to-send/clear-to-send* (RTS/CTS) mechanism for transmitting data packets whose destination is the BS. That reduces delay even more.

If the density of nodes within a network is high, collisions are very likely to occur. In order to reduce collisions, we propose an algorithm to compute time schedules such that collisions should not occur.

Synchronization for our protocol has also been designed to be simple and robust. We intend to lower the frequency of synchronization losses in the network. Furthermore, the synchronization is unique for the whole network given that only the base station starts and maintains synchronization while the other nodes only broadcast synchronization packets generated previously.

30.3.2. *Time schedule*

We can identify three main communication patterns in sensor network applications. The first involves local data exchange among nearby nodes. The second involves the dispatch of control and synchronization packets from the BS to nodes. The third and most significant traffic pattern in WSN is data gathering from sensor nodes to the sink BS. We have proposed delay and collision reduction techniques for the third type of traffic pattern and created a separate active time slot for control packets.

Our protocol uses a schedule in which nodes only wake up when a sample from environment is taken. No periodic sleep/listen schedule will be necessary as it was proposed in most existing protocols, including S-MAC,[1] T-MAC[3] or D-MAC.[4] Furthermore, it will not be necessary to have a short wake-up tone for senders to guarantee rendezvous as it was in SCP-MAC[2] since nodes know in advance when they have to turn on its radio to sample monitoring variables.

An example of the proposed scheduling scheme is shown in Fig. 30.1. In the proposed time schedule, we stagger the schedule to lower the delay in the network, which is similar to the protocol proposed in Ref. 4. Furthermore, we design our time

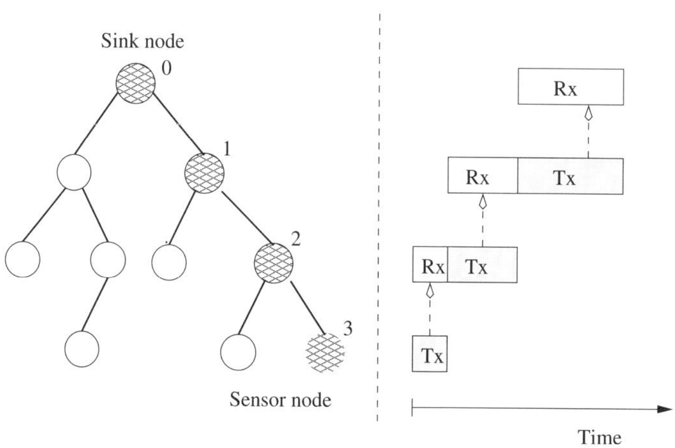

Fig. 30.1. An example of the proposed scheduling scheme.

Table 30.1. List of parameters used for the scheduling algorithm.

Parameter	Description
$t_{TX,i,j}$	Duration of transmitting slot of node i within route j
$t_{RX,i,j}$	Duration of receiving slot of node i within route j
$t_{SP,i,j}$	Duration of sleeping slot of node i within route j
$\|R_j\|$	number of nodes on route j
t_B	Time to transmit or receive a byte
L_{DATA}	length of data packet in bytes
L_{SYNC}	length of synchronization packet in bytes
L_{ACK}	length of ACK packet in bytes
P_{TX}	power for transmitting
P_{RX}	power for receiving
P_L	power for listening
P_{SP}	power in sleeping
T_{DATA}	transmission duration of data packet
T_{SYNC}	transmission duration of synchronization packet
r_{DATA}	rate for transmitting a data packet
r_{SYNC}	rate for transmitting a synchronization packet
t_{TX}	the average duration that a node is transmitting.
t_{RX}	the average duration that a node is receiving.
t_{SP}	the average duration that a node is sleeping.

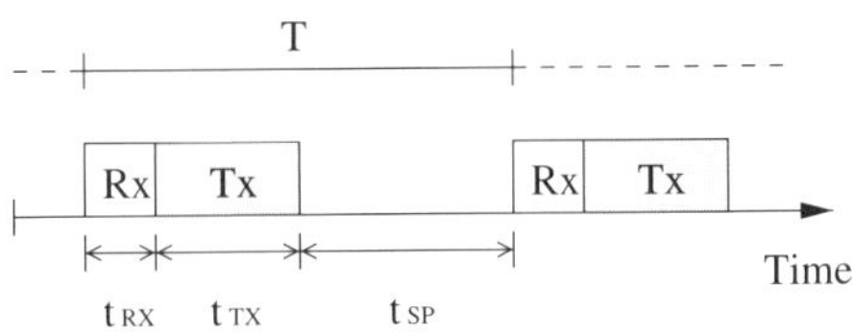

Fig. 30.2. Scheduling parameters.

schedule in such a way that all data gathered from sensor nodes be delivered to the sink in just one active period, i.e., a node would only wake up once in a period to receive and transmit packets destined to the sink.

Figure 30.1 shows that, as a node approaches the sink, its receiving and transmitting intervals get larger. This happens because the closer a node is to the sink, the more data it receives from other nodes and the more packets it has to relay.

To facilitate further discussion, we define a number of parameters in Table 30.1.

In our protocol, the time schedule of a node is shown in Fig. 30.2. Within a period (T), a node has a slot to receive packets (t_{RX}), a slot to transmit packets (t_{TX}), and a slot to sleep (t_{SP}). We denote the duration of an active slot as t_{LP} which is the sum of t_{RX} and t_{TX}.

As stated above, t_{TX}, t_{RX} and t_{SP} (schedule parameters) are not supposed to get the same value for all nodes within a route. Their values depend on the position of a node within a particular route. To simplify the discussion, we index all nodes in a route such that the index of the sink is 0, and the node connected to the sink is 1, as illustrated in Fig. 30.1. Values of schedule parameters for a particular node within a route are given by the following expressions:

$$t_{TX,i,j} = t_B \times L_{DATA} \times (|R_j| - i + 1), \tag{30.1}$$

$$t_{RX,i,j} = t_B \times L_{DATA} \times (|R_j| - i), \tag{30.2}$$

$$t_{SP,i,j} = t - t_{TX,i,j} - t_{RX,i,j}. \tag{30.3}$$

30.3.3. *Route partition*

To further reduce the delay and to reduce collisions, we propose a mechanism, namely, *route partition*. Route partition is a mechanism through which only one route is active at a time. When only one route is active at a time and using the staggered time schedule described in the previous subsection, our protocol nullifies the *hidden terminal* problem without using the RTS/CTS packet exchange or the virtual carrier sensing.[1] Figure 30.3 shows an example of route partition.

In our protocol, the sink computes the time schedule that every node in the network will follow. A node within the network can be involved in more than one route and consequently will follow more than one schedule.

Route partition has two states: *initialization* and *maintenance*. Nodes are in initialization state right after the network has been deployed in field, while nodes are

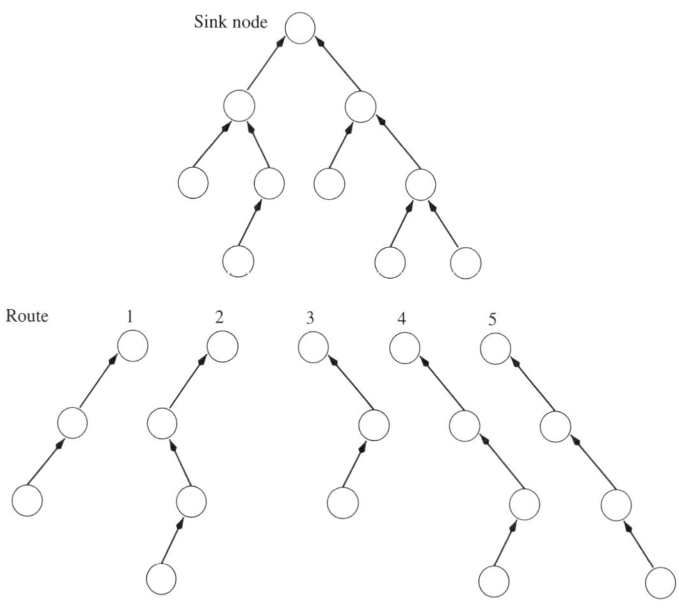

Fig. 30.3. Route partition mechanism.

running in the maintenance state continuously after the network has converged. At the beginning of the initialization state, sensor nodes dispatch *route advertisement* (RA) packets to the sink. Since nodes are contending to send their respective RA packets, RTS/CTS mechanism is used temporarily to avoid collisions. Moreover, a suitable routing protocol is used during the initialization state. As RA packets traverse the network, each node will add its address into the packet. In this way, each RA originated by a sensor node contains the complete route from the node to the sink. Once the sink has received RA packets from all sensor nodes, it runs an algorithm to compute time schedules of all sensor nodes. Time schedules will be disseminated through *schedule dissemination* (SD) packets. Again, RTS/CTS mechanism is used in this state to prevent collisions. Upon receiving SD packets, nodes will start to follow their respective time schedule and will enter the maintenance state. As part of the maintenance state, sensor nodes may send RA packets and the sink broadcasts SD packets periodically to adapt to possible changes.

Due to the staggered time schedule that we proposed in our protocol, nodes start their active periods at different times depending on their position within a route. As shown in Fig. 30.1, nodes that are farther from the sink start transmitting earlier than those closer to the sink. We denote the offset in time between the start of transmission of furthest node from the sink in route j and the start of transmission of node i within the same route as $\phi_{i,j}$. Figure 30.4 depicts the concept of offset within a route. The sink, when broadcasting SD packets for a particular route, includes the sampling period (T), the time when a node starts to follow the time schedule of a particular route (TS), and the route size $|R_j|$. Then, every sensor node computes its own offset $\phi_{i,j}$ according to the following expressions:

$$\phi_{i,j} = \phi_{1,j} - (i-1)|R_j| + \frac{i(i+1)}{2} - 1, \tag{30.4}$$

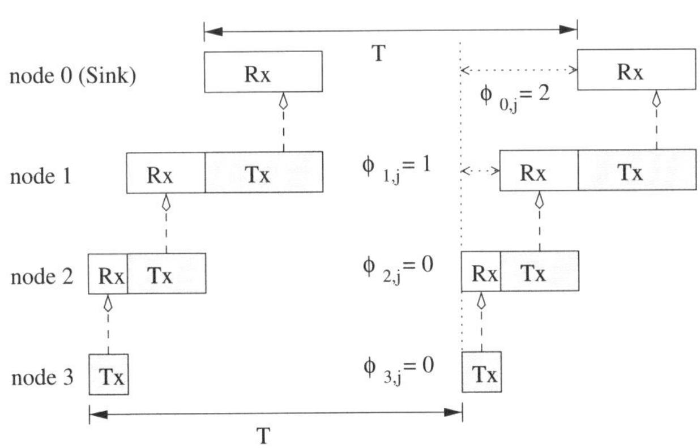

Fig. 30.4. An example of the offset time at each node.

Algorithm 30.1 Time schedule algorithm at sensor node.

SD packet received
if Destination address = My address **then**
  Compute $t_{TX,i,j}$, $t_{RX,i,j}$, T and ϕ_{ij}
  if I am not the last node on the route. **then**
    Forward SD packet
  end if
end if
Idle

Algorithm 30.2 Path computation algorithm at the sink node.

RA from all nodes received
for All unused routes
  Add a route to the list of routes to be disseminate
  Tag all subpaths as used
end for
The list of routes to be disseminated is complete

and

$$\phi_{1,j} = \frac{|R_j|^2}{2} - \frac{3|R_j|}{2} + 1. \tag{30.5}$$

Upon receiving SD packets, sensor nodes follow Algorithm 30.3.3, whereby time schedule can be computed for each route a sensor node belongs to. The assumptions that we take into account are the following:

- Sensor nodes are fixed without mobility.
- Route to the sink are durable and are established by a suitable routing protocol.
- The sink is the only destination of data packets.

As stated in previous paragraphs, the sink receives RA packets from all sensor nodes within the network. Consequently, after some time interval, the sink should have N packets (number of nodes in the network). Then, the sink builds up a matrix of routes called R in which every column represents the path from a sensor node to the sink. A particular element of R, $r_{i,j}$ is the address of a node that is $i-1$ nodes away from the sink that belongs to route j. We denote a path j as P^j which is a set of all node addresses belonging to a column j of R. In this way, $P^j = \{r_{i,j} | 1 \leq i \leq |R_j|, \forall j\}$. A path P^k will be called a subpath of P^j if $P^k \subset P^j$. In this case, we say that P^j contains P^k and only P^j should be broadcasted in a SD packet. Algorithm 30.3.3 is the proposed algorithm to compute the set of routes which will be broadcasted in SD packets. The algorithm will output a matrix R' which will be used by the sink to broadcast all remaining useful routes in SD packets.

30.3.4. *Energy consumption analysis*

We consider a network of j paths, which correspond to the number of columns of matrix R', and which is the output of Algorithm 30.3.3. We compute the energy consumed in the whole network as the sum of the energy consumed in every path. Clearly, the expression for energy consumption is:

$$E_T = \sum_{j=1}^{N'} \sum_{i=0}^{|R_j|+1} E_{i,j}. \tag{30.6}$$

In Eq. (30.6), $E_{i,j}$ is the energy consumed by node i in path j. The energy consumed at each node includes the energy consumed in transmitting, receiving, and sleeping. Each term can be expressed as the average power in that state multiplied by the time that the node is on that state. Consequently, for a sensor node that is not the end node of any path, we can derive the energy consumed as:

$$\begin{aligned} E_{i,j} &= E_{TX,i,j} + E_{RX,i,j} + E_{SP,i,j} + E_{IL} \\ &= P_{TX}t_{TX,i,j} + P_{RX}t_{RX,i,j} + P_{SP}t_{SP,i,j}. \end{aligned} \tag{30.7}$$

Taking into account that in our protocol there is no energy consumption in idle listening and using the idea of Eq. (30.1) and Eq. (30.2), we get:

$$\begin{aligned} E_{i,j} &= P_{TX}t_B(L_{ACK} + L_{DATA,i,j})(|R_j| - i + 1) \\ &\quad + P_{RX}t_B(L_{ACK} + L_{DATA,i,j})(|R_j| - i) + P_{SP}t_{SP,i,j}. \end{aligned} \tag{30.8}$$

Similarly, we can derive the energy consumption for the sink and for nodes that are most distant from the sink in every path:

$$E_{SINK} = P_{TX}t_BL_{ACK} + P_{RX}t_BL_{DATA,i,j}|R_j|, \tag{30.9}$$

and

$$E_{|R_j|} = P_{RX}t_BL_{ACK} + P_{TX}t_BL_{DATA,i,j}. \tag{30.10}$$

The sleeping time ($t_{SP,i,j}$) in sensor nodes is not constant and depends on the position of the nodes within a path and the number of paths a sensor node belongs to within the network. However, P_{SL} is significantly less than P_{RX} or P_{TX}. Consequently, we consider that $E_{SP,i,j}$ is negligible in our analysis. We can now derive the total energy consumption as:

$$E_T = \sum_{j=1}^{N'} \left(E_{SINK} + \left(\sum_{i=1}^{|R_j|} E_{i,j} \right) + E_{|R_j|} \right). \tag{30.11}$$

Taking average on both sides we finally get:

$$E[E_T] = N' t_B \Bigg((L_{ACK} + L_{DATA}) P_{TX} \left(\frac{\sigma^2 + |\bar{R}_j|^2 + 2\bar{R}_j + 2}{2} \right)$$

$$+ P_{RX} \left(\frac{\sigma^2 + |\bar{R}_j|^2 - |\bar{R}_j|}{2} \right) + P_{RX} \left(L_{ACK} + |\bar{R}_j| L_{DATA} \right) \Bigg), \quad (30.12)$$

where:

$$|\bar{R}_j| = \textit{Average route size}$$
$$\sigma^2 = \textit{Variance of the route size.} \quad (30.13)$$

30.3.5. *Synchronization procedure*

In our scheme, the sink is the only node that can start and maintain synchronization. All other nodes only disseminate synchronization packets in a multihop environment. The dissemination of synchronization packets is similar to that of data packets, i.e., only one route is active at a single time instant so that nodes do not contend with each other. For every route, the sink dispatches synchronization packets at a synchronization rate r_{SYNC}. To synchronize, sensor nodes do not follow the staggered time schedule proposed to cope with third type of communication traffic described briefly in subsection 30.3.2. Instead, nodes set their time offset to 0 and then forward synchronization packets from the sink to the furthest node. Once sensor nodes have received the synchronization packet and have successfully relayed it to the next node within a path, they go to sleep. Figure 30.5 shows the proposed time schedule for synchronization.

30.3.6. *Protocol state machine*

As stated previously, the sink node is responsible for route partition. In other words, it needs to pre-compute the time schedule for each node in the network based on the

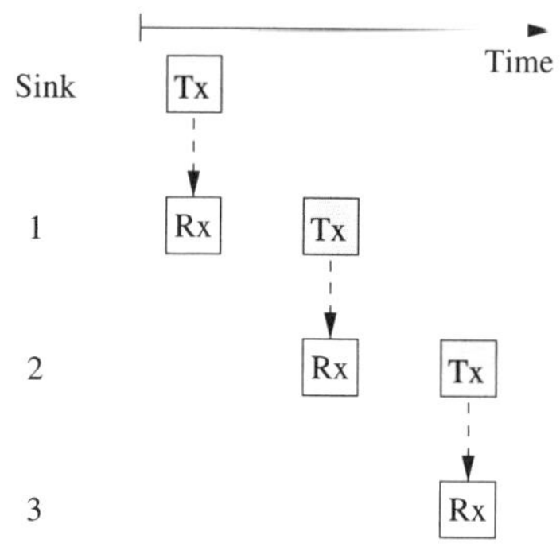

Fig. 30.5. Synchronization time schedule.

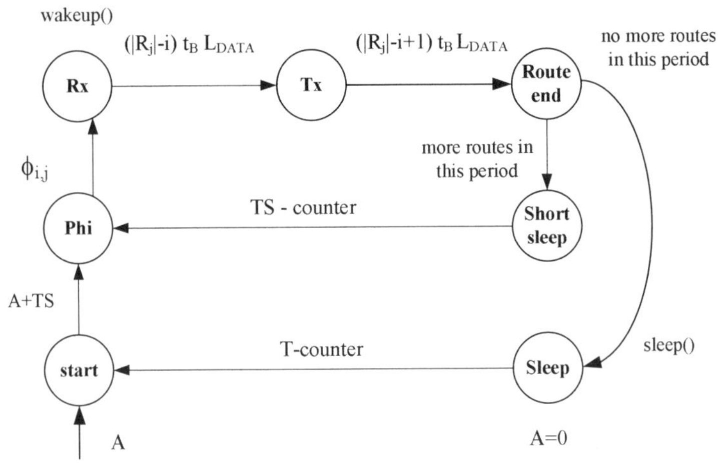

Fig. 30.6. Protocol state machine.

Table 30.2. List of symbols used in time schedule state machine.

Symbol	Meaning
$\phi_{i,j}$	Offset in time between the start of transmission of furthest node from the sink in route j and the start of transmission of node i within the same route
TS	Offset in time between the start of transmission of furthest node from the sink in route j and the start of transmission of node i within the same route
counter	counter in each node [ms]
$\|R_j\|$	Size of route j
i	Position of node from the sink
wakeup()	Turn on radio
sleep()	Turn off radio
A	Time to start to follow time schedule

RA packets received from every one of them. After the calculation, the sink node will disseminate RD packets through the network whose payload contains data used by nodes to calculate their own time schedule. The time schedule that each node follows has many states which are depicted in the state transition diagram, shown in Fig. 30.6. The notations used in Fig. 30.6 are listed in Table 30.2.

30.4. Experimental Results

30.4.1. *Previous experiments*

Our proposed protocol inherits some beneficial features of our previous work (SEA-MAC), i.e., reduction of idle listening. In the following paragraphs we show the results obtained comparing SEA-MAC performance against that of S-MAC and SCP-MAC.

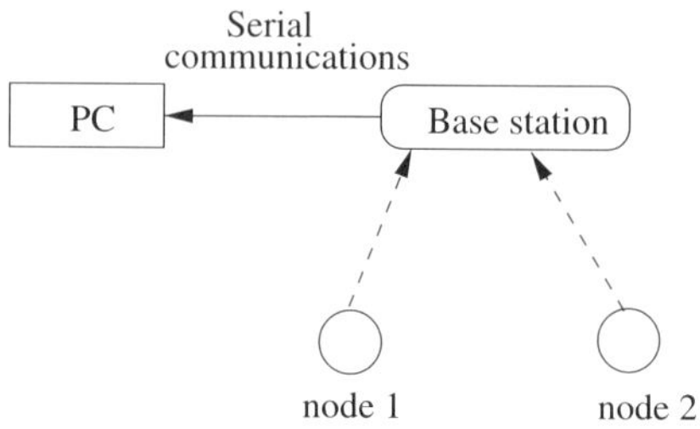

Fig. 30.7. Network configuration (each node sends data every 60 seconds).

We implemented SEA-MAC protocol in mica2 motes running TinyOS.[9] The network configuration we used for the tests is shown in Fig. 30.7. Our goal was to build an application to emulate real applications. For this purpose, we made nodes to periodically sample physical variables such as humidity and barometric pressure and include such data into packets that must be conveyed to the BS. In our configuration, nodes 1 and 2 sample environmental variables periodically and generate corresponding packets, which have to reach the BS.

We added NesC components from Crossbow[10] to SEA-MAC, S-MAC and SCP-MAC C++ code such that nodes are able to sense environmental variables. In addition, we also added NesC components to the BS code to transmit packets to the PC through the UART. Finally, we stored sampled data in files together with voltage measures and the time the packets were received.

In our tests, we monitored the battery voltage in each mica2 mote every time they sent a packet. This information is then forwarded in packets together with sampled data. Nodes 1 and 2 send a data packet every 60 seconds. Upon receiving the packets, the BS sends them to the PC through the UART. Further, the information about the sampled data is stored in files for further analysis. In this test, we intended to find out which protocol consumes less energy by determining which protocol produces the least voltage drop in 48 hours of continuous test. The results are shown in Fig. 30.8. The results show that the SEA-MAC protocol can outperform existing protocols in terms of energy consumption.

30.4.2. *Energy consumption, delay and packet loss*

To evaluate the new protocol proposed in this chapter, we have conducted simulation analysis using the network simulator NS-2.[8] In our simulation, we consider a WSN with 10 nodes, where the sink is placed in the middle of the network and all other 9 nodes are placed randomly around the sink, as shown in Fig. 30.9. We use AODV[11] routing protocol in the initialization state of the route partition algorithm. To simplify the discussion, we skip the maintenance and synchronization operations in the protocol, and keep only the initialization and data transmission operations. In the simulation, the data rate at the physical layer is 20 kbps (i.e., $t_B = 0.4\,\text{ms}$)

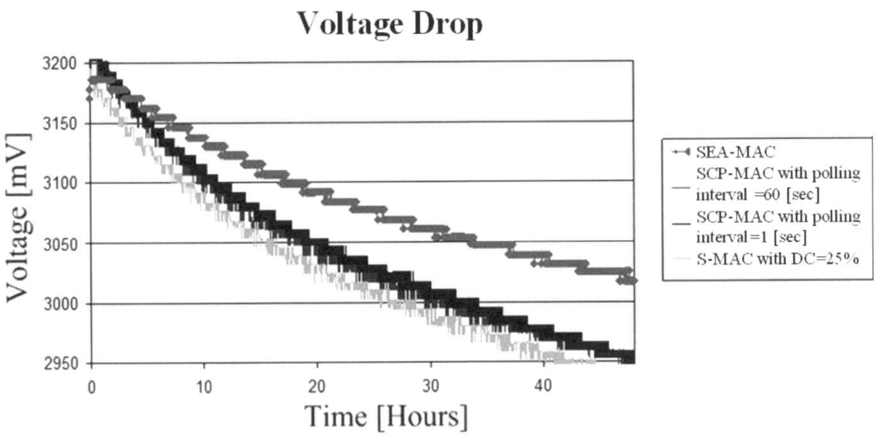

Fig. 30.8. Energy efficiency comparison.

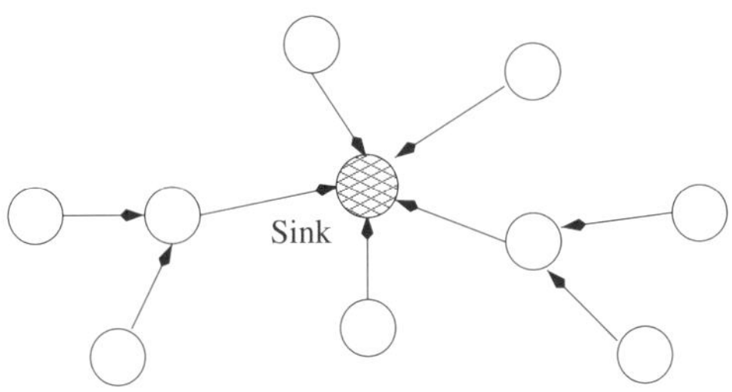

Fig. 30.9. Network topology used in the experiment.

and the packet size is fixed to 50 bytes. Because of other overheads, the payload at the MAC layer is 105 bytes.

Figure 30.10 shows the simulation results for the proposed protocol in terms of energy consumption, average packet delay, and packet loss rate. Note that the transmission interval is the time between transmissions of sensor nodes. As expected, the energy consumption increases as the transmission interval decreases, as shown in Fig. 30.10(a). Figure 30.10(b) shows that the average delay of data packets in our protocol remains practically constant for different values of the transmission interval. Although our protocol is expected not to have any packet loss, Fig. 30.10(c) illustrates that a very low percentage of data packets are actually dropped if transmission interval is less than 60 seconds.

30.4.3. *Scalability*

To evaluate the scalability of the scheme, we have also tested our protocol to see how it behaved as the density of nodes increased. We used a network configuration where the sink is the node that is placed at the center of a 500 by 500 m^2 area.

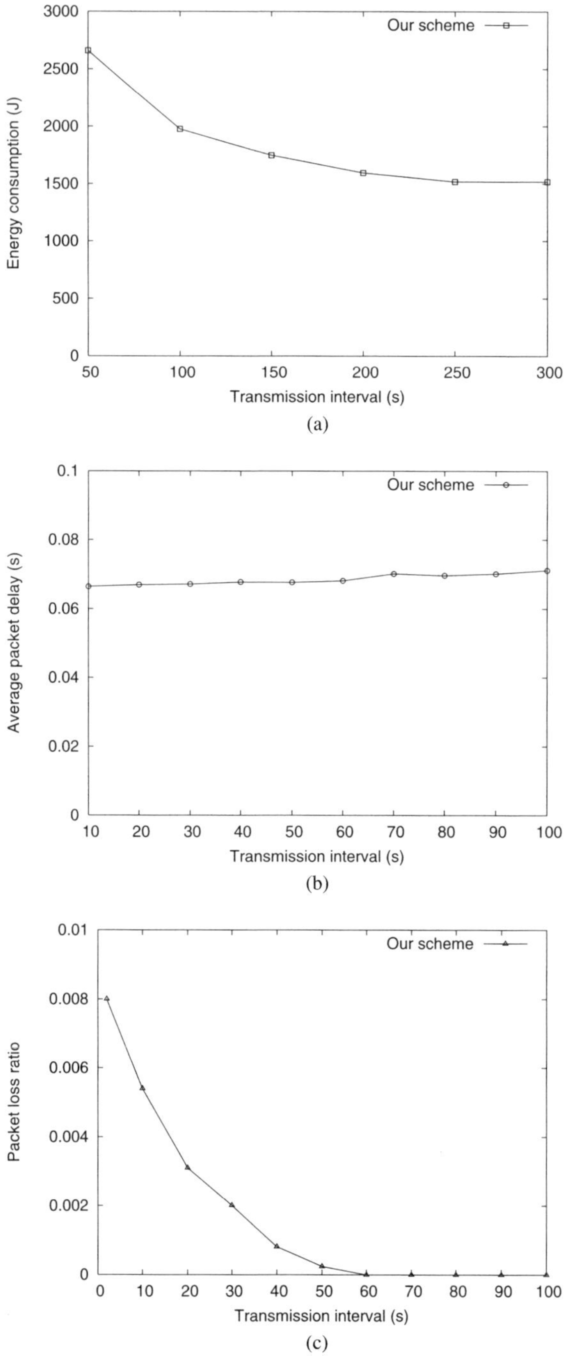

Fig. 30.10. Performance of the proposed MAC protocol. (a) Energy consumption. (b) Delay and (c) packet loss.

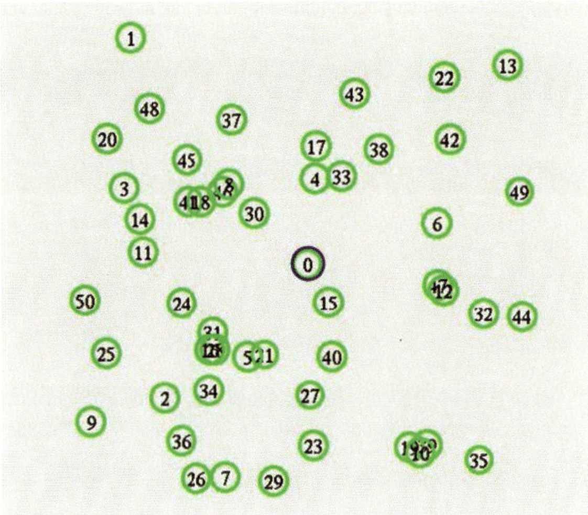

Fig. 30.11. Network topology used in the experiment.

The network configuration is shown in Fig. 30.11. The results obtained are shown in Fig. 30.12 for 2 different values of buffer size in each node. Note that the buffer size is the number of packets a node can hold. Here we include the buffer size in the tests to explore the impact of it.

Figure 30.12(a) and (b) show that the percentage of packets successfully received by the sink is greater than 99% for densities smaller than 200 nodes/km^2. For a density of 200 nodes/km^2, there is a slight degradation of the performance of our protocol due to the drop of packets successfully received. For densities higher than 200, our protocol exhibited problem to compute time schedules for all nodes. In the future, we intend to run some routes in parallel to lessen this characteristic.

30.4.4. *Performance comparison*

Figure 30.13 compares the performance of our protocol with S-MAC. In our simulation, the duty cycle of the S-MAC is set to 50% to obtain an acceptable network connectivity. In fact, a lower value of duty cycle may lead to excessive packets loss. The results show that our protocol significantly outperforms S-MAC, in terms of energy consumption, delay, and packet loss. Note in Fig. 30.13(b), how the delay of S-MAC increases dramatically when the transmission interval is less than 10 seconds.

30.5. Conclusions

In this book chapter, we have proposed a new MAC protocol to reduce energy consumption, delay, and packet loss for periodic monitoring applications in wireless

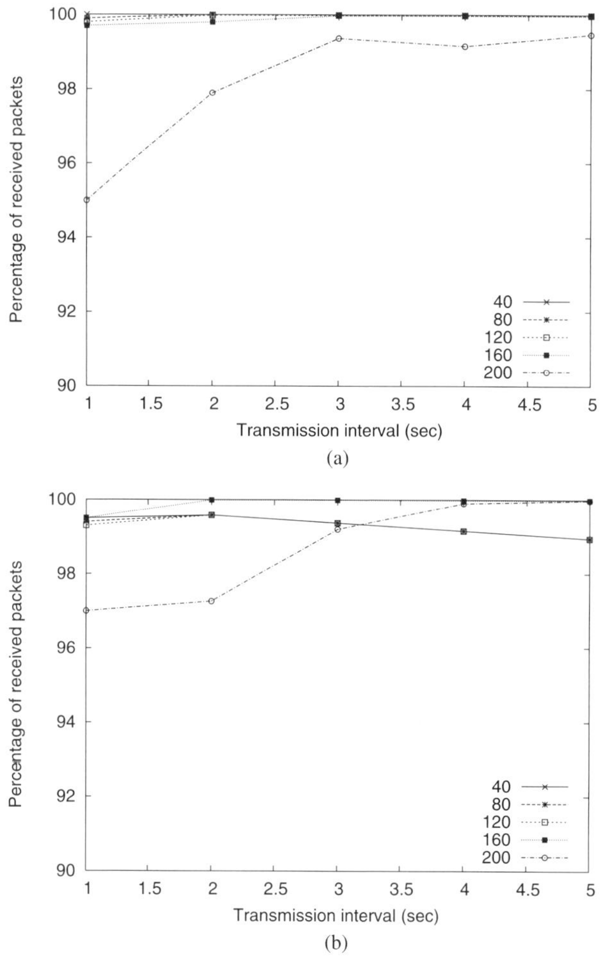

Fig. 30.12. Performance of the protocol with different node density. (a) Buffer size = 20 and (b) buffer size = 40.

sensor networks. The key feature of our protocol is that an efficient scheduling mechanism can make nodes to wake up only when a sample is taken. In this way, transmission collision is avoided and idle listening is reduced. Moreover, energy consumption is further reduced by making nodes to follow only one synchronization source. Simulation results show that our protocol significantly outperforms S-MAC in terms of energy consumption, packet delay and loss.

Acknowledgment

This work was supported in part by US National Science Foundation (NSF) under Award Number CNS0424546.

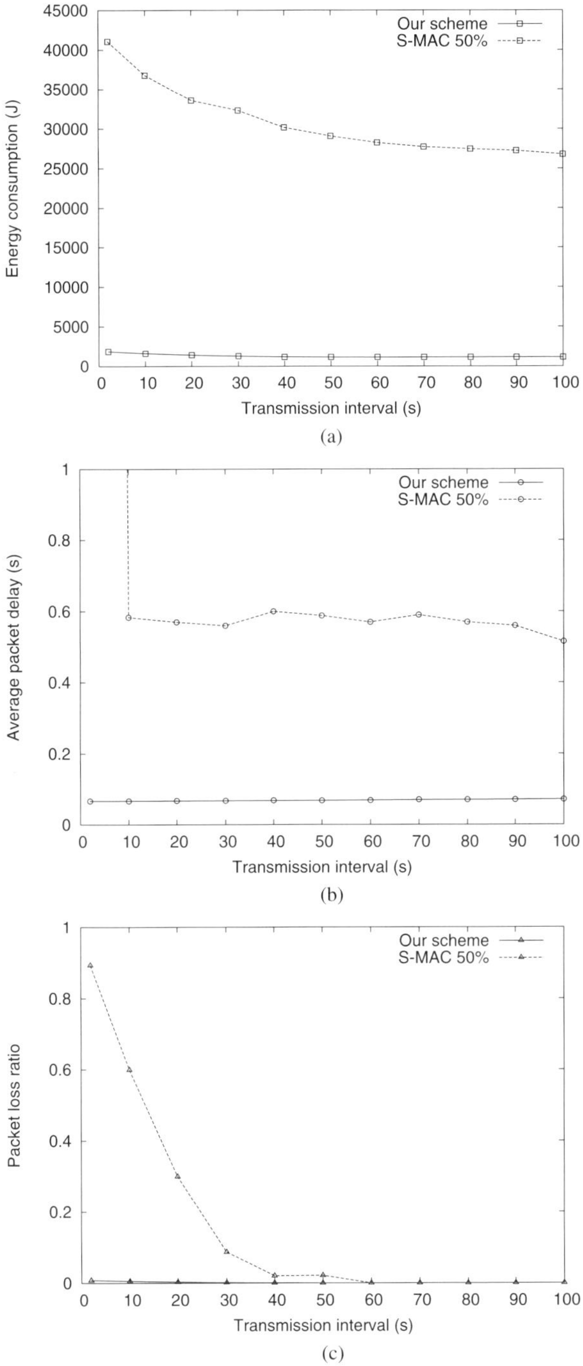

Fig. 30.13. Performance comparison. (a) Energy consumption, (b) delay and (c) packet loss.

References

1. W. Ye, J. Heidemann and D. Estrin, Medium access control with coordinated adaptive sleeping for wireless sensor networks, *IEEE/ACM Transactions on Networking*, **12**(3), 493–506 (June 2004).
2. W. Ye, F. Silva and J. Heidemann, Ultra-low duty cycle MAC with scheduled channel polling, *ACM SenSys 2006* (November 2006).
3. T. van Dam and K. Langendoen, An adaptive energy-efficient mac protocol for wireless sensor networks, *Proc. of the First ACM Conference on Embedded Networked Sensor Systems*, 171–180, Los Angeles, California, USA (November 2003).
4. G. Lu, B. Krishnamachari and C. S. Raghavendra, An adaptive energy-efficient and low-latency MAC for data gathering in wireless sensor networks, *Proc. of IPDPS'2004* (April 2004).
5. A. Mainwaring, J. Polastre, R. Szewczykt, D. Culler and J. Anderson, Wireless sensor networks for habitat monitoring, *First ACM Workshop on Wireless Sensor Networks and Applications*, Atlanta, GA, USA (September 2002).
6. M. A. Erazo and Y. Qian, SEA-MAC: Simple energy aware MAC protocol for wireless sensor networks for environmental monitoring, *Proc. of ISWPC'2007*, San Juan, PR (February 2007).
7. A. Boukerche, R. W. N. Pazzi and R. B. Araujo, HPEQ A hierarchical periodic, event-driven and query-based wireless sensor network protocol, *The IEEE Conference on Local Computer Networks* (November 2005).
8. The ns-2 simulator, URL: http://www.isi.edu/nsnam/ns/.
9. TinyOS: http://www.tinyos.net/.
10. Crossbow: http://www.xbow.com/
11. C. E. Perkins and E. M. Royer, Ad hoc on-demand distance vector routing, *Proc. of the 2nd IEEE Workshop on Mobile Computing Systems and Applications*, New Orleans, LA, 90–100 (February 1999).

Chapter 31

Deadline-Driven Data Gathering in Periodic Monitoring Sensor Networks

S. Selvakennedy

School of Information Technologies J12
University of Sydney, NSW 2006, Australia
s.kennedy@usyd.edu.au

There are numerous quality of service schemes in use for both wired and wireless networks. However, due to the unique wireless sensor application needs, most of them are not directly applicable. Recently, there are several sensor network specific proposals that aim to support delay-constrained transmissions for real-time communications both at the link and network levels. In most considered scenarios, all sensor readings are treated equally. In some applications however, the semantic significance of sensor readings also differs even if their modality is the same. In this chapter, we propose a new quality of service scheme aimed for wireless sensor networks. It uses a dynamic overlay structure to deliver high priority readings within certain application delay bound. Contrary to typical approaches, it uses *on the fly* reservation to facilitate data transmission with minimal delay. Through analysis and simulations, we demonstrate how this unique QoS design achieves the required communication requirements.

31.1. Introduction

The integration of sensing and wireless communications are proving to be a very useful combination with many original applications being envisioned that were previously not possible with the traditional wired sensing technology. Moreover, using a hierarchical organization, wireless sensor networks (WSNs) at scale of thousands of nodes are already shown to be feasible through the ExScal project.[1] In most applications, sensors are stationary and gather single or multi-modal data such as thermal, humidity, light and seismic measurements. The nodes communicate typically using a single shared frequency channel, and are mainly powered by limited non-renewable batteries.

In certain types of applications, there seem to exist a natural ordering of sensor readings in terms of their importance. For instance, in a monitoring application for chemical leaks in a chemical processing facility, readings from sensors in an *affected* region of a chemical spill are naturally more critical than sensor readings from elsewhere in the network. Furthermore, even within the affected region, it may be more critical to deliver the *boundary* or *edge* readings of the phenomenon earlier to activate an automated or semi-automated actuation mechanism to prevent any possible human casualties. The notion of an event edge or boundary in WSNs was initially coined by Chintalapudi *et al.*[2] and Nowak and Mitra,[3] independently. It is readily apparent that a phenomenon spanning across an area can be observed in many monitoring applications such as seismic disturbances, contaminant flows and fire emergencies. Thus, during periodic data collections, it might be necessary to forward these edge readings with their locations to the processing center (i.e., the sink) earlier than the other readings. Such a need demands for the provision of quality of service (QoS). In some sensor networks with actuators, it may also be necessary to provide a prompt response to external stimuli. The end-to-end delay needs to be bounded, as late data arrivals would be useless and excluded from any subsequent user decision and/or actuation mechanism. As such, a QoS scheme should aim to meet such delay constraints. While achieving this design goal, it is also vital to be energy-efficient considering the constraints of sensor nodes.

Since there is a wealth of information on QoS schemes for wired and other wireless networks, it might be tempting to adopt them directly for WSNs too. However, there are some key differences that might suggest otherwise. Firstly, the data sources in WSNs might generate *interesting* readings spontaneously, which need to be delivered within certain delay bound. Since we are not able to predict the occurrence of such events *a priori* to make any reasonable resource reservation, the use of classical traffic control schemes such as admission control, usage monitoring and sophisticated weighted queuing schemes, are rather inappropriate. Secondly, sensor messages are typically in the order of a few tens of bytes against hundreds to thousands of bytes per packet on the Internet. The overhead involved in these classical QoS schemes is an order of magnitude larger than sensor messages themselves, which further amplifies their irrelevance. Thirdly, the composition and intensity of the Internet traffic is beyond the control of any network or service providers, even collectively. On the contrary, the environment sampling rate and data collection frequency of the sensors are either predetermined at compile time or through subsequent limited user queries. Finally, a WSN is typically singly owned for some specific tasks. As such, sensor readings of lower significance could be completely suppressed or forwarded after data aggregation at appropriate nodes. Such schemes are inconceivable for the Internet traffic, as even the best effort traffic must be delivered *as is*. Therefore, we need to devise QoS schemes in an orthogonal manner for WSNs with possible compile-time support according to the application needs.

Most existing data gathering protocols for WSNs, such as Directed Diffusion[4] and HEED[5] (and references therein) do not consider any QoS issues. In Ref. 6, the authors proposed a data gathering protocol with multiple mobile sinks. Their protocol uses geographic multicasting to minimize end-to-end delay to sinks. However, all sensor readings are treated equally. Similarly there only are a handful of QoS-enhanced routing and MAC protocols for WSNs that offer differentiated services for any sensor data. The very first proposal in this space is RAP,[7] which appeared in 2002. RAP uses a form of packet scheduling that is aware of distance and message deadline to prioritize real-time traffic, and enforces such prioritization through a differentiated MAC layer. An adaptive MAC layer rate control is proposed by Woo and Culler[8] to achieve fairness among nodes with varying distances to the base station. These approaches work well by locally throttling certain low-priority traffic. On the contrary, SPEED[9] and MMSPEED[10] use cross layer information of MAC and network layers to schedule packets based on per-hop delay and end-to-end deadline. However, these protocols require acknowledged communications to estimate the delivery speed, which contributes towards increased overhead. Moreover, MMSPEED may lead to significant overhead in guaranteeing delivery to support its reliability service as it uses multiple paths to carry redundant packets.

In this chapter, we propose a new QoS scheme that supplements a data gathering protocol to provide differentiated treatment for data of same modality based on their semantics. The data gathering protocol is based on a biologically inspired dynamic clustering protocol from the literature termed T-ANT, which supports a fixed number of clusterheads and facilitates good clusterhead distribution.[11] However, the proposed QoS scheme is applicable to *any* data gathering protocol that employs a clustered topology with uniform clusterhead distribution. A clustered environment is considered here mainly due to its scalability. Accordingly, our QoS scheme exploits the existence of hierarchy in such a clustered network. A minimum spanning tree overlay is formed among the clusterheads with the sink as its root. For data forwarding, priority queuing is adopted at these clusterheads. High priority messages are forwarded using the overlay structure, whereas low priority messages are briefly suppressed, aggregated and forwarded using standard routing protocol. Based on our analysis and simulations, it is demonstrated that the proposed localized QoS protocol is appropriate for real-time communications with better than soft real-time guarantees.

The rest of the chapter is organized as follows. Section 2 further describes some related QoS-enhanced proposals in the literature. In Sec. 3, our proposed QoS scheme is described and analyzed for its theoretical basis. The simulation framework and some adopted implementation decisions are presented in Sec. 4. Section 5 discusses the comparative performance of our proposal against a benchmarking protocol. The concluding remarks are made in Sec. 6.

31.2. Related Work

There are many unique properties specific to WSNs that makes it different from other wireless technologies. Even the number of nodes in a typical deployment is much greater than in other wireless networks. The typical problem of multihop wireless networks is significantly exacerbated here. Fortunately though, the traffic dynamics in WSNs is less unpredictable as sensors employ specific timers to control environment sampling and collection frequency (mostly at compile time). Thus, this relatively new wireless technology affords interesting challenges as well as opportunities to manage them in its own unique way. Classical communication paradigms need to be modified or new ones invented to be useable here. There have been some proposals in recent years on new paradigms and solutions for WSNs.

There are several attempts to enable delay-constrained communications at the link layer. A MAC proposal based on Earliest Deadline First scheduling is employed in Ref. 12. The network is however assumed to have *cellular* structure that benefits from channel spatial reuse to mitigate inter-cell interference problems. At higher layers, many data gathering and routing protocols have been proposed for WSNs. Directed Diffusion[4] is a data-centric gathering protocol, where certain paths are gradually reinforced based on the interests of sinks. Only data of interest is forwarded, and uninteresting readings are completely suppressed. Another data gathering protocol that considers both delay and energy is PEGASIS.[13] It uses a composite metric of energy and delay to construct an efficient data aggregation tree. DEED[6] is a data gathering protocol for networks with mobile sinks, and new sinks are allowed to join the network at later times. Due to the possibility of many sinks, the problem is addressed like a multicast communication based on the geographic routing approach. DEED dynamically builds an overlay Steiner tree using the average delay metric, while ensuring energy efficiency. As the underlying MAC protocol is based on contention-based access rather than reservation-based, the authors aimed to provide a soft real-time guarantee on end-to-end delay. SPEED[9] is a routing protocol that supplements geographic routing with delay-awareness and non-deterministic forwarding. The latter feature in SPEED allows the protocol to avoid congesting shorter paths to the sink. By relying on MAC layer feedbacks, it attempts to forward packets to achieve a constant average speed of propagation towards the sink. With these features, this protocol is able to support soft real-time transmission guarantees. It is apparent in all the above proposals that the nature of data criticalness itself is not distinguished apart from its statistical redundancy.

In this chapter, we argue for the need to provide differentiated services to sensor readings according to their semantic contribution. Based on the fact that sensor traffic has more predictability than the Internet traffic, we propose the use of a minimum spanning tree overlay exploiting the availability of clusterheads, and on the fly reservation for high priority traffic. Furthermore, similar to data timers used to control data sampling and collection frequencies, we utilize a suppression timer to facilitate the forwarding of higher priority traffic. The details of the proposed scheme are described next.

31.3. The Localized QoS Scheme

Before we describe the scheme, we make the following assumptions about the system:

- All sensor nodes are stationary and a single sink is used to collect data from the network. (The multi-sink scenario is considered in our further extension. This mainly involves groups of clusterheads (CHs) to be associated to different sinks.)
- The network is clustered with uniformly distributed CHs. Both static and dynamic clustering can be employed here.
- Each sensor node has a transceiver with multiple transmit power levels.
- Each node is aware of its own geographic location, and builds a neighbor table with neighboring nodes' locations.

The second assumption is made about the CH distribution to allow the selection of an appropriate radio range to ensure connectivity among them as in HEED. Each CH should reach its neighboring CHs at a higher transmit power level, which is available in commonly used sensor platforms such as Mica2. To ensure that this CH connectivity, the CH transmits at the higher power level, r_h. What is the minimum range r_h such that, with high probability p, no CH in the network is isolated (i.e., each CH has at least one CH neighbor)? Based on *nearest neighbor methods*, a tight lower bound on the radio range for a large network was derived and proved to avoid isolated nodes in Ref. 14. Assuming a homogenous CH density, we apply this probabilistic bound theorem to compute the bound on r_h as:

$$r_h \geq \sqrt{\frac{-M^2 \times \ln(1 - p^{1/n_a})}{\pi n_a}}, \tag{31.1}$$

where M is one side of a square terrain and n_a is the number of CHs.

In order to provide QoS for some readings against others, we exploit this connectivity among CHs. To this end, an efficient overlay structure is necessary that simultaneously meets the delay constraint of the application. We choose to form a minimum weight spanning tree, as polynomial algorithms are available and readily extendable to a localized application.

31.3.1. *The CH overlay*

Consider a graph where the CHs are the nodes and their connectivity represents the edges. We need to construct a delay-aware overlay on this graph to support deadline-driven transmissions for high priority traffic. In order to be energy efficient as well as delay aware, the edge weight of the CH graph should be appropriately determined. Since our focus here is to bound the delivery deadline, a suitable weight function should consider transmission delay across edges between pairs of CHs. Also, to create a localized implementation of this overlay, the weight function should be convex. This can be achieved by using cumulative delay to the sink for edge weight rather than the pair-wise delay.

To use the delay measure for the edge, it is necessary to estimate the delay between node pairs. This per-hop delay is influenced by numerous factors such as queuing, access, processing, transmission, propagation and retransmission delays. It is however apparent that this measure tends to be dynamic, and quite difficult to capture accurately with the resource constraints. Furthermore, achieving fine-grain time synchronization is quite expensive in WSNs. Fortunately, it may not be necessary to accurately represent it as network situation may change, for instance, due to an event break-out or dynamic clustering. In large-scale sensor deployments, the geometric pair-wise distance is a reliable proportional measure of delay between nodes. Furthermore, as energy usage is at least in the quadratic order with distance, minimizing distance would result in lower average delay as well as energy reduction. It is rather redundant to consider node residual energy here, as such a consideration is typically made when the CHs are elected. Moreover, in a static clustering scenario, the CHs are usually nodes with richer resources than other sensor nodes. Since estimating per-hop delay directly for all pairs is expensive, we instead extrapolate delay from average node degree and node distance. Further details about this estimation are given in the following subsection.

Since estimating per-hop delay directly for all pairs is expensive, we instead extrapolate the transmission latency and propagation delay from average node degree and node distance, respectively. The former component is estimated assuming a fair share of the medium, which reduces the available data rate by node degree. With a fixed message size, transmission latency can be readily computed. This approximation broadly captures variable delay components such as queuing and access delays. For the latter delay component, we just use the RF signal propagation speed and node distance to estimate the propagation delay. The sum of these components then gives the per-hop delay.

Using this CH graph, we can then construct a delay-bounded minimum spanning tree (DMST) as the overlay with minimum delay paths. As the base station acts as the sink for all traffic, especially high priority traffic, this node is a natural choice for the root. To initiate the DMST construction, the sink broadcasts a beacon with its edge weight, w (which is 0), location, l and an application delay bound, b at r_h transmit range. The application delay bound can be excluded from the beacon, if it is fixed and is known prior to deployment. The first-hop CHs compute their edge cost to the sink by estimating its per-hop delay as above, say d_i. The cost to the sink is then the sum of weights giving $w_i = w_0 + d_i$. This beacon is further broadcasted using the new weight and location of the sender. Each node just needs to store its upstream node id to be part of this overlay. If the computed weight is greater than the application delay bound, further beacon broadcast is suppressed for this leaf node. Due to the convexity of the weight function, it is guaranteed to find a loop free tree. This minimal spanning tree formation algorithm is summarized in Algorithm 31.1.

Algorithm 31.1. The DMST construction algorithm.

if (node n_i is the sink) **then**
{
  $w_i = 0$
  broadcast a beacon with w_i, location l_i and bound, b
}
else if (node n_i is a CH **and** receives beacon (w_j, l_j, b)) **then**
{
  estimate pair-wise delay to j, d_{ij}
  $w_i = w_j + d_{ij}$
if ($w_i <$ best_weight and $w_i < b$) **then** {
  best_weight $= w_i$
  best_parent $= j$
  broadcast a beacon with w_i, location l_i and bound, b
  }
}

This algorithm is operationally similar to Prim's algorithm, as the minimum weight edge is added to the tree only if the corresponding sender node is already on the tree. Thus, using a similar proof as for Prim's algorithm, we could show that the above algorithm finds a minimum spanning tree. Moreover, as the edge weights are considered in ascending order as a heap structure and each beacon is broadcasted instead of unicast, the worst-case message complexity is just linear of the number of CHs. The analysis of the rest of DMST properties is given in the following subsection.

This overlay structure is used only for the transmission of critical (i.e., high priority) messages. For the forwarding of normal messages, lossy data aggregation is performed first at the CHs to reduce redundant information due to their spatial proximity prior to transmission. Then, the aggregated data is forwarded using a standard routing protocol for energy efficiency. In order to provide this service differentiation, a form of priority queuing is required at the CHs, and it is described in Sec. 31.3.3.

31.3.2. *Analysis of DMST*

To understand the theoretical basis of the proposed algorithm, we start by defining the following terms. The overlay topology is constructed under the common radio range r_h as an undirected simple graph $G = (V, E)$, where V is the set of CHs and

$E = \{(u, v) : \text{dist}(u, v) \leq r_h, u, v \in V\}$ is the edge set with $\text{dist}(u, v)$ represents the distance between nodes u and v.

To build a DMST, the weight of an edge can be associated to per-hop delay between the two nodes. As stated earlier, it is however difficult to determine this dynamic measure accurately. Instead, we will approximate this measure by subdividing it into two components, namely *transmission latency* and propagation delay. The former component is roughly used to capture the delays of packet transmission, queuing and access. Since the nodes are uniformly distributed, their node degree is nearly constant. Node degree affects the shared medium access delay, which consequently affects the available bandwidth for each node. Its effect is assumed to enforce fair access, and is captured by assigning equally reduced bandwidth. The latter propagation delay component, the ratio of nodes' distance and signal speed, is a strictly increasing function of the Euclidean distance. Together, they can be utilized to estimate per-hop delay. Even though this is a simple delay estimation, it is found sufficient in the simulations to bound the delay on the overlay in the absence of the event knowledge.

Definition 1 (Per-Hop Delay). The per-hop delay h between nodes u and v is roughly estimated based on transmission latency and propagation delay as:

$$h = \frac{l \cdot n_d}{W} + \frac{\text{dist}(u, v)}{c}, \tag{31.2}$$

where l is packet size, n_d is the node degree, W is bandwidth and c is the RF propagation speed. Maximum per-hop delay $h_{\max}$ is readily obtainable by replacing the distance function with r_h. To bound the height of the spanning tree against an application deadline b, we should use the cumulative delay to the root as the weight function.

Definition 2 (Weight Function). Given an edge (u, v), the weight function represents the cumulative delay from node u to the root u_0 of the spanning tree through node v. Given two edges (v_0, v_1) and (v_0, v_2), the weight function $d : E \mapsto R$ is defined as:

$$\begin{aligned} d(v_0, v_1) > d(v_0, v_2) \Rightarrow \text{dist}(v_0, v_1) &> \text{dist}(v_0, v_2) \\ \text{or } \text{dist}(v_0, v_1) &\leq \text{dist}(v_0, v_2)\&\& \\ d(v_1, u_0) &> d(v_2, u_0) \end{aligned} .$$

The weight function d guarantees that in each step of the proposed DMST algorithm, the choice on the minimum weight edges result in minimum distance to the root implying a minimum delay tree construction.

To facilitate further discussion, we define neighbor relation and overlay topology.

Definition 3 (Neighbor). Node v is a neighbor of node u, denoted $u \rightarrow v$, if an only if $(u, v) \in E(G)$.

Definition 4 (Overlay). The topology G^* derived under the proposed DMST is a directed minimum spanning tree $G^* = (V^*, E^*)$, where $V^* = V$ and $E^* = \{(u, v) : u \to v, u, v \in V(G)\}$.

We now state and prove several desirable properties of the overlay derived by DMST.

Lemma 1. *Given three nodes $u, v, w \in V(G^*)$ satisfying $d(u, v) > d(u, w)$ and $d(u, v) > d(v, w)$, then $u \to v$.*

Proof. Assume $u \to v$. Then $(u, v) \in E(G^*)$. Thus, only one of the two edges (u, w) and (v, w) can be in $E(G^*)$ to avoid a cycle. Without loss of generality, assume $(u, w) \in E(G^*)$. Since $(v, w) \notin E(G^*)$ and $d(v, w) < d(u, v)$, replacing edge (u, v) with edge (v, w) and keeping all other edges unchanged forms another spanning tree of G with a lower weight. This contradicts the fact that G^* is the minimum spanning tree of G. □

For any node $u \in V(G^*)$, node u is connected to the root node u_0 (denoted by $u \Rightarrow u_0$) if there exists a path $(v_0 = u, v_1, \ldots, v_{m-1}, v_m = u_0)$, where $v_k \in V(G^*)$, $k = 0, 1, \ldots, m$.

Lemma 2. *Given the root node is located at the network center of an $M \times M$ area and an application deadline $b > (M/\sqrt{2}r_h)h_{\max}$, for any node $u \in V(G^*)$ and the root node u_0, if $d(u, u_0) < b$, then $u \Rightarrow u_0$.*

Proof. We prove this by determining the edge weight of the furthest leaf node u. Let k be this maximum number of hops. According to the DMST construction, a k-hop path must have been extended from a $(k-1)$-hop path, which itself is from a $(k-2)$-hop path and so on until the root is reached. Let $(v_0 = u, v_1, \ldots, v_{k-1}, v_k = u_0)$ represent this longest path. Since $d(v_{k-1}, u_0) < d(v_{k-2}, u_0) < \cdots < d(u, u_0)$, we just need to show $d(u, u_0) < b$. Since each hop length $\leq r_h$, the number of hops from the furthest leaf node u to node u_0 is $(M/\sqrt{2}r_h)$ (see Fig. 31.1).

$$\therefore d(u, u_0) = k \cdot h = (M/\sqrt{2}r_h) \cdot h \leq (M/\sqrt{2}r_h) \cdot h_{\max} < b$$

Since $d(u, u_0) < b$, $u \Rightarrow u_0$. □

Corollary 1. *The height of G^* is bounded by $(M/\sqrt{2}r_h)$ and delay of the longest path is bounded by $(M/\sqrt{2}r_h) \cdot h_{\max}$, i.e., delay on G^* is bounded by b.*

Theorem 1. *G^* preserves the connectivity of G.*

Proof. Suppose G is connected. We prove this by contradiction. Assume G^* is not connected. Among all node pairs $[u, u_0]$ satisfying $u \Rightarrow u_0$, there exists a node pair with the minimum delay, i.e., say $d(v_0, u_0) = \min_{u \in V(G^*)}\{d(u, u_0) : u \Rightarrow u_0\}$. Since G is connected, node v_0 cannot be more than $(M/\sqrt{2}r_h)$ hops from node u_0 by Corollary 1. By Lemma 2, $v_0 \Rightarrow u_0$, which leads to a contradiction. □

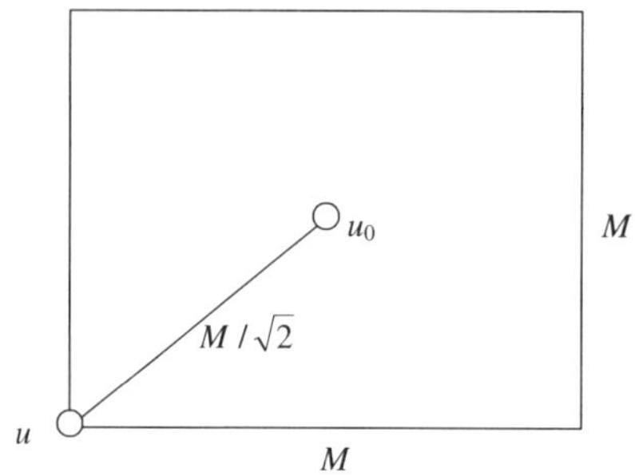

Fig. 31.1. The maximum distance between the root and any node u.

31.3.3. *Priority queuing*

In the proposed approach, we exploit the existence of CHs to support the QoS provision in a localized manner. To decide the type of queuing policy to adopt between strict priority against any weighted fair queuing approaches, let's consider the likely traffic composition and intensity. On the Internet, the number of flows with QoS needs is typically not known *a priori* and largely unbounded. As such, a policy strictly favoring such flows would very likely starve the best-effort flows. On the contrary, traffic intensity on a WSN is mainly determined at compile time where the sampling and data collection frequencies are determined based on the application need and network capacity. When priority readings are generated, even their collective intensity would be well within the network capacity as the sources are finite. And to address the real-time communication need of some applications, the end-to-end latency is the most critical consideration. In view of this, it is apparent that the most suitable queuing policy for WSNs would be strict priority queuing, where the best bounds in delay is achievable. Furthermore, as the high priority traffic load is always bounded in WSNs, the lower priority traffic will not starve.

Accordingly, two queues are utilized at each CH for the high and low priority traffic, respectively. Forwarding precedence is always given to the high priority queue. When a node determines that it has an *interesting* data, it immediately sends the reading to its CH. For this purpose, we employ the edge detection test to classify the data, and this is described in the following section. Any neighboring node with low priority data will briefly *suppress* its transmission upon hearing any critical node to facilitate the forwarding of high priority traffic and reduce the competition for the shared medium. None of the nodes require a large buffer size to store any suppressed readings, as the messages are mostly individually buffered at the sources. To ensure the smooth flow of higher priority messages upstream on the spanning tree overlay towards the sink, the CH includes its high priority queue length in such a message, before forwarding it to an upstream node (c.f. sink-to-node is downstream). When such a message is received by the upstream CH, it stores a reservation counter of the number of messages pending downstream, and accordingly abstains from transmitting any queued low priority messages. Any subsequent priority transmission from this node shall decrement the reservation counter. Such on the fly reservation ensures that there is limited interruption on the high priority flows at the intermediate nodes while propagating towards the sink. Any low priority messages in the forwarding queue are suppressed until the reservation counter is back to zero. By avoiding the usage of the common broadcast channel, high priority messages are smoothly forwarded towards the sink. Nodes that are far from the affected region will continue forwarding their readings without suppression, as their transmissions will have limited interference.

31.4. The Simulation Framework

The simulator is extended based on the framework given in Ref. 11. The radio module adopts the *Free Space* propagation model. At the MAC layer, it uses the CSMA protocol as does most implementations. For routing purposes, minimum hop routing is used. The proposed QoS mechanism completes the network layer by providing hierarchy and QoS. Since it is based on T-ANT clustering, we term our QoS scheme *differentiated* T-ANT or DT-ANT for convenience. For the application layer, we needed to identify a suitable application that could generate different priority traffic. To this end, there are different event detection and processing applications in the literature that may meet this requirement. Here, we adopted the event edge detection application using the T-Fit algorithm proposed in Ref. 15, which is a localized algorithm and shown to have the best accuracy in the boundary estimation. For the sake of completeness, we briefly describe it here.

In a monitoring scenario, when an interesting phenomenon occurs, a number of affected nodes discover its significance using simple rule based test against an application-defined threshold. Subsequently, they broadcast an urgent message to allow the nodes to learn about the extent of the phenomenon. Based on this direct neighborhood information, an affected node classifies its affected neighbors into four quadrants on a Cartesian system with the current node as the origin. The node is on the edge of a convex region, if the angle between the reference node as the vertex and its *farthest* two neighbors is smaller than π radian. As the nodes are classified into four quadrants, if the affected neighbors are only populated in two quadrants, this node is definitely on the edge. However, if the neighbors are populated in all four quadrants, such a node is surely not on the edge. When the neighboring nodes are populated in either one or three quadrants, more careful considerations are required. The former situation might represent an isolated erroneous sensor reading, whereas the latter might imply an edge node if the neighbors are inside the tangent. Using basic trigonometry, the angle between these nodes is readily determined. Figure 31.2 visualizes the outcome of the execution of this algorithm for a circular event region. In our implementation, the edge nodes are considered to be more critical than the rest of the nodes, and thus considered high priority. A high priority reading is

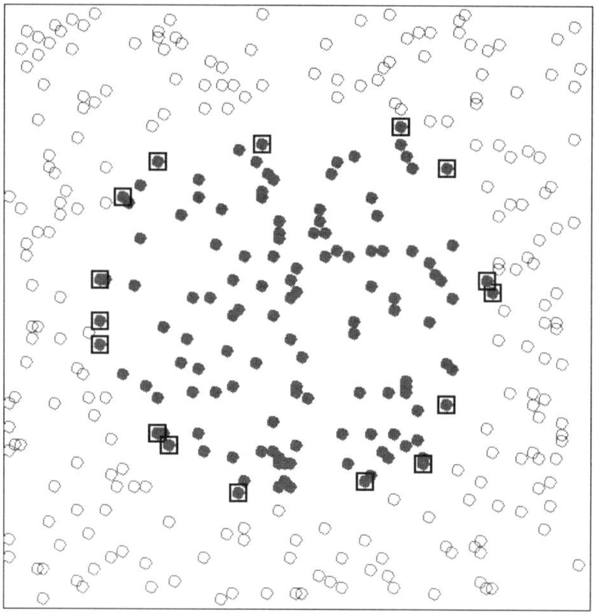

Fig. 31.2. Event visualization for a network with 350 nodes at 15-m radio range, affected by a circular event region with 35-m radius. The affected nodes are shaded, and the edge nodes are bounded with a square.

forwarded as is by its CH using the overlay, whereas the lower priority readings are aggregated at the CHs and then forwarded on the routing tree.

In order to benchmark our proposal, DT-ANT's performance is compared against SPEED, which is one of the pioneering proposals in this space. In its original specification,[9] SPEED does not cater for different traffic classes. To ensure fairness in our comparison, we adopted the same priority regime as above and strict priority queuing as in DT-ANT for SPEED's implementation. Moreover, to ensure the same load level is handled by SPEED, similar clustering technique is adopted to allow aggregation and forwarding from the CHs.

Since SPEED supports a form of geographic forwarding function, the choice of appropriate forwarding nodes is crucial for its performance. The forwarding node set is mainly determined based on the location and hop delay information. Per-hop delay is estimated based on the weighted average of acknowledged MAC communications. Furthermore, SPEED aims to distribute load among these forwarding nodes to avoid overloading the best forwarding path by probabilistically choosing the next-hop node; hence its non-deterministic geographic forwarding nature. To support multi-priority traffic, SPEED is modified here to support differentiated forwarding decisions. If a high priority packet is pending for transmission, the next-hop neighbor is selected from the forwarding set such that it can support at least the desired speed, $S_{setpoint}$. When a low priority packet is pending, the next-hop node is randomly chosen from the forwarding set irrespective of the speed it affords. With these modifications, we are now ready to present the comparative performance of DT-ANT and SPEED in the following section.

31.5. Results and Discussions

Extensive simulations are performed to quantify the performance of DT-ANT. In most scenarios, there are 100 sensor nodes deployed uniformly at random in a square $M \times M$ region with $M = 100\,\text{m}$. The sink is located at the center of the terrain. To quantify the energy efficiency of these algorithms, the transceiver energy parameters are set as: $\text{E}_{\text{elec}} = 50\,\text{nJ/bit}$ and $\varepsilon_{\text{fs}} = 10\,\text{pJ/bit/m}^2$. The energy for data aggregation is set to $\text{E}_{\text{DA}} = 5\,\text{nJ/bit}$ per signal. The data message size is fixed at 30 bytes. The basic radio range is fixed at 30 m, whereas the higher radio range (r_h) for the overlay communication is thrice longer. The monitored phenomenon is assumed to be circular with a 30-m radius. There are two types of traffic present. Only the edge node readings are given high priority. The low priority readings of neighboring nodes are suppressed for 50 ms. An application delivery deadline of 25 ms is chosen for most investigations. For SPEED, the desired speed $\text{S}_{\text{Setpoint}}$ is computed based on the ratio of maximum distance to the sink and the application deadline, i.e., 2.92 m/msec. Unless otherwise stated, all the following investigations adopt these values as their system parameters. For all simulation results in this chapter, each experiment is repeated 10 times and 95% confidence interval is obtained, and shown on the plots. Mostly, the confidence intervals for SPEED show higher variability due to its non-deterministic nature with its probabilistic forwarding.

For ease of exposition, different sets of results are presented in the following order:

- The impact of node density;
- The impact of application delivery deadline;
- The impact of event region size;

These are the performance metrics utilized in our investigations:

- *Average Delay*: The latency involved in the reporting of event data to the sink. It is the time elapsed from the edge node detection test to the packet reception by the sink.
- *Message Deadline Miss Ratio*: The ratio of the number of high priority messages missing the deadline to the number of messages received by the sink.[6] For SPEED, if none of its forwarding nodes can support $\text{S}_{\text{Setpoint}}$, the packet is dropped.
- *Total Energy*: This metric represents the energy dissipated by all sensors from the moment an event is detected to the delivery of all these readings to the sink.

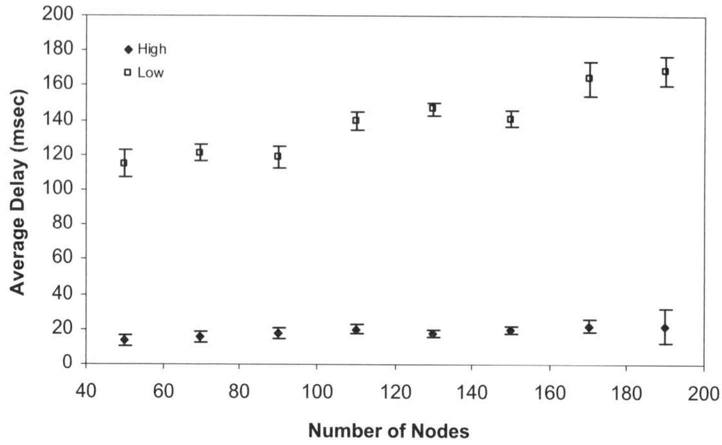

Fig. 31.3. Average delay of high and low priority traffic against number of nodes for DT-ANT.

31.5.1. *Impact of node density*

To investigate the impact of node density, we increased the number of sensor nodes for the same sensing terrain. Figure 31.3 depicts the average delay of both types of traffic. For high priority traffic, its average delay is barely affected even with a triple increase in the number of nodes from 50 to 150. As for low priority traffic, there is a linear increase in delay along with node density. This is an encouraging performance for both traffic types even when strict priority queuing is employed. Even though low priority traffic is suppressed to facilitate high priority transmission, its delay is still bounded mainly due to the finite number of either traffic sources. The delay also did not increase exponentially as the overall traffic intensity is predictable and always controlled to be within the maximum network capacity, unlike the Internet traffic. Such disparity between high and low priority traffic is also observed against other system parameters. For all subsequent results, the plots only show high priority traffic performance.

For the same scenario, the performance of high priority traffic in DT-ANT is compared against SPEED. In Fig. 31.4(a), even though both exhibited similar behavior at lower densities, it is evident that DT-ANT outperformed SPEED at higher node densities. As the network becomes larger, non-deterministic forwarding of SPEED forces the use of more paths. When high priority traffic becomes distributed across these paths and with each forwarding decision is independent, the bandwidth contention can get quite acute toward the sink. Although the use of load balancing is useful, this could be quite detrimental in real-time communications. On the contrary, DT-ANT exploits the existence of CHs to form limited paths towards the sink, which minimizes the bandwidth contention. The corresponding miss ratio metric plot is given in Fig. 31.4(b). Even with 170 nodes, less than 45% of high

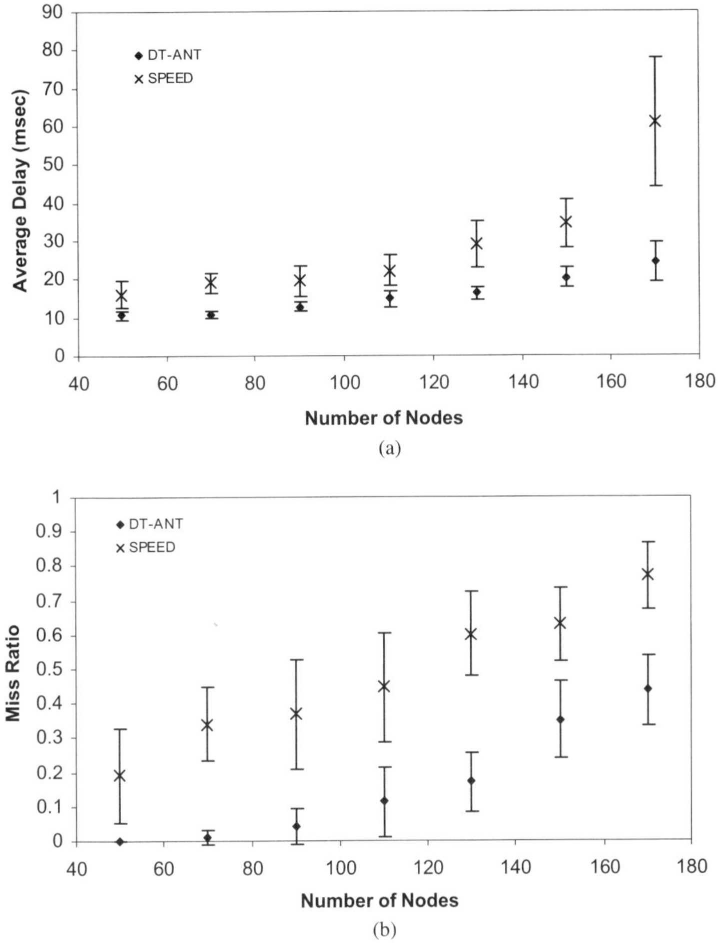

Fig. 31.4. Average delay and message miss ratio of high priority traffic against number of nodes; (a) average delay and (b) message miss ratio.

priority messages missed their deadlines with DT-ANT, whereas SPEED reported more than 50% misses for higher node densities. This is mainly due to the use of weighted average delay in its speed estimation, which does not efficiently anticipate and accommodate a sudden event break-out reporting.

It might appear odd that even though DT-ANT uses a delay-bounded spanning tree for its high priority traffic transmission, it still experiences deadline misses. In Sec. 31.3, DT-ANT is shown to bound delay only if the application deadline is within certain limit. For the above scenario, we plotted the minimum delay bound as per Lemma 2 against the number of nodes in Fig. 31.5. The current selected application deadline (i.e., 25 ms) is also shown. For this application deadline, DT-ANT is able

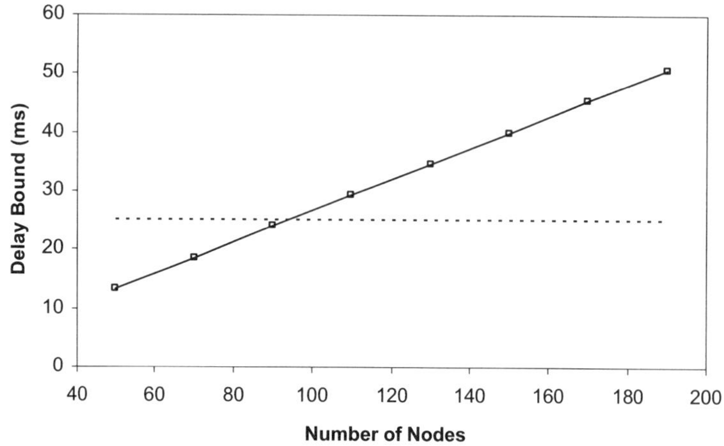

Fig. 31.5. Required minimum delay bound against number of nodes. The current application deadline is shown as dotted.

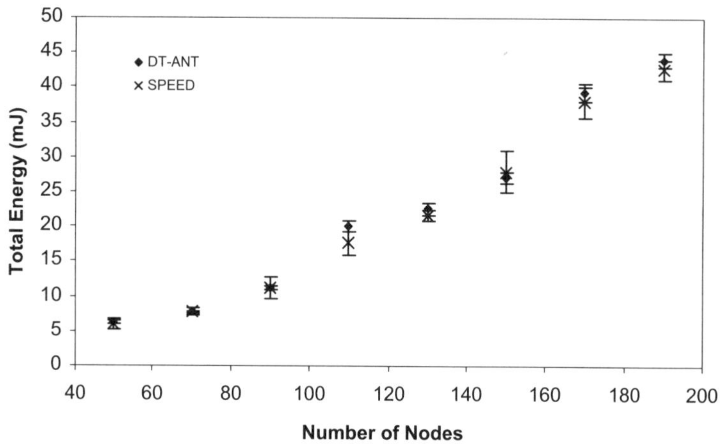

Fig. 31.6. Total energy dissipated for event information delivery against number of nodes.

to guarantee deadline-limited delivery for up to 90 nodes, i.e., at the line crossing of Fig. 31.5. Compared to Fig. 31.4(b), this is a rather accurate estimation as the deadline misses becomes significant only beyond 90 nodes. Even though the event knowledge is unavailable during DMST construction, the estimated bound seems to be sufficient.

To be appropriate for use in WSNs, it is crucial for a protocol proposal to be energy efficient as well. Thus, for the same scenario as above, we investigated the energy dissipation behavior of both protocols for different node density. Figure 31.6 shows both approaches exhibit rather similar energy usage. Even though DT-ANT needs to form and maintain an overlay structure, it is efficient in terms of message overhead, and the overlay formation is only repeated with the change of the CHs. Moreover, even though long links may be present on the overlay, the number of hops and re-forwarding is reduced. The energy consumed for these long-link transmissions at higher transmit level is then offset by the reduced hops. Thus, it has only a minor impact of the overall energy usage.

31.5.2. *Impact of application delivery deadline*

On selecting a suitable deadline, it is necessary to consider both the application need as well as the network limitation. For instance, readings have to be gathered every 10 ms for an inter-vehicular sensor network for an acceptable speed estimate and crash prevention. Also, depending on the network and node configuration, there is also an absolute minimum lower limit. For this study, we fixed the phenomenon size and varied the deadline. Figure 31.7 depicts message miss ratio of DT-ANT and SPEED. For deadlines close to the given network limit (< 30 ms), both protocols faced high misses in a contention-based network. However, for deadlines beyond 30-ms, it is evident that DT-ANT ensured almost zero deadline misses. This is mainly due to its on-the fly reservation technique on the overlay, which facilitates subsequent high priority forwarding with minimal queuing upstream (i.e., source-to-sink). SPEED could still be employed for some applications, where a larger than 40-ms bound is acceptable.

31.5.3. *Impact of the monitored phenomenon*

To study the impact of number of priority sources in a network, we varied the affected region radius to extend coverage up to about 60% of the monitored terrain.

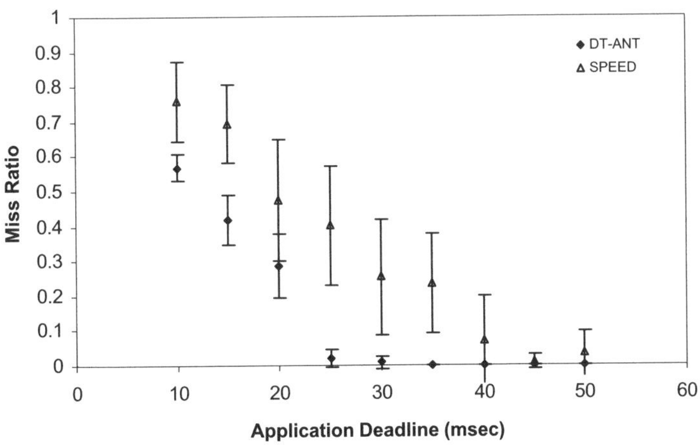

Fig. 31.7. Message miss ratio of high priority traffic against application deadline.

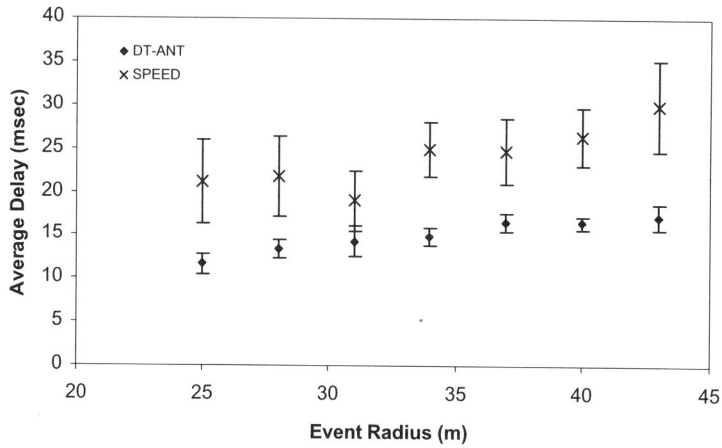

(a)

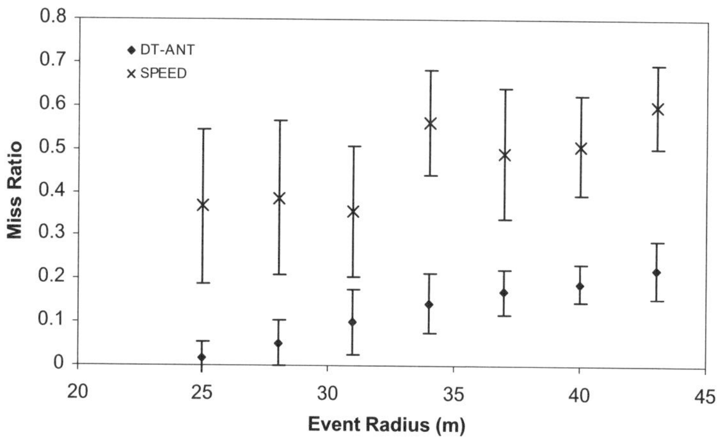

(b)

Fig. 31.8. Average delay and message miss ratio of high priority traffic against event radii; (a) average delay and (b) message miss ratio.

The application delay bound is fixed at 25 ms, as before. In Fig. 31.8(a), average delay of both approaches increased rather linearly against event size. This is due to the linear increase in the number of edge nodes (actually, this number varies in $O(\sqrt{n})$ where n is the number of nodes,[3] but for relatively small n, linear approximation is reasonable). Again, DT-ANT supports lower average delay than SPEED. For the same scenario, Fig. 31.8(b) depicts message miss ratio against event size, which also increases linearly for both approaches. Even with larger event sizes, DT-ANT is able to deliver more than 80% of its high priority messages within their deadline. This performance could be improved if the low priority messages can tolerate longer delay, which is controlled through the suppression timer. Since some of the event characteristics can be known *a priori*, such domain knowledge is useful in guiding the configuration of certain application specific parameters for an optimal protocol operation.

31.6. Conclusion

There are many wireless sensor network applications that are likely to treat data of same modality with different preference due to their semantics. This calls for the provision of quality of service (QoS) in sensor networks. In this chapter, we argued that although a wealth of literature with different QoS schemes is available, they are not directly applicable for sensor networks. Orthogonal approaches to the current schemes are necessary to tackle the unique needs of sensor network applications. Also, clustering is a commonly adopted data gathering technique for a scalable solution.

Accordingly, we proposed the DT-ANT protocol that forms a minimum spanning tree overlay for high priority, if one exists, among the clusterheads. Using a strict priority queuing policy, the clusterheads ensure that the high priority messages are delivered within the application deadline. Moreover, we also introduced *on the fly* reservation that is used to reserve access at the upstream nodes, when a high priority message is received. We further suppress the lower priority readings briefly at the sources to further facilitate the transmission of high priority messages. This is contrary to current Internet approaches, where a hard or soft resource reservation is made prior to data transmission. Even with such a strict policy, it is demonstrated that this protocol does not starve the low priority traffic, as its traffic intensity is bounded and cannot be oversubscribed unlike the Internet traffic. Through analysis, it is proved that DT-ANT guarantees deadline-driven delivery by constructing a delay-bounded minimum spanning tree if the application deadline is greater than certain limit.

Acknowledgments

This work was supported in part by grant ARC Discovery Project DP0664782.

References

1. A. Arora, *7th International Conference on Mobile Data Management* (*Keynote*), Nara, Japan (2006).
2. K. K. Chintalapudi and R. Govindan, *IEEE International Workshop on Sensor Network Protocols and Applications*, Anchorage, AK, USA, 59–70 (2003).
3. R. Nowak and U. Mitra, *Information Processing in Sensor Networks*, Palo Alto, CA, USA, 80–95 (2003).
4. C. Intanagonwiwat, R. Govindan and D. Estrin *et al.*, *IEEE/ACM Transactions on Networking*, **11**(1), 2–16 (2003).

5. O. Younis and S. Fahmy, *IEEE Transactions on Mobile Computing*, **3**(4), 366–379 (2004).
6. H. S. Kim, T. Abdelzaher and W. H. Kwon, *ACM Transactions on Embedded Computing Systems*, **4**(3), 679–706 (2005).
7. C. Lu, B. M. Blum and T. E. Abdelzaher *et al.*, *Eighth IEEE Real-Time and Embedded Technology and Applications Symposium*, San Jose, CA, USA, 55–66 (2002).
8. A. Woo and D. Culler, *7th Annual International Conference on Mobile Computing and Networking*, Rome, Italy, 221–235 (2001).
9. T. He, J. A. Stankovic and C. Lu *et al.*, *23rd International Conference on Distributed Computing Systems*, Providence, RI, USA, 46–55 (2003).
10. E. Felemban, C.-G. Lee and E. Ekici *et al.*, *INFOCOM*, 2646–2657 (2005).
11. S. Selvakennedy, S. Sinnappan and Y. Shang, *Elsevier Computer Communications*, **30**(14–15), 2786–2801 (2007).
12. T. L. Crenshaw, A. Tirumala, S. Hoke *et al.*, *17th Euromicro Conference on Real-Time Systems*, Palma de Mallorca, Spain, 177–186 (2005).
13. S. Lindsey, C. Raghavendra and K. M. Sivalingam, *IEEE Transactions on Parallel and Distributed Systems*, **13**(9), 924–935 (2002).
14. C. Bettstetter, *3rd ACM International Symposium on Mobile Ad Hoc Networking & Computing*, Lausanne, Switzerland, 80–91 (2002).
15. S. Selvakennedy, *Mobile Ad-hoc and Sensor Networks*, LCNS, Springer, Berlin/ Heidelberg, **4325**, 588–599 (2006).

Part X

Various Good Things

Chapter 32

Wireless Passive Sensor Networks: Research Challenges

Ozgur B. Akan and M. Talha Isik

Next generation Wireless Communications Laboratory (NWCL)
Department of Electrical and Electronics Engineering
Middle East Technical University, 06531 Ankara, Turkey
akan@eee.metu.edu.tr

In the near future, networks of small intelligent sensor nodes will be deployed almost everywhere to monitor the environment. The primary challenge in the design of these networks is the energy constraint due to the finite-capacity of the batteries. Therefore, the vast majority of research efforts thus far have focused on the development of energy-efficient communication algorithms and computation techniques. This chapter describes the concept of Wireless Passive Sensor Networks (WPSN) which aims to eliminate the limitation on the system lifetime of sensor networks. In WPSN, power is externally supplied to the sensor network node via an external RF source. Hence, the lifetime of the system is no longer determined by the lifetime of the batteries. An alternative communication scheme, modulated backscattering, is also discussed to be utilized in WPSN. The feasibility of the proposed system is investigated along with the challenges for reliable communication and networking in WPSN.

32.1. Introduction

The most challenging design problem of conventional Wireless Sensor Networks (WSN) which consist of low-cost, low-power multifunctional sensor nodes,[1] is the energy scarcity. The sensor nodes run on batteries with limited size and hence limited energy capacity. Moreover, recharging the batteries is not an option for most of the WSN scenarios. Therefore, the vast literature on the design of WSN mostly consists of techniques, protocols and algorithms which aim to prolong the lifetime of the network.[1] However, the finite capacity of the batteries deplete sooner or later and the operations of WSN cease.

Obviously, the reason for limited life span is the limited capacity of the batteries. After the batteries of the majority of the nodes are depleted, the deployed nodes become inoperable, thus redundant in the environment. In conclusion, a WSN operated by batteries is a disposable system, the use of which is strictly limited by the life span of the batteries on board of the sensor nodes.

Alternative sources of power, particularly sources without limited capacity, should be considered for WSN. Such a network, i.e., a WSN with unlimited power, is no more a disposable system, hence, more functional and feasible. External radio frequency (RF) power, in this regard, stands as a promising source of power for WSN. In this chapter, we analyze and show that it is practical to remotely feed the sensor nodes with this power source.

With regard to remote feeding, RFID emerges as a promising technology.[2] Accordingly, RFID tags completely depend on external RF power to function. A passive tag converts the incident RF power to DC power and operates its circuity. Moreover, the tag transmits information back to the transmitter by employing Modulated Backscattering (MB) technique which is basically modulating information onto the reflected signal by switching the antenna impedance. Since the switching operation is also powered from the harvested RF power, this communication technique does not involve active communication. Hence, power consumption is very low for RFID tags. However, the range of these systems are very short (e.g. usually not exceeding 10 m).[2]

The passive RFID tags generally transmit the stored identification information. On the other hand, sensor nodes are more complicated devices, that transmit the data gathered about the environment. In this regard, the development of wireless, remotely powered telemetry systems,[3,4] is an encouraging progress which permits a sensor node store RF power and then consume it to run a temperature sensor with a transmitter. On the other hand, another implementation consists of several passive sensors which communicate through MB from a maximum range of 15 m and at a target rate of 10 bps.[5] The sensor nodes are ultra low-cost and do not possess any receivers and transmitters. They constantly backscatter the readings of their sensors. Other preliminary studies intend to integrate RFID with sensor networks in order to improve the sensing capabilities.[6,7] However, to the best of our knowledge, there has been no effort which addresses the energy limitation problem of WSN from a fundamentally different approach.

This chapter presents Wireless Passive Sensor Networks (WPSN), a completely new sensor networking paradigm. WPSN is not constrained by the limited capacity of the batteries. *The objective of this work is to analyze the promise of battery-free WSN, present the fundamentals of WPSN and point out the challenges for reliable communication in WPSN and discuss the open research issues.* WPSN run as long as power is delivered to the sensor nodes. When not, the system remains idle but ready to operate. WPSN do not have lifetime limitation and hence is no more a disposable system making it more functional and cost efficient.

The chapter is organized as follows. In Sec. 32.2, the overview of the WPSN system model, the communication architecture and several possible topologies are presented. In Sec. 32.3, the theoretical background of the analysis on WPSN, related derivations and calculations are presented. Section 32.4 discusses alternative communication schemes. In Sec. 32.5, the communication protocol suite for WPSN are elaborated along with the open research challenges. Finally, the chapter is concluded in Sec. 32.6.

32.2. WPSN Topologies and Node Architecture

In this section, possible WPSN topologies and a WPSN model are introduced. The architecture of a WPSN node and its operation are described.

32.2.1. *WPSN topologies*

A possible WPSN topology includes a single RF source, feeding all of the WPSN nodes in the network. Alternatively, WPSN nodes may be fed by multiple RF sources spread in the network. In this approach, RF sources may be static or mobile. Depending on application requirements, using multiple mobile RF sources is advantageous in terms of data transportation and network operations. These issues are discussed in the following section.

32.2.1.1. *Single RF source*

In contrast to conventional WSNs, WPSN are fed by RF sources. A possible network topology for WPSN is shown in Fig. 32.1(a). An RF source with unlimited power feeds the WPSN nodes with RF power, and voltage is induced on the receivers of the WPSN nodes. The induced voltage is then converted to DC. The DC power is used to wake up and operate the node, however, the converted DC power can also be kept in a charge capacitor for future use. As in conventional WSNs, WPSN nodes are

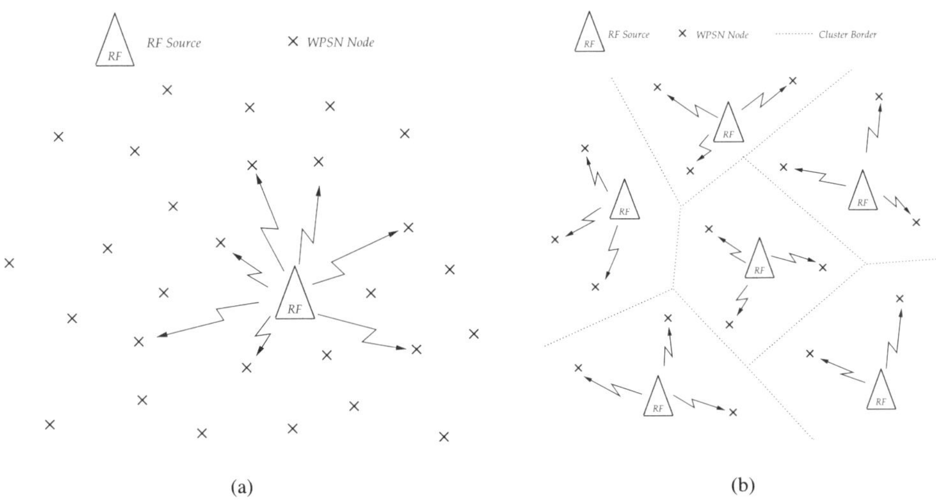

Fig. 32.1. A typical proposed WPSN topology with passive sensor nodes fed by (a) an RF source and (b) multiple RF sources in clustered architecture.

assumed to be randomly deployed. The RF source transmits[a] RF power to be used by the passive nodes in sensing, processing, receiving and transmitting. The antenna of the RF source is either omnidirectional or directional. To feed the network in a homogeneous manner, omnidirectional antennas should be used for equal power radiation. If it is required to concentrate power radiation in specific directions, directional antennas are appropriate to feed the network from distant locations.

32.2.1.2. *Cluster-based topology with multiple RF sources*

The alternative to single-source topology is using multiple RF sources, as illustrated in Fig. 32.1(b). WPSN nodes are fed by more than one RF source. As described in the next section, the communication range of WPSN nodes communicating at a specific frequency depends on the RF output power of the sources feeding the network. The analytical study presented in Ref. 8 shows that as the number of deployed RF sources increases, the required RF output power decreases. This result is shown in Fig. 32.2. Hence, the communication connectivity of the WPSN is increased by using more than one RF source.[8] With this deployment, it is more probable that a passive node is able to communicate only with one of the RF sources, and RF sources

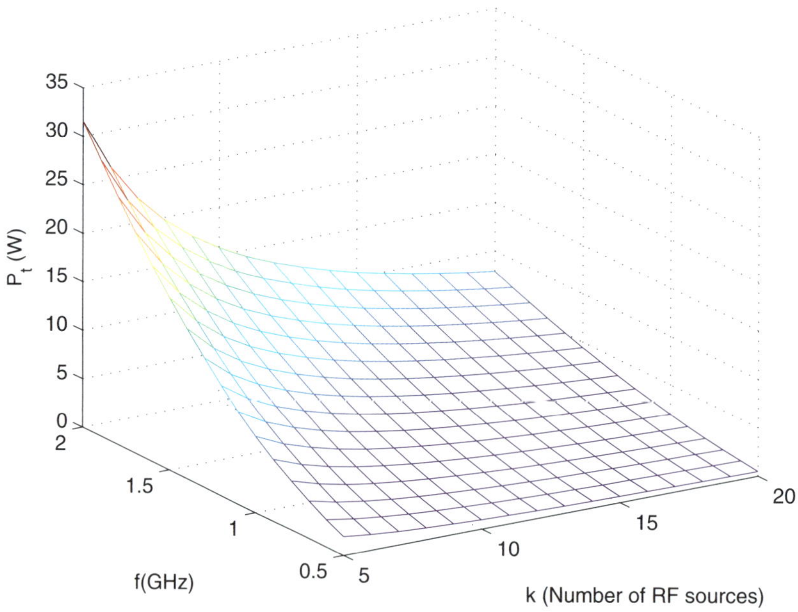

Fig. 32.2. Variation of the required RF output power with the number of RF sources and RF frequency.

[a]The RF source continuously or periodically feeds the WPSN according to the application requirements.

transmit at lower output power levels to avoid negative effects on communication such as interference.

32.2.1.3. *Multiple mobile RF sources*

Similar to the topology illustrated in Fig. 32.1(b), the RF sources in a WPSN may also be mobile. The mobility of RF sources brings advantages in sensing the event field, data communication, and energy usage. Some portions of the whole network may be more active according to the events sensed by the WPSN nodes. As a result, nodes in the active region need more energy for sensing and data processing. With mobile RF sources, power is delivered to those active regions with a higher priority. Moreover, for communication coverage and network connectivity, all WPSN nodes should sense the environment and communicate the collected data.[8] Obviously, they should be supplied with the required energy to successfully perform these duties. Therefore, efficient energy distribution is a critical issue in WPSN. To achieve fair and efficient energy distribution in WPSN, directional antennas may also be used on mobile RF sources.

32.2.1.4. *Hybrid topology with active nodes and multiple RF sources*

There are many different design alternatives for WPSN with these topologies. A promising design alternative is multi-hop data transport with network clustering. The operation of WPSN is based on the energy provided by RF sources, and clustering may be achieved by either passive or active nodes, as studied in Ref. 9. Multi-hop communication is possible through the usage of only passive nodes or by adding some active nodes into the WPSN. When all nodes are passive, the output power of the sources or the number of RF sources should be increased in order to make passive sensors store enough energy to sense events and transmit data even when they are not fed by RF sources. With the stored energy, passive nodes are able to receive and process data. After receiving data packets and processing the data, they transmit by using MB, and data is transported hop-by-hop to the sink.

32.2.2. *WPSN node architecture and operation*

A typical WPSN node hardware structure is shown in Fig. 32.3(a). The WPSN node resembles a conventional WSN node except for the *power unit* and the *transceiver*. The *power unit* of a conventional WSN node is a battery, and an additional unit *power generator* is also offered as a supporting device. In a WPSN node, the *power generator*, which is an RF-to-DC converter, is an inherent part of the *power unit* and it is the unique power source for the node. The *power unit* delivers the power received from the RF-to-DC converter to the operational units of the WPSN node and stores extra power, if available.

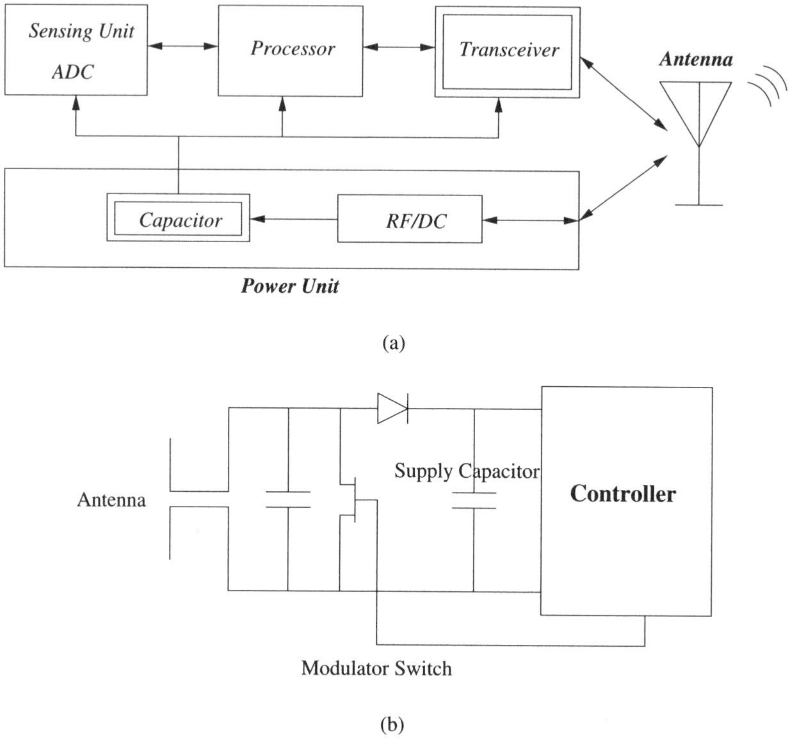

Fig. 32.3. Building blocks of a typical WPSN node and MB circuitry.

The *transceiver* of a WSN node is usually a short range RF transceiver with a considerably high power consumption when compared to the other units of the node. Hence, in this work, we study MB[10] as the communication architecture for WPSN, since it is a passive and less power consuming technique. In this model, a signal on the antenna of a WPSN node incident from the RF source is reflected back by the WPSN node. The node passively modulates the signal by changing the impedance of its antenna, thereby transmits its data by reflecting the signal back to the RF source[b] passively. The data is gathered from the *sensing unit* of the node and is processed by the *processing unit*.

Compared to the conventional RF transceiver used in WSN, the *transceiver* used for MB is much less power consuming and less complex. The receiver structures for both network architectures are similar, however, the transmitter of the MB is simply an antenna impedance switching circuitry, as seen in Fig. 32.3(b).

Using the MB technique, double sideband signals are generated, and data signals lie on both sides of the main carrier frequency. The original RF source signal is at the

[b]The RF source may also operate as the sink in WPSN.

main carrier frequency. The data rate of the WPSN node is determined by the data switching frequency, which is the difference between the frequencies of main carrier and data signal. Furthermore, the communication range of a WPSN node using MB depends both on the intensity of the incident signal, and the sensitivity of the RF signal receiver. Thus, long range communication in WPSN node is theoretically possible without increasing the power consumption, as long as a sensitive receiver and a powerful RF source exists in the network.

On the other hand, it is possible that conventional RF transceivers are employed in the WPSN nodes if sufficient power for data receiving and transmission is available on the node. In that regard, hybrid architectures based on the cooperative operation of MB hardware and RF transceivers on WPSN nodes may also be considered. Practical communication techniques that can be considered for WPSN are discussed in Sec. 32.4.

In the analysis presented in this work, randomly deployed WPSN nodes are assumed to be equipped with omnidirectional antennas, with nondirectional radiation pattern in the horizontal plane and directional radiation pattern in the vertical plane. Furthermore, the antenna is preferred to be low cost. According to these constraints, a cheap and basic omnidirectional half-wave dipole antenna is considered together with high gain omnidirectional antennas.

32.3. WPSN Model

A good understanding of the fundamental physical parameters of WPSN paradigm is essential. In this section, we look at various basic issues that arise in the design of WPSN. We first investigate the capabilities of WPSN nodes to harvest energy sufficient to power their circuitry in Sec. 32.3.1. Then we study the attainable communication ranges of the Modulated Backscattering (MB) technique in Sec. 32.3.2.

32.3.1. *Power interception characteristics of the WPSN node*

In WPSN, all the required power is supplied by the RF sources. Therefore, we first investigate whether sufficient amount of power can be intercepted by the sensor nodes of the WPSN from reasonable ranges. To estimate the power incident on the nodes, the Friis transmission equation[11] is given by

$$\frac{P_r}{P_t} = \left(\frac{\lambda}{4\pi R}\right)^2 G_t G_r, \tag{32.1}$$

where P_r is the received signal power, P_t is the power transmitted from the source, G_t is the gain of the transmitting antenna, G_r is the gain of the receiving antenna, λ is the wavelength of the signal, and R is the distance between the antennas.

WPSN nodes employ RF-to-DC converters to rectify the incident RF power to DC. The RF-to-DC converter can rectify the RF power into DC as long as 100 mV voltage is induced.[3] Hence, to start intercepting power the threshold level of 100 mV should be exceeded on the node's antenna. In this regard, the relation between the induced voltage, frequency and range is expressed by[11]

$$\frac{G\lambda^2}{4\pi} = \frac{|V_t|^2}{8W_i}\left[\frac{1}{R_r + R_L}\right], \tag{32.2}$$

where V_t is the voltage induced, W_i is the incident power density, R_r is the radiation resistance and R_L is the load resistance.

According to Eq. (32.2), the emitted power from the RF source is an important parameter. We will use two different power levels to investigate the effect of RF source. First, the maximum EIRP allowed by FCC on WLAN, 4 W, is considered. Then, we recall that for military purposes output power levels beyond FCC regulations have been commonly used, e.g., 100 W tactical radio.[12] With this regard, monitoring borders or tactically sensitive areas on an irregular basis can be provided by WPSN. For such purposes, increasing the EIRP level above the regulations may guarantee the safety of the monitoring troops. In such scenarios, the FCC regulations are most likely to be ignored, and the EIRP level is increased to keep the soldiers secure. Regarding such situations, the WPSN feasibility analysis is repeated for 0.5 W output power with the 30 dBi directional source antenna.

According to Eq. (32.2), the gain of the receiver antenna is another important parameter on power interception characteristics of the WPSN node as higher antenna gain provides better power interception capability. A 8.5 dBi gain omnidirectional antenna is assumed to be used on WPSN nodes. The radiation and load resistances are 50Ω.

The results of the first analysis are shown in Fig. 32.4(a) where we plot the maximum distance to induce 100 mV on the antennae of the nodes by using Eqs. (32.1) and (32.2). The RF output power is 4 W EIRP. Accordingly, at 2 GHz the distance

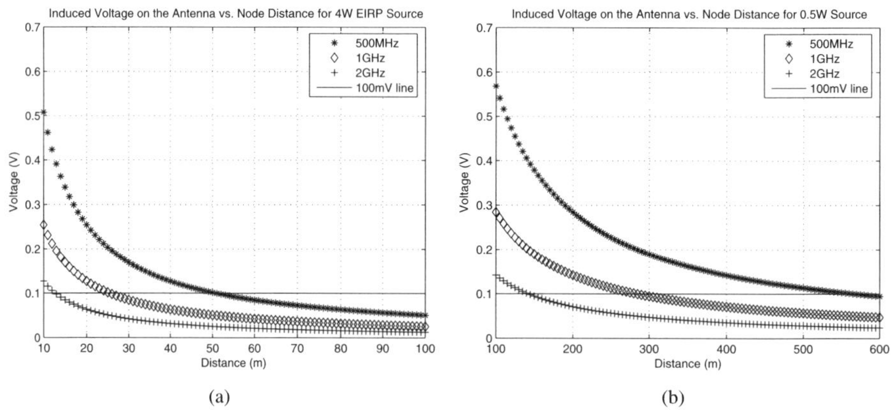

Fig. 32.4. Induced voltage on the antenna for 3 different frequencies with (a) 4 W EIRP source and (b) 0.5 W source and 30 dBi antenna.

between a sensor node and an RF source is at most 13 m. This distance increases to 26 m at 1 GHz and 51 m at 500 MHz. We conclude that it is possible to transmit sufficient energy to the WPSN nodes while also meeting the RF emission regulations. However, the maximum distance of 26 m at 1 GHz means that the RF source must come close to the WPSN in order to transmit power, requiring 4 W EIRP source to be mobile.

The same inspection is now repeated for the high output power case. The results are presented in Fig. 32.4(b) where the RF source emits 0.5 W with a 30 dBi directional antenna. Accordingly, 100 mV can be induced on the antennae from 142 m at 2 GHz, 284 m at 1 GHz and 569 m at 500 MHz which is a promising result, demonstrating the feasibility of WPSN paradigm for high power military applications, i.e., the troops may feed the WPSN from distant secure locations, given high RF power is emitted.

A conventional sensor node consumes approximately 10 mW to operate the sensor hardware, the microprocessor and the RF transceiver.[13] Therefore, we next inspect the distance from which a passive sensor node can harvest 10 mW power from the electromagnetic signals emitted from an RF source. We employ Eq. (32.1) and first perform the analysis again assuming 4 *W* EIRP source case. Accordingly, the maximum distance to transmit 10 mW power to the WPSN node at 1 GHz is 1.27 m. This result is expected since the permitted power emission levels limit the power transmission range. The solution to operate the WPSN node is either to store the transmitted power or to reduce the power consumption of the WPSN node. These options are discussed in the following sections.

For the high output power case, we employ first an omnidirectional antenna with a gain of 12 dBi and then a directional antenna emitting 10 W is used where we consider the requirement of power transmission for tactical operations. The results are shown in Fig. 32.5(a).

We observe that for the case where the RF source employs an omnidirectional antenna, the maximum range from which the sensor nodes are able to intercept 10 mW at 1 GHz operating frequency is 8 m. On the other hand, the range increases to 63.5 m for the directional antenna case illustrating the benefits of directional antennae. However, the directional antenna emits power only to a small portion of WPSN. Use of a mobile and rotating RF source with a directional antenna might be a solution. We conclude from Fig. 32.5(a) that the power incident on WPSN nodes are sufficiently high in order to power themselves from reasonable distances.

Part or all of the harvested RF power could be stored in the node. This way, the nodes become capable of operating even when no or insufficient amount of RF power is incident on the node. In this regard, the use of ultracapacitor technology is promising due to their increased lifetime, short charging time and high power density.[14–16] A 3 V, 10 F ultracapacitor with 1.0 s time constant weighs only 6.6 g. For an average power consumption of 10 mW a WPSN node runs approximately

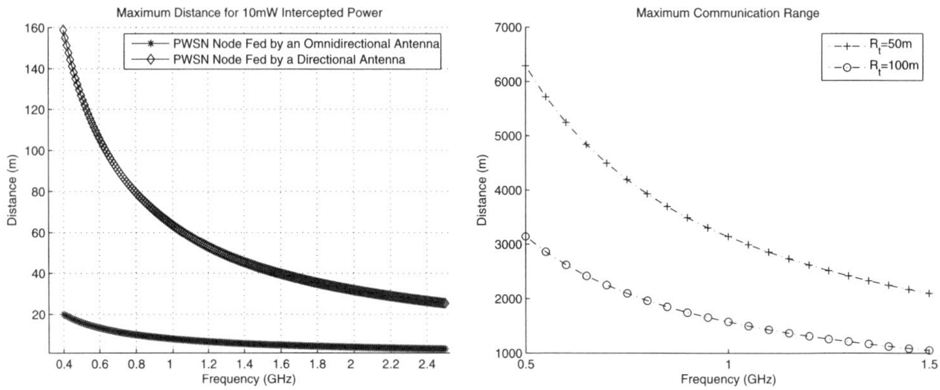

(a) (b)

Fig. 32.5. Maximum communication distance for (a) 10 mW intercepted power versus frequency for the node fed by omnidirectional and directional antennas and (b) with modulated backscattering for the half-wave dipole.

30 minutes for an operation range of 1 V.[3] According to these results, a WPSN node can function with just like a conventional WSN node for significant durations which is discussed in more detail in Sec. 32.4.

We conclude that the distances required to transmit and store power (142 m and 63.5 m respectively, at 1 GHz) are promising and demonstrate the feasibility of WPSN. The results of the investigation show that a sensor node can harvest and store RF power, and operate without batteries.

32.3.2. *Modulated backscattering*

We now consider communication through Modulated Backscattering and calculate the ranges over which an RF source can extract the information in the reflected signals from the sensor nodes. For this purpose, we use[11]

$$P_r = \frac{P_t G \sigma A_e}{(4\pi)^2 R^4}, \tag{32.3}$$

where P_r is the received reflected signal power, P_t is the power transmitted from the source, G is the gain of the antenna, σ is the radar cross section of the reflector, A_e is the effective aperture of the receiving antenna and R is the distance from the source to the reflector. The radar cross section (σ) characterizes the backscattering properties of an object. The effective aperture (A_e) of an antenna is the area, which gives the power delivered to the antenna, when multiplied by the incident power density on the antenna itself.[11]

The results are shown in Fig. 32.5(b). The RF source emits 4 W EIRP with an omnidirectional antenna of 12 dBi gain. The receiver sensitivity of the RF source is taken as $-100\,\text{dBm}$, a typical value.[11] According to the results, the maximum distance of communication at 1 GHz is around 396 m.

These results imply that the sensor nodes harvesting power from the electromagnetic signals emitted from an RF source can form a network realizing the WPSN paradigm. A detailed discussion on the possible approaches for communication in PWSN are presented next.

32.4. Communication in WPSN

The discussion in Sec. 32.2 shows that WPSN is feasible and practical. Therefore, the communication techniques to be used in WPSN should be examined, and their applicability to certain WPSN conditions should be discussed. In this section, firstly, the adaptability of conventional communication schemes employing active transmission is investigated. Secondly, MB is discussed for WPSN. Finally, some hybrid architectures are considered for WPSN applications.

32.4.1. *Active RF transmission*

WPSN nodes may employ conventional active transmitters if they have sufficient power for sensing, processing, and communication. The operation may or may not be continuous, and this depends on the amount of intercepted and stored power. The discussion on continuous and discontinuous operation is as follows:

32.4.1.1. *Continuous operation*

With this type of operation, WPSN is analogous to conventional WSN, with the unique difference of being powered by RF signals instead of batteries. The network should still be fed continuously by an omnidirectional antenna. As shown in Fig. 32.5(a), only nodes that are closer than 4 m to the RF source may be provided with RF power continuously. Hence, such a system does not satisfy a sufficient network coverage. For better network coverage, high RF power levels are required from the sources, which is not practical. RF emission regulations limit the RF power level for civilian applications. Moreover, transmitting at high power levels in tactical and military applications is dangerous, since high RF power levels make the network easily noticeable by enemy forces.

32.4.1.2. *Discontinuous operation*

Discontinuous scheme of active transmission is based on "store-and-transmit" type of operation. In this type of operation WPSN nodes do not receive enough power to operate continuously, but they store RF power in a capacitor. With stored RF power, this scheme enables increased network coverage, however, due to the storage issues, it may fail in time-critical applications. This scheme becomes more feasible with the development of ultracapacitors, which enable the WPSN nodes to operate for considerably longer durations with no need for RF sources.

32.4.2. *Modulated backscattering for communication in WPSN*

Another alternative for WPSN communication architecture design is Modulated Backscattering. As illustrated in Fig. 32.5(b), the communication range between a halfwave dipole and an isotropic RF source emitting 4 W EIRP at a frequency of 1 GHz is approximately 396 m. The power consumption of the WPSN node is only due to the antenna impedance switching. *Communication with WPSN nodes at mid and long distances is achievable by using MB technique at low RF output power compared to that of active RF transmission. However, this approach requires comprehensive investigation and development of a WPSN communication protocol stack.*

All nodes in WPSN can establish long-distance communication, and any node in the PSWN can possibly act as the data sink providing data flow from the WPSN to the user. To increase the flexibility and security of the link between the sink and the user, the sink assignment may be shifted among the WPSN nodes.

Another alternative to be considered is to feed the nodes by a mobile RF source. A mobile RF source with a directional antenna feeds the nodes in its range with its RF power and collects the sensing data from the event field. Directive antenna increases the maximum source-to-node range. This fact is illustrated in Fig. 32.5(a). Furthermore, with this alternative, there is no continuous high-power RF transmission over the event field, and hence the network becomes less noticeable by possible jammers and eavesdroppers in tactical operations.

32.4.3. *Hybrid methods*

In addition to the many advantages of MB, the advances in ultracapacitor technology enable nodes to operate without the need for RF sources in their neighborhood. In this regard, using both methods in a *hybrid architecture* utilizes the advantages of both architectures, and this might be a very promising communication method for WPSN. With a *hybrid architecture*, WPSN nodes sense events and process collected data even if no RF power signal is present. Therefore, the nodes may be capable of communicating with RF sources or the sink even when no RF signal is incident on their antennas. This way, they are able to report an urgent event to the data sink and request RF power from the sources for continuous operation in the event field.

32.5. WPSN Communication Protocol Suite

The investigation of the WPSN protocol suite and the applicability of existing WSN protocols to WPSN are mainly determined by the communication technique.

If active RF transmission is used with continuous operation, WPSN act similar to conventional WSN. The only difference is the RF power source used to feed the network. Thus, with this technique, the communication protocols used for conventional WSN protocols are applicable to WPSN. In this section, we mainly discuss WPSN with communication techniques which cannot be adapted from conventional WSN, that is, active transmission with discontinuous operation, MB and hybrid communication schemes. The adaptability of existing protocols to WPSN and the communication requirements of WPSN are investigated. Possible challenges for networking in WPSN are discussed.

32.5.1. *Physical layer*

The physical layer requirements of WPSN are much different from those of the conventional WSN, since the two networking paradigms differ in the communication and power circuitry. The conventional physical layer solutions are inapplicable to the WPSN domain, and hence the physical layer in WPSN should be investigated separately.

One of the most important issues at the physical layer of WPSN is the development of RF power induction and storing systems. For power efficiency, certain optimizations should be carried out for antenna design, signal waveform, and bandwidth. Another important consideration for power efficiency is the RF-to-DC conversion of the intercepted power. Low-level power transmission should be enabled and the RF-to-DC converters should become more efficient. Moreover, increasing the capacity and decreasing the charging time and leakage current of ultracapacitors would also lead to an improvement in the performance and lifetime of WPSN.

MB is an effective solution for WPSN owing to the simple transmitter circuitry. However, a certain receiver sensitivity is required to receive the reflected MB signals. The other important parameters which should be investigated for the receiver are power consumption, size and complexity.

Finally, in order to simplify the receiver circuitry and to increase the performance of WPSN nodes, modulation techniques should be investigated. After data is gathered by a WPSN node, it is passed through the A/D converter, and finally it is processed before being put into the format for transmission. The data to be sent is transmitted as a bit stream when the node captures the channel according to the medium access mechanism in use.

32.5.2. *Data link layer*

The data link layer challenges of WPSN are different from conventional WSN issues. First of all, error control mechanisms should be investigated thoroughly. A possible method of error control is based on the signal-to-noise ratio, that is changing the output power of the transmitter. However, physical layer based power control schemes are not applicable to WPSN employing MB, because WPSN nodes are not capable of varying the intensity of the incident signal coming from the RF source. To use a power control scheme, WPSN nodes should have active transmission capability (as in Sec. 32.4.1 and Sec. 32.4.3). Therefore, for WPSN with MB, alternative error control mechanisms, i.e., *Automatic Repeat reQuest* (*ARQ*) and *Forward Error Correction* (*FEC*) should be considered. Retransmission of data in *ARQ* based schemes, may not be practical at the presence of a mobile RF source. Therefore, the power consumption due to *FEC-based* schemes and the reliability added to the network should be tested in a real WPSN environment. According to our expectations, because of the low power levels of reflected signals from passive nodes, there is a need for error control coding for packets backscattered from the nodes. With this discussion in mind, convolutional codes could be used, since they are highly capable of error control and consume low energy for encoding.[17] Therefore, error control in WPSN is also related to the physical layer issues.

Another critical issue in WPSN is the medium access control. There are currently two groups of MAC layer solutions for conventional WSN, namely *reservation-based* and *contention-based* protocols.[1] These two groups of protocols should be analyzed separately for medium access in WPSN.

32.5.2.1. *Reservation-based protocols*

This group of protocols usually use time division multiple access (TDMA) technique, and require a cluster-based architecture for time slot assignment. There are several advantages of using reservation-based protocols. Since WPSN nodes share the same medium and the same signals incident from RF sources, a TDMA approach may avoid contention at the RF sources. However, for some TDMA-based medium access and scheduling solutions for RFID,[18] delay is a drawback in time-critical application scenarios. Additionally, a setup phase for contention is necessary for the cluster-heads to assign the time slots. Furthermore, there is a need for time synchronization, and synchronization is hard to achieve for the WPSN nodes which are dependent on RF sources and run out of power so often.

32.5.2.2. *Contention-based protocols*

In contention-based protocols, WPSN nodes listen to the channel and access the medium accordingly. For time-critical applications, contention based protocols cause a low delay, and they are preferable. Since there is no time slot assignment, no cluster hierarchy is required. On the other hand, with increasing node density, collision probability is increased. Therefore, the collision problem of nodes modulating and backscattering the same signal should be analyzed. Moreover, the physical layer properties should be investigated for the collision problem, because of the high power RF signals which may lead to interference with the low power reflected signals.

WPSN is theoretically capable of medium-range and long-range communication, and MB is a novel approach to the WSN paradigm as discussed in Sec. 32.4.2.

32.5.3. *Network layer*

Currently, there are many routing protocols proposed for conventional WSN.[1,19] The proposed solutions are grouped as *data-centric and flat-architecture*, *hierarchical*, *location-based* and *QoS-based* protocols.[1] The applicability of these protocols are investigated and WPSN requirements are discussed in this part.

32.5.3.1. *Data-centric and flat-architecture protocols*

Although simple, these protocols assume a static and slowly changing network environment, and they do not seem to be applicable to WPSN. WPSN operate in a dynamic network environment, since the power level at the nodes is a rapidly varying parameter.

32.5.3.2. *Hierarchical protocols*

If multiple RF sources communicate with multiple nodes as in Fig. 32.1(b), employing hierarchical protocols is appropriate for WPSN. With hierarchical approach, the power consumption and the delay caused by the routing setup phase are avoided. Dynamic clustering may also be needed if RF sources are mobile.

32.5.3.3. *Location-based protocols*

This group of protocols use the location information of all WPSN nodes. However, location finding hardware (e.g., GPS receiver) is expensive, power-consuming, and complicated, and hence the installation of such hardware on every WPSN node is not feasible. On the other hand, if RF sources use directive antenna in a WPSN, assuming the RF sources have location finding capability, WPSN nodes are able to get their angular position relative to different reference points. Therefore, collaborative processing of data from all WPSN nodes results in a more feasible location finding method, and location-based protocols might be used in WPSN.

32.5.3.4. *QoS-based protocols*

As a quality-of-service metric, in general, energy consumption of the network is minimized.[1] This minimization is modified in Ref. 20, considering the power flow into the WSN to fit the problem into WPSN. When MB is applied to WPSN, communication capability of the network is determined by the RF source. For active RF communication and hybrid architectures, existing protocols should be modified such that WPSN nodes require power from the RF source when needed. This approach brings a completely new routing protocol design. Moreover, with a novel multi-hop routing protocol, mid-range and long-range communication can be employed over short-range hop-by-hop links.

32.5.4. *Transport layer*

Existing transport protocols for conventional WSN are all based on active RF transmission and are not applicable to WPSN based on MB and hybrid methods. In a WPSN, the transmission of passive nodes is in correlation with the RF beam and the available power. Reliability of data delivery in WPSN is determined by certain factors such as the location of the RF beam and the power available at WPSN nodes. Hence, reliability and congestion avoidance characteristics differ largely from that of a conventional WSN. Therefore, reliability and congestion should be defined after a thorough investigation of the lower layer, i.e., physical, data link and network layer, characteristics. After then, a dedicated mechanism to control the newly defined congestion should be developed. Moreover, interaction with other layers should be analyzed to develop cross-layer solutions.

32.6. Conclusion

In this chapter, Wireless Passive Sensor Network (WPSN) is introduced. WPSN does not have any energy constraints theoretically, and hence it has an infinite lifetime. WPSN nodes are fed by external RF power sources and Modulated Backscattering is employed as a new communication technique. Possible WPSN topologies are discussed, and the feasibility of the proposed paradigm is investigated. The communication requirements and characteristics of WPSN are analyzed, adaptability of existing protocols to WPSN and communication requirements of WPSN are investigated. Possible challenges for networking in WPSN are also discussed. It is observed that WPSN is theoretically practical and is a novel approach to the design of WSN. There are many research challenges to be investigated for the development of WPSN. In addition to the research challenges discussed in this chapter, the physical layer characteristics and the applicability aspects of WPSN design remain to be investigated.

References

1. I. F. Akyildiz, W. Su, Y. Sankarasubramaniam and E. Cayirci, A survey on sensor networks, *IEEE Communications Magazine*, **40**(8), 102–114 (2002).
2. K. Finkenzeller, *RFID Handbook*, John Wiley and Sons (2003).
3. F. Kocer, P. M. Walsh and M. P. Flynn, Wireless, remotely powered telemetry in 0.25 μm CMOS, *RFIC* (2004).
4. S. Nambi, S. Nyalamadugu, S. M. Wentworth and B. A. Chin, On scheduling transmissions for hidden terminal problems in dynamic RFID system, *7th World Multiconf. on Systemics, Cybernetics and Informatics* (July 2003).
5. G. Vanucci, A. Bletsas and D. Leigh, Implementing backscatter radio for wireless sensor networks, *IEEE PIMRC* (2007).

6. M. Philipose, J. R. Smith, B. Jiang, A. Mamishev, S. Roy and K. Sundara-Rajan, Battery-free wireless identification and sensing, *IEEE Pervasive Computing*, **4**(5), 37–45 (January 2005).
7. D. C. Ranasinghe, K. S. Leong, M. L. Ng, D. W. Engels and P. H. Cole, A distributed architecture for a ubiquitous RFID sensing network, *Intelligent Sensors, Sensor Networks and Info. Processing Conf.* (2005).
8. A. Bereketli and O. B. Akan, *Communication Coverage in Wireless Passive Sensor Networks*, **13**(2), 133–135 (February 2009).
9. M. T. Isik and O. B. Akan, *PADRE: Modulated Backscattering-based PAssive Data REtrieval in Wireless Sensor Networks, IEEE Wireless Communications and Networking Conference*, (April 2009).
10. H. Stockman, "Communication by Means of Reflected Power," Proc. I. R. E, **36**, 1196–1204, (1948).
M. Kossel, H. R. Benedickter, R. Peter and W. Bächtold, Microwave backscatter modulation systems, *2000 IEEE MTT-S Digest*, 1427–1430, (June 2000).
11. C. A. Balanis, *Antenna Theory: Analysis and Design* (2nd ed.), John Wiley and Sons Inc. (1997).
12. J. F. Keating, The MXF-400 series of radios-communications for the 21st century, *Proc. IEEE Tactical Communications Conference*, 449–458, (May 1994).
13. S. Hollar, *COTS Dust*, M.Sc. Thesis, UC Berkeley, (December 2000).
14. A. Burke, Ultracapacitors: Why, how, and where is the technology, *Journal of Power Sources (Elsevier)*, **91**(1), 37–50 (2000).
15. Y. Li, H. Yu, B. Su and Y. Shang, Hybrid micropower source for wireless sensor network, *IEEE Sensor Journal*, **8**(6), 678–681 (June 2008).
16. S. Roundy, P. K. Wright and J. M. Rabaey, *Energy Scavenging for Wireless Sensor Networks with Special Focus on Vibrations*, Springer (2003).
17. E. Shih, B. H. Calhoun, S. Cho and A. Chandrakasan, "Energy-efficient link layer for wireless microsensor networks, *Proceedings IEEE Computer Society Workshop on VLSI 2001*, 16–21, (April 2001).
18. J. Waldrop, D. W. Engels and S. E. Sarma, Colorwave: A MAC for RFID reader networks, *IEEE Wireless Communications and Networking Conference (WCNC03)*, 1701–1704 (March 2003).
19. K. Akkaya and M. Younis, A survey of routing protocols in wireless sensor networks, *Ad Hoc Networks Journal (Elsevier)*, **3**(3), 325–349 (May 2005).
20. A. Kansal and M. B. Srivastava, An environmental energy harvesting framework for sensor networks, *International Symposium on Low Power Electronics and Design*, 481–486, (August 2003).

Chapter 33

Location Management in Multi-Hop Wireless Sensor Networks

Stefano Basagni* and Maurizio A. Nanni†

Department of Electrical and Computer Engineering
Northeastern University
Boston, MA, USA
**basagni@ece.neu.edu*
†mnanni@ece.neu.edu

The chapter concerns solutions about the problems of managing the location information of nodes of ad hoc and wireless sensor networks (WSNs). Once nodes know about their location, solutions for location management take care of disseminating this important information to all or some of the other network nodes that need it for routing or other purposes. The chapter covers first the solutions that have been proposed for mobile ad hoc networks, where research in this area has started along geographic routing over a decade ago. We then describe solutions in the still largely uncharted territory of WSNs. In particular, we survey methods for location management that have been proposed for different application scenarios, emphasizing how location information is managed, i.e., proactively, reactively, or through dedicated nodes (location servers), which nodes move, and the different communication models adopted. Our review of the solutions currently proposed reveals that further research is needed for providing efficient location management protocols, especially for WSNs, and that the evaluation of their effectiveness for location aware applications and geographic routing is needed for truly identify new protocol design guidelines and improved network performance.

33.1. Localization and Location Management in Ad Hoc and Wireless Sensor Networks

Since the renewed interest in *mobile ad hoc networks*[1,2] in the mid 1990s, it has become clear that *geographically enabled ad hoc routing* (or just *geo routing*)[3,4] is a viable and effective solution for data communications in multi-hop networks with node dynamics and mobility. The reasons are multi-fold. First of all, the routes from source to destination do not have to depend on the identity of intermediate nodes, as it happens in both *proactive* and *reactive* approaches to ad hoc routing.[5] For instance, in a proactive ad hoc routing protocol nodes maintain next-hop information about every possible destination continuously updated in their routing tables. When a packet for a given destination arrives, the table is checked to determine which is the next node to send the packet to in order to progress toward that destination. If the table is not updated and that node is no longer there (e.g., it has moved, a typical ad hoc event), an exception has to be triggered to solve this situation and the packet is either highly likely to be discarded or it is for sure sensibly delayed. Similarly, in a reactive setting, i.e., where routes are sought between source and destination at the time a packet needs to be forwarded, the packet itself carries the exact route it should go through (source routing). If one of the nodes in that route has moved, the packet suffers either discarding or long delays. In the case of geo routing, it is enough for some nodes to be in between source and destination at the time the packet needs to be forwarded. When a node generates or receives a packet for forwarding, it looks for *any* node in the direction of the destination, independently of its identity, which is instead a key information for proactive and reactive routing. Furthermore, in general ad hoc networks, geo-routing is considered more scalable than non-geo routing given that source nodes have to just store or look for the coordinates of the destination location (usually represented by few bytes) instead of keeping large routing tables updated or caching routes. Location awareness enables also a host of new (ad hoc and non ad hoc) applications. Typical examples include automatic device reconfiguration depending on the current location of the user/device, securing application usage/access (e.g., some features are usable only from specified locations), tracking the current position of a user/resource/device, enabling the computation of travel times depending on current position and final destination, providing traffic information based on predetermined routes, and so on.

The use of location information is even more compelling in *wireless sensor networks* (WSNs), where a large number of generally resource constrained devices (the *sensor nodes*) are deployed for providing an interface with the physical environment. These devices either *observe* the environment, or even *interact* with it (in this case they are called *actor nodes*, and the network is also called a WSAN, for wireless sensor and actor network). Specifically, each sensor node has a sensing component that performs monitoring tasks, some computational capabilities (for manipulating the sensed data) and a communication interface (usually wireless, often radio) through which it interconnects to nodes within its own transmission range to form a multi-hop network. Routes are built and maintained from the (many) sensors to few data collectors (the *sinks*), and vice-versa. Communications sensors-to-sinks serve the purpose of gathering the data at the collection points for further forwarding (for instance, over the Internet) or for processing/storage; The second direction of communication is used to communicate to the sensors what they should sense (*interest dissemination*) or, in case of a WSAN, what are the actions that (some of) the actor nodes should perform in response to some specific events. It is clear that whenever an event of interest is detected by a sensor node, the location where the event happens should be part of the information to be delivered to the sinks. Furthermore, as for ad hoc networks, geographic forwarding has been shown to be a very effective way for data dissemination and gathering in WSNs. For instance, protocols like GeRaF[6,7] or ALBA–R,[8] use nodal location and the knowledge of the current location of the sink to determine the next hop relay for a data packet. These protocols have been shown to be among the most effective routing solutions for WSNs, being able to meet their most crucial requirements, which include routing reliability, scalability, high throughput, low latency and especially energy conservation.

In order to implement geo routing in ad hoc and WSNs, and, more generally, for enabling location aware applications, two fundamental network operations must be efficiently implemented and readily available.

(1) *Localization.* Nodes needs to continuously know where they are. Mechanisms, technologies and protocols must be provided for each node to be able to determine its current position with respect to an absolute, relative or a virtual set of coordinates.
(2) *Location management.* Once a node knows where it is, there should be an efficient way to let the other nodes know its current location every time it is required.

The problem of localizing ad hoc or WSN nodes has been investigated quite widely. The US Global Positioning System (GPS), the Russian GLObal'naya NAvigatsionnaya Sputnikovaya Sistema (GLONASS) and the more recent and still "under construction" EU Galileo Positioning System[9] are nowadays a relatively easy and inexpensive solution for this problem. GPS technology is commonplace in cars, and more recently even in the most advanced cellphones. When, however, satellite-based systems cannot be used because of environmental limitations (e.g., indoor or in "urban canyons") or because of energy constraints (e.g., a tiny battery-powered sensor mote), protocols must be provided that determine and maintain a node aware of where it currently is with respect to the selected reference system. A host of protocols have been presented in the last decade for both ad hoc and WSNs. The reader is referred to Ref. 10 and Refs. 11 and 12, respectively, for further details and references.

Differently from localization, location management has not being extensively investigated, especially for wireless sensor networks. It is the aim of this chapter to provide a description of what has been done for this important field of research. We will start by presenting a brief summary of location management protocols in the general setting of mobile ad hoc networks, where research on the topic started. We then explore location management solutions for WS(A)Ns, and present the different scenarios and protocols that have been investigated and proposed so far in the literature.

33.2. Ad Hoc Location Management

The management of location information in multi-hop ad hoc networks has been mostly investigated for supporting geo routing. The first general solutions for managing location information were presented with the first geo routing protocols specifically designed for ad hoc networking, namely, *DREAM* (Distance Routing Effect Algorithm for Mobility)[13] and Location Aided Routing (*LAR*).[14]

The world according to DREAM is one where, once retrieved its location (e.g., geodetic coordinates obtained through GPS), a node *proactively* spreads it around so that every other node that might want to send it a message knows (approximately) where it is. Flooding location updates, however, can be detrimental for the network performance, especially when nodes are highly mobile (e.g., in a *vehicular ad hoc network*, or VANET[15]). Therefore, DREAM describes an efficient mechanism for location updates dissemination that is based on two simple, but very effective ideas. The first is termed the *distance effect*, and it is inspired by the concept that closer mobile objects seems to "move more" than objects farther away moving at the same speed. In other words, with respect to the same observer, the direction of the closer object changes more than that of the one that is away. In order to take advantage of the distance effect, packet carrying a location update are assigned a time-to-live based on the distance they have traveled (geographic, or in number of hops): Only few of them will actually flood the whole network. Most of them will only reach closer nodes, since these are the nodes that most need to know that the source of the update has changed location. The second idea that allows DREAM to keep location table well updated is based on the even simpler observation that if a node does not move, or moves slowly, it needs to send out location updates less frequently than nodes that are moving often or at higher speed. In other words, the sending of location updates is mobility-dependent. Once a node receives a data packet for a given destination, it checks the location of the destination carried by the packet, and it also checks its own location table to see if it has a more recent information about the destination whereabouts. The packet is then forwarded to those neighbors that are in the direction of the destination, i.e., through *directional routing*. The closer the packet gets to its destination, the more updated and accurate the location of the destination (because of the distance effect), the faster and less overhead-generating the routing.

The LAR concept takes a more reactive approach to geo routing in the sense that location is used in this case to reduce the overhead of route discovery, typical of reactive ad hoc routing protocols (that usually use flooding for route finding[5]). Based on the knowledge of the location of the destination of a data packet at a certain time, and also of its speed (and direction, if available), the source node estimates where the destination can possibly be, i.e., its *expected zone*. Based on this zone, the source sends a route request that is forwarded only by the nodes of a *request zone*. This eventually allows nodes to route request packets to the expected zone of the destination and to the destination itself. Once the routing probe reaches the destination, the destination sends back a route reply packet, as in non-geo reactive routing protocols. While data routing is of the reactive type, location information for other nodes is maintained at each node in a proactive fashion, although not periodically or based on nodal mobility as in DREAM. When a source node seeks for a route to the destination, it piggybacks its own current location to its route request packet. All the nodes that receive this packet update their entry for that source node. The same is done by the destination when it sends back a route reply packet to the source. In general, location information can be propagated by using any packet. Similarly, a node may propagate its own current speed and, if available, the direction of its movement (or its destination, if known).

Whether to deliver data (DREAM) or to seek a route (LAR) to the intended recipient of a packet, the two protocols employ a reduced (directional) form of flooding, which becomes full flooding when, for some reasons the destination cannot be found. Such situation arises, for instance, when while progressing toward the known direction of the destination, packets get stuck at a so-called *dead end node*, i.e., a node that does not have neighbors in the direction of the final recipient of the packet. Rather than resorting to flooding, Bose *et al.*[16,17] proposed *GEDIR* plus face routing (and then Karp and Kung[18] propose *greedy perimeter stateless routing*, GPSR), for which a packet gets out of a dead end node by routing around the perimeter of the region where greedy forwarding is impossible. In both cases, the protocol assumes that the nodes have access to an ideal, efficient, location database that provides them with the location of the destination. However, in the GPSR paper the increased overhead of accessing an actual location database is discussed, and the authors claim that research has started to solve the location management problem efficiently. In fact, at the same ACM MobiCom 2000, Li *et al.*[19] presented GLS, a distributed scalable location service for geo routing. A small set of the mobile ad hoc nodes act as location servers, i.e., maintain the location of the other nodes. Each node periodically updates the location servers with its current location. Queries for a mobile node location are sent by source nodes to the location servers, that reply back with the latest whereabouts of the destination. Once a source node receives the location information about the destination, it can forward the data packets by following the rules of one of the geo routing protocols seen above.

It is interesting to notice that GLS is a hybrid approach with respect to the proactive/reactive classification of location management schemes. Methods à la GLS are often referred to as *rendezvous* methods, in that the destinations proactively send their current coordinates to the location servers, the sources reactively query the servers for the destination position, and these two operations *meet* "in the middle," i.e., at the servers. Another characteristic of GLS is that a node sends its current position to the servers without knowing their actual identity. This is made possible by a predefined order of node IDs and by a spatial (geographical) hierarchy, also predefined. More specifically, the network deployment area is partitioned into a hierarchy of *grids* (whence the name GLS, for *grid location service*) with grid cells (squares) of increasing sizes. A precise order among the squares is defined so that a hierarchical organization of them is obtained that avoids overlapping. This order and the induced hierarchy are such that each node belongs to exactly one square of each size. More specifically, four smallest squares (order-1 squares) make up an order-2 square. Four of these make up an order-3 square, and so on, with the restriction that a lower order square is part of only one upper order square, not four. (This creates a tree-kind of hierarchy.) A node X determines which are its location servers according to its own ID and the predetermined grid hierarchy. The strategy is based on choosing for location servers those nodes whose ID is "close" to X's. In particular, once defined the *closest* node to X as the node that has the least ID greater than X's (the IDs are organized circularly), X chooses the three closest nodes from each of the three square siblings of the one that contains it. Similarly, it chooses three location servers for each level of the grid hierarchy. A node Y that needs to find the location of X uses geo routing to send a request to the node whose ID is the least greater than or equal than X's ID of which Y knows the location. That node forwards the location query in the same way and so on. Since the query contains Y's location, X can reply directly to Y (using geo routing). The whole GLS mechanism is based on a bootstrapping technique that takes care of X's initial selection of location servers. (The reader is referred to the GLS paper[19] for further details and the GLS performance analysis.)

As the initiator of rendezvous-based approaches to location management, GLS has inspired many other works. Xue *et al.*[20] deal with the problem of location management by proposing a *Distributed Location Management* (DLM) scheme aimed at addressing some of what they consider GLS shortcomings. Specifically, the authors argue that a GLS node can potentially scan an entire, large higher order grid before finding its closest location server in that area. Furthermore, when the location server of a node moves away from the grid cell it belongs to, another location server should be selected, and this would impose periodic location server selection, with the corresponding non-negligible overhead. Overall, the authors conclude, GLS performs well in more static environments, and some other method should better take care of mobility. DLM is based on a different partition of the network deployment area. The whole area is called the 0-order region. A first partition of this area into squares creates the 1-order regions, which are further partitioned into 2-order regions, and so on, according to a top-down partitioning (GLS implements a bottom-up one) that uses rectangles of equal size instead of squares. As in GLS, a node X should select location servers only based on its unique ID, since that is the only thing that a potential sender Y knows about X. DLM nodes select location servers as follows. The ID of X is mapped into a set of locations. Any node currently at that location can act as location server for X. Therefore, the crucial operation here is the mapping from X's ID to the locations. In DLM this is performed by using a simple hash function that takes as input the order of a region, the number of rectangles into which that region is partitioned, and X's ID. For each of the regions at a given level of the partition, based on its ID, X can choose any of the nodes in that region to act as its location server. (This process is optimized to avoid the selection of too many servers[20]). A node Y that wants to get ahold of X's current location uses X's ID to get the location server in its own region, and queries that server for the current location of X. Once the server has provided the information requested, Y can reach X directly, and X can provide more accurate information about its whereabouts. Location updates are sent by X to its servers every time it moves from its current region. When a selected server for a node X moves out of a region R, two possible solutions are suggested. Either the server itself selects another node in that region to act as a server for X and passes X's information to the newly selected node, or X itself could check whether its location server for region R is still there, and if not it selects a new server by using the selection algorithm. Other works based on the GLS idea are those by Sucec and Marsic[21] and more recently by Wang and Wang.[22] In the first case the authors address the problem of fair distribution of location management responsibilities to the location servers, so that none of them become too much of a hot spot, degrading the network performance. Furthermore, through their *Virtual Hierarchy Location Management* (VHLM) they also discuss the communication overhead associated to location registration events that happens every time a node moves. In the case of the paper by the two Wang,[22] their *Modified Grid Location Service* (MGLS) focuses on finding a different (in this case binary) grid partitioning scheme. MGLS is shown to reduce the overhead associated with location updates.

Woo and Singh[23] define the *Scalable Location Update-based Routing Protocol* (SLURP). The SLURP[a] location management is conceptually similar to that used for roaming by Mobile IP.[24] Each node is associated with a home region (a subdivision of the network deployment area, a rectangular region in the paper) by a mapping of its own unique ID (the mapping is static and known to all nodes in the network). When a node moves from a region to another it always informs the nodes in its own home region about its new coordinates (mobility triggered updates). This message is broadcast to all nodes in the node home region. When a node Y has a message for node X, it determines the home region of X and then it sends a request to the nodes in that region. The first node in X's home region that receives the request sends back X's current region to Y, and the rest of the communication happens from Y to X directly, via geo routing. In other words, the nodes in the home region of a node X act as the location servers where X's (approximate) location is proactively maintained.

[a] Note that SLURP is an ad hoc geo routing protocol, not just its location management mechanism. In the chapter however we will make no distinction between the two.

Another rendezvous-based method, termed SLALoM (for *ScaLable Ad-hoc Location Management*), has been introduced by Cheng *et al.*[25] The starting points for SLALoM are the location management solution presented for SLURP[23] and the GLS[19] protocol described above. The latter two protocols have different ways for selecting location servers, with clear pros and cons. The SLURP concept of home region makes the servers independent of the current location of the destination node X. This has the advantage that a source node Y always knows where to retrieve X's location. At the same time, if Y is far from X's home region it could wait a long time before receiving X's location, even when X is close. GLS, on the other hand, does not have a static association between a node ID and a particular region of the network deployment area, and selects servers depending on the current location of X. The density of GLS location servers is higher closer to X, which achieves the advantage that the distance traveled by the location query is proportional to the path length between X and Y. Unfortunately, however, every time X moves all the servers have to be re-appointed, which generates mobility dependent overhead (oftentimes non-negligible). The authors of SLALoM set out to define a protocol that joins the advantages of SLURP and GLS without keeping their drawback. The solution is fairly simple: Instead of having one home region, a node has many of them, uniformly distributed in the network deployment area. This renders the Y's waiting for X's location shorter than *SLURP*'s. However, many home regions require higher traffic for updates. In order to keep this traffic at bay, they use the GLS concept that nodes in those among X's home regions that are close to the current location of X should be receiving X's update, while farther home regions should be updated less frequently (à la distance effect of DREAM).

A similar approach (multiple home regions) is described by Dolev *et al.*[26] The paper defines a geo routing protocol based on the *Virtual Stationary Automata* (VSA) programming abstraction. Said abstraction consists of mobile nodes, the VSAs acting as virtual timed machines, and a local broadcast mechanism for communications among mobile nodes and VSAs. The substantial difference between this paper and previous papers on the topic is that the VSAs are statically deployed, and provide a virtual infrastructure for the communications among the nodes, having broadcast capabilities. Each VSA represents a predetermined geographic area. The location management scheme presented in this paper is based on hash tables and on the VSA-to-VSA routing service. More precisely, a mobile node unique ID hashes to one (or more, for increased reliability and fault tolerance) VSA, which represents the mobile node home region and maintain its location up-to-date.

The techniques for location management described so far, from that of DREAM to those based on location servers, involve all the network nodes for spreading out location updates. The involvement of all nodes brings with it a mobility-dependent, sometimes unbearably high, location update overhead. In order to mitigate this problem Sivavakeesar and Pavlou[27] deploy a geographically-based clustering scheme through which they define a network backbone (the usual *dominating set*[28]) that is used for location updates. More specifically, every node is assigned to a home zone (basically a virtual cluster with a unique ID) and whenever it moves it is required to update its location with any of the nodes in their home zone (by using the backbone).

Hierarchically-based location management is also explored by Philip *et al.*[29] The authors define *HGRID*, a hierarchical grid location management which, as seen so far, is based on a partitioning of the network deployment area into squares, grouped to form the different layers of the hierarchy. The first layer, formed by these unit squares, is called L_0. The grouping is performed recursively so that the leaders of the world at level L_i are chosen among the elements of the hierarchy at level L_{i-1} based on their position. Location management in HGRID is triggered every time a node crosses an L_0 grid boundary. Location updates are broadcast through the new region and also sent to both the old L_1 grid containing the previous L_0 one (if different from the current) and to the new L_1 grid. These location updates are processed at each level of the hierarchy, so that level leaders maintain a consistent vision of where the network nodes are. When a node Y needs to know the location of a node X a location query packet is sent to Y's L_1 leader. The query climbs up the hierarchy until it reaches a level L_i that contains both Y and X. At this time the location server of the ith level returns X location to Y. The location update analysis performed in the paper shows that the average per node signaling overhead grows only logarithmically with the number of nodes in the network. Simulation-based comparison with SLURP and SLALoM shows that HGRID achieves greater scalability with respect to network size and that it also adapts better to node mobility.

A hierarchically organized system of *pointers* is used for location retrieval by Flury and Wattenhofer.[30] This location management system is called MLS (this acronym is not spelled out in the paper). The MLS world is a big square with land (the region where the nodes are densely deployed) and lakes (regions with no nodes), called level-M of the lookup system. Similarly to what seen in many solutions so far, and to geographic hash tables,[31] each node has a designated (home) position on land where its current location is maintained. Instead of its (estimated) location, however, a node stores in which one of the four sub-squares of the world it resides. Recursively, each selected square stores a pointer to its sub-square that contains the node. The lookup terminates when a square is reached with a predetermined side ρ. The pointers to each square are stored at nodes in that area. The selection of the location server in this case is determined by the vicinity of a node to a specific position in the area. (The presence of such a node is "guaranteed" by the assumption of high nodal density.) Any hash function mapping a node unique ID to a position on land is a suitable function for this mechanism. Node updates and node lookup are similar to the rendezvous protocols seen so far.

At the end of this section we want to mention a method that addresses the problem to determine the current location of a node for a purpose different than that of enabling geo routing. This is the case of the joint solution to the problems of mobility management and location management addressed by Haas and Liang.[32] Although geared toward ad hoc networking, this work has a more "cell phone network" flavor, in that it considers location databases and discusses how to extend and distribute the concepts of *home location register* and *visitor location register* to work well in the ad hoc setting. Nodal location is sought for by the network so that calls to a node can be efficiently delivered to it, and the location of a node is actually defined based on its vicinity to a location database (in the specific case illustrated in the paper the location of a node is the ID of its nearest location database, although other location indications are possible). In this sense this work is much more a work on mobility management for ad hoc network than a solution for location management to support geographic routing. Some of the network nodes act as location databases and organize themselves into a virtual backbone that is maintained as the nodes move. Location searches are performed through the backbone, while once a node location is determined, routing happens in the flat network (i.e., the network with no hierarchical organization) and packets do not have to necessarily go through backbone nodes. (The routing itself does not need to be geo routing.) The location databases are organized as a class of *uniform quorum systems*, i.e., sets of databases every two of which intersect at a constant number of databases (and no quorum contains another). When a location update or a call for a mobile node arrives at a database the mobile ID is stored or read from all the databases of a quorum, chosen non-deterministically. The details of the method are conveyed in the paper, which also describes how to partition the ad hoc network so that each node has a database suitably close, even in presence of mobility. As mentioned, although the selection and use of the location databases could be used for location management as intended in this chapter, the actual aim of this paper is to implement efficient mobility management à la cellular networks.

Performance comparisons among different techniques for ad hoc location management as well as among specific location management protocols has been performed by Camp *et al.*[33] as well as by Das *et al.*[34]

Further information and references on location management for ad hoc networks can be found in the surveys by Ivan Stojmenovic[35] and by Mauve *et al.*[36] The reader is also referred to the paper by Friedman and Kliot[37] for a survey on the more general topic of *location services* for (hybrid) ad hoc networks.

33.3. Location Management in Wireless Sensor Networks

As a specialized paradigm of the general ad hoc networking model where nodes are generally heavily resource constrained, wireless sensor networks (WSNs) have been initially investigated with a strong emphasis on energy conservation rather than mobility. In fact, mobility has not been a problem at all in early WSNs research, since most of the investigated scenarios concerned networks where a large number of *static* wireless sensor nodes would self-configure into a multi-hop network and would deliver data to a small number (usually equal to 1) of *static* data collectors (the *sinks*). A host of protocol stack solutions, new technologies and techniques have been presented in the past decade that focus on how to prolong the lifetime of tiny, resource limited *motes* that are usually battery powered and deployed in regions where recharging their batteries or changing them is not viable, or impossible all-together. Only recently, after so many physical, MAC and network layer solutions have been defined and tested for static wireless sensor networks, an interest in the mobility of some of the network components has arisen. Two are the main research directions. The first and perhaps most investigated concerns the *exploitation* of the mobility of the devices for the betterment of network performance.[38–50] In particular, research have explored ways of moving through the network the least constrained nodes (such as the sinks, or resource-rich relays acting as middle-men between the sensors and the sinks) so to prolong network lifetime. A thorough survey of this kind of mobility is beyond the scope of this chapter, and the interested reader is referred to works by Basagni *et al.*[50–52] and Ekici *et al.*[53] The other direction is similar to that of ad hoc networks, where basically all nodes can move, and there is the need to define protocols that know how to handle routing toward the (possibly mobile) sinks.

With device mobility comes the need to manage their changing location, and therefore the need to define location management protocols that take into account the different requirements of wireless sensor networking applications. In fact, applications for these networks have requirements so specific that each of them defined a different scenario. This is quite different from ad hoc networking. For instance, while in ad hoc networks all nodes are mobile and they have overall the same characteristics and importance, in WSNs devices are very heterogeneous: Sensors are different from sinks, which in turn might be different from relay nodes (e.g., as in the data MULEs scenario[39]). The application mandates which network component is necessary. Ad hoc nodes can all be source and destination of communications (peer-to-peer model). As a consequence, they all query for the location or other nodes, or maintain up-to-date information about it at location servers. The WSN model of communication is greatly application dependent: For environmental monitoring, for instance, data goes from the sensors to one sink (many-to-one model) and from the sink to all sensors (e.g., for interest dissemination; one-to-all model). As a consequence, if a sink moves, the sensors need to query where the sink is, and not the sinks themselves.[50] In tracking applications, the objects to be tracked (humans, robots, resources) can be roaming through the network, and either themselves or the closest sensors should take care of updating their location at the location servers. In case of a WSAN (wireless sensor and actor network), actors can have completely different requirements than those of sensors or sinks. They might need to retrieve the location of the sensor that has sensed the occurrence of a given event. Or they might make their own location known to the sensors or to the sinks, so that they can be reached in case they are needed.

Because of this variety, we present the mechanisms for WSN location management one by one, and for each one we focus on the description of following characteristics:

- The application scenario, with a particular emphasis on which network components move.
- How location information is managed: Proactively, reactively or through location servers (rendezvous).
- Which network components need to be aware of their location.
- The communication model.

The description of the protocols follows. The section concludes with a table that lists all the major protocol characteristics (Table 33.1).

33.3.1. *GMRE: The greedy maximum residual energy protocol and its proactive location management*

GMRE[50,54] is a distributed heuristic designed for WSNs where a large number of sensors are deployed either on a grid or randomly and uniformly, and one sink roams through the network and sojourns at specified *sink sites*. The sink moves in order to drain energy from the nodes evenly, which obtains longer network lifetime. Balanced energy consumption is achieved by making the sink aware that somewhere else in the network there are nodes with a higher level of energy. At that time the sink greedily moves to the neighborhood with the maximum residual energy. Since when the sink is in transit from a site to the next one nodes cannot send their data packets to it, GMRE mandates that before moving the sink floods the networks with a "stop" packet, which makes the nodes buffer all their data packets, and that upon arriving to the next site the sink sends a "resume" packet that has the twofold effect of building new routes to the current position of the sink, and to resume packet transmission. Therefore, the location of the sink (which is its coordinates only if the routing from the sensor to the sink is geo routing, but that in general is just a route to it) is proactively maintained at the sensor nodes, without them having to query for it. However, sensors and sink need to be aware of their own position,[50] which can be obtained via GPS, or, when not possible, by executing a WSN localization algorithm.[11] Once routes are set up, and the sensors know the new position of the sink, the communication flow is from the sensors to the sink.

Basagni *et al.*[52] also describe a solution for a similar scenario with multiple sinks where the GMRE proactive location management is used for route management as described above. As noticed for DREAM and LAR (Sec. 33.2), using flooding can be too expensive in terms of energy consumption and nodal overhead, and therefore, methods based on intermediate nodes that can provide cheaper mechanism have been developed.

33.3.2. *ACT: Actors location management in Wireless Sensor and Actors Networks (WSANs)*

Wireless Sensor and Actor Networks (WSANs)[55] are distributed wireless systems of heterogeneous devices referred to as *sensors* and *actors*. Actors collect and process data produced and sent by the sensors and consequently perform actions. In general, actors are considered devices with high battery life, good processing capabilities and also high transmission power. It is also assumed that they can easily communicate among themselves, e.g., through wireless access points or the like. In the scenario depicted by Akyildiz *et al.*[55] actors are the only mobile nodes in the network, and because of this mobility, sensors need a mechanism to retrieve their location. Based on the sensor data, actors identify an *action area*, for instance, a place where an event has happened and there might be the need of their presence. Based on the event and on the recognized action area, actors coordinate and some of them move to the area. In such a scenario, both *sensor-actor* and *actor-actor* coordination needs to be efficiently handled. To this purpose, Melodia *et al.*[56] introduce a hybrid location management scheme to handle the mobility of actors requiring minimal energy expenditure to the sensors. This solution is proactive given that it is based on update packets sent by mobile actors to sensors to keep them updated about where they are (à la GMRE). The network deployment area is partitioned according to the Voronoi diagram technique,[57] a well known method for partitioning the plane according to predetermined points. The Voronoi tessellation is performed with respect to the actors, and therefore there is an actor in each Voronoi cell (Fig. 33.1). Each actor node is responsible for the nodes located in the cell where it resides and these nodes are made aware to the presence of their actor based on a periodic broadcast from

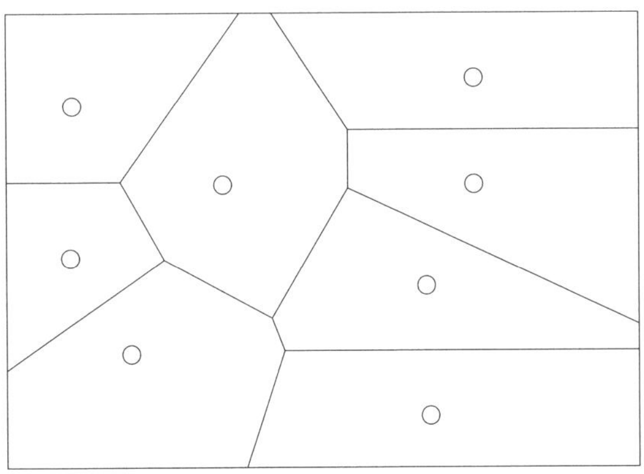

Fig. 33.1. Example of a Voronoi diagram generated by actor nodes (the empty bullets).

it, carrying its position. Location updates are sent by the actors to the sensors locally. By using Kalman filters[58] both at the actors and at the sensor nodes it is also possible to reduce the number of location updates. At each step, by using the filters each actor emulates the prediction procedure performed at the sensor nodes in its cell. It calculates its new position and broadcasts it if and only if a sensor in its cell is not able to estimate it within a maximum error e_{max}. A sensor that does not receive a location update assumes that the predicted position is a good estimation for the position of the actor. Therefore, when a sensor node needs to send some data to the actor node, it either uses the location update it has received (if any) or it uses the estimated position. A mechanism for congestion control is also introduced according to which when an actor a_k detects low reliability (e.g., high packet delays or high packet drop rate), it redirects half of the sensors-actor traffic to another actor. The selection of the alternative actor is performed considering congestion of the other actors and their current position. For further details about the congestion control mechanism and the actor-actor coordination mechanism (for which no location management service is needed), the reader is referred to Ref. 55.

33.3.3. *MT: Object tracking and position retrieving with a multi-tree structure*

Let us consider a WSN scenario in which users know the presence of some objects in the network and may request the location of some of them by querying the sensor nodes. To this purpose, the sensors need to send out a location query in order to retrieve the object position and possibly start a communication with it. For such a scenario Lin *et al.*[59] propose a location management scheme that falls in the flooding-based reactive protocols category. In order to limit the "broadcast storm"[60] which is typical of flooding, the extent of the broadcast of the query packet is contained by defining a multi-tree structure over the flat organization of the network nodes. In order to track the objects, a simple *nearest-sensor tracking* model is adopted. The space is partitioned by using Voronoi diagrams (see above), based on the sensors, i.e., there is a Voronoi cell for each sensor in the network. Each sensor is in charge for the cell containing it. Given a WSN with n sensor nodes, $m \leq n$ are designed as sinks $(\sigma_1, \ldots, \sigma_m)$. A multi-tree construction protocol is then initiated for building m trees each routed at one of the designated sinks. The trees are build with the precise aim of minimizing the cost of location updates. The paper explores two different multi-tree construction protocols: A first one, termed MT-HW (multi-tree construction with high-weight-first property), selects the tree edges based on the weight of the links. In this case the weight is given by the event rate between a node and each of its neighbors. A second algorithm, termed MT-EO (multi-tree construction with edge-overlap-first property), is designed to increase the level of overlap among links of different trees. Both solutions have the property that each of the constructed tree is a shortest-path tree.

Concerning the location update mechanism, every node X maintains a *Detected_List* DL_x that contains an entry for the objects detected by the sensor X itself, and an entry for each neighbor Y that contains all the objects detected by the nodes of the subtrees rooted at Y of some T_{σ_i} (the tree rooted at the sink σ_i). This implies that if a node Z is tracking a certain object o, and Y is an ancestor of Z, then a third node X can find out the position of o by asking Y. It follows that for each sink σ_i, the list DL_{σ_i} contains all the objects tracked by the network. The goal of the location update is to ensure that the *Detected_Lists* of the sensors are updated. The idea behind the location update is that when an object o moves from a sensor X to a sensor Y, for each sink σ_i, the update messages should be sent from X to Y up along T_{σ_i}. This is because the DL of the common ancestor nodes that are two hops away in T_{σ_i} are not affected by this movement. Furthermore, since in a network with m trees the number of neighbors of X may be smaller than m, some of the neighbor nodes are parents in more than one tree and as such they can be updated together. Let us consider the multi-tree structure in Fig. 33.2, where one tree is represented by solid links and the other by dashed ones. The figure shows two trees, T_A and T_B, rooted at the two sink nodes A and B, respectively. The two objects O_1 and O_2 are tracked respectively by the nodes X and F, respectively. If the object O_1 moves from the Voronoi cell of node X to that of node Y, the only nodes that need to be updated are the nodes in the path from X to Y in the trees. Nodes B, D, E, and F do not contain the object O_1 in their DL, and they do not contain it after it moves from X to Y. Node A does not need to update its tables, since object O_1 is still tracked by one of the nodes in the subtree rooted at its descendant node C. The only node that needs to perform the update is node C, which has to move the object O_1 from the subtree rooted in X to the subtree rooted in Y. In other words, the update can be limited to the first common ancestor. For

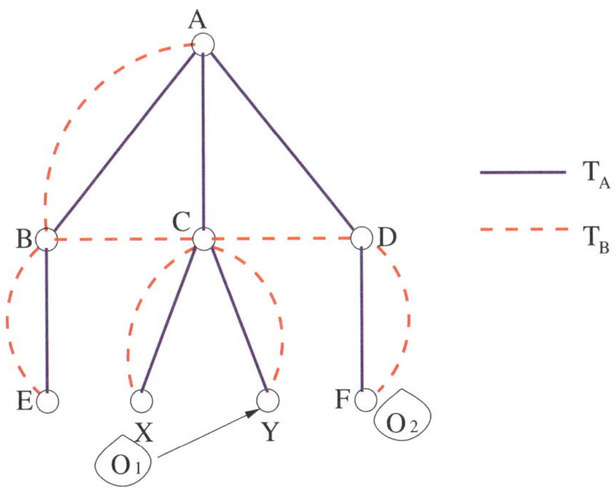

Fig. 33.2. The location update limited to the closest common ancestor in the tree structure.

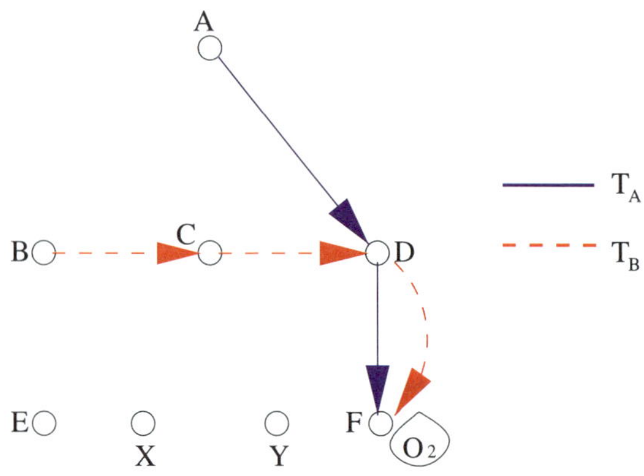

Fig. 33.3. Query graph, and O_2 retrieval.

what concerns the location query mechanism, a user can issue a query from any sensor. When a node X receives a query about an object O, we have two possible cases: (1) O does not appear in any of the entries in DL_X. In this case the query is forwarded to the closest sink. (2) The object O appears in at least one of the entries of DL_X. In this case, given an object O we can define the directed *query graph* $G_O = (V_O, E_O)$ where a directed edge $(u, v) \in E_O$ if and only if $O \in DL_u(v)$. If X forwards the query along the query graph G_O the object O is always reachable. In Fig. 33.3 we show the query graph for the object O_2 of the multi-tree of Fig. 33.2. When the query reaches the sensor that is currently tracking the object, the tracking node replies to the source sensor with the position of the object through the graph. The source sensor is then able to communicate to the object by sending the packets via geo routing.

33.3.4. *ALS: Anchor location service for mobile sinks scenarios*

The WSNs and scenarios considered by the *Anchor Location Service* (ALS)[61] are similar to those of GMRE. In this case, however, multiple sinks are allowed to move throughout the network deployment area. The substantial difference with GMRE is that the ALS protocol is a rendezvous kind of location management: There are nodes (sensors) that keep the location of the closer sink. The *ALS* sensing field is a plane divided into cells of equal size (a grid), similar to that used by GLS[19] for ad hoc networks. The crossing points of the grid are called *grid points*. For each grid point, the nearest sensor node to such grid point is referred to as *grid node*. (For each grid point we have exactly one grid node.) Grid nodes are elected in a distributed manner during the *global grid setup process*. Grid points and grid nodes are depicted in Fig. 33.4. Once grid nodes are selected, each sink selects the nearest grid node as its *sink agent*. The sink agent selects some grid nodes as *anchors* and builds an anchor system, i.e., a set of grid nodes that act as location

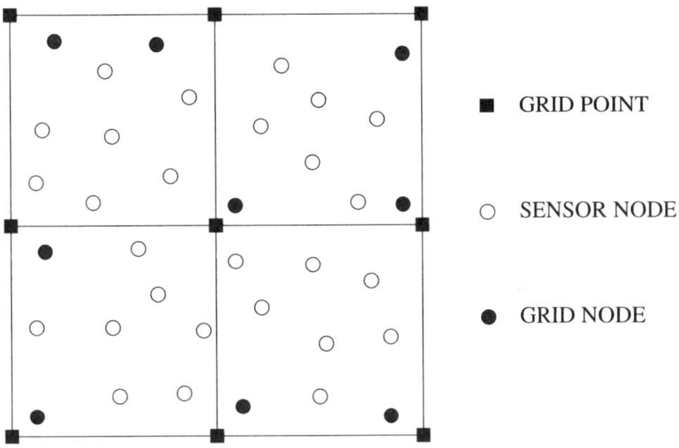

Fig. 33.4. The ALS grid, with grid points and grid nodes.

servers for that sink. Anchors are selected in a distributed manner in such a way that they will be distributed along the entire network and on the border of the void areas (i.e., area where there are no sensors). In general, a sink agent starts the *anchor selection process* sending four *first stage anchor setup packets* toward four orthogonal directions, say, North, East, West, South. All the grid nodes along the path are recruited as anchors. When one of these messages arrives at the border of the deployment area or at that of a void, two *second stage anchor setup messages* are created and routed following the right-hand rule and the left-hand rule[18] with the aim of routing the packets around the void. This mechanism is better explained with an example (Fig. 33.5). The sink agent is located on the bottom border of the grid. It sends out four first stage packets. The packet heading North reaches the node located at point P, in the proximity of a void (dark solid area). The node checks its neighborhood list and realizes that the packet can not be further forwarded North. Therefore, two second stage packets are generated and forwarded East and West according to the the left-hand and to right-hand rules. When a second stage packet reaches the line $x = 5$ in the point P' the packet is divided again into two new second phase messages. In particular, one message keep heading East until it reaches the point P'', while the other is routed North along the line $x = 5$. If some grid node in the network receives some anchor setup messages that it has already received, the node stops propagating that message (as it is the case at points P'' and P''').

Once every sink agent has performed the anchor setup phase, normal communication sensor-to-sink may start. In particular, when a sensor node needs to send out some data to a sink, it sends a request to the nearest grid node (its source agent). The source agent sends out four query packets along four orthogonal directions, as in the anchor system setup process, to find the location of the sink agent. Once the source agent gets back the location of the sink agent from one of the anchor nodes,

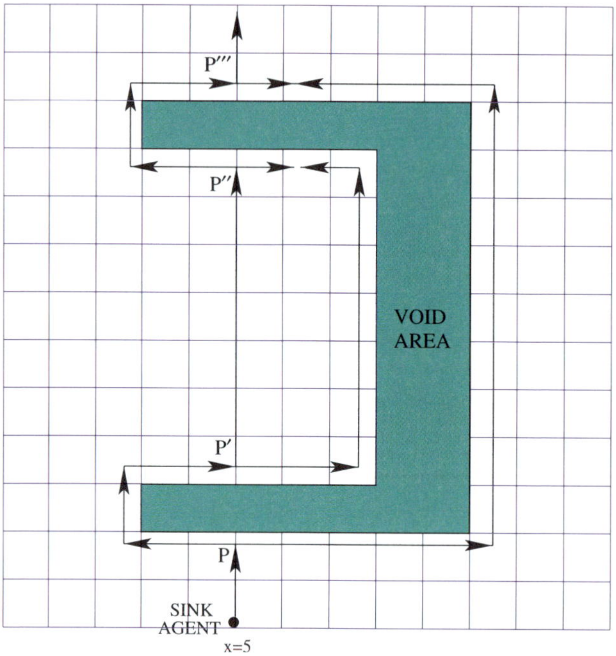

Fig. 33.5. Dealing with voids.

it sends it to the source node. The source node can then send out data packets to the sink agent using any existing geo routing.

33.3.5. *MANY: Manycast communications from a fixed source S*

Zhu and Gupta[62] consider a scenario in which a static source node S wants to perform a manycast communication to a subset D of mobile destination nodes. The authors introduce a solution, termed MANY, which falls into the rendezvous-based category. The deployment area is divided into grids (similar to GLS[19]), and a distributed protocol is introduced for selecting location servers. For each of the equally-sized cell of the grid, a certain number of nodes are elected to be *grid leaders*. The leaders are in charge of maintaining the location information of the destinations in their cell. Destination nodes know their own position and report it to the grid leaders when they switch from a cell to a neighboring one. This update requires the cell size to be fine-tuned. In fact, on one hand, the grid size should be large enough to avoid too many location updates. On the other hand, very large cells may lead to inefficient routing between the grid leaders and the destinations. Furthermore, the few grid leaders in the cell may result to be bottlenecks in the network. Grid leaders are elected in such a way that central nodes in the cell are more likely to be selected. In particular, a node X select itself to be grid leader if

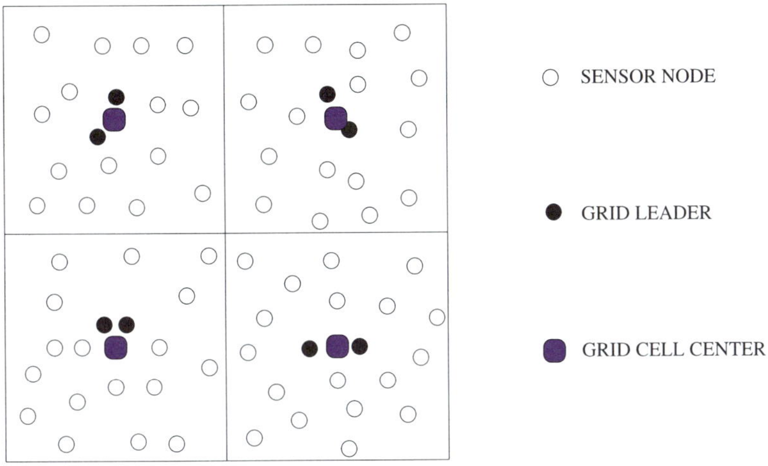

Fig. 33.6. The MANY grid scenario ($l = 2$).

at most $l - 1$ of its neighbors are closer to the geometric center of the cell than X. The value l is chosen based on the network density and it determines the number of grid leaders in each cell. In Fig. 33.6 we show an example of a sensor network organized following the MANY grid structure. In the example, $l = 2$, i.e., the two nodes that are the closest to the centroid of the grid cell are selected as grid leaders. When a destination walks into a new cell, it sends out a location update toward the center of the cell, using geo routing. The destination also includes in the packet its speed and movement direction. Assuming that the destination will move on a straight line for a short period of time, a grid leader may estimate when the destination will leave its cell. Each grid leader uses this information to estimate the number of destinations in its cell. Leaders periodically update the source node S about the number of destinations in their cell. The actual manycast communication happens via a protocol defined in the paper and called *GridTree*. The idea of GridTree is that of optimizing the overall transmission cost by using grid leaders as backbone and routing the data packets through a tree formed based on the grid leaders.

33.3.6. *RNNS: Reverse nearest neighbor and objects-to-objects communications*

Tseng *et al.*[63] investigate the in-network processing of *reverse nearest neighbor* (RNN) queries for moving objects in sensor networks. Let us consider a sensor network in which sensor nodes are employed for detecting the presence of objects in the sensing field. Given a set of objects and a query object, a RNN query retrieves all the objects whose nearest neighbor is the query object. To this purpose, a rendezvous-based location management scheme has been developed. The sensing field is divided

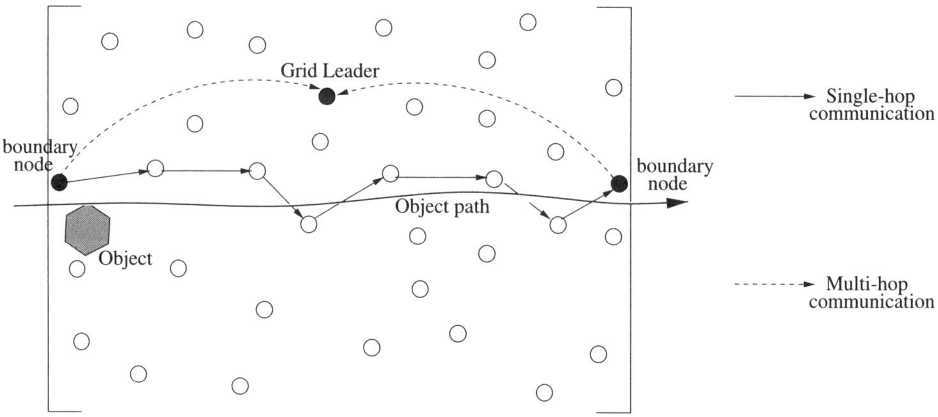

Fig. 33.7. A grid cell, boundary nodes and the grid leader.

into grid cells. The sensor node closest to the centroid of a grid cell is referred to as the *grid leader* and it serves as the location server for the objects tracked in the grid cell. Nodes close to the boundary of the grid cell are called *boundary nodes*: These nodes are responsible of detecting any object entering or leaving the grid cell and of reporting any change to the grid leader. In order to distinguish whether an object is entering or leaving the grid cell, the sensor nodes in the grid cell track the path followed by the object inside the cell, broadcasting a packet every time a sensor node detects the object. The packet carries the ID of the node and all the information collected about it. In so doing, when the object reaches a boundary node and leaves the grid cell, the boundary node has already received information about that object, therefore realizing that the object is leaving the cell. This event is signaled to the grid leader. This mechanism is shown in Fig. 33.7. In the example we can see an object entering and leaving the grid cell. As soon as the object gets into the grid cell, the boundary node signals its presence to the grid leader. (This phase is called *link initialization.*) The intermediate sensor nodes keep tracking the presence of the object, broadcasting information as they detect it. (This phase is called *link construction* and the link chain is referred to as *forwarding link.*) In the picture the forwarding link is represented by the arrow chain from the left boundary node to the right boundary node. When the object reaches the boundary of the grid cell, the boundary node is aware of the fact the object is actually leaving the grid cell, and this is what it communicates to the grid leader. (This phase is called *link reset.*)

In order to perform a reverse nearest neighbor (RNN) query, two phases are defined: A *filtering phase* in which objects that cannot be RNNs are pruned, and a *verification phase*, in which the remaining objects are verified to be RNNs. When a query object needs to inject a query in the network, i.e., when it needs to know which objects are "close" to it, a query packet is geographically routed toward the

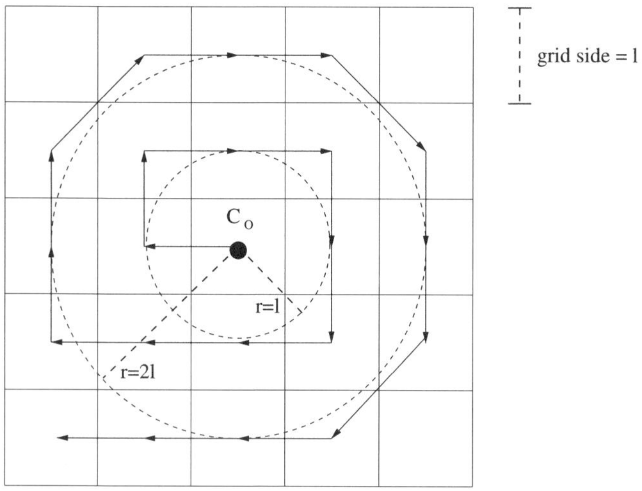

Fig. 33.8. Query forwarding: Spiral routing.

centroid of the actual grid cell C_o, i.e., toward the grid leader of C_o. The grid leader is responsible for performing the RNN query and for returning the query result to the query object. The cells surrounding C_o are sequentially visited in a spiral routing fashion, as shown in Fig. 33.8. In particular, at each round i, the grid cells intersecting the circle centered in C_o and with radius $l * i$, where l is the side of a grid cell, are visited in clockwise order. Each grid leader knows exactly who is the next grid leader to which the message has to be forwarded. When a grid leader receives a query packet, it searches for candidate objects in its own grid cell. In particular, if a candidate object appears in its tables, a packet is sent through the forwarding link until the last sensor node in the chain is encountered. Then, a packet with the location of this sensor is sent back to the grid leader, returning the current position of the inquired object. After the grid node has retrieved the position of all the candidate objects in its grid cell, some objects are discarded via the filtering phase, based on the distance of the objects in the grid cell from the query object. In particular, an object o_i in the grid cell is discarded if $dist(o_i, o_q) > dist(o_i, o_j)$, where o_q is the query object and o_j is another object in the grid cell. If this is the case, o_i cannot be an object such that the query object is the nearest one. After the filtering phase, the query packet is forwarded to the next grid cell. When a cell leader has no more neighbor cells to which to forward the packet, a packet containing the set of the candidate objects is sent back to the grid leader of the cell C_o for the verification phase. During the verification phase, the node analyzes each candidate object o_c. In particular, an object o_c is discarded if, considering a circle of radius $dist(o_c, o_q)$, there exists at least one candidate object inside that circle. The objects that survive the verification phase are RNN objects and such list is sent to the query object.

33.3.7. *SERV: Service localization in static WSNs*

Let us consider a static WSN scenario in which some of the nodes are capable to provide some services, such as providing the locations of other nodes or resources in the network, to other sensor nodes. In order to use one of these services, a sensor node needs to retrieve the location of the node that offers it, i.e., a services localization scheme is required. This is the problem tackled by Nidito *et al.*[64] They propose a rendezvous-based service management scheme, in which each node providing one or more services (also referred as *server nodes*) are mapped to some special nodes (*server locators*) that know the location of server nodes and the services they provide. Each server node registers its services to some server locators. The location of the locator is obtained employing some *Geographic Hash Tables* (GHT).[31] This hash tables perform two basic operations, namely, *put* and *get*. The hash function takes as input a *key* and return a pair of coordinates (x, y). The actual GHT algorithm employed in this solution is called Q-NiGHT,[65] which includes mechanisms for providing some QoS, fault-tolerance and a better balancing of the service requests among the nodes. In particular, in Q-NiGHT the information is stored at the Q nodes that are closest to the point returned by the GHT. Therefore, the information can survive $Q - 1$ faults. Furthermore, Q-NiGHT uses a hash function that considers the distribution of the sensors on the sensing area, and distribute data according to such distribution. Therefore, dense regions store a higher amount of data, while sparse regions store only few entries. This approach guarantees a better balancing of the request traffic among the sensor nodes. The algorithm works as follows. At the beginning each server node registers its service(s) to the server locators using the hashing function provided by Q-NiGHT. In particular, each server hashes the name of each of its services obtaining a pair of coordinates (x, y). Then, the node sends a *PUT* packet to each of the server locators routing the packet via geo routing. In this way, servers make server locators aware of their position. When a sensor node needs a service s_i, it hashes the service name obtaining the spatial location (x, y) of s_i. Then, the node sends a *GET* packet to the server locator in order to retrieve the position of the server of the service s_i. The node also caches the location for that service for future uses and maintains this information for a period τ. If the same service is offered by several server nodes, the server locator chooses one of the servers according to some policy (for instance in a round robin fashion) with the aim of balancing the query load among the different servers. In order to obtain a certain level of fault-tolerance, server nodes keep providing their position periodically (every τ seconds) to the server locators. The server locator removes the service from its tables if no *PUT* packet has been received for 2τ seconds. If a sensor node contacts a dead server using the cached information, the previous neighbor of the server responds to the querying sensor with an error packet. Then, the node remove the information from the cache and perform a *GET* to the service

Table 33.1. A bird's eye view of the characteristics of location management protocols for WSNs.

Protocol	Type	Who moves	Who queries	Who is located	Communication flow	Location awareness
GMRE[50]	proactive	sink	no query	sink	sensors to sink	sensors and sinks
ACT[56]	proactive	actors	no query	actors	sensors to actors actors to actors	sensors and actors
MT[59]	reactive	objects	users through any sensor node	objects	sensors to objects	sensors, sinks and objects
ALS[61]	rendezvous	sinks	sensors	sinks	sensors to sinks	sensors and sinks
MANY[62]	rendezvous	a set D of destination nodes	fixed source S	destination nodes	node S to a set $D' \subseteq D$ of destinations	sensors and destinations
RNNS[63]	rendezvous	objects	objects	objects	objects to objects	sensors
SERV[64]	rendezvous	none	sensors	servers	sensors to servers	servers

locator. Once the querying node obtain the server location, it can start using the service routing packets via some geographic routing algorithm.

33.3.8. *Table summary*

The main characteristics of the protocols described in this section are summed up in Table 33.1.

33.4. Conclusions

In this chapter we have discussed the importance of mechanisms for location management in multi-hop networks and especially in wireless sensor networks. We have briefly reviews location management schemes proposed for mobile ad hoc networks, with an emphasis on those that enable geo routing. We have then described recent solutions for wireless sensor networking, where location management is a crucial tools for the requirements of very specific and very different applications. Our survey of the proposed methods reveal that for both ad hoc and WSNs research is still needed about the impact that the location management schemes have on the performance of geo routing, and in general of all location aware or location based application. Further insights are also necessary about the interaction of mobility and location management. These insights are expected to provide new and more efficient design guideline for location management as well as for more efficient WSN protocol stacks.

Acknowledgments

This work was supported in part by the NSF grant #CNS-0737720. The first author is also thankful to Michael J. Roncarati for useful comments.

References

1. S. Basagni, M. Conti, S. Giordano and I. Stojmenovic, (eds.), *Mobile Ad Hoc Networking*, IEEE Press and John Wiley & Sons, Inc., Piscataway, NJ and Hoboken, NJ, (April 2004).
2. O. K. Tonguz and G. Ferrari, *Ad Hoc Wireless Networks*, John Wiley & Son., LTD, West Sussex, UK (2006).
3. I. Stojmenovic, Position based routing in ad hoc networks, *IEEE Communication Magazine*, **40**(7), 128–134 (July 2002).
4. S. Giordano and I. Stojmenovic, Position-based routing algorithms for ad hoc networks: A taxonomy, (eds.) X. Cheng, X. Huang and D.-Z. Du, *Ad Hoc Wireless Networking, Network Theory and Applications*, chapter 4, 103–136, Springer, New York, NY (2004).
5. E. M. Belding-Royer, Routing approaches in mobile ad hoc networks, (eds.) S. Basagni, M. Conti, S. Giordano and I. Stojmenovic, *Mobile Ad Hoc Networking*, chapter 10, 275–300. IEEE Press and John Wiley & Sons, Inc., Piscataway, NJ and Hoboken, NJ (April 2004).

6. M. Zorzi and R. R. Rao, Geographic random forwarding (GeRaF) for ad hoc and sensor networks: Multihop performance, *IEEE Transactions on Mobile Computing*, **2**(4), 337–348 (October–December 2003).
7. M. Zorzi and R. R. Rao, Geographic random forwarding (GeRaF) for ad hoc and sensor networks: Energy and latency performance, *IEEE Transactions on Mobile Computing*, **2**(4), 349–365 (October–December 2003).
8. P. Casari, M. Nati, C. Petrioli and M. Zorzi, Efficient non-planar routing around dead ends in sparse topologies using random forwarding, *Proceedings of the IEEE International Conference on Communications, ICC 2007*, Glasgow, Scotland (June 24–28, 2007).
9. N. Samama, *Global Positioning: Technologies and Performance*, Wiley Survival Guides in Engineering and Science, Wiley and Sons, Inc., Hoboken, NJ (2008).
10. A. Savvides and M. B. Srivastava, Location discovery, (eds.) S. Basagni, M. Conti, S. Giordano and I. Stojmenovic, *Mobile Ad Hoc Networking*, chapter 8, 231–254. IEEE Press and John Wiley and Sons, Inc., Piscataway, NJ and New York, NY (April 2004).
11. M. Battelli and S. Basagni, Localization for wireless sensor networks: Protocols and perspectives, *Proceedings of IEEE CCECE 2007*, 1074–1077, Vancouver, Canada (April 22–26, 2007).
12. V. Chandrasekhar, W. K. G. Seah, Y. S. Choo and H. Ee. Localization in underwater sensor networks — Survey and challenges, *Proceedings of the 1st ACM International Workshop on UnderWater Networks, WuWNet 2006*, Los Angeles, CA (September 25, 2006).
13. S. Basagni, I. Chlamtac, V. R. Syrotiuk and B. A. Woodward. A distance routing effect algorithm for mobility (DREAM) *Proceedings of the 4th Annual ACM/IEEE International Conference on Mobile Computing and Networking, MobiCom 98*, 76–84, Dallas, TX (October 25–30, 1998).
14. Y.-B. Ko and N. H. Vaidya, Location-aided routing (LAR) in mobile ad hoc networks, *ACM/Kluwer Wireless Networks*, **6**(4), 307–321 (July 2000).
15. H. Hartenstein and K. P. Laberteaux, Topics in ad hoc and sensor networks — A tutorial survey on vehicular ad hoc networks, *IEEE Communications Magazine*, **46**(6), 164–171 (June 6 2008).
16. P. Bose, P. Morin, I. Stojmenovic and J. Urrutia. Routing with guaranteed delivery in ad hoc wireless networks, *Proceedings of the 3rd International Workshop on Discrete Algorithms and Methods for Mobile Computing and Communications, DIAL M '99*, 48–55, Seattle, WA (1999).
17. P. Bose, P. Morin, I. Stojmenovic and J. Urrutia, Routing with guaranteed delivery in ad hoc wireless networks, *ACM/Kluwer Wireless Networks*, **7**(6), 609–616 (November 2001).
18. B. K. and H. T. Kung. GPSR: Greedy perimeter stateless routing for wireless networks, *Proceedings of the 6th ACM Annual International Conference on Mobile Computing and Networking, MobiCom 2000*, 243–254, Boston, Massachusetts, (2000), ACM. ISBN 1-58113-197-6. doi: http://doi.acm.org/10.1145/345910.345953.
19. J. Li, J. Jannotti, D. S. J. De Couto, D. R. Karger and R. Morris. A scalable location service for geographic ad hoc networks, *Proceedings of the 6th ACM Annual International Conference on Mobile Computing and Networking, MobiCom 2000*, 120–130, Boston, MA (August 6–11, 2000).
20. Y. Xue, B. Li and K. Nahrstedt, A scalable location management scheme in mobile ad-hoc networks, *Proceedings of the 26th Annual IEEE Conference on Local Computer Networks, LCN 2001*, 102–111, Tampa, FL (November 14–16, 2001).

21. J. Sucec and I. Marsic, Location management for hierarchically organized mobile ad hoc networks, *Proceedings of the IEEE Wireless Communications and Networking Conference, WCNC 2002*, **2**, 603–607, Orlando, FL (March 17–21, 2002).
22. H.-H. Wang and S.-D. Wang, The modified grid location service for mobile ad-hoc networks, *Proceedings of the 2nd International Conference on Grid and Pervasive Computing, GPC 2007*, **4459**, *LNCS*, 334–347, Paris, France (May 2–4, 2007).
23. S.-C. M. Woo and S. Singh, Scalable routing protocol for ad hoc networks, *ACM/Kluwer Wireless Networks*, **7**(5), 513–529 (September 2001) ISSN 1022-0038, doi: http://dx.doi.org/10.1023/A:1016726711167.
24. C. Perkins and I. P. Mobile, *IEEE Communications Magazine*, **35**(5), 84–99 (May 1997).
25. C. T. Cheng, H. L. Lamberg, S. J. Philip, E. van der Berg and T. Zhang. SLALoM: A scalable location management scheme for large mobile ad-hoc networks. In *Proceedings of the 2002 IEEE Wireless Communication and Networking Conference, WCNC 2002*, **2**, 574–578, Orlando, FL (March 17–21, 2002).
26. S. Dolev, L. Lahiani, N. Lynch and T. Nolte. Self-stabilizing mobile node location management and message routing, *Proceedings of the 7th International Symposium on Self-stabilizing Systems, SSS 2005*, LNCS 3764, 96–112, Barcelona, Spain (October 26–27, 2005).
27. S. Sivavakeesar and G. Pavlou, Scalable location services for hierarchically organized mobile ad hoc networks, *Proceedings of the 6th ACM International Symposium on Mobile Ad Hoc Networking and Computing, MobiHoc 2005*, 217–228, Urbana-Champaign, IL (May 25–28, 2005).
28. S. Basagni, M. Mastrogiovanni, A. Panconesi and C. Petrioli, Localized protocols for ad hoc clustering and backbone formation: A performance comparison, *IEEE Transactions on Parallel and Distributed Systems, Special Issue on Localized Communication and Topology Protocols for Ad Hoc Networks* (*S. Olariu, D. Simplot-Ryl, and I. Stojmenovic, editors*). **17**(4), 292–306 (April 2006).
29. S. J. Philip, J. Ghosh and C. Qiao, Performance evaluation of a hierarchical location management protocol for ad hoc networks, *Computer Communications, Special issue on Performance Issues of Wireless LANs, PANs, and Ad Hoc Networks*, **8**(10), 1110–1122 (2005).
30. R. Flury and R. Wattenhofer, MLS: An efficient location service for mobile ad hoc networks, *Proceedings of the 7th ACM International Symposium on Mobile Ad Hoc Networking and Computing, MobiHoc 2006*, 226–237, Florence, Italy (May 22–25, 2006). ISBN 1-59593-368-9. doi: http://doi.acm.org/10.1145/1132905.1132931.
31. S. Ratnasamy, B. Karp, S. Shenker, D. Estrin, R. Govindan, L. Yin and F. Yu, Data-centric storage in sensornets with GHT, a geographic hash table, *ACM/Kluwer Mobile Networks and Applications*, **8**(4), 427–442 (August 2003).
32. Z. J. Haas and B. Liang, Ad hoc mobility management with uniform quorum systems, *IEEE/ACM Transactions on Networking*, **7**(2), 228–240 (April 1999).
33. T. Camp, J. Boleng and L. Wilcox, Location information services in mobile ad hoc networks, *Proceedings of the IEEE International Conference on Communications, ICC 2002*, **5**, 3318–3324, New York, NY (April 28–May 2, 2002).
34. S. M. Das, H. Pucha and Y. C. Hu, Performance comparison of scalable location services for geographic ad hoc routing, *Proceeding of the 24th IEEE Infocom 2005*, **2**, 1228–1239, Miami, FL (March 13–17, 2005).

35. I. Stojmenovic, Location updates for efficient routing in ad hoc wireless networks, (ed.) I. Stojmenovic, *Handbook of Wireless Networks and Mobile Computing*, chapter 21, 451–471. John Wiley and Sons, Inc., Hoboken, NJ (April 2002).
36. M. Mauve, A. Widmer and H. Hartenstein, A survey on position-based routing in mobile ad hoc networks, *IEEE Network*, **15**(6), 30–39 (November–December, 2001).
37. R. Friedman and G. Kliot. Location services in wireless ad hoc and hybrid networks: A survey. Technical Report CS-2006-10, Department of Computer Science, Technion, Haifa, Israel (April 24, 2006).
38. A. Howard, M. J. Matarić and G. S. Sukhatme, An incremental deployment algorithm for mobile sensor networks, *Kluwer Autonomous Robots, Special Issue on Intelligent Embedded Systems* (*G. S. Sukhatme, editor*). **13**(2), 113–126 (September 2002).
39. R. C. Shah, S. Roy, S. Jain and W. Brunette. Data MULEs: Modeling a three-tier architecture for sparse sensor networks, *Proceedings of the First IEEE International Workshop on Sensor Network Protocols and Applications, SNPA 2003*, 30–41, Anchorage, AK (May 11, 2003).
40. R. Rao and G. Kesidis, Purposeful mobility for relaying and surveillance in mobile ad hoc sensor networks, *IEEE Transactions on Mobile Computing*, **3**(3), 225–232 (July–September, 2004).
41. G. Wang, G. Cao and T. F. La Porta, Movement-assisted sensor deployment. *Proceedings of IEEE INFOCOM 2004*, **4**, 2469–2479, Hong Kong (March 7–11, 2004).
42. G. Wang, G. Cao and T. F. La Porta Proxy-based sensor deployment for mobile sensor networks, *Proceedings of the First IEEE International Conference on Mobile Ad Hoc and Sensor Systems, MASS 2004*, 493–502, Fort Lauderdale, FL (October 25–27, 2004).
43. A. Kansal, A. A. Somasundara, D. D. Jea, M. B. Srivastava and D. Estrin, Intelligent fluid infrastructure for embedded networks, *Proceedings of the* 2*nd ACM/SIGMOBILE International Conference on Mobile Systems, Applications, and Services, MobySys 2004*, 111–124, Boston, MA (June 6–9, 2004).
44. W. Wang, V. Srinivasan and K.-C. Chua. Using mobile relays to prolong the lifetime of wireless sensor networks, *Proceedings of the* 11*th Annual ACM/SIGMOBILE International Conference on Mobile Computing and Networking, MobiCom 2005*, 270–283, Cologne, Germany (August 28–September 2, 2005).
45. S. R. Gandham, M. Dawande, R. Prakash and S. Venkatesan, Energy efficient schemes for wireless sensor networks with multiple mobile base stations, *Proceedings of IEEE Globecom 2003*, **1**, 377–381, San Francisco, CA (December 1–5, 2003).
46. I. Papadimitriou and L. Georgiadis, Maximum lifetime routing to mobile sink in wireless sensor networks, *Proceedings of the 2005 International Conference on Software, Telecommunications and Computer Networks, SoftCOM 2005*, Split, Croatia (September 15–17, 2005).
47. J. Luo and J.-P. Hubaux, Joint mobility and routing for lifetime elongation in wireless sensor networks, *Proceedings of IEEE Infocom 2005*, **3**, 1735–1746, Miami, FL (March 13–17, 2005).
48. A. P. Azad and A. Chockalingam, Mobile base station placement and energy aware routing in wireless sensor networks, *Proceeding of the IEEE Wireless Communications and Networking Conference, WCNC 2006*, **1**, 264–269, Las Vegas, NV (April 3–6, 2006).

49. S. Basagni, A. Carosi, E. Melachrinoudis, C. Petrioli and M. Z. Wang, A new MILP formulation and distributed protocols for wireless sensor networks lifetime maximization, *Proceedings of the IEEE International Conference on Communications, ICC 2006*, **8**, 3517–3524, Istanbul, Turkey (June 11–15, 2006).
50. S. Basagni, A. Carosi, E. Melachrinoudis, C. Petrioli and Z. M. Wang, Controlled sink mobility for prolonging wireless sensor networks lifetime, *ACM/Springer Wireless Networks*. (2008). Published online on February 7, 2007.
51. S. Basagni, A. Carosi and C. Petrioli, Mobility in wireless sensor networks. In ed. A. Boukerche, *Algorithms and Protocols for Ad Hoc and Sensor Networks*, chapter 10, 267–305, John Wiley & Sons, Inc., Hoboken, NJ (2008).
52. S. Basagni, C. Carosi, C. Petrioli and C. A. Phillips, Moving multiple sinks through wireless sensor networks for lifetime maximization, *Proceedings of the 5th IEEE International Conference on Mobile Ad Hoc and Sensor Systems, MASS 2008*, Atlanta, GA (September 29–October 2, 2008).
53. E. Ekici, Y. Gu and D. Bozdag, Mobility-based communications in wireless sensor networks, *IEEE Communications Magazine*, **44**(7), 56–62 (July 2006).
54. S. Basagni, A. Carosi, E. Melachrinoudis, C. Petrioli and Z. M. Wang, Protocols and model for sink mobility in wireless sensor networks, *ACM Mobile Computing and Communication Review*, MC^2R, **10**(4), 28–30 (October 2006).
55. I. Akyildiz and I. Kasimoglu, Wireless sensor and actor networks: Research challenges, *Ad Hoc Networks Journal*, **2**(4), 351–367 (October 2004).
56. T. Melodia, D. Pompili and I. F. Akyldiz, A communication architecture for mobile wireless sensor and actor networks, *Proceedings of the 3rd Annual EEE International Conference on Sensor, Mesh and Ad Hoc Communications and Networks, SECON 2006*, 109–118, Reston, VA, USA (September 25–28, 2006).
57. F. Aurenhammer, Voronoi diagrams — a survey of a fundamental geometric data structure, *ACM Computing Surveys*, **23**(3), 345–405 (1991).
58. R. G. Brown and P. Y. C. Hwang, *Introduction to Random Signals and Applied Kalman Filtering*, John Wiley & Sons, Inc., Hoboken, NJ (1996), 3rd edition.
59. C. Y. Lin, Y. C. Tseng and T. H. Lai, Message-efficient in-network location management in a multi-sink wireless sensor network, *Proceedings of the IEEE International Conference on Sensor Networks, Ubiquitous, and Trustworthy Computing, SUTC 2006*, 496–505, Taichung, Taiwan (June 5–7, 2006).
60. Y.-C. Tseng, S.-Y. Ni, Y.-S. Chen and J.-P. Sheu, The broadcast storm problem in a mobile ad hoc network, *ACM/Kluwer Wireless Networks*, **8**(2/3), 153–167 (March–May, 2002).
61. R. Zhang, H. Zhao and M. A. Labrador, The anchor location service (ALS) protocol for large-scale wireless sensor networks, *Proceedings of the 1st International Conference on Integrated Internet Ad Hoc and Sensor Networks, InterSense 2006*, 18, Nice, France (May, 30–31, 2006).
62. X. Zhu and H. Gupta, Fault-tolerant manycast to mobile destinations in sensor networks, *Proceedings of the IEEE International Conference on Communications, ICC 2007*, 3596–3603, Glasgow, Scotland (June 24–28, 2007).
63. Y. C. Tseng, C. C. Chen, C. Lee and Y. K. Huang. Incremental in-network RNN search in wireless sensor networks, *Proceedings of the 2007 International Conference on Parallel Processing Workshops, ICPPW 2007*, 64, Xi'an, China (September 10–14, 2007).
64. F. Nidito, M. Battelli and S. Basagni, Fault-tolerant and load balancing localization of services in wireless sensor networks. In *Proceedings of the 67th Semi-Annual IEEE*

Vehicular Technology Conference, VTC 2007 Fall, 382–386, Baltimore, MD (September 30–October 3, 2007).

65. M. Albano, S. Chessa, F. Nidito and S. Pelagatti, Q-NiGHT: Adding QoS to data centric storage in non-uniform sensor networks, *Proceedings of the 8th International Conference on Mobile Data Management, MDM 2007)*, 166–173, Mannheim, Germany (May 7–11, 2007).

Chapter 34

Sensor Network Economics

S. Buchegger* and S. Krishnamurthy†

Deutsche Telekom Laboratories, Ernst-Reuter-Platz 7
D-10587 Berlin, Germany
**sonja.@ieee.org*
†krishnadots@gmail.com

Sensor networks pose many challenges that stem from the trade-off between the utility of sensing, computation, and communication tasks fulfilled on the benefit side and the constraints on the capacity to carry out those tasks, e.g., power and location, on the cost side. Economics provides a theoretical foundation and methods for such problems. In this chapter we bring these two domains together, showcase some examples where economics have already been applied to sensor networks and discuss some areas that could still benefit from insights gained by economics. To this end, we also give an introduction of some relevant concepts in economics targeted at the sensor networks research community.

34.1. Introduction

In recent years, the networking community has shown an increased interest in applying tools and methods from economics to inform the design of protocols and networks and to evaluate and estimate node behavior.

In this chapter we give an overview over some of these applications and widen the scope of economics that can be applied to networking questions in general and address the challenges of sensor networks in particular. While some areas, such as game theory, have been widely used, there are methods and tools from economics that still await their application in networking.

Economics deals with the distribution of finite and scarce resources. This overall purpose is pursued with a variety of methods, tools, and principles, which can come from different schools of thought regarding fairness or efficiency. For instance, the trade-off between individual well-being (or utility-maximization) and the collective welfare of society is weighed in various, sometimes contradicting ways, when concerning human society. An important assumption underlying economics is the rationality of behavior. We thus have a body of theory about (a) resource allocation among (b) rational entities in (c) constrained environments, with (d) methods and metrics for the benefit of the system in total. We now describe the corresponding counterparts of these properties in the context of sensor networks.

Sensor networks are collections of nodes with constrained resources such as computational power, battery energy, bandwidth, storage, and sensing capacity. While it sounds like an anthropomorphism to speak about node welfare, there are similarities to human society with respect to economics. The collective welfare of the nodes, i.e., of the network as a whole, can differ from that for the individual node. As an example, let us take battery power. Sensor nodes have a limited battery size and thus limited energy. Once deployed, it can be difficult or even impossible to change batteries. For the life-time of an individual node it is thus best to conserve as much energy as possible. The network as a whole should keep its main functionality as long as possible, the so-called life-time of the network should be maximized. Yet carrying out the functions of sensing, computing, and communicating consumes power. For the life-time of the entire network, providing functionality and reducing power consumption are trade-offs that can vary with the distribution of tasks (and therefore power usage) to individual nodes. Individual and total utility or welfare are not necessarily pulling in the same direction. Economics deals with such resource constraints and contradictions between individual and overall system preferences.

Sensor network nodes execute programs, they can be made to act rationally in the economics sense of utility maximization. Although the assumption of rational behavior in humans is not justified in many cases, it has served as a useful abstraction to make economic analysis tractable. In sensor networks, this assumption is more reasonable, given the programmability of nodes.

As in other domains of economics applications, we can formulate goals that maximize the welfare of a sensor network. Such goals include maximized life-time, functionality (including robustness and data fidelity, maintaining coverage), and minimized cost of device, deployment, maintenance as well as obtaining of relevant information. Metrics for functionality are accuracy and latency.

These goals are addressed by striving for a suitable topology, physical location, proximity to phenomenon of interest, algorithms and protocols, and self-adaption (in response to changes in the environment or other node behavior) and organization. Algorithms are needed for resource allocation (and task allocation and scheduling, sampling rates), power management and power control, local organization (e.g., cluster-head election), global organization (e.g., routing, data processing such as aggregation), ensuring of data fidelity, robustness to device failure or malicious attacks. Economics provides additional tools to address these issues.

One way of using an economics perspective is to see nodes as agents in a market. Nodes are viewed not as self-interested agents in the pure game-theoretic sense, but still as participants in a market, making local decisions. While the concept of selfishness comes from intentional behavior and docs not quite fit the scenario of nodes in sensor network that is under a single authority that programed the nodes, an assumption of node rationality or self-interest helps to keep node behavior predictable in an environment where global knowledge is not available. If nodes had the global information necessary to act optimally, the rationality assumption would not be needed. In the case of sensor networks, however, it is not only easily fulfilled but also useful for decision making.

In the rest of this chapter we give brief introductions to topics in economics that have either been applied to sensor networks or have the potential to help address remaining issues in sensor network research and design. Specifically, we introduce game theory, mechanism design, fair division and equity. We then pick some problems in sensor networks and explain them in more detail, and, where appropriate, discuss samples of the application of economics to address them. The first of these topics in sensor networks is resource allocation, which we complement with a brief discussion of market-based approaches. Another important topic, especially regarding the goal of life-time maximization is power. We discuss both power management and power control issues, they have been addressed by game-theoretic approaches. The third topic we explore is that of information routing. Finally, we elaborate on the data fidelity problem and discuss decision-theoretic approaches using reputation systems. The concluding section also provides an outlook on the application of insights from economics to open problems in sensor networks.

34.2. Economic Tools and Methods

34.2.1. *Game theory*

Game theory[1] is a mathematical tool for analyzing the interaction of two or more decision makers. A (strategic) game consists of three components: a set of players, the strategy set for each player and a utility (payoff) function for each player measuring the degree of happiness of the player.

Game theory, extensively used in economics, is concerned primarily with the general analysis of strategic interactions in conflicting situations among economic agents where these agents can interact in a variety of ways with different strategies. The main purpose of game theory is to consider situations where instead of agents making decisions as reactions to exogenous circumstances, their decisions are strategic reactions to other agents' actions. An agent is faced with a set of moves he can play and will form a strategy, a best response to his environment, which he will play. Strategies can either be pure (i.e., play a particular move with certainty) or mixed (play moves with randomization).

Cooperative games in game theory are games where the players can make agreements beforehand. This is not allowed in non-cooperative games. In this way the players can come to an outcome were all players have the highest possible payoff given the best responses of the others, called the equilibrium of the system. Two-player games have only two players and the possible outcomes are known, based on the outcome function and the available strategies. If the game is played repetitively, the game can turn from a non-cooperative game into a cooperative one where the players use the outcome of previous games to decide their next strategy.

The users' interaction in a wireless network can be modeled as a game in which the users' terminals are the players in the game competing for network resources (i.e., bandwidth and energy). Any action taken by a user affects the performance of other users in the network. Game theory is the natural tool for studying this interaction. Since our focus in this article is on distributed schemes, we will concentrate on non-cooperative games. Let $G = [K, A_k, u_k]$ represent a game where $K = 1, \ldots, K$ is the set of players/users, A_k is the set of actions (strategies) available to user k, and u_k is the utility (payoff) function for user k. In a non-cooperative game, each user seeks to choose its strategy in such a way as to maximize its own utility, i.e.,

$$\max_{a_k \in A_k} u_k \quad \text{for } k = 1, \ldots, K. \tag{34.1}$$

For such a game, we first need to define two important concepts, namely, a Nash equilibrium and Pareto optimality. A Nash equilibrium (NE) is a set of strategies, $(a_1^*, \ldots, a_K^*)$, such that no user can unilaterally improve its own utility, that is, $u_k(a_k^*, a_{-k}^*) = u_k(a_k, a_{-k}^*) \forall a_k \in A_k$ and $k = 1, \ldots, K$, where $a_{-k}^* = (a_1^*, \ldots, a_{k-1}^*, a_{k+1}^*, \ldots, a_K^*)$. A Nash equilibrium is a stable outcome of G. At NE, no user has any incentive to change its strategy. A set of strategies, $(\tilde{a}_1, \ldots, \tilde{a}_K)$ is Pareto-optimal, if there exists no other set of strategies for which one or more users can improve their utilities without reducing the utilities of other users.

Game theory has widely been used for ad-hoc networks due to the decentralized nature of nodes, independently adapting their operation based on perceived or measured statistics and the existence of interactive decision makers: the decision of one node affects the others.

Nodes in the network are the players. The adaptations are the set of actions. The adaptation algorithm involves two steps: (1) finding the preferences which is equivalent to the utility function and (2) decision update algorithm which constitutes the learning process.

When applying game theory to sensor networks, one first has to develop a game-theoretic model: the solution of the game's Nash equilibrium provides information about the steady state and convergence of the network. Questions such as the following are addressed: Does a steady state exist? Is it optimal? Do nodes converge to it? Is it stable? Does the steady-state scale?

Sensor network problems that can be modeled by game theory include

- Power control at physical layer: Adjust transmit power levels. Objective: To achieve a target signal-to-interference-to-noise ratio.
- Setting probability of packet transmission at MAC layer. Objective: To maximize individual throughput.
- Node participation at network layer: deciding the sleep state. Objective: increase lifetime of nodes by reducing participation, increase throughput by participating.

Determine the optimal sleep duration of a node and study the impact of varying level of participation on a routing protocol.

34.2.2. *Fair division and equity*

Fair Division[2] and Equity[3] are topics from economics that deal with the distribution of goods (or *bads*, such as cost). Fair division is often exemplified with the cake-cutting problem,[2] how to divide a piece of cake among people (with subjective evaluations of parts of the cake) such that no one envies another. While the problem is quite trivial for two (one cuts, the other chooses), it becomes complicated with several participants.

Methods for fair division are the most valuable in the presence of different preferences and different valuation of the same good. In the context of sensor networks, this means that nodes would for instance value units of power differently from one another. This can happen when nodes are in a different state in their power consumption, i.e., when they become heterogeneous due to the difference in battery power they have left at a particular time. A unit of power is more costly to a node whose battery is about to run out than to a node with a fully charged battery. Different valuations can thus lead to different prices for a single good in a market environment, as well as to different evaluations of bundles of goods or bads. An example of a bundle of bads would be a task that requires certain amounts of battery power in terms of computation, sensing, or communications. How to allocate tasks, simple tasks or more complex combinations of tasks, can therefore be viewed as fair division problems.

When dividing goods or bads, we need to measure how fair or equitable an outcome is. A simple tool to measure equity is the Gini coefficient. In economics, it has mainly been used to compare the income distributions across countries. Complete income equality, i.e., every one earning the same, would be a zero in the Gini coefficient. To compare how much equal another distribution is, one plots the cumulative income distribution and subtracts it from the one for complete equality. The latter is simply a line with a slope of 45 degree, originating at 0, meaning that income is exactly proportional to the number of earners. The area of the difference between these two curves, the total equality one and the actual one (also called the Lorenz curve when plotted in percentages), yields the number used for the Gini coefficient. This way, countries with different populations can be compared with a single number. This tool can also be used in systems, to evaluate how evenly distributed a good, such as a resource, or a bad, such as power consumption in sensor networks, is and compare the result across different networks with different protocols. We hereby gain a metric to evaluate a distribution in a simple way. Since power is an important and scarce resource in sensor networks, it is helpful to know the distribution of power consumption over all nodes. The life-time of the sensor network overall is shortened by uneven distributions of power consumption when it means that nodes critical for the operation of the sensor network are overloaded and run out of power. A more even distribution can prolong the life-time of the network, and the Gini coefficient (or, as we shall see) other economics methods and tools for fair distribution, can help evaluate protocols and the design of sensor networks to that end.

While the Gini coefficient and other metrics help us assess the equity of outcomes, we also need constructive mechanisms of how to divide goods or bads. One such way of fair division is the Shapley value.[4] It can be applied to fairly allocate gains (or losses) to a coalition of participants that contributed differently from a given situation. A simple real-world example is the division of costs of a common good that people benefit from in different quantities, such as splitting the cost of building an elevator in an apartment building among the people on different floors in a fair way, such that all the costs are covered, people who do not have use of the service do not pay (e.g., living on the ground floor), etc. The Shapley value has desirable properties that address these concerns. In sensor networks, it could be used to allocate sensing and communication tasks to nodes according to their location in the network topology and relative to the phenomenon of interest.

34.2.3. *Mechanism design*

While game theory analyzes an existing game (or protocol, in the networking sense) and aims at finding equilibria of the system, taking into account individual player (or node) behavior, (Algorithmic) mechanism design[5] takes the reverse approach. Given the assumptions of node behavior from game theory, mechanism design aims at creating a game/protocol/system that elicits desirable behavior by making it attractive. This can be done by designing incentives to make certain kinds of behavior pay off more than others. The resulting game can, in turn, be analyzed using game theory, even in an iterative fashion.

Mechanism design[6] tries to find a way of balancing the following basic goals: efficiency, budget balance (no money needs to be inserted into the system), and incentive compatibility (truthfulness, strategyproof), since one cannot achieve all of the above simultaneously. Other goals include fairness, Pareto efficiency, maximizing revenue for an auction holder, resisting harmful coalitions (group strategyproof).

Incentive compatible means that it is in the own interest of every participant to truthfully reveal any private information asked for by the mechanism, to reveal private preferences. An example of such a mechanism is a second-price auction, where the bidder with the highest bid gets the item (the best social choice) but pays the price equal to the bid of the second highest bidder. There is no advantage gained in bidding higher or lower than the true preference.

Regarding truthfulness (incentive compatibility), an important result is the *revelation principle*, stating that if there is a mechanism that implements a social choice function in dominant strategies, then there is also a direct truthful (or incentive compatible) mechanism implementing the same function.

At the root of the need for incentives lies what is called *moral hazard* in economics.[7] This refers to a state of information asymmetry. Hidden information and hidden action are providing this asymmetry. This is formulated in the principal-agent problem, where the agent is acting on behalf of the principal, but also has a utility function that may differ from that of the principal. The behavior, or in game-theoretic terms the strategy, of the agent can thus differ from what the principal wants if the behavior cannot be observed, i.e., there is hidden action. The difference of utility function and intended strategy is an instance of hidden information.

Applying principal-agent terminology and concepts to sensor network, the deployer or owner of a sensor network would be the principal and the sensor network nodes can be seen as agents, being deployed to fulfill the purpose intended by the principal.

Game Theory makes sense when there is intentional behavior of players with potentially conflicting interests. In a sensor network under a single authority (the owner, the deployer, the designer of the network), the sensors just follow the protocol however they are programmed. There is no strategic behavior in the human sense in a regular sensor network. This changes when there are several users of a sensor network or several entities that deploy sensor nodes. In any case, even if there is no strategic behavior, the model of strategic behavior remains useful for predictability of behavior around which mechanisms can be designed.

Among the applications of mechanism design there have been several areas, such as the creation of markets, auctions (for single goods or combinatorial auctions for bundles of goods), matching algorithms, taxation and distribution of public goods.

In sensor networks research, auctions have been proposed for task allocation and combinatorial auctions have been used for finding paths in networks. Matching algorithms could be used to match nodes to tasks, pairing up nodes that can perform a particular sensing, communication or computation task given their capacity constraints, task suitability and power consideration, with the right workload, subject to overall network goals. Using prices[8] as signals to influence behavior can make sensor networks adapt to varying conditions without having to reprogram the nodes. Sensor network research has been making use of market-based approaches, as detailed in the next section.

34.3. Sensor Networks Economics

34.3.1. *Resource allocation*

Resource allocation in sensor networks poses a unique challenge, which is that how can we achieve efficient global behavior, despite the constrained resources of the nodes, dynamic and uncertain network conditions, and the infeasibility of having an entity in the network that has a global view of the entire network continuously. In such environments, there is a need to guide large collections of locally-controlled, asynchronous and concurrent nodes to make decisions based on local and imperfect information, in order to interact with an unpredictable environment. Consider a typical sensor network application, such as real-time vehicular surveillance.[9] In this application, nodes must take periodic sensor readings, combine readings with other nearby nodes, and report aggregated values in real-time to a base station. The periodicity with which each node performs sensing, computation, and communication impacts the overall lifetime of the network and the accuracy of the surveillance system. The system must also adapt these rates in response to changes in the target vehicles location and velocity. Currently, there are few automated mechanisms that aid application programmers to dynamically allocate the resources of a sensor network, in order to meet the energy and accuracy targets. Dynamically reprogramming a sensor network through an external base station by updating the code on the sensor nodes, in order to reconfigure their resources in real-time is not a feasible solution. Instead, these dynamic resource allocation decisions need to be made by the nodes deployed in the network. Market-based programming provides a high-level programming environment that can be used by the system to achieve globally efficient resource allocation under dynamic conditions, subject to certain constraints. Using market-based mechanisms, systems are modeled along the lines of some economic model in which participating entities act toward increasing their personal profit or utility. System-wide parameters are modeled in a manner similar to macroeconomic variables, such as economic growth, while the parameters of the individual entities correspond to microeconomic parameters. The main issue in using such an approach for resource allocation is to select suitable parameter values and market interaction rules, so that desired system goals, both local and global, are achieved. Market devices, such as auctions and prices, have been used to facilitate resource management in other types of distributed systems. For example, Spawn[10] is a market-based computational system for a distributed network of heterogeneous high-performance workstations, which uses a microeconomic approach for resource management in concurrent programs. Buyers use an auction-based approach to buy slices of CPU time on various workstations for computation from sellers who auction their workstation's idle processing resources.

Market-based techniques for sensor networks

Market-based techniques are appealing for programming sensor networks, because they provide a method for nodes to locally assess the impact of their actions on global behavior and make decisions to meet certain criteria. Furthermore, market-based techniques can be used to adapt the resource allocation in a network of embedded sensor nodes by modeling the network as a self-organizing system consisting of producers and consumers that interact through markets to adapt the prices on the basis of which they buy and sell virtual goods. Market-based macroprogramming requires a specification of the actions that each sensor node may take, as well as the local utility function that guides the decision-making of each node. Typical actions that are relevant to a sensor node include sampling a local sensor reading, transmitting data, listening for incoming messages, sleeping for some interval, and aggregating multiple sensor readings into a single value. Each action produces some virtual goods (e.g., data), but in the process consumes some resources. Each of the goods has an associated price that may be adjusted at runtime to coordinate the actions of the nodes. The utility function represents the tradeoff between the profit obtained as a result of taking an action and the cost associated with the resources consumed, such as energy and bandwidth, as a result of performing that action. Nodes continuously monitor prices and select actions to maximize their local utility, given the availability of local resources such as energy, sensor data, and pending messages to forward. Depending on the application, a sensor network may have end-users, in which case they are represented as external agents with an associated utility function. This utility function allows the users to induce the network to take certain actions. Thus, market-based techniques also provide a way for multiple users to share the sensor network by offering differing payments for node actions. We now provide a concrete example of a system that employs market-based techniques for resource allocation in sensor networks.

Example — SORA

Self-Organizing Resource Allocation (SORA)[11,12] adopts concepts from reinforcement learning and market-based macroprogramming for decentralized resource allocation in sensor networks. SORA models the network as a virtual market in which every action by a node consumes some energy and produces some goods, which the node can then sell at a specific price. Given a set of actions, goods produced by those actions, price for each good, and energy cost for each action, each node operates as follows. Individual sensor nodes are modeled as self-interested agents that attempt to maximize their utility for performing local actions subject to energy constraints, in response to globally-advertised price information. Each node monitors its local resources and the global price vector, and selects the action A that maximizes its utility. The nodes use a simple utility function $u(A)$ for an action A, which is defined as:

$$u(A) = B(A)p(A), \text{ if the action is available} = 0 \text{ otherwise},$$

where $p(A)$ is the current price for action A, and $B(a)$ is the estimated probability of payment for that action, which is a parameter that is learned by the nodes. Prices may be determined by the client of the sensor network, who consumes the data produced by the network and sets prices to meet certain objectives. A node receives a virtual payment based on the value that its goods contribute to the network's overall operation. For example, in a surveillance application, a node may be paid for transmitting a sensor reading that accurately indicates the presence of a vehicle in its neighborhood at a given time, but will not be paid, if the reading is a false positive and there is no vehicle there in reality. Sensor nodes individually adapt their actions over time in response to feedback from payments, using reinforcement learning. Using this learning technique, nodes continuously learn which actions are most profitable and thereby have the most value to the sensor network as a whole. Each node thereby, attempts to maximize its utility, subject to its resource constraints, such as energy.

The price for each action can be dynamically updated to meet system-wide goals, such as network lifetime, data fidelity, or latency in response to changing network conditions. In addition, nodes use the payment they receive for their goods as a continuous form of feedback to adapt their actions. Both of these mechanisms allow the nodes to dynamically reallocate their resources to changing network conditions, energy budgets, and external stimuli. Thus, by using the SORA virtual market model, network retasking is accomplished by adjusting prices instead of pushing new code to sensor nodes. Market-based techniques, such as those employed in SORA, can also be extended for addressing issues that arise when multiple competing users wish to share a sensor network. In such a case, each user advertises its demand for taking certain actions on its behalf, and equilibrium prices are calculated to maximize the utility of the sensor nodes and users in the system. One of the challenges that needs to be addressed in this scenario is to ensure that the pricing results in a competitive equilibrium condition that leads to an optimal resource allocation.

34.3.2. *Power management*

Sensor networks consist of spatially distributed inexpensive sensor nodes that are typically powered by batteries. On account of the limited battery life and the complexity of replacing batteries in a large-scale sensor network, efficient power management is critical for lengthening the lifetime of a sensor network, especially in untethered environments. While energy harvesting from natural resources, such as solar and wind energy, are being explored as alternative energy sources for sensor nodes that are deployed in outdoor environments,[13] these technologies are still in their infancy and need hardware support. Instead, we look at some of the approaches that exploit the redundancy in sensor networks for efficient power management. Power management is concerned with which set of nodes should be turned on/off and for how long, for the purpose of constructing an energy saving topology to prolong the network lifetime. For example, in a highly dense deployment, not all of the sensor nodes in a neighborhood need to remain awake all the time, because powering on too many nodes creates interference and diminishes network capacity. Instead, the nodes can take turns to wake up and sleep, even though such a strategy may reduce the overall sensing capability. Therefore, finding an optimal trade-off between energy usage and sensing capability needs to be considered when designing schemes for efficient power management. Many of the previous power management approaches for sensor networks are based on heuristics that typically work well for very specific scenarios,[14] but lack a more general theoretical basis for their performance. We now look at how economic theories can be applied to model distributed power management in sensor networks.

Game theoretical approach to power management

The problem of distributed power management can be modeled as a game-theoretic problem. Limited bilateral communication proscribes bargaining and the formation of coalitions, which are the subject of study of cooperative game theory. Instead, the paradigm of independent decision making and limited communication fits better into the framework of non-cooperative game theory, yet in a game where all players ultimately share the same objective, although they might not have the global knowledge to optimize for it.

For example, a game-theoretic approach has been used[15] to quantify the trade-off between energy usage and sensing capability by modeling it as a non-cooperative game. Nodes try to save energy by maximizing their individual utility, while finding a minimal sensor coverage configuration. A sensor is considered covered, if all points within its sensing radius are covered by the sensor itself or by other active sensors.

34.3.3. *Power control*

While power management, which was described in the previous section, enables the sensor nodes to reduce their power consumption by deciding how long they need to keep their radios turned on, another approach to reduce power consumption in a wireless sensor node is power control. Typically, a node wants to transmit at a high power to increase the probability of success of packet transmission. However, transmitting at high power creates interference to the other nodes for whom the transmission is not intended. So power control is used for interference management and resource allocation in wireless networks and deals with the issue of who or what will control the transmission power levels of the nodes. The conventional approach has been to model power control as a constrained optimization problem, where the total transmit power is minimized under the constraint that the end-to-end QoS requirements are satisfied. However, in sensor networks, power control has to use a more distributed approach, where each node takes into account its local topology and resource constraints to make power control decisions.

As in the case of power management, distributed power control in sensor networks can also be modeled using game-theoretic approaches. In the case of power control games, the players have incomplete information, because the sensor nodes only have information about their own power levels, their perceived signal to interference and noise ratio, and their own channel conditions. The decision-making can be formulated as a non-cooperative game in which every node chooses the best response that tries to maximize its own utility, while trying to meet a specific network objective. To make power control decisions, a node may use a utility function that measures the number of reliable bits that are transmitted per joule of energy consumed,[16] while the overall network objective could be to either increase the longevity or the reliability of the network. The state at which the system achieves power stability corresponds to the existence of a Nash equilibrium of the non-cooperative power control game, in which the players are making decisions under incomplete information.

34.3.4. *Information routing*

Information routing in sensor networks is primarily data-centric in nature.[17,18] Interest queries originating from sink nodes are disseminated over the network, which then result in responses from those sensors whose sensed information matches the query. However, in order to route responses from the sensor nodes to the querying entities, several factors need to be considered. First, since sensor networks are intended for unattended deployment, they need to be able to manage their limited energy resources efficiently. If many sensor nodes are active simultaneously, it leads to increased energy consumption and competition for communication resources. Second, in certain applications, sensor nodes are deployed in hazardous and hostile environments in which they may fail or suffer damage with certain probabilities. For example, consider seismic sensor networks for monitoring earthquakes or chemical sensors that monitor toxic environments. In such scenarios, the sensor nodes must be able to detect reliable paths to route strategic and time-critical information. Third, while making these information routing decisions, the sensor nodes should be able to decide how they can cooperate to maximize information utility and meet overall network objectives, while attempting to optimize the use of their individual resources. Also, in traditional networks, the routing paths are chosen based on their ability to meet certain end-to-end quality of service (QoS) requirements. Such end-to-end concepts may not be sufficient to make routing decisions in sensor networks, where we also need to capture the contributions of the individual sensor nodes, in order to compare the merits of different routing paths. Currently, few systematic approaches have been used to compare and quantify the merits of routing paths under the above constraints. We now look at how economic theories can help in formally modeling these situations, thereby obviating the need for ad-hoc decision making on the part of the sensor nodes.

Game theoretic approaches for information routing

In a paper by Kannan *et al.*,[19] a game theoretic approach has been used to model data-centric information routing combined with data aggregation in an unattended, untethered sensor environment, where the sensor nodes are prone to fail with a certain probability. The precise problem addressed by the model is the following: given that data transmission in the network is costly and nodes are not fully reliable, how can we induce the formation of a maximally reliable data aggregation tree from the reporting sensors to the querying node, where every sensor is motivated by self-interest and knows how to trade-off individual costs with network-wide benefits. The game-theoretic model assumes the sensor nodes to behave as rational players in an N-player routing game, where they tradeoff individual communication and other costs with network-wide benefits. The model solves the problem by designing a routing game with payoff functions to characterize the contributions of individual sensors, such that the Nash equilibrium of the N-player routing game corresponds to the optimally reliable data aggregation tree.

The game-theoretic approach consists of modeling the strategies and payoffs. We now describe the model used in Ref. 19 in more detail. Let $S = s_1, \ldots, s_n$ denote the set of sensors, that represent the players in a routing game and let ij denote an ordered pair $(i, j) \in S \times S$. Let sensor s_i be a node that has information of value v_i, which it wishes to send to the sink node $s_q = s_n$ in response to a query, where $v_i \in R+$ represents an abstract quantification of the value of the event sensed at node $s_i, 1 \leq i \leq n$. $v_i = 0$ for nodes whose sensed information does not satisfy the specified attributes of the query. Information is routed to s_q through an optimally chosen subset of intermediate nodes by forming neighbor communication links. Link formation occurs by a process of simultaneous reasoning at each node leading to a path from each s_i with nonzero value v_i to the destination s_q. For untethered sensor networks, communication energy costs are a significant constraint, which need to be modeled. Each node incurs a cost $c_{ij} > 0$ for each link ij that it establishes. This link cost is an abstraction of message transmission costs in terms of required transmission power or available sensor battery life. The model assumes that each node can only establish one link. The strategy of each node is a vector $l_i = (l_{i1}, \ldots, l_{ii-1}, l_{ii+1}, \ldots, l_{in})$ and $l_{ij} \in \{0, 1\}$ for each $j \in S - \{i\}$. The value $l_{ij} = 1$ means that nodes i and j have a link initiated by i whereas $l_{ij} = 0$ means that sensor i does not send information to j. The set of all pure strategies of player i is denoted by L_i. Given that node i has the option of forming or not forming a link with each of the remaining $n - 1$ nodes, the number of strategies available to node i is $|L_i| = 2^{n-1}$. The strategy space of all nodes is given by $L = L_1 \times \cdots \times L_n$. Each strategy profile $l = (l_1, \ldots, l_n)$ is essentially a reverse routing tree T, rooted at the sink s_q. These different routing paths have to then be compared and evaluated for their optimality from a game-theoretic perspective.

Modeling the payoffs in a cooperative sensor network using game-theoretic approaches is challenging. In a standard non-cooperative game, players are assumed to be selfish and only interested in maximizing their own benefits. However, in order to make information routing decisions in a decentralized sensor network, the sensor nodes need to behave in a collaborative manner to achieve a joint goal, while taking individual operation costs into account. In Kannan's paper,[19] the common goal that nodes strive for is to establish reliable paths for data transmission. Hence, in order to model the payoffs, the benefits to a player is modeled as a function of path reliability, while the cost of communication is modeled as the cost incurred by the nodes to establish individual links, as follows. Given a strategy profile $l = (l_i, l_{-i})$ that results in a tree T rooted at s_q, where l_{-i} denotes the strategy chosen by all the other players except player i, every sensor that receives data has an incentive in its reaching s_q. Hence, the payoff to any player s_i on T must be a function of the path reliability from s_i onwards as well as the expected value of information at s_i. The payoff for a player s_i is modeled in the paper[19] as $\prod_i(l) = g_i(v_1, \ldots, v_{n-1})R_i - c_{ij}$, if $s_i \in T$ and 0 otherwise, where R_i denotes the path reliability from s_i onwards to s_q and g_i is the expectation function.

The expected value of the information depends on the data aggregation that happens while routing along the tree. To model this, let $V_i = g_i(v_1, \ldots, v_{n-1})$ denote the expected value of the data at node i and $D(i)$ be the set of its downlink nodes in the tree, from whom node i receives data for routing to the sink. Since sensor nodes may be deployed in harsh environments and may fail, a node s_i along the routing tree gets information from its downlink nodes, only if they are operational. So if we assume that a node s_j can fail independently with a probability $(1 - p_j) \in [0, 1]$, then the expected value of the data at node i is $V_i = v_i + \sum_{j \in D(i)} p_j V_j$. Hence, the expected benefit to sensor s_i depends on the survival probability of the downlink players of i and is given by $V_i R_i$. The total payoff to s_i, taking into the account the communication cost is therefore, $\prod_i = R_i V_i - c_{ij}$. Now that a node has a way to compute its payoff for a strategy, each node chooses the best response to the strategies chosen by the other players. A strategy l_i is a best response of player i to l_{-i}, if it maximizes the payoff for i, i.e., $\prod_i(l_i, l_{-i}) \geq \prod_i(l'_i, l_{-i})$ for all $l'_i \in L_i$. The optimal routing tree is then formed by a strategy profile l_{opt} that consists of the best responses of each player, i.e., $l_{opt} = (l_1, \ldots, l_n)$, where l_i is a best response of i to l_{-i} for each i. In order to choose the optimal strategy, each node determines the optimal tree formed by each of its possible successors on receiving its data. A node i then selects as next hop neighbor in the optimal routing tree, that node routing through which results in the highest payoff for i. In other words, the payoff to a node on the optimal tree is the highest possible, given optimal behavior by all other nodes. A node may get higher payoffs by selecting a different neighbor on another tree, however in doing so, it results in lower payoffs to some other nodes. This optimal routing tree therefore, denotes the state in which the sensors are in a Nash equilibrium. The game-theoretic model in Ref. 19 can also be used to model situations where a certain proportion of the nodes switch themselves off to conserve energy and for selecting routing paths based on the urgency or importance of the information being routed. Thus, the model allows sensor nodes to rationally decide on the basis of their individual payoffs, whether or not to participate in routing information of a given significance.

34.3.5. *Data fidelity*

The utility of sensor networks lies in their ability to automatically gather data from the environments in which they are deployed. Typical real-world sensor network deployments make use of a large number of sensor nodes that are implemented using relatively inexpensive hardware components. Hence, the information gathered by individual sensor nodes may have some degree of unreliability. Moreover, some of the nodes may exhibit inconsistent behavior by behaving well at one point in time, but producing incorrect readings at another point in time. Such inconsistent behavior may be a result of faulty hardware or due to the effects of the physical environments in which they are embedded. For example, during the development of the Vigilnet system[9] for real-time vehicle tracking, some of the sensor nodes that behaved normally in an indoor environment produced incorrect readings when they were deployed in very humid outdoor environments. Faulty behavior also results when some of the sensor nodes get stuck in their values for a period of time. For example, during the Vigilnet deployment, some of the magnetic sensors continuously reported the presence of a vehicle, long after the vehicle had passed by their location. Similar examples of faulty behavior have also been reported[20] in other real-world sensor deployments. The consequences of lack of data integrity are especially dire in deployments where the readings are not monitored in real-time. In such scenarios, if the inconsistencies are detected during offline analysis of the collected data, then it may be too late to rectify the errors.

The above real-world observations motivate the need for mechanisms that can detect inconsistencies and improve the data fidelity and trustworthiness of the data collected by the sensor nodes. However, we need to understand the challenges before describing the techniques that can be used to improve the data fidelity in sensor networks. First, the uncertainty and lack of control over the physical world and faulty nodes makes it hard to detect and isolate data integrity errors in a large deployment. Second, in sensor networks, information from multiple nodes is aggregated when it is being routed to the sink node. So if an incorrect sensor measurement is not detected locally, then it may corrupt other sensor readings and make the final outcome less trustworthy. Third, if the incorrect readings are outside the expected threshold, then it is possible to detect the incorrect readings using a simple range check. However, in some cases, the faulty nodes may produce incorrect measurements that are well within the expected threshold, in which case a simple range check will not reveal the fault. To overcome these challenges, we need an approach that allows the sensor nodes in the network to themselves assess how trustworthy is the data they collect before the data reaches an external user.

Reputation systems have been widely used in several domains to evaluate the trustworthiness within a social community. In a reputation system, the trust between two individuals evolves based on their actions over time. When there is a need to make decisions under uncertainty, individuals trust and rely on the actions and opinions of others who have behaved well in the past. Decision theory is a tool also used in economics to maximize expected utility and that has been used as a basis for building reputation systems. To improve the data fidelity in a sensor network in the presence of some of the faulty behavior that were illustrated above, reputation-based mechanisms may be employed, by regarding sensor networks as a cooperative, social community in which there is more interaction among the nodes within a neighborhood than among the nodes across distant neighborhoods. One such system that illustrates the use of reputation-based mechanisms to improve data fidelity in a sensor network is RFSN[20] that applies techniques used for misbehavior detection in mobile ad-hoc networks such as a Bayesian reputation system for trust evaluation[21] and observation[22] to the sensor networks context.

34.4. Conclusions

Economics offers a vast array of theories, methods, and tools for assessing and increasing utility for rational individuals and the overall system, called collective welfare, in an environment with resource constraints. Sensor networks have many of the characteristics that make economics applicable, e.g., the constraint of sensing, computation, storage, communication, and power capacity; sensor networks being systems with interacting rational (by programming) agents. As discussed in this paper, some insights from economics have already been applied to sensor networks, addressing issues of resource allocation, power control and management, information routing, data fidelity, etc. Beyond what we discussed in this chapter, there are other issues in sensor networks that can benefit from economics, such as security, topology, and self-organization. There is still potential for research in the area of sensor network economics, applying more solutions of economics to more problems of sensor networks. Applying fair division insights to resource allocation, equity and fairness theories to power management, game theory to security, combinatorial auctions to task distribution, network formation games[23] for topology, are just a few examples of possible and potentially beneficial future research directions.

References

1. M. J. Osborne and A. Rubinstein, *A Course in Game Theory*, The MIT Press (1994).
2. S. J. Brams and A. D. Taylor, *Fair Division. From Cake-Cutting to Dispute Resolution.* Cambridge University Press (1996).
3. H. P. Young, *Equity in Theory and Practice*, Princeton University Press (1995).
4. Hervé J. Moulin, *Fair Division and Collective Welfare*, The MIT Press (2003).
5. E. N. Nisan, T. Roughgarden, E. Tardos and V. Vazirani, *Algorithmic Game Theory.* Cambridge University Press (2007).
6. D. C. Parkes, *Classical Mechanism Design, Iterative Combinatorial Auctions: Achieving Economic and Computational Efficiency*, Chapter 2. Dissertation at the Department of Computer and Information Science, University of Pennsylvania (2001).
7. R. S. Pindyck and D. L. Rubinfeld, *Microeconomics, 6th Edition*, Prentice Hall (2005).
8. C. Courcoubetis and R. Weber, *Pricing Communication Networks. Economics, Technology and Modelling* (Wiley 2003).
9. T. He *et al.*, Vigilnet: An integrated sensor network system for energy-efficient surveillance, *ACM Transactions on Sensor Networks* (2006).

10. C. A. Waldspurger, T. Hogg, B. A. Huberman, J. O. Kephart and W. S. Stornetta, Spawn: A distributed computational economy, *Software Engineering*, **18**(2), 103–117 (1992).
11. G. Mainland, D. C. Parkes and M. Welsh, Decentralized, adaptive resource allocation for sensor networks, *Symposium on Networked Systems Design and Implementation* (2005).
12. L. Kang, S. Lahaie, G. Mainland, D. C. Parkes and M. Welsh, Using virtual markets to program global behavior in sensor networks, *Proc. 11th ACM SIGOPS European Workshop* (September 2004).
13. A. Kansal and M. B. Srivastava, *Energy Harvesting Aware Power Management, Wireless Sensor Networks: A System Perspective.* N. Bulusu and S. Jha (2005).
14. B. Chen, K. Jamieson, H. Balakrishnan and R. Morris, Span: An energy-efficient coordination algorithm for topology maintenance in ad hoc wireless networks, *ACM Wireless Networks*, **8**(5) (September 2002).
15. E. Nanez, A. Garcia and C. Li, A game-theoretic approach to efficient power management in sensor networks, *Operations Research* (2007).
16. F. Meshkati, V. Poor and S. Schwartz, *Energy-Efficient Resource Allocation in Wireless Networks: An Overview of Game-Theoretic Approaches*, *CoRR*. abs/0705.1787, (2007). URL http://arxiv.org/abs/0705.1787.
17. B. Krishnamachari, D. Estrin and S. Wicker, Modelling data-centric routing in wireless sensor networks, *IEEE Infocom* (2002).
18. C. Intanagonwiwat, R. Govindan and D. Estrin, Directed diffusion: A scalable and robust communication paradigm for sensor networks, *Proc. of Mobile Computing and Networking* (*MOBICOM*), 56–67 (August 2000).
19. R. Kannan, S. Sarangi, S. S. Iyengar and L. Ray, Sensor-centric quality of routing in sensor networks, *IEEE Infocom* (2003).
20. S. Ganeriwal and M. B. Srivastava, Reputation-based framework for high integrity sensor networks, *ACM Transactions on Sensor Networks* (September 2007).
21. S. Buchegger and J.-Y. L. Boudec, The effect of rumor spreading in reputation systems in mobile ad-hoc networks, Wiopt'03, Sofia-Antipolis (March 2003).
22. S. Marti, T. Giuli, K. Lai and M. Baker, Mitigating routing misbehavior in mobile ad hoc networks, *Proceedings of MOBICOM 2000*, 255–265 (2000).
23. S. Goyal, *Connections. An Introduction to the Economics of Networks*, Princeton University Press (2007).

Chapter 35

Low-Power Circuit Design for Cardiac Data Mining in Medical Sensor Networks

Fei Hu*, Alexandru Samachisa*, Marcin Lukowiak*,
Daniel Philips† and Yang Xiao‡

**Department of Computer Engineering, RIT, Rochester, New York, USA*

†Electrical Engineering, RIT, Rochester, New York, USA

‡Department of Computer Science
The University of Alabama, Tuscaloosa, AL 35487-0290, USA

Medical Sensor Networks are becoming an important tele-healthcare information infrastructure due to their low-power, low-cost, large-scale wireless sensor deployment and flexible data collection and processing. For a long term, ECG data mining is based on pure software implementation, which needs significant calculation time. To speed up the local ECG data processing in a medical sensor, this work proposes the chip design approach to make a dedicate VLSI chip for ECG data pattern recognition. We will provide the detailed circuit design principle for complex Wavelet-based data classification algorithms. Especially we target low-power design.

35.1. Introduction

Cardiovascular diseases (CVDs) are the number one underlying cause of death in most advanced countries in the world. Timely detection of CVDs can prevent later complications. This means constant heart monitoring needs to be extended to more than just hospitalized patients in critical condition, or patients that are known to suffer from CVDs. This kind of monitoring is mostly intended to monitor patients at home, without influencing the patient's day-to-day life, while still keeping a fast response time in the event medical intervention is needed.

An important step in this direction was taken with the introduction of Medical Sensor Networks (MSN) technology in medical applications. The leading research in this area is done under the name CodeBlue at Harvard University.[1] The portable ECG sensors designed can transmit the patient's heart data through the wireless connection for recording and/or further analysis. The recording of the data allows the medics to diagnose patients based on their heart activity history, while real time processing can provide a way to detect if immediate medical intervention is needed.

Besides the functionality provided, such a system needs to be scalable to meet the need for monitoring a large number of patients.

A top concern in wireless sensor network (WSN) design is to reduce the power consumption at the nodes, in order to increase their portability by increasing their battery life. The general approach to increase the bandwidth and reduce power in WSN is to reduce the amount of data being transmitted by preprocessing or compression the data. It is thus beneficial to remove normal data from the ECG signal before transmission over the wireless connection, and only transmit data which can be considered irrelevant to the diagnosis of the patient. This approach would introduce another level of processing at each node, but reduce the amount of data traveling through the network. The necessary bandwidth will be reduced, making the system more scalable. The power consumption of the wireless transmitter will be decreased at the cost of adding the power requirements of the new processing stage. This modification will be most beneficial if the monitoring is extended to patients with no signs of CVDs, since these will have regular heartbeats most of the time and, thus, will ideally have no need to transmit data over the network.

Our approach to reduce the ECG data (i.e., only send abnormal data) is to identify abnormal patterns based on feature extraction and type classification. We use wavelet analysis to extract the ECG features. Although the pattern recognition could be implemented in pure software (which is what most of the current works do), it can have serious delay performance issues. For instance, it can take 100s microseconds to accurately identify heart diseases from a 30-minute of ECG stream.[2]

Therefore, we seek to implement ECG data processing from a dedicated chip instead of software approach. The circuit's location is shown in Fig. 35.1. The chip takes the incoming digital ECG signal, isolates the individual beats, detects as many of the normal beats as possible and only enables transmission of the abnormal beats that would require further analysis. This can be combined with another more complex software classifier at the receiving end to process the signal further and decide whether human attention is required or not. In order to achieve the highest power savings and integration, the entire system could be implemented on a single VLSI chip as a very low power solution.

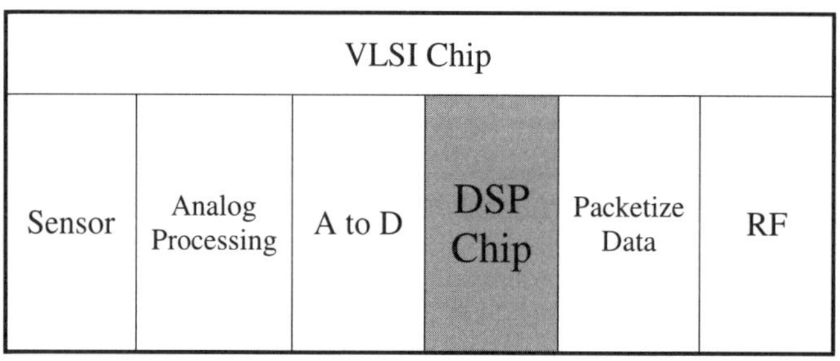

Fig. 35.1. ECG data mining chip (shown as shaded part).

The rest of the chapter will be organized as follows. In Sec. 35.2, we will provide the background on ECG data mining in MSN. Section 35.3 will explain our circuit implementation for each math component. The performance analysis will be discussed in Sec. 35.4. Section 35.5 concludes this chapter.

35.2. ECG Data Mining

35.2.1. *Medical sensor networks*

A simple MSN scenario is shown in Fig. 35.2 (top). Each patient's ECG signal could be automatically collected and processed (such as Analog-to-Digital conversion) by a small ECG sensor, and then be wirelessly sent to a remote ECG server for analysis purpose (such as using data classification to find out arrhythmia). If an ECG sensor reports any abnormal heart beat signals, an emergency communication channel established between the physician's office and the patient's wireless device (such as a beeper or cellular phone), will be used to send out alerts to provide the patient some medical suggestions (such as taking drugs or performing other further processing). In a more advanced MSN, shown in Fig. 35.2 (bottom), a patient's ECG sensor can even use a neighbor sensor to relay its data if his/her distance is too far away from the ECG server. This communication mode is called "Multi-hop" wireless transmission. Multi-hop MSN not only extends communication distance but also saves the energy consumption of an ECG sensor since direct sensor-server long distance wireless communication is avoided through hop-to-hop relay.

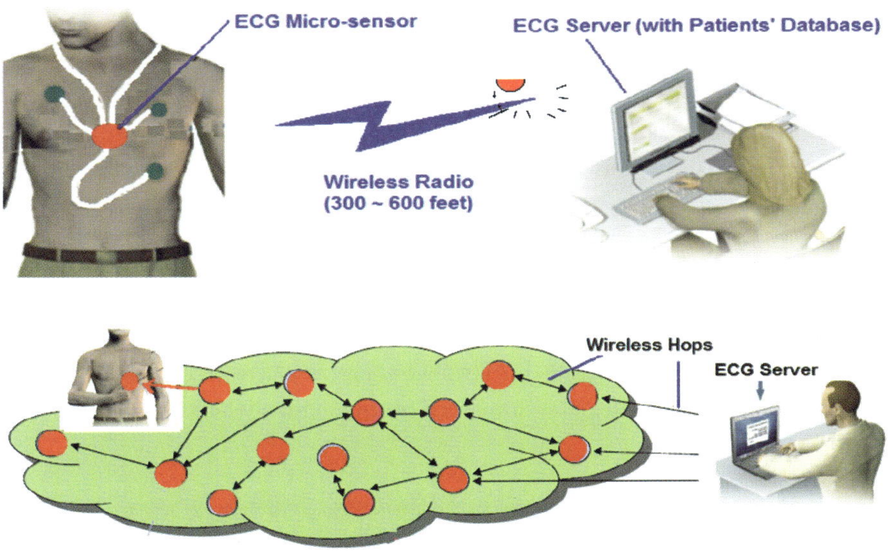

Fig. 35.2. Medical Sensor Networks (MSNs): (top): one-hop case; (bottom) multi-hop case.

Fig. 35.3. Mobile platform appearance (includes ECG sensor + RF mote).

Our MSN hardware mainly includes tiny ECG sensors and RF communication boards. The manufacturing cost for all the components of a sensor (such as resistors, amplifiers, etc.) is less than \$80 each. If produced in large amount (> 1000), the cost will be less than \$50. Because of our low-power design (through voltage scaling, low duty cycle, less RF collisions, and sleep control), the two AA batteries could provide the entire ECG sensor board for 13 months of lifetime. Compared to the current commercial ECG measurement devices, our design is much lighter (< 250 g), much cheaper (< \$80), more portable without nurse's help), and more power-efficient (no AC power outlet is needed). Moreover, our MSN includes a new RF board design, which saves more manufacturing cost than current medical sensor networks (such as CodeBlue[1]).

Our MSN consists of large amount of wireless ECG communication units. Each unit is called a "mobile platform" in this work. These mobile platforms are essentially the wearable ECG devices that would be distributed among cardiac patients in order to offer continuous monitoring of the patients' vital signs. As shown in Fig. 35.3, each platform is composed of a customized ECG sensor board providing connections to a 3-Lead ECG monitoring system, which is housed on a wireless communication board (also called RF motes). While the ECG sensor board gathers useful patient ECG data, the RF mote provides limited local signal processing capabilities (such as ECG noise filtering), and more importantly wireless communication for transmitting the ECG signals back to the server for feature extraction.

Figure 35.4 shows the logic architecture components of the MASN mobile platform in Fig. 35.3.

35.2.2. *ECG signals*

The standard for analyzing heart activity over time is the electrocardiogram (ECG or EKG). The ECG is a graphic illustration of the electric heart activity, which

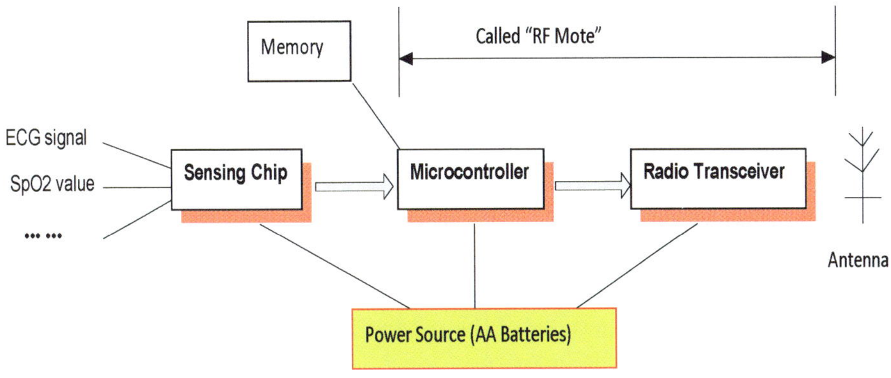

Fig. 35.4. MSN mobile platform: logic architecture.

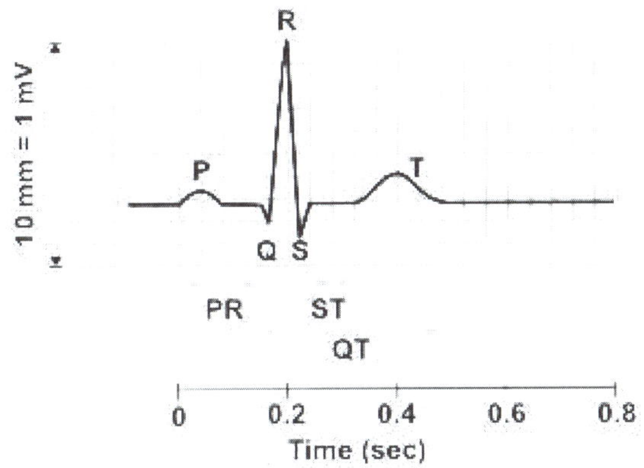

Fig. 35.5. Typical ECG heart beat waveform.

is obtained by measuring the electrical potential differences between points of the body. In order to perform an ECG, up to 12 self-adhesive electrodes are attached to fixed predefined locations on clear skin. Each measurement between two points is called a lead. Each lead is defined by end points of the measurement. For example, Lead I measures the electric potential difference between the left leg (+) and the right arm (−). Based on these locations, each lead records the heart's electrical potential from a particular vantage point and can contain extra information than what is given by all the other leads. The optimal compromise between time-efficiency and completeness of the ECG was set to 12 leads, which is considered the standard ECG. The 12 leads are: I, II, III, aVR, aVL, aVF, V1, V2, V3, V4, V5 and V6.

Figure 35.5 shows a typical ECG beat. A beat is composed of a P wave, a QRS complex and a T wave, and sometimes a U wave following the T wave. Each change in voltage levels is detected by the ECG and the shape represented graphically depends on the orientation of the lead with respect to the direction of the polarization wave. The waves are a pure reflection of the heart's electrical activity, but from a medical perspective, the actual mechanical events are important in diagnosis as well. These events are defined as segments on the ECG. Some of the useful segments from the analysis point of view are the PR, ST and QT segments, which are also shown in Fig. 35.5. The PR interval is measured from the onset of the P wave to the beginning of the QRS complex. The ST segment is defined as the duration from the end of the QRS until the onset of the T wave, while the QT is the ST segment plus the QRS complex. All the waves and segment lengths contain information about the state of the heart and can be used to detect any abnormalities in the heart activity of the patient being observed. For example, the P wave rate is what gives the heart rate, which is considered normal only when it lies between 60 and 100 beats per minute with less than 10% variation.

One of the most important problems in ECG analysis is automatic beat delineation. This is needed in many cases ranging from simple heart rate computations to serving as the first stage of complex automatic diagnosis. Beat delineation techniques have to start by identifying features in the ECG signal that can constantly be detected in each heart beat. Simply by looking at an ECG plot, it can be noticed that the QRS complex is the predominant feature in every beat. The other features of the ECG signal, like the P wave and T wave, are sometimes too small to be detected, or have characteristics too close to those of noise. This makes the QRS complex the feature that can yield the best detection accuracy. As an example, Cuiwei obtained an accuracy of over 99.8% in detecting the QRS complexes over the entire MIT-BIH in Ref. 3, through the use of wavelets. The high reliability of its detection made the QRS detection the basis for all the automated ECG signal analysis from simple heart rate determination to complex classification schemes of the cardiac cycles. Most beat delineation techniques use the QRS as a starting point. For example, one possible approach is selecting a fixed interval before and after the detected QRS for further analysis.[4]

The next step in ECG analysis is to further process the extracted beats to determine the state of the patient. The beat classification problem is defined as successfully detecting what type of beat is being analyzed upon its extraction from the ECG signal. This problem can be solved through one of the many classification algorithms available. Most of the existing algorithms were successfully used in ECG classification. These include Artifical Neural Networks,[5] Block-Based Neural Networks,[6] Hidden Markov models,[7] and Support Vector Machines.[8] Besides the algorithm, the features chosen for the classifiers are also of great importance. In the case of ECG, the features can be directly extracted from the samples from the ECG signal, morphological descriptors, time-frequency descriptors, or a combination of the types.[9] The morphological features are usually features extracted from the segmentation of the ECG beat, for example the ST length, while the time frequency descriptors can be coefficients of the Discrete Wavelet Transform of the ECG beat.

35.2.3. *Wavelets analysis*

The first step in performing signal analysis is choosing the domain to be used. The frequency domain would be useful because of the possibility of removing noise that has specific frequency bands. For example, baseline drift, a low frequency type of noise, and muscular contractions, a high frequency type of noise, are very common in ECG signals.[2] Unfortunately, this approach would lose all the time information, which sometimes is the only sign of a problem (e.g., accelerated heart rhythm). The time domain would keep the location in time of the points of interest, but it could make the feature detection harder, due to noise and ECG variance. The ECG varies across different patients and even across different beats from the same patient. An example of the latter is shown in Fig. 35.6, where the amplitude and shapes are different from one beat to the next, even though all the beats are normal activity beats.

A middle ground is provided by wavelets, which work in both time and frequency domain. Wavelets can decompose the signal into different frequency scales, but at the same time keep the time information, thus making them a perfect tool for ECG analysis. This is noticeable from the many results obtained in ECG analysis using wavelets. A wavelet is a waveform of effectively limited duration that has an average value of zero. A sample wavelet is presented in Fig. 35.7. The wavelet chosen for the wavelet transform is also known as *the mother wavelet.* The use of wavelets is similar to Fourier's idea of representing functions by superposing sines and cosines. The Fourier transform contains the frequency information of the signal, independent

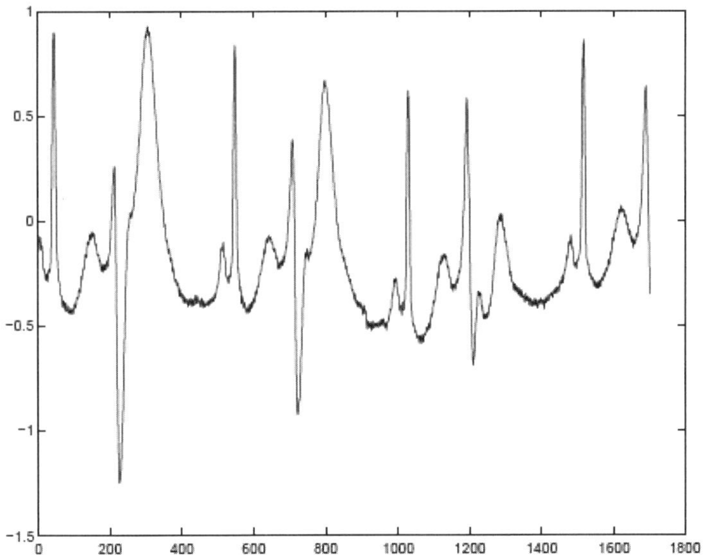

Fig. 35.6. ECG signals with noise.

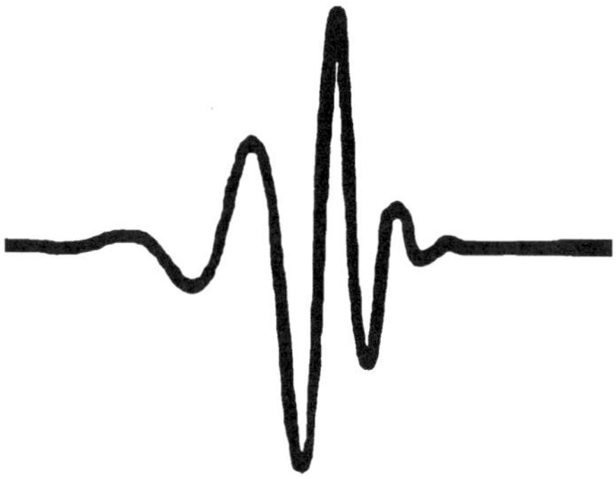

Fig. 35.7. Mother wavelet example.

of the time at which the frequencies occur. Wavelets moved from Fourier's frequency analysis to scale analysis. This means the signal is divided in scales of resolution rather than different frequencies. This is achieved by superposing shifted and scaled versions of the mother wavelet to approximate the signal. The wavelet transform can be continuous (CWT) or discrete (DWT), just like the Fourier transform. The general formula for the CWT is presented as follows[10]:

$$\mathrm{DWT}_f(m,n) = \frac{1}{\sqrt{|a_0^m|}} \int_{-\infty}^{\infty} f(t)\Psi\left(\frac{t - nb_0a_0^m}{a_0^m}\right) dt, \tag{35.1}$$

where the two parameters a and b describe the shifting and scaling of the wavelet $\psi(t)$ respectively. As a change, different frequency ranges are covered and as b changes, the time localization center is moved.

The DWT formula is presented in (35.2), which is obtained from (35.1) by simply restricting a and b to discrete values.

$$\mathrm{CWT}_f(b,a) = \frac{1}{\sqrt{|a|}} \int_{-\infty}^{\infty} f(t)\Psi\left(\frac{t-b}{a}\right) dt, \tag{35.2}$$

$a = a_0^m$ and $b = nb_0a_0^m$, where $a_0 > 1$, $b_0 > 0$, and m and n range over Z.

Based on Eqs. (35.1) and (35.2), the general steps in finding the wavelet transform of a given signal can be described as the following 4 steps: (1) Start at the beginning of the signal and compare it with the mother wavelet by correlation; (2) Shift the wavelet to the right and go back to step one. Continue until the entire signal is covered; (3) Scale (stretch) the mother wavelet and repeat steps (1) and (2). (4) Repeat steps (1) through (3) for as many scales as needed. The 4 steps described above can be applied in continuous fashion or in discrete steps. The CWT following the steps above would produce a two dimensional continuous domain of coefficients indexed by scaling and shifting (a and b), while the DWT will have discrete scaling and shifting (m and n), thus producing a discrete two dimensional domain.

However, in practice, a different method for obtaining the DWT is used. The method involves using a low pass and a high pass filters at each level to obtain

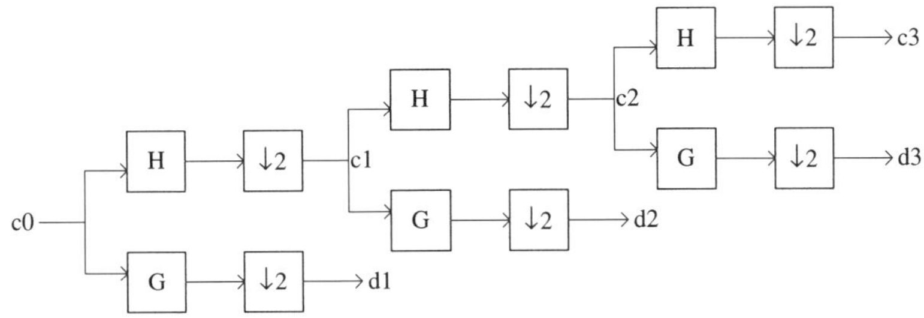

Fig. 35.8. General schematic of a practical implementation of the DWT.

the coefficients at the next scale. This can be explained because small values of $|a|$ in Eq. (35.1) correspond to high frequencies or very fine scale, while large values correspond to low frequencies. The equation for these transformations is as follows, where j is the scale, H is the low pass filter and G is the high pass filter.

$$\begin{aligned} c_{j+1}(k) &= \sum H(m-2k)c_j(m) \\ d_{j+1}(k) &= \sum G(m-2k)c_j(m) \end{aligned}. \tag{35.3}$$

The choice of scales chosen for this approach is the dyadic scale. In order to obtain the next dyadic scale according to the Eq. (35.3), the signals have to be down sampled and then passed through the same filters over and over as shown in Fig. 35.8, where c_0 is the signal to be processed. Based on the use of the low pass and high pass filters, the d_i coefficients can be interpreted as the details of the signal in a specific frequency band, defined by the chain of filters leading to d_i.

The DWT can be modeled using FIR filters, whose coefficients can be computed based on the mother wavelet used. The mother wavelet used in this work is a quadratic spline wavelet, successfully used for the first time to process ECG signals in Ref. 3. The wavelet is defined by its Fourier transform in (35.4).

$$\hat{\Psi}(\omega) = j\omega\left(\frac{\sin(\omega/4)}{\omega/4}\right)^4. \tag{35.4}$$

The filters needed to implement the DWT based on the qudratic spline wavelet are $H(w)$ and $G(w)$, as defined by their frequency response in Eq. (35.5). The two filter responses lead to the transfer functions defined in Eq. (35.6). These equations give the coefficients for the two FIR filters needed to be implemented, as well as the delays introduced by each filter.

$$\begin{aligned} H(\omega) &= e^{j\omega/2}\left(\cos\frac{\omega}{2}\right)^3 \\ G(\omega) &= 4ie^{j\omega/2}\left(\sin\frac{\omega}{2}\right) \end{aligned}, \tag{35.5}$$

$$\begin{aligned} H(z) &= \frac{1}{8}z^2 + \frac{3}{8}z + \frac{3}{8} + \frac{1}{8}z^{-1} \\ G(z) &= 2z - 2 \end{aligned}. \tag{35.6}$$

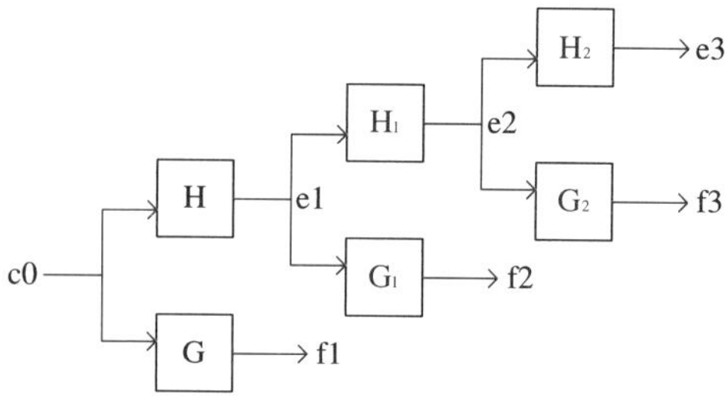

Fig. 35.9. Modified DWT design.

The downsampling by a factor of two followed by filtering with a filter F is the same as filtering a filter F_1 obtained by introducing zeros between the coefficients of F and then downsampling. Due to this we can modify the filters to include the downsampling. The new cascaded design is shown in Fig. 35.9, where H_p and G_p are filters obtained by introducing $(2p - 1 - 1)$ zero coefficients between all the coefficients of H and G, respectively. The difference is that the new outputs e_i and f_i have the same sampling rate as the original signal. The old outputs c_i and d_i can be obtained by simply downsampling the new ones by the appropriate factor.

35.2.4. *Wavelets analysis*

An Artificial Neural Network (ANN) is a processing system that attempts to emulate a biological neural network, in an attempt to gain its performance characteristics. The ANN is composed of nodes (neurons) and weighted links among them, which are used to multiply the signal transmitted through that link and thus simulate a simplified neuron interactions model.

The input units are the chosen features for the classification. These features are multiplied by the weights associated with all the links and act as inputs to the next layer. Let the input feature vector be $x = (x_1; \ldots; x_i; \ldots; x_n)$ and let the weight of the link connecting x_i to z_j be v_{ij}. This means the input to the hidden node z_j is given by:

$$z\_in_j = v_{0j} + \sum x_i v_{ij}. \tag{35.7}$$

Each neuron layer has an activation function associated with it. A typical activation function is a sigmoid like the one defined below. The sigmoid shape is showed in Fig. 35.10.

$$f(x) = \frac{1}{1 + e^{-x}}. \tag{35.8}$$

Based on the chosen activation function the output value form each node is computed as shown below, where f is the chosen activation function:

$$z_j = f(z\_in_j). \tag{35.9}$$

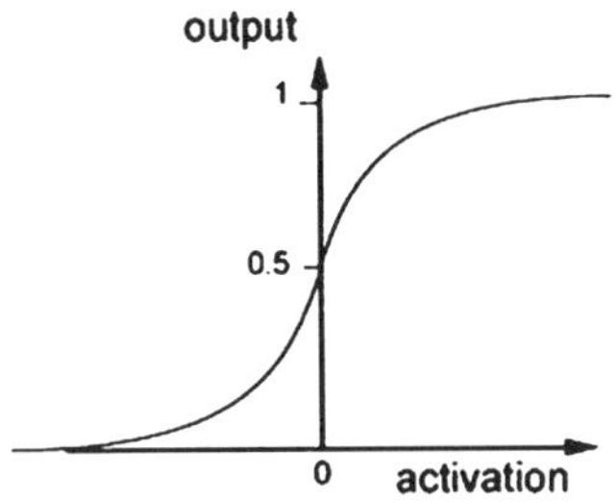

Fig. 35.10. ANN activation function.

The next steps are computing the value at the inputs of the output nodes y_ink as shown in Eq. (35.10), and the output values based on the activation functions of these output nodes y_k as shown in Eq. (35.11), where w_{ij} is the weight of the link connecting hidden node z_i to output node y_j. The output values y_k form the response of the ANN to the input vector.

35.3. Circuit Design

After implementing the ECG waveform QRS detection and beat classification algorithms in MATLAB and testing their accuracy over the MIT-BIH database, a VHDL (Very high-speed Integrated circuit Hardware Description Language) implementation to match the MATLAB model is needed. The VHDL model needs to be synthesizable, so that the power consumption, delay and area estimates can be extracted from the synthesized design.

35.3.1. *Top-level design: low-power circuit*

One of the main goals of this work is to reduce the power consumption at the node, and thus the chip should be designed to consume as little power as possible. The power consumption of a VLSI chip can be divided into dynamic power consumption and static power consumption. The dynamic power is defined in Ref. 11 as:

$$P_{avg} = P_{switching} + P_{shortcircuit} + P_{leakage} = \alpha C_L V_{dd}^2 f_{dk} + I_{sc} * V_{dd} + I_{leak} * V_{dd} \tag{35.12}$$

where α is the activity factor, which can take a value between 0 and 1. The activity factor describes the probability of switching in a clock period. As an example, the clock has an activity factor of 1. C_L is the capacitance that needs to be charged/discharged in the event of a switch. Sometimes another term is defined as Ceffective $= \alpha^* \ C_L$, which is the effective capacitance to be charged/discharged per clock period. I_{sc} is the short circuit current, which appears in the middle of the transition, when neither of the pull up and pull down networks are completely closed. I_{leak} is the leakage current that appears across a transistor in its off state.

There are many techniques that can be used to reduce any of the components of P_{avg}. Many techniques of reducing the power consumption are presented in Ref. 11. Out of these, a few were implemented in the current work and namely clock gating, resource sharing and multiplication with constants.

The clock gating technique allows reducing the dynamic power by disabling the clock for the structures that are not in use. This reduces the activity factor (α) for that part of the circuit. In the current design, clock gating is used for the classifier, since this is only needed when a successful QRS detection is made. A successful QRS detection is used as an enable signal for the classifier as shown in Fig. 35.11, which will load the new features and compute the result of the classification. When in standby, the classifiers inputs are held at the last known value and thus no switching will occur inside the classifier.

The resource sharing technique is a technique to use the same hardware and performing different computations in different cycles instead of multiplying the hardware and execute everything in parallel. In the current design, if the ANN were to be designed to compute the result in one cycle, 432 multipliers would be required. Due to the fact that speed is not as important as power in the current design, only 43 multipliers were shared at the cost of computing the classification result in Ref. 43 (to be discussed later).

The multiplication with constants is a circuit level technique to reduce both dynamic and static power. The method consists in replacing multiplications by shifts and adds whenever possible. This approach leads to less hardware. This reduces the dynamic power because the switching capacitance is less and also the static power simply due to less devices, and thus less sources for leaking. Due to the values of the coefficients of the filters used for computing the DWT transforms, the

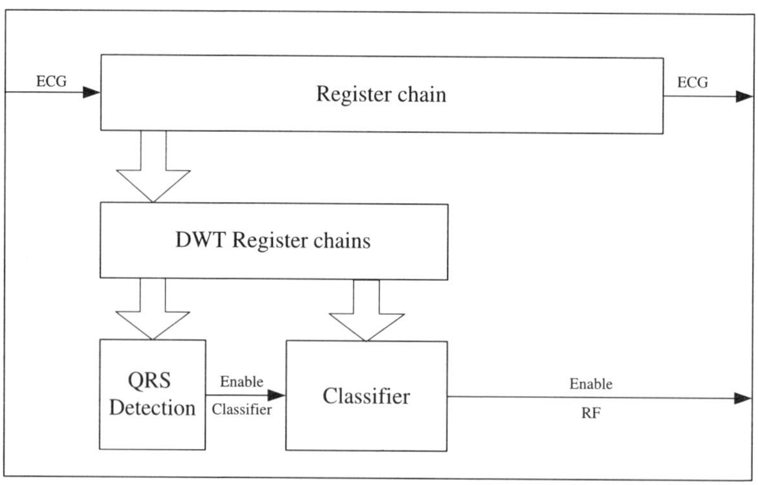

Fig. 35.11. Top level circuit design.

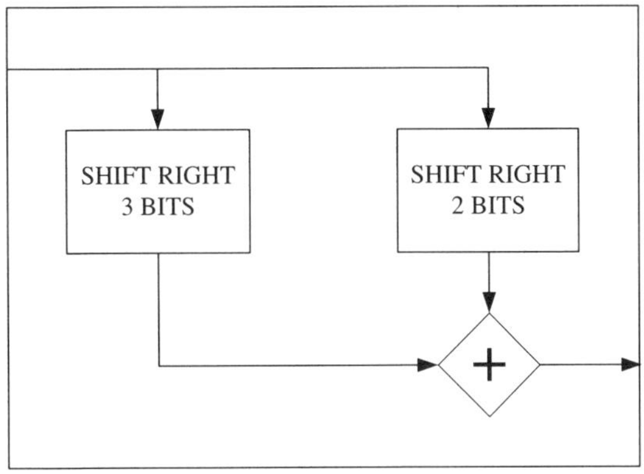

Fig. 35.12. Design of the multiplication with 3/8 based on the representation in (35.13).

Table 35.1. Replacing the multiplication operations.

Operation needed	Design to replace multipliers
$x * 1/8$	$x \gg 3$
$x * 3/8$	$x \gg 3 + x \gg 3$
$x * 2$	$x \ll 1$
$x * (-2)$	$(\text{not}(x) + 1) \ll 1$

multiplications with these coefficients can be successfully replaced with shift and addition operations. For example, the coefficient 3/8 can be written as shown below. The design for multiplications with 3/8 is shown in Fig. 35.12.

$$\frac{3}{8} = \frac{1}{8} + \frac{1}{4} = 2^{-3} + 2^{-2}. \tag{35.13}$$

Following this technique, the representation for all the coefficients needed is shown in Table 35.1, which can be designed without the use of multipliers. The symbols $\ll$ and $\gg$ are used to denote shifting to the left and right by the number of bits immediately following the symbols, respectively.

Even with these techniques, the main technique to reduce the dynamic power consumption (Pswitching) is to design the chip to work at a very low frequency fclk. This frequency was chosen to be 360 Hz, which is also the sampling frequency of the ECG signal. This would allow for the entire chip to work on the same clock as the A to D converter that samples the ECG signal. The static power reduction techniques are mostly circuit level techniques, and none were applied due to the lack of special libraries needed for these techniques. One method that will certainly reduce the static power consumption is to use high threshold devices across the entire chip. The introduction of high threshold devices slows down the circuit at the cost of reduced static power consumption, but due to the extremely low frequency of the chip (360 Hz), speed is not a concern.

The first decision to be made about the number representation is between the fixed-point and the floating point representation. One advantage of fixed-point arithmetic is that it requires significantly less hardware than the floating-point arithmetic. This advantage reduces the area and thus the power consumption of the chip, making the fixed-point representation a better candidate for the current work. Due to the extra bits used to represent the mantissa, the fixed point representation can also be capable of higher accuracies. This advantage is useful if all the numbers are represented using the same common magnitude, or they can be normalized and scaled to meet this criteria. However the accuracy advantage is lost quickly if numbers of different magnitudes have to be manipulated. This means a common magnitude in which all the values can be represented needs to be found.

After analyzing the possible values used inside the chip, it was observed that all the values are located inside the interval [−31:31]. The only value outside this interval is the RRinterval feature, which is a value that can be located in the interval [200:350]. The decision was made to use RRinterval = 256 as the feature, and thus be able to represent all the numbers in the given interval. The 256 value was chosen because it reduces the [200:350] interval to the [0.78:1.37], and because it is a power of two and thus can be implemented in hardware as a simple shift to the left by 8 bits. The final representation of the numbers was chosen as shown in Fig. 35.13, where 1 bit is used for the sign, 5 bits for the integer part to match the interval [−31:31], and 18 bits for the fractional part.

Due to multiplication operations inside the classifier the number representation in some parts of the classifier will change to the representation seen in Fig. 35.13, but this representation will not be visible from anywhere outside the chip. The only representation visible from outside the chip is the one presented in Fig. 35.14, which is the format in which the ECG signal will enter and exit the chip.

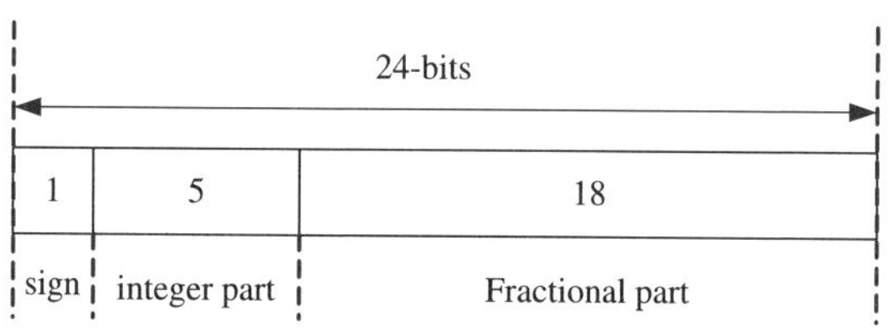

Fig. 35.13. Chosen number representation: 24-bit fixed point.

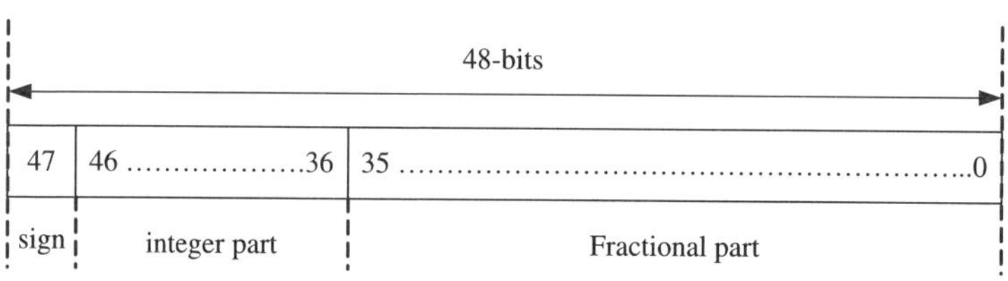

Fig. 35.14. Alternative representation: 48-bit fixed point.

35.3.2. *Wavelet circuit*

The computation of the DWT is equivalent with the design of a series of FIR filters already described in Sec. 35.2. Table 35.2 shows the filters that are required for each DWT scale needed, while Table 35.3 shows the coefficients of the filters present in Table 35.3.

The computation hardware for each of the DWT scales can be designed using Tables 35.2 and 35.3. Figure 35.15 shows the implementation of the second scale of the DWT. The top signal is the ECG signal passing through the pipelined registers. The second row is the implementation of the H filter with its corresponding coefficients. Each of the multiplications with a coefficient, symbolized here by a block with the coefficient value inside, is realized using only shift and add operations as already described before. After the first filter, the resulting signal is pipelined again and then the second filter is applied, in this case G_1. The zero coefficient is simply designed by not connecting the corresponding sample. The result is the second scale of the DWT of the ECG signal, which is pipelined for further processing.

The fact that the higher DWT scales use intermediate results from the computations of the lower scales leads to the idea of sharing parts of the hardware when computing all the scales, in order to reduce the total amount of hardware needed. For example, the third DWT scale passes the signal through H, H_1 and G_2, while the third scale can take the intermediate signal from the output of H_1 and pass it through H_2 and G_3 instead of replicating the first two filters. The design of the computation of all the first 4 scales of the DWT is shown in Fig. 35.16. The inset shows the output filters hardware that need to be connected on each row to obtain the DWT at each scale. The two shaded registers on each row correspond to the two registers in the inset. The outputs from the G_i filters shown in the inset are the DWT coefficients, which are pipelined to be used further for QRS detection and beat classification.

Table 35.2. Filters needed for each DWT scale.

DWT scale	Filters
2^1	G
2^2	$H\ G_1$
2^3	$H\ H_1\ G_2$
2^4	$H\ H_1\ H_2\ G_3$

Table 35.3. Coefficients of the required filters.

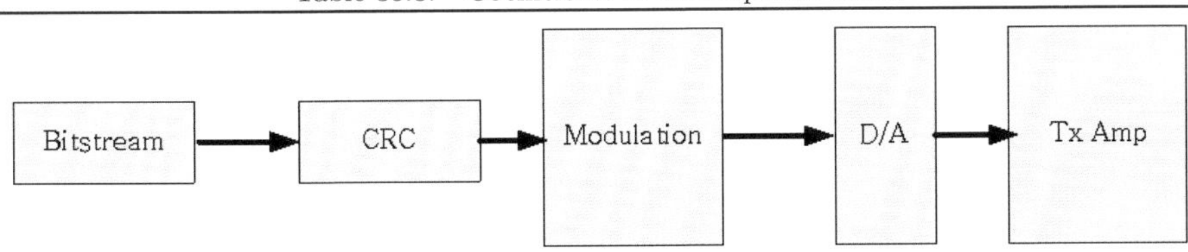

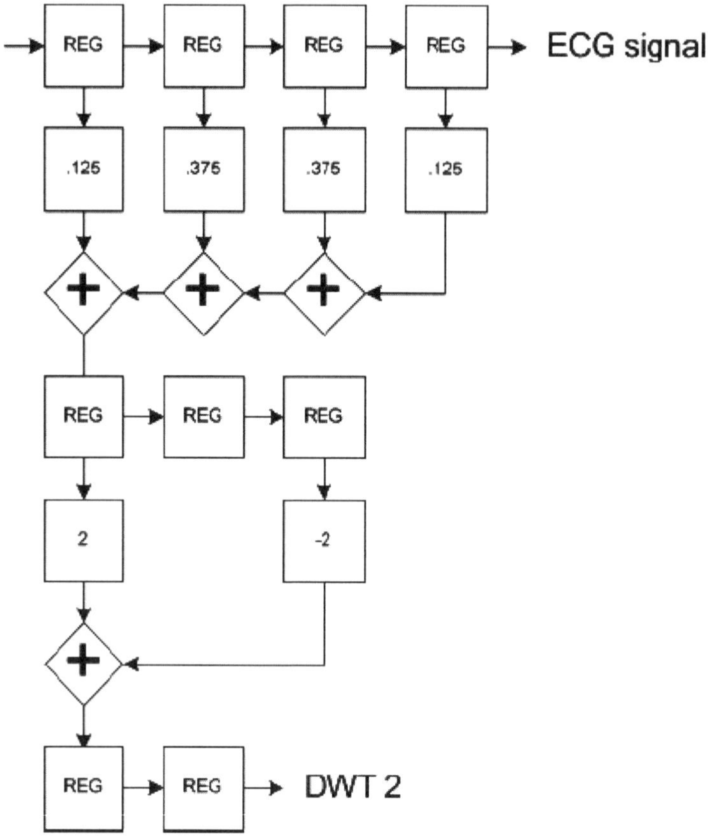

Fig. 35.15. Design of the scale 22 of the DWT.

The QRS detection algorithm needed to be implemented in hardware consists of detecting matching zero crossings that are flanked by opposite sign peaks across the first 4 DWT scales of the signals, as described before. The first step is to detect the zero crossings at each scale. Figure 35.17 shows the circuitry that needs to be added to each of the DWT scales pipelines. The figure shows two comparators in the middle that are used to localize a zero crossing and 2 comparators on the sides used to check for peaks.

The symmetric hardware on top and bottom of Fig. 35.17 accounts for the two cases: (1) positive peak followed by negative peak or (2) negative peak followed by positive peak. The check for peaks is shown in Fig. 35.17 to be 2 samples away from the zero crossing, but the distance is different with every scale. This distance also needs to include a few neighbors in the check in order to account for asymmetric QRS shapes. If either the hardware above the DWT chain or the one below evaluates as true, a zero crossing is assumed to be detected and pipeline for further processing.

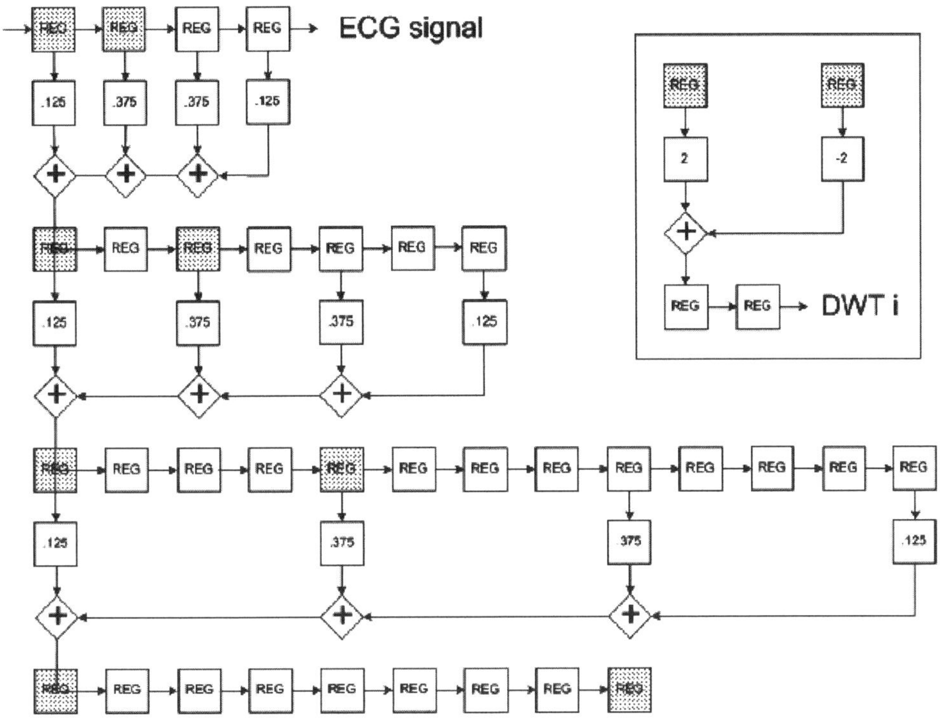

Fig. 35.16. Combined design for the first 4 scales of the DWT.

After the 4 zero crossings pipelines are generated, the hardware in Fig. 35.18 is used to detect the R waves.

The delays introduced by the hardware designed to perform the DWT computations and the zero crossings detection has to be taken into account in each scale, so that the connection can be made accordingly. Table 35.4 shows the delays needed for each of the DWT scales with respect to the ECG signal. The first column shows the delay introduced by the theoretical computation of the DWT for a symmetric R wave as calculated in Ref. 3, the second column the added delay of the particular design used in the work, the third column shows the delay accuracy, while the last column shows the total delay and accuracy.

In order to implement the delay in the last column, the connection is made to the zero crossings pipelines as many stages later with respect to the ECG point analyzed as the delay shows. This delay is represented in Fig. 35.18 by the long vertical dashed lines. The accuracy is needed because if the wave is not symmetric, the actual delay will be different from the delay present here, and thus this error needs to be taken into account in order to detect non symmetric R waves. The values for the accuracy were chosen empirically. It was decided to fix the detection on the fourth scale of the DWT because it is less affected by noise and set a delay a

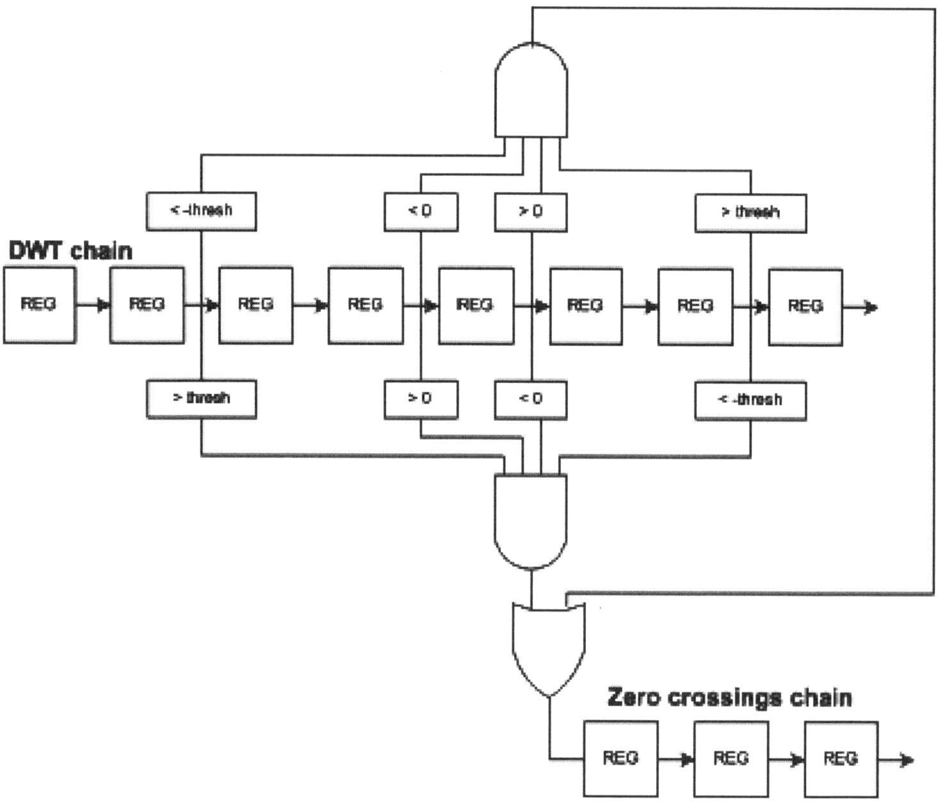

Fig. 35.17. Design of obtaining the zero crossing at each DWT scale.

margin error of ±5 on the other scales. Figure 35.18 shows how the ±5 error margin is taken into account by making connections to all the neighboring 5 stages before and after the zero crossing. Note that only 4 of these neighbors are shown at each scale, the rest are hidden by the short vertical dashed lines.

If the result of the logic in Fig. 35.18 evaluates as true, the QRS is assumed to be 20 samples before the zero crossing detected on the 4th scale of the DWT. The detection is then pipelined and will be used to trigger the classification of the beat when the entire beat is inside the chip.

35.3.3. *Control circuitry for missed beats*

The proposed chip needs to ensure that if no QRS complex is detected over a certain period of time the transmission is enabled, because something abnormal might be happening, and by definition all abnormal activity needs transmitted to the base station. This can be ensured by measuring the time since the last R wave detection. If a wave is not detected after the maximum RR interval length allowed, the RF

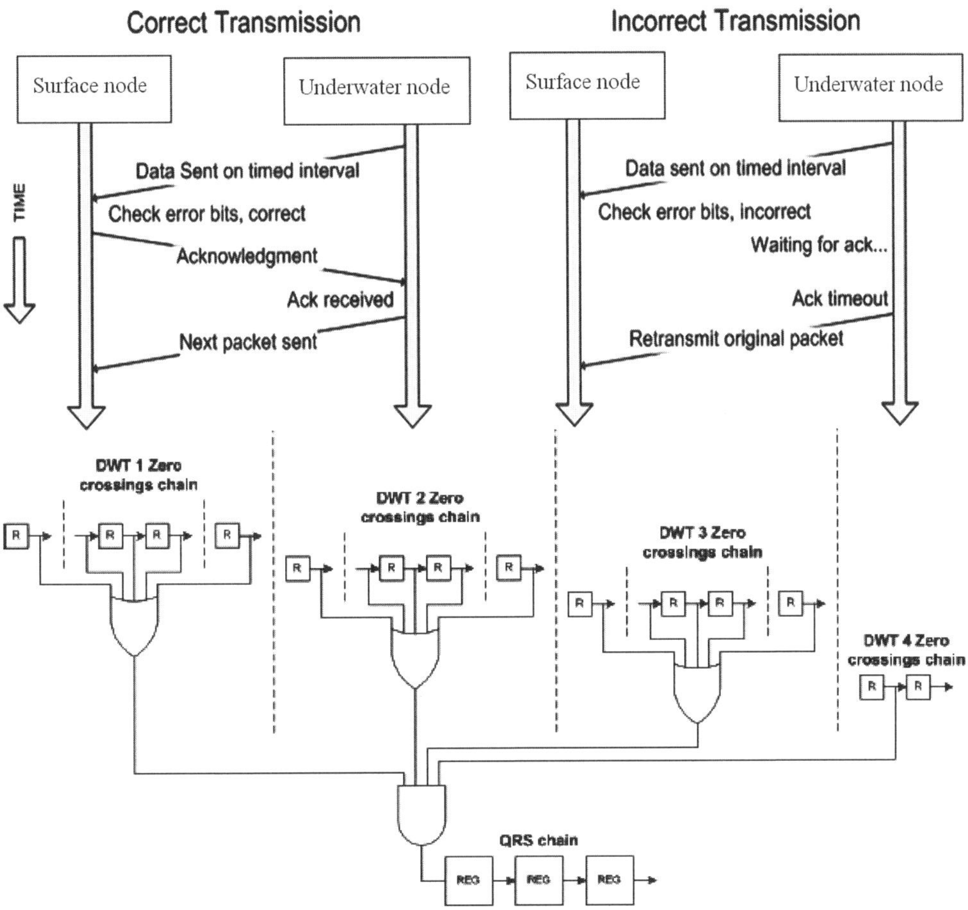

Fig. 35.18. Design of the QRS detection from the zero crossings across the scales.

Table 35.4. Delays for each DWT scale in samples.

DWT scale	Theroetical delay	Delay added by design	Delay accuracy	Total
2^1	1	2	± 5	3 ± 5
2^2	3	3	± 5	6 ± 5
2^3	7	4	± 5	11 ± 5
2^4	15	5	± 0	20

will be turned on so that the signal can be transmitted. Figure 35.19 shows the implementation of this part of the chip.

The desired behavior in the case of abnormal beats is to ensure their transmission. Assuming the QRS detection algorithm fails to detect the R peak of an abnormal beat, the beat will still be sent due to the missed beat logic, which is

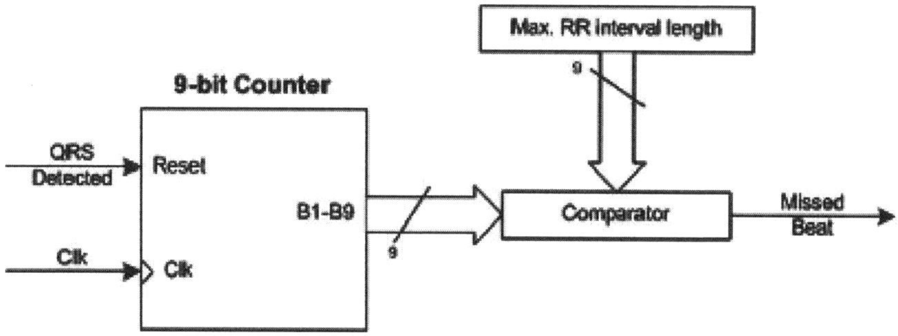

Fig. 35.19. Logic to ensure transmission of missed beats.

also the desired behavior in this case. This means that the QRS algorithm can be relaxed because the accuracy of detecting the QRS in the case of abnormal beats has no importance for the current work due to the missed beat detection circuitry.

35.3.4. *ANN circuit*

The classifier chosen is a neural network with 43 input nodes, 1 hidden layer composed of 43 nodes and one output nodes, as described before. The training of the classifier is performed off line, using MATLAB, and the computed weights are hard coded into the design. From the digital perspective, the classifier is thus composed of the feed forward network, the memory to store the weights, and the control logic for the two units. The main bottlenecks of a digital VLSI implementation of a Neural Network are the nonlinearity of the activation function, the large amount of memory needed for the weights and the large number of interconnects and multipliers in the case of large networks.[4]

One of the main problems in hardware implementation of a neural network is the nonlinearity of the activation function. This function is usually a sigmoid. One of the most common sigmoid functions, which is also used in the current work, is defined in Eq. (35.8). The most common approaches for hardware implementation of the activation function are approximation functions that are more suitable for digital implementation.

The most straight-forward approach is the use of a look-up table. The problems with using the look-up table are the size of this look-up table, which is directly proportional to the accuracy of the function approximation, and the fact that it is unfeasible to have a lookup table at each node that uses the activation function in the case of large networks. The problem with sharing one common large look-up table is that the parallelism advantage of a hardware neural network is lost.

A better alternative from a hardware perspective is the approximation of the sigmoid by a piecewise linear function. The most common approximation from this category is the one proposed by Alippi and Storti-Gajani in Ref. 12, which is also the approach chosen in this work. The idea for this approximation is to split the Y domain into an integer number of intervals, and define a linear function over each interval. The attractiveness of this proposed approach is that the entire function can be designed using only shifters and a counter. This was made possible by selecting the interval limits as powers of two (e.g., 0.5, 0.25). The function is defined below, where $\hat{x}$ represents the signed fractional part of x, and (x) represents the integer part of x.

$$f(x) = \frac{\hat{x}+2}{2|(x)|+2} = \frac{\frac{\hat{x}}{4}+\frac{1}{2}}{2|(x)|}. \tag{35.14}$$

This function is a very good approximation of the sigmoid defined in Eq. (35.8). In order to increase hardware classification accuracy, the function defined in Eq. (35.14) is used in the backpropagation training of the neural network, replacing the default functions defined in the MATLAB neural network toolbox. This will ensure that the hardware implementation will work exactly like the MATLAB model. Figure 35.20 shows the hardware design of the function proposed in Ref. 12.

The advantage of a hardware neural network is its speed. This is due to the fact that it can execute all the multiplications needed for each hidden layer in parallel. However, the cost of this speed is a large number of interconnects and multipliers required. For example, for the current work, the straight forward implementation of the feed forward network would require 432 24-bit multipliers, which is the number of connections from the input layer to the hidden layer.

The proposed design is shown in Fig. 35.21. The main difference is that only 43 multipliers are used to compute all the values leading to one hidden layer node each

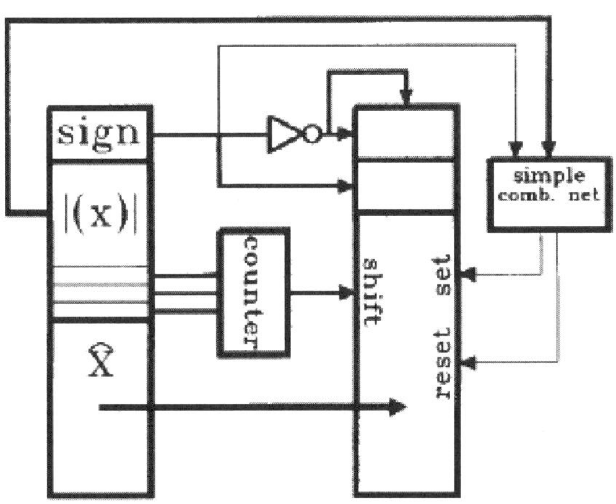

Fig. 35.20. Hardware design of the activation function from Ref. 12.

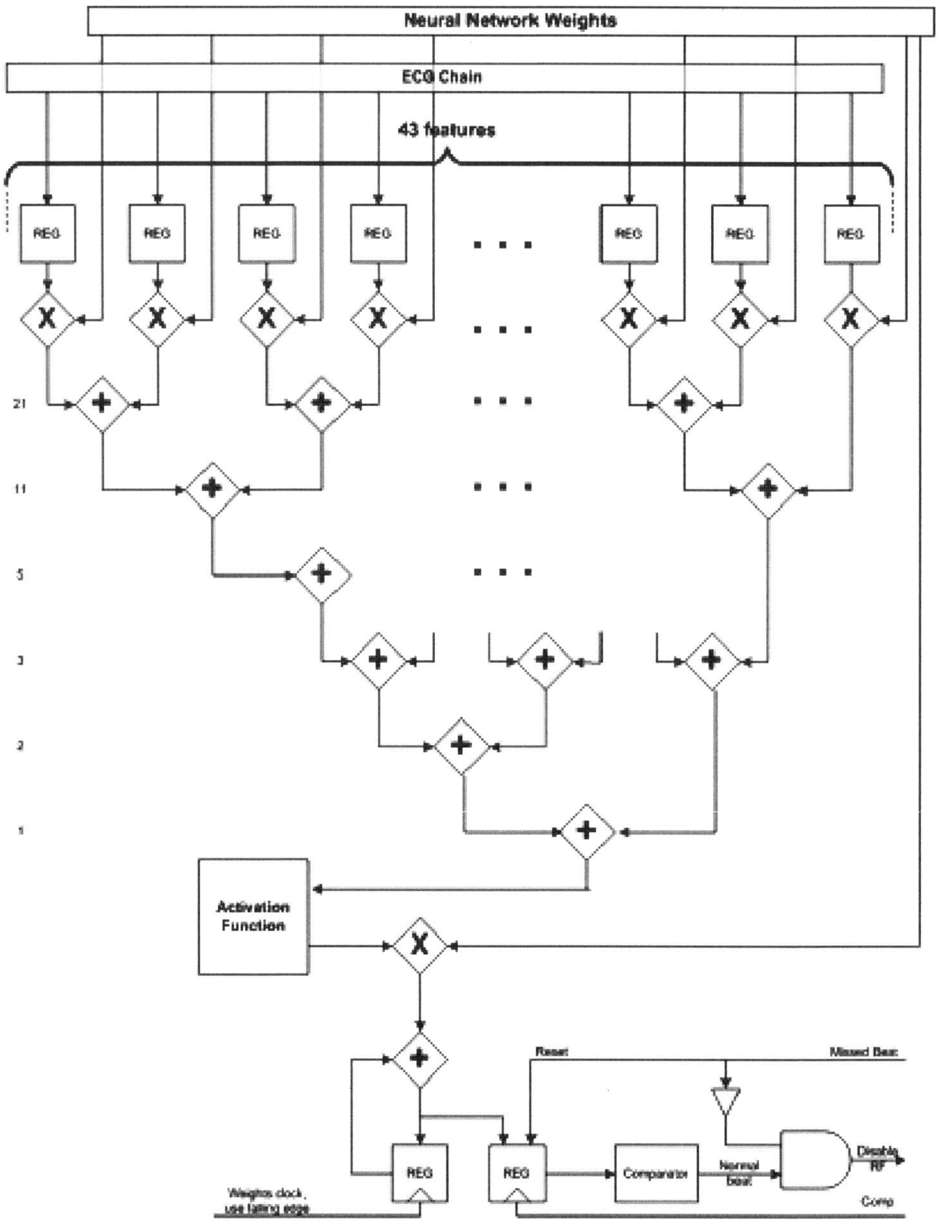

Fig. 35.21. ANN design.

cycle and keep accumulating the results as shown in Fig. 35.21. This means that at least 43 cycles are needed to compute the result of one classification. The speed advantage of the neural network was thus traded for less power consumption due to significantly less hardware, which is the one of the main goals in the current work.

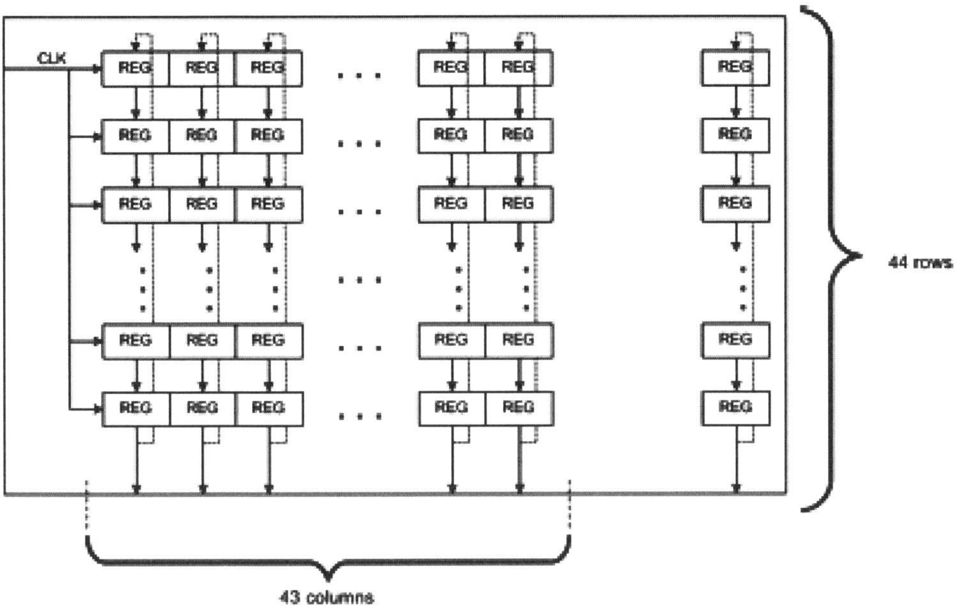

Fig. 35.22. Memory design.

The 43 multipliers receive the 43 features as one of the inputs and each cycle the 43 weights corresponding to a hidden layer node as the second input. The results are added and passed through the activation function. This result is multiplied by the weight corresponding to the connection for the current node to the output and then accumulated into the result register.

The offset for the output layer also needs to be added to the accumulated result. This is done by setting all the weights in the 44th cycle to zero, except for the last one. This one needs to be set to twice the value of the actual offset value because setting all the features to zero will return 0.5 at the output of the activation function, instead of a 1.

This means the memory has to be designed in such way that it will supply 44 weights each clock cycle for 44 cycles. The memory design is presented in Fig. 35.22, memory that has 44 lines and 44 rows. Each weight is a 24-bit number, so the total memory needed to store the weights is 46464 bits.

The control logic needed for both the memory and the feed forward network is shown in Fig. 35.23. The main clock is gated in order to save power as already described before. The gated clock stops the memory from changing its output. The feed forward network is stopped from switching because the feature registers at the top of Fig. 35.21 are loaded only on a successful QRS detection. The entire classifier is only active for 44 cycles after a successful QRS detection, after which no switching occurs in the classifier until the next QRS is detected.

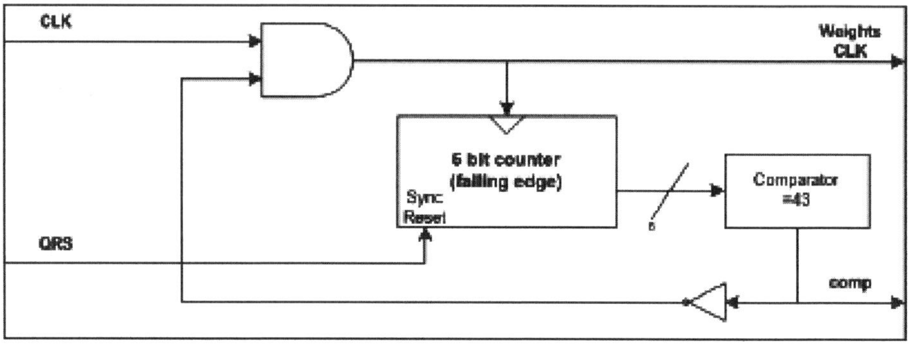

Fig. 35.23. ANN control logic circuit.

35.4. Circuit Design Test and Analysis

The MATLAB model was used as a reference for testing the VHDL model and ensure the functionality of the two models is identical. There are however differences between the two models. The most important difference is that the VHDL model uses a different number representation and thus does not have the accuracies MATLAB has. The VHDL model was tested by selecting random sequences from the ECG signals present in the MIT-BIH database and compare the classification results to the classification results to the results obtained from running the same sequence through the MATLAB model.

An example of a typical ECG signal extracted is shown in Fig. 35.24. The waveform resulted from running the ECG signal shown in Fig. 35.24 is shown in Fig. 35.25. Some of the functionality of the designed described in this chapter can be identified in this figure. For example, it can be seen that many zero crossings are detected across the 4 DWT scales, but only 3 of them aligned with the appropriate delays to form a QRS detection. It can also be seen how the classifier clock is activated only when a QRS is detected and lasts until the classification is completed. The delay seen from the point where the zero crossings aligned to the classification activation is the delay introduced so that the entire beat is inside the chip. When the classification is complete, the wireless transmission is enabled or disabled based on the result of the classification and the previous state. In the current scenario, the first three beats were successfully detected as normal beats and it can be seen that the wireless transmission is disabled for the duration of these three beats. In the case of the last beat, the QRS was missed, no classification was performed, but the missed beat circuitry (described before) detected this and enabled the transmission. All the tests ran matched perfectly the MATLAB functionality.

After building and verifying the synthesizable VHDL model, the next step is to synthesize it in order to obtain power and delay estimations. The tool used for this step is Design compiler from Synopsis. The model was synthesized without using

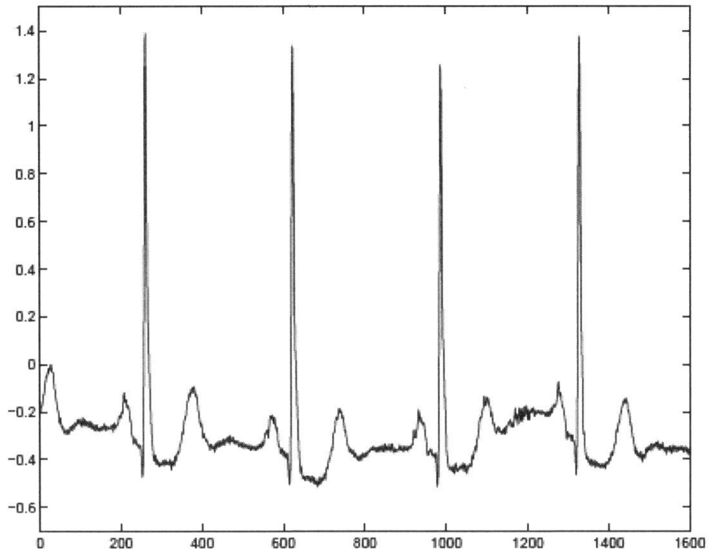

Fig. 35.24. Sample of ECG portion used for testing the VHDL model.

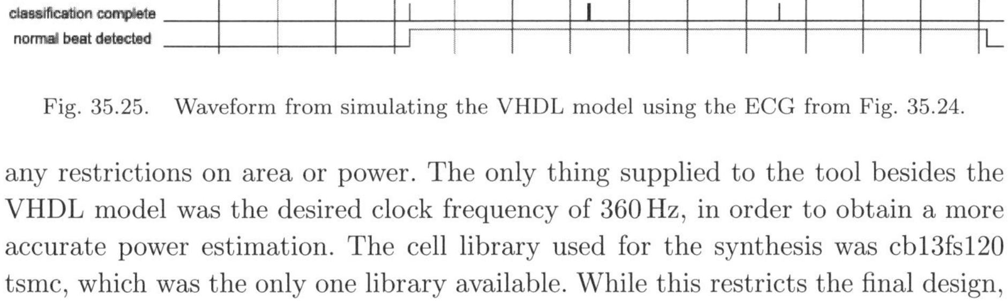

Fig. 35.25. Waveform from simulating the VHDL model using the ECG from Fig. 35.24.

any restrictions on area or power. The only thing supplied to the tool besides the VHDL model was the desired clock frequency of 360 Hz, in order to obtain a more accurate power estimation. The cell library used for the synthesis was cb13fs120 tsmc, which was the only one library available. While this restricts the final design, it is sufficient to obtain power and delay estimates. If a more accurate estimate is desired, more accurate tools should be used after the synthesis step. For example, NanoSim could be used for power estimations and Pathmill for critical path delay, which are already proven to be more accurate than Design compiler in estimating power and delay.

We then present the chip characteristics as extracted from the synthesized VHDL code. The first results are the power estimation results for the proposed chip, which are presented in Table 35.5. These results show that the power consumption is being

Table 35.5. Overall design results.

File number	Normal beats removed	Normal beats sent	Abnormal beats sent	Abnormal beats removed
100	2211	2	3	30
101	1823	12	3	3
103	2040	17	0	2
105	1963	534	109	8
106	1435	49	515	4
107	0	0	2012	100
108	121	1598	19	4
109	0	0	2442	60
111	0	0	2066	33
112	2487	19	0	2
113	1742	26	7	0
114	1185	621	56	4
115	1854	75	0	0
116	1991	285	104	4
117	18	1497	1	0
118	0	0	2252	0
119	1522	1	443	3
121	1727	112	1	1
122	2445	2	0	0
123	1424	70	2	0
124	0	0	1591	11
200	1681	37	803	51
202	1578	463	72	2
203	1490	1010	460	48
205	2520	18	75	10
207	0	0	1847	16
208	1249	319	1219	141
209	2549	37	302	80
210	2199	197	215	12
212	915	2	1799	1
213	2560	50	466	141
214	0	0	2228	8
215	3051	106	161	6
217	231	11	1930	11
219	1784	275	57	13
220	1930	2	58	34
221	1992	14	392	0
222	416	1620	357	63
223	1356	646	548	25
228	970	694	357	6
230	1443	781	1	0
231	1	312	1237	0
233	2074	125	839	3
234	2666	1	36	18
Total	60643	11640	27085	958

dominated by the leakage power. This is explained by the very low clock frequency of 360 Hz. Another important thing to notice is that the classifier accounts for more than half of the total power consumption, despite the large number of registers used to pipeline the ECG signal and its DWT transform.

Due to the magnitude of the static power consumed compared to the dynamic power consumed, implementation of static power reduction techniques can reduce the chip's power consumption. The most common technique to reduce the static power consumption is the use of high thresholds devices. These devices would replace the normal devices and reduce their leakage current at the cost of increasing delay. However, the timing analysis of the circuit, shows that there is plenty of room to increase the delay. The critical path of the chip was identified to have a delay of 41 μs inside the classifier, when the maximum delay allowed is $1,389\,\mu$s. This means that the entire chip can be implementing using only high threshold devices, which will decrease the static current consumption, without affecting the functionality due to the large amount of slack available. Unfortunately, no high threshold libraries were available for synthesis to verify how much will the static power be reduced by this technique.

According to Ref. 11, the energy consumption breaks into the different phases of the radio transmission and the different states of the radio. The power consumption estimation proposed in Ref. 11 is greatly simplified in this work. The assumptions for the simplification were that the power in all other states other than the transmission state and is zero, the 1power needed to switch between states is zero, and there is no need for retransmission. The resulting power estimation formula is shown below.

$$\text{TxActualPower} = \text{TxSpecPower} * \text{DataRate} = \text{TransmissionDataRate} \quad (35.15)$$

where the TxActualPower is the actual power consumed in transmitting the ECG signal as is, the TransmissionDataRate is the transmission rate of the used transmitter, the TxSpecPower is the given transmission power for the transmitter, and the DataRate the data rate of the signal being transmitted. For this work it was assumed that the ECG signal is sampled at 360 Hz, using 24 bits per sample, which leads to a DataRate of 8.64 kbps.

Based on the power results given in Table 35.6, a power savings analysis is performed in Table 35.7, for several commonly used motes. In order to assess the transmission power consumed by transmitting the ECG signal present in the 3rd row of Table 35.6, Eq. (35.15) is used.

Table 35.6. Power consumption estimates.

Circuit	Internal power (μW)	Net switching power (μW)	Total dynamic power (μW)	Leakage power (mW)	Total power (mW)
Classifier	—	—	0.7915	0.7423	0.7431
Entire Chip	12.2546	16.2985	28.5531	1.2576	1.2862

Table 35.7. Power savings.

Row	Wireless type	WeC	Rene	Rene2	Dot	Mica	Mica2Dot	Mica2	Telos
1	Data rate (kbps)	10	10	10	10	40	38.4	38.4	250
2	Tx spec power (mW)	36	36	36	36	36	42	42	35
3	Tx actual power (mW)	31.10	31.10	31.10	31.10	7.78	9.45	9.45	1.21
4	Tx savings (mW)	19.10	19.10	19.10	19.10	4.77	5.80	5.80	0.74
5	Total savings (%)	57.27	57.27	57.27	57.27	44.86	47.79	47.79	−44.92

Table 35.8. Potential power savings.

Assumptions		Mote types							
Percentage removed	Chip power (mW)	WeC	Rene	Rene2	Dot	Mica	Mica2Dot	Mica2	Telos
95	1.286	90.87	90.87	90.87	90.87	78.46	81.39	81.39	−11.32
61.4	0.74	59.02	59.02	59.02	59.02	51.88	53.57	53.57	0.22
95	0.74	92.62	92.62	92.62	92.62	85.48	87.17	87.17	33.82

The power savings in the 4th row of Table 35.7 are computed as a percentage of the transmission power from the 3rd row. This percentage is the percentage of normal beats found by the current design over the MIT-BIH database, which is 61.4%. The 5th row savings are calculated as a percentage of the total savings by adding the estimated power requirements of the proposed circuit to the values from the 4th row.

The results show consistent power improvements except for the Telos motes, which due to its higher bandwidth does not see any improvement from the proposed chip, and its power consumption is worsened.

Table 35.8 shows potential savings assuming different percentages of normal beats detected, as well as a case where the power consumption of the chip were to be reduced to a value of 0.74 mW by implementing several static power reduction techniques on the current design. The value of 0.74 was chosen because it's the limit where the Telos motes can also see power improvements evet at the detection rate given by the current chip over the MIT-BIH database of 61.4%. The 95% detection rate was chosen as the normal beat detection rate in the case of a relatively healthy.

Due to the processing power of the proposed chip, the existing microcontroller on each of the motes can be removed altogether and thus improve the power savings even further.

35.5. Conclusions

The goal of investigating the improvements given by an ECG pre-classifying chip was accomplished in this chapter. The chip was shown to be able to remove 61.4% of the data from the MIT-BIH database. This data can be dropped from transmission, and thus save the same percentage of bandwidth available at a node. The power savings are also significant. The chip will perform differently based on the percentage of normal beats in the patient's ECG heartbeat. The higher this percentage, which is very close to 100% in the case of patients with no heart problems, the higher the bandwidth and power savings of the design are. This means that an investigation of the actual savings should be performed in each case where the chip is intended to be used, because its performance is directly affected by the data being monitored.

As directions for future work, there are many possible improvements of the current design: The accuracy of the classifier should be increased in the sense that no abnormal data should be dropped from transmission, attempting at the same time to also improve or at least not incur a significant loss in the accuracy of detecting the normal beats. This could be done either by handpicking a better training set for the current classification scheme, or replacing the current classification scheme altogether. Due to the variations in the ECG signal, morphological features could improve the classification accuracy, but the detection algorithm should be changed as well in order to detect the new features. The power of the current chip can be further reduced using static power reduction techniques. There is plenty of room to increase the delay due to the low frequency of the chip, which is usually the trade-off in most power savings techniques. The easiest one to implement that would be ideal for the current chip is to use high threshold devices in the entire chip, which will reduce the leakage current and thus the static power consumption. The power can be estimated using more accurate tools, such as NanoSim. The dynamic power can be more accurate even using Design compiler by including a switching profile. This was not necessary in the current work due power consumption being dominated by the static power. The power consumption of the wireless transmitter should also be analyzed in more detail, maybe even using actual measurements from one of the currently existing ECG monitoring motes.

Acknowledgment

The work is supported in parts by the US National Science Foundation (NSF) under grants CNS-0716211 and CNS-0716455.

References

1. V. Shnayder, B. Chen, K. Lorincz, T. R. F. Fulford-Jones and M. Welsh, *Sensor Networks for Medical Care*, Technical report, Harvard University (2005).
2. K. Grauer, *A Practical Guide to ECG Interpretation.* Mosby, St. Louis, 2nd edition (1998).
3. L. Cuiwei, Z. Chongxun and Y. Chaowei, Detection method of ECG using wavelet transform. *Chinese Journal of Biomedical Engineering*, **14**(1), 59–66 (1995).

4. O. T. Inan, L. Giovangrandi and G. T. A. Kovacs, Robust neural-network-based classification of premature ventricular contractions using wavelet transform and timing interval features, *IEEE Transactions on Biomedical Engineering*, **53**(12), 2507–2515 (2006).
5. W. Jiang, S. G. Kong and G. D. Peterson, ECG signal classification using block-based neural networks, *International Joint Conference on Neural Networks, IJCNN 2005, Jul 31–Aug 4 2005*, **1**, 326–331 (2005).
6. R. V. Andreao, B. Dorizzi and J. Boudy, ECG signal analysis through hidden Markov models. *IEEE Transactions on Biomedical Engineering*, **53**(8), 1541–1549 (2006).
7. Z. Qibin and Z. Liqing, ECG feature extraction and classification using wavelet transform and support vector machines, *2005 International Conference on Neural Networks and Brain Proceedings, ICNNB'05*, **2**, 1089–1092 (2005).
8. I. Christov, G. Gomez-Herrero, V. Krasteva, I. Jekova, A. Gotchev and K. Egiazarian, Comparative study of morphological and time-frequency ECG descriptors for heartbeat classification. *Medical Engineering and Physics*, **28**(9), 876–887 (2006).
9. J. P. Martinez, R. Almeida, S. Olmos, A. P. Rocha and P. Laguna, A wavelet-based ECG delineator evaluation on standard databases, *IEEE Transactions on Biomedical Engineering*, **51**(4), 570–581 (2004).
10. D. F. Mix and K. J. Olejniczak, *Elements of Wavelets for Engineers and Scientists*, Wiley-Interscience, Hoboken, NJ (2003).
11. A. P. Chandrakasan and R. W. Brodersen, Minimizing power consumption in digital CMOS circuits, *Proceedings of the IEEE*, **83**(4), 498–523 (1995).
12. C. Alippi and G. Storti-Gajani, Simple approximation of sigmoidal functions: Realistic design of digital neural networks capable of learning, *Proceedings — IEEE International Symposium on Circuits and Systems*, **3**, 1505–1508 (1991).